Chambers
students' dictionary

Chambers
students' dictionary

Chambers

CHAMBERS
An imprint of Chambers Harrap Publishers Ltd
7 Hopetoun Crescent, Edinburgh, EH7 4AY

First published by Chambers Harrap Publishers Ltd 2006
Reprinted 2007

A CIP catalogue record for this book is available from the British Library.

ISBN 978 0550 10212 6

Designed and typeset by Chambers Harrap Publishers Ltd, Edinburgh
Printed and Bound in Germany by Bercker

Contents

Contributors

Project Editor
Mary O'Neill

Editors
Pat Bulhosen
Alice Grandison

Editorial Assistance
Ian Brookes

Publishing Manager
Patrick White

Subject Consultants
Neil DeMarco
Anne and Patrick Fullick
Ros Hyde
Andrew Owen

Supplement
Andrew Holmes

Prepress
Susan Lawrie
Clair Simpson

Preface

In *Chambers Students' Dictionary* you will find all the traditional and essential features of a good, comprehensive dictionary – how to spell words, what they mean, what their different forms are and, if the words are unusual or particularly difficult, how to pronounce them. To help consolidate or distinguish between meanings, many words are illustrated by phrases and sentences in which they may occur.

However, *Chambers Students' Dictionary* has been specially compiled to offer much more. It focuses on the requirements of students aged 15+, with thorough coverage of vocabulary from various subjects at GCSE and Scottish Standard Grade level and beyond. Included are over 1,000 words from the sciences, 500 terms from mathematics and hundreds more from geography, history, religious studies and ICT. The definitions elucidate the concepts but do not oversimplify.

To provide further practical help, words which are often confused with each other, for example *complement* and *compliment*, or *flounder* and *founder*, have a warning note at the relevant entry. There are concise notes on word origins at the end of many entries and, in addition, there are more than 200 boxes throughout the book featuring more detailed information on the history of some of the words.

The benefits of this dictionary to the student do not end there. Also included is *Working with English*, a specially written supplement that puts the focus on using language in academic contexts and beyond. Accessible in style and attractive in design, the information it provides will help students to convey their knowledge skilfully and communicate effectively.

Chambers Students' Dictionary has been thoroughly researched and compiled with the expert advice and editorial input of teachers, ensuring that it reflects the modern syllabus and meets the *real* needs of students today.

How to use the dictionary

Entry word

attentive *adjective* **1** giving or showing attention **2** polite ♦ **attentively** *adverb*

attenuate *verb* **1** to make or become thin or weak **2** to reduce the value or something **3** *physics* of sound, radiation, etc: to decrease in intensity after passing through a medium ♦ **attenuation** *noun*

Definition

attest *verb* **1** to affirm or be proof of the truth of something **2** (**attest to**) to certify that something is so, especially by giving a sworn statement ⓞ Comes from Latin *attestari*, from *ad* meaning 'to' + *testari* meaning 'to bear witness'

attic *noun* a room just under the roof of a house

Word history

ⓞ From *Attica* in ancient Greece, famous for a type of square architectural column used in upper storeys of classical buildings

Usage information

attire *formal,* *verb* to dress ➤ *noun* clothing

attitude *noun* **1** a way of thinking or feeling: *a positive attitude* **2** a position of the body

Where the word is used

attorney *noun* (*plural* **attorneys**) **1** someone with legal power to act for another **2** *US* a lawyer

attract *verb* **1** to draw to or towards **2** to arouse liking or interest

attraction *noun* **1** the power of attracting **2** something which attracts visitors etc: *a tourist attraction* **3** *physics* a force that pulls two objects together, eg that between opposite electric charges

Subject label

attractive *adjective* **1** good-looking, likeable **2** pleasing: *attractive price*

Part of speech:
noun, verb, etc

attribute *verb* (pronounced a-**trib**-yoot) **1** to state or consider as the source or cause of: *attribute the accident to human error* **2** to state as the author or originator of: *attributed to Rembrandt* ➤ *noun* (pronounced **a**-trib-yoot) **1** a quality or characteristic, often with positive connotations: *one of her many attributes/attributes of power* **2** *computing* an item of information about a file stored by the operating system, eg the date and time last saved ♦ **attributable** *adjective*

Pronunciation

attributive *adjective* **1** expressing an attribute **2** *grammar* of an adjective: placed immediately before or immediately after the noun it describes, eg 'pretty' ('the pretty girl')

Usage information

ⓘ Most adjectives can be used in this 'attributive' way. The opposite of attributive (meaning 2) is 'predicative'. An example of an adjective which is only ever used in a predicative way is 'asleep', because you cannot use it to make phrases like 'the asleep girl'.

bicycle *noun* a vehicle with two wheels, driven by foot-pedals

bid¹ *verb* (**bidding, bade** or **bid, bidden** or **bid**) ──────── Tenses of verb
1 to offer a price (for) **2** to make an attempt to achieve something ➤ *noun* **1** an offer of a price **2** a bold attempt: *a bid for freedom*

bid² *verb* (**bidding, bade** or **bid, bidden** or **bid**)
1 to tell, say: *bidding her farewell* **2** to command ──────── Example of use
3 to invite

biddable *adjective* compliant; obedient; docile

bidding *noun* **1** a command, request or invitation **2** the offers at an auction **3** *cards* the act of making bids • **do someone's bidding** to ──────── Phrase containing the entry word
obey their orders

bide *verb* (**biding, bided** or **bode**), *Scot* or *old* **1** to wait or stay **2** to dwell or reside; to stay, especially temporarily **3** to endure or tolerate • **bide your time** to wait patiently for the right moment ○ Comes from Anglo-Saxon *bidan* ──────── Word origin

---

contemptible *adjective* deserving scorn, worthless

❗ Do not confuse: **contemptible** and **contemptuous**.
Contemptible is formed from **contempt** + **-ible** meaning 'able to be scorned, worthy of scorn'. It is used in phrases like *a contemptible little tell-tale*. ──────── Note on words easily confused with each other

contemptuous *adjective* scornful

❗ Do not confuse: **contemptuous** and **contemptible**.
Contemptuous means 'full of contempt' (for something or someone). Use it in phrases like *a contemptuous laugh* or *He was contemptuous of my achievement*.

contend *verb* **1** to struggle against **2** to hold firmly to a belief; maintain (that) ◆ **contender** ──────── Related word
noun someone taking part in a contest

content¹ (*pronounced* kon-**tent**) *adjective* happy, satisfied ➤ *noun* happiness, satisfaction ➤ *verb* to make happy, satisfy ──────── Different words spelt the same way

content² (*pronounced* **kon**-tent) *noun* **1** (often **contents**) what is contained in something **2** the subject matter of a book, speech, etc **3** the proportion in which an ingredient is present: *a diet with a high starch content* **4** (**contents**) (a list of) the chapters in a book

Pronunciation guide

This dictionary gives you help when the pronunciation of a word may be tricky. Pronunciations are given in brackets, signalled by the word *pronounced*, for example:

obligatory (*pronounced* ob-**lig**-at-*o*-ri)

The way the pronunciations are shown is designed to be easily understandable. The syllables are separated by hyphens, and the stressed syllable (that is, the syllable pronounced with most emphasis) is shown in thick black type. Any vowel (or group of vowels) that is pronounced with an unemphasized 'uh' sound is shown in italic type.

A few sounds are difficult to show in normal English letters. Here is a guide to the letter combinations that are used to show these sounds:

Consonants
'ng'   shows the sound as in ri**ng**
'ngg'   shows the sound as in fi**ng**er
'th'   shows the sound as in **th**in
'dh'   shows the sound as in **th**is
'sz'   shows the sound as in deci**s**ion, mea**s**ure
'kh'   shows the sound as in lo**ch**

Vowels
'uw'   shows the sound as in b**oo**k, p**u**t
'oo'   shows the sound as in m**oo**n, l**o**se
'ah'   shows the sound as in **ar**m, d**a**nce
'aw'   shows the sound as in s**aw**, ign**o**re
'er'   shows the sound as in f**er**n, b**ir**d, h**ear**d
'ei'   shows the sound as in d**ay**, s**a**me
'ai'   shows the sound as in m**y**, p**i**ne
'oi'   shows the sound as in b**oy**, s**oi**l
'oh'   shows the sound as in b**o**ne, n**o**, th**ough**
'ow'   shows the sound as in n**ow**, b**ough**

Sound combinations
'eer'   shows the sound as in n**ear**, b**eer**, t**ier**
'eir'   shows the sound as in h**air**, c**are**, th**ere**
'oor'   shows the sound as in p**oor**, s**ure**
'air'   shows the sound as in f**ire**, h**igher**

Abbreviations used in the dictionary

The dictionary also has some labels in full (for example *informal* and *music*) which show you the way in which a word or meaning is used, or its subject area.

abbrev	abbreviation
Aust	Australian English
Brit	British English
E	East
eg	for example
esp	especially
etc	and so on, and other things
ie	that is
N	North
N Am	North American English
S	South
Scot	Scottish English
TV	television
UK	United Kingdom
US	United States English
USA	United States of America
W	West

Aa

A[1] *noun* **1** *music* the sixth note in the scale of C major **2** *medicine* the name of a blood group
A[2] *symbol* ampere
a or **an** *adjective* **1** one: *a knock at the door* **2** any: *an ant has six legs* **3** in, to or for each: *four times a day*

> ℹ The form **a** is used before words beginning with a consonant sound, eg a *knock*; **an** is used before words beginning with a vowel sound, eg *an ant, an hour*.

a- see **an-**
aardvark *noun* a nocturnal African mammal with a large snout
AB *noun* the name of a blood group
aback *adverb*: **taken aback** surprised or slightly shocked
abacus (*pronounced* ab-a-kus) *noun* (*plural* **abacuses**) a frame with columns of beads for counting
abandon *verb* **1** to leave, without intending to return **2** to give up (an idea etc): *abandon hope* ➤ *noun* lack of inhibition: *dancing with gay abandon* ◆ **abandoned** *adjective* ◆ **abandonment** *noun*
abase *verb, formal* to make humble: *abase yourself before God* ◆ **abasement** *noun*
abashed *adjective* embarrassed, confused
abate *verb* to make or grow less: *wait for the storm to abate* ◆ **abatement** *noun*
abattoir (*pronounced* ab-a-twahr) *noun* a slaughterhouse
abbess *noun* the female head of an abbey or a convent
abbey *noun* (*plural* **abbeys**) **1** a monastery or convent run by an abbot or an abbess **2** the church now or formerly attached to such a monastery or convent
abbot *noun* the male head of an abbey
abbreviate *verb* to shorten (a word, phrase, etc) ◷ Comes from Latin *brevis* meaning 'short'
abbreviation *noun* a shortened form of a word or group of words, either with some letters missing, eg *maths* for *mathematics*, or with each word represented by its first letter, eg *BBC* for *British Broadcasting Corporation*
abdicate (*pronounced* ab-di-kayt) *verb* to give up (a position or responsibility, especially that of king or queen) ◆ **abdication** *noun*
abdomen (*pronounced* ab-dom-en) *noun* **1** the part of the body between the chest and the hips containing the stomach, bowels and reproductive organs **2** the rear part of an insect's body ◆ **abdominal** (*pronounced* ab-**dom**-in-al) *adjective*
abduct *verb* **1** to take away by force or fraud **2** of a muscle: to draw a part of the body (such as an arm or finger) away from another or away from the centre line of the body (*compare with*: **adduct**) ◆ **abduction** *noun* ◆ **abductor** *noun*
aberration *noun* an often temporary change from what is normal
abet *verb* (**abetting, abetted**) to help or encourage to do wrong, especially to commit a crime: *He was aided and abetted by his partner in crime*
abeyance *noun*: **in abeyance** not being used or dealt with for the time being
abhor *verb* (**abhorring, abhorred**) to hate, or regard with horror ◆ **abhorrence** *noun* ◆ **abhorrent** *adjective*
abide *verb* to put up with, tolerate • **abide by** to keep, act according to: *abide by a decision*
abiding *adjective* lasting
ability *noun* (*plural* **abilities**) **1** power or means to do something **2** talent ◷ Comes from Latin *habilitas* meaning 'skill'
abject (*pronounced* ab-jekt) *adjective* miserable, degraded ◆ **abjectly** *adverb*
ablation *noun, geography* the melting of ice
ablaze *adjective & adverb* **1** on fire **2** gleaming like fire: *a house ablaze with lights*
able *adjective* **1** having the power or means (to do something) **2** clever: *more able students*
able-bodied *adjective* **1** fit and healthy **2** not disabled
ablutions *plural noun, formal* washing of the body
ably *adverb* in an efficient or competent way
abnormal *adjective* **1** not normal (in behaviour etc) **2** unusual
abnormality *noun* (*plural* **abnormalities**) **1** something which is abnormal **2** the condition of being abnormal
abnormally *adverb* unusually; unnaturally
aboard *adverb & preposition* on (to) or in(to) (a ship or aeroplane)
abode *noun* a formal word for a dwelling: *of no fixed abode*
abolish *verb* to stop or put an end to (eg a

custom, law, etc) ♦ **abolition** noun

abolitionist noun someone who tries to put an end to something, especially slavery or capital punishment ♦ **abolitionism** noun

abominable adjective **1** hateful **2** very bad, terrible • **the Abominable Snowman** another name for the **Yeti** ♦ **abominably** adverb (meaning 2): behave abominably

abominate verb to hate very much

abomination noun **1** great hatred **2** anything hateful

Aboriginal (pronounced a-bor-**ij**-i-nal) or **Aborigine** (pronounced a-bor-**ij**-i-nee) noun a member of the people who were the original inhabitants of Australia ♦ **Aboriginal** adjective ⊕ Comes from Latin ab meaning 'from', and origo meaning 'beginning'

abort verb **1** to stop (a plan etc) before its completion **2** to end a pregnancy deliberately by having an abortion **3** biology to fail to grow or develop to maturity **4** computing to stop the execution of (a program) before it has been completed

abortion noun an operation to end an unwanted or dangerous pregnancy

abortion pill noun a drug used to end a pregnancy

abortive adjective coming to nothing, unsuccessful: an abortive attempt

abound verb to be very plentiful • **abounding in** full of, having many

about preposition **1** on the subject of: a programme about dinosaurs **2** around: look about you **3** near (in time, size, etc): about ten o'clock **4** here and there in: scattered about the room ➤ adverb **1** around: stood about waiting **2** in motion or in action: running about **3** in the opposite direction: turned about and walked away • **about to** on the point of (doing something)

above preposition **1** over, in a higher position than: above your head **2** greater than: above average **3** too good for: above criticism ➤ adverb **1** at, in or to a higher position, rank, etc **2** earlier on (in a letter etc): see above for details ⊕ Comes from Old English bufan meaning 'above'

above board adjective open; without fraud or deception ➤ adverb openly; without fraud or deception

abrasion noun **1** the action of rubbing off **2** a graze on the body **3** geography (also called: **corrasion**) erosion caused by rocks and other material in a river or glacier scraping the surfaces they are in contact with

abrasive adjective **1** rough and scratchy **2** having a harsh and rude manner ➤ noun something used for rubbing or polishing ♦ **abrasively** adverb (meaning 2)

abreast adverb side by side • **abreast of** up to date with: keep abreast of current affairs

abridge verb to shorten (a book, story, etc) ♦ **abridgement** or **abridgment** noun

abroad adverb **1** in another country **2** formal outside: witches go abroad after dark

abrupt adjective **1** sudden, without warning **2** of speech or behaviour: bad-tempered or snappy ♦ **abruptly** adverb ♦ **abruptness** noun

abscess (pronounced **ab**-ses) noun (plural **abscesses**) a boil or other swelling filled with pus

abscissa noun (plural **abscissas** or **abscissae** – pronounced ab-**sis**-ee), maths in Cartesian co-ordinates: the distance of a point from the vertical or y-axis (see also: **ordinate**) ⊕ Comes from Latin abscissus meaning 'cut off'

abscond verb to run away secretly: absconded with the money

abseil (pronounced **ab**-sayl) verb to let yourself down a rock face using a double rope ⊕ Comes from German ab meaning 'down', and Seil meaning 'rope'

absence noun the state of being away

absent adjective (pronounced **ab**-sent) away, not present ➤ verb (pronounced ab-**sent**): **absent yourself** to keep away

absentee noun someone who is absent

absenteeism noun continual absence from school or work

absently adverb in a dreamy way: 'I suppose so,' he replied absently

absent-minded adjective forgetful ♦ **absent-mindedly** adverb

absolute adjective complete, not limited by anything: absolute power

absolute error noun, maths the difference between the measured or predicted value of a quantity and its actual value

absolutely adverb **1** completely, certainly **2** (as an informal enthusiastic reply) yes, I agree

absolute majority noun, politics a vote gained by a candidate which is greater than the total number of votes for all other candidates

absolute value noun, maths the value of a number irrespective of whether it is positive or negative, eg the absolute value of -5 is 5

absolute zero noun, physics the lowest possible temperature of matter, equal to $-273.15°C$

absolution noun formal forgiveness of sins, especially by a priest

absolutism noun government by someone who has total power ♦ **absolutist** adjective & noun

absolve verb, formal to pardon: absolve me of my sins

absorb verb **1** to soak up (liquid) **2** to take up the whole attention of: *He was totally absorbed in his book* **3** *physics* to take up (energy) without reflecting or emitting it ♦ **absorbing** *adjective*

absorbent *adjective* able to soak up liquid etc ♦ **absorbency** *noun* (*plural* **absorbencies**)

absorption *noun* **1** the act of absorbing **2** complete mental concentration

abstain *verb* **1** to refuse to cast a vote for or against **2** (**abstain from something** or **from doing something**) to hold yourself back from it or from doing it

abstemious (*pronounced* ab-**steem**-i-us) *adjective* taking food, alcohol, etc in very small amounts

abstention *noun* **1** the act of choosing not to do something, especially not to take food or alcohol **2** a refusal to vote

abstinence (*pronounced* **ab**-stin-ens) *noun* abstaining from alcohol etc

abstinent *adjective* keeping oneself from indulgence, especially in alcohol

abstract *adjective* **1** existing only as an idea, not as a real thing **2** as a representation of reality, rather than a real thing **3** of art: using shapes and patterns to represent things ➤ *noun* a summary of the main points of a book, speech, etc

abstraction *noun* **1** a thing existing only as an idea or as a representation of reality: *No-one really has 1.7 children. It's a statistical abstraction* **2** the quality of being based on an idea rather than reality: *the increasing abstraction of his arguments* **3** absent-mindedness: *an air of abstraction* **4** the process of taking something from a source: *abstraction of water from rivers*

abstruse (*pronounced* ab-**stroos**) *adjective* difficult to understand

absurd *adjective* clearly inappropriate, unsuitable or wrong; ridiculous ♦ **absurdity** *noun* (*plural* **absurdities**) ♦ **absurdly** *adverb*

abundance *noun* a plentiful supply

abundant *adjective* plentiful ♦ **abundantly** *adverb* to a great degree, extremely: *abundantly obvious*

abuse *verb* (*pronounced* a-**byooz**) **1** to use wrongly **2** to insult or speak unkindly to; treat badly ➤ *noun* (*pronounced* a-**byoos**) **1** wrongful use **2** insulting language or behaviour **3** bad or cruel treatment: *sexual abuse/child abuse*

abusive *adjective* insulting or rude ♦ **abusively** *adverb*

abut *verb* (**abutting, abutted**) to lean on or touch something

abysmal (*pronounced* a-**biz**-mal) *adjective* **1** very bad; terrible **2** bottomless ♦ **abysmally** *adverb* (meaning 1)

abyss (*pronounced* a-**bis**) *noun* (*plural* **abysses**) a bottomless depth

AC *abbreviation* alternating current (*compare with*: **DC**)

Ac *symbol, chemistry* actinium

acacia (*pronounced* a-**kay**-sha) *noun* any member of a family of thorny shrubs and trees

academic *adjective* **1** concerned with theoretical education or complicated ideas: *academic qualifications* **2** not practical: *purely of academic interest* **3** of a university etc ➤ *noun* a university or college teacher ♦ **academically** *adverb* (meaning 1): *He's not academically bright, but he's got a lot of common sense*

academy *noun* (*plural* **academies**) **1** a college for special study or training **2** a society for encouraging science or art **3** in Scotland, a senior school

⊙ Comes from Greek *Akademeia*, which was Plato's school of philosophy, named after the garden outside Athens where Plato taught

acanthus *noun* (*plural* **acanthuses**) a Mediterranean ornamental shrub

a cappella (*pronounced* ah ka-**pel**-a) *adjective & adverb, music* sung without accompaniment by musical instruments

accede (*pronounced* ak-**seed**) *verb* (**accede to**) *formal* to agree to

accelerando (*pronounced* ak-sel-er-**an**-doh) *adverb, music* increasingly faster

accelerate *verb* to increase in speed ⊙ Comes from Latin *celer* meaning 'swift'

acceleration *noun* **1** an increasing of speed; the rate of increase of speed **2** *physics* the rate of increase of velocity (velocity/time), equal to force divided by mass

accelerator *noun* **1** a lever or pedal used to increase the speed of a car etc **2** *physics* a piece of equipment designed to increase the velocity of charged particles **3** *chemistry* a substance that increases the rate at which a process occurs, eg a catalyst

accent *noun* **1** (a mark indicating) stress on a syllable or word **2** a mark used in written French and other languages to show the quality of a vowel **3** emphasis: *The accent must be on hard work* **4** the way in which words are pronounced in a particular area etc: *a Scottish accent* **5** *music* emphasis placed on certain notes or chords

accentuate (*pronounced* ak-**sen**-choo-ayt) *verb* to make more obvious; emphasize ♦ **accentuation** *noun*

accept *verb* **1** to take something offered **2** to agree or submit to

❗ Do not confuse with: **except**

acceptable *adjective* satisfactory; pleasing ♦ **acceptably** *adverb*

acceptance *noun* **1** the act of accepting: *total*

acceptance of the situation **2** an official statement that someone or something has been accepted: *an acceptance from Stirling University*

access (*pronounced* **ak**-ses) *noun* **1** a means of approach or entry **2** the right to approach or enter **3** *computing* the right to log on to a system, and to read and edit files that held in it ➤ *verb, computing* to locate or retrieve (information in the memory of a computer)

! Do not confuse with: **excess**

accessibility *noun* **1** being accessible **2** *geography* how easy it is to enter a settlement

accessible (*pronounced* ak-**ses**-i-bl) *adjective* easily approached or reached

accession (*pronounced* ak-**sesh**-on) *noun* the act of taking up a new office, or of becoming king or queen: *accession to the throne*

accessory (*pronounced* ak-**ses**-or-i) *noun* (*plural* **accessories**) **1** an item chosen to match or complement a piece of clothing or an outfit, eg a piece of jewellery, a handbag, etc **2** a helper, especially in crime

accident *noun* **1** an unexpected event causing injury: *a road accident* **2** a mishap: *I had a little accident with the cream* **3** chance: *I came upon the book by accident*

accidental *adjective* happening by chance ➤ *noun, music* a sign, eg sharp or flat, put in front of a note to show it is played higher or lower than indicated by the key signature ◆ **accidentally** *adverb*

accident-prone *adjective* often causing or involved in accidents, usually minor ones

acclaim *verb* to praise enthusiastically ➤ *noun* enthusiastic praise: *met with critical acclaim*

acclaimed *adjective* highly praised: *an acclaimed television drama*

acclamation *noun* noisy signs of approval

acclimatization or **acclimatisation** *noun* becoming accustomed to a new climate or environment

acclimatize or **acclimatise** *verb* to become accustomed to another climate or situation

accolade *noun* a sign or expression of great praise or approval

accommodate *verb* **1** to find room for: *A few families are being accommodated in hotels* **2** to make suitable: *hours which accommodate part-time workers* **3** to be helpful to; supply (with): *We will accommodate any requests from guests on special diets*

accommodating *adjective* making an effort to be helpful

accommodation *noun* **1** a place to live or to stay, lodgings: *student accommodation* **2** *biology* adjustment of the shape of the lens of the eye, in order to focus on distant or nearby objects

accompaniment *noun* **1** something that accompanies **2** the music played while a singer sings etc

accompanist *noun* someone who plays an accompaniment

accompany *verb* (**accompanies, accompanying, accompanied**) **1** to go or be with **2** to play an instrument (eg a piano) while a singer sings etc

accomplice *noun* someone who helps another person, especially to commit a crime

accomplish *verb* **1** to complete **2** to manage to do

accomplished *adjective* **1** completed **2** skilled, talented

accomplishment *noun* **1** completion **2** a personal talent or skill

accord *verb* **1** to agree (with): *These results do not accord with our previous data* **2** to give, grant: *The village elders should always be accorded proper respect* ➤ *noun* an official agreement: *an international accord on nuclear disarmament* • **of your own accord** of your own free will

accordance *noun* agreement: *I am acting in accordance with his wishes*

according *adverb*: **according to 1** as told by: *according to Tom* **2** in relation to: *paid according to your work*

accordingly *adverb* **1** in a way which suits what has just been said or what is happening: *You know your duty, and I expect you to act accordingly* **2** therefore: *She won her case, and accordingly received full compensation*

accordion *noun* a musical instrument with bellows, a keyboard and metal reeds

accordionist *noun* an accordion player

accost *verb* to approach and speak to in a forceful or threatening way

account *verb*: **account for 1** to give a reason (for): *He's had bad news? That would account for his silence* **2** to make up: *Tax accounts for most of the price of a bottle of whisky* ➤ *noun* **1** a bill **2** (*often* **accounts**) a record of finances **3** a description of events etc; an explanation **4** an arrangement by which a bank or building society lets someone have banking or credit facilities • **on account of** because of

accountable *adjective* answerable, responsible: *be accountable for your actions*

accountant *noun* a keeper or inspector of financial accounts ◆ **accountancy** *noun*

accoutrements (*pronounced* a-**koo**-tre-ments) *plural noun* dress and equipment, especially military

accredited *adjective* having official status, or

the official power to act: *an accredited member of the diplomatic delegation*

accrue (*pronounced a-***kroo**) *verb* **1** to accumulate, collect: *The account accrued no interest* **2** to be given or added to: *the benefits that could accrue to the town* ♦ **accrued** *adjective*

accumulate *verb* **1** to collect: *accumulate a large sum of money* **2** to increase: *Income from investments accumulates rapidly*

accumulation *noun* **1** a collection **2** a mass or pile

accumulator *noun* a type of battery used in a car etc

accuracy *noun* exactness

accurate *adjective* correct, exact ♦ **accurately** *adverb*

accursed *adjective* **1** *formal* under a curse **2** hateful

accusation *noun* **1** the act of accusing **2** a statement accusing someone of something

accusative *grammar, noun* in certain languages, eg Latin, Greek and German: the form or case of a noun, pronoun or adjective when it is the object of an action or the point towards which something is moving ➤ *adjective* belonging to or in this case

accuse *verb* (**accuse someone of something** or **of doing something**) to claim that someone has done something wrong ♦ **the accused** *noun* (*plural* **the accused**) the person charged with a crime etc

accuser *noun* a person who accuses or blames

accustomed *adjective* **1** used to: *accustomed to travel* **2** usual: *his accustomed walk along the river bank*

ace *noun* **1** the number one in a pack of playing-cards **2** an expert: *a computer ace* **3** *tennis* an unreturned first serve ➤ *adjective, informal* excellent ⊕ The adjective is a new sense of 'ace', first used in the mid 20th century

acetaldehyde (*pronounced ah-si-***tal**-di-haid) *noun, chemistry* a colourless, pungent liquid used as a solvent and reducing agent (*also called*: **ethanal**)

acetate *noun* (*pronounced* **ah**-se-teit) **1** *chemistry* a salt or ester of acetic acid **2** any of various synthetic fibres that are made from cellulose acetate

acetic acid *noun, chemistry* a clear colourless liquid with acidic properties, present in vinegar (*also called*: **ethanoic acid**)

acetone (*pronounced* **ah**-se-tohn) *noun, chemistry* a colourless, pungent liquid used as a solvent and reducing agent (*also called*: **propanone**)

acetylene (*pronounced a-***set**-il-een) *noun, chemistry* a colourless, flammable gas used for

giving light and heat (*also called*: **ethyne**)

ache *noun* a continuous pain ➤ *verb* to be in continuous pain

achieve *verb* **1** to get (something) done, accomplish **2** to win

achievement *noun* **1** the gaining of something, usually after working hard for it **2** something that has been done or gained by effort

Achilles' heel (*pronounced a-***kil**-eez) *noun* a person's weak or vulnerable point

---

⊕ Named after Achilles, a hero in Homer's *Iliad*, who was invulnerable to weapons except in his heel

---

Achilles' tendon (*pronounced a-***kil**-eez) *noun, anatomy* the tendon situated at the back of the ankle, that connects the calf muscles to the heelbone

acid *noun* **1** *chemistry* a substance that dissolves in water to produce hydrogen ions and which can react with bases to form salts (*contrasted with*: **alkali**) **2** *slang* the drug LSD ➤ *adjective* **1** *chemistry* having the properties of an acid **2** of taste: sharp **3** sarcastic ♦ **acidic** *adjective*

acidify *verb* (**acidifies, acidifying, acidified**) to make or become acid

acidity *noun* (*plural* **acidities**) **1** the state of being acid **2** *chemistry* the extent to which a substance is acid, indicated by its pH value

acid rain *noun* rain containing sulphur and nitrogen compounds and other pollutants

acid test *noun* a decisive test to determine whether something is genuine or valid

---

⊕ From a test using acid to determine whether a substance contained gold

---

acknowledge *verb* **1** to admit the truth of something **2** to admit that you know or are aware of something **3** to (write to) say you have received something **4** to express gratitude or thanks ♦ **acknowledgement** or **acknowledgment** *noun*

acme (*pronounced* **ak**-mi) *noun, formal* the highest point, perfection

acne (*pronounced* **ak**-ni) *noun, medicine* a common skin disease with pimples, caused by overactive sebaceous glands

acorn *noun* the fruit of the oak tree

acoustic (*pronounced a-***koo**-stik) *adjective* **1** of hearing or sound **2** played without an amplifier: *an acoustic guitar*

acoustics (*pronounced a-***koo**-stiks) *noun* **1** *singular* the study of sound **2** *plural* the characteristics of a room etc which affect the way sound is heard in it

acquaint *verb* (**acquaint with**) to make someone familiar with: *Are you acquainted with the facts?*

acquaintance *noun* **1** slight knowledge **2** someone whom you know slightly

acquiesce (*pronounced* ak-wi-**es**) *verb* (**acquiesce to** or **in**) to agree to: *acquiesce to their demands/acquiesce in the terms of this agreement* ♦ **acquiescence** *noun* ♦ **acquiescent** *adjective*

acquire *verb* to obtain, get ♦ **acquired** *adjective* gained; not something you were born with or have inherited

acquisition *noun* **1** the act of getting **2** something obtained: *This painting is the art gallery's most recent acquisition*

acquisitive *adjective* eager to get things, especially desirable items to add to your property

acquit *verb* (**acquitting, acquitted**) to declare (someone) innocent of a crime: *the decision to acquit him of the crime* • **acquit yourself badly** to do badly, be unsuccessful • **acquit yourself well** to do well, be successful

acquittal *noun* a legal judgement of 'not guilty'

acre *noun* a land measure of 4840 square yards or about 4000 square metres

acreage *noun* the number of acres in a piece of land

acrid (*pronounced* **ak**-rid) *adjective* harsh, bitter

acrimonious (*pronounced* ak-rim-**oh**-ni-*us*) *adjective* bitter; accusing

acrimony (*pronounced* **ak**-rim-on-i) *noun* bitterness of feeling or speech

acro- *prefix* tip, point ⊙ Comes from Greek *acron* meaning 'tip'

acrobat *noun* someone who performs gymnastic tricks, tightrope-walking, etc

acrobatic *adjective* able to perform gymnastic tricks; agile

acronym (*pronounced* **ak**-ron-im) *noun* a word formed from the initial letters of other words, eg *radar* for *radio detecting and ranging* ⊙ A word invented in the mid 20th century, and formed from the prefix *acro-*, and Greek *onyma* meaning 'name'

across *adverb & preposition* to or at the other side (of): *swam across the river/winked at him across the table* • **across the board** involving everyone or everything; sweeping

acrostic (*pronounced* a-**kros**-tik) *noun* a poem or puzzle in which the first or last letters of each line, taken in order, spell a word or words

acrylic (*pronounced* a-**kril**-ik) *noun* **1** a synthetically produced fibre **2** paint containing acrylic material ➤ *adjective* made with this fibre

act *verb* **1** to do something **2** to behave in a particular way: *act tough* **3** to play a dramatic role on stage, film, etc ➤ *noun* **1** something done **2** a law passed by a government **3** a section of a play **4** a short piece of entertainment or the

person doing it **5** behaviour that is not a sincere reflection of feelings: *Her shyness is just an act* • **act up** *informal* to behave or act naughtily or badly ⊙ Comes from Latin *actum* meaning 'a thing which has been done'

acting *adjective* temporarily doing someone else's job or duties: *the acting chairman*

actinide series *noun* a series of radioactive elements from atomic number 89 upwards

actinium *noun, chemistry* (symbol **Ac**) a radioactive element found in uranium ores ⊙ Comes from Greek *aktis* meaning 'ray' (from its being radioactive)

action *noun* **1** a deed, an act **2** a law case **3** dramatic events portrayed in a film, play, etc

actionable *adjective* giving reasonable grounds for legal action: *an actionable statement*

action painting *noun, art* a form of painting in which paint is dripped, splattered or smeared on the canvas

action potential *noun, biology* the change in electrical potential across the membrane of a nerve cell when an impulse is being conducted (*compare with:* **resting potential**)

activate *verb* to start (a machine) working

activation energy *noun, chemistry* the least amount of energy needed for a chemical reaction to occur

active *adjective* **1** busy; lively **2** able to perform physical tasks **3** *grammar* describing the form of a verb in which the subject performs the action of the verb, eg 'the dog bit the postman' (*compare with:* **passive**) ♦ **actively** *adverb* in a way which involves doing things: *actively involved in nature conservation*

activist *noun* an active member of something such as a political group: *animal rights activists*

activity *noun* (*plural* **activities**) **1** the state of being active: *The office was a hive of activity* **2** anything that you do, either for pleasure or as part of an organized programme: *outdoor activities/the gang's criminal activities* **3** *physics* the rate at which the atoms of a radioactive substance disintegrate

Act of Parliament *noun, Brit* a statute that has passed through both the House of Commons and the House of Lords, and received royal assent

actor *noun* someone who acts a part in a play or film

actress *noun* (*plural* **actresses**) a female actor

actual *adjective* real, existing in fact

actuality *noun* fact; reality

actually *adverb* really, in fact, as a matter of fact

actuarial (*pronounced* ak-choo-**eir**-i-al) *adjective* relating to actuaries or their work

actuary (*pronounced* **ak**-choo-ar-i) *noun* (*plural* **actuaries**) someone who works out the price of insurance using statistics to assess risk

actuate *verb* to put into action: *a radar detector, actuated by certain frequencies of radio waves*

actuator *noun* a person or device that puts something into action

acumen (*pronounced* **ak**-yuw-men) *noun* quickness of understanding: *He owes his success to his keen business acumen*

acupuncture (*pronounced* ak-yuw-pungk-cher) *noun* a method of treating illness by piercing the skin with needles at specific pressure points ♦ **acupuncturist** *noun* ⊙ Comes from Latin *acus* meaning 'needle'

acute *adjective* **1** quick at understanding **2** sudden and severe: *acute back pain/acute difficulties/acute appendicitis* (*compare with*: **chronic**) **3** *maths* of an angle: less than 90° (*compare with*: **obtuse, reflex**) • **acute accent** a forward-leaning stroke (´) placed over letters in some languages to show their pronunciation ♦ **acutely** *adverb* extremely, painfully: *an acutely embarrassing situation/He was acutely aware that he was being observed* ♦ **acuteness** *noun* the quality of being acute, used especially about mental perception

AD *abbreviation* in the year of our Lord (from Latin *anno Domini*). Used with a date, eg AD1900, to show that it refers to the time after, and not before, the birth of Christ (*compare with*: **BC**)

ad *noun, informal* an advertisement

adage (*pronounced* **a**-dij) *noun* an old saying, a proverb

adagio (*pronounced* a-**dah**-jee-oh) *noun* (*plural* **adagios**), *music* a slow-paced piece of music ⊙ In Italian *ad agio* means 'at ease'

adamant (*pronounced* **ad**-am-ant) *adjective* not going to change your mind or opinion

Adam's apple *noun* the natural lump which sticks out from a man's throat, a projection of the thyroid cartilage

adapt *verb* (**adapt to**) to make suitable for; alter so as to fit

adaptable *adjective* easily altered to suit new conditions

adaptation *noun* **1** a change in the form of something to make it suitable for another situation or purpose: *a popular television adaptation of this classic novel* **2** *biology* a change in the structure or behaviour of a living organism that improves its chances of survival in its environment

adaptor *noun* a device allowing an electrical plug to be used in a socket for which it was not designed, or several plugs to be used on the same socket

A/D converter *noun, computing* an analogue-to-digital converter

add *verb* **1** to make one thing join another to give a sum total or whole **2** to mix in: *add water to the dough* **3** to say further • **add up 1** to combine, grow to a large quantity: *add up the different quantities/All these expenses soon add up* **2** to make sense, seem logical: *His story just doesn't add up*

addendum (*pronounced* a-**den**-dum) *noun* (*plural* **addenda**) something added

adder *noun* the common name of the viper, a poisonous snake

addict (*pronounced* **a**-dikt) *noun* **1** someone who is dependent on a drug **2** *informal* someone who is extremely fond of a hobby: *a chess addict*

addicted (*pronounced* a-**dik**-tid) *adjective* (**addicted to**) unable to do without

addiction *noun* dependency on a drug etc

addictive (*pronounced* a-**dikt**-iv) *adjective* more and more difficult to do without, the more often it is used

addition *noun* **1** the act of adding **2** something added

additional *adjective* extra; more than usual ♦ **additionally** *adverb* as well as that: *William was not happy at home. Additionally, he was bullied at school*

additive *noun* a chemical etc added to another substance

address *verb* **1** to speak to **2** to write the address on (a letter etc) ➤ *noun* (*plural* **addresses**) **1** the name of the house, street and town where someone lives, works, etc **2** *computing* a name and location where you can be contacted by e-mail **3** *computing* the place where a particular piece of information is stored in memory **4** a formal speech

address book *noun* **1** a notebook in which names and addresses can be entered **2** *computing* a facility on a computer for storing details of e-mail addresses

addressee *noun* the person to whom a letter etc is addressed

adduct *verb* of a muscle: to bring a part of the body (such as an arm or finger) towards another or towards the centre line of the body (*compare with*: **abduct** sense 2) ♦ **adduction** *noun* ♦ **adductor** *noun*

adenoids (*pronounced* **a**-de-noydz) *plural noun, anatomy* a pair of lymph glands at the back of the nose which can swell and make it difficult to breathe ♦ **adenoidal** *adjective*

adept (*pronounced* a-**dept**) *adjective* very skilful

adequacy *noun* being adequate; sufficiency

adequate *adjective* sufficient, enough ♦ **adequately** *adverb*

adhan see **azan**

adhere *verb* **1** to stick (to): *adhere to a clean, dry* *surface* **2** to give support (to), follow: *adhere to a strict dress code*

adherent *adjective* sticking (to) ➤ *noun* a follower or supporter of a cause etc
♦ **adherence** *noun*

adhesion *noun* **1** the act of sticking (to) **2** *medicine* a band of connective tissue that develops between structures that are normally separate, especially after injury or surgery

adhesive *adjective* sticky, gummed ➤ *noun* something which makes things stick to each other

ad hoc *adjective* set up for a particular purpose only

Adi-Granth (*pronounced* **uh**-dhee grunt) *noun* the Guru Granth Sahib, the holy book of the Sikh religion

ad infinitum (*pronounced* ad in-fi-**nai**-tum) *adverb* for ever

adipose tissue *noun, anatomy* body tissue that stores fat and provides insulation and an energy reserve

adjacent (*pronounced* a-**jei**-sent) *adjective* (**adjacent to**) lying next to

adjacent angles *plural noun, maths* a pair of angles that have the same vertex and one side in common

adjective *noun* a word which tells something about a noun, eg 'the *black* cat,' 'times are *hard*'
♦ **adjectival** *adjective*

adjoin *verb* to be joined to: *A large shed adjoins the house* ♦ **adjoining** *adjective*

adjourn *verb* **1** to stop (a meeting etc) with the intention of continuing it at another time or place **2** (**adjourn to**) to go to another place: *adjourn to the lounge* ♦ **adjournment** *noun*

adjudicate *verb* **1** to give a judgement on (a dispute etc) **2** to act as a judge at a competition
♦ **adjudication** *noun*

adjudicator *noun* someone who adjudicates

adjunct (*pronounced* **aj**-ungkt) *noun* something joined or added

adjust *verb* to rearrange or alter to suit the circumstances ♦ **adjustable** *adjective*
♦ **adjustment** *noun*

ad-lib *verb* (**ad-libbing, ad-libbed**) to speak without any plan or preparation ➤ *adjective* without preparation

administer *verb* **1** to manage or govern: *South Pacific islands administered by France* **2** to carry out (the law etc) **3** to give (help, medicine, etc): *A qualified doctor must administer the drug to patients*

administrate *verb* to manage or govern

administration *noun* **1** management **2** (the body that carries on) the government of a country etc

administrative *adjective* having to do with

management or government

administrator *noun* someone involved in the administration of a country etc

admirable *adjective* worthy of being admired
♦ **admirably** *adverb*

admiral *noun* the commander of a navy

Admiralty *noun* (**the Admiralty**) the government office which manages naval affairs

admire *verb* **1** to think very highly of **2** to look at with pleasure ♦ **admiration** *noun* ♦ **admirer** *noun*

admissible *adjective* allowable: *admissible evidence*

admission *noun* **1** (the price of) being let in **2** anything admitted

admit *verb* (**admitting, admitted**) **1** to let in **2** to acknowledge the truth of, confess **3** (**admit of**) to leave room for, allow: *admits of no other explanation*

admittance *noun* the right or permission to enter

admittedly *adverb* as I must admit: *Admittedly my work could be better*

admonish *verb* **1** to warn **2** to rebuke, scold

admonition *noun* a warning ♦ **admonitory** *adjective*

ad nauseam (*pronounced* ad **naw**-zi-am) *adverb* to a tiresome degree

ado (*pronounced* a-**doo**) *noun* trouble, fuss

adolescent *noun* someone between a child and an adult in age ➤ *adjective* of this age
♦ **adolescence** *noun*

adopt *verb* **1** to take as your own (especially a child of other parents) **2** to take (eg precautions), choose formally: *adopt certain new measures in the fight against crime* ♦ **adoption** *noun*

adoptive *adjective* adopted, taken as your own: *her adoptive country*

adorable *adjective* very loveable

adoration *noun* **1** worship **2** great love

adore *verb* **1** to love very much **2** to worship

adorn *verb* to decorate (with ornaments etc): *Her head was adorned with flowers*

adornment *noun* ornament

ADP *abbreviation* **1** *computing* automatic data processing **2** *chemistry* adenosine diphosphate, an organic compound formed by the breakdown of ATP

adrenal (*pronounced* a-**dree**-nal) *noun, anatomy* **1** to do with the kidneys **2** on or near the kidneys **3** to do with the adrenal glands

adrenal gland *noun, anatomy* either of two glands, one above each kidney, producing adrenaline

adrenaline or **adrenalin** (*pronounced* a-**dren**-a-lin) *noun* a hormone produced in response to fear, anger, etc, which causes an increase in heartbeat and diverts blood towards the muscles

adrift *adverb* drifting, floating

adroit (*pronounced a-***droit**) *adjective* skilful

ADSL *abbreviation, computing* Asymmetric Digital Subscriber Line, a fast Internet connection over a phone line

adsorb *verb* of a solid or a liquid: to accumulate a thin film of the molecules of a gas or liquid on its surface ◆ **adsorbent** *adjective* ◆ **adsorption** *noun*

adulation (*pronounced* ad-yuw-**lei**-shun) *noun* great flattery ◆ **adulatory** *adjective*

adult *adjective* grown up ➤ *noun* a grown-up person

adulterate *verb* to make impure by adding something else ◆ **adulteration** *noun*

adultery *noun* unfaithfulness to a husband or wife ◆ **adulterer** or **adulteress** *noun*

adulthood *noun* the state of being an adult

adult literacy *noun* the percentage of the adult population in a given area who are able to read and write

advance *verb* **1** to go forward **2** to put forward (a plan etc): *He advanced a number of proposals* **3** to help the progress of: *research which has advanced our treatment of cancer* **4** to pay before the usual or agreed time: *Could you advance me £50 and take it off my next pay cheque?* ➤ *noun* **1** movement forward **2** improvement **3** a loan of money • **in advance** beforehand

advanced *adjective* **1** having progressed well: *advanced for her age* **2** modern: *advanced technology*

advancement *noun* progress

advantage *noun* **1** a better position, superiority **2** gain or benefit ➤ *verb* to help, benefit • **take advantage of** to make use of (a situation, person, etc) in such a way as to benefit yourself

advantageous *adjective* profitable; helpful

advent (*pronounced* ad-vent) *noun* **1** coming, arrival: *before the advent of television* **2** (**Advent**) in the Christian church, the four weeks before Christmas

adventitious *adjective* **1** happening by chance **2** *biology* denoting tissues or organs that grow in an unusual position, eg a root growing upwards from a stem

adventure *noun* a bold or exciting undertaking or experience

adventure playground *noun* a playground with things for children to climb on etc

adventurer *noun* **1** someone who takes risks, especially in the hope of making a lot of money **2** a mercenary soldier

adventurous *adjective* taking risks, liking adventure

adverb *noun* a word which adds something to the meaning of a verb, adjective or other adverb, eg 'eat *slowly*,' '*extremely* hard,' '*very* carefully' ◆ **adverbial** *adjective*

adversary (*pronounced* **ad**-ver-sar-i) *noun* (*plural* **adversaries**) an enemy; an opponent

adverse (*pronounced* **ad**-vers) *adjective* unfavourable: *adverse criticism*

⚠ Do not confuse with: **averse**

adversity *noun* (*plural* **adversities**) misfortune

advert *noun, informal* an advertisement

advertise *verb* **1** to make known to the public **2** to stress the good points of (a product for sale)

advertisement *noun* a photograph, short film, etc intended to persuade the public to buy a particular product

advice *noun* **1** something said to help someone trying to make a decision etc **2** a formal notice

⚠ Do not confuse with: **advise**. To help you remember: 'ice' is a noun, 'ise' is not.

advisable *adjective* wise, sensible ◆ **advisability** *noun*

advise *verb* **1** to give advice to **2** to recommend (an action etc) ◆ **adviser** or **advisor** *noun*

⚠ Do not confuse with: **advice**. To help you remember: 'ice' is a noun, so 'ise' must be the verb.

advisedly *adverb* after careful thought; on purpose

advisory *adjective* giving advice

advocate *noun* (*pronounced* **ad**-vo-kat) **1** someone who supports or recommends a proposal, cause, etc **2** in Scotland, a lawyer who pleads cases in court ➤ *verb* (*pronounced* **ad**-vo-keit) to argue for or recommend: *I do not advocate the use of force* ◆ **advocacy** *noun*

aegis (*pronounced* **ee**-jis) *noun* protection; patronage

aeolian deposits (*pronounced* ee-**oh**-li-an) *plural noun, geography* sediments carried and deposited by wind, eg desert sands, loess, etc

aeon or **eon** (*pronounced* **ee**-on) *noun* **1** a very long period of time, an age **2** a very large division of time used in geology

aerate (*pronounced* **eir**-eit) *verb* to put air or another gas into (a liquid)

aerial *adjective* **1** of, in or from the air: *aerial photography* **2** placed high up or overhead: *aerial railway* ➤ *noun* a wire or rod (or a set of these) by which radio or television signals are received or sent

aero- *prefix* of air or aircraft ⊕ Comes from Greek *aer* meaning 'air'

aerobatics *plural noun* stunts performed by an aircraft

aerobe *noun, biology* any organism that requires oxygen to survive (*compare with*: **anaerobe**)

aerobic *adjective* **1** *biology* of an organism: requiring oxygen in order to obtain energy by respiration (*compare with*: **anaerobic**) **2** relating to aerobics **3** of some forms of physical exercise, eg walking, jogging, swimming: producing an increase in the rate at which the body uses oxygen

aerobic respiration *noun, biology* the process in which cells use oxygen to break down foodstuffs, especially carbohydrates, releasing energy and creating carbon dioxide and water (*compare with*: **anaerobic respiration**)

aerobics *singular noun* a system of physical exercise which aims to strengthen the heart and lungs by increasing the body's oxygen consumption

aerodrome *noun* a landing and maintenance station for aircraft

aerodynamic *adjective* designed to promote more efficient movement through air

aerodynamics *singular noun* the study of the movement of air relative to moving objects, eg aircraft, cars, etc

aeronautics *singular noun* the science or art of navigation in the air

aeroplane or *US* **airplane** *noun* a flying machine with fixed wings and an engine (*short form* **plane**)

aerosol *noun* a container of liquid and gas under pressure, from which the liquid is squirted as a mist

aerospace *adjective* referring to the design and development of aircraft and spacecraft: *the aerospace industry*

aesthetic (*pronounced* ees-**thet**-ik) *adjective* **1** having to do with beauty or its appreciation **2** artistic, pleasing to the eye ♦ **aesthetically** *adverb*

aestivation or *US* **estivation** (*pronounced* es-ti-vei-shon *noun, biology* **1** in certain animals, eg tropical amphibians: a state of inactivity that enables them to survive prolonged periods of heat or drought **2** the arrangement of the petals and sepals in a flower bud

aetiology or *US* **etiology** (*pronounced* ee-ti-ol-oj-i) *noun* (the study of) the causes or origins of a disease

afar *adverb, formal* a long way away

affable *adjective* pleasant, easy to speak to ♦ **affability** *noun*

affair *noun* **1** events etc connected with one person or thing: *the Watergate affair* **2** (**affairs**) personal concerns, transactions, etc: *His affairs*

seemed to be in order **3** business, concern: *that's not your affair* **4** a love affair

affect *verb* **1** to act upon **2** to have an effect on; make feel strong emotions **3** to pretend to feel etc: *affect an air of indifference* ⊙ Meanings 1 and 2 come from Latin *afficere* meaning 'to do something to'; meaning 3 comes from Latin *affectare* meaning 'to strive after'

! Do not confuse with: **effect**.
Affect is usually a verb. **Effect** is usually a noun.
To **affect** means 'to have an **effect** on'.

affectation *noun* pretence

affected *adjective* **1** feeling emotional **2** not natural, sham

affecting *adjective* emotionally moving

affection *noun* a strong liking

affectionate *adjective* loving

affidavit (*pronounced* af-i-**dei**-vit) *noun, law* a written statement made on oath

affiliated *adjective* (**affiliated with** or **to**) connected with or attached to ♦ **affiliation** *noun*

affinity *noun* (*plural* **affinities**) a close likeness or agreement

affirm *verb* to state firmly: *He affirmed that they had an excellent safety record* ♦ **affirmation** *noun*

affirmative *adjective* saying 'yes'

affix *verb* to attach to

afflict *verb* to cause pain or suffering to: *What sadness afflicts him?*

affliction *noun* great suffering, misery

affluent (*pronounced* **af**-luw-ent) *adjective* wealthy ♦ **affluence** *noun*

afford *verb* **1** to be able to pay for **2** *formal* to give, provide with: *I hoped the situation would afford me a chance to speak to him*

afforest *verb* to cover land with forest ♦ **afforestation** *noun*

affray *noun* a fight, a brawl

affront *verb* to insult openly ➤ *noun* an insult

aflatoxin *noun, biology* a toxic substance, produced by a fungus, which contaminates stored corn, soya beans, peanuts, etc in warm, humid regions

afloat *adverb & adjective* floating

afoot *adverb* happening or about to happen: *I could tell something was afoot*

aforesaid (*pronounced* a-**fawr**-sed) *adjective, formal* said or named before: *the aforesaid person*

afraid *adjective* **1** frightened **2** *informal* sorry to have to admit that: *I'm afraid there are no tickets left*

afresh *adverb* once again, anew

African National Congress *noun* a political movement in South Africa that played an important part in ending apartheid

Afro *noun* (*plural* **Afros**) a hairstyle consisting of thick bushy curls standing out from the head

Afro- *prefix* African: *Afro-American*

aft (*pronounced* ahft) *adverb* near or towards the stern of a vessel

after *preposition* **1** later in time than: *after dinner* **2** following: *arrived one after another/day after day* **3** in memory or honour of: *named after his father* **4** in pursuit of: *run after the bus* **5** about: *asked after her health* **6** despite: *After all my efforts, it still didn't work* **7** in the style of: *after Rubens* ➤ *adverb* later in time or place: *We left soon after* ➤ *conjunction* later than the time when: *After she arrived, things improved* • **after all 1** all things considered: *After all, he's still young* **2** despite everything said or done before: *I went after all*

after- *prefix* later in time or place: *aftertaste/ afterthought*

afterbirth *noun* the placenta and membranes expelled from the uterus after giving birth

after-effect *noun* a circumstance or event, often an unpleasant one, that follows as the result of something

afterlife *noun* the continued existence of the spirit or soul after death

aftermath *noun* the bad results of something: *the aftermath of the election*

> ⊙ Originally a second mowing after the main harvest

afternoon *noun* the time between noon and evening ➤ *adjective* taking place in the afternoon

aftershave *noun* a lotion used on the face after shaving

aftershock *noun* a small earthquake that follows the main shock of a large earthquake

afterthought *noun* a later thought

afterwards *adverb* later

Ag *symbol, chemistry* silver ⊙ Comes from Latin *argentum* meaning 'silver'

again *adverb* **1** once more: *Say that again* **2** in or into the original state, place, etc: *there and back again* **3** on the other hand: *Again, I might be wrong* **4** *informal* at another later time: *See you again*

against *preposition* **1** in opposition to: *against the law/fight against injustice* **2** in the opposite direction to: *against the wind* **3** on a background of: *clouds against the sky* **4** close to, touching: *lean against the wall* **5** as protection from: *guard against infection*

agape[1] *adjective* **1** of the mouth: gaping; open wide **2** of a person: very surprised

agape[2] (*pronounced* ag-a-pei) *noun, Christianity* Christian brotherly love ⊙ Comes

from Greek, literally meaning 'love'

agaric (*pronounced* a-ga-rik) *noun, botany* a type of fungus that has a vertical stem supporting a cap, eg a mushroom

age *noun* **1** a long period of time **2** the time someone or something has lived or existed ➤ *verb* (**ageing** or **aging, aged**) to grow or make visibly older: *He has aged ten years* (= seems to have grown ten years older) *in the past six months/That hat ages her* (= makes her look older) • **of age** legally an adult

aged *adjective* **1** (*pronounced* **eij**-id) old **2** (*pronounced* eijd) of the age of: *aged five*

ageism *noun* discrimination on grounds of age ♦ **ageist** *adjective*

agency *noun* (*plural* **agencies**) **1** the office or business of an agent **2** action; means by which something is done

agenda *noun* a list of things to be done, especially at a meeting

agent *noun* **1** someone who acts for another **2** someone or something that causes an effect **3** a spy **4** a substance that can cause a chemical reaction (*compare with:* **reagent**)

agent provocateur (*pronounced* **ah**-szong praw-vaw-ka-**toor**) *noun* (*plural* **agents provocateurs** – *pronounced* **ah**-szong praw-vaw-ka-**toor**) someone employed to lead others in illegal acts for which they will be punished

age of consent *noun* the age at which a person is old enough to agree to sexual intercourse without breaking the law

age of criminal responsibility *noun* the age at which a person is old enough to be charged with and punished for a crime

agglutinate *verb* **1** to stick or glue together **2** *biology* of red blood cells, bacteria, etc: to clump together and form a visible precipitate ♦ **agglutination** *noun* ⊙ Comes from Latin *agglutinare* meaning 'to glue together'

aggrandize or **aggrandise** *verb* to make greater

aggrandizement or **aggrandisement** (*pronounced* a-**gran**-diz-ment) *noun* the process of making yourself seem greater or more powerful: *You should not enter politics for self-aggrandizement*

aggravate *verb* **1** to make worse **2** *informal* to annoy ♦ **aggravating** *adjective* ♦ **aggravation** *noun*

aggregate (*pronounced* ag-ri-gat) *noun* a total

aggressive *adjective* **1** ready to attack first **2** quarrelsome ♦ **aggression** *noun* ♦ **aggressively** *adverb* ♦ **aggressor** *noun*

aggrieved (*pronounced* a-**greevd**) *adjective* hurt, upset

aghast (*pronounced* a-**gahst**) *adjective* struck with horror

agile *adjective* able to move, change direction, etc quickly and easily ♦ **agility** *noun*

aging population or **ageing population** *noun, geography* a population where there is a high proportion of elderly people (*also:* **greying population**)

agitate *verb* **1** to stir up **2** to excite, disturb ♦ **agitated** *adjective* ♦ **agitation** *noun*

agitator *noun* someone who stirs up others: *political agitators*

agnostic (*pronounced* ag-**nos**-tik) *noun* someone who believes it is impossible to know whether God exists or not ▸ *adjective* having this belief ♦ **agnosticism** *noun*

ago *adverb* in the past, earlier: *That happened five years ago*

agog (*pronounced* a-**gog**) *adjective* eager, excited

agonist *noun* a muscle the relaxation of which opposes the contraction of another muscle (the **antagonist**)

agonize or **agonise** *verb* (to cause) to worry intensely or suffer great anxiety about something

agonized or **agonised** *adjective* showing great pain or suffering: *an agonized expression*

agonizing or **agonising** *adjective* causing great pain or suffering

agony *noun* (*plural* **agonies**) great pain

agoraphobia (*pronounced* ag-ra-**foh**-bi-a) *noun* great fear of open spaces

agoraphobic (*pronounced* ag-ra-**foh**-bik) *noun & adjective* (someone) suffering from agoraphobia

agrarian *adjective* of farmland or farming

agree *verb* **1** to be alike in opinions, decisions, etc **2** to say that you will do something: *Toby has agreed to play us a tune* **3** (**agree with**) to suit **4** (**agree with**) to cause no problems in digestion: *The fish didn't agree with me* **5** to be the same or consistent, fit together: *I'd like to believe them both, but their stories don't agree* **6** (often **agree with**) *grammar* of words in a phrase, clause or sentence: to be in forms representing the same number, person, gender or case

agreeable *adjective* **1** pleasant **2** ready to agree ♦ **agreeably** *adverb*

agreement *noun* **1** likeness (especially of opinions) **2** a written statement making a bargain **3** *grammar* the situation where words in a phrase, clause or sentence are in forms representing the same number, person, gender or case

agri- *prefix* of fields, land use, or farming ⊙ Comes from Latin *ager* meaning 'field'

agribusiness *noun* all the operations involved in supplying the market with farm produce, including growing, providing farm machinery, distribution, etc

Agricultural Revolution *noun, history* the gradual movement in Britain, in the eighteenth and nineteenth centuries, away from subsistence farming towards intensive farming

agriculture *noun* the cultivation of the land, farming ♦ **agricultural** *adjective*

agro- *prefix* of fields, land use or farming: *agrobiology* (= the study of plant nutrition)/ *agrochemical* (= a chemical used in farming the land) ⊙ Comes from Greek *agros* meaning 'field'

agroforestry *noun* the cultivation of trees and shrubs and the raising of agricultural crops or animals on the same land

aground *adjective & adverb* stuck on the bottom of the sea or a river: *run aground*

ahead *adverb* in front; in advance: *finishing ahead of time*

-aholic or **-oholic** *suffix* having an addiction to: *workaholic/chocaholic* ⊙ Comes from the ending of the word alc*oholic*

AI *abbreviation* artificial intelligence

aid *verb* to help, assist ▸ *noun* **1** help **2** money, equipment, etc given to people in need, eg in developing countries

aide (*pronounced* eid) *noun* an assistant or adviser to a government leader

AIDS or **Aids** *abbreviation, medicine* Acquired Immune Deficiency Syndrome, a disease which destroys the immune system

aikido (*pronounced* ai-**kee**-doh) *noun* a Japanese martial art using pressure against the joints

ail *verb, old* to be or make ill: *My poor father is ailing/What ails thee?*

ailing *adjective* **1** troubled, in a bad state: *the ailing steel industry* **2** ill

ailment *noun* an illness: *minor ailments*

aim *verb* **1** to point (a gun etc) (at) **2** to intend to do: *We were aiming to get there early* **3** to have as your purpose ▸ *noun* **1** the act of, or skill in, aiming **2** the point aimed at, goal, intention

aimless *adjective* without aim or purpose ♦ **aimlessly** *adverb*

air *noun* **1** the mixture of gases (mainly oxygen and nitrogen) which we breathe; the atmosphere **2** a light breeze **3** fresh air **4** space overhead **5** a tune **6** the look or manner (of a person) ▸ *verb* **1** to expose to the air **2** to make known (an opinion etc) • **on the air** broadcasting

airbag *noun* a bag which automatically inflates inside a car on impact to protect the driver or passenger from injury

airbed *noun* a mattress which can be inflated

air bladder *noun, biology* **1** a cavity or sac

containing air **2** a swim bladder

airborne *adjective* in the air, flying

airbrush *verb* a device for painting that uses compressed air to form a spray ➤ *verb* to improve (a picture of someone or something) by masking defects

air-conditioned *adjective* equipped with a system for filtering and controlling the temperature of the air ♦ **air-conditioner** *noun* ♦ **air-conditioning** *noun*

aircraft *noun* (*plural* **aircraft**) a flying machine

aircraft carrier *noun* a warship that aircraft can take off from and land on

airfield *noun* an expanse of land used by aircraft for landing and take-off

air force *noun* the branch of the armed forces using aircraft

airgun *noun* a gun worked by means of compressed air

airhead *noun informal* an idiot

airily *adverb* in a light and not very serious way

airing *noun* **1** the act of exposing to the air: *give the room an airing* **2** the act of talking about something openly: *give your views an airing*

airless *adjective* stuffy, with no circulation of fresh air

airlift *noun* the transporting of large numbers of people or large amounts of goods in aircraft when other routes are blocked ➤ *verb* to transport (people, goods, etc) in this way: *They were airlifted to safety*

airline *noun* a company which provides travel by aeroplane

airlock *noun* **1** a bubble in a pipe obstructing the flow of a liquid **2** a compartment with two doors for entering and leaving an airtight spaceship etc

air mass *noun, meteorology* a vast horizontal body of air

airplane US for **aeroplane**

air pocket *noun* an area of reduced pressure in the air, or a downward current, which can cause an aircraft to suddenly lose height

airport *noun* a place where aircraft land and take off, with buildings for customs, waiting-rooms, etc

air raid *noun* an attack by aircraft

airship *noun* a large balloon which can be steered and driven

airstream *noun* a flow of air

airtight *adjective* made so that air cannot pass in or out

airway *noun* **1** a passage for air **2** in the body: the route by which air enters the lungs **3** a route used by aircraft

airy *adjective* (**airier, airiest**) **1** of or like the air **2** well supplied with fresh air **3** light-hearted

aisle (*pronounced* ail) *noun* **1** the side part of a

church **2** a passage between seats in a theatre etc

ajar *adverb* partly open: *leave the door ajar*

aka (*pronounced* ei-kei-**ei**) *abbreviation* also known as: *Stevens, aka The Fly*

akimbo *adverb* (*placed after the noun*) with hand on hip and elbow bent outward

⊙ From an Old Norse term meaning 'bowed' or 'curved'

akin *adjective* similar

Al *symbol, chemistry* aluminium

alabaster *noun* a type of white stone used for ornaments etc

à la carte *adjective & adverb* with each dish chosen and priced separately ⊙ Comes from French, meaning 'according to the menu'

alack *interjection, old* alas

alacrity *noun* briskness; cheerful readiness

alarm *noun* **1** sudden fear **2** something which makes someone take action or warns of danger ➤ *verb* to frighten ♦ **alarming** *adjective*

alarmist *noun* someone who frightens others needlessly

alas *interjection* a cry showing grief or disappointment

albatross *noun* (*plural* **albatrosses**) a type of large seabird

albinism *noun, biology* the inherited lack of pigmentation, which in vertebrates is caused by a lack of the enzyme responsible for the production of melanin

albino (*pronounced* ahl-**been**-oh or US ahl-**bain**-oh) *noun* (*plural* **albinos**), *biology* **1** an animal or human having an abnormal lack of pigmentation in the hair, skin and eyes **2** a plant having a total or partial lack of chlorophyll or other pigments ⊙ Comes from Portuguese, originally from Latin *albus* meaning 'white'

album *noun* **1** a book with blank pages for holding photographs, stamps, etc **2** a record, CD, etc with multiple tracks

albumen (*pronounced* **al**-byuw-men) *noun* the white of eggs

albumin (*pronounced* **al**-byuw-min) *noun, chemistry* a water-soluble protein found in egg white, milk, blood serum, etc

alchemist *noun* someone who practised alchemy

alchemy *noun* an early form of chemistry aimed at changing other metals into gold

alcohol *noun* **1** *chemistry* a compound containing one or more hydroxyl groups and used in dyes, perfumes, etc **2** the compound ethanol, as found in alcoholic drinks **3** drink containing ethanol

alcoholic *adjective* of or containing alcohol ➤ *noun* someone addicted to alcohol

alcoholism *noun* physical dependence on or addiction to alcohol

alcove *noun* a recess in a room's wall

alder *noun* a type of tree which grows beside ponds and rivers

alderman *noun* 1 *history* a councillor next in rank to the mayor of a town etc 2 *US* a member of the governing body of a city

ale *noun* a drink made from malt, hops, etc; beer

alert *noun* signal to be ready for action ➤ *verb* to make alert, warn: *alert them to the dangers of the job* ➤ *adjective* 1 watchful 2 quick-thinking • **on the alert** on the watch (for)

alfresco *adverb & adjective* in the open air ☺ Comes from Italian *al fresco* meaning 'in the fresh air'

algae (*pronounced* al-gi or al-ji) *plural noun* (*singular* **alga**) a group of simple water plants which includes seaweed

algebra *noun* a part of mathematics in which letters and signs are used to represent numbers

-algia *suffix* forms nouns relating to pain: *neuralgia/nostalgia* ☺ Comes from Greek *algos* meaning 'pain'

algorithm *noun, maths* a procedure involving a logical series of steps to find the solution to a problem ♦ **algorithmic** *adjective*

alias *adverb* also known as: *Mitchell alias Grassic Gibbon* ➤ *noun* (*plural* **aliases**) a false name

alibi *noun* 1 *law* the plea that someone charged with a crime was elsewhere when it was done 2 the state or fact of being elsewhere when a crime was committed

alien *adjective* 1 foreign 2 (**alien to**) not in keeping with: *alien to her nature* ➤ *noun* 1 a foreigner 2 a being from elsewhere in the universe

alienate *verb* to make someone unfriendly, probably by causing them to feel unwanted or rejected: *We must be careful not to alienate our old supporters*

alight¹ *verb* (**alighting, alighted**) 1 to climb etc down: *alight from the train* 2 to settle, land

alight² *adjective & adverb* on fire, burning

align (*pronounced* a-**lain**) *verb* 1 to put in line or bring into line: *Align the text with the margin* 2 to take sides in an argument etc: *align yourself with environmentalists*

alignment *noun* arrangement in a line

alike *adjective* like one another, similar ➤ *adverb* in the same way, similarly

alimentary *adjective* of food

alimentary canal *noun, anatomy* the passage in the body, beginning at the mouth and ending at the anus, through which food passes

alimony *noun* an allowance paid by a husband to his wife, or a wife to her husband, when they are legally separated

aliphatic *adjective, chemistry* of an organic compound: with carbon atoms arranged in chains rather than rings (*compare with*: **aromatic** sense 2)

alive *adjective* 1 living 2 full of activity • **alive to** aware of

alkali *noun* (*plural* **alkalis** or **alkalies**), *chemistry* a substance that dissolves in water to produce hydroxide ions, and neutralizes acids to form salts (*compare with*: **acid**)

alkali metal *noun, chemistry* a metal, eg sodium or potassium, that forms an alkaline solution in water

alkaline *adjective, chemistry* having the properties of an alkali

alkaline-earth metal *noun, chemistry* a metallic element, such as magnesium or calcium, that is only found in nature in compounds

alkalinity *noun* (*plural* **alkalinities**) 1 the state of being alkaline 2 *chemistry* the extent to which a substance is alkaline, indicated by its pH value

alkaloid *noun, chemistry* one of many organic compounds containing nitrogen, with toxic or medicinal properties

alkane *noun, chemistry* a hydrocarbon whose carbon atoms form chains linked by single bonds

alkene *noun, chemistry* a hydrocarbon whose carbon atoms form chains linked by one or more double bonds

all *adjective & pronoun* 1 every one (of): *We are all invited/All letters will be answered* 2 the whole (of): *painted all the house* ➤ *adverb* wholly, completely: *dressed all in red* • **all in** 1 with everything included: *all-in price* 2 *informal* exhausted: *I felt completely all in* • **all over** 1 over the whole of 2 everywhere 3 finished, ended • **all ready** totally ready

❗ Do not use this as an alternative spelling for 'already'.

all right *adjective* in a normal state; not hurt, unhappy or feeling strange

❗ It is best to avoid the spelling 'alright', since some people say it is incorrect.

all together *adverb* together as a group

❗ Do not use this as an alternative spelling for 'altogether'.

all ways *adverb* in every way possible

❗ Do not use this as an alternative spelling for 'always'.

Allah *noun, Islam* God

allay *verb* 1 to make less, relieve: *tried to allay my fears* 2 to calm

allege verb to say without proof: allege that this man was involved in the crime ♦ **allegation** noun

alleged adjective claimed to be: the alleged criminal ♦ **allegedly** adverb

allegiance noun loyalty

allegory noun (plural **allegories**) a story or fable which deals with a subject in a way which is meant to suggest a deeper, more serious subject ♦ **allegorical** adjective

allegretto music, adverb quick and lively, but less so than allegro ➤ noun (plural **allegrettos**) a piece of music to be played in a fairly quick and lively way ⊙ Comes from Italian, diminutive of allegro

allegro music, adverb in quick and lively way ➤ noun (plural **allegros**) a piece of music to be played in a quick and lively way ⊙ Comes from Italian, meaning 'lively'

allele noun any of the alternative forms of a particular gene, of which each individual inherits two (one from each parent), different combinations of which produce different characteristics

allergen noun, medicine any substance that causes an allergic reaction in someone

allergy noun (plural **allergies**), medicine abnormal sensitiveness of the body to certain substances (**allergens**): an allergy to cow's milk ♦ **allergic** adjective

alleviate verb to make lighter, lessen: alleviate their suffering ♦ **alleviation** noun

alley noun (plural **alleys**) 1 a narrow passage or lane 2 an enclosure for bowls or skittles

alliance noun a joining together of two people, nations, etc for a common cause

allied adjective joined by an alliance

alligator noun a large reptile like a crocodile but with a broader head and blunter snout

alliteration noun the repetition of the same sound at the beginning of two or more words close together, eg 'round and round the rugged rock' or 'sing a song of sixpence' ♦ **alliterative** adjective

allo- prefix other, different, from outside ⊙ Comes from Greek allos meaning 'other'

allocate verb to allot, share out, reserve for a particular purpose: The task of collecting the data has been allocated to you ♦ **allocation** noun

allopathic adjective of medicine: conventional; treating disease with drugs which have an effect on the body which is opposite to that of the disease (contrasted with: **homeopathic**)

allot verb (**allotting, allotted**) to give each person a share of: A ten-minute slot will be allotted to each candidate

allotment noun 1 the act of allotting 2 a small plot of ground for growing vegetables etc

allotrope noun, chemistry any of the two or more structural forms in which some elements can exist, eg graphite and diamond (allotropes of carbon) ♦ **allotropic** adjective ♦ **allotropy** (pronounced a-**lot**-ro-pi) noun

allow verb 1 to let (someone do something) 2 (**allow for**) to take into consideration (in sums, plans, etc) 3 to admit, confess: I will allow that we could have handled the situation better 4 to give, especially at regular intervals: She allows him £40 a week ♦ **allowable** adjective

allowance noun a fixed sum or amount given regularly • **make allowances for** to treat differently by taking into consideration special circumstances etc

alloy noun a mixture of two or more metals

allude verb (**allude to**) to refer to indirectly or in passing ⊙ Comes from Latin ad ludere meaning 'to play at'

! Do not confuse with: **elude**

allure verb to tempt, draw on by promises etc ♦ **allurement** noun ♦ **alluring** adjective

allusion noun an indirect reference

! Do not confuse with: **delusion** and **illusion**. An **allusion** is a comment which **alludes to** something.

allusive adjective referring indirectly, hinting

! Do not confuse with: **elusive** and **illusive**. **Allusive** is related to the verb **allude** and the noun **allusion**.

alluvium noun (plural **alluvia**) earth, sand, etc brought down and left by flowing rivers ♦ **alluvial** adjective

ally verb (**allies, allying, allied**) to join with someone else, especially by an alliance or treaty: a small organization seeking to ally itself with larger ones ➤ noun (plural **allies**) someone in alliance with another; a friend

almanac noun a calendar for any year, with information about the phases of the moon etc

almighty adjective having a lot of power • **the Almighty** God

almond (pronounced **ah**-mond) noun a flat, tear-shaped nut, the kernel of the fruit of the almond tree

almost adverb very nearly but not quite: almost five years old/almost home

alms (pronounced ahmz) plural noun gifts to the poor

aloft adverb 1 on high 2 upward

alone adjective not accompanied by others, solitary: alone in the house ➤ adverb 1 only,

without anything else: *That alone is bad enough*
2 not accompanied by others: *Do you live
alone?* • **leave alone** to leave undisturbed

along *preposition* **1** by the side of or near:
Flowers grew along the roadside **2** over the
length of: *walk along the road* ➤ *adverb* onward:
Come along! • **along with** together with

alongside *preposition* beside ➤ *adverb* near a
ship's side

aloof *adjective & adverb* **1** at a distance, apart **2**
showing no interest in others

alopecia (*pronounced* a-lo-**peesh**-i-a) *noun*
loss of hair

aloud *adverb* so as to be heard

alpha *noun* the first letter of the Greek alphabet
➤ *adjective* **1** *chemistry* denoting one of the
isomers of a compound **2** *sociology, zoology*
referring to the most dominant member of a
group

alphabet *noun* the letters of a language given in
a fixed order

⊙ From *alpha* and *beta*, the first two letters of
the Greek alphabet

alphabetical or **alphabetic** *adjective* in the
order of the letters of the alphabet

alpha decay *noun, physics* a form of
radioactive decay in which a radioactive nucleus
emits an alpha particle

alphanumeric or **alphanumerical**
adjective, computing denoting characters,
codes or data that consist of letters of the
alphabet and numerals, but do not include
punctuation marks or special characters

alpha particle *noun, physics* a positively
charged particle consisting of two protons and
two neutrons, identical to a helium nucleus

alpha test *noun, computing* a first test of a
product (eg new computer software) by its
developers before being released (*compare
with*: **beta test**) ◆ **alpha testing** *noun*

alpine *adjective* of the Alps or other high
mountains

alps *plural noun* high mountains • **the Alps** a
mountain range in Switzerland and
neighbouring countries

already *adverb* **1** before this or that time: *I've
already done that* **2** now, before the expected
time: *You can't have finished already*

❗ If you write 'all ready' as two words, it has the
very different meaning of 'totally ready':
Are you all ready for the big day?

❗ **alright** It is best to spell this as two words: 'all
right'. Some people consider the spelling
'alright' to be incorrect.

Alsatian *noun* a German shepherd dog

also *adverb* in addition, besides, too: *I also need
to buy milk*

also-ran *noun* someone or something that
competed (as in a race) but was not among the
winners

altar *noun* **1** a raised place for offerings to a god **2**
in Christian churches, the communion table

❗ Do not confuse: **altar** and **alter**

alter *verb* to change ◆ **alteration** *noun*

altercation *noun* an argument or quarrel

alter ego *noun* **1** someone's alternative
character **2** a trusted friend, a confidant(e)

alternate *verb* (*pronounced* **ol**-ter-neit) of two
things: to do or happen in turn: *Meetings
alternate between my house and hers*
➤ *adjective* (*pronounced* ol-**tern**-at) **1**
happening etc in turns **2** every other; one out of
two: *on alternate days* **3** *botany* of leaves, petals,
etc: appearing singly and regularly at either side
of a stem ◆ **alternation** *noun*

❗ Do not confuse: **alternate** and **alternative**.
To **alternate** is to move between two things.
Alternate is the adjective from this verb:
We visit on alternate days.

alternate angles *plural noun, maths* a pair of
angles on opposite sides and at opposite ends of
a transversal that cuts two parallel lines

alternating current *noun* (*abbrev* **AC**) an
electric current that reverses its direction at
regular intervals (*compare with*: **direct current**)

alternation of generations *noun, biology*
the occurrence within the life cycle of certain
living organisms, eg ferns and mosses, of a
sexually reproducing generation alternating
with an asexually reproducing generation

alternative *adjective* offering a second
possibility: *an alternative solution* ➤ *noun* a
second possibility, a different course of action: *I
had no alternative but to agree*

❗ Do not confuse with: **alternate**

alternative energy *noun* energy derived
from sources other than nuclear power or the
burning of fossil fuels, eg solar energy

alternative medicine *noun* the treatment of
diseases and disorders using procedures that are
not traditionally used in orthodox medicine, eg
acupuncture

alternator *noun* a generator producing
alternating current

although *conjunction* though, in spite of the
fact that

altimeter (*pronounced* al-**tim**-i-ter or **al**-ti-
mee-ter) *noun* an instrument for measuring
height above sea level

altitude *noun* **1** height above sea level **2** *maths* in a plane or solid figure: the distance from a vertex to the side opposite the vertex (the **base**)

alto noun (plural **altos**), music **1** the male singing voice of the highest pitch **2** (also called: **contralto**) the female singing voice of the lowest pitch **3** a singer with such a voice

altogether adverb **1** considering everything, in all: There were 20 of us altogether **2** completely: not altogether satisfied

❗ If you write 'all together' as two words, it has the very different meaning of 'together in a group':
It's great to be all together for Christmas.

altruism noun unselfish concern for the other people's wellbeing ♦ **altruistic** adjective

ALU abbreviation, computing arithmetic logic unit

alum noun, chemistry a sulphate of aluminium and potassium, used in dyeing and tanning, and in medicine to stop bleeding

alumina noun, chemistry a white crystalline compound that is the main ingredient of bauxite

aluminium (pronounced al-yuw-**min**-i-um) or US **aluminum** (pronounced a-**loo**-min-um) noun, chemistry (symbol **Al**) a silvery-white, light, metallic element that forms strong alloys

alveolus (pronounced al-**vi**-o-lus) noun (plural **alveoli** – pronounced al-**vi**-o-lai) anatomy **1** any of the millions of tiny air sacs in the lungs **2** a tooth socket in the jaw bone ♦ **alveolar** adjective

always adverb **1** for ever: He'll always remember this day **2** every time: She always gets it wrong

❗ If you write 'all ways' as two words, it has the very different meaning of 'in every way possible':
I've tried all ways to tell her, but she just won't listen.

Alzheimer's disease (pronounced alts-hai-merz) noun an illness affecting the brain and causing dementia in middle-aged and elderly people

AM abbreviation **1** amplitude modulation (compare with: **FM**) **2** Assembly Member (of the National Assembly of Wales)

Am symbol, chemistry americium

am[1] abbreviation before noon (from Latin ante meridiem)

am[2] see **be**

amalgam noun **1** a mixture (especially of metals) **2** medicine an alloy of mercury with other metals that forms a soft paste on mixing but later hardens and is used by dentists to fill holes in teeth

amalgamate verb **1** to join together, combine: the company recently amalgamated with a large

French firm **2** to mix ♦ **amalgamation** noun

amanita (pronounced a-ma-**nai**-ta) noun (plural **amanitas**), biology any mushroom of a genus that includes many poisonous varieties

amass verb to collect in large quantities: amass a lot of furniture over the years

amateur noun someone who takes part in a sport, activity, etc because they enjoy it and without being paid for doing it (contrasted with: **professional**)

amateurish adjective not done properly; not skilful

amaze verb to surprise greatly ♦ **amazed** adjective ♦ **amazement** noun ♦ **amazing** adjective ♦ **amazingly** adverb

ambassador noun **1** an official sent to another country to look after the interests of their country and government **2** a representative

amber noun a hard yellowish fossil resin used in making jewellery ➤ adjective **1** made of amber **2** of the colour of amber

ambi- prefix **1** both, on both sides **2** round ⏱ Comes from Latin ambo meaning 'both'

ambidextrous adjective able to use both hands with equal skill

ambience noun environment, atmosphere

ambient adjective: **ambient temperature** the temperature of the air in an enclosed space, eg a room

ambiguity noun (plural **ambiguities**) uncertainty in meaning

ambiguous adjective **1** having two possible meanings **2** not clear ⏱ Comes from Latin ambiguus meaning 'changing from one to another'

❗ Do not confuse with: **ambivalent**

ambition noun the desire for success, power, fame, etc ♦ **ambitious** adjective ♦ **ambitiously** adverb

ambivalent adjective having two contrasting feelings or attitudes towards something ♦ **ambivalence** noun ⏱ Comes from the prefix ambi-, and Latin valens meaning 'strong'

❗ Do not confuse with: **ambiguous**

amble verb to walk in an unhurried, relaxed way ➤ noun an unhurried walk

ambrosia noun the mythological food of the Greek gods, which gave eternal youth and beauty

ambulance noun a vehicle for carrying people who are ill or injured

ambush noun (plural **ambushes**) **1** the act of lying hidden in order to make a surprise attack **2** the people hidden in this way **3** the place where they hide ➤ verb to lie in wait for someone and attack them suddenly

amenable (*pronounced* a-**meen**-a-bl) *adjective* open to advice or suggestion
♦ **amenability** *noun* ♦ **amenably** *adverb*
amend *verb* **1** to correct; improve (a text or statement) by making small additions **2** to alter (a text or statement) slightly by making small additions ➤ *noun*: **make amends** to make up for having done wrong

❗ Do not confuse with: **emend**.
Amending involves making changes or improvements. **Emending** consists simply of getting rid of errors.

amendment *noun* a change, often in something written: *an amendment to the constitution*
amenity (*pronounced* a-**meen**-i-ti or a-**men**-i-ti) *noun* (*plural* **amenities**) a pleasant or convenient feature of a place etc
americium (*pronounced* am-e-**ris**-i-um) *noun, chemistry* (symbol **Am**) a silvery-white, radioactive, metallic element that occurs naturally in trace amounts and is produced artificially by bombarding plutonium with neutrons

🕐 Named after America (where it was discovered by G T Seaborg, R A James and L O Morgan)

amethyst *noun* a precious stone of a bluish-violet colour
amiable *adjective* likeable; friendly
♦ **amiability** *noun* ♦ **amiably** *adverb*
amicable *adjective* friendly ♦ **amicably** *adverb*
amid or **amidst** *preposition* in the middle of, surrounded by: *staying calm amidst all the confusion* 🕐 Comes from Old English *on middan* meaning 'in middle'
amide *noun, chemistry* **1** a compound that contains a $CONH_2$ group **2** a compound that contains an NH_2^- ion
amine (*pronounced* a-meen) *noun, chemistry* an organic compound in which one or more of the hydrogen atoms of ammonia has been replaced by an organic group
amino acid *noun, chemistry* a compound which contains the $-NH_2$ group, and joins with others to form proteins
amiss *adverb* wrongly; badly
ammeter *noun* a device for measuring electrical current
ammonia *noun* **1** *chemistry* a colourless strong-smelling gas, a compound of hydrogen and nitrogen **2** a solution of ammonia in water, used in bleach
ammonite *noun* the fossilized shell of a type of extinct mollusc
ammonium *noun, chemistry* a positively

charged ion (NH_4^+) formed by the reaction of ammonia with acid
ammunition *noun* gunpowder, shot, bullets, bombs, etc
amnesia *noun* loss of memory
amnesiac *noun* & *adjective* (someone) suffering from amnesia
amnesty *noun* (*plural* **amnesties**) a general pardon of wrongdoers
amniocentesis (*pronounced* am-nee-oh-sen-**tee**-sis) *noun, medicine* a procedure in which a hollow needle is inserted into the uterus of a pregnant woman to draw off a small quantity of fluid that can be tested for abnormalities in the foetus
amnion *noun* (*plural* **amnia**), *biology* the innermost membrane surrounding the embryo of mammals, birds and reptiles
amniotic fluid *noun, biology* the clear fluid surrounding the embryo of mammals, birds and reptiles
amoeba (*pronounced* a-**mee**-ba) *noun* (*plural* **amoebas** or **amoebae** – *pronounced* a-**mee**-bi or a-**mee**-bai) a microscopic, single-celled creature with no fixed shape, found in ponds etc
amok or **amuck** *adverb*: **run amok** to go mad and do a lot of damage, run riot

🕐 From a Malay word meaning 'fighting frenziedly'

among or **amongst** *preposition* **1** surrounded by or in the middle of: *among friends* **2** giving each a part: *Divide it amongst yourselves* **3** in the group of: *Among all her novels, this is the best* 🕐 Comes from Old English *on-gemang* meaning 'in mixture or crowd'

ℹ️ Use **among** when there is a notion of distributing or sharing:
Share the sweets among yourselves.
Use **between** when individual people or things are named:
Duties are shared between John, James and Catherine.

amoral (*pronounced* ei-**mo**-ral) *adjective* incapable of distinguishing between right and wrong ♦ **amorality** *noun* 🕐 Comes from Greek prefix a- meaning 'the opposite of', and Latin *moralis* meaning 'moral'

❗ Do not confuse with: **immoral**.
An **amoral** person behaves badly because they do not understand the difference between right and wrong. An **immoral** person behaves badly in the full knowledge that what they are doing is wrong.

amorous *adjective* loving; ready or inclined to love or make love

amorphous *adjective* **1** without definite shape or structure **2** *chemistry* of rocks, chemicals, etc: without a crystalline structure ☉ Comes from Greek *amorphos* meaning 'shapeless'

amortize or **amortise** (*pronounced* a-**mawr**-taiz or a-**mawr**-tiz) *verb* **1** to gradually pay off (a debt) by regular payments of money **2** to gradually write off (the initial cost of an asset) in accounts over a period

amount *noun* **1** total, sum **2** a quantity ▸ *verb* : **amount to** to add up to

amp *noun* **1** an ampere **2** *informal* an amplifier

ampere *noun* (symbol **A**) the standard unit of electric current

ampersand *noun* the character (&) representing *and*

> ☉ From the phrase *and per se and*, 'and by itself *and*'

amphetamine (*pronounced* am-**fet**-a-min) *noun, medicine* a potentially addictive synthetic drug, often used illegally as a stimulant (*see also*: **speed**)

amphi- *prefix* **1** both; on both sides or ends **2** around ☉ Comes from Greek *amphi* meaning 'on both sides' or 'around'

amphibian *noun* **1** a cold-blooded vertebrate, eg a frog, toad or newt, that lives partly on land and returns to water to lay eggs **2** a vehicle for use on land and in water ▸ *adjective* living on land and water

amphibious *adjective* living or operating on land and water

amphitheatre *noun* a theatre with seats surrounding a central arena

amphora (*pronounced* amf-o-ra)*noun* (*plural* **amphoras** or **amphorae** – *pronounced* amf-o-ree or amf-o-rei) a large Greek or Roman jar with a handle on either side, used for storing liquids such as wine or oil

ample *adjective* **1** plenty (of) **2** large enough ♦ **amply** *adverb*

amplification *noun* **1** the process or product of making something louder, larger or more detailed **2** *genetics* the formation of multiple copies of a particular gene or DNA sequence

amplifier *noun* an electrical device for increasing loudness

amplify *verb* (**amplifies, amplifying, amplified**) **1** to make louder **2** to make more pronounced

amplitude *noun* **1** largeness **2** abundance **3** *maths* the height of a wave from a centre line **4** *physics* the maximum displacement of a periodic cycle

amputate *verb* to cut off (especially a human limb) ♦ **amputation** *noun*

amputee *noun* someone who has had a limb amputated

amrit *noun, Sikhism* **1** a ceremonial drink made of sugar and water **2** the initiation ceremony in which amrit is drunk

amuck another spelling of **amok**

amulet *noun* a small object, charm or jewel worn to protect the wearer from witchcraft, evil, disease, etc

amuse *verb* **1** to make someone laugh **2** to make someone enjoy himself or herself ♦ **amusement** *noun*

amusing *adjective* **1** funny **2** enjoyable

amylase (*pronounced* am-i-leiz) *noun, chemistry* an important enzyme present in digestive juices

an see **a**

an- or **a-** *prefix* without, not, opposite to: *anaerobic/anodyne* (= without pain) ☉ Comes from Greek a- meaning 'without' or 'not'

ana- or **an-** *prefix* up, back, again: *anabolic/aneurism* ☉ Comes from Greek prefix *ana-* with the same meaning

anabolic steroids *plural noun* synthetic male sex hormones used to increase the build-up of body tissue, especially muscle

anabolism (*pronounced* a-**nab**-o-lizm) *noun, chemistry* the synthesis of complex molecules from smaller ones, eg in food (*compare with*: **catabolism**) ♦ **anabolic** *adjective*

anachronism (*pronounced* a-**nak**-ro-nizm) *noun* the mistake of referring to, showing, etc something which did not exist or was not yet invented at the time spoken about or depicted ♦ **anachronistic** *adjective*

anaconda *noun* a large South American water snake

anaemia or *US* **anemia** (*both pronounced* a-**nee**-mi-a) *noun, medicine* a shortage of red cells in the blood

anaemic or *US* **anemic** (*both pronounced* a-**nee**-mik) *adjective* **1** *medicine* suffering from anaemia **2** pale or ill-looking

anaerobe (*pronounced* an-e-rohb) *noun, biology* any organism that does not require oxygen for respiration, or that cannot survive in the presence of oxygen (*compare with*: **aerobe**)

anaerobic *adjective, biology* of an organism, especially a bacterium: not requiring oxygen in order to obtain energy by respiration, or unable to survive in the presence of oxygen (*compare with*: **aerobic**)

anaerobic respiration *noun, biology* a form of respiration in which oxygen is not required to break down carbohydrates (*compare with*: **aerobic respiration**)

anaesthesia or *US* **anesthesia** (*both pronounced* an-es-**thee**-zi-a) *noun, medicine* loss of feeling or sensation

anaesthetic or US **anesthetic** (*both pronounced* an-es-**thet**-ik) *noun, medicine* a substance which produces lack of feeling for a time in a part of the body, or which makes someone unconscious

anaesthetist (*pronounced* an-**ees**-the-tist) or US **anesthetist** (*pronounced* an-**es**-the-tist) *noun, medicine* a doctor trained to administer anaesthetics ♦ **anaesthetize** or **anaesthetise** or US **anesthetize** *verb*

anagram *noun* a word or sentence formed by reordering the letters of another word or sentence, eg *veil* is an anagram of *evil*

anal *adjective* **1** of the anus **2** *psychology* having personality traits such as obsessiveness, attention to detail, and obstinacy

analgesia *noun* a reduction in pain

analgesic *adjective* relieving pain

analogous *adjective* **1** similar, alike in some way **2** *biology* denoting plant or animal structures that are similar in function, but have evolved independently of each other in different groups, eg the wings of insects and birds (*compare with*: **homologous**)

analogue or US **analog** *noun* **1** something regarded in terms of its similarity to something else **2** *biology* any part of an animal or plant that is similar in function, though not in origin, to a part in a different organism ➤ *adjective* (*compare with*: **digital**) **1** of data: in a form that is changing continuously rather than in a series of digits **2** of a device: with divisions and pointers on a dial showing information

analogue-to-digital converter or **A/D converter** *noun, computing* a device which allows a computer to accept and convert data in analogue form (*also called*: **digitizer**)

analogy *noun* (*plural* **analogies**) a likeness; resemblance in certain ways

analyse or US **analyze** *verb* **1** to break down, separate into parts **2** to examine in detail

analysis *noun* (*plural* **analyses**) **1** a breaking up of a thing into its parts **2** a detailed examination of something ♦ **analytical** *adjective*

analysis of variance *noun, maths* a procedure to separate the different factors which cause variance

analyst *noun* **1** someone who analyses **2** a psychiatrist or psychologist **3** *computing* a systems analyst

analytical geometry same as **co-ordinate geometry**

analyze US spelling of **analyse**

anapaest (*pronounced* **ahn**-a-pest) *noun, poetry* a metrical foot consisting of two short or unstressed syllables followed by a long or stressed one ♦ **anapaestic** *adjective*

anaphylaxis (*pronounced* an-a-fil-**aks**-is) *noun, medicine* a sudden severe hypersensitive reaction to a particular substance or antigen ♦ **anaphylactic** *adjective*

anarchic or **anarchical** *adjective* **1** refusing to obey any rules **2** in a state of disorder or confusion

anarchist *noun* someone who believes in anarchy (meaning 1) ♦ **anarchism** *noun*

anarchy *noun* **1** lack or absence of government **2** disorder or confusion

anathema (*pronounced* a-**nath**-e-ma) *noun* **1** a curse **2** a hated person or thing: *Opera is anathema to him*

anatomist *noun* a person who specializes in the study of the human body

anatomy *noun* (*plural* **anatomies**) **1** the study of the parts of the body **2** the body

ANC *abbreviation* African National Congress

ancestor *noun* a person from whom someone is descended by birth; a forefather ♦ **ancestral** *adjective*

ancestry *noun* (*plural* **ancestries**) a line of ancestors

anchor *noun* a heavy piece of iron, with hooked ends, for holding a ship fast to the bed of the sea etc ➤ *verb* **1** to fix by anchor **2** to let down the anchor **3** to fix securely ● **weigh anchor** to pull up the anchor

anchorage *noun* a place where a ship can anchor

anchorman or **anchorwoman** *noun* the main presenter of a television news programme etc

anchovy *noun* (*plural* **anchovies**) a type of small fish of the herring family with a very strong flavour

ancient *adjective* **1** very old **2** of times long past

ancient monument *noun* a building, grave, etc remaining from ancient times

ancillary *adjective* serving or supporting something more important

and *conjunction* **1** used to join two statements, pieces of information, etc: *black and white film/ Add milk and stir* **2** in addition to: *2 and 2 make 4*

andante (*pronounced* an-**dan**-ti) *adverb, music* in a slow, steady manner ♦ *noun* a piece of music to be played in a slow, steady way ⊙ Comes from Italian *andare* meaning 'to go'

AND gate *noun, computing* a circuit that gives out a signal when it receives two or more signals *compare with*: **NOT gate**, **OR gate**)

andro- or **andr-** *prefix* having to do with men, male ⊙ Comes from Greek *aner, andros* meaning 'man' or 'male'

androecium (*pronounced* an-**dree**-shi-um or an-**dree**-si-um) *noun* (*plural* **androecia**), *botany* the stamens of a flowering plant considered collectively

androgen *noun, biology* a male sex hormone that controls the functioning of the male sex organs

androgynous (*pronounced* **an**-droj-*i*-nus) *adjective* **1** *biology* denoting an animal or plant that shows both male and female characteristics, especially one that possesses both male and female sex organs **2** showing both male and female traits, eg referring to a woman who resembles a man in appearance ◑ Comes from Greek *aner, andros* meaning 'man' + *gyne* meaning 'woman'

android *noun* a robot in human form

anecdote *noun* a short, interesting or amusing story, usually true ✦ **anecdotal** *adjective*

anemo- *prefix* of the wind ◑ Comes from Greek *anemos* meaning 'wind'

anemometer *noun* an instrument for measuring the speed of the wind

anemone (*pronounced* a-**nem**-o-ni) *noun* **1** a type of woodland or garden flower **2** a sea anemone

aneroid barometer *noun* a barometer which measures air pressure without the use of mercury

aneurism (*pronounced* an-yoo-rizm) *noun* **1** *medicine* a swelling in the wall of an artery **2** abnormal enlargement

anew *adverb* **1** once more, again **2** in a different way

angel *noun* **1** a messenger or attendant of God or Allah **2** a very good or beautiful person ✦ **angelic** *adjective* as perfectly sweet and good as an angel

angelica *noun* a plant whose candied leaf-stalks are used as cake decoration

anger *noun* a bitter feeling against someone; annoyance, rage ➤ *verb* to make angry

angina (*pronounced* an-**jai**-na) *noun, medicine* a form of heart disease causing acute chest pains

angle *noun* **1** the V-shape made by two lines meeting at a point **2** a corner **3** a point of view ➤ *verb* to try to get by hints etc: *angling for a job*

angle of incidence *noun, physics* the angle between the point where a ray strikes a reflecting surface, and a line drawn perpendicular to the surface at that point

angle of reflection *noun, physics* the angle between the point where a ray leaves a reflecting surface, and a line drawn perpendicular to the surface at that point

angle of refraction *noun, physics* the angle between the point where a ray is refracted at an interface between two different media, eg water and glass, and a line drawn perpendicular to the surface at that point

angler *noun* someone who fishes with a rod and line

Anglican *adjective* of the Church of England ➤ *noun* a member of the Church of England ✦ **Anglicanism** *noun*

anglicize or **anglicise** *verb* **1** to turn into the English language **2** to make English in character ✦ **anglicization** *noun*

angling *noun* the sport of fishing with a rod and line

Anglo-Saxon *noun* **1** a member of any of the Germanic tribes who settled in England in the 5th century **2** any English-speaking White person **3** Old English **4** plain, short English words, including rude words ➤ *adjective* **1** to do with the Anglo-Saxons **2** to do with Old English **3** of English speech or writing: blunt and to the point **4** relating to the shared cultural, political, etc aspects of British and American life

angry *adjective* (**angrier, angriest**) feeling or showing anger ✦ **angrily** *adverb*

angst *noun* a feeling of apprehension or anxiety

anguish *noun* very great pain or distress

anguished *adjective* in or showing misery and suffering: *an anguished look*

angular *adjective* **1** having angles **2** thin, bony **3** measured by an angle: *angular distance* ✦ **angularity** *noun*

angular momentum *noun, physics* for a particle moving about an axis: the product of its angular velocity and its moment of inertia about the axis of rotation

angular velocity *noun, physics* the rate at which an object rotates round a fixed point or axis

anhydride *noun, chemistry* a compound formed by removing water from another compound, especially an acid

anhydrous *adjective, chemistry* denoting a chemical compound that contains no water

animal *noun* **1** one of the kingdom of organisms that can make voluntary movement and have specialized sense organs that respond quickly to stimuli **2** an animal other than a human ➤ *adjective* of or like an animal

animal kingdom *noun, biology* the rank in the classification of living organisms which includes all animals

animal rights *plural noun* the rights of animals to exist without being exploited by humans

animate *verb* (*pronounced* **an**-im-eit) **1** to give life to **2** to make lively **3** *cinema* to record (drawings) on film in such a way as to make the images seem to move **4** *computing* to make (an image) move ➤ *adjective* (*pronounced* **an**-im-at) living

animated *adjective* **1** lively **2** made to move as if alive ✦ **animatedly** *adverb*

animation *noun* 1 liveliness 2 *cinema* a film made from a series of drawings that give the illusion of movement when shown in sequence 3 *cinema* the techniques used to record still drawings on film in such a way as to make the images seem to move 4 *computing* the process of making an image move

animator *noun, cinema* an artist who works in animation

animatronics *singular noun, cinema* in film-making: the art of animating a lifelike figure of a person, animal, etc by means of computer technology

animosity *noun* (*plural* **animosities**) bitter hatred, enmity

anion (*pronounced* an-ai-on) *noun, chemistry* a negatively charged ion, which moves towards the anode during electrolysis (*compare with*: **cation**)

aniseed *noun* a seed with a flavour like that of liquorice

ankle *noun* the joint connecting the foot and leg

annals *plural noun* yearly historical accounts of events

annelid *noun, zoology* an invertebrate animal with a long cylindrical body composed of many ring-shaped segments, eg the earthworm

annex *verb* 1 to take possession of (land) 2 to add, attach ➤ *noun* (*also spelled*: **annexe**) a building added to another ♦ **annexation** *noun*

annihilate (*pronounced* a-nai-i-leit) *verb* 1 to destroy completely 2 *physics* of a particle: to be destroyed by a collision with its corresponding antiparticle ♦ **annihilation** *noun*

anniversary *noun* (*plural* **anniversaries**) the date on which something happened in a previous year

annotate *verb* 1 to make notes upon 2 to add notes or explanation to ♦ **annotation** *noun*

announce *verb* to make publicly known ♦ **announcement** *noun*

announcer *noun* someone who announces programmes on TV etc, or reads the news

annoy *verb* to make rather angry; irritate ♦ **annoyance** *noun*

annual *adjective* yearly ➤ *noun* 1 a plant that lives for only one year (*compare with*: **biennial**, **perennial**) 2 a book published yearly

annually *adverb* every year

annuity *noun* (*plural* **annuities**) a yearly payment made for a certain period or for life

annul *verb* (**annulling, annulled**) 1 to put an end to 2 to declare no longer valid ♦ **annulment** *noun*

annulus (*pronounced* an-juw-lus) *noun* (*plural* **annuli** (*pronounced* an-juw-lai), *maths* the figure formed by two concentric circles, ie a disc with a central hole ⊙ Comes from Latin meaning

'a ring or ring-shaped object'

anode *noun* the positive electrode in a battery or other electronic device (*contrasted with*: **cathode**)

anodize or **anodise** *verb* to coat (an object made of metal, especially aluminium) with a thin protective oxide film by making it the anode in a cell to which an electric current is applied

anodyne *adjective* 1 soothing, relieving pain 2 bland and harmless: *a fairly anodyne comment*

anoint *verb* to smear with ointment or oil ♦ **anointment** *noun*

anomaly *noun* (*plural* **anomalies**) something unusual, not according to a rule ♦ **anomalous** *adjective*

anon *abbreviation* anonymous

anonymous *adjective* without the name of the author, giver, etc being known or given ♦ **anonymously** *adverb*

anorak *noun* a hooded waterproof jacket

anorexia *noun, medicine* an emotional illness causing the sufferer to refuse food and become sometimes dangerously thin (*also called*: **anorexia nervosa**)

anorexic *adjective, medicine* of or suffering from anorexia ➤ *noun* someone suffering from anorexia

another *adjective* 1 a different (thing or person): *moving to another job* 2 one more of the same kind: *Have another biscuit* ➤ *pronoun* an additional thing of the same kind: *Do you want another?*

Anschluss (*pronounced* an-shloos) *noun, history* the political union of Germany and Austria in 1938

answer *verb* 1 to speak, write, etc in return or reply 2 to find the result or solution (of a sum, problem, etc) ➤ *noun* 1 something said, written, etc in return or reply 2 a solution • **answer back** to give a cheeky or aggressive answer to someone in authority • **answer for** 1 to be responsible for 2 to suffer for, be punished for

answerable *adjective* 1 responsible: *answerable for her actions* 2 able to be answered

ant *noun* a very small insect which lives in organized colonies • **have ants in your pants** to be impatient or restless

antacid *noun, medicine* an alkaline substance able to dissolve excess acid in the stomach's digestive juices

antagonism *noun* 1 hostility, opposition, enmity 2 the opposing action between one muscle or group of muscles and another 3 *chemistry* interference with the growth or action of one organism or substance by another

antagonist *noun* 1 an enemy 2 an opponent 3 a muscle the contraction of which opposes the relaxation of another muscle (the **agonist**) 4 *chemistry* a substance or organism that interferes with the growth or action of another

antagonistic *adjective* opposed (to), unfriendly, hostile

antagonize or **antagonise** *verb* to make an enemy of, cause dislike

Antarctic *adjective* of the South Pole or regions round it

ante- *prefix* before ○ Comes from Latin *ante* meaning 'before'

anteater *noun* an American animal with a long snout which feeds on ants and termites

antecedent (*pronounced* ant-i-**see**-dent) *adjective* going before in time ► *noun* **1** someone who lived at an earlier time; an ancestor **2** (**antecedents**) previous conduct, history, etc

antedate *verb* **1** to be earlier in date than **2** to put a date on a document which is earlier than the day you are actually writing it

antediluvian *adjective* very old or old-fashioned

○ From Latin, literally 'before the flood', in allusion to the story of Noah in the Bible and Koran

antelope *noun* a graceful, swift-running animal like a deer

antenatal *adjective* **1** before birth **2** relating to pregnancy: *antenatal clinic*

antenna *noun* **1** (*plural* **antennae** – *pronounced* an-**ten**-ee) an insect's feeler **2** (*plural* **antennas**) an aerial

anterior *adjective* **1** earlier in time **2** at or nearer the front **3** *zoology* at or near the head **4** *botany* growing away from the main stem (*compare with*: **posterior**)

anteroom *noun* a room leading into a large room

anthem *noun* **1** a piece of music for a church choir **2** any song of praise

anther *noun, botany* the structure at the tip of the stamen which contains the pollen sacs where pollen grains are produced

ant-hill *noun* an earth mound built by ants as a nest

antho- *prefix* of or relating to flowers: *anthology/anthomania* (= a craze for flowers) ○ Comes from Greek *anthos* meaning 'flower'

anthology *noun* (*plural* **anthologies**) a collection of specially chosen poems, stories, etc ○ Comes from Greek *anthos* meaning 'flower', and *logia* meaning 'collection'

anthracite *noun* coal that burns with a hot, smokeless flame

anthrax *noun, medicine* an infectious disease of cattle, sheep, etc, sometimes transferred to humans

anthropo- or **anthrop-** *prefix* of or relating to humans ○ Comes from Greek *anthropos* meaning 'human being'

anthropoid *adjective* of apes: resembling humans

anthropology *noun* the study of mankind
 ♦ **anthropological** *adjective*
 ♦ **anthropologist** *noun*

anthropomorphism *noun* (*pronounced* anthrop-o-**mawr**-fizm) ascribing human characteristics or feelings to animals, gods, objects, etc ♦ **anthropomorphic** *adjective*

anti- *prefix* against, opposite: *anti-terrorist* ○ Comes from Greek *anti* meaning 'against'

antibiotic *noun, medicine* a medicine taken to kill bacteria that cause disease

antibody *noun* (*plural* **antibodies**) a substance produced in the human body to fight bacteria etc

anticipate *verb* **1** to look forward to, expect **2** to see or know in advance **3** to act before (someone or something) ♦ **anticipation** *noun*
 ♦ **anticipatory** *adjective*

anticlerical *adjective* opposed to the clergy and their influence in politics ♦ **anticlericalism** *noun*

anticlimax *noun* (*plural* **anticlimaxes**) a dull or disappointing ending

anticlockwise *adjective & adverb* in the opposite direction to the hands of a clock

antics *plural noun* tricks, odd or amusing actions

anticyclone *noun* a circling movement of air round an area of high air pressure, causing calm weather

antidote *noun* something given to act against the effect of poison

antifreeze *noun* a chemical with a low freezing point, added to a car radiator to prevent freezing

antigen *noun* a substance, eg a bacterium or virus, that stimulates the production of antibodies

antihero *noun* (*plural* **antiheroes**) a principal character in a novel, play, film, etc who lacks the conventional qualities of a hero

antihistamine *noun, medicine* a medicine used to treat an allergy

antimony (*pronounced* **an**-ti-mo-ni) *noun, chemistry* (symbol **Sb**) a brittle bluish-white metallic element used to increase the hardness of lead alloys

anti-natalist policy *noun* (*also*: **birth control policy**) a government policy designed to limit the number of children people have

antinode *noun, physics* a point halfway between the nodes in a standing wave, indicating a position of maximum displacement

antioxidant *noun, chemistry* a substance, especially an additive, that slows down the oxidation of other substances

antiparticle *noun, physics* a subatomic particle which has the opposite electrical charge and magnetism from another of the same mass, eg as the positron is the antiparticle of the electron

antipathy *noun* (*plural* **antipathies**) extreme dislike

antiperspirant *noun* a substance applied to the body to reduce sweating

antiphon *noun, music* a hymn sung alternately by two groups of singers ✦ **antiphonal** *adjective*

antipodes (*pronounced* an-**tip**-od-eez) *plural noun* places on the earth's surface exactly opposite each other, especially Australia and New Zealand in relation to Europe
✦ **antipodean** *adjective*

antiquarian *noun* a dealer in antiques or rare books

antiquated *adjective* grown old, or out of fashion

antique *noun* an old, interesting or valuable object from earlier times ➤ *adjective* **1** old, from earlier times **2** old-fashioned

antiquity *noun* (*plural* **antiquities**) **1** ancient times, especially those of the Greeks and Romans **2** great age **3** (**antiquities**) objects from earlier times

anti-Semitism *noun* hatred of the Jews or their perceived influence ✦ **anti-Semitic** *adjective*

antiseptic *adjective* germ-destroying ➤ *noun* a chemical etc which destroys germs

antisocial *adjective* **1** not fitting in with other people or harmful to them **2** disliking the company of other people

antithesis *noun* (*plural* **antitheses** – *pronounced* an-**ti**-the-seez) the exact opposite: *the antithesis of good taste* ✦ **antithetical** *adjective*

antler *noun* the horn of a deer

antonym *noun* a word which means the opposite of another, eg 'big' and 'small', or 'brave' and 'cowardly'

anus (*pronounced* **ei**-nus) *noun, anatomy* the lower opening of the bowel through which faeces pass

anvil *noun* a metal block on which blacksmiths hammer metal into shape

anxiety *noun* (*plural* **anxieties**) worry about what may happen

anxious *adjective* **1** worried **2** full of worry or uncertainty **3** eager, keen: *anxious to please* ✦ **anxiously** *adverb*

any *adjective* **1** some: *Is there any milk?* **2** every, no matter which: *Any day will suit me* ➤ *pronoun* some: *There aren't any left* ➤ *adverb* at all: *I can't work any faster* • **at any rate** in any case, whatever happens

anybody *pronoun* any person

anyhow *adverb* **1** in any case: *I think I'll go anyhow* **2** carelessly: *scattered anyhow over the floor*

anyone *pronoun* any person

anything *pronoun* something of any kind

anyway *adverb* at any rate

anywhere *adverb* in any place

aorta (*pronounced* ei-**awr**-ta) *noun, anatomy* the main artery in the body, which carries oxygenated blood from the heart to the smaller arteries

apart *adverb* **1** separated by a particular distance or time: *The villages are five miles apart* **2** in or into pieces: *came apart in my hands* **3** to or on one side: *set apart for special occasions* **4** in opposite directions • **apart from 1** separate, or separately, from **2** except for: *Who else knows apart from us?*

apartheid (*pronounced* a-**paht**-heit or a-**paht**-hait) *noun* the political policy of keeping people of different races apart, especially as formerly practised in South Africa

apartment *noun* **1** a room in a house **2** *US* a flat

apathy *noun* lack of feeling or interest
✦ **apathetic** *adjective*

apatosaurus *noun* a huge dinosaur that had massive limbs, a small head, a long neck and a whip-like tail (*former name*: **brontosaurus**)

ape *noun* a member of a group of animals related to monkeys, but larger, tailless and walking upright ➤ *verb* to imitate

aperitif (*pronounced* a-pe-ri-**teef**) *noun* a drink taken before a meal

aperture *noun* an opening, a hole

apex *noun* (*plural* **apexes** or **apices** – *pronounced* **ei**-pi-seez) **1** the highest point **2** *maths* the highest point of a plane or solid figure in relation to a plane or line

aphid (*pronounced* **ei**-fid) *noun* a small insect which feeds on plants

aphrodisiac *noun* a drug, food, etc that increases sexual desire ➤ *adjective* causing increased sexual desire

apiarist (*pronounced* **ei**-pi-a-rist) *noun* someone who keeps or studies bees

apiary (*pronounced* **ei**-pi-a-ri) *noun* (*plural* **apiaries**) a place where bees are kept

apiece *adverb* to or for each one: *three chocolates apiece*

aplomb *noun* self-confidence

apo- or **ap-** *prefix* from, off, away, quite ☉ Comes from Greek prefix *apo-* with the same meaning

apocalypse *noun* **1** (**the Apocalypse**) the last book of the New Testament, which describes the end of the world (*also called*: **Revelation**) **2** any revelation of the future, especially future destruction ◆ **apocalyptic** adjective ⊕ Comes from Greek apocalypsis meaning 'uncovering'

Apocrypha (pronounced a-**pok**-rif-a) plural noun (**the Apocrypha**) those books of the Bible included in the ancient Greek and Latin versions of the Old Testament but not in the Hebrew version ⊕ Comes from Greek apocryphos meaning 'hidden'

apocryphal (pronounced a-**pok**-rif-al) adjective unlikely to be true

apogee (pronounced **ap**-o-jee) noun **1** a culmination, a climax **2** the point of an orbit furthest from the earth

apologetic adjective expressing regret ◆ **apologetically** adverb

apologize or **apologise** verb to express regret, say you are sorry

apology noun (plural **apologies**) an expression of regret for having done wrong

apoplexy noun sudden loss of ability to feel, move, etc; a stroke ◆ **apoplectic** adjective

a posteriori (pronounced ei post-er-i-**aw**-rai or a post-er-i-**aw**-ri) adjective & adverb working from effect to cause or from particular cases to general principles (compare with: **a priori**)

apostle noun a religious preacher, especially one of the disciples of Christ

apostolic (pronounced ap-os-**tawl**-ik) adjective **1** relating to the apostles in the early Christian Church **2** relating to the teaching that the church was founded by Christ's apostles, and that the Pope is the successor to the Apostle Peter

apostrophe noun **1** a mark (') indicating possession: the minister's cat **2** the same mark indicating that a letter etc has been missed out, eg isn't for is not

apothecary noun (plural **apothecaries**) old a chemist or pharmacist

appal verb (**appalling, appalled**) to horrify, shock

appalling adjective shocking

apparatus noun (plural **apparatuses** or **apparatus**) **1** an instrument or machine **2** instruments, tools or material required for a piece of work

apparel noun a formal or literary word for clothing

apparent adjective easily seen, evident ◆ **apparently** adverb it appears that: 'But I thought they were going out together.' 'Apparently not.'

apparition noun **1** something remarkable which appears suddenly **2** a ghost

appeal verb **1** to ask earnestly (for help etc): appeal to the public for information **2** law to take a case that has been lost to a higher court **3** (**appeal to**) to be attractive to someone ▶ noun

1 a request for help **2** law the taking of a case that has been lost to a higher court

appealing adjective arousing liking or sympathy

appear verb **1** to come into view **2** to arrive **3** to seem

appearance noun **1** an act of appearing **2** the way something looks **3** a pretence

appease verb to soothe or satisfy, especially by giving what was asked for: nothing would appease his anger

appeasement noun **1** the act of appeasing **2** a political policy of achieving peace by making concessions

append verb to add or attach to a document

appendage noun **1** anything added or attached to a larger or more important part **2** zoology a part or organ, eg a leg, antenna, etc, that extends from the body of animals such as insects, crustaceans, etc **3** botany an offshoot, eg a branch, leaf, etc, that sprouts from the stem of a plant

appendectomy noun (plural **appendectomies**), medicine surgical removal of the appendix

appendicitis noun, medicine inflammation of the appendix

appendix noun (plural **appendices** or **appendixes**) **1** a part added at the end of a book or document containing extra information, notes, etc **2** anatomy a small tube-shaped sac at the junction of the small and large intestines

appertain verb (**appertain to**), formal **1** to belong to **2** to be relevant to

appetite noun **1** desire for food **2** taste or enthusiasm (for): no appetite for violence

appetizer or **appetiser** noun a snack taken before a main meal

appetizing or **appetising** adjective tempting to the appetite

applaud verb **1** to show that you approve of something by clapping your hands **2** to express strong approval of and admiration for: I applaud the Prime Minister's decision

applause noun a show of approval by clapping

apple noun a round firm fruit, usually red or green • **the apple of someone's eye** a person or thing that someone loves very much

applet noun, computing a small program that runs within another application

appliance noun a tool, instrument, machine, etc

applicable (pronounced **ap**-li-ka-bl or ap-**li**-ka-bl) adjective **1** able to be applied **2** suitable, relevant

applicant noun someone who applies or asks

application noun **1** the act of applying **2** something applied, eg an ointment **3** a formal request, usually on paper **4** hard work, close attention **5** *computing* (*full form*: **application program**) a computer program which performs a special function, such as word processing, Web browsing, spreadsheet, image editing, etc (*compare with*: **operating system**)

applicator *noun* a tool or device for applying something

applied *adjective* used practically and not just in theory: *applied science*

appliqué (*pronounced* ap-**leek**-ei) *noun* needlework in which cut pieces of fabric are sewn on to a background to form patterns

apply *verb* (**applies, applying, applied**) **1** to put on (an ointment etc) **2** to use: *Apply these rules in each case* **3** to ask formally (for): *apply for a job* **4** to be suitable or relevant • **apply to** to have an effect on • **apply yourself** to work hard

appoint *verb* **1** to fix (a date etc) **2** to place in a job: *She was appointed manager* ♦ **appointed** *adjective* (meaning 1): *fail to arrive at the appointed time*

appointment *noun* **1** the act of appointing **2** a job, a post **3** an arrangement to meet someone

apportion *verb* to divide in fair shares: *The blame must be apportioned among several different people*

apposite (*pronounced* **ap**-o-zit) *adjective* suitable, appropriate

appraise *verb* to estimate the value or quality of: *appraise someone's work* ♦ **appraisal** *noun*

appreciable *adjective* noticeable, considerable

appreciate *verb* **1** to see or understand the good points, beauties, etc of: *appreciate art* **2** to understand: *I appreciate your point* **3** to rise in value ♦ **appreciation** *noun*

apprehend *verb* **1** to arrest: *The escaped prisoner was apprehended early today* **2** *formal* to understand

apprehension *noun* **1** arrest **2** fear or nervousness **3** *formal* understanding

apprehensive *adjective* afraid

apprentice *noun* someone who is learning a trade ♦ **apprenticeship** *noun*

approach *verb* **1** to come near **2** to be nearly equal to **3** to speak to in order to ask for something ➤ *noun* (*plural* **approaches**) **1** a coming near to **2** a way leading to a place

approachable *adjective* **1** able to be reached **2** easy to speak to, friendly

approbation *noun* good opinion, approval

appropriate *adjective* (*pronounced* a-**proh**-pri-at) suitable, fitting ➤ *verb* (*pronounced* a-**proh**-pri-eit) **1** to take possession of: *She seems to have appropriated certain items of my clothing* **2** to set (money etc) apart for a purpose: *Funds must be appropriated for this work* ♦ **appropriately** *adverb*: *the appropriately named 'Wall of Death'* ♦ **appropriation** *noun*

ⓘ 'to appropriate' (meaning 1) is often used as a euphemism for 'to steal'

---

appropriate technology *noun* the development of industries and use of equipment most appropriate for a particular locality, eg weaving, pottery, etc in developing countries (*see also*: **intermediate technology**)

approval *noun* **1** permission **2** satisfaction, favourable judgement • **on approval** on trial, for return to a shop if not bought

approve *verb* **1** to agree to, permit **2** to think well (of)

approximate *adjective* (*pronounced* ap-**rok**-sim-at) more or less accurate ➤ *verb* (*pronounced* ap-**rok**-sim-eit) (**approximate to**) to be or come near to ♦ **approximately** *adverb*

approximation *noun* a rough estimate

apricot (*pronounced* **ei**-pri-kot) *noun* an orange-coloured fruit like a small peach

April *noun* the fourth month of the year

⏲ From a Latin word meaning 'open', because spring flowers start to open their buds around April

---

a priori (*pronounced* ei prai-**aw**-rai or a pri-**aw**-ri) *adjective* based on accepted principles or arguments (*compare with*: **a posteriori**)

apron *noun* **1** a garment worn to protect the front of the clothes **2** a hard surface for aircraft to stand on

apron stage *noun* the part of the stage in front of the curtains in a theatre

apropos (*pronounced* a-pro-**poh**) *adverb*: **apropos of** in connection with, concerning

apse *noun* a rounded domed section, especially at the east end of a church

apt *adjective* **1** likely (to): *apt to change his mind* **2** suitable, fitting ♦ **aptly** *adverb*

aptitude *noun* talent, ability

aptness *noun* suitability

aqua- *prefix* of or relating to water ⏲ Comes from Latin *aqua* meaning 'water'

aqualung *noun* a breathing apparatus worn by divers

aquamarine *noun* **1** a type of bluish-green precious stone **2** a bluish-green colour ➤ *adjective* bluish-green

aquaplane *verb* of a vehicle: to skid out of control on a thin film of water

aquarium *noun* (*plural* **aquaria** or **aquariums**) a tank or tanks for keeping fish or water animals

Aquarius *noun* **1** the eleventh sign of the zodiac, represented by the water carrier **2**

someone born under this sign, between 21 January and 19 February

aquatic *adjective* living, growing or taking place in water

aqueduct *noun* a bridge for taking a canal etc across a valley

aqueous (*pronounced* **ei**-kwi-us) *adjective* **1** relating to water **2** dissolved in water

aqueous humour *noun, anatomy* the clear liquid between the lens and the cornea of the eye

aqueous solution *noun, chemistry* a solution in which the solvent is water

aquiline *adjective* **1** like an eagle **2** of a nose: curved or hooked

Ar *symbol, chemistry* argon

Arab *noun* a member of a Semitic people living in the Middle East and N Africa ➤ *adjective* of or relating to the Arabs

Arabic *noun* the language of the Arabs ➤ *adjective* of or relating to Arabs or their language

Arabic numeral *noun* one of the numbers 1, 2, 3, 4, 5, 6, 7, 8, 9, 0, based on Arabic characters

arable *adjective* of land: used for growing crops

arachnid (*pronounced* a-**rak**-nid) *noun* any eight-legged invertebrate animal belonging to the class which includes spiders and scorpions

arachnoid *adjective* **1** relating to or resembling an arachnid **2** resembling a spider's web **3** *botany* covered in, or made up of, thin delicate fibres

arbiter *noun* **1** a judge, an umpire; someone chosen by opposing parties to decide between them **2** someone who sets a standard or has influence: *arbiter of good taste*

arbitrage *noun* the practice of buying goods etc in one market and selling in another to make a profit

arbitrary *adjective* **1** fixed according to opinion or whim rather than by objective rules **2** occurring haphazardly ✦ **arbitrarily** *adverb*

arbitrate *verb* to act as a judge between people or their claims etc: *arbitrate between the different parties/It falls to me to arbitrate this case* ✦ **arbitration** *noun* ✦ **arbitrator** *noun*

arboreal (*pronounced* ah-**bawr**-ri-al) *adjective* of trees; living in trees

arboretum (*pronounced* ahr-bo-**ree**-tum) *noun* (*plural* **arboreta**) a garden where trees and shrubs are grown for display

arbour *noun* a seat in a garden shaded by trees etc

arc *noun* **1** part of a curve or of the circumference of a circle **2** something that appears curved in shape ➤ *verb* (**arcing, arced**) **1** to form an arc **2** to move in an arc

arcade *noun* a covered walk, especially one with shops on both sides

arcane *adjective* mysterious or secret; difficult to understand ☉ Comes from Latin *arcanus*, from *arcere* meaning 'to shut up'

arch *noun* (*plural* **arches**) the curved part above people's heads in a gateway or the curved support for a bridge, roof, etc ➤ *adjective* mischievous, roguish ➤ *verb* to raise or curve in the shape of an arch

arch- *prefix* chief, main: *arch-enemy* ☉ Comes from Greek *archos* meaning 'chief'

i Arch- is usually pronounced *ahch* (as in 'March'), but in *archangel* it is pronounced *ahk* (like 'ark').

-arch (*pronounced* ahrk) *suffix* chief, ruler: *monarch/matriarch* ☉ Comes from Greek *arche* meaning 'rule'

Archaean *adjective* of the geological era from the formation of the earth to 2500 million years ago

archaebacterium (*pronounced* ahr-ki-bak-**teer**-i-um) *noun* (*plural* **archaebacteria**), *biology* any of various micro-organisms which resemble ordinary bacteria in size and structure but which evolved separately, so that the organization of their molecules is unique

archaeo- *prefix* of or relating to ancient or primitive things ☉ Comes from Greek *archaios* meaning 'ancient'

archaeology *noun* the study of the people of earlier times from the remains of their buildings etc ✦ **archaeological** *adjective* ✦ **archaeologist** *noun*

archaic (*pronounced* ahrk-**ei**-ik) *adjective* no longer used, old-fashioned

archaism (*pronounced* **ahrk**-ei-izm) *noun* an old-fashioned word etc

archangel *noun* a chief angel

archbishop *noun* a chief bishop

archdeacon *noun* a clergyman next in rank below a bishop

archduke *noun, history* the title of the ruling princes of Austria

archer *noun* someone who shoots arrows from a bow

archery *noun* the sport of shooting with a bow and arrows

archetype (*pronounced* **ahrk**-i-taip) *noun* **1** the original pattern or model from which copies are made **2** a perfect example ✦ **archetypal** *adjective*

Archimedes' principle (*pronounced* ahrk-i-**mee**-deez) *noun, physics* the law that, when a body is immersed in a liquid, the weight of the fluid displaced by the body is equal to the weight of the body

ⓘ Named after the Greek philosopher, mathematician and scientist *Archimedes* (c.287–212 BC)

archipelago (*pronounced* ahrk-i-**pe**-la-goh) *noun* (*plural* **archipelagoes** or **archipelagos**) a group of small islands

ⓘ From an ancient Greek term meaning 'chief sea', referring to the Aegean Sea, which contains many small islands

architect *noun* someone who plans and designs buildings

architecture *noun* **1** the study or profession of designing and constructing buildings **2** the style of a building ♦ **architectural** *adjective*

archive *noun* **1** archives **2** *computing* a place on a computer for storing files that are rarely used

archives *plural noun* **1** historical papers, written records, etc **2** a building etc in which these are kept

archway *noun* a passage or road beneath an arch

-archy *suffix* forms nouns describing different types of government: *monarchy/oligarchy* ⓘ Comes from Greek *arche* meaning 'rule'

arc lamp or **arc light** *noun* a bright lamp lit by a special kind of electric current

Arctic or **arctic** *adjective* **1** (*usually* **Arctic**) of the district round the North Pole **2** (*usually* **arctic**) very cold

ardas (*pronounced* uhr-**das**) *noun, Sikhism* a short direct prayer to God ⓘ Comes from Punjabi meaning 'supplication'

ardent *adjective* eager, passionate ♦ **ardently** *adverb* ♦ **ardour** *noun*

arduous *adjective* difficult, needing a lot of work or effort: *an arduous climb to the top*

are see **be**

area *noun* **1** the extent of a surface measured in square metres etc **2** a region, a piece of land or ground

arena *noun* **1** any place for a public contest, show, etc **2** *history* the centre of an amphitheatre etc where gladiators fought

ⓘ From a Latin word meaning 'sand', after the sand-covered arenas in which Roman gladiators fought

areola (*pronounced* a-ree-**oh**-la) *noun* (*plural* **areolae** – *pronounced* a-ree-**oh**-lee – or **areolas**), *anatomy* **1** a ring of pigmented tissue surrounding a nipple **2** the part of the iris surrounding the pupil of the eye

arête (*pronounced* a-**ret**) *noun, geography* a ridge on the side of a mountain, between two corries ⓘ Comes from French, from Latin *arista* meaning 'ear of corn' or 'fish bone'

Argand diagram (*pronounced* **ahr**-gand) *noun, maths* a graph representing complex numbers, with real numbers shown on the x-axis and imaginary numbers shown on the y-axis

argon *noun, chemistry* (symbol **Ar**) a colourless, odourless, inert gas, one of the noble gases

arguable *adjective* that can be argued as being true

arguably *adverb* in certain people's opinion (although this opinion could be disagreed with): *This is arguably the best Scottish film of the decade*

argue *verb* **1** to quarrel in words **2** to try to prove by giving reasons (that) **3** (**argue for** or **against something**) to give reasons for or against something as a way of persuading people

argument *noun* **1** a heated discussion, quarrel **2** reasoning (for or against something) **3** *maths, computing* a quantity or element to which a function, operation, etc applies **4** *maths* a variable on which another depends

argumentative *adjective* fond of arguing

aria *noun* a song for a solo voice in an opera

arid *adjective* **1** dry **2** of climate: hot and dry ♦ **aridity** or **aridness** *noun*

Aries *noun* **1** the first sign of the zodiac, represented by the ram **2** someone born under this sign, between 21 March and 20 April

arise *verb* (**arising, arose, arisen**) **1** to rise up **2** to come into being

aristocracy *noun* people of the nobility and upper class

aristocrat *noun* a member of the aristocracy

aristocratic *adjective* of the aristocracy

arithmetic *noun* a way of counting and calculating by using numbers ♦ **arithmetical** *adjective*

arithmetic logic unit *noun, computing* (*abbrev* **ALU**) in the central processing unit of a computer: the circuit or set of circuits that performs arithmetic operations and logical operations

arithmetic mean *noun, maths* the result obtained by adding several amounts and dividing the total by the number of amounts, eg the arithmetic mean of 3, 7, 9, 13 is 8 $(32 \div 4)$

arithmetic progression or **arithmetic sequence** *noun, maths* a sequence of numbers in which each number differs from the preceding and following ones by a constant amount, eg 4, 10, 16, 22

ark *noun* (**the Ark**) the covered boat used by Noah in the story of the Flood in the Bible and the Koran

arm *noun* **1** the part of the body between the shoulder and the hand **2** anything jutting out like this **3** the sleeve of a garment **4** (**arms**) weapons ➤ *verb* to equip with weapons • **chance your arm** to say or do something which, though a bit

risky, could possibly get you what you want
• **twist someone's arm** to persuade someone forcefully

armada *noun* a fleet of armed ships

armadillo *noun* (*plural* **armadillos**) a small American animal whose body is protected by bony plates

⊙ From a Spanish word meaning 'armed man', because of the animal's weapon-like plates

armageddon *noun* a final battle or devastation, an apocalypse

armaments *plural noun* equipment for war, especially the guns of a ship, tank, etc

armchair *noun* a comfortable chair with arms at each side

armed *adjective* carrying a weapon, now especially a gun

armed forces *plural noun* the military forces of a country

armistice *noun* a halt in fighting during war, a truce

armour *noun, history* a protective suit of metal worn by knights

armoured *adjective* of a vehicle: protected by metal plates

armoury *noun* (*plural* **armouries**) a store for military arms

armpit *noun* the hollow under the arm at the shoulder

army *noun* (*plural* **armies**) **1** a large number of soldiers armed for war **2** a great number of people, animals, etc

aroma *noun* a sweet smell

aromatherapy *noun* a healing therapy involving massage with plant oils

aromatic *adjective* **1** having a strong but pleasant smell **2** *chemistry* of an organic compound: with carbon atoms arranged in one or more rings rather than chains (*compare with*: **aliphatic**)

arose past tense of **arise**

around *preposition* **1** in a circle about **2** on all sides of, surrounding **3** all over, at several places in: *papers scattered around the room* **4** somewhere near in time, place, amount: *I left him around here/Come back around three o'clock* ➤ *adverb* all about, in various places: *People stood around watching* • **get around 1** of a story: to become known to everyone **2** to be active • **get around to something** or **get around to doing something** to do something eventually or reluctantly

arousal *noun* **1** the state of being stimulated or excited, especially sexually **2** awakening (of feelings)

arouse *verb* **1** to awaken **2** to stir, move (a feeling or person)

arpeggio (*pronounced* ahr-**ped**-jee-oh) *noun, music* a chord with the notes played in rapid succession, not at the same time

arrange *verb* **1** to put in some order **2** to plan, settle

arrangement *noun* **1** a pattern or particular order **2** an agreed plan

array *noun* **1** order, arrangement **2** clothing **3** *maths* a set of numbers, counters, etc ordered in rows and columns ➤ *verb* **1** to put in order: *a collection of insects, arrayed in glass cases* **2** to dress, adorn: *arrayed in fantastic plumage*

arrears *plural noun*: **in arrears** not up to date; behind with payments

arrest *verb* **1** to seize, capture, especially by power of the law **2** to stop **3** to catch (the attention etc) **4** *medicine* to suffer a cardiac arrest ➤ *noun* **1** capture by the police **2** stopping ♦ **arresting** *adjective* striking, capturing the attention

arrival *noun* **1** the act of arriving **2** someone or something that arrives

arrive *verb* to reach a place • **arrive at** to reach, come to (a decision etc)

arrogant *adjective* proud, haughty, self-important ♦ **arrogance** *noun* ♦ **arrogantly** *adverb*

arrow *noun* **1** a straight, pointed weapon shot from a bow **2** an arrow shape, eg on a road sign, showing direction

arrowhead *noun* **1** the pointed metal part at the top of an arrow **2** a concave four-sided figure that has one reflex angle

arsenal *noun* a factory or store for weapons, ammunition, etc

arsenic *noun, chemistry* (symbol **As**) a metalloid element that occurs in three different forms, the commonest and most stable of which is a toxic, grey, shiny solid

arson *noun* the crime of setting fire to a house etc on purpose ♦ **arsonist** *noun*

art *noun* **1** drawing, painting, sculpture, etc **2** cleverness, skill; cunning **3** (**arts**) non-scientific school or university subjects

artefact or **artifact** *noun* a human-made object

arterial *adjective* of or like arteries

arterial road *noun* a main road carrying traffic

arteriole *noun, anatomy* a small artery

arteriosclerosis *noun* (*plural* **arterioscleroses**), *medicine* a thickening of the artery walls

artery *noun* (*plural* **arteries**), *anatomy* a tube which carries blood from the heart all around the body

artesian well *noun* a well in which water rises to the surface by natural pressure

artful *adjective* wily, cunning ♦ **artfully** *adverb*

arthritis *noun, medicine* a condition causing swollen and painful joints ♦ **arthritic** *adjective*

arthropod *noun* an invertebrate animal of the phylum that includes insects, crustaceans and arachnids

arti *noun, Hinduism* a ceremony in which incense and lamps are offered to a deity

artichoke *noun* a thistle-like plant with an edible flowerhead

article *noun* **1** a thing, object **2** a piece of writing in a newspaper, journal, etc **3** a section of a document **4** *grammar* one of the words *the, a, an,* or any similar word in other languages ➤ *verb* to bind (an apprentice etc) by articles of a contract

articulate *adjective* (*pronounced* ah-**tik**-yuw-lat) **1** speaking clearly **2** expressing thoughts clearly **3** *biology* having joints ➤ *verb* (*pronounced* ah-**tik**-yuw-leit) **1** to express clearly **2** *biology* to be attached by a joint: *The carpals articulate with the metacarpals* ♦ **articulation** *noun*

articulated lorry *noun* a lorry with a cab which can turn at an angle to the main part of the lorry, making cornering easier

artifact another spelling of **artefact**

artifice *noun* **1** a clever trick; a crafty plan or ploy **2** clever trickery; cunning ☉ Comes from Latin *artificium*, from *ars, artis* meaning 'art' + *facere* meaning 'to make'

artificial *adjective* not natural; man-made ♦ **artificiality** *noun* ♦ **artificially** *adverb*

artificial insemination *noun* the insertion of sperm into the uterus by means other than sexual intercourse

artificial intelligence *noun* (*abbrev* **AI**) the ability of computers to perform actions thought to require human intelligence, eg problem solving

artificial respiration *noun* the starting and maintaining of breathing manually or mechanically, by forcing air in and out of the lungs

artillery *noun* **1** big guns **2** an army division that uses these

artisan *noun* someone who does skilled work with their hands

artist *noun* **1** someone who paints pictures **2** someone skilled in anything **3** an artiste

artiste (*pronounced* ah-**teest**) *noun* a performer in a theatre, circus, etc

artistic *adjective* **1** of artists: *the artistic community* **2** having a talent for art

artistry *noun* skill as an artist

artless *adjective* simple, frank

As *symbol, chemistry* arsenic

as *adverb & conjunction* in phrases expressing comparison or similarity: *as good as his brother/ the same as this one* ➤ *conjunction* **1** while, when: *happened as I was walking past* **2** because, since: *We stayed at home as it was raining* **3** in the same way that: *He thinks as I do* ➤ *adverb* for instance: *large books, as this one* ➤ *preposition* in the role of something: *speaking as a friend* • **as for** concerning, regarding • **as if** or **as though** as it would be if • **as to** regarding • **as well (as)** too, in addition (to)

asbestos *noun* a thread-like mineral which can be woven and will not burn

asbestosis *noun, medicine* a lung disease caused by inhaling asbestos dust

ASBO (*pronounced* **ahz**-boh) *abbreviation* Anti-Social Behaviour Order

ascend *verb* **1** to climb, go up **2** to rise or slope upwards • **ascend the throne** to be crowned king or queen

ascendancy or **ascendency** *noun* control (over)

ascendant or **ascendent** *adjective* rising

ascension *noun* **1** an act of climbing or moving upwards **2** (**the Ascension**) *Christianity* Christ's passing into heaven on the fortieth day after the Resurrection

ascent *noun* **1** an upward move or climb **2** a slope upwards; a rise

ascertain *verb* **1** to find out **2** to make certain

ascetic *noun* someone who keeps away from all kinds of pleasure

ASCII (*pronounced* **as**-ki) *abbreviation, computing* American Standard Code for Information Interchange, a binary code representing characters and used by VDUs, printers, etc

ascomycete (*pronounced* as-koh-**mai**-seet) *noun, biology* any member of a large subdivision of fungi characterized by the formation of asci, eg truffles, morels, most yeasts and many parasitic fungi

ascorbic acid *noun* vitamin C

ascribe *verb* (**ascribe to**) to think of as belonging to or due to that person or thing: *ascribing the blame to parents*

ascus *noun* (*plural* **asci** – *pronounced* **as**-ai or **ask**-ai), *botany* an enlarged cell in which usually eight spores are formed

asexual reproduction (*pronounced* ei-**seks**-yoo-al) *noun, biology* reproduction in which new individuals are produced from a single parent and not from the union of male and female reproductive cells (*compare with*: **sexual reproduction**)

ash *noun* (*plural* **ashes**) **1** a type of hardwood tree with silvery bark **2** (**ashes**) what is left after anything is burnt • **rise from the ashes** to develop and flourish after experiencing ruin or disaster

ashamed *adjective* feeling shame

ashen *adjective* very pale

Ashkenazim *plural noun* the Polish and German Jews (as distinguished from the Sephardim, the Spanish and Portuguese Jews) ➤ *adjective* of the Ashkenazim

Ashkenazi *noun* a member of the Ashkenazim

ashen *adjective* very pale

ashore *adverb* on or on to the shore

ashram *noun, Hinduism* **1** a hermitage for a holy man **2** a place of retreat for a religious community **3** a religious community in an ashram

ashrama *noun, Hinduism* any one of the four stages of life which a man of the upper three castes should pass through: pupil, householder, hermitage-dweller, and wanderer

ashtray *noun* a small dish for the ash from cigarettes

Ash Wednesday *noun, Christianity* the first day of Lent, so called because of the practice of putting ashes on the heads of penitents

aside *adverb* on or to one side; apart ➤ *noun* words spoken in a play which the other actors are not supposed to hear

asinine *adjective* **1** of an ass **2** stupid

ask *verb* **1** to request information about: *asked for my address* **2** to invite: *We've asked over twenty people to come* • **ask after someone** to make enquiries about someone's health and wellbeing

askance *adverb* sideways • **look askance at** to look at with suspicion or disapproval

askew *adverb* not straight, to one side

asleep *adjective* **1** sleeping **2** of limbs: numbed

asp *noun* a small poisonous snake

asparagus *noun* a plant whose young shoots are eaten as a vegetable

aspartame (*pronounced* a-**spahr**-teim) *noun* an artificial sweetener

aspect *noun* **1** look, appearance **2** view, point of view **3** the direction in which something, eg the side of a building or a piece of land, faces

aspen *noun* a kind of poplar tree

asperity *noun* harshness, sharpness of temper

asphalt *noun* a tarry mixture used to make pavements, paths, etc

asphyxia (*pronounced* as-**fik**-si-a) *noun, medicine* suffocation by smoke or other fumes

asphyxiate *verb* to suffocate ✦ **asphyxiation** *noun*

aspidistra *noun* a kind of pot plant with large leaves

aspiration *noun* a goal which you hope to achieve

aspire *verb* (**aspire to** or **after**) to try to achieve or reach something difficult, ambitious, etc

aspirin *noun, medicine* a pain-killing drug

aspiring *adjective* trying or wishing to be: *an aspiring director*

ass *noun* (*plural* **asses**) **1** a donkey **2** a stupid person

assail *verb* to attack

assailant *noun* an attacker

assassin *noun* someone who assassinates, a murderer

⊙ Literally 'hashish eater', after an Islamic sect during the Crusades who took the drug

assassinate *verb* to murder (especially a politically important person) ✦ **assassination** *noun*

assault *noun* an attack, especially a sudden one ➤ *verb* to attack

assault course *noun* a series of physical obstacles to be jumped, climbed, etc

assegai (*pronounced* **as**-eg-ai) *noun* a South African spear, tipped with metal

assemblage *noun* a collection, a gathering

assemble *verb* **1** to bring (people) together **2** to put together (a machine, piece of furniture, etc) **3** to meet together

assembler *noun* **1** someone who or something that assembles **2** *computing* a program that converts a program from assembly language to machine code

assembly *noun* (*plural* **assemblies**) **1** a putting together **2** a gathering of people, especially for a special purpose

assembly language *noun, computing* a programming language used for programs controlling the processor's basic operations

assembly line *noun* a series of machines and workers that an article passes along in each stage of its manufacture

assent *verb* to agree: *The committee assents to your request* ➤ *noun* agreement

assert *verb* **1** to state firmly: *She asserts that she did not take the money* **2** to insist on (a right etc): *women asserting their right to equal pay with men* • **assert yourself** to make yourself noticed, heard, etc ✦ **assertion** *noun*

assertive *adjective* forceful, inclined to assert yourself

assess *verb* **1** to estimate the value, power, etc of **2** to fix an amount (to be paid in tax etc) ✦ **assessment** *noun*

assessor *noun* someone who assesses

asset *noun* **1** an advantage, a help **2** (**assets**) the property of a person, company, etc

assiduous *adjective* persevering; hard-working

assign (*pronounced* a-**sain**) *verb* **1** to give to someone as a share or task: *I've assigned these jobs to you* **2** to fix (a time or place): *assign a date for the meeting*

assignation (*pronounced* as-ig-**nei**-shun) *noun* an appointment to meet

assignment *noun* **1** an act of assigning **2** a task given, especially an essay set for students

assimilate (*pronounced* a-**si**-mi-leit) *verb* **1** to take in and understand (facts etc): *assimilate all the information* **2** to become part of, or make (people) part of, a larger group **3** *biology* of a plant or animal: to manufacture complex organic compounds from simple molecules obtained from the environment or from digested food ▸ *noun* (*pronounced* a-**si**-mi-lat), *biology* an organic compound produced by green plants and certain bacteria that manufactures complex molecules from simple molecules obtained from the environment ♦ **assimilation** *noun*

assist *verb* to help ♦ **assistance** *noun*

assistant *noun* **1** a helper, eg to a senior worker **2** someone who serves in a shop etc

assisted suicide *noun* helping someone to commit suicide because they cannot do so unaided, eg because they are very ill

assizes *plural noun* formerly the name of certain law courts in England and Wales

associate *verb* (*pronounced* a-**soh**-shi-eit) **1** (**associate with**) to keep company with **2** (**associate yourself with**) to join with in partnership or friendship: *associated himself with the radicals* **3** to connect in your mind: *associates gardening with hard work* ▸ *adjective* (*pronounced* as-**oh**-shi-at) joined or connected (with) ▸ *noun* (*pronounced* as-**oh**-shi-at) a friend, partner, companion

association *noun* **1** a club, society, union, etc **2** a partnership, friendship **3** a connection made in the mind

associative *adjective, maths* of an arithmetical process: resulting in the same answer no matter which way the elements are grouped together, as in multiplication, eg $3 \times 2 = 2 \times 3$

assonance *noun* the repetition of the same vowel sound in the same word or in two or more words close together, eg 'my life is fine'

assorted *adjective* various, mixed

assortment *noun* a variety, a mixture

assuage (*pronounced* a-**sweidj**) *verb* to soothe, ease (pain, hunger, etc)

assume *verb* **1** to take upon yourself: *assume responsibility for the errors* **2** to take as true without further proof, take for granted **3** to put on (a disguise etc)

assumed *adjective* false or pretended: *an assumed air of confidence/an assumed name*

assumption *noun* **1** the act of assuming **2** something taken for granted

assurance *noun* **1** a feeling of certainty; confidence **2** a promise **3** insurance

assure *verb* **1** to make (someone) sure: *I assured* *him of my intention to return to work* **2** to state positively (that)

assured *adjective* certain; confident

astatine (*pronounced* **as**-ta-teen) *noun, chemistry* (symbol **At**) a radioactive chemical element, the heaviest of the halogens ⊙ Comes from Greek *astatos* meaning 'unstable'

asterisk *noun* a star (*) used in printing for various purposes, especially to point out a footnote or insertion

astern *adverb* at or towards the back of a ship

asteroid *noun* one of thousands of small, rocky objects that orbit the sun

asthma (*pronounced* **as**-ma) *noun, medicine* an illness causing breathing difficulty, coughing, etc

asthmatic (*pronounced* as-**mat**-ik) *medicine, adjective* suffering from asthma ▸ *noun* someone with asthma

astigmatism (*pronounced* a-**stig**-ma-tizm) *noun, medicine* abnormal curvature of the lens or cornea of the eye, causing distortion of the image of an object

astonish *verb* to surprise greatly ♦ **astonished** *adjective* ♦ **astonishing** *adjective*

astonishment *noun* amazement, wonder

astound *verb* to surprise greatly, amaze ♦ **astounding** *adjective*

astral *adjective* of the stars

astray *adverb* out of the right way, straying

astride *adverb* with legs apart ▸ *preposition* with legs on each side of

astringent *noun* a lotion etc used for closing up the skin's pores ▸ *adjective* **1** used for closing the pores **2** of manner: sharp, sarcastic

astro- or **astr-** *prefix* of or relating to stars or outer space ⊙ Comes from Greek *astron* meaning 'a star'

astrology *noun* the study of the stars and planets and their supposed influence over people's lives ♦ **astrologer** *noun*

astronaut *noun* someone who travels in space

astronomical *adjective* **1** of astronomy **2** of a number: very large

astronomy *noun* the study of the stars and their movements ♦ **astronomer** *noun*

astute *adjective* cunning, clever ♦ **astutely** *adverb*

asunder *adverb* a literary word meaning 'apart' or 'into pieces'

asylum *noun* **1** refuge given in a country to someone from a country where they may be in danger **2** *old* a home for the mentally ill

asylum seeker *noun* someone who has fled their native country in search of asylum in another

asymmetrical (*pronounced* ei-si-**met**-rik-al) *adjective, adjective* displaying asymmetry;

lopsided in appearance ♦ **asymmetrically** *adverb*

asymmetry *noun* the inequality in size, shape or position of two halves on either side of a dividing line (*contrasted with*: **symmetry**)

asymptote (*pronounced* **as**-im-toht) *noun, maths* a straight line which is continually approached by a curve that never actually meets the line ♦ **asymptotic** *adjective* ⊕ Comes from Greek *asymptotos* meaning 'not falling together'

asystole (*pronounced* a-**sis**-to-li) *adjective, noun, medicine* absence or stopping of the heartbeat

At *symbol, chemistry* astatine

at *preposition* **1** showing position, time, etc: *I'll be at home/Come at 7 o'clock* **2** towards: *working at getting fit* • **at all** in any way: *not worried at all*

ataxia *noun, medicine* inability to control movement of the limbs

ate past tense of **eat**

atheism *noun* belief that there is no God

atheist *noun* someone who does not believe in God ♦ **atheistic** *adjective*

atheroma *noun* (*plural* **atheromas** or **atheromata**), *medicine* in atherosclerosis: a fatty deposit that develops on the artery walls

atherosclerosis *noun* (*plural* **atheroscleroses**), *medicine* a form of arteriosclerosis in which fatty deposits develop on the artery walls

athlete *noun* someone good at sport, especially running, gymnastics, etc

athlete's foot *noun* a fungal condition which affects the feet

athletic *adjective* **1** of athletics **2** good at sports; strong, powerful

athletics *noun* running, jumping, etc or competitions in these

-athon or **-thon** *suffix* forms nouns describing events, usually for charity, which are long in terms of time or endurance: *telethon* (= a very long television programme)/*talkathon* (= a long talking-session) ⊕ Comes from the ending of mara*thon*

atlas *noun* (*plural* **atlases**) a book of maps

⊕ After a mythological giant called *Atlas*, who was pictured on early books of maps supporting the heavens on his shoulders

ATM *abbreviation* automatic teller machine

atman *noun, Buddhism, Hinduism* (also *Buddhism* **atta**, *Hinduism* **atma**) the soul, the real self

atmosphere *noun* **1** the air round the earth **2** any surrounding feeling or mood: *friendly atmosphere*

atmospheric *adjective* **1** in or of the atmosphere **2** of a place, piece of art, etc: conveying a mood or impression

atmospheric circulation *noun* the movement of air and areas of pressure in the atmosphere

atmospheric pressure *noun* the pressure exerted by the atmosphere at the earth's surface, due to the weight of the air

atmospherics *plural noun* air disturbances causing crackling noises on the radio etc

atoll *noun* a coral island or reef

atom *noun* **1** *chemistry* the smallest part of an element, consisting of protons and neutrons **2** anything very small

atom bomb or **atomic bomb** *noun* a bomb in which the explosion is caused by nuclear energy

atomic *adjective* **1** relating to an atom or atoms **2** using nuclear energy: *atomic bombs*

atomic clock *noun, physics* a precise clock regulated by the movements of individual atoms or molecules

atomic energy *noun* nuclear energy

atomicity *noun, chemistry* **1** existence in the form of atoms **2** the number of atoms in a molecule of an element

atomic mass short for **relative atomic mass**

atomic mass unit *noun, chemistry* a unit of mass equal to that of a twelfth of a carbon-12 atom, used to denote the masses of atoms or molecules

atomic number *noun, chemistry* (symbol **Z**) the number of protons in the nucleus of an atom

atomic theory *noun, chemistry* the theory that all matter can be formed by the union of atoms

atomic weight see **relative atomic mass**

atomizer or **atomiser** *noun* an instrument for releasing liquids in a fine spray

atonal (*pronounced* ei-**toh**-nal) *adjective* of music: not written in a particular key ♦ **atonality** *noun*

atone *verb* to make up for wrongdoing

atonement *noun* **1** an act of making amends for a wrongdoing **2** (**the Atonement**) *Christianity* the reconciliation of God and humanity through Christ

⊕ Comes from the earlier phrase *at onement*, meaning 'in harmony'

ATP *abbreviation, chemistry* adenosine triphosphate, a compound that is the main source of energy in living organisms (*compare with*: **ADP**)

atrium *noun* (*plural* **atria** or **atriums**) **1** a central court or entrance hall in an ancient Roman house **2** a court in a public space, with galleries around it **3** *anatomy* either of the two upper chambers of the heart that receive blood from the veins

atrocious *adjective* **1** cruel or wicked **2** *informal* very bad

atrocity *noun* (*plural* **atrocities**) **1** a terrible crime **2** *informal* something very ugly

atrophy (*pronounced* **aht**-rof-i) *verb* (**atrophies, atrophying, atrophied**)**1** to make or become weak and thin through lack of use or nourishment **2** to diminish or die away; to cause to diminish or die away: *Respect had atrophied with the passing years* ➤ *noun* the process of atrophying ⊕ Comes from Greek *atrophia* meaning 'lack of nourishment', from *trephein* meaning 'to feed'

attach *verb* **1** to fasten or join (to) **2** to think of (something) as having: *Don't attach any importance to it*

attaché (*pronounced* a-**tash**-ei) *noun* a junior member of an embassy staff

attaché case *noun* small case for papers etc

attached *adjective* **1** fastened **2** (**attached to**) fond of

attachment *noun* **1** something attached: *a vacuum cleaner attachment* **2** a joining by love or friendship **3** *computing* an electronic file sent with an e-mail message

attack *verb* **1** to suddenly or violently try to hurt or damage **2** to speak or write against ➤ *noun* **1** an act of attacking **2** a bout (of an illness etc)

attain *verb* to reach; gain

attainable *adjective* able to be attained

attainment *noun* the act of attaining; the thing attained, an achievement or accomplishment

attempt *verb* to try ➤ *noun* a try or effort: *a first attempt*

attend *verb* **1** to be present at **2** (**attend to**) to pay attention to **3** (**attend to**) to wait on, look after someone **4** to accompany

attendance *noun* **1** the fact of being present: *My attendance was expected* **2** the number of people present: *good attendance at the first night*

attendant *noun* someone employed to look after a public place, shop, etc: *a cloakroom attendant* ➤ *adjective* accompanying, related: *stress and its attendant health problems*

attention *noun* **1** careful notice: *pay attention* **2** concentration **3** care **4** *military* a stiffly straight standing position: *stand to attention*

attentive *adjective* **1** giving or showing attention **2** polite ♦ **attentively** *adverb*

attenuate *verb* **1** to make or become thin or weak **2** to reduce the value or something **3** *physics* of sound, radiation, etc: to decrease in intensity after passing through a medium ♦ **attenuation** *noun*

attest *verb* **1** to affirm or be proof of the truth of something **2** (**attest to**) to certify that something is so, especially by giving a sworn statement ⊕ Comes from Latin *attestari*, from *ad* meaning 'to' + *testari* meaning 'to bear witness'

attic *noun* a room just under the roof of a house

⊕ From *Attica* in ancient Greece, famous for a type of square architectural column used in upper storeys of classical buildings

attire *formal, verb* to dress ➤ *noun* clothing

attitude *noun* **1** a way of thinking or feeling: *a positive attitude* **2** a position of the body

attorney *noun* (*plural* **attorneys**) **1** someone with legal power to act for another **2** *US* a lawyer

attract *verb* **1** to draw to or towards **2** to arouse liking or interest

attraction *noun* **1** the power of attracting **2** something which attracts visitors etc: *a tourist attraction* **3** *physics* a force that pulls two objects together, eg that between opposite electric charges

attractive *adjective* **1** good-looking, likeable **2** pleasing: *attractive price*

attribute *verb* (*pronounced* a-**trib**-yoot) **1** to state or consider as the source or cause of: *attribute the accident to human error* **2** to state as the author or originator of: *attributed to Rembrandt* ➤ *noun* (*pronounced* **a**-trib-yoot) **1** a quality or characteristic, often with positive connotations: *one of her many attributes/attributes of power* **2** *computing* an item of information about a file stored by the operating system, eg the date and time last saved ♦ **attributable** *adjective*

attributive *adjective* **1** expressing an attribute **2** *grammar* of an adjective: placed immediately before or immediately after the noun it describes, eg 'pretty' ('the pretty girl')

ⓘ Most adjectives can be used in this 'attributive' way. The opposite of attributive (meaning 2) is 'predicative'. An example of an adjective which is only ever used in a predicative way is 'asleep', because you cannot use it to make phrases like 'the asleep girl'.

attrition *noun* **1** wearing down, especially by constant attacks: *a war of attrition* **2** *geography* erosion involving rocks scraping against each other and being worn down

atypical (*pronounced* ei-**tip**-i-kal) *adjective* not typical, representative, usual, etc ♦ **atypically** *adverb*

Au *symbol, chemistry* gold ⊕ Comes from Latin *aurum* meaning 'gold'

aubergine (*pronounced* **oh**-ber-szeen) *noun* an oval, dark purple fruit, eaten as a vegetable

auburn *adjective* of hair: reddish-brown in colour

auction *noun* a public sale in which articles are

sold to the highest bidder ➤ *verb* to sell by auction

auctioneer *noun* someone whose job is to sell things by auction

audacious *adjective* daring, bold ◆ **audacity** *noun*

audible *adjective* able to be heard ◆ **audibility** *noun*

audience *noun* **1** a number of people gathered to watch or hear a performance etc **2** the person reading or listening to a piece of writing or speech **3** a formal interview with someone important: *an audience with the Pope*

audio *noun* the reproduction of recorded or radio sound ➤ *adjective* relating to such sound: *an audio tape*

audio- *prefix* of or relating to sounds which can be heard ◷ Comes from Latin *audio* meaning 'I hear'

audio-typist *noun* a typist able to type from a recording on a tape recorder

audiovisual *adjective* concerned with hearing and seeing at the same time • **audiovisual aids** films, recordings, etc used in teaching

audit *verb* to examine accounts officially ➤ *noun* an official examination of a company's accounts

audition *noun* a short performance to test whether an actor, singer, etc is suitable for a particular role

auditor *noun* someone who audits accounts

auditorium *noun* (*plural* **auditoria** *or* **auditoriums**) the part of a theatre etc where the audience sits

auditory *adjective* of hearing

augment *verb* to increase in size, number or amount ◆ **augmentation** *noun*

augmentative *adjective* having the quality or power of increasing in size, number or amount

augur *verb*: **augur ill** to be a bad sign for the future • **augur well** to be a good sign for the future

August *noun* the eighth month of the year

> ◷ Named in honour of the Roman emperor *Augustus* Caesar

august (*pronounced* aw-**gust**) *adjective* full of dignity, stately

Aum or **Om** *noun*, *Hinduism* a sacred syllable intoned as part of Hindu devotion and contemplation

aunt *noun* a father's or a mother's sister, or an uncle's wife

au pair *noun* a foreign person, usually a girl, who does domestic work in someone's home in return for board, lodging and pocket money

aura *noun* (**auras** or **aurae** – *pronounced* aw-ree) **1** a distinctive character or quality around a

person or in a place **2** an faint light supposedly coming from and surrounding the body **3** *medicine* an unusual sensation that precedes eg a migraine or epileptic seizure ◷ Comes from Greek, meaning 'breeze'

aural *adjective* relating to the ear ◷ Comes from Latin *auris* meaning 'ear'

> ❗ Do not confuse with: **oral**.
> **Oral** means 'relating to the mouth'. It may help to think of the 'O' as looking like an open mouth; and to remember that many words related to listening start with 'au', like 'audition' and 'auditorium'.

auricle *noun*, *anatomy* the outer part of the ear

aurora *noun* (**auroras** or **aurorae** – *pronounced* aw-**raw**-ree), *astronomy* the appearance of bands of coloured lights in the night sky, most often observed from the Arctic and Antarctic regions ◷ Comes from Latin meaning 'dawn'

aurora australis *noun* the aurora visible in the southern hemisphere (*also called*: **the southern lights**) ◷ Comes from Latin meaning 'southern dawn'

aurora borealis *noun* the aurora visible in the northern hemisphere (*also called*: **the northern lights**) ◷ Comes from Latin meaning 'northern dawn'

Ausgleich (*pronounced* **ows**-glaix) *noun*, *history* the agreement establishing a dual monarchy for Austria and Hungary in 1867 ◷ Comes from German, meaning 'settlement'

auspices *plural noun*: **under the auspices of** with the support or guidance of

auspicious *adjective* favourable; promising luck

austere *adjective* **1** severe **2** without luxury; simple, sparse ◆ **austerity** *noun*

autarchy (*pronounced* **aw**-tahr-ki) *noun* (*plural* **autarchies**) government of a country by a ruler who has absolute power ◷ Comes from Greek *autarchos* meaning 'an absolute ruler'

autarky (*pronounced* **aw**-tahr-ki) *noun* (*plural* **autarkies**) **1** a system or policy of economic self-sufficiency in a country, state, etc, with strict limits on international trade **2** a country, state, etc that operates this kind of economic system or policy ◷ Comes from Greek *autarkeia* meaning 'self-sufficiency'

authentic *adjective* true, real, genuine ◆ **authentically** *adverb* ◆ **authenticity** *noun*

authenticate *verb* to show to be true or real ◆ **authentication** *noun*

author *noun* the writer of a book, poem, play, etc

authoritarian *adjective* insisting on or characterized by strict authority ➤ *noun* a

person who insists on having strict authority
♦ **authoritarianism** noun

authoritative adjective stated by an expert or someone in authority

authority noun (plural **authorities**) **1** the power or right to control others **2** someone whose opinion is reliable, an expert **3** someone or a body of people having control (over something) **4** (**the authorities**) people in power

authorize or **authorise** verb **1** to give (a person) the power or the right to do something: I have authorized him to carry out these tasks **2** to give permission (for something to be done): The proposed renovation work has been authorized ♦ **authorization** noun

autism noun a disability affecting a person's ability to relate to and communicate with other people ♦ **autistic** adjective

auto- or **aut-** prefix **1** self: autobiography **2** self-caused or automatic **3** of or relating to cars ⊙ Comes from Greek autos meaning 'self' or 'same'

autobiographer noun the writer of an autobiography

autobiography noun (plural **autobiographies**) the story of someone's life, written or told by themselves
♦ **autobiographical** adjective

autocatalysis noun, chemistry a catalytic reaction that is catalysed by one of the products of the reaction

autocracy noun (plural **autocracies**) government by an autocrat, or a country ruled by an autocrat

autocrat noun a ruler who has complete power

autocratic adjective expecting complete obedience

autocue noun, television a screen hidden from the camera which slowly shows a script line by line, so that the newscaster or speaker can read it

autogamy noun, botany in flowering plants: self-fertilization

autograph noun **1** someone's own signature **2** someone's own handwriting ➤ verb to write your own name on: autograph the book

autoimmunity noun, biology the production by the body of antibodies that attack constituents of its own tissues ♦ **autoimmune** adjective

autolysis (pronounced aw-**tol**-i-sis) noun, biology the breakdown of cells or tissues by enzymes produced within them

automate verb to make automatic by introducing machines etc

automatic adjective **1** of a machine etc: working on its own **2** of an action: unconscious, without thinking ➤ noun **1** something automatic

(eg an automatic washing-machine) **2** a kind of self-loading gun ♦ **automatically** adverb: Second-time offenders will automatically lose their licence

automatic pilot or **autopilot** noun a device which can be set to control an aircraft on a course • **on automatic pilot** or **on autopilot** (doing something) without thinking, as when bored, distracted, etc

automatic teller machine or **autoteller** noun (abbrev **ATM**) an electronic panel set into the wall of a bank etc from which customers can obtain cash etc

automation noun the use of machines for controlling other machines in factories etc

automaton (pronounced aw-**tom**-a-ton) noun (plural **automata**) **1** a mechanical toy or machine made to look and move like a human **2** someone who acts mindlessly, like a machine

automobile noun, US a car

autonomic nervous system noun, biology a system of nerve fibres, muscles, glands, etc whose actions are automatic

autonomy noun the power or right of a country to govern itself ♦ **autonomous** adjective

autopilot see **automatic pilot**

autopsy noun (plural **autopsies**) an examination of the internal organs of a body after death

autoradiography noun, physics, biology a photographic technique for showing the positions of radioactive molecules in a specimen

autosome noun, genetics a chromosome other than a sex chromosome ♦ **autosomal** adjective

autoteller see **automatic teller machine**

autotrophic adjective, biology of an organism such as a plant: manufacturing complex organic compounds from simple inorganic substances such as carbon dioxide and nitrogen
♦ **autotroph** noun an autotrphic organism
♦ **autotrophism** or **autotrophy** noun

autumn noun the season of the year following summer, when leaves change colour and fruits are ripe

autumnal adjective **1** relating to autumn **2** like that or those of autumn: autumnal colours

auxiliary adjective supplementary, additional ➤ noun (plural **auxiliaries**) a helper, an assistant

auxiliary verb noun, grammar a short verb, eg 'be', 'do', 'have' or 'can', used with other verbs to show tense etc, eg 'has' in 'he has gone' (also called: **helping verb**)

auxin noun, botany a hormone that promotes and regulates plant growth

avail verb: **avail yourself of** to make use of: avail yourself of this opportunity ➤ noun: **to no avail** without any effect, of no use

available *adjective* able or ready to be made use of ◆ **availability** *noun*

avalanche *noun* **1** a mass of snow and ice sliding down from a mountain **2** a great amount: *an avalanche of work*

avant-garde *adjective* ahead of fashion, very modern

avarice *noun* greed, especially for riches ◆ **avaricious** *adjective*

avatar *noun* **1** *Hinduism* the appearance of a god, especially Vishnu, in human or animal form **2** the visual manifestation of something abstract **3** an icon or other visual image representing a person in virtual reality or cyberspace ⊕ Comes from Sanskrit *ava* meaning 'down' + *tarati* meaning 'he passes over'

avenge *verb* to take revenge for (a wrong): *avenge his sister's death/determined to avenge herself*

avenue *noun* **1** a tree-lined street or drive up to a house **2** a means, a way: *avenue of escape*

average *noun* the result obtained by adding several amounts and dividing the total by the number of amounts, eg the average of 3, 7, 9, 13 is 8 (32 ÷ 4) ➤ *adjective* **1** ordinary, usual; of medium size etc **2** obtained by working out an average: *The average cost will be £10 each* ➤ *verb* **1** to form an average **2** to find the average of

averse *adjective* not fond of, opposed (to)

❗ Do not confuse with: **adverse**

aversion *noun* **1** extreme dislike or distaste: *an aversion to sprouts* **2** something that is hated

avert *verb* **1** to turn away or aside: *avert your eyes* **2** to prevent from happening: *avert the danger*

aviary *noun* (*plural* **aviaries**) a place for keeping birds

aviation *noun* **1** the practice of flying or piloting aircraft **2** the business of designing and producing aircraft

aviator *noun* an aircraft pilot

avid *adjective* eager, greedy: *an avid reader* ◆ **avidity** *noun*

avocado *noun* (*plural* **avocados**) **1** a pear-shaped fruit with a rough peel and rich, creamy flesh **2** a light, yellowish-green colour

Avogadro's constant or **Avogadro's number** *noun, chemistry* the number of atoms, molecules or ions that are present in a mole of any substance

Avogadro's law or **Avogadro's rule** *noun, chemistry* the law which states that, at the same temperature and pressure, equal volumes of all gases contain the same number of molecules

⊕ Named after the Italian scientist, Amedeo *Avogadro* (1776–1856), who proposed the law

avoid *verb* to escape, keep clear of ◆ **avoidable** *adjective* ◆ **avoidance** *noun*

avoirdupois (*pronounced* av-wahr-dyoo-**pwah**) *noun* the system of measuring weights in pounds and ounces (*compare with*: **metric system**)

avow *verb, formal* to declare openly ◆ **avowal** *noun* ◆ **avowed** *adjective*

avuncular (*pronounced* a-**vung**-kyoo-lar) *adjective* relating to or like an uncle, especially in being kind and caring ⊕ Comes from Latin *avunculus* maning 'maternal uncle', from *avus* meaning 'grandfather'

await *verb* to wait for

awake *verb* **1** to rouse from sleep **2** to stop sleeping ➤ *adjective* not asleep

awaken *verb* **1** to awake **2** to arouse (interest etc)

awakening *noun* the act or process of waking up or coming into existence: *the awakening of unfamiliar feelings/a rude awakening* (= an event which brings someone sharply out of a dreamlike state and into the world of harsh reality)

award *verb* **1** to give, grant (a prize etc) **2** to grant legally: *awarded custody of the children* ➤ *noun* something that is awarded, a prize etc

aware *adjective* **1** having knowledge (of), conscious (of): *aware of the dangers* **2** alert ◆ **awareness** *noun*

away *adverb* **1** to or at a distance from the speaker or person spoken to: *Throw that ball away* **2** in the proper place: *Put the toys away* **3** in the opposite direction: *He turned away and left* **4** into nothing: *The sound died away* **5** constantly: *working away* • **do away with** to abolish, get rid of • **get away with** to do (something) without being punished • **make away with** to steal and escape with • **right** or **straight away** immediately

awe *noun* wonder or admiration mixed with fear ➤ *verb* to fill with awe: *awed by the occasion*

awesome *adjective* **1** causing awe **2** *informal* remarkable, admirable

awestruck *adjective* full of awe

awful *adjective* **1** *informal* bad: *an awful headache* **2** *informal* very great: *an awful lot* **3** terrible: *I feel awful about this*

awfully *adverb, informal* very, extremely: *awfully good of you*

awkward *adjective* **1** clumsy, not graceful **2** difficult to deal with: *awkward customer* ◆ **awkwardly** *adverb* ◆ **awkwardness** *noun*

awl *noun* a pointed tool for boring small holes

awning *noun* a covering of canvas etc providing shelter

awry (*pronounced* a-**rai**) *adjective & adverb* **1** not according to plan, wrong **2** crooked

axe *noun* a tool for chopping ➤ *verb* **1** to cancel (a plan etc) **2** to reduce greatly (costs, services, etc) • **have an axe to grind** to have a strong point of view or resentful feelings which you tend to express at any opportunity

axil *noun, botany* the angle between a leaf and the stem of plant or a branch and the trunk of a tree

axiom *noun* **1** a self-evident truth **2** an accepted principle **3** an assumption made for the purpose of argument ♦ **axiomatic** *adjective*

axis *noun* (*plural* **axes**) **1** the line, real or imaginary, on which a thing turns **2** the axis of the earth, from North to South Pole, around which the earth turns **3** *maths, geography* a fixed line taken as a reference to map points on a graph, eg the horizontal x-axis and the vertical y-axis **4** an alliance of powerful nations **5** *history* (**Axis**) the political alliance made in 1936 by Germany and Italy

axis of symmetry *noun, maths* a line through a figure on which the opposite sides are symmetrical

axle *noun* the rod on which a wheel turns

ayatollah *noun* a religious leader of the Shiah sect of Islam

aye *adverb* yes ➤ *noun* a vote in favour of something

azan or **adhan** *noun, Islam* the call to prayer made five times a day by a muezzin

Aztec *noun* **1** a group of Mexican peoples whose enpire was overthrown by the Spanish in the 16th century **2** someone belonging to this group of peoples **3** the language of this group of peoples ♦ *adjective* belonging or referring to this group or their language

azure (*pronounced* **ei**-szur) *adjective* sky-coloured, clear blue

B¹ *noun* **1** *music* the seventh note in the scale of C major **2** the name of a blood group

B² *symbol, chemistry* boron

BA *abbreviation* **1** British Airways **2** Bachelor of Arts

Ba *symbol, chemistry* barium

babble *verb* to talk indistinctly or foolishly ➤ *noun* indistinct or foolish talk

babe *noun* **1** *old* a baby **2** *informal* a girl or young woman

babel (*pronounced* **bei**-bel) *noun* **1** a confused sound of voices **2** a scene of noise and confusion

---

① Comes from Hebrew *Babel*, the place where, according to the biblical account, God caused people to speak different languages

---

baboon *noun* a large monkey with a dog-like snout

baby *noun* (*plural* **babies**) a very young child, an infant ➤ *verb* (**babies, babying, babied**) to treat like a baby

babyhood *noun* the time when someone is a baby

babysit *verb* (**babysitting, babysat**) to look after a child while its parents are out

babysitter *noun* someone who looks after a child while its parents are out

baccalaureate (*pronounced* bak-a-**law**-ree-at) *noun* **1** *formal* a Bachelor's degree **2** a diploma of a lower status than a degree ① Comes from French *baccalauréat*, from Latin *baccalaureus* meaning 'bachelor'

bachelor *noun* **1** an unmarried man **2** (**Bachelor**) someone who has passed examinations at a certain level in subjects at a university; a person who has taken a first university degree: *Bachelor of Science*

bacillus (*pronounced* ba-**sil**-us) *noun* (*plural* **bacilli** – *pronounced* ba-**sil**-ai), *biology* a rod-shaped germ found in soil and air

back *noun* **1** the part of the human body from the neck to the base of the spine **2** the upper part of an animal's body **3** the part of anything situated behind: *sitting at the back of the bus* **4** *football etc* a player positioned behind the forwards ➤ *adjective* of or at the back ➤ *adverb* **1** to or in the place from which someone or something came: *back at the house/walked back home* **2** to or in a former time or condition: *thinking back to*

their youth ➤ *verb* **1** to move backwards **2** to bet on (a horse etc) **3** (often **back up**) to help or support ♦ **backer** *noun* • **back down** to change your opinion etc • **back out 1** to move out backwards **2** to excuse yourself from keeping to an agreement • **back someone up** to support or assist them • **back something up** to copy (computer data) onto a disk or tape (*see also*: **backup**) • **put your back into** to work hard at • **put someone's back up** to irritate someone • **with your back to the wall** in desperate difficulties ① Comes from Old English *bæc*

back bench *noun* a seat in the House of Commons for members who do not hold an official position in the government or in the opposition (*compare with*: **front bench**) ♦ **backbencher** *noun*

backbone *noun* **1** the spine **2** the main support of something **3** firmness, resolve

backcloth or **backdrop** *noun, drama* the painted cloth at the back of a stage, forming part of the scenery

backcomb *verb* to comb (the hair) towards the roots to make it look thicker

back-cross *noun, genetics* a cross between a hybrid and a parent

backdate *verb* **1** to put a date on (a document etc) which is earlier than the actual date **2** to make effective from a date in the past

backdoor *adjective* of an activity: done secretly and often dishonestly: *a backdoor deal*

backdrop see **backcloth**

backfire *verb* **1** of a vehicle: to make an explosive noise in the exhaust pipe **2** of a plan: to go wrong

backgammon *noun* a game similar to draughts, played with dice

background *noun* **1** the space behind the principal figures or objects in a picture **2** details that explain something **3** someone's family, upbringing and education

background radiation *noun, physics* naturally occurring radiation on Earth, resulting from cosmic rays and from natural radioactive substances, eg certain rocks

backhand *noun, tennis etc* a stroke played with the back of the hand facing the ball (*compare with*: **forehand**)

backhanded compliment *noun* a

compliment with a second, unflattering meaning

backing *noun* **1** support, especially financial support **2** material used on the back of a picture etc **3** a musical accompaniment on a recording

backing store *noun, computing* a large data store supplementary to a computer's main memory

backlog *noun* a pile or amount of uncompleted work etc

backpack *noun* a rucksack ➤ *verb* to travel about with your belongings in a backpack

backspace *verb, computing* to move a computer cursor back one or more spaces

backstage *drama, adverb* behind a theatre stage ➤ *adjective* not seen by the public

backstreet *noun* a street away from a town's main streets ➤ *adjective* secret or illicit: *a backstreet abortion*

backstroke *noun* a stroke used in swimming on the back

backtrack *verb* **1** to return in the direction from which you came **2** to reverse your previous opinion or course of action

backup *noun* **1** support, assistance **2** *computing* a procedure for copying data onto a disk or tape for security purposes, or a copy so made

backward *adjective* **1** to or towards the back: *a backward glance* **2** slow in learning or development

backwards *adverb* **1** towards the back **2** with your back facing the direction of movement: *walked backwards out of the room* **3** in a reverse direction; back to front: *written backwards* **4** towards the past

backwash *noun* a backward current, such as one caused by an outgoing wave (*contrasted with*: **swash**)

backwater *noun* **1** a river pool separate from the main stream **2** *derogatory* an isolated place not affected by what is happening in the outside world

bacon *noun* the flesh of a pig, salted and dried and used as food

bacteria (*pronounced* bak-**teer**-i-a) *plural noun* (*singular* **bacterium**) a diverse group of microscopic and usually single-celled organisms found in air, water, and living and dead bodies, and responsible for decay, fermentation and a number of diseases ♦ **bacterial** *adjective*

bacteriology *noun* the scientific study of bacteria and their effects ♦ **bacteriologist** *noun*

bacteriophage (*pronounced* bak-**tee**-ri-oh-feidj) *noun, biology* any virus whose function is to destroy bacteria (*short form*: **phage**) ⊘ Comes from Greek *phagein* meaning 'to eat'

bad *adjective* (**worse, worst**) **1** not good;

wicked **2** not of a good standard: *bad workmanship/bad at maths* **3** (often **bad for**) harmful: *Smoking is bad for you* **4** of food: rotten, decaying **5** severe, serious: *a bad dose of flu* • **not bad** *informal* quite good

badge *noun* a mark or sign or brooch-like ornament giving some information about the wearer

badger *noun* a black and white burrowing animal of the weasel family which comes out at night ➤ *verb* to pester or annoy

badly *adverb* (**worse, worst**) **1** not well **2** seriously: *badly hurt* **3** very much: *He badly wanted to win* • **badly off** poor

badminton *noun* a game resembling tennis, played with shuttlecocks

⊘ The game was first played in its modern form at *Badminton* House in SW England

baffle *verb* to be too difficult for; puzzle or confound ♦ **baffling** *adjective*

bag *noun* **1** a holder or container, often of a soft material **2** (*also*: **bagful**) the amount a bag can hold: *a bag of crisps* **3** a quantity of fish or game caught **4** (**bags**) *informal* a large amount: *bags of confidence* ➤ *verb* (**bagging, bagged**) **1** to put in a bag **2** to secure possession of, claim: *bag a seat* **3** to kill (an animal) in a hunt

bagatelle *noun* a board game in which balls are struck into numbered holes

bagel or **beigel** (*pronounced* **bei**-gel) *noun* a hard, ring-shaped bread roll ⊘ Comes from Yiddish *beygel*

baggage *noun* luggage

baggy *adjective* (**baggier, baggiest**) of clothes: large and loose

bag lady *noun* a homeless woman who carries her belongings with her in shopping bags

bagpipes *plural noun* a wind instrument made up of a bag and several pipes

baguette *noun* a long narrow French loaf

bail[1] *noun* money given to bail out a prisoner ♦ **bail out** *verb* to obtain temporary release of (an untried prisoner) by giving money which will be forfeited if they do not return for trial ⊘ Comes from Old French *bail* meaning 'custody'

❗ Do not confuse with: **bale**

bail[2] *verb*: **bail out** to bale out

bail[3] *noun, cricket* one of the crosspieces on the top of the wickets ⊘ Probably comes from Old French *baillier* meaning 'to enclose', or from Latin *baculum* meaning 'stick'

❗ Do not confuse with: **bale**

bailiff *noun* **1** an officer who works for a sheriff **2** a landowner's agent

bain-marie (*pronounced* ban-ma-**ree**) *noun*

(plural **bain-maries**) a vessel of hot or boiling water into which another vessel is placed to cook slowly or keep hot

---

Ⓛ A French word meaning 'Mary's bath', named after Mary the sister of Moses, and originally referring to an alchemist's pot

---

bairn noun, Scottish a child

Baisakhi (pronounced bai-**sak**-ee) or **Vaisakhi** noun, Sikhism a festival commemorating the founding of the Khalsa Ⓛ From Hindi Baisakh meaning 'April'

bait noun **1** food put on a hook to make fish bite, or in a trap to attract animals **2** something tempting or alluring ➤ verb **1** to put bait on a hook etc **2** to worry, annoy

---

❗ Do not confuse: **baited** and **bated**, as in the phrase bated breath

---

baize (pronounced beiz) noun a coarse woollen cloth

bake verb **1** to cook in an oven **2** to dry or harden in the sun or in an oven

baked beans plural noun haricot beans baked in tomato sauce and tinned

baker noun someone who bakes or sells bread etc

bakery or **bakehouse** noun (plural **bakeries** or **bakehouses**) **1** a place used for baking in **2** a shop where baked products are sold

baking powder noun a mixture of tartaric acid and sodium bicarbonate, used in baking for raising

baking soda noun bicarbonate of soda

balaclava or **balaklava** noun a knitted covering for the head and neck

---

Ⓛ After the battle of Balaklava in 1854, during the Crimean War, when such headgear was first worn

---

balalaika (pronounced bal-a-**lai**-ka) noun a Russian musical instrument with a triangular body and normally three strings

balance noun **1** physical stability in which the weight of a body is evenly distributed: I lost my balance and fell over **2** the money needed to make the two sides of an account equal **3** a weighing device ➤ verb **1** to be the same in weight **2** to make both sides of an account the same **3** to make or keep steady: She balanced it on her head

balance of trade noun, economics the difference in value of a country's imports and exports

balcony noun (plural **balconies**) **1** a platform built out from the wall of a building **2** an upper floor or gallery in a theatre etc

bald adjective **1** without hair **2** plain, frank: a

bald statement ◆ **baldness** noun

balding adjective going bald

bale¹ noun a large tight bundle of cotton, hay, etc Ⓛ Perhaps comes from Old High German balla, palla meaning 'ball'

❗ Do not confuse with: **bail**

---

bale² verb: **bale out** or **bail out 1** to escape by parachute from an aircraft in an emergency **2** to scoop water out of a boat

baleful adjective harmful, evil: baleful influence

Balfour Declaration noun, history the statement made in November 1917 by Arthur Balfour, the British Foreign Secretary, that Britain was in favour of establishing a home for the Jewish people in Palestine

balk verb **1** to hinder or block **2** (**balk at**) to refuse to do something

ball¹ noun **1** anything round: a ball of wool **2** the round or roundish object used in playing many games • **on the ball** informal in touch with a situation, alert • **play ball** informal to play along, cooperate

ball² noun a formal party at which dancing takes place • **have a ball** informal to have a great time, enjoy yourself

ballad noun **1** a narrative poem with a simple rhyme scheme, usually in verses of four lines **2** a slow romantic song

ballast noun sand, gravel, etc put into a ship to steady it

ball-bearings plural noun small steel balls that sit loosely in grooves and ease the movement of one machinery part over another

ballcock noun a floating ball that rises and falls with the water level in a tank or cistern and controls the inflow of water

ballerina noun a female ballet dancer

ballet noun a form of stylized dancing which tells a story by mime

ballistic missile noun a self-guided missile which falls on to its target

ballistics singular noun the scientific study of the movement of projectiles such as bullets, rockets and missiles ◆ **ballistic** adjective

balloon noun a bag filled with gas to make it float in the air, especially one made of thin rubber used as a toy etc ➤ verb to puff or swell out

ballot noun a way of voting in secret by marking a paper and putting it into a special box ➤ verb (**balloting, balloted**) to collect votes from (people) by ballot

ballpark noun, US a sports field for ball games ➤ adjective rough, estimated: a ballpark figure

ballpoint noun a pen with a tiny ball as the writing point

ballroom *noun* a large room used for public dances etc

balm (*pronounced* bahm) *noun* **1** something soothing **2** a sweet-smelling healing ointment

balmy *adjective* (**balmier, balmiest**) **1** mild, gentle; soothing: *balmy air* **2** sweet-smelling

balsa (*pronounced* **bawl**-sa) *noun* a very light wood, from a tropical American tree (*also called*: **balsawood**)

balsam (*pronounced* **bawl**-sam) *noun* an oily sweet-smelling substance obtained from certain trees

balti (*pronounced* **bawl**-ti) *noun* a style of Indian curry in which the food is cooked in a two-handled wok-like dish ⏱ Comes from Hindi, meaning 'bucket' or 'scoop'

balustrade (*pronounced* **bal**-us-treid) *noun* a row of pillars on a balcony etc, joined by a rail

bamboo *noun* the woody, jointed stem of a type of very tall grass

bamboozle *verb* to puzzle or confuse

ban *noun* an order forbidding something ➤ *verb* (**banning, banned**) to forbid officially (the publication of a book etc)

banal (*pronounced* ba-**nahl**) *adjective* lacking originality or wit; commonplace ◆ **banality** *noun*

banana *noun* the long curved yellow fruit of a type of tropical tree

band *noun* **1** a group of people **2** a group of musicians playing together **3** a strip of some material to put round something **4** a stripe (of colour etc) **5** a group of wavelengths for radio broadcasts ➤ *verb* to join together

bandage *noun* a strip of cloth for winding round a wound

bandana or **bandanna** *noun* a large brightly coloured cotton or silk square, folded and worn around the neck or head

B and B or **B & B** or **b & b** *noun* (*plural* **B and B's** or **B & B's** or **b & b's**) a bed and breakfast

bandit *noun* an outlaw or robber, especially a member of a gang of robbers

bandstand *noun* an outdoor platform with a roof, where bands play music

bandwagon *noun*: **jump** or **climb on the bandwagon** to join something because it is successful or popular

bandwidth *noun* **1** the width of a band of radio or television frequencies **2** *computing* the amount of information that can be conveyed in a link between computers

bandy¹ *adjective* (**bandier, bandiest**) of legs: bent outwards at the knee

bandy² *verb* (**bandies, bandying, bandied**): **bandy words** to argue

bane *noun* a cause of ruin or trouble: *the bane of my life*

bang *noun* **1** a sudden, loud noise **2** a heavy blow ➤ *verb* **1** to close with a bang, slam **2** to hit, strike: *banged his head*

banger *noun* **1** a type of firework that bangs **2** *informal* a sausage **3** *informal* an old car

bangle *noun* a large ring worn on an arm or leg

banish *verb* **1** to order (someone) to leave a country **2** to drive away (doubts, fear, etc)
◆ **banishment** *noun*

banister *noun* the posts and handrail of a staircase

banjo *noun* (*plural* **banjoes** or **banjos**) a stringed musical instrument like a guitar, with a long neck and a round body

bank *noun* **1** a mound or ridge of earth etc **2** the edge of a river **3** a place where money is lent, put for safety, etc **4** a place where blood etc is stored till needed **5** a public bin for collecting items for recycling: *a bottle bank* • **bank on** to depend on, count on

bank account *noun* an arrangement by which you keep money in a bank and take it out when needed

bank card *noun* a cash card, cheque card or debit card

banker *noun* someone who manages a bank

bankfull *noun, geography* the limit to the height of the water in a river before it bursts its banks

bank holiday *noun* a day on which all banks and many shops etc are closed

banking *noun* the business conducted by banks

banknote *noun* a piece of paper money issued by a bank

bankrupt *noun* someone who has no money to pay their debts ➤ *adjective* **1** unable to pay debts **2** utterly lacking in: *bankrupt of ideas*
◆ **bankruptcy** *noun* (*plural* **bankruptcies**)

banner *noun* **1** a large flag carried in processions etc, often hung between two poles **2** any flag **3** *computing* an advertisement or graphic across the width of a Web page

banns *plural noun* a public announcement of a forthcoming marriage

banquet *noun* a ceremonial dinner

banshee *noun* in Scottish and Irish folklore, a female spirit whose wailing warns of a death in a house ⏱ Comes from Irish Gaelic *bean sídhe* meaning 'woman of the fairies'

bantam *noun* a small kind of hen

banter *verb* to tease in fun ➤ *noun* light teasing

Bantu *noun* **1** a group of languages spoken in southern and central Africa **2** the peoples who speak these languages

bap *noun, Scottish & N English dialect* a large flat bread roll

Baptist *noun* a member of the Baptist Church, a Christian group which believes that only adult believers should be baptized, by complete immersion in water

baptize or **baptise** *verb* **1** to dip in, or sprinkle with, water as a sign of admission into the Christian Church **2** to christen, give a name to ♦ **baptism** *noun* ♦ **baptismal** *adjective*

bar *noun* **1** a rod of solid material **2** a broad line or band **3** a piece, a cake: *a bar of soap* **4** a hindrance, a block **5** *geography* a raised area of sand, mud, stones, etc at the mouth of a river or on a beach **6** a room, or counter, where drinks are served in a public house, hotel, etc **7** a public house **8** *law* the rail at which prisoners stand for trial **9** *law* the lawyers who plead in a court **10** *music* a time division ► *preposition* except: *All the runners, bar Ian, finished the race* ► *verb* (**barring, barred**) **1** to fasten with a bar **2** to exclude, shut out: *barred from the competition*

barb *noun* **1** the backward-pointing spike on an arrow, fish-hook, etc **2** *zoology* one of the threadlike structures forming a feather's web

barbarian *noun* an uncivilized person ► *adjective* uncivilized

barbaric *adjective* **1** uncivilized **2** extremely cruel ♦ **barbarity** *noun*

barbecue *noun* **1** a frame on which to grill food over an open fire **2** an outdoor party providing food from a barbecue ► *verb* to cook (food) on a barbecue

⊙ From a Haitian creole term for a wooden grid or frame

barbed *adjective* having a barb or barbs

barbed wire *noun* wire with regular clusters of sharp points, used for fencing etc

barbell *noun* a bar with heavy metal weights at each end, used for weightlifting exercises

barber *noun* a men's hairdresser

barbiturate (*pronounced* bahr-**bit**-yuw-rat) *noun* a type of sedative drug

barbule *noun, zoology* any of the hairlike filaments on the barb of a bird's feather

bar chart *noun* a chart or graph which uses horizontal or vertical blocks or bars to show amounts

barcode *noun* a series of numbers and parallel lines, used on product labels, which provides information about the product for sales checkouts etc

bar code reader *noun* a device that reads a bar code into a computer system

bard *noun, literary* a poet

bare *adjective* **1** uncovered, naked **2** plain, simple **3** empty ► *verb* to uncover, expose ♦ **barely** *adverb* hardly, scarcely

bareback *adverb & adjective* on a horse without a saddle

barefaced *adjective* impudent, unashamed: *a barefaced lie*

barefoot or **barefooted** *adjective & adverb* not wearing shoes or socks

bargain *noun* **1** an agreement, especially about buying or selling **2** something bought cheaply ► *verb* to argue about a price etc ● **bargain for** to expect: *more than he bargained for* ● **into the bargain** in addition, besides

barge *noun* a flat-bottomed boat used on rivers and canals ► *verb* **1** to rush clumsily **2** to push or bump (into) **3** to push your way (into) rudely

baritone *noun, music* **1** a male singing voice between tenor and bass **2** a singer with such a voice

barium *noun, chemistry* (symbol **Ba**) a soft, silvery-white, metallic element, soluble compounds of which burn with a green flame ⊙ Comes from Greek *baris* meaning 'heavy'

bark¹ *noun* the noise made by a dog, fox, etc ► *verb* **1** to give a bark **2** to speak sharply or angrily

bark² *noun* the rough protective outer covering of a tree's trunk and branches

barley *noun* a grain used for food and for making beer and whisky

barley sugar *noun* sugar candied by melting and cooling to make a sweet

barmaid *noun* a woman serving drinks at a bar

barman *noun* (*plural* **barmen**) a man serving drinks at a bar

bar mitzvah (*pronounced* bahr **mits**-va) *noun* a Jewish ceremony to mark a boy's coming of age

barmy *adjective* (**barmier, barmiest**) *informal* crazy; mentally unsound

barn *noun* a building in which grain, hay, etc is stored

barnacle *noun* a type of shellfish which sticks to rocks, ships' hulls, etc

barometer (*pronounced* ba-**rom**-it-er) *noun* an instrument which measures the weight or pressure of the air and shows changes in the weather

baron *noun* **1** a nobleman of the lowest rank in the British peerage **2** a powerful person, especially in a business: *drug baron* ♦ **baronial** *adjective* (meaning 1)

baroness *noun* (*plural* **baronesses**) a baron's wife or a female baron

baronet *noun* a man holding the lowest title that can be passed on to an heir ♦ **baronetcy** *noun* the rank of baronet

baroque (*pronounced* ba-**rok**) *adjective* extravagantly ornamented

barracks *singular* or *plural noun* a place for housing soldiers

barracuda (*pronounced* bar-a-**koo**-da) *noun* a large tropical sea fish which feeds on other fish

barrage *noun* **1** heavy gunfire against an enemy

2 an overwhelming number: *a barrage of questions* **3** a bar across a river to make the water deeper

barrage balloon *noun* a large balloon attached to the ground by a cable and often with a net hanging from it, used to prevent attack by low-flying aircraft

barre *noun* a rail fixed to a wall at waist level, which ballet dancers use to balance themselves while exercising ⊕ Comes from French, meaning 'bar'

barrel *noun* **1** a wooden cask with curved sides **2** the metal tube of a gun through which the shot is fired

barren *adjective* **1** not able to reproduce, infertile **2** of land or soil: not able to produce crops or fruit

barricade *noun* a barrier put up to block a street etc ▸ *verb* **1** to block or strengthen against attack **2** to shut behind a barrier

barrier *noun* **1** a strong fence etc used for enclosing or keeping out **2** an obstacle

barring *preposition* except for

barrister *noun* a lawyer who pleads cases in English or Irish courts

barrow¹ *noun* a small hand-cart

barrow² *noun* a mound built over an ancient grave

barter *verb* to give one thing in exchange for another ▸ *noun* trading by exchanging goods without using money

baryon (*pronounced* ba-ri-on) *noun, physics* a heavy subatomic particle composed of three quarks bound by gluon

basalt (*pronounced* bas-alt *or* bas-awlt) *noun* a hard, dark-coloured rock thrown up as lava from volcanoes

base¹ *noun* **1** something on which a thing stands or rests **2** the lowest part **3** a place from where an expedition, military action, etc is carried out **4** *chemistry* a compound that contains hydroxyl ions and can neutralize acids **5** *maths* the number of different symbols used in a counting system, eg in the binary number system the base is two, because the symbols 0 and 1 are used **6** *maths* in logarithms: the number that, when raised to a certain power has a logarithm equal in value to that power **7** *maths* the line or surface on which a geometric figure rests ▸ *verb* to use as a foundation: *based on the facts*

base² *adjective* worthless, cowardly

baseball *noun* a North American ball game in which players make a circuit of four stations (**bases**) on a field

base flow *noun, geography* groundwater that discharges to a river, or that part of the discharge that is groundwater

baseless *adjective* without foundation; untrue

base level *noun, geography* the lowest level to which land in a riverbed or seabed can be eroded by water

basement *noun* a storey below ground level in a building

base 2 *noun* binary

bash *informal, verb* to hit hard ▸ *noun* (*plural* **bashes**) a heavy blow • **have a bash** to make an attempt

bashful *adjective* lacking confidence; shy; self-conscious ◆ **bashfully** *adverb* ◆ **bashfulness** *noun*

BASIC *or* **Basic** *noun* a computer programming language using a combination of simple English and algebra

⊕ An acronym from *Beginner's All-purpose Symbolic Instruction Code*

basic *adjective* **1** of or forming a base **2** necessary, fundamental ◆ **basically** *adverb* fundamentally, essentially

basidium (*pronounced* ba-**sid**-i-um) *noun, biology* in fungi: a club-shaped reproductive structure which contains spores

basil *noun* an aromatic herb used in cooking

basilica (*pronounced* ba-**sil**-i-ka) *noun* a church with a rounded wall at one end and a large central hall

basilisk (*pronounced* **bas**-i-lisk) *noun* **1** a mythological reptile with a deadly look and poisonous breath **2** a type of American lizard

basin *noun* **1** a wide, open dish **2** a washhand basin **3** a large hollow in the ground holding water **4** the land drained by a river and its tributaries

basis *noun* (*plural* **bases** – *pronounced* **bei**-seez) **1** something on which a thing rests, a foundation: *the basis of their friendship* **2** the main ingredient

bask *verb* **1** to lie in warmth **2** to enjoy, feel great pleasure (in): *basking in glory*

basket *noun* **1** a container made of strips of wood, rushes, etc woven together **2** the raised horizontal hoop and attached open net, used for scoring in basketball **3** a goal scored in basketball

basketball *noun* a team game in which goals are scored by throwing a ball into a raised horizontal hoop with a net attached

basmati *or* **basmati rice** (*pronounced* bas-**mat**-i) *noun* a type of aromatic long-grain rice, eaten especially with Indian food

bas-relief (*pronounced* ba-ri-**leef**) *noun, art* a method of caving in which the figures stand out only slightly from the stone or wood on which they are carved (*see also*: **relief**, meaning 6) ⊕ Comes from French, from Italian *basso rilievo* meaning 'low relief'

bass¹ (*pronounced* beis) *noun* (*plural* **basses**), *music* **1** the low part in music **2** the male singing voice of the lowest pitch **3** a singer with such a voice ➤ *adjective* low or deep in tone

bass² (*pronounced* bas) *noun* (*plural* **bass** or **basses**) a kind of fish of the perch family

bass clef *noun* a musical sign (`𝄢`) placed on a stave to fix the pitch of the notes

bassoon *noun* a musical wind instrument with low notes

bastard *noun* **1** *old, often offensive* a child born to parents who are not married to each other **2** *slang* a general term of abuse

baste¹ *verb* to spoon fat over (meat) while roasting to keep (it) from drying out

baste² *verb* to sew loosely together with big stitches; tack

bastion *noun* **1** a defensive position, a preserve: *the last bastions of male power* **2** a tower on a castle etc

bat¹ *noun* a shaped piece of wood etc for striking a ball in some games ➤ *verb* (**batting, batted**) to use the bat in cricket etc

bat² *noun* a mouse-like flying animal, active at night

bat³ *verb* (**batting, batted**) to flutter (the eyelids etc)

batch *noun* (*plural* **batches**) a quantity of things made etc at one time

batch file *noun, computing* a text file containing a series of commands which are executed in order

batch processing *noun, computing* a method of processing data in which similar items of data are collected for processing at one time

bated *adjective*: **with bated breath** anxiously

bath *noun* **1** a vessel which holds water in which to wash the body **2** the water in which to wash **3** a washing of the body in water **4** (**baths**) a public swimming pool ➤ *verb* to wash (oneself or another person) in a bath

bathchair *noun* an old-fashioned wheelchair

bathe *verb* **1** to swim in water **2** to wash gently: *bathe your eyes* **3** to take a bath ➤ *noun* the act of bathing: *We went for a bathe in the sea* • **bathed in** covered with

bathos (*pronounced* bei-thos) *noun* in speech or writing: a sudden change from a very serious or beautiful tone or content to a very ordinary or trivial one ♦ **bathetic** *adjective* ⊙ From Greek, meaning 'depth'

> ⚠ Do not confuse with: **pathos**

bathrobe *noun* a loose towelling coat used especially before and after taking a bath

bathroom *noun* a room containing facilities for washing yourself and usually a lavatory

bat mitzvah (*pronounced* bat **mits**-va) *noun* a Jewish ceremony to mark a girl's coming of age

baton *noun* **1** a small wooden stick **2** a light stick used by a conductor of music

> ⚠ Do not confuse with: **batten**

baton round *noun, formal* a plastic or rubber bullet

batsman, batswoman *noun* (*plural* **batsmen** or **batswomen**) someone who bats in cricket etc

battalion *noun* a part of a regiment of foot soldiers

batten *noun* **1** a piece of sawn timber **2** a strip of wood used to fasten down a ship's hatches during a storm ➤ *verb*: **batten down** to fasten down firmly

> ⚠ Do not confuse with: **baton**

batter¹ *verb* to hit repeatedly ♦ **battered** *adjective* **1** beaten, ill-treated **2** worn out by use

batter² *noun* a beaten mixture of flour, milk and eggs, for cooking ♦ **battered** *adjective* dipped in batter and fried

battering-ram *noun, history* a heavy beam used as a weapon for breaking through walls etc

battery *noun* (*plural* **batteries**) **1** a number of large guns **2** a device for storing and transmitting electricity **3** a series of cages etc in which hens are kept for egg-laying

battle *noun* a fight, especially between armies ➤ *verb* to fight

battle-axe *noun* **1** *informal* a fierce and domineering older woman **2** *history* a large broad-bladed axe

battlefield *noun* the site of a battle

battlement *noun* a wall on the top of a building, with openings or notches for firing

battleship *noun* a heavily armed and armoured warship

bauble *noun* a brightly coloured ornament of little value

baud or **baud rate** *noun, computing* the number of bits that can be transmitted between computers per second

> ⊙ Named after French inventor J M E *Baud*ot (died 1903)

bauxite *noun* a clay-like compound which is the main ore of aluminium

bawdy *adjective* (**bawdier, bawdiest**) of language or writing etc: containing coarsely humorous references to sex ♦ **bawdily** *adverb* ♦ **bawdiness** *noun*

bawl *verb* to shout or cry out loudly ➤ *noun* a loud cry

bay¹ *noun* a wide inlet of the sea in a coastline

bay² *noun* **1** a space in a room which is set back, a recess **2** a compartment in an aircraft: *the bomb bay*

bay³ *noun* the laurel tree

bay⁴ *verb* of dogs: to bark • **hold at bay** to fight off • **stand at bay** to stand and face attackers etc

bayonet *noun* a steel stabbing blade that can be fixed to the muzzle of a rifle ➤ *verb* (**bayoneting, bayoneted**) to stab with this

bay window *noun* a window that forms a recess

bazaar *noun* **1** a sale of goods for charity etc **2** an Eastern marketplace **3** a shop

bazooka (*pronounced* ba-**zoo**-ka) *noun* a portable anti-tank gun which fires small rockets

BBC *abbreviation* British Broadcasting Corporation

BC *abbreviation* before Christ. Used with a date, eg 55 BC, to show that it refers to the time before, and not after, the birth of Christ (*compare with:* **AD**)

BCC or **Bcc** *abbreviation* blind carbon copy, used to mark a copy of a message sent without the knowledge of the main recipient

BCG *abbreviation* bacillus Calmette-Guérin, a vaccine that prevents tuberculosis

Be *symbol, chemistry* beryllium

be *verb* **1** to live, exist: *There may be some milk left* **2** to have a position, quality, etc: *She wants to be a dentist/If only you could be happy*

ⓘ **be** → *present form* **am**, **are**, **is**, *past form* **was**, **were**, *past participle* **been**
The present tense comes from Anglo-Saxon *beon*, to live or exist; the past tense comes from Anglo-Saxon *weran*, to be

---

be- *prefix* used **1** to add to words the sense of: around, in all directions, thoroughly: *besiege* **2** to form verbs from adjectives and nouns: *befriend/belittle* **3** to make intransitive verbs (eg *fall*) into transitive verbs (*befall someone*)

beach *noun* (*plural* **beaches**) the shore of the sea etc, especially when sandy or pebbly ➤ *verb* to drive or haul (a boat etc) up on the beach

beachcomber *noun* someone who searches beaches for useful articles or things to sell

beach nourishment or **beach replenishment** *noun, geography* making or improving a beach by artificial means such as bringing in sand from elsewhere

beach profile *noun, geography* a measurement of the height, length and steepness of a beach

beacon *noun* **1** a flashing light or other warning signal **2** *history* a fire on a hill used as a signal of danger

bead *noun* **1** a small pierced ball of glass, plastic, etc, used in needlework or jewellery-making **2** a

drop of liquid: *beads of sweat*

beadle *noun* an officer of a church or college

beagle *noun* a small hunting hound

beak *noun* **1** the hard, horny part of a bird's mouth with which it gathers food **2** a point, a projection

beaker *noun* a tall cup or glass, usually without a handle, especially one used in laboratory work

beam *noun* **1** a long straight piece of wood or metal **2** a shaft of light **3** a radio signal **4** the greatest breadth of a ship **5** *physics* a directed flow of electromagnetic radiation or particles ➤ *verb* **1** to shine **2** to smile broadly **3** to send out or transmit (rays of light, radio waves, etc)

bean *noun* **1** any of various pod-bearing plants **2** the seed of this used as food

bean bag *noun* **1** a small cloth bag filled with dried beans, used like a ball in children's games **2** a very large cushion filled with polystyrene chips etc, kept on the floor as seating

beansprout or **beanshoot** *noun* a young shoot of the mung bean plant eaten as a vegetable, especially in Chinese food

bear¹ *noun* a heavy animal with shaggy fur and hooked claws

bear² *verb* (**bearing, bore, borne**) **1** *formal* to carry **2** to endure, put up with **3** to produce (fruit, children, etc) • **bear in mind** to remember, take into account • **bear out** to confirm: *This bears out my suspicions* • **bear with** to be patient with • **bring to bear** to bring into use

---

ⓘ **Born** is used for the past participle when referring to the birth of a child, idea, etc:
When were you born?
This form is also used in the passive, unless it is followed by the word **by**:
The child was born last week.
Otherwise the form is **borne**:
the baby borne by Ms Smith/I couldn't have borne it any longer.

---

bearable *adjective* able to be borne or endured

beard *noun* the hair that grows on a man's chin and cheeks ➤ *verb* to face up to, defy

bearer *noun* a carrier or messenger

bear hug *noun, informal* a rough, tight embrace

bearing *noun* **1** behaviour **2** the direction of a line or point from a reference point, expressed as an angle measured in degrees clockwise from the north **3** (**bearings**) *informal* a sense or awareness of your own position or surroundings **4** relevance: *It has no bearing on the issue* **5** part of a machine supporting a moving part

beast *noun* **1** a four-footed animal **2** a brutal person ♦ **beastly** *adjective* (**beastlier, beastliest**) **1** behaving like an animal **2** *informal* horrible **3** *informal* unpleasant

beat *verb* (**beating, beat, beaten**) **1** to hit violently and repeatedly **2** to overcome, defeat **3** of a pulse or the heart: to move or throb in the normal way **4** to mark (time) in music **5** to stir (a mixture etc) with quick movements **6** to strike (bushes etc) to rouse birds for shooting ➤ *noun* **1** a pulse, eg of the heart **2** the regular round of a police officer etc ♦ **beaten** *adjective* **1** of metal: shaped **2** of earth: worn smooth by treading **3** defeated ● **beat up** *informal* to injure by repeated hitting, kicking, etc

beatific (*pronounced* bee-a-**tif**-ik) *adjective* of, or showing, great happiness

beatify (*pronounced* bee-**at**-if-ai) *verb* (**beatifies, beatifying, beatified**) **1** *RC Church* to declare someone who has died as holy **2** to make supremely happy ♦ **beatification** *noun*

beau (*pronounced* boh) *noun* (*plural* **beaux** or **beaus** – *both pronounced* bohz), *US* or *dated Brit* a boyfriend or male lover

Beaufort scale (*pronounced* **boh**-fort) *noun*, *meteorology* a system for estimating wind speeds without using instruments

> ⊙ Named after Sir Francis *Beaufort* (1774–1857), the British naval officer and scientist who devised it

beautiful *adjective* very attractive or pleasing in appearance, sound, etc ♦ **beautifully** *adverb*

beautify *verb* (**beautifies, beautifying, beautified**) to make beautiful

beauty *noun* (*plural* **beauties**) **1** very attractive or pleasing appearance, sound, etc **2** a very attractive person, especially a woman

beauty therapist *noun* someone who gives beauty treatments, especially to women ♦ **beauty therapy** *noun*

beaver *noun* **1** an animal that can gnaw through wood and dam streams **2** a member of the most junior branch of the Scout Association

becalmed *adjective* of a sailing ship: unable to move for lack of wind

because *conjunction* for the reason that: *We didn't go because it was raining* ➤ *preposition* (**because of**) on account of: *Because of the holiday, the bank will be shut*

beck *noun*: **at someone's beck and call** obeying all their orders or requests

beckon *verb* to make a sign (with the finger) to summon someone

become *verb* **1** to come to be: *She became angry* **2** to suit: *That tie becomes you* ♦ **becoming** *adjective* **1** suiting someone well **2** of behaviour: appropriate, suitable

becquerel (*pronounced* **bek**-e-rel) *noun*, *physics* (symbol **Bq**) the standard unit of measure of radioactivity, equivalent to one disintegration of a radioactive source per second

> ⊙ Named after the French physicist A H *Becquerel* (1852–1908)

bed *noun* **1** a place on which to rest or sleep **2** a plot for flowers etc in a garden **3** the bottom of a river etc ➤ *verb* (**bedding, bedded**) **1** to plant in soil etc **2** to provide a bed for **3** *informal* to have sexual intercourse with

bed and breakfast (*abbrev* **B and B** or **B & B** or **b & b**) *noun* **1** at a guesthouse, hotel, etc: overnight accommodation with breakfast included in the price **2** a guesthouse etc that provides accommodation and breakfast

bedclothes *plural noun* sheets, blankets, etc for a bed

bedding *noun* **1** mattress, bedclothes, etc **2** straw etc for cattle to lie on

bedlam *noun* a place full of uproar and confusion

> ⊙ After St Mary of *Bethlehem* Hospital, a former mental asylum in London

bed linen *noun* sheets and pillowcases

Bedouin (*pronounced* **bed**-oo-in) *noun* (*plural* **Bedouin** or **Bedouins**) a member of a nomadic tent-dwelling Arab tribe that lives in the deserts of the Middle East ⊙ Comes from French *beduin*, from Arabic *badawi* meaning 'desert-dweller'

bedpan *noun* a wide shallow pan used as a toilet by someone unable to get out of bed

bedraggled *adjective* wet and untidy

bedridden (*pronounced* **bed**-rid-en) *adjective* kept in bed by weakness, illness, etc

bedrock *noun* the solid rock under the soil

bedroom *noun* a room for sleeping

bedside manner *noun* a doctor's way of talking to and dealing with a patient

bedsore *noun* an ulcer on a person's skin, caused by lying in bed for long periods (*also called*: **pressure sore**)

bedspread *noun* a top cover for a bed

bedstead *noun* a frame supporting a bed

bee¹ *noun* a winged insect that makes honey in wax cells

bee² *noun* a group of people who gather together for some activity: *a spelling bee*

beech *noun* (*plural* **beeches**) a forest tree with grey, smooth bark

beef *noun* the flesh of an ox or cow, used as food

beefburger *noun* a flattened cake of minced beef, grilled or fried

beefeater *noun* **1** a guardian of the Tower of London **2** a member of the Queen's or King's Guard

beefy (**beefier, beefiest**) *adjective* stout and muscular

beehive *noun* a dome or box in which bees are kept

beeline *noun*: **make a beeline for** to go directly towards

Beelzebub (*pronounced* bi-**el**-zib-ub) *noun, old* the Devil, Satan

been see **be**

beep *noun* a short high-pitched sound, like that made by a car horn ➤ *verb* to produce a beep

beer *noun* an alcoholic drink flavoured with hops

beeswax *noun* a solid yellowish substance produced by bees to make the cells in which they live

beet *noun* a plant with a carrot-like root, one type (**sugar beet**) used as a source of sugar, the other (**beetroot**) used as a vegetable

beetle *noun* an insect with four wings, the front pair forming hard covers for the back pair

beetling *adjective* **1** of cliffs etc: overhanging **2** of eyebrows: heavy, frowning

BEF *abbreviation* British Expeditionary Force

befall *verb* (**befalling, befell, befallen**) *formal* to happen to, strike: *A disaster befell them*

befit *verb* (**befitting, befitted**) *formal* to be suitable or right for ♦ **befitting** *adjective*

before *preposition* **1** in front of: *before the entrance to the tunnel* **2** earlier than: *before three o'clock* **3** rather than, in preference to: *I'd die before telling him* ➤ *adverb* **1** in front **2** earlier ➤ *conjunction* earlier than the time that: *before he was born*

beforehand *adverb* previously, before the time when something else is done

befriend *verb* to become a friend of, help

beg *verb* (**begging, begged**) **1** to ask for money etc from others **2** to ask earnestly: *He begged her to stay* • **beg the question** to take as being proved the very point that needs to be proved

began past tense of **begin**

beget *verb* (**begetting, begat, begotten**) *formal* **1** to be the father of **2** to cause

beggar *noun* someone who begs for money ♦ **beggarly** *adjective* poor; worthless • **beggar belief** to be beyond belief, be incredible

begin *verb* (**beginning, began, begun**) to make a start on ♦ **beginner** *noun* ♦ **beginning** *noun*

begone *interjection, old* be off, go away!

begonia *noun* a tropical plant with brightly-coloured waxy flowers

begrudge *verb* to grudge, envy: *He begrudged me my success*

beguile *verb* to captivate • **beguile into** or **out of** to trick (someone) into or out of (something)

begun past participle of **begin**

behalf *noun*: **on behalf of 1** as the representative of: *on behalf of my client* **2** in aid of: *collecting on behalf of the homeless*

behave *verb* **1** to act (in a certain way): *He always behaves badly at parties* **2** to conduct yourself well: *Can't you behave for just a minute?* ♦ **behaviour** *noun*

behead *verb* to cut off the head of

behemoth (*pronounced* be-**hee**-moth) *noun* something huge or monstrous

⊙ The word comes from the name of an animal described in the Bible, thought to be the hippopotamus

behest *noun, formal* command

behind *preposition* **1** at or towards the back of: *behind the door* **2** in support of, encouraging: *behind him all the way* ➤ *adverb* **1** at the back **2** not up to date: *behind with his work*

behold *verb, old* to look (at), see

beholden *adjective*: **beholden to** grateful to because of a good turn

behove *verb, formal*: **it behoves you to** you ought to

beige (*pronounced* beisz) *noun* a light brown colour

beigel see **bagel**

being *noun* **1** existence **2** a living person or thing

belabour *verb* **1** to argue about or discuss something at excessive length: *belabour the point* **2** to attack or batter thoroughly

belated *adjective* arriving late ♦ **belatedly** *adverb*

belch *verb* **1** to bring up wind from the stomach through the mouth **2** of a fire etc: to send up (smoke) violently

beleaguer (*pronounced* be-**leeg**-er) *verb* to besiege

belfry (*pronounced* **bel**-fri) *noun* (*plural* **belfries**) the part of a steeple or tower in which the bells are hung

belie (*pronounced* bi-**lai**) *verb* (**belies, belying, belied**) **1** to show something to be untrue: *The new figures belied previous reports* **2** to give a false idea or impression of something: *Her cheerful face belied the seriousness of the situation* ⊙ Comes from Anglo-Saxon *beleogan* meaning 'to deceive by lying'

belief *noun* **1** what someone thinks to be true **2** faith

believable *adjective* able to be believed; possible

believe *verb* **1** to think of as true or as existing **2** to trust (in) **3** to think or suppose • **make believe** to pretend

Belisha beacon (*pronounced* be-**lee**-sha) *noun, Brit* a pole with an orange globe on top, marking a pedestrian crossing

belittle *verb* to make seem small or unimportant

bell *noun* a hollow metal object which gives a ringing sound when struck by the clapper inside

bellicose *adjective* inclined to fight, quarrelsome ◆ **bellicosity** *noun*

belligerent *adjective* quarrelsome, aggressive ◆ **belligerence** or **belligerency** *noun*

bellow *verb* to roar like a bull > *noun* a deep roar

bellows *plural noun* an instrument for making a blast of air, eg to increase a fire

belly *noun* (*plural* **bellies**) 1 the abdomen 2 the underpart of an animal's body 3 the bulging part of anything > *verb* (**bellies, bellying, bellied**) to swell or bulge out

belly button *noun, informal* the navel

belly dance *noun* a sensuous dance performed by women, with circling movements of the stomach and hips ◆ **belly-dancer** *noun*

belly flop *noun* a dive into water in which the body hits the surface flat, instead of at an angle

belong *verb* 1 to be someone's property: *This book belongs to me* 2 to be a member of (a club etc) 3 to be born in or live in: *I belong to Glasgow* 4 of an object: to have its place in: *Those glasses belong in the kitchen* ◆ **belongings** *plural noun* what someone possesses

beloved *adjective* much loved, very dear > *noun* someone much loved

below *preposition* lower in position, amount, etc than: *Her skirt reached below her knees/40 degrees below zero* > *adverb* 1 in a lower position: *looking down at the street below* 2 further on in a book etc

belt *noun* 1 a strip of leather, cloth, etc worn around the waist 2 a continuous band on a machine for conveying objects in a factory etc 3 a broad strip, eg of land > *verb* 1 to put a belt round 2 to beat with a belt 3 *informal* to beat, hit ● **belt out** *informal* to sing or say very loudly

bemoan *verb* to weep about, mourn

bemused *adjective* bewildered; confused

bench *noun* (*plural* **benches**) 1 a long seat 2 a worktable 3 (**the bench**) the judges of a court

benchmark *noun* 1 anything used as a standard or point of reference 2 *surveying* a permanent mark cut on a post, building, etc giving the height above sea level of the land at that spot 3 *computing* a standard program used to compare the performance of different makes of computer

bench test *noun* a test carried out on something, eg computer hardware or software, before it is installed or released

bend *verb* (**bending, bent**) 1 to curve 2 to stoop > *noun* 1 a curve 2 a turn in a road

beneath *preposition* 1 under, in a lower position than: *sitting beneath the tree reading a book* 2 covered by: *wearing a black dress beneath her coat* 3 considered too low a task etc for: *Sweeping floors was beneath him* > *adverb* below

benediction *noun, Christianity* a blessing at the end of worship

benefactor *noun* someone who does good to others

beneficial *adjective* bringing gain or advantage (to)

beneficiary *noun* (*plural* **beneficiaries**) someone who receives a gift, an advantage, etc

benefit *noun* 1 something good to receive or have done to you 2 money received from social security or insurance schemes: *unemployment benefit* > *verb* (**benefiting, benefited**) 1 to do good to 2 to gain advantage: *benefited from the cut in interest rates*

benefit society see **friendly society**

benevolence *noun* 1 tendency to do good; kindliness 2 a kind act ◆ **benevolent** *adjective* kindly

benign (*pronounced* bi-**nain**) *adjective* 1 gentle, kindly 2 of disease: not causing death (*contrasted with*: **malignant**)

Benioff zone *noun, geography* an earthquake zone generated by collision between plates

⊙ Named after Hugo *Benioff* (1899–1968), American geophysicist

bent *noun* a natural liking or aptitude (for something) > *adjective* 1 curved, crooked 2 *informal* dishonest ● **be bent on** to be determined to > *verb* past form of **bend**

benthos *noun, biology* the living organisms that are found at the bottom of the sea or a lake ◆ **benthic** *adjective* (*compare with*: **pelagic**)

benzene *noun, chemistry* an inflammable colourless liquid hydrocarbon, used as a solvent and in the manufacture of plastics, dyes, drugs, etc

benzene ring *noun, chemistry* a molecule consisting of six linked carbon atoms, as in a molecule of benzene

bequeath (*pronounced* bi-**kweedh**) *verb* to leave by will

bequest *noun* money, property, etc left in a will

berate *verb* to scold severely

bereaved *adjective* suffering from the recent death of a relative or friend ◆ **bereavement** *noun*

bereft *adjective* lacking, deprived (of)

beret (*pronounced* **be**-rei) *noun* a flat, round hat

beriberi *noun, medicine* a disease, most common in the tropics, caused by lack of thiamine, resulting in inflammation of the nerves and paralysis of the limbs ⊙ Comes from Sinhalese *beri* meaning 'weakness'

berkelium *noun, chemistry* (symbol **Bk**) an

artificially produced radioactive metallic element

🕐 It was first produced at *Berkeley*, California

Berlin Wall *noun, history* a wall separating East Berlin, Germany, from the part of the city occupied by Western powers, built in 1961 to stop emigration from East to West, but mostly taken down when Germany was reunified in 1990

berm *noun* **1** a narrow ledge or path beside an embankment, road, canal, etc **2** *geography* a ridge of sand or stones on a beach, formed by incoming tides

Bermuda shorts or **Bermudas** *plural noun* knee-length shorts

berry *noun* (*plural* **berries**) a small juicy fruit enclosing seeds

berserk *adverb* in a frenzy, mad

berth *noun* **1** a room for sleeping in a ship etc **2** the place where a ship is tied up in a dock ➤ *verb* to moor (a ship) • **give a wide berth to** to keep well away from

beryl *noun* a type of precious stone such as an emerald or aquamarine

beryllium *noun, chemistry* (symbol **Be**) a silvery-grey metallic element, obtained from the mineral beryl

beseech *verb* (**beseeching, besought** or **beseeched**) to ask earnestly

beset *verb* (**besetting, beset**) to attack from all sides; surround

beside *preposition* **1** by the side of, near: *the building beside the station* **2** compared with: *Beside her sister she seems quite shy* • **be beside yourself** to lose self-control • **beside the point** irrelevant

besides *preposition* **1** in addition to: *He has other friends, besides me* **2** other than, except: *nothing in the fridge besides some cheese* ➤ *adverb* **1** also, moreover: *Besides, it was your idea* **2** in addition: *plenty more besides*

besiege *verb* (**besieging, besieged**) **1** to surround (a town etc) with an army **2** to crowd round; overwhelm: *besieged with letters*

besotted *adjective* (**besotted with**) foolishly fond of

besought past form of **beseech**

bespoke *adjective* **1** of clothes: ordered to be made **2** *computing* of software: specially created for a specific situation

best *adjective* good in the most excellent way ➤ *adverb* in the most excellent way ➤ *verb* to defeat • **at best** under the most favourable circumstances • **do your best** to try as hard as you can • **make the best of** to do as well as possible with 🕐 Comes from Old English *betst/betest*

bestial *adjective* like a beast, beastly

best man *noun* someone who attends a man who is being married

bestow *verb, formal* to give

best part *noun* the largest or greatest part

bestseller *noun* a book etc which sells exceedingly well

bet *noun* money put down to be lost or kept depending on the outcome of a race etc ➤ *verb* (**betting, bet** or **betted**) to place a bet

beta-blocker (*pronounced* **bee**-ta) *noun* a drug that slows the heartbeat, used to treat high blood pressure, angina and abnormal heart rhythms

beta decay (*pronounced* **bee**-ta) *noun, physics* radioactive decay in which a neutron in an atomic nucleus breaks up into a proton and an electron

beta particle (*pronounced* **bee**-ta) *noun, physics* a high-speed electron or positron emitted by an atomic nucleus undergoing beta decay

beta test (*pronounced* **bee**-ta) *noun, computing* a second round of tests run on new software before it is marketed, designed to recreate normal working conditions (*compare with*: **alpha test**) ♦ **beta testing** *noun*

bête noire (*pronounced* bet **nwahr**) *noun* (*plural* **bêtes noires** – *pronounced* bet **nwahrz**) a particular dislike

betray *verb* **1** to give up (secrets, friends, etc) to an enemy **2** to show signs of: *His face betrayed no emotion* ♦ **betrayal** *noun*

betroth (*pronounced* bi-**trohdh**) *verb, formal* to promise in marriage ♦ **betrothal** *noun* • **betrothed to** engaged to be married to

better *adjective* **1** good to a greater degree, of a more excellent kind **2** healthier **3** completely recovered from illness: *Don't go back to work until you're better* ➤ *adverb* in a more excellent way ➤ *verb* to improve • **better off** *adjective* in a better position, wealthier • **get the better of** to defeat, overcome • **had better** ought to, must • **think better of** to change your mind about 🕐 Comes from Old English *betera*

between *preposition* **1** in or through the space dividing two people or things: *There was an empty seat between us/between 3 o'clock and 6 o'clock* **2** in parts, in shares to: *Divide the chocolates between you* **3** from one thing to another: *the road between Edinburgh and Glasgow* **4** comparing one to the other: *The only difference between them is the price*

ℹ️ Use **between** when individual people or things are named:
Duties are shared between John, James and Catherine.
Use **among** when there is a notion of

distrubuting or sharing:
Share the sweets among yourselves.

---

bevel *noun* a slanting edge ➤ *verb* (**bevelling, bevelled**) to give a slanting edge to ◆ **bevelled** *adjective*

beverage *noun* a drink

Beveridge Report *noun, history* a proposal for social reform made in 1942 by William Beveridge, a British economist, that was the basis for the creation of the welfare state

bevy[1] *noun* (*plural* **bevies**) **1** a group of women or girls **2** a flock of quails

bevy[2] or **bevvy** *noun* (*plural* **bevies** or **bevvies**) *Brit informal* **1** an alcoholic drink **2** a drinking session

bewail *verb* to mourn loudly over

beware *verb* to watch out for (something dangerous): *Beware of the dog*

bewilder *verb* to puzzle, confuse ◆ **bewildering** *adjective* ◆ **bewilderment** *noun* confusion

bewitch *verb* to put under a spell; charm ◆ **bewitching** *adjective* charming; very beautiful

beyond *preposition* **1** on the far side of: *beyond the next set of traffic lights* **2** later than: *beyond January* **3** more than: *beyond the call of duty* **4** too far gone for: *beyond repair* **5** too difficult or confusing for: *It's beyond me!* ➤ *adverb* on or to the far side, further away

Bh *symbol, chemistry* bohrium

bhajan *noun, Hinduism* a devotional hymn

bhakti *noun, Hinduism* loving devotion to God

bhangra (*pronounced* **bung**-ru) *noun* a style of pop music created from a mix of traditional Punjabi and Western pop ⊙ Comes from Punjabi, the name of a traditional harvest dance

bhikkhu or **bhikshu** *noun, Buddhism* a Buddhist monk

bhikkhuni or **bhikshuni** *noun, Buddhism* a Buddhist nun

bhindi see **bindi**

Bi *symbol, chemistry* bismuth

bi- *prefix* **1** having two: *biped/bipolar* (= having two poles or extremities)/*bicycle* **2** occurring twice in a certain period, or once in every two periods: *bi-monthly* **3** *chemistry* indicating a salt or compound with twice the amount of the given acid etc: *bicarbonate* **4** *chemistry* indicating a compound with two identical hydrocarbon groups: *biphenyl* ⊙ Comes from Latin *bis* meaning 'twice' or 'two'

biannual *adjective* happening twice a year ⊙ Comes from Latin *bi-* meaning 'two' or 'twice', and *annus* meaning 'year'

⚠ Do not confuse with: **biennial**

bias *noun* **1** the favouring of one person or point of view over any others **2** a tendency to move in a particular direction **3** a weight on or in an object making it move in a particular direction **4** *statistics* an unevenness in a sample due to systematic error ➤ *verb* (**biases** or **biasses, biasing** or **biassing, biased** or **biassed**) to give a bias to ◆ **biased** or **biassed** *adjective*

bib *noun* **1** a piece of cloth put under a child's chin to protect their clothes from food stains etc **2** a part of an apron, dungarees, etc above the waist, covering the chest

Bible *noun* the holy book of the Christian Church ◆ **Biblical** *adjective*

biblio- *prefix* of or relating to books ⊙ Comes from Greek *biblion* meaning 'book'

bibliographer *noun* someone who compiles bibliographies, or who studies book classification

bibliography *noun* (*plural* **bibliographies**) **1** a list of books (about a subject) **2** the art of classifying books

bibliophile (*pronounced* **bib**-li-oh-fail) *noun* a lover of books

bicameral *adjective* of a legislative body: made up of two chambers ⊙ Comes from Latin *camera* meaning 'a chamber'

bicarbonate *noun, chemistry* a salt of carbonic acid

bicarbonate of soda *noun* sodium bicarbonate, a white crystalline compound used in baking powder or as a digestive remedy (*also called*: **baking soda**)

bicentenary (*pronounced* bai-sen-**tee**-na-ri) *noun* (*plural* **bicentenaries**) the two-hundredth year after an event, eg someone's birth

biceps *singular noun, anatomy* the muscle in front of the upper part of the arm

bicker *verb* to quarrel over small matters

biconcave *adjective, physics* of a lens: concave on both sides

biconvex *adjective, physics* of a lens: convex on both sides

bicycle *noun* a vehicle with two wheels, driven by foot-pedals

bid[1] *verb* (**bidding, bade** or **bid, bidden** or **bid**) **1** to offer a price (for) **2** to make an attempt to achieve something ➤ *noun* **1** an offer of a price **2** a bold attempt: *a bid for freedom*

bid[2] *verb* (**bidding, bade** or **bid, bidden** or **bid**) **1** to tell, say: *bidding her farewell* **2** to command **3** to invite

biddable *adjective* compliant; obedient; docile

bidding *noun* **1** a command, request or invitation **2** the offers at an auction **3** *cards* the act of making bids • **do someone's bidding** to obey their orders

bide *verb* (**biding, bided** or **bode**), *Scot* or *old* **1**

to wait or stay **2** to dwell or reside; to stay, especially temporarily **3** to endure or tolerate • **bide your time** to wait patiently for the right moment ⊙ Comes from Anglo-Saxon *bidan*

bidet (*pronounced* **beed**-ei) *noun* a low wash-basin for washing the genital area and feet

biennial *adjective* happening once every two years ➤ *noun* **1** *botany* a plant that takes two years to complete its life cycle (*compare with*: **annual**, **perennial**) **2** an event taking place or celebrated every two years ⊙ Comes from Latin *biennium* meaning 'two years'

! Do not confuse with: **biannual**

bier (*pronounced* beer) *noun* a carriage or frame for carrying a dead body

bifid (*pronounced* **bai**-fid or **bi**-fid) *adjective, biology* divided into two parts by a deep split

bifocal (*pronounced* bai-**foh**-kal) *adjective* of spectacle or contact lenses: having two separate sections with different focal lengths, one for near vision, and one for viewing distant objects

bifocals *plural noun* a pair of glasses with bifocal lenses

bifurcate (*pronounced* **bai**-fer-keit) *verb, formal* of roads etc: to divide into two parts or branches; to fork ➤ *adjective* forked or branched into two parts ✦ **bifurcation** *noun* ⊙ Comes from Latin *bifurcatus*, from *furca* meaning 'fork'

big *adjective* (**bigger, biggest**) **1** large in size, amount, extent, etc **2** important **3** boastful: *big ideas*

bigamy *noun* (*plural* **bigamies**) the crime or fact of having two wives or two husbands at once ✦ **bigamist** *noun* ✦ **bigamous** *adjective*

big game *noun* large animals, such as lions, tigers, and elephants, hunted for sport

bight *noun* a small bay

bigot *noun* someone with narrow-minded, prejudiced beliefs ✦ **bigoted** *adjective* prejudiced ✦ **bigotry** *noun*

big top *noun* the main tent of a circus

bike *noun, informal* a bicycle

bikini *noun* (*plural* **bikinis**) a woman's brief two-piece bathing suit

⊙ Named after *Bikini* Atoll atomic test site, because of its supposedly 'explosive' effect on men

bilateral *adjective* **1** having two sides **2** affecting two sides, parties, etc: *bilateral agreement* ✦ **bilaterally** *adverb*

bilberry *noun* (*plural* **bilberries**) a type of plant with an edible dark-blue berry

bile *noun* **1** *biology* a thick alkaline fluid produced by the liver, used in the digestion of fats **2** anger, irritability or bad temper

⊙ The second meaning arose because in early medicine, an excess of bile in the body was thought to produce irritability

bilge *noun* **1** the broadest part of a ship's bottom **2** bilgewater **3** *informal* nonsense

bilgewater *noun* water which lies in the ship's bottom

bilharzia *noun, medicine* a tropical disease caused by infestation with parasitic flukes which circulate in the blood

⊙ Named after Theodor *Bilharz* (1825–62), the German parisitologist who discovered the flukes

bilingual *adjective* using or fluent in two languages

bilious (*pronounced* **bil**-i-us) *adjective* **1** ill with too much bile; nauseated **2** greenish-yellow in colour

bill[1] *noun* a bird's beak

bill[2] *noun* **1** an account for money **2** an early version of a law before it has been passed by parliament **3** a printed sheet of information

billet *noun* a lodging, especially for soldiers ➤ *verb* to lodge (soldiers) in private houses

billiards *singular noun* a game played with a cue and balls on a table

billion *noun* **1** a million millions (1,000,000,000,000) **2** *US* (now often in Britain) a thousand millions (1,000,000,000)

billionaire or **billionairess** *noun* someone who owns money and property worth over a billion pounds, dollars, etc

billow *noun* **1** a great wave **2** a mass of something such as smoke rising on or being swept along by the wind ➤ *verb* to be filled and swelled with, or moved along by, the wind: *sheets on a washing-line billowing in the wind/a billowing sail/billowing smoke* ✦ **billowy** *adjective* giving the impression of billowing: *billowy clouds*

billposter *noun* someone who puts up advertising posters on walls, hoardings, etc ✦ **billposting** *noun*

billy (*plural* **billies**) or **billycan** *noun, Brit and Australian* a container for cooking, making tea, etc outdoors

billy goat *noun* a male goat

bimbo *noun* (*plural* **bimbos**) *slang* a young woman who is physically attractive but empty-headed

bimodal *adjective, statistics* having two modes ✦ **bimodality** *noun*

bin *noun* a container for storing goods or rubbish ➤ *verb* (**binning, binned**) **1** to put in a bin **2** to throw away

binary (*pronounced* **bai**-na-ri) *adjective* **1** made up of two parts or components **2** *computing,* *maths* denoting a system that consists of two components, especially the numbers 0 and 1

binary digit *noun, computing, maths* **1** either of the two digits 0 and 1, used in binary systems **2** (*usually in short form* **bit**) the smallest unit of information

binary number *noun, computing, maths* a number represented by a combination of the digits 0 and 1

binary system *noun, computing, maths* a mathematical system in which numbers are expressed by two digits only, 1 and 0

bind *verb* (**binding, bound**) **1** to tie with a band **2** to fasten together **3** to make to promise **4** to fasten the sections and put a cover on (a book)

bindi or **bhindi** (*pronounced* **bin**-dee) *noun* a circular mark, usually red, traditionally worn by Hindu women as a decoration on the face

binding *noun* **1** anything that binds **2** the cover, stitching, etc which holds a book together

binge *verb* (**bingeing** or **binging, binged**) to eat and drink too much ➤ *noun* a spell of overeating or drinking too much

bingo *noun* a popular gambling game using numbers

bin-liner *noun* a disposable plastic bag used as a lining inside a rubbish bin

binoculars *plural noun* a small double telescope

binomial *noun* **1** *maths* an expression that contains two variables, eg $6x - 3y$ **2** *biology* a two-part name for an animal or plant, made up of the genus name and then the species name, eg *Homo sapiens* ➤ *adjective* **1** *maths* containing two variables **2** consisting of two names or terms ⊙ Comes from **bi-** + *nomen* meaning 'name'

binomial distribution *noun, statistics* the frequency distribution of the total number of outcomes of a particular kind in a predetermined number of trials, with the probability of the outcome being constant at each trial because only two outcomes are possible, eg in tossing a coin

binomial theorem *noun, maths* a formula for finding any power of a binomial without lengthy multiplication, eg $(a+b)^2 = (a^2 = 2ab + b^2)$

bio- *prefix* of or relating to life or living organisms ⊙ Comes from Greek *bios* meaning 'life'

bioassay *noun, biology* assessing the concentration of a chemical substance by testing its effect on a living organism, eg its effect on plant growth

bioavailability *noun, biology* the extent to which, and rate at which, a drug is taken up by the body and reaches the tissues and organs it is intended for

biochemistry *noun* the study of the chemical composition and processes of living matter

biocontrol short for **biological control**

biodegradable *adjective* able to be broken down into parts by bacteria

biodiversity *noun, biology* the variety of organisms found in a specified geographical region

bioenergetics *singular noun, biology* the scientific study of the use of energy by living organisms, including its conversion from one form to another

bioengineering *noun* **1** *medicine* the application of engineering technology to biology and medicine, especially the manufacture of artificial limbs, heart pacemakers, etc **2** *biology* the application of engineering technology to the synthesis of plant and animal products

bioethics *singular noun* the study of ethics in biological and medical research and health care

bioflavonoid *noun*, vitamin P, a vitamin important for the capillaries, found in citrus fruit, blackcurrant and rosehips (*also called:* **citrin, flavonoid**)

biogenesis *noun, biology* the theory that living matter always arises from other, pre-existing, living matter (*compare with:* **spontaneous generation**) ♦ **biogenetic** *adjective*

biogeography *noun* the scientific study of the distributions of plants and animals

biographer *noun* someone who writes a biography

biography *noun* (*plural* **biographies**) a written account of someone's life ♦ **biographical** *adjective*

biological *adjective* **1** relating to the way that living organisms grow and behave: *What is the biological explanation for the ageing process?/ biological washing powder* (= containing enzymes which break down certain types of dirt) **2** relating to biology

biological clock *noun* the system in living things that controls the cycle of functions such as sleep or photosynthesis

biological control *noun, biology* the control of plant or animal pests by the introduction of natural predators or parasites etc, or by interfering with their reproductive behaviour (*short form:* **biocontrol**)

biological warfare *noun* war using as weapons germs which can cause disease

biology *noun* the study of living things ♦ **biologist** *noun*

bioluminescence *noun, biology* emission of light by living organisms, eg fireflies and certain fungi

biomass *noun* **1** *biology, geography* all the living things in a given habitat **2** organic materials, eg plants and manure, that can be converted into fuel

biome *noun, biology* a large community of plants and animals characterized by the main vegetation in the region where they live, eg grassland biome, desert biome

bionics *singular noun* the use of natural systems as models for artificial systems ♦ **bionic** *adjective*

biophysics *singular noun* the application of the laws of physics to the study of biological processes ♦ **biophysicist** *noun*

biopsy *noun* (*plural* **biopsies**) the removal of a sample of body tissue for medical examination

biorhythm *noun, biology* a periodic change in the behaviour or physiology of many animals and plants (eg hibernation and migration)

BIOS (*pronounced* **bai**-os) *abbreviation, computing* Basic Input-Output System, an essential part of a computer operating system on which more complex functions are based

biosphere *noun, biology* the parts of the land, sea and atmosphere in which organisms live

biotechnology *noun, biology* the use of living organisms or biological substances to perform an industrial process or manufacture a product

biotin *noun, chemistry* vitamin H

biped (*pronounced* **bai**-ped) *noun* an animal with two feet, eg a bird or a human being

biplane *noun* an early type of aeroplane with two sets of wings, one above the other

bipolar *adjective* having two poles or extremes ♦ **bipolarity** *noun*

birch *noun* (*plural* **birches**) **1** a type of hardwood tree **2** a bundle of birch twigs, used for beating ➤ *verb* to beat with a birch

bird *noun* a feathered, egg-laying creature • **get the bird** *slang* to be booed or hissed at; be dismissed

bird of paradise *noun* (*plural* **birds of paradise**) any of various brilliantly-coloured birds native to New Guinea and Australia

bird of prey *noun* (*plural* **birds of prey**) a bird (eg a hawk) which kills and eats small animals or birds

bird's-eye view *noun* a wide view, as would be seen from above

birdwatching *noun* the study of birds in their natural surroundings ♦ **birdwatcher** *noun*

biriani or **biryani** (*pronounced* bir-**yah**-ni) *noun, cookery* a type of spicy Indian dish consisting mainly of rice, with meat or fish and vegetables etc

birl *verb, Scottish* to spin round, whirl

Biro *noun, trademark* a type of ballpoint pen

⏱ After László *Bíró* (1899–1985), a Hungarian journalist who invented it

birth *noun* the very beginning of someone's life

birth certificate *noun* an official document that records a person's birth, stating the date and place, the parents, etc

birth control *noun* the prevention of pregnancy, especially by means of contraception

birth control policy see **anti-natalist policy**

birthday *noun* **1** the day on which someone is born **2** the date of this day each year

birthmark *noun* a mark on the body from birth

birthplace *noun* the place where someone was born: *Shakespeare's birthplace*

birth rate *noun* (sometimes **crude birth rate**) the number of live births occurring over a period of a year in a given area per thousand inhabitants

birthright *noun* the right which someone may claim because of their parentage

biscuit *noun* dough baked hard in a small cake

bisect *verb, maths etc* to divide into two equal parts ♦ **bisector** *noun* a line that divides an angle etc into two equal parts

bisexual *noun* someone who is sexually attracted to both males and females ➤ *adjective* sexually attracted to both males and females ♦ **bisexuality** *noun*

bishop *noun* a high-ranking member of the clergy (next below an archbishop) in the Roman Catholic Church, the Church of England and some other churches ♦ **bishopric** *noun* the district ruled by a bishop

bismuth *noun, chemistry* (symbol **Bi**) a hard, silvery-white, metallic element with a pinkish tinge, used to make alloys and in medicine

bison *noun* (*plural* **bison**) a large wild ox with shaggy hair and a large hump

bistro (*pronounced* **beest**-roh) *noun* (*plural* **bistros**) a small bar or restaurant

bit[1] *noun* a small piece • **bit by bit** gradually • **do your bit** to do your required share • **to bits** apart, in pieces

bit[2] *noun* **1** a small tool for boring **2** the part of the bridle which the horse holds in its mouth

bit[3] *noun, computing* a binary digit, the smallest unit of information a computer can process

bit[4] past tense of **bite**

bitch *noun* (*plural* **bitches**) **1** a female dog, wolf, etc **2** *slang* an unpleasant woman

bitchy *adjective* (**bitchier, bitchiest**) *informal* catty, malicious

bite *verb* (**biting, bit, bitten**) to grip, cut or tear with the teeth ➤ *noun* **1** a grip with the teeth **2** the part bitten off **3** a nibble at a fishing bait **4** a wound caused by an animal's or insect's bite

biting *adjective* **1** bitterly and painfully cold **2** of a remark: sharp and hurtful; sarcastic

bitmap *computing, noun* a method of screen display where the colours of each small element (**pixel**) are assigned bits of memory ➤ *verb* (**bitmapping, bitmapped**) to display using this method ◆ **bitmapped** *adjective* ◆ **bitmapping** *noun*

bit-part *noun* a small acting part in a play or film

bits per second *noun, computing* (*abbrev* **bps**) a measurement for the rate of transmission of bits

bitten past participle of **bite**

bitter *adjective* **1** unpleasant to the taste; sour **2** harsh: *bitter cold* **3** resentful; angry through disappointment

bittern *noun* a bird resembling a heron

bitterness *noun* **1** the quality of being bitter: *the bitterness of the drink* **2** bitter feelings: *the bitterness I used to feel towards him*

bittersweet *adjective* pleasant and unpleasant at the same time: *a bittersweet love story*

bitty *adjective* (**bittier, bittiest**) piecemeal, scrappy

bitumen *noun* a black solid or tarry substance composed of an impure mixture of hydrocarbons, either occurring naturally or obtained by the distillation of petroleum, and used for surfacing roads etc

bivalve *zoology, adjective* said of a mollusc: having a shell composed of two valves hinged together by a ligament ➤ *noun* one of many mainly marine species of mollusc with such a shell, eg clam, mussel and scallop

bivariate *adjective, maths* involving two variables

bivouac (*pronounced* **biv**-oo-ak) *noun* an overnight camp outdoors without a tent ➤ *verb* (**bivouacking, bivouacked**) to sleep outdoors without a tent

bi-weekly *adjective* happening twice a week or once every two weeks

bizarre *adjective* odd, strange

Bk *symbol, chemistry* berkelium

blab *verb* (**blabbing, blabbed**) **1** to talk a lot **2** to let out a secret

Black *adjective* **1** of people: dark skinned, especially of African, West Indian or Australian Aboriginal origin **2** belonging or relating to Black people ➤ *noun* a dark-skinned person, especially of African, West Indian or Aboriginal origin

black *adjective* **1** dark and colourless, like coal **2** without any light **3** of tea or coffee: without added milk **4** angry, threatening: *black looks* **5** dirty, soiled **6** sad or gloomy: *black despair* ➤ *noun* **1** the colour of coal **2** black clothes worn for mourning • **black out** to become unconscious • **in the black** in credit; out of debt

black-and-blue *adjective informal* badly bruised

blackball *verb* to ostracize, exclude from (a club etc)

black belt *noun* an award for skill in judo, karate, and other martial arts

blackberry *noun* (*plural* **blackberries**) a blackish-purple soft fruit growing on a prickly stem

blackbird *noun* a bird of the thrush family, the male of which is black

blackboard *noun* a dark-coloured board for writing on in chalk

black body *noun, physics* a hypothetical body that absorbs all the radiation that falls on it, and reflects none

black box *noun* a **flight recorder** in an aircraft

Black Codes *plural noun, history* laws passed by Southern states of the USA in 1865–6, which restricted the rights of the slaves freed after the American Civil War

blackcurrant *noun* a widely cultivated shrub or one of the small round black fruits it produces

Black Death *noun, history* a deadly epidemic of bubonic plague that swept over Asia and Europe in the 14th century

black economy *noun* unofficial business or trade etc, not declared for tax purposes

blacken *verb* **1** to make black or dark **2** to dishonour, defame: *blackening his name*

black eye *noun* a bruised area round the eye as the result of a blow

blackguard (*pronounced* **blag**-ahrd) *noun, old* a wicked person

blackhead *noun* a small black spot on the skin caused by sweat blocking one of the skin's tiny pores

black hole *noun* a region in space with such a strong gravitational pull that not even light can escape from it

black ice *noun* a thin transparent layer of ice on a road

blackleg *noun, derogatory* someone who works when other workers are on strike

blacklist *noun* a list of people to be refused credit, jobs, etc ➤ *verb* to put on a blacklist

black magic *noun* magic performed for an evil purpose; witchcraft

blackmail *noun* the crime of threatening to reveal secrets unless money is paid ➤ *verb* to threaten by blackmail ◆ **blackmailer** *noun*

black market *noun* illegal or dishonest buying and selling

Black Muslims see **Nation of Islam**

blackout *noun* **1** total darkness caused by putting out or covering all lights **2** a temporary loss of consciousness

black pepper *noun* pepper produced from the dried fruits of the pepper plant ground without removing their dark outer covering

Black Power *noun, history* a militant movement to increase the political influence of black people, especially in the USA

black pudding *noun* sausage made with pig's blood

black sheep *noun* someone who is considered a failure or outsider in a group

Blackshirt *noun, history* a member of a Fascist organization, especially in the Nazi SS and in Italy during World War II, named after the colour of the uniform

blacksmith *noun* someone who makes or repairs iron goods, especially horseshoes

black spot *noun, chiefly Brit* **1** a dangerous stretch of road where accidents often occur **2** an area where an unfortunate social condition is common: *an unemployment black spot*

black tie *noun* formal evening dress

black widow *noun* a very poisonous American spider, the female of which often eats her mate

bladder *noun* **1** *anatomy* the hollow organ in which urine collects in the body **2** any hollow organ in which liquid or gas is stored, eg the swim bladder of fish **3** a bag made of thin leather, which expands when filled with air or liquid **4** a hollow, sac-like structure in some plants

bladderwrack *noun* a common seaweed with air bladders on its strands

blade *noun* **1** the cutting part of a knife, sword, etc **2** a leaf of grass or wheat

blag *verb* (**blagging, blagged**), *slang* **1** to rob or steal **2** to get (something) for nothing: *blagged his way into the club*

blame *verb* to find fault with; consider responsible for ➤ *noun* fault; responsibility for something bad ◆ **blameless** *adjective*

blameworthy *adjective* deserving blame

blanch *verb* **1** to make white by removing the colour **2** to become pale, especially out of fear **3** *cookery* to prepare (vegetables or meat) by boiling in water for a few seconds **4** *cookery* to remove the skins from (almonds etc) by soaking in boiling water ◎ Comes from French *blanc* meaning 'white'

blancmange (*pronounced* bla-**monsz**) *noun* a jelly-like pudding made with milk ◎ Comes from French *blanc* meaning 'white' + *manger* meaning 'food'

bland *adjective* **1** mild, not strong or irritating: *bland taste* **2** dull, insipid

blandishments *plural noun* acts or words meant to flatter

blank *adjective* **1** clear, unmarked: *a blank sheet of paper* **2** expressionless: *a blank look* ➤ *noun* **1** an empty space **2** a cartridge without a bullet ➤ *verb* **1** to ignore (someone): *I tried to blank the incident from my mind* ◆ **blankly** *adverb*

blank cheque *noun* **1** a cheque which has been signed but on which the amount to be paid has been left blank **2** complete freedom or authority

blanket *noun* **1** a bedcovering of wool etc **2** a widespread, soft covering: *a blanket of snow* ➤ *adjective* covering a group of things: *a blanket agreement* ➤ *verb* (**blanketing, blanketed**) to cover widely or thickly

blanket bombing *noun* bombing from the air over a widespread area

blank verse *noun* non-rhyming poetry, especially in a metre of five feet per line

blare *verb* to sound loudly ➤ *noun* a loud sound, eg on a trumpet

blasé (*pronounced* blah-**zei**) *adjective* indifferent, unconcerned, especially because of being already familiar with something ◎ Comes from French *blaser* meaning 'to cloy'

blaspheme *verb* **1** to speak irreverently of a god **2** to swear, curse ◆ **blasphemer** *noun* ◆ **blasphemous** *adjective* ◆ **blasphemy** *noun* (*plural* **blasphemies**) **1** the act of speaking irreverently of a god **2** a swear-word: *uttering foul blasphemies*

blast *noun* **1** a blowing or gust of wind **2** a loud note, eg on a trumpet **3** an explosion ➤ *verb* **1** to break (stones, a bridge, etc) by explosion **2** to produce a loud noise **3** *formal* to wither, destroy ➤ *interjection* damn! • **at full blast** as quickly, strongly, etc as possible

blast furnace *noun* a furnace used in iron-smelting into which hot air is blown

blast-off *noun* the moment of the launching of a rocket

blastula *noun* (*plural* **blastulas** or **blastulae** *pronounced* **blast**-juw-lee), *biology* a hollow sphere of cells, one cell thick, formed during the division process early in the development of a multicellular embryo (*also called*: **blastosphere**)

blatant (*pronounced* **bleit**-ant) *adjective* very obvious; shameless: *blatant lie* ◆ **blatantly** *adverb*

blaze *noun* a rush of light or flame ➤ *verb* **1** to burn with a strong flame **2** to throw out a strong light

blazer *noun* a light jacket often worn as part of a uniform

bleach *verb* to whiten, remove the colour from ➤ *noun* (*plural* **bleaches**) a substance which bleaches, used for cleaning, whitening clothes, etc

bleak *adjective* dull and cheerless; cold, unsheltered ◆ **bleakly** *adverb* sadly, wistfully ◆ **bleakness** *noun*

bleary *adjective* (**blearier, bleariest**) of eyes: tired and inflamed ◆ **blearily** *adverb* with tired-looking, watery eyes: *He opened his eyes and looked at me blearily*

bleat *verb* **1** to cry like a sheep **2** to complain in an irritating or whining way ➤ *noun* **1** a sheep's cry **2** an irritating whine

bleed *verb* (**bleeding, bled**) **1** to lose blood **2** to draw blood from

bleeding *noun* a flow of blood

bleep *noun* a high-pitched intermittent sound ➤ *verb* to give out such a sound

bleeper *noun* an electronic device using a bleep as a signal

blemish *noun* (*plural* **blemishes**) a stain; a fault or flaw ➤ *verb* to stain, spoil

blend *verb* to mix together ➤ *noun* a mixture

blender *noun* an electric machine which mixes thoroughly and liquidizes food

bless *verb* **1** to wish happiness to **2** to make happy **3** to make holy ◆ **blessed** (*pronounced* **bles**-id) or (in poetry etc) **blest** *adjective* **1** happy; fortunate **2** made holy, consecrated

blessing *noun* **1** a wish or prayer for happiness **2** a source of happiness or relief: *The extra money was a blessing to them* • **blessing in disguise** something unexpectedly useful or beneficial

blether *verb, Scottish* to chatter; talk nonsense

blew past tense of **blow**

blight *noun* **1** a disease which makes plants wither **2** a cause of destruction ➤ *verb* to destroy

blind *adjective* unable to see ➤ *noun* **1** a window screen **2** a deception, a trick ➤ *verb* **1** to make blind **2** to dazzle ◆ **blindness** *noun*

blind alley *noun* a street open only at one end; anything which leads nowhere

blind date *noun* **1** a date with a person whom you have not met before **2** the person met on such a date

blindfold *noun* a bandage or cover which is put over a person's eyes to prevent them from seeing ➤ *adjective* with the eyes bandaged or covered, so as not to see ➤ *verb* to apply a blindfold to

blindly *adverb* without knowledge or direction: *stumbling around blindly*

blindman's buff *noun* a game in which a blindfold person tries to catch others

blind spot *noun* **1** a small area in the eye from which no visual images can be transmitted **2** a place where vision is obscured **3** any subject which a person refuses to try to understand

blink *verb* to close the eyes for a moment; shine unsteadily ➤ *noun* an act of blinking

blinkers *plural noun* pieces of leather over a horse's eyes to prevent it seeing in any direction except in front

blip *noun* **1** a sudden sharp sound produced by a machine such as a monitor or radar screen **2** a spot of bright light on a radar screen, showing

the position of an object **3** a short interruption or pause in the expected course of something **4** an unforeseen phenomenon which is claimed or expected to be temporary

bliss *noun* very great happiness ◆ **blissful** *adjective* bringing feelings of great happiness; lovely: *a blissful holiday*

blister *noun* a thin bubble on the skin full of watery matter ➤ *verb* to rise up in a blister

blithe (*pronounced* blaidh) *adjective* happy, merry ◆ **blithely** *adverb*: *He blithely imagines he'll pass his exams without studying*

blitz *noun* (*plural* **blitzes**) **1** (also **blitzkreig**) an air attack **2** (**the Blitz**) the series of air-raids on British cities by the German air force in 1940–41 **3** (also **blitzkreig**) a sudden violent attack **4** *informal* a burst of intensive activity or work to achieve something

blizzard *noun* a fierce storm of wind and snow

bloated *adjective* swollen, puffed out

bloater *noun* a type of smoked herring

blob *noun* **1** a drop of liquid **2** a round spot

bloc *noun* a group of countries or people that have a common interest, purpose or policy

block *noun* **1** a lump of wood, stone, etc **2** a connected group of buildings **3** an obstruction: *a road block* **4** an engraved piece of wood or metal for printing **5** *history* the wood on which people were beheaded **6** *computing* a group of data units treated as a complete unit for transfer or modification ➤ *verb* to hinder, prevent from progress

blockade *verb* to surround (a fort or country) so that food etc cannot reach it ➤ *noun* the surrounding of a place in this way

blockage *noun* **1** anything that causes a pipe, roadway, etc to be blocked **2** the state of being blocked

block capitals or **block letters** *plural noun* capital letters

blog *computing, informal, noun* short for **weblog** ➤ *verb* (**blogged, blogging**) to write a **weblog** ◆ **blogger** *noun* ◆ **blogging** *noun*

bloke *noun, Brit informal* a man or chap ◆ **blokeish** or **blokey** *adjective* (**blokier, blokiest**)

blond *adjective* of a man: having fair skin and light-coloured hair

blonde *adjective* of a woman: having fair skin and light-coloured hair ➤ *noun* a woman with this colouring

blood *noun* **1** the red liquid which flows in the bodies of human beings and animals **2** someone's descent or parentage: *royal blood*

blood cell *noun* a cell contained in the blood

blood clot *noun* a clot formed at a bleeding wound or in a blood vessel

bloodcurdling *adjective* causing chilling fear

blood donor *noun* someone who gives blood which is stored and given to others in transfusions etc

blood group *noun* any one of the types into which human blood is classified

bloodhound *noun* a breed of large dog with a good sense of smell

bloodless *adjective* without bloodshed: *bloodless revolution*

blood plasma *noun* the clear, liquid part of blood

blood poisoning *noun* a serious condition caused by bacteria in the bloodstream

blood pressure *noun* the pressure of the blood in the vessels, especially in the arteries

bloodshed *noun* violent loss of life, slaughter

bloodshot *adjective* of eyes: inflamed with blood

blood sports *plural noun* sports that involve the killing of animals, eg fox-hunting

bloodstream *noun* the flow of blood around the body

bloodthirsty *adjective* (**bloodthirstier, bloodthirstiest**) cruel, eager to kill

blood transfusion *noun, medicine* the introduction of donated blood directly into a person's bloodstream

blood vessel *noun, anatomy* a tube in the body through which blood circulates, eg a vein or artery

bloody *adjective* (**bloodier, bloodiest**) **1** covered with blood **2** extremely violent, gory **3** *slang* terrible, awful ◆ **bloodiness** *noun*

bloom *verb* **1** of a plant: to flower **2** to be in good health ➤ *noun* **1** a flower **2** flowers or blossoms collectively **3** rosy colour **4** freshness, perfection **5** a powder on the skin of fresh fruits **6** *biology* a rapid increase in the growth rate of certain algae in lakes, ponds, etc

bloomer *noun, informal* an embarrassing mistake

bloomers *plural noun* **1** loose underpants with legs gathered above the knee **2** in the past, a woman's outfit of a jacket, skirt and baggy knee-length trousers

⊙ After Amelia *Bloomer*, 19th-century US feminist who promoted the use of the outfit for women

blossom *noun* **1** a flower **2** the flowers on a fruit tree ➤ *verb* **1** to produce flowers **2** to open out, develop, flourish

blot *noun* **1** a spot of ink **2** a stain ➤ *verb* (**blotting, blotted**) **1** to spot, stain **2** to dry (writing) with blotting paper ● **blot out** to remove from sight or memory

blotch *noun* (*plural* **blotches**) a spot or patch of colour ➤ *verb* to mark with blotches ◆ **blotched**

adjective ◆ **blotchy** *adjective* (**blotchier, blotchiest**) with skin or another surface which is temporarily an uneven colour: *Her face was blotchy from crying*

blotting paper *noun* thick paper for absorbing spilled or excess ink

blouse *noun* a woman's loose piece of clothing for the upper body

blow[1] *verb* (**blowing, blew, blown**) **1** of wind: to move around **2** to drive air upon or into **3** to sound (a wind instrument) **4** to breathe hard or with difficulty ● **blow over** to pass and be forgotten ● **blow up** to destroy or be destroyed by explosion

blow[2] *noun* **1** a hard stroke or knock, eg with the fist **2** *informal* a sudden piece of bad luck

blow-dry *verb* (**blow-dries, blow-drying, blow-dried**) to dry (hair) in a particular style using a hand-held hairdryer ➤ *noun* (*plural* **blow-dries**) an act of blow-drying

blowfly *noun* (*plural* **blowflies**) a kind of fly whose eggs are laid in rotting flesh or excrement

blowhole *noun* **1** a hole in an area of surface ice, where marine mammals, eg seals, can go to breathe **2** *zoology* a hole or modified nostril on top of a whale's head **3** *geography* a natural vent from the roof of a sea cave up to the ground surface, through which air and water are forced by breaking waves

blowout another term for a **deflation hollow**

blowtorch or **blowlamp** *noun* a tool for aiming a very hot flame at a particular spot, used for paint-stripping etc

blowy *adjective* (**blowier, blowiest**) windy

blubber *noun* the fat of whales and other sea animals

bludgeon *noun* a short stick with a heavy end ➤ *verb* to hit with a heavy object

blue *noun* the colour of a clear sky ➤ *adjective* **1** of this colour **2** unhappy, depressed **3** containing sexual material: *blue film* ● **out of the blue**

bluebell *noun* **1** the wild hyacinth **2** in Scotland, the harebell

blueberry *noun* (*plural* **blueberries**) **1** a deciduous shrub, native to N America, with white or pinkish flowers and edible berries **2** the bluish-black edible berry produced by this plant

bluebird *noun* a bird of the thrush family, the male of which has bright blue plumage on its back

blue blood *noun* royal or aristocratic blood

bluebottle *noun* a large fly with a blue abdomen

blue cheese *noun* cheese with veins of blue mould running through it

blue-chip *adjective* of a business company: reliable for investment; prestigious

blue-collar *adjective* referring ro workers

doing manual or unskilled work (*compare with*: **white collar**)

blue-green alga *noun, biology* the common name for any of a group of single-celled, photosynthetic organisms, often blue in colour

Blue Peter *noun* a blue flag with a white centre, raised when a ship is about to sail

blueprint *noun* a plan of work to be done

blues *plural noun*: **the blues 1** a slow, sad song **2** low spirits, depression

blue tit *noun* a small bird which has a bright blue crown, wings and tail, and yellow underparts

blue whale *noun* a rare, bluish whale, which is the largest living animal

bluff[1] *verb* to try to deceive by pretending self-confidence ➤ *noun* deception, trickery • **call someone's bluff** to challenge someone to prove their claim or promise

bluff[2] *adjective* **1** rough and cheerful in manner **2** frank, outspoken ➤ *noun* a steep bank overlooking the sea or a river

blunder *verb* to make a bad mistake ➤ *noun* a bad mistake

blunderbuss *noun* (*plural* **blunderbusses**), *history* a short handgun with a wide mouth

blunt *adjective* **1** having an edge or point that is not sharp **2** rough in manner ➤ *verb* to make less sharp or less painful ◆ **bluntly** *adverb* frankly, straightforwardly

blur *noun* an indistinct area of something; a smudge, a smear ➤ *verb* (**blurring, blurred**) to make indistinct, smudge ◆ **blurred** *adjective*

blurb *noun* a brief description of a book printed on the jacket in order to promote it

blurt *verb*: **blurt out** to speak suddenly and without thinking

blush *noun* (*plural* **blushes**) **1** a red glow on the face caused by embarrassment etc **2** a reddish glow ➤ *verb* to go red in the face

bluster *verb* **1** to blow strongly **2** to boast loudly ➤ *noun* **1** a strong wind **2** empty boasting ◆ **blustery** *adjective* very windy

BMA *abbreviation* British Medical Association

boa *noun* a long scarf of fur or feathers

boa constrictor *noun* a large snake which kills its prey by winding itself round it and crushing it

boar *noun* **1** a male pig **2** a wild pig

board *noun* **1** a sheet of wood **2** a group of people who run a business: *a board of directors* **3** stiff card used to bind books **4** food: *bed and board* ➤ *verb* **1** to cover with boards **2** to receive or supply with food and lodging **3** to enter (a ship, aeroplane, etc) ◆ **boarder** *noun* someone who receives food and lodging

board game *noun* a game played with pieces or counters that are moved on a specially designed board

boarding house *noun* a house in which

people live and take meals as paying guests

boarding school *noun* a school in which food and lodging is given

boast *verb* **1** to talk proudly about yourself **2** to have (something worth being proud of): *The hotel boasts magnificent views* ➤ *noun* an act of boasting

boastful *adjective* with a tendency to boast

boat *noun* **1** a vessel for sailing or rowing; a ship **2** a boat-shaped dish: *a sauce boat* ➤ *verb* to sail about in a boat

boater *noun* a straw hat with a brim

boatman or **boatwoman** *noun* (*plural* **boatmen** or **boatwomen**) **1** someone who is in charge of a boat **2** a rower

boat people *plural noun* refugees who have fled their country by boat

boatswain or **bosun** (*both pronounced* **boh**-sun) *noun* an officer who looks after a ship's boats, rigging, etc

bob[1] *verb* (**bobbing, bobbed**) to move up and down rapidly ➤ *noun* a bobbing action

bob[2] *verb* (**bobbing, bobbed**) to cut (hair) to about neck level ➤ *noun* a bobbed haircut

bob[3] *noun* a bobsleigh

bobbin *noun* a reel or spool on which thread is wound

bobble *noun* **1** a woolly ball for decorating hats etc **2** a little ball on the surface of fabric

bobby *noun* (*plural* **bobbies**), *Brit informal* a police officer

---

⊕ After Sir *Robert* Peel, who introduced the Metropolitan Police Force when Home Secretary in 1828

---

bobsleigh *noun* a long sledge or two short sledges joined together with one long seat

bode[1] *verb*: **bode ill** to be a bad sign • **bode well** to be a good sign

bode[2] past tense of **bide**

Bodhisattva *noun, Buddhism* a future Buddha who postpones entry into nirvana in order to help others

bodhi tree or **bo tree** *noun, Buddhism* the holy tree of the Buddhists, under which Buddha found enlightenment

bodice *noun* the close-fitting part of a woman's or a child's dress above the waist

bodily *adjective* of the body

bodkin *noun, old* a large blunt needle

body *noun* (*plural* **bodies**) **1** the whole or main part of a human being or animal **2** a corpse **3** the main part of anything **4** a mass of people **5** a solid object **6** *informal* a bodystocking

body-building *noun* physical exercise designed to develop the muscles ◆ **body-builder** *noun*

bodyguard *noun* someone or a group of

people whose job is to protect an important person from harm or attack

body language *noun* communication by means of conscious or unconscious gestures, attitudes, facial expressions, etc

body piercing *noun* **1** the practice of piercing parts of the body other than the earlobes **2** a piece of jewellery inserted through a pierced body part

bodystocking *noun* a one-piece woman's undergarment

bodywarmer *noun* a padded sleeveless jacket

bodywork *noun* the outer shell of a motor vehicle

boffin *noun, informal* a research scientist

> ⏱ Said to come from a scientist who gave his colleagues nicknames from Dickens, Mr Boffin being a character in *Our Mutual Friend*

bog *noun* **1** a marsh **2** *slang* a toilet ♦ **boggy** *adjective* (**boggier, boggiest**) marshy • **bog down** to prevent from making progress

bogey *noun* (*plural* **bogeys**) something greatly feared

boggle *verb* to be astonished at

bogus *adjective* false

bohemian (*pronounced* boh-**hee**-mi-an) *noun* someone who lives outside social conventions, especially an artist or writer > *adjective* of the lifestyle of a bohemian

bohrium *noun, chemistry* (symbol **Bh**) an artificially produced radioactive element

> ⏱ Named after Danish physicist Niels *Bohr* (1885–1962)

boil¹ *verb* **1** of a liquid: to reach the temperature at which it turns to vapour **2** to bubble up owing to heat **3** *informal* to be hot **4** *informal* to be angry

boil² *noun* a kind of inflamed swelling

boiler *noun* a container in which water is heated or steam is produced

boilersuit *noun* a one-piece suit worn over normal clothes to protect them while doing manual work

boiling point *noun* the temperature at which a liquid turns to vapour (eg, for water, 100°C)

boisterous *adjective* **1** wild, noisy **2** of weather: stormy

bold *adjective* **1** daring, full of courage **2** cheeky **3** striking, well-marked: *bold colours* **4** of printing type: thick and clear ♦ **boldly** *adverb* (meanings 1, 2 and 3)

bollard *noun* **1** a post to which ropes are fastened on a ship or quay **2** a short post on a street used for traffic control

Bolshevik *noun* **1** *history* a member of the

Extreme Socialist Party in revolutionary Russia **2** *derogatory* a communist

> ⏱ A Russian word based on *bolshe* 'greater', either because of the majority held by the Bolsheviks in the Social Democratic Congress of 1903, or because of their more extreme programme

bolshy *adjective* (**bolshier, bolshiest**), *informal* awkward, unco-operative

> ⏱ Originally a shortening of **Bolshevik**

bolster *noun* a long cylindrical pillow or cushion • **bolster up** to support

bolt *noun* **1** a small metal sliding bar used to fasten a door etc **2** a large screw or pin **3** a roll of cloth > *verb* **1** to fasten with a bolt **2** to swallow (food) hurriedly **3** to rush away, escape **4** of a plant: to flower and produce seeds too early > *adverb*: **bolt upright** sitting with a very straight back

bomb *noun* **1** a case containing explosive or other harmful material thrown, dropped, timed to go off automatically, etc **2** (**the bomb**) the nuclear bomb > *verb* to drop bombs on

bombard *verb* **1** to attack with artillery **2** to overwhelm (with): *bombarded with letters* **3** *physics* to subject (a target) to a stream of high-energy particles ♦ **bombardment** *noun*

bombast *noun* pompous language ♦ **bombastic** *adjective* using pompous language

bomber *noun* **1** an aeroplane built for bombing **2** someone who throws or plants bombs

bombshell *noun* **1** a startling piece of news **2** a stunningly attractive woman

bona fide (*pronounced* bohn-a **fai**-dei) *adjective* real, genuine: *a bona fide excuse*

> ⏱ In Latin, *bona fide* means 'in good faith'

bond *noun* **1** something which binds, eg a rope **2** something which brings people together: *Music was a bond between them* **3** a promise to pay or do something **4** *chemistry* the strong force of attraction that holds together two atoms in a molecule • **in bond** in a bonded warehouse

bondage *noun* slavery

bonded warehouse *noun* a warehouse where goods are kept until taxes have been paid on them

bond energy *noun, chemistry* the energy released or absorbed during the formation of a chemical bond

bone *noun* **1** a hard material forming the skeleton of animals **2** one of the connected pieces of a skeleton: *the hip bone* > *verb* to take the bones out of (meat etc)

bonfire *noun* a large fire in the open air

bongo *noun* (*plural* **bongos** or **bongoes**) each of a pair of small drums held between the knees and played with the hands

bonk *noun* 1 the sound of a blow 2 *slang* an act of sexual intercourse ➤ *verb*, *slang* to have sexual intercourse with

bonnet *noun* 1 a decorative woman's hat, fastened under the chin 2 the covering over a car engine

bonny (**bonnier, bonniest**) *adjective* good-looking; pretty

bonsai (*pronounced* **bon**-sai) *noun* a miniature or dwarf tree created by special pruning, or the art of growing such trees

bonus *noun* (*plural* **bonuses**) 1 an extra payment in addition to wages 2 something extra

bony *adjective* (**bonier, boniest**) 1 full of bones 2 not fleshy, thin 3 made of bone or a bone-like substance

boo *verb* to make a sound of disapproval ➤ *noun* a sound of disapproval

boob[1] *noun*, *informal* a mistake

boob[2] *noun*, *slang* a woman's breast

booby *noun* (*plural* **boobies**) an idiot

booby prize *noun* a prize for the person who is last in a competition

booby trap *noun* a device hidden or disguised as something harmless, intended to injure the first person to come near it

boogie (*pronounced* **boo**-gi) *informal*, *verb* (**boogieing** or **boogying, boogied**) to dance to pop, rock or jazz music ➤ *noun* a dance to pop, rock or jazz music

book *noun* 1 a number of pages bound together 2 a written work which has appeared, or is intended to appear, in the form of a book ➤ *verb* 1 to order (places etc) beforehand 2 of a police officer or other official: to record the details of (someone who is being charged with an offence)

bookcase *noun* a piece of furniture with shelves for books

book group *noun* a group of people who meet regularly to discuss books

book-keeping *noun* the keeping of accounts ♦ **book-keeper** *noun*

booklet *noun* a small paperback book

bookmaker *noun* someone who takes bets and pays winnings

bookmark *noun* 1 something inserted in the pages of a book to mark a place 2 *computing* a record of the location of a favourite Internet site, web page, etc ➤ *verb*, *computing* to make an electronic record of (a favourite Internet site etc)

bookworm *noun* 1 *informal* an avid reader 2 a grub which eats holes in books

Boolean algebra (*pronounced* **boo**-li-an)

noun a form of algebra used to work out the logic for computer programs

⊙ This form of algebra was devised by British mathematician George *Boole* (1815–64)

Boolean expression (*pronounced* **boo**-li-an) *noun* an expression containing any of the Boolean operators 'NOT', 'AND' and 'OR', used extensively in computing

Boolean operators (*pronounced* **boo**-li-an) *plural noun*, *computing* the words 'NOT', 'AND' and 'OR', used extensively in computing (*also called*: **Boolean connectors**)

boom[1] *verb* to make a hollow sound or roar ➤ *noun* a loud, hollow sound

boom[2] *verb* to increase in prosperity, success, etc ➤ *noun* a rush or increase of trade, prosperity, etc: *oil boom/property boom*

boom[3] *noun* a pole along which a sail is streched

boomerang *noun* a curved piece of wood which when thrown returns to the thrower, a traditional hunting weapon of Australian Aboriginals

boon *noun* something to be grateful for, a blessing

boon companion *noun* a close friend who is good company

boor *noun* a rough or rude person ♦ **boorish** *adjective*

boost *verb* to push up, raise, increase: *boost the sales figures* ➤ *noun* an increase, a rise

booster *noun* 1 a device for increasing the power of a machine etc 2 the first of several stages of a rocket 3 (*also called*: **booster shot**) a dose of vaccine that is given in order to increase the immune response to a previous dose of the same vaccine

boot[1] *noun* 1 a heavy shoe covering the foot and lower part of the leg 2 *Brit* a place for stowing luggage in a car 3 *computing* the starting of a computer from its start-up programs 4 a kick ➤ *verb* to kick ● **boot up** *computing* to start (a computer) by running its start-up programs

boot[2] *noun*: **to boot** in addition, as well

bootee *noun* a knitted boot for a baby

booth *noun* 1 a covered stall, eg at a market 2 a small compartment for telephoning, voting, etc

bootleg *verb* (**bootlegging, bootlegged**) 1 to make or deal in (illicit goods such as unofficial recordings of copyright music) 2 to make or sell (alcoholic drink) illegally ➤ *noun* 1 illegally produced, sold or transported goods, especially alcoholic drink or recorded material 2 the leg of a high boot ♦ **bootlegger** *noun* ♦ **bootlegging** *noun*

⊙ In the past, a *bootlegger* would conceal bottles of illegal alcoholic drink in his bootlegs

booty *noun* plunder, gains taken in war etc

booze *slang, noun* alcoholic drink ➤ *verb* to drink a lot of alcohol ♦ **boozer** *noun*

borax *noun, chemistry* a mineral found on alkaline lake shores

border *noun* **1** the edge or side of anything **2** the boundary of a country **3** a flowerbed in a garden ➤ *verb*: **border on** to be near to: *bordering on the absurd*

borderline *noun* **1** the line dividing two countries etc **2** the line dividing two things: *the borderline between passing and failing* ➤ *adjective* on the borderline between one thing and another: *a borderline pass*

bore[1] *verb* to make a hole by piercing ➤ *noun* **1** a pierced hole **2** the size across the tube of a gun

bore[2] *verb* to weary, be tiresome to: *This book bores me* ➤ *noun* a tiresome person or thing ♦ **bored** *adjective*

bore[3] *noun* a wave that rushes up a river mouth at high tide

bore[4] past tense of **bear**[2]

boreal forest another term for **taiga**

boredom *noun* lack of interest, weariness

boric acid *noun, chemistry* a soluble white or colourless crystalline solid obtained from borax, used in pharmaceutical products

boring *adjective* not at all interesting ♦ **boringly** *adverb*

born *adjective* by birth, natural: *a born actor* • **be born 1** of a baby: to come out of the mother's womb **2** to come into existence

! Do not confuse: **born** and **borne**. **Born** is used for the past participle of **bear** when referring to the birth of a child, idea, etc; otherwise the form is **borne**: *I couldn't have borne it any longer.*

born-again *adjective* converted or re-converted, especially to an evangelical Christian faith

borne past participle of **bear**[2]

! Do not confuse: **borne** and **born**

boron *noun, chemistry* (symbol **B**) a non-metallic element found only in compounds

borough *noun* **1** *history* a town with special privileges granted by royal charter **2** a town that elects Members of Parliament

borrow *verb* to get on loan ♦ **borrower** *noun*

borzoi *noun* a large breed of dog with a long soft coat ⊙ Comes from Russian, meaning 'swift'

bosom *noun* **1** the breast **2** midst, centre: *in the bosom of her family* ➤ *adjective* of a friend: close, intimate

boss *noun* (*plural* **bosses**) a manager, a chief ➤ *verb* to order about in a high-handed way

bossy *adjective* (**bossier, bossiest**) tending to boss others, domineering

bosun see **boatswain**

botanic garden *noun* a large public garden containing plants and trees from different countries

botanist *noun* someone who studies botany

botany *noun* the study of plants ♦ **botanic** or **botanical** *adjective*

botch *verb* to mend clumsily; do badly ➤ *noun* (*plural* **botches**) a badly done piece of work

both *adjective & pronoun* the two, the one and the other: *We're both going to Paris/Both the men are dead* ➤ *adverb* equally, together: *both willing and able*

bother *verb* **1** to be a nuisance to: *Stop bothering me!* **2** to take time or trouble over something: *Don't bother with the dishes* ➤ *noun* trouble, inconvenience

bothy *noun* (*plural* **bothies**), *Scot* **1** a hut to give shelter to hillwalkers **2** a simply furnished hut for farm workers

bottle *noun* **1** a hollow narrow-necked vessel for holding liquids **2** *slang* courage, nerve or confidence ➤ *verb* to put in a bottle • **bottle out** *slang* to lose your courage and decide not to do something • **bottle up** to keep in, hold back (feelings)

bottle bank *noun* a skip collecting empty glass containers for recycling

bottleneck *noun* **1** a narrow part of a road likely to become crowded with traffic **2** a stage in a process where progress is held up

bottom *noun* **1** the lowest part or underside of anything **2** the buttocks

bottomless *adjective* extremely deep

bottom line *noun* (**the bottom line**) **1** *informal* the most important factor in a situation **2** the last line of a financial statement, showing profit or loss

botulism (*pronounced* bot-yuw-lizm) *noun, medicine* a severe form of food poisoning, caused by bacteria in poorly preserved foods

boudoir (*pronounced* bood-wahr) *noun, old* a lady's private room

bough *noun* a branch of a tree

bought past form of **buy**

boulder *noun* a large stone

boulder clay *noun, geography* a glacial deposit consisting of boulders of different sizes embedded in hard clay

boulevard (*pronounced* boo-le-vahrd) *noun* a broad street in a town or city, especially one lined with trees

⊙ Came into English from French, but is originally from German *Bollwerk* meaning 'bulwark'. The term was originally applied to a road built on a town's demolished fortifications

bounce *verb* **1** to jump up after striking the ground etc **2** to make (a ball etc) do this ➤ *noun* a jumping back up • **bounce back** to recover after a setback or trouble

bouncer *noun* someone employed to force troublemakers to leave a club etc

bouncing *adjective* full of life, lively

bouncy *adjective* (**bouncier, bounciest**) **1** tending to bounce **2** able to be bounced on: *an inflatable bouncy castle* **3** lively

bound¹ past form of **bind** ➤ *adjective* obliged • **bound to** certain to

bound² *adjective*: **bound for** on the way to

bound³ *noun* **1** (**bounds**) borders, limits **2** *maths* a number which shows the upper (the **upper bound**) and lower (the **lower bound**) values in range of possible values ➤ *verb* to enclose, surround • **out of bounds** beyond the permitted limits

bound⁴ *verb* to jump, leap ➤ *noun* a leap, a jump

boundary *noun* (*plural* **boundaries**) **1** an edge, a limit **2** a line etc marking an edge

boundless *adjective* having no limit, vast

bountiful or **bounteous** *adjective* **1** generous **2** plentiful

bounty *noun* (*plural* **bounties**) **1** a gift **2** generosity **3** a reward

bouquet (*pronounced* boo-**kei**) *noun* **1** a bunch of flowers **2** a scent, eg of wine

bouquet garni (*pronounced* **boo**-kei **gahr**-nee) *noun* (*plural* **bouquets garnis** – *pronounced* **boo**-kei **gahr**-nee) *cookery* a small packet or bunch of mixed herbs used eg in stews to add flavour

bourgeois (*pronounced* **boorsz**-wah) *adjective* of the middle class ♦ **bourgeoisie** *noun* (**the bourgeoisie**) a rather insulting name for middle-class people who have a comfortable but unimaginative lifestyle

bout *noun* **1** a round in a contest **2** a spell, a fit: *a bout of flu*

boutique *noun* a small shop selling fashionable clothes etc

bovine (*pronounced* **boh**-vain) *adjective* **1** of or like cattle **2** *derogatory* stupid

bow¹ (*pronounced* bow) *verb* **1** to bend **2** to nod the head or bend the body in greeting **3** to give in: *bow to pressure* ➤ *noun* **1** a bending of the head or body **2** the front part of a ship

bow² (*pronounced* boh) *noun* **1** anything in the shape of a curve or arch **2** a weapon for shooting arrows, made of a stick of springy wood bent by a string **3** a looped knot, usually decorative **4** a wooden rod with horsehair stretched along it, by which the strings of a violin etc are played

bowdlerize or **bowdlerise** (*pronounced* **bowd**-ler-aiz) *verb* to censor heavily

ⓘ After Thomas *Bowdler*, who produced a heavily censored edition of Shakespeare in the 19th century

bowels *plural noun* **1** the large and small intestines **2** the innermost or deepest parts of anything: *in the bowels of the earth*

bower (*pronounced* **bow**-er) *noun* a shady spot in a garden

bowl¹ *noun* **1** a basin for holding liquids **2** a basin-shaped hollow

bowl² *noun* **1** a heavy wooden ball, used in bowling etc **2** (**bowls**) a game played on a green with specially weighted bowls ➤ *verb* **1** to play at bowls **2** to move speedily like a bowl **3** *cricket* to send (the ball) at the wicket **4** *cricket* to put out by knocking the wicket with the ball • **bowl over 1** to knock down **2** to surprise greatly

bow-legged *adjective* having legs curving outwards

bowler¹ *noun* **1** someone who plays bowls **2** someone who bowls in cricket

bowler² *noun* a hat with a rounded top

bowling *noun* **1** the game of bowls **2** the game of tenpin bowling

bow tie *noun* a neck tie with two loops and a knot

bow window *noun* a window built in a curve

box¹ *noun* (*plural* **boxes**) **1** a case for holding anything **2** an enclosure of private seats in a theatre ➤ *verb* **1** to put in a box **2** to confine in a small space

box² *verb* **1** to punch **2** to engage in the sport of boxing

box³ *noun* **1** a hardwood tree **2** an evergreen shrub

box and whisker plot see **box-plot**

boxer *noun* **1** someone who boxes as a sport **2** a breed of large smooth-haired dog with a head like a bulldog's

boxer shorts *plural noun* loose-fitting men's underpants

boxing *noun* the sport of fighting with the fists wearing padded gloves

Boxing Day *noun* the first weekday after Christmas Day

box number *noun* the number of a box at a newspaper office, post office, etc to which mail may be sent

box office *noun* an office where theatre tickets etc may be bought

box-plot *noun, statistics* a type of diagram representing a set of numerical data, in which each interquartile range is represented by a box (*also called*: **box and whisker plot**)

boxroom *noun, chiefly Brit* a small room, used especially for storage

boy *noun* a male child

boycott *verb* to refuse to do business or trade with ➤ *noun* a refusal to trade or do business

⊙ After Charles *Boycott*, British estate manager ostracized by the Irish Land League in the 19th century

boyfriend *noun* a male friend, especially in a romantic relationship

boyhood *noun* the time of being a boy

boyish *adjective* 1 of a girl: having an appearance or behaviour which gives an impression of masculinity 2 of a man: having an appearance or behaviour which gives an impression of youthfulness

Boyle's law *noun, physics* the law which states that the volume of a mass of gas at a constant temperature is inversely proportional to its pressure

⊙ Named after Robert *Boyle* (1627–91), Irish chemist

bps *abbreviation, computing* bits per second

Bq *symbol, physics* becquerel

Br *symbol, chemistry* bromine

bra *noun* an article of women's underwear for supporting the breasts

brace *noun* 1 an instrument which draws things together and holds them firmly 2 a piece of wire fitted over teeth to straighten them 3 a pair of pheasant, grouse, etc when shot 4 a carpenter's tool for boring 5 (**braces**) shoulder-straps for holding up trousers ➤ *verb* to strengthen, give firmness to

bracelet *noun* 1 a circular ornament placed around the wrist 2 *slang* a handcuff

brachiate (*pronounced* **brei**-ki-eit) *adjective* 1 *botany* having widely spreading branches 2 *zoology* having arms

brachiopod (*pronounced* **brei**-ki-o-pod) *noun, zoology* a marine invertebrate animal with a shell consisting of two valves, and a short fleshy stalk at the rear of the shell

bracing *adjective* giving strength

bracken *noun* a coarse kind of fern

bracket *noun* 1 a support for something fastened to a wall 2 each of a pair of written or printed marks, eg (), [ ], used to group together several words, figures, etc 3 a grouping, category: *in the same age bracket* ➤ *verb* 1 to enclose in brackets 2 to group together

brackish *adjective* of water: rather salty

bract *noun, botany* a small leaf that develops a flower in its axil

brag *verb* (**bragging, bragged**) to boast ➤ *noun* a boast

braggart *noun* someone vain and boastful

Brahma *noun, Hinduism* the first god of the Trimurti, the creator of the universe

Brahman *noun, Hinduism* 1 the guiding principle beneath all reality 2 a Brahmin

Brahmin or **Brahman** *noun* (*plural* **Brahmins** or **Brahmans**) one of the highest-ranking groups of Hindus, from which priests come

braid *verb* to plait (the hair) ➤ *noun* 1 a plait of hair 2 decorative ribbon used as trimming

braided channel *noun, geography* a channel divided into several shallow interconnected channels

braille *noun* a system of raised marks on paper which blind people can read by feeling

⊙ Named after its inventor Louis *Braille* (1809–52), a teacher in France

brain *noun* the part of the body inside the skull, the centre of feeling and thinking ➤ *verb* to hit hard on the head

brainchild *noun* a person's particular and original theory, idea or plan

brainstem *noun, anatomy* the part of the brain that is connected to the tip of the spinal cord

brainstorm *noun* 1 *informal* a sudden loss of the ability to think clearly and act sensibly 2 *US informal* a brainwave

brainwash *verb* to force (someone) to believe something by using constant pressure
  ♦ **brainwashing** *noun*

brainwave *noun* a good idea

brainy *adjective* (**brainier, brainiest**) *informal* clever

braise *verb* to stew (meat) in a small amount of liquid

brake *noun* a part of a vehicle used for stopping or slowing down ➤ *verb* to slow down by using the brake(s)

bramble *noun* 1 the blackberry bush 2 its fruit

bran *noun* the inner husks of wheat etc, separated from flour after grinding

branch *noun* (*plural* **branches**) 1 an arm-like limb of a tree 2 a small shop, bank, etc belonging to a bigger one ➤ *verb* to spread out like branches • **branch out** to develop different interests or projects etc

brand *noun* 1 a make of goods with a special trademark 2 a burning piece of wood 3 a permanent mark made by a red-hot iron ➤ *verb* 1 to mark with a brand 2 to mark permanently; impress deeply 3 to mark with disgrace: *branded as a thief*

brandish *verb* to wave (a weapon etc) about

brand-new *adjective* absolutely new

Brandt line *noun* a hypothetical line dividing the world into the economically developed countries of the north and the less economically developed countries of the south

⊙ The concept of the line was put forward in the 'Brandt report', a report on international development by a commission chaired by Willy Brandt, in 1980

brandy *noun* (*plural* **brandies**) an alcoholic spirit made from wine

brash *adjective* **1** very loud, flashy or showy **2** rude; impudent, overbearingly forward
♦ **brashness** *noun*

brass *noun* (*plural* **brasses**) **1** a metal made by mixing copper and zinc **2** *music* brass wind instruments, eg trumpets and horns ➤ *adjective* **1** made of brass **2** playing brass musical instruments: *the brass section*

brass band *noun* a musical band consisting mainly of brass wind instruments

brasserie *noun* a small and usually inexpensive restaurant, serving food, and originally beer ⊙ Comes from French, meaning 'brewery'

brassière *noun* a bra

brassy *adjective* (**brassier, brassiest**) **1** like brass **2** of a voice: harsh **3** *slang* of a person: loudly confident and rude **4** flashy or showy

brat *noun* a disapproving name for a child

bravado (*pronounced* bra-**vah**-doh) *noun* a show of bravery; bold pretence

brave *adjective* ready to meet danger, pain, etc without showing fear; courageous, noble ➤ *verb* to face or meet boldly and without fear ➤ *noun* a Native American warrior

bravery *noun* the quality of being brave and acting with courage

bravo *interjection* well done!

bravura (*pronounced* bra-**voor**-a) *noun* **1** a display of great spirit or daring **2** *music* especially in vocal music: spirit or brilliance in performance

brawl *noun* a noisy quarrel; a fight ➤ *verb* to quarrel or fight noisily

brawn *noun* muscle power ♦ **brawny** *adjective* (**brawnier, brawniest**) big and strong

bray *noun* **1** a cry like that of an ass **2** a pin pressing against a string on a harp to produce a buzzing effect ➤ *verb* to cry like an ass

brazen *adjective* **1** impudent, shameless: *brazen hussy* **2** of or like brass ♦ **brazenly** *adverb*
• **brazen it out** to face a difficult situation with bold impudence

brazier (*pronounced* **breiz**-i-er) *noun* an iron basket for holding burning coals

breach *noun* (*plural* **breaches**) **1** a break, a gap **2** a breaking of a law, a promise, etc **3** a quarrel ➤ *verb* to make a gap or opening in • **breach of the peace** a breaking of the law by noisy, offensive behaviour

bread *noun* food made of flour or meal mixed with water etc and baked

breadline *noun*: **on the breadline** having hardly enough food and money to live on

breadth *noun* **1** distance from side to side, width **2** extent: *breadth of knowledge*

breadwinner *noun* someone who earns a living for a family

break *verb* (**breaking, broke, broken**) **1** to (cause to) fall to pieces or apart **2** to fracture a bone in (a limb etc) **3** to act against (a law, promise, etc) **4** to interrupt (a silence) **5** to tell (news) **6** to check, soften the effect of (a fall) **7** to cure (a habit) **8** of a boy's voice: to drop to a deep male tone at puberty ➤ *noun* **1** an opening **2** a pause **3** *informal* a lucky chance • **break down 1** to divide into parts **2** of an engine: to fail **3** to be overcome with weeping or nervous exhaustion **4** to be unsuccessful and come to an end: *talks broke down* • **break in** to tame, train (a wild horse etc) • **break into** to enter by force • **break out 1** to appear suddenly **2** to escape • **break out in something** to become covered (with a rash etc) • **break up 1** to (cause to) fall to pieces or apart **2** to separate, leave one another
♦ **breakable** *adjective*

breakage *noun* **1** the act of breaking **2** something broken

breakdown *noun* **1** a division into parts **2** a collapse from nervous exhaustion etc

breaker *noun* a large wave

breakfast *noun* the first meal of the day ➤ *verb* to eat this meal

break-in *noun* illegal forced entry of a house etc with intent to steal

breaking point *noun* the point at which a person or relationship can no longer stand up to a stress or strain and breaks down

breakthrough *noun* a sudden success after some effort

breakwater *noun* a barrier to break the force of waves

breast *noun* **1** either of the milk-producing glands on a woman's body **2** the front part of a human or animal body between neck and belly **3** a part of a jacket or coat which covers the breast • **make a clean breast** to make a full confession

breastbone *noun* the bone running down the middle of the breast; the sternum

breastfeed *verb* (**breastfeeding, breastfed**) to feed (a baby) with milk from the breast

breastplate *noun* a piece of armour for the breast

breaststroke *noun* a stroke used in swimming where the arms and legs are pushed forwards then sideways

breath (*pronounced* breth) *noun* **1** the air drawn into and then sent out from the lungs **2** an instance of breathing **3** a very slight breeze

⚠ Do not confuse: **breath** and **breathe**

Breathalyser *noun, trademark* a device into which someone breathes to indicate the amount of alcohol in their blood ◆ **breathalyse** *verb*

breathe (*pronounced* breedh) *verb* (**breathing, breathed**) **1** to draw in and send out air from the lungs **2** to whisper

! Do not confuse: **breathe** and **breath**

breather *noun* a rest or pause

breathing-space *noun* a short time allowed for rest

breathless *adjective* **1** breathing very fast, panting **2** excited

breathtaking *adjective* very surprising or impressive

bred past form of **breed**

breech *noun* (*plural* **breeches**) the back part, especially of a gun

breeches (*pronounced* **brich**-iz) *plural noun* trousers reaching to just below the knee

breed *verb* (**breeding, bred**) **1** to produce offspring **2** to mate and rear (animals) **3** to cause: *Dirt breeds disease* ➤ *noun* **1** a group of animals etc descended from the same ancestor **2** type, sort: *a new breed of salesmen* ◆ **breeder** *noun* someone who breeds certain animals

breeding *noun* **1** *biology* controlling the reproduction of plants or animals so that certain characteristics are passed on **2** the act of producing or rearing **3** good manners; education and training

breeze *noun* a gentle wind

breeze block *noun* a type of large, grey brick used in building

breezy *adjective* (**breezier, breeziest**) **1** windy, gusty **2** bright, lively ◆ **breezily** *adverb* (meaning 2)

brethren *plural noun, old* brothers

breve (*pronounced* breev) *noun* a mark (˘) sometimes put over a vowel to show that it is short or unstressed

brevity (*pronounced* **brev**-i-ti) *noun* shortness, conciseness

brew *verb* **1** to make beer **2** to make (tea etc) **3** to be gathering or forming: *There's trouble brewing* **4** to plot, plan: *brewing mischief* ◆ **brewer** *noun* someone who brews beer etc

brewery *noun* (*plural* **breweries**) a place where beer is made

Brezhnev Doctrine *noun, history* the Soviet doctrine which arose during the leadership of Leonid Brezhnev (died 1982), that the Soviet Union could intervene in the affairs of another communist country to counter a supposed threat to socialism

briar or **brier** *noun* **1** the wild rose **2** a heather plant whose wood is used for making tobacco pipes

bribe *noun* a gift of money etc given to persuade someone to do something ➤ *verb* to offer a bribe to

bribery *noun* the act of bribing someone to do something

bric-à-brac *noun* small odds and ends

brick *noun* **1** a block of baked clay for building **2** a toy building-block of wood etc

brickbat *noun* an insult or criticism

bricklayer *noun* someone whose job it is to build with bricks

bridal *adjective* of a bride or a wedding

! Do not confuse with: **bridle**

bride *noun* a woman about to be married, or newly married

bridegroom *noun* a man about to be married, or newly married

bridesmaid *noun* a woman who attends the bride at a wedding

bridge[1] *noun* **1** a structure built to carry a track or road across a river etc **2** the captain's platform on a ship **3** the bony part of the nose **4** a thin piece of wood holding up the strings of a violin etc **5** *computing* a piece of hardware that connects networks or parts of a network ➤ *verb* **1** to be a bridge over; span **2** to build a bridge over **3** to get over (a difficulty)

bridge[2] *noun* a card game for two pairs of players

bridle *noun* the harness on a horse's head to which the reins are attached ➤ *verb* **1** to put on a bridle **2** to toss the head indignantly

! Do not confuse with: **bridal**

bridle path *noun* a path for horse-riders

brief *adjective* short; taking a short time ➤ *noun* a set of notes giving information or instructions, especially to a lawyer about a law case ➤ *verb* to instruct or inform ● **in brief** in a few words ◆ **briefly** *adverb*

briefcase *noun* a flat case for carrying papers

briefs *plural noun* close-fitting underpants

brier another spelling of **briar**

brigade *noun* a body of soldiers, usually two battalions

brigadier (*pronounced* brig-a-**deer**) *noun* a senior army officer

brigand (*pronounced* **brig**-and) *noun, old* a robber, a bandit

bright *adjective* **1** shining; full of light **2** clever **3** cheerful

brighten *verb* to make or grow bright

brilliant *adjective* **1** very clever **2** sparkling **3** *informal* very good, excellent ◆ **brilliance** *noun* ◆ **brilliantly** *adverb*: *brilliantly intelligent/The* *edges of the diamond gleamed brilliantly/He did brilliantly in his exams*

brim *noun* **1** the edge of a cup etc: *filled to the brim* **2** the protruding lower edge of a hat or cap ➤ *verb* (**brimming, brimmed**) to be full

brimful *adjective* full to the brim

brimstone *noun, old* sulphur

brine *noun* salt water ♦ **briny** *adjective* (**brinier, briniest**)

bring *verb* (**bringing, brought**) **1** to fetch, lead or carry (to a place) **2** to cause to come: *The medicine brings him relief* • **bring about** to cause • **bring home to** to make (someone) realize (something) • **bring off** to do (something) successfully • **bring to** to revive • **bring up 1** to rear, feed and educate: *brought up three children single-handed* **2** to mention: *I'll bring it up at the meeting* **3** *informal* to vomit ◑ Comes from Old English *bringan* meaning 'to carry' or 'to bring'

brink *noun* the edge of a cliff etc • **on the brink of** almost at the point of, on the verge of: *on the brink of tears*

bris or **brith** *noun, Judaism* a circumcision ceremony

brisk *adjective* **1** moving quickly: *a brisk walk* **2** lively and efficient: *a brisk manner* ♦ **briskly** *adverb*

brisket *noun* meat from the breast of a bull or cow

bristle *noun* a short, stiff hair on an animal, a brush, etc ➤ *verb* **1** of hair etc: to stand on end **2** to show anger and indignation: *He bristled at my remark* ♦ **bristly** *adjective* (**bristlier, bristliest**) having bristles; rough

brith see **bris**

British Expeditionary Force *noun, history* (*abbrev* **BEF**) an army established to support the left wing of the French armies under German attack during World War I and again in World War II

Briton *noun* a British person

brittle *adjective* hard but easily broken

broach *verb* **1** to begin to talk about: *broached the subject* **2** to open, begin using (eg a cask of wine)

❗ Do not confuse with: **brooch**

broad *adjective* **1** wide, extensive **2** of an accent etc: strong, obvious ♦ **broadly** *adverb* **1** widely: *smile broadly* **2** generally: *Broadly speaking, we're all afraid of the same things*

broadband *adjective* **1** of telecommunications: operating across a wide range of frequencies (*compare with:* **narrowband**) **2** *computing* accommodating data from a wide range of sources, eg telephone, television, etc

broad bean *noun* **1** an annual plant of the bean family **2** one of the large pale green edible seeds growing in pods on this plant

broadcast *verb* to transmit (a programme etc) on radio or television ➤ *noun* a programme transmitted on radio or television

♦ **broadcaster** *noun*

broaden *verb* to make or grow broader

broad-gauge *adjective* of a railway: having the distance between rails greater than the standard gauge (4 feet 8 inches or 1.435 metres) (*compare with:* **narrow-gauge**)

broad-minded *adjective* tolerant and liberal

broadsheet *noun* a large-format newspaper, usually with in-depth news coverage (*compare with:* **tabloid**)

broadside *noun* **1** a strong attack in an argument etc **2** a shot by all the guns on one side of a ship

brocade *noun* a silk cloth on which fine patterns are sewn

broccoli *noun* a hardy variety of cauliflower with small green or purple flower-heads

brochure (*pronounced* broh-**shoor** or broh-shur) *noun* a booklet, a pamphlet: *a holiday brochure*

broderie anglaise (*pronounced* **brod**-ree ong-**glez**) *noun* open embroidery used for decorating cotton and linen ◑ Comes from French, meaning 'English embroidery'

brogue[1] (*pronounced* brohg) *noun* a strong shoe

brogue[2] (*pronounced* brohg) *noun* a broad accent in speaking: *Irish brogue*

broil *verb* **1** to make or be very hot **2** *US* to grill

broke past tense of **break** ➤ *adjective, informal* having no money

broken past participle of **break**

broken-hearted *adjective* deeply hurt emotionally, or overwhelmed with sadness or grief

broker *noun* someone who buys and sells stocks and shares for others ➤ *verb* **1** to act as a broker **2** to negotiate on behalf of others: *broker a deal*

brolly *noun* (*plural* **brollies**), *chiefly Brit informal* an umbrella

bromide *noun* **1** a chemical compound used as a sedative **2** a monochrome photographic print

bromine *noun, chemistry* (symbol **Br**) a non-metallic element consisting of a dark-red, highly corrosive liquid with a pungent smell, used in photographic film and in manufacturing ◑ Comes from Greek *bromos* meaning 'stink'

bronchial (*pronounced* **brong**-ki-al) *adjective* relating to either of the two main airways to the lungs, known as the bronchi

bronchiole (*pronounced* **brong**-ki-ohl) *noun, anatomy* any of the tiny branches of the bronchi

bronchitis (*pronounced* brong-**kait**-is) *noun, medicine* inflammation of the mucous membrane of the bronchi, causing difficulty in breathing ♦ **bronchitic** *adjective & noun*

bronchus (*pronounced* brong-kus) *noun* (*plural* **bronchi** – *pronounced* **brong**-kai) *anatomy* either of the two tubes leading from the windpipe to the lungs

bronco *noun* (*plural* **broncos**) *US* a half-tamed horse

brontosaurus *noun* the old name for an apatosaurus

⊙ Based on two Greek words, literally meaning 'thunder lizard'

bronze *noun* a golden-brown mixture of copper and tin ➤ *adjective* of this colour ♦ **bronzed** *adjective* suntanned

bronze medal *noun* a medal given to a competitor who comes third

brooch (*pronounced* brohch) *noun* (*plural* **brooches**) an ornament pinned to the clothing

❗ Do not confuse with: **broach**

brood *verb* 1 of a hen etc: to sit on eggs 2 to think anxiously for some time ➤ *noun* 1 a number of young birds hatched at one time 2 young animals or children of the same family

broody *adjective* (**broodier, broodiest**) 1 moody, thoughtful 2 *informal* of a woman: eager to have a baby

brook¹ *noun* a small stream

brook² *verb, formal* to put up with, endure: *I shall brook no criticism*

broom *noun* 1 a type of shrub with yellow flowers 2 a brush for sweeping

broomstick *noun* the handle of a broom

brose *noun, Scottish* a liquid food of boiling water poured on oatmeal etc

broth *noun* 1 water in which vegetables and meat, etc have been boiled, used as soup 2 *science* a similar liquid used as a medium for the culture of bacteria

brothel *noun* a house where prostitution is practised

brother *noun* 1 a male born of the same parents as yourself 2 a companion, a fellow-worker

brotherhood *noun* 1 comradeship between men 2 a men's association

brother-in-law *noun* (*plural* **brothers-in-law**) 1 the brother of your husband or wife 2 the husband of your sister or sister-in-law

brotherly *adjective* like a brother; affectionate

brought past form of **bring**

brow *noun* 1 a forehead 2 an eyebrow 3 the edge of a hill

browbeat *verb* to bully

brown *noun* a dark colour made by mixing red, yellow, black, etc ➤ *adjective* 1 of this colour 2 *informal* suntanned

brown alga *noun, biology* any member of a class of mainly marine algae, eg kelp, characterized by the presence of a brown pigment which masks the green pigment chlorophyll

brownfield site *noun* an area which has been redeveloped for another use (*compare with*: **greenfield site**)

Brownian motion or **Brownian movement** *noun, physics* the random movement of small particles in a liquid or gas, caused by the continual bombardment of the particles by molecules of the liquid or gas

brownie *noun* 1 a helpful fairy or goblin 2 a Brownie Guide

Brownie Guide *noun* a junior Guide

brownie point or **Brownie point** *noun, informal, usually ironic* an imaginary mark of approval awarded for doing something good or helpful

brown rice *noun* unpolished rice from which only the fibrous husk has been removed

Brownshirt *noun, history* a member of the Nazi militia before and during World War II, named after the colour of the uniform

browse *verb* 1 to glance through a range of books, shop merchandise, etc 2 of deer etc: to feed on the shoots or leaves of plants 3 *computing* to examine information (in a database etc)

browser *noun, computing* a computer program used for searching and managing data from the World Wide Web

bruise *noun* a discoloured area on the skin, the surface of fruit, etc, where it has been struck ➤ *verb* to cause bruises (to)

brunch *noun* (*plural* **brunches**), *informal* a meal which combines breakfast and lunch, eaten around midday or late morning ⊙ From *breakfast* + *lunch*

brunette *noun* a woman with dark brown hair

brunt *noun*: **bear** or **take the brunt** to take the chief strain

brush *noun* (*plural* **brushes**) 1 an instrument with tufts of bristles, hair, etc for smoothing the hair, cleaning, painting, etc 2 a disagreement, a brief quarrel: *a brush with the law* 3 the tail of a fox 4 undergrowth ➤ *verb* 1 to pass a brush over 2 to remove by sweeping 3 to touch lightly in passing

brushwood *noun* 1 broken branches, twigs, etc 2 undergrowth

brusque (*pronounced* broosk) *adjective* blunt and often impolite; curt ♦ **brusquely** *adverb* ♦ **brusqueness** *noun* ⊙ Comes from Italian *brusco* meaning 'sour' or 'rough'

Brussels sprout *noun* a type of vegetable with sprouts like small cabbages on the stem

brutal *adjective* cruel or violent ◆ **brutality** *noun* ◆ **brutally** *adverb*

brutalize or **brutalise** *verb* **1** to make brutal **2** to treat brutally ◆ **brutalization** *noun*

brute *noun* **1** an animal **2** a cruel person

brutish *adjective* like a brute, savage, coarse

BSc *abbreviation* Bachelor of Science

BSE *abbreviation* bovine spongiform encephalopathy, a brain disease of cattle (*often called*: **mad cow disease**)

Bt *abbreviation* baronet

bubble *noun* **1** a thin ball of liquid blown with air **2** a small ball of air in anything ➤ *verb* to rise in bubbles

bubble chamber *noun, physics* a device for detecting the movement of charged subatomic particles through a liquid

bubble gum *noun* a type of chewing gum which can be blown into bubbles

bubble jet printer *noun* a type of printer in which droplets of heated ink are projected onto the paper

bubbly *adjective* (**bubblier, bubbliest**) **1** full of bubbles **2** lively, vivacious ➤ *noun, informal* champagne; sparkling wine

bubo (*pronounced* **byoo**-boh) *noun* (*plural* **buboes**), *medicine* a swollen lymph node

bubonic plague (*pronounced* byoo-**bon**-ik) *noun, medicine* the commonest form of plague, transmitted to humans via fleas carried by rats, characterized by fever and the development of buboes

buccaneer *noun, old* a pirate ◆ **buccaneering** *adjective* like a pirate

buck[1] *noun* the male of the deer, goat, hare or rabbit ➤ *verb* of a horse etc: to attempt to throw (a ride) by rapid jumps into the air

buck[2] *noun, US informal* a dollar

bucket *noun* a container for water etc

buckle *noun* a clip for fastening straps or belts ➤ *verb* to fasten with a buckle

buckminsterfullerene *noun, chemistry* a ball-shaped molecule containing 60 carbon atoms linked together in hexagons and pentagons to form a closed, near spherical structure

⊕ Named after *Buckminster Fuller* (1895–1983), a US engineer who designed a geodesic dome for the 1967 Montreal Expo

buckyball *noun, chemistry* a name for buckminsterfullerene

bucolic (*pronounced* byoo-**kol**-ik) *adjective* of the countryside; pastoral, rural

bud *noun* **1** *biology* in a plant: a knob-like shoot that will eventually develop into a leaf or flower

2 a flower or leaf not fully open **3** *biology* in yeasts and simple animals, eg hydras: a small outgrowth from the parent that detaches and develops into a new individual **4** *biology* an outgrowth in an embryo from which a limb develops ➤ *verb* (**budding, budded**) to produce buds

Buddhism *noun* a religion founded in the 6th century BC by Buddha ('the enlightened one'), based on spiritual purity and freedom from human concerns and desires ◆ **Buddhist** *noun & adjective*

budding *adjective* showing signs of becoming: *budding author*

buddy *noun* (*plural* **buddies**) **1** *informal, esp US* a friend or companion **2** someone who volunteers to care for a person suffering from AIDS

budge *verb* to move slightly, stir

budgerigar *noun* a kind of small parrot often kept as a pet

budget *noun* **1** a government plan for the year's spending **2** any plan of their future spending ➤ *verb* to allow for in a budget: *The project has been budgeted for* ⊕ Comes from French *bougette* meaning 'a little bag'

budgie *noun, informal* a budgerigar

buff *noun* **1** a light yellowish-brown colour **2** an enthusiast, a fan: *a film buff* ➤ *verb* to polish

⊕ The later meaning of 'enthusiast' derives from the *buff*-coloured uniforms once used by volunteer firefighters in New York

buffalo *noun* (*plural* **buffaloes**) **1** a large Asian ox, used to draw loads **2** the North American bison

buffer *noun* **1** something which lessens the force of a blow or collision **2** *chemistry* a solution that maintains a constant pH level when an acid or alkali is added to it **3** *computing* a temporary storage area for data that is being sent from the CPU to an output device

buffer state or **buffer zone** *noun* a neutral country or zone which is situated between two others which are hostile towards each other

buffet[1] (*pronounced* **buf**-it) *verb* (**buffeting, buffeted**) to strike, knock about ➤ *noun* a slap or a blow

buffet[2] *noun* (*pronounced* **buwf**-ei) **1** a counter or café serving food and drink **2** a range of dishes set out at a party etc for people to serve themselves

buffoon *noun* a clown, fool ◆ **buffoonery** *noun* silly behaviour, clowning around

bug *noun* **1** a small, especially irritating, insect **2** a disease germ: *a tummy bug* **3** a tiny hidden microphone for recording conversations **4** *computing* a problem in a computer program causing errors in its execution ➤ *verb* (**bugging, bugged**) **1** to conceal a microphone in (a room etc) **2** to record with a hidden microphone **3** *informal* to annoy, harass

bugbear *noun* something that frightens or annoys

buggy *noun* (*plural* **buggies**) a child's pushchair

bugle *noun* a small military trumpet ◆ **bugler** *noun* someone who plays the bugle

build *verb* (**building, built**) to put together the parts of anything ➤ *noun* physique; physical character: *a man of heavy build* ◆ **builder** *noun*

building *noun* **1** the act or trade of building (houses etc) **2** a house or other built dwelling etc

building society *noun* an institution like a bank which accepts investments and whose main business is to lend people money to buy a house

built-up *adjective* of an area: containing houses and other buildings

bulb *noun* **1** the rounded part of the stem of an onion, tulip, etc, in which it stores its food **2** a glass globe surrounding the element of an electric light ◆ **bulbous** *adjective* bulb-shaped

bulge *noun* **1** a swelling **2** a noticeable increase ➤ *verb* to swell out

bulimia (*pronounced* buw-**lim**-i-a) *noun, medicine* an eating disorder in which bingeing is followed by self-induced vomiting or purging ◆ **bulimic** *adjective* suffering from bulimia

bulk *noun* **1** large size **2** the greater part: *the bulk of the population*

bulkhead *noun* a wall in the inside of a ship, meant to keep out water if the hull is damaged

bulky *adjective* (**bulkier, bulkiest**) taking up a lot of room ◆ **bulkily** *adverb*

bull *noun* the male of animals of the ox family, also of the whale, elephant, etc

bulldog *noun* a breed of strong, fierce-looking dog

bulldoze *verb* **1** to use a bulldozer on **2** to force: *bulldozed his way into the room*

bulldozer *noun* a machine for levelling land and clearing away obstacles

bullet *noun* **1** the piece of metal fired from a gun **2** a small shape, such as a circle or square, highlighting each of the various points on a list

bulletin *noun* a report of current news, someone's health, etc

bulletin board *noun, computing* an electronic data system containing messages and programs accessible to a number of users

bullet-proof *adjective* not able to be pierced by bullets

bullfight *noun* a public entertainment in Spain etc, in which a bull is baited and usually killed ◆ **bullfighter** *noun*

bullfinch *noun* (*plural* **bullfinches**) a small pink-breasted bird

bullion (*pronounced* **buwl**-yon) *noun* gold or silver in the form of bars etc

bullock *noun* a young bull

bullring *noun* an arena where bullfights take place

bull's-eye *noun* **1** the mark in the middle of a target **2** a striped sweet

bull terrier *noun* a breed of dog with a heavy body and a short, smooth coat

bully *noun* (*plural* **bullies**) someone who unfairly uses their size and strength to hurt or frighten others ➤ *verb* (**bullies, bullying, bullied**) to act like a bully towards ◆ **bullying** *noun*

bulrush (*pronounced* **buwl**-rush) *noun* (*plural* **bulrushes**) a large strong reed which grows on, in, or near water

bulwark (*pronounced* **buwl**-wark) *noun* **1** a strong defensive wall **2** a prop, a defence

bum[1] *noun, Brit informal* the buttocks

bum[2] *US informal, noun* a tramp ➤ *adjective* useless, dud

bumbag *noun* a carrying pouch strapped round the waist

bumblebee *noun* a type of large bee

bumf another spelling of **bumph**

bump *verb* **1** to strike heavily **2** to knock by accident ➤ *noun* **1** the sound of a heavy blow **2** an accidental knock **3** a raised lump ◆ **bumpy** *adjective* (**bumpier, bumpiest**)

bumper *noun* a bar round the front and back of a car's body to protect it from damage ➤ *adjective* large: *a bumper crop*

bumph or **bumf** *noun, Brit informal* miscellaneous uninteresting papers, leaflets, etc

⏱ Originally short for 'bum-fodder', ie toilet paper

bumpkin *noun, informal* a clumsy, awkward, country person

bumptious *adjective* self-important

bun *noun* **1** a sweet roll made of egg dough **2** hair wound into a rounded mass

bunch *noun* (*plural* **bunches**) a number of things tied together or growing together ➤ *verb* to crowd together

bundle *noun* a number of things loosely bound together ➤ *verb* **1** to tie in a bundle **2** to push roughly: *bundled the children into the car*

bung *noun* the stopper of the hole in a barrel, bottle, etc ➤ *verb* **1** to stop up with a bung **2** *informal* to throw or put somewhere in a careless way

bungalow *noun* a one-storey detached house

bungee jumping (*pronounced* **bun**-ji) *noun* the sport of jumping from a height with strong rubber ropes attached to the ankles so that the jumper bounces up before reaching the ground

bungle *verb* **1** to do badly or clumsily **2** to mishandle, mismanage ➤ *noun* a clumsy or mishandled action

bunion *noun* a lump or swelling on the joint of the big toe

bunk *noun* a narrow bed, eg in a ship's cabin

bunk bed *noun* one of a pair of narrow beds one above the other

bunker *noun* **1** a sandpit on a golf course **2** an underground shelter **3** a large box for keeping coal

bunkum *noun* nonsense

⊙ From *Buncombe* county in N Carolina, whose representative once gave a rambling speech in Congress

bunny *noun* (*plural* **bunnies**) a child's name for a rabbit

Bunsen burner *noun* a gas-burner used in laboratories

bunting¹ *noun* **1** a thin cloth used for making flags **2** flags

bunting² *noun* any of various birds of the finch family

buoy (*pronounced* boi) *noun* **1** a floating mark acting as a guide or warning for ships **2** a float, eg a lifebuoy

buoyant *adjective* **1** able to float **2** cheerful, bouncy ♦ **buoyancy** *noun*

bur another spelling of **burr**

burden *noun* **1** a load **2** something difficult to bear, eg poverty or sorrow **3** *old* the chorus of a song ♦ **burdensome** *adjective*

bureau (*pronounced* **byoo**-roh) *noun* (*plural* **bureaux** or **bureaus** – *both pronounced* **byoo**-rohz) **1** a writing table **2** an office

⊙ **Bureau** is a French word, and comes from the name of a type of coarse cloth (*burel*) which was used as a cover for writing tables

bureaucracy (*pronounced* byoo-**rok**-ra-si) *noun* government by officials ♦ **bureaucrat** *noun* an administrative official ♦ **bureaucratic** *adjective* **1** involving bureaucracy **2** full of complicated and irritating official procedures

burette (*pronounced* byuw-**ret**) *noun* a long vertical glass tube with a tap and marked with a scale for measuring volumes of liquid run off

burgeon (*pronounced* **ber**-jon) *verb* **1** to grow or develop quickly; to flourish **2** of a plant: to bud or sprout

burger *noun* a hamburger

burgh *noun* in Scotland, a borough

burglar *noun* someone who breaks into a house to steal

burglary *noun* (*plural* **burglaries**) a break-in

into a house by a person who wants to steal things

burgle *verb* to commit burglary

burgundy *noun* (*plural* **burgundies**) **1** a French wine made in the Burgundy region, especially a red wine **2** a deep or purplish red colour ➤ *adjective* deep or purplish red in colour

burial *noun* the placing of a body under the ground after death

burlesque *noun* a piece of writing, acting, etc making fun of somebody

burly *adjective* (**burlier, burliest**) broad and strong

burn¹ *verb* (**burning, burnt** or **burned**) **1** to set fire to **2** to be on fire, or scorching **3** to injure by burning **4** *computing* to record data onto (a compact disc) ➤ *noun* an injury or mark caused by fire

burn² *noun, Scottish* a small stream

burner *noun* **1** the part of a lamp or gas jet from which the flame rises **2** *computing* a CD burner

burnish *verb* to polish ➤ *noun* polish

burnt past form of **burn¹**

burp *verb, informal* to bring up wind through the mouth from the stomach

burr or **bur** *noun* the prickly seedcase or head of certain plants

burrow *noun* a hole or passage in the ground dug by certain animals for shelter ➤ *verb* to make a passage beneath the ground

bursary *noun* (*plural* **bursaries**) especially in Scotland and New Zealand: an award or grant of money made to a student

burst *verb* (**bursting, burst**) **1** to break suddenly (after increased pressure) **2** to move, speak, etc suddenly or violently ➤ *noun* **1** an instance of something breaking suddenly **2** a sudden activity: *a burst of gunfire*

bury *verb* (**buries, burying, buried**) **1** to place (a dead body etc) under the ground **2** to cover, hide

bus *noun* (*plural* **buses**) **1** a large road vehicle, often used for public transport **2** *computing* a channel or path along which data can be transmitted to and from computer hardware

busby *noun* (*plural* **busbies**) a tall fur hat worn by soldiers in certain regiments

bush *noun* (*plural* **bushes**) **1** a growing thing between a plant and a tree in size **2** wild, unfarmed country in Africa etc

bushbaby *noun* (*plural* **bushbabies**) an African primate with thick fur, large eyes and a long tail

bush telegraph *noun* the quick passing-on of news from person to person

bushy *adjective* (**bushier, bushiest**) **1** growing thickly: *bushy eyebrows* **2** full of bushes ♦ **bushiness** *noun*

business noun (plural **businesses**) **1** someone's work or job **2** trade, commerce: Business is booming **3** a matter of personal interest or concern: none of your business

business card noun a card carried by a person in business showing their name and business details

businesslike adjective practical, methodical, alert and prompt

businessman or **businesswoman** noun (plural **businessmen** or **businesswomen**) someone who works in commerce

business park noun an area, usually on the edge of a town, designed to accommodate business offices and light industry

busk verb to play or sing in the street for money
♦ **busker** noun

bus stop noun an official stopping place for buses

bust noun **1** a woman's breasts **2** a sculpture of someone's head and shoulders

bustard noun a large, fast-running bird similar to a turkey

bustier (pronounced **buws**-tyei) noun a short tight-fitting strapless bodice for women ☉ Comes from French, meaning 'bodice'

bustle¹ verb to busy oneself noisily ➤ noun noisy activity, fuss

bustle² noun, history a stuffed pad worn at the back under a woman's full skirt

busy adjective (**busier, busiest**) having a lot to do ➤ verb (**busies, busying, busied**): **busy yourself with** to occupy yourself with
♦ **busily** adverb

busybody noun (plural **busybodies**) someone nosey about others

but conjunction **1** showing a contrast between two ideas etc: My brother can swim but I can't/That paint isn't black but brown **2** except that, without that: It never rains but it pours ➤ preposition except, with the exception of: No one but Tom had any money/Take the next road but one (= the second road) ➤ adverb only: We can but hope ● **but for** were it not for; without: But for your car, we would have been late

butch adjective, slang of a woman: looking or behaving in a masculine way

butcher noun someone whose work is to carve up meat and sell it ➤ verb **1** to kill and carve up (an animal) for food **2** to kill cruelly

butchery noun great or cruel slaughter

butler noun the chief male servant in a household

butt noun **1** a large cask, a barrel **2** someone of whom others make fun **3** the thick heavy end of a rifle etc **4** the end of a finished cigarette or cigar **5** a push with the head **6** US slang the buttocks

➤ verb to strike with the head ● **butt in** to interrupt, interfere

butte (pronounced byoot) noun a flat-topped, isolated hill

butter noun a fatty food made by churning cream ➤ verb to spread over with butter
● **butter up** to flatter, soften up

butter bean noun any of several varieties of bean plants, or one of their large edible seeds

buttercup noun a plant with a cup-like yellow flower

butterfingers noun, informal someone who often drops things, or who fails to catch things

butterfly noun (plural **butterflies**) **1** a kind of insect with large, often patterned wings **2** a swimming stroke where the arms are swung forwards in a circling motion

buttermilk noun the milk that is left after butter has been made

butterscotch noun a hard toffee made with butter

buttocks plural noun the two fleshy parts of the body on which you sit

button noun **1** a knob or disc of metal, plastic, etc used to fasten clothing **2** a knob pressed to work an electrical device ➤ verb to fasten by means of buttons

buttonhole noun a hole through which a button is passed ➤ verb to catch the attention of (someone) and force them to listen

buttress noun (plural **buttresses**) a support on the outside of a wall ➤ verb to support, prop up

buxom adjective plump and pretty

buy verb (**buying, bought**) to get in exchange for money ➤ noun a purchase: a good buy

buyer noun **1** a person who buys; a customer **2** a person employed by a large shop or firm to buy goods on its behalf

buzz verb **1** to make a humming noise like bees **2** informal to call, telephone **3** of aircraft: to fly close to ➤ noun (plural **buzzes**) **1** a humming sound **2** informal a phone call

buzzard noun a large bird of prey

buzzer noun a signalling device which makes a buzzing noise

buzzword noun a word well established in a particular jargon, its use suggesting up-to-date specialized knowledge

by adverb **1** near: A crowd stood by, watching **2** past: People strolled by **3** aside: money put by for an emergency ➤ preposition **1** next to, near: standing by the door **2** past: going by the house **3** through, along, across: We came by the main road **4** indicating the person who does something: written by Burns/played by a young actor **5** of time: not after: It'll be ready by four o'clock **6** during the time of: working by night **7** by means of: by train **8** to the extent of: taller by a _head_ **9** used to express measurements, compass directions, etc: _6 metres by 4 metres/north by northwest_ **10** in the quantity of: _sold by the pound/paid by the week_

bye¹ or **bye-bye** _interjection, informal_ goodbye

bye² _noun, cricket_ **1** a ball bowled past the wicket **2** a run made from this

by-election _noun_ an election for parliament during a parliamentary session

bygone _adjective_ past ▸ _noun_ (**bygones**) old grievances or events that have been, or should be, forgotten

by-law or **bye-law** _noun_ a local (not a national) law

⊙ **By-law** probably comes from the obsolete word _byrlaw_ meaning 'local custom', originally from Norse _byjar-log_ which means 'town law'

byline _noun_ **1** a line under the title of a newspaper or magazine article which gives the name of the author **2** _football_ the touchline

bypass _noun_ a road built round a town etc so that traffic need not pass through it

by-product _noun_ **1** something useful obtained during the manufacture of something else **2** an unexpected or extra result; a side effect

byroad or **byway** _noun_ a secondary or side road

bystander _noun_ someone who stands watching an event or accident

byte (_pronounced_ bait) _noun, computing_ a unit of eight bits, used to measure data or memory

byword _noun_ someone or something well known for a particular quality

Byzantine (_pronounced_ bi-**zan**-tain or bai-**zan**-teen) **1** relating to Byzantium, a city in ancient Greece, now Istanbul, Turkey **2** relating to the Byzantine Empire, the Greek (or Eastern Roman) Empire from 295 to 1453 AD **3** relating to the style of architecture of the Byzantine Empire, with domes, arches, mosaics, etc **4** of a system etc: rigid and inflexible **5** intricate, over-complicated ▸ _noun_ an inhabitant of Byzantium

Cc

C¹ *noun* **1** *music* the musical note on which the Western system of music is based **2** *computing* a widely used programming language

C² *symbol* **1** *chemistry* carbon **2** coulomb **3** the Roman numeral for 100

°C *abbreviation* degree(s) Celsius or centigrade

Ca *symbol, chemistry* calcium

CAB *abbreviation* Citizens Advice Bureau, an organization people can go to for free advice about legal, financial or social problems

cab *noun* **1** a taxi **2** in the past, a hired carriage

cabal (*pronounced* ka-**bal**) *noun* **1** a small group plotting in secret **2** a political plot or conspiracy ➤ *verb* (**caballed, caballing**) **1** to form a cabal **2** to plot

cabaret (*pronounced* **kab**-a-rei) *noun* **1** an entertainment consisting of variety acts **2** a restaurant with a cabaret

cabbage *noun* a type of vegetable with tightly packed edible green leaves

cabbala, cabala, kabala or **kabbala** (*pronounced* ka-**bahl**-a) *noun* a mystical Jewish lore, based on interpreting hidden meanings in the Old Testament

caber (*pronounced* **kei**-ber) *noun* a heavy pole tossed in competition at Scottish Highland games

cabin *noun* **1** a wooden hut **2** a small room used for living quarters in a ship **3** the part of a commercial aircraft containing passenger seating

cabin crew *noun* the flight attendants on a commercial airline

cabinet *noun* **1** a cupboard which has shelves and doors **2** a similar container for storage or display **3** a wooden case with drawers **4** a selected number of government ministers who decide on policy

cabinet-maker *noun* a maker of fine furniture

cable *noun* **1** a strong rope or thick metal line **2** a line of covered telegraph wires laid under the sea or underground **3** a telegram sent by such a line **4** an underground wire **5** *informal* cable television ➤ *verb* to telegraph by cable

cable car *noun* a small carriage suspended from a moving cable

cable modem *noun* a modem that transmits data using digital television cables

cable television *noun* a service transmitting television programmes to individual subscribers by underground cable

caboodle *noun, informal*: **the whole caboodle** the whole lot, everything

cacao *noun* a tree from whose seeds cocoa and chocolate are made

cache (*pronounced* kash) *noun* **1** a store or hiding place for ammunition, treasure, etc **2** things hidden ⊕ Comes from French *cacher* meaning 'to hide'

cache memory *noun, computing* an extremely fast part of the main store of computer memory

cachet (*pronounced* ka-**shei**) *noun* **1** prestige, credit **2** an official stamp or seal

cackle *noun* **1** the sound made by a hen or goose **2** a laugh which sounds like this ➤ *verb* to make such a sound

caco- *prefix* bad, incorrect ⊕ Comes from Greek *kakos* meaning 'bad'

cacophonous *adjective* noisy and unpleasant-sounding: *a cacophonous wailing*

cacophony *noun* (*plural* **cacophonies**) an unpleasant noise

cactus *noun* (*plural* **cactuses** or **cacti** – *pronounced* **kak**-tai) a type of prickly plant

CAD *abbreviation, technology* computer-aided design

cad *noun, old* a mean, despicable person

cadaver (*pronounced* ka-**dav**-er) *noun* a human corpse

cadaverous *adjective* corpse-like, very pale and thin

caddie *noun* an assistant who carries a golfer's clubs

caddy *noun* (*plural* **caddies**) a box for keeping tea fresh

cadence *noun* **1** a fall of the voice, eg at the end of a sentence **2** *music* a group of chords ending a piece of music

cadenza *noun, music* a musical passage at the end of a movement, concerto, etc

cadet (*pronounced* ka-**det**) *noun* **1** an officer trainee in the armed forces or police service **2** a school pupil who takes military training

cadge *verb* (**cadging, cadged**) to scrounge without paying ◆ **cadger** *noun*

cadmium *noun, chemistry* (symbol **Cd**) a soft, bluish-white, metallic element used in alloys, corrosion-resistant plating, nuclear reactors and batteries

caecum or US **cecum** (*pronounced* **see**-kum) *noun* (*plural* **caeca** or **ceca**) a pouch at the junction of the small and large intestines

Caesarean (*pronounced* se-**zeir**-i-an) *medicine, adjective* of a birth: involving delivery by cutting through the walls of the mother's abdomen ➤ *noun* (*also called*: **Caesarean section**) a Caesarean birth or operation

⊙ After Julius *Caesar*, who was supposed to be the first child delivered by this method

caesium or US **cesium** *noun, chemistry* (symbol **Cs**) a soft, silvery-white, metallic element formed by the fission of uranium ⊙ Comes from Latin, from *caesius* meaning 'bluish-grey'

caesura or **cesura** (*pronounced* si-**zyuwr**-a) *noun* (**caesuras** or **caesurae** – *pronounced* si-**zyuwr**-ee) a pause near the middle of a line of verse ⊙ Comes from Latin *caedere, caesum* meaning 'to cut'

café *noun* a small restaurant serving coffee, tea, snacks, etc

cafeteria *noun* a self-service restaurant

cafetière (*pronounced* kaf-e-**tyeir**) *noun* a coffee-pot with a plunger for separating the grounds from the liquid

caffeine *noun* a stimulating drug found in coffee and tea

caftan or **kaftan** *noun* a long-sleeved, ankle-length Middle-Eastern garment

cage *noun* **1** a barred enclosure for birds or animals **2** a lift used by miners ➤ *verb* (**caging, caged**) to close up in a cage

cagey or **cagy** *adjective* (**cagier, cagiest**) unwilling to speak freely; wary ♦ **caginess** *noun*

cagoule *noun* a lightweight anorak

cahoots *plural noun*: **in cahoots with** in collusion with

cairn *noun* **1** a heap of stones marking a grave, or on top of a mountain **2** a breed of small terrier

cairngorm *noun* a brown or yellow variety of quartz, used for brooches etc

cajole *verb* to coax by flattery ♦ **cajolery** *noun*

cake *noun* **1** a baked piece of dough made from flour, eggs, sugar, etc **2** something pressed into a lump: *a cake of soap* ➤ *verb* to become dry and hard: *boots caked with mud* • **have your cake and eat it** to enjoy both of two alternative things

CAL *abbreviation, technology* computer-aided learning

calamine lotion *noun* a pink lotion containing a zinc salt, used to soothe the skin

calamitous *adjective* extremely unfortunate, disastrous

calamity *noun* (*plural* **calamities**) a great disaster, a misfortune

calciferous (*pronounced* kal-**sif**-er-*us*) *adjective* **1** *biology* containing or producing calcium or calcium salts **2** *chemistry* containing lime

calcify *verb* (**calcified, calcifying**) **1** to harden as a result of a deposit of calcium salts **2** to change or be changed into lime ♦ **calcification** *noun*

calcium *noun, chemistry* (symbol **Ca**) a silvery-white metallic element which forms the chief part of lime and is a basic component of teeth and bones

calcium carbonate *noun, chemistry* a white powder or colourless crystals, occurring naturally as limestone, marble, chalk, etc, and also found in the bones and shells of animals

calcium hydroxide *noun, chemistry* a white crystalline powder that forms an alkaline solution which is used in the manufacture of cement, bleaching powder and water softeners, and to reduce acidity in soil

calcium oxide *noun, chemistry* (also **lime, quicklime**) a white chemical compound used in producing other calcium compounds, and as an alkali to reduce acidity in soil

calculable *adjective* able to be counted or measured

calculate *verb* **1** to count, work out by mathematics **2** to think out in an exact way

⊙ Based on a Latin word meaning 'stone', from the use of stones in the past as an aid to counting

calculating *adjective* thinking selfishly

calculation *noun* a mathematical reckoning, a sum

calculator *noun* a machine which makes mathematical calculations

calculus *noun* a mathematics concerned with **differentration** and **integration**

calendar *noun* a table or list showing the year divided into months, weeks and days

calf[1] *noun* (*plural* **calves**) **1** the young of a cow or ox **2** the young of certain other mammals, eg an elephant or whale **3** calf's skin cured as leather

calf[2] *noun* (*plural* **calves**) the back of the lower part of the leg

calibrate *verb* **1** to mark the scale on (a measuring instrument) **2** to check or adjust the scale of (a measuring instrument)

calibre or US **caliber** *noun* **1** the measurement across the opening of a tube or gun **2** of a person: quality of character, ability

ⓘ This is one of a large number of words which are spelled with an **-re** ending in British English, but with an **-er** in American English, eg *centre/center, metre/meter, lustre/luster*.

calico *noun* a patterned kind of cotton cloth

◎ Originally *Calicut cloth*, after the port in SW India from where it was exported

calif another spelling of **caliph**

californium *noun, chemistry* (symbol **Cf**) a synthetic, radioactive, metallic element of the actinide series, produced by bombarding an isotope of curium with alpha particles

◎ Named after *California*, USA, where the element was first made

calipers another spelling of **callipers**

caliph, calif, kalif, khalifa, or **khalifah** *noun* a former title of a chief Muslim civil and religious leader ◎ Comes from Arabic *khalifah* meaning 'successor' (of Muhammad)

call *verb* **1** to cry aloud **2** to name: *What is your cat called?* **3** to summon: *call the doctor/call for help* **4** to make a short visit: *I'll call on my way home* **5** to telephone **6** *computing* to transfer control of (a function) to a different part of a program ➤ *noun* **1** a loud cry **2** a short visit **3** a telephone conversation • **call off** to cancel • **on call** of a doctor: available if needed, eg to deal with an emergency

call centre *noun* a building where workers provide services to a company's customers by telephone

calligram *noun* a poem or word written or printed so that its appearance on the page represents its meaning or subject, eg a poem about growth where the size of the letters gets bigger

calligraphy *noun* the art of handwriting

calling *noun* a vocation

callipers or **calipers** *plural noun* **1** an instrument like compasses, used to measure thickness **2** (**calliper**) a splint to support the leg, made of two metal rods

callous *adjective* cruel, hardhearted ♦ **callously** *adverb* ♦ **callousness** *noun* ◎ Comes from Latin *callosus* meaning 'thick-skinned'

⚠ Do not confuse with: **callus**

callow *adjective* not mature; inexperienced, naive ♦ **callowly** *adverb*

callus *noun* (*plural* **calluses**) an area of thickened or hardened skin ◎ Comes from Latin *callus* meaning 'hardened skin'

⚠ Do not confuse with: **callous**

calm *adjective* **1** still or quiet **2** not anxious or flustered ➤ *noun* **1** absence of wind **2** quietness, peacefulness ➤ *verb* to make peaceful ♦ **calmly** *adverb* ♦ **calmness** *noun*

calorie *noun* **1** a measure of heat **2** a measure of the energy-giving value of food

calumny *noun* (*plural* **calumnies**) a false accusation or lie about a person

calve *verb* to give birth to a calf

calypso *noun* (*plural* **calypsos**) a West Indian improvised song

calyx (*pronounced* **keil**-iks or **kal**-iks) *noun* (*plural* **calyces** – *pronounced* **keil**-i-seez or **kal**-i-seez – or **calyxes**) the outer covering or cup of a flower, enclosing the petals, stamens and carpels

CAM *abbreviation, technology* computer-aided manufacturing or manufacture

cam *noun, engineering* an projection on a wheel or rotating shaft that transmits regular movement to another part in contact with it ◎ Comes from Dutch *kam* meaning 'comb'

camaraderie *noun* comradeship, fellowship

camber *noun* a slight curve on a road etc making the middle higher than the sides

Cambrian *adjective* of the geological period from 580 million to 505 million years ago

camcorder *noun* a hand-held device combining a video camera and video recorder

came past tense of **come**

camel *noun* an animal native to Asia and Africa, with a humped back, used for transport

cameo *noun* (*plural* **cameos**) a gem or stone with a figure carved in relief

camera¹ *noun* an instrument for taking photographs

camera² *noun:* **in camera** in private

◎ A Latin phrase meaning 'in a room'

camera phone *noun* a mobile phone with which you can take photographs to display on the phone's screen

camisole (*pronounced* **kam**-i-sohl) *noun* a woman's undervest with thin shoulder straps

camomile *noun* a plant with pale yellow flowers, used as a medicinal herb

camouflage (*pronounced* **kam**-o-flahsz) *noun* **1** the disguising of the appearance of something to blend in with its background **2** natural protective colouring in animals ➤ *verb* to disguise by camouflage

camp *noun* **1** a group of tents, caravans, etc forming a temporary settlement **2** fixed military quarters ➤ *verb* **1** to pitch tents **2** to set up a temporary home ♦ **camper** *noun*

campaign *noun* **1** organized action in support of a cause or movement **2** a planned series of battles or movements during a war ➤ *verb* **1** to organize support: *campaigning against the poll tax* **2** to serve in a military campaign ♦ **campaigner** *noun*

camp bed *noun* a small portable folding bed

camphor *noun* a pungent solid oil obtained

from a cinnamon tree, or a synthetic substitute for it, used to repel insects etc

campion noun a plant with pink or white star-shaped flowers

campsite noun an area set aside for pitching tents

campus noun (plural **campuses**) the grounds and buildings of a university or college

campylobacter (pronounced **kam**-pil-o-bak-ter) noun, biology a spiral-shaped bacterium that occurs in the reproductive and digestive tracts of humans and animals, causing diarrhoea and gastritis in humans, and genital diseases in cattle and sheep

camshaft noun, engineering a shaft to which one or more cams are attached

can[1] verb (**can, could**) **1** to be able to (do something): Can anybody here play the piano? **2** to have permission to (do something): asked if I could have the day off • **can but** can only: We can but hope ☺ Comes from Old English cunnan meaning 'to know how to' or 'to be able'

can[2] noun a sealed tin container for preserving food or liquids ➤ verb (**canning, canned**) to put into a sealed tin to preserve

canal noun **1** an artificial waterway for boats **2** biology a tube-shaped channel or passage: the alimentary canal

canary noun (plural **canaries**) a songbird with yellow plumage, kept as a pet

canasta noun a card game similar to rummy played by two teams of two people

cancan noun a high-kicking dance performed by women

cancel verb (**cancelling, cancelled**) **1** to put off permanently, call off: cancel all engagements for the week **2** to mark for deletion by crossing with lines ✦ **cancellation** noun • **cancel out** to make ineffective by balancing each other

Cancer noun **1** the fourth sign of the zodiac, represented by the crab **2** someone born under this sign, between 22 June and 23 July

cancer noun a serious disease in which cells in the body grow rapidly into lumps which can spread and may cause death ✦ **cancerous** adjective

candela noun, physics (symbol **cd**) the standard unit of measurement luminous intensity

candelabrum noun (plural **candelabrums** or **candelabra**; also singular **candelabra**, plural **candelabras**) a decorative candle-holder with branches for several candles ☺ Comes from Latin, meaning 'candlestick'

candid adjective frank, open, honest ✦ **candidly** adverb

candida (pronounced **kan**-did-a) noun, medicine an infection caused by a yeastlike fungus

candidacy or **candidature** noun the state of being a candidate for something

candidate noun **1** an entrant for an examination, or competitor for a job, prize, etc **2** an entrant in a political election

☺ From a Latin word meaning 'dressed in white', because of the white togas worn by electoral candidates in ancient Rome

candied adjective cooked or coated in sugar

candle noun a stick of wax containing a wick, used for giving light • **not worth the candle** not worth the effort or expense needed

candlestick noun a holder for a candle

candour or US **candor** noun frankness, honesty

candy noun **1** sugar crystallized by boiling **2** US (plural **candies**) sweets, chocolate

candy floss noun a fluffy mass of spun sugar served on a stick

cane noun **1** the woody stem of bamboo, sugar cane, etc **2** a walking stick ➤ verb to beat with a cane

cane sugar noun sugar extracted from sugar cane

canine (pronounced **kei**-nain) adjective of dogs

canine tooth noun a sharp-pointed tooth found on each side of the upper and lower jaw

canister noun a tin or other container for tea etc

canker noun **1** a spreading sore **2** a disease in trees, plants, etc

cannabis noun a narcotic drug obtained from the hemp plant

canned music noun pre-recorded bland music often played in public places

cannibal noun **1** someone who eats human flesh **2** an animal that eats its own kind
✦ **cannibalism** noun ✦ **cannibalistic** adjective

cannibalize or **cannibalise** verb to take parts from (a machine, vehicle, etc) for use in repairing another

cannon noun a large gun mounted on a wheel-carriage ☺ Comes from Italian canna meaning 'reed' or 'tube'

❗ Do not confuse with: **canon**

cannonball noun a solid metal ball shot from a cannon

cannot verb **1** used with another verb to express inability to do something: I cannot understand this **2** used to refuse permission: He cannot see me today

canny adjective (**cannier, canniest**) wise, shrewd, cautious ✦ **cannily** adverb

canoe noun a light narrow boat moved along by paddles

canon noun **1** a rule used as a standard to judge by **2** the books of the Bible accepted as the standard by the Jewish or Christian faiths **3** a member of the Roman Catholic or Anglican clergy connected with a cathedral **4** a list of saints **5** an accepted or established list: *not in the literary canon* **6** *music* a piece of music in which parts follow each other repeating the melody ⊙ Comes from Greek *kanon* meaning 'a straight rod'

❗ Do not confuse with: **cannon**

canonical *adjective* part of an accepted canon: *the canonical text*

canonize or **canonise** *verb* make (someone) a saint ◆ **canonization** *noun*

canopy *noun* (*plural* **canopies**) **1** a canvas or cloth covering suspended over a bed etc **2** *geography, botany* the topmost layer of a forest, consisting of the uppermost leaves and branches of trees

cant¹ *noun* **1** the slang or vocabulary of a particular group: *thieves' cant* **2** insincere talk

cant² *noun* a slope, an incline ➤ *verb* to tilt from a level position

can't short form of **cannot**

cantaloup or **cantaloupe** *noun* a type of melon with a thick ridged skin and orange-coloured flesh

cantankerous *adjective* crotchety, bad-tempered, quarrelsome

cantata *noun* a short piece of music for a choir

canteen *noun* **1** a place serving food and drink in a workplace etc **2** a water-flask **3** *Brit* a case for storing cutlery

canter *verb* to move at an easy gallop ➤ *noun* an easy gallop

⊙ Originally *Canterbury gallop*, referring to the pace at which pilgrims rode to the town

cantilever *noun* a large projecting bracket used to support a balcony or staircase

cantilever bridge *noun* a bridge consisting of upright piers with cantilevers extending to meet one another

canton *noun* a federal state in Switzerland

canvas *noun* (*plural* **canvases**) **1** coarse, strong cloth used for sails, tents, etc **2** a piece of this stretched and used for painting on **3** a painting on canvas

❗ Do not confuse: **canvas** and **canvass**

canvass *verb* to go round asking for votes, money, etc ◆ **canvasser** *noun*

canyon *noun* a deep, steep-sided river valley

cap *noun* **1** a peaked soft hat **2** a lid, a top **3** a contraceptive diaphragm **4** a protective or cosmetic covering fitted over a damaged or decayed tooth ➤ *verb* (**capping, capped**) **1** to put a cap on **2** to set a limit to (a budget etc) **3** to

do better than, improve on: *No-one can cap this story* **4** to select for a national sports team **5** to confer a university degree on

capability *noun* (*plural* **capabilities**) the ability, potential or skill to do something: *He has the capability to do it, but does he have the commitment?*

capable *adjective* able to cope with difficulties without help ● **capable of 1** able or likely to achieve, produce, etc: *capable of a better performance* **2** having the temperament to do something: *When he loses his temper he's capable of anything*

capably *adverb* in an efficient and confident way

capacious *adjective* roomy, wide ◆ **capaciously** *adverb* ◆ **capaciousness** *noun*

capacitance *noun, physics* the ability of the conductors in a capacitor to store electric charge, measured in farads

capacitor *noun* a device for collecting and storing electricity

capacity *noun* (*plural* **capacities**) **1** power of understanding **2** ability to do something: *capacity for growth* **3** the amount that something can hold **4** post, position: *in her capacity as leader* ● **to capacity** to the greatest extent possible: *filled to capacity*

cape¹ *noun* a thick shawl or covering for the shoulders

cape² *noun, geography* a point of land running into the sea

caper¹ *verb* to leap, dance about ➤ *noun* **1** a leap **2** *informal* a prank, an adventure

caper² *noun* the flower-bud of a shrub, pickled or salted for eating

capillary *noun* (*plural* **capillaries**) **1** a type of narrow blood vessel that forms a network connecting arteries with veins **2** a very fine tube ➤ *adjective* very fine, like a hair

capital *adjective* **1** chief, most important **2** punishable by death: *a capital offence* **3** *informal, old* excellent **4** of a letter: written or printed in upper case, eg A, B or C ➤ *noun* **1** the chief city of a country: *Paris is the capital of France* **2** an upper-case letter **3** money for running a business **4** money invested; accumulated wealth ● **make capital out of** to turn to your advantage

capital-intensive *adjective, economics, geography* of an industry: requiring a large amount of capital for machinery etc compared to the amount of labour involved (*compare with*: **labour-intensive**)

capitalism *noun* a system in which a country's wealth is owned by individuals, not by the State

capitalist *noun* someone who supports or practises capitalism ◆ **capitalistic** *adjective*

capitalize or **capitalise** *verb* **1** to write in capital letters **2** (**capitalize on**) to turn to your advantage ♦ **capitalization** *noun*

capital punishment *noun* punishment by death

capitulate *verb* to give in to an enemy or to persuasion ♦ **capitulation** *noun*

capon (*pronounced* **kei**-pon) *noun* a young castrated cock, fattened for eating

cappuccino (*pronounced* kap-u-**chee**-no-h) *noun* (*plural* **cappuccinos**) coffee made with frothy milk

caprice (*pronounced* kap-**rees**) *noun* a sudden, impulsive change of mind or mood

capricious *adjective* full of caprice; impulsive, fickle ♦ **capriciously** *adverb* in a way which is characterized by mood swings or unpredictable behaviour: *The car has been behaving a bit capriciously*

Capricorn *noun* **1** the tenth sign of the zodiac, represented by the goat **2** someone born under this sign, between 23 December and 20 January

capsize *verb* of a boat: to upset, overturn

capstan *noun* a device used for winding in heavy ropes on a ship or quay

capsule *noun* **1** a small gelatine case containing a dose of medicine etc **2** a self-contained, detachable part of a spacecraft **3** *biology* a membranous structure that surrounds an organ or tissue, eg the capsule that surrounds the lens of the eye **4** *biology* a dry seed-pod on a plant **5** *biology* a jelly-like envelope of protein or polysaccharide that surrounds certain bacteria

captain *noun* **1** the commander of a company of soldiers, a ship or an aircraft **2** the leader of a sports team, club, etc ➤ *verb* to lead

captaincy *noun* (*plural* **captaincies**) the rank of captain

caption *noun* **1** a piece of text below a newspaper article, photograph, cartoon, etc, explaining it **2** *computing* the wording on an object on the screen, eg on a command button

captious *adjective* quick to find fault; judgemental

captivate *verb* to charm, fascinate

captive *noun* a prisoner ➤ *adjective* **1** taken or kept prisoner **2** not able to get away: *a captive audience*

captivity *noun* **1** the state of being a prisoner **2** the enclosure of an animal in a zoo etc, not in the wild

captor *noun* someone who takes a prisoner

capture *verb* **1** to take by force **2** to get hold of; seize: *capture the imagination* ➤ *noun* **1** the act of capturing **2** something captured **3** data capture

car *noun* **1** a small enclosed motor vehicle **2** *US* a train carriage

carafe (*pronounced* ka-**raf**) *noun* a bottle for serving wine, water, etc

caramel *noun* **1** sugar melted and browned **2** a sweet made with sugar and butter

carapace *noun*, *zoology* the hard thick shell covering the upper part of the body of some tortoises, turtles and crustaceans ⊙ Comes from Spanish *carapacho*

carat *noun* **1** a measure of purity for gold **2** a measure of weight for gemstones ⊙ Perhaps from Greek *keration* meaning 'a carob-seed, used as a weight'

❗ Do not confuse with: **carrot**

caravan *noun* **1** a covered vehicle with living accommodation drawn behind a car **2** a number of travellers etc crossing the desert together

caraway *noun* a plant with spicy seeds used in cooking

carbide *noun*, *chemistry* a chemical compound consisting of carbon and another element (except for hydrogen), usually a metallic one

carbohydrate *noun*, *biology*, *chemistry* a compound of carbon, hydrogen and oxygen formed in green plants during photosynthesis, eg sugar or starch

carbolic acid see **phenol**

carbon *noun*, *chemistry* (symbol **C**) an element that is found in all organic compounds and occurs in various forms, such as coal, coke and charcoal, and as two allotropes, diamond and graphite ⊙ Comes from French *carbone*, from Latin *carbo* meaning 'charcoal'

carbonaceous *adjective* containing large amounts of, or resembling, carbon

carbonate *noun*, *chemistry* a compound which contains the group CO_3 ➤ *verb* to add carbon dioxide to something eg to make a fizzy drink ♦ **carbonated** *adjective*

carbon black *noun* a form of fine carbon used in pigments and printer's ink

carbon copy *noun* **1** a copy of a document made by using carbon paper **2** an exact copy

carbon cycle *noun*, *biology* the continuous process by which carbon is exchanged between organisms and the environment

carbon dating *noun* a technique for estimating the age of an organic material from the amount of a radioactive carbon isotope in it (*also called:* **radiocarbon dating**)

carbon dioxide *noun*, *chemistry* an odourless tasteless gas, present in the air and formed during respiration

carbon fixation *noun*, *biology* the process by which carbon is converted into carbon compounds by plants and algae

carbonic *adjective* of a compound: containing carbon

carboniferous *adjective* **1** producing or containing coal or carbon **2** (**Carboniferous**) of the geological period 360 million to 290 million years ago, characterized by swampy forests which subsequently formed coal deposits

carbonize or **carbonise** *verb* **1** to convert or reduce (a substance) into carbon chiefly by heating or fossilization **2** to coat (a substance) with a layer of carbon ♦ **carbonization** *noun*

carbon monoxide *noun, chemistry* a poisonous, odourless gas formed by the incomplete combustion of carbon, eg in car exhausts

carbon paper *noun* paper coated with ink, interleaved between ordinary paper when typing to produce exact copies

carbonyl group (*pronounced* **kahr**-bon-il) *noun, chemistry* in certain organic chemical compounds: the C=O group, consisting of a carbon atom joined to an oxygen atom by a double bond

carborundum *noun, trademark, chemistry* an extremely hard, black, crystalline substance that is used as an abrasive and semiconductor

carboxyl group (*pronounced* kahr-**bok**-sil) *noun, chemistry* in certain organic chemical compounds: the -COOH group

carboxylic acid *noun, chemistry* an organic acid containing a carboxyl group bonded to hydrogen or a hydrocarbon, eg methanoic acid

carbuncle *noun* **1** a fiery-red precious stone **2** an inflamed swelling under the skin

carburettor or **carburetter** or *US* **carburetor** *noun* the part of a car engine which changes the petrol into vapour

carcass or **carcase** *noun* (*plural* **carcasses** or **carcases**) the dead body (of an animal)

carcinogen (*pronounced* kahr-**sin**-o-jen) or **kahr**-sin-o-jen) *noun* a substance that encourages the growth of cancer

carcinogenic *adjective* causing cancer

carcinoma (*pronounced* kah-si-**noh**-ma) *noun* (*plural* **carcinomas** or **carcinomata**) a cancerous growth

card *noun* **1** pasteboard or very thick paper **2** an illustrated, folded square of paper sent in greeting etc **3** a tool for combing wool etc **4** (**cards**) any of the many types of games played with a pack of special cards **5** a small rectangular piece of stiff plastic issued by a bank, shop, etc to a customer, used when making payments, as a guarantee for a cheque, for operating a cash machine, etc (*see also*: **cash card**, **credit card**, **debit card**) **6** *computing* a printed circuit board ➤ *verb* to comb (wool etc)

cardamom or **cardamum** or **cardamon** *noun* the dried aromatic seeds of a tropical shrub, which are used as a spice

cardboard *noun* stiff material made from pulped paper

cardiac *adjective* of the heart: *cardiac failure* ◐ Comes from Greek *kardia* meaning 'heart'

cardiac arrest *noun* the stopping of the heartbeat

cardiac muscle *noun* muscle that can contract and expand without tiring, found only in the walls of the heart

cardigan *noun* a knitted woollen jacket

◐ Named after the 7th Earl of *Cardigan*, who advocated the use of buttonable woollen jackets

cardinal *adjective* **1** principal, important **2** of a sin: very bad (*compare with*: **venial**) ➤ *noun* the highest rank of priest in the Roman Catholic Church, from which the Pope is selected

cardinal number *noun* a number which expresses quantity, eg 1, 2, 3 (*contrasted with*: **ordinal number**)

cardiology *noun, medicine* the branch of medicine concerned with the study of the structure, function and diseases of the heart ♦ **cardiologist** *noun*

cardiopulmonary *adjective* relating to the heart and lungs

cardiovascular *adjective* relating to the heart and blood vessels

care *noun* **1** close attention **2** worry, anxiety **3** protection, keeping: *in my care* ➤ *verb* to be concerned or worried: *I don't care what happens now* • **care for 1** to look after **2** to feel affection or liking for **3** to have a wish for: *Would you care for a drink?* • **care of** at the house of (often written as **c/o**) • **take care** to be careful; watch out • **take care of** to look after

career *noun* **1** life work; trade, profession **2** course, progress through life **3** a headlong rush ➤ *verb* to run rapidly and wildly: *careering along the road*

careerist *noun* someone who is chiefly interested in the advancement of their career: *politicians who are just careerists*

carefree *adjective* having no worries

careful *adjective* attentive, taking care ♦ **carefully** *adverb*

careless *adjective* paying little attention; not taking care ♦ **carelessly** *adverb*

carer *noun* a person who looks after someone who cannot look after themselves

caress *verb* to touch or stroke gently and lovingly ➤ *noun* (*plural* **caresses**) a gentle touch

caretaker *noun* someone who looks after a building ➤ *adjective* in charge temporarily; interim: *a caretaker government*

careworn *adjective* worn out by anxiety

carfuffle another spelling of **kerfuffle**

cargo *noun* (*plural* **cargoes**) a ship's load

caribou *noun* (*plural* **caribou** or **caribous**) the North American reindeer

caricature *noun* a picture of someone which exaggerates certain of their features ➤ *verb* to draw a caricature of ♦ **caricaturist** *noun*

caries (*pronounced* **kei**-ri-eez) *noun* (*plural* **caries**) decay, especially of the teeth

caring *adjective* **1** showing concern for others **2** professionally concerned with medical, social or personal welfare: *the caring professions*

carmine *noun* a bright red colour ➤ *adjective* of this colour

carnage *noun* slaughter, killing

carnal *adjective* bodily or sexual, as opposed to spiritual or intellectual

carnassial tooth *noun* a molar or premolar tooth that is adapted for tearing flesh

carnation *noun* a type of garden flower, often pink, red or white

carni- or **carn-** *prefix* of or relating to meat or flesh: *carnivore/carnage*

carnival *noun* a celebration with festivities, processions, etc

carnivore *noun* a flesh-eating animal

carnivorous *adjective* eating meat or flesh

carol *noun* a hymn or song sung at Christmas

caroller *noun* a person who sings carols

carolling *noun* the singing of carols

carotene *noun, biochemistry* any of a number of reddish-yellow pigments found in plants that are converted to vitamin A in the body

carotid or **carotid artery** (*pronounced* ka-**rot**-id) *noun, anatomy* either of the two major arteries that supply blood to the head and neck

carousal (*pronounced* ka-**row**-zal) *noun* a bout of drinking, a noisy party

carouse *verb* to take part in a drinking bout

carousel (*pronounced* kar-u-**sel**) *noun* **1** *US* a merry-go-round **2** a rotating conveyor belt for luggage at an airport etc

carp[1] *noun* a freshwater fish found in ponds

carp[2] *verb* to find fault with small errors; complain about nothing

carpal *noun, anatomy* any of the eight small bones that form the wrist

car park *noun* a place where cars etc may be left for a time

carpe diem *interjection* a Latin phrase meaning 'seize the day' (ie make the most of the present)

carpel *noun, botany* the female part of a flower, consisting of a stigma, style and ovary

carpenter *noun* a worker in wood, eg for building

carpentry *noun* the trade of a carpenter

carpet *noun* the woven covering of floors, stairs, etc ➤ *verb* to cover with a carpet

carpetbagger *noun* **1** *history, US derogatory* someone from the Northern states who travelled to the South after the American Civil War, to make money from its reconstruction **2** *derogatory* someone who uses a place or organization with which he or she has no connection for personal gain

car pool *noun* **1** a number of cars owned by a business for use by employees **2** an arrangement between car owners to take turns at driving each other to work etc

carriage *noun* **1** a vehicle for carrying people **2** the act or cost of carrying **3** a way of walking; bearing

carrier *noun* **1** someone who carries goods **2** a machine or container for carrying **3** someone who passes on a disease

carrier pigeon *noun* a pigeon used to carry messages

carrion *noun* rotting animal flesh

carrot *noun* a vegetable with an edible orange-coloured root ℗ Comes from French *carotte*

❗ Do not confuse with: **carat**

carry *verb* (**carries, carrying, carried**) **1** to pick up and take to another place **2** to contain and take to a destination: *cables carrying electricity* **3** to bear, have as a mark: *carry a scar* **4** of a voice: to be able to be heard at a distance **5** to win, succeed: *carry the day* **6** to keep for sale: *We don't carry cigarettes* **7** to be the means of spreading a disease: *Mosquitos carry malaria* • **carried away** overcome by emotion; overexcited • **carry on** to continue (doing) • **carry out** to accomplish; succeed in doing • **carry the can** to accept responsibility for an error • **carry weight** to have force or authority

carrycot *noun* a light box-like bed with handles, for carrying a baby

carrying capacity *noun, geography* the maximum number of people or animals that a given area of land can support

carry-on *noun* a fuss, a to-do

carry-out *noun* a takeaway meal or alcoholic drink

cart *noun* **1** a horse-drawn vehicle used for carrying loads **2** a small, wheeled vehicle pushed by hand ➤ *verb* **1** to carry by cart **2** to drag, haul: *carted off the stage*

carte blanche (*pronounced* kahrt **blonsh**) *noun* freedom of action; a free hand

℗ In French, **carte blanche** means 'white card', and the expression refers to a blank piece of paper which a person has signed and given to you, thus giving you their official advance permission for whatever you wish to write on the paper

cartel *noun* a group of firms that agree, often

illegally, on similar fixed prices for their products, so as to reduce competition and keep profits high

Cartesian co-ordinates *plural noun, maths* a set of co-ordinates specifying the position of a point in a plane or in space by its distances from two or three intersecting axes

carthorse *noun* a large, heavy working horse

cartilage *noun* a strong, elastic material that surrounds the joints of humans and animals; gristle

cartography *noun* the science of map-making ♦ **cartographer** *noun*

carton *noun* a small container made of cardboard, plastic, etc

cartoon *noun* **1** a comic drawing, or strip of drawings, often with a caption **2** an animated film **3** a drawing used as the basis for a large painting etc

cartoonist *noun* someone who draws cartoons

cartridge *noun* **1** a case holding the powder and bullet fired by a gun **2** a spool of film or tape enclosed in a case **3** a tube of ink for loading a pen **4** the part of a record-player which holds the stylus **5** a container of ink for a printer

cartwheel *noun* **1** the wheel of a cart **2** a sideways somersault with hands touching the ground

cartwright *noun* someone who makes carts

carve *verb* **1** to make or shape by cutting **2** to cut up (meat) into slices

cascade *noun* **1** a waterfall **2** an abundant hanging display: *a cascade of curls* ➤ *verb* to fall like or in a waterfall

case[1] *noun* a container or outer covering ◑ Comes from Latin *capsa* meaning 'a holder' or 'a box'

case[2] *noun* **1** that which happens, an occurrence **2** a statement of facts; a set of arguments **3** a matter requiring investigation **4** a trial in a law-court: *a murder case* **5** *grammar* the relationship of a noun, pronoun or adjective to other words in a sentence ◑ Comes from Latin *casus* meaning 'a falling'

case history *noun* a record of details from someone's past kept by a doctor, social worker, etc

casement *noun* **1** a window-frame **2** a window that swings on hinges

cash *noun* money in the form of coins and notes ➤ *verb* to turn into, or change for, money • **cash in on** to profit from

cash-and-carry *noun* (*plural* **cash-and-carries**) a large, often wholesale, shop where customers pay for goods in cash and take them away immediately

cashback *noun* **1** a facility whereby a person paying for goods by debit card may also withdraw cash **2** money offered as an incentive to someone to enter into a financial agreement, eg a mortgage

cash card *noun* a card issued by a bank etc that allows the holder to use a cash dispenser

cash crop *noun, geography* a crop that is grown for sale rather than for consumption by the farmer's household or by livestock

cash dispenser *noun* a cash machine

cashew *noun* a kidney-shaped nut produced by a tropical tree

cashier *noun* someone who looks after the receiving and paying of money ➤ *verb, military* to dismiss (an officer) in disgrace

cash machine *noun* an electronic machine, often in the outside wall of a bank, from which one can obtain cash using a cash card

cashmere *noun* fine soft goat's wool from the Kashmir goat

cash point *noun* a cash machine

cash register *noun* a machine for holding money that records the amount put in

casino (*pronounced* ka-**see**-noh) *noun* (*plural* **casinos**) a building in which gambling takes place

cask *noun* a barrel for wine etc

casket *noun* **1** a small box for holding jewels etc **2** *US* a coffin

cassava *noun* a tropical plant with roots from which tapioca is obtained

casserole *noun* **1** a covered dish for cooking and serving food **2** food cooked in a casserole

cassette *noun* **1** a small case for film, magnetic recording tape, etc **2** the magnetic tape itself

cassock *noun* a long robe worn by priests

cast *verb* (**casting, cast**) **1** to throw, fling **2** to throw off; drop, shed: *The snake cast its skin* **3** to shape in a mould **4** to choose (actors) for a play or film **5** to give a part to (an actor etc) **6** to project, cause to appear: *cast a shadow* **7** to give or record (a vote) ➤ *noun* **1** something shaped in a mould **2** plaster encasing a broken limb **3** the actors in a play **4** a small heap of earth thrown up by a worm **5** a type: *cast of mind* **6** an eye squint ♦ **cast down** *adjective* depressed ♦ **cast off** *adjective* used by someone else, second-hand • **cast off** to finish off and remove (stitches or knitting) from the needles • **cast on** to form (stitches or knitting) by looping and securing wool over the needles

castanets *plural noun* hollow shells of ivory or hard wood, clicked together to accompany a dance

◑ From a Spanish word for 'chestnuts', because of their shape

castaway *noun* a deserted or shipwrecked person

caste *noun* a class or rank of people, especially in the Indian subcontinent

caster another spelling of **castor**

castigate *verb* to scold, punish ◆ **castigation** *noun*

castle *noun* a fortified house or fortress

castor or **caster** *noun* a small wheel, eg on the legs or bottom of furniture

castor oil or **caster oil** *noun* a kind of palm oil used medicinally

castor sugar or **caster sugar** *noun* very fine granulated sugar

castrate *verb* to remove the testicles of

casual *adjective* 1 happening by chance: *a casual encounter* 2 not regular, temporary: *casual labour* 3 informal: *casual clothes* 4 not careful, unconcerned: *a casual attitude to work* ◆ **casually** *adverb*

casualty *noun* (*plural* **casualties**) 1 someone who is killed or wounded 2 a casualty department

casualty department *noun* a hospital department for treating accidental injuries, emergencies, etc

cat *noun* 1 a sharp-clawed, furry animal kept as a pet 2 an animal of a family which includes lions, tigers, etc

cata- or **cath-** *prefix* down: *catastrophe* (= a turning down)/*cathode* (= a going down) ⊕ Comes from Greek *kata* meaning 'down'

catabolism *noun, biochemistry* the process whereby complex organic compounds in living organisms are broken down by the body into simple molecules

cataclysm *noun* 1 a violent change; an upheaval 2 a great flood of water

catacombs *plural noun* an underground burial place

catalogue *noun* an ordered list of names, books, objects for sale, etc ➤ *verb* 1 to list in order 2 to compile details of (a book) for a library catalogue

catalyst *noun* 1 *chemistry* a substance which alters the rate of a chemical reaction without itself changing 2 something that speeds up or brings about a change ◆ **catalyse** or *US* **catalyze** *verb* ◆ **catalysis** *noun*

catalytic converter *noun* a device containing catalysts, attached to car engines to reduce the polluting gases produced

catamaran *noun* a boat with two parallel hulls

catapult *noun* 1 a small forked stick with a piece of elastic attached, used for firing small stones 2 *history* a weapon for throwing heavy stones in warfare

cataract *noun* 1 a waterfall 2 *medicine* a disease in which the lens in the eye becomes opaque, producing blurring of vision

catarrh *noun* inflammation of the lining of the nose and throat causing a discharge

catastrophe (*pronounced* kat-**as**-tro-fi) *noun* a sudden disaster

catastrophic (*pronounced* kat-as-**trof**-ik) *adjective* disastrous, absolutely terrible

catatonia *noun* a mental state characterized either by stupor or by excessive excitement and violent activity ◆ **catatonic** *adjective*

cat burglar *noun* a burglar who breaks into houses by climbing walls etc

catch *verb* (**catching, caught**) 1 to take hold of, capture 2 to become infected with (a disease): *catch a cold* 3 to be in time for: *catch the last train* 4 to surprise (in an act): *caught him stealing* 5 to manage to hear or understand: *I didn't catch what you said* ➤ *noun* 1 a haul of fish etc 2 something you are lucky to have got or won 3 a hidden flaw or disadvantage: *Where's the catch?* 4 a fastening: *a window catch* ◆ **catchy** *adjective* (**catchier, catchiest**) of a tune: easily remembered ● **catch on** to become popular ● **catch-22** an absurd situation with no way out ● **catch up on** 1 to draw level with, overtake 2 to get up-to-date with (work etc)

catching *adjective* infectious

catchment *noun* 1 the area served by a particular school, hospital, etc 2 another term for a **drainage basin**

catchphrase *noun* a phrase which is popular for a while

catchword *noun* a word which is popular for a while

catechism (*pronounced* **kat**-e-kizm) *noun* a series of questions and answers about the Christian religion, used for instruction

catechize or **catechise** (*pronounced* **kat**-e-kaiz) *verb* 1 to instruct someone in the Christian religion, especially by using a catechism 2 to question someone very thoroughly

categorical *adjective* allowing no doubt or argument: *a categorical denial*

categorically *adverb* in such a sure way that there can be no discussion or argument: *He has stated quite categorically that he is not interested*

categorize or **categorise** *verb* to divide into categories

category *noun* (*plural* **categories**) a class or group of similar people or things

catena (*pronounced* ka-**teen**-a) *noun, geography* the differences in the moisture, acidity, etc of soil along a slope

cater *verb* 1 to provide food 2 to supply what is required: *cater for all tastes*

caterer *noun* someone whose job is to provide

ready-prepared food and drinks for people

caterpillar *noun* an insect larva that feeds on plant leaves ➤ *adjective* moving on rotating metal belts: *a caterpillar tractor*

> ⊙ Based on an Old French phrase which translates as 'hairy cat'

caterwaul *verb* to howl or yell like a cat

cat flap *noun* a small door set in a larger door to allow a cat to go in and out

catgut *noun* cord made from sheep's stomachs, used to make strings for violins, harps, etc

cathedral *noun* **1** the church of a bishop **2** the chief church in a bishop's district

catherine-wheel *noun* a firework which spins as it burns

catheter (*pronounced* **kath**-i-ter) *noun, medicine* a slender flexible tube that can be introduced into the body in order to drain off a liquid, usually urine

cathode *noun* the negative electrode in a battery or other electronic device (*contrasted with*: **anode**)

cathode ray tube *noun* a device in a television set etc, which causes a narrow beam of electrons to strike against a screen

catholic *adjective* **1** wide, comprehensive: *a catholic taste in literature* **2** (**Catholic**) of the Roman Catholic Church ➤ *noun* (**Catholic**) a member of the Roman Catholic Church

Catholic Emancipation *noun, history* a concession granted by the British government in 1829 that Roman Catholics could become MPs, or take on an office of state in Ireland

cation (*pronounced* **kat**-ai-on) *noun, chemistry* a positively charged ion, which moves towards the cathode during electrolysis (*compare with*: **anion**)

catkin *noun* a tuft of small flowers adapted for wind pollination on certain trees, eg the willow and hazel

cat-o'-nine-tails *noun* a whip with nine lashes

CAT scanner or **CT scanner** *noun* an X-ray machine that produces three-dimensional images

> ⊙ An acronym of computed (or computerized) axial tomography

cat's cradle *noun* a children's game of creating patterns by winding string around the fingers

Catseye *noun, trademark* a small mirror fixed in a road surface to reflect light from vehicles at night

cattle *plural noun* oxen, bulls and cows, and other grass-eating animals of this family

catty *adjective* (**cattier, cattiest**) **1** like a cat **2** spiteful ◆ **cattiness** *noun*

catwalk *noun* the narrow raised stage along which models walk at a fashion show

Caucasian (*pronounced* kaw-**kei**-szi-an) *adjective* belonging to one of the light- or white-skinned races of mankind ➤ *noun, loosely* a white-skinned person

caucus (*pronounced* **kaw**-kus) *noun* (*plural* **caucuses**), *US* a meeting of members of a political party to nominate candidates for election etc

caudal *adjective, biology* relating to the tail or the tail end of the body

caught past form of **catch**

cauldron *noun* a large pan

cauliflower *noun* a kind of cabbage with a head made up of edible white florets

causality or **causation** *noun* **1** the relationship between cause and effect **2** the idea that everything has been brought about by something else

cause *noun* **1** something that makes something happen **2** a reason for action: *cause for complaint* **3** an aim for which a group or person works: *the cause of peace* ➤ *verb* to make happen

causeway *noun* a raised road over wet ground or shallow water

caustic *adjective* **1** of a chemical substance: strongly alkaline and corrosive to living tissue **2** sarcastic, bitter, severe: *caustic wit*

caustic soda see **sodium hydroxide**

cauterize or **cauterise** *verb* to burn away flesh with a hot iron etc in order to make a wound heal cleanly

caution *noun* **1** carefulness because of potential danger: *approach with caution* **2** a warning ➤ *verb* to warn

cautionary *adjective* giving a warning

cautious *adjective* careful, showing caution

cavalcade *noun* a procession on horseback, in cars, etc

cavalier *noun, history* (**Cavalier**) a supporter of the king in the English Civil War of the 17th century (*compare with*: **Roundhead**) ➤ *adjective* offhand, careless: *in a cavalier fashion*

cavalry *noun* soldiers mounted on horses

cave *noun* a hollow place in the earth or in rock ➤ *verb*: **cave in** to fall or collapse inwards

caveat (*pronounced* **kav**-i-at) *noun* a warning

caveman or **cavewoman** *noun* (*plural* **cavemen** or **cavewomen**) a prehistoric cave-dweller

cavern *noun* a deep hollow place in the earth

cavernous *adjective* **1** huge and hollow **2** full of caverns

caviar or **caviare** *noun* the pickled eggs of the sturgeon, eaten as a delicacy

cavil *verb* (**cavilling, cavilled**) to make

objections over small, unimportant details

cavitation another word for **hydraulic action**

cavity noun (plural **cavities**) **1** a hollow place, a hole **2** a decayed hollow in a tooth

cavort verb to dance or leap around

caw verb to call like a crow ➤ noun a crow's call

CBD or **cbd** abbreviation, geography central business district

CC or **Cc** abbreviation carbon copy, used to mark a copy of a message sent to people other than the main recipient

cc abbreviation cubic centimetre(s)

CCTV abbreviation closed-circuit television

CD abbreviation compact disc

Cd symbol, chemistry cadmium

cd symbol candela

CD burner or **CD recorder** noun a device used to record data onto compact discs

CDI or **CD-i** abbreviation compact disc interactive, a type of CD-ROM that responds intelligently to a user's instructions

CD-R abbreviation compact disc recordable, a CD that can be written to

CD-ROM abbreviation compact disc read-only memory, a CD that lets you look at but not alter text

CD-RW abbreviation compact disc rewritable, a CD that can be recorded on many times

Ce symbol, chemistry cerium

cease verb to come to or bring to an end

ceasefire noun **1** an order to stop firing weapons **2** an agreed, although maybe temporary, end to active hostilities

ceaseless adjective without stopping

cedar noun a large evergreen tree with a hard, sweet-smelling wood

cede verb to yield, give up

cedilla (pronounced si-**dil**-a) noun **1** in French and Portuguese: a mark put under c in some words, eg façade, to show that it is to be pronounced like s, not k **2** the same mark used under other letters in other languages to indicate various sounds ⊙ From Spanish meaning 'little c'

ceilidh or Irish **ceilí** (pronounced **kei**-li) noun an event involving traditional Scottish or Irish dancing, sometimes combined with musical performances

ceiling noun **1** the inner roof of a room **2** an upper limit

celandine noun a small yellow wild flower

celebrate verb to commemorate an event (eg a birthday or marriage) by going out, having a party, etc ◆ **celebrated** adjective famous ◆ **celebration** noun ◆ **celebratory** adjective

celebrity noun (plural **celebrities**) **1** a famous person, a star **2** fame

celeriac (pronounced si-**le**-ri-ak) noun the swollen base of the stem of a variety of celery, which is eaten raw in salads or cooked as a vegetable

celery noun a type of vegetable with edible fibrous stalks

celestial adjective **1** of the sky: celestial bodies (= stars and planets) **2** heavenly

celibacy noun a lifestyle without sexual intercourse ◆ **celibate** adjective abstaining from sexual intercourse

cell noun **1** a small room in a prison, monastery, etc **2** biology the smallest basic structural unit of living things, consisting of a mass of protein material composed of the cytoplasm and usually a nucleus **3** electronics a device consisting of two electrodes immersed in an electrolyte, for converting chemical energy into electrical energy **4** a compartment in a honeycomb or in a similar structure **5** a location on a computerized spreadsheet

cellar noun an underground room used for storing coal, wine, etc

cellist (pronounced **chel**-ist) noun someone who plays the cello

cell membrane noun (also called: **plasma membrane**) the surface membrane enclosing the cytoplasm of a cell, which separates it from its environment and controls how substances pass in and out

cello (pronounced **chel**-oh) noun (short for: **violoncello**) a stringed musical instrument, similar in shape to a violin but much larger

cellophane noun, trademark a thin transparent wrapping material

cellphone noun a mobile phone

cellular adjective made of or having cells

cellulite noun deposits of fat which give the skin a dimpled, pitted appearance

celluloid noun, trademark a very hard, elastic substance used for making photographic film etc

cellulose noun a complex carbohydrate found in plants and wood, used to make paper, textiles, etc

cellulose acetate noun, chemistry a tough thermoplastic resin, prepared by treating cellulose with acetic acid and used to make photographic film, magnetic tape, lacquers and acetate fibres, eg rayon

cellulose nitrate noun, chemistry a flammable, pulpy solid, prepared by treating cellulose with concentrated nitric acid and used as an explosive and propellant

cell wall noun the outermost layer of cells in plants, bacteria, etc

Celsius (pronounced **sel**-si-us) adjective **1** of a temperature scale: consisting of a hundred degrees, on which water freezes at 0° and boils at 100° **2** of a degree: measured on this scale: 10° Celsius

Celtic *adjective & noun* **1** of the Celts, a group of ancient peoples of Europe, or their descendants in Wales, Scotland and Ireland **2** (of) their languages

cement *noun* **1** the mixture of clay and lime used to secure bricks in a wall **2** something used to make two things stick together ➤ *verb* **1** to put together with cement **2** to join firmly, fix: *cemented their friendship*

cemetery *noun* (*plural* **cemeteries**) a place where the dead are buried

cenotaph *noun* a monument to someone or a group buried elsewhere

Cenozoic *adjective* of the geological era from 65 million years ago to the present day

censer *noun* a container for burning incense in a church ☉ Comes from Latin *incendere* meaning 'to burn'

⚠ Do not confuse: **censer, censor** and **censure**

censor *noun* someone whose job is to examine books, films, etc with the power to delete any of the contents or forbid them to be shown or released ➤ *verb* to examine (books etc) in this way ☉ Comes from Latin *censor*

⚠ Do not confuse: **censor, censer** and **censure**

censorious *adjective* fault-finding; judgemental

censorship *noun* the activity of censoring

censure *noun* blame; expression of disapproval ➤ *verb* to blame, criticize ☉ Comes from Latin *censura* meaning 'censorship'

⚠ Do not confuse: **censure, censer** and **censor**

census *noun* (*plural* **censuses**) a periodical official count of the people who live in a country ☉ Comes from Latin *census* meaning 'a register'

⚠ Do not confuse with: **consensus**

cent *noun* a coin which is the hundredth part of a larger coin, eg of a euro or a US dollar ☉ Comes from Latin *centum* meaning 'a hundred'

centaur *noun* a mythological creature, half man and half horse

centenarian *noun* someone a hundred or more years old

centenary *noun* (*plural* **centenaries**) a hundredth anniversary; the hundredth year since an event took place

centennial *adjective* **1** having lasted a hundred years **2** happening every hundred years ➤ *noun* a centenary

centi- or **cent-** *prefix* hundred; a hundredth part of ☉ Comes from Latin *centum* meaning 'a hundred'

centigrade *adjective* **1** of a temperature scale: consisting of a hundred degrees **2** measured on this scale: *5° centigrade* **3** Celsius

centigram or **centigramme** *noun* (*abbrev* **cg**) a hundredth part of a gram

centilitre *noun* (*abbrev* **cl**) a hundredth part of a litre

centimetre *noun* (*abbrev* **cm**) a hundredth part of a metre

centipede *noun* a small crawling insect with many legs

central *adjective* **1** belonging to the centre **2** chief, main: *the central point of the argument*

central business district *noun, geography* (*abbrev* **CBD** or **cbd**) the area of a town or city containing most of the business and commerce, usually the town or city centre

central government *noun* administration of the affairs of a whole country (*compare with:* **local government**)

central heating *noun* heating of a building by water, steam or air from a central point

centralize or **centralise** *verb* **1** to group in a single place **2** to bring (eg a government department, an industry, etc) under one central control ✦ **centralization** *noun*

central limit theorem *noun, statistics* the theorem that the distribution of a sample mean is approximately normal provided the sample size is large enough, and that variance of the distribution of the sample mean equals the variance of the sample mean divided by the sample size

central locking *noun* a system whereby all the doors of a vehicle are locked by the locking of the driver's door

central nervous system *noun* the brain and spinal cord

Central Powers *plural noun, history* the allied countries of Germany, Austria-Hungary, Turkey, and later Bulgaria, in World War I

central processing unit *noun, computing* (*abbrev* **CPU**) the part of a computer that controls all the other parts and performs arithmetical and logical operations on data

central reservation *noun* a narrow strip of grass, concrete, etc dividing the two sides of a dual carriageway or motorway

centre or *US* **center** *noun* **1** the middle point or part **2** a building used for some special activity: *sports centre/shopping centre* ➤ *verb* (**centring, centred**) to put in the centre

ⓘ This is one of a large number of words which are spelled with an **-re** ending in British English, but with an **-er** in American English eg *metre/meter, calibre/caliber, lustre/luster.*

centre of gravity *noun, physics* a theoretical

point in an object about which its weight is evenly distributed

centrifugal (*pronounced* sen-tri-**fyoo**-gal or sen-**trif**-yoo-gal) *adjective* moving away from a centre or an axis of rotation (*contrasted with*: **centripetal**)

centriole *noun, biology* in animal cells: a tiny cylindrical structure that plays an important role in cell division

centripetal (*pronounced* sen-**trip**-i-tal or sen-tri-**peet**-al) *adjective* moving towards a centre or an axis of rotation (*contrasted with*: **centrifugal**)

centrist *adjective* having moderate, non-extreme political opinions ▸ *noun* someone holding such opinions ♦ **centrism** *noun*

centurion *noun, history* a commander of 100 Roman soldiers

century *noun* (*plural* **centuries**) **1** a hundred years **2** *cricket* a hundred runs

cephalopod (*pronounced* **sef**-al-o-pod) *noun* a sea mollusc with a highly developed brain and sense organs, eg squid, octopus

ceramic *adjective* **1** made of pottery **2** of pottery-making ▸ *noun* **1** something made of pottery **2** (**ceramics**) the art of pottery

cereal *noun* **1** grain used as food **2** a breakfast food prepared from grain

cerebellum *noun* (*plural* **cerebella**) a part of the brain that controls the body's movement

cerebral *adjective* of the brain

cerebral palsy *noun* a disorder caused by brain injury at birth, causing poor muscle control

cerebrum *noun* (*plural* **cerebrums** or **cerebra**) the largest part of the brain, which controls thinking, emotions and personality

ceremonial *adjective* with or of ceremony ♦ **ceremonially** *adverb*

ceremonious *adjective* full of ceremony, formal ♦ **ceremoniously** *adverb*

ceremony *noun* (*plural* **ceremonies**) the formal acts that accompany an important event: *the marriage ceremony*

cerise (*pronounced* se-**reez** or se-**rees**) *noun* a bright cherry-red colour ▸ *adjective* cerise-coloured ☉ Comes from French meaning 'cherry'

cerium *noun, chemistry* (symbol **Ce**) a soft, silvery-grey, metallic element belonging to the lanthanide series, used in catalytic converters

⊙ Named after the asteroid *Ceres*

certain *adjective* **1** sure; not to be doubted **2** fixed, settled **3** particular but unnamed: *stopping at certain places/a certain look*

certainly *adverb* **1** definitely, without any doubt **2** of course

certainty *noun* (*plural* **certainties**) **1** a sure

thing: *It's almost a certainty that he will be re-elected* **2** the quality of being certain: *I can tell you this with absolute certainty*

certificate *noun* a written or printed statement giving details of a birth, passed examination, etc

certify *verb* (**certifies, certifying, certified**) to put down in writing as an official promise or statement etc

cervical (*pronounced* ser-**vai**-kal or **ser**-vi-kal) *adjective* of the cervix

cervix *noun* (*plural* **cervixes** or **cervices** – *pronounced* **ser**-vi-seez or ser -**vai**-seez) the neck of the womb

cessation *noun* a ceasing or stopping; an ending

cesspool *noun* a pool or tank for storing liquid waste or sewage

cetane (*pronounced* **see**-tein) *noun* a colourless liquid hydrocarbon found in petroleum, used as a solvent ☉ Comes from Latin *cetus* whale

Cf *symbol, chemistry* californium

cf *abbreviation* compare (from Latin *confer*)

CFC *abbreviation* chlorofluorocarbon

cg *abbreviation* centigram(s)

CGI *noun* computer-generated imagery, often used in animated films

chador (*pronounced* **chud**-er) *noun* a thick veil worn by Muslim women

chafe *verb* **1** to make hot or sore by rubbing **2** to wear away by rubbing **3** to become annoyed

chaff *noun* **1** husks of corn left after threshing **2** something of little value **3** good-natured teasing ▸ *verb* to tease jokingly

chaffinch *noun* (*plural* **chaffinches**) a small songbird of the finch family

chagrin (*pronounced* **sha**-grin or sha-**green**) *noun* annoyance, irritation

chain *noun* **1** a number of metal links or rings passing through one another **2** (**chains**) these links used to tie a prisoner's limbs; fetters **3** a number of connected things: *a mountain chain* **4** a group of shops owned by one person or company **5** *chemistry* a number of atoms of an element joined together ▸ *verb* to fasten or imprison with a chain

chain letter *noun* a letter containing promises or threats, requesting the recipient to send a similar letter to several other people

chain mail *noun* armour made of iron links

chain reaction *noun* **1** *physics* a nuclear reaction that is self-sustaining, eg nuclear fission **2** *chemistry* a chemical process in which each change in a molecule causes change in other molecules **3** a series of events, each causing the next

chainsaw *noun* a power-driven saw with teeth on a rotating chain

chain-smoke *verb* to smoke (cigarettes etc) continuously ♦ **chain-smoker** *noun*

chain store *noun* one of several shops under the same ownership

chair *noun* **1** a seat for one person with a back to it **2** a university professorship: *the chair of French literature* **3** a chairman or chairwoman

chairlift *noun* a row of chairs on a rotating cable for carrying people up mountains etc

chairman, chairperson or **chairwoman** *noun* (*plural* **chairmen, chairpersons** or **chairwomen**) someone who presides at or is in charge of a meeting

chaise longue (*pronounced* sheiz **long**) *noun* (*plural* **chaises longues** – *pronounced* sheiz **long** or sheiz **longz**) a long seat with a back and one armrest, on which one can recline at full length ⊙ Comes from French

chalet (*pronounced* **shal**-ei) *noun* **1** a small wooden house used by holidaymakers **2** a summer hut used by Swiss herdsmen in the Alps

chalice *noun* a cup for wine, used eg in church services

chalk *noun* **1** a type of limestone **2** a compressed stick of coloured powder used for writing or drawing ➤ *verb* to mark with chalk

chalky *adjective* (**chalkier, chalkiest**) **1** of chalk **2** white, pale

challenge *verb* **1** to question another's right to do something **2** to ask (someone) to take part in a contest, eg to settle a quarrel ➤ *noun* **1** a questioning of another's right **2** a call to a contest **3** a problem or task that is stimulating and interesting

challenged *adjective* a supposedly neutral term denoting some kind of handicap, impairment or disability: *visually challenged*

challenger *noun* someone who challenges a person such as a champion or holder of an important position to a competition for their status

challenging *adjective* interesting but difficult

chamber (*pronounced* **cheim**-ber) *noun* **1** a room **2** a place where a parliament meets **3** a room where legal cases are heard by a judge **4** an enclosed space or cavity **5** the part of a gun that holds the cartridges

chamberlain *noun* an officer appointed by the crown or a local authority to carry out certain duties

chamber music *noun* music for a small group of players, suitable for performance in a room rather than a large hall

chamberpot *noun* a receptacle for urine etc, used in the bedroom

chameleon (*pronounced* ka-**meel**-yon) *noun* a small lizard able to change its colour to match its surroundings

chamois *noun* **1** (*pronounced* **sham**-wah) a goat-like deer living in mountainous country **2** (*pronounced* **sham**-i) a soft leather formerly made from chamois skin, now from the skins of sheep and goats (*also spelled*: **shammy**)

champ *verb* to chew noisily • **champing at the bit** impatient to act

champagne (*pronounced* sham-**pein**) *noun* a type of white sparkling wine

champion *noun* **1** someone who has beaten all others in a competition **2** a strong supporter of a cause: *a champion of free speech* ➤ *verb* to support the cause of

championship *noun* **1** the act of championing **2** a contest to find a champion

chance *noun* **1** a risk, a possibility **2** something unexpected or unplanned **3** an opportunity ➤ *verb* **1** to risk **2** to happen by accident ➤ *adjective* happening by accident • **by chance** not by arrangement, unexpectedly • **chance upon** to meet or find unexpectedly

chancel *noun* the part of a church near the altar

chancellor *noun* **1** a high-ranking government minister **2** the head of a university • **Chancellor of the Exchequer** the minister in the British cabinet in charge of government spending

chancy *adjective* (**chancier, chanciest**) risky

chandelier (*pronounced* shan-de-**leer**) *noun* a fixture hanging from the ceiling with branches for holding lights

change *verb* **1** to make or become different **2** to give up or leave (a job, house, etc) for another **3** to put on different clothes **4** to give (money of one kind) in exchange for (money of another kind) ➤ *noun* **1** the act of making or becoming different **2** another set of clothing **3** money in the form of coins **4** money returned when a buyer gives more than the price of an article • **the change of life** the menopause

changeable *adjective* likely to change; often changing

changeling *noun* in stories: a fairy child secretly left in place of a human one

channel *noun* **1** a watercourse; the bed of a stream, canal or river **2** a passage for ships through an area of water **3** a wide stretch of water between an island and a continent, or linking two seas **4** a groove; a gutter **5** a band of frequencies for a radio or television signal ➤ *verb* (**channelling, channelled**) to direct into a particular course

channel efficiency *noun, geography* the energy required by a channel of water to flow, controlled by the amount of contact between the flow and the bed and banks of the channel

chant *verb* to recite in a singing manner ➤ *noun* a singing recitation

Chanukkah see **Hanukkah**

chaos (*pronounced* **kei**-os) *noun* **1** disorder, confusion **2** *physics* a state of irregularity between highly ordered motion and entirely random motion

chaotic *adjective* disordered, confused ◆ **chaotically** *adverb*

chap *noun, informal* a man

chapati or **chapatti** (*pronounced* cha-**paht**-ee) *noun* a round of unleavened Indian bread

chapel *noun* **1** a small church **2** a small part of a larger church

chaperon or **chaperone** (*pronounced* shap-e-rohn) *noun* a woman who accompanies a younger one when she goes out in public ➤ *verb* to act as a chaperon to

chaplain *noun* a member of the clergy accompanying an army, navy, etc

chapped *adjective* of skin: cracked by cold or wet weather

chapter *noun* **1** a division of a book **2** a branch of a society or organization ● **chapter of accidents** a series of accidents

char¹ *verb* (**charring, charred**) to burn until black

char² *verb* to do odd jobs of housework, cleaning, etc ➤ *noun, informal* a charwoman

character *noun* **1** the nature and qualities of someone **2** the good and bad points which make up a person's nature **3** self-control, firmness **4** someone noted for eccentric behaviour **5** someone in a play, story or film **6** a letter, number or other written or printed symbol

characteristic *noun* a typical and noticeable feature of someone or something ➤ *adjective* typical

characteristically *adverb* typically, as always: *His suggestions were characteristically tactful*

characterization or **characterisation** *noun* the creation and development of the different characters in a book, story or piece of drama: *Jane Austen's power of characterization*

characterize or **characterise** *verb* **1** to be typical of **2** to describe (as)

charade (*pronounced* sha-**rahd** or sha-**reid**) *noun* **1** a ridiculous pretence **2** (**charades**) a game in which players have to guess a word from gestures representing its sound or meaning

charcoal *noun* wood burnt black, used for fuel or sketching

charge *verb* **1** to accuse: *charged with murder* **2** to ask (a price) **3** to ask to do; give responsibility for **4** to load (a gun) **5** to make (a battery) fill up with electricity: *charge a mobile phone* **6** to attack in a rush ➤ *noun* **1** accusation for a crime **2** a price, a fee **3** an attack **4** the gunpowder in a shell or bullet **5** an accumulation of electricity **6** care, responsibility **7** someone looked after by another person ◆ **charged** *adjective, physics*

holding or receiving electrical charge ● **in charge** in command or control ● **take charge of** to take command of

charge card *noun* a plastic card issued by a store, which entitles the holder to buy goods on credit

charger *noun* a horse used in battle

chariot *noun, history* a wheeled carriage used in battle

charioteer *noun* a chariot-driver

charisma (*pronounced* ka-**riz**-ma) *noun* a personal quality that impresses others

charismatic *adjective* **1** full of charisma or charm **2** denoting a Christian movement based on belief in God-given gifts of unconsciously speaking in unknown languages, healing, etc

charitable *adjective* **1** giving to the poor; kindly **2** of a charity: *charitable status* ◆ **charitably** *adverb* (meaning 1)

charity *noun* (*plural* **charities**) **1** donation of money to the poor etc **2** an organization which collects money and gives it to those in need **3** kindness, humanity

charlatan (*pronounced* **shahr**-lat-an) *noun* someone who claims greater powers or abilities than they really have

Charles's law *noun, physics* the law which states that at a constant pressure the volume of a mass of gas is directly proportional to its temperature

⊙ Named after Jacques *Charles* (1746–1823), French physicist

charm *noun* **1** something thought to have magical powers **2** a magical spell **3** personal power to attract **4** a small ornament worn on a bracelet ➤ *verb* **1** to please greatly, delight **2** to put under a spell

charming *adjective* lovely, delightful

chart *noun* **1** a table or diagram giving particular information: *a temperature chart* **2** a geographical map of the sea **3** a rough map **4** (**the charts**) a weekly list of the top-selling recordings ➤ *verb* to make into a chart; plot

charter *noun* a written paper showing the official granting of rights, lands, etc ➤ *verb* to hire (a boat, aeroplane, etc) ➤ *adjective* hired for a special purpose: *a charter flight*

chartered *adjective* **1** qualified under the regulations of a professional body: *a chartered surveyor* **2** hired for a purpose

Chartism *noun, history* a movement in England supporting political reform, most active between 1838 and 1849, which presented 'the People's Charter' twice to parliament ◆ **Chartist** *noun & adjective*

charwoman *noun* (*plural* **charwomen**) a woman hired to do domestic cleaning etc

chary (*pronounced* **cheir**-i) *adjective* (**charier, chariest**) cautious, careful (of)

chase *verb* **1** to run after, pursue **2** to hunt ➤ *noun* a pursuit, a hunt

chasm (*pronounced* **ka**-zm) *noun* **1** a steep drop between high rocks etc **2** a wide difference; a gulf

chassis (*pronounced* **shas**-i) *noun* (*plural* **chassis** – *pronounced* **shas**-iz) **1** the frame, wheels and machinery of a car **2** an aeroplane's landing carriage

chaste *adjective* **1** pure, virtuous **2** modest, decent

chastely *adverb* in a pure, virtuous way

chasten *verb* **1** to make humble **2** to scold

chastened *adjective* humble or sorry, as a result of receiving a scolding

chastise *verb* to punish, especially by beating ♦ **chastisement** *noun*

chastity *noun* sexual purity and virtue

chat *verb* (**chatting, chatted**) to talk in an easy, friendly way ➤ *noun* a friendly conversation

chateau (*pronounced* **shat**-oh) *noun* (*plural* **chateaux** – *pronounced* **shat**-ohz) a French castle or country house

chat room *noun, computing* a place on the Internet where people can exchange messages

chat show *noun* a radio or TV programme in which personalities talk informally with their host

chattels *plural noun* movable possessions • **goods and chattels** personal possessions

chatter *verb* **1** to talk idly or rapidly; gossip **2** of teeth: to rattle together because of cold

chatterbox *noun* (*plural* **chatterboxes**) someone who talks a great deal

chatty *adjective* (**chattier, chattiest**) willing to talk, talkative ♦ **chattily** *adverb*

chauffeur (*pronounced* **shoh**-fer) *noun* someone employed to drive a car ➤ *verb* to act as a driver for someone else

chauvinism (*pronounced* **shoh**-vin-izm) *noun* **1** extreme nationalism or patriotism **2** sexism towards women ♦ **chauvinist** *noun* ♦ **chauvinistic** *adjective*

⊙ After Nicholas *Chauvin*, Napoleonic French soldier and keen patriot

cheap *adjective* **1** low in price, inexpensive **2** of little value, worthless **3** nasty or unfair: *a cheap trick*

cheapen *verb* to make cheap

cheaply *adverb* for a low price: *You can see that this skirt was cheaply made*

cheat *verb* **1** to deceive **2** to act dishonestly to gain an advantage ➤ *noun* **1** someone who cheats **2** a dishonest trick • **cheat on** *informal* to be unfaithful to (a sexual partner)

check *verb* **1** to bring to a stop **2** to hold back, restrain **3** to see if (a total etc) is correct or accurate **4** to see if (a machine etc) is in good condition or working properly ➤ *noun* **1** a sudden stop **2** a restraint **3** a test of correctness or accuracy **4** a square, eg on a draughtboard **5** a pattern of squares **6** US spelling of **cheque** • **check in** or **check out** to record your arrival at or departure from (a hotel etc)

❗ Do not confuse with: **cheque**

check box *noun, computing* a square on a screen which the user can click the mouse on to activate a feature

checked *adjective* patterned with squares

checkered another spelling of **chequered**

checkers another spelling of **chequers**

checkmate *noun, chess* a position from which the king cannot escape

checkout *noun* a place where payment is made in a supermarket

checkpoint *noun* a place, eg at a frontier, where vehicles, etc are stopped and travel documents checked

check-up *noun* a medical examination

cheek *noun* **1** the side of the face below the eye **2** a buttock **3** insolence, disrespectful behaviour

cheeky *adjective* (**cheekier, cheekiest**) impudent, insolent ♦ **cheekily** *adverb*

cheep *verb* to make a faint sound like a small bird ➤ *noun* the sound of a small bird

cheer *noun* a shout of approval or welcome ➤ *verb* **1** to shout approval **2** to encourage, urge on **3** to comfort, gladden • **cheer up** to make or become less gloomy

cheerful *adjective* happy, in good spirits ♦ **cheerfully** *adverb* ♦ **cheerfulness** *noun*

cheerio *interjection* goodbye!

cheerless *adjective* sad, gloomy

cheers *interjection* **1** good health! **2** regards, best wishes

cheery *adjective* (**cheerier, cheeriest**) lively and merry ♦ **cheerily** *adverb*

cheese *noun* a solid food made from milk

cheesecake *noun* a cake with a biscuit base topped with sweet cream cheese

cheesecloth *noun* loosely woven thin cotton cloth

cheesy *adjective* (**cheesier, cheesiest**) **1** tasting of cheese **2** of a smile: broad **3** *informal* inferior, cheap

cheetah *noun* a member of the cat family with a spotted coat, the fastest land mammal

chef *noun* a cook in a restaurant

chef d'oeuvre (*pronounced* shei **der**-vr) *noun* (*plural* **chefs d'oeuvre** *pronounced* shei **der**-vr) a masterpiece; a life's work

Cheka (*pronounced* **chei**-ka) *noun, history* a

secret police force formed in Russia in 1917 to investigate and punish anti-Bolshevik activities

chemical *adjective* relating to the reactions between elements etc ➤ *noun* a substance formed by or used in a chemical process

chemical weathering *noun, geography* the decomposition of rock caused by the action of sea water or rainwater, or by a chemical change within the rock (*compare with*: **mechanical weathering**)

chemise (*pronounced* she-**meez**) *noun* a woman's shirt or loose-fitting dress ⏱ Comes from French, ultimately from Latin *camisa* meaning 'shirt'

chemist *noun* **1** someone who studies chemistry **2** someone who makes up and sells medicines; a pharmacist **3** a shop selling medicines, toiletries, cosmetics, etc

chemistry *noun* the study of the elements and the ways they combine or react with each other

chemoreceptor (*pronounced* keem-oh-ri-**sep**-tor) *noun, biology* any sense organ that responds to stimulation by chemical substances

chemotaxis (*pronounced* keem-oh-**tak**-sis) *noun, biology* the movement of a whole organism in response to chemical stimulus

chemotherapy (*pronounced* keem-oh-**the**-rap-i) *noun* treatment of infectious diseases or cancer using chemical compounds

cheque or *US* **check** *noun* a written order to a banker to pay money from a bank account to another person

❗ Do not confuse with: **check**

cheque book *noun* a book containing cheques

cheque card *noun* a card issued to customers by a bank, guaranteeing payment of their cheques

chequered or **checkered** *adjective* **1** marked like a chessboard **2** partly good, partly bad: *a chequered career*

chequers or **checkers 1** *plural noun* a pattern of squares, eg on a chessboard **2** *singular noun* the game of draughts

cherish *verb* **1** to protect and treat with fondness or kindness **2** to keep in your mind or heart: *cherish a hope*

cherry *noun* (*plural* **cherries**) **1** a small bright-red fruit with a stone **2** the tree that produces this fruit

cherry-picking *noun* the practice of choosing only the best among assets, staff members, etc, and discarding the rest

cherub *noun* (*plural* **cherubs** or **cherubim** *pronounced* **cher**-u-bim or **cher**-yoo-bim) **1** an angel with a plump, childish face and body **2** a beautiful child

chervil *noun* a plant cultivated for its aromatic leaves that are used in cooking

chess *noun* a game for two players in which pieces are moved in turn on a board marked in alternate black and white squares

chessboard *noun* the board on which you play chess

chessman or **chesspiece** *noun* (*plural* **chessmen** or **chesspieces**) any of the little figures which you move on a chessboard when playing chess

chest *noun* **1** a large strong box **2** the part of the body between the neck and the stomach
• **chest of drawers** a piece of furniture fitted with a set of drawers

chesterfield *noun* a kind of sofa

chestnut *noun* **1** a reddish-brown edible nut (**sweet chestnut**), or the tree that produces it **2** a reddish-brown inedible nut (**horse chestnut**), or the tree that produces it **3** a reddish-brown horse **4** an old joke

chevron *noun* (*pronounced* **shev**-ron) a V-shape, eg on a badge or road sign

chew *verb* **1** to break up (food) with the teeth before swallowing **2** to reflect or ponder (on)

chewy *adjective* (**chewier, chewiest**) needing a lot of chewing

chiaroscuro (*pronounced* kyar-oh-**skoo**-roh) *noun* (*plural* **chiaroscuros**) *art* **1** the management of light and shade in a picture **2** a painting in black and white ⏱ Comes from Italian, from *chiaro* meaning 'clear' + *oscuro* meaning 'dark'

chic (*pronounced* sheek) *adjective* smart and fashionable ➤ *noun* style; fashionable elegance

chicane (*pronounced* shi-**kein**) *noun* on a motor-racing circuit: a series of sharp bends ⏱ Comes from French meaning 'quibble'

chicanery (*pronounced* shi-**kein**-e-ri) *noun* dishonest cleverness

chick *noun* **1** a chicken **2** *slang* a girl, a young woman

chicken *noun* **1** the young of birds, especially of domestic poultry **2** *informal* a coward ➤ *adjective, informal* cowardly

chickenfeed *noun* **1** food for poultry **2** something paltry or worthless

chicken-hearted *adjective* cowardly

chickenpox *noun* an infectious disease which causes red, itchy spots

chickpea *noun* a plant of the pea family with a yellow-brown edible seed

chicory *noun* **1** a plant with sharp-tasting leaves eaten in salads **2** its root, roasted and ground to mix with coffee

chide *verb* to scold with words

chief *adjective* **1** main, most important **2** largest ➤ *noun* **1** a leader or ruler **2** the head of a department, organization, etc

chiefly *adverb* mainly, for the most part

chieftain *noun* the head of a clan or tribe

chiffon (*pronounced* **shif**-on) *noun* a thin, flimsy material made of silk or nylon

chihuahua (*pronounced* chi-**wah**-wah) *noun* a breed of very small dog, originally from Mexico

chilblain *noun* a painful swelling on hands and feet, caused by constricted blood vessels in cold weather

child *noun* (*plural* **children**) **1** a young human being **2** a son or daughter: *She has two children* ⏱ Comes from Old English *cild*

childbirth *noun* the process of giving birth to a child

childhood *noun* the time of being a child

childish *adjective* **1** of or like a child **2** silly, immature ◆ **childishly** *adverb*

childlike *adjective* innocent

childminder *noun* a person who is paid to look after other people's children in his or her home

chili *noun* another spelling of **chilli**

chill *noun* **1** coldness **2** an illness that causes fever and shivering **3** lack of warmth or enthusiasm ➤ *adjective* cold ➤ *verb* **1** to make cold **2** to refrigerate

chilli or **chili** *noun* (*plural* **chillis** or **chillies**) **1** the hot-tasting pod of a kind of pepper, sometimes dried for cooking **2** a dish or sauce made with this

chilly *adjective* (**chillier, chilliest**) cold

chime *noun* **1** the sound of bells ringing **2 chimes** a set of bells, eg in a clock ➤ *verb* **1** to ring **2** of a clock: to strike

chimera (*pronounced* kai-**meer**-a or ki-**meer**-a) *noun* **1** a wild or impossible idea **2** a beast made up from various different animals **3** *biology* an organism made up of two or more genetically distinct tissues

chimney *noun* (*plural* **chimneys**) a passage allowing smoke or heated air to escape from a fire

chimneypot *noun* a metal or earthenware pipe placed at the top of a chimney

chimneystack *noun* **1** a tall chimney, eg in a factory **2** a number of chimneys built in a brick or stone structure on a roof

chimneysweep *noun* someone employed to clean chimneys

chimpanzee *noun* a type of African ape

chin *noun* the part of the face below the mouth

china *noun* **1** fine kind of earthenware; porcelain **2** articles made of this

china clay same as **kaolin**

chinchilla *noun* **1** a small S American mammal with a thick soft grey coat **2** the thick soft fur of this animal

chink *noun* **1** a narrow opening **2** the sound of coins etc striking together

chintz *noun* (*plural* **chintzes**) a cotton cloth with brightly coloured patterning

⏱ From a Hindi word for painted or multicoloured cotton

chip *verb* (**chipping, chipped**) to break or cut small pieces (from or off) ➤ *noun* **1** a small piece chipped off **2** a part damaged by chipping **3** a long thin piece of fried potato **4** *US* a potato or corn crisp **5** in football, golf: a short high kick or shot **6** in gambling: a plastic counter used as a money token **7** *see* **integrated circuit**

chip and PIN *noun* a system where the user of a credit or debit card types in a secret number on a device in a shop

chipboard *noun* board made from compressed wood chips

chipmunk *noun* a kind of small N American squirrel

chipolata *noun* a type of small sausage

chiropodist (*pronounced* ki-**rop**-o-dist) *noun* someone who treats minor disorders and diseases of the feet

chiropody (*pronounced* ki-**rop**-o-di) *noun* the profession of caring for people's feet and treating minor foot problems such as corns

chiropractic (*pronounced* kai-ro-**prak**-tik) *noun, medicine* a method of treating pain by manual adjustment of the spinal column, etc, so as to release pressure on the nerves ◆ **chiropractor** *noun*

chirp or **chirrup** *verb* of a bird: to make a sharp, shrill sound

chirpy *adjective* merry, cheerful

chisel *noun* a metal tool to cut or hollow out wood, stone, etc ➤ *verb* (**chiselling, chiselled**) to cut with a chisel

chit *noun* **1** a short note **2** a child, a young woman: *chit of a girl*

chit-chat *noun* gossip, talk ➤ *verb* to gossip, talk

chitin (*pronounced* **kai**-tin) *noun, biology* a complex carbohydrate substance that strengthens the tough outer covering of insects and crustaceans and the cell walls of many fungi ◆ **chitinous** *adjective* ⏱ Comes from French *chitine*, ultimately from Greek *chiton* meaning 'tunic'

chivalrous (*pronounced* **shiv**-al-rus) *adjective* gallant, showing traditional good manners especially to women

chivalry (*pronounced* **shiv**-al-ri) *noun* **1** kindness, especially towards women or the weak **2** *history* the standard of behaviour expected of knights in medieval times

chive *noun* an onion-like herb used in cooking

chlamydia (*pronounced* kla-**mid**-i-a) *noun* a sexually transmitted disease

chlorate *noun, chemistry* a salt containing the ion ClO_3^-

chloride *noun, chemistry* **1** a compound which contains chlorine and another element **2** a salt or ester of hydrochloric acid

chlorinate *verb* **1** *chemistry* to cause (an organic compound) to combine with chlorine **2** to add chlorine to ◆ **chlorination** *noun*

chlorinated *adjective* mixed with chlorine or containing chlorine

chlorine (*pronounced* **klaw**-reen) *noun, chemistry* (symbol **Cl**) a yellowish-green gas with a sharp smell, obtained from deposits of sodium chloride or potassium chloride and from sea water, and widely used as a disinfectant and bleach

chlorofluorocarbon *noun, chemistry* (*abbrev* **CFC**) a compound of chlorine, fluorine and carbon, formerly used as an aerosol propellant and refrigerant, but now banned by many countries as a result of its damaging effects on the ozone layer

chloroform *noun, chemistry* a colourless liquid whose vapour causes unconsciousness if inhaled

chlorophyll *noun* a green pigment in some plants and algae that traps light energy to use in photosynthesis

chloroplast *noun* a tiny structure in the cells of green algae and green plants that contains chlorophyll

chock-a-block *adjective* completely full or congested

chockfull *adjective* completely full

chocolate *noun* **1** a sweet made from the seeds of the cacao tree **2** a drink made from these seeds ➤ *adjective* dark brown in colour

chocolatey *adjective* tasting of chocolate

choice *noun* **1** the act or power of choosing **2** something chosen **3** a variety of things available: *a wide choice of goods* ➤ *adjective* of a high quality: *choice vegetables*

choir *noun* **1** a group or society of singers **2** a part of a church where a choir sits ☉ Comes from Latin *chorus* meaning 'a band of singers and dancers'

choke *verb* **1** to stop or partly stop the breathing of **2** to block or clog (a pipe etc) **3** to have your breathing stopped or interrupted, eg by smoke ➤ *noun* a valve in a petrol engine which controls the inflow of air

cholera (*pronounced* **kol**-e-ra) *noun* an infectious intestinal disease, causing severe vomiting and diarrhoea

choleric *adjective* irritable, bad-tempered

cholesterol (*pronounced* ko-**lest**-er-ol) *noun* a substance found in body cells which carries fats through the bloodstream

chomp *verb, informal* to munch noisily

choose *verb* (**choosing, chose, chosen**) **1** to select and take from two or several things: *Choose whichever book you like* **2** to decide, prefer to: *We chose to leave before the film began*

choosy *adjective* (**choosier, choosiest**) difficult to please; fussy

chop *verb* (**chopping, chopped**) **1** to cut into small pieces **2** to cut with a sudden blow ➤ *noun* **1** a chopping blow **2** a slice of meat containing a bone: *a mutton chop* • **chop and change** to keep changing

chopper *noun* **1** a knife or axe for chopping **2** *informal* a helicopter

choppy *adjective* (**choppier, choppiest**) of the sea: not calm, having small waves

chopsticks *plural noun* a pair of small sticks of wood, ivory, etc used for eating Chinese food

☉ Literally 'quick sticks', from Pidgin English *chop* for 'quick'

choral *adjective* sung by or written for a choir

chord *noun* **1** a musical sound made by playing several notes together **2** *maths* a straight line joining any two points on a curve

☉ Meaning 1 of **chord** comes from the word 'accord', while meaning 2 comes from the Greek *chorde* meaning 'a string'. From this you might expect meaning 1 to be spelt without an 'h', but through the influence of meaning 2 their spellings have become identical.

❗ Do not confuse with: **cord**

chordate *noun, biology* any animal that has a skeletal rod (a **notochord**) supporting its body at some stage of its development

chore *noun* **1** a dull, boring job **2** (**chores**) housework

choreographer (*pronounced* kor-ei-**og**-ra-fer) *noun* a person who designs dances and dance steps, usually for a team of dancers eg in a ballet or a musical ◆ **choreograph** *verb*

choreography (*pronounced* kor-ei-**og**-ra-fi) *noun* the arrangement of dancing and dance steps

chorister *noun* a member of a choir

choroid (*pronounced* **kaw**-roid) *noun* a layer of coloured cells in front of the retina in the eye

choropleth map (*pronounced* **ko**-ro-pleth) *noun* a map in which colour or shading indicate eg different populations or temperatures in an area, by having darker colour for higher figures

chortle *verb* to laugh, chuckle

chorus *noun* (*plural* **choruses**) **1** a band of singers and dancers **2** a choir or choral group **3** a part of a song repeated after each verse

chose past tense of **choose**

chosen past participle of **choose**

chrism noun consecrated oil used in some religious ceremonies

christen verb 1 to baptize in the name of Christ 2 to give a name to

christening noun, Christianity the ceremony of baptism

Christian noun a believer in Christianity ▷ adjective of Christianity

Christianity noun the religion which follows the teachings of Christ

Christian name noun a first or personal name

Christmas noun an annual Christian holiday or festival, in memory of the birth of Christ, held on 25 December

Christmas Eve noun 24 December

Christmassy adjective typical of, or suitable for, Christmas

Christmas tree noun an evergreen tree hung with lights, decorations and gifts at Christmas

chromatic adjective 1 of colours 2 coloured 3 music of or written in a scale in which each note is separated from the next by a semitone

chromatin noun, biology in a cell nucleus: the loose network of thread-like material, composed of DNA, RNA and proteins, which becomes organized into chromosomes at the time of cell division

chromatography noun, chemistry a technique for separating the components of a mixture in order to analyse them

chrome noun chromium, especially when it is used as a silvery plating for other metals

chromium noun, chemistry (symbol **Cr**) a hard metallic element that is resistant to corrosion, used in electroplating and to make stainless steel

chromosome noun, biology a rod-like part of a cell that contains, in the form of DNA, all the genetic information needed for the development of the cell and the whole organism

chronic adjective 1 of a disease: long-term and progressing slowly (compare with: **acute**) 2 informal very bad ◆ **chronically** adverb

chronicle noun a record of events in the order they happened ▷ verb to write down events in order ◆ **chronicler** noun

chrono- or **chron-** prefix of or relating to time: chronological ⊕ Comes from Greek chronos meaning 'time'

chronological adjective arranged in the order of the time of happening ◆ **chronologically** adverb

chronology noun the arrangement of events in the order they occurred

chronometer noun an instrument for measuring time

chrysalis (pronounced **kri**-sa-lis) noun (plural chrysalises) an insect (especially a butterfly or moth) in its early stage of life, with no wings and encased in a soft cocoon

chrysanthemum (pronounced kri-**san**-the-mum or kri-**zan**-the-mum) noun a type of colourful garden flower with a large bushy head

chubby adjective (**chubbier, chubbiest**) plump

chuck verb 1 to throw, toss 2 to pat gently under the chin • **chuck out** informal 1 to throw away, get rid of 2 to expel

chuckle noun a quiet laugh ▷ verb to laugh quietly

chuffed adjective, informal very pleased

chug verb (**chugging, chugged**) of a vehicle: to move along making a thudding noise

chum noun, informal a close friend

chummy adjective (**chummier, chummiest**) very friendly

chump noun 1 informal an idiot 2 a piece of lamb or mutton cut from the loin • **off your chump** informal off your head; mad

chunk noun a thick piece

chunky adjective (**chunkier, chunkiest**) heavy, thick

church noun (plural **churches**) 1 a building for public, especially Christian, worship 2 any group of people who meet together for worship

churchyard noun a burial ground next to a church

churlish adjective bad-mannered, rude

churn noun a machine for making butter from milk ▷ verb 1 to make (butter) in a churn 2 to shake or stir about violently: My stomach was churning

chute (pronounced shoot) noun 1 a sloping trough for sending water, parcels, etc to a lower level 2 a sloping structure for children to slide down, with steps for climbing back up

chutney noun (plural **chutneys**) a pickle made with vegetables or fruit and vinegar

chutzpah (pronounced **khoot**-spa) noun self-assurance bordering on rudeness

chyle (pronounced kail) noun, biology a milky fluid containing fats that have been absorbed from the small intestine during digestion

chyme (pronounced kaim) noun, biology partially digested food that passes into the duodenum and small intestine from the stomach

CIA abbreviation Central Intelligence Agency, a US government organization that collects secret political, military, etc information about other countries

ciabatta (pronounced cha-**bat**-a) noun (a loaf of) Italian bread with an open texture, made with olive oil

CID abbreviation Criminal Investigation Department, the police department in the UK

-cide *suffix* forms words describing murder or killing, or a person or thing that murders or kills: *suicide/homicide/insecticide* ⊙ Comes from Latin *caedere* meaning 'to kill'

cider *noun* an alcoholic drink made from fermented apple juice

cigar *noun* a roll of tobacco leaves for smoking

cigarette *noun* a tube of fine tobacco enclosed in thin paper

ciliary muscle *noun* a muscle that controls the curvature of the lens of the eye

cilium *noun* (*plural* **cilia**) a hair-like growth found in certain cells and micro-organisms, used eg for movement or the removal of foreign bodies

cinder *noun* a burnt-out piece of coal

cine camera *noun* a hand-held camera for making films

cinema *noun* **1** a place where films are shown **2** films as an art form or industry

cinematography *noun* the art of making motion pictures ♦ **cinematographer** *noun*

cinnamon *noun* a yellowish-brown spice obtained from tree bark

cipher (*pronounced* **sai**-fer) *noun* **1** a secret writing, a code **2** nought, zero **3** someone of no importance

⊙ Originally meaning 'zero' and later 'number', because of the early use of numbers in encoded documents

circa *preposition* about (in dates): *circa 1900*

circadian *adjective, biology* relating to a biological rhythm that is more or less on a 24-hour cycle, eg the pattern of sleeping and waking in adult humans ⊙ Comes from Latin *circa* meaning 'around' + *dies* meaning 'day'

circle *noun* **1** a figure formed from an endless curved line **2** something in the form of a circle; a ring **3** a society or group of people **4** a tier of seats in a theatre etc ▸ *verb* **1** to enclose in a circle **2** to move round in a circle

circuit *noun* **1** a movement in a circle **2** a connected group of places, events, etc: *the American tennis circuit* **3** the path of an electric current

circuitous (*pronounced* sir-**kyoo**-i-tus) *adjective* not direct, roundabout: *by a circuitous route*

circular *adjective* round, like a circle ▸ *noun* a letter sent round to a number of people

circular function *noun, maths* a trigonometric function

circulate *verb* **1** to move round **2** to send round: *circulate a memo*

circulation *noun* **1** the act of circulating **2** the movement of the blood through the body **3** the

total sales of a newspaper or magazine

circulatory system *noun* the system that circulates blood through the body; the heart and blood vessels

circum- or **circu-** *prefix* round: *circumnavigate/circuit* ⊙ Comes from Latin *circum* meaning 'all around'

circumcentre *noun, maths* the centre of a circle circumscribing another figure

circumcircle *noun, maths* a circle drawn round another figure, especially round a triangle and touching all its points

circumcise *verb* **1** to cut away the foreskin of the penis, for medical or religious reasons **2** to cut away the clitoris, especially as a religious rite ♦ **circumcision** *noun*

circumduction *noun* the circular movement of a limb around a joint

circumference *noun, maths* **1** the outside line of a circle or closed curve **2** the length of this line

circumflex *noun* (*plural* **circumflexes**) in some languages, eg French: a mark placed over a vowel, eg ô, û, as an indication of pronunciation or the omission of a letter formerly pronounced

circumlocution *noun* a roundabout way of saying something

circumnavigate *verb* to sail or fly right round something ♦ **circumnavigator** *noun*

circumscribe *verb* **1** to draw a line round **2** *maths* to draw (a figure) around another figure so that they touch at as many points as possible but do not intersect (*compare with*: **inscribe**)

circumscribed *adjective, maths* of a figure: enclosing another figure

circumscription *noun* **1** a limitation **2** an inscription or line running round something

circumspect *adjective* wary, cautious

circumspection *noun* caution

circumstance *noun* **1** a condition of time, place, etc which affects a person, an action or an event **2** (**circumstances**) the state of someone's financial affairs

circumstantial *adjective* of evidence: pointing to a conclusion without giving absolute proof

circumstantiate *verb* to prove by giving details

circumvent *verb* **1** to get round (a difficulty) **2** to outwit ♦ **circumvention** *noun*

circus *noun* (*plural* **circuses**) a travelling company of clowns, acrobats, etc

cirque (*pronounced* sirk) another word for a **corrie**

cirrhosis (*pronounced* si-**roh**-sis) *noun, medicine* a disease of the liver

cirrocumulus (*pronounced* si-roh-**kyoo**-myuw-lus) *noun* (*plural* **cirrocumuli** – *pronounced* si-roh-**kyoo**-myuw-lai), *meteorology* a type of high cloud which consists of small masses of white clouds that form a rippled pattern

cirrostratus (*pronounced* si-roh-**strah**-tus) *noun* (*plural* **cirrostrati** – *pronounced* si-roh-**strah**-tai), *meteorology* a type of high cloud which forms a thin whitish layer

cirrus (*pronounced* **si**-rus) *noun* (*plural* **cirri** – *pronounced* **si**-rai), a fleecy kind of cloud

cissy *noun* (*plural* **cissies**), *informal* an effeminate person

cistern *noun* a tank for storing water

citadel *noun* a fortress within a city

citation *noun* **1** something quoted **2** a summons to appear in court **3** official recognition of an achievement or action

cite *verb* **1** to quote as an example or as proof **2** to summon to appear in court ⏱ Comes from Latin *citare* meaning 'to call'

❗ Do not confuse with: **sight** and **site**

citizen *noun* **1** someone who lives in a city or town **2** a native of a country, or a naturalized member of it

citizenry *noun* the inhabitants of a city or state

citizenship *noun* **1** the rights or state of being a citizen **2** the duties and responsibilities of being a citizen

citrate *noun, chemistry* a salt or ester of citric acid

citric acid *noun, chemistry* a sharp-tasting organic acid found in citrus fruits

citrin *noun* bioflavonoid

citron *noun* a fruit similar to a lemon

citrus fruit *noun* any of a group of fruits including the orange, lemon and lime

city *noun* (*plural* **cities**) **1** a large town **2** a town with a cathedral **3** (**the City**) the part of London regarded as the centre of British financial affairs

civic *adjective* relating to a city or citizens

civics *singular noun* the study of people's duties as citizens

civil *adjective* **1** relating to a community **2** non-military, civilian **3** polite

civil engineer *noun* an engineer who plans bridges, roads, etc

civilian *noun* someone who is not in the armed forces ➤ *adjective* non-military

civility *noun* politeness, good manners

civilization or **civilisation** *noun* **1** making or becoming civilized **2** life under a civilized system **3** a particular culture: *a prehistoric civilization*

civilize or **civilise** *verb* to bring (a people) under a regular system of laws, education, etc

civilized or **civilised** *adjective* living under a system of laws, education, etc; not savage

civil law *noun* law concerned with citizens' rights, not criminal acts (*compare with*: **criminal law**)

civil liberties *plural noun* the right to exercise personal freedom of thought, speech, action, etc

civil list *noun* the expenses of the royal household

civil marriage *noun* a marriage which does not take place in church

civil rights *noun* the rights of a citizen to freedom and equality, regardless of race, religion, sex or sexuality

civil servant *noun* someone who works in the civil service

civil service *noun* the paid administrative officials of the country, excluding the armed forces

civil war *noun* war between citizens of the same country

CJD *abbreviation, medicine* Creutzfeldt-Jakob disease, a rare degenerative brain disease, characterized by dementia, wasting of muscle tissue and various neurological abnormalities

Cl *symbol, chemistry* chlorine

cl *abbreviation* centilitre(s)

clad *adjective, literary* clothed: *clad in leather from head to toe*

claim *verb* **1** to demand as a right **2** to state as a truth; assert (that) ➤ *noun* an act of claiming

claimant *noun* someone who makes a claim

clairvoyant *adjective* able to see into the future, or to contact the spirit world ➤ *noun* someone with clairvoyant powers
 ◆ **clairvoyance** *noun*

clam *noun* a large shellfish with two shells hinged together

clamber *verb* to climb awkwardly or with difficulty

clammy *adjective* (**clammier, clammiest**) moist and sticky

clamorous *adjective* noisy

clamour *noun* a loud, continuous noise or outcry ➤ *verb* **1** to cry aloud **2** to make a loud demand (for)

clamp *noun* a piece of metal, wood, etc used to fasten things together ➤ *verb* to bind with a clamp • **clamp down on** to suppress firmly

clan *noun* **1** a number of families with the same surname, traditionally under a single chieftain **2** a sect, a clique

⏱ From Scottish Gaelic *clann* meaning 'children'

clandestine (*pronounced* klan-**des**-tin) *adjective* hidden, secret, underhand

clang *verb* to make a loud, deep ringing sound ➤ *noun* a loud, deep ring

clank *noun* a sound like that made by metal hitting metal ➤ *verb* to make this sound

clansman or **clanswoman** *noun* (*plural*

clansmen or **clanswomen**), a member of a clan

clap *noun* **1** the noise made by striking together two things, especially the hands **2** a burst of sound, especially thunder ➤ *verb* (**clapping, clapped**) **1** to strike noisily together **2** to strike the hands together to show approval **3** *informal* to put suddenly, throw: *clap in jail*

clapper *noun* the tongue of a bell

claptrap *noun* meaningless words, nonsense

claret *noun* a type of red wine

clarify *verb* (**clarifies, clarifying, clarified**) **1** to make clear and understandable **2** to make (butter, fat) clear and pure by heating

clarinet *noun* a musical wind instrument, usually made of wood

clarinettist *noun* someone who plays the clarinet

clarion *noun, old* **1** a kind of trumpet **2** a shrill, rousing noise

clarion call *noun* a clear call to action

clarity *noun* clearness

clash *noun* (*plural* **clashes**) **1** a loud noise made by striking swords etc **2** a disagreement, a fight ➤ *verb* **1** to bang noisily together **2** to disagree **3** of events: to take place at the same time **4** of two colours etc: not to look well together

clasp *noun* **1** a hook or pin for fastening: *a hair clasp* **2** a handshake **3** an embrace ➤ *verb* **1** to hold closely; grasp **2** to fasten

class *noun* (*plural* **classes**) **1** a rank or order of people or things **2** a group of schoolchildren or students taught together **3** *biology* any of the groups, eg mammals, into which a phylum in the animal kingdom or a division in the plant kingdom is divided, which is in turn subdivided into orders ➤ *verb* **1** to place in a class **2** to arrange in some order

classic *noun* **1** a great book or other work of art **2** something typical and influential of its kind **3** (**classics**) the study of ancient Greek and Latin literature ➤ *adjective* **1** excellent **2** standard, typical of its kind: *a classic example* **3** simple and elegant in style: *a classic black dress*

classical *adjective* **1** of a classic or the classics **2** of music: serious, not light

classification *noun* **1** the activity of arranging things into classes or categories **2** the label or name that you give something in order to indicate its class or category

classify *verb* (**classifies, classifying, classified**) **1** to arrange in classes **2** to put into a class or category **3** to declare (information) to be secret ♦ **classified** *adjective*

class interval *noun, statistics* any of the subsets that represent a range of values of a variable

classmate *noun* a fellow pupil or student in your class

classroom *noun* a room in a school or college where lessons take place

classy *adjective* (**classier, classiest**) elegant, stylish

clatter *noun* a noise of plates etc banged together

clause *noun* **1** *grammar* a group of words that contains a subject and its related verb **2** a part of a will, act of parliament, etc

claustrophobia (*pronounced* klos-tro-**foh**-bi-a) *noun* an abnormal fear of enclosed spaces

claustrophobic *adjective* **1** suffering from or affected by claustrophobia: *She can't go in because she'll get claustrophobic* **2** causing feelings of anxiety related to being in an enclosed space or to feeling trapped or enclosed in some other way: *a claustrophobic little room*

clavichord (*pronounced* **klav**-i-kawrd) *noun* an early keyboard instrument with a soft tone

clavicle *noun, anatomy* in vertebrates: either of two short slender bones linking the shoulder-blades with the top of the breastbone

claw *noun* **1** an animal's or bird's foot with hooked nails **2** a hooked nail on one of these feet ➤ *verb* to scratch or tear

clay *noun* soft, sticky earth, often used to make pottery, bricks, etc ♦ **clayey** *adjective*

clean *adjective* **1** free from dirt; pure **2** neat, complete: *a clean break* **3** completely: *got clean away* ➤ *verb* to make clean; free from dirt ♦ **cleanly** *adverb* (meaning 2)

cleaner *noun* **1** someone employed to clean a building etc **2** a substance which cleans

cleanliness (*pronounced* **klen**-li-nes) *noun* the quality of being free from dirt

cleanse (*pronounced* klenz) *verb* to make clean

cleanser *noun* a substance that cleanses, especially the skin

clear *adjective* **1** bright, undimmed **2** free from mist or cloud: *clear sky* **3** transparent **4** free from difficulty or obstructions **5** easy to see, hear or understand **6** evident, obvious **7** after deductions and charges have been made: *clear profit* **8** without a stain **9** without touching: *clear of the rocks* ➤ *verb* **1** to make clear **2** to empty **3** to free from blame **4** to leap over without touching **5** of the sky: to become bright ● **clear out** or **clear off** to go away ♦ **clearness** *noun* (adjective, meanings 1, 2, 3, 4 and 5)

clearance *noun* **1** the activity of getting rid of all the things which are in a certain place so that a new start can be made: *a clearance sale* (= a cut-price sale in a shop to get rid of all the old stock)/ *the Highland Clearances* (= the removal of tenant farmers from the Scottish Highlands by landowners in the 19th century) **2** (**the Clearances**) see **Highland Clearances 3**

permission to do something: *receive official clearance for the project*

clear-cut *adjective* distinct, obvious

clearing *noun* land free of trees

clearly *adverb* **1** obviously **2** in a clear way

cleavage *noun* **1** splitting **2** the way in which two things are split or divided **3** the hollow between a woman's breasts

cleave *verb* (**cleaving, clove** or **cleft** or **cleaved, cloven** or **cleft** or **cleaved**) **1** to divide, split **2** to crack **3** to stick (to)

cleaver *noun* a heavy knife for splitting meat carcasses etc

clef *noun* a musical sign, 𝄞 (**treble clef**) or 𝄢 (**bass clef**), placed on a stave to fix the pitch of the notes

cleft *noun* an opening made by splitting; a crack ➤ *verb* past form of **cleave**

cleft palate *noun* a deformity in the roof of the mouth, present in some people at birth

clemency *noun* readiness to forgive; mercy

clement *adjective* mild; merciful

clementine (*pronounced* **klem**-en-teen or **klem**-en-tain) *noun* a citrus fruit like a small orange

clench *verb* to press firmly together: *clenching his teeth*

clergy *plural noun* the ministers of the Christian church

clergyman or **clergywoman** *noun* (*plural* **clergymen** or **clergywomen**) a Christian minister

cleric *noun* a member of the clergy

clerical *adjective* **1** relating to office work **2** of the clergy

clericalism *noun* the power or influence of the church

clerihew *noun* a humorous poem about a famous person, consisting of two short couplets

⊕ Named after E *Clerihew* Bentley (1875–1956), the English journalist and novelist who invented it

clerk *noun* an office worker who writes letters, keeps accounts, etc ➤ *verb* to act as clerk

clever *adjective* **1** quick in learning and understanding **2** intelligent, skilful: *a clever answer* ♦ **cleverly** *adverb*

cliché (*pronounced* **klee**-shei) *noun* an idea, phrase, etc that has been used too much and has little meaning

⊕ From a French word for 'stereotype', in the sense of a fixed printing plate

click *noun* a short sharp sound like a clock's tick ➤ *verb* **1** to make this sound **2** *computing* to press and release a button on a mouse to select an option on the screen

client *noun* **1** a customer of a shop etc **2** someone who goes to a lawyer etc for advice **3** *computing* a program used to contact and download data from a server

clientele (*pronounced* klee-en-**tel** or klai-en-**tel**) *noun* the customers of a lawyer, shopkeeper, etc

cliff *noun* a very steep, rocky slope, especially by the sea

cliffhanger *noun* **1** a story that keeps you in suspense until the end **2** the ending of an episode of a serial story which leaves the audience in suspense

climacteric (*pronounced* klai-**mak**-te-rik or klai-mak-**te**-rik) *noun, biology* **1** in living organisms: a period of changes, especially those associated with the menopause in women, and with a reduction in sexual desire in men **2** in plants: an increase in respiration rate associated with the ripening of fruit

climactic *adjective* most important or intense, of the climax: *the climactic moment of the play*

climate *noun* **1** the weather conditions of a particular area **2** general condition or situation: *in the present cultural climate* ♦ **climatic** *adjective* (meaning 1)

climate change *noun* change in the Earth's climate, especially global warming caused by the greenhouse effect

climax *noun* (*plural* **climaxes**) **1** the point of greatest interest or importance in a situation **2** a sexual orgasm

climax vegetation *noun, geography* the final stage of the development of vegetation in a particular area, when it remains relatively stable under the prevailing environmental conditions

climb *verb* **1** to go to the top of **2** to go up using hands and feet **3** to slope upward ➤ *noun* an act of climbing

climber *noun* **1** someone who climbs **2** a plant which climbs up walls etc

clinch *verb* **1** to grasp tightly **2** to settle (an argument, bargain, etc) ➤ *noun* (*plural* **clinches**) **1** *boxing* a position in which the boxers hold each other with their arms **2** a passionate embrace

clincher *noun* the thing which settles an argument, bargain, etc

cline *noun, biology* a gradual change in the form of an animal or plant species across different parts of its geographical or environmental range

cling *verb* (**clinging, clung**) to stick or hang on (to) ♦ **clingy** *adjective* (**clingier, clingiest**)

clingfilm *noun* thin transparent plastic material used to wrap food

clinic *noun* a place or part of a hospital where a particular kind of treatment is given

clinical *adjective* **1** of a clinic **2** based on

observation: *clinical medicine* **3** objective, cool and unemotional: *a clinical approach*

clinically *adverb* **1** according to medical diagnosis: *clinically depressed* **2** as an object of medical observation: *His skin condition is clinically interesting*

clink *noun* a ringing sound of knocked glasses etc ➤ *verb* to make such a sound

clip *verb* (**clipping, clipped**) **1** to cut (off) **2** to fasten with a clip ➤ *noun* **1** something clipped off **2** a small fastener **3** *informal* a smart blow

clipboard *noun* **1** a firm board with a clip at the top for holding paper, which can be used as a portable writing surface **2** *computing* a temporary store for text or graphics being transferred between documents or programs

clipper *noun* **1** a fast-sailing ship **2** (**clippers**) large scissors for clipping

clique (*pronounced* kleek) *noun* a small group of people who help each other but keep others at a distance

clitoris (*pronounced* **klit**-or-is) *noun* (*plural* **clitorises**), *anatomy* a small highly sensitive structure at the front of the external female sex organs ♦ **clitoral** *adjective*

cloaca (*pronounced* kloh-**ei**-ka) *noun* (*plural* **cloacae** – *pronounced* kloh-**ei**-see or kloh-**ei**-kai) in many animals (but not mammals): a part of the gut into which the alimentary canal and the urinary and reproductive systems open ♦ **cloacal** *adjective* ① Comes from Latin meaning 'sewer'

cloak *noun* **1** a loose outer garment with no sleeves **2** something which hides: *under the cloak of darkness* ➤ *verb* **1** to cover as with a cloak **2** to hide

cloakroom *noun* a place where coats, hats, etc may be left for a time

cloche (*pronounced* klosh) *noun* a transparent frame for protecting plants

clock *noun* a machine for measuring time • **clock in** or **clock out** to record your time of arrival at, or departure from, work

clockwise *adjective* turning or moving in the same direction as the hands of a clock

clockwork *adjective* worked by machinery such as that of a clock • **like clockwork** smoothly, without difficulties

clod *noun* **1** a thick lump of turf **2** a stupid man

clodhopper *noun* a stupid, clumsy person ♦ **clodhopping** *adjective*

clog *noun* a shoe with a wooden sole ➤ *verb* (**clogging, clogged**) to block (pipes etc)

cloister *noun* **1** a covered-in walk in a monastery or convent **2** a monastery or convent ♦ **cloistered** *adjective* **1** shut up in a monastery etc **2** sheltered

clone *noun* **1** *biology* any of a group of

genetically identical cells or organisms produced by asexual reproduction from a single ancestor **2** *genetics* any of a large number of identical copies of a gene produced by genetic engineering **3** *computing* a copy of a software, etc ➤ *verb* **1** *biology* to produce a set of identical cells or organisms from (a single parent cell or organism) **2** *genetics* to produce many identical copies of (a gene) by genetic engineering

close[1] (*pronounced* klohs) *adjective* **1** near in time, place, etc **2** shut up, with no opening **3** without fresh air, stuffy **4** narrow, confined **5** mean **6** secretive **7** beloved, very dear: *a close friend* **8** decided by a small amount: *a close contest* ➤ *noun* **1** a street with houses that is a dead end **2** a narrow passage off a street **3** the gardens, walks, etc near a cathedral

close[2] (*pronounced* klohz) *verb* **1** to shut **2** to finish **3** to come closer to and fight (with) ➤ *noun* the end

closed *adjective, maths* **1** of a curve: having no end points, as in a circle **2** of a set: having as members the results of an operation (eg addition) on other members of the set

closed-circuit television *noun* (*abbrev* **CCTV**) a system of television cameras and receivers for use in shops etc

closed interval *noun, maths* an interval that includes its end points

closed skill *noun* a physical skill that is not affected by external forces, eg swimming

close-knit *adjective* of a group, community, etc: closely bound together

closely *adverb* **1** carefully: *observe something closely/listen closely* **2** strongly, intimately: *He was closely involved in these activities* **3** in a way that brings things close together: *objects packed closely together in a box*

closet *noun, US* a cupboard ➤ *verb* to take into a room for a private conference • **closeted with** in private conference with

close-up *noun* a film or photograph taken very near the subject

clostridium *noun* (*plural* **clostridia**), *biology* a rod-shaped bacterium that occurs in soil and in the digestive tract of humans and animals, and which can cause botulism and tetanus ① Comes from Greek *kloster* meaning 'spindle'

closure *noun* the act of closing

clot *noun* **1** a lump that forms in blood, cream, etc **2** *informal* an idiot ➤ *verb* (**clotting, clotted**) to form into clots

cloth *noun* **1** woven material of cotton, wool, silk, etc **2** a piece of this

clothe *verb* **1** to put clothes on **2** to provide with clothes **3** to cover

clothes *plural noun* things worn to cover the body and limbs, eg shirt, trousers, skirt

clothing *noun* clothes

cloud *noun* **1** a mass of tiny drops of water or ice floating in the sky **2** a mass of anything: *a cloud of bees* ➤ *verb* to become dim or blurred ♦ **clouded** *adjective* ♦ **cloudless** *adjective* (noun, meaning 1)

cloudburst *noun* a sudden heavy fall of rain

cloud chamber *noun, physics* a device for detecting the movement of charged subatomic particles through a gas

cloud forest *noun, geography* a mountain forest that is continuously covered by cloud

cloudy *adjective* (**cloudier, cloudiest**) **1** darkened with clouds **2** not clear or transparent

clout *noun, informal* **1** a blow **2** influence, power ➤ *verb, informal* to hit

clove[1] *noun* **1** a flower bud of the clove tree, used as a spice **2** a small section of a bulb of garlic

> ⊙ The spice gets its name from French *clou* meaning 'nail' because of its shape

clove[2] past tense of **cleave**

cloven past participle of **cleave**

cloven-hoofed *adjective* having a divided hoof like an ox, sheep, etc

clover *noun* a field plant with leaves usually in three parts • **in clover** in luxury

clown *noun* **1** a comedian with a painted face and comical clothes in a circus **2** a fool

clowning *noun* silly or comical behaviour

clownish *adjective* like a clown; awkward

cloy *verb* of something sweet: to become unpleasant when too much is taken

cloying *adjective* over-sweet, sickly

club *noun* **1** a heavy stick **2** a stick used to hit the ball in golf **3** a group of people who meet for social events etc **4** the place where these people meet **5** a nightclub **6** (**clubs**) one of the four suits in playing-cards ➤ *verb* (**clubbing, clubbed**) **1** to beat with a club **2** to go to nightclubs ♦ **clubber** *noun* ♦ **clubbing** *noun* • **club together** to put money into a joint fund for some purpose

cluck *noun* a sound like that made by a hen ➤ *verb* to make this sound

clue *noun* a sign or piece of evidence that helps to solve a mystery

clump *noun* a cluster of trees or shrubs ➤ *verb* to walk heavily

clumsy *adjective* (**clumsier, clumsiest**) **1** awkward in movement or actions **2** tactless, thoughtless: *a clumsy apology* ♦ **clumsily** *adverb*

clung past form of **cling**

cluster *noun* **1** a bunch of fruit etc **2** a crowd ➤ *verb* to group together in clusters

clutch *verb* **1** to hold firmly **2** to seize, grasp ➤ *noun* (*plural* **clutches**) **1** a grasp **2** part of a car

engine used for changing gears **3** a brood of chickens

clutter *noun* **1** a muddled or disordered collection of things **2** disorder, confusion, untidiness ➤ *verb* **1** to crowd together untidily **2** (often **clutter up**) to fill or cover in an untidy, disordered way

Cm *symbol, chemistry* curium

cm *abbreviation* centimetre(s)

CND *abbreviation* Campaign for Nuclear Disarmament, a British organization whose aim is to persuade countries to get rid of nuclear weapons

CO *abbreviation* **1** carbon monoxide **2** Commanding Officer

Co[1] *abbreviation* **1** Company **2** County

Co[2] *symbol, chemistry* cobalt

co- also **col-, com-, con-, cor-** *prefix* **1** joint, working with, together with: *co-author/co-driver/connect/compound/collision/correspond* **2** sometimes just gives extra emphasis to a word: *corroborate/commemorate* ⊙ Comes from Latin *cum* meaning 'with'

c/o *abbreviation* care of

coach *noun* (*plural* **coaches**) **1** a bus for long-distance travel **2** a closed, four-wheeled horse carriage **3** a railway carriage **4** trainer or instructor ➤ *verb* to train or help to prepare for an examination, sports contest, etc

coagulate (*pronounced* koh-**ag**-yuw-leit) *verb* to thicken; clot

coal *noun* a black substance dug out of the earth and used for burning, making gas, etc

coalesce (*pronounced* koh-a-**les**) *verb* to come together and unite

coalfield *noun* an area where there is coal to be mined

coal gas *noun* the mixture of gases obtained from coal, used for lighting and heating

coalition (*pronounced* koh-a-**li**-shun) *noun* a joining together of different parts or groups

coalmine *noun* a mine from which coal is dug ♦ **coalminer** *noun*

coal tar *noun* a thick black liquid obtained as a by-product during the manufacture of coke

coarse *adjective* **1** not fine in texture; rough, harsh **2** vulgar

coarsen *verb* to make coarse

coast *noun* the border of land next to the sea ➤ *verb* **1** to sail along or near a coast **2** to move without the use of power on a bike, in a car, etc

coastal *adjective* of or on the coast

coastguard *noun* someone who acts as a guard along the coast to help those in danger in boats etc

coastline *noun* the shape of the coast, especially as seen from the sea or air

coat *noun* **1** an outer garment with sleeves **2** an animal's covering of hair or wool **3** a layer of paint ► *verb* to cover with a coat or layer • **coat of arms** the badge or crest of a family

coating *noun* a covering

coax *verb* to persuade to do what is wanted without using force

coaxial (*pronounced* koh-**aks**-i-al) *adjective* **1** having a common axis **2** *electronics* of a cable: consisting of a conductor in the form of a metal tube surrounding and insulated from a second conductor

cob *noun* **1** a head of corn **2** a male swan

cobalt (*pronounced* koh-**bawlt**) *noun* **1** *chemistry* (symbol **Co**) a hard silvery-white metallic element used in alloys to produce cutting tools and magnets **2** a blue colouring obtained from this

⊙ Comes from German *Kobold* meaning 'goblin of the mines', the name given to the metal by frustrated miners who were looking for silver

cobble *noun* (*also called*: **cobblestone**) a rounded stone used in paving roads ► *verb* **1** to mend (shoes) **2** to repair roughly or hurriedly

cobbled *adjective* of streets: paved with cobbles

cobbler *noun* someone who mends shoes

cobra (*pronounced* koh-bra *or* ko-bra) *noun* a poisonous snake found in India and Africa

cobweb *noun* a spider's web

cocaine *noun, medicine* an addictive narcotic drug, used medicinally as a local anaesthetic and illegally as a stimulant

coccus (*pronounced* **kok**-us) *noun* (*plural* **cocci** – *pronounced* **kok**-sai), *biology* a spherical bacterium ⊙ Comes from Latin, ultimately from Greek *kokkos* meaning 'berry'

coccyx (*pronounced* **kok**-siks) *noun* (*plural* **coccyges** – *pronounced* kok-**sai**-jeez), *anatomy* a small triangular bone at the base of the spine ⊙ Comes from Latin, from Greek *kokkyx* meaning 'cuckoo', from its triangular beak

cochlea (*pronounced* **kok**-li-a) *noun* (*plural* **cochleae** – *pronounced* **kok**-li-ee), *anatomy* in the inner ear: a hollow coiled structure which converts the vibrations of sound waves into nerve impulses, which are then interpreted by the brain as sound ⊙ Comes from Latin, meaning 'snail' or 'snail shell', from Greek *kochlias* meaning 'snail with a spiral shell' ♦ **cochlear** *adjective*

cock *noun* **1** the male of most kinds of bird, especially of the farmyard hen **2** a tap or valve for controlling the flow of liquid **3** a hammer-like part of a gun which fires the shot **4** a small heap of hay **5** *slang* the penis ► *verb* **1** to draw back the cock of a gun **2** to set (the ears) upright to listen **3** to tilt (the head) to one side

cockatoo *noun* a kind of parrot

cockerel *noun* a young cock

cocker spaniel *noun* a breed of small spaniel

cockle *noun* a type of shellfish • **warm the cockles of the heart** to make someone feel happy and contented

cockleshell *noun* the shell of a cockle

cockney *noun* (*plural* **cockneys**) **1** someone born in the East End of London **2** the speech characteristic of this area

⊙ Literally 'cock's egg', an old word for a misshapen egg, which was later applied to an effeminate person, and so to a soft-living city-dweller

cockpit *noun* **1** the space for the pilot or driver in an aeroplane or small boat **2** a pit where game cocks fight

cockroach *noun* (*plural* **cockroaches**) a type of large insect that infests houses etc

cocksure *adjective* very confident, often without cause

cocktail *noun* a mixed alcoholic drink

cock-up *noun, slang* a mess or muddle caused by incompetence

cocky *adjective* (**cockier, cockiest**) conceited, self-confident

cocoa *noun* a drink made from the ground seeds of the cacao tree

coconut *noun* **1** the large, hard-shelled nut of a type of palm tree **2** the sweet white flesh of this nut

⊙ Based on a Portuguese word meaning 'grimace', because of the resemblance of the three marks on the base of the fruit to a human face

cocoon *noun* a protective covering of silk spun by the larva of a butterfly, moth, etc

cod *noun* (*plural* **cod**) a fish often eaten as food, found in the northern seas

coddle *verb* **1** to pamper, over-protect **2** to cook (an egg) gently over hot water

code *noun* **1** a way of signalling or sending secret messages, using letters etc agreed beforehand **2** a book or collection of laws, rules, etc **3** *computing* a set of symbols that represent numbers, letters, etc in binary form **4** *computing* the set of written statements that make up a computer program ► *verb* to put into a code

codeine (*pronounced* **koh**-deen) *noun, medicine* a drug that relieves pain and has a sedative effect

codger (*pronounced* **koj**-er) *noun* an old, sometimes eccentric man

codicil (*pronounced* **kod**-i-sil *or* **kohd**-i-sil) *noun* a note added to a will or treaty

codify *verb* (**codifies, codifying, codified**) to arrange in an orderly way, classify

codomain *noun, maths* the set of results of a function on the values specified (*also called*: **target**)

coed (*pronounced* koh-**ed**) *adjective, informal* coeducational

coeducation *noun* the education of boys and girls together ♦ **coeducational** *adjective*

coefficient *noun* **1** *maths* a number appearing before a variable, eg 5 in *5x*, showing the variable is to be multiplied by that number **2** *physics* a number or other constant that is a measure of a property of a particular substance under certain conditions

coelenterate (*pronounced* si-**len**-ter-eit) *noun* an invertebrate with a single body opening, eg jellyfish and corals ⊕ Comes from Greek *koilos* meaning 'hollow' + *enteron* meaning 'intestine'

coeliac disease (*pronounced* **see**-li-ak) *noun* a condition in which the body cannot digest and absorb food properly due to abnormal sensitivity to gluten

coerce *verb* to force, compel ♦ **coercion** *noun* ♦ **coercive** *adjective*

coeval (*pronounced* koh-**ee**-val) *adjective* of the same age or time

coexist *verb* to exist at the same time ♦ **coexistence** *noun* ♦ **coexistent** *adjective*

coffee *noun* **1** a drink made from the roasted, ground beans of the coffee shrub **2** a pale brown colour

coffee table *noun* a small, low table

coffer *noun* a chest for holding money, gold, etc

cofferdam *noun* a watertight chamber used when carrying out construction under water

coffin *noun* a box in which a dead body is buried or cremated

cog *noun* a tooth on a wheel

cogent (*pronounced* **koh**-jent) *adjective* convincing, believable ♦ **cogency** *noun*

cogitate *verb* to think carefully ♦ **cogitation** *noun*

cognac (*pronounced* **kon**-yak) *noun* a kind of French brandy

cognate *adjective* **1** descended from a common ancestor **2** of words or languages: derived from the same original form **3** related ➤ *noun* something that is related to something else

cognition *noun* the mental processes enabling humans to experience things, process knowledge, etc

cognizant or **cognisant** (*pronounced* **kog**-ni-zant or **ko**-ni-zant) *adjective* aware of something or having knowledge of it ♦ **cognizance** or **cognisance** *noun*

cognomen *noun* (**cognomens** or

cognomina) **1** a nickname **2** a surname **3** *Roman history* a Roman's third name, often an epithet or nickname, which became their family name

cognoscenti (*pronounced* ko-nyoh-**shen**-tee) *plural noun* knowledgeable people

cogwheel *noun* a toothed wheel

cohabit *verb* to live together as husband and wife, usually without being married ♦ **cohabitation** *noun*

cohere *verb* to stick together

coherence *noun* connection between thoughts, ideas, etc

coherent *adjective* **1** sticking together **2** clear and logical in thought or speech **3** *physics* of two or more waves, eg light waves: having the same frequency and the same phase difference

cohesion *noun* the act of sticking together

cohesive *adjective* of a group: consisting of members who are closely linked together or associated with each other

cohort *noun* **1** *history* a tenth part of a Roman legion **2** a group of people who share a belief **3** a follower or companion

coil *verb* to wind in rings; twist ➤ *noun* **1** a wound arrangement of hair, rope, etc **2** a contraceptive device fitted in the uterus

coin *noun* a piece of stamped metal used as money ➤ *verb* **1** to make metal into money **2** to make up (a new word etc)

coinage *noun* **1** the system of coins used in a country **2** a newly made word

coincide *verb* (often **coincide with**) **1** to be the same as: *Their interests coincide/His story coincides with mine* **2** to happen at the same time as: *coincided with his departure*

coincidence *noun* the occurrence of two things simultaneously without planning

coincidental *adjective* happening by chance, the result of a coincidence: *Any resemblance to real people is purely coincidental* ♦ **coincidentally** *adverb*

coke *noun* **1** a type of fuel made by heating coal till the gas is driven out **2** *informal* cocaine

col- see **co-**

cola *noun* a soft drink made with flavouring from the nuts of a tropical tree

colander (*pronounced* **kol**-an-der) *noun* a bowl with small holes in it for straining vegetables, pasta, etc

cold *adjective* **1** low in temperature **2** lower in temperature than is comfortable **3** unfriendly ➤ *noun* **1** the state of being cold **2** an infectious disease causing shivering, running nose, etc ♦ **coldly** *adverb* (adjective, meanings 2 and 3) ♦ **coldness** *noun*

cold-blooded *adjective* **1** of fishes etc: having a body temperature that varies with the temperature of the surrounding environment **2** cruel; lacking in feelings

cold calling *noun* the contacting of potential business contacts etc without an appointment

cold feet *plural noun* lack of courage

cold front *noun, geography* the leading edge of an advancing mass of cold air moving under a retreating mass of warm air

cold sore *noun* a blister on or near the mouth, caused by a contagious virus

cold turkey *noun* a way of curing an addiction by suddenly and completely stopping the use of the drug

cold war *noun* **1** a power struggle between nations without open warfare **2** (**the Cold War**) tension between the former USSR and the Western powers, especially the USA, from after World War II until around 1990

coleslaw *noun* a salad made from finely sliced raw cabbage, onion and carrot, mixed together in mayonnaise

colic *noun* a severe stomach pain

collaborate *verb* **1** to work together (with) **2** to work with (an enemy) to betray your country ✦ **collaboration** *noun* ✦ **collaborator** *noun* ⊙ Comes from Latin *col-* meaning 'together with', and *laborare* meaning 'to work'

collage (*pronounced* ko-**lahsz**) *noun* a design made of scraps of paper, cloth, etc pasted on wood, card, etc

collagen (*pronounced* **ko**-la-jen) *noun* a tough, fibrous protein found in skin, bone, teeth, etc and used in skin cream or plastic surgery to make the skin look younger

collapse *verb* **1** to fall or break down **2** to cave or fall in **3** to become unable to continue ➤ *noun* a falling down or caving in

collapsible *adjective* of a chair etc: able to be folded up

collar *noun* **1** a band, strip, etc worn round the neck **2** part of a garment that fits round the neck ➤ *verb, informal* to seize

collarbone *noun* either of two bones joining the breast bone and shoulderblade

collate *verb* **1** to examine and compare **2** to gather together and arrange in order: *collate the pages for the book*

collateral *noun* assets offered as additional security for repayment of a debt

collation *noun* **1** a light, often cold meal **2** a comparison

colleague *noun* someone who works in the same company etc as yourself

collect *verb* **1** to bring together **2** to gather together: *collect stamps* **3** to call for at a place: *collect a package/I'll collect you from the airport*

collected *adjective* **1** gathered together **2** calm, composed

collection *noun* **1** the act of collecting **2** a number of objects or people **3** money gathered from a group of people, eg for a present or at a church service

collective *adjective* **1** acting together **2** of several things or people, not of one: *a collective decision* ➤ *noun* a business etc owned and managed by the workers ✦ **collectively** *adverb* together; as a whole

collective farming *noun,* **1** *geography* the running of a farm by a group of individuals, with profits shared by the whole group **2** *history* in the former Soviet bloc: state-controlled farming, usually on large farms formed by the merging of several smaller privately owned farms

collective noun *noun* a singular noun which refers to a group of people, animals, things, etc, such as *cast, flock, gang*

collectivization or **collectivisation** *noun* **1** the grouping of farms, factories, etc into larger units under state control and ownership **2** *history* the process initiated by Stalin in the USSR of forcing peasants to give up their private land and work in large communal farms ✦ **collectivize** *verb*

collector *noun* someone who collects a particular group of things: *stamp collector*

colleen *noun, Irish* a young woman, a girl

college *noun* **1** a building housing students, forming part of a university **2** a higher-education institute (*see also:* **sixth-form college**): *art college*

collegiate *adjective* (*pronounced* ko-**lee**-ji-at) of a university: divided into colleges

collide *verb* to come together with great force; clash

collie *noun* a breed of long-haired dog with a pointed nose

collier *noun* **1** a coalminer **2** a ship that carries coal

colliery *noun* (*plural* **collieries**) a coalmine

collision *noun* **1** a crash between two moving vehicles etc **2** a disagreement, clash of interests, etc

collocate *verb* **1** to arrange or group in some kind of order **2** *grammar* of a word: to occur frequently alongside another word, eg *different* collocates with *from* and *to*, and sometimes with *than* ⊙ Comes from Latin *collocare* meaning 'to place together'

collocation *noun* **1** grouping together in a certain order **2** *grammar* the habitual co-occurrence of certain words

colloid *noun, chemistry* a mixture in which particles larger than those in a solution and smaller than those in a suspension are dispersed through a liquid

colloquial *adjective* used in everyday speech but not in formal writing or speaking
♦ **colloquially** *adverb*

colloquialism *noun* an example of colloquial speech

collude *verb* to plot secretly with someone

collusion *noun* a secret or clandestine agreement

cologne (*pronounced* ko-**lohn**) *noun* light perfume made with plant oils and alcohol

colon[1] *noun* a punctuation mark (:) used eg to introduce a list of examples

colon[2] *noun, anatomy* the part of the large intestine between the caecum and the rectum
♦ **colonic** *adjective*

colonel (*pronounced* **ker**-nel) *noun* a senior army officer in charge of a regiment

colonial *adjective* of colonies abroad

colonialism *noun* the policy of setting up colonies abroad

colonialist *noun* someone who supports the policy of setting up and maintaining colonies abroad ➤ *adjective* related to colonialism

colonist *noun* a settler

colonize or **colonise** *verb* 1 to set up a colony in 2 to settle (people) in a colony
♦ **colonization** *noun*

colonnade *noun* a row of columns or pillars

colony *noun* (*plural* **colonies**) 1 a group of settlers or the settlement they make in another country 2 a group of people, animals, etc of the same type living together 3 *biology* a group of bacteria growing on a culture medium

colossal *adjective* huge, enormous

colossus *noun* (*plural* **colossuses** or **colossi** – *pronounced* ko-**los**-ai), an enormous statue

colostomy *noun* (*plural* **colostomies**), *surgery* an operation in which part of the colon is brought to the surface of the abdomen, forming an opening through which the colon can be emptied

colostomy bag *noun* a device worn over the opening created by a colostomy, into which waste is passed

colour or *US* **color** *noun* 1 a quality that an object shows in the light, eg redness, blueness, etc 2 a shade or tint 3 vividness, brightness 4 (**colours**) a flag or standard ➤ *verb* 1 to put colour on 2 to blush 3 to influence: *coloured my attitude to life*

colour-blind *adjective* unable to distinguish between certain colours, eg red and green

coloured *adjective* 1 having colour 2 an old-fashioned and offensive word meaning 'not white-skinned'

ⓘ It is generally considered more correct to say 'black' for meaning 2.

colourful *adjective* 1 brightly coloured 2 vivid, interesting

colouring *noun* 1 shade or combination of colours 2 complexion 3 a substance used to colour food etc

colourless *adjective* 1 without colour 2 dull, bland

colt *noun* a young horse

column *noun* 1 an upright stone or wooden pillar 2 something of a long or tall, narrow shape 3 a vertical line of print, figures, etc on a page 4 a regular feature in a newspaper 5 an arrangement of troops etc one behind the other

columnist (*pronounced* **ko**-lum-nist or **ko**-lum-ist) *noun* someone who writes a regular newspaper column

com- see **co-**

coma (*pronounced* **koh**-ma) *noun* unconsciousness lasting a long time

comatose *adjective* 1 in or of a coma 2 drowsy, sluggish

comb *noun* 1 a toothed instrument for separating or smoothing hair, wool, etc 2 the fleshy crest of certain birds 3 a collection of cells for honey ➤ *verb* 1 to arrange or smooth with a comb 2 to search through thoroughly

combat *verb* to fight or struggle against ➤ *noun* a fight or struggle

combatant *noun* someone who is fighting ➤ *adjective* fighting

combative *adjective* quarrelsome; fighting

combat trousers *plural noun* loose-fitting trousers with side pockets

combination *noun* 1 a joining together of things or people 2 a set of things or people combined 3 a series of letters or figures dialled to open a safe, lock, etc 4 *maths* arranging a set of numbers or objects into groups regardless of the order of selection (*compare with*: **permutation** meaning 3) 5 *maths* any of the groups resulting from combination 6 *chemistry* a union of chemical substances that forms a new compound

combine *verb* to join together ➤ *noun* a number of traders etc who join together

combine harvester *noun* a machine that both cuts and threshes crops

combo box *noun, computing* a box on screen attached to an arrow and containing a choice of options in a list

combustible *adjective* liable to catch fire and burn ➤ *noun* anything that will catch fire

combustion *noun* 1 catching fire and burning 2 *chemistry* a chemical reaction in which a gas, liquid or solid is rapidly oxidized, producing heat and light

come *verb* (**coming, came, come**) 1 to move towards this place: *Come here!* 2 to draw near:

Christmas is coming **3** to arrive: *We'll have tea when she comes* **4** to happen, occur: *The index comes at the end* • **come about** to happen • **come across** or **come upon** to meet or find accidentally • **come by** to obtain • **come into** to inherit • **come of age** to reach the age at which you become an adult for legal purposes • **come out 1** to become known or public **2** to go on strike **3** to state openly that you are homosexual • **come round** or **come to** to recover from a faint etc • **come upon** see **come across** • **to come** in the future: *in years to come* ○ Comes from Old English *cuman*

comedian *noun* a performer who tells jokes, acts in comedy, etc

comedown *noun* **1** a decline in social status **2** an anticlimax

comedy *noun* (*plural* **comedies**) **1** a light-hearted or amusing play or film **2** such plays as a genre (*contrasted with*: **tragedy**)

comely *adjective* (**comelier, comeliest**) good-looking, pleasing ♦ **comeliness** *noun*

comet *noun* a rock-like body which orbits the sun and has a tail of light

comfort *verb* to help, soothe (someone in pain or distress) ➤ *noun* **1** ease; quiet enjoyment **2** something or someone that brings ease and happiness

comfortable *adjective* **1** at ease; free from trouble, pain, etc **2** giving comfort **3** having enough money for a pleasant lifestyle **4** of a hospital patient: in a stable condition

comfortably *adverb* **1** easily, happily, or without any problems: *At this rate, he'll win comfortably* **2** in a way which involves no pain or physical irritation: *Are you sitting comfortably?* **3** financially well: *comfortably off*

comfrey (*pronounced* **kum**-fri) *noun* a plant with hairy leaves, used in herbal medicine

comfy *adjective* (**comfier, comfiest**), *informal* comfortable

comic *adjective* **1** of or to do with comedy **2** amusing, funny ➤ *noun* **1** a professional comedian **2** a magazine with illustrated stories, strip cartoons, etc

comical *adjective* funny, amusing ♦ **comically** *adverb*

comic strip *noun* a strip of small pictures outlining a story

comma *noun* a punctuation mark (,) indicating a pause in a sentence

command *verb* **1** to give an order **2** to be in charge of **3** to look over or down upon: *commanding a view* ➤ *noun* **1** an order **2** control: *in command of the situation*

commandant *noun* an officer in command of a place or of troops

commandeer *verb* to seize (something)

especially for the use of an army

commander *noun* **1** someone who commands **2** a naval officer next in rank below captain **3** a high-ranking police officer

commandment *noun* an order or command

commando *noun* (*plural* **commandoes**) a soldier in an army unit trained for special tasks

commemorate *verb* **1** to honour the memory of (a person or event) with a ceremony etc **2** to serve as a memorial to ♦ **commemoration** *noun* ♦ **commemorative** *adjective*

commence *verb* to begin

commencement *noun* the start or beginning

commend *verb* **1** to praise **2** to give into the care of

commendable *adjective* praiseworthy

commendation *noun* **1** praise **2** an official award given to someone for bravery, good service, etc

commendatory *adjective* praising

commensalism *noun*, *biology* a close association of two organisms of different species, with one gaining from the relationship, and the other remaining unaffected by it (*compare with*: **mutualism, parasitism**) ♦ **commensal** *adjective*

commensurate *adjective* in equal proportion to something; equal in extent, quantity, etc

comment *noun* **1** a remark **2** a criticism ➤ *verb* to remark on; criticize

commentary *noun* (*plural* **commentaries**) **1** a description of an event etc by someone who is watching it **2** a set of explanatory notes for a book etc

commentator *noun* someone who gives or writes a commentary

commerce *noun* the buying and selling of goods between people or nations; trade, dealings

commercial *adjective* **1** of or to do with commerce **2** paid for by advertisements: *commercial radio* ➤ *noun* an advertisement on radio, TV, etc

commercialize or **commercialise** *verb* to develop something in order to make a profit, especially by sacrificing quality ♦ **commercialization** *noun*

commercially *adverb* **1** in a way which can make money: *a commercially attractive proposal* **2** as a large-scale industrial process: *A home-made gift is more personal than a commercially produced one* **3** on the open market: *It will be a while before these gadgets are commercially available*

commis or **commis chef** (*pronounced* **kom**-ee) *noun* (*plural* **commis** – *pronounced* **kom**-eez – or **commis chefs**) a trainee chef

commiserate *verb* to sympathize (with)

commiseration *noun* pity ♦ **commiserations** *plural noun* an expression of sympathy when someone has failed to do or achieve something

commission *noun* **1** the act of committing **2** a document giving authority to an officer in the armed forces **3** an order for a work of art **4** a fee or percentage for doing business on another's behalf **5** a group of people appointed to investigate something ➤ *verb* to give a commission or power to ● **in** or **out of commission** in or not in use

commissionaire (*pronounced* ko-mi-shon-**eir**) *noun* a uniformed doorkeeper

commissioner *noun* **1** someone with high authority in a district **2** a member of a commission

commit *verb* (**committing, committed**) **1** to give or hand over; entrust **2** to make a promise to do: *committed to finishing this book* **3** to do, bring about: *commit a crime* **4** to have someone put in a mental institution or prison

commitment *noun* **1** a promise **2** a task that must be done

committal *noun* the act of committing

committed *adjective* strong in belief or support: *a committed socialist*

committee *noun* a number of people chosen from a larger body, eg a club, to perform certain tasks on its behalf

commodious *adjective* roomy, spacious

commodity *noun* (*plural* **commodities**) **1** an article to be bought or sold **2** (**commodities**) goods, produce

commodore *noun* an officer next above a captain in the navy

common *adjective* **1** shared by all or many: *common belief* **2** seen or happening often: *a common occurrence* **3** ordinary, normal: *the common cold* **4** publicly owned: *common land* ➤ *noun* **1** land belonging to the people of a town, parish, etc **2** (**the Commons**) the House of Commons

commoner *noun* someone who is not a noble

common factor *noun, maths* a factor shared by two or more numbers, eg 5 is a common factor of 15 and 20

common fraction another term for **vulgar fraction**

common law *noun* unwritten law based on custom or previous court judgements

common-law *adjective* denoting the relationship between two people who have lived together as husband and wife for some years but who have not been through a civil or religious marriage ceremony

common multiple *noun, maths* a multiple shared by two or more numbers, eg 18 is a common multiple of 2, 3, 6 and 9

common noun *noun, grammar* a name for any one of a class of things (*contrasted with*: **proper noun**)

commonplace *adjective* ordinary

common ratio *noun, maths* a constant that is the quotient of successive numbers in a geometric sequence

common room *noun* a sitting room for the students or staff in a school, university, etc

common sense *noun* practical good sense

commonwealth *noun* **1** an association of self-governing states **2** (**the Commonwealth**) an association of countries or states which were formerly ruled by Britain (*full form*: **the Commonwealth of Nations**)

commotion *noun* a disturbance among several people

communal *adjective* common, shared ♦ **communally** *adverb*

commune *noun* **1** a group of people living together, sharing work, etc **2** in some European countries, eg France, the smallest administrative unit of local government ➤ *verb* **1** to talk together **2** to relate to spiritually: *communing with nature*

communicable *adjective* able to be passed on to others: *a communicable disease*

communicate *verb* **1** to make known, tell **2** to pass on **3** to get in touch (with) **4** to have a connecting door

communication *noun* **1** a means of conveying information **2** a message **3** a way of passing from place to place **4** the process of communicating

communicative *adjective* willing to give information, talkative

communion *noun* **1** the act of sharing thoughts, feelings, etc; fellowship **2** (**Communion**) in the Christian Church, the celebration of the Lord's supper

communion table *noun, Christianity* the table in a church from which communion is served

communiqué (*pronounced* kom-**yoon**-ik-ei) *noun* an official announcement

communism *noun* a form of socialism in which industry is controlled by the state

communist *adjective* of communism ➤ *noun* someone who believes in communism

community *noun* (*plural* **communities**) **1** a group of people living in one place **2** the public in general **3** *biology* a group of different plant or animal species that occupy the same habitat and interact with each other

commutative *adjective, maths* of an arithmetical process: performed on two numbers, the order of which does not affect the result, eg addition and multiplication (but not subtraction or division)

commute *verb* **1** to travel regularly between

two places, eg between home and work **2** to change (a punishment) for one less severe: *commute a sentence*

commuter *noun* someone who travels regularly some distance from their home to work

commuter village *noun, geography* a village within travelling distance of a large city or town, from which people commute to work

compact *adjective* **1** fitted or packed closely together **2** small, but containing all the essentials: *a compact flat* **3** of a quality newspaper: in a small format ➤ *noun* **1** a bargain or agreement **2** a small case for women's face powder, usually with a mirror

compact disc or *computing* **compact disk** *noun* a small disc on which digitally recorded sound, graphics or text can be read by a laser beam

companion *noun* **1** someone or something that accompanies; a friend **2** in the past: a woman employed to live or travel with another woman and keep her company

companionable *adjective* friendly

companionship *noun* friendship; the act of accompanying someone

company *noun* (*plural* **companies**) **1** a gathering of people **2** a business firm **3** a part of a regiment **4** a ship's crew **5** companionship **6** guests or visitors: *expecting company* ⏲ Comes from French *compagnie* meaning 'company' or 'a gathering of people'

comparable (*pronounced* **kom**-pa-ra-bl or kom-**pa**-ra-bl) *adjective* roughly similar or equal in some way: *The two films are comparable in terms of quality*

comparative *adjective* **1** judged by comparing with something else; relative: *comparative improvement* **2** near to being: *a comparative stranger* **3** *grammar* the degree of an adjective or adverb between positive and superlative, eg *blacker, better, more courageous*
♦ **comparatively** *adverb* in comparison to others: *The test was comparatively easy*

compare *verb* **1** to look at things together to see how similar or different they are **2** to liken
● **beyond compare** much better than all rivals

comparison *noun* the act of comparing

compartment *noun* a separate part or division, eg of a railway carriage

compass *noun* (*plural* **compasses**) **1** an instrument with a magnetized needle for showing direction **2** (**compasses**) an instrument with one fixed and one movable leg for drawing circles

compassion *noun* pity for another's suffering; mercy

compassionate *adjective* pitying, merciful
♦ **compassionately** *adverb*

compatibility *noun* **1** the natural tendency for two or more people or groups to get on well together **2** the ability of pieces of electronic equipment, computer software, etc to be connected and used together

compatible *adjective* **1** able to live with, agree with, etc **2** of pieces of electronic equipment, computer software, etc: able to be used together
♦ **compatibly** *adverb*

compatriot *noun* (*pronounced* kom-**pat**-ri-ot or kom-**peit**-ri-ot) a fellow-countryman or -countrywoman

compel *verb* (**compelling, compelled**) to force to do something

compelling *adjective* **1** convincing: *compelling arguments* **2** fascinating: *a compelling TV series*

compendium *noun* (*plural* **compendiums** or **compendia**) **1** a concise summary **2** a collection of board games, puzzles, etc

compensate *verb* to make up for wrong or damage done, especially by giving money
♦ **compensation** *noun*

compère *noun* someone who introduces acts as part of an entertainment ➤ *verb* to act as compère

compete *verb* **1** to try to beat others in a race, contest, etc **2** to try to be more successful than other companies or businesses

competent *adjective* **1** capable, efficient **2** skilled; properly trained or qualified **3** *geography* of rock: hard and relatively stable, and less likely to be eroded (*contrasted with*: **incompetent**) ♦ **competence** *noun*
♦ **competently** *adverb*

competition *noun* **1** a contest between rivals **2** rivalry **3** *biology* the demand for the same limited resource, eg light or water, among organisms or species in a community

competitive *adjective* **1** of sport: based on competitions **2** wanting to win or be more successful than others

competitor *noun* someone who competes; a rival

compilation *noun* **1** a collection of several short, related pieces of writing, music or information **2** the activity of compiling something

compile *verb* to make (a book etc) from information that has been collected

compiler *noun* **1** a person whose job consists of compiling **2** *computing* a program that translates high-level-language instructions into machine-code instructions

complacency or **complacence** *noun* a lazy attitude resulting from an exaggerated belief in your own security

complacent *adjective* self-satisfied and with a tendency to be lazy ♦ **complacently** *adverb*

complain *verb* **1** to express dissatisfaction about something **2** to grumble

complaint *noun* **1** a statement of dissatisfaction **2** an illness

complement *noun* **1** something which completes or fills up **2** the full number or quantity needed to fill something **3** *maths* the angle that must be added to a given angle to make up a right angle **4** *grammar* a word or phrase that tells you about the subject of a verb, eg *dark* in *It grew dark* **5** *biology* a group of proteins in blood serum that combine with antibodies in an immune response

! Do not confuse with: **compliment**. Remember **COMPLEM**ent and **COMPLETE** are related in meaning, and the first six letters of both words are the same.

complementary *adjective* **1** together making up a whole **2** *maths* of angles: making up a right angle

! Do not confuse with: **complimentary**. Complementary is related to the noun **complement**.

complete *adjective* **1** having nothing missing; whole **2** finished ➤ *verb* **1** to finish **2** to make whole **3** to fill in (a form) ♦ **completion** *noun*

completely *adverb* totally, absolutely

complex *adjective* **1** made up of many parts **2** complicated, difficult ➤ *noun* (*plural* **complexes**) **1** a set of repressed emotions and ideas which affect someone's behaviour **2** an exaggerated reaction, an obsession: *She has a complex about her height/an inferiority complex* **3** a group of related buildings: *sports complex*

complexion *noun* **1** the colour or look of the skin of the face **2** appearance

complexity *noun* (*plural* **complexities**) the quality of being complicated or difficult: *the complexity of this problem*

complex number *noun, maths* the sum of a real and an imaginary number

complex sentence *noun, grammar* a sentence made up of a main clause joined by a subordinating conjunction to at least one subordinate clause (*compare with*: **compound sentence**, **simple sentence**)

compliance *noun* the act of complying; agreement with another's wishes

compliant *adjective* yielding, giving agreement

complicate *verb* to make difficult

complicated *adjective* difficult to understand; detailed

complication *noun* **1** a difficulty **2** a second disease or disorder that arises during the course of, and often as a result of, an existing one

complicity *noun* (*plural* **complicities**) a shared involvement in a crime or other misdeed

compliment *noun* **1** an expression of praise or flattery **2** (**compliments**) good wishes ➤ *verb* to praise, congratulate: *complimented me on my cooking*

! Do not confuse with: **complement**. Remember, if you make a **compLIment**, you are being **poLIte**, and an 'I' comes after the 'L' in both words.

complimentary *adjective* **1** flattering, praising **2** given free: *complimentary ticket*

! Do not confuse with: **complementary**. Complimentary is related to the noun **compliment**.

comply *verb* (**complies, complying, complied**) to agree to do something that someone else orders or wishes; obey a rule or law

component *adjective* forming one of the parts of a whole ➤ *noun* one of several parts, eg of a machine

compose *verb* **1** to put together or in order; arrange **2** to create (a piece of music, a poem, etc) **3** to calm (oneself)

composed *adjective* quiet, calm

composer *noun* someone who writes music

composite *adjective* **1** made up of parts **2** *geography* of a volcano: volcanoes, with steep sides formed from layers of ash and lava (*also*: **strato**) **3** of a plant: having a flower head consisting of a crowd of tiny florets

composition *noun* **1** the act of composing **2** a created piece of writing or music **3** a mixture of things **4** the way something is made up **5** *art* the arrangement of elements in a work

compos mentis *adjective* sane, rational ☉ Comes from Latin, literally meaning 'of sound mind'

compost *noun* a mixture of rotted organic material used to enrich soil and nourish plants

composure *noun* calmness, self-possession

compound *adjective* (*pronounced* **kom**-pownd) **1** made up of a number of different parts **2** not simple ➤ *noun* (*pronounced* **kom**-pownd) **1** *chemistry* a substance formed from two or more elements in fixed proportions **2** an enclosure round a building **3** a word made up of two or more words, eg *tablecloth* ➤ *verb* (*pronounced* kom-**pownd**) to make (something bad) worse

compound eye *noun* an eye, eg of an insect or crustacean, consisting of hundreds or thousands of light-sensitive parts

compound interest *noun* interest calculated on the original sum of money borrowed and also on any interest already accumulated (*compare with*: **simple interest**)

compound sentence *noun, grammar* (*also called*: **co-ordinate sentence**) a sentence made up of two or more simple sentences joined by a co-ordinating conjunction (*compare with*: **complex sentence, simple sentence**)

comprehend *verb* **1** to understand **2** to include ♦ **comprehension** *noun* (meaning 1)

comprehensible *adjective* able to be understood

comprehensive *adjective* taking in or including much or all

comprehensive school *noun* a state-funded school providing all types of secondary education

compress *verb* (*pronounced* kom-**pres**) **1** to press together **2** to force into a narrower or smaller space **3** *computing* to pack (data) into the minimum possible space in memory ➤ *noun* (*pronounced* **kom**-pres) a pad used to create pressure on a part of the body or to reduce inflammation ♦ **compression** *noun*

comprise *verb* **1** to include, contain **2** to consist of

> ! Do not confuse with: **consist**

> ⓘ Remember, you do not need the word 'of' after **comprise**. You say *the exam comprises three parts*, but *the exam consists of three parts*.

compromise *noun* an agreement reached by both sides giving up something ➤ *verb* **1** to make a compromise **2** to put in a difficult or embarrassing position by being indiscreet

compulsion *noun* an irresistible urge driving someone to do something

compulsive *adjective* unable to stop yourself, obsessional: *a compulsive liar*

> ! Do not confuse: **compulsive** and **compulsory**

compulsory *adjective* **1** requiring to be done **2** forced upon someone

> ! Do not confuse: **compulsory** and **compulsive**

compunction *noun* regret

computation *noun* counting, calculation

compute *verb* to count, calculate

computer *noun* an electronic machine that stores information of various kinds and sorts it very quickly

computerize or **computerise** *verb* **1** to transfer (a system or procedure) to computer control **2** to install computers in (a place) ♦ **computerization** *noun*

computer-literate *adjective* able to use computers, software programs, etc

computer science *noun* the study of the design and operation of computers

comrade *noun* **1** a companion, a friend **2** a fellow communist or socialist ♦ **comradeship** *noun*

con *verb* (**conning, conned**) to trick, play a confidence trick on ➤ *noun* a trick, a deceit (*see also*: **pros and cons**)

con- see **co-**

concatenate *verb* (**concatenating, concatenated**) to link up, especially into a connected series ♦ **concatenation** *noun* a series of items linked together in a chain-like way

concave *adjective* hollow or curved inwards (*contrasted with*: **convex**) ♦ **concavity** *noun* (*plural* **concavities**)

conceal *verb* to hide, keep secret ♦ **concealment** *noun*

concede *verb* **1** to give up, yield **2** to admit the truth of something: *I concede that you may be right*

conceit *noun* a too high opinion of yourself; vanity

conceited *adjective* full of conceit; vain

conceivable *adjective* able to be imagined ♦ **conceivably** *adverb*

conceive *verb* **1** to form in the mind, imagine **2** to become pregnant

concentrate *verb* **1** to direct all your attention or effort towards something **2** to bring together to one place **3** *chemistry* to increase the strength of (a dissolved substance in a solution) **4** *chemistry* to make (a substance) denser or purer ➤ *noun* a concentrated liquid or substance

concentrated *adjective* made stronger or less dilute

concentration *noun* **1** intense mental effort **2** the act of concentrating or the state of being concentrated **3** *chemistry* the number of molecules or ions of a substance present in unit volume or weight of a solution or mixture **4** a concentrate

concentration camp *noun* a prison camp for civilians, especially in the Nazi regime

concentric *adjective, maths* of circles: placed one inside the other with the same centre point (*contrasted with*: **eccentric**)

concept *noun* a general idea about something ♦ **conceptual** *adjective*

conception *noun* **1** the act of conceiving **2** *biology* the fertilization of an ovum by a sperm, starting pregnancy **3** an idea

conceptualize or **conceptualise** *verb* to form an idea of something ♦ **conceptualization** *noun*

concern *verb* **1** to have to do with **2** to make

uneasy **3** to interest, affect ➤ *noun* **1** anxiety **2** a cause of anxiety, a worry **3** a business • **concern yourself with** to be worried about

concerning *preposition* about: *concerning your application*

concert *noun* a musical performance • **in concert** together

! Do not confuse with: **consort**

concerted *adjective* planned or performed together

concertina *noun* a type of musical wind instrument, with bellows and keys

concerto (*pronounced* kon-**cher**-toh) *noun* (*plural* **concertos**) a long piece of music for a solo instrument with orchestral accompaniment

concession *noun* **1** a granting or allowing of something: *a concession for oil exploration* **2** something granted or allowed **3** a reduction in the price of something for children, the unemployed, senior citizens, etc **4** the right to conduct a business from within a larger concern

conch (*pronounced* kongk or konch) *noun* (*plural* **conchs** or **conches**) **1** any of a family of large tropical sea snails with large colourful shells **2** the shell of this animal, used as a trumpet ⊙ Comes from Latin *concha*, from Greek *konche* meaning 'cockle' or 'mussel'

concierge (*pronounced* kon-see-**ersz**) *noun* a warden or caretaker of a block of flats

conciliate *verb* to win over (someone previously unfriendly or angry)

conciliation *noun* the act or process of making peace with a person or group

conciliatory *adjective* having the aim of making peace: *a conciliatory gesture*

concise *adjective* brief, using few words ⊙ Comes from Latin *concisus* meaning 'cut up'

! Do not confuse with: **precise**

conclave *noun* the group of cardinals gathered to elect a new pope

conclude *verb* **1** to end **2** to reach a decision or judgement; settle

concluding *adjective* last, final

conclusion *noun* **1** an end **2** a decision, judgement

conclusive *adjective* of evidence etc: convincing, leaving no room for doubt: *conclusive proof*

conclusively *adverb* in a way which leaves no doubt: *prove conclusively that there is no other life in the solar system*

concoct *verb* **1** to mix together (a dish or drink) **2** to make up, invent: *concoct a story* ♦ **concoction** *noun*

concord *noun* agreement

concordant coast *noun*, *geography* a coast with bands of resistant and less resistant rock parallel to the coastline (*contrasted with*: **discordant coast**)

concourse *noun* **1** a crowd **2** a large open space in a building etc

concrete *adjective* **1** solid, real **2** made of concrete ➤ *noun* a mixture of gravel, cement, etc used in building

concrete poem *noun* a poem written or printed so that its appearance on the page represents its subject, eg a poem about growth where the size of the letters gets bigger

concur *verb* (**concurring, concurred**) to agree

concurrence *noun* agreement

concurrent *adjective* **1** happening together **2** agreeing ♦ **concurrently** *adverb* (meaning 1)

concuss *verb* to cause concussion in

concussion *noun* temporary harm done to the brain from a knock on the head

condemn *verb* **1** to blame **2** to sentence to (a certain punishment) **3** to declare (a building) unfit for use ♦ **condemnation** *noun* (meaning 1)

condemned cell *noun* a cell for a prisoner condemned to death

condensation *noun* **1** the act of condensing **2** *chemistry* the process in which a gas or vapour turns into a liquid as a result of cooling **3** drops of liquid formed from vapour

condense *verb* **1** to make (a substance) go into a smaller space **2** of steam: to turn to liquid **3** to express something more briefly; summarize

condenser *noun* **1** a **capacitor** **2** *chemistry* an apparatus for changing a vapour into a liquid by cooling it and allowing it to condense **3** in a microscope, film projector, etc: a lens used to concentrate a light source

condescend *verb* to act towards someone as if you are better than them ♦ **condescending** *adjective* ♦ **condescension** *noun*

condiment *noun* a seasoning for food, especially salt or pepper

condition *noun* **1** the state in which anything is: *in poor condition* **2** something that must happen before some other thing happens **3** a point in a bargain, treaty, etc **4** a restriction **5** a disorder or ailment: *a heart condition* ➤ *verb* **1** to train to behave or react in a particular way **2** to improve (the physical state of hair, skin, fabrics, etc) by applying a special substance

conditional *adjective* depending on certain things happening ♦ **conditionally** *adverb*

conditioner *noun* a substance that improves the condition of something, eg hair, fabric, etc

condolence *noun* **1** sharing in another's sorrow; sympathy **2 condolences** an expression of sympathy: *offer my condolences*

condom *noun* a rubber sheath worn on the

penis during sexual intercourse to prevent conception and the spread of sexually transmitted diseases

condominium *noun, US* a building in which each apartment is individually owned and the common areas are commonly owned, or an apartment in such a block

condone *verb* to allow (an offence) to pass unchecked

conducive *adjective* helping, favourable (to): *conducive to peace*

conduct *verb* (pronounced kon-**dukt**) **1** to lead, guide **2** to control, be in charge of **3** *music* to direct (an orchestra or choir) **4** to transmit (electricity etc) **5** to behave: *conducted himself correctly* ➤ *noun* (pronounced **kon**-dukt) behaviour

conductance *noun* the ability of a material to conduct electricity, measured in siemens

conduction *noun* transmission of heat, electricity, etc

conductor *noun* **1** someone who directs an orchestra or choir **2** someone who collects fares on a bus etc **3** something that transmits heat, electricity, etc

conduit (pronounced **kon**-dit or **kon**-dyuw-it) *noun* a channel or pipe to carry water, electric wires, etc

cone *noun* **1** a shape that is circular at the bottom and comes to a point **2** the fruit of a pine or fir tree etc **3** an ice-cream cornet **4** *anatomy* a type of cell in the retina of the eye that detects colour

confection *noun* any sweet food, eg a cake, sweet, etc

confectioner *noun* someone who makes or sells sweets, cakes, etc

confectionery *noun* **1** sweets, cakes, etc **2** the shop or business of a confectioner

confederacy *noun* (plural **confederacies**) **1** a league, an alliance **2** (**the Confederacy**) *US history* the union of Southern states in the American Civil War

confederate *adjective* **1** joined together by treaty **2** *US history* supporting the Confederacy ➤ *noun* someone acting in an alliance with others

confederation *noun* a union, a league

confer *verb* (**conferring, conferred**) **1** to talk together **2** to give, grant: *confer a degree*

conference *noun* an organized meeting for discussion of matters of common interest

confess *verb* **1** to own up, admit to (wrong) **2** to declare (your sins) to a priest in order to be absolved

confessed *adjective* admitted, not secret

confession *noun* **1** an admission of wrongdoing **2** the act of confessing your sins to a priest
♦ **confessional** *adjective*

confetti *plural noun* small pieces of coloured paper thrown at weddings or other celebrations

confidant or *feminine* **confidante** (*pronounced* con-fi-**dont**) *noun* someone trusted with a secret

! Do not confuse with: **confident**

confide *verb*: **confide in 1** to tell secrets to **2** *formal* to hand over to someone's care

confidence *noun* **1** trust, belief **2** self-assurance, boldness **3** something told privately

confidence interval *noun, statistics* an interval that can with reasonable confidence be expected to contain the true value of an unknown variable

confidence trick *noun* a trick to get money etc from someone by first gaining their trust

confident *adjective* **1** very self-assured **2** certain of an outcome: *confident that they would win* ♦ **confidently** *adverb*

! Do not confuse with: **confidant** and **confidante**

confidential *adjective* **1** to be kept as a secret: *confidential information* **2** entrusted with secrets ♦ **confidentially** *adverb*

confiding *adjective* trusting

configuration *noun* **1** the positioning of the parts of something, relative to each other **2** an outline or external shape ⓞ Comes from Latin *configuratio*, from *configurare* meaning 'to form or fashion'

confine *verb* **1** to shut up, imprison **2** to keep within limits

confinement *noun* **1** the state of being confined **2** imprisonment **3** the time of a woman's labour and childbirth

confines (*pronounced* **kon**-fainz) *plural noun* limits

confirm *verb* **1** to make firm, strengthen: *confirm a booking* **2** to make sure **3** to show to be true **4** to admit into full membership of a church

confirmation *noun* **1** a making sure **2** proof **3** the ceremony by which someone is made a full member of a church

confirmed *adjective* settled in a habit etc: *a confirmed bachelor*

confiscate *verb* to take away, as a punishment ♦ **confiscation** *noun*

conflagration *noun* a large, widespread fire

conflate *verb* to blend or combine (two things) into a single whole ♦ **conflation** *noun*

conflict *noun* (*pronounced* **kon**-flikt) **1** a struggle, a contest **2** a battle **3** disagreement ➤ *verb* (*pronounced* kon-**flikt**) of statements etc: to contradict each other ♦ **conflicting** *adjective*

confluence (*pronounced* **kon**-fluw-ens) *noun, geography* a place where rivers, streams, etc join and flow together

conform *verb* to follow the example of most people in behaviour, dress, etc

conformation *noun* the way something is made up from different parts; structure

conformity *noun* (*plural* **conformities**) **1** likeness **2** the act of conforming

confound *verb* to puzzle, confuse

confront *verb* **1** to face, meet: *confronted the difficulty* **2** to bring face to face (with): *confronted with the evidence*

confrontation *noun* a situation in which two people or groups are challenging each other openly

confuse *verb* **1** to mix up, disorder **2** to puzzle, bewilder ♦ **confusion** *noun*

confusing *adjective* puzzling, bewildering

conga *noun* a dance that originated in Cuba, of three steps and a kick, performed by people moving in single file

congeal *verb* **1** to become solid, especially by cooling: *congealed blood* **2** to freeze

congenial *adjective* agreeable, pleasant ♦ **congenially** *adverb*

congenital *adjective* of a disease: present in someone from birth

conger (*pronounced* **kong**-ger) *noun* a kind of large sea-eel

congested *adjective* **1** overcrowded, especially with traffic **2** clogged **3** of part of the body: too full of blood ♦ **congestion** *noun*

conglomerate *noun* a business group made up of a number of rims with different interests

conglomeration *noun* a heap or collection

congratulate *verb* to express joy to (someone) at their success

congratulations *plural noun* an expression of joy at someone's success

congratulatory *adjective* expressing congratulations

congregate *verb* to come together in a crowd

congregation *noun* a gathering, especially of people in a church

Congregationalism *noun, Christianity* a form of church government in which each congregation manages its own affairs ♦ **Congregationalist** *adjective & noun*

congress *noun* (*plural* **congresses**) **1** a large meeting of people from different countries etc for discussion **2** (**Congress**) the parliament of the United States, consisting of the Senate and the House of Representatives

congressman or **congresswoman** *noun* (*plural* **congressmen** or **congresswomen**) someone who is a member of the US Congress, especially the House of Representatives

congruent *adjective* **1** (often **congruent with**) agreeing or corresponding: *skills congruent with the job* **2** *maths* of figures: identical in size and shape ♦ **congruence** *noun*

congruous *adjective* (often **congruous with**) **1** corresponding **2** fitting; suitable ♦ **congruity** *noun* ♦ **congruously** *adverb* ☉ Comes from Latin *congruus*, from *congruere* meaning 'to meet together'

conic or **conical** *adjective* cone-shaped

conic section *noun, maths* the curved figure produced when a plane intersects a cone

conifer (*pronounced* **kon**-i-fer or **kohn**-i-fer) *noun* an evergreen tree that produces its seeds in cones, eg pine, spruce, etc ♦ **coniferous** *adjective*

conjecture *noun* a guess ➤ *verb* to guess ♦ **conjectural** *adjective*

conjoined twins *plural noun* twins joined by their flesh, and sometimes their internal organs, at birth

conjugal *adjective* of marriage

conjugate *verb* **1** *grammar* to give the different grammatical parts of (a verb), indicating number, person, tense, mood and voice **2** *biology* to reproduce by conjugation ➤ *adjective* **1** joined, connected **2** *maths* reciprocally related

conjugation *noun* **1** *grammar* the inflection of a verb to indicate number, person, tense, voice and mood **2** a joining or fusing **3** *biology* a method of sexual reproduction which involves the fusion of gametes

conjunction *noun* **1** *grammar* a word that joins sentences or phrases, eg *and, but* **2** a union, a combination • **in conjunction with** together with, acting with

conjunctiva (*pronounced* kon-jungk-**tai**-va) *noun* (*plural* **conjunctivas** or **conjunctivae** – *pronounced* kon-jungk-**tai**-vee) the thin membrane that lines the eyelids and covers the exposed surface of the eyeball ♦ **conjunctival** *adjective*

conjunctivitis *noun* inflammation of the conjunctiva

conjure *verb* to perform tricks that seem magical

conjuror or **conjurer** *noun* someone who performs conjuring tricks

conker *noun* **1** a horse chestnut **2** (**conkers**) a game in which conkers are tied on strings and players try to hit and break each other's

con man *noun* someone who regularly plays confidence tricks on people in order to cheat them out of money

connect *verb* to join or fasten together ♦ **connector** or **connecter** *noun*

connection *noun* **1** something that connects **2** a state of being connected **3** a train, aeroplane, etc which takes you on the next part of a journey **4** an acquaintance, a friend • **in connection with** concerning

connective adjective serving to connect ➤ noun **1** something which connects **2** grammar a word which links phrases, clauses, other words, etc

connective tissue noun, anatomy any of several tissues that provide the body and its internal organs with structural support, eg bone, cartilage, tendons, ligaments

conning-tower noun the place on a warship or submarine from which orders for steering are given

connive verb to conspire or plot • **connive at** to disregard (a misdeed) ✦ **connivance** noun

connoisseur (pronounced kon-o-**ser**) noun someone with an expert knowledge of a subject: a wine connoisseur

connotation noun **1** a meaning **2** what is suggested by a word in addition to its simple meaning ✦ **connotative** adjective ✦ **connote** verb ⊙ Comes from Latin connotare meaning 'to mark in addition'

conquer verb **1** to gain by force **2** to overcome: conquered his fear of heights ✦ **conqueror** noun

conquest noun **1** something won by force **2** an act of conquering

conquistador (pronounced kong-**kees**-ta-dawr or kong-**kwis**-ta-dawr) noun (plural **conquistadores** – pronounced kong-kees-ta-**dawr**-ez – or **conquistadors** – pronounced kong-**kwis**-ta-dawrz) an adventurer or conqueror, especially one of the 16th-century Spanish conquerors of Peru and Mexico ⊙ Comes from Spanish, meaning 'conqueror'

conscience noun an inner sense of what is right and wrong

conscientious adjective careful and diligent in work etc ✦ **conscientiously** adverb

conscious adjective **1** aware of yourself and your surroundings; awake **2** aware, knowing: I was conscious that someone was watching me **3** deliberate, intentional: a conscious effort ✦ **consciously** adverb ✦ **consciousness** noun: lose consciousness

conscript noun (pronounced **kon**-skript) someone obliged by law to serve in the armed forces ➤ verb (pronounced kon-**skript**) to compel to serve in the armed forces ✦ **conscription** noun

consecrate verb to set apart for sacred use ✦ **consecration** noun

consecutive adjective coming in order, one after the other

consensus noun an agreement of opinion ⊙

Comes from Latin consensus meaning 'agreement'

❗ Do not confuse with: **census**

consent verb to agree (to) ➤ noun **1** agreement **2** permission • **age of consent** the age at which someone is legally able to consent to sexual intercourse

consequence noun **1** something that follows as a result **2** importance

consequent adjective following as a result ✦ **consequently** adverb

❗ Do not confuse with: **subsequent**. **Consequent** means happening after something, **subsequent** means happening after something, but not necessarily as a result of it.

consequential adjective **1** following as a result **2** important

conservation noun the maintaining of old buildings, the countryside, etc in an undamaged state

conservation area noun an area that is legally protected from any changes that might spoil its character

conservationist noun someone who encourages and practises conservation

conservation law noun, physics the law that in the interaction between particles, certain quantities, eg mass, energy, charge, etc, remain unchanged

conservative adjective **1** resistant to change **2** moderate, not extreme: conservative estimate **3** (**Conservative**) relating to the Conservative Party ➤ noun **1** someone of conservative views **2** (**Conservative**) a supporter of the Conservative Party

Conservative Party noun one of the chief political parties of the UK, supporting established customs and institutions, and free enterprise

conservative plate boundary or **conservative plate margin** noun, geography (also called: **transform plate boundary**) a type of boundary between tectonic plates which pass each other, which does not create new crust but can cause earthquakes (see also: **constructive plate boundary, destructive plate boundary**)

conservatory (pronounced kon-**ser**-vat-ri) noun (plural **conservatories**) a glasshouse for plants, or a similar room used as a lounge, attached to and entered from, the house

conserve verb to keep from being wasted or lost; preserve

consider verb **1** to think about carefully **2** to think of as, regard as: I consider her a friend **3** to pay attention to the wishes of (someone)

considerable *adjective* fairly large, substantial

considerably *adverb* substantially, quite a lot: *He got considerably more votes than I did*

considerate *adjective* taking others' wishes into account; thoughtful

consideration *noun* **1** serious thought **2** thoughtfulness for others **3** a small payment

considering *preposition* taking into account: *considering your age*

consign (*pronounced* kon-**sain**) *verb* to give into the care of

consignment (*pronounced* kon-**sain**-ment) *noun* a load, eg of goods

consist *verb* to be made up (of)

⚠ Do not confuse with: **comprise**

ℹ You need the word 'of' after **consist**, but not after **comprise**. You say *the exam consists of three parts*, but *the exam comprises three parts*.

consistency *noun* (*plural* **consistencies**) **1** thickness, firmness: *the consistency of double cream* **2** the quality of always being the same

consistent *adjective* **1** not changing, regular **2** of statements etc: not contradicting each other ♦ **consistently** *adverb*

consolation *noun* something that makes trouble etc more easy to bear

consolation prize *noun* a prize sometimes given to someone coming second in a competition

console *verb* to comfort, cheer up

consolidate *verb* **1** to make or become strong **2** to unite ♦ **consolidation** *noun*

consonance *noun* **1** the state of agreement **2** *music* a pleasant-sounding combination of musical notes **3** the repetition of sounds occupying the same position in a sequence of words

consonant *noun* a letter of the alphabet that is not a vowel, eg b, c, d

consort *noun* (*pronounced* **kon**-sawrt) **1** a husband or wife **2** a companion ➤ *verb* (*pronounced* kon-**sawrt**): **consort with** to keep company with

⚠ Do not confuse with: **concert**

consortium *noun* (*plural* **consortiums** or **consortia**) an association of banks, businesses, etc working together for a specific purpose

conspicuous *adjective* clearly seen, noticeable ♦ **conspicuously** *adverb*

conspiracy *noun* (*plural* **conspiracies**) a plot by a group of people

conspirator *noun* someone who takes part in a conspiracy

conspire *verb* to plan or plot together

constable (*pronounced* **kun**-sta-bl or **kon**-sta-bl) *noun* **1** a policeman **2** *history* a high officer of state

constabulary *noun* the police force

constant *adjective* **1** never stopping **2** never changing **3** faithful ➤ *noun, maths* a symbol representing a value that does not vary (*compare with*: **variable**) ♦ **constancy** *noun*

constantly *adverb* always

constellation *noun* a group of stars

consternation *noun* dismay, astonishment

constipated *adjective* suffering from constipation

constipation *noun, medical* a condition in which solid waste becomes hard and is difficult to pass out of the body

constituency *noun* (*plural* **constituencies**) **1** a district which has a member of parliament **2** the voters in such a district

constituent *adjective* **1** making or forming: *constituent parts of the brain* **2** having the power to create or change a constitution: *a constituent assembly* ➤ *noun* **1** a necessary part **2** a voter in a constituency

constitute *verb* **1** to set up, establish **2** to form, make up **3** to be the equivalent of: *This action constitutes a crime*

constitution *noun* **1** the way in which something is made up **2** the natural condition of a body in terms of health etc: *a weak constitution* **3** a set of laws or rules governing a country or organization

constitutional *adjective* of a constitution ➤ *noun* a short walk for the sake of your health

constrain *verb* to force to act in a certain way

constraint *noun* **1** compulsion, force **2** restraint, repression **3** a condition that limits a process or action

constrict *verb* **1** to press together tightly **2** to surround and squeeze

constrictor *noun* **1** a snake that kills by coiling around its prey and squeezing it until it suffocates **2** *anatomy* any muscle that narrows an opening

construct *verb* **1** to build, make **2** *maths* to draw (a figure)

construction *noun* **1** the act of constructing **2** something built **3** *maths* a figure drawn by following certain conditions, eg only using a ruler and compass **4** *grammar* the arrangement of words in a sentence **5** meaning

constructive *adjective* **1** of construction **2** helping to improve: *constructive criticism* ♦ **constructively** *adverb* (meaning 2)

constructive plate boundary or **constructive plate margin** *noun, geography* (*also called*: **divergent plate**

boundary) a type of boundary between tectonic plates which move apart, creating new crust and sometimes causing earthquakes, volcanoes, and the formation of mid-ocean ridges (*see also*: **conservative plate boundary, destructive plate boundary**)

constructive wave *noun, geography* a type of wave, found in calm conditions, which carries and deposits material on the shore (*compare with*: **destructive wave**)

construe *verb* **1** to interpret or explain **2** to deduce or infer

consul *noun* **1** someone who looks after their country's affairs in a foreign country **2** *history* a chief ruler in ancient Rome ♦ **consular** *adjective* ♦ **consulate** *noun* **1** the official residence of a consul **2** the duties and authority of a consul

consult *verb* to seek advice or information from: *consult your doctor/consult a dictionary*

consultant *noun* **1** someone who gives professional or expert advice **2** the senior grade of hospital doctor

consultation *noun* **1** the activity of looking in eg reference books for information **2** a meeting with someone to exchange ideas and opinions **3** discussion

consulting room *noun* a room where a doctor sees patients

consume *verb* **1** to eat up **2** to use or use up **3** to destroy

consumer *noun* someone who buys, eats or uses goods, energy, resources, etc

consumer durables *plural noun* goods that are designed to last quite a long time, eg furniture, kitchen appliances, etc

consummate *verb* (*pronounced* **kon**-sum-eit or **kon**-syoo-meit) **1** to complete **2** to make (marriage) legally complete by sexual intercourse ➤ *adjective* (*pronounced* **kon**-syoo-mat or kon-**sum**-at) complete, perfect: *a consummate dancer*

consumption *noun* **1** the act of consuming **2** an amount consumed **3** *old* tuberculosis

cont or **contd** *abbreviation* continued

contact *noun* **1** touch **2** meeting, communication **3** an acquaintance; someone who can be of help: *business contacts* **4** someone who has been with someone suffering from an infectious disease ➤ *verb* to get into contact with

contact lens *noun* a plastic lens worn in contact with the eyeball

contact process *noun, chemistry* the process by which sulphuric acid is manufactured by the oxidation of sulphur dioxide in the presence of a catalyst

contagious *adjective* **1** of a disease: spreading easily from person to person by ordinary contact

(*compare with*: **infectious**) **2** spreading easily: *Her enthusiasm is contagious*

contain *verb* **1** to hold or have inside **2** to hold back: *couldn't contain her anger*

container *noun* a box, tin, jar, etc for holding anything

contaminate *verb* to make impure or dirty ♦ **contaminated** *adjective* ♦ **contamination** *noun*

contd another spelling of **cont**

contemplate (*pronounced* **kon**-temp-leit) *verb* **1** to look at or think about attentively **2** to consider as a possibility: *contemplating suicide* ♦ **contemplation** *noun*

contemplative (*pronounced* kon-**temp**-lat-iv) *adjective* quiet and absorbed in thought: *in contemplative mood*

contemporary *adjective* belonging to the same time ➤ *noun* (*plural* **contemporories**) someone of roughly the same age as yourself

contempt *noun* complete lack of respect; scorn • **contempt of court** deliberate disobedience to and disrespect for the law and those who carry it out

contemptible *adjective* deserving scorn, worthless

! Do not confuse: **contemptible** and **contemptuous**.
Contemptible is formed from **contempt** + **-ible** meaning 'able to be scorned, worthy of scorn'. It is used in phrases like a *contemptible little tell-tale.*

contemptuous *adjective* scornful

! Do not confuse: **contemptuous** and **contemptible**.
Contemptuous means 'full of contempt' (for something or someone). Use it in phrases like a *contemptuous laugh* or *He was contemptuous of my achievement.*

contend *verb* **1** to struggle against **2** to hold firmly to a belief; maintain (that) ♦ **contender** *noun* someone taking part in a contest

content¹ (*pronounced* kon-**tent**) *adjective* happy, satisfied ➤ *noun* happiness, satisfaction ➤ *verb* to make happy, satisfy

content² (*pronounced* **kon**-tent) *noun* **1** (often **contents**) what is contained in something **2** the subject matter of a book, speech, etc **3** the proportion in which an ingredient is present: *a diet with a high starch content* **4** (**contents**) (a list of) the chapters in a book

contented *adjective* happy, content

contention *noun* **1** an opinion strongly held **2** a quarrel, a dispute

contentious *adjective* **1** quarrelsome **2** likely to cause an argument: *a contentious issue*

contentment *noun* happiness, content

contest *verb* (*pronounced* kon-**test**) to fight for, argue against ▸ *noun* (*pronounced* **kon**-test) a fight, a competition

contestant *noun* someone who takes part in a contest

context *noun* **1** the place in a book etc to which a certain part belongs **2** the background of an event, remark, etc

contiguous *adjective* touching, close
  ♦ **contiguity** *noun*

continent *noun* **1** any of the seven large divisions of the earth's land surface (Europe, Asia, Africa, Antarctica, Australia, North America, South America) **2** (**the Continent**) *Brit* the mainland of Europe

continental *adjective* **1** of a continent **2** *Brit* European **3** *geography* of climate: with low rainfall and warm in summer and cool in winter, because of being inland

continental crust *noun, geography* the part of the earth's crust lying underneath the large landmasses

continental drift *noun* the gradual movement of the earth's continents

continental shelf *noun* the edge of a continent where it is submerged in shallow sea

contingency *noun* (*plural* **contingencies**) a chance happening

contingency plan *noun* a plan of action in case something does not happen as expected

contingent *adjective* depending (on) ▸ *noun* a group, especially of soldiers

continual *adjective* happening again and again at close intervals

! Do not confuse with: **continuous**. Something which is **continual** happens often, but there are short breaks when it is not happening. Something which is **continuous** happens all the time without stopping. So you could talk about, for example, *continual interruptions*, but the *continuous* lapping of waves on a beach.

continually *adverb* all the time, repeatedly

continuation *noun* **1** the act of continuing **2** a part that continues, an extension

continue *verb* to keep on, go on (doing something)

continuity *noun* the state of having no gaps or breaks

continuous *adjective* coming in a steady stream without any gap or break
  ♦ **continuously** *adverb*

! Do not confuse with: **continual**

continuous data *noun, statistics* data from measurements on a continuous variable such as people's heights (*compare with*: **discrete data**)

continuum *noun* (**continua** or **continuums**) a continuous sequence; an unbroken progression

contort *verb* to twist or turn violently
  ♦ **contorted** *adjective* ♦ **contortion** *noun*

contortionist *noun* someone who can twist their body into strange shapes

contour *noun* (often **contours**) outline, shape

contour line *noun, geography* a line drawn on a map through points all at the same height above sea level

contra- see **counter-**

contraband *noun* **1** goods legally forbidden to be brought into a country **2** smuggled goods

contraception *noun* the deliberate prevention of pregnancy using natural or artificial methods

contraceptive *adjective* used to prevent the conceiving of children ▸ *noun* a contraceptive device or drug

contract *verb* (*pronounced* kon-**trakt**) **1** to become or make smaller **2** to bargain for **3** to promise in writing ▸ *noun* (*pronounced* **kon**-trakt) a written agreement

contraction *noun* **1** a shortening **2** a shortened form of a word **3** a muscle spasm, eg during childbirth

contractor *noun* someone who promises to do work, or supply goods, at an arranged price

contradict *verb* to say the opposite of; deny
  ♦ **contradiction** *noun*

contradictory *adjective* **1** contradicting something **2** of two pieces of information: contradicting each other

contraflow *noun* two lines of traffic going in opposite directions on the same side of a main road

contralto *noun* (*plural* **contraltos**), *music* **1** the female singing voice of the lowest pitch **2** a singer with such a voice

contraption *noun* a machine, a device

contrapuntal *adjective, music* involving the combination of two or more melodies to make a piece of music: *Bach's music tends to be contrapuntal*

contrary[1] (*pronounced* **kon**-tra-ri) *adjective* opposite ▸ *noun* (*plural* **contraries**) the opposite ● **on the contrary** just the opposite

contrary[2] (*pronounced* kon-**treir**-ri) *adjective* always doing or saying the opposite, perverse

contrast *verb* (*pronounced* kon-**trast**) **1** to compare so as to show differences **2** to show a marked difference from ▸ *noun* (*pronounced* **kon**-trast) a difference between (two) things

contravene *verb* to break (a law etc)
  ♦ **contravention** *noun*

contretemps (*pronounced* **kon**-tre-tom) *noun* a mishap at an awkward moment

contribute *verb* **1** to give (money, help, etc) along with others **2** to supply (articles etc) for a publication **3** to help to cause: *contributed to a nervous breakdown*

contribution *noun* something given or supplied • **make a contribution** to give or supply something, play a part

contributor *noun* a person or thing that contributes

contributory *adjective* contributing to, or playing a part in some result: *a contributory factor*

con-trick *noun* short for **confidence trick**

contrite *adjective* very sorry for having done wrong ♦ **contrition** *noun*

contrivance *noun* an act of contriving; an invention

contrive *verb* **1** to plan **2** to bring about, manage: *contrived to be out of the office*

contrived *adjective* unconvincingly artificial: *The plot seemed contrived*

contro- see **counter-**

control *noun* **1** authority to rule, manage, guide, etc **2** (often **controls**) means by which a driver keeps a machine powered or guided **3** (also **control experiment**) a scientific experiment performed to provide a standard of comparison for other experiments ➤ *verb* **1** to exercise control over **2** to have power over **3** to regulate or limit ♦ **controllable** *adjective* ♦ **controlled** *adjective* ♦ **controller** *noun*

control group *noun* a group of people or things used as a standard of comparison when analysing the results of an experiment

control tower *noun* an airport building from which landing and take-off instructions are given

controversial *adjective* likely to cause argument

controversy (*pronounced* kon-tro-ver-si or kon-**trov**-er-si) *noun* (*plural* **controversies**) an argument, a disagreement

conundrum *noun* a riddle, a question

conurbation *noun* a group of towns forming a single built-up area

convalesce *verb* to recover health gradually after being ill ♦ **convalescence** *noun*

convalescent *noun* someone convalescing from illness

convection *noun* **1** the spreading of heat by movement of heated air or water **2** *geography* the movement of hot currents of molten rock in the earth's mantle, causing the plates on its crust to move

convectional rainfall *noun, meteorology* heavy rainfall caused by the rising of water vapour and air heated by the sun, which then cools and condenses to form large clouds (*compare with*: **frontal rainfall, relief rainfall**)

convector *noun* a heater which works by convection

convene *verb* to call or come together

convener *noun* **1** someone who calls a meeting **2** the chairman or chairwoman of a committee

convenience *noun* **1** suitableness, handiness **2** a means of giving ease or comfort **3** *informal* a public lavatory • **at your convenience** when it suits you best

convenient *adjective* easy to reach or use, handy ♦ **conveniently** *adverb*

convent *noun* a building accommodating an order of nuns

convention *noun* **1** a way of behaving that has become usual, a custom **2** a large meeting, an assembly: *a Star Trek convention* **3** a treaty or agreement

conventional *adjective* **1** done by habit or custom **2** having traditional attitudes and behaviour ♦ **conventionally** *adverb*

converge *verb* to come together, meet at a point

convergent *adjective* **1** meeting, coming together **2** *maths* of an infinite sequence, series, etc: having a limit ♦ **convergence** *noun*

convergent evolution *noun, biology* the development of similarities in unrelated species of plants or animals, eg the wings of birds and insects

convergent plate boundary another term for **destructive plate boundary**

converging lens *noun, physics* a lens that causes light rays to converge to a focus, eg a convex lens (*compare with*: **diverging lens**)

conversant *adjective* (usually **conversant with**) having knowledge of

conversation *noun* talk, exchange of ideas, news, etc

conversational *adjective* **1** to do with conversation **2** talkative

converse¹ *verb* (*pronounced* kon-**vers**) to talk ➤ *noun* (*pronounced* **kon**-vers), *formal* conversation

converse² (*pronounced* **kon**-vers) *noun* the opposite ➤ *adjective* **1** opposite **2** reverse

convert *verb* (*pronounced* kon-**vert**) **1** to change (from one thing into another) **2** to turn from one religion to another ➤ *noun* (*pronounced* **kon**-vert) someone who has been converted ♦ **conversion** *noun*

convertible *adjective* able to be changed from one thing to another ➤ *noun* a car with a folding roof

convex *adjective* curving outwards (*contrasted with*: **concave**) ♦ **convexity** *noun* (*plural* **convexities**)

convey *verb* **1** to carry, transport **2** to send **3** *law* to hand over: *convey property*

conveyance *noun* **1** the act of conveying **2** a vehicle

conveyancing *noun, law* the process of handing over from one party to another the legal ownership of property

conveyor or **conveyor belt** *noun* an endless moving mechanism for conveying articles, especially in a factory

convict *law, verb* (*pronounced* kon-**vikt**) to declare or prove that someone is guilty ➤ *noun* (*pronounced* **kon**-vikt) someone found guilty of a crime and sent to prison

conviction *noun* **1** *law* the passing of a guilty sentence on someone in court **2** a strong belief

convince *verb* **1** to make (someone) believe that something is true **2** to persuade (someone) by showing ♦ **convinced** *adjective*

convivial *adjective* jolly, festive ♦ **conviviality** *noun*

convoluted *adjective* complicated, difficult to understand

convoy *verb* to go along with and protect ➤ *noun* **1** merchant ships protected by warships **2** a line of army lorries with armed guard

convulse *verb* to cause to shake violently: *convulsed with laughter*

convulsion *noun* **1** a sudden stiffening or jerking of the muscles **2** a violent disturbance ♦ **convulsive** *adjective*

coo *noun* a sound like that of a dove ➤ *verb* to make this sound

cook *verb* **1** to prepare (food) by heating **2** *informal* to alter (accounts etc) dishonestly ➤ *noun* someone who cooks and prepares food

cooker *noun* a stove for cooking

cookery *noun* the art of cooking

cookie *noun* **1** a biscuit **2** *computing* a small piece of basic information on a user, sent to a web browser when a certain web page is accessed by them

cool *adjective* **1** slightly cold **2** calm, not excited **3** *informal* acceptable **4** *informal* good, fashionable ➤ *verb* to make or grow cool; to calm ♦ **coolness** *noun* (adjective, meanings 1 and 2)

coolly *adverb* **1** in a calm way **2** in a slightly unfriendly way

coop *noun* a box or cage for hens etc ➤ *verb* to shut (up) as in a coop

co-op see **co-operative society**

cooper *noun* someone who makes barrels

co-operate *verb* to work or act together ♦ **co-operation** *noun*

co-operative *noun* a business or farm etc owned by the workers

co-operative society or **co-op** *noun* a trading organization in which the profits are shared among members

co-opt *verb* to choose (someone) to join a committee or other body

co-ordinate *verb* (*pronounced* koh-**awrd**-in-eit) to make things fit in or work smoothly together ➤ *noun* (*pronounced* koh-**awrd**-in-at), *maths* one of a set of numbers used to indicate the position of a point, line or surface in relation to a system of axes

co-ordinate geometry *noun, maths* a system of geometry in which points, lines and surfaces are located in two-dimensional or three-dimensional space by co-ordinates (*also called:* **analytical geometry**)

co-ordinate sentence see **compound sentence**

co-ordination *noun* **1** the activity or skill of co-ordinating things **2** the ability to move and use the different parts of your body smoothly together: *You must have good co-ordination if you want to be a dancer* **3** *grammar* the linking of words, phrases or clauses in a sentence by using conjunctions

coot *noun* a water bird with a white forehead

cop *noun, slang* a police officer ➤ *verb* (**copping, copped**) to catch, seize ● **cop it** to land in trouble ● **cop out** to avoid responsibility

cope *verb* to struggle or deal successfully (with), manage

co-pilot *noun* the assistant pilot of an aircraft

coping *noun* the top layer of stone in a wall

coping-stone *noun* the top stone of a wall

copious *adjective* plentiful ♦ **copiously** *adverb*

cop-out *noun, slang* an avoidance of a responsibility

copper *noun* **1** *chemistry* (symbol **Cu**) a soft, reddish-brown, metallic element that also occurs in various ores **2** a reddish-brown colour **3** a coin made from copper **4** a large vessel made of copper, for boiling water ⊘ Comes from Anglo-Saxon *coper*, from Latin *cuprum*, from *Cyprium aes* meaning 'metal of Cyprus'

copperplate *noun* a style of very fine and regular handwriting

copper sulphate *noun, chemistry* a blue compound that tends to absorb moisture from the atmosphere, used in electroplating and as an antiseptic and pesticide

coppice or **copse** *noun* a group of low-growing trees

copra *noun* the dried kernel of the coconut, yielding coconut oil

copulate *verb* to have sexual intercourse

copy *noun* (*plural* **copies**) **1** an imitation **2** a print or reproduction of a picture etc **3** an individual example of a certain book etc ➤ *verb* (**copies, copying, copied**) **1** to make a copy of **2** to imitate

copy and paste *verb, computing* to copy text

or data from one document or program to another

copycat *noun, informal* a person who copies what someone else does

copyright *noun* the right of one person or body to publish a book, perform a play, print music, etc ► *adjective* of or protected by the law of copyright

copywriter *noun* someone who writes text for advertisements

coquette (*pronounced* ko-**ket**) *noun* a flirtatious woman

coquettish *adjective* flirtatious

cor- see co-

coral *noun* **1** a hard substance made from the skeletons of tiny animals, used to make jewellery **2** a pinkish-orange colour

coral reef *noun* a rock-like mass of coral built up gradually from the seabed

cor anglais (*pronounced* kawr-**ong**-glei) *noun* (*plural* **cors anglais** – *pronounced* kawrz-**ong**-glei) *music* a woodwind instrument similar to, but lower in pitch than, the oboe ⊙ Comes from French meaning 'English horn'

cord *noun* **1** thin rope or strong string **2** a thick strand of anything **3** *anatomy* a long flexible structure: *the spinal cord* ⊙ Comes from French *corde* meaning 'a rope'

❗ Do not confuse with: **chord**

cordial *adjective* cheery, friendly ► *noun* a concentrated fruit drink that is usually diluted before it is drunk ♦ **cordiality** *noun*

cordless *adjective* of a piece of electrical equipment: powered by a battery rather than being connected to the mains: *a cordless phone*

cordon *noun* a line of guards, police, etc to keep people back

cordon bleu (*pronounced* kawr-dong **bler**) *adjective* of a cook or cooking: first-class, excellent

⊙ Literally 'blue ribbon' in French, after the ribbon worn by the Knights of the Holy Ghost

corduroy *noun* a ribbed cotton cloth resembling velvet

core *noun* **1** the inner part of anything, especially fruit **2** the magnetic centre of the earth **3** *geography* the most economically important and prosperous part of a country or region (*contrasted with*: **periphery**) ► *verb* to take out the core of (fruit)

corgi *noun* a breed of short-legged dog

coriander *noun* a plant whose leaves and seeds are used to flavour food

cork *noun* **1** the outer bark of a type of oak found in southern Europe etc **2** a stopper for a bottle etc made of cork or other material ► *adjective*

made of cork ► *verb* to plug or stop up with a cork

corkscrew *noun* a tool with a screw-like spike for taking out corks ► *adjective* shaped like a corkscrew

corm *noun* the bulb-like underground stem of certain plants, eg the crocus

cormorant *noun* a type of big seabird with black or dark brown plumage and a long neck

corn *noun* **1** wheat, oats or maize **2** a small lump of hard skin, especially on a toe

cornea (*pronounced* **kawr**-ni-a) *noun* the transparent covering of the eyeball

corned beef *noun* salted tinned beef

corner *noun* **1** the point where two walls, roads, etc meet **2** a small secluded place **3** *informal* a difficult situation **4** in football, a free kick from the corner of the field ► *verb* **1** to force into a position from which there is no escape **2** to go around a corner: *The car corners well*

cornerstone *noun* **1** the stone at the corner of a building's foundations **2** something upon which a lot depends

cornet *noun* **1** a musical instrument like a small trumpet **2** an ice-cream in a cone-shaped wafer

cornflakes *plural noun* toasted flakes of maize, usually eaten as a breakfast cereal

cornflour *noun* finely ground maize flour

cornflower *noun* a type of plant with a blue flower

cornice *noun* an ornamental border round a ceiling

Corn Laws *plural noun, history* legislation passed in Britain in the 18th and 19th centuries, especially that which put high import duties on corn

cornucopia *noun* (*plural* **cornucopias**) **1** (*also called*: **horn of plenty**) *art* in painting etc: a horn overflowing with fruit etc, used as a symbol of abundance **2** an abundant supply ⊙ Comes from Latin *cornu* meaning 'horn' + *copiae* meaning 'abundance'

corny *adjective* (**cornier, corniest**) of a joke: old and stale

corolla *noun, botany* the petals of a flower

corollary *noun* (*plural* **corollaries**) **1** something that directly follows from another thing that has been proved **2** a natural or obvious consequence

corona *noun* **1** a halo of luminous gases around the sun **2** *physics* a glowing region of air surrounding a high-voltage conductor **3** *botany* in some plants, eg daffodil: a trumpet-like outgrowth from the petals

coronary *adjective* encircling a part of the body, used especially of the vessels supplying blood to the heart: *coronary arteries* ► *noun* (*plural* **coronaries**) (*short for* **coronary thrombosis**) a heart disease caused by blockage of one of the arteries supplying the heart

coronation *noun* the crowning of a king or queen

coroner *noun* a government officer who holds inquiries into the causes of sudden or accidental deaths

coronet *noun* **1** a small crown **2** a crown-like head-dress

corporal[1] *noun* the rank next below sergeant in the British army

corporal[2] *adjective* of the body

corporal punishment *noun* physical punishment by beating

corporate *adjective* **1** of or forming a whole; united **2** to do with a corporation: *a corporate uniform*

corporation *noun* a body of people acting as one for administrative or business purposes

corporeal (*pronounced* kawr-**paw**-ri-al) *adjective* **1** relating to the body as distinct from the soul **2** relating to material things ⊕ Comes from Latin *corporeus*, from *corpus* meaning 'body'

corps (*pronounced* kawr) *noun* (*plural* **corps** – *pronounced* kawrz) **1** a division of an army **2** an organized group

! Do not confuse: **corps** and **corpse**

corpse *noun* a dead body

corpulence *noun* obesity, fatness

corpulent *adjective* fat

corpus *noun* (*plural* **corpora**) a collection of writing etc

corpuscle *noun*, *anatomy* **1** a very small particle **2** a red or white blood cell ♦ **corpuscular** *adjective*

corral *noun*, *US* a fenced enclosure for animals ➤ *verb* (**corralling, corralled**) to enclose, pen

corrasion see **abrasion**

correct *verb* **1** to remove errors from **2** to set right **3** to punish ➤ *adjective* **1** having no errors **2** true **3** suitable and acceptable

correction *noun* **1** the putting right of a mistake **2** punishment

corrective *adjective* with the purpose of putting right some fault or of punishing someone

correlate *verb* **1** of two or more things: to have a connection: *Your prediction does not correlate with the result* **2** to combine or compare (information, reports, etc) ➤ *noun* either of two related things

correlation *noun* **1** a connection **2** an act of correlating **3** *statistics* the strength of the relationship between two random variables, eg **positive correlation**, where if one variable has a high or low value so does the other, and **negative correlation**, where if one variable has

a high value, the other has a low value

correlation coefficient *noun*, *statistics* a number between −1 and 1 calculated to represent the degree of correlation between two variables

correspond *verb* **1** to write letters to **2** to be similar (to), match

correspondence *noun* **1** letters **2** likeness, similarity

correspondent *noun* **1** someone who writes letters **2** someone who contributes reports to a newspaper etc ⊕ Comes from Latin *cor* meaning 'with' and *respondere* meaning 'to answer'

corresponding angles *plural noun*, *maths* angles that are in a similar position and the same side of the line when two straight lines are intersected by a transversal

corridor *noun* a passageway

corrie *noun*, *geography* a deep hollow on a mountain slope, caused by erosion by snow and ice (*also called*: **cirque, cwm**)

corroborate *verb* to give evidence which strengthens evidence already given ♦ **corroboration** *noun* ♦ **corroborative** *adjective* ⊕ Comes from Latin *cor-* giving emphasis, and *roborare* meaning 'to make strong'

corrode *verb* **1** *chemistry* of a metal or alloy: to gradually wear away through corrosion, to rust **2** to eat away at, erode ⊕ Comes via French from Latin *corrodere* meaning 'to gnaw away'

corrosion *noun* **1** *chemistry* the gradual wearing away of a metal or alloy as a result of oxidation by air, water or chemicals **2** a corroded part **3** *geography* another word for **solution** (meaning 2)

corrosive *adjective* **1** able to destroy or wear away materials such as metal by reacting chemically with them: *Nitric acid is highly corrosive* **2** having the effect of gradually wearing down or destroying something

corrugated (*pronounced* **kor**-u-gei-tid or **kor-**juw-gei-tid) *adjective* folded or shaped into ridges: *corrugated iron*

corrupt *verb* **1** to make evil or rotten **2** to make dishonest, bribe **3** *computing* to introduce errors into (a program or data) so that it is no longer reliable or usable ➤ *adjective* **1** dishonest, taking bribes **2** bad, rotten **3** *computing* said of a program or data: containing errors and no longer reliable or usable

corruptible *adjective* able to be corrupted, usually because of being innocent or naive

corruption *noun* **1** dishonesty, often involving the taking of bribes **2** the process of taking away someone's innocence or goodness: *corruption of the mind* **3** the unconscious changing of a word in speech or text, or a word which has changed in this way: *'Yeah' is a corruption of the word 'yes'*

corsage (*pronounced* kawr-**sasz**) *noun* **1** a small spray of flowers for pinning to the bodice of a dress **2** the bodice of a dress

corsair *noun, old* **1** a pirate **2** a pirate ship

corset *noun* a tight-fitting undergarment worn to support the body

cortège (*pronounced* kawr-**tesz**) *noun* a funeral procession

cortex *noun, anatomy* the outer layer of an organ or tissue, eg the brain ♦ **cortical** *adjective* ⊙ Comes from Latin meaning 'tree bark'

cortisone *noun* a naturally occurring steroid hormone which, in synthetic form, is used to treat rheumatoid arthritis and certain other disorders

cos¹ or **cos lettuce** (*pronounced* kos) *noun* a type of lettuce with crisp slender leaves

cos² (*pronounced* koz) *abbreviation, maths* cosine

cosec (*pronounced* **koh**-sek) *abbreviation, maths* cosecant

cosecant (*pronounced* koh-**see**-kant) *noun, maths* (*abbrev* **cosec**) for an angle in a right-angled triangle: a function that is the ratio of the length of the hypotenuse to that of the side opposite the angle

cosh *noun* (*plural* **coshes**) a short heavy stick ➤ *verb* to hit with a cosh

cosine *noun, maths* (*abbrev* **cos**) for an angle in a right-angled triangle: a function that is the ratio of the length of the side adjacent to the angle to that of the hypotenuse

cosine rule *noun, maths* a rule for calculating the sides and angles of a triangle ($c^2 = a^2 + b^2 - 2ab \cos C$)

cosmetic *noun* something designed to improve the appearance, especially of the face ➤ *adjective* **1** applied as a cosmetic **2** superficial, for appearances only

cosmic *adjective* **1** of the universe or outer space **2** *informal* excellent

cosmology *noun* astronomy that deals with the evolution of the universe

cosmonaut *noun* an astronaut of the former USSR

cosmopolitan *adjective* **1** including people from many countries **2** familiar with, or comfortable in, many different countries

cosmos *noun* the universe

cosset *verb* to treat with too much kindness, pamper

cost *verb* (**costing, cost**) **1** to be priced at **2** to cause the loss of: *The war cost many lives* **3** (past form **costed**) to calculate the cost of ➤ *noun*

what must be spent or suffered in order to get something

cost-effective *adjective* giving a good financial return in exchange for what is spent

costly *adjective* (**costlier, costliest**) high-priced, valuable ♦ **costliness** *noun*

costume *noun* **1** a set of clothes **2** clothes to wear in a play **3** fancy dress **4** a swimsuit

costume jewellery *noun* inexpensive, imitation jewellery

cosy *adjective* (**cosier, cosiest**) warm and comfortable ➤ *noun* (*plural* **cosies**) a covering to keep a teapot etc warm

cot¹ *noun* **1** a small high-sided bed for children **2** *US* a small collapsible bed; a camp bed

cot² *abbreviation, maths* cotangent

cotangent *noun, maths* (*abbrev* **cot**) for an angle in a right-angled triangle: a function that is the ratio of the length of the side adjacent to the angle to the length of the side opposite it

cot death *noun* the sudden unexplained death in sleep of an apparently healthy baby (*see also:* **sudden infant death syndrome**)

cottage *noun* a small house, especially in the countryside or a village

cottage cheese *noun* a soft, white cheese made from skimmed milk

cottage industry *noun* a craft industry such as knitting or weaving, employing workers in their own homes

cotton *noun* **1** a soft fluffy substance obtained from the seeds of the cotton plant **2** cloth made of cotton ➤ *adjective* made of cotton

cotton wool *noun* cotton in a fluffy state, used for wiping or absorbing

cotyledon (*pronounced* kot-i-**lee**-don) *noun, botany* one of the leaves produced by the embryo of a flowering plant

couch *noun* (*plural* **couches**) a sofa ➤ *verb* to express verbally: *couched in archaic language*

couch grass (*pronounced* kowch or kooch) *noun* a kind of grass, a troublesome weed

couch potato *noun* (*plural* **couch potatoes**) someone who spends their free time watching TV, playing computer games, etc

cougar *noun, US* the puma

cough *noun* a noisy effort of the lungs to throw out air, mucus, etc from the throat ➤ *verb* to make this effort

could *verb* **1** the form of the verb **can¹** used to express a condition: *He could afford it if he tried/ I could understand a small mistake, but this is ridiculous* **2** past form of the verb **can¹** ⊙ Comes from Old English *cuthe* meaning 'was able'

coulomb *noun* (symbol **C**) the standard unit of electric charge

council *noun* a group of people elected to discuss or give advice about policy, government, etc ⏱ Comes from Latin *concilium* meaning 'a calling together'

! Do not confuse with: **counsel**

councillor *noun* a member of a council

counsel *noun* **1** advice **2** *US* someone who gives legal advice; a lawyer ➤ *verb* (**counselling, counselled**) to give advice to ◆ **counselling** *noun* ⏱ Comes from Latin *consilium* meaning 'advice'

! Do not confuse with: **council**

counsellor *noun* someone who gives advice

count[1] *verb* **1** to find the total number of, add up **2** to say numbers in order (1, 2, 3, etc) **3** to think, consider: *Count yourself lucky!* ➤ *noun* **1** the act of counting **2** the number counted, eg of votes at an election **3** a charge, an accusation **4** a point being considered ◆ **count on** to rely on, depend on

count[2] *noun* a nobleman in certain countries

countable noun or **count noun** *noun, grammar* a noun which can be qualified in the singular by the indefinite article and can also be used in the plural, eg *car* (as in *a car* or *cars*) but not *furniture* (*compare with:* **mass noun**)

countdown *noun* a count backwards to zero, the point where the action takes place

countenance *noun* **1** the face **2** the expression on someone's face ➤ *verb* to tolerate, encourage

counter[1] *verb* to answer or oppose (a move, act, etc) by another ➤ *adverb* in the opposite direction ➤ *adjective* opposed; opposite

counter[2] *noun* **1** a token used in counting or gambing instead of a coin **2** a small plastic disc used in games such as ludo etc **3** a table across which payments are made in a shop

counter- also **contra-, contro-** *prefix* **1** against, opposing: *counter-argument* **2** opposite ⏱ Comes from Latin *contra* meaning 'against'

counteract *verb* to block or defeat (an action) by doing the opposite

counterattack *noun* an attack made by the defenders upon an attacking enemy ➤ *verb* to launch a counterattack

counter-example *noun* an example that disproves a statement or theory

counterfeit *adjective* **1** not genuine, not real **2** made in imitation for criminal purposes: *counterfeit money* ➤ *verb* to make a copy of

counterfoil *noun* a part of a cheque, postal order, etc kept by the payer or sender

countermand *verb* to give an order which goes against one already given

counterpane *noun* a top cover for a bed

counterpart *noun* someone or something which is just like or which corresponds to another person or thing

counterpoint *noun* the combining of two or more melodies to make a piece of music

counterpoise *noun* a weight which balances another weight

counter-productive *adjective* **1** tending to undermine productivity and efficiency **2** having the opposite effect to that intended

Counter-Reformation *noun* (**the Counter-Reformation**), *history* a reform and missionary movement in the Roman Catholic Church in the 16th century, following and counteracting the Reformation

countersign *verb* to sign your name after someone else's signature to show that a document is genuine

counter-tenor *noun, music* **1** the highest alto male singing voice **2** a singer with such a voice

counterurbanization *noun, geography* the movement of people away from towns into the countryside

countess *noun* (*plural* **countesses**) **1** a woman of the same rank as a count or earl **2** the wife or widow of a count or earl

countless *adjective* too many to be counted, very many

count noun another term for **countable noun**

country *noun* (*plural* **countries**) **1** a nation **2** a land under one government **3** the land in which someone lives **4** a district which is not in a town or city **5** an area or stretch of land ➤ *adjective* belonging to the country ⏱ Comes from Old French *contrée* meaning 'a stretch of land'

countryman or **countrywoman** *noun* (*plural* **countrymen** or **countrywomen**) **1** someone who lives in a rural area **2** someone who belongs to the same country as you

countryside *noun* the parts of a country other than towns and cities

county *noun* (*plural* **counties**) a division of a country

county court *noun* a local court dealing with non-criminal cases

coup (*pronounced* koo) *noun* **1** a sudden outstandingly successful move or act **2** a coup d'état

coup d'état (*pronounced* koo dei-**tah**) *noun* (*plural* **coups d'état** – *pronounced* koo dei-**tah**) a sudden and violent change in government

coupé (*pronounced* koo-**pei**) *noun* a car with two doors and a sloping rear

couple *noun* **1** a pair, two of a kind together **2** a husband and wife **3** *physics* a pair of equal but opposite forces applied to different points on the same object, producing a turning effect ➤ *verb* to join together

couplet *noun* two consecutive lines of verse,

especially ones which rhyme and have the same metre

coupling *noun* a link for joining railway carriages etc

coupon *noun* a piece of paper which may be exchanged for goods or money

courage *noun* bravery, lack of fear

courageous *adjective* brave, fearless

courgette *noun* (*pronounced* koor-**szet**) a type of small marrow

courier *noun* **1** someone who acts as a guide for tourists **2** a messenger

course *noun* **1** a path in which anything moves **2** movement from point to point **3** a track along which athletes etc run **4** a direction to be followed: *The ship held its course* **5** line of action: *the best course to follow* **6** a part of a meal **7** a number of things following each other: *a course of twelve lectures/a course of treatment* **8** one of the rows of bricks in a wall ➤ *verb* **1** to move quickly **2** to hunt • **in due course** after a while, in its proper time • **in the course of** during ⊕ Comes from French *cours* meaning 'course', 'lesson' or 'currency'

coursework *noun* work that makes up a course of study

coursing *noun* the hunting of hares with hounds

court *noun* **1** an open space surrounded by houses **2** an area marked out for playing tennis etc **3** the people who attend a monarch etc **4** a royal residence **5** *law* a room or building where legal cases are heard or tried ➤ *verb* **1** to try to win someone's love **2** to try to gain: *courting her affections* **3** to come near to achieving: *courting disaster*

courteous *adjective* polite; obliging ♦ **courteously** *adverb*

courtesy *noun* (*plural* **courtesies**) **1** politeness **2** a courteous action or remark

courtier *noun* a member of a royal court

courtly *adjective* having fine manners

court-martial *noun* (*plural* **courts-martial** or **court-martials**) a court held within the armed forces to try those who break military laws ➤ *verb* to try in a court-martial

Court of Appeal *noun, law* in England and Wales: a court with civil and criminal divisions which hears appeals from other courts

courtship *noun* the act or time of courting or wooing

courtyard *noun* a court or enclosed space beside a house

couscous *noun* a type of crushed semolina that is steamed and served with vegetables, chicken, etc

cousin *noun* the son or daughter of an uncle or aunt

covalency *noun, chemistry* the union of two or more atoms by sharing one or more pairs of electrons ♦ **covalent** *adjective* ♦ **covalently** *adverb*

covalent bond *noun* a chemical bond formed in which a pair of electrons are shared by two atoms

cove *noun* a small inlet on the sea coast; a bay

coven (*pronounced* **kuv**-en) *noun* a gathering of witches

covenant *noun* **1** an important agreement between people to do or not to do something **2** an engagement between God and a person or a people

cover *verb* **1** to put or spread something on or over **2** to hide **3** to stretch over: *The hills were covered with heather/My diary covers three years* **4** to include, deal with: *covering the news story* **5** to be enough for: *Five pounds should cover the cost* **6** to travel over: *covering 3 kilometres a day* **7** to point a weapon at: *had the gangster covered* ➤ *noun* something that covers, hides or protects • **cover up 1** to cover completely **2** to conceal deliberately

coverage *noun* **1** an area covered: *a mobile phone network with good coverage* **2** the extent of news covered by a newspaper etc **3** the amount of protection given by an insurance policy

coverlet *noun* a bed cover ⊕ Comes from French *couvrir* meaning 'to cover', and *lit* meaning 'bed'

cover note *noun* a temporary insurance certificate used until the actual policy is issued

covert (*pronounced* **kuv**-ert or **koh**-vert) *adjective* secret, not done openly ➤ *noun* (*pronounced* **kuv**-ert) a hiding place for animals or birds when hunted

cover-up *noun* a deliberate concealment, especially by people in authority

covet (*pronounced* **kuv**-it) *verb* to long to have, especially something belonging to another person

covetous *adjective* having a tendency to want things, especially things which belong to other people ♦ **covetously** *adverb* ♦ **covetousness** *noun*

covey (*pronounced* **kuv**-i) *noun* (*plural* **coveys**) a flock of birds, especially partridges

cow[1] *noun* **1** the female of various types of ox, bred by humans for giving milk **2** the female of an elephant, whale, etc

cow[2] *verb* to frighten, subdue

coward *noun* someone who has no courage and shows fear easily ♦ **cowardly** *adjective*

cowardice *noun* lack of courage

cowboy *noun* **1** a man who works with cattle on a ranch **2** *slang* someone who does building or other work without proper training or qualifications and does a bad job

cowed *adjective* frightened, subdued

cower *verb* to crouch down or shrink back through fear

cowgirl *noun* a woman who works with cattle on a ranch

cowherd *noun* someone who looks after cows

cowl *noun* 1 a hood, especially that of a monk 2 a cover for a chimney

cowslip *noun* a yellow wild flower

cox *noun* (*plural* **coxes**) *short for* **coxswain** ➤ *verb* to act as a coxswain

coxcomb *noun* 1 in the past, a head-covering notched like a cock's comb, worn by a jester 2 a vain or conceited person

coxswain (*pronounced* **kok**-sun) *noun* 1 someone who steers a boat 2 an officer in charge of a boat and crew

coy *adjective* too modest or shy

coyote (*pronounced* koi-**oh**-ti or kai-**oh**-ti) *noun* (*plural* **coyote** or **coyotes**) a type of small North American wolf

coypu (*pronounced* **koi**-poo) *noun* a large, beaverlike animal living in rivers and marshes

CPU *abbreviation, computing* central processing unit

Cr *symbol, chemistry* chromium

crab *noun* 1 a sea creature with a shell and five pairs of legs, the first pair of which have large claws 2 (**crabs**) pubic lice

crab apple *noun* a type of small, bitter apple

crabbed (*pronounced* **krab**-id) *adjective* bad-tempered

crabwise *adverb* sideways like a crab

crack *verb* 1 to (cause to) make a sharp, sudden sound 2 to break partly without falling to pieces 3 to break into (a safe) 4 to decipher (a code) 5 to gain unauthorized access to (computer files) 6 to break open (a nut) 7 to make (a joke) 8 *chemistry* to break down long-chain molecules into smaller molecules, as in the refining of crude oil ➤ *noun* 1 a sharp sound 2 a split, a break 3 a narrow opening 4 *informal* a sharp, witty remark 5 *informal* a pure form of cocaine ➤ *adjective* excellent: *a crack tennis player* • **crack up** 1 to have an emotional breakdown 2 to collapse with laughter

crackdown *noun* firm action taken to stop a particular type of activity

cracked *adjective* 1 split, damaged 2 *informal* mad, crazy

cracker *noun* 1 a hollow paper tube containing a small gift, which breaks with a bang when the ends are pulled 2 a thin, crisp biscuit 3 *informal* something excellent: *a cracker of a story*

cracking *adjective, informal* 1 very good: *a cracking story* 2 very fast: *a cracking pace* ➤ *noun, chemistry* the breaking down of

crude oil into smaller molecules

crackle *verb* to make a continuous cracking noise ➤ *noun* a continuous cracking noise

crackling *noun* 1 a cracking sound 2 the rind or outer skin of roast pork

-cracy *suffix* forms nouns describing different types of government, or the members of a ruling group: *democracy/aristocracy* ⊙ Comes from Greek *kratos* meaning 'power'

cradle *noun* 1 a baby's bed, especially one which can be rocked 2 a frame under a ship that is being built

craft *noun* 1 an artistic activity involving construction as opposed to drawing etc 2 a trade, a skill 3 a boat, a small ship 4 slyness, cunning

craftsman or **craftswoman** *noun* (*plural* **craftsmen** or **craftswomen**) someone who works at a trade, especially with their hands

craftwork *noun* 1 creative artistic activity 2 the result of this activity

crafty *adjective* (**craftier, craftiest**) cunning, sly ◆ **craftily** *adverb*

crag *noun* a rough steep rock

craggy *adjective* (**craggier, craggiest**) 1 rocky 2 of a face: well-marked, lined

cram *verb* (**cramming, crammed**) 1 to fill full, stuff 2 to learn up facts for an examination in a short time

cramp *noun* 1 a painful stiffening of the muscles 2 (**cramps**) an acute stomach pain ➤ *verb* 1 to confine in too small a space 2 to hinder, restrict

cramped *adjective* 1 overcrowded, without enough room 2 of handwriting: small and closely written

cranberry *noun* (*plural* **cranberries**) a type of red, sour berry

crane *noun* 1 a large wading bird with long legs, neck and bill 2 a machine for lifting and moving heavy weights ➤ *verb* to stretch out (the neck) to see round or over something

cranefly *noun* (*plural* **craneflies**) a long-legged, two-winged insect (*also called*: **daddy-long-legs**)

cranium (*pronounced* **krei**-ni-um) *noun, anatomy* (*plural* **crania** or **craniums**) the skull

crank *noun* 1 a handle for turning an axle 2 a lever which converts a horizontal movement into a rotating one 3 an eccentric ➤ *verb* to start (an engine) with a crank

crankshaft *noun* the main shaft of an engine or other machine, with one or more cranks, used to transmit power from the cranks to the connecting rods

cranky *adjective* (**crankier, crankiest**) 1 odd, eccentric 2 cross, irritable

cranny *noun* (*plural* **crannies**) a small opening or crack

crape another spelling of **crêpe**

crash noun (plural **crashes**) **1** a noise of heavy things breaking or banging together **2** a collision causing damage, eg between vehicles **3** the failure of a business ▸ adjective short but intensive: a crash course in French ▸ verb **1** to be involved in a crash **2** of a business: to fail **3** of a computer program: to break down, fail **4** (also: **gatecrash**) informal to attend (a party) uninvited

crash-helmet noun a protective covering for the head worn by motorcyclists etc

crash-land verb to land (an aircraft) in an emergency, causing some structural damage ♦ **crash-landing** noun

crass adjective stupid ♦ **crassly** adverb

crate noun a container for carrying goods, often made of wooden slats

crater noun **1** the bowl-shaped mouth of a volcano **2** a hole made by an explosion

craton (pronounced **krei**-ton) noun, geography a relatively rigid and stable area of rock in the Earth's crust (also called: **shield**)

cravat (pronounced kra-**vat**) noun a scarf worn in place of a tie

> ⏱ From a French word for 'Croat', because of the linen neck-bands worn by 17th-century Croatian soldiers

crave verb to long for (something) ♦ **craving** noun

craven adjective, old cowardly

craw another word for **crop** (meaning 2)

crawl verb **1** to move on hands and knees **2** to move slowly: The traffic was crawling **3** to be covered (with): crawling with wasps **4** to be obsequious; fawn ▸ noun **1** the act of crawling **2** a swimming stroke of kicking the legs and alternating the arms

crawler noun **1** informal an obsequious, fawning person **2** computing a web crawler

crayon noun a coloured pencil or stick of wax for drawing

craze noun a temporary fashion or enthusiasm

crazy adjective (**crazier, craziest**) mad, unreasonable ♦ **crazily** adverb ♦ **craziness** noun

crazy paving noun paving with stones of irregular shape

creak verb to make a sharp, grating sound like a hinge in need of oiling ♦ **creaky** adjective (**creakier, creakiest**)

cream noun **1** the fatty substance which forms on milk **2** something like this in texture: cleansing cream/shaving cream **3** the best part: the cream of society ▸ verb **1** to take the cream from **2** to take away (the best part)

creamy adjective (**creamier, creamiest**) full of or like cream

crease noun **1** a mark made by folding **2** cricket a line showing the position of a batsman and bowler ▸ verb **1** to make creases in **2** to become creased

create verb **1** to bring into being; make **2** informal to make a fuss

creatine phosphate (pronounced **kree**-at-in or **kree**-at-een) noun a substance found in limited amounts in muscle, used as a short-term source of energy during bursts of activity

creation noun **1** the act of creating **2** something created

creative adjective having the ability to create, artistic ♦ **creativity** noun

creator noun **1** the person who has created something **2** (**the Creator**) God

creature noun an animal or person

crèche (pronounced kresh) noun a nursery for children

credentials plural noun documents carried as proof of identity, character, etc

credible adjective able to be believed ♦ **credibility** noun

> ❗ Do not confuse with: **credulous**

credit noun **1** recognition of good qualities, achievements, etc: Give him credit for some common sense **2** good qualities **3** a source of honour: a credit to the family **4** trustworthiness in ability to pay for goods **5** the sale of goods to be paid for later **6** the side of an account on which payments received are entered **7** a sum of money in a bank account **8** belief, trust **9** (**credits**) the naming of people who have helped in a film etc ▸ verb **1** to believe **2** to enter on the credit side of an account **3** (**credit someone with**) to believe them to have: I credited him with more sense

creditable adjective bringing honour or good reputation to

creditably adverb in a way which can be approved of or admired

credit card noun a card allowing the holder to pay for purchased articles at a later date

creditor noun someone to whom money is owed

credulity noun willingness to believe things which may be untrue

credulous adjective believing too easily

> ❗ Do not confuse with: **credible**

creed noun a summary of belief, especially religious belief

creek noun **1** a small inlet or bay on the sea coast **2** a short river

creep verb (**creeping, crept**) **1** to move slowly and silently **2** to move with the body close to the ground **3** to shiver with fear or disgust: makes your flesh creep **4** of a plant: to grow along the ground or up a wall etc ➤ noun **1** a move in a creeping way **2** informal an unpleasant person **3** (**the creeps**) informal a feeling of disgust or fear • **creep up on** to approach silently from behind

creeper noun a plant growing along the ground or up a wall etc

creepy adjective (**creepier, creepiest**) unsettlingly sinister

cremate verb to burn (a dead body) ♦ **cremation** noun

crematorium noun (plural **crematoria** or **crematoriums**) a place where dead bodies are burnt

crème fraîche (pronounced krem **fresh**) noun cream thickened with a culture of bacteria, used in cooking

creosote (pronounced **kree**-o-soht) noun an oily liquid made from wood tar, used to keep wood from rotting

crêpe (pronounced kreip or krep) noun **1** a type of fine, crinkly material **2** a thin pancake

crêpe paper noun paper with a crinkled appearance

crept past form of **creep**

crepuscular (pronounced kri-**pus**-yuw-lar) adjective **1** relating to or like twilight **2** denoting animals that are active before sunrise or at dusk, eg bats, rabbits, deer ◐ Comes from Latin crepusculum meaning 'twilight'

crescendo (pronounced kri-**shen**-doh) noun (plural **crescendos**) **1** music a musical passage that becomes increasingly loud **2** a climax

crescent adjective shaped like the new or old moon; curved ➤ noun **1** something in a curved shape **2** a curved road or street

cress noun a plant with small, slightly bitter-tasting leaves, used in salads

crest noun **1** a tuft on the head of a cock or other bird **2** the top of a hill, wave, etc **3** feathers on top of a helmet **4** a badge

crestfallen adjective downhearted, discouraged

Cretaceous adjective of the geological period from 140 million to 65 million years ago

cretin noun, informal an idiot, a fool

crevasse (pronounced kre-**vas**) noun a deep split in snow or ice

❗ Do not confuse: **crevasse** and **crevice**

crevice (pronounced **krev**-is) noun a crack, a narrow opening

crew¹ noun **1** the people who man a ship, aircraft, etc **2** a gang, a mob ➤ verb to act as a member of a crew

crew² past form of **crow** (meaning 1)

crewcut noun an extremely short hairstyle

crib noun **1** a manger **2** a child's bed **3** a ready-made translation of a school text etc ➤ verb (**cribbing, cribbed**) to copy someone else's work

cribbage noun a card game in which the score is kept with a pegged board

crick noun a sharp pain, especially in the neck ➤ verb to produce a crick in

cricket¹ noun a game played with bats, ball and wickets, between two sides of eleven players each

cricket² noun an insect similar to a grasshopper

cricketer noun someone who plays cricket

crime noun an act or deed which is against the law

criminal adjective **1** forbidden by law **2** very wrong ➤ noun someone guilty of a crime

criminal law noun the branch of law dealing with unlawful acts (compare with: **civil law**)

crimp verb to press into small ridges: Crimp the edges of the pastry

crimson noun a deep red colour ➤ adjective of this colour

cringe verb **1** to crouch or shrink back in fear **2** to behave in too humble a way

crinkle verb **1** to wrinkle, crease **2** to make a crackling sound

crinkly adjective wrinkled

crinoline (pronounced **krin**-o-lin) noun a wide petticoat or skirt shaped by concentric hoops

cripple noun, offensive a disabled person ➤ verb **1** to make lame **2** to make less strong, less efficient, etc: Their policies crippled the economy ♦ **crippled** adjective

crisis noun (plural **crises**) **1** a deciding moment, a turning point **2** a time of great danger or suspense

crisp adjective **1** stiff and dry; brittle **2** cool and fresh: crisp air **3** firm and fresh: crisp lettuce **4** sharp ➤ noun a thin, crisp piece of fried potato eaten cold ♦ **crispness** noun ♦ **crispy** adjective

criss-cross adjective having a pattern of crossing lines ➤ verb to move across and back: Railway lines criss-cross the landscape

◐ Based on the phrase Christ's cross

criterion (pronounced krai-**tee**-ri-on) noun (plural **criteria**) a means or rule by which something can be judged; a standard

ⓘ **Criteria** is a plural form. A criteria is wrong.

critic noun **1** someone whose job is to review books, films, etc **2** someone who finds faults in a thing or person

critical adjective **1** fault-finding **2** using analysis and assessment: a critical commentary/critical thinking **3** to do with or at a crisis **4** very ill **5** serious, very important **6** physics denoting a state or value at which there is a significant change in a system's properties

critical mass *noun, physics* the smallest amount of a fissile material that is needed to sustain a nuclear chain reaction

critical point *noun, maths* a point at which the derivative of a function is zero or infinite

critical region *noun, statistics* in testing a hypothesis: the set of values which would disprove the null hypothesis and prove the alternative hypothesis

critical temperature *noun, physics* **1** the temperature above which a gas cannot be liquefied by pressure alone **2** the temperature above which a magnetic material loses its magnetic properties

criticism *noun* **1** finding faults **2** reasoned analysis and assessment, especially of art, literature, music, etc **3** the act of criticizing

criticize or **criticise** *verb* **1** to find fault with **2** to give an opinion or judgement on

croak *verb* to make a low, hoarse sound like a frog ➤ *noun* a low, hoarse sound ◆ **croaky** *adjective* (**croakier, croakiest**)

crochet (*pronounced* **kroh**-shei) *noun* a form of knitting done with one hooked needle ➤ *verb* to work in crochet

crock *noun* **1** an earthenware pot or jar **2** an old and decrepit person or thing

crockery *noun* china or earthenware dishes

crocodile *noun* **1** a large reptile found in rivers in Asia, Africa, etc **2** a procession of children walking two by two

crocodile tears *plural noun* a show of pretended grief

crocus *noun* (*plural* **crocuses**) a yellow, purple or white flower which grows from a corm

croft *noun* a small farm with a cottage, especially in the Scottish Highlands

crofter *noun* someone who farms on a croft

crofting *noun* farming on a croft

croissant (*pronounced* **krwah**-song) *noun* a curved flaky roll of rich bread dough

crone *noun* an ugly old woman

crony *noun* (*plural* **cronies**) *informal* a close friend

crook *noun* **1** a shepherd's or bishop's stick bent at the end **2** a criminal ➤ *verb* to bend or form into a hook

crooked (*pronounced* **kruwk**-id) *adjective* **1** bent, hooked **2** dishonest, criminal

croon *verb* to sing or hum in a low voice ◆ **crooning** *noun*

crop *noun* **1** natural produce gathered for food from fields, trees or bushes **2** (*also called*: **craw**) a pouch in a bird's stomach where food is stored before digestion **3** a riding whip **4** the hair on the head **5** a short haircut ➤ *verb* (**cropping,**

cropped) **1** to cut short **2** to cut off the top, ends, margins, etc of **3** to gather a crop (of wheat etc) • **crop up** to happen unexpectedly

cropper *noun*: **come a cropper 1** to fail badly **2** to have a bad fall

croquet (*pronounced* **kroh**-kei) *noun* a game in which players use long-handled mallets to drive wooden balls through hoops in the ground

cross *noun* (*plural* **crosses**) **1** a shape (×) or (+) formed of two lines intersecting in the middle **2** a structure on which criminals were executed in ancient times **3** *Christianity* a monument, symbol, etc in the shape (†) that represents the cross on which Christ was executed; a crucifix **4** a medal etc in the shape of a cross **5** a place where there is a crossroads **6** the result of breeding an animal or plant with one of another kind: *a cross between a horse and a donkey* **7** a trouble that must be endured **8** in sports, especially football: a pass from the wing to the centre or the opposite wing of the pitch ➤ *verb* **1** to mark with a cross **2** to go to the other side of (a room, road, etc) **3** to lie or pass across **4** to meet and pass **5** to go against the wishes of **6** to draw two lines across to validate (a cheque) **7** to breed (one kind) with (another) **8** in sports, especially football: to pass (the ball) from the wing to the centre or the opposite wing of the pitch ➤ *adjective* bad-tempered, angry • **cross out** to delete (something) by drawing a line through it

crossbar *noun* **1** a horizontal bar between posts, especially goalposts **2** the horizontal bar on a man's bicycle

crossbow *noun* a bow fixed to a wooden stand with a device for pulling back the string

cross-breed *biology, verb* to mate (two animals or plants of different breeds) in order to produce offspring with the best characteristics of both parents ➤ *noun* an animal or plant bred from two different pure breeds

crosscheck *verb* to verify (information) from an independent source

cross-country *adjective* of a race: across fields etc, not on roads

cross-dress *verb* especially of men: to dress in the clothes of the opposite sex

cross-examine *verb* to question closely in court to test the accuracy of a statement etc ◆ **cross-examination** *noun*

cross-eyed *adjective* having a squint

crossfire *noun* gunfire coming from different directions

crosshatching *noun* shading consisting of sets of lines drawn across each other ◆ **crosshatch** *verb*

crossing *noun* **1** a place where a street, river, etc may be crossed **2** a journey over the sea

crossly *adverb* angrily

crossness *noun* bad temper, sulkiness

crosspiece *noun* a piece that lies across another

cross-pollination *noun, botany* the transfer of pollen from the anther of one flower to the stigma of another of the same species

cross-purposes *plural noun* confusion in a conversation through misunderstanding

cross-reference *noun* a statement in a reference book directing the reader to further information in another section

crossroads *singular noun* a place where roads cross each other

cross-section *noun* 1 a section made by cutting across something 2 a sample taken as representative of the whole: *a cross-section of voters*

crossword *noun* a puzzle in which letters are written into blank squares to form words in answer to numbered clues

crotch *noun* (*plural* **crotches**) the area between the tops of the legs

crotchet *noun* a musical note (♩) equivalent to a quarter of a whole note or semibreve

crotchety *adjective* bad-tempered

crouch *verb* 1 to stand with the knees well bent 2 of an animal: to lie close to the ground

croup[1] (*pronounced* kroop) *noun* a children's disease causing difficulty in breathing and a harsh cough

croup[2] (*pronounced* kroop) *noun* the hindquarters of a horse

crow *noun* 1 a large bird, generally black 2 the cry of a cock 3 the happy sounds made by a baby ➤ *verb* (**crowing, crew** or **crowed**) 1 (past tense **crew**) to cry like a cock 2 to boast 3 of a baby: to make happy noises • **as the crow flies** in a straight line

crowbar *noun* a large iron bar used as a lever

crowd *noun* a number of people or things together ➤ *verb* 1 to gather into a crowd 2 to fill too full 3 to keep too close to, impede: *Don't crowd me!*

crown *noun* 1 a jewelled headdress worn by monarchs on ceremonial occasions 2 the top of the head 3 the highest part of something 4 *Brit* an old coin worth five shillings ➤ *verb* 1 to put a crown on 2 to make a monarch 3 *informal* to hit on the head 4 to reward, finish happily: *crowned with success*

crown courts *plural noun* in England and Wales: the courts dealing with serious crimes

crow's-nest *noun* a sheltered and enclosed platform near the masthead of a ship from which a lookout is kept

crucial *adjective* extremely important, critical: *crucial question* ♦ **crucially** *adverb*

crucible *noun* a small container for melting metals etc

crucifix *noun* (*plural* **crucifixes**) a figure or picture of Christ fixed to the cross

crucifixion *noun* 1 the act of crucifying 2 death on the cross, especially that of Christ

crucify *verb* (**crucifies, crucifying, crucified**) to put to death by fixing the hands and feet to a cross

crude *adjective* 1 not purified or refined: *crude oil* 2 roughly made or done 3 vulgar, blunt, tactless: *a crude joke* ♦ **crudely** *adverb* ♦ **crudity** *noun*

crude birth rate and **crude death rate** see **birth rate** and **death rate**

cruel *adjective* (**crueller, cruellest**) 1 deliberately causing pain or distress 2 having no pity for others' sufferings ♦ **cruelly** *adverb* ♦ **cruelty** *noun* (*plural* **cruelties**)

cruet (*pronounced* **kroo**-it) *noun* 1 a small jar for salt, pepper, mustard, etc 2 two or more such jars on a stand

cruise *verb* to travel by car, ship, etc at a steady speed ➤ *noun* a journey by ship made for pleasure

cruiser *noun* a middle-sized warship

crumb *noun* a small bit of anything, especially bread: *a crumb of comfort*

crumble *verb* 1 to break into crumbs or small pieces 2 to fall to pieces ➤ *noun* a dish of stewed fruit etc topped with crumbs

crumbly *adjective* (**crumblier, crumbliest**) having a tendency to fall to pieces

crumpet *noun* a soft, flat cake, baked on a griddle

crumple *verb* 1 to crush into creases or wrinkles 2 to become creased 3 to collapse

crunch *verb* 1 to chew hard so as to make a noise 2 to crush ➤ *noun* (*plural* **crunches**) 1 a noise of crunching 2 (**the crunch**) *informal* a testing moment, a turning-point ♦ **crunchy** *adjective* (**crunchier, crunchiest**)

crusade *noun* 1 a movement undertaken for some good cause 2 *history* a Christian expedition to regain the Holy Land from the Turks

crusader *noun* someone who goes on a crusade

crush *verb* 1 to squeeze together 2 to beat down, overcome: *crush the opposition to the bill* 3 to crease, crumple ➤ *noun* (*plural* **crushes**) 1 a violent squeezing 2 a pressing crowd of people 3 a drink made by squeezing fruit

crushed *adjective* 1 squeezed, squashed 2 completely defeated or miserable

crust *noun* 1 a hard outside coating, eg on bread, a cut in the skin, etc 2 the solid outermost layer of the earth, consisting mainly of sedimentary rocks over ancient igneous rocks

crustacean (*pronounced* krus-**tei**-shun) *noun*

any of a large group of invertebrate animals which typically has two pairs of antennae and a hard shell, including crabs, lobsters, shrimps, etc

crusty adjective (**crustier, crustiest**) **1** having a crust **2** cross, irritable

crutch noun (plural **crutches**) **1** a stick held under the armpit or elbow, used for support in walking **2** a support, a prop

crux noun (plural **cruxes**) the most important or difficult part of a problem

cry verb (**cries, crying, cried**) **1** to make a loud sound in pain or sorrow **2** to weep **3** to call loudly ➤ noun (plural **cries**) a loud call • **cry off** to cancel • **cry over spilt milk** to be worried about a misfortune that is past

crying adjective **1** weeping **2** calling loudly **3** requiring notice or attention: a crying need

cryogenics singular noun the branch of physics concerned with phenomena occurring at very low temperatures

cryonics singular noun the preservation of human corpses by freezing them, with the idea that advances in science will enable them to be revived at a later date

cryopreservation noun, biology the preservation by freezing of living cells, eg blood, eggs, sperm, etc

crypt noun an underground cell or chapel, especially one used for burial

cryptic adjective mysterious, difficult to understand: a cryptic remark • **cryptically** adverb

crypto- or **crypt-** prefix hidden: cryptic ☺ Comes from Greek kryptos meaning 'hidden'

cryptography noun the art of coding and reading codes

crystal noun **1** very clear glass often used for making drinking glasses etc **2** the regular shape taken by each small part of certain substances, eg salt or sugar **3** chemistry any solid substance consisting of a regularly repeating arrangement of atoms, ions or molecules

crystal lattice noun, physics the orderly arrangement of points around which atoms or ions in a crystal are centred

crystalline adjective **1** made up of crystals **2** chemistry displaying the properties of crystals, eg the regular internal arrangement of atoms

crystallize or **crystallise** verb **1** chemistry to form into crystals **2** to take a form or shape, become clear • **crystallization** noun

Cs symbol, chemistry caesium

CS gas noun an irritant vapour which causes a burning sensation in the eyes, choking, and vomiting, used for riot control

⊙ Named from the initials of its US inventors, B Corson and R Stoughton

CT scanner see **CAT scanner**

Cu symbol, chemistry copper

cub noun **1** the young of certain animals, eg foxes **2** a Cub Scout

cube noun **1** a solid body having six equal square sides **2** maths the answer to a sum in which a number is multiplied by itself twice: 8 is the cube of 2

cube root noun, maths the number which, multiplied by itself and then by itself again, gives a certain other number (eg 2 is the cube root of 8)

cubic adjective **1** of cubes **2** in the shape of a cube **3** maths involving the cube of a variable: a cubic equation **4** in volume: a cubic metre

cubicle noun a small room closed off in some way from a larger one

Cubism (pronounced **kyoob**-izm) noun, art a 20th-century movement which represented natural objects as geometric shapes ◆ **Cubist** noun & adjective

cuboid noun, maths a solid body having six rectangular faces, the opposite faces of which are equal

Cub Scout noun a junior Scout

cuckoo noun a bird which visits Britain in summer and lays its eggs in the nests of other birds

cucumber noun a creeping plant with a long green fruit used in salads

cud noun food regurgitated by certain animals, eg sheep and cows

cuddle verb to put your arms round, hug ➤ noun a hug, an embrace ◆ **cuddly** adjective (**cuddlier, cuddliest**) pleasant to cuddle: cuddly kittens

cudgel noun a heavy stick, a club ➤ verb (**cudgelling, cudgelled**) to beat with a cudgel

cue[1] noun **1** a sign to tell an actor when to speak etc **2** a hint, an indication

cue[2] noun the stick used to hit a ball in pool, billiards and snooker

cuff noun **1** the end of a sleeve near the wrist **2** US the turned-back part of a trouser leg **3** a blow with the open hand ➤ verb to hit with the hand • **off the cuff** without planning or rehearsal

cufflinks plural noun a pair of ornamental buttons etc used to fasten a shirt cuff

cuisine (pronounced kwi-**zeen**) noun **1** the art of cookery **2** a style of cooking: Mexican cuisine

cul-de-sac (pronounced **kul**-de-sak) noun (plural **cul-de-sacs** or **culs-de-sac**) a street closed at one end

culinary adjective of or used for cookery

cull verb **1** to gather **2** to choose from a group **3** to pick out (seals, deer, etc) from a herd and kill for the good of the herd ➤ noun such a killing

culminate verb **1** to reach the highest point **2** to reach the most important or greatest point, end (in): *an investigation culminating in several arrests* ♦ **culmination** *noun*

culpable *adjective* guilty, blameworthy

culprit *noun* **1** someone who is to blame for something **2** *English law, US law* a prisoner accused but not yet tried

cult *noun* **1** a religious sect **2** a general strong enthusiasm for something: *the cult of physical fitness*

cultivate *verb* **1** to grow (vegetables etc) **2** to plough, sow: *cultivate the land* **3** to try to develop and improve: *cultivated my friendship* ♦ **cultivation** *noun*

cultivated *adjective* **1** farmed, ploughed **2** educated, informed

cultivator *noun* **1** a person who cultivates the land **2** a machine or tool that you use for cultivating

cultural *adjective* **1** to do with a culture: *cultural differences* **2** to do with the arts: *a cultural visit to the gallery*

Cultural Revolution *noun, history* a mass movement in China from 1966 to 1976, aimed at overthrowing the bourgeoisie, that resulted in social and political turmoil

culture *noun* **1** a type of civilization with its associated customs: *ancient Greek culture* **2** development of the mind by education **3** educated tastes in art, music, etc **4** cultivation of plants **5** *biology* a population of bacteria, cells or tissues grown for scientific study

cultured *adjective* well-educated in literature, art, etc

culture medium *noun* a solid or liquid nutrient in which micro-organisms, cells or tissues can be grown in a laboratory

culture shock *noun* disorientation caused by a change from a familiar environment, culture, etc, to another that is very different

culvert *noun* an arched drain for carrying water under a road or railway

cum *preposition* used for both of two stated purposes: *a newsagent-cum-grocer*

cumbersome *adjective* awkward to handle

cumin (*pronounced* **kum**-in or **kyoom**-in) or **cummin** (*pronounced* **kum**-in) *noun* a Mediterranean plant whose seeds are used to flavour food

cummerbund *noun* a broad sash worn around the waist

cumulative *adjective* increasing with additions: *cumulative effect*

cumulative frequency *noun, maths* a measure of frequency obtained by adding frequencies in succession

cumulative frequency diagram *noun, maths* a graph showing cumulative frequency in

which the number of frequencies up to a given point is shown on the horizontal axis, and the sum of their values is represented by its vertical co-ordinate

cumulative sum *noun, maths* a sequence of sums from a given sequence, eg *a, a + b, b + c, … from a, b, c, …*

cumulus *noun* (*plural* **cumuli** – *pronounced* **kyoo**-myuw-lai) a kind of cloud made up of rounded heaps

cunning *adjective* **1** sly, clever in a deceitful way **2** skilful, clever ➤ *noun* **1** slyness **2** skill, knowledge

cup *noun* **1** a hollow container holding liquid for drinking **2** an ornamental vessel given as a prize in sports events ➤ *verb* (**cupping, cupped**) to make (hands etc) into the shape of a cup

cupboard *noun* a shelved recess, or a box with drawers, used for storage

cupful *noun* (*plural* **cupfuls**) as much as fills a cup

Cupid (*pronounced* **kyoop**-id) *noun* the Roman god of sexual love

cupidity (*pronounced* kyoo-**pid**-it-i) *noun* greed

cupola (*pronounced* **kyoop**-ol-a) *noun* a curved ceiling or dome on the top of a building

cupric (*pronounced* **kyoop**-rik) *adjective, chemistry* denoting any compound of copper in which the element has a valency of two

cuprous (*pronounced* **kyoop**-rus) *adjective, chemistry* denoting any compound of copper in which the element has a valency of one

cup-tie *noun* a game in a sports competition for which the prize is a cup

cur *noun* **1** a dog of mixed breed **2** a cowardly person

curable *adjective* able to be treated and cured

curate *noun* a member of the Church of England clergy assisting a rector or vicar

curative *adjective* likely to cure

curator *noun* someone who has charge of a museum, art gallery, etc

curb *verb* to hold back, restrain ➤ *noun* a restraint

⚠ Do not confuse with: **kerb**

curd *noun* **1** milk thickened by acid **2** the clotted protein formed when milk curdles and from which cheese is made (*compare with*: **whey**)

curdle *verb* to turn into curd

cure *noun* **1** freeing from disease, healing **2** something which frees from disease ➤ *verb* **1** to heal **2** to get rid of (a bad habit etc) **3** to preserve by drying, salting, etc

curfew *noun* an order forbidding people to be out of their houses after a certain time

curio *noun* (*plural* **curios**) an article valued for its oddness or rarity

curiosity *noun* (*plural* **curiosities**) **1** strong desire to find something out **2** something unusual, an oddity

curious *adjective* **1** anxious to find out **2** unusual, odd ♦ **curiously** *adverb*

curium *noun, chemistry* (symbol **Cm**) a radioactive element formed by bombarding plutonium with alpha particles

⊙ Named after the French physicists Marie (1867–1934) and Pierre (1859–1906) *Curie*

curl *verb* **1** to twist (hair) into small coils **2** of hair: to grow naturally in small coils **3** of smoke: to move in a spiral **4** to twist, form a curved shape **5** to play at the game of curling ➤ *noun* a small coil or roll, eg of hair

curler *noun* **1** something used to make curls **2** someone who plays the game of curling

curlew *noun* a wading bird with very long slender bill and legs

curliness *noun* the quality of being curled or of having lots of curls

curling *noun* a game played by throwing round, flat stones along a sheet of ice

curly *adjective* having curls

curmudgeon *noun* a bad-tempered or mean person

currant *noun* **1** a small black raisin **2** a berry of various kinds of soft fruit: *redcurrant*

❗ Do not confuse: **currant** and **current**

currency *noun* (*plural* **currencies**) **1** the money used in a particular country **2** the state of being generally known: *The story gained currency*

current *adjective* belonging to the present time: *the current year/current affairs* ➤ *noun* a stream of water, air or electrical power moving in one direction

❗ Do not confuse: **current** and **currant**

current account *noun* a bank account from which money may be withdrawn at any time by cheque or bank card, used for regular credits and debits (*compare with*: **deposit account**)

curriculum *noun* (*plural* **curriculums** or **curricula**) the course of study at a university, school, etc

curriculum vitae (*pronounced* ku-**rik**-yuw-lum **vee**-tai) *noun* (*plural* **curricula vitae**) (*abbrev* **CV**) a brief account of a person's education and career, used for job applications

curry[1] *noun* (*plural* **curries**) a dish containing a mixture of spices with a strong, peppery flavour ➤ *verb* (**curries, currying, curried**) to make into a curry by adding spices

curry[2] *verb* (**curries, currying, curried**) to rub down (a horse) • **curry favour** to try hard to gain someone's favour

curry powder *noun* a selection of ground spices used in making curry

curse *verb* **1** to use swear-words **2** to wish evil towards ➤ *noun* **1** a wish for evil or a magic spell **2** an evil or a great misfortune or the cause of this

cursed *adjective* **1** (*pronounced* kerst) under a curse **2** (*pronounced* **ker**-sid) hateful

cursive *adjective* of handwriting: with the letters in the words joined to one another, as opposed to separate

cursor *noun* a flashing symbol that appears on a VDU screen to show the position for entering data

cursorily *adverb* briefly, hurriedly, without taking a lot of care

cursory *adjective* hurried

curt *adjective* of someone's way of speaking: clipped and unfriendly ♦ **curtly** *adverb*

curtail *verb* to make less, reduce ♦ **curtailment** *noun*

curtain *noun* a piece of material hung to cover a window, stage, etc

curtsy or **curtsey** *noun* (*plural* **curtsies** or **curtseys**) a bow made by bending the knees ➤ *verb* (**curtsies, curtsying, curtsied** or **curtseys, curtseying, curtseyed**) to perform such a bow

curvaceous *adjective* of a woman: having a shapely figure

curvature *noun* **1** a curving or bending **2** a curved piece **3** *medicine* an abnormal curving of the spine

curve *noun* **1** a rounded line, like part of the edge of a circle **2** a bend: *a curve in the road*

cushion *noun* **1** a fabric casing stuffed with feathers, foam, etc, for resting on **2** a soft pad

cushy *adjective, informal* (**cushier, cushiest**) easy and comfortable: *a cushy job*

cusp *noun* **1** a point **2** *maths* a point formed by the meeting of two curves, corresponding to the point where the two tangents coincide **3** *anatomy* a sharp raised point on the grinding surface of a molar **4** *astrology* a division between signs of the zodiac

custard *noun* a sweet sauce made from eggs, milk and sugar

custodian *noun* **1** a keeper **2** a caretaker, eg of a museum

custody *noun* **1** care, guardianship **2** arrest or imprisonment: *taken into custody*

custom *noun* **1** something done by habit **2** the regular or frequent doing of something; habit **3** the buying of goods at a shop **4** (**customs**) taxes on goods coming into a country **5** (**customs**) the government department that collects these

customary *adjective* usual

custom-built *adjective* built to suit a particular purpose

customer *noun* **1** someone who buys from a shop **2** *informal* a person: *an awkward customer*

customize or **customise** *verb* to make changes to (something) to suit particular needs or tastes

cut *verb* (**cutting, cut**) **1** to make a slit in, remove or divide, with a blade: *cut a hole/cut a slice of bread* **2** to wound **3** to trim with a blade etc: *cut the grass/My hair needs cutting* **4** to reduce in amount **5** to shorten (a play, book, etc) by removing parts **6** to refuse to acknowledge (someone you know) **7** to divide (a pack of cards) in two **8** to stop filming **9** *informal* to play truant from (school) ➤ *noun* **1** a slit made by cutting **2** a wound made with something sharp **3** a stroke, a blow **4** a thrust with a sword **5** the way something is cut **6** the shape and style of clothes **7** a piece of meat • **cut down 1** to take down by cutting **2** to reduce • **cut down on** to reduce the intake of • **cut in** to interrupt • **cut off 1** to separate, isolate: *cut off from the mainland* **2** to stop: *cut off supplies* • **cut out 1** to shape (a dress etc) by cutting **2** *informal* to stop: *Cut it out* **3** of an engine: to fail

cut-and-dried *adjective* settled beforehand; decided

cut and paste *verb, computing* to take a graphic or text out of one document and put it into another

cutback *noun* a reduction in spending, use of resources, etc

cute *adjective* **1** smart, clever **2** pretty and pleasing

cut glass *noun* glass with ornamental patterns cut on the surface

cuticle *noun* **1** *anatomy* the epidermis, the thin protective outer later of the skin **2** the hard skin around the bottom and side edges of finger and toe nails

cutlass *noun* (*plural* **cutlasses**) a short, broad sword

cutlery *noun* knives, forks, spoons, etc

cutlet *noun* a slice of meat with the bone attached

cut-price *adjective* sold at a price lower than usual

cut-throat *adjective* fiercely competitive: *cut-throat business* ➤ *noun* a ruffian

cutting *noun* **1** a piece cut from a newspaper **2** a trench cut in the earth or rock for a road etc **3** a shoot of a tree or plant ➤ *adjective* wounding, hurtful: *a cutting remark*

cuttlefish *noun* a type of sea creature like a squid

cut-up *adjective* distressed

CV *abbreviation* curriculum vitae

cwm (*pronounced* cuwm) another word for a **corrie**

cwt *abbreviation* hundredweight

cyan (*pronounced* **sai**-an) *noun* a blue ink used as a primary colour in printing

cyanide *noun* a kind of poison

cyanocobalamin *noun* vitamin B_{12}

cyanosis *noun, medicine* a bluish discoloration of the skin, usually caused by lack of oxygen in the blood

cyber- (*pronounced* **saib**-er) *prefix* relating to computers or electronic media: *cyberspace/ cyber-selling*

ⓘ This prefix was taken from the word **cyber**netics, meaning 'the study of communication or control systems'. Its origin is the Greek word *kybernetes*, meaning 'the person who steers a boat or ship'

---

cybercafé *noun* a place which serves snacks and also has several personal computers linked to the Internet for use by customers

cyberspace *noun* the three-dimensional artificial environment of virtual reality

cycle *noun* **1** a bicycle **2** a round of events following on from one another repeatedly: *the cycle of the seasons* **3** *physics* one of a regularly repeated set of changes, eg in the movement of a wave **4** a series of poems, stories, etc written about a single person or event ➤ *verb* **1** to ride a bicycle **2** to move in a cycle; rotate

cycle lane *noun* a section of road marked off for cyclists to use

cyclic or **cyclical** *adjective* **1** relating to, containing, or moving in a cycle **2** recurring in cycles **3** arranged in a ring or rings **4** *chemistry* an organic chemical compound whose molecules contain one or more closed rings of atoms, eg benzene ♦ **cyclically** *adverb*

cyclic quadrilateral *noun, maths* a four-sided figure whose vertices lie on a circle

cyclist *noun* someone who rides a bicycle

cyclo- *prefix* **1** circle, ring, cycle: *cyclometer* **2** *chemistry* denoting a cyclic compound: *cyclopropane*

cycloid *noun, maths* the curve traced by a point on the circumference of a circle as the circle rolls along a straight line (*compare with*: **trochoid**) ♦ **cycloidal** *adjective*

cyclone *noun* **1** (*also called*: **hurricane, typhoon**) a violent tropical windstorm **2** an area of low atmospheric pressure in which winds spiral inwards towards the centre ♦ **cyclonic** *adjective* ⓘ Comes from Greek *kyklon* meaning 'a whirling round'

cyclotron *noun, physics* a circular type of particle accelerator

cygnet (*pronounced* **sig**-net) *noun* a young swan ① Comes from Latin *cygnus* meaning 'swan'

! Do not confuse with: **signet**

cylinder *noun* **1** a solid or hollow tube-shaped object **2** in machines, car engines, etc: the hollow tube in which a piston works

cylindrical *adjective* shaped like a cylinder

cymbals (*pronounced* **sim**-balz) *plural noun* brass, plate-like musical instruments, beaten together in pairs

cynic (*pronounced* **sin**-ik) *noun* someone who believes the worst about people ♦ **cynicism** *noun*

cynical (*pronounced* **sin**-i-kal) *adjective* sneering; believing the worst of people ♦ **cynically** *adverb*

! Do not confuse with: **sceptical**.
A **cynical** person is suspicious of apparently good things, a **sceptical** person is cautious about accepting something to be true.

cypress *noun* a type of evergreen tree

cyst (*pronounced* sist) *noun* **1** *medicine* an abnormal liquid-filled blister within the body or just under the skin **2** *anatomy* a normal sac in the body, eg the bladder **3** a tough outer membrane surrounding certain organisms, eg bacteria, protozoa, etc, during the resting stage in their life cycle

cystic fibrosis *noun, medicine* a hereditary disease which is present at birth or appears in early childhood, and causes breathing problems

cystitis *noun, medicine* inflammation of the bladder, often caused by infection

-cyte (*pronounced* sait) *suffix* forms nouns describing different types of cell in the body: *leucocyte/phagocyte* ① Comes from Latin *kytos* meaning 'container' or 'hollow vessel'

cytoplasm *noun* the jelly-like material, enclosed by the cell membrane, that makes up most of a cell

cytoskeleton *noun, biology* a network of protein filaments in the cytoplasm that forms the structural framework of the cell

cytosol *noun, biology* the soluble component of cytoplasm

cytotoxic *adjective, biology* denoting a drug that destroys or prevents the division of cells, used in chemotherapy to treat various forms of cancer

czar another spelling of **tsar**

czarina another spelling of **tsarina**

Dd

D¹ *noun, music* the second note in the scale of C major

D² *symbol* **1** *chemistry* deuterium **2** the Roman numeral for 500

dabble *verb* **1** to play in water with hands or feet **2** to do in a half-serious way or as a hobby: *He dabbles in computers*

dab hand *noun, informal* an expert: *a dab hand at decorating*

dachshund (*pronounced* **daks**-huwnt or **daks**-huwnd) *noun* a breed of dog with short legs and a long body ⊙ Comes from German *Dachs* meaning 'badger', and *Hund* meaning 'dog'

dactyl (*pronounced* **dak**-til) *noun, poetry* a metrical foot consisting of one long or stressed syllable followed by two short or unstressed ones ◆ **dactylic** *adjective*

⊙ Comes from Greek *daktylos* meaning 'finger', from the similarity between the lengths of the syllables in a dactyl and the lengths of the bones in a finger (one long and two short)

dad or **daddy** *noun* (*plural* **dads** or **daddies**) *informal* a father

Dada or **Dadaism** *noun, art, literature* a movement from 1916 to 1920 which aimed to abandon all artistic form and tradition ◆ **Dadaist** *noun* ◆ **Dadaistic** *adjective*

daddy-long-legs *noun* (*plural* **daddy-long-legs**), *informal* a cranefly

daffodil *noun* a yellow trumpet-shaped flower which grows from a bulb

daft *adjective, informal* silly • **daft about** or **on something** enthusiastic about it; keen on it

dagger *noun* a short sword for stabbing

dahl *see* **dal**

dahlia (*pronounced* **deil**-i-a) *noun* a type of garden plant with large flowers

⊙ Named after Anders *Dahl*, 18th-century Swiss botanist

Dáil or **Dáil Eireann** (*pronounced* doil **e**-ran) the lower house of parliament in the Republic of Ireland ⊙ Irish Gaelic, literally meaning 'assembly' (of Ireland)

daily *adjective & adverb* every day ➤ *noun* (*plural* **dailies**) **1** a paper published every day **2** *informal* someone employed to clean a house regularly

daily bread *noun* necessary food, means of living

dainty *adjective* (**daintier, daintiest**) **1** small and neat **2** pleasant-tasting ➤ *noun* (*plural* **dainties**) a tasty morsel of food ◆ **daintily** *adverb* (adjective, meaning 1)

dairy *noun* (*plural* **dairies**) **1** a building for storing milk and making butter and cheese **2** a shop which sells milk, butter, cheese, etc

dairy cattle *plural noun* cows kept for their milk, not their meat

dairy farm *noun* a farm concerned with the production of milk, butter, etc

dairymaid *noun* an old-fashioned name for a woman working in a dairy (meaning 1)

dairyman *noun* (*plural* **dairymen**) an old-fashioned name for a man working in a dairy (meaning 1)

dairy products *plural noun* food made of milk, butter, or cheese

dais (*pronounced* **dei**-is) *noun* (*plural* **daises**) a raised floor at the upper end of a hall

daisy *noun* (*plural* **daisies**) a small common flower with white petals

⊙ From an Old English name meaning 'day's eye', so called because of its opening during the day

daisy chain *noun* a string of daisies threaded through each other's stems

daisy-wheel *noun* a flat printing wheel with characters at the end of spokes

dal, dahl or **dhal** (*pronounced* dahl) *noun* a cooked dish made of edible dried split pea-like seeds ⊙ Comes from Hindi

dalai lama (*pronounced* **dal**-ai **lah**-ma) *noun* the spiritual leader of Tibetan Buddhism

dale *noun* low ground between hills

dalliance (*pronounced* **dal**-i-ans) *noun* **1** flirtation **2** idle time-wasting

dally *verb* (**dallies, dallying, dallied**) **1** to waste time idling or playing **2** to play (with)

Dalmatian *noun* a breed of large spotted dog

dam *noun* **1** a wall of earth, concrete, etc to keep back water **2** water kept in like this ➤ *verb* (**damming, dammed**) **1** to keep back by a dam **2** to hold back, restrain (tears etc)

damage *noun* **1** hurt, injury **2** (**damages**) money paid by one person to another to make up for injury, insults, etc ➤ *verb* to spoil, make less effective or unusable

damask (*pronounced* **dam**-ask) *noun* silk, linen, or cotton cloth, with figures and designs in the weave

⊙ After *Damascus* in Syria, from where it was exported in the Middle Ages

dame *noun* **1** a comic woman in a pantomime, played by a man in drag **2** *US slang* a woman **3** (**Dame**) the title of a woman of the same rank as a knight

damn *verb* **1** to sentence to unending punishment in hell **2** to condemn as wrong, bad, etc ➤ *interjection* an expression of annoyance

damnable (*pronounced* **dam**-na-bl) *adjective* **1** deserving to be condemned **2** hateful

damnably (*pronounced* **dam**-na-bli) *adverb* extremely

damnation *noun* **1** unending punishment in hell **2** condemnation

damning *adjective* leading to conviction or ruin: *damning evidence*

damp *noun* **1** moist air **2** wetness, moistness ➤ *verb* **1** to wet slightly **2** to make (emotions, interest, etc) less fierce or intense ➤ *adjective* moist, slightly wet

damp-course *noun* a layer of damp-proof material inside a wall or under a floor

dampen *verb* **1** to make or become damp; moisten **2** to lessen (enthusiasm etc)

damper *noun, music* a pad which touches the strings inside a piano, silencing each note after it has been played • **put a damper on something** to make it less cheerful

dampness *noun* the quality of being damp

damp-proof *adjective* not allowing wetness through ➤ *verb, building* to make damp-proof

damp-proof course *noun* a damp-course

damsel *noun, old* a girl or young woman

damson *noun* a type of small dark-red plum

dance *verb* to move in time to music ➤ *noun* **1** a sequence of steps in time to music **2** a social event with dancing ♦ **dancer** *noun* ♦ **dancing** *noun & adjective*

dandelion *noun* a type of common plant with a yellow flower

⊙ From the French phrase *dent de lion*, meaning 'lion's tooth'

dandruff *noun* dead skin which collects under the hair and falls off in flakes

dandy *noun* (*plural* **dandies**), *old* a man who pays great attention to his dress and looks

danger *noun* **1** something potentially harmful: *The canal is a danger to children* **2** potential harm: *unaware of the danger*

dangerous *adjective* **1** unsafe, likely to cause harm **2** full of risks ♦ **dangerously** *adverb*

dangle *verb* to hang loosely

Danish blue *noun* a strong-tasting white cheese with streaks of bluish mould through it

Danish pastry *noun* a flat cake of rich light pastry, with a sweet filling or topping

dank *adjective* moist, wet, and cold

dapper *adjective* small and neat

dappled *adjective* marked with spots or splashes of colour

dare *verb* **1** to be brave or bold enough (to): *I didn't dare tell him* **2** to lay yourself open to, risk: *daring his wrath* **3** to challenge: *dared him to cross the railway line* ➤ *noun* a challenge to do something dangerous etc • **I dare say** I suppose: *I dare say you're right*

daredevil *noun* a rash person fond of taking risks ➤ *adjective* rash, risky

daring *adjective* bold, fearless ➤ *noun* boldness ♦ **daringly** *adverb*

dark *adjective* **1** without light **2** black or near to black **3** gloomy **4** evil: *dark deeds* ➤ *noun* absence of light, nightfall ♦ **darkness** *noun* • **in the dark** knowing nothing about something • **keep dark** to keep (something) secret

darken *verb* to make or grow dark or darker

dark horse *noun* someone about whom little is known

darkroom *noun* a room with no ordinary light, used for developing photographs

darling *noun* **1** a word showing affection **2** someone dearly loved; a favourite

darn *verb* to mend (clothes) with crossing rows of stitches ➤ *noun* a patch mended in this way

dart *noun* **1** a pointed weapon for throwing or shooting **2** something which pierces **3** a fold sewn into a piece of clothing ➤ *verb* to move quickly and suddenly

dartboard *noun* the board used in playing the game of darts

darts *singular noun* a game in which small darts are thrown at a board marked off in circles and numbered sections

Darwinism *noun, biology* the theory that plants and animals evolved by the process of natural selection

dash *verb* **1** to throw or knock violently, especially so as to break **2** to ruin (hopes) **3** to depress, sadden (spirits) **4** to rush with speed or violence ➤ *noun* (*plural* **dashes**) **1** a rush **2** a short race **3** a small amount of a drink etc **4** liveliness **5** a short line (–) to show a break in a sentence etc

dashboard *noun* a panel with dials, switches, etc in front of the driver's seat in a vehicle

dashing *adjective* **1** hasty **2** smart, elegant

dastardly *adjective, formal* cowardly

DAT *abbreviation* digital audio tape

data (*pronounced* **dei**-ta or **dah**-ta) *noun*

(*singular* **datum**) **1** available facts from which conclusions may be drawn **2** *computing* unprocessed information stored in a computer

ⓘ Although **data** is strictly a plural of **datum**, it is now often used as a singular noun: *The data was entered into the computer.*

database *noun, computing* a collection of systematically stored files that are often connected with each other

data capture *noun, computing* changing information into a form which can be fed into a computer

data compression *noun, computing* the altering of the form of data in order to reduce its storage space

data logging *noun, computing* collecting and recording data, especially on a computer

data mining *noun, computing* the gathering of electronically stored information, eg about shopping patterns from loyalty cards

data processing *noun, computing* the processing of data by a computer system

data protection *noun* safeguards to protect the privacy and security of data held on computer

data set *noun, computing* a collection of data that fulfils a set of search conditions and can be used for research

date¹ *noun* **1** a statement of time in terms of the day, month and year, eg 23 December 1995 **2** the time at which an event occurs **3** the period of time to which something belongs **4** *informal* an appointment ▸ *verb* **1** to give a date to **2** to belong to a certain time: *dates from the 12th century* **3** to become old-fashioned: *That dress will date quickly* **4** to go out with someone, especially regularly for romantic reasons

date² *noun* **1** a type of palm tree **2** its blackish, shiny fruit with a hard stone

datum singular of **data**

daub *verb* **1** to smear **2** to paint roughly

daughter *noun* a female child, considered in relation to her parents ▸ *adjective, biology* of a cell: formed by division

daughter cell *noun, biology* either of two new cells formed as a result of cell division

daughter-in-law *noun* (*plural* **daughters-in-law**) a son's wife

daughter nucleus *noun, biology* either of the two nuclei that are produced when the nucleus of a living cell splits into two parts during mitosis

daunt *verb* **1** to frighten **2** to be discouraging

dauntless *adjective* unable to be frightened

Davy lamp *noun* an early kind of lamp used by coalminers

dawdle *verb* to move slowly ◆ **dawdler** *noun*

dawn *noun* **1** daybreak **2** a beginning: *the dawn*

of a new era ▸ *verb* **1** to become day **2** to begin to appear • **dawn on** to become suddenly clear to (someone)

dawn chorus *noun* the singing of birds at dawn

dawning *noun* a rather poetic way of saying 'dawn'

day *noun* **1** the time of light, from sunrise to sunset **2** twenty-four hours, from one midnight to the next **3** the time or hours spent at work **4** (often **days**) a particular time or period: *in the days of steam* • **day in, day out** on and on, continuously ◷ Comes from Old English *dæg*

daybreak *noun* dawn; the time of day when the sun rises

day care *noun* supervision and care given to young children, the elderly, or handicapped people during the day

day centre or **day care centre** *noun* a place which provides day care and social activities for the elderly, the handicapped, etc

daydream *noun* an imagining of pleasant events while awake ▸ *verb* to imagine in this way

dayglo *adjective* luminously bright in colour

daylight *noun* **1** the light of day, sunlight **2** a clear space

day-release *noun* time off from work for training or education

day return *noun* a ticket at a reduced price for a journey to somewhere and back again on the same day

day trader *noun* a person who buys and sells stocks and shares on the same day in the hope of making quick profits

daze *verb* **1** to stun with a blow **2** to confuse, bewilder ▸ *noun* a confused, forgetful or inattentive state of mind

dazzle *verb* **1** to shine on so as to prevent from seeing clearly **2** to shine brilliantly **3** to fascinate, impress deeply

Db *symbol, chemistry* dubnium

dB *abbreviation* decibel

DC *abbreviation* **1** District of Columbia (US) **2** detective constable **3** direct current (*compare with:* **AC**)

DDT *noun* dichlorodiphenyltrichloroethane, an insecticide that is also poisonous to humans and animals

deacon *noun* **1** the lowest rank of clergy in the Church of England **2** a church official in other churches

deaconess *noun* (*plural* **deaconesses**) a woman deacon

deactivate *verb* to remove the capacity of (something such as a bomb) to function or work

dead *adjective* **1** not living, without life **2** cold and cheerless **3** numb **4** not working; no longer in use **5** complete, utter: *dead silence* **6** exact: *the dead centre* **7** certain: *a dead shot* ▸ *adverb*

1 completely: *dead certain* **2** suddenly and completely: *stop dead* ➤ *noun* **1** those who have died: *speak well of the dead* **2** the time of greatest stillness etc: *the dead of night*

dead-and-alive *adjective* dull, having little life

dead-beat *adjective* having no strength left

deaden *verb* to lessen (pain etc)

dead end *noun* **1** a road etc closed at one end **2** a job etc not leading to promotion

dead heat *noun* a race in which two or more runners finish equal

deadline *noun* a date by which something must be done

⊙ Originally a line in a military prison. The penalty for crossing it was death

deadlock *noun* a standstill resulting from a complete failure to agree

deadly (**deadlier, deadliest**) *adjective* **1** likely to cause death, fatal **2** intense, very great: *a deadly hush* ➤ *adverb* intensely, extremely: *deadly dull* ♦ **deadliness** *noun*

deadpan *adjective & adverb* without expression on the face

dead ringer *noun, informal* someone looking exactly like someone else

deaf *adjective* **1** unable to hear **2** refusing to listen: *deaf to her pleas*

deafblind *adjective* both deaf and blind

deafen *verb* **1** to make deaf **2** to be unpleasantly loud **3** to make (walls etc) soundproof

deafening *adjective* extremely loud

deaf-mute *often considered offensive, noun* someone who can neither hear nor speak ➤ *adjective* unable to hear or speak

deal¹ *noun* **1** an agreement, especially in business **2** an amount or quantity: *a good deal of paper* **3** the dividing out of playing-cards in a game ➤ *verb* (**dealing, dealt** – *pronounced* delt) **1** to divide, give out **2** to trade (in) **3** to do business (with) • **deal with** to take action concerning, cope with

deal² *noun* a kind of softwood

dealer *noun* **1** someone who deals out cards at a game **2** a trader **3** a stockbroker

dealings *plural noun* **1** your manner of acting towards others **2** business etc contacts and transactions

dean *noun* **1** the chief religious officer in a cathedral church **2** the head of a faculty in a university

dear *adjective* **1** high in price **2** highly valued; much loved ➤ *noun* **1** someone who is loved **2** someone who is lovable or charming ➤ *adverb* at a high price: *It cost them dear*

dearly *adverb* **1** very much, sincerely: *love someone dearly* **2** involving a great cost, either

financially or in some other way: *His freedom was dearly bought*

dearth (*pronounced* derth) *noun* a scarcity, shortage

death *noun* **1** the state of being dead, the end of life **2** the end of something: *the death of steam railways* • **done to death** too often repeated

deathbed *noun* the bed in which a person died or is about to die

deathblow *noun* **1** a blow that causes death **2** an event that causes something to end

death certificate *noun* a certificate stating the time and cause of someone's death

death knell (*pronounced* **deth** nel) *noun* **1** a bell announcing a death **2** something indicating the end of a scheme, hope, etc

deathly *adjective* **1** very pale or ill-looking **2** deadly

death mask *noun* a plaster cast taken of a dead person's face

death penalty *noun* punishment for a crime by death

death rate *noun* (sometimes **crude death rate**) the number of deaths occurring over a period of a year in a given area per thousand inhabitants

death rattle *noun* a rattling in the throat sometimes heard before someone dies

death wish *noun* a conscious or unconscious desire to die

debacle or **débâcle** (*pronounced* dei-**bah**-kel) *noun* total disorder, defeat, collapse of organization, etc ⊙ Comes from French

debar *verb* (**debarring, debarred**) to keep from, prevent

debase *verb* **1** to lessen in value **2** to make bad, wicked, etc ♦ **debased** *adjective* ♦ **debasement** *noun*

debatable *adjective* arguable, doubtful: *a debatable point* ♦ **debatably** *adverb*

debate *noun* **1** a discussion, especially a formal one before an audience **2** an argument ➤ *verb* to engage in debate, discuss

debauched *adjective* inclined to debauchery

debauchery *noun* excessive indulgence in drunkenness, lewdness, etc

debilitate *verb* to make weak ♦ **debilitated** *adjective*

debility *noun* weakness of the body

debit *noun* an amount owed, spent, or deducted from a bank account ➤ *verb* (**debiting, debited**) to mark down as a debit

debit card *noun* a plastic card which transfers money directly from a purchaser's account to a retailer's

debonair (*pronounced* deb-o-**neir**) *adjective* especially of a man: of pleasant and cheerful appearance and behaviour

debrief *verb* to gather information from an astronaut, spy, etc after a mission ♦ **debriefing** *noun*

debris (*pronounced* **deb**-ree) *noun* 1 the remains of something broken, destroyed, etc 2 rubbish

debt (*pronounced* det) *noun* something that is owed, usually money ● **in debt** owing money ● **in someone's debt** under an obligation to them

debtor (*pronounced* **det**-or) *noun* someone who owes a debt

debug *verb* (**debugging, debugged**) 1 to remove secret microphones from (a room etc) 2 *computing* to remove faults in (a computer program)

debunk *verb* to show (someone's claims, good reputation, etc) to be false or unjustified

debut or **début** (*pronounced* **dei**-byoo) *noun* the first public appearance, eg of an actor ➤ *adjective* first before the public: *debut concert*

debutante or **débutante** (*pronounced* **dei**-byuw-tont) *noun* a young woman making her first formal appearance as an adult in upper-class society

deca- or **dec-** *prefix* ten, multiplied by ten: *decathlon* ⓞ Comes from Greek *deka* meaning 'ten'

decade *noun* 1 a period of ten years 2 a set or series of ten

decadence (*pronounced* **dek**-a-dens) *noun* a falling from high to low standards in morals, the arts, etc

decadent (*pronounced* **dek**-a-dent) *adjective* wicked, throwing away moral standards for the sake of pleasure

decaff (*pronounced* **dee**-kaf) *informal, adjective* decaffeinated ➤ *noun* decaffeinated coffee

decaffeinated (*pronounced* dee-**kaf**-i-neit-id) *adjective* with the caffeine removed

decagon *noun* a figure with ten sides

decahedron (*pronounced* dek-a-**hee**-dron) *noun* (*plural* **decahedrons** or **decahedra**) a solid figure with ten faces

decamp *verb* to run away

decant *verb* to pour (wine etc) from a bottle into a decanter

decanter *noun* an ornamental bottle with a glass stopper for wine, whisky, etc

decapitate *verb* to cut the head from ♦ **decapitation** *noun*

decapod *noun, zoology* 1 a crustacean with ten limbs, including pincers, eg a crab or prawn 2 a cephalopod with ten arms, eg a squid

decathlon *noun* an athletic contest comprising ten events (*compare with*: **heptathlon, pentathlon**) ♦ **decathlete** *noun*

decay *verb* 1 to become bad, worse or rotten 2 *physics* of a radioactive substance: to break down spontaneously into one or more isotopes ➤ *noun* 1 the process of rotting or worsening 2 *physics* the spontaneous breakdown of a nucleus of a radioactive substance into one or more isotopes ♦ **decayed** *adjective*

decease *noun, formal* death

deceased *formal, adjective* dead ➤ *noun* (**the deceased**) a dead person

deceit *noun* the act of deceiving

deceitful *adjective* inclined to deceive; lying ♦ **deceitfully** *adverb*

deceive *verb* to tell lies to so as to mislead ♦ **deceiver** *noun*

decelerate *verb* to slow down ♦ **deceleration** *noun*

December *noun* the twelfth month of the year

ⓞ From a Latin word meaning 'tenth', because December was originally the tenth month of the year, before January and February were added

decent *adjective* 1 respectable 2 good enough, adequate: *decent salary* 3 kind: *decent of you to help* ♦ **decency** *noun* (meanings 1 and 3) ♦ **decently** *adverb*

decentralize or **decentralise** *verb* to change (eg a government department, an industry, etc) from having one central place of control into several smaller and less central positions ♦ **decentralization** *noun*

deception *noun* 1 the act of deceiving 2 something that deceives or is intended to deceive

deceptive *adjective* misleading: *Appearances may be deceptive* ♦ **deceptively** *adverb*

deci- *prefix* one-tenth: *decimal/decimate* ⓞ Comes from Latin *decimus* meaning 'tenth'

decibel (*pronounced* **des**-i-bel) *noun* (*abbrev* **dB**) a unit of loudness of sound

decide *verb* 1 to make up your mind to do something: *I've decided to take your advice* 2 to settle (an argument etc)

decided *adjective* 1 clear: *a decided difference* 2 with your mind made up: *He was decided on the issue*

decidedly *adverb* definitely

deciduous (di-**sid**-yuw-us) *adjective* 1 of a tree: having leaves that fall in autumn 2 of a forest: comprising deciduous trees 3 *biology* denoting a structure that is lost after a period of growth, eg milk teeth

decimal *adjective* 1 numbered by tens 2 of ten parts or the number 10 ➤ *noun, maths* a decimal fraction

decimal currency *noun* a system of money in which each coin or note is either a tenth of another or ten times another in value

decimal fraction *noun, maths* a fraction expressed in tenths, hundredths, thousandths, etc, separated by a decimal point

decimalize or **decimalise** *verb* to convert (figures or currency) to decimal form ♦ **decimalization** *noun*

decimal place *noun, maths* a digit to the right of a decimal point, eg in 0.26, 2 is in the first decimal place

decimal point *noun, maths* a dot used to separate units from decimal fractions, eg $0.1 = \frac{1}{10}$, $2.33 = \frac{233}{100}$

decimate *verb* to make much smaller in numbers by destruction

> ⊙ Literally 'reduce by a tenth'; from Latin *decem* meaning ten

decipher (*pronounced* di-**sai**-fer) *verb* **1** to translate (a code) into ordinary, understandable language **2** to make out the meaning of: *can't decipher his handwriting*

decision *noun* **1** the act of deciding **2** clear judgement, firmness: *acting with decision*

decisive *adjective* **1** final, putting an end to a contest etc: *a decisive defeat* **2** showing decision and firmness: *a decisive manner* ♦ **decisively** *adverb*

deck¹ *noun* **1** a platform forming the floor of a ship, bus, etc **2** a pack of playing-cards **3** the turntable of a record-player • **clear the decks** to get rid of old papers, work, etc before starting something fresh

deck² *verb* to decorate, adorn

deckchair *noun* a collapsible chair of wood and canvas etc

declaim *verb* **1** to make a speech in impressive, dramatic language **2** to speak violently (against) ♦ **declamation** *noun*

declamatory *adjective* of a speech or announcement: impressive and dramatic

declare *verb* **1** to make known (goods or income on which tax is payable) **2** to announce formally or publicly: *declare war* **3** to say firmly **4** *cricket* to end an innings before ten wickets have fallen ♦ **declaration** *noun*

declension *noun, grammar* **1** in certain languages, eg Latin: any of various sets of different forms taken by nouns, adjectives or pronouns to indicate case, number and gender **2** the act of stating these forms **3** a group of nouns or adjectives showing the same pattern of forms

declination *noun* **1** *astronomy* the angular distance of a star or planet north or south of the celestial equator **2** *geography* the angle between true north and magnetic north (*also called*: **angle of declination**)

decline *verb* **1** to say 'no' to, refuse: *I had to*

decline his offer **2** to weaken, become worse **3** to slope down **4** *grammar* to state the declension of (a noun etc) ➤ *noun* **1** a downward slope **2** a gradual worsening of health etc

decode *verb* to translate (a coded message) into ordinary, understandable language

decolonize or **decolonise** *verb* to grant independence to (a colony) ♦ **decolonization** *noun*

decommission *verb* to take out of operation (eg a warship, atomic reactor, or weapons used in a war)

decompose *verb* **1** to rot, decay **2** to separate in parts or elements ♦ **decomposition** *noun*

decomposer *noun, biology* an organism that feeds on and breaks down dead matter

decongestant (*pronounced* dee-kon-**jest**-ant) *noun, medicine* a drug which eases a blocked nose

decontaminate *verb* to remove poisons, radioactivity, etc from ♦ **decontamination** *noun*

décor (*pronounced* **dei**-kawr) *noun* the decoration of, and arrangement of objects in, a room etc

decorate *verb* **1** to add ornament to **2** to paint or paper the walls of (a room etc) **3** to pin a badge or medal on (someone) as a mark of honour ♦ **decoration** *noun*

decorative *adjective* **1** ornamental **2** pretty

decorator *noun* someone who decorates houses, rooms, etc

decorous *adjective* behaving in an acceptable or dignified way

decorum (*pronounced* di-**kaw**-rum) *noun* good behaviour

decoy *verb* to lead into a trap or into evil ➤ *noun* something or someone intended to lead another into a trap

decrease *verb* (*pronounced* di-**krees**) to make or become less in number ➤ *noun* (*pronounced* **dee**-krees) a growing less

decreasing function *noun, maths* any function that results in a variable which was previously lower in value than a second variable becoming higher in value than the second variable (*contrasted with*: **increasing function**)

decree *noun* **1** an order, a law **2** *law* a judge's decision ➤ *verb* (**decreeing, decreed**) to give an order

decrepit *adjective* **1** weak and infirm because of old age **2** in ruins or disrepair ♦ **decrepitude** *noun*

decriminalize or **decriminalise** *verb, law* to make (something) no longer a criminal offence ♦ **decriminalization** *noun*

decrypt *verb* to convert information (eg computer data or TV signals) from a coded into a

readable form (*contrasted with*: **encrypt**)
♦ **decryption** *noun*

dedicate *verb* **1** to devote yourself (to): *dedicated himself to music* **2** to set apart for a special or sacred purpose **3** to inscribe or publish (a book etc) in tribute to someone or something: *I dedicate this book to my father*
♦ **dedicated** *adjective* ♦ **dedication** *noun*

deduce *verb* to find out by putting together all that is known

! Do not confuse: **deduce** and **deduct**

deduct *verb* to subtract, take away (from)

deduction *noun* **1** a subtraction **2** finding something out using logic, or a thing which has been found out in this way

deductive *adjective* using logic or known principles

deed *noun* **1** something done, an act **2** *law* a signed statement or bargain

deed poll *noun* (*plural* **deeds poll**) a document by which someone legally changes their name

(ⓘ From an old meaning of *poll* as 'cut' or 'trimmed', because these were written on paper with cut edges)

deem *verb*, *formal* to judge or consider: *deemed unsuitable for children*

deep *adjective* **1** being or going far down **2** hard to understand; cunning **3** involved to a great extent: *deep in debt/deep in thought* **4** intense, strong: *a deep red colour/deep affection* **5** low in pitch ➤ *noun* (**the deep**) the sea • **in deep water** in serious trouble

deepen *verb* to make or become deep or deeper

deep-freeze *noun* a low-temperature refrigerator that can freeze food and preserve it frozen for a long time

deep-fry *verb* to fry by completely submerging in hot fat or oil

deep-seated *adjective* firmly fixed, not easily removed

deep-vein thrombosis *noun* (*abbrev* **DVT**) a blood clot in a deep vein, usually in the leg

deer *noun* (*plural* **deer**) an animal with antlers in the male, eg the reindeer

de-escalate *verb* to reduce in scale or intensity: *The conflict is de-escalating*
♦ **de-escalation** *noun*

deface *verb* to spoil the appearance of, disfigure
♦ **defacement** *noun*

defamatory (*pronounced* di-**fam**-a-to-ri) *adjective* intended to harm, or having the effect of harming, someone's reputation

defame *verb* to try to harm the reputation of
♦ **defamation** *noun*

default *verb* to fail to do something you ought to

do, eg to pay a debt ➤ *noun* **1** failure to do something you ought to do **2** *computing* a preset action taken by a computer system unless a user's instruction overrides it ♦ **defaulter** *noun*
• **by default** because of a failure to do something

defeat *verb* to beat, win a victory over ➤ *noun* a win, a beating

defeatist *adjective* inclined to accept defeat
♦ **defeatism** *noun*

defecate (*pronounced* **def**-e-keit) *verb* to empty waste matter from the bowels
♦ **defecation** *noun*

defect *noun* (*pronounced* **dee**-fekt) a lack of something needed for completeness or perfection; a flaw ➤ *verb* (*pronounced* di-**fekt**) to desert a country, political party, etc to join or go to another

defection *noun* **1** failure in duty **2** desertion

defective *adjective* faulty; incomplete

! Do not confuse with: **deficient**

defence or *US* **defense** *noun* **1** the act of defending against attack **2** a means or method of protection **3** *law* the argument defending the accused person in a case (*contrasted with*: **prosecution**) **4** *law* the lawyer(s) putting forward this argument

defenceless *adjective* without defence

defend *verb* **1** to guard or protect against attack **2** *law* to conduct the defence of **3** to support against criticism

defendant *noun* **1** someone who resists attack **2** *law* the accused person in a law case

defense *US* spelling of **defence**

defensible *adjective* able to be defended

defensive *adjective* **1** used for defence **2** expecting criticism, ready to justify actions • **on the defensive** prepared to defend yourself against attack or criticism

defer *verb* (**deferring, deferred**) **1** to put off to another time **2** to give way (to): *He deferred to my wishes*

deference *noun* **1** willingness to consider the wishes etc of others **2** the act of giving way to another

deferential *adjective* showing deference, respectful

defiance *noun* open disobedience or opposition ♦ **defiant** *adjective* ♦ **defiantly** *adverb*

deficiency *noun* (*plural* **deficiencies**) **1** lack, need **2** an amount lacking

deficient *adjective* lacking in what is needed

! Do not confuse with: **defective**

deficit (*pronounced* **def**-i-sit) *noun* an amount

by which a sum of money etc is too little

defile *verb* **1** to make dirty, soil **2** to corrupt, make bad ♦ **defilement** *noun*

define *verb* **1** to fix the bounds or limits of **2** to outline or show clearly **3** to state the exact meaning of

definite *adjective* **1** having clear limits, fixed **2** exact **3** certain, sure

definite article *noun, grammar* the name given to the word *the*

definite integral see **integral**

definitely *adverb* certainly, without doubt

definition *noun* **1** an explanation of the exact meaning of a word or phrase **2** sharpness or clearness of outline

definitive *adjective* **1** fixed, final **2** not able to be bettered: *the definitive biography*
♦ **definitively** *adverb* (meaning 1)

deflate *verb* **1** to let the air out of (a tyre etc) **2** to reduce in self-importance or self-confidence

deflation *noun* **1** *economics* a reduction of the amount of money in circulation in a country, resulting in a lower level of industrial activity, industrial output, and employment, and a lower rate of increase in wages and prices **2** *geography* the movement of fine particles, eg sand, by the wind **3** the letting out of air (from eg a tyre) **4** the feeling of sadness or disappointment which you get eg when your hopes have been dashed

deflationary *adjective, economics* having the purpose of creating economic deflation

deflation hollow *noun, geography* a shallow depression from which fine material, eg sand, has been blown by wind (*also called*: **blowout**)

deflect *verb* to turn aside (from a fixed course)
♦ **deflection** *noun*

deforestation *noun* the removal of all or most of the trees in a forested area

deform *verb* **1** to spoil the shape of **2** to make ugly

deformed *adjective* badly or abnormally formed

deformity *noun* (*plural* **deformities**) **1** something abnormal in shape **2** the fact of being badly shaped

defragment or **defrag** *verb* (**defragging,** **defragged**), *computing* to move files or parts of files together on a hard disk

defraud *verb* **1** to cheat **2** (**defraud someone of something**) to take or keep it from them by cheating or fraud

defray *verb, formal* to pay for (expenses)

defrock *verb* to remove (a priest) from office

defrost *verb* to remove frost or ice from; thaw

deft *adjective* clever with the hands, handy
♦ **deftly** *adverb*

defunct *adjective* no longer active or in use

defuse *verb* **1** to remove the fuse from (a bomb etc) **2** to make (a situation etc) harmless or less dangerous

❗ Do not confuse with: **diffuse**

defy *verb* (**defies, defying, defied**) **1** to dare to do something, challenge **2** to resist openly **3** to make impossible: *Its beauty defies description*

degenerate *adjective* (*pronounced* di-**jen**-e-rat) **1** having become immoral or very bad **2** *biology* having lost former structure, or changed to a simpler form ➤ *verb* (*pronounced* di-**jen**-e-reit) **1** to become or grow bad or worse **2** *biology* to lose former structure, or change to a simpler form ♦ **degenerative** *adjective* **1** tending to degenerate **2** causing degeneration

degeneration *noun* **1** the process or act of degenerating **2** *biology* the breakdown, death or decay of cells, nerve fibres, etc **3** *biology* an evolutionary change from a complex structural form to an apparently simpler form

degradation *noun* humiliation, loss of dignity

degrade *verb* **1** to lower in grade or rank **2** to disgrace

degrading *adjective* humiliating and embarrassing

degree *noun* **1** a step or stage in a process **2** rank or grade **3** amount, extent: *a degree of certainty* **4** a unit of temperature used eg in the Celsius, Fahrenheit and Kelvin scales **5** a unit by which angles are measured, one 360th part of the circumference of a circle **6** a certificate given by a university, gained by examination or given as an honour **7** *grammar* a level of comparison (*positive, comparative,* or *superlative*) for adjectives and adverbs

dehiscent (*pronounced* di-**his**-ent) *adjective, botany* denoting a fruit or an anther that bursts open when mature to release seeds or pollen

dehydrate *verb* **1** to remove water from (food etc) **2** to lose excessive water from the body

dehydrated *adjective* **1** weak and exhausted as a result of losing too much water from your body **2** dried (food etc)

dehydration *noun* a lack of sufficient water in the body

de-ice *verb* to make or keep free of ice ♦ **de-icer** *noun*

deign (*pronounced* dein) *verb* to act as if doing a favour: *She deigned to answer us*

deindustrialize or **deindustrialise** *verb* **1** of a country: to experience a decline in the importance of its industry **2** to reduce the industrial organization and potential of (a country, region, etc) ♦ **deindustrialization** *noun*

deionization or **deionisation** *noun, chemistry* a process involving exchange of ions that is used to purify a solution

deity (*pronounced* **dei**-it-i) *noun* (*plural* **deities**) a god or goddess

déjà vu (*pronounced* dei-szah **voo**) *noun* the feeling of having experienced something before

dejected *adjective* gloomy, dispirited
♦ **dejection** *noun*

delay *verb* 1 to put off, postpone 2 to keep back, hinder ➤ *noun* 1 a postponement 2 a hindrance

delectable *adjective* delightful, pleasing
♦ **delectably** *adverb*

delectation *noun, formal* delight, enjoyment

delegate *verb* (*pronounced* **del**-ig-eit) to give (a task) to someone else to do ➤ *noun* (*pronounced* **del**-ig-at) someone acting on behalf of another; a representative

delegation *noun* a group of delegates

delete *verb* to rub or strike out (eg a piece of writing) ♦ **deletion** *noun*

deli (*pronounced* **del**-i) *noun, informal* a **delicatessen**

deliberate *verb* (*pronounced* di-**lib**-e-reit) to think carefully or seriously (about) ➤ *adjective* (*pronounced* di-**lib**-e-rat) 1 intentional, not accidental 2 slow in deciding 3 not hurried
♦ **deliberately** *adverb*

deliberation *noun* 1 careful thought 2 calmness, coolness 3 (**deliberations**) *formal* discussions

delicacy *noun* (*plural* **delicacies**) 1 tact 2 something delicious to eat

delicate *adjective* 1 not strong, frail 2 easily damaged 3 fine, dainty: *delicate features* 4 pleasant to taste 5 tactful 6 requiring skill or care: *a delicate operation*

delicatessen (*pronounced* del-i-ka-**tes**-en) *noun* a shop selling eg cheeses, cooked meats, and unusual or imported foods

delicious *adjective* 1 very pleasant to taste 2 giving pleasure ♦ **deliciously** *adverb*

delight *verb* 1 to please greatly 2 to take great pleasure (in) ➤ *noun* great pleasure

delighted *adjective* very pleased

delightful *adjective* very pleasing
♦ **delightfully** *adverb*

delineate (*pronounced* di-**lin**-i-eit) *verb* 1 to show by drawing 2 to describe in words
♦ **delineation** *noun* ⊙ Comes from Latin *delineare* meaning 'to sketch out'

delinquency *noun* 1 wrongdoing, misdeeds 2 failure in duty

delinquent *adjective* 1 guilty of an offence or misdeed 2 not carrying out your duties ➤ *noun* 1 someone, especially a young person, guilty of an offence 2 someone who fails in their duty

deliquesce (*pronounced* de-li-**kwes**) *verb, chemistry* of salts: to dissolve slowly in water absorbed from the air ♦ **deliquescence** *noun*

delirious (*pronounced* di-**lir**-i-us) *adjective* 1 raving, wandering in the mind 2 wildly excited
♦ **deliriously** *adverb*

delirium (*pronounced* di-**lir**-i-um) *noun* 1 a delirious state, especially caused by fever 2 wild excitement

delirium tremens (*pronounced* **trem**-enz) *noun* a delirious disorder of the brain caused by drinking alcohol excessively

deliver *verb* 1 to hand over 2 to give out (eg a speech, a blow) 3 to set free, rescue 4 to assist at the birth of (a child) ♦ **deliverance** *noun* (meaning 3)

delivery *noun* (*plural* **deliveries**) 1 a handing over, eg of letters 2 the birth of a child 3 a style of speaking

dell *noun* a small valley or hollow

delphinium (*pronounced* del-**fin**-i-um) *noun* a branching garden plant with blue flowers

⊙ From a Greek word translating as 'little dolphin', because of the shape of the flower-heads

delta *noun, geography* the flat, triangular stretch of land at the mouth of a river, where it splits into branches

⊙ From the fourth letter of the Greek alphabet, which was triangular in shape

delude *verb* to deceive ⊙ Comes from Latin *deludere* meaning 'to play false'

deluge (*pronounced* **del**-yooj) *noun* 1 a great flood of water 2 an overwhelming amount: *a deluge of work* ➤ *verb* 1 to flood, drench 2 to overwhelm

delusion *noun* a false belief, especially as a symptom of mental illness

❗ Do not confuse with: **allusion** and **illusion**. **Delusion** comes from the verb **delude**

de luxe or **deluxe** *adjective* 1 very luxurious or elegant 2 with special features or qualities ⊙ Comes from French, meaning 'of luxury'

delve *verb* 1 to dig 2 to rummage, search through: *delved in her bag for her keys*

demagogue (*pronounced* **dem**-a-gog) *noun, derogatory* someone who tries to win power or support by appealing to the emotions

demand *verb* 1 to ask, or ask for, firmly 2 to insist: *I demand that you listen* 3 to require, call for: *demanding attention* ➤ *noun* 1 a forceful request 2 an urgent claim: *many demands on his time* 3 a need for certain goods etc

demanding *adjective* 1 requiring a lot of effort, ability, etc 2 needing or expecting a lot of attention

demarcation *noun* 1 the marking out of limits or boundaries 2 the strict separation of the types of work to be done by the members of the various trade unions in a factory etc

deme (*pronounced* deem) *noun, biology* a group of plants or animals that are closely related and live in a distinct locality

demean *verb* to lower, degrade

demeanour *noun* behaviour, conduct

demented *adjective* mad, insane

dementia (*pronounced* di-**men**-sha) *noun* a loss of normal mental ability and functioning, especially in the elderly ◐ Comes from Latin *de* meaning 'from' + *mens* meaning 'mind'

demerara or **demerara sugar** (*pronounced* dem-e-**rei**-ra or dem-e-**rah**-ra) *noun* a form of crystallized brown sugar

demise *noun, formal* death

demob *Brit informal, verb* (**demobbed, demobbing**) to demobilize ➤ *noun* demobilization

demobilize or **demobilise** *verb* **1** to break up an army after a war is over **2** to free (a soldier) from army service ◆ **demobilization** *noun*

democracy *noun* a form of government in which the people govern themselves or elect representatives to govern them ◐ Comes from Greek *demos* meaning 'the people', and *kratos* meaning 'strength'

democrat *noun* **1** someone who believes in democracy **2** (**Democrat**) *US* a supporter of the Democratic Party

democratic *adjective* of or governed by democracy ◆ **democratically** *adverb*

Democratic Party *noun* one of the two chief political parties in the USA, generally inclining to left of centre (*compare with:* **Republican Party**)

demographic transition model *noun, geography* a graph showing changes in a population over time

demography *noun* the study of population statistics, eg births, deaths, etc ◆ **demographer** *noun* ◆ **demographic** *adjective*

demolish *verb* **1** to destroy completely **2** to pull down (a building etc) ◆ **demolition** *noun*

demon *noun* an evil spirit, a devil ◆ **demonic** *adjective*

demonstrable (*pronounced* **dem**-on-stra-bl) *adjective* able to be shown clearly ◆ **demonstrably** *adverb*

demonstrate *verb* **1** to show clearly; prove **2** to show (a machine etc) in action **3** to express an opinion by marching, showing placards, etc in public

demonstration *noun* **1** a showing, a display **2** a public expression of opinion by a procession, mass meeting, etc

demonstrative (*pronounced* di-**mon**-stra-tiv) *adjective* **1** pointing out; proving **2** inclined to show feelings openly

demonstrator *noun* **1** a person who takes part in a public demonstration to express their opinion about something **2** a person who explains how something works, or shows you how to do something

demoralize or **demoralise** *verb* to take away the confidence of ◆ **demoralization** *noun*

demote *verb* to reduce to a lower rank or grade ◆ **demotion** *noun*

demur (*pronounced* di-**mer**) *verb* (**demurring, demurred**) to object, say 'no'

demure *adjective* shy and modest ◆ **demurely** *adverb*

den *noun* **1** the lair of a wild animal **2** a small private room for working etc

denary (*pronounced* **deen**-a-ri) *adjective* containing or having the number 10 as a basis

denationalize or **denationalise** *verb* to transfer (an industry) from government ownership to private ownership ◆ **denationalization** *noun*

denature or **denaturize** or **denaturise** *verb, biology* to change the structure of (a protein, eg an enzyme), by exposing it to high temperatures, certain chemicals or extremes of acidity and alkalinity

denial *noun* the act of denying • **in denial** doggedly refusing to accept something

denier (*pronounced* **den**-i-er) *noun* a unit of weight of nylon, silk, etc

denigrate (*pronounced* **den**-i-greit) *verb* to attack the reputation of, defame

denim *noun* a hard-wearing cotton cloth used for jeans, overalls, etc

◐ **Denim** was first manufactured in the town of Nîmes in the south of France, and this is how it got its name (*de Nîmes* means 'from Nîmes')

denizen (*pronounced* **den**-i-zen) *noun* **1** a dweller, an inhabitant **2** *biology* a species of animal or plant established in a place to which it is not native and into which it has been introduced

denomination *noun* **1** name, title **2** a value of a coin, stamp, etc **3** a religious sect ◆ **denominational** *adjective*

denominator *noun, maths* the lower number in a vulgar fraction by which the upper number is divided, eg the 3 in $\frac{2}{3}$ (*compare with:* **numerator**)

denote *verb* to mean, signify ◆ **denotation** *noun* ◐ Comes from Latin *denotare* meaning 'to mark out'

dénouement (*pronounced* dei-**noo**-mong) *noun* the ending of a story where mysteries etc are explained

◐ Literally 'untying' or 'unravelling', from French

denounce *verb* **1** to accuse publicly of a crime **2** to inform against: *denounced him to the enemy*

dense *adjective* **1** closely packed together; thick **2** very stupid ◆ **densely** *adverb* (meaning 1)

density *noun* (*plural* **densities**) **1** thickness **2** weight in proportion to volume **3** *computing* the extent to which data can be held on a floppy disk

dent *noun* a hollow made by a blow or pressure ➤ *verb* to make a dent in

dental *adjective* of or for a tooth or teeth

dental floss *noun* a soft thread used for cleaning between the teeth

dental surgeon *noun* a dentist

dentine (*pronounced* **den**-teen) *noun*, *anatomy* a hard yellowish-white material that forms the bulk of the tooth

dentist *noun* a doctor who examines teeth and treats dental problems

dentistry *noun* the work of a dentist

dentures *plural noun* a set of false teeth

denude *verb* to make bare, strip: *denuded of leaves* ◆ **denudation** *noun*

denunciation *noun* a strongly expressed public criticism or condemnation

deny *verb* (**denies, denying, denied**) **1** to declare to be untrue: *He denied that he did it* **2** to refuse, forbid: *He was denied the right to appeal* ● **deny yourself** to do without things you want or need

deodorant *noun* something that hides unpleasant smells, especially body smells such as perspiration

deoxygenate *verb*, *chemistry* to remove oxygen from

deoxyribonucleic acid see **DNA**

depart *verb* **1** to go away **2** to turn aside (from): *departing from the plan*

department *noun* a self-contained section within a shop, university, government, etc

department store *noun* a large shop with many departments selling a wide variety of goods

departure *noun* **1** the act of leaving or going away **2** a break with something expected or traditional ● **a new departure** a new course of action

depend *verb* (**depend on**) **1** to rely on **2** to receive necessary financial support from **3** to be controlled or decided by: *It all depends on the weather*

dependable *adjective* able to be trusted

dependant *noun* someone who is kept or supported by another

! Do not confuse: **dependant** and **dependent**

dependence or **dependency** *noun* the state of being dependent

dependency ratio *noun* the ratio of people of working age to those not of working age in an area

dependent *adjective* relying or depending (on)

! Do not confuse: **dependent** and **dependant**

dependent clause another name for a **subordinate clause**

dependent event *noun*, *maths* an event the probability of which depends on the result of some other event (*compare with*: **independent event**)

dependent variable *noun*, *maths* a variable in an equation, the value of which depends on that of another variable (the **independent variable**)

depict *verb* **1** to draw, paint, etc **2** to describe

deplete *verb* to make smaller in amount or number ◆ **depletion** *noun*

deplorable *adjective* regrettable; very bad

deplore *verb* to disapprove of, regret: *deplored his use of language*

deploy *verb* to place in position ready for action ◆ **deployment** *noun*

depolarize or **depolarise** *verb*, *physics* to reduce or remove the polarity of something

depopulate *verb* to reduce greatly in population ◆ **depopulated** *adjective* ◆ **depopulation** *noun*

deport *verb* to send (someone) out of a country ◆ **deportation** *noun*

deportment *noun* behaviour, bearing

depose *verb* to remove from a high position, especially a monarch from a throne ◆ **deposition** *noun*

deposit *verb* (**depositing, deposited**) **1** to put or set down **2** to put in for safe keeping, eg money in a bank ➤ *noun* **1** money paid in part payment of something **2** money put in a bank account **3** a solid that has settled at the bottom of a liquid **4** a layer of coal, iron, etc occurring naturally in rock

deposit account *noun* a bank account with a higher interest rate than a **current account**, used for savings

deposition (*pronounced* dep-o-**zish**-on) *noun* **1** the removal of someone from a high position, especially a monarch from a throne **2** a written piece of evidence **3** *geography* the laying down of eroded material, eg rocks, that has been transported by wind, rivers, glaciers, avalanches, etc

depository *noun* (*plural* **depositories**) a place where anything is deposited

depot (*pronounced* **dep**-oh) *noun* **1** a storehouse **2** a building where railway engines, buses, etc are kept and repaired

deprave *verb* to make wicked

depraved *adjective* wicked

depravity (*pronounced* di-**prav**-i-ti) *noun* wickedness

deprecate (*pronounced* **dep**-ri-keit) *verb* to show disapproval of, condemn ☉ Comes from Latin *de* meaning 'away', and *precari* meaning 'to pray'

❗ Do not confuse: **deprecate** and **depreciate**

deprecating or **deprecatory** *adjective* disapproving, extremely critical

deprecation *noun* the act or process of disapproving of, devaluing or condemning something: *self-deprecation* (= bringing yourself down, being too self-critical)

depreciate (*pronounced* dip-**ree**-shi-eit) *verb* **1** to lessen the value of **2** to fall in value
   ♦ **depreciation** *noun* ☉ Comes from Latin *de* meaning 'down', and *pretium* meaning 'price'

❗ Be careful. **Depreciate** is most frequently used to refer to a fall or a bringing down in financial value. Don't use it when you really mean **deprecate**.

depredations *plural noun* damage or violent robbery

depress *verb* **1** to make gloomy or unhappy **2** to press down **3** to make lower in value or intensity

depressant *medicine, adjective* of a drug: able to reduce mental or physical activity ➤ *noun* a depressant drug

depressed *adjective* gloomy, in low spirits

depressing *adjective* having the effect of making you gloomy or unhappy

depression *noun* **1** low spirits, gloominess **2** a hollow **3** a lowering in value **4** a low period in a country's economy with unemployment, lack of trade, etc **5** (**the Depression**) another term for **the Great Depression 6** a region of low atmospheric pressure that is associated with unsettled weather **7** *maths* (*also called*: **angle of depression**) an angle measuring a point below a horizontal line (*compare with*: **elevation** meaning 5)

depressive *adjective* **1** depressing **2** of a person: suffering frequently from depression ➤ *noun* someone who suffers frequently from depression

depressor *noun* **1** something that depresses **2** *anatomy* a muscle that draws down the part it is connected to

deprivation *noun* hardship caused by being deprived of necessities, rights, etc

deprive *verb* (**deprive of**) to take away from

deprived *adjective* suffering from hardship; disadvantaged

Dept *abbreviation* department

depth *noun* **1** deepness **2** a deep place **3** the deepest part: *from the depth of her soul* **4** the

middle: *the depth of winter* **5** intensity, strength: *depth of colour* • **in depth** thoroughly, carefully • **out of your depth** concerned in problems too difficult to understand

deputation *noun* a group of people chosen and sent as representatives

deputize or **deputise** *verb* to take another's place, act as substitute

deputy *noun* (*plural* **deputies**) **1** a delegate, a representative **2** a person appointed to act for another person in their absence

derail *verb* to cause (a train etc) to leave the rails
   ♦ **derailment** *noun*

derange *verb* to put out of place, or out of working order

deranged *adjective* mad, insane

derangement *noun* an old-fashioned word meaning 'madness' or 'insanity'

derby (*pronounced* **dahr**-bi) *noun* (*plural* **derbies**) a sports event between two teams from the same area

derelict (*pronounced* **de**-re-likt) *adjective* broken-down, abandoned

dereliction *noun* neglect of what should be attended to: *dereliction of duty*

deride *verb* to laugh at, mock

de rigueur (*pronounced* di ri-**ger**) *adjective* required by custom or fashion

derision *noun* mockery

derisive (*pronounced* di-**rai**-siv) *adjective* mocking

❗ Do not confuse: **derisive** and **derisory**

derisory (*pronounced* di-**rai**-so-ri) *adjective* so small or inadequate as to be not worth taking seriously, laughable: *He offered me a derisory* (= ridiculously small) *sum for the work I'd done*

derivative (*pronounced* di-**riv**-a-tiv) *adjective* not original ➤ *noun* **1** a word formed on the base of another word, eg *fabulous* from *fable* **2** *maths* (*also called*: **differential coefficient**) the rate of change of one variable quantity in relation to small changes in another

derive *verb* **1** to be descended or formed (from) **2** to trace (a word) back to the beginning of its existence **3** to receive, obtain: *derive satisfaction*
   ♦ **derivation** *noun*

dermatitis *noun* inflammation of the skin

dermato- also **dermat-, -derm-** *prefix & word particle* of or relating to the skin: *dermatology/dermatitis/hypodermic/ pachyderm/taxidermist*

dermatology *noun* the study and treatment of skin diseases ♦ **dermatologist** *noun*

dermis *noun, anatomy* the thick lower layer of skin beneath the epidermis

derogatory *adjective* **1** harmful to reputation, dignity, etc **2** scornful, belittling, disparaging

derrick *noun* **1** a crane for lifting weights **2** a framework over an oil well that holds the drilling machinery

○ Named after *Derrick*, a famous 17th-century hangman in Tyburn, England

derring-do (*pronounced* de-ring-**doo**) *noun old* daring action, boldness

○ Based on a misprint of a medieval English phrase *dorring do*, meaning 'daring to do'

dervish *noun* a member of an austere Islamic sect

descant (*pronounced* **des**-kant) *noun, music* a tune played or sung above the main tune

descend *verb* **1** to go or climb down **2** to slope downwards **3** to go from a better to a worse state • **descend from** to have as an ancestor: *claims he's descended from Napoleon*

descendant *noun* someone descended from another

descent *noun* **1** an act of descending **2** a downward slope

describe *verb* **1** to give an account of in words **2** to draw the outline of, trace

description *noun* **1** the act of describing **2** an account of something in words **3** sort, kind: *people of all descriptions* ♦ **descriptive** *adjective* (meaning 1)

desecrate (*pronounced* **des**-i-kreit) *verb* **1** to spoil (something sacred) **2** to treat without respect ♦ **desecration** *noun*

⚠ Do not confuse with: **desiccate**. Remember that **desecRate** and **sacRed** are related, and they both contain an **R**.

desegregate *verb* to end segregation, especially racial segregation in (public places, schools, etc) ♦ **desegregation** *noun*

desert¹ (*pronounced* di-**zert**) *verb* **1** to run away from (the army) **2** to leave, abandon: *deserted his wife/His courage deserted him* ♦ **deserter** *noun* (meaning 1) ♦ **desertion** *noun*

desert² (*pronounced* **dez**-ert) *noun* a stretch of barren country with very little rainfall ○ Comes from Latin *desertum* meaning 'deserted'

⚠ Do not confuse with: **dessert**

desertification (*pronounced* dez-er-ti-fi-**keish**-on) *noun, geography* the transformation of fertile land into desert

desert island *noun* an uninhabited island in a tropical area

deserts (*pronounced* de-**zerts**) *plural noun*: **just deserts** what you deserve, usually something bad

deserve *verb* to have earned as a right, be worthy of: *You deserve a holiday*

deservedly (*pronounced* di-**zer**-vid-li) *adverb* justly

deserving *adjective* worthy of being rewarded or helped • **be deserving of** to deserve

desiccate (*pronounced* **des**-i-keit) *verb* **1** to dry up **2** to preserve by drying: *desiccated coconut* ○ Comes from Latin *desiccare* meaning 'to dry up'

⚠ Do not confuse with: **desecrate**. Remember that **desecRate** and **sacRed** are related, and they both contain an **R**.

design *verb* **1** to make a plan of (eg a building or an article of clothing) before it is made **2** to intend ➤ *noun* **1** a plan, a sketch **2** a painted picture, pattern, etc **3** an intention • **by design** intentionally • **have designs on** to plan to get for yourself

designate *verb* (*pronounced* **dez**-ig-neit) **1** to point out, indicate **2** to name **3** to appoint, select ➤ *adjective* (*pronounced* **dez**-ig-nat) (*placed after the noun*) appointed to a post but not yet occupying it: *the director designate*

designation (*pronounced* dez-ig-**nei**-shon) *noun* a name, a title

designer *noun* someone who makes plans, patterns, drawings, etc ➤ *adjective* designed by and bearing the name of a famous fashion designer: *designer dresses*

designing *adjective* crafty, cunning

desirable *adjective* pleasing; worth having ♦ **desirability** *noun*

desire *verb* to wish for greatly ➤ *noun* **1** a longing for **2** a wish

desist *verb, formal* to stop (doing something)

desk *noun* a table for writing, reading, etc

desktop *adjective* small enough to fit on the top of a desk ➤ *noun* **1** a desktop computer **2** *computing* a screen showing the files and programs available for working with

desktop computer *noun* a computer designed for use on a desk, usually with CPU, VDU, keyboard and mouse

desktop publishing *noun* the preparation and production of typeset material using a desktop computer and printer

desolate *adjective* **1** deeply unhappy **2** empty of people, deserted **3** barren

desolation *noun* **1** deep sorrow **2** barren land **3** ruin

despair *verb* to give up hope ➤ *noun* **1** lack of hope **2** a cause of despair: *She was the despair of her mother*

despairing *adjective* in despair

despatch another spelling of **dispatch**

desperado (*pronounced* des-pe-**rah**-doh) *noun* (*plural* **desperadoes** or **desperados**) a violent criminal

desperate *adjective* **1** without hope, despairing **2** very bad, awful **3** reckless; violent

desperately *adverb* very much, very intensely: *desperately proud of his baby daughter/missing you desperately*

desperation *noun* the feeling you have when your situation is so bad that you are prepared to do anything to get out of it

despicable *adjective* contemptible, hateful

despise *verb* to look on with contempt

despite *preposition* in spite of: *We had a picnic despite the weather*

despoil *verb* to rob, plunder ✦ **despoliation** *noun*

despondent *adjective* downhearted, dejected ✦ **despondency** *noun*

despot (*pronounced* **des**-pot) *noun* a ruler with unlimited power, a tyrant ✦ **despotic** *adjective* ✦ **despotism** *noun*

dessert (*pronounced* de-**zert**) *noun* fruits, sweets, etc served at the end of a meal ⓞ Comes from Old French *dessert* meaning 'the clearing of the table'

⚠ Do not confuse with: **desert**

dessertspoon *noun* **1** a spoon about twice the size of a teaspoon, used for eating desserts **2** (also **dessertspoonful**) the amount a dessertspoon will hold

destination *noun* the place to which someone or something is going

destine *verb* to set apart for a certain use

destined *adjective* **1** bound (for) **2** intended (for) by fate: *destined to succeed*

destiny *noun* (*plural* **destinies**) what is destined to happen; fate

destitute *adjective* **1** in need of food, shelter, etc **2** (**destitute of**) completely lacking in: *destitute of wit*

destitution *noun* the state of having nothing, not even food and shelter

destroy *verb* **1** to pull down, knock to pieces **2** to ruin **3** to kill

destroyer *noun* **1** someone who destroys **2** a type of fast warship

destructible *adjective* able to be destroyed

destruction *noun* **1** the act of destroying or being destroyed **2** ruin **3** death

destructive *adjective* **1** doing great damage **2** of criticism: pointing out faults without suggesting improvements

destructive plate boundary or **destructive plate margin** *noun*, *geography* (*also called*: **convergent plate boundary**) a type of boundary between tectonic plates in which the plates collide, and which can cause violent earthquakes and volcanoes and the formation of ocean trenches and fold mountains (*see also*: **conservative plate boundary, constructive plate boundary**)

destructive wave *noun*, *geography* a strong wave, found in storm conditions, which removes material from the shore and causes coastal erosion (*compare with*: **constructive wave**)

desultory (*pronounced* **dez**-ul-to-ri) *adjective* **1** moving from one thing to another without a fixed plan **2** changing from subject to subject, rambling

detach *verb* to unfasten, remove (from)

detachable *adjective* able to be taken off: *a detachable lining*

detached *adjective* **1** standing apart, by itself: *a detached house* **2** not personally involved, showing no emotion

detachment *noun* **1** the state of being detached **2** a body or group (eg of troops on special service)

detail *noun* a small part, fact, item, etc ➤ *verb* **1** to describe fully, give particulars of **2** to set to do a special job or task: *detailed to keep watch* • **in detail** giving attention to details, item by item

detailed *adjective* with nothing left out

detain *verb* **1** to hold back **2** to keep late **3** to keep under guard

detect *verb* **1** to discover **2** to notice ✦ **detection** *noun*

detector *noun* a device for detecting the presence of something

detective *noun* someone who tries to find criminals or watches suspects

détente (*pronounced* dei-**tont**) *noun* a lessening of tension, especially between countries ⓞ Comes from French

detention *noun* **1** imprisonment **2** a forced stay after school as a punishment

detention centre *noun* a place where young criminals are kept for a short time by order of a court

deter *verb* (**deterring, deterred**) to discourage or prevent through fear

detergent *noun* a soapless substance used with water for washing dishes etc

deteriorate *verb* to grow worse: *Her health is deteriorating rapidly* ✦ **deterioration** *noun*

determinant *noun* **1** *maths* the sum of all the products obtained by taking one from each row and column of a square matrix of quantities **2** *biology* in an antigen molecule: a region or regions that enable it to be recognized and bound by an antibody

determination *noun* **1** the fact of being determined **2** stubbornness, firmness of purpose

determine *verb* **1** to decide (on) **2** to fix, settle: *determined his course of action*

determined *adjective* **1** firmly decided; having a strong intention: *determined to succeed* **2** fixed, settled

determiner *noun, grammar* a word that comes before a noun and limits its meaning in some way, eg *a, the, this, every, some*

deterrent *noun* something, especially a threat of some kind, which deters or discourages people from a particular course of action ♦ **deterrence** *noun*

detest *verb* to hate greatly

detestable *adjective* very hateful

detestation *noun* great hatred

detonate *verb* to (cause to) explode

detonation *noun* an explosion

detonator *noun* something which sets off an explosive

detour *noun* a circuitous route

detract *verb* to take away (from), lessen ♦ **detraction** *noun*

> ⚠ Do not confuse: **detract from** and **distract from**

detriment *noun* harm, damage, disadvantage

detrimental *adjective* disadvantageous (to), causing harm or damage

detritus (*pronounced* di-**trai**-tus) *noun* **1** loosened fragments, especially of rock **2** *biology* dead plants or animals, or debris from living organisms

deuce (*pronounced* dyoos) *noun* **1** a playing-card with two pips **2** *tennis* a score of forty points each

deuterium *noun, chemistry* (symbol **D** or ^{2}**H**) one of the three isotopes of hydrogen

deuterium oxide *noun, chemistry* a compound of deuterium and oxygen, used to slow down neutrons in nuclear reactors

deuteron *noun, physics* the nucleus of an atom of deuterium, composed of a proton and a neutron

devalue or **devaluate** *verb* **1** to reduce the value of (a currency) in relation to other currencies **2** to make (a person, action, etc) seem less valuable or important ♦ **devaluation** *noun*

devastate *verb* **1** to lay in ruins **2** to overwhelm with grief etc ♦ **devastation** *noun*

develop *verb* (**developing, developed**) **1** to (cause to) grow bigger or more advanced **2** to acquire gradually: *developed a taste for opera* **3** to become active or visible **4** to unfold gradually **5** to use chemicals to make (a photograph) appear

developer *noun* a chemical mixture used to make an image appear from a photograph

Developing World *noun* a name for the underdeveloped countries in Africa, Asia and Latin America (*also called*: **the Third World**)

development *noun* **1** growth in size or sophistication **2** work done on studying and improving on previous or basic models, designs, or techniques **3** improvement of land so as to make it more fertile, useful or profitable **4** an area of housing built by a developer **5** an occurrence that affects or influences a situation **6** the gradual unfolding of something, eg a story **7** the process of using chemicals to make a photograph appear

deviate *verb* to turn aside, especially from a standard course

deviation *noun* **1** something which is different, or which departs from the normal course **2** *statistics* the amount of difference between the average of a group of numbers and one of the numbers in that group

device *noun* **1** a tool, an instrument **2** a plan **3** a design on a coat of arms

> ⚠ Do not confuse with: **devise**.
> To help you remember: 'ice' is a noun, 'ise' is not!

devil *noun* **1** an evil spirit **2** Satan **3** a wicked person

devilish *adjective* very wicked

devil-may-care *adjective* not caring what happens

devilment or **devilry** *noun* mischief

devil's advocate *noun* someone who argues against a proposal in order to test it

devious *adjective* **1** not direct, roundabout **2** not straightforward

devise *verb* **1** to make up, put together **2** to plan, plot

> ⚠ Do not confuse with: **device**.
> To help you remember: 'ice' is a noun … so 'ise' must be the verb!

devoid *adjective* (**devoid of**) empty of, free from: *devoid of curiosity*

devolution *noun* the act of devolving, especially of giving certain powers to a regional government by a central government

devolutionist *noun* a supporter of devolution

devolve *verb* **1** to fall as a duty (on) **2** to delegate (power) to a regional or national assembly

Devonian *adjective* of the geological period 410 million to 360 million years ago

devote *verb* to give up wholly (to)

devoted *adjective* **1** loving and loyal **2** given up (to): *devoted to her work*

devotee (*pronounced* dev-oh-**tee**) *noun* a keen follower

devotion *noun* **1** great love **2** religious enthusiasm ♦ **devotional** *adjective* expressing devotion

devour *verb* **1** to eat up greedily **2** to destroy

devout *adjective* **1** earnest, sincere **2** religious
♦ **devoutly** *adverb*

dew *noun* tiny drops of water which form from the air as it cools at night

dewy *adjective* (**dewier, dewiest**) covered in dew; moist

dexterity *noun* skill, quickness ♦ **dexterous** or **dextrous** *adjective*

dextrin or **dextrine** *noun, chemistry* a substance produced during the breakdown of starch, used as a thickener in foods and adhesives

dextrose *noun* a type of glucose

dhal see **dal**

dharma *noun* **1** *Buddhism* truth as laid down in the scriptures, law **2** *Hinduism* the universal laws, especially the moral laws to be followed by each individual ℗ Comes from Sanskrit, meaning 'decree' or 'custom'

dhoti (*pronounced* **doh**-ti) *noun* (*plural* **dhotis**) a piece of cloth worn around the hips by some Hindu men

di-¹ *prefix* **1** two, twice, or double **2** *chemistry* containing two atoms of the same type: *carbon dioxide* ℗ Comes from Greek *dis* meaning 'two', 'twice' or 'double'

di-² see **dis-**

diabetes (*pronounced* dai-a-**bee**-teez) *noun* a disease in which there is too much sugar in the blood

diabetic *noun & adjective* (someone) suffering from diabetes

diabolical or **diabolic** *adjective* devilish, very wicked ♦ **diabolically** *adverb*

diadem *noun* a kind of crown

diagnose *verb* to identify (a cause of illness) after making an examination

diagnosis *noun* (*plural* **diagnoses**) **1** the identification (of the cause of illness in a patient) by examination **2** *biology* a formal description, eg of a plant, and its characteristics

diagnostic *adjective* having the purpose of identifying the cause of illness or a fault

diagonal *adjective* going from one corner to the opposite corner ▸ *noun* a line from one corner to the opposite corner ♦ **diagonally** *adverb*

diagram *noun* a drawing to explain something

diagrammatic or **diagrammatical** *adjective* in the form of a diagram

diakinesis (*pronounced* dai-a-kai-**nee**-sis or dai-a-ki-**nee**-sis) *noun, biology* the final stage of prophase during meiosis

dial *noun* **1** the face of a clock or watch **2** a rotating disc over the numbers on some telephones ▸ *verb* (**dialling, dialled**) to call (a number) on a telephone using a dial or buttons

dialect *noun* a way of speaking found only in a certain area or among a certain group of people

dialogue *noun* a talk between two or more people

dialogue box *noun, computing* a small box which appears on screen to prompt the user to give information or enter an option

dial-up *adjective, computing* of a connection: using a modem to connect to another computer or to the Internet

dialysis (*pronounced* dai-**al**-i-sis) *noun* **1** *medicine* removal of impurities from the blood by a kidney machine **2** *chemistry* the separation of particles of different sizes in a solution

diamanté (*pronounced* dee-a-**mon**-tei) *adjective* decorated with small sparkling ornaments ℗ Comes from French, meaning 'decorated with diamonds'

diameter (*pronounced* dai-**am**-i-ter) *noun* *maths* a line which dissects a circle, passing through its centre, and which is equal to twice its radius

diamond *noun* **1** a very hard, precious stone **2** an elongated, four-cornered shape (◊) **3** a playing-card with red diamond pips

diamond wedding *noun* the sixtieth anniversary of a marriage

diapause *noun, biology* a pause in the development of an insect, until conditions become more favourable

diaper *noun, US* a baby's nappy

> ℗ Originally a kind of decorated white silk. The current US meaning was used in British English in the 16th century

diaphragm (*pronounced* **dai**-a-fram) *noun* **1** *anatomy* a layer of muscle separating the abdomen from the chest **2** a thin dividing layer **3** a contraceptive device that fits over the neck of the womb

diarrhoea (*pronounced* dai-a-**ree**-a) *noun* frequent emptying of the bowels, with too much liquid in the faeces

diary *noun* (*plural* **diaries**) **1** a record of daily happenings **2** a book detailing these

Diaspora (*pronounced* dai-**as**-po-ra) *noun* (**the Diaspora**) **1** the scattering of the Jewish people to various countries after their exile in Babylon in the 6th century BC **2** the resulting new communities of Jews in various countries ℗ Comes from Greek *dia* meaning 'through' + *speirein* meaning 'to scatter'

diatomic *adjective, chemistry* denoting a molecule that consists of two identical atoms

diatribe *noun* an angry attack in words

diazo compound (*pronounced* dai-**az**-oh) *noun, chemistry* a compound containing two adjacent nitrogen atoms, only one of which is attached to a carbon atom, used in dyes and drugs

dibasic *adjective, chemistry* denoting an acid that contains two replaceable atoms, allowing the formation of two types of salt, the normal and the acid salt

dice *noun* (*plural* **dice**) (*also called*: **die**) a small cube with numbered sides or faces, used in certain games ➤ *verb* to cut (food) into small cubes

dichotomy (*pronounced* **dai**-kaw-to-mi) *noun* (*plural* **dichotomies**) a division or separation into two groups or parts, especially when these are sharply contrasted ⊙ Comes from Greek *dicha* meaning 'in two' + *tome* meaning 'cut'

dicotyledon (*pronounced* dai-kot-i-**lee**-don) *noun, botany* a flowering plant with an embryo that has two cotyledons (*compare with*: **monocotyledon**)

dictate *verb* (*pronounced* dik-**teit**) 1 to speak the text of (a letter etc) for someone else to write down 2 to give firm commands ➤ *noun* (*pronounced* **dik**-teit) an order, a command

dictation *noun* the act of dictating

dictator *noun* an all-powerful ruler

dictatorial *adjective* like a dictator; domineering

dictatorship *noun* government by a dictator

diction *noun* 1 manner of speaking 2 choice of words

dictionary *noun* (*plural* **dictionaries**) 1 a book giving the words of a language in alphabetical order, together with their meanings 2 any alphabetically ordered reference book: *a medical dictionary* 3 *computing* a dictionary contained on the disk that a program can check against for spelling errors in text

did see **do**[1]

didactic (*pronounced* di-**dak**-tik or dai-**dak**-tik) *adjective* 1 intended to teach or instruct 2 *derogatory* too eager or too obviously intended to instruct ⊙ Comes from Greek *didaskein* meaning 'to teach' ◆ **didacticism** *noun*

didgeridoo *noun, music* a native Australian musical instrument, consisting of a long tube which you blow into to produce a low, droning sound

die[1] *verb* (**dying, died**) 1 to lose life 2 to wither • **die down** to become less intense

die[2] *noun* 1 a stamp or punch for making raised designs on money etc 2 another word for **dice**

diehard *noun* an obstinate or determined person

dielectric *physics, noun* a non-conducting material used as a component of capacitors ➤ *adjective* denoting such material

diesel (*pronounced* **dee**-zel) *noun* 1 an internal combustion engine in which heavy oil is ignited by heat generated by compression 2 liquid fuel for use in a diesel engine

diet[1] *noun* 1 food 2 a course of recommended foods, eg to lose weight ➤ *verb* (**dieting, dieted**) to eat certain kinds of food only, especially to lose weight ◆ **dieter** *noun*

diet[2] *noun* a council, an assembly

dietary *adjective* concerning a **diet**[1]

dietetic *adjective* 1 concerning a **diet**[1] 2 for use in a special medical diet

dif- another form of **dis-**

differ *verb* (**differing, differed**) to disagree • **differ from** to be unlike

difference *noun* 1 a point in which things differ 2 the amount by which one number is greater than another 3 a disagreement

different *adjective* 1 varying, not the same 2 unusual 3 (**different from**) unlike

---

ⓘ Both **different to** and **different from** can be used in British English, although some people consider only **different from** to be correct:
You are different to your brother.
In American English, **different than** is also used.

---

differential *adjective* 1 being, showing, relating to or based on a difference 2 *maths* to do with a minute difference in values ➤ *noun* 1 something that differentiates two things 2 a difference in pay between one category of worker and another in the same industry or company 3 *maths* a minute difference in values

differential calculus *noun, maths* a branch of calculus concerned with finding derivatives, used to find velocities, gradients of curves, etc (*see also*: **differentiation**)

differential coefficient same as **derivative** (meaning 2)

differential equation *noun, maths* an equation involving derivatives

differential erosion *noun, geography* different rates of erosion in the same piece of rock, where some parts are softer than other parts

differentiate *verb* 1 to make a difference or distinction between 2 *maths* to use the process of differentiation to find the derivative of (a function or variable) 3 *biology* of a cell: to become increasingly specialized in structure and function, eg during the development of a muscle fibre

differentiation *noun* 1 making a distinction 2 *biology* the process by which unspecialized cells or tissues develop a specialized structure and function 3 *maths* a method used in calculus to calculate the rate of change of one variable quantity produced by small changes in another, ie to find the derivative of a function or variable (*compare with*: **integration**)

difficult *adjective* **1** not easy, hard to do, understand or deal with **2** hard to please

difficulty *noun* (*plural* **difficulties**) **1** lack of easiness, hardness **2** anything difficult **3** anything which makes something difficult; an obstacle, hindrance, etc **4** (**difficulties**) troubles

diffident *adjective* shy, not confident
♦ **diffidence** *noun*

diffract *verb, physics* to cause diffraction in

diffraction *noun, physics* **1** the change in direction of a light or sound wave when it encounters an obstacle **2** the spreading of a light or sound wave when it emerges from a small opening

diffuse *verb* (*pronounced* dif-**yooz**) to spread in all directions ➤ *adjective* (*pronounced* dif-**yoos**) widely spread

⚠ Do not confuse with: **defuse**

diffusion *noun* **1** the reflection of light in all directions **2** the way light passes through a transparent substance **3** *physics* the movement of ions or molecules from an area of higher concentration to a lower one

dig *verb* (**digging, dug**) **1** to turn up (earth) with a spade etc **2** to make (a hole) by this means **3** to poke or push (something) into ➤ *noun* **1** a poke, a thrust **2** an archaeological excavation

digest[1] (*pronounced* dai-**jest**) *verb* **1** to break down (food) in the stomach into a form that the body can make use of **2** to think over **3** *chemistry* to soften or disintegrate in heat or moisture

digest[2] (*pronounced* **dai**-jest) *noun* **1** a summing-up **2** a collection of written material

digestible *adjective* able to be digested

digestion *noun* the act or power of digesting

digestive *adjective* aiding digestion

digestive tract *noun* the system of organs in the body, including the stomach and intestines, that breaks down food

digger *noun* a machine for digging

digit *noun* **1** a finger or toe **2** any of the numbers 0–9

digital *adjective* (*compare with*: **analogue**) **1** of data: in the form of a series of binary digits **2** of a device: showing information in the form of digits rather than with pointers on a dial **3** using information supplied and stored as binary digits
♦ **digitally** *adverb*

digital audio tape *noun* (*abbrev* **DAT**) a magnetic audio tape on which sound has been recorded digitally

digital camera *noun* a camera which records photographic images in digital form to be viewed on a computer

digitalis (*pronounced* di-ji-**teil**-is) *noun* **1**

botany a plant of the genus that includes the foxglove **2** *medicine* a type of drug that stimulates the heart, originally made from the leaves of the foxglove

digital recording *noun* the recording of sound by storing electrical pulses representing the audio signal on compact disc, digital audio tape, etc

digital television or **digital TV** *noun* a method of TV broadcasting, using digital rather than traditional analogue signals

digitate *adjective, botany* of leaves: consisting of several finger-like sections

digitize or **digitise** *verb, computing, maths* to convert (data) into binary digits

digitizer or **digitiser** *noun, computing* a device that converts analogue signals to digital codes (*also called*: **analogue-to-digital converter, A/D converter**)

diglossia *noun* the existence of both a colloquial and a formal or literary form of a language in a community

dignified *adjective* stately, serious

dignitary *noun* (*plural* **dignitaries**) someone of high rank or office

dignity *noun* **1** manner showing a sense of your own worth or the seriousness of the occasion **2** high rank

digraph (*pronounced* **dai**-grahf) *noun* two letters representing a single sound, eg *ph* in *digraph*

digress *verb* to wander from the point in speaking or writing ♦ **digression** *noun*

digs *plural noun, Brit informal* lodgings

dihedral (*pronounced* dai-**hee**-dral) *maths, adjective* formed or bounded by two planes ➤ *noun* the figure made by two intersecting planes ⊙ Comes from Greek *di-* meaning 'twice' + *hedra* meaning 'seat'

dike or **dyke** *noun* **1** a wall; an embankment **2** a ditch

dilapidated *adjective* falling to pieces, needing repair

dilate *verb* to make or grow larger, swell out
♦ **dilatation** or **dilation** *noun*

dilatory (*pronounced* **dil**-at-o-ri) *adjective* slow to act, inclined to delay

dilemma *noun* a situation offering a difficult choice between two options

diligent *adjective* hard-working, industrious
♦ **diligence** *noun* ♦ **diligently** *adverb*

dill *noun* a herb used in flavouring

dilly-dally *verb* (**dilly-dallies, dilly-dallying, dilly-dallied**) to loiter, waste time

diluent (*pronounced* **dil**-yuw-ent) *noun, chemistry* any solvent used to dilute a solution

dilute (*pronounced* dai-**loot** or di-**loot**) *verb* **1** to lessen the concentration of (a liquid etc), especially by adding water **2** to lessen the influence or effect of something ➤ *adjective* of a solution: with a relatively low concentration: *a dilute form of the same substance* ✦ **diluted** *adjective* ✦ **dilution** *noun*

dim *adjective* (**dimmer, dimmest**) **1** not bright or clear **2** not understanding clearly, stupid ➤ *verb* (**dimming, dimmed**) to make or become dim

dime *noun* a tenth of a US or Canadian dollar, ten cents

dimension *noun* **1** a measurement of length, width or thickness **2** (**dimensions**) size, measurements

dimer (*pronounced* **dai**-mer) *noun, chemistry* a chemical compound composed of two monomers

diminish *verb* to make or grow less

diminuendo *noun* (*plural* **diminuendoes** or **diminuendos**), *music* a fading or falling sound

diminution *noun* a lessening

diminutive *adjective* very small

dimly *adverb* vaguely, not brightly or clearly

dimmer or **dimmer switch** *noun* a control used to make a light brighter or dimmer

dimness *noun* haziness, half-light, lack of clarity

dimorphism *noun* **1** *biology* the occurrence of two distinct forms within a species of living organism, eg male and female **2** *chemistry* the crystallization of a chemical element or compound into two different crystalline forms that have the same chemical composition ✦ **dimorphic** or **dimorphous** *adjective*

dimple *noun* a small hollow, especially on the cheek or chin

dim sum (*pronounced* dim **sum**) *noun* a selection of Chinese foods, usually including steamed filled dumplings, served as an appetizer

din *noun* a loud, lasting noise ➤ *verb* (**dinning, dinned**) to put (into) someone's mind by constant repetition

dine *verb* to eat dinner

diner *noun* **1** someone who dines **2** a restaurant car on a train **3** *US* a small, cheap restaurant

dinghy (*pronounced* **ding**-i or **ding**-gi) *noun* (*plural* **dinghies**) a small rowing boat

dingo *noun* (*plural* **dingoes**) an Australian wild dog

dingy (*pronounced* **din**-ji) *adjective* (**dingier, dingiest**) dull, faded or dirty-looking ✦ **dinginess** *noun*

dining room *noun* a room in a house, hotel, etc used for eating in

dinner *noun* **1** a main evening meal **2** a midday meal, lunch

dinner jacket *noun* a black jacket worn by men at formal social gatherings, especially in the evening

dinosaur *noun* any of various types of extinct giant reptile

⊘ Coined in the 19th century, from Greek words which translate as 'terrible lizard'

dint *noun* a hollow made by a blow, a dent • **by dint of** by means of

diocese (*pronounced* **dai**-o-sis) *noun* a bishop's district

diode *noun, electronics* an electronic device containing two electrodes, an **anode** and a **cathode**, that allows current to flow in one direction only ⊘ Comes from Greek *di-* meaning 'twice' + *hodos* meaning 'way'

dioecious (*pronounced* dai-**ee**-shus) *adjective, biology* **1** of a plant: having male and female flowers on different plants **2** with the male and female sexual organs in separate individuals or creatures (*compare with*: **monoecious**)

dioxide *noun, chemistry* a compound formed by combining two oxygen atoms with one atom of another element

dip *verb* (**dipping, dipped**) **1** to plunge into a liquid quickly **2** to lower (eg a flag) and raise again **3** to slope down **4** to look briefly (into a book etc) ➤ *noun* **1** a liquid in which anything is dipped **2** a creamy sauce into which biscuits etc are dipped **3** a downward slope **4** a hollow **5** a short bathe or swim

dipeptide *noun, chemistry* a peptide formed by combining two amino acids

diphtheria (*pronounced* dif-**theer**-i-a) *noun* an infectious throat disease

diphthong *noun* two vowel sounds pronounced as one syllable (for example the *ow* sound in *out*)

diploid (*pronounced* **dip**-loid) *biology, adjective* of a cell: having two sets of chromosomes, one from each parent (*compare with*: **haploid**) ➤ *noun* a diploid cell or organism

diploma *noun* a document certifying that you have passed a certain examination or completed a course of study

⊘ From a Greek word meaning a letter folded double

diplomacy *noun* **1** the business of making agreements, treaties, etc between countries **2** skill in making people agree, tact

diplomat *noun* someone engaged in diplomacy

diplomatic *adjective* **1** of diplomacy **2** tactful

dipole *noun, physics* two equal and opposite electric charges separated by a small distance ✦ **dipolar** *adjective*

dipstick *noun* **1** a stick used to measure the level

of oil in a car engine, etc **2** *slang* a stupid person

dire *adjective* dreadful: *in dire need*

direct *adjective* **1** straight, not roundabout **2** frank, outspoken ▸ *verb* **1** to point or aim at **2** to show the way **3** to order, instruct **4** to control, organize **5** to put a name and address on (a letter)

direct current *noun* (*abbrev*: **DC**) an electric current flowing in one direction (*compare with*: **alternating current**)

direct debit *noun* an order to your bank which allows someone else to withdraw sums of money from your account, especially for payment of bills

direction *noun* **1** the act of directing **2** the place or point to which someone moves, looks, etc **3** an order **4** guidance **5** (**directions**) instructions on how to get somewhere ♦ **directional** *adjective*

directly *adverb* **1** straight away, immediately: *I shall do it directly* **2** straight: *I looked directly at him* **3** just, exactly: *directly opposite*

directness *noun* frankness, with no effort to be tactful

direct object *noun, grammar* the noun, phrase or pronoun which is directly affected by the action of a verb, eg *the dog* in *the boy kicked the dog* (*compare with*: **indirect object**)

director *noun* **1** a manager of a business etc **2** the person who controls the shooting of a film etc

directory *noun* (*plural* **directories**) **1** a book of names and addresses etc **2** *computing* a named group of files on a computer disk

directrix *noun* (*plural* **directrices** – pronounced dai-**rek**-tri-seez), *maths* a straight line from which the distance to any point on a conic section is in a constant ratio to the distance between that point and the focus

direct speech *noun* speech reported in the speaker's exact words (*contrasted with*: **indirect speech**)

dirge *noun* a lament; a funeral hymn

dirk *noun* a kind of dagger ⊙ Scots

dirt *noun* any unclean substance, such as mud, dust, dung, etc

dirt track *noun* an earth track for motorcycle racing

dirty *adjective* (**dirtier, dirtiest**) **1** not clean, soiled **2** obscene, lewd ▸ *verb* (**dirties, dirtying, dirtied**) to soil with dirt ♦ **dirtily** *adverb*

dis- also **dif-, di-** *prefix* **1** apart: *disjointed/divide* **2** not: *dislike* ⊙ Comes from Latin prefix *dis-, di-* with the same meaning

disability *noun* (*plural* **disabilities**) something which disables

disable *verb* **1** to take away power or strength

from **2** to make (eg a machine) unable to work

disabled *adjective* having a severely restricted lifestyle as the result of an injury, or a physical or mental illness or handicap

---

ⓘ Avoid referring to disabled people as **the disabled**. It is better to use 'people with a disability'.

---

disablement *noun* the state of being, or the process of becoming, disabled

disaccharide *noun, chemistry* a carbohydrate consisting of two monosaccharides joined together, eg sucrose

disadvantage *noun* an unfavourable circumstance, a drawback

disadvantaged *adjective* suffering a disadvantage, especially poverty or homelessness

disadvantageous *adjective* not advantageous

disaffected *adjective* dissatisfied and no longer loyal or committed

disagree *verb* **1** (often **disagree with**) to hold different opinions (from) **2** to quarrel **3** (**disagree with**) of food: to make (someone) feel ill

disagreeable *adjective* unpleasant

disagreement *noun* a difference of opinion or quarrel

disallow *verb* to not allow

disappear *verb* to go out of sight, vanish ♦ **disappearance** *noun*

disappoint *verb* **1** to fail to come up to the hopes or expectations (of) **2** to fail to fulfil

disappointed *adjective* sad because your hopes or expectations have not been fulfilled

disappointment *noun* **1** something which disappoints you **2** the feeling of being disappointed

disapprove *verb* to have an unfavourable opinion (of) ♦ **disapproval** *noun*

disarm *verb* **1** to take a weapon away from **2** to get rid of war weapons **3** to make less angry, charm

disarmament *noun* the removal or disabling of war weapons

disarming *adjective* gaining friendliness, charming: *a disarming smile*

disarray *noun* disorder

disaster *noun* an extremely unfortunate happening, often causing great damage or loss ♦ **disastrous** *adjective* ♦ **disastrously** *adverb*

disband *verb* to break up, separate: *The gang disbanded* ♦ **disbandment** *noun*

disbelief *noun* inability to believe something

disbelieve *verb* to not believe ♦ **disbeliever** *noun*

disburse verb to pay out ♦ **disbursement** noun

disc noun 1 a flat, round shape 2 anatomy a pad of cartilage between vertebrae 3 a gramophone record or compact disc 4 computing see **disk**

discard verb to throw away as useless

disc brakes plural noun vehicle brakes which use pads that are hydraulically forced against discs on the wheels

discern verb to see, realize

discernible adjective noticeable: no discernible difference

discerning adjective quick at noticing; discriminating: a discerning eye

discernment noun good taste, ability to judge between good and bad things

discharge verb (pronounced dis-**chahrj**) 1 to unload (cargo) 2 to set free 3 to dismiss 4 to fire (a gun) 5 to perform (duties) 6 to pay (a debt) 7 to give off (eg smoke) 8 to let out (pus) 9 of a device: to lose or cause to lose electrical charge ➤ noun (pronounced **dis**-chahrj) 1 a discharging 2 dismissal 3 pus etc discharged from the body 4 performance (of duties) 5 payment 6 the release of stored electric charge from a battery 7 physics a flow of electric current through a gas 8 geography the volume of water passing a specific point in river over a specific amount of time

disciple (pronounced di-**sai**-pl) noun 1 someone who believes in another's teaching 2 one of the followers of Christ

disciplinarian noun someone who insists on strict discipline

disciplinary adjective relating to the enforcement of rules and discipline, and the punishment of disobedience and other offences

discipline noun 1 training in an orderly way of life 2 order kept by means of control 3 punishment 4 a subject of study or training ➤ verb 1 to bring to order 2 to punish

disc jockey noun someone who introduces and plays recorded music on the radio, at a club, etc

disclaim verb to refuse to have anything to do with, deny

disclaimer noun 1 a written statement denying legal responsibility 2 a denial

disclose verb to uncover, reveal, make known

disclosure noun 1 the act of disclosing 2 something disclosed

disco noun (plural **discos**) an event or place where recorded music is played for dancing

discolour or US **discolor** verb to spoil the colour of; stain ♦ **discoloration** noun

discomfit verb (**discomfiting, discomfited**) 1 to disconcert 2 to thwart, defeat

discomfiture noun a feeling of slight embarrassment

discomfort noun lack of comfort, uneasiness

disconcert verb to upset, confuse

disconnect verb to separate, break the connection between

disconnected adjective 1 separated, no longer connected 2 of thoughts etc: not following logically, rambling

disconsolate adjective sad, disappointed

discontent noun dissatisfaction

discontented adjective dissatisfied, cross

discontinue verb to stop, cease to continue

discontinuous adjective with breaks or interruptions ♦ **discontinuity** noun

discord noun 1 disagreement, quarrelling 2 music a jarring of notes

discordant adjective 1 music made up of notes which do not make pleasant harmonies, creating a strange or unpleasant effect 2 strange or unpleasant because not made up of parts which fit well together

discordant coast noun, geography a coast where bands of resistant and less resistant rock are perpendicular to the coastline (contrasted with: **concordant coast**)

discotheque noun, old a place where discos are held

discount noun (pronounced **dis**-kownt) a small sum taken off the price of something: 10% discount ➤ verb (pronounced dis-**kownt**) 1 to leave out, not consider: completely discounted my ideas 2 to allow for exaggeration in (eg a story)

discourage verb 1 to take away the confidence, hope, etc of 2 to try to prevent by showing dislike or disapproval: discouraged his plan ♦ **discouragement** noun

discouraging adjective giving little hope or encouragement

discourse noun (pronounced **dis**-kawrs) 1 a speech, a lecture 2 an essay 3 a conversation ➤ verb (pronounced dis-**kawrs**) to talk, especially at some length

discourse marker noun a word or phrase which is a guideline to the structure of a text or argument, eg later, however, on the other hand

discourteous adjective not polite; rude ♦ **discourteously** adverb ♦ **discourtesy** noun (plural **discourtesies**)

discover verb 1 to find out 2 to find by chance, especially for the first time ♦ **discoverer** noun

discovery noun (plural **discoveries**) 1 the act of finding or finding out 2 something discovered

discredit verb (**discrediting, discredited**) 1 to refuse to believe 2 to cause to doubt 3 to disgrace ➤ noun 1 disgrace 2 disbelief

discreditable adjective disgraceful

discreet adjective wisely cautious, tactful ♦ **discreetly** adverb

❗ Do not confuse with: **discrete**

discrepancy noun (plural **discrepancies**) a difference or disagreement between two things: *some discrepancy in the figures*

discrete adjective separate, distinct

❗ Do not confuse with: **discreet**.
It may help you to think of **Crete**, which is an island separate from the rest of Greece.

discrete data noun, *statistics* data from measurements on a discrete, fixed unit such as shoe size (*compare with*: **continuous data**)

discretion noun wise caution, tact • **at someone's discretion** according to that person's own judgement

discriminant noun, *maths* an expression within a quadratic equation, the value of which gives information about the roots of the equation

discriminate verb 1 to make differences (between), distinguish 2 to treat (people) differently because of their gender, race, etc

discriminating adjective showing good judgement

discrimination noun 1 ability to discriminate 2 unfair treatment on grounds of gender, race, etc

discursive adjective involving discussion: *a discursive essay*

discus noun (plural **discuses**) a heavy disc thrown in an athletic competition

discuss verb to talk about ♦ **discussion** noun

disdain verb 1 to look down on, scorn 2 to be too proud to do ➤ noun scorn ♦ **disdainful** adjective

disease noun illness

diseased adjective affected by disease

disembark verb to put or go ashore ♦ **disembarkation** noun

disembodied adjective of a soul etc: separated from the body

disembowel verb (**disembowelling, disembowelled**) to remove the internal organs of

disenchanted adjective dissatisfied or discontented ♦ **disenchantment** noun

disengage verb to separate, free ♦ **disengaged** adjective

disentangle verb to free from entanglement, unravel

disfavour or US **disfavor** noun dislike, disapproval

disfigure verb to spoil the beauty or appearance of ♦ **disfigurement** noun

disgorge verb 1 to throw out 2 to vomit

disgrace noun the state of being out of favour; shame ➤ verb to bring shame on

disgraceful adjective shameful; very bad ♦ **disgracefully** adverb

disgruntled adjective discontented, sulky

disguise verb 1 to change the appearance of 2 to hide (feelings etc) ➤ noun 1 a disguised state 2 a costume etc which disguises

disgust noun 1 strong dislike, loathing 2 indignation ➤ verb 1 to cause loathing, revolt 2 to make indignant ♦ **disgusted** adjective

disgusting adjective sickening; causing disgust

dish noun (plural **dishes**) 1 a plate or bowl for food 2 food prepared for eating 3 a saucer-shaped aerial for receiving information from a satellite ➤ verb 1 to serve (food) 2 to deal (out), distribute

dishcloth noun a cloth for washing or drying dishes

dishearten verb to take away courage or hope from ♦ **disheartened** adjective ♦ **disheartening** adjective

dishevelled (*pronounced* di-**shev**-eld) adjective untidy, with hair etc disordered

dishonest adjective not honest, deceitful ♦ **dishonesty** noun

dishonour or US **dishonor** noun disgrace, shame ➤ verb to cause shame to ♦ **dishonourable** adjective

dishwasher noun a machine that washes and dries dishes

disillusion verb to take away a false belief from

disillusioned adjective unhappy and disappointed after your happy impressions of something have been destroyed ♦ **disillusionment** noun

disinclined adjective unwilling

disinfect verb to destroy disease-causing germs in

disinfectant noun a substance that kills germs

disinformation noun 1 false information intended to deceive or mislead 2 the act of supplying false information

disingenuous adjective not entirely sincere; creating a false impression of frankness ♦ **disingenuousness** noun

disinherit verb to take away the rights of (an heir) ♦ **disinheritance** noun

disintegrate verb 1 to fall into pieces; break down 2 *physics* to undergo or make a substance undergo nuclear fission

disintegration noun 1 the act of breaking down into pieces 2 the state of being breaking down 3 *physics* the breakdown of an atomic nucleus

disinterested adjective unbiased, not influenced by personal feelings

! Do not confuse with: **uninterested**. It is generally a positive thing to be **disinterested** (= fair), especially if you are trying to make an unbiased decision. It is generally a negative thing to be **uninterested** (= bored).

disjointed *adjective* of speech etc: not well connected together

disk *noun* **1** US spelling of **disc 2** *computing* a flat round magnetic plate used for storing data

disk drive *noun, computing* the part of a computer that records data on to and retrieves data from disks

diskette *noun, computing* a floppy disk

disk operating system *noun, computing* (*abbrev* **DOS**) software that manages the storage and retrieval of information on disk

dislike *verb* to not like, disapprove of ➤ *noun* disapproval

dislocate *verb* **1** to put (a bone) out of joint **2** to upset, disorder ♦ **dislocation** *noun*

dislodge *verb* **1** to drive from a place of rest, hiding, or defence **2** to knock out of place accidentally

disloyal *adjective* not loyal, unfaithful ♦ **disloyalty** *noun*

dismal *adjective* gloomy; sorrowful, sad

⊙ Based on a Latin phrase *dies mali* 'evil days', referring to two days each month which were believed to be unusually unlucky

dismantle *verb* **1** to remove fittings, furniture, etc from **2** to take to pieces

dismay *verb* to make to feel hopeless, upset ➤ *noun* hopelessness or discouragement: *watching in dismay*

dismember *verb* **1** to tear to pieces **2** to cut the limbs from

dismiss *verb* **1** to send or put away **2** to remove (someone) from a job, sack **3** to close (a law case) ♦ **dismissal** *noun*

dismount *verb* to come down off a horse, bicycle, etc

disobedient *adjective* refusing or failing to obey

disobey *verb* to neglect or refuse to do what is commanded ♦ **disobedience** *noun*

disorder *noun* **1** lack of order, confusion **2** things out of place **3** a disease or illness ➤ *verb* to throw out of order ♦ **disordered** *adjective*

disorderly *adjective* **1** out of order **2** behaving in a lawless and noisy manner ♦ **disorderliness** *noun*

disorganize or **disorganise** *verb* to disturb the order of; to throw into confusion ♦ **disorganization** *noun* ♦ **disorganized** *adjective*

disorientate or **disorient** *verb* to make (someone) lose all sense of position, direction or time ♦ **disorientation** *noun*

disown *verb* to deny having any relationship to, or connection with

disparage *verb* to speak of as being of little worth or importance; belittle ♦ **disparagement** *noun* ♦ **disparaging** *adjective*

disparity *noun* (*plural* **disparities**) great difference, inequality

dispassionate *adjective* **1** favouring no one, unbiased **2** calm, cool ♦ **dispassionately** *adverb*

dispatch or **despatch** *verb* **1** to send off (a letter etc) **2** to kill, finish off **3** to do or deal with quickly ➤ *noun* (*plural* **dispatches** or **despatches**) **1** the act of sending off **2** a report to a newspaper **3** speed in doing something **4** killing **5** (**dispatches**) official papers (especially military or diplomatic)

dispatch box *noun* **1** a case for official papers **2** the box beside which members of parliament stand to make speeches in the House of Commons

dispatch rider *noun* a courier who delivers military dispatches by motorcycle

dispel *verb* (**dispelling, dispelled**) to drive away, make disappear

dispensable *adjective* able to be done without

dispensary *noun* (*plural* **dispensaries**) a place where medicines are given out

dispensation *noun* special leave to break a rule etc

dispense *verb* **1** to give out **2** to prepare (medicines) for giving out **3** (**dispense with**) to do without

dispenser *noun* **1** a machine that issues something to you **2** a holder or container from which you can get something one at a time or in measured quantities

dispersal *noun* a scattering

disperse *verb* **1** to scatter; spread **2** to (cause to) vanish **3** *physics* of white light: to break up into the colours of the spectrum

dispersion *noun* **1** a scattering **2** *statistics* the range of deviation of values of a variable from the average value **3** *physics* the breaking-up of white light into the colours of the spectrum

dispirited *adjective* sad, discouraged

displace *verb* **1** to put out of place **2** to disorder, disarrange **3** to put (someone) out of office ♦ **displacement** *noun*

displaced person *noun* someone forced to leave his or her own country because of war, political reasons, etc

display *verb* to set out for show ➤ *noun* a show, exhibition

displease *verb* to offend, annoy

displeasure *noun* annoyance, disapproval

disposable *adjective* intended to be thrown away

disposal *noun* the act or process of getting rid of something • **at your disposal** available for your use

dispose *verb* **1** to arrange, settle **2** to get rid (of): *They disposed of the body*

disposed *adjective* inclined, willing • **be well disposed towards someone** to favour them and be inclined to treat them well

disposition *noun* **1** arrangement **2** nature, personality **3** *law* the handing over of property etc to another

disproportionate *adjective* too big or too little in comparison to something else ♦ **disproportion** *noun*

disprove *verb* to prove to be false

disputable *adjective* not certain, able to be argued about

disputation *noun* an argument

dispute *verb* to argue about ➤ *noun* an argument, quarrel

disqualification *noun* the act of disqualifying someone or the state of being disqualified

disqualify *verb* (**disqualifies, disqualifying, disqualified**) **1** to put out of a competition for breaking rules **2** to take away a qualification or right

disquiet *noun* uneasiness, anxiety

disregard *verb* to pay no attention to, ignore ➤ *noun* neglect

disrepair *noun* a state of bad repair

disreputable (*pronounced* dis-**rep**-uw-ta-bl) *adjective* having a bad reputation, not respectable

disrepute *noun* bad reputation

disrespect *noun* rudeness, lack of politeness ♦ **disrespectful** *adjective*

disrupt *verb* **1** to break up **2** to throw (a meeting etc) into disorder

disruption *noun* an obstacle or disturbance

disruptive *adjective* causing disorder

dissatisfaction *noun* displeasure, annoyance

dissatisfy *verb* (**dissatisfies, dissatisfying, dissatisfied**) to bring no satisfaction, displease ♦ **dissatisfied** *adjective*

dissect (*pronounced* dai-**sekt**) *verb* **1** to divide into parts **2** to cut into parts for the purposes of examination **3** to study and criticize ♦ **dissection** *noun*

dissemble *verb* to hide, disguise intentions etc

disseminate *verb* to scatter, spread ♦ **dissemination** *noun*

dissent *verb* **1** to have a different opinion **2** to break away, especially from an established church ➤ *noun* **1** disagreement **2** separation, especially from an established church

dissenter *noun* **1** someone who disagrees **2** (**Dissenter**) someone, especially a Protestant, who refuses to conform to the established church

dissertation *noun* a long piece of writing or talk on a particular (often academic) subject

disservice *noun* harm, a bad turn

dissident *noun* someone who disagrees, especially with a political regime

dissimilar *adjective* not the same ♦ **dissimilarity** *noun* (*plural* **dissimilarities**)

dissipate *verb* **1** to (cause to) disappear **2** to waste, squander ♦ **dissipation** *noun* overindulgence in extravagant living

dissipated *adjective* overindulging in extravagant living

dissociate *verb* **1** to separate **2** *chemistry* of a chemical substance: to break down into constituent molecules, atoms or ions • **dissociate yourself from** to refuse to be associated with

dissolute *adjective* having loose morals; debauched

dissolution *noun* **1** the breaking up of a meeting or assembly, eg Parliament **2** the ending of a formal partnership, eg a marriage or business **3** abolition, eg of the monarchy **4** the process of breaking up into parts **5** debauched behaviour

dissolve *verb* **1** to melt **2** to break up **3** to put an end to **4** to dismiss (an assembly, such as Parliament)

dissonance *noun* **1** *music* discord, especially used deliberately for musical effect **2** disagreement ♦ **dissonant** *adjective*

dissuade *verb* to persuade not to do something: *We dissuaded her from leaving school* ♦ **dissuasion** *noun*

distaff *noun* a stick used to hold flax or wool being spun

distal *adjective, biology* denoting the part of an organ or limb that is furthest from the point of attachment to the body (*compare with:* **proximal**) ♦ **distally** *adverb*

distance *noun* **1** the space between things **2** a far-off place or point: *in the distance* **3** coldness of manner

distant *adjective* **1** far off or far apart in place or time: *distant era/distant land* **2** not close: *distant cousin* **3** cold in manner

distantly *adverb* **1** with a dreamy or cold manner **2** not closely: *distantly related*

distaste *noun* dislike

distasteful *adjective* disagreeable, unpleasant

distemper *noun* **1** a kind of paint used chiefly for walls **2** a viral disease of dogs, foxes, etc ➤ *verb* to paint with distemper

distend *verb* to swell; stretch outwards
♦ **distension** *noun*

distil *verb* (**distilling, distilled**) **1** to purify (liquid) by heating it to a vapour and condensing it **2** to extract the spirit or essence from **3** to (cause to) fall in drops ♦ **distillation** *noun*
♦ **distiller** *noun*

distillery *noun* (*plural* **distilleries**) a place where whisky, brandy, etc is distilled

distinct *adjective* **1** clear; easily seen or noticed: *a distinct improvement* **2** different: *The two languages are quite distinct*

! Do not confuse: **distinct** and **distinctive**

distinction *noun* **1** a difference **2** outstanding worth or merit

distinctive *adjective* different, special, easily recognizable: *That singer has a very distinctive voice* ♦ **distinctively** *adverb*

! Do not confuse: **distinctive** and **distinct**

distinguish *verb* **1** to recognize a difference (between) **2** to mark off as different **3** to recognize **4** to give distinction to

distinguished *adjective* **1** outstanding, famous **2** dignified

distort *verb* **1** to twist out of shape **2** to turn or twist (a statement etc) from its true meaning **3** to make (a sound) unclear and harsh ♦ **distortion** *noun*

distract *verb* **1** to divert (the attention) **2** to trouble, confuse **3** to make mad

! Do not confuse with: **detract**

distracted *adjective* mad with pain, grief, etc

distraction *noun* **1** something which diverts your attention **2** anxiety, confusion **3** amusement **4** madness

distraught *adjective* extremely agitated or anxious

distress *noun* **1** pain, trouble, sorrow **2** a cause of suffering ➤ *verb* to cause pain or sorrow to
♦ **distressed** *adjective* ♦ **distressing** *adjective*

distributary *noun* (*plural* **distributaries**), *geography* a branch that flows off from a river

distribute *verb* **1** to divide among several **2** to spread out widely

distribution *noun* **1** the process of distributing or being distributed **2** the pattern of things spread out **3** *statistics* a set of measurements or values, and the observed or predicted frequencies with which they occur

distributive *adjective*, *maths* following the law that the same result is gained by multiplying a set of numbers as multiplying each individual member of the set, so that $a \times (x+y+z+ \dots)$ $=(a \times x)+(a \times y)+(a \times z)+ \dots$

distributor *noun* a person or company that distributes goods, especially between manufacturer and retailer

district *noun* a region of a country or town

district nurse *noun* a nurse who treats patients in their homes

distrust *noun* lack of trust, suspicion ➤ *verb* to have no trust in ♦ **distrustful** *adjective*

disturb *verb* **1** to confuse, worry, upset **2** to interrupt

disturbance *noun* **1** an outbreak of violent behaviour, especially in public **2** an act of disturbing, agitating or disorganizing **3** psychological damage or illness

disturbed *adjective* **1** mentally or emotionally ill or damaged **2** full of trouble and anxiety **3** (**disturbed about**) very anxious about

disuse *noun* the state of being no longer used

disused *adjective* no longer used

disyllable (*pronounced* dai-**sil**-a-bl) or **dissyllable** (*pronounced* di-**sil**-a-bl) *noun* a word with two syllables ♦ **disyllabic** or **dissyllabic** *adjective*

ditch *noun* (*plural* **ditches**) a long, narrow, hollow trench dug in the ground, especially to carry water

dither *verb* **1** to hesitate, be undecided **2** to act in a nervous, uncertain manner ➤ *noun* a state of indecision

ditto *noun* (often written as **do**) **1** the same as already written or said **2** a character (") written below a word in a text, meaning it is to be repeated

ditty *noun* (*plural* **ditties**) a simple, short song

diva (*pronounced* **dee**-va) *noun* (*plural* **divas** or **dive** – *pronounced* **dee**-vei) a great female singer, especially in opera ☉ Comes from Latin, meaning 'goddess'

divalent *adjective*, *chemistry* of an atom: able to combine with two atoms of hydrogen

divan (*pronounced* di-**van**) *noun* **1** a long, low couch without a back **2** a bed without a headboard

dive *verb* (**diving, dived** or *US* **dove**) **1** to plunge headfirst into water **2** to swoop through the air **3** to go down steeply and quickly ➤ *noun* an act of diving

dive-bomb *verb* to bomb from an aircraft in a steep downward dive ♦ **dive-bomber** *noun*

diver *noun* **1** someone who works under water using special breathing equipment **2** a type of diving bird

diverge *verb* to separate and go in different directions; differ ♦ **divergence** *noun*
♦ **divergent** *adjective*

divergent plate boundary another term for **constructive plate boundary**

divergent series *noun, maths* a series that increases indefinitely

diverging lens *noun, physics* a lens that causes light rays to spread out, eg a concave lens (*compare with*: **converging lens**)

diverse *adjective* different, various

diversify *verb* (**diversifies, diversifying, diversified**) to make or become different or varied

diversion *noun* **1** turning aside **2** an alteration to a traffic route **3** an amusement

diversity *noun* difference; variety

divert *verb* **1** to turn aside, change the direction of **2** to entertain, amuse

diverting *adjective* entertaining, amusing

divest *verb* to strip or deprive (of): *divested him of his authority*

divide *verb* **1** to separate into parts **2** to share (among) **3** to (cause to) go into separate groups **4** *maths* to find out how many times one number contains another

dividend *noun* **1** *maths* an amount to be divided (*compare with*: **divisor**) **2** a share of profits from a business

dividers *plural noun* measuring compasses, used in geometry to measure lengths

divine *adjective* **1** of a god; holy **2** *informal* splendid, wonderful ➤ *verb* **1** to guess **2** to foretell, predict ♦ **divination** *noun*

diviner *noun* someone who claims special powers in finding hidden water or metals

diving board *noun* a narrow platform from which swimmers can dive into a pool

divinity *noun* (*plural* **divinities**) **1** a god **2** the nature of a god **3** religious studies

divisible (*pronounced* di-**viz**-i-bl) *adjective* able to be divided ♦ **divisibility** *noun*

division *noun* **1** the act of dividing **2** a barrier, a separator **3** a section, especially of an army **4** separation **5** disagreement **6** *biology* any of the major groups into which the plant kingdom is divided and which in turn is subdivided into one or more classes

divisional *adjective* of a division

divisive (*pronounced* di-**vai**-siv) *adjective* tending to cause disagreement or conflict

divisor (*pronounced* di-**vai**-sor) *noun, maths* the number by which another number (the **dividend**) is divided

divorce *noun* **1** the legal ending of a marriage **2** a complete separation ➤ *verb* **1** to end a marriage with **2** to separate (from)

divorcee *noun* someone who has been divorced

divot (*pronounced* **div**-ot) *noun* a piece of grass and earth

divulge (*pronounced* dai-**vulj** or di-**vulj**) *verb* to let out, make known (a secret etc)

Diwali (*pronounced* dee-**wah**-lee), **Dewali** or **Divali** (*pronounced* dee-**vah**-lee) *noun* the Hindu and Sikh festival of lamps, celebrated in October or November

Dixie *noun* a name given to southern states of the USA (*also called*: **Dixieland**)

Dixiecrat *noun, US history* one of a group of 35 Southern Democrats who opposed the Democratic Party's extension of civil rights and formed a third party in 1948

DIY *abbreviation* do-it-yourself

dizygotic (*pronounced* dai-zai-**got**-ik) *adjective, biology* developed from two zygotes or fertilized eggs (*compare with*: **monozygotic**)

dizzy *adjective* (**dizzier, dizziest**) **1** experiencing or causing a spinning sensation in the head **2** *informal* silly; not reliable or responsible **3** *informal* bewildered ♦ **dizzily** *adverb*

DJ *abbreviation* disc jockey

djinn (*pronounced* jeen or jin) *plural noun* (*singular* **djinni** – *pronounced* **jeen**-i or jin-**ee**) a group of spirits in Islamic folklore

DNA *abbreviation* deoxyribonucleic acid, a compound of which the chromosomes and genes of almost all living things are composed, carrying genetic instructions for passing on hereditary characteristics

DNA fingerprinting *noun* examining a sample of a person's DNA to find out their identity

DNS *abbreviation, computing* domain name server

do¹ *verb* (**does, doing, did, done**) **1** to carry out, perform (a job etc) **2** to perform an action on, eg clean (dishes), arrange (hair), etc **3** *slang* to swindle **4** to act: *Do as you please* **5** to get on: *I hear she's doing very well/How are you doing?* **6** to be enough: *A pound will do* **7** used to avoid repeating a verb: *I seldom see him now, and when I do, he ignores me* **8** used with a more important verb in questions: *Do you see what I mean?* **9** used with a more important verb in sentences with **not**: *I don't know* **10** used with a more important verb for emphasis: *I do hope she'll be there* ➤ *noun* (*plural* **dos**) *informal* a social event, a party ● **do away with** *informal* to put an end to, destroy ● **do down** to get the better of ● **do in** *informal* **1** to exhaust, wear out **2** to murder ● **do or die** a desperate final attempt at something whatever the consequences ● **do out of** to swindle out of ● **do up 1** to fasten **2** to renovate ⊙ Comes from Old English *don*

do² *abbreviation* ditto

do³ same as **doh**

Dobermann pinscher (*pronounced* **doh-**

ber-man **pin**-sher) or **Dobermann** *noun* a
large breed of dog with a smooth black-and-tan
coat ⊙ Comes from Ludwig *Dobermann*, the
breeder + German *Pinscher* meaning 'terrier'

docile (*pronounced* **doh**-sail) *adjective* tame,
easy to manage ♦ **docilely** *adverb* ♦ **docility**
noun

dock¹ *noun* (often **docks**) a deepened part of a
harbour where ships go for loading, repair, etc
➤ *verb* **1** to put in or enter a dock **2** of a
spacecraft: to join on to another craft in space

dock² *verb* to clip or cut short (an animal's tail)

dock³ *noun* a weed with large leaves

dock⁴ *noun* the box in a law court where the
accused person stands

docker *noun* someone who works in the
docks

docket *noun* a label listing the contents of
something

dockyard *noun* a naval harbour with docks,
stores, etc

doctor *noun* **1** someone trained in and licensed
to practise medicine **2** someone with the
highest university degree in any subject ➤ *verb* **1**
to treat as a patient **2** to tamper with, alter

doctrinaire *adjective, derogatory* adhering
rigidly to theories or principles, even if they are
impractical

doctrine (*pronounced* **dok**-trin) *noun* a belief
that is taught ♦ **doctrinal** (*pronounced* dok-
trai-nal) *adjective*

document *noun* **1** a written statement giving
proof, information, etc **2** *computing* a file of text
produced and read by a computer, especially a
word processor

documentary *noun* (*plural* **documentaries**) a
film giving information about real people or
events ➤ *adjective* **1** of or in documents:
documentary evidence **2** of a documentary

documentation *noun* **1** documents or
documentary evidence **2** the provision or
collection of these

document reader *noun, computing* an
optical character reader which converts printed
characters into a digital code to allow them to be
stored on a computer

dodder *verb* to shake, tremble, especially as a
result of old age

doddery *adjective* shaky or slow because of old
age

doddle *noun, informal* an easy task

dodecagon (*pronounced* doh-**dek**-a-gon)
noun, maths a flat figure with twelve sides

dodecahedron (*pronounced* doh-dek-a-**hee**-
dron) *noun, maths* a solid figure with twelve
faces

dodge *verb* to avoid by a sudden or clever
movement ➤ *noun* a trick

dodgy *adjective* (**dodgier, dodgiest**), *informal*
1 difficult or risky **2** untrustworthy or dishonest **3**
unstable or broken

dodo *noun* (*plural* **dodoes** or **dodos**) a type of
large, extinct bird

doe *noun* the female of certain animals, eg a
deer, rabbit or hare

doer *noun* an active person who does a lot of
things

doff *verb* to take off (a hat) in greeting

dog *noun* **1** a four-footed animal often kept as a
pet **2** a member of the dog family which includes
wolves, foxes, etc ➤ *adjective* of certain animals:
male ➤ *verb* (**dogging, dogged**) **1** to follow and
watch constantly **2** to hamper, plague: *dogged
by ill health* ● **dog in the manger** someone
who stands in the way of a plan or proposal ● **go
to the dogs** *informal* to be ruined

dog collar *noun* **1** a collar for dogs **2** the stiff
white collar worn by certain members of the
clergy

dog-eared *adjective* of a page: turned down at
the corner

dog-eat-dog *adjective* viciously competitive

dogfight *noun* a fight between aeroplanes at
close quarters

dogfish *noun* a kind of small shark

dogged (*pronounced* **dog**-id) *adjective*
determined, stubborn: *dogged refusal*
♦ **doggedly** *adverb*

doggerel *noun* badly written poetry

doggy *adjective* (**doggier, doggiest**) of or for
dogs ➤ *noun, informal* a child's name for a dog

doggy-bag *noun* a bag to take away leftover
food from a restaurant meal

doggy-paddle or **dog-paddle** *noun* a
simple style of swimming

dog-leg *noun* a sharp bend

dogma *noun* an opinion, especially religious,
accepted or fixed by an authority

dogmatic *adjective* **1** of dogma **2** stubbornly
forcing your opinions on others
♦ **dogmatically** *adverb*

do-gooder *noun* someone who tries to help
others in a self-righteous way

dog-paddle see doggy-paddle

dogsbody *noun* (*plural* **dogsbodies**), *informal*
someone who is given unpleasant or dreary
tasks to do

dog's breakfast or **dog's dinner** *noun* a
complete mess

dog's life *noun* a life of misery

dog-tag *noun* **1** a dog's identity disc **2** an
identity disc worn by soldiers etc

dog-tired *adjective, informal* completely worn
out

doh or **do** *noun, music* in sol-fa notation: the
first note of the major scale

doily or **doyley** *noun* (*plural* **doilies** or **doyleys**) a perforated paper napkin put underneath cakes etc

⊙ Originally a light summer fabric, named after *Doily*'s drapery shop in 17th-century London

doings *plural noun* actions

do-it-yourself *noun* (*abbrev* **DIY**) the practice of doing your own household repairs etc without professional help

Dolby *noun, trademark* a system for reducing background noise, used in recording music or soundtracks

doldrums *plural noun* low spirits: *in the doldrums*

⊙ The *doldrums* take their name from an area of the ocean about the equator famous for calms and variable winds

dole *verb* to deal (out) in small amounts ➤ *noun, informal* a payment made by the state to unemployed people

doleful *adjective* sad, unhappy ✦ **dolefully** *adverb*

doll *noun* a toy in the shape of a small human being

dollar *noun* the main unit of currency in several countries, eg the USA, Canada, Australia and New Zealand

⊙ From a shortened form of *Joachimsthaler*, the name of a silver coin produced at Joachimsthal in what is now the Czech Republic

dollop *noun, informal* a small, shapeless mass

dolmen *noun* an ancient tomb in the shape of a stone table

dolphin *noun* a type of sea animal like a porpoise

dolt *noun* a stupid person ✦ **doltish** *adjective*

domain *noun* 1 a kingdom 2 a country estate 3 an area of interest or knowledge 4 *maths* the set of values specified for a function or dependent variable

domain name *noun, computing* in e-mail and website addresses: the name and location of the server

domain name server *noun, computing* (*abbrev* **DNS**) software that searches domain names

dome *noun* 1 the shape of a half sphere or ball 2 the roof of a building etc in this shape ✦ **domed** *adjective*

domestic *adjective* 1 of the home or house 2 of an animal: tame, domesticated 3 not foreign, of your own country: *domestic products* ➤ *noun* 1 *informal* a fight between members of a household 2 a live-in maid etc

domesticated *adjective* 1 of an animal: tame,

used for farming etc 2 fond of doing housework, cooking, etc

domesticity *noun* home life

domestic science *noun, old* cookery, needlework, etc, taught as a subject (now called **home economics**)

domicile (*pronounced* **dom**-i-sail) *noun* the country etc in which someone lives permanently

dominant *adjective* 1 ruling; most powerful or important 2 *biology* denoting a gene in a pair that produces a trait in an individual even when it is inherited from one parent only (*compare with*: **recessive**) 3 *biology* denoting the most prevalent plant or animal species in a particular community ✦ **dominance** *noun*

dominate *verb* 1 to have command or influence over 2 to be most strong, or most noticeable 3 to tower above, overlook: *The castle dominates the skyline* ✦ **domination** *noun*

domineering *adjective* overbearing, like a tyrant

dominion *noun* 1 rule, authority 2 an area with one ruler or government

domino *noun* (*plural* **dominoes**) a piece used in the game of dominoes

dominoes *singular noun* a game played on a table with pieces marked with dots, each side of which must match a piece placed next to it

domino theory *noun, politics* the theory, first used by US President Eisenhower in 1954 of the spread of Communism, that a political event can cause a series of similar events in neighbouring areas

don *noun* a college or university lecturer ➤ *verb* (**donning, donned**) to put on (a coat etc)

donate *verb* to present a gift

donation *noun* a gift of money or goods

done past participle of **do**[1] ➤ *adjective* finished

doner kebab (*pronounced* **don**-er) *noun* thin slices of minced and seasoned lamb grilled on a spit and eaten on unleavened bread ⊙ Comes from Turkish *döner* meaning 'rotating' + **kebab**

donkey *noun* (*plural* **donkeys**) a type of animal with long ears, related to the horse (*also called*: **ass**)

donor *noun* 1 a giver of a gift 2 someone who agrees to let their body organs be used for transplant operations

donor card *noun* a card that states that the carrier is willing, in the event of sudden death, to have their organs removed for transplantation

don't short for **do not**

doodle *verb* to scrawl or scribble aimlessly and meaninglessly ➤ *noun* a meaningless scribble

doom *noun* 1 judgement; fate 2 ruin

doomed *adjective* 1 destined, condemned 2 bound to fail or be destroyed

doomsday *noun* the last day of the world

door *noun* **1** a hinged barrier which closes the entrance to a room or building **2** the entrance itself

doorman *noun* (*plural* **doormen**) a man employed to guard the entrance to a hotel, club, etc

doorstep *noun* the step in front of the door of a house

doorstop *noun* **1** a wedge for holding a door open **2** a device, eg a fixed knob, for preventing a door opening too far

doorway *noun* the space filled by a door, the entrance

dopa (*pronounced* **doh**-pa) *noun, chemistry* a substance that plays an important role in the production of adrenaline and dopamine

dopamine (*pronounced* **doh**-pa-meen) *noun, chemistry* an important compound that functions as a neurotransmitter

dope *noun, informal* **1** a drug, especially one taken illegally by an athlete or by an addict **2** the drug cannabis **3** an idiot ➤ *verb* to drug (someone or something), especially illegally ♦ **doping** *noun*

Doppler effect or **Doppler shift** *noun, physics* the change in wavelength observed when the distance between a source of waves and the observer is changing, eg the sound change perceived as an aircraft passes by

---
🕓 Named after the Austrian physicist Christian *Doppler* (1803–53)
---

dormant *adjective* **1** sleeping, inactive: *a dormant volcano* **2** *biology* in a resting state, especially to survive a period of unfavourable conditions

dormitory *noun* (*plural* **dormitories**) **1** a room with beds for several people **2** *geography* a small town or a suburb from which most residents commute to work elsewhere

dormouse *noun* (*plural* **dormice**) a small, mouse-like, furry-tailed rodent which hibernates 🕓 Probably from Latin *dormire* meaning 'to sleep', and English *mouse*

dorsal *adjective* of the back: *a dorsal fin* (*compare with*: **ventral**)

DOS (*pronounced* dos) *abbreviation, computing* disk operating system

dosage *noun* the proper size of dose: *The dosage for adults is 1-2 tablets*

dose *noun* **1** a quantity of medicine to be taken at one time **2** a bout of something unpleasant: *a dose of flu* ➤ *verb* to give medicine to

doss *verb, informal* to lie down to sleep somewhere temporary

dossier (*pronounced* **dos**-i-ei) *noun* a set of papers containing information about a certain person or subject

dot *noun* a small, round mark ➤ *verb* (**dotting, dotted**) **1** to mark with a dot **2** to scatter • **on the dot** exactly on time

dotage (*pronounced* **doh**-tij) *noun* the foolishness and childishness of old age

dotcom *adjective* of a company: trading on the Internet ➤ *noun* a dotcom company

dote *verb* (**dote on**) to be foolishly fond of

dot matrix printer *noun, computing* a computer printer using arrangements of pins from a matrix to form the printed characters

double *verb* **1** to multiply by two **2** to fold ➤ *noun* **1** twice as much: *Whatever he is offering, I'll pay you double* **2** someone so like another as to be mistaken for them ➤ *adjective* **1** containing twice as much: *a double dose/double the amount* **2** made up of two of the same sort **3** folded over **4** ambiguous: *a double meaning* • **at the double** very quickly • **double back** to turn sharply and go back the way you have come • **double up 1** to writhe in pain **2** to share accommodation (with)

double agent *noun* a spy paid by two rival countries, but loyal to only one

double-barrelled or *N Am* **double-barreled** *adjective* **1** of a gun: having two barrels **2** of a surname: made up of two names

double bass *noun* a type of large stringed musical instrument played by plucking the strings

double bond *noun, chemistry* a covalent bond formed by the sharing of two pairs of electrons between two atoms

double-breasted *adjective* of a coat: with one half of the front overlapping the other

double-check *verb* to check twice or again

double-click *verb, computing* to click the button of a mouse two times in rapid succession

double-cross *verb* to cheat

double-dealer *noun* a deceitful, cheating person ♦ **double-dealing** *noun*

double-decker *noun* a bus with two floors

double-Dutch *noun* incomprehensible talk, gibberish

double glazing *noun* two sheets of glass in a window to keep in the heat or keep out noise

double-jointed *adjective* having extraordinarily flexible body joints

double negative *noun, grammar* an expression containing two negative words where only one is needed, eg *He hasn't never asked me*

doublet *noun* in the past, a man's close-fitting jacket

double-take *noun* a second look at something surprising or confusing

double-time *noun* payment for overtime work etc at twice the usual rate

doubling time *noun, geography* the time it takes for a population to double

doubly *adverb* **1** extra, especially: *Check the door to make doubly sure you have locked it* **2** in two ways: *He's doubly responsible for the mess we're in*

doubt (*pronounced* dowt) *verb* **1** to be unsure or undecided about **2** to think unlikely: *I doubt that we'll be able to go* ➤ *noun* a lack of certainty or trust; suspicion • **no doubt** probably, surely

doubtful *adjective* **1** unlikely, uncertain or unreliable **2** strange; raising suspicion
• **doubtful about something** unsure about it

doubtless *adverb* probably

dough *noun* **1** a mass of flour, moistened and kneaded **2** *informal* money

doughnut *noun* a ring-shaped cake fried in fat

doughty (*pronounced* **dowt**-i) *adjective* (**doughtier, doughtiest**) strong; brave

dour (*pronounced* door) *adjective* dull, humourless

douse or **dowse** *verb* **1** to throw water over something or plunge something into water **2** to extinguish (a light or fire)

dove¹ (*pronounced* duv) *noun* **1** a type of pigeon **2** this bird as an emblem of peace **3** *politics* someone who favours peace rather than hostility (*contrasted with:* **hawk**)

dove² (*pronounced* dohv) *US* past form of **dive**

dovecote *noun* a small building for housing pigeons

dovetail *verb* to fit one thing exactly into another

dowdy *adjective* (**dowdier, dowdiest**) not smart, badly dressed

down¹ *adverb* **1** towards or in a lower position: *fell down/sitting down* **2** to a smaller size: *grind down* **3** to a later generation: *handed down from mother to daughter* **4** on the spot, in cash: *£10 down* ➤ *preposition* **1** towards or in the lower part of: *rolled back down the hill* **2** along: *strolling down the road* ➤ *adjective* going downwards: *the down escalator* • **go down with** or **be down with** to become or be ill with

down² *noun* light, soft feathers

down-and-out *adjective* homeless and penniless ➤ *noun* a down-and-out person

down-at-heel *adjective* worn down, shabby

downcast *adjective* sad

downfall *noun* ruin, defeat

downhearted *adjective* discouraged

downhill *adverb* **1** downwards **2** to or towards a worse condition ➤ *adjective* downwardly sloping ➤ *noun* a ski race down a hillside • **go downhill** to deteriorate

download *computing, verb* (*pronounced* down-**lohd**) to transfer (information from the Internet) from one computer to another ➤ *noun*

(*pronounced* **down**-lohd) **1** an act of downloading **2** something downloaded

down payment *noun* a deposit

downpour *noun* a heavy fall of rain

downright *adjective* utter: *downright idiocy* ➤ *adverb* utterly

downs *plural noun* low, grassy hills

downside *noun informal* a negative aspect; a disadvantage

Down's syndrome *noun* a disorder which results in mental impairment, flattened facial features and slight slanting of the eyes

downstairs *adjective* on a lower floor of a building ➤ *adverb* to a lower floor

downstream *adverb* further down a river, in the direction of its flow

down-to-earth *adjective* sensible and practical

downtrodden *adjective* kept in a lowly, inferior position

downwards or **downward** *adverb* moving or leading down

downy *adjective* (**downier, downiest**) soft, feathery

dowry *noun* (*plural* **dowries**) money and property brought by a woman to her husband on their marriage

dowse another spelling of **douse**

-dox *suffix* forms words related to opinions or beliefs: *orthodox/heterodox* ℗ Comes from Greek *doxa* meaning 'opinion'

doyley another spelling of **doily**

doze *verb* to sleep lightly ➤ *noun* a light, short sleep

dozen *noun* twelve

dpi or **DPI** *abbreviation, computing* dots per inch

Dr *abbreviation* Doctor

drab *adjective* (**drabber, drabbest**) dull, monotonous

draconian *adjective* of a law etc: harsh; severe

℗ Named after *Draco*, a 7th-century BC statesman in Athens

draft *noun* **1** a rough outline, a sketch **2** a group of people selected for a special purpose **3** *US* conscription into the army **4** an order for payment of money **5** *US* spelling of **draught** ➤ *verb* **1** to make a rough plan **2** to select for a purpose **3** *US* to conscript

❗ Do not confuse with: **draught**

draftsman or **draftswoman** *US* spellings of **draughtsman** or **draughtswoman**

drag *verb* (**dragging, dragged**) **1** to pull roughly **2** to move slowly and heavily **3** to trail along the ground **4** *computing* to move (an icon or file) across a screen by using a mouse with its key pressed down **5** to search (a riverbed etc) with a net or hook ➤ *noun* **1** a dreary task **2** *informal* a tedious person **3** *informal* clothes for one sex worn by the other **4** *physics* a force that slows down movement through a liquid or gas • **drag your feet** or **drag your heels** to be slow to do something

drag and drop *verb, computing* to move an icon, file, etc across the screen using a mouse and release it in a different place

dragon *noun* **1** an imaginary fire-breathing, winged reptile **2** a fierce, intimidating person, especially a woman

dragonfly *noun* (*plural* **dragonflies**) a winged insect with a long body and double wings

dragoon *noun* a heavily armed horse soldier ➤ *verb* to force or bully (into)

drain *verb* **1** to clear (land) of water by trenches or pipes **2** to drink the contents of (a glass etc) **3** to use up completely ➤ *noun* a channel or pipe used to carry off water etc

drainage *noun* the drawing-off of water by rivers, pipes, etc

drainage basin *noun, geography* an area from which a river or reservoir draws its water supply (also called: **catchment area**)

drained *adjective* **1** emptied of liquid **2** sapped of strength

drake *noun* a male duck

drama *noun* **1** a play for acting in the theatre **2** exciting or tense action

dramatic *adjective* **1** relating to plays **2** exciting, thrilling **3** unexpected, sudden ♦ **dramatically** *adverb*

dramatis personae (*pronounced* **dram**-a-tis per-**soh**-nai) *plural noun* the characters in a play

dramatist *noun* a playwright

dramatize or **dramatise** *verb* **1** to turn into a play for the theatre **2** to make vivid or sensational ♦ **dramatization** *noun*

drank past tense of **drink**

drape *verb* to arrange (cloth) to hang gracefully ➤ *noun* (**drapes**) *US* curtains

draper *noun* a dealer in cloth

drapery *noun* (*plural* **draperies**) **1** cloth goods **2** a draper's shop

drastic *adjective* severe, extreme ♦ **drastically** *adverb*

draught (*pronounced* drahft) or *US* **draft** *noun* **1** a current of air **2** the act of drawing or pulling **3** something drawn out **4** a drink taken all at once **5** (**draughts**) a game for two, played by moving pieces on a board marked with squares (a **draughtboard**)

⚠ Do not confuse with: **draft**

draughtsman or **draughtswoman** *noun*

(*plural* **draughtsmen** or **draughtswomen**) **1** someone employed to draw plans **2** someone skilled in drawing

draughty *adjective* (**draughtier, draughtiest**) full of air currents, chilly

draw *verb* (**drawing, drew, drawn**) **1** to make a picture with pencil, crayons, etc **2** to pull after or along **3** to attract: *drew a large crowd* **4** to obtain money from a fund: *drawing a pension* **5** to require (a depth) for floating: *This ship draws 20 feet* **6** to approach, come: *Night is drawing near* **7** to score equal points in a game ➤ *noun* **1** an equal score **2** a lottery • **draw a blank** to get no result • **draw a conclusion** to form an opinion from evidence heard • **draw on 1** to approach **2** to use as a resource: *drawing on experience* • **draw out 1** to lengthen **2** to persuade (someone) to talk and be at ease • **draw the line at** to refuse to allow or accept • **draw up 1** to come to a stop **2** to move closer **3** to plan, write out (a contract etc)

drawback *noun* a disadvantage

drawbridge *noun* a bridge at the entrance to a castle which can be drawn up or let down

drawer *noun* **1** someone who draws **2** (*pronounced* drawr) a sliding box fitting into a chest, table, etc

drawing *noun* a picture made by pencil, crayon, etc

drawing pin *noun* a pin with a large flat head for fastening paper on a board etc

drawing room *noun* a sitting room

drawl *verb* to speak in a slow, lazy manner ➤ *noun* a drawling voice

drawn past participle of **draw** • **drawn and quartered** *history* disembowelled and cut in pieces after being hanged

drawstring *noun* a cord sewn inside a hem on a bag or piece of clothing, closing up the hem when pulled

dread *noun* great fear ➤ *verb* to be greatly afraid of ♦ **dreaded** *adjective*

dreadful *adjective* **1** terrible **2** *informal* very bad ♦ **dreadfully** *adverb*

dreadlocks *plural noun* thin braids of hair tied tightly all over the head, especially worn by a Rastafarian

dreadnought *noun, history* a kind of battleship

dream *noun* **1** a series of images and sounds in the mind during sleep **2** something imagined, not real **3** something very beautiful **4** a hope, an ambition: *Her dream was to go to Mexico* ➤ *verb* (**dreaming, dreamt** – *pronounced* dremt – or **dreamed** – *pronounced* dremt or dreemd) to have a dream • **dream up** to invent

dreamy *adjective* (**dreamier, dreamiest**) **1** sleepy, half-awake **2** vague, dim **3** *informal* beautiful or handsome ♦ **dreamily** *adverb*

dreary *adjective* (**drearier, dreariest**) gloomy, cheerless ✦ **drearily** *adverb*

dredge[1] *verb* to drag a net or bucket along a river bed or seabed to bring up fish, mud, etc ➤ *noun* an instrument for dredging a river etc

dredge[2] *verb* to sprinkle (with sugar or flour)

dredger[1] *noun* a ship which digs a channel by lifting mud from the bottom

dredger[2] *noun* a perforated jar for sprinkling sugar or flour

dregs *plural noun* **1** sediment on the bottom of a liquid: *dregs of wine* **2** last remnants **3** worthless or contemptible elements: *the dregs of society*

drench *verb* to soak

dress *verb* **1** to put on clothes or a covering **2** to prepare (food etc) for use **3** to arrange (hair) **4** to treat and bandage (wounds) ➤ *noun* (*plural* **dresses**) **1** clothes **2** a one-piece woman's garment combining skirt and top **3** a style of clothing: *formal dress* ➤ *adjective* of clothes: for formal use: *a dress shirt*

dresser *noun* a kitchen sideboard for dishes

dressing *noun* **1** a covering **2** a seasoned sauce poured over salads etc **3** a bandage

dressing-gown *noun* a loose, light coat worn indoors over pyjamas etc

dressing room *noun* **1** *theatre* a room backstage where a performer can change clothing, apply make-up, etc **2** any room used when changing clothing

dressing table *noun* a piece of bedroom furniture with drawers and a large mirror

dressmaking *noun* making women's clothes ✦ **dressmaker** *noun*

dress rehearsal *noun* the final rehearsal of a play etc, in which the actors wear their costumes

dressy *adjective* (**dressier, dressiest**) stylish, smart

drew past tense of **draw**

drey *noun* (*plural* **dreys**) a squirrel's nest

dribble *verb* **1** to (cause to) fall in small drops **2** to let saliva run down the chin **3** *football, hockey, etc* to move the ball forward little by little

drift *noun* **1** a pile of snow, sand, etc driven by the wind **2** the direction in which something is driven **3** the general meaning of someone's words **4** continental drift ➤ *verb* **1** to go with the tide or current **2** to be driven into heaps by the wind **3** to wander about **4** to live aimlessly

drifter *noun* **1** someone who drifts **2** a fishing boat that uses drift nets

drift net *noun* a fishing net which stays near the surface of the water

driftwood *noun* wood driven on to the seashore by winds or tides

drill *verb* **1** to make a hole in **2** to make with a drill **3** to exercise (soldiers) **4** to sow (seeds) in rows ➤ *noun* **1** a tool for making holes in wood etc **2**

military exercise **3** a row of seeds or plants

drily another spelling of **dryly**

drink *verb* (**drinking, drank, drunk**) **1** to swallow (a liquid) **2** to take alcoholic drink, especially excessively ➤ *noun* **1** liquid to be drunk **2** alcoholic liquids • **drink in** to listen to eagerly • **drink to** to drink a toast to • **drink up** to finish a drink

drink-driving *noun* the act of driving while under the influence of alcohol

drip *verb* (**dripping, dripped**) **1** to fall in drops **2** to let (water etc) fall in drops ➤ *noun* **1** a drop **2** a continual dropping, eg of water **3** a device for adding liquid slowly to a vein etc

drip and stem flow or **stem flow** *noun* the movement of precipitation along the stem of a plant into the ground

drip-dry *verb* to dry (a garment) by hanging it up to dry without wringing it first

dripping *noun* fat from roasting meat

drive *verb* (**driving, drove, driven**) **1** to control or guide (a car etc) **2** to go in a vehicle: *driving to work* **3** to force or urge along **4** to hurry on **5** to hit (a ball, nail, etc) hard **6** to bring about: *drive a bargain* ➤ *noun* **1** a journey in a car **2** a private road to a house **3** an avenue or road **4** energy, enthusiasm **5** a campaign: *a drive to save the local school* **6** a games tournament: *a whist drive* **7** a hard stroke with a club or bat • **what are you driving at?** what are you suggesting or implying?

drive-in *noun, US* a cinema where the audience watches the screen while staying in their cars

drivel *informal, noun* nonsense ➤ *verb* (**drivelling, drivelled**) to talk nonsense

driven past participle of **drive**

driver *noun* **1** someone who drives a car etc **2** a wooden-headed golf club **3** *computing* software connecting a peripheral device to a computer

drizzle *noun* light rain ➤ *verb* to rain lightly ✦ **drizzly** *adjective*

droll *adjective* **1** funny, amusing **2** odd

dromedary (*pronounced* **drom**-e-da-ri) *noun* (*plural* **dromedaries**) an Arabian camel with one hump

drone *verb* **1** to make a low humming sound **2** to speak in a dull, boring voice ➤ *noun* **1** a low humming sound **2** a dull, boring voice **3** the low-sounding pipe of a bagpipe **4** a male bee **5** a lazy, idle person

drool *verb* **1** to produce saliva **2** to show uncontrolled admiration for

droop *verb* **1** to hang down: *Your hem is drooping* **2** to grow weak or discouraged

drop *noun* **1** a small round or pear-shaped blob of liquid **2** a small quantity: *a drop of whisky* **3** a fall from a height: *a drop of six feet* **4** a small, flavoured sweet: *a pear drop* ➤ *verb* (**dropping, dropped**) **1** to fall suddenly **2** to let fall **3** to fall in drops **4** to set down from a car etc: *Drop me at the corner* **5** to give up, abandon (a friend, habit, etc) • **drop back** to fall behind others in a group • **drop in** to pay a brief visit • **drop off** to fall asleep • **drop out** to withdraw from a class, from society, etc

drop-dead *adverb, slang* stunningly or breathtakingly: *drop-dead gorgeous*

drop-down menu *noun, computing* a menu on a computer screen viewed by making a single click on a button on the toolbar (*compare with:* **pull-down menu**)

drop goal *noun, rugby* a goal scored by a drop kick

drop-in *adjective* of a day centre, clinic, etc: where clients are free to attend casually

drop kick *rugby, noun* a kick made when the ball rebounds from the ground after being dropped from the hands ➤ *verb* (**drop-kick**) to kick in this way

droplet *noun* a tiny drop

droppings *plural noun* animal or bird faeces

drop-shot *noun, tennis, badminton, etc* a shot hit so that it drops low and close to the net

dross *noun* **1** scum produced by melting metal **2** waste material, impurities **3** coal dust **4** anything worthless

drought *noun* a prolonged period of time when no rain falls

drove *noun* **1** a number of moving cattle or other animals **2** (**droves**) a great number of people ➤ *past tense* of **drive**

drover *noun* someone who drives cattle

drown *verb* **1** to die by suffocating in water **2** to kill in this way **3** to flood or soak completely **4** to block out (a sound) with a louder one

drowsy *adjective* (**drowsier, drowsiest**) sleepy ◆ **drowsily** *adverb*

drubbing *noun* a thrashing

drudge *verb* to do very humble or boring work ➤ *noun* someone who does such work

drudgery *noun* hard, uninteresting work

drug *noun* **1** a substance used in medicine to treat illness, kill pain, etc **2** a stimulant or narcotic substance taken habitually for its effects ➤ *verb* (**drugging, drugged**) **1** to administer drugs to **2** to make (someone) lose consciousness by drugs

druggist *noun, US* a chemist

drugstore *noun, US* a shop selling newspapers, soft drinks, etc as well as medicines

druid or **Druid** *noun* a member of a Celtic order of priests in pre-Christian times

drum *noun* **1** a musical instrument of skin etc stretched on a round frame and beaten with sticks **2** a cylindrical container: *an oil drum/ biscuit drum* ➤ *verb* (**drumming, drummed**) **1**

to beat a drum **2** to tap continuously with the fingers ◆ **drummer** *noun*

drumbeat *noun* the sound of a drum being hit

drumstick *noun* **1** a stick for beating a drum **2** the lower part of the leg of a cooked chicken etc

drunk *adjective* showing the effects (giddiness, unsteadiness, etc) of drinking too much alcohol ➤ *noun* someone who is drunk, or habitually drunk ➤ *past participle* of **drink**

drunkard *noun* a drunk

drunken *adjective* **1** habitually drunk **2** caused by too much alcohol: *a drunken stupor* **3** involving much alcohol: *a drunken spree* ◆ **drunkenness** *noun*

drupe *noun, botany* a fleshy fruit with a stone containing a seed, eg cherry, plum

dry *adjective* (**drier, driest**) **1** not moist or wet **2** thirsty **3** uninteresting: *makes very dry reading* **4** reserved, matter-of-fact **5** of wine: not sweet **6** of a sense of humour: funny in a quiet, subtle way ➤ *verb* (**dries, drying, dried**) to make or become dry

dryad (*pronounced* **drai**-ad) *noun* a mythological wood nymph

dry cell *noun, chemistry* an electrolytic cell in which the electrolyte is a moist paste instead of a liquid

dry-clean *verb* to clean (clothes etc) with chemicals, not with water

dry ice *noun* solid carbon dioxide used as a refrigerating agent and also in drama etc for creating special effects

dryly or **drily** *adverb* **1** in a reserved, matter-of-fact, emotionless way **2** with quiet, subtle humour

dryness *noun* the quality of being dry

dry rot *noun* **1** a disease caused by fungus, which reduces wood to a dry and crumbly mass **2** *botany* a fungal disease of plants such as potatoes or fruit

dry run *noun* a rehearsal, practice or test

dry-stone *adjective* of a wall: built of stone without cement or mortar

DSL *abbreviation, computing* Digital Subscriber Line, a fast Internet connection over an analogue phone line

DTI *abbreviation* Department of Trade and Industry

DTP *abbreviation* desktop publishing

dual *adjective* double; made up of two

❗ Do not confuse with: **duel**

dual carriageway *noun* a road divided by a central barrier or boundary, with each side used by traffic moving in one direction

dual-purpose *adjective* able to be used for two purposes

dub[1] *verb* (**dubbing, dubbed**) **1** to declare (a

man) a knight by touching each shoulder with a sword **2** to name or nickname

dub² *verb* (**dubbing, dubbed**) **1** to add sound to (a film) **2** to give (a film) a new soundtrack in a different language ➤ *noun* a type of reggae music in which drums and bass are prominent

dubbin or **dubbing** *noun* a grease for softening or waterproofing leather

dubiety (*pronounced* juw-**bai**-i-ti) *noun* doubt

dubious (*pronounced* **dyoo**-bi-us) *adjective* **1** doubtful, uncertain **2** probably dishonest: *dubious dealings*

dubnium *noun, chemistry* (symbol **Db**) an artificially produced radioactive element, formerly called unnilpentium, joliotium and hahnium

⊙ First produced in *Dubna*, Russia

ducal (*pronounced* **joo**-kal) *adjective* of a duke

ducat (*pronounced* **duk**-at) *noun, history* an old European gold coin

duchess *noun* (*plural* **duchesses**) **1** a woman of the same rank as a duke **2** the wife or widow of a duke

duchy *noun* (*plural* **duchies**) the land owned by a duke or duchess

duck¹ *noun* **1** a web-footed bird, with a broad, flat beak **2** *cricket* a score of no runs

⊙ The meaning in cricket comes from the use of 'duck's egg' to mean a nought on a scoring sheet

duck² *verb* **1** to lower the head quickly as if to avoid a blow **2** to push (someone's head) under water • **duck out (of)** to avoid responsibility (for)

duck-billed platypus see **platypus**

duckling *noun* a baby duck

duct *noun* **1** *anatomy* any tube in the body **2** a pipe for carrying liquids, electric cables, etc

ductile *adjective* **1** yielding, not liable to breaking **2** easily led ♦ **ductility** *noun*

dud *noun* **1** a counterfeit article **2** a bomb, firework, etc that fails to go off **3** *informal* any useless or ineffectual person or thing ➤ *adjective, informal* useless, broken

dude (*pronounced* dood) *noun, US slang* **1** a man **2** a man preoccupied with dressing smartly

dudgeon *noun*: **in high dudgeon** very angry, indignant

due *adjective* **1** owed, needing to be paid: *The rent is due next week* **2** expected to arrive etc: *They're due here at six* **3** proper, appropriate: *due care* ➤ *adverb* directly: *due south* ➤ *noun* **1** something you have a right to: *Give him his due, he did own up in the end* **2** (**dues**) the amount of money charged for belonging to a club etc • **due to** brought about by, caused by

duel *noun* a formalized fight with pistols or swords between two people ➤ *verb* (**duelling, duelled**) to fight in a duel

❗ Do not confuse with: **dual**

duellist *noun* someone who fights in a duel

duet (*pronounced* dyoo-**et**) *noun* a piece of music for two singers or players

duff *adjective, informal* useless, broken

duffel bag *noun* a cylindrical canvas bag tied with a drawstring

duffel coat *noun* a heavy woollen coat, fastened with toggles

⊙ After *Duffel*, a town in Belgium where the fabric was first made

duffer *noun, informal* a stupid or incompetent person

dug past form of **dig**

dugout *noun* **1** a boat made by hollowing out the trunk of a tree **2** a rough shelter dug out of a slope or bank or in a trench **3** *football* a bench beside the pitch for team managers, trainers and substitutes

duke *noun* a nobleman next in rank below a prince

dukedom *noun* the title, rank or lands of a duke

dulcet (*pronounced* **dul**-sit) *adjective* pleasant-sounding, melodious

dulcimer *noun* a musical instrument with stretched wires which are struck with small hammers

dull *adjective* **1** not lively **2** slow to understand or learn **3** not exciting or interesting **4** of weather: cloudy, not bright or clear **5** not bright in colour **6** of sounds: not clear or ringing **7** blunt, not sharp **8** of pain: present in the background, but not acute ➤ *verb* to make dull ♦ **dullness** *noun* ♦ **dully** *adverb* (adjective, meanings 1, 5, 6 and 8)

duly *adverb* at the proper or expected time; as expected: *He duly arrived*

duma (*pronounced* **doo**-ma) *noun, history* the Russian parliament before the Russian Revolution

dumb *adjective* **1** without the power of speech **2** silent **3** *informal* stupid

dumbbell *noun* a short metal bar with a weight on each end, used in muscle-developing exercises

dumb down *verb* to present (information etc) in a less sophisticated form

dumbfounded *adjective* astonished

dumbly *adverb* in silence

dumb show *noun* acting without words

dumbstruck *adjective* silent with astonishment or shock

dummy *noun* (*plural* **dummies**) **1** a mock-up of

something used for display **2** a model used for displaying clothes etc **3** an artificial teat used to comfort a baby **4** *slang* a stupid person

dummy run *noun* a try-out, a practice

dump *verb* **1** to throw down heavily **2** to unload and leave (rubbish etc) **3** to sell at a low price **4** *computing* to transfer (data) from a computer's memory onto a printout, disk or tape ➤ *noun* **1** a place for leaving rubbish **2** *computing* a copy of the contents of a computer's memory on a printout, disk or tape **3** *informal* a dirty or messy place • **in the dumps** *informal* feeling low or depressed

dumpling *noun* a cooked ball of dough

dumpy *adjective* (**dumpier, dumpiest**) short and thick or fat

dun¹ *adjective* greyish-brown, mouse-coloured

dun² *verb* (**dunning, dunned**) to press for payment

dunce *noun* a stupid or slow-learning person

Ⓘ Originally a term of abuse applied to followers of the medieval Scottish philosopher, John *Duns Scotus*

---

dunderhead *noun, informal* a stupid person

dune *noun* a low hill of sand caused by drifting

dung *noun* animal faeces, manure

dungarees *plural noun* trousers made of coarse, hard-wearing material with a bib

dungeon *noun* a dark underground prison

dunk *verb* **1** to dip (eg a biscuit) into a drink **2** to submerge or be submerged **3** *basketball* to jump up and push (the ball) down through the basket

duo *noun* (*plural* **duos**) **1** a pair of musicians or performers **2** people considered a pair

duodenum (*pronounced* joo-oh-**dee**-num) *noun* (*plural* **duodena** or **duodenums**) the first part of the small intestine, into which food passes from the stomach

DUP *abbreviation* Democratic Unionist Party, a Protestant loyalist party of Northern Ireland

dupe *noun* someone easily cheated ➤ *verb* to deceive, trick

duplicate *adjective* (*pronounced* **joo**-pli-kat) exactly the same ➤ *noun* (*pronounced* **joo**-pli-kat) an exact copy ➤ *verb* (*pronounced* **joo**-pli-keit) to make a copy or copies of ♦ **duplication** *noun*

duplicity *noun* deceit, double-dealing ♦ **duplicitous** *adjective*

durable *adjective* lasting, able to last; wearing well ♦ **durability** *noun*

duration *noun* the time a thing lasts • **for the duration** *informal* **1** for a long time, for ages **2** for as long as the activity, situation, etc continues

duress (*pronounced* dyoo-**res**) *noun* illegal force used to make someone do something

• **under duress** under the influence of force, threats, etc

during *preposition* **1** throughout all or part of: *We lived here during the war* **2** at a particular point within: *She died during the night*

dusk *noun* twilight, partial dark

dusky *adjective* (**duskier, duskiest**) dark-coloured ♦ **duskiness** *noun*

dust *noun* **1** fine grains or specks of earth, sand, etc **2** fine powder ➤ *verb* **1** to remove dust from: *dusted the table* **2** to sprinkle lightly with powder

dustbin *noun, geography* a container for household rubbish

dust bowl *noun, geography* an area of land from which the topsoil has been eroded by strong winds and drought

duster *noun* a cloth for removing dust

dust jacket *noun* a paper cover on a book

dustman *noun* (*plural* **dustmen**) someone employed to collect household rubbish

dustpan *noun* a handled container into which dust is swept, like a flattish open-ended box with a shovel edge

dusty *adjective* (**dustier, dustiest**) covered with dust

Dutch courage *noun* artificial courage gained by drinking alcohol

Dutch elm disease *noun* a serious disease of elm trees, caused by a fungus

dutiful *adjective* obedient ♦ **dutifully** *adverb*

duty *noun* (*plural* **duties**) **1** something a person ought to do **2** an action required to be done **3** a tax **4** (**duties**) the various tasks involved in a job

duty-free *adjective* not taxed

duvet (*pronounced* **doo**-vei) *noun* a quilt stuffed with feathers or synthetic material, used instead of blankets

DVD *abbreviation* digital versatile disc or digital video disc, a CD that can store large amounts of audio and visual content

DVD-ROM *abbreviation* digital versatile disc read only memory, a type of disk capable of holding a greater amount of video or audio data than a conventional CD

DVT *abbreviation* deep-vein thrombosis

dwarf *noun* (*plural* **dwarfs** or **dwarves**) an undersized person, animal or plant ➤ *verb* to make to appear small by comparison ➤ *adjective* not growing to full or usual height: *a dwarf cherry tree*

dwell *verb* to live, inhabit, stay • **dwell on** to think habitually about something: *dwelling on the past*

dwelling *noun, formal* a place of residence

dwindle *verb* to grow less, waste away

DWP *abbreviation* Department for Work and Pensions

Dy *symbol, chemistry* dysprosium

dye *verb* (**dyeing, dyed**) to give a colour to (fabric etc) ➤ *noun* a powder or liquid for colouring ◆ **dyeing** *noun*

dying present participle of **die¹**

dyke another spelling of **dike**

dynamic *adjective* forceful, energetic ◆ **dynamically** *adverb*

dynamics *singular noun* the scientific study of movement and force (also called: **kinetics**)

dynamite *noun* a type of powerful explosive

dynamo *noun* (*plural* **dynamos**) a device for turning mechanical energy into electricity

dynasty (*pronounced* **din**-as-ti) *noun* (*plural* **dynasties**) a succession of monarchs, leaders, etc of the same family ◆ **dynastic** *adjective*

dys- (*pronounced* dis) *prefix* forms words which describe disorders of some part of the body or of the mind: *dyslexia/dyspepsia/dysentery* ⊙ Comes from Greek prefix *dys-* meaning 'badly'

dysentery (*pronounced* **dis**-en-te-ri) *noun* a severe infectious disease of the intestine causing fever, pain and diarrhoea

dysfunction *noun* abnormality of functioning ◆ **dysfunctional** *adjective*

dyslexia *noun* difficulty in learning to read and write and in spelling

dyslexic *noun & adjective* (someone) suffering from dyslexia

dyspepsia *noun* indigestion ◆ **dyspeptic** *adjective*

dysprosium *noun, chemistry* (symbol **Dy**) a soft, silvery-white, metallic element that is one of the most magnetic substances known ⊙ Comes from Greek *dysprositos* meaning 'difficult to reach'

Ee

E¹ *noun* **1** *music* the third note in the scale of C major **2** *informal* a tablet of the drug Ecstasy

E² *abbreviation* **1** east; eastern **2** *informal* the drug Ecstasy **3** electronic: *e-commerce*

e *symbol, maths* the base of the natural system of logarithms, with an approximate value of 2.718281828 …

each *adjective* of two or more things: every one taken individually: *There is a postbox on each side of the road/She was late on each occasion* ► *pronoun* every one individually: *Each of them won a prize* • **each other** used when an action takes place between two people: *We don't see each other very often*

eager *adjective* keen, anxious to do or get (something) ♦ **eagerly** *adverb*

eagle *noun* a kind of large bird of prey

eaglet *noun* a young eagle

ear *noun* **1** the part of the body through which you hear sounds **2** a head (of corn etc) • **a good ear** the ability to tell one sound from another • **lend an ear** to listen

eardrum *noun* the membrane in the middle of the ear (*also called:* **tympanic membrane**)

earl *noun* a member of the British aristocracy between a marquis and a viscount

earldom *noun* the lands or title of an earl

earlobe *noun* the soft fleshy part at the bottom of the human ear

early *adjective* (**earlier, earliest**) **1** in good time **2** at or near the beginning: *in an earlier chapter* **3** sooner than expected: *You're early!* ► *adverb*: *The bus left early* ♦ **earliness** *noun*

early bird *noun* **1** an early riser **2** someone who gains an advantage by acting more quickly than rivals

earmark *verb* to mark or set aside for a special purpose

earmuffs *plural noun* two pads of warm material joined by a band across the head, which you use to cover your ears to stop them getting cold

earn *verb* **1** to receive (money) for work **2** to deserve

earnest *adjective* serious, serious-minded ► *noun* **1** seriousness **2** money etc given to make sure that a bargain will be kept • **in earnest** meaning what you say or do ♦ **earnestly** *adverb*

earnings *plural noun* pay for work done

earphones *plural noun* a pair of tiny speakers fitting in or against the ear for listening to a radio etc

earpiece *noun* the part of a telephone or hearing aid etc placed at or in the ear

ear-piercing *adjective* very loud or shrill

earplugs *plural noun* a pair of plugs placed in the ears to block off outside noise

earring *noun* a piece of jewellery worn on the ear

earshot *noun* the distance at which a sound can be heard

earth *noun* **1** the third planet from the sun; our world **2** its surface **3** soil **4** the hole of a fox, badger, etc **5** an electrical connection with the ground ► *verb* to connect electrically with the ground

earthenware *noun* pottery, dishes made of clay

earthily *adverb* in a coarse, natural, unrefined way

earthiness *noun* coarseness, naturalness, lack of refinement

earthly *adjective* of the earth as opposed to heaven

earthquake *noun* a movement of the earth's crust, causing the surface to shake

earth science *noun* any of the sciences concerned with the earth, eg geology or meteorology

earthshattering *adjective* of great importance

earthworm *noun* the common worm

earthy *adjective* (**earthier, earthiest**) **1** like soil **2** covered in soil **3** coarse and natural, not refined

earwig *noun* a type of insect with pincers at its tail

ease *noun* **1** freedom from difficulty: *finished the race with ease* **2** freedom from pain, worry or embarrassment **3** rest from work ► *verb* **1** to make or become less painful or difficult **2** to move carefully and gradually: *Ease the stone into position* • **at ease** comfortable, relaxed • **stand at ease** to stand with your legs apart and arms behind your back

easel *noun* a stand for an artist's canvas while painting etc

easily *adverb* **1** without difficulty **2** without pain, worry or discomfort **3** obviously, clearly, beyond doubt or by a long way: *He's easily the most* accomplished actor in Britain today **4** more quickly or more readily than most people **5** very possibly: *He could easily be out for a couple of hours*

easiness *noun* the quality of being or feeling easy

east *noun* the direction from which the sun rises, one of the four main points of the compass ➤ *adjective* **1** in or to the east **2** of the wind: from the east ➤ *adverb* in, to or towards the east: *We headed east*

Easter *noun* **1** the Christian celebration of Christ's rising from the dead **2** the weekend when this is celebrated each year, sometime in spring

easterly *adjective* **1** of the wind: coming from or facing the east **2** in or towards the east

eastern *adjective* of the east

Eastern question *noun, history* (**the Eastern question**) a set of diplomatic problems affecting Europe in the 18th, 19th, and 20th centuries, created by the decline of the Ottoman Empire and the scramble for power in south-east Europe

eastward or **eastwards** *adjective & adverb* towards the east

easy *adjective* (**easier, easiest**) **1** not hard to do **2** free from pain, worry or discomfort

eat *verb* (**eating, ate, eaten**) **1** to chew and swallow (food) **2** to destroy gradually, waste away

eatable *adjective* fit to eat, edible

eaves *plural noun* the edge of a roof overhanging the walls

eavesdrop *verb* (**eavesdropping, eavesdropped**) to listen secretly to a private conversation ◆ **eavesdropper** *noun*

ebb *noun* **1** the flowing away of the tide after high tide **2** a lessening, a worsening ➤ *verb* **1** to flow away **2** to grow less or worse

ebony *noun* a type of black, hard wood ➤ *adjective* **1** made of ebony **2** black

ebullient *adjective* **1** very high-spirited, cheerful or enthusiastic **2** boiling ⊕ Comes from Latin *ebullire* meaning 'to boil out' ◆ **ebullience** or **ebulliency** *noun*

eccentric *adjective* **1** odd, acting strangely **2** of circles: not having the same centre (*contrasted with*: **concentric**)

eccentricity *noun* (*plural* **eccentricities**) oddness of manner or conduct

ecclesiastic or **ecclesiastical** *adjective* of the church or clergy

ecdysis *noun, biology* the shedding of the exoskeleton by insects, crustaceans, etc so that growth can occur

ECG *abbreviation* **1** an electrocardiogram: the diagram or tracing produced by an

electrocardiograph **2** an electrocardiograph: a machine that registers the electrical variations of the beating heart as a diagram or tracing

echo *noun* (*plural* **echoes**) **1** the repetition of a sound caused by its striking a surface and coming back **2** something that evokes a memory: *echoes of the past* ➤ *verb* **1** to send back sound **2** to repeat (a thing said) **3** to imitate

éclair (*pronounced* ei-**kleir**) *noun* an oblong sweet pastry filled with cream

⊕ From a French word meaning literally 'lightning', perhaps because it is eaten quickly

eclampsia *noun, medicine* a toxic condition which can develop in the last three months of pregnancy, causing convulsions and swelling

eclectic *adjective* taking material or ideas from a wide range of sources

eclipse *noun* **1** the covering of the whole or part of the sun (**solar eclipse**) or moon (**lunar eclipse**), eg when the moon comes between the sun and the earth **2** loss of position or prestige ➤ *verb* **1** to throw into the shade **2** to blot out (someone's achievement) by doing better

eco- *prefix* relating to the environment: *ecofriendly/eco-summit*

eco-friendly *adjective* not harmful to or threatening the environment

E. coli *abbreviation* for *Escherichia coli*, a species of bacterium that lives naturally in the intestines of vertebrates including humans, and sometimes causes food poisoning

ecological *adjective* **1** having to do with plants, animals, etc and their natural surroundings **2** concerned with protecting and preserving plants, animals and the natural environment ◆ **ecologically** *adverb*

ecological footprint *noun, geography* a measure of the effect that someone or something has on the environment by eg producing waste, emitting carbon dioxide, etc

ecologist *noun* someone who studies, or is an expert in, ecology

ecology *noun* the study of plants, animals, etc in relation to their natural surroundings ⊕ Comes from Greek *oikos* meaning 'house', and *logos* meaning 'discourse'

e-commerce *noun, computing* the buying and selling of goods on the Internet

economic *adjective* **1** concerning economy **2** making a profit

❗ Do not confuse: **economic** and **economical**

economical *adjective* thrifty, not wasteful

economic migrant *noun* someone who has left their native country because of poverty rather than for political reasons etc

economics *singular noun* the study of how money is created and spent

economist *noun* someone who studies or is an expert on economics

economize or **economise** *verb* to be careful in spending or using

economy *noun* (*plural* **economies**) **1** the management of a country's finances **2** the careful use of something, especially money

ecosystem *noun* a community of living things and their relationship with their environment

ecoterrorism *noun* **1** violence carried out to draw attention to environmental issues **2** acts causing deliberate environmental damage ♦ **ecoterrorist** *noun*

Ecstasy *noun* a powerful hallucinatory drug

ecstasy *noun* (*plural* **ecstasies**) very great joy or pleasure ♦ **ecstatic** *adjective* ♦ **ecstatically** *adverb*

ectomorph *noun* a person of thin light body build (*compare with*: **endomorph**, **mesomorph**) ♦ **ectomorphic** *adjective*

-ectomy see **-tomy**

ectopic pregnancy *noun, medicine* the development of a fetus outside the uterus, especially in a fallopian tube ☾ Comes from Greek *ek* meaning 'out of' + *topos* meaning 'place'

ecumenism *noun* a movement concerned with the unity of the whole Christian church ♦ **ecumenical** *adjective*

eczema (*pronounced* **ek**-sim-a) *noun* a skin disease causing itching red patches on the skin ♦ **eczematic** *adjective*

eddy *noun* (*plural* **eddies**) a circling current of water or air running against the main stream ➤ *verb* to flow in circles

edelweiss (*pronounced* **eid**-el-vais) *noun* an Alpine plant with white flowers ☾ Comes from German *edel* meaning 'noble', and *weiss* meaning 'white'

edge *noun* **1** the border of anything, farthest from the middle **2** a line joining two vertices in a figure **3** sharpness: *put an edge on my appetite* **4** advantage: *Brazil had the edge at half-time* ➤ *verb* **1** to put a border on **2** to move little by little: *edging forward* • **on edge** nervous, edgy • **set someone's teeth on edge** to grate on their nerves, make them wince

edgeways *adverb* sideways

edging *noun* a border, a fringe

edgy *adjective* (**edgier, edgiest**) unable to relax, irritable

edible *adjective* fit to be eaten

edict *noun* an order, a command

edification *noun* mental and spiritual improvement

edifice *noun* a large building

edify *verb* (**edifies, edifying, edified**) to improve the mind, enlighten ♦ **edifying** *adjective*

edit *verb* **1** to prepare (a text, film, etc) for publication or broadcasting **2** to be in overall charge of producing (a newspaper etc) **3** to prepare (data) for processing by a computer

edition *noun* **1** the form in which a book etc is published after being edited **2** the copies of a book, newspaper, etc printed at one time **3** a special issue of a newspaper, eg for a local area

editor *noun* **1** someone who edits a book, film, etc **2** the chief journalist of a newspaper or section of a newspaper: *the sports editor*

editorial *adjective* of editing ➤ *noun* a newspaper column written by or on behalf of the chief editor, giving an opinion on a topic

educate *verb* to teach (people), especially in a school or college

educated *adjective* knowledgeable and cultured, as a result of receiving a good education

educated guess *noun* a guess based on knowledge of the subject involved

education *noun* **1** the process or system of teaching in schools and other establishments **2** the development of a person's knowledge **3** an experience from which you think you have learnt something

educational *adjective* **1** concerned with formal teaching **2** concerned with giving information, rather than simply entertaining or amusing **3** interesting from the point of view of teaching you something which you did not know before

Edwardian *adjective* relating to or characteristic of the period of reign of a King Edward, especially Edward VII (1901–1910) ➤ *noun* someone who lived in such a period

eel *noun* a long, ribbon-shaped fish

EEPROM (*pronounced* **ee**-prom) *abbreviation, computing* electrically erasable programmable read-only memory

eerie *adjective* causing fear of the unknown ♦ **eerily** *adverb*

☾ Originally a Scots word meaning 'afraid' or 'cowardly'

efface *verb* to rub out • **efface yourself** to avoid drawing attention to yourself

effect *noun* **1** the result of an action **2** strength, power: *The pills had little effect* **3** an impression produced: *the effect of the sunset* **4** general meaning **5** use, operation: *That law is not yet in effect* **6** (**effects**) goods, property ➤ *verb* to bring about ☾ Comes from Latin *effectus* meaning 'finished'

! Do not confuse with: **affect**.
Effect is usually a noun. **Affect** is usually a verb.
To **affect** means 'to have an **effect** on'.

effective adjective **1** producing the desired effect **2** actual

effector biology, adjective causing a response to stimulus ➤ noun an organ or substance with this property

effectual adjective able to do what is required ✦ **effectually** adverb

effeminate adjective unmanly, womanish

efferent noun, anatomy of a nerve: carrying impulses from the brain ⊙ Comes from Latin efferre meaning 'to carry out'

effervesce verb **1** to froth up **2** to be very lively, excited, etc ✦ **effervescence** noun
✦ **effervescent** adjective

effete adjective weak, feeble

efficacious adjective effective ✦ **efficacy** noun

efficient adjective able to do things well; capable ✦ **efficiency** noun ✦ **efficiently** adverb

effigy noun (plural **effigies**) a likeness of a person carved in stone, wood, etc

effloresce verb, biology to produce flowers ✦ **efflorescence** noun

effluent noun **1** a stream flowing from another stream or lake **2** liquid industrial waste; sewage

effort noun **1** an attempt using a lot of strength or ability **2** hard work

effrontery noun impudence

effusive adjective speaking freely, gushing ✦ **effusively** adverb

EFL abbreviation English as a foreign language

EFTPOS (pronounced **eft**-pos) abbreviation electronic funds transfer at point of sale, a system of paying for goods by using a plastic card to transfer money from your account to the seller's

eg abbreviation for example (from Latin exempli gratia)

egalitarian adjective relating to or believing in the principle that all human beings are equal and should have the same rights ➤ noun a person who believes in this principle ⊙ Comes from French égalitaire, from égal meaning 'equal' ✦ **egalitarianism** noun

egg noun **1** an oval shell containing the embryo of a bird, insect or reptile **2** (also called: **ovum**) a human reproductive cell **3** a hen's egg used for eating • **egg on** to urge, encourage

eggplant noun, US an aubergine

ego noun (plural **egos**) **1** the conscious self **2** self-conceit, egotism

egocentric adjective interested only in oneself

egoism or **egotism** noun the habit of considering only your own interests, selfishness

✦ **egoist** or **egotist** noun ✦ **egoistic** or **egotistic** adjective

Eid or **Eid-ul-Fitr** see **Id-ul-Fitr**

eiderdown noun **1** soft feathers from the eider, a type of northern sea-duck **2** a feather quilt

eight noun the number 8 ➤ adjective 8 in number

eighteen noun the number 18 ➤ adjective 18 in number

eighteenth adjective the last of a series of eighteen ➤ noun one of eighteen equal parts

eighth adjective the last of a series of eight ➤ noun one of eight equal parts

eighties plural noun (also **80s, 80's**) **1** the period of time between eightieth and ninetieth birthdays **2** the range of temperatures between eighty and ninety degrees **3** the period of time between the eightieth and ninetieth years of a century

eightieth adjective the last of a series of eighty ➤ noun one of eighty equal parts

eighty noun the number 80 ➤ adjective 80 in number

einsteinium noun, chemistry (symbol **Es**) an element produced artificially from plutonium

⊙ Named after German-born physicist Albert Einstein (1879–1955)

either adjective & pronoun **1** one or other of two: Either bus will go there/Either of the dates would suit me **2** each of two, both: There is a crossing on either side of the road ➤ conjunction used with **or** to show alternatives: Either he goes or I do ➤ adverb any more than another: That won't work either

ejaculate verb **1** to emit semen **2** to shout out, exclaim ✦ **ejaculation** noun

eject verb **1** to throw out **2** to force to leave a house, job, etc ✦ **ejection** noun

eke verb: **eke out 1** to make (a supply) go further or last longer by adding to it or using it carefully: eked out the stew with more vegetables **2** to make a living with difficulty

elaborate verb (pronounced i-**lab**-o-reit) **1** to work out in detail: You must elaborate your escape plan **2** (often **elaborate on**) to explain fully ➤ adjective (pronounced i-**lab**-o-rat) highly detailed or decorated ✦ **elaboration** noun

élan noun impressive and energetic style ⊙ Comes from French

elapse verb of time: to pass

elastic adjective able to stretch and spring back again, springy ➤ noun a piece of cotton etc interwoven with rubber to make it springy ✦ **elasticity** noun

elated adjective in high spirits, very pleased ✦ **elation** noun

elbow *noun* the joint where the arm bends ➤ *verb* to push with the elbow, jostle

elbow-grease *noun, informal* 1 vigorous rubbing 2 hard work, effort

elbow-room *noun* plenty of room to move

elder[1] *adjective* older ➤ *noun* 1 someone who is older 2 an office-bearer in the Presbyterian church

elder[2] *noun* a type of tree with purple-black berries

elderberry *noun* (*plural* **elderberries**) a berry from the elder tree

elderly *adjective* nearing old age

eldest *adjective* oldest

elect *verb* 1 to choose by voting 2 to choose (to) ➤ *adjective* 1 chosen 2 (*placed after the noun*) chosen for a post but not yet in it: *president elect*

election *noun* the choosing by vote of people to sit in parliament, hold an official position, etc

elector *noun* someone who has the right to vote at an election ✦ **electoral** *adjective*

electorate *noun* all those who have the right to vote

electric or **electrical** *adjective* produced or worked by electricity

electrician *noun* someone skilled in working with electricity

electricity *noun* a form of energy used to give light, heat and power

electric shock *noun* a violent jerking of the body caused by an electric current passing through it

electrify *verb* (**electrifies, electrifying, electrified**) 1 to supply with electricity 2 to excite greatly

electro- *prefix* electric, of or by electricity ⊙ Comes from Greek *elektro-*, a form of *elektron* meaning 'amber'

electrocute *verb* to kill by an electric current ✦ **electrocution** *noun*

electrode *noun* a conductor through which an electric current enters or leaves a battery etc

electrolysis *noun* 1 *chemistry* the decomposition of a chemical in a liquid or solution form by passing an electric current through it 2 the removal of tumours or hair roots using an electric current

electrolyte *noun, chemistry* a solution of chemical salts which can conduct electricity, eg in a battery, and helps keep a balance of fluids in the body ✦ **electrolytic** *adjective*

electromagnet *noun* a piece of soft metal magnetized by an electric current ✦ **electromagnetic** *adjective* ✦ **electromagnetism** *noun*

electromagnetic wave *noun, physics* a wave of energy produced by the acceleration of an electric charge

electromotive *adjective, physics* producing an electric current

electromotive force *noun, physics* the energy which causes a current to flow in an electrical circuit

electron *noun* a very light particle with the smallest possible charge of electricity, which orbits the nucleus of an atom (*see also:* **neutron, proton**)

electronegative *adjective, physics* 1 carrying a negative charge 2 tending to gain electrons and form negative ions ✦ **electronegativity** *noun*

electronic *adjective* of or using electrical circuits

electronics *singular noun* a branch of physics dealing with electrical circuits and their use in machines etc ➤ *plural noun* the electronic parts of a machine or system

electronvolt *noun, physics* a unit of energy equal to that acquired by an electron when accelerated by a potential of one volt

electroplating *noun* using an electric current to coat an object with metal

electropositive *adjective, physics* 1 carrying a positive charge 2 tending to release electrons and form positive ions ✦ **electropositivity** *noun*

electrostatic *adjective* to do with electricity at rest

elegant *adjective* 1 graceful, well-dressed, fashionable 2 of clothes etc: well-made and tasteful ✦ **elegance** *noun* ✦ **elegantly** *adverb*

elegy *noun* (*plural* **elegies**) a poem written on someone's death

element *noun* 1 a part of anything 2 a substance that cannot be split chemically into simpler substances, eg oxygen, iron, etc 3 a slight amount 4 a heating wire carrying the current in an electric heater or kettle 5 (**elements**) basic facts or skills 6 (**elements**) the powers of nature, the weather • **in your element** in the surroundings you find enjoyable or natural

elemental *adjective* of the elements

elementary *adjective* 1 at the first stage 2 simple

elementary particle *noun, chemistry, physics* any of the particles (eg **electrons, protons** and **neutrons**) which make up an atom

elephant *noun* a very large animal with a thick skin, a trunk and two ivory tusks

elephantiasis *noun, medicine* a tropical disease, caused by parasitic worms, in which the skin becomes thicker and the limbs are enlarged

elephantine (*pronounced* el-i-**fan**-tain) *adjective* big and clumsy

elevate *verb* 1 to raise to a higher position 2 to cheer up 3 to improve (the mind)

elevation *noun* **1** the act of raising up **2** rising ground **3** height **4** a drawing of a building as seen from the side **5** *maths* (*also called*: **angle of elevation**) an angle measuring a point above a horizontal line (*compare with*: **depression** meaning 7)

elevator *noun*, *US* a lift in a building

eleven *noun* **1** the number 11 **2** a team of eleven players, eg for cricket ➤ *adjective* 11 in number

elevenses *plural noun* coffee, biscuits, etc taken around eleven o'clock in the morning

eleventh *adjective* the last of a series of eleven ➤ *noun* one of eleven equal parts

elf *noun* (*plural* **elves**) a tiny, mischievous supernatural creature that looks like a little human being

elfin, elfish or **elvish** *adjective* like an elf

elicit *verb* to draw out (information etc) ⓛ Comes from Latin *elicit-*, a form of *elicere* meaning 'to lure out'

! Do not confuse with: **illicit**

elide *verb* **1** *grammar* to omit (a vowel or syllable) at the beginning or end of a word **2** to omit (a part of anything) ♦ **elision** *noun* ⓛ Comes from Latin *elidere* meaning 'to strike out'

eligible *adjective* **1** fit or worthy to be chosen, especially for marriage **2** having a right to something: *eligible to enter/eligible for compensation* ♦ **eligibility** *noun*

eliminate *verb* **1** to get rid of **2** to exclude, omit ♦ **elimination** *noun*

élite or **elite** (*pronounced* ei-**leet**) *noun* a part of a group selected as, or believed to be, the best

elitism *noun* **1** the belief in the natural social superiority of some people **2** an awareness of, or pride in, belonging to an elite group in society ♦ **elitist** *adjective*

elixir (*pronounced* e-**liks**-eer) *noun* a liquid believed to give eternal life, or to be able to turn iron etc into gold

elk *noun* a very large deer found in N Europe and Asia, related to the moose

ellipse *noun* (*plural* **ellipses**) an oval shape

ellipsis *noun* **1** *grammar* when a word or words needed for the sense or grammar are omitted but understood in written text: a set of three dots (…) that indicates the omission of a word or words, eg in a long quotation

ellipsoid *noun*, *maths* a surface or solid object of which every plane is an ellipse or a circle ♦ **ellipsoidal** *adjective*

elliptic or **elliptical** *adjective* **1** oval **2** having part of the words or meaning left out

elm *noun* a tree with a rough bark and leaves with saw-like edges

El Niño (*pronounced* ell **nee**-nyo) *noun*, *meteorology* a periodic large-scale warming of the surface of the Eastern Pacific Ocean, which causes extreme weather in the Pacific region (*compare with*: **La Niña**)

> ⓛ A Spanish term, short for *El Niño de Navidad* meaning 'the Christ Child', originally referring to a warm current observed at Christmas

elocution *noun* **1** the art of what is thought to be correct speech **2** style of speaking

elongate *verb* to stretch out lengthwise, make longer ♦ **elongation** *noun*

elope *verb* to run away from home to get married ♦ **elopement** *noun*

eloquent *adjective* **1** good at expressing thoughts in words **2** persuasive ♦ **eloquence** *noun*

else *adverb* otherwise: *Come inside or else you will catch cold* ➤ *adjective* other than the person or thing mentioned: *Someone else has taken her place*

elsewhere *adverb* in or to another place

elucidate *verb* to make (something) easy to understand

elude *verb* **1** to escape by a trick **2** to be too difficult to remember or understand ⓛ Comes from Latin *eludere* meaning 'to outplay'

! Do not confuse with: **allude**

elusive *adjective* hard to catch

! Do not confuse with: **allusive** and **illusive**. **Elusive** comes from the verb **elude**.

elvish see **elfin**

em- see **in-**

emaciated *adjective* very thin, like a skeleton

e-mail or **email** *noun* electronic mail, messages exchanged across a network of computers

emanate *verb* to flow, come out from ♦ **emanation** *noun*

emancipate *verb* to set free, eg from slavery or repressive social conditions ♦ **emancipation** *noun*

embalm *verb* to preserve (a dead body) from decay by treating it with spices or drugs

embankment *noun* a bank of earth or stone to keep back water, or carry a railway over low-lying places

embargo *noun* (*plural* **embargoes**) an official order forbidding something, especially trade with another country

embark *verb* to go on board ship • **embark on** to start (a new career etc) ♦ **embarkation** *noun*

embarrass *verb* to make (someone) feel uncomfortable and self-conscious ♦ **embarrassed** *adjective* ♦ **embarrassing** *adjective* ♦ **embarrassment** *noun*

embassy *noun* (*plural* **embassies**) the offices

and staff of an ambassador in a foreign country

embed *verb* (**embedding, embedded**) to set or fix something in another thing

embellish *verb* 1 to decorate 2 to add details to (a story etc) ♦ **embellishment** *noun*

ember *noun* a piece of wood or coal glowing in a fire

embezzle *verb* to use for yourself money entrusted to you ♦ **embezzlement** *noun*

embittered *adjective* feeling resentful and angry about your lack of good fortune

emblazon *verb* 1 to decorate, adorn 2 to show in a brightly coloured or conspicuous way

emblem *noun* 1 an image which represents something: *The dove is the emblem of peace/ The leek is the emblem of Wales* 2 a badge

embodiment *noun* a person or thing that perfectly symbolizes some idea or quality

embody *verb* (**embodies, embodying, embodied**) 1 to include 2 to express, give form to: *embodying the spirit of the age*

embolism *noun, medicine* the blocking of a blood vessel by an air bubble, blood clot, etc

emboss *verb* to make a pattern in leather, metal, etc, which stands out from a flat surface ♦ **embossed** *adjective*

embrace *verb* 1 to throw your arms round in affection 2 to include 3 to accept, adopt eagerly ➤ *noun* an affectionate hug

embrocation *noun* an ointment for rubbing on the body, eg to relieve stiffness

embroider *verb* 1 to decorate with designs in needlework 2 to add false details to (a story)

embroidery *noun* 1 the art or practice of sewing designs on to cloth 2 the designs sewn on to cloth

embroil *verb* 1 to get (someone) into a quarrel, or into a difficult situation 2 to throw into confusion

embryo *noun* (*plural* **embryos**), *biology* 1 the young of an animal until hatching or birth 2 in humans: the developing organism the first seven weeks after conception (*compare with*: **fetus**) 3 a plant in its earliest stages of development

embryo dune *noun, geography* a low sand dune formed from an accumulation of blown sand

embryonic *adjective* in an early stage of development

emend *verb* a rather formal word meaning 'to remove faults or errors from' ♦ **emendation** *noun*

> **!** Do not confuse with: **amend**.
> **Emending** consists simply of deleting errors. **Amending** involves making changes or improvements.

emerald *noun* a bright green precious stone

emerge *verb* 1 to come out 2 to become known or clear ♦ **emergence** *noun*

emergency *noun* (*plural* **emergencies**) an unexpected event requiring very quick action

emergency exit *noun* a way out of a building for use in an emergency

emergent *adjective* 1 arising 2 newly formed or newly independent: *emergent nation*

emery *noun* a very hard mineral, used for smoothing and polishing

emetic *adjective* causing vomiting ➤ *noun* an emetic medicine

emigrant *noun* someone who emigrates

emigrate *verb* to leave your country to settle in another ♦ **emigration** *noun* ℗ Comes from Latin *emigrare*, from e meaning 'from', and *migrare* meaning 'to remove'

> **!** Do not confuse with: **immigrate**.
> You are **emigrating** when you leave your home country (the E comes from the Latin meaning 'from'). You **immigrate** to the country where you plan to start living (the IM comes from the Latin meaning 'into').

émigré (*pronounced* ei-mee-**grei**) *noun* someone who is forced to emigrate for political reasons

eminence *noun* 1 distinction, fame 2 a title of honour 3 a hill

eminent *adjective* famous, notable ℗ Comes from Latin *eminens* meaning 'standing out'

> **!** Do not confuse with: **imminent**

eminently *adverb* very, obviously: *eminently suitable*

emir *noun* a title given to various Muslim rulers

emissary *noun* (*plural* **emissaries**) 1 a person sent on a mission, especially on behalf of a government 2 a person sent with a message

emit *verb* (**emitting, emitted**) to send or give out (light, sound, etc) ♦ **emission** *noun*

emolument *noun, formal* wages, salary

emoticon *noun, computing* a combination of characters used in e-mails to express an emotional reaction, eg :-) for happiness or laughter

emotion *noun* a feeling that disturbs or excites the mind, eg fear, love, hatred

emotional *adjective* 1 moving the feelings 2 of a person: tending to show feelings easily or excessively ♦ **emotionally** *adverb*

emotive *adjective* causing emotion rather than thought

empathize or **empathise** *verb* to share another person's feelings etc

empathy *noun* the ability to share another person's feelings etc

emperor *noun* the ruler of an empire

emphasis *noun* **1** stress placed on a word or part of a word in speaking **2** greater attention or importance: *The emphasis is on playing, not winning*

emphasize or **emphasise** *verb* to put emphasis on; call attention to

emphatic *adjective* spoken strongly: *an emphatic 'no'* ♦ **emphatically** *adverb*

emphysema (*pronounced* em-fi-**seem**-a) *noun* a disease in which the lung or another body part is abnormally enlarged with air

empire *noun* **1** a group of nations etc under the same ruling power **2** a large business organization including several companies

empirical *adjective* based on experiment and experience, not on theory alone ♦ **empiricism** *noun*

empirical formula *noun, chemistry* a formula showing the simplest possible ratio of atoms in a molecule

employ *verb* **1** to give work to **2** to use **3** to occupy the time of ➤ *noun* employment

employee *noun* someone who works for someone else in return for payment

employer *noun* someone who gives work to employees

employment *noun* work, occupation

employment structure *noun, geography* in a given area: the number of people in various types of job

emporium *noun* (*plural* **emporia** or **emporiums**) a large shop; a market

empower *verb* **1** to authorize **2** to give self-confidence to

empress *noun* the female ruler of an empire

empty *adjective* (**emptier, emptiest**) **1** containing nothing or no one **2** unlikely to result in anything: *empty threats* ➤ *verb* (**empties, emptying, emptied**) to make or become empty ➤ *noun* (*plural* **empties**) an empty bottle etc ♦ **emptiness** *noun*

empty-handed *adjective* bringing or gaining nothing

empty-headed *adjective* flighty, irresponsible

EMU *abbreviation* European Monetary Union

emu *noun* a type of Australian bird which cannot fly

emulate *verb* **1** to try to do as well as, or better than **2** to imitate **3** *computing* of a computer or a program: to imitate the internal design of another device ♦ **emulation** *noun*

emulator *noun* **1** someone or something that emulates **2** *computing* a computer or program that imitates the internal design of another device

emulsifier or **emulsifying agent** *noun* a chemical substance that coats the surface of

droplets of one liquid so that they can remain dispersed throughout a second liquid, forming an emulsion

emulsify *verb* (**emulsifies, emulsifying, emulsified**) to make or become an emulsion

emulsion *noun* a milky liquid (eg that made by mixing oil and water), in which small droplets of one liquid are dispersed uniformly throughout the other

en- see **in-**

enable *verb* **1** to make it possible for, allow: *The money enabled him to retire* **2** *computing* to activate: *enable the sound card*

enact *verb* **1** to act, perform **2** to make a law

enamel *noun* **1** a glassy coating fired on to metal **2** a paint with a glossy finish **3** the smooth white coating of the teeth ➤ *verb* (**enamelling, enamelled**) to coat or paint with enamel ♦ **enamelling** *noun*

enamoured *adjective* (**enamoured of**) fond of

encampment *noun* **1** a large group of tents **2** a military camp

encapsulate *verb* to capture the essence of; describe briefly and accurately

encephalitis (*pronounced* en-sef-a-**lai**-tis) *noun, medicine* inflammation of the brain

enchant *verb* **1** to delight, please greatly **2** to put a spell or charm on ♦ **enchanter**, ♦ **enchantress** *noun* (meaning 2)

enchanting *adjective* delightful, charming

enchantment *noun* **1** a feeling of delight and wonder **2** a spell or charm

encircle *verb* to surround, or form a circle round, something ♦ **encirclement** *noun*

enclave *noun* an area enclosed within foreign territory

enclose *verb* **1** to put inside an envelope with a letter etc **2** to put (eg a wall) around

enclosure *noun* **1** the act of enclosing **2** something enclosed eg with a letter **3** a small field with a high fence or wall round it **4** *history* the division of shared land into privately owned plots, as took place in Britain in the 18th century

encode *verb* to express in code or convert into code

encompass *verb* to surround; to include

encore (*pronounced* **ong**-kawr) *noun* **1** an extra performance of a song etc in reply to audience applause **2** a call for an encore

encounter *verb* **1** to meet by chance **2** to come up against (a difficulty, enemy, etc) ➤ *noun* a meeting, a fight

encourage *verb* **1** to give hope or confidence to **2** to urge (to do) ♦ **encouragement** *noun* ♦ **encouraging** *adjective* (meaning 1)

encroach *verb* to go beyond your rights or land and interfere with someone else's ♦ **encroachment** *noun*

encrypt *verb* to put information (eg computer data or TV signals) into a coded form (*contrasted with*: **decrypt**) ✦ **encryption** *noun*

encumber *verb* to burden, load down

encumbrance *noun* a heavy burden, a hindrance

encyclopedia or **encyclopaedia** *noun* a reference book containing information on many subjects, or on a particular subject

encyclopedic or **encyclopaedic** *adjective* giving complete information

encyst *verb, biology* to enclose or become enclosed in a cyst ✦ **encystation** *noun*

end *noun* **1** the last point or part **2** death **3** the farthest point of the length of something: *at the end of the road* **4** a result aimed at **5** a small piece left over ➤ *verb* to bring or come to an end ● **on end 1** standing on one end **2** in a series, without a stop: *go for days on end without eating* ⊙ Comes from Old English *ende*

endanger *verb* to put in danger or at risk

endangered species *noun* a plant or animal in danger of becoming extinct

endear *verb* to make dear or more dear

endearing *adjective* appealing

endearment *noun* an expression of love

endeavour *verb* to try hard (to) ➤ *noun* a determined attempt

endemic *adjective, biology* **1** of a disease: found regularly in a certain area **2** of a plant or animal: native to a certain area

ending *noun* the last part

endocarp *noun, biology* the inner layer of the pericarp of a fruit

endocrine *adjective, biology* of a gland: secreting hormones directly into the bloodstream (*see also*: **exocrine**) ✦ **endocrinal** or **endocrinic** *adjective*

endometrium *noun, anatomy* the mucous membrane lining the uterus

endomorph *noun* a person of rounded or plump body build (*compare with*: **ectomorph**, **mesomorph**) ✦ **endomorphic** *adjective*

endophyte *noun, biology* a plant that lives on another plant for support

endorphin *noun, biology, chemistry* any of a group of chemical compounds that occur naturally in the brain and relieve pain in a similar way to morphine

endorse *verb* **1** to give your support to something said or written **2** to sign the back of a cheque to confirm receiving money for it **3** to indicate on a motor licence that the owner has broken a driving law ✦ **endorsement** *noun*

endoskeleton *noun, biology* an internal skeleton made of bone or cartilage

endosperm *noun, biology* nutritive tissue in the seed of some plants ✦ **endospermic** *adjective*

endothermic *adjective, chemistry* of a process, especially a reaction: involving the absorption of heat (*contrasted with*: **exothermic**)

endow *verb* **1** to give money for the buying and upkeep of: *He endowed a bed in the hospital* **2** to give a talent, quality, etc to: *Nature endowed her with a good brain* ✦ **endowment** *noun*

endurable *adjective* bearable

endurance *noun* the ability to withstand long periods of pressure, hardship, etc

endure *verb* to bear without giving way; last

end-user *noun* the person, company, etc who is or will be the recipient or user of a product

enema (*pronounced* en-im-a) *noun* the injection of fluid into the rectum, to clean out the bowels or introduce medication

enemy *noun* (*plural* **enemies**) **1** someone hostile to another; a foe **2** someone armed to fight against another **3** someone who is against something: *an enemy of socialism* ➤ *adjective* hostile; belong to a hostile force or nation

energetic *adjective* active, lively ✦ **energetically** *adverb*

energize or **energise** *verb* to stimulate, invigorate or enliven

energy *noun* (*plural* **energies**) **1** strength to act, vigour **2** forcefulness **3** a form of power, eg electricity, heat, etc **4** *physics* the capacity to do work

energy level *noun, physics* one of the fixed amounts of energy that an electron can have at any given time

enervate *verb* **1** to take strength or energy from something **2** to deprive someone of moral or mental vigour ✦ **enervating** *adjective* ✦ **enervation** *noun*

enfold *verb* to enclose, embrace

enforce *verb* to cause (a law etc) to be carried out ✦ **enforcement** *noun*

enfranchise *verb* **1** to set free **2** to give the right to vote to

engage *verb* **1** to begin to employ (workers etc) **2** to book in advance **3** to take or keep hold of (someone's attention etc) **4** to be busy with, be occupied (in) **5** of machine parts: to fit together **6** to begin fighting

engaged *adjective* **1** bound by a promise of marriage **2** busy with something **3** of a telephone, room: in use

engagement *noun* **1** a promise of marriage **2** an appointment to meet **3** a fight: *naval engagement*

engaging *adjective* pleasant, charming

engender *verb* to produce or cause (especially feelings or emotions) ⊙ Comes from French engendrer, from Latin generare meaning 'to generate'

engine noun **1** a machine which converts heat or other energy into motion **2** the part of a train which pulls the coaches

engineer noun **1** someone who works with, or designs, engines or machines **2** someone who designs or makes bridges, roads, etc ➤ verb to bring about by clever planning

engineering noun the science of designing machines, roadmaking, etc

engorged adjective **1** crammed full **2** medicine congested with blood

engrave verb **1** to draw with a special tool on glass, metal, etc **2** to make a deep impression on: engraved on his memory

engraving noun a print made from a cut-out drawing in metal or wood

engross verb to take up the whole interest or attention

engulf verb to swallow up wholly

enhance verb to improve, make greater or better

enigma noun something or someone difficult to understand, a mystery ♦ **enigmatic** adjective

enjoy verb **1** to take pleasure in **2** to experience, have (something beneficial): enjoying good health • **enjoy yourself** to have a pleasant time

enjoyable adjective pleasant and satisfying

enjoyment noun **1** pleasure and satisfaction **2** the experiencing or having (of something beneficial)

enlarge verb **1** to make larger **2** **enlarge on** to say much or more about something

enlargement noun **1** an increase in size **2** a larger photograph made from a smaller one **3** maths a transformation that produces a larger figure with its dimensions in the same ratio (compare with: **reflection**, **rotation**, **translation**)

enlighten verb **1** to give more knowledge or information to **2** to correct the false beliefs of

enlightenment noun **1** new understanding or awareness **2** (**The Enlightenment**) a European philosophical movement of the 18th century, which believed in human progress and questioned tradition and authority

enlist verb **1** to join an army etc **2** to obtain the support and help of

enliven verb to make more active or cheerful

en masse (pronounced on **mas**) adverb all together, in a body

enmity noun hostility

enormity noun **1** hugeness **2** extreme wickedness

enormous adjective very large

enormously adverb **1** very greatly, a great deal: enjoy yourself enormously **2** extremely: enormously confident

enough adjective & pronoun (in) the number or amount wanted or needed: I have enough coins/ Do you have enough money? ➤ adverb as much as is wanted or necessary: She's been there often enough to know the way

enquire see **inquire**

enquiring see **inquiring**

enquiry see **inquiry**

enrage verb to make angry

enrich verb **1** to make something richer in quality or value **2** to make more wealthy ♦ **enriched** adjective

enrol or **enroll** verb (**enrolling, enrolled**) to enter (a name) in a register or list, eg as a member or student ♦ **enrolment** noun

en route (pronounced on **root**) adverb on the way

ensconce verb: **ensconce yourself** to settle yourself comfortably

ensemble noun **1** the parts of a thing taken together **2** an outfit of clothes **3** a group of musicians

enshrine verb **1** to enter and protect (a right, idea, etc) in the laws of a state, constitution of an organization, etc **2** to treat as sacred, cherish

ensign noun **1** the flag of a nation, regiment, etc **2** history a young officer who carried the flag

enslave verb to make a slave of

ensue verb **1** to follow, come after **2** to result (from)

en suite adverb & adjective forming a single unit or set: an en suite bathroom ➤ noun an en suite bathroom ◐ Comes from French, meaning 'in sequence'

ensure verb to make sure

! Do not confuse with: **insure**

entail verb **1** to bring as a result, involve: The job entailed extra work **2** to leave land so that the heir cannot sell any part of it

entangle verb **1** to make tangled or complicated **2** to involve (in difficulties) ♦ **entanglement** noun

entente (pronounced on-**tont**) noun a friendly agreement or relationship between countries

entente cordiale (pronounced on-**tont** kawrd-ee-**al**) noun a friendly agreement made between Britain and France in 1904 ◐ Comes from French, meaning 'cordial understanding'

Entente powers see **Triple Entente**

enter verb **1** to go or come in or into **2** to put (a name etc) on to a list **3** to take part (in) **4** to begin (on) **5** computing to send (an instruction etc) to a processor ➤ noun an enter key on a computer keyboard

enteric *adjective, anatomy* to do with the intestines

enteritis *noun, medicine* inflammation of the intestines, especially the small intestine

enter key *noun, computing* a key on a computer keyboard that you press to end a line of text or carry out a command (*also called:* **return**)

enterovirus *noun, medicine* a virus infecting the intestine

enterprise *noun* **1** an undertaking, especially if risky or difficult **2** boldness in trying new things **3** a business concern

enterprise zone *noun* an economically depressed area in which the government encourages companies to invest by giving them financial incentives to do so

enterprising *adjective* inventive, clever, original, go-ahead

entertain *verb* **1** to amuse **2** to receive as a guest **3** to give a party **4** to consider (eg a suggestion) **5** to hold in the mind: *entertain a belief*

entertainer *noun* someone who entertains professionally

entertaining *adjective* amusing

entertainment *noun* **1** performances and activities that amuse and interest people **2** a performance or activity organized for the public

enthral *verb* (**enthralling, enthralled**) to hold the attention or give great delight to

enthralpy *noun, chemistry* the amount of heat energy a substance has per unit mass

enthuse *verb* to be enthusiastic (about)

enthusiasm *noun* great interest and keenness

enthusiast *noun* someone who is very keen on a certain activity

enthusiastic *adjective* greatly interested, very keen ♦ **enthusiastically** *adverb*

entice *verb* to attract with promises, rewards, etc

enticement *noun* a bribe, an attractive promise

enticing *adjective* very attractive and tempting

entire *adjective* whole, complete

entirely *adverb* utterly, wholly, fully, absolutely

entirety *noun* whole and complete state

entitle *verb* **1** to give a name to (a book etc) **2** to give (someone) a right to ♦ **entitlement** *noun*

entity *noun* (*plural* **entities**) something which exists; a being

entomology *noun* the study of insects ♦ **entomologist** *noun*

entourage (*pronounced* **ong**-too-rahsz) *noun* a group of followers or assistants accompanying a famous or important person

entrails *plural noun* the inner parts of an animal's body, the bowels

entrance[1] (*pronounced* **en**-trans) *noun* **1** a place for entering, eg a door **2** the act of coming in **3** the right to enter

entrance[2] (*pronounced* in-**trahns**) *verb* **1** to delight, charm **2** to bewitch ♦ **entrancing** *adjective*

entrant *noun* someone who goes in for a race, competition, etc

entreat *verb* to ask earnestly; to beg

entreaty *noun* (*plural* **entreaties**) an earnest request or plea

entrenched *adjective* **1** firmly established **2** unmoving, inflexible

entrepreneur (*pronounced* on-tre-pre-**ner**) *noun* someone who undertakes an enterprise, often involving financial risk

entrepreneurial (*pronounced* ong-tre-pre-**ner**-i-al or ong-tre-pre-**nyoo**-ri-al) *adjective* of an entrepreneur

entropy *noun, physics* a measure of the amount of energy in a system that is unavailable for doing work ♦ **entropic** *adjective*

entrust or **intrust** *verb* to place in someone else's care

entry *noun* (*plural* **entries**) **1** the act of entering **2** a place for entering, a doorway **3** a name or item in a record book

entry-level *adjective* of a job: suitable for someone with no previous experience who is seeking to make a career in that industry

entwine *verb* to wind or twist (two or more things) together

E-number *noun* an identification code for food additives, eg E102 for tartrazine

enumerate *verb* **1** to count **2** to mention individually ♦ **enumeration** *noun*

enunciate *verb* **1** to pronounce distinctly **2** to state formally ♦ **enunciation** *noun*

envelop (*pronounced* in-**vel**-op) *verb* **1** to cover by wrapping **2** to surround entirely: *enveloped in mist*

envelope *noun* **1** a sealable paper cover, especially for a letter **2** any wrapper or cover **3** *biology* a plant or animal structure that contains or encloses something

enviable *adjective* worth envying, worth having

envious *adjective* feeling envy ♦ **enviously** *adverb*

environment *noun* **1** the particular surroundings, circumstances, etc in which a person or an animal lives **2** the natural features which make up the earth, eg land, plants, animals, water, etc ♦ **environmental** *adjective*

environmental audit *noun* an investigation into the extent to which an organization's activities pollute the environment

environmentalist *noun* someone who is concerned about the harmful effects of human activity on the environment ♦ **environmentalism** *noun*

environmentally sensitive area *noun, Brit* (*abbrev* **ESA**) an area recognized by the government as having a landscape, wildlife or historic feature of national importance

environs (*pronounced* in-**vai**-ronz) *plural noun* surrounding area, neighbourhood

envisage *verb* **1** to visualize, picture in the mind **2** to consider, contemplate

envoy (*pronounced* **en**-voi) *noun* a messenger, especially one sent to deal with a foreign government

envy *noun* (*plural* **envies**) greedy desire for someone else's property, qualities, etc ➤ *verb* (**envies, envying, envied**) to feel envy for

enzyme *noun, biology, chemistry* a specialized molecule which acts as a catalyst for chemical reactions in living cells

Eocene *adjective* of the geological epoch 54 million to 38 million years ago

eon another spelling of **aeon**

epaulet or **epaulette** *noun* a shoulder ornament on a uniform

ephedrine *noun* a drug with similar effects to adrenaline, used to relieve hay fever and asthma

ephemeral *adjective* **1** very short-lived, fleeting **2** *biology* denoting a plant or animal that completes its life cycle within weeks, days or hours ♦ **ephemerality** *noun*

epi- or **ep-** *prefix* upon or over: *epidermis* ☉ Comes from Greek *epi* meaning 'on' or 'over'

epic *noun* a long poem, story, film, etc about heroic deeds ➤ *adjective* **1** of an epic; heroic **2** large-scale, impressive

epicene *noun* common to both sexes

epicentre or *US* **epicenter** *noun* the point on the earth's surface directly over the point of origin of an earthquake

epicure *noun* a person who appreciates fine food and drink ♦ **epicurean** *adjective*

epidemic *noun* a widespread outbreak of a disease etc

epidemiology (*pronounced* ep-i-deem-i-**awl**-lodj-i) *noun, biology* the study of the distribution, effects and causes of diseases in populations ♦ **epidemiological** *adjective* ♦ **epidemiologist** *noun*

epidermis *noun* the top covering of the skin ♦ **epidermal** or **epidermic** *adjective*

epididymis *noun* (*plural* **epididymides**) *biology* a coiled tube in the testis that stores sperm and carries it to the vas deferens

epidural *noun* (*short for* **epidural anaesthetic**) the injection of anaesthetic into the spine to ease pain in the lower half of the body, especially during childbirth

epiglottis *noun, anatomy* the flap of cartilage at the back of the tongue which closes the windpipe during swallowing

epigram *noun* a short, witty saying ♦ **epigrammatic** *adjective*

epilate *verb* to remove (hair) by any method ♦ **epilation** *noun*

epilepsy *noun, medicine* a disorder of the nervous system causing attacks of unconsciousness and convulsions

epileptic *adjective* **1** suffering from epilepsy **2** of epilepsy: *an epileptic fit* ➤ *noun* someone suffering from epilepsy

epilogue or *US* **epilog** *noun* **1** the very end part of a book, programme, etc **2** a speech at the end of a play

epiphany *noun* **1** (**Epiphany**) a Christian festival celebrated on 6 January commemorating the showing of Christ to the three wise men **2** a sudden revelation or insight

episcopacy *noun* **1** church government by bishops **2** the position or period of office of a bishop

episcopal *adjective* of or ruled by bishops

episcopalian *adjective* belonging to a church ruled by bishops

episode *noun* **1** one of several parts of a story etc **2** an interesting event

episodic *adjective* happening at irregular intervals

epistle *noun* a formal letter, especially one from an apostle of Christ in the Bible

epistolary *adjective* written in the form of letters: *an epistolary novel*

epitaph *noun* words on a gravestone about a dead person

epithelium *noun* (*plural* **epithelia**), *anatomy* a layer of tissue covering the external surfaces of the body, and lining all hollow structures apart from blood vessels and lymph vessels ♦ **epithelial** *adjective*

epithet *noun* a word used to describe someone; an adjective

epitome (*pronounced* i-**pit**-om-i) *noun* **1** a perfect example or representative of something: *the epitome of good taste* **2** a summary of a book etc

epitomize or **epitomise** *verb* to be the epitome of something

epoch (*pronounced* **eep**-ok) *noun* an extended period of time, often marked by a series of important events ♦ **epochal** (*pronounced* **ep**-ok-al) *adjective*

epoch-making *adjective* marking an important point in history

eponymous *adjective* of a character in a story, film, etc: having the same name as the title: *the eponymous heroine of 'Harriet the Spy'*

EPOS (*pronounced* **ee**-pos) *abbreviation* electronic point of sale

EPROM (*pronounced* **eep**-rom) *abbreviation,*

computing erasable programmable read-only memory, a special kind of memory in which stored data can be erased and reprogrammed

equ- *prefix* of or relating to horses: *equine/equestrian* ⏱ Comes from Latin *equus* meaning 'horse'

equable *adjective* **1** of calm temper **2** of climate: neither very hot nor very cold

equal *adjective* **1** of the same size, value, quantity, etc **2** evenly balanced **3** (**equal to**) able, fit for: *not equal to the job* ➤ *noun* someone of the same rank, cleverness, etc as another ➤ *verb* (**equalling, equalled**) **1** to be or make equal to **2** to be the same as ♦ **equally** *adverb*

equality *noun* equal treatment for all the people in a group or society

equalize or **equalise** *verb* **1** to make equal **2** in sports such as football: to score a goal which makes your team's score the same as that of the opposing team

equalizer or **equaliser** *noun* a goal etc which draws the score in a game

equal opportunities *plural noun* the principle of equal treatment for all employees or prospective employees, irrespective of race, religion, sex, etc

equanimity *noun* evenness of temper, calmness

equate *verb* **1** to regard or treat as the same **2** to state as being equal

equation *noun* **1** a statement or belief that two things are equal **2** *maths* a statement that two expressions involving constants and variables are equal **3** *chemistry* a formula expressing a chemical reaction and the proportions of the substances involved

equator *noun* an imaginary line around the earth, halfway between the North and South Poles

⏱ From a Latin word meaning literally 'something that makes equal', because night and day are of equal length there

equatorial *adjective* on or near the equator

equerry *noun* (*plural* **equerries**) ➤ *noun* a royal attendant

equestrian *adjective* **1** of horse-riding **2** on horseback ➤ *noun* a horse-rider

equi- *prefix* equal *equidistant/equilateral* ⏱ Comes from Latin *aequus* meaning 'equal'

equidistant *adjective* equally distant ♦ **equidistance** *noun*

equilateral *adjective, maths* of a triangle or other polygon: with all sides equal (*see also:* **isosceles**)

equilibrium *noun* **1** *physics* equal balance between weights, forces, etc, so there is no

tendency to move **2** a balanced state of mind or feelings

equine *adjective* of or like a horse

equinox *noun* either of the times (about 21 March and 23 September) when the sun crosses the equator, making night and day equal in length ♦ **equinoctial** *adjective*

equip *verb* (**equipping, equipped**) to supply with everything needed for a task

equipage (*pronounced* **ek**-wip-eij) *noun* attendants, retinue

equipment *noun* a set of tools etc needed for a task; an outfit

equipoise *noun* balance

equitable *adjective* fair, just

equity *noun* **1** fairness, just dealing **2** (**Equity**) the trade union for the British acting profession

equivalent *adjective* equal in value, power, meaning, etc ➤ *noun* something that is the equal of another

equivocal *adjective* having more than one meaning; ambiguous, uncertain ♦ **equivocally** *adverb*

equivocate *verb* to use ambiguous words in order to mislead ♦ **equivocation** *noun*

Er *symbol, chemistry* erbium

era *noun* **1** a period in history: *the Jacobean era/the era of steam* **2** a division of time used in geology

eradicate *verb* to get rid of completely ♦ **eradication** *noun*

erase *verb* **1** to rub out **2** to remove ♦ **erasable** *adjective*

eraser *noun* something which erases, a rubber

erasure *noun* **1** a letter or word that has been rubbed out **2** the complete removal or destruction of something

erbium *noun, chemistry* (symbol **Er**) a soft silvery metallic element that is highly resistant to electricity

⏱ The name comes from *Ytterby* in Sweden, where it was first discovered

ere *preposition & conjunction, poetic* before: *ere long*

erect *verb* **1** to build **2** to set upright ➤ *adjective* **1** standing straight up **2** of the penis, clitoris or nipples: enlarged and rigid through swelling with blood, usually as a result of sexual excitement

erectile *adjective, physiology* of an organ of the body etc: capable of becoming erect

erection *noun* **1** the act of erecting **2** something erected or erect **3** a man's penis when it becomes enlarged and rigid as a result of sexual excitement

ergonomics *singular noun* the study of the relationship between people and their working environment, including machinery, computer systems, etc ♦ **ergonomic** *adjective* ℗ Comes from Greek *ergon* meaning 'work'

ermine (*pronounced* **er**-min) *noun* **1** a stoat **2** its white fur

℗ From *Armenia*, because the ermine was known to the Romans as the 'Armenian mouse'

erode *verb* to wear away, destroy gradually

erogenous *adjective* of areas of the body, usually called **erogenous zones**: sensitive to sexual stimulation ℗ Comes from Greek *eros* meaning 'love'

erosion *noun* **1** a gradual destruction: *the erosion of my confidence* **2** *geography* the gradual wearing away of land by water, wind, ice, etc

erotic *adjective* of or arousing sexual desire

erotica *plural noun* erotic art or literature

err *verb* **1** to make a mistake **2** to sin

errand *noun* a short journey to carry a message, buy something, etc

errant *adjective* **1** doing wrong **2** *old* wandering in search of adventure: *knight errant*

erratic *adjective* **1** irregular, not following a fixed course **2** not steady or reliable in behaviour ➤ *noun, geography* a mass of rock transported by ice and deposited elsewhere ♦ **erratically** *adverb*

erroneous *adjective* wrong, mistaken ♦ **erroneously** *adverb*

error *noun* **1** a mistake **2** wrongdoing **3** *maths* the difference between an estimate or calculation of a quantity and the true value

ersatz (*pronounced* **er**-zats) *adjective* substitute; imitation ℗ Comes from German *ersetzen* meaning 'to substitute'

erudite *adjective* well-educated or well-read, learned ♦ **erudition** *noun*

erupt *verb* to break out or through

eruption *noun* **1** an outburst from a volcano **2** a rash or spot on the skin

erythrocyte (*pronounced* e-**rith**-roh-sait) *noun, biology* a red blood corpuscle

Es *symbol, chemistry* einsteinium

escalate *verb* to increase in amount, intensity, etc ♦ **escalation** *noun*

escalator *noun* a moving stairway

escalope *noun* a thin slice of boneless meat, eg veal or turkey

escapade *noun* an adventure

escape *verb* **1** to get away safe or free **2** of gas etc: to leak **3** to slip from memory: *His name escapes me* ➤ *noun* the act of escaping

escapee *noun* someone who has escaped, especially from prison

escape key *noun, computing* a function key on some keyboards, used to cancel commands, leave a program, etc

escape velocity *noun, physics* the minimum velocity needed to escape from the gravitational field of a body such as the earth

escapism *noun* the tendency to escape from reality by daydreaming etc ♦ **escapist** *noun & adjective*

escarpment *noun* a steep side of a hill or rock (*also called*: **scarp**)

eschew *verb, formal* to avoid, keep away from, or abstain from something

escort *noun* someone who accompanies others for protection, courtesy, etc ➤ *verb* to act as escort to

Eskimo *noun* (*plural* **Eskimos**) Inuit

℗ Based on a Native American name meaning 'eaters of raw flesh'

ⓘ Although Eskimo is the established name in English, the people themselves prefer the name **Inuit**.

esoteric (*pronounced* ees-oh-**ter**-ik) *adjective* understood only by the few people with the necessary special knowledge; secret or mysterious

ESP *abbreviation* extrasensory perception, the supposed ability to perceive things without the normal senses, eg what someone is thinking or what will happen in the future

espadrille *noun* a light canvas shoe with a sole made of rope or other plaited fibre

especial *adjective* **1** special, extraordinary **2** particular

especially *adverb* particularly

❗ Do not confuse with: **specially**.
Especially means 'particularly, above all':
I like making cakes, especially for birthdays.
Specially means 'for a special purpose':
I made this cake specially for your birthday.

Esperanto *noun* an international language created in the 19th century

espionage *noun* spying, especially by one country to find out the secrets of another

esplanade *noun* a level roadway, especially along a seafront

espouse *verb* to adopt, embrace (a cause)

espresso *noun* strong coffee made by extraction under high pressure

espy (*pronounced* es-**pai**) *verb, old* to watch, observe

Esq *abbreviation* or **Esquire** *noun* a courtesy title written after a man's name: *Robert Brown, Esq*

essay *noun* (*pronounced* **es**-ei) **1** a written

composition **2** an attempt ➤ *verb* (*pronounced* es-**ei**) to try

essence *noun* **1** the most important part or quality of something **2** a concentrated extract from a plant etc: *vanilla essence*

essential *adjective* absolutely necessary ➤ *noun* an absolute requirement

essentially *adverb* **1** basically **2** necessarily

essential oil *noun* a mixture of oils with distinctive, characteristic odours, obtained from aromatic plants, used to make perfumes and in aromatherapy

establish *verb* **1** to settle in position **2** to found, set up **3** to show to be true, prove (that)

established *adjective* **1** firmly set up **2** accepted, recognized **3** of a church: officially recognized as national

establishment *noun* **1** a place of business, residence, etc **2** (**The Establishment**) the people holding influential positions in a community

estate *noun* **1** a large piece of private land **2** someone's total possessions **3** land built on with houses, factories, etc: *housing estate/industrial estate*

estate agent *noun* someone who sells and leases property for clients

estate car *noun* a car with an inside luggage compartment and a rear door

esteem *verb* to think highly of; value ➤ *noun* high value or opinion

esteemed *adjective* respected, valued

ester *noun, chemistry* an organic chemical compound formed by the reaction of an alcohol with an organic acid

estimate *verb* (*pronounced* es-tim-eit) to judge roughly the size, amount or value of something ➤ *noun* (*pronounced* es-tim-at) a rough judgement of size etc

estimation *noun* opinion, judgement

estranged *adjective* no longer friendly; separated

estuary *noun* (*plural* **estuaries**) the wide lower part of a river, up which the tide travels

etc or **&c** *abbreviation* and other things of the same sort ☉ from Latin *et cetera*

etch *verb* to draw on metal or glass by eating out the lines with acid

etching *noun* a picture printed from an etched metal plate

eternal *adjective* **1** lasting for ever **2** seemingly endless

eternally *adverb* for ever

eternity *noun* **1** time without end **2** the time or state after death

ethanal another word for **acetaldehyde**

ethane *noun, chemistry* a colourless odourless flammable gas found in natural gas

ethanoic acid same as **acetic acid**

ethanol *noun, chemistry* a colourless flammable compound used in alcoholic drinks

ethene another word for **ethylene**

ether *noun* a colourless liquid used as an anaesthetic, or to dissolve fats

ethereal (*pronounced* i-**theer**-ri-al) *adjective* delicate, airy, spirit-like ✦ **ethereality** *noun* ✦ **ethereally** *adverb*

Ethernet *noun, computing* a system for networking computers

ethical *adjective* having to do with right behaviour, justice, duty; right, just, honourable ✦ **ethically** *adverb*

ethics *singular noun* **1** the study of right and wrong **2** (belief in) standards leading to right, ethical behaviour

ethnic *adjective* **1** of race or culture **2** of the culture of a particular race or group ✦ **ethnically** *adverb*

ethnic cleansing *noun* the removal of the members of less powerful ethnic groups by the most powerful ethnic group living in an area

ethnicity *noun* racial or cultural character

ethnic minority *noun* a section of a society belonging to a different racial group than the majority

ethnocentric *adjective* believing in the superiority of your own culture ✦ **ethnocentrism** *noun*

ethnocide *noun* the extermination of a racial or cultural group

ethnology *noun* the study of human cultures and civilizations ✦ **ethnological** *adjective* ✦ **ethnologist** *noun*

ethology *noun* the study of animal behaviour, especially in their natural habitats

ethos *noun* the typical spirit, character or attitudes of a group or community

ethyl *noun, chemistry* in organic compounds: the C_2H_5- group

ethylene *noun, chemistry* a colourless flammable gas with a sweet smell (*also called*: **ethene**)

ethyne another word for **acetylene**

etiolated *adjective* of a plant: yellow through lack of sunlight ✦ **etiolation** *noun*

etiquette *noun* rules governing correct social behaviour

etymology *noun* (*plural* **etymologies**) **1** the study of the history of words **2** the history of a word ✦ **etymological** *adjective*

EU *abbreviation* European Union

Eu *symbol, chemistry* europium

eucalyptus *noun* (*plural* **eucalyptuses** or **eucalypti**) a large Australian evergreen tree whose leaves produce a pungent oil

Eucharist *noun* **1** the Christian sacrament of the

Lord's Supper **2** bread and wine etc taken as a sacrament

eukaryote *noun, biology* an organism in which the cells have a distinct nucleus containing the genetic material and separated from the cytoplasm by a nuclear membrane ✦ **eukaryotic** *adjective*

eulogize or **eulogise** *verb* to praise greatly

eulogy *noun* (*plural* **eulogies**) a speech, poem, etc in praise of someone

eunuch (*pronounced* **yoo**-nuk) *noun* a castrated man

euphemism (*pronounced* **yoof**-e-mizm) *noun* a vague word or phrase used to refer to an unpleasant subject, eg 'passed on' for 'died' ✦ **euphemistic** *adjective*

euphonium *noun* a brass musical instrument with a low tone

euphoria *noun* a feeling of great happiness, joy ✦ **euphoric** *adjective*

Euro- *prefix* of Europe or the European community: *Euro-budget/Eurocrat*

euro *noun* the unit of currency of some members of the European Union, made up of 100 cents

European Parliament *noun* a legislative body forming laws that apply to members of the European Union

European Union *noun* (*abbrev* **EU**) an economic and political association of European states

europium *noun, chemistry* (symbol **Eu**) a soft silvery metallic element of the lanthanide series

> ⊙ Named after *Europe*

Eurosceptic *noun & adjective, Brit* (someone) opposed to strengthening the powers of the European Union

Eustachian tube *noun, anatomy* a tube connecting the middle ear with the pharynx, and which equalizes the pressure on either side of the eardrum

> ⊙ Named after the Italian anatomist B *Eustachio* (died 1574)

eustatic adjustment *noun, geography* changes in shoreline levels, probably caused by the rise or fall of the sea level and not by changes in land levels (*compare with*: **isostatic adjustment**)

euthanasia *noun* the killing of someone painlessly, especially to end suffering ⊙ Comes from Greek, from *eu-* meaning 'good' + *thanatos* meaning 'death'

eutrophication *noun, geography* the process by which a body of water becomes over-enriched with nutrients, from sewage, agricultural fertilizers, etc, resulting in

overgrowth of algae and depleted oxygen levels, and the death of aquatic animals ✦ **eutrophic** *adjective*

evacuate *verb* **1** to (cause to) leave, especially because of danger **2** to empty (the bowels) **3** *physics* to create a vacuum in (a vessel) ✦ **evacuation** *noun*

evacuee *noun* someone who has been evacuated (from danger)

evade *verb* to avoid or escape, especially by cleverness or trickery

evaluate *verb* to find or state the value or worth of ✦ **evaluation** *noun*

evangelical *adjective* **1** of Christian groups: stressing the authority of the Bible **2** strongly supporting and speaking for some cause

evangelist *noun* **1** a person who spreads Christian teaching **2** (**Evangelist**) an author of a Gospel, especially Matthew, Mark, Luke or John **3** a person who supports and speaks for some cause ✦ **evangelism** *noun* ✦ **evangelistic** *adjective*

evaporate *verb* **1** of water: to change into vapour **2** to vanish ✦ **evaporation** *noun*

evapotranspiration *noun, geography* the loss of water from the earth's surface to the atmosphere as a result of evaporation and transpiration from plants

evasion *noun* **1** the act of evading **2** an attempt to avoid the point of an argument or accusation

evasive *adjective* with the purpose of evading; not straightforward: *an evasive answer*

eve *noun* **1** the evening or day before a festival: *New Year's Eve* **2** the time just before an event: *the eve of the revolution*

even *adjective* **1** level, smooth **2** equal **3** of a number: able to be divided by 2 without a remainder (*contrasted with*: **odd**) **4** calm ➤ *adverb* **1** used to emphasize another word: *even harder than before/even a child would understand* **2** exactly, just ➤ *verb* to make even or smooth • **even out** to become equal • **get even with** to get revenge on

even-handed *adverb* fair, unbiased

evening *noun* the last part of the day and early part of the night

evenly *adverb* **1** levelly, smoothly **2** equally **3** calmly

evenness *noun* the quality of being even

evensong *noun* an evening service in the Anglican church

event *noun* **1** anything which happens, an occurrence **2** an important or memorable happening **3** an item in a programme of sports etc

eventful *adjective* exciting

eventual *adjective* **1** final **2** happening as a result

eventuality *noun* (*plural* **eventualities**) a possible happening

eventually *adverb* at last, finally

ever *adverb* **1** always, for ever **2** at any time, at all: *I won't ever see her again* **3** that has existed, on record: *the best ever*

evergreen *noun* a tree with green leaves all the year round

everlasting *adjective* lasting for ever, eternal

evermore *adverb, old* forever

every *adjective* each of several things without exception • **every other** one out of every two, alternate

everybody or **everyone** *pronoun* each person without exception

everyday *adjective* **1** daily **2** common, usual

everything *pronoun* all things

everywhere *adverb* in every place

evict *verb* to force (someone) out of their house, especially by law ◆ **eviction** *noun*

evidence *noun* **1** a clear sign; proof **2** information given in a law case

evident *adjective* easily seen or understood

evidently *adverb* seemingly, obviously

evil *adjective* wicked, very bad; malicious ➤ *noun* wickedness ◆ **evilly** *adverb*

eviscerate *verb* to tear out the bowels of a person or animal; to gut ◆ **evisceration** *noun*

evocative *adjective* evoking memories or atmosphere

evoke *verb* to draw out, produce: *evoking memories of their childhood*

evolution *noun* **1** gradual development **2** *biology* changes in the characteristics of living organisms from generation to generation, resulting in the development of new types of organism over long periods of time ◆ **evolutionary** *adjective*

evolve *verb* **1** to develop gradually **2** to work out (a plan etc) **3** *chemistry* to give off (heat etc)

ewe *noun* a female sheep

ewer *noun* a large jug with a wide spout

ex *noun, informal* a former husband, wife or lover

ex- *prefix* **1** no longer, former: *ex-husband/ex-president* **2** outside, not in: *ex-directory number* ⊙ Comes from Latin *ex* meaning 'out of' or 'from'

exacerbate *verb* to make worse or more severe ⊙ Comes from Latin *acerbare* meaning 'to embitter'

! Do not confuse with: **exasperate**

exact *adjective* **1** accurate, precise **2** punctual **3** careful ➤ *verb* to compel to pay, give, etc: *exacting revenge*

exacting *adjective* **1** asking too much **2** wearying, tiring

exactly *adverb* **1** precisely **2** as a reply to something someone has said: 'that's right' or 'I agree'

exactness *noun* accuracy, correctness

exaggerate *verb* to make (something) seem larger or greater than it really is ◆ **exaggeration** *noun*

exalt *verb* **1** to raise in rank **2** to praise **3** to make joyful

exaltation *noun* **1** joy **2** the act of praising and glorifying someone or something

exam *noun* an examination

examination *noun* **1** a formal test of knowledge or skill **2** an inspection of someone's health by a doctor **3** a close inspection or inquiry **4** formal questioning

examine *verb* **1** to put questions to (pupils etc) to test knowledge **2** to question (a witness) **3** to look at closely, inquire into **4** to look over (someone's body) for signs of illness ◆ **examiner** *noun* (meaning 1)

example *noun* **1** something taken as a representative of its kind: *an example of an early computer game* **2** a warning: *make an example of someone*

exasperate *verb* to make very angry ◆ **exasperation** *noun* ⊙ Comes from Latin *asperare* meaning 'to make rough'

! Do not confuse with: **exacerbate**

excavate *verb* **1** to dig, scoop out **2** to uncover by digging

excavation *noun* **1** the act of digging out **2** a hollow made by digging

excavator *noun* a machine used for excavating

exceed *verb* to go beyond, be greater than ⊙ Comes from Latin *ex-* meaning 'beyond', and *cedere* meaning 'to go'

exceedingly *adverb* very

excel *verb* (**excelling, excelled**) **1** to do very well **2** to be better than

excellence *noun* the fact of being excellent, very high quality

Excellency *noun* (*plural* **Excellencies**) a title of ambassadors etc

excellent *adjective* unusually or extremely good

except *preposition* leaving out, not counting ➤ *conjunction* with the exception (that) ➤ *verb* to leave out, not to count • **except for** with the exception of

excepting *preposition* except

exception *noun* **1** something left out **2** something unlike the rest: *an exception to the rule* • **take exception to** to object to, be offended by ⊙ Comes from Latin *exceptio* meaning 'an exception, restriction or objection'

exceptional *adjective* standing out from the rest

exceptionally *adverb* very, extremely

excerpt (*pronounced* **ek**-sert) *noun* a part chosen from a whole work: *excerpt from a play* ○ Comes from Latin *excerptum* meaning 'picked out'

● Do not confuse with: **exert**

excess *noun* (*pronounced* ik-**ses**) **1** a going beyond what is usual or proper **2** the amount by which one thing is greater than another **3** (**excesses**) very bad behaviour ➤ *adjective* (*pronounced* **ek**-ses) beyond the amount allowed ○ For origin, see **exceed**

● Do not confuse with: **access**

excessive *adjective* too much, too great, etc ◆ **excessively** *adverb*

exchange *verb* to give (one thing) and get another in return ➤ *noun* **1** the act of exchanging **2** exchanging money of one country for that of another **3** the difference between the value of money in different places: *rate of exchange* **4** a central office or building: *telephone exchange* **5** a place where business shares are bought and sold

exchequer *noun* a government office concerned with a country's finances
• **Chancellor of the Exchequer** see **chancellor**

○ From the chequered cloth formerly used on the tables of tax offices, and on which accounts were recorded

excise[1] *verb* to cut off or out ◆ **excision** *noun*

excise[2] *noun* tax on goods etc made and sold within a country and on certain licences etc

excitable *adjective* easily excited

excite *verb* **1** to make (someone) feel pleasant expectation or thrill **2** to rouse the feelings of **3** to move to action **4** *physics* to raise (a nucleus, atom or molecule) to a higher energy level

excited *adjective* **1** unable to be calm because of extreme feelings of happiness, impatience or arousal **2** in a state of great activity **3** *physics* (of a molecule etc): having higher energy than that of the ground state ◆ **excitedly** *adverb*

excitement *noun* the state of being excited

exciting *adjective* creating feelings of excitement

excitor *noun, anatomy* a nerve that brings impulses to the brain to stimulate a part of the body

exclaim *verb* to cry or shout out

exclamation *noun* a sudden shout

exclamation mark *noun* a punctuation mark (!) used for emphasis, or to indicate surprise etc

exclamatory (*pronounced* iks-**klam**-at-ri) *adjective* exclaiming, emphatic

exclude *verb* **1** to shut out **2** to prevent from sharing or taking part: *He was excluded from school* **3** to leave out of consideration ◆ **exclusion** *noun*

excluding *preposition* not including or counting

exclusive *adjective* **1** only open to certain people, select: *an exclusive club* **2** not obtainable elsewhere: *exclusive offer* **3** (**exclusive of**) not including

excommunicate *verb* to expel from membership of a church ◆ **excommunication** *noun*

excrement *noun* the waste matter passed out of the body by humans or animals

excrescence *noun* an unwelcome growth, eg a wart

excreta *plural noun* discharged waste products

excrete *verb* to discharge (waste matter) from the body ◆ **excretion** *noun*

excruciating *adjective* **1** of pain etc: very severe **2** painfully bad: *an excruciating performance*

exculpate *verb* to absolve from a crime; vindicate ◆ **exculpation** *noun* ◆ **exculpatory** *adjective*

excursion *noun* an outing for pleasure, eg a picnic

excusable *adjective* pardonable

excuse *verb* (*pronounced* eks-**kyooz**) **1** to forgive, pardon **2** to set free from a duty or task ➤ *noun* (*pronounced* eks-**kyoos**) an explanation for having done something wrong

execrable *adjective* very bad

execrate *verb* to curse, denounce

executable *verb* **1** able to be executed **2** *computing* able to be run by computer: *executable file* ➤ *noun, computing* an executable file or program

execute *verb* **1** to perform: *execute a dance step* **2** to carry out: *execute instructions* **3** to put to death legally

execution *noun* **1** a doing or performing: *execution of a duty* **2** killing by order of the law

executioner *noun* someone with the job of putting condemned prisoners to death

executive *adjective* having power to act or carry out laws ➤ *noun* **1** the part of a government with such power **2** a business manager

executor *noun* someone who sees that the requests stated in a will are carried out

exemplary *adjective* **1** worth following as an example: *exemplary conduct* **2** acting as a warning: *exemplary punishment*

exemplify *verb* (**exemplifies, exemplifying, exemplified**) **1** to be an example of **2** to demonstrate by example

exempt *verb* to grant freedom from an

unwelcome task, payment, etc ➤ *adjective* free (from), not liable for payment, etc ✦ **exemption** *noun*

exercise *noun* **1** a task for practice **2** a physical routine for training muscles etc ➤ *verb* **1** to give exercise to **2** to use: *exercise great care* ☉ Comes from Latin *exercere* meaning 'to make thoroughly effective'

⚠ Do not confuse with: **exorcize**

exert *verb* to bring into action, use: *exerting great influence* • **exert yourself** to make a great effort ☉ Comes from Latin *exsert-*, a form of *exserere* meaning 'to thrust out'

⚠ Do not confuse with: **excerpt**

exertion ➤ *noun* or **exertions** ➤ *plural noun* effort(s); hard work

exeunt *verb* of more than one person: leave the stage (a direction printed in the script of a play): *exeunt Rosencrantz and Guildenstern*

exfoliate *verb* to rub the skin with an abrasive substance in order to remove dead cells
✦ **exfoliation** *noun* ✦ **exfoliative** *adjective* ☉ Comes from Latin *exfoliare* meaning 'to strip of leaves'

ex gratia (*pronounced* eks **grei**-shi-a) *adjective & adverb* given as a favour and not in recognition of any obligation: *an ex gratia payment*

exhale *verb* to breathe out ✦ **exhalation** *noun*

exhaust *verb* **1** to tire out **2** to use up completely: *We've exhausted our supplies* **3** to say all that can be said about (a subject etc)
➤ *noun* a device for expelling waste fumes from internal combustion engines

exhausted *adjective* **1** tired out **2** emptied; used up ✦ **exhaustion** *noun*

exhaustive *adjective* extremely thorough: *exhaustive research* ✦ **exhaustively** *adverb*

exhibit *verb* to show; put on public display
➤ *noun* something on display in a gallery etc

exhibition *noun* a public show, an open display

exhibitionism *noun* a tendency to try to attract people's attention

exhibitionist *noun* someone who tries to get people's attention all the time, a show-off

exhibitor *noun* a person who has presented something belonging to them for display at an exhibition

exhilarate *verb* to make joyful or lively, refresh
✦ **exhilarating** *adjective* ✦ **exhilaration** *noun*

exhort *verb* to urge (to do) ✦ **exhortation** *noun*

exhume *verb* to dig out (a buried body)
✦ **exhumation** *noun*

exile *noun* **1** someone who lives outside their own country, by choice or unwillingly **2** a period of living in a foreign country ➤ *verb* to drive

(someone) away from their own country; banish

exist *verb* **1** to be, have life; live **2** to live in poor circumstances

existence *noun* life, being

existent *adjective* existing at the moment

existentialism *noun* a philosophy that emphasizes freedom of choice and responsibility for one's own actions, which create one's own moral values and determine one's future ✦ **existentialist** *adjective & noun*

exit *noun* **1** a way out **2** the act of going out: *a hasty exit*

exocrine *adjective, biology* of a gland, eg a sweat gland: discharging its secretions through a duct (*see also*: **endocrine**) ✦ **exocrinal** or **exocrinic** *adjective*

exodus *noun* a going away of many people (especially those leaving a country for ever)

exon *noun, genetics* a segment of DNA in a gene that is transcribed onto messenger RNA and then into protein

exonerate *verb* to free from blame
✦ **exoneration** *noun*

exorbitant *adjective* going beyond what is usual or reasonable: *exorbitant price*
✦ **exorbitance** *noun*

exorcism *noun* the act of driving away evil spirits

exorcist *noun* a person who drives evil spirits away

exorcize or **exorcise** *verb* **1** to drive out (an evil spirit) **2** to free (a place, person) from possession by an evil spirit ☉ Comes from Greek *ex* meaning 'out', and *horkos* meaning 'an oath'

⚠ Do not confuse with: **exercise**

exoskeleton *noun* in some invertebrates: an external skeleton that forms a rigid covering

exothermic *adjective, chemistry* of a process, especially a reaction: involving the release of heat (*contrasted with*: **endothermic**)

exotic *adjective* **1** coming from a foreign country **2** unusual, colourful

expand *verb* **1** to grow wider or bigger **2** to open out **3** *maths* to multiply out (terms in brackets)

expanse *noun* a wide stretch of land etc

expansion *noun* **1** a growing, stretching or spreading **2** *maths* the result of multiplying out terms in brackets

expansion card or **expansion board** *noun, computing* a printed circuit board which can be inserted into a computer to add extra facilities

expansionism *noun* the practice of gaining territory or political influence, usually at the expense of other nations or bodies
✦ **expansionist** *noun & adjective*

expansion slot *noun, computing* a connector

for an expansion card on the motherboard of a computer

expansive *adjective* **1** spreading out **2** talkative; open and eager to talk ◆ **expansively** *adverb*

expat *noun, informal* an expatriate

expatriate *adjective* living outside your native country ➤ *noun* someone living abroad

expect *verb* **1** to think of as likely to happen or arrive soon: *What did you expect her to say?* **2** to think, assume: *I expect he's too busy*

expectancy *noun* the feeling of excitement that you get when you know something good is about to happen

expectant *adjective* **1** hopeful, expecting **2** waiting to become: *expectant mother*

expectation *noun* a firm belief or hope that something will happen

expecting *adjective, informal* pregnant

expedience or **expediency** *noun* speed or convenience in a particular situation, rather than fairness or truth

expedient *adjective* done for speed or convenience rather than fairness or truth ➤ *noun* something done to get round a difficulty

expedite *verb* to hasten, hurry on

expedition *noun* **1** a journey with a purpose, often for exploration **2** people making such a journey

expeditionary *adjective* of or forming an expedition

expeditious *adjective* swift, speedy ◆ **expeditiously** *adverb*

expel *verb* (**expelling, expelled**) **1** to drive or force out **2** to send away in disgrace, eg from a school

expend *verb* to spend, use up

expendable *adjective* **1** able to be given up or sacrificed for some purpose or cause **2** not worth keeping

expenditure *noun* an amount spent or used up, especially money

expense *noun* **1** cost **2** something money is spent on: *The house was a continual expense* **3** (**expenses**) money spent in carrying out a job etc

expensive *adjective* costing a lot of money ◆ **expensively** *adverb*

experience *noun* **1** an event in which you are involved: *a horrific experience* **2** knowledge gained from events, practice, etc ➤ *verb* to go through, undergo

experienced *adjective* skilled, knowledgeable

experiment *noun* a trial, a test (of an idea, machine, etc) ➤ *verb* to carry out experiments ◆ **experimentation** *noun*

experimental *adjective* of something new: being done for the first time, to see how successful it will be ◆ **experimentally** *adverb*

expert *adjective* highly skilful or knowledgeable (in a particular subject) ➤ *noun* someone who is highly skilled or knowledgeable ◆ **expertly** *adverb*

expertise (*pronounced* eks-per-**teez**) *noun* skill

expert system *noun, computing* a program designed to solve problems by using human knowledge and reasoning

expiate (*pronounced* **ek**-spi-eit) *verb* to make up for (a crime etc) ◆ **expiation** *noun*

expire *verb* **1** to come to an end, become invalid: *Your visa has expired* **2** to breathe out **3** to die ◆ **expiration** *noun*

expiry *noun* the end or finish

explain *verb* **1** to make clear **2** to give reasons for: *Please explain your behaviour*

explanation *noun* a statement which makes clear something difficult or puzzling; a reason (eg for your behaviour)

explanatory (*pronounced* eks-**plan**-at-ri) *adjective* intended to make clear

expletive *noun* an exclamation, especially a swear word

explicable *adjective* able to be explained

explicit *adjective* plainly stated or shown; outspoken, frank ◆ **explicitly** *adverb*: *I explicitly told you not to touch that!*

explode *verb* **1** to blow up like a bomb with loud noise **2** to prove to be wrong or unfounded: *That explodes your theory*

exploit *noun* (*pronounced* **eks**-ploit) a daring deed; a feat ➤ *verb* (*pronounced* eks-**ploit**) **1** to make use of selfishly **2** to make good use of (resources etc) ◆ **exploitation** *noun*

exploration *noun* **1** travel for the sake of discovery **2** the act of searching or searching for something thoroughly

exploratory (*pronounced* eks-**plo**-rat-ri) *adjective* **1** of talks etc: having the purpose of establishing procedures or ground rules **2** of surgery: aiming to establish the nature of a complaint rather than to treat it

explore *verb* **1** to make a journey of discovery **2** to think about very carefully, research ◆ **explorer** *noun* (meaning 1)

explosion *noun* **1** a sudden violent increase in pressure, which generates heat and shock waves **2** the sudden loud noise accompanying an explosion **3** a sudden outburst or surge

explosive *adjective* **1** liable to explode **2** hot-tempered ➤ *noun* something that will explode, eg gunpowder

expo *noun* (*plural* **expos**), a large public exhibition ◷ Comes from **exposition**

exponent *noun* **1** someone who shows skill in a particular art or craft: *an exponent of karate* **2** someone who explains and promotes (a particular theory or belief) **3** *maths* an upper number which shows how many times a number is multiplied by itself (eg 4^3 means $4 \times 4 \times 4$) (*also called*: **index**)

exponential *noun, maths* a function, equation, curve, etc that involves numbers raised to exponents ➤ *adjective* **1** *maths* to do with or involving numbers that are exponents **2** having an increasingly steep rate of increase
♦ **exponentially** *adverb* **1** according to an exponent, eg if $y = a^x$, then y varies exponentially with x **2** very rapidly

exponential curve *noun, maths* a curve expressed by an exponential equation in which the variable occurs in the exponent of one or more terms

exponential function *noun, maths* a quantity with a variable exponent (*also called*: **exponential**)

export *verb* (*pronounced* eks-**pawt**) **1** to sell goods etc in a foreign country **2** *computing* to send data from one computer, program, etc to another ➤ *noun* (*pronounced* **eks**-pawt) **1** an act of exporting **2** something exported
♦ **exportation** *noun*

expose *verb* **1** to place in full view **2** to show up (a hidden crime etc) **3** to lay open to the sun or wind **4** to allow light to reach and act on (a film)

exposé (*pronounced* ehks-**po**-zei) *noun* an article or programme that exposes a public scandal, crime, etc

exposition *noun* **1** an in-depth account **2** a large public exhibition ⊕ Comes from Latin *expositio* meaning 'a setting out'

expostulate (*pronounced* eks-**pos**-chuwl-eit) *verb* to protest ♦ **expostulation** *noun*

exposure *noun* **1** the state of being allowed to experience something or be affected by something **2** appearance or mention in public, eg on television or in newspapers **3** the extremely harmful effects of severe cold on a person's body **4** the fact of revealing something about someone, usually something unpleasant, that has been kept secret **5** a single photograph or frame on a film

expound *verb* to explain fully

express *verb* **1** to show by action **2** to put into words **3** to press or squeeze out ➤ *adjective* **1** clearly stated: *express instructions* **2** sent in haste: *express messenger* ➤ *noun* a fast train, bus, etc

expression *noun* **1** the look on someone's face: *expression of horror* **2** showing meaning or emotion through language, art, etc **3** a show of emotion in an artistic performance etc **4** a word or phrase: *idiomatic expression* **5** *maths* a symbol or combination of symbols **6** pressing or squeezing out

expressive *adjective* expressing meaning or feeling clearly

expulsion *noun* **1** the act of driving or forcing a person or thing out **2** the sending away of someone in disgrace, eg from a school

expunge *verb* to rub out, remove

expurgate (*pronounced* **eks**-pu-geit) *verb* **1** to revise (a book) by removing offensive words or passages **2** to remove (offensive words or passages)

exquisite (*pronounced* **eks**-kwiz-it or iks-**kwiz**-it) *adjective* **1** extremely beautiful **2** excellent **3** very great, utter: *exquisite pleasure*

extemporize or **extemporise** (*pronounced* iks-**tem**-po-raiz) *verb* to make up on the spot, improvise

extend *verb* **1** to stretch, make longer **2** to hold out: *extended a hand* **3** to last, carry over: *My holiday extends into next week*

extended family *noun* a family unit comprising not only a couple and their children but other relatives, eg aunts, uncles and grandparents (*compare with*: **nuclear family**)

extension *noun* **1** the act of extending or state of being extended **2** a part added, eg to a building **3** an additional amount of time on a schedule, holiday, etc **4** an additional telephone connected with a main one **5** *computing* a file extension

extensive *adjective* **1** wide; covering a large space **2** happening in many places **3** wide-ranging, sweeping: *extensive changes*
♦ **extensively** *adverb*

extensor *noun, anatomy* a muscle that straightens out a part of the body (*compare with*: **flexor**)

extent *noun* **1** the space something covers **2** degree: *to a great extent*

extenuate *verb* **1** to lessen **2** to make (something) seem less bad: *extenuating circumstances* ♦ **extenuation** *noun*

exterior *adjective* on the outside; outer: *exterior wall* ➤ *noun* the outside of a building etc

exterior angle *noun, maths* the angle between any extended side and the adjacent side of a polygon

exterminate *verb* to kill off completely (a race, a type of animal, etc), wipe out
♦ **extermination** *noun*

external *adjective* **1** outside; on the outside **2** not central: *external considerations*

externalize or **externalise** *verb* to express (thoughts, feelings, etc) in words

extinct *adjective* **1** of an old volcano: no longer erupting **2** no longer in existence: *The dodo is now extinct*

extinction *noun* making or becoming extinct

extinguish *verb* **1** to put out (fire etc) **2** to put an end to

extinguisher *noun* a spray containing chemicals for putting out fires

extirpate *verb* to destroy completely, exterminate ☉ Comes from Latin *exstirpare* meaning 'to pluck up by the root'

⚠ Do not confuse with: **extricate** and **extrapolate**

extol *verb* (**extolling, extolled**) to praise greatly

extort *verb* to take by force or threats ◆ **extortion** *noun*

extortionate *adjective* of a price: much too high

extra *adjective* more than is usual or necessary; additional ➤ *adverb* unusually; more than is average: *extra large* ➤ *noun* **1** something extra **2** someone employed to be one of a crowd in a film

extra- *prefix* outside, beyond ☉ Comes from Latin *extra* meaning 'outside'

extracellular *adjective, biology* located or happening outside a cell

extract *verb* (*pronounced* eks-**trakt**) **1** to draw or pull out, especially by force: *extract a tooth* **2** to remove selected parts of a book etc **3** to draw out from a mixture by pressure or chemical action ➤ *noun* (*pronounced* **eks**-trakt) **1** an excerpt from a book etc **2** a substance obtained by extracting: *vanilla extract*

extraction *noun* **1** the act of extracting **2** someone's descent or lineage: *of Irish extraction*

extractive industry *noun* an industry such as mining, forestry, agriculture, etc which draws out natural resources and processes them for manufacturing industries

extracurricular *adjective* done outside school or college hours

extradite *verb* to hand over (someone wanted for trial) to the police of another country ◆ **extradition** *noun*

extramarital *adjective* happening outside a marriage: *extramarital affair*

extramural *adjective* of a university department: teaching courses which are not part of the regular degree courses

extraneous *adjective* having nothing to do with the subject: *extraneous information*

extranet *noun, computing* a restricted network, eg in a company, which allows some access from users outside

extraordinaire *adjective* (*placed after the noun*) outstanding in a particular skill or area: *linguist extraordinaire* ☉ Comes from French

extraordinary *adjective* **1** not usual, exceptional **2** very surprising **3** specially

employed: *ambassador extraordinary* ◆ **extraordinarily** *adverb* (meanings 1 and 2)

extrapolate *verb* **1** to take known facts and use them to infer or predict things which are beyond what is known **2** *maths* to estimate (a value outside the known values), usually by means of a graph ◆ **extrapolation** *noun*

⚠ Do not confuse with: **extirpate** and **extricate**

extrasensory *adjective* beyond the range of the ordinary senses: *extrasensory perception*

extraterrestrial *adjective* from outside the earth ➤ *noun* a being from another planet

extravagant *adjective* **1** spending too freely; wasteful **2** too great, overblown: *extravagant praise* ◆ **extravagance** *noun* ◆ **extravagantly** *adverb*

extravaganza *noun* an extravagant creation or production

extreme *adjective* **1** far from the centre **2** far from the ordinary or usual **3** very great: *extreme sadness* ➤ *noun* an extreme point

extremely *adverb* very, exceptionally

extreme sport *noun* an unconventional and dangerous sport, such as bungee jumping

extremist *noun* someone who carries ideas foolishly far ◆ **extremism** *noun*

extremity (*pronounced* eks-**trem**-it-i) *noun* (*plural* **extremities**) **1** a part or place furthest from the centre **2** the quality of being extreme **3** (**extremities**) the hands and feet

extricate *verb* to free from (difficulties etc); to disentangle ☉ Comes from Latin *extricare* meaning 'to disentangle'

⚠ Do not confuse with: **extirpate** and **extrapolate**

extrovert *noun* an outgoing, sociable person (*contrasted with*: **introvert**)

extrude *verb* to squeeze or force out

extrusive *noun, geography* of rock: formed from molten rock material such as magma or lava

exuberant *adjective* in very high spirits ◆ **exuberance** *noun* ◆ **exuberantly** *adverb*

exudate *noun, biology* **1** any substance released from a plant or animal through a gland, pore, or membrane, eg resin and sweat **2** the fluid containing proteins and white blood cells that is discharged through small pores in membranes

exude *verb* to give off in large amounts: *exuding sweat/exuded happiness*

exult *verb* to be very glad, rejoice greatly: *exulting in their victory* ◆ **exultant** *adjective* ◆ **exultation** *noun*

eye *noun* **1** the part of the body with which you see **2** the ability to notice: *an eye for detail* **3** sight **4** something the shape of an eye, eg the hole in a needle **5** the bud of a tuber such as a potato ➤ *verb* (**eyeing, eyed**) to look at with interest: *eyeing the last slice of cake*

eyeball *noun* the round part of the eye; the eye itself (the part between the eyelids)

eyebrow *noun* the hairy ridge above the eye

eye-catching *adjective* drawing attention; striking

eyelash *noun* one of the hairs on the edge of the eyelid

eyelet *noun* a small hole for a shoelace etc

eyelid *noun* the skin covering of the eye

eyeliner *noun* make-up used to outline the eyes

eye-opener *noun* an unexpected or revealing sight, experience, etc

eyeshadow *noun* coloured make-up used on the eyelids

eyesight *noun* the ability to see

eyesore *noun* anything that is ugly (especially a building)

eye tooth *noun* a canine tooth

eyewash *noun* **1** a liquid for soothing the eyes **2** *informal* nonsense; false or deceptive talk

eyewitness *noun* someone who sees a thing done (eg a crime committed)

eyrie (*pronounced* **ee**-e-ri) *noun* the nest of an eagle or other bird of prey

e-zine or **ezine** (*pronounced* **ee**-zeen) *noun, computing* a journal available only in electronic form on a computer network

Ff

F¹ *noun, music* the fourth note in the scale of C major

F² *abbreviation, physics* force

F³ *symbol* **1** *chemistry* fluorine **2** *physics* farad **3** *biology* a filial generation (F_1 is the first filial generation etc)

°F *abbreviation* degree(s) Fahrenheit

FA *abbreviation, Brit* Football Association

fa same as **fah**

Fabian (*pronounced* **fei**-bi-an) *noun* a member of the **Fabian Society**, favouring the gradual introduction and spread of socialism ➤ *adjective* to do with the Fabian Society ♦ **Fabianism** *noun*

fable *noun* a story about animals etc, including a lesson or moral

fabric *noun* **1** cloth **2** orderly structure: *the fabric of society*

fabricate *verb* to make up (lies) ♦ **fabrication** *noun*

fabulous *adjective* **1** *informal* very good, excellent **2** imaginary, mythological

fabulously *adverb* extremely, unbelievably: *fabulously rich*

façade (*pronounced* fa-**sahd**) *noun* **1** the front of a building **2** a deceptive appearance or act; a mask

face *noun* **1** the front part of the head **2** the front of anything **3** appearance **4** one of the flat surfaces of a solid figure ➤ *verb* **1** to turn or stand in the direction of **2** to stand opposite to **3** to put an additional surface on • **face up to** to meet or accept boldly: *facing up to responsibilities*

facelift *noun* **1** a surgical operation to smooth and firm the tissues of the face **2** any procedure for improving the external appearance of something

face pack *noun* a cosmetic paste applied to the face and left to dry before being peeled or washed off

facepowder *noun* cosmetic powder for the face

facet (*pronounced* **fas**-it) *noun* **1** a side of a many-sided object, eg a cut gem **2** an aspect; a characteristic

facetious (*pronounced* fa-**see**-shus) *adjective* not meant seriously; joking ♦ **facetiously** *adverb*

face value *noun* the apparent meaning, eg of a statement, which may not be the same as its real meaning

facial *adjective* of the face ♦ **facially** *adverb*

facile (*pronounced* **fas**-ail) *adjective* **1** not deep or thorough; superficial, glib **2** fluent ♦ **facilely** *adverb*

facilitate *verb* to make easy

facility *noun* (*plural* **facilities**) **1** ease **2** skill, ability **3** (**facilities**) buildings, equipment, etc provided for a purpose: *sports facilities*

facsimile (*pronounced* fak-**sim**-i-li) *noun* **1** an exact copy **2** (*often shortened to:* **fax**) electronic copying of a document and its transmission by telephone line **3** a copy made by facsimile

fact *noun* **1** something known or held to be true **2** reality **3** *law* a deed • **in fact** actually, really ☉ Comes from Latin *factum* meaning 'something done or accomplished'

faction *noun* a group that is part of a larger group: *rival factions*

fact of life *noun* (*plural* **facts of life**) **1** an unavoidable truth, especially if unpleasant **2** (**the facts of life**) basic information on sexual matters and reproduction

factor *noun* **1** something affecting the course of events **2** someone who does business for another **3** *maths* a number which exactly divides into another (eg 3 is a factor of 6)

factorial *maths, noun* the number resulting when a whole number and all whole numbers below it are multiplied together, eg $5 \times 4 \times 3 \times 2 \times 1 = 120$ ➤ *adjective* relating to a factor or a factorial

factorize or **factorise** *verb, maths* to find the factors of (a number or expression) ♦ **factorization** *noun*

factory *noun* (*plural* **factories**) a building or buildings with equipment for the large-scale manufacture of goods

factory farming *noun* farming in which animals are reared usually with a minimum of space and which uses highly industrialized machinery etc, in order to achieve maximum production

factotum *noun* someone employed to do a large number of different jobs

factual *adjective* consisting of facts; real, not fictional: *factual account* ♦ **factually** *adverb*

facultative *adjective, biology* able to live under different conditions

faculty *noun* (*plural* **faculties**) **1** power of the mind, eg reason **2** a natural power of the body, eg hearing **3** ability, aptitude **4** a department of study in a university: *Faculty of Arts*

fad *noun* **1** an odd like or dislike **2** a temporary fashion ♦ **faddy** *adjective*

fade *verb* **1** to lose colour or strength or cause to lose colour or strength **2** to disappear gradually, eg from sight or hearing

faeces or *US* **feces** (*pronounced* **fees**-eez) *plural noun* solid excrement

faff *verb, informal* to dither, fumble: *Don't faff about*

fag *noun* **1** tiring work **2** *slang* a cigarette **3** *Brit, informal* a young schoolboy forced to do jobs for an older one

fag end *noun, informal* **1** a cigarette butt **2** the very end, the tail end

fagged out *adjective, informal* exhausted, tired out

faggot or *US* **fagot** *noun* **1** a bundle of sticks **2** a meatball

fah or **fa** *noun, music* in sol-fa notation: the fourth note of the major scale

Fahrenheit *noun* a temperature scale on which water freezes at 32° and boils at 212° ➤ *adjective* measured on this scale: *70° Fahrenheit*

fail *verb* **1** to (declare to) be unsuccessful **2** to break down, stop **3** to lose strength **4** to be lacking or insufficient **5** to disappoint • **without fail** certainly, for sure

failing *noun* a fault; a weakness

fail-safe *adjective* made to correct automatically, or be safe, if a fault occurs

failure *noun* **1** the act of failing **2** someone or something that fails

fain *adverb, old* willingly: *I would fain go with you*

faint *adjective* **1** lacking in strength, brightness, etc **2** about to lose consciousness: *feel faint* ➤ *verb* to fall down unconscious ➤ *noun* a loss of consciousness

❗ Do not confuse with: **feint**

faint-hearted *adjective* cowardly, timid

faintly *adverb* **1** dimly, not clearly **2** slightly: *not even faintly amusing*

faintness *noun* **1** lack of strength, brightness, etc **2** a feeling of weakness, as if you were about to lose consciousness

fair[1] *adjective* **1** of a light colour: *fair hair* **2** of weather: clear and dry **3** unbiased, just: *fair assessment* **4** good enough but not excellent **5** *old* beautiful

fair[2] *noun* **1** a large market held at fixed times **2** an exhibition of goods from different producers etc: *craft fair* **3** a travelling collection of merry-go-rounds, stalls, etc ◷ Comes from Late Latin *feria* meaning 'market'

❗ Do not confuse with: **fare**

fairground *noun* the piece of land on which sideshows and amusements are set up for a fair

fair-haired *adjective* having light-coloured hair; blond

fairly *adverb* **1** in a just and reasonable way **2** rather, reasonably **3** only moderately, to a limited extent **4** *informal* absolutely: *She fairly flung herself at me*

fairness *noun* the quality of being reasonable or just in your treatment of people

fair trade *noun* a system of trade in which fair prices are paid for goods, especially those produced in developing countries

fairway *noun* **1** *golf* the mown part on a golf course, between the tee and the green **2** the deep-water part of a river

fair-weather friend *noun* someone who is a friend only when things are going well

fairy *noun* (*plural* **fairies**) a small imaginary creature, human in shape, with magical powers

fairy light *noun* a small coloured or white light for decorating Christmas trees etc

fairy story or **fairy tale** *noun* **1** a traditional story of fairies, giants, etc **2** *informal* a lie

fait accompli (*pronounced* feit a-**kom**-plee) *noun* (*plural* **faits accomplis**) an established fact ◷ Comes from French, meaning 'accomplished fact'

faith *noun* **1** trust **2** belief in a religion or creed **3** loyalty to a promise: *kept faith with them*

faithful *adjective* **1** loyal; keeping your promises **2** true, accurate: *faithful account of events* **3** believing in a particular religion or creed **4** having sex only with your spouse or partner ♦ **faithfully** *adverb* (meanings 1 and 2) ♦ **faithfulness** *noun*

faith healing *noun* the curing of illness through religious faith rather than medical treatment ♦ **faith healer** *noun*

faithless *adjective* **1** untrustworthy, inconstant **2** without faith or belief, especially in God or Christianity

fake *adjective* not genuine, forged ➤ *noun* **1** someone who is not what they pretend to be **2** a forgery ➤ *verb* to make an imitation or forgery of

fakir (*pronounced* **fei**-keer) *noun* an Islamic or Hindu holy man

falcon *noun* a kind of bird of prey

falconry *noun* the training of falcons for hunting ♦ **falconer** *noun*

fall *verb* (**falling, fell, fallen**) **1** to drop down **2** to become less **3** of a fortress etc: to be captured **4** to die in battle **5** to happen, occur: *Christmas falls on a Monday this year* ➤ *noun* **1** a dropping down **2** something that falls: *a fall of snow* **3** lowering in value etc **4** *US* autumn **5** an accident involving falling **6** ruin, downfall, surrender **7** (**falls**) a waterfall • **fall in love** to begin to be in love • **fall out with** to quarrel with • **fall through** of a plan: to fail, come to nothing

fallacious adjective wrong, because based on false information or on faulty reasoning

fallacy noun (plural **fallacies**) a false belief; something believed to be true but really false

fall guy noun informal a scapegoat

fallible adjective liable to make a mistake or to be wrong ♦ **fallibility** noun

falling limb noun, geography plotting on a hydrograph showing a decrease in river discharge (contrasted with: **rising limb**)

Fallopian tubes plural noun two tubes along which egg cells pass from a woman's ovaries to her uterus

fallout noun radioactive dust resulting from the explosion of an atomic bomb etc

fallow[1] adjective of land: left unsown for a time after being ploughed

fallow[2] adjective of a yellowish-brown colour

fallow deer noun a type of yellowish-brown deer

false adjective **1** untrue **2** not real, fake **3** not natural: false teeth

false alarm noun an alarm given unnecessarily

falsehood noun a lie, an untruth

falseness or **falsity** noun quality of being false

false start noun **1** a failed attempt to begin something **2** an invalid start to a race, in which one or more competitors begin before the signal is given

falsetto noun a singing voice forced higher than its natural range

falsify verb (**falsifies, falsifying, falsified**) to make false, alter for a dishonest purpose: falsified his tax forms

falsity see falseness

falter verb to stumble or hesitate

fame noun the quality of being well-known, renown

famed adjective famous

familiar adjective **1** well-known **2** seen, known, etc before **3** well-acquainted (with) **4** over-friendly, cheeky ♦ **familiarity** noun

familiarize or **familiarise** verb to make quite accustomed or acquainted (with)

family noun (plural **families**) **1** a couple and their children **2** the children alone **3** a group of people related to one another **4** biology any of the groups of animals into which an order is divided and which in turn is subdivided into one or more genera **5** a group of languages with common characteristics ☉ Comes from Latin familia meaning 'the slaves in a household'

family planning noun the control of the number and spacing of children, especially by using contraceptives

family tree noun the relationships within a family throughout the generations, or a diagram showing these

famine noun a great shortage of food, usually caused by an increase in population or failure of food crops

famished adjective, informal very hungry

famous adjective well-known, having fame

famously adverb, informal very well: get along famously

fan[1] noun **1** a device or appliance for making a rush of air **2** a small hand-held device for cooling the face ➤ verb (**fanning, fanned**) **1** to cause a rush of air with a fan **2** to increase the strength of: fanning her anger • **fan out** to spread out in the shape of a fan

fan[2] noun an admirer, a devoted follower: a fan of traditional music

fanatic noun someone who is over-enthusiastic about something ➤ adjective fanatical

fanatical adjective wildly or excessively enthusiastic ♦ **fanatically** adverb

fancier noun someone whose hobby is to keep prize animals, birds, etc: a pigeon fancier

fanciful adjective **1** inclined to have fancies **2** imaginary, not real ♦ **fancifully** adverb

fancy noun (plural **fancies**) **1** a sudden liking or desire: He had a fancy for ice-cream **2** imagination **3** something imagined ➤ adjective (**fancier, fanciest**) not plain, elaborate ➤ verb (**fancies, fancying, fancied**) **1** to picture, imagine **2** to have a liking or a sudden wish for **3** informal to be physically attracted to **4** to think without being sure ♦ **fanciable** adjective

fancy dress noun an elaborate costume worn eg for a party, often representing a famous character

fanfare noun a loud flourish from a trumpet or bugle

fang noun **1** a long tooth of a wild animal **2** the poison-tooth of a snake

fanlight noun a window above a door, usually semicircular

fantasize or **fantasise** verb to indulge in pleasurable fantasies or daydreams

fantastic adjective **1** very unusual, strange **2** informal very great **3** informal excellent

fantasy noun (plural **fantasies**) **1** an imaginary scene, story, etc **2** an idea not based on reality

fanzine (pronounced **fan**-zeen) noun, informal **1** a magazine for a particular group of fans **2** a small-circulation magazine

FAO abbreviation for the attention of

FAQ or **faq** (pronounced fak) abbreviation, computing frequently asked question(s), a question or list of common questions relating to a particular topic

far (**farther**, **farthest**) *adverb* **1** at or to a long way: *far off* **2** very much: *far better* ➤ *adjective* **1** a long way off, distant: *a far country* **2** more distant: *the far side* (see also **further**)

farad *noun, physics* (symbol **F**) the standard unit of measurement of capacitance

⏲ Named after British physicist Michael Faraday (1791–1867)

farce *noun* **1** a play with far-fetched characters and plot **2** a ridiculous situation

⏲ Based on a French word meaning 'stuffing', after humorous scenes that were performed in between the acts of a play

farcical *adjective* absurd, ridiculous
fard *noun, Islam* obligatory duty
fare *verb, formal* to get on (either well or badly): *They fared well in the competition* ➤ *noun* **1** the price of a journey **2** a paying passenger in a taxi etc **3** food ⏲ Comes from Old English *faran*

❗ Do not confuse with: **fair**

farewell *interjection & noun old* goodbye
far-fetched *adjective* very unlikely: *a far-fetched story*
far-flung *adjective* extending over a great distance
farm *noun* **1** an area of land for growing crops, breeding and feeding animals, etc **2** a place where certain animals, fish, etc are reared: *a salmon farm* ➤ *verb* to work on a farm • **farm out** to give (work) to others to do for payment
farmer *noun* the owner or tenant of a farm
farmers' market *noun* a market where farmers sell their produce directly to the public
farmhouse *noun* the house attached to a farm
farmstead *noun* a farm and farmhouse
farmyard *noun* the yard surrounded by farm buildings
farrow *noun* a litter of baby pigs ➤ *verb* to give birth to a litter of pigs
far-sighted *adjective* foreseeing what is likely to happen and preparing for it
farther and **farthest** see **far**
farthing *noun* an old coin, worth $\frac{1}{2}$ of an old penny
fartlek *noun, athletics* alternate fast and slow running, done as training for long-distance races ⏲ Comes from Swedish, from *fart* meaning 'speed' + *lek* meaning 'play'
fascia (*pronounced* **fei**-shi-a) *noun* (*plural* **fasciae** or **fascias**) the board above a shop entrance, with the shop name and logo
fascinate *verb* **1** to charm, attract irresistibly **2** to hypnotize

fascinating *adjective* extremely interesting
fascination *noun* an intense and deep interest
fascism (*pronounced* **fash**-iz-em)*noun* a form of authoritarian government characterized by extreme nationalism and suppression of individual freedom

⏲ From the *fasces*, a bundle of rods with an axe in the middle, carried before magistrates in ancient Rome to symbolize their power to inflict punishment

fascist (*pronounced* **fash**-ist) *noun* **1** a supporter of fascism **2** a right-wing extremist
fashion *noun* **1** the style in which something is made, especially clothes **2** a way of behaving or dressing which is popular for a time **3** a manner, a way: *acting in a strange fashion* ➤ *verb* to shape, form • **after a fashion** to some extent, in a way • **in fashion** fashionable
fashionable *adjective* up-to-date, agreeing with the latest style
fast[1] *adjective* **1** quick-moving **2** of a clock: showing a time in advance of the correct time **3** of dyed colour: fixed, not likely to wash out ➤ *adverb* **1** quickly **2** firmly: *stand fast* **3** soundly, completely: *fast asleep* • **in the fast lane** having an exciting but stressful lifestyle
fast[2] *verb* to go without food voluntarily, eg for religious reasons or as a protest ➤ *noun* a period of fasting
fasten *verb* to fix; make firm by tying, nailing, etc ♦ **fastener** or **fastening** *noun*
fast food *noun* cooked food, such as hamburgers, fried fish, chips, etc, either to be eaten in the restaurant or taken away
fastidious *adjective* difficult to please, liking things properly done in every detail
fastidiously *adverb* extremely thoroughly, taking much care
fastidiousness *noun* the quality of being fastidious
fast neutron *noun, physics* a neutron produced by nuclear fission that travels too fast to cause further fission, but is used to sustain nuclear chain reactions
fast-track *adjective* of a career: liable for quick promotion
fat *noun* an oily substance made by the bodies of animals and by plants ➤ *adjective* **1** having a lot of fat; plump **2** thick, wide
fatal *adjective* causing death or disaster
fatalism *noun* **1** the belief that all events are predestined and humans cannot alter them **2** a defeatist attitude or outlook ♦ **fatalist** *noun* ♦ **fatalistic** *adjective*
fatality *noun* (*plural* **fatalities**) a death, especially caused by accident or disaster
fate *noun* **1** what the future holds; fortune, luck **2**

end, death: *met his fate bravely*

fated *adjective* doomed

fateful *adjective* with important consequences; crucial, significant

father *noun* **1** a male parent **2** a priest **3** the creator or inventor of something: *Poe is the father of crime fiction* ➤ *verb* to be the father of

father figure *noun* an older man who is respected and admired

fatherhood *noun* the state of being a father

father-in-law *noun* (*plural* **fathers-in-law**) the father of someone's husband or wife

fatherland *noun* someone's native country

fatherly *adjective* kind and protective

fathom *noun* a measure of depth of water (6 feet, 1.83 metres) ➤ *verb* to understand, get to the bottom of

fatigue (*pronounced* fa-**teeg**) *noun* **1** great tiredness after physical or mental effort **2** *biology* a decreased response to stimulus, resulting from effort **3** weakness or strain caused by use: *metal fatigue* ➤ *verb* to tire out

fatten *verb* to make or become fat

fatty *adjective* (**fattier, fattiest**) containing a lot of fat

fatty acid *noun* one of a group of acids found in animal and vegetable fats

fatuous (*pronounced* **fat**-yoo-us) *adjective* very foolish ♦ **fatuously** *adverb*

fatwa or **fatwah** (*pronounced* **fat**-wa) *noun* a formal decree issued by a Muslim authority ⊙ Comes from Arabic, meaning 'a legal decision'

faucet (*pronounced* **faw**-set) *noun, US* a water tap

fault *noun* **1** a mistake **2** a flaw, something bad or wrong, eg with a machine **3** a long crack in the earth's surface where a section of the rock layer has slipped

faultless *adjective* perfect ♦ **faultlessly** *adverb*

faultline *noun, geology* a surface along which faults have occurred, or are likely to occur

faulty *adjective* (**faultier, faultiest**) having a fault or faults

faun *noun* a mythological creature, half human and half animal

❗ Do not confuse with: fawn

fauna *noun* the animals of a district or country as a whole

faux pas (*pronounced* foh **pah**) *noun* (*plural* **faux pas**) an embarrassing mistake, a blunder

favour or *US* **favor** *noun* **1** a kind action **2** goodwill, approval **3** a gift, a token ➤ *verb* **1** to show preference for **2** to be an advantage to: *The darkness favoured our escape* • **in favour of 1** in support of **2** for the benefit of

favourable *adjective* **1** showing approval

2 advantageous, helpful (to)

favourably *adverb* in a positive or advantageous way • **compare favourably with** to be better than, or at least as good as (the other thing or things mentioned)

favourite *adjective* best liked ➤ *noun* **1** a liked or best-loved person or thing **2** a competitor, horse, etc expected to win a race

favouritism *noun* showing favour towards one person etc more than another

fawn¹ *noun* **1** a young deer **2** a light yellowish-brown colour ➤ *adjective* of this colour

fawn² *verb* **1** to show affection as a dog does **2** **fawn on** to flatter in a grovelling fashion

❗ Do not confuse with: faun

fax *noun* (*plural* **faxes**) **1** a machine that scans a document electronically and transfers the information by a telephone line to a receiving machine that produces a corresponding copy **2** a document copied and sent in this way ➤ *verb* **1** to send by fax **2** to send a fax message to

faze *verb, informal* to disturb, worry, or fluster

FBI *abbreviation, US* Federal Bureau of Investigation

FE *abbreviation* Further Education

Fe *symbol, chemistry* iron

fear *noun* an unpleasant feeling caused by danger, evil, etc

fearful *adjective* **1** timid, afraid **2** terrible **3** *informal* very bad: *a fearful headache*

fearfully *adverb* **1** timidly, showing fear **2** extremely, dreadfully

fearless *adjective* brave, daring ♦ **fearlessly** *adverb*

fearsome *adjective* causing fear, frightening

feasible *adjective* able to be done, likely ♦ **feasibility** *noun* ♦ **feasibly** *adverb*

feast *noun* **1** a rich and plentiful meal **2** a festival day commemorating some event ➤ *verb* to eat or hold a feast

feat *noun* a deed requiring some effort

feather *noun* one of the growths which form the outer covering of a bird

feathery *adjective* **1** covered in feathers **2** soft **3** light

feature *noun* **1** an identifying mark, a characteristic **2** a special article in a newspaper etc **3** the main film in a cinema programme **4** a special attraction **5** (**features**) the various parts of someone's face, eg eyes, nose, etc ➤ *verb* **1** to have as a feature **2** to take part (in) **3** to be prominent in

febrile *adjective* relating to fever; feverish ⊙ Comes from Latin *febris* meaning 'fever'

February *noun* the second month of the year

⊙ From a Latin name for a feast of purification

feckless *adjective* 1 helpless; clueless 2 irresponsible; aimless

fecund (*pronounced* **fek**und) *adjective* fertile; richly productive

fed past form of **feed**

federal *adjective* joined by treaty or agreement

federation *noun* a group of states etc joined together for a common purpose, a league

fed up *adjective* tired, bored and disgusted

fee *noun* a price paid for work done, or for a special service

feeble *adjective* weak ♦ **feebly** *adverb*

feed *verb* (**feeding, fed**) 1 to give food to 2 to eat food 3 to supply with necessary materials ➤ *noun* food for animals: *cattle feed*

feedback *noun* 1 responses and reactions (to something) 2 *biology* in living organisms: the return of information about the performance of an action to the part performing it, in order to regulate following action 3 *computing* the process in which part of the output of a system is returned to the input, in order to regulate the following output 4 in a public-address system: the return of some of the output sound to the microphone, producing a whistle or howl

feel *verb* (**feeling, felt**) 1 to explore by touch 2 to experience, be aware of: *He felt no pain* 3 to believe, consider 4 to think (yourself) to be: *I feel ill* 5 to be sorry (for): *We felt for her in her grief* ➤ *noun* an act of touching • **feel like** to want, have an inclination for: *Do you feel like going out tonight?*

feeler *noun* one of two thread-like parts on an insect's head for sensing danger etc

feelgood *adjective informal* causing a feeling of comfort or security: *feelgood movie*

feeling *noun* 1 sense of touch 2 emotion: *spoken with great feeling* 3 affection 4 an impression, belief

feelings *plural noun* what someone feels inside; emotions

feet plural of **foot**

feign (*pronounced* fein) *verb* to pretend to feel or be: *feigning illness*

feint¹ (*pronounced* feint) *noun* 1 a pretence 2 a move to put an enemy off guard ➤ *verb* to make a feint

❗ Do not confuse with: **faint**

feint² *adjective* of paper: ruled with faint lines: *narrow feint* (= having lines which are close together)

feisty (*pronounced* **fai**-sti-er) *adjective* (**feistier, feistiest**) *informal* 1 spirited 2 irritable, touchy

felicitous *adjective* 1 lucky 2 well-chosen, suiting well

felicity *noun* happiness

feline (*pronounced* **fee**-lain) *adjective* 1 of or relating to cats 2 like a cat

fell¹ *noun* a barren hill

fell² *verb* to cut down (a tree)

fell³ *adjective, old* cruel, ruthless • **in one fell swoop** in one quick operation

fell⁴ past tense of **fall**

fellow *noun* 1 an equal 2 one of a pair 3 a member of an academic society, college, etc 4 a man, a boy

fellowship *noun* 1 comradeship, friendship 2 an award to a university graduate

felon (*pronounced* **fel**-on) *noun* someone who commits a serious crime

felony (*pronounced* **fel**-o-ni) *noun* (*plural* **felonies**) a serious crime

felt¹ *noun* a type of rough cloth made of rolled and pressed wool

felt² past form of **feel**

felt pen or **felt-tip pen** or **felt tip** *noun* a pen with a nib made of felt

female *adjective* of the sex which produces children ➤ *noun* a human or animal of this sex

feminine *adjective* 1 of or relating to women 2 characteristic of women 3 *grammar* of the gender to which words denoting females belong

femininity *noun* 1 the circumstance of being a woman 2 the quality of being feminine, or of having physical and mental characteristics traditionally thought suitable and essential for women

feminism *noun* a belief or movement advocating women's rights and opportunities, particularly equal rights with men ♦ **feminist** *noun & adjective*

femur (*pronounced* **fee**-mer) *noun* the thigh bone

fen *noun* low marshy land, often covered with water

fence *noun* 1 a railing, hedge, etc for closing in animals or land 2 *slang* a receiver of stolen goods ➤ *verb* 1 to close in with a fence 2 to fight with swords 3 to give evasive answers when questioned

fencing *noun* 1 material for fences 2 the sport of fighting with swords, using blunted weapons

fend *verb*: **fend for yourself** to look after and provide for yourself • **fend off** to defend yourself from (blows, questions, etc)

fender *noun* 1 a low guard round a fireplace to keep in coal etc 2 a piece of matting over a ship's side acting as a buffer against the quay 3 *US* the bumper of a car

fenestra *noun, biology* 1 a small opening, especially between the middle and inner ear 2 a translucent spot, eg on a moth's wing

feng shui (*pronounced* fung **shwei**) *noun* positioning furniture, buildings, etc in a way thought to bring good fortune or happiness ⊙ Comes from Chinese, from *feng* meaning 'wind' + *shui* meaning 'water'

fennel *noun* a strong-smelling plant, whose seeds and leaves are used in cooking

feral (*pronounced* **fe**-ral) *adjective* of domesticated animals or cultivated plants: living or growing wild ⊙ Comes from Latin *fera* meaning 'wild beast'

ferment *verb* (*pronounced* fe-**ment**) **1** to change by fermentation **2** to stir up (trouble etc) ➤ *noun* (*pronounced* **fer**-ment) **1** a state of agitation or excitement **2** a substance that causes fermentation ⊙ Comes from Latin *fermentum* meaning 'yeast'

⚠ Do not confuse with: **foment**

fermentation *noun* **1** a reaction caused by bringing certain substances together, eg by adding yeast to dough in bread-making **2** great excitement or agitation

fermium *noun, chemistry* (symbol **Fm**) an artificially produced metallic radioactive element

⊙ Named after Italian-born physicist Enrico *Fermi* (1901–54)

fern *noun* a plant with no flowers and feather-like leaves

ferocious *adjective* fierce, savage
♦ **ferociously** *adverb* ♦ **ferocity** *noun*

-ferous *suffix* forms adjectives related to the idea of carrying or containing: *coniferous* (= producing cones) ⊙ Comes from Latin *ferre* meaning 'to carry'

ferret *noun* a small weasel-like animal used to chase rabbits out of their warrens ➤ *verb* to search busily and persistently

ferric *adjective, chemistry* **1** referring or relating to iron in its trivalent state **2** denoting a compound that contains iron in its trivalent state (*compare with:* **ferrous**) ⊙ Comes from Latin *ferrum* meaning 'iron'

Ferris wheel *noun* a giant fairground wheel that turns vertically, with seats hanging from its rim

⊙ Named after G W G *Ferris* (1859–96), the US engineer who designed it

ferrite *noun, chemistry* any of a group of materials composed of oxides of iron and some other metal

ferrous *adjective, chemistry* **1** referring or relating to iron in its divalent state **2** denoting a compound that contains iron in its divalent state (*compare with:* **ferric**) ⊙ Comes from Latin *ferrum* meaning 'iron'

ferry *verb* (**ferries, ferrying, ferried**) to carry

over water by boat, or overland by aeroplane ➤ *noun* (*plural* **ferries**) **1** a crossing place for boats **2** a boat which carries passengers and cars etc across a channel

fertile *adjective* **1** of land, soil, etc: containing the nutrients required to produce crops, plants, etc **2** able to produce children or young **3** full of ideas, creative, productive ♦ **fertility** *noun*

fertilize or **fertilise** *verb* **1** to make (soil etc) fertile **2** to start the process of reproduction in (an egg or plant) by combining them with sperm or pollen ♦ **fertilization** *noun*

fertilizer or **fertiliser** *noun* manure or chemicals used to make soil more fertile

fervent *adjective* very eager; intense
♦ **fervently** *adverb*

fervour or *US* **fervor** *noun* ardour, zeal

fest or **-fest** *noun & suffix* a gathering or festival around some subject: *news-fest/trade fest* ⊙ Comes from German *Fest* meaning 'a festival'

fester *verb* **1** of a wound: to produce pus because of infection **2** of resentment or anger: to become more bitter, usually over time

festival *noun* **1** a celebration; a feast **2** a season of musical, theatrical, or other performances

festive *adjective* **1** of a feast **2** in a happy, celebrating mood

festivity *noun* (*plural* **festivities**) a celebration, a feast

festoon *verb* to decorate with chains of ribbons, flowers, etc

fetal or **foetal** *adjective* relating to a fetus

fetch *verb* **1** to go and get **2** to bring in (a price): *fetched £100 at auction*

fetching *adjective, informal* of appearance: attractive, charming

fete or **fête** *noun* a public event with stalls, competitions, etc to raise money ➤ *verb* to entertain lavishly, make much of

fetid or **foetid** (*pronounced* **feet**-id or **fet**-id) *adjective* having a strong disgusting smell ⊙ Comes from Latin *fetere* meaning 'to stink'

fetish *noun* (*plural* **fetishes**) **1** a sacred object believed to carry supernatural power **2** an object of excessive fixation or (especially sexual) obsession ♦ **fetishist** *noun* ♦ **fetishistic** *adjective*

fetlock *noun* the part of a horse's leg just above the foot

fetters *plural noun, formal* chains for imprisonment

fettle *noun*: **in fine fettle** in good health or condition

fettuccine or **fettucine** or **fettucini** (*pronounced* fet-oo-**chee**-ni) *noun* pasta made in long ribbons ⊙ Comes from Italian, from *fettucia* meaning 'slice' or 'ribbon'

fetus or **foetus** *noun* (*plural* **fetuses** or

foetuses) 1 the embryo of some mammals during the later stages of development in the uterus **2** a young human being in the womb, from the end of the eighth week after conception until birth (*compare with*: **embryo**)

feud (*pronounced* fyood) *noun* a private, drawn-out war between families, clans, etc

feudal (*pronounced* **fyood**-al) *adjective, history* of a social system under which tenants were bound to give certain services to the overlord in return for their tenancies
♦ **feudalism** *noun* ♦ **feudalist** *adjective*

fever *noun* an above-normal body temperature and quickened pulse

fevered *adjective* **1** having a fever **2** very excited

feverish *adjective* **1** having a slight fever **2** excited **3** too eager, frantic: *feverish pace*

few *adjective* (**fewer, fewest**) not many: *only a few tickets left* • **a good few** or **quite a few** several, a considerable number

---

ℹ️ **Fewer** should be used with plurals:
There are fewer cars on the roads.
However, **less** should be used with amounts, and with measurements:
There are less than twelve hours to go.
People aged twenty or less.
Less should also be used with *than*:
Less than twenty of them made it back.

---

fey *adjective* **1** strangely fanciful or whimsical **2** able to foresee future events ⏱ Comes from Anglo-Saxon *fæge* meaning 'doomed to die'

fez *noun* (*plural* **fezzes**) a brimless flowerpot-shaped hat, usually with a top tassel

---

⏱ Named after the city of *Fez* in Morocco, where such hats were made

---

fiancé (*pronounced* fi-**on**-sei) *noun* the man a woman is engaged to marry

fiancée (*pronounced* fi-**on**-sei) *noun* the woman a man is engaged to marry

fiasco *noun* (*plural* **fiascos**) a complete failure

⏱ Based on an Italian phrase *far fiasco* 'make a bottle', meaning forget your lines on stage

---

fib *verb* (**fibbing, fibbed**) to lie about something unimportant ➤ *noun* an unimportant lie ♦ **fibber** *noun*

Fibonacci numbers, sequence or **series** (*pronounced* fee-boh-**nah**-tchee) *noun, maths* the infinite series of numbers (0, 1, 1, 2, 3, 5, 8, etc) in which each term is the sum of the preceding two terms

---

⏱ Named after its discoverer, the mathematician Leonardo Fibonacci of Pisa, Italy (c.1170–c.1230)

---

fibre or *US* **fiber** *noun* **1** a single thread or string

of a substance **2** a material composed of fibres **3** the indigestible parts of plants or seeds, that help food move through the body • **to the fibre of your being** deeply, fundamentally

fibreboard *noun* strong board made from compressed wood chips

fibreglass *noun* a lightweight material made of very fine threads of glass, used for building boats etc

fibre-optic *adjective* of a cable: made of glass or plastic filaments which transmit light signals

fibrin *noun, biology, chemistry* a soluble protein produced from fibrinogen when blood clots

fibrinogen *noun, biology, chemistry* a soluble protein plasma involved in the blood-clotting process

fibroid *adjective* fibrous ➤ *noun, medicine* a benign tumour which can develop in the walls of the uterus

fibrosis *noun, medicine* an abnormal amount of fibrous connective tissue forming on a body part

fibrous *adjective* thread-like, stringy

fickle *adjective* changeable; not stable or loyal

fiction *noun* **1** stories about imaginary characters and events **2** a lie ⏱ Comes from Latin *fictio* meaning 'a forming'

fictional *adjective* imagined, created for a story: *fictional character* ⏱ For origin, see **fiction**

❗ Do not confuse: **fictional** and **fictitious**

---

fictitious *adjective* **1** not real, imaginary **2** untrue ⏱ Comes from Latin *ficticius* meaning 'counterfeit'

fiddle *noun* **1** a violin **2** a tricky or delicate operation **3** *informal* a cheat, a swindle ➤ *verb* **1** to play the violin **2** to play aimlessly (with) **3** to interfere, tamper (with) **4** *informal* to falsify (accounts etc) with the intention of cheating

fiddly *adjective* (**fiddlier, fiddliest**) needing delicate or careful handling

fidelity *noun* **1** faithfulness **2** truth, accuracy

fidget *verb* (**fidgeting, fidgeted**) to move about restlessly

field *noun* **1** a piece of enclosed ground for pasture, crops, sports, etc **2** an area of land containing a natural resource: *goldfield/coalfield* **3** a branch of interest or knowledge **4** those taking part in a race **5** *physics* a region of space in which one object exerts force on another: *force field* **6** *maths* a collection of numbers or elements on which binary operations of addition, subtraction, multiplication, and division can be performed **7** *computing* a unit of information (eg a name) that is part of a database record **8** *computing* an area in a database or screen display in which information may be entered ➤ *verb*, **1** *cricket*, rounders, etc to catch the ball and return it **2** to deal with a succession of (inquiries etc)

field day noun a day of unusual activity or success

fielder noun someone whose role is to catch and return the ball in cricket, rounders, etc

fieldglasses plural noun binoculars

field marshal noun the highest ranking army officer

fieldwork noun practical work done outside the classroom or home

fiend noun **1** an evil spirit **2** informal a wicked person **3** informal an extreme enthusiast: a crossword fiend

fiendish adjective **1** evil or wicked **2** extremely bad **3** very complicated or clever

fierce adjective **1** very angry-looking, hostile, likely to attack **2** intense, strong: fierce competition ♦ **fiercely** adverb

fiery adjective (**fierier, fieriest**) **1** like fire **2** quick-tempered, volatile ♦ **fieriness** noun

fiesta noun a religious festival or carnival

fife noun a small flute

fifteen noun the number 15 ➤ adjective 15 in number

fifteenth adjective the last of a series of fifteen ➤ noun one of fifteen equal parts

fifth adjective the last of a series of five ➤ noun one of five equal parts

fifth column noun a body of citizens prepared to co-operate with an invading enemy ♦ **fifth columnist** noun

⊙ Originally applied to General Franco's sympathizers in Madrid during the Spanish Civil War (1936–9) who were prepared to join the four columns marching against the city

fifties plural noun (also **50s, 50's**) **1** the period of time between fiftieth and sixtieth birthdays **2** the range of temperatures between fifty and sixty degrees **3** the period of time between the fiftieth and sixtieth years of a century

fiftieth adjective the last of a series of fifty ➤ noun one of fifty equal parts

fifty noun the number 50 ➤ adjective 50 in number

fifty-fifty adjective **1** of a chance: equal either way **2** half-and-half ➤ adverb divided equally between two; half-and-half

fig noun **1** a soft roundish fruit with thin, dark skin and red pulp containing many seeds **2** the tree which bears it

fight verb (**fighting, fought**) **1** to struggle with fists, weapons, etc **2** to quarrel **3** to go to war with ➤ noun a struggle; a battle

fighter noun **1** someone who fights **2** a fast military aircraft that attacks other aircraft

fig leaf noun **1** the leaf of a fig tree **2** art a

representation of a fig leaf covering the genitals of a figure in a statue or painting

figment noun an imaginary story or idea

figurative adjective of a word: used not in its ordinary meaning but to show likenesses, eg 'she was a tiger' for 'she was as ferocious as a tiger'; metaphorical (contrasted with: **literal**)
♦ **figuratively** adverb

figure noun **1** outward form or shape **2** a number **3** a geometrical shape **4** an unidentified person: A shadowy figure approached **5** the shape of a person's body **6** a diagram or drawing on a page **7** a set of movements in skating etc ➤ verb to appear, take part: He figures in the story ● **figure out** to work out, understand

figured adjective marked with a design: figured silk

figurehead noun **1** a carved wooden figure fixed to the prow of a ship **2** a leader who has little real power

figure of speech noun a device such as a metaphor, simile, etc that enlivens language

figure skating noun skating in which set patterns are performed on the ice ♦ **figure skater** noun

figurine (pronounced fig-yuw-**reen**) noun a small carved or moulded figure, usually representing a human form

filament (pronounced **fil**-a-ment) noun **1** a slender thread or fibre **2** a fine wire that emits heat and light when an electric current passes through it, eg in a light bulb **3** botany the stalk of a stamen, bearing the anther

filch verb, informal to steal

file[1] noun **1** a loose-leaf book etc to hold papers **2** computing an amount of computer data held under a single name **3** a line of soldiers etc walking one behind another ➤ verb **1** to put (papers etc) in a file **2** to walk in a file

file[2] noun a steel tool with a roughened surface for smoothing wood, metal, etc ➤ verb to rub with a file

file extension noun, computing the 2- or 3-letter suffix, eg doc, bmp, xls, that follows the dot at the end of a computer filename and gives the file type

filename noun, computing a name or reference used to specify a file stored in a computer

filial (pronounced **fil**-i-al) adjective **1** of or characteristic of a son or daughter **2** biology denoting any successive generation following a parental generation (abbreviated to F1, F2, etc)

filibuster noun a long speech given in parliament to delay the passing of a law

filigree noun very fine gold or silver work in lace or metal

filing cabinet noun a set of drawers, usually metal, for holding papers and documents

fill *verb* **1** to put (something) into until there is no room for more: *Fill the bucket with water* **2** to become full: *Her eyes filled with tears* **3** to satisfy, fulfil (a requirement etc) **4** to occupy: *fill a post* **5** to appoint someone to (a job etc): *Have you filled the vacancy?* **6** to put something in (a hole) to stop it up ➤ *noun* as much as is needed to fill: *We ate our fill* • **fill in 1** to fill (a hole) **2** to complete (a form etc) **3** to do another person's job while they are absent: *I'm filling in for Anne* • **fill up** to fill completely

filler *noun* **1** a funnel for pouring liquids through **2** a substance added to increase bulk **3** a material used to fill up holes in wood, plaster, etc

fillet *noun* a piece of meat or fish with bones removed ➤ *verb* (**filleting, filleted**) to remove the bones from

filling *noun* something used to fill a hole or gap ➤ *adjective* of food: satisfying

filling-station *noun* a garage which sells petrol

filly *noun* (*plural* **fillies**) a young female horse

film *noun* **1** a thin skin or coating **2** a strip of celluloid coated with chemicals, on which photographs are taken **3** a narrative photographed on celluloid and shown in a cinema, on television, etc ➤ *verb* **1** to photograph on celluloid **2** to develop a thin coating: *His eyes filmed over*

film star *noun* a famous actor or actress in films

filmy *adjective* (**filmier, filmiest**) of a fabric etc: thin, light and transparent

filo or **phyllo** (*pronounced* fee-loh) *noun* (*in full*: **filo pastry**) a type of Greek flaky pastry made in thin sheets ⊙ Comes from Modern Greek *phyllon* meaning 'leaf'

Filofax *noun* (*plural* **Filofaxes**), *trademark* a personal organizer

filter *noun* **1** a substance that allows liquid and gas through but traps solid matter **2** a device containing such a substance, for removing impurities from liquids or gases **3** a transparent disc used to reduce the strength of certain frequencies in the light entering a camera or emitted by a lamp **4** a device for suppressing radio waves of unwanted frequencies **5** *computing* a device for blocking access to certain websites or e-mail addresses **6** a green arrow on a traffic light signalling one lane of traffic to move while the main stream is held up ➤ *verb* (**filtering, filtered**) **1** to strain through a filter **2** to move or arrive gradually: *The news filtered through* **3** of cars etc: to join a stream of traffic gradually **4** of a lane of traffic: to move in the direction shown by a filter

filter paper *noun* a porous paper through which a liquid is passed to separate out any solid particles suspended in it

filth *noun* **1** dirt **2** obscene words or pictures

filthily *adverb* dirtily or obscenely

filthiness *noun* extreme dirtiness or obscenity

filthy *adjective* (**filthier, filthiest**) **1** very dirty **2** obscene, lewd

filtrate *noun, chemistry* the clear liquid obtained after filtration

filtration *noun* filtering

fin *noun* a flexible projecting part of a fish's body used for balance and swimming

final *adjective* **1** last **2** allowing of no argument: *The judge's decision is final* ➤ *noun* the last contest in a competition: *World Cup final*

finale (*pronounced* fi-**nah**-li) *noun* the last part of anything (eg a concert)

finalist *noun* someone who reaches the final round in a competition

finality *noun* the quality of being final and decisive

finalize or **finalise** *verb* to put (eg plans) in a final or finished form

finally *adverb* in the end, at last, eventually, lastly

final solution *plural noun, history* (**the final solution**) the translation of the German name for the Nazi policy of exterminating European Jews

finance *noun* **1** money affairs **2** the study or management of these **3** (**finances**) the money someone has to spend ➤ *verb* to supply with sums of money ♦ **financial** *adjective* (*noun, meaning* 1) ♦ **financially** *adverb* (*noun, meaning* 1)

financier *noun* someone who manages (public) money

finch *noun* (*plural* **finches**) a small bird

find *verb* (**finding, found**) **1** to come upon accidentally or after searching: *I found an earring in the street* **2** to discover **3** to judge to be: *finds it hard to live on her pension* ➤ *noun* something found, especially something of interest or value • **find out** to discover, detect ⊙ Comes from Old English *findan*

fine¹ *adjective* **1** made up of very small pieces, drops, etc **2** not coarse: *fine linen* **3** thin, delicate **4** slight: *a fine distinction* **5** beautiful, handsome **6** of good quality; pure **7** bright, not rainy **8** well, healthy

fine² *noun* money to be paid as a punishment ➤ *verb* to compel to pay (money) as punishment

fine art *noun* **1** art produced for its aesthetic value **2** (**fine arts**) painting, drawing, sculpture, and architecture

finery *noun* splendid clothes etc

finesse (*pronounced* fi-**nes**) *noun* cleverness and subtlety in handling situations etc

finger *noun* one of the five branching parts of the hand ➤ *verb* to touch with the fingers

fingering *noun* **1** the positioning of the fingers

in playing a musical instrument **2** the showing of this by numbers

fingerprint *noun* the mark made by the tip of a finger, used by the police as a means of identification

finicky *adjective* **1** too concerned with detail **2** of a task: intricate, tricky **3** fussy, faddy

finish *verb* **1** to end or complete the making of **2** to stop: *When do you finish work today?* ➤ *noun* (*plural* **finishes**) **1** the end (eg of a race) **2** the last coating of paint, polish, etc

finished *adjective* **1** ended, complete **2** of a person: ruined, not likely to achieve further success etc

finite *adjective* **1** having an end or limit **2** *maths* having a fixed, countable number of elements

finite verb *noun* a verb in a form that indicates person, number, tense or mood, as opposed to an infinitive or a participle

fiord or **fjord** (*pronounced* **fee**-awd) *noun* a long narrow sea inlet between steep hills, especially in Norway

fir *noun* a kind of cone-bearing tree

fir cone *noun* one of the small, woody cones which grow on a fir tree and hold its seeds

fire *noun* **1** the heat and light given off by something burning **2** a mass of burning material, objects, etc **3** a heating device: *electric fire* **4** eagerness, keenness ➤ *verb* (**firing, fired**) **1** to set on fire **2** to make eager: *fired by his enthusiasm* **3** to make (a gun) explode, shoot

fire alarm *noun* a device to sound a bell etc as a warning of fire

firearm *noun* a gun, eg a pistol

firebomb *noun* an incendiary bomb ➤ *verb* to attack or destroy with firebombs

firebrand *noun* **1** a piece of burning wood **2** someone who stirs up unrest

fire brigade *noun* a company of firefighters

firedamp *noun* a dangerous gas found in coal mines

fire-eater *noun* a performer who pretends to swallow fire from flaming torches

fire engine *noun* a vehicle carrying firefighters and their equipment

fire escape *noun* a means of escape from a building in case of fire

fire extinguisher *noun* a device containing water, foam, etc, for spraying on to a fire to put it out

firefighter *noun* someone whose job it is to put out fires

firefly *noun* (*plural* **fireflies**) a type of insect which glows in the dark

fireguard *noun* a framework of iron placed in front of a fireplace for safety

fireman or **firewoman** *noun* (*plural* **firemen** or **firewomen**) a firefighter

fireplace *noun* a recess in a room below a chimney for a fire

firewall *noun, computing* a piece of software which stops unauthorized access to a computer network

firewood *noun* wood for burning on a fire

fireworks *plural noun* **1** devices which, when lit, produce coloured sparks, flares, etc, often with accompanying loud bangs **2** *informal* angry behaviour

firing squad *noun* a group of soldiers with the job of shooting a condemned person

firm *adjective* **1** not easily moved or shaken **2** with mind made up ➤ *noun* a business company

firmament *noun, formal* the heavens, the sky

firmware *noun, computing* a software program which cannot be altered and is held in a computer's read-only memory

first *adjective & adverb* before all others in place, time, or rank ➤ *adverb* before doing anything else

first-aid *noun* treatment of a wounded or sick person before the doctor's arrival

first-born *noun* the eldest child in a family

first-class *adjective* of the highest standard, best kind, etc

first-degree *adjective* **1** *medicine* denoting the least severe type of burn in which only the outer layer of the skin is damaged **2** *N Am law* denoting the most serious of the two levels of murder, ie with intent and premeditation

first-hand *adjective* direct • **at first hand** directly from the source

First Minister *noun* the leader of the parliament in Scotland or the assembly in Northern Ireland or Wales

first name *noun* a person's name that is not their surname

first-past-the-post *adjective, politics* referring to an electoral system in which voters have one vote only and whoever gets most votes wins

first person *noun, grammar* a class into which pronouns and verb forms fall, denoting the speaker or writer (or the speaker or writer and others, eg *I* and *we*) ◆ **first-person** *adjective*

first-rate *adjective* first-class

firth *noun* especially in Scotland, a narrow arm of the sea, especially at a river mouth

fiscal *adjective* **1** of the public revenue **2** of financial matters

fish *noun* (*plural* **fish** or **fishes**) a kind of animal that lives in water, and breathes through gills ➤ *verb* **1** to try to catch fish with rod, nets, etc **2** to search (for): *fishing for a handkerchief in her bag* **3** to try to obtain: *fish for compliments*

fisherman *noun* (*plural* **fishermen**) a man who fishes, especially for a living

fish finger *noun* an oblong piece of filleted or minced fish coated in breadcrumbs

fishmonger (*pronounced* **fish**-mung-ger) *noun* someone who sells fish for eating

fishnet *noun* a net for catching fish ► *adjective* of clothes: having an open mesh, like netting: *fishnet tights*

fish slice *noun* a kitchen utensil with a flat slotted head, for turning food in a frying pan etc

fishy *adjective* (**fishier, fishiest**) **1** like a fish **2** doubtful, arousing suspicion

fissile *adjective* **1** *geography* of certain rocks: capable of being split or tending to split **2** *physics* (also **fissionable**) capable of undergoing nuclear fission

fission *noun* **1** splitting into pieces **2** *biology* the reproduction of some single-cell organisms from a single parent by the division of the cell into two more or less equal parts **3** nuclear fission ♦ **fissionable** *adjective, physics* capable of nuclear fission

fissure *noun* **1** a crack **2** *geography* a long narrow crack or fracture in rock, the earth's surface or a volcano **3** *anatomy* a narrow groove dividing an organ (eg the brain) into lobes

fist *noun* a tightly shut hand

fisticuffs *plural noun, old* a fight with the fists

fistula *noun, medicine* an abnormal connection between body parts ⓞ Comes from Latin meaning 'tube' or 'pipe'

fit¹ *adjective* (**fitter, fittest**) **1** suited to a purpose; proper **2** in good training or health **3** *informal* very attractive ► *verb* (**fitting, fitted**) **1** to be of the right size or shape for **2** to be suitable for

fit² *noun* a sudden attack or spasm of laughter, illness, etc

fitful *adjective* coming or doing in bursts or spasms ♦ **fitfully** *adverb*

fitment *noun* a piece of equipment or furniture which is fixed to a wall, floor, etc

fitness *noun* good physical health and strength

fitting *adjective* suitable ► *noun* something fixed or fitted in a room, house, etc

five *noun* the number 5 ► *adjective* 5 in number ⓞ Comes from Old English *fif*

fives *plural noun* a handball game played in a walled court

fix *verb* **1** to make firm; fasten **2** to mend, repair **3** *informal* to arrange (the result of a race, trial, etc) dishonestly ► *noun, informal* **1** a situation which is difficult to escape from **2** act of arranging the result of a race, trial, etc dishonestly

fixation *noun* **1** an (often abnormal) attachment, preoccupation, or obsession **2** *biology* the procedure whereby cells or tissues have their shape and structure preserved with suitable chemical agents before being examined

3 *chemistry* the conversion of a substance into a form that does not evaporate **4** see **nitrogen fixation**

fixative (*pronounced* **fik**-sa-tiv) *noun* a liquid used to preserve and protect a drawing, painting, or photograph or to hold eg dentures in place

fixed *adjective* settled; set in position

fixed dune *noun, geography* a large sand dune that has become a permanent feature, in which sand has turned to soil and on which vegetation has grown

fixedly (*pronounced* **fik**-sid-li) *adverb* steadily, intently: *staring fixedly*

fixture *noun* **1** a piece of furniture etc fixed in position **2** an arranged sports match or race

fizz *verb* to make a hissing sound ► *noun* (*plural* **fizzes**) a hissing sound

fizzle *verb*: **fizzle out** to fail, coming to nothing

fizzy *adjective* (**fizzier, fizziest**) of a drink: forming bubbles on the surface

fjord another spelling of **fiord**

flabbergasted *adjective, informal* very surprised

flabby *adjective* (**flabbier, flabbiest**) not firm, soft, limp; weak, feeble ♦ **flabbiness** *noun*

flaccid (*pronounced* **flak**-sid) *adjective* **1** hanging loosely **2** limp, not firm

flag¹ *noun* a banner, standard, or ensign

flag² *verb* (**flagging, flagged**) to become tired or weak

flag³ *noun* a flat paving-stone (*also called*: **flagstone**)

flagellate (*pronounced* flaj-i-**leit**) *verb* to whip yourself or someone ► *adjective* **1** *biology* relating to or having flagella **2** whiplike ► *noun, biology* any of a group of single-celled protozoan animals possessing one or more flagella

flagellum (*pronounced* fla-**jel**-um) *noun* (*plural* **flagella**), *biology* **1** the long whip-like structure that projects from the surface of sperm, and certain bacteria, algae and protozoans, used to move the cell through a liquid **2** a long thin shoot of a plant

flagon *noun* a large container for liquid

flagrant *adjective* **1** conspicuous **2** openly wicked ♦ **flagrancy** *noun* ♦ **flagrantly** *adverb*

flagship *noun* **1** the ship that carries and flies the flag of the fleet commander **2** the leading ship in a shipping line **3** a commercial company's leading product, model, etc

flagstone see **flag³**

flail *verb* to wave or swing in the air ► *noun, old* a tool for threshing corn

flair *noun* talent, skill: *a flair for languages*

flak *noun* **1** anti-aircraft fire **2** *informal* strong criticism

flake noun 1 a thin slice or chip of anything 2 a very small piece of snow etc ▸ verb to form into flakes • **flake off** to break off in flakes

flaky adjective (**flakier, flakiest**) 1 forming flakes, crumbly: flaky pastry 2 US informal eccentric

flamboyant adjective 1 splendidly coloured 2 too showy, gaudy

flame noun the bright leaping light of a fire ▸ verb 1 to burn brightly 2 computing slang to send abusive electronic mail to

flamenco noun 1 a stirring type of Spanish Gypsy music, usually played on the guitar 2 the dance performed to it ⊙ Comes from Spanish, meaning 'flamingo'

flaming adjective 1 burning 2 red 3 informal violent: a flaming temper

flamingo noun (plural **flamingos** or **flamingoes**) a type of long-legged bird with pink or white plumage

flammable adjective easily set on fire

ⓘ **Flammable** and **inflammable** mean the same thing.

flan noun a flat, open tart

flank noun the side of an animal's body, of an army, etc ▸ verb 1 to go by the side of 2 to be situated at the side of

flannel noun 1 loosely woven woollen fabric 2 a small towel or face cloth

flap noun 1 anything broad and loose-hanging: tent flap 2 the sound of a wing etc moving through air 3 informal a panic: getting in a flap over nothing ▸ verb (**flapping, flapped**) 1 to hang down loosely 2 to move with a flapping noise 3 informal to get into a panic

flapjack noun 1 Brit a biscuit made with rolled oats, butter, and sugar 2 US a pancake

flare verb (**flaring, flared**) 1 to blaze up 2 to widen towards the edge ▸ noun 1 a bright light, especially one used at night as a signal, to show the position of a boat in distress etc 2 (**flares**) informal trousers with legs which widen greatly below the knee ♦ **flared** adjective

flash noun (plural **flashes**) 1 a quick burst of light 2 a moment, an instant 3 a distinctive mark on a uniform ▸ verb 1 to shine out suddenly 2 to pass quickly • **in a flash** very quickly or suddenly

flashback noun especially in a film, novel, etc: a scene showing events which happened before the current ones

flashbulb noun a small light bulb used to produce a brief bright light in photography

flash flood noun a sudden, severe, and brief flood caused by a heavy rainstorm

flashlight noun 1 a burst of light in which a photograph is taken 2 US an electric torch

flash point noun 1 a stage in a tense situation at which people become angry or violent 2 an area in the world where violence is liable to break out 3 chemistry the lowest temperature at which the vapour in the air above a volatile liquid will ignite momentarily when a small flame is applied

flashy adjective (**flashier, flashiest**) showy, gaudy

flask noun 1 a narrow-necked bottle 2 a small flat bottle 3 an insulated bottle or vacuum flask

flat[1] adjective (**flatter, flattest**) 1 level: a flat surface 2 of a drink: no longer fizzy 3 leaving no doubt, downright: a flat denial 4 music a semitone below the right musical pitch 5 of a tyre: punctured 6 dull, uninteresting ▸ adverb stretched out: lying flat on her back ▸ noun 1 music a sign (♭) which lowers a note by a semitone 2 a punctured tyre • **fall flat** informal to fail to achieve the hoped-for effect • **flat out** informal as fast as possible, with as much effort as possible

flat[2] noun an apartment on one storey of a building

flatfish noun a flat-bodied fish with its eyes on the upper surface, eg a sole

flatly adverb in a definite or emphatic way: He flatly refused to help

flatness noun the quality of being flat

flat race noun a race over level ground

flat rate noun a rate which is the same in all cases

flatten verb to make or become flat

flatter verb to praise insincerely ♦ **flattery** noun

flattish adjective fairly flat

flatulence noun wind in the stomach ♦ **flatulent** adjective

flaunt (pronounced flawnt) verb to display in an obvious way: flaunted his wealth

❗ Do not confuse with: **flout**.
Remember that the use of **flaunt** is perfectly illustrated in the well-known phrase 'if you've got it, **flaunt** it'. On the other hand, when you **flout** something, you treat it with contempt instead of showing it off, eg you might 'flout the rules' or 'flout tradition'.

flautist (pronounced **flawt**-ist) noun a flute player

flavonoid noun bioflavonoid

flavour or US **flavor** noun 1 taste: lemon flavour 2 quality or atmosphere: an exotic flavour ▸ verb to give a taste to

flavouring noun an ingredient used to give a particular taste: chocolate flavouring

flaw noun a fault, an imperfection

flawless adjective with no faults or blemishes ♦ **flawlessly** adverb

flax *noun* a plant whose fibres are woven into linen cloth

flaxen *adjective* **1** made of or looking like flax **2** of hair: fair

flay *verb* to strip the skin off

flea *noun* a small, wingless, blood-sucking insect with great jumping power

flea market *noun, informal* a street market that sells second-hand goods or clothes

fleck *noun* a spot, a speck

flecked *adjective* marked with spots or patches

fled past form of **flee**

fledgling *noun* a young bird with fully grown feathers

flee *verb* (**fleeing, fled**) to run away from danger etc

fleece *noun* **1** a sheep's coat of wool **2** a garment for the upper body which is made of fluffy, warm fabric ➤ *verb* **1** to clip wool from **2** *slang* to rob by cheating

fleecy *adjective* (**fleecier, fleeciest**) soft and fluffy like wool

fleet¹ *noun* **1** a number of ships **2** a number of cars or taxis

fleet² *adjective, poetic* swift; nimble, quick in movement

fleeting *adjective* passing quickly: *fleeting glimpse* ♦ **fleetingly** *adverb*

fleetness *noun, poetic* swiftness

Fleet Street *noun* British newspapers or journalism collectively

---

🕔 Named after the street in London where many newspapers were formerly produced and published

---

flesh *noun* **1** the soft tissue which covers the bones of humans and animals **2** meat **3** the body as distinct from the soul or spirit **4** the soft eatable part of fruit • **flesh and blood 1** relations, family **2** human, mortal

fleshy *adjective* (**fleshier, fleshiest**) fat, plump

flew past tense of **fly²**

flex¹ *verb* **1** to bend **2** to contract or tighten (a muscle) so as to bend a joint

flex² *noun* (*plural* **flexes**) a length of covered wire attached to electrical devices

flexible *adjective* **1** easily bending **2** of a joint: able to move **3** willing to adapt to new or different conditions ♦ **flexibility** *noun*

flexion *noun* the bending of a limb or joint, especially a flexor muscle

flexitime *noun* a system in which an agreed number of hours' work is done at times chosen by the worker

flexor *noun, anatomy* a muscle that causes bending of a limb or other body part (*compare with*: **extensor**)

flick *verb* **1** to strike lightly with a quick movement **2** to remove (dust etc) with a movement of this kind ➤ *noun* a quick, sharp movement: *a flick of the wrist*

flicker *verb* **1** to flutter **2** to burn unsteadily ➤ *noun* **1** a brief or unsteady light **2** a fleeting appearance or occurrence: *a flicker of hope*

flight¹ *noun* **1** the act of flying **2** a journey by plane **3** a flock (of birds) **4** a number (of steps)

flight² *noun* the act of fleeing or escaping

flight attendant *noun* a member of the cabin crew on a passenger aircraft

flightless *adjective* of certain birds or insects: unable to fly

flight recorder *noun* a device on an aircraft which records information about the craft's functioning, used in finding out the cause of an air crash

flighty *adjective* (**flightier, flightiest**) changeable, impulsive

flimsy *adjective* (**flimsier, flimsiest**) **1** thin; easily torn or broken etc **2** weak: *a flimsy excuse*

flinch *verb* to move or shrink back in fear, pain, etc

fling *verb* (**flinging, flung**) to throw ➤ *noun* **1** a throw **2** a casual attempt **3** *informal* a period of time devoted to pleasure **4** *informal* a brief romantic affair

flint *noun* a kind of hard stone ➤ *adjective* made of flint

flip *verb* (**flipping, flipped**) to toss lightly ➤ *noun* a light toss or stroke

flip-flop *noun, informal* a sandal consisting of a sole held on to the foot by a thong that separates the big toe from the other toes

flippant *adjective* joking, not serious ♦ **flippancy** *noun* ♦ **flippantly** *adverb*

flipper *noun* **1** a limb of a seal, walrus, etc **2** a webbed rubber shoe worn by divers

flip side *noun, informal* the converse of anything

flirt *verb* to behave in a playful sexual manner ➤ *noun* someone who flirts • **flirt with** to take an interest in (something) without committing yourself seriously to it • **flirt with danger** to take unnecessary risks ♦ **flirtation** *noun*

flirtatious *adjective* fond of flirting

flit *verb* (**flitting, flitted**) **1** to move quickly and lightly from place to place **2** *Scottish* to move house

float *verb* **1** to keep on the surface of a liquid without sinking **2** to set going: *float a fund* ➤ *noun* **1** a cork etc on a fishing line **2** a raft **3** a van delivering milk etc **4** a large lorry for transporting cattle **5** a platform on wheels, used in processions **6** a sum of money set aside for giving change

flock¹ *noun* **1** a number of animals or birds together **2** a large number of people **3** the congregation of a church ➤ *verb* to go (to) in large numbers or in a large crowd • **flock together** to gather in a crowd

flock² *noun* **1** a shred or tuft of wool **2** wool or cotton waste

floe (*pronounced* floh) *noun* a sheet of floating ice

flog *verb* (**flogging, flogged**) **1** to beat, lash **2** *slang* to sell ✦ **flogging** *noun* (meaning 1)

flood *noun* **1** a great flow, especially of water **2** the rise or flow of the tide **3** a great quantity: *a flood of letters* ➤ *verb* **1** to (cause to) overflow **2** to cover or fill with water

floodgate *noun* a gate for controlling the flow of a large amount of water • **open the floodgates** to remove all restraints or controls

floodlight *verb* (**floodlighting, floodlit**) to illuminate with floodlighting ➤ *noun* a light used to floodlight

floodlighting *noun* strong artificial lighting to illuminate an exterior or stage

flood plain *noun, geography* an extensive level area beside a river, corresponding to the part of the river valley which becomes covered with water when the river floods

floor *noun* **1** the base level of a room on which people walk **2** a storey of a building: *a flat on the third floor* ➤ *verb* **1** to make a floor **2** *informal* to knock flat **3** *informal* to puzzle: *floored by the question*

flop *verb* (**flopping, flopped**) **1** to sway or swing about loosely **2** to fall or sit down suddenly and heavily **3** to move about clumsily **4** *informal* to fail badly ➤ *noun* **1** an act of flopping **2** *informal* a complete failure

floppy *adjective* (**floppier, floppiest**) flopping, soft, and flexible

floppy disk *noun, computing* a flexible computer disk, often in a harder case, used to store data

flora *noun* the plants of a district or country as a whole

floral *adjective* (made) of flowers

florescence *noun* the process, state or period of flowering

floret (*pronounced* **flor**-it) *noun, botany* **1** one of the single flowers in the head of a composite flower, such as a daisy or sunflower **2** each of the branches in the head of a cauliflower or of broccoli

florid *noun* of a complexion: pink or ruddy

florist *noun* a seller or grower of flowers

floss *noun* **1** fine silk thread **2** thin, often waxed thread for passing between the teeth to clean them ➤ *verb* to clean (teeth) with dental floss

flotilla *noun* a fleet of small ships

flotsam *noun* floating objects washed from a ship or wreck

flounce¹ *verb* to walk away suddenly and impatiently, eg in anger

flounce² *noun* a gathered decorative strip sewn on to the hem of a dress

flounder¹ *verb* **1** to struggle to move your legs and arms in water, mud, etc **2** to have difficulty in speaking or thinking clearly, or in acting efficiently

---

ⓘ **Flounder** was probably formed by a gradual blending of 'blunder' and 'founder'

❗ Do not confuse with: **founder**

flounder² *noun* a small flatfish

flour *noun* **1** finely ground wheat **2** any grain crushed to powder: *rice flour*

flourish *verb* **1** to be successful, especially financially **2** to grow well, thrive **3** to be healthy **4** to wave or brandish as a show or threat ➤ *noun* (*plural* **flourishes**) **1** a fancy stroke in writing **2** a sweeping movement with the hand, a sword, etc **3** showy splendour **4** an ornamental passage in music

floury *adjective* **1** covered with flour **2** powdery

❗ Do not confuse with: **flowery**

flout *verb* to treat with contempt, defy openly: *flouted the speed limit* ⊙ Probably comes from *floute*, a form found in Middle English meaning 'to play the flute'

❗ Do not confuse with: **flaunt**

flow *verb* **1** to run, as water **2** to move or come out in an unbroken run **3** of the tide: to rise ➤ *noun* a smooth or unbroken run: *flow of ideas* ✦ **flowing** *adjective*

flow chart *noun* a diagram showing a sequence of operations

flower *noun* **1** the part of a plant or tree from which fruit or seeds grow **2** the best of anything ➤ *verb* **1** of plants etc: to produce a flower **2** to be at your best, flourish

flowerhead *noun, botany* a group of florets growing at the tip of a stem

flowering *noun* of plants: producing flowers

flowery *adjective* **1** full of or decorated with flowers **2** using fine-sounding, fancy language: *flowery prose style*

❗ Do not confuse with: **floury**

flown past participle of **fly²**

fl. oz. *abbreviation* fluid ounce

flu *noun, informal* influenza

fluctuate *verb* **1** to vary in number, price, etc **2** to be always changing ✦ **fluctuation** *noun*

flue *noun* a passage for air and smoke in a stove or chimney

fluent *adjective* finding words easily in speaking or writing without any awkward pauses ◆ **fluency** *noun*

fluff *noun* soft, downy material ➤ *verb* **1** to spoil something by doing it badly or making a mistake **2** to shake or arrange into a soft mass: *She fluffed up her hair* ◆ **fluffy** *adjective*

fluid *noun* a substance whose particles can move about freely, a liquid or gas ➤ *adjective* **1** flowing **2** not settled or fixed: *My plans for the weekend are fluid*

fluid ounce *noun* **1** UK a unit of liquid measurement, equal to one twentieth of a British or imperial pint **2** US a unit of liquid measurement, equal to one sixteenth of a US pint

fluke¹ *noun* an accidental or unplanned success

fluke² *noun* a small parasitic worm which can infest sheep, cattle and humans

fluke³ *noun* the part of an anchor which holds fast in sand

flume *noun* a water chute at a leisure pool

flummox *verb informal* to bewilder, confuse totally

flung past form of **fling**

flunk *verb, slang* to fail

flunkey or **flunky** *noun* (*plural* **flunkeys** or **flunkies**) **1** a uniformed manservant, eg a footman **2** *derogatory* a slavish follower **3** *US* a person doing a humble or menial job

fluorescence *noun* the emission of light by an object when exposed electrons or radiation of another wavelength, especially ultraviolet light ◆ **fluorescent** *adjective*

fluorescent light *noun* a glass tube containing a gas that emits ultraviolet radiation, absorbed by phosphors coating the inner part of the tube which emit light by fluorescence

fluoride *noun* any chemical compound consisting of fluorine and another element, especially sodium fluoride, which is added to water or toothpaste to prevent tooth decay

fluoridize, fluoridise or **fluoridate** *verb* to add fluoride to

fluorine *noun, chemistry* (symbol **F**) a highly corrosive poisonous yellow gas that is the most reactive chemical element

fluorocarbon *noun, chemistry* a compound of carbon and fluorine, formerly used in aerosols and refrigerators, but now banned by many countries as a result of its damaging effects on the ozone layer (*see also*: **chlorofluorocarbon**)

flurry *noun* (*plural* **flurries**) a sudden rush of wind etc ➤ *verb* (**flurries, flurrying, flurried**) to excite

flush¹ *noun* (*plural* **flushes**) **1** a reddening of the face **2** freshness, glow ➤ *verb* **1** to become red in the face **2** to clean by a rush of water

flush² *adjective* **1** having the surface level with the surface around **2** *informal* well supplied with money

fluster *noun* excitement caused by hurry ➤ *verb* to harass, confuse

flute *noun* **1** a high-pitched musical wind instrument **2** a tall narrow wine glass

fluted *adjective* decorated with grooves

flutter *verb* to move (eyelids, wings, etc) back and forth quickly ➤ *noun* **1** a quick beating of the pulse etc **2** nervous excitement: *in a flutter* **3** *informal* a small bet

flux *noun* **1** a flow **2** constant change: *in a state of flux* **3** *physics* the rate of flow of particles, energy or mass

fly¹ *noun* (*plural* **flies**) **1** a small winged insect **2** a fish-hook made to look like a fly to catch fish

fly² *verb* (**flies, flying, flew, flown**) **1** to move through the air on wings or in an aircraft **2** *informal* to run away ➤ *noun* (usually **flies**) a flap of material with buttons or a zip, especially at the front of trousers

flyer *noun* a small poster or advertising sheet

flying colours *plural noun* triumphant success: *She passed the exam with flying colours*

flying picket *noun* a picket travelling from place to place to support local pickets during a strike

flying saucer *noun* a disc-shaped object believed to be an alien spacecraft

flying squad *noun* a group of police officers organized for fast action or movement

flying start *noun*: **get off to a flying start** to begin promisingly or with a special advantage

flyover *noun* a road built on pillars to cross over another

flysheet *noun* the outer covering of a tent

flywheel *noun* a heavy wheel which enables a machine to run at a steady speed

FM *abbreviation* frequency modulation (*compare with*: **AM**)

Fm *symbol, chemistry* fermium

foal *noun* a young horse ➤ *verb* to give birth to a foal

foam *noun* a mass of small bubbles on liquids ➤ *verb* to produce foam ◆ **foamy** *adjective*

foam rubber *noun* a sponge-like form of rubber for stuffing chairs, mattresses, etc

fob¹ *noun* **1** *history* a small watch pocket **2** an ornamental chain hanging from such a pocket

fob² *verb* (**fobbing, fobbed**) to force to accept (something worthless): *I won't be fobbed off with a silly excuse*

focaccia (*pronounced* fo-**kach**-a) *noun* a flat round of Italian bread made with olive oil and herbs or spices

focal *adjective* central, pivotal: *focal point*

fo'c'sle another spelling of **forecastle**

focus *noun* (*plural* **focuses** *or* **foci** – pronounced **foh**-sai) **1** the meeting point for rays of light **2** the point to which light, a look, or someone's attention is directed **3** *maths* a fixed point on a conic section from where the distance between it and any point on the curve is in a constant ratio to the distance between that point and the **directrix 4** the location of the centre of an earthquake, where the fracture takes place under the ground and from which the waves radiate outward ▸ *verb* (**focusing, focused**) **1** to meet or make something meet at a focus **2** to adjust (the lens of the eye or an optical instrument) to get the clearest possible image **3** to direct (one's attention etc) to one point

focus group *noun* a small group of people brought together to examine some topic

fodder *noun* dried food, eg hay or oats, for farm animals

foe *noun, formal* an enemy

foetal another spelling of **fetal**

foetid another spelling of **fetid**

foetus another spelling of **fetus**

fog *noun* thick mist ▸ *verb* (**fogging, fogged**) **1** to cover in fog **2** to bewilder, confuse ◆ **foggy** *adjective*

foghorn *noun* a horn used as a warning to or by ships in fog

fogy *or* **fogey** *noun* (*plural* **fogies** *or* **fogeys**) someone with old-fashioned views

foible *noun* a slight personal weakness or eccentricity ⊙ Comes from French, variant of *faible* meaning 'feeble' or 'weak'

foil¹ *verb* to defeat, disappoint

foil² *noun* **1** metal in the form of paper-thin sheets **2** a dull person against whom someone else seems brighter

foil³ *noun* a blunt sword with a button at the end, used in fencing practice

foist *verb* **1** to pass off as genuine **2** to palm off (something undesirable) on someone

fold *noun* **1** a part laid on top of another **2** an enclosure for sheep etc **3** a bend in stratified rocks as a result of the movement of the Earth's crust ▸ *verb* to lay one part on top of another

folder *noun* **1** a cover to hold papers **2** *computing* another name for a **directory**

fold mountain *noun, geography* a mountain formed by part of the Earth's crust being pushed up by the collision of tectonic plates

foliage *noun* leaves

foliate *adjective* leaflike or having leaves ⊙ Comes from Latin *foliatus* meaning 'leafy'

folic acid *noun, biology, chemistry* a member of the vitamin B complex found in many foods, eg green leafy vegetables, required for the manufacture of DNA and RNA and red blood cells

folio *noun* (*plural* **folios**) **1** a leaf (two pages back to back) of a book **2** a page number **3** a sheet of paper folded once

folk *plural noun* **1** people **2** a nation, race **3** (*also:* **folks**) family or relations ▸ *singular noun informal* folk music

folklore *noun* the study of the customs, beliefs, stories, etc of a people

folk music *noun* traditional music of a particular culture

folk song *noun* a traditional song passed on orally

follicle *noun, anatomy* a small cavity or sac in a body part, eg the pit surrounding a root of hair ◆ **follicular** *or* **folliculose** *adjective* ⊙ Comes from Latin *folliculus* meaning 'a small bag'

follow *verb* **1** to go or come after **2** to happen as a result **3** to act according to: *Follow your instincts* **4** to understand: *I don't follow you* **5** to work at (a trade)

follower *noun* **1** someone who follows **2** a supporter, disciple: *a follower of Jung*

following *noun* supporters: *The team has a large following* ▸ *adjective* next in time: *We left the following day* ▸ *preposition* after, as a result of: *Following the fire, the house collapsed*

follow-up *noun* further action or investigation

folly *noun* (*plural* **follies**) **1** foolishness **2** a purposeless building

foment (*pronounced* foh-**ment**) *verb* to stir up, encourage growth of (a rebellion etc) ⊙ Comes from Latin *fomentum* meaning 'a warm lotion' or 'a poultice'

⚠ Do not confuse with: **ferment**

fond *adjective* **1** loving; tender **2** *old* foolish ● **fond of** having a liking for

fondant *noun* a soft sweet or paste made with sugar and water ⊙ Comes from French, from *fondre* meaning 'to melt'

fondle *verb* to caress

fondly *adverb* **1** with fondness **2** foolishly

fondness *noun* **1** affection, love, tenderness **2** liking

font¹ *noun* **1** a basin holding water for baptism **2** a main source: *a font of knowledge*

font² *or* **fount** *noun* a particular style of letters and characters

fontanelle *noun, anatomy* a soft membranous gap between the bones of a baby's or young animal's skull

food *noun* substances which living beings eat

food chain *noun* the sequence in which food is transferred from one living thing to another in an ecosystem, eg plants are eaten by herbivores, which may then be eaten by carnivores

food processor *noun* an electrical appliance for chopping, blending, etc food

foodstuff *noun* something used for food

food web *noun* a group of interrelated food chains

fool *noun* **1** a silly person **2** *history* a court jester **3** a dessert made of fruit, sugar, and whipped cream ➤ *verb* to deceive • **fool about** to behave in a playful or silly manner

foolery *noun* silliness, foolish behaviour

foolhardy *adjective* rash, taking foolish risks

foolish *adjective* unwise, ill-considered ♦ **foolishly** *adverb*

foolproof *adjective* unable to go wrong

foolscap *noun* paper for writing or printing, 43 × 34 cm (17 × 13 inches)

> ⊙ Referring to the original watermark used on this size of paper, showing a jester's cap and bells

fool's gold same as **pyrites**

foot *noun* (*plural* **feet**) **1** the part of the leg below the ankle **2** the lower part of anything **3** (*plural* **feet** or **foot**) twelve inches, 30 cm ➤ *verb*: **foot the bill** to pay up • **my foot!** an interjection used to express disbelief • **not put a foot wrong** to make no mistakes, behave well

footage *noun* a clip from a film etc

football *noun* **1** a game played by two teams of 11 on a field with a round ball **2** *US* a game played with an oval ball which can be handled or kicked **3** a ball used in football

football coupon *noun* a form on which people guess the results of football matches in the hope of winning money

football pools same as **pools**

footer *noun* **1** a line of information at the foot of a page **2** *informal* football

foothill *noun* a smaller hill at the foot of a mountain

foothold *noun* **1** a place to put the foot in climbing **2** a firm position from which to begin something

footing *noun* balance; degree of friendship, seniority, etc

footlight *noun* a light at the front of a stage, which shines on the actors

footloose *adjective* **1** unattached, with no responsibilities **2** of an industry: not dependent on factors found only in a specific location, and therefore able to set up anywhere

footman *noun* (*plural* **footmen**) a male attendant of eg a nobleman

footnote *noun* a note at the bottom of a page

footpath *noun* **1** a path or track for walkers **2** a pavement

footplate *noun* a driver's platform on a railway engine

footprint *noun* a mark of a foot

footsore *adjective* tired out from too much walking

footstep *noun* the sound of someone's foot when walking

footwear *noun* shoes, boots, etc

fop *noun* a man who is vain about the way he dresses ♦ **foppish** *adjective*

for *preposition* **1** sent to or to be given to: *There is a letter for you* **2** towards: *headed for home* **3** during (an amount of time): *waited for three hours* **4** on behalf of: *for me* **5** because of: *for no good reason* **6** as the price of: *£5 for a ticket* **7** in order to obtain: *only doing it for the money*

for- *prefix* forms words containing a notion of 'loss' or of 'not having or not doing something': *forbid/forget* ⊙ Comes from Latin *foris* meaning 'outside'

> ❗ Note that **for-** has a different meaning from the prefix **fore-** (which is connected with 'be**fore**', 'in front of' or 'be**fore**hand'). There are a few words which do not fit this general rule of thumb: note the spelling of 'foreclose' and 'forward'. See also the note at 'forgo'

forage (*pronounced* for-ij) *noun* food for horses and cattle ➤ *verb* to search for food, fuel, etc

foramen *noun* (*plural* **foramina** or **foramens**), *anatomy* a naturally occurring small opening, especially in a bone

foray (*pronounced* for-ei) *noun* **1** a raid **2** a brief journey

forbade past tense of **forbid**

forbearance *noun* control of temper

forbid *verb* (**forbidding, forbade, forbidden**) to order not to

forbidden *adjective* not allowed

forbidding *adjective* rather frightening

force *noun* **1** strength, power **2** compulsion, especially with threats or violence **3** strength or validity: *the force of her argument* **4** *physics* (symbol **F**) an agent that produces a state of motion in an object in a state of rest, or changes the speed or direction of a moving object **5** a group of workers, soldiers, etc **6** (**the forces**) those in the army, navy, and air force **7** (**the force**) the police ➤ *verb* **1** to make, compel: *forced him to go* **2** to get by violence: *force an entry* **3** to break open **4** to hurry on **5** to make (vegetables etc) grow more quickly

forced *adjective* done unwillingly, with effort: *a forced laugh*

forceful *adjective* **1** acting with power **2** persuasive, convincing, powerful ♦ **forcefully** *adverb* ♦ **forcefulness** *noun*

forceps (*pronounced* faw-seps) *noun* (*plural*

forceps) surgical pincers for holding or lifting

forcible *adjective* **1** done by force **2** strong and effective **3** powerful ♦ **forcibly** *adverb*

ford *noun* a shallow crossing-place in a river ➤ *verb* to cross (water) on foot

fore- *prefix* **1** before **2** beforehand **3** in front ⊕ Comes from the Old English prefix *fore-*

❗ Note that **fore-** has a different meaning from the prefix **for-** (which usually indicates some notion of 'loss' or 'not having or not doing something'). There are a few words which do not fit this general rule of thumb: note the spelling of 'foreclose' and 'forward'. See also the note at 'forgo'

forearm¹ (*pronounced* **faw**-rahm) *noun* the part of the arm between elbow and wrist

forearm² (*pronounced* faw-**rahm**) *verb* to prepare beforehand

foreboding *noun* a feeling of coming evil

forebrain *noun, anatomy* the largest part of the brain in vertebrates

forecast *verb* (**forecasting, forecast**) to tell about beforehand, predict ➤ *noun* a prediction

forecastle or **fo'c'sle** (*both pronounced* **fohk**-sl) *noun* **1** a raised deck at the front of a ship **2** the part of a ship under the deck containing the crew's quarters

foreclose *verb* **1** to prevent, preclude **2** to bar from redeeming (a mortgage)

forecourt *noun* a paved area in front of a building, eg a petrol station

forefather *noun, formal* an ancestor

forefinger *noun* the finger next to the thumb (*also called*: **index finger**)

forefront *noun* the very front

foregoing *adjective* preceding, going before

foregone *adjective*: **a foregone conclusion** a result that can be guessed rightly in advance (*see also*: **forgo**)

foreground *noun* the part of a view or picture nearest the person looking at it

forehand *noun, tennis etc* a stroke played with the front of the hand facing the ball (*compare with*: **backhand**)

forehead *noun* the part of the face above the eyebrows

foreign *adjective* **1** belonging to another country **2** not belonging naturally in a place etc: *a foreign body in an eye* **3** not familiar

foreigner *noun* **1** someone from another country **2** someone unfamiliar

foreleg *noun* an animal's front leg

forelock *noun* the lock of hair next to the forehead

foreman *noun* (*plural* **foremen**) **1** an overseer of a group of workers **2** the leader of a jury

foremast *noun* a ship's mast nearest the bow

foremost *adjective* the most famous or important

forensic *adjective* relating to courts of law or criminal investigation

forensic medicine *noun* the branch of medicine concerned with finding causes of injury and death

forerunner *noun* an earlier example or sign of what is to follow: *the forerunner of cinema*

foresee *verb* (**foreseeing, foresaw, foreseen**) to see or know beforehand

foreshadow *verb* to give an indication of (something) in advance

foreshore *noun* the part of the shore between high and low tidemarks

foresight *noun* **1** ability to see what will happen later **2** a fitting on the front of the barrel of a gun to help the aim

foreskin *noun, anatomy* the fold of skin that covers the end of the penis

forest *noun* **1** a large piece of land dominated by trees, which form an unbroken canopy **2** a stretch of country kept for game

forestall *verb* to upset someone's plan by acting earlier than they expect

forester *noun* a worker in a forest

forestry *noun* the science of forest-growing

foretaste *noun* a sample of what is to come

foretell *verb* (**foretelling, foretold**) to tell in advance, prophesy

forethought *noun* thought or care for the future

foretold past form of **foretell**

forever or **for ever** *adverb* **1** for all time **2** continually: *forever complaining* ➤ *noun* **1** an endless period of time **2** *informal* a very long time

forewarn *verb* to warn beforehand ♦ **forewarning** *noun*

foreword (*pronounced* **faw**-werd) *noun* a piece of writing at the beginning of a book

❗ Do not confuse with: **forward**. It is helpful to remember that the foreWORD in a book is made up of WORDs

forfeit *verb* to lose (a right) as a result of doing something: *forfeit the right to appeal* ➤ *noun* something given in compensation or punishment for an action, eg a fine

forfeiture *noun* the loss of something as a punishment

forge¹ *noun* **1** a blacksmith's workshop **2** a furnace in which metal is heated ➤ *verb* (**forging, forged**) **1** to hammer (metal) into shape **2** to imitate (a signature, banknote, etc) for criminal purposes ♦ **forger** *noun* (verb, meaning 2)

forge^2 *verb* to move steadily on: *forged ahead with the plan*

forgery *noun* (*plural* **forgeries**) **1** something imitated for criminal purposes **2** the act of criminal forging

forget *verb* (**forgetting, forgot, forgotten**) to lose or put away from the memory

forgetful *adjective* likely to forget, having a tendency to forget things ♦ **forgetfully** *adverb*

forget-me-not *noun* a plant with small blue flowers

forgive *verb* (**forgiving, forgave, forgiven**) **1** to be no longer angry with **2** to overlook (a fault, debt, etc)

forgiveness *noun* pardon

forgiving *adjective* merciful, willing to forgive other people for their faults

forgo *verb* (**forgoes, forgoing, forwent, forgone**) to give up, do without

❗ It is possible to spell **forgo** and many of its forms with an 'e' – 'forego', 'forewent', etc. However, it is probably less confusing to stick to the basic spellings shown above when you are writing, and to keep the 'e' spelling for **forego** meaning 'to go before' (most commonly used in the expression 'a foregone conclusion'). See also prefix entries **for-** and **fore-**

forgot and **forgotten** see **forget**

fork *noun* **1** a pronged tool for piercing and lifting things **2** the point where a road, tree, etc divides into two branches ➤ *verb* to divide into two branches etc

fork-lift truck *noun* a small vehicle with two horizontal prongs that can be raised and lowered to move or stack goods

forlorn *adjective* pitiful, unhappy

forlorn hope *noun* a wish which seems to have no chance of being granted

form *noun* **1** shape or appearance **2** the way language appears or structured, as opposed to the role it plays (*contrasted with*: **function**) **3** kind, type **4** a paper with printed questions and space for answers **5** a long seat **6** a school class **7** the nest of a hare ➤ *verb* **1** to give shape to **2** to make

formal *adjective* **1** done according to custom or convention: *formal dress* **2** stiffly polite **3** valid, official: *a formal agreement* **4** of language: strictly correct with regard to grammar, style and choice of words ♦ **formally** *adverb*

formaldehyde (*pronounced* for-**mal**-di-haid) *noun, chemistry* a colourless strong-smelling gas used as a disinfectant and as a preservative for biological specimens

formalin *noun, chemistry* a solution of formaldehyde in water used as a disinfectant and as a preservative for biological specimens

formality *noun* (*plural* **formalities**) **1** something which must be done but has little meaning: *the nomination was only a formality* **2** cold correctness of manner

formalize or **formalise** *verb* **1** to make precise or give definite form to **2** to make official, eg by putting in writing

format *noun* **1** the size, shape, etc of a printed book **2** the design or arrangement of an event, eg a television programme **3** *computing* the way data is, or is to be, arranged in a file, on a card, disk, tape, etc ➤ *verb* (**formatting, formatted**) **1** to arrange into a specific format **2** *computing* to arrange (data) for use on a disk **3** *computing* to prepare (a disk) for use by dividing it into sectors

formation *noun* **1** the act of forming **2** arrangement, eg of aeroplanes in flight

formative (*pronounced* **faw**-ma-tiv) *adjective* **1** relating to development or growth: *the formative years* **2** having an effect on development

former *adjective* **1** of an earlier time **2** of the first-mentioned of two (*contrasted with*: **latter**)

formerly *adverb* in earlier times; previously

formic *adjective* relating to ants

formica (*pronounced* for-**mai**-ka) *noun, trademark* a tough, heat-resistant material used for covering work surfaces

formic acid *noun, chemistry* a colourless toxic acid found in ant bites and nettle stings

formidable *adjective* **1** fearsome, frightening **2** difficult to overcome

formula *noun* (*plural* **formulas** or **formulae** – *pronounced* **faw**-myuw-lee) **1** a set of ingredients in a substance **2** a set of rules to be followed **3** *chemistry* a combination of symbols representing the chemical composition of a substance, eg H_2O = water **4** *maths, physics* an equation or expression that represents the relationship between various quantities

formulate *verb* **1** to set down clearly: *formulate the rules* **2** to make into a formula

fornicate *verb* to have sexual intercourse outside marriage ♦ **fornication** *noun* ♦ **fornicator** *noun*

forsake *verb* (**forsaking, forsook, forsaken**) to desert

forsaken *adjective* deserted; miserable

forswear *verb* (**forswearing, forswore, forsworn**) *formal* to give up

fort *noun* a place of defence against an enemy

forte (*pronounced* **for**-tei) *noun* someone's particular talent or speciality

forth *adverb* forward, onward

forthcoming *adjective* **1** happening soon **2** willing to share knowledge; friendly and open

forthright *adjective* outspoken, straightforward

forthwith *adverb* immediately

forties *plural noun* (also **40s, 40's**) **1** the period of time between fortieth and fiftieth birthdays **2** the range of temperatures between forty and fifty degrees **3** the period of time between the fortieth and fiftieth years of a century

fortieth *adjective* the last of a series of forty ➤ *noun* one of forty equal parts

fortifications *plural noun* walls etc built to strengthen a position

fortify *verb* (**fortifies, fortifying, fortified**) to strengthen against attack

fortitude *noun* courage in meeting danger or bearing pain

fortnight *noun* two weeks

fortnightly *adjective & adverb* once a fortnight

FORTRAN (*pronounced* **faw**-tran) *noun* a computer language

fortress *noun* (*plural* **fortresses**) a fortified place

fortuitous *adjective* happening by chance ◆ **fortuitously** *adverb*

fortunate *adjective* lucky ◆ **fortunately** *adverb*

fortune *noun* **1** luck (good or bad) **2** large sum of money

fortune-teller *noun* a person who claims to be able to tell people their destinies ◆ **fortune-telling** *noun*

forty *noun* the number 40 ➤ *adjective* 40 in number

forty winks *plural noun, informal* a short sleep

forum *noun* (*plural* **fora**) **1** a public place where speeches are made **2** a meeting to talk about a particular subject **3** a discussion group on the Internet for people with a shared interest **4** *history* a marketplace in ancient Rome

forward *adjective* **1** advancing: *a forward movement* **2** near or at the front **3** of fruit: ripe earlier than usual **4** *derogatory* too quick to speak or act, pert ➤ *verb* **1** to help towards success: *forwarded his plans* **2** to send on (letters) ➤ *adverb* forwards

! Do not confuse with: **foreword**.
It is helpful to remember that for**WARD** is an indication of direction, similar to back**WARD**s and home**WARD**s.

forwards *adverb* onward, towards the front

forwent *past tense of* **forgo**

fossil *noun* the hardened remains of the shape of a plant or animal found in rock

fossil fuel *noun* a fuel derived from the remains of ancient plants and animals, eg coal and natural gas

fossilize or **fossilise** *verb* to change into a fossil ◆ **fossilization** *noun*

foster *verb* **1** to bring up or nurse (a child not your own) **2** to help on, encourage

foster-child *noun* a child fostered by a family

foster-parent *noun* someone who brings up a fostered child

fought *past form of* **fight**

foul *adjective* **1** very dirty **2** smelling or tasting bad **3** stormy: *foul weather/in a foul temper* ➤ *verb* **1** to become entangled with **2** to dirty **3** to play unfairly ➤ *noun* a breaking of the rules of a game

foul-mouthed *adjective* using offensive or obscene language

foul play *noun* a criminal act

found[1] *verb* to establish, set up

found[2] *verb* to shape by pouring melted metal into a mould

found[3] *past form of* **find**

foundation *noun* **1** the basis on which anything rests **2** (**foundations**) the underground structure supporting a building **3** a sum of money left or set aside for a special purpose **4** an organization etc supported in this way

foundation course *noun* an introductory course, usually taken as a preparation for more advanced studies

founder[1] *verb* **1** of a ship: to sink **2** of a horse: to stumble, go lame ☉ Comes from Old French *fondrer* meaning 'to fall in'

! Do not confuse with: **flounder**

founder[2] *noun* someone who founds

foundling *noun* a child abandoned by its parents

foundry *noun* (*plural* **foundries**) a workshop where metal founding is done

fount *see* **font**[2]

fountain *noun* **1** a rising jet of water **2** the pipe or structure from which it comes **3** the beginning of anything

fountain pen *noun* a pen with a metal nib and a cartridge of ink

four *noun* the number 4 ➤ *adjective* 4 in number ☉ Comes from Old English *feower*

four-poster *noun* a large bed with a post at each corner to support curtains and a canopy

fourteen *noun* the number 14 ➤ *adjective* 14 in number

Fourteen points *plural noun, history* the peace programme outlined by US President Wilson in 1918, at the end of World War I

fourteenth *adjective* the last of a series of fourteen ➤ *noun* one of fourteen equal parts

fourth *adjective* the last of a series of four ➤ *noun* **1** one of four equal parts **2** *music* an interval of four notes

fowl *noun* (*plural* **fowls** or **fowl**) a bird, especially a domestic cock or hen

fox *noun* (*plural* **foxes**) **1** a wild animal related to the dog, with reddish-brown fur and a long bushy tail **2** *US slang* an attractive woman ➤ *verb* **1** to trick by cleverness **2** to puzzle, baffle

foxglove *noun* a tall wild flower

foxhound *noun* a breed of dog trained to chase foxes

foxtrot *noun* a ballroom dance made up of walking steps and turns

foxy *adjective* (**foxier, foxiest**) **1** cunning **2** *slang* of a woman: sexually attractive

foyer (*pronounced* **foi**-ei) *noun* an entrance hall to a theatre, hotel, etc

Fr *symbol, chemistry* francium

fracas (*pronounced* **frak**-ah) *noun* (*plural* **fracas**) **1** uproar **2** a noisy quarrel

fraction *noun* **1** a part, not a whole number, eg $\frac{4}{5}$ **2** a small part **3** *chemistry* a group of compounds with boiling points in a narrow range, which can be separated into components by fractional distillation ♦ **fractional** *adjective*

fractional distillation *noun, chemistry* the separation of the components of a mixture of liquids by heating and condensing at their various boiling points

fractious *adjective* cross, quarrelsome

fracture *noun* a break in something hard, especially in a bone of the body

fragile *adjective* easily broken ♦ **fragility** *noun*

fragment *noun* (*pronounced* **frag**-ment) a part broken off; something not complete ➤ *verb* (*pronounced* frag-**ment**) to break into pieces

fragmentary *adjective* consisting of small pieces, not amounting to a connected whole

fragmentation *noun* breaking up, division into fragments

fragrance *noun* sweet scent

fragrant *adjective* sweet-smelling

frail *adjective* **1** physically weak **2** easily tempted to do wrong

frailty *noun* (*plural* **frailties**) weakness

frame *verb* (**framing, framed**) **1** to put a frame round **2** to put together, construct **3** *slang* to make (someone) appear to be guilty of a crime ➤ *noun* **1** a case or border round anything **2** build of human body **3** one of the pictures that make up a strip of film or a comic strip **4** *computing* an independent section on a web page **5** state (of mind)

frame of mind *noun* (*plural* **frames of mind**) a mood; state of mind

framework *noun* the outline or skeleton of something

franc *noun* **1** the standard unit of money in Switzerland, Liechtenstein, etc **2** the former standard unit of money in France, Belgium, and Luxembourg, replaced in 2002 by the euro

franchise *noun* **1** the right to vote in a general election **2** a right to sell the goods of a particular company ➤ *verb* to give a business franchise to

francium *noun, chemistry* (symbol **Fr**) a radioactive metallic element which is the heaviest of the alkali metals

⊙ Named after *France*, the country where it was discovered

Franco- *prefix* of France, French: *Francophile*

frank *adjective* open, speaking your mind ➤ *verb* to mark (a letter) by machine to show that postage has been paid

frankfurter *noun* a type of spicy smoked sausage ⊙ Short for German *Frankfurter Wurst* meaning 'Frankfurt sausage'

frankincense *noun* a sweet-smelling resin used as incense

frankly *adverb* **1** openly **2** to be honest, I tell you

frankness *noun* the quality of being frank

frantic *adjective* wildly excited or anxious ♦ **frantically** *adverb*

frater- or **fratri-** *prefix* brother: *fraternize with someone* (= to behave towards them with brotherly friendliness)/*fratricide* ⊙ Comes from Latin *frater* meaning 'brother'

fraternal *adjective* brotherly; of a brother ♦ **fraternally** *adverb*

fraternity *noun* (*plural* **fraternities**) **1** a society, a brotherhood **2** a North American male college society (*compare with:* **sorority**)

fraternize or **fraternise** *verb* to make friends (with)

fratricide *noun* **1** the murder of a brother **2** someone who murders their brother

fraud *noun* **1** deceit, dishonesty **2** an impostor; a fake

fraudulence or **fraudulency** *noun* deceitful or dishonest nature

fraudulent *adjective* deceitful, dishonest ♦ **fraudulently** *adverb*

fraught *adjective* anxious, tense • **fraught with** filled with: *fraught with danger*

fray¹ *verb* to wear away

fray² *noun* a fight, a brawl

freak *noun* **1** an unusual event **2** an odd or eccentric person **3** *informal* a keen fan: *film freak* ➤ *adjective* abnormal: *freak storms* ♦ **freaky** *adjective*

freckle *noun* a small brown spot on the skin ♦ **freckled** *adjective*

free *adjective* (**freer, freest**) **1** not bound or shut in **2** not restricted or controlled: *free trade* **3** costing nothing **4** open or available to all **5** *chemistry* not combined with another chemical element ➤ *verb* (**freeing, freed**) to make or set free • **free someone from something** or **free someone of something** to get rid of it for them ⊙ Comes from Old English *freo*

-free adjective (added to another word) not containing or involving: a*dditive-free/cruelty-free*

freebie noun, informal a free event, performance, etc

free church noun **1** the branch of Presbyterians in Scotland which left the established church in 1843 **2** in England: a Nonconformist church

freedom noun the state of being free; liberty

free face noun, geography a slope at an angle of 45 degrees or more, therefore too steep for eroded material or debris to lie on

free-for-all noun a fight, argument, or discussion in which everybody present feels free to join

freehand adjective of drawing: done without the help of rulers, tracing, etc

freehold adjective of an estate: belonging to the holder or their heirs for all time

free kick noun, football a kick awarded to one side with no tackling from the other, following an infringement of the rules

freelance or **freelancer** noun someone working independently (such as a writer who is not employed by any one newspaper)

⊙ Originally referring to a medieval knight who would fight for anyone who paid him

free-living adjective, biology not parasitic or symbiotic

freeload verb informal to eat, live, enjoy oneself, etc at someone else's expense
♦ **freeloader** noun

Freemason noun a member of a certain men's society, sworn to secrecy

freephone or **freefone** noun, trademark a telephone service whereby calls made to an organization are charged to that organization rather than to the caller

free radical noun, chemistry a group of atoms containing at least one unpaired electron, capable of starting a range of chemical reactions

free-range adjective **1** of poultry: allowed to move about freely and feed out of doors **2** of eggs: laid by free-range poultry

freesia (pronounced **free**-sza) noun a plant of the iris family with sweet-smelling trumpet-shaped flowers

free speech noun the right to express opinions of any kind

free-standing adjective not attached to or supported by a wall or other structure

freestyle adjective of swimming, skating, etc: in which any style may be used

free trade noun free or unrestricted trade; free interchange of goods without import duties

free verse noun poetry with no regular pattern of rhyme, rhythm or line length

freeware noun, computing software programs offered to the public at no cost

freeway noun, US a road for high-speed traffic

freewheel verb to travel on a bicycle or car, especially downhill, without using mechanical power

freeze verb (**freezing, froze, frozen**) **1** to turn into ice **2** to make (food) very cold in order to preserve **3** to go stiff with cold, fear, etc **4** to fix (prices or wages) at a certain level

freezer noun a refrigerated cabinet in which food is made, or kept, frozen

freeze-thaw noun, geography erosion caused by the alternate freezing and thawing of water in cracks in rock, and the subsequent widening and contraction of the cracks (also called: **ice wedging**)

freezing point noun the point at which liquid becomes a solid (of water, 0°C)

freight noun **1** load, cargo **2** a charge for carrying a load ‣ verb to load with goods

freighter noun a ship or aircraft that carries cargo

freight train noun a goods train

French bean noun a species of bean plant whose pods and unripe seeds are eaten together as a vegetable

French bread or **French loaf** or **French stick** noun white bread in the form of a long narrow loaf with tapered ends and a thick crisp crust

French dressing noun a salad dressing made from oil, herbs, and lemon juice or vinegar

French fries plural noun US potato chips

French horn noun an orchestral wind instrument made of brass

French leave noun: **take French leave** to go or stay away without permission

French polish noun a kind of varnish for furniture

French toast noun bread dipped in egg and fried

French window noun a long window also used as a door

frenetic adjective frantic

frenzied adjective mad ♦ **frenziedly** adverb

frenzy noun **1** a fit of madness **2** wild excitement

frequency noun (plural **frequencies**) **1** the rate at which something happens **2** physics the number of times a wave is repeated per unit time **3** statistics the number of values, items, etc that occur within a specified category

frequency distribution noun, statistics a set of data that includes values for the frequencies of different scores or results, ie the number of times that each particular score or result occurs

frequency polygon noun, statistics a frequency table with intervals shown on the x-axis and the scores for each interval shown on the y-axis, and in which the points are joined to form a polygon

frequency table noun, statistics a table showing a frequency distribution

frequent adjective (pronounced **free**-kwent) happening often ➤ verb (pronounced fri-**kwent**) to visit often

fresco noun (plural **frescoes** or **frescos**) a picture painted on a wall while the plaster is still damp

fresh adjective **1** new, unused: fresh sheet of paper **2** newly made or picked; not preserved: fresh fruit **3** cool, refreshing: fresh breeze **4** not tired **5** informal cheeky, impertinent ➤ adverb newly: fresh-laid eggs ◆ **freshness** noun

freshen verb **1** to make fresh **2** of a wind: to grow strong • **freshen up** to get washed and tidy

freshly adverb newly, recently

freshwater adjective of inland rivers, lakes, etc, not of the sea

fret¹ verb (**fretting, fretted**) to worry or show discontent

fret² noun one of the ridges on the fingerboard of a guitar

fretful adjective showing feelings of worry or discontent ◆ **fretfully** adverb

fretsaw noun a narrow-bladed, fine-toothed saw for fretwork

fretwork noun decorative cut-out work in wood

Freudian slip (pronounced **froi**-di-an) noun an error, especially a slip of the tongue, taken as revealing an unconscious thought

⊙ After Austrian psychiatrist Sigmund Freud (1895–1982), who first noted it

friar noun a member of one of the Roman Catholic brotherhoods, especially someone who has vowed to live in poverty

friary noun (plural **friaries**) a building where friars live

friction noun **1** rubbing of two things together **2** physics the force that opposes the relative motion of one body in contact with another **3** quarrelling, bad feeling

Friday noun the sixth day of the week

⊙ After Freya, the Norse goddess of love

fridge noun, informal refrigerator

fried see **fry¹**

friend noun **1** someone who knows another person well and likes them **2** sympathizer, helper ◆ **friendless** adjective ⊙ Comes from Old English freon meaning 'to love'

friendly adjective (**friendlier, friendliest**) **1** kind **2** on good terms (with) ➤ noun (plural **friendlies**) a sports match that is not part of a competition ◆ **friendliness** noun

-friendly adjective (added to another word) **1** not harmful towards: dolphin-friendly **2** compatible with or easy to use for: child-friendly

friendly society noun, Brit an organization which gives support to members in sickness, old age, widowhood, etc, in return for regular financial contributions (also called: **benefit society**)

friendship noun the state of being friends; mutual affection

fries see **fry¹**

frieze noun **1** a part of a wall below the ceiling, often ornamented with designs **2** a picture on a long strip of paper etc, often displayed on a wall

frigate (pronounced **frig**-at) noun a small warship

fright noun sudden fear: gave me a fright/took fright and ran away

frighten verb to make afraid ◆ **frightened** adjective ◆ **frightening** adjective

frightful adjective **1** causing terror **2** informal very bad

frightfully adverb **1** very badly **2** informal extremely

frigid (pronounced **frij**-id) adjective **1** frozen, cold **2** cold in manner **3** sexually unresponsive ◆ **frigidity** noun ◆ **frigidly** adverb

frill noun **1** an ornamental edging **2** an unnecessary ornament ◆ **frilly** adjective

fringe noun **1** a border of loose threads **2** hair cut to hang over the forehead **3** a border of soft material, paper, etc ➤ verb to edge round

Frisbee noun, trademark a plastic plate-like object skimmed through the air as a game

⊙ Based on the name of the Frisbie bakery in Connecticut, whose lightweight pie tins inspired the invention

frisk verb **1** to skip about playfully **2** informal to search (someone) closely for concealed weapons etc

frisky adjective (**friskier, friskiest**) lively, playful, and keen to have fun ◆ **friskily** adverb

frisson (pronounced **free**-son) noun a shiver of fear or excitement

fritter noun a piece of fried batter containing fruit etc

fritter away verb to waste, squander

frivolity noun (plural **frivolities**) levity, lack of seriousness

frivolous adjective playful, not serious ◆ **frivolously** adverb

frizz noun of hair: a mass of tight curls ➤ verb to form or make (something) form a frizz

frizzy adjective (**frizzier, frizziest**) of hair: massed in small curls

fro adverb: **to and fro** forwards and backwards

frock *noun* **1** a woman's or girl's dress **2** a monk's wide-sleeved garment

frock-coat *noun* a man's double-breasted coat that reaches down to the knees

frog *noun* a small greenish jumping animal living on land and in water

frogman *noun* (*plural* **frogmen**) *informal* an underwater diver with flippers and breathing apparatus

frogmarch *verb* to seize (someone) from behind and push them forward while holding their arms tight behind their back

frogspawn *noun* a mass of frogs' eggs encased in a protective jelly

frolic *noun* a merry, light-hearted playing ➤ *verb* (**frolicking, frolicked**) to play light-heartedly

frolicsome *adjective* in the mood for, or fond of, frolicking

from *preposition* **1** used before the place, person, etc that is the starting point of an action etc: *sailing from England to France/The office is closed from Friday to Monday* **2** used to show separation: *Warn them to keep away from there*

fromage frais (*pronounced* from-ahsz **frei**) *noun* a creamy low-fat cheese with the consistency of whipped cream ⊙ Comes from French meaning 'fresh cheese'

frond *noun, botany* a leaf-like growth, especially a branch of a fern or palm

front *noun* **1** the part of anything nearest the person who sees it **2** the part which faces the direction in which something moves **3** the fighting line in a war **4** the boundary between two air masses that have different temperatures (*see also:* **cold front, occluded front, warm front**) ➤ *adjective* at or in the front • **in front of** at the head of, before

frontage *noun* the front part of a building

frontal *adjective* **1** relating to the front **2** aimed at the front **3** *anatomy* to do with the forehead **4** *meteorology* to do with a **front** (sense 4): *frontal system*

frontal rainfall *noun, meteorology* rainfall caused by a warm air mass being forced upwards by a cooler air mass, then cooling and condensing

front bench *noun* a seat in the House of Commons for members who hold an official position in the government or in the opposition (*compare with:* **back bench**) ♦ **front-bencher** *noun*

frontier *noun* a boundary between countries

frontispiece *noun* a picture at the very beginning of a book

frost *noun* **1** frozen dew **2** the coldness of weather needed to form ice ➤ *verb* **1** to cover with frost **2** *US* to ice (a cake)

frostbite *noun* damage to the body tissues, especially the nose, fingers, or toes, caused by exposure to very low temperatures

frosted *adjective* having an appearance as if covered in frost, eg glass with a specially roughened surface

frosting *noun, US* icing on a cake etc

frosty *adjective* (**frostier, frostiest**) **1** of weather: cold enough for frost to form **2** cold, unwelcoming: *gave me a frosty look*

froth *noun* foam on liquids ➤ *verb* to throw up foam ♦ **frothy** *adjective*

frown *verb* to wrinkle the brows in deep thought, disapproval, etc ➤ *noun* **1** a wrinkling of the brows **2** a disapproving look • **frown on** to look upon with disapproval

froze and **frozen** see **freeze**

fructify *verb* (**fructifies, fructifying, fructified**) to bear fruit or make bear fruit

fructose *noun* a natural sugar found in honey and fruit

frugal *adjective* **1** careful in spending, thrifty **2** costing little, small: *a frugal meal* ♦ **frugality** *noun*

frugally *adverb* in a way which reduces spending to a minimum

fruit *noun* **1** the part of a plant containing the seed **2** result: *All their hard work bore fruit* ♦ **fruity** *adjective*

fruitarian *noun* someone who eats only fruit

fruiterer *noun* someone who sells fruit

fruitful *adjective* **1** producing plenty of fruit **2** producing good results: *a fruitful meeting*

fruition (*pronounced* froo-**ish**-on) *noun* **1** ripeness **2** a good result

fruitless *adjective* useless, done in vain

fruit machine *noun* a gambling machine into which coins are put

frump *noun* a plain, badly or unfashionably dressed woman ♦ **frumpish** *adjective* ♦ **frumpy** *adjective*

frustrate *verb* **1** to make to feel powerless **2** to bring to nothing: *frustrated his wishes*

frustration *noun* **1** a feeling of irritation and annoyance as a result of being powerless or unable to do something **2** the bringing to nothing or spoiling of something

frustum *noun, maths* (*plural* **frustums** or **frusta**) a part of a cone between two parallel planes

fry[1] *verb* (**fries, frying, fried**) to cook in hot fat ➤ *noun* (*plural* **fries**) food cooked in hot fat

fry[2] *plural noun* a young fish • **small fry** unimportant people or things

frying pan *noun* a shallow long-handled pan for frying food in • **out of the frying pan into the fire** from a bad situation into an even worse one

FSA *abbreviation* **1** Financial Services Authority, a body that regulates financial markets **2** Food Standards Agency

FTP *abbreviation, computing* file-transfer protocol, a means of transferring data across a computer network

fuchsia (*pronounced* **fyoo**-sha) *noun* a plant with long hanging flowers

fuddle *verb* to confuse, muddle

fudge¹ *noun* a soft, sugary sweet

fudge² *verb* to cheat ➤ *noun* a cheat

fuel *noun* a substance such as coal, gas, or petrol, used to keep a fire or engine going

fuel cell *noun* a device that produces electricity by converting the chemical energy released by oxidizing a fuel

fugitive *adjective* running away, on the run ➤ *noun* someone who is running away from the police etc: *a fugitive from justice*

fugue (*pronounced* fyoog) *noun* a piece of music in which a theme is introduced in one part and developed as other parts take it up

-ful *suffix* **1** full of: *joyful* **2** causing: *wonderful/ stressful* **3** forming nouns referring to the amount a container will hold: *spoonful*

fulcrum (*pronounced* **fuwl**-krum) *noun* (*plural* **fulcrums** *or* **fulcra**) the point on which a lever turns, or a balanced object rests

fulfil *or US* **fulfill** *verb* (**fulfilling, fulfilled**) to carry out (a task, promise, etc)

fulfilment *noun* **1** successful completion, accomplishment **2** satisfaction with things achieved

full *adjective* **1** holding as much as can be held **2** plump: *a full face* ➤ *adverb* (used with *adjectives*) fully: *full-grown* • **full of** having a great deal or plenty of

fullback *noun* a defensive player in football etc, the nearest to their team's goal-line

full-blown *adjective* having all the features of the specified thing: *a full-blown war*

full moon *noun* the moon when it appears at its largest

full stop *noun* a punctuation mark (.) placed at the end of a sentence

full-time *adjective* for the whole of the working week: *a full-time job* (*compare with*: **part-time**)

fully *adverb* **1** entirely, completely **2** at least

fully-fledged *adjective* **1** of a person: completely trained or qualified **2** of a bird: old enough to have grown feathers

fulmar (*pronounced* **fuwl**-mar) *noun* a white sea bird

fulsome *adjective, formal* overdone: *fulsome praise*

fumble *verb* **1** to use the hands awkwardly **2** to drop (a thrown ball etc)

fume *verb* **1** to give off smoke or vapour **2** to be in a silent rage

fumes *plural noun* smoke, vapour

fumigate *verb* to kill the germs in (a place) by means of strong fumes ♦ **fumigation** *noun*

fun *noun* enjoyment, a good time: *Are you having fun?* • **make fun of** to tease, make others laugh at

function *noun* **1** a special job, use, or duty of a machine, person, part of the body, etc **2** the part played by a word etc in a phrase, sentence, etc or by language in general, as opposed to its appearance (*contrasted with*: **form**) **3** *computing* any of the basic operations of a computer, usually corresponding to a single operation **4** an organized event such as a party, reception, etc **5** *maths* the relation of every element in a set (the **domain**) to a single element of a second set (the **codomain**), shown by $y = f(x)$, where x is an element of the first set and y is an element of the second ➤ *verb* **1** to work, operate: *The engine isn't functioning properly* **2** to carry out usual duties: *I can't function at this time in the morning*

functional *adjective* **1** designed to be efficient rather than decorative; plain **2** in working order

functional group *noun, chemistry* in a molecule of a substance: a combination of two or more bonded atoms that tend to act as a single unit, eg the hydroxyl group

functionalism *noun* **1** the practical application of ideas **2** the idea that the form of something should be determined by its function or use ♦ **functionalist** *noun*

functionality *noun, computing* **1** the capacity that a thing, idea, etc has to be functional or practical **2** the application of a computer program

fund *noun* **1** a sum of money for a special purpose: *charity fund* **2** a store or supply

fundamental *adjective* **1** of great or far-reaching importance **2** basic, essential: *fundamental to her happiness* ➤ *noun* **1** a necessary part **2** (**fundamentals**) the groundwork, the first stages

fundamentalism *noun* in religion, politics, etc: strict adherence to the traditional teachings of a particular religion or doctrine ♦ **fundamentalist** *noun*

fundamental particle *noun, physics* an elementary particle

fundamental unit *noun* a unit in a system of measurement from which all other units are derived, eg metre as a unit of length and second as a unit of time

fundraiser *noun* **1** someone engaged in fundraising for a charity etc **2** an event held to raise money for a cause ♦ **fundraising** *noun*

fundus *noun* (*plural* **fundi** – *pronounced* **fun**-dai) *anatomy* the bottom of a hollow organ

funeral *noun* the ceremony of burial or cremation

funeral director *noun* an undertaker

funeral parlour *noun* an undertaker's place of business

funereal (*pronounced* fyoo-**neer**-i-al) *adjective* mournful

funfair *noun* an amusement park

fungicide *noun* a chemical that kills or limits the growth of fungi ♦ **fungicidal** *adjective*

fungoid *adjective* resembling a fungus

fungus *noun* (*plural* **fungi** – *pronounced* fung-gee) **1** a soft, spongy plant-like growth, eg a mushroom, that lives on other organisms or matter **2** disease-growth on animals and plants ♦ **fungal** *adjective* ♦ **fungoid** *adjective* like a fungus ♦ **fungous** *adjective* **1** like a fungus **2** growing suddenly

funk¹ *noun, informal* funky music

funk² *noun, informal* fear, panic

funky *adjective* (**funkier, funkiest**), *informal* **1** of jazz and pop music: unsophisticated, earthy and soulful, like early blues **2** fashionable, trendy **3** odd, eccentric

funnel *noun* **1** a cone ending in a tube, for pouring liquids into bottles **2** a tube or passage for escape of smoke, air, etc ➤ *verb* (**funnelling, funnelled**) to pass through a funnel; channel

funny *adjective* (**funnier, funniest**) **1** amusing **2** odd ♦ **funnily** *adverb*

funny bone *noun* part of the elbow which gives a prickly feeling when knocked

fur *noun* **1** the short fine hair of certain animals **2** their skins covered with fur **3** a coating on the tongue, on the inside of kettles, etc ➤ *verb* (**furring, furred**) to line or cover with fur

furbish *verb* to rub until bright; burnish

furcate (*pronounced* **fer**-keit or fer-**keit**) *verb* to branch or divide like a fork ➤ *adjective* (*pronounced* **fer**-keit or **fer**-kat) forked ⊙ Comes from Latin *furca* meaning 'fork'

furious *adjective* **1** extremely angry **2** stormy **3** fast, energetic and rather disorganized ♦ **furiously** *adverb*

furl *verb* of flags, sails or umbrellas: to roll up

furlong *noun* one-eighth of a mile (220 yards, 201.17 metres)

furlough (*pronounced* **fer**-loh) *noun* leave of absence, especially for military duty

furnace *noun* a very hot oven for melting iron ore, making steam for heating etc

furnish *verb* **1** to fit up (a room or house) completely **2** to supply: *furnished with enough food for a week*

furnishings *plural noun* fittings, furniture

furniture *noun* movable articles in a house, eg tables, chairs

furore (*pronounced* fyoo-**raw**-ri) *noun* uproar; excitement

furrier (*pronounced* **fu**-ri-er) *noun* someone who trades in or works with furs

furrow *noun* **1** a groove made by a plough **2** a deep groove **3** a deep wrinkle ➤ *verb* **1** to cut deep grooves in **2** to wrinkle: *furrowed brow*

furry *adjective* (**furrier, furriest**) covered with fur

further *adverb & adjective* to a greater distance or degree; in addition ➤ *verb* to help on or forward

further education *noun* education after secondary school other than at a university (*compare:* **higher education**)

furthermore *adverb* in addition to what has been said

furthest *adverb* to the greatest distance or degree

furtive *adjective* stealthy, sly: *furtive glance* ♦ **furtively** *adverb*

fury *noun* violent anger

furze another name for **gorse**

fuse *verb* (**fusing, fused**) **1** to melt **2** to join together **3** to put a fuse in (a plug etc) **4** of a circuit etc: to stop working because of the melting of a fuse ➤ *noun* **1** a wire which melts when an electric current exceeds a certain value, put in an electric circuit for safety **2** any device for causing an explosion to take place automatically

fuselage (*pronounced* **fyoo**-ze-lahsz) *noun* the body of an aeroplane

fusible *adjective* able to be fused or melted

fusillade (*pronounced* **fyoo**-zi-lad) *noun* **1** a simultaneous or continuous discharge of firearms **2** an onslaught, eg of criticism ⊙ Comes from French *fusillade*, from *fusiller* meaning 'to shoot'

fusion *noun* **1** *chemistry* melting, changing from a solid to a liquid **2** a merging, a joining together: *a fusion of musical traditions* **3** nuclear fusion

fuss *noun* **1** unnecessary activity, excitement or attention, often about something unimportant: *making a fuss about nothing* **2** strong complaint ➤ *verb* **1** to be unnecessarily concerned about details **2** to worry too much

fussy *adjective* (**fussier, fussiest**) **1** over-elaborate **2** choosy, finicky **3** partial, in favour of one thing over another: *Either will do; I'm not fussy* ♦ **fussily** *adverb* (meanings 1 and 2) ♦ **fussiness** *noun* (meanings 1 and 2)

fusty *adjective* (**fustier, fustiest**) mouldy; stale-smelling

futile *adjective* useless; having no effect

futility *noun* uselessness

futon (*pronounced* **foo**-ton) *noun* a sofa bed with a low frame and detachable mattress

future *adjective* happening later in time ➤ *noun* **1** the time to come: *foretell the future* **2** the part of your life still to come: *planning for their future* **3** *grammar* the future tense • **in future** far from now

future tense *noun, grammar* the tense of a verb which indicates that something will take place in the future, in English formed with the auxiliary verb *will* and infinitive without *to*, as in *She will see him tomorrow*

futurism *noun* an artistic movement of the 20th century concerned with making use of modern technology ♦ **futurist** *noun & adjective*

futuristic *adjective* of design etc: so modern or original as to seem appropriate to the future

fuzz *noun* **1** fine, light hair or feathers **2** *Brit slang* the police

fuzzy *adjective* (**fuzzier, fuzziest**) **1** covered with fuzz, fluffy **2** tightly curled: *fuzzy hairdo*

fx *abbreviation, film & TV* effects

Gg

G *noun, music* the fifth note in the scale of C major

g *abbreviation* gram(s)

Ga *symbol, chemistry* gallium

gabble *verb* to talk fast, chatter ➤ *noun* fast talk

gaberdine *noun* **1** a heavy overcoat **2** a heavy wool or cotton fabric

gable *noun* the triangular area of wall at the end of a building with a ridged roof

gadabout *noun* someone who loves going out or travelling

gadget *noun* a small simple machine or tool: *a gadget to unlock your mobile phone*

gadolinium *noun, chemistry* (symbol **Gd**) a soft silvery-white metallic element, belonging to the lanthanide series, which is highly magnetic at low temperatures

> ⊙ Named after Finnish mineralogist Johan Gadolin (1760–1852)

Gaelic *noun* **1** (*pronounced* **ga**-lik) the language of the Scottish Highlands **2** (*pronounced* **gei**-lik) the Irish language ➤ *adjective* written or spoken in Gaelic

gaff *noun* **1** a large hook used for landing fish, such as salmon **2** a spar made from a mast, for raising the top of a sail • **blow the gaff** *informal* to let out a secret

gag *verb* (**gagging, gagged**) to silence someone by putting something over their mouth ➤ *noun* **1** a piece of cloth etc put in or over someone's mouth to silence them **2** *informal* a joke

gaggle *noun* a flock of geese

gaiety and **gaily** see gay

gain *verb* **1** to win; earn **2** to reach **3** to get closer, especially in a race: *gaining on the leader* **4** of a clock: to go ahead of correct time **5** to take on (eg weight) ➤ *noun* **1** something gained **2** profit

gait *noun* way or manner of walking

> ❗ Do not confuse with: **gate**

gaiter *noun* a cloth ankle-covering, fitting over the shoe, sometimes reaching to the knee

gala *noun* **1** a public festival **2** a sports meeting: *swimming gala*

galactic *adjective* relating to a galaxy or the Galaxy

galactose *noun, chemistry* a soluble sugar obtained from lactose

galaxy *noun* (*plural* **galaxies**) **1** a system of stars **2** an impressive gathering **3** (**the Galaxy**) the Milky Way

gale *noun* a strong wind

gall (*pronounced* gawl) *noun* **1** (**the gall**) *informal* the impudence, cheek: *he had the gall to suggest I was cheating* **2** a growth caused by insects on trees and plants **3** bitterness of feeling **4** *old* bile, a bitter fluid produced by the liver and stored in the **gall bladder** ➤ *verb* to annoy

gallant *adjective* **1** brave; noble **2** polite or attentive towards women ➤ *noun* a gallant man

gallantry *noun* gallant behaviour

gall bladder *noun, anatomy* a small muscular pear-shaped organ lying beneath the liver that stores bile and releases it into the intestine

galleon *noun, history* a large Spanish sailing ship

gallery *noun* (*plural* **galleries**) **1** a long passage **2** the top floor of seats in a theatre **3** a room or building for showing artworks **4** a balcony along an inside upper wall, eg of a church or hall, often reserved for musicians etc: *minstrels' gallery*

galley *noun* (*plural* **galleys**) **1** *history* a long, low-built ship driven by oars **2** a ship's kitchen

galley-slave *noun, history* a prisoner condemned to row in a galley

galling *adjective* annoying, frustrating: *it was galling to lose by only one point*

gallium *noun, chemistry* (symbol **Ga**) a soft silvery metallic element used in alloys with low melting points

> ⊙ Comes from Latin *gallus* meaning 'cock', a translation of the name of the element's French discoverer, *Lecoq* de Boisbaudran (1838–1912)

gallivant *verb* to travel or go out for pleasure

gallon *noun* a measure for liquids (8 pints, 4.546 litres)

gallop *verb* **1** to move by leaps **2** to (cause to) move very fast ➤ *noun* a fast pace

gallows *singular noun* a wooden framework on which criminals were hanged

gallstone *noun, medicine* a small hard mass that is formed in the gall bladder or one of its ducts

galore *adverb* (*placed after the noun*) in plenty: *whisky galore*

> ⊙ Based on an Irish Gaelic phrase *go leor*, meaning 'sufficient'

galoshes or **goloshes** *plural noun* waterproof shoes worn over other shoes

galvanic *adjective* relating to electricity produced by the action of acids or other chemicals on metal ♦ **galvanism** *noun*

> ⊙ Named after the Italian physicist, Luigi *Galvani*

galvanize or **galvanise** *verb* **1** to stir into activity **2** to stimulate by electricity **3** to coat (iron etc) with zinc

gambit *noun* **1** *chess* a first move involving sacrificing a piece to make the player's position stronger **2** an opening move in a transaction, or an opening remark in a conversation

gamble *verb* **1** to play games for money **2** to risk money on the result of a game, race, etc **3** to take a wild chance ➤ *noun* a risk; a bet on a result

gambol *verb* (**gambolling, gambolled**) to leap playfully

game *noun* **1** a contest played according to rules **2** (**games**) athletic competition **3** wild animals and birds hunted for sport • **give the game away** to reveal the truth ➤ *adjective* **1** plucky **2** of a limb: lame

gamekeeper *noun* someone who looks after game birds, animals, fish, etc

gamelan (*pronounced* **gam**-e-lan) *noun, music* **1** a musical instrument similar to a xylophone **2** an orchestra of SE Asia consisting chiefly of percussion

gamer *noun* someone who plays computer games

game show *noun* a TV quiz or other game, usually with prizes

gamete *noun* in sexually reproducing organisms: a specialized sex cell, especially an **ovum** or **sperm**, which fuses with another gamete of the opposite type during fertilization (*also called*: **germ cell**)

gamine (*pronounced* ga-**meen**) *noun* a girl or young woman with a boyish appearance ➤ *adjective* of a girl or young woman: boyish in appearance ⊙ Comes from French, literally meaning 'a female urchin'

gaming *noun & adjective* **1** gambling **2** playing computer games

gamma globulin *noun, biology* any of various proteins in blood plasma that bring about passive immunity to certain diseases

gamma ray *noun* an electromagnetic ray that is stronger than an X-ray

gammon *noun* leg of a pig, salted and smoked

gamut *noun* **1** the whole range or extent of anything **2** the range of notes of an individual voice or musical instrument

> ⊙ From the name of a medieval 6-note musical scale, two notes of which were *gamma* and *ut*

gander *noun* a male goose

gang *noun* **1** a group of people who meet regularly: *I'm going out for a drink with the gang tonight* **2** a team of criminals **3** a number of labourers: *a gang of bricklayers*

gangling or **gangly** *adjective* (**ganglier, gangliest**) tall and thin, and often awkward in movement: *gangling teenagers*

ganglion *noun* (*plural* **ganglia** or **ganglions**) **1** *anatomy* a group of nerve cells, usually enclosed in a capsule **2** *medicine* a swelling that forms on the tissue surrounding a tendon

Gang of Four *noun, history* a term given to a group of four of Mao Zedong's leading advisers during the Cultural Revolution

gangrene *noun, medicine* the death and decay of a part of the body when blood cannot reach it because of an injury, disease, or frostbite ♦ **gangrenous** *adjective*

gangster *noun* a member of a gang of criminals

gangway *noun* **1** a passage between rows of seats, eg on a plane or in a theatre **2** a movable bridge leading from a quay to a ship

ganja *noun* marijuana ⊙ Comes from Hindi *ganjha* meaning 'hemp'

gannet *noun* a large white sea bird

gantry *noun* (*plural* **gantries**) a platform or structure for supporting a travelling crane etc

gaol another spelling of **jail**

gaoler another spelling of **jailer**

gap *noun* an opening or space between things

gape *verb* **1** to open the mouth wide (as in surprise) **2** to be wide open

gap year *noun* a year spent by a student between school and university doing non-academic activities

garage *noun* **1** a building for storing a car or cars **2** a shop which carries out car repairs and sells petrol, oil, etc

garb *formal, noun* dress ➤ *verb* to clothe

garbage *noun* rubbish

garble *verb* to mix up, muddle: *garbled account of events*

> ⊙ Originally meaning 'sift', which gradually developed into the sense of confusing by leaving out too much

garden *noun* a piece of ground on which flowers or vegetables are grown ➤ *verb* to work in a garden

garden centre *noun* a place where plants, seeds, garden tools, etc are sold

gardener *noun* someone who tends a garden

gardening *noun & adjective* working in a garden

garden party *noun* a large tea party, held out of doors

gargantuan *adjective* extremely large, huge

🕐 Named after *Gargantua*, a giant with an enormous appetite in a 16th-century French novel by Rabelais

gargle *verb* to rinse the throat with a liquid, without swallowing

gargoyle *noun* a grotesque carving of a human or animal head, jutting out from a roof

garish *adjective* tastelessly over-bright: *garish book cover*

garland *noun* flowers or leaves tied or woven into a circle

garlic *noun* an onion-like plant with a strong smell and taste, used in cooking

garment *noun* an article of clothing

garner *verb, formal* to gather; collect and store

garnet *noun* a semi-precious stone, usually red in colour

garnish *verb* to decorate (a dish of food) ➤ *noun* (*plural* **garnishes**) a decoration on food
♦ **garnishing** *noun*

garret *noun* an attic room

garrison *noun* a group of troops for guarding a fortress

garrotte *verb* to strangle someone by tightening a noose etc round their neck (originally by tightening an iron collar, also called a **garrotte**)

garrulous *adjective* fond of talking ♦ **garrulity** *noun*

garter *noun* a broad elastic band to keep a stocking up

gas *noun* (*plural* **gases**) **1** a substance like air (though you can smell some gases) **2** a natural or manufactured form of this which will burn and is used as a fuel **3** *US* petrol ➤ *verb* (**gassing**, **gassed**) to poison with gas

gaseous *adjective* in gas form

gash *noun* (*plural* **gashes**) a deep, open cut ➤ *verb* to cut deeply into

gasket *noun* a layer of padding used to make airtight or gas-tight joints

gas mask *noun* a covering for the face to prevent breathing in poisonous gas

gasoline *noun, US* petrol

gasometer *noun* a tank for storing gas

gasp *noun* the sound made by a sudden intake of breath ➤ *verb* **1** to breathe with difficulty **2** to say breathlessly **3** *informal* to want badly: *gasping for a cup of tea*

gastric *adjective* relating to the stomach: *gastric ulcer*

gastric juice *noun, chemistry* a strongly acidic fluid produced in the stomach during digestion

gastroenteritis *noun, medicine* inflammation of the lining of the stomach and intestine

gastronomy *noun* the appreciation and enjoyment of good food and wine

gastropod *noun, biology* any of a class of invertebrate animals which typically have a large flattened muscular foot and a single spirally coiled shell, eg snail, slug, whelk

gasworks *noun* place where gas is made

gate *noun* **1** a door across an opening in a wall, fence, etc **2** the number of people at a football match **3** the total entrance money paid by the people at a football match **4** an electronic circuit whose output is controlled by the combination of inputs it receives (*see also:* **logic gate**)

⚠ Do not confuse with: **gait**

gateau (*pronounced* **gat**-oh) *noun* (*plural* **gateaus** *or* **gateaux**) a rich cake, usually layered and filled with cream

gatecrash *verb* to go to a party uninvited
♦ **gatecrasher** *noun*

gateway *noun* **1** an opening containing a gate **2** an entrance **3** *computing* a connection between networks

gather *verb* **1** to bring together, or meet, in one place **2** to pick (flowers etc) **3** to increase in: *gather speed* **4** to learn, come to the conclusion (that): *I gather you don't want to go* **5** to pull (material) into small folds

gathering *noun* a crowd

gauche (*pronounced* gohsh) *adjective* awkward and clumsy in people's company

🕐 Taken from the French word for 'left', because of the supposed awkwardness of using the left hand

gaudy *adjective* showy; vulgarly bright in colour
♦ **gaudily** *adverb*

gauge (*pronounced* geij) *verb* **1** to measure **2** to make a guess ➤ *noun* a measuring device: *a rain gauge*

gaunt *adjective* thin, haggard

gauntlet[1] *noun* **1** a long glove (often of leather) with a guard for the wrist, used for some sports etc: *the falcon landed on his leather gauntlet* **2** *history* an iron glove worn with armour • **take up the gauntlet** to accept a challenge • **throw down the gauntlet** to offer a challenge

gauntlet[2] *noun*: **run the gauntlet** to expose yourself to criticism, hostility, etc

🕐 The *gauntlet* was an old military punishment of being made to run past a line of soldiers armed with sticks; the word is of Swedish origin and unrelated to **gauntlet**[1].

gauze *noun* thin cloth that you can see through

gawky *adjective* (**gawkier, gawkiest**) awkward

gay *adjective* **1** homosexual **2** lively; merry, full of fun **3** brightly coloured ➤ *noun* a homosexual

♦ **gaiety** noun (meaning 2) ♦ **gaily** adverb (meanings 2 and 3)

gaze verb to look steadily ➤ noun a fixed look

gazelle noun a small deer

gazette noun a newspaper, especially one having lists of government notices

gazetteer noun a geographical dictionary

GB, Gb or **Gbyte** abbreviation, computing gigabyte(s)

GBH or **gbh** abbreviation, law grievous bodily harm, the crime of deliberately causing someone a serious physical injury

Gbit abbreviation, computing gigabit(s)

GCSE abbreviation **1** General Certificate of Secondary Education, an examination in one of a range of subjects taken around the age of 16 in British schools **2** a pass gained in such an examination

Gd symbol, chemistry gadolinium

GDP abbreviation gross domestic product

Ge symbol, chemistry germanium

gear noun **1** clothing and equipment needed for a particular job, sport, etc **2** a connection by means of a set of toothed wheels between a car engine and the wheels ➤ verb: **gear to** to adapt to, design for what is needed

gearbox noun (plural **gearboxes**) the system of gears that transmits power from the engine to the road wheels in a vehicle

Geddes axe noun, history the term given to cuts in public and welfare expenditure in Britain in 1922

⊙ The committee which recommended the cuts was chaired by Sir Eric *Geddes*, then Minister for Transport

geese plural of **goose**

Geiger counter (pronounced **gai**-ger) noun, physics an instrument that detects and measures the intensity of radiation

⊙ Named after German physicist Hans *Geiger* (1882–1945)

gel (pronounced jel) noun a jelly-like substance, especially one used for styling the hair

gelatine noun a jelly-like substance made from hooves, animal bones, etc, and used to make food set

gelatinous (pronounced jel-**at**-in-us) adjective jelly-like

geld verb to castrate (an animal)

gelding noun a castrated horse

gem noun **1** (also called: **gemstone**) a precious stone, especially when cut **2** someone or something greatly valued

Gemini noun **1** the third sign of the zodiac, represented by the twins **2** someone born under this sign, between 21 May and 21 June

gender noun **1** the condition of being male or female **2** grammar a classification of words roughly corresponding to the sex they refer to: masculine, feminine or neuter

gene noun the basic unit of heredity responsible for passing on specific characteristics from parents to offspring

genealogical adjective relating to genealogy

genealogy noun (plural **genealogies**) **1** the history of families from generation to generation **2** a personal family history

gene mapping noun, genetics the determination of the positions and relative distances of genes on chromosomes

general adjective **1** not detailed, broad: a general idea of the person's interests **2** involving everyone: a general election **3** to do with several different things: general knowledge **4** of most people: the general opinion **5** (**in general**) generally ➤ noun a high-ranking army officer

general anaesthetic noun, medicine a drug that causes loss of consciousness (compare with: **local anaesthetic**)

generalize or **generalise** verb to make a broad general statement, meant to cover all individual cases ♦ **generalization** noun

generally adverb **1** usually, in most cases **2** by most people: generally known

general practitioner noun a doctor who treats most ordinary illnesses

general strike noun **1** a national strike involving most of a country's workforce **2** history (**the General Strike**) the general strike that took place in Britain from 4–12 May 1926

generate verb to produce, bring into being: generate electricity/generate good will

generation noun **1** creation, making **2** a step in family descent **3** the average period between the birth of a person or animal and their offspring **4** people born at about the same time: the generation who were teenagers in the 90s **5** a stage in development: the next generation of mobile phones

generator noun a machine that converts mechanical energy into electrical energy

generic adjective **1** general, applicable to any member of a group or class **2** of a drug, software, etc: not sold as a specific brand **3** biology belonging or relating to a genus

generous adjective giving plentifully; kind ♦ **generosity** noun ♦ **generously** adverb

genesis noun beginning, origin

gene therapy noun replacing defective genes with healthy ones

genetic adjective **1** relating to genes **2** inherited through genes: genetic disease ♦ **genetically** adverb

genetically modified adjective (abbrev **GM**)

of an organism: having had its genes artificially altered so it has fewer defects

genetic code *noun* the system by which genes pass on instructions to pass on features inherited from previous generations

genetic engineering or **genetic manipulation** *noun* the science of altering the genetic structure of an organism to change its characteristics

genetic fingerprinting *noun* the analysis of DNA from body tissues or fluids in order to establish a person's identity

genetics *singular noun* the study of the way characteristics are passed from one generation to the next ♦ **geneticist** *noun*

genial *adjective* good-natured ♦ **geniality** *noun* ♦ **genially** *adverb*

genie *noun* (*plural* **genii** – *pronounced* **jeen**-i-ai) a guardian spirit

genitals *noun plural* the organs of sexual reproduction ♦ **genital** *adjective*

genius *noun* (*plural* **geniuses**) **1** unusual cleverness **2** someone who is unusually clever

genocide *noun* the deliberate extermination of a race of people ♦ **genocidal** *adjective*

genome *noun* the full set of chromosomes of an organism, or the total number of genes in the set

genomics *singular noun* the study of genomes

genotype *noun* **1** the genetic make-up of an organism **2** a group containing all the individual organisms that have the same genetic make-up

genre (*pronounced* szahn-re) *noun* **1** a particular type or kind of literature, music or other artistic work **2** (*full form:* **genre painting**) *art* a painting of scenes from everyday life ℗ Comes from French *genre* meaning 'kind' or 'type'

gent *noun, informal* a man

genteel *adjective* good-mannered, especially excessively

gentile (*pronounced* **jen**-tail) *noun* a non-Jew

gentility *noun* **1** aristocracy **2** good manners, refinement, often in excess

gentle *adjective* **1** mild-mannered, not brutal **2** mild, not extreme: *gentle breeze* **3** having a pleasant light or soft quality, not harsh or forceful ♦ **gentleness** *noun* ♦ **gently** *adverb*

gentleman *noun* (*plural* **gentlemen**) **1** a man, especially one of noble birth **2** a well-mannered man

gentlemanly *adjective* behaving in a polite manner

gentrification *noun, geography* the movement of middle-class people into a formerly working-class area, and the consequent changes in the character of the area

gentry *noun* a wealthy, land-owning class of people

gents *singular noun* (**the gents**) *informal* a men's public toilet

genuine *adjective* **1** real, not fake or pretended: *genuine antique/She may have been lying, but her distress was genuine* **2** honest and straightforward ♦ **genuinely** *adverb* (meaning 1) ♦ **genuineness** *noun*

genus (*pronounced* **jee**-nus)*noun* (*plural* **genera**: *pronounced* **jen**-e-ra) a category of organisms into which a family is divided, and which in turn is subdivided into species

geo- *prefix* of or relating to the earth: *geography/geometry* (= a branch of mathematics originally concerned with measuring the earth) ℗ Comes from Greek *ge* meaning 'earth'

geodesic dome *noun* a dome whose surface is composed of a large number of triangles or other elements with straight lines

geodesic line *noun, maths* a line on a plane or curve that represents the shortest distance between two points

geographer *noun* someone who studies geography

geographic information system *noun* (*abbrev* **GIS**) a computer system that captures and analyses geographical data from a location

geography *noun* the study of the surface of the earth and its inhabitants ♦ **geographic** or **geographical** *adjective*

geologist *noun* someone who studies geology

geology *noun* the study of the earth's history as shown in its rocks and soils ♦ **geological** *adjective*

geometric or **geometrical** *adjective* **1** relating to geometry **2** of a shape or pattern: made up of angles and straight lines

geometric mean *noun, maths* the nth root of the product of *n* quantities or numbers, eg the geometric mean of 2 and 3 is the second (ie square) root of 6

geometric progression or **geometric sequence** *noun, maths* a sequence of numbers in which the ratio between one term and the next remains constant, eg 1, 2, 4, 8, …

geometry *noun* the branch of mathematics which deals with the study of lines, angles, and figures

geomorphology *noun* the study of the nature and history of the landforms on the surface of the Earth ♦ **geomorphological** *adjective* ♦ **geomorphologist** *noun*

geophysics *singular noun* the scientific study of the Earth's physical properties ♦ **geophysicist** *noun*

Georgian *adjective* relating to or characteristic of the period of reign of a King George, especially the first four collectively (from 1714 to

1830) ➤ *noun* someone who lived in such a period

geotropism *noun, botany* the growth of the roots or shoots of plants in response to gravity (eg roots show **positive geotropism** because they grow in the direction of gravity)

geranium *noun* a plant with thick leaves and bright red or pink flowers

gerbil (*pronounced* **jerb**-il) *noun* a small, rat-like desert animal, often kept as a pet

geriatric *adjective* **1** dealing with old people **2** *informal* very old

geriatrics *singular noun* the health and care of the elderly

germ *noun* **1** a small living organism which can cause disease **2** the earliest or initial form of something, eg a fertilized egg **3** that from which anything grows: *germ of an idea*

germanium *noun, chemistry* (symbol **Ge**) a hard greyish-white element, used as a semiconductor in electronic devices

⊙ Named after *Germany*, the native country of its discoverer, C A Winkler (1838–1904)

German measles *singular noun* rubella

German shepherd *noun* a breed of large wolf-like dog (*also called*: **alsatian**)

germ cell *noun* the reproductive cell of a plant or animal (*also called*: **gamete**)

germicide *noun* a germ-killing substance

germinate *verb* **1** *biology* of a seed or spore: to show the first signs of development **2** to make (a seed, an idea, etc) begin to grow **3** to come into being ♦ **germination** *noun*

gerrymander *verb* to rearrange (voting districts etc) to suit a political purpose ♦ **gerrymandering** *noun*

⊙ After US governor, Elbridge *Gerry*, who rearranged the map of Massachusetts in 1811 to a shape resembling that of a sala*mander*

gerund *noun* an action noun with the ending -ing, eg watch*ing*, wait*ing*

Gestapo (*pronounced* gi-**sta**-po) *noun, history* the secret police in Nazi Germany ⊙ Comes from German *Geheime Staatspolizei* meaning 'secret state police'

gestate *verb* **1** of mammals: to carry young in the uterus **2** to be carried in the uterus and develop physically **3** to develop slowly in the mind ⊙ From Latin *gestare* meaning 'to carry'

gestation *noun* in mammals: the period of time when a young animal develops in the uterus

gesticulate *verb* to wave the hands and arms about in excitement etc ♦ **gesticulation** *noun*

gesture *noun* **1** a meaningful action with the hands, head, etc **2** an action expressing your feelings or intent: *gesture of good will*

get *verb* (**getting, got** *US* **getting, got, gotten**) **1** to go and find, take hold of, obtain: *get a carton of milk on the way home/I'll get you, you rascal!/I'm at the station. Can you come and get me?* **2** to go or move **3** to cause to be done: *get your hair cut* **4** to receive: *get a letter* **5** to cause to be in some condition: *get the car started* **6** to arrive: *what time did you get home?* **7** to catch or have (a disease): *I think I've got flu* **8** to become: *get rich* • **get at 1** to reach **2** to hint at: *what are you getting at?* **3** to criticize continually: *stop getting at me* • **get away with** to escape punishment for • **get on with** to be on friendly terms with • **get over** to recover from • **get up 1** to stand up **2** to get out of bed ⊙ Comes from Old Norse *geta*

❗ **Get** is one of the most overused words in the English language. Make sure you don't use it too much!

geyser (*pronounced* **geez**-er) *noun* **1** a natural hot spring **2** a device which heats domestic water when the tap is turned on

ghastly *adjective* **ghastlier, ghastliest 1** *informal* very ill: *feeling ghastly* **2** horrible, ugly **3** very pale, death-like **4** *informal* very bad ♦ **ghastliness** *noun*

gherkin *noun* a small pickled cucumber

ghetto *noun* (*plural* **ghettos** *or* **ghettoes**) a poor residential part of a city in which a certain group (especially of immigrants) lives

ghost *noun* the spirit of a dead person ➤ *verb* to ghost-write (books, speeches, etc)

ghostly *adjective* like a ghost

ghost-write *verb* (**ghost-writing, ghost-wrote, ghost-written**) to write (books, speeches, etc) for another person who is credited as the author ♦ **ghost-writer** *noun*

ghoul (*pronounced* gool) *noun* **1** an evil spirit which robs dead bodies **2** someone unnaturally interested in death and disaster ♦ **ghoulish** *adjective*

GHz *abbreviation* gigahertz, a unit of frequency equal to one thousand hertz

giant *noun* **1** an imaginary being, like a human but enormous **2** a very tall or large person ➤ *adjective* huge

giantess *noun* a female giant

gibber *verb* **1** to speak nonsense **2** to make meaningless noises; babble

gibberish *noun* words without meaning; rubbish

gibbet *noun, history* a gallows where criminals were executed, or hung up after execution

gibbon *noun* a large, tailless ape

gibe another spelling of **jibe**

giblets (*pronounced* **jib**-lets) *plural noun* organs from the inside of a chicken or other fowl

giddy *adjective* **giddier, giddiest 1** unsteady, dizzy **2** causing dizziness: *from a giddy height* ♦ **giddiness** *noun* (meaning 1)

GIF *abbreviation, computing* graphic interchange format, a standard image file format

gift *noun* **1** something freely given, eg a present **2** a natural talent: *a gift for music* **3** *informal* something easily done: *the exam paper was a gift* • **look a gift horse in the mouth** to find fault with a gift

gifted *adjective* having special natural power or ability

gig *noun* a pop, jazz or folk concert

gigabit *noun* (*abbrev* **Gbit**) a measure of computer data or memory, approximately 10^9 (one billion) bits

gigabyte *noun* (*abbrev* **GB, Gb** or **Gbyte**) a measure of computer data or memory, equal to 1024 megabytes

gigahertz *noun* (*abbrev* **GHz**) gigahertz, a unit of frequency equal to one billion hertz

gigantic *adjective* huge, of giant size

gigantism (*pronounced* jai-**gant**-ism) *noun, biology* excessive size or growth

giggle *verb* to laugh in a nervous or silly manner ► *noun* a nervous or silly laugh

GIGO *abbreviation, computing* garbage in garbage out, ie incorrect input results in incorrect output

gild (*pronounced* gild) *verb* **1** to cover with beaten gold **2** to make bright • **gild the lily** to try to improve something already beautiful enough ⊕ Comes from Old English *gyldan* which is related to *gold*

⚠ Do not confuse with: **guild**

gill (*pronounced* gil) *noun* one of the openings on the side of a fish's head through which it breathes

gillie (*pronounced* **gil**-i) *noun* an assistant and guide to someone fishing or shooting on a Scottish estate

gilt (*pronounced* gilt) *noun* beaten gold used for gilding ► *adjective* **1** covered with thin gold **2** gold in colour

⚠ Do not confuse with: **guilt**. **Gilt** is a past participle of the verb 'gild'.

gilt-edged *adjective* not risky, safe to invest in: *gilt-edged stocks*

gimlet (*pronounced* **gim**-lit) *noun* a small tool for boring holes by hand

gimmick *noun* something meant to attract attention

gin[1] *noun* an alcoholic drink made from grain, flavoured with juniper berries

gin[2] *noun* a trap or snare

ginger *noun* a hot-tasting root, used as a seasoning in food ► *adjective* **1** flavoured with ginger: *ginger biscuits* **2** reddish-brown in colour: *ginger hair*

gingerbread *noun* cake flavoured with ginger

gingerly *adverb* very carefully and gently: *opened the door gingerly*

ginormous *adjective, informal* exceptionally huge ⊕ Comes from **gigantic** + **enormous**.

ginseng *noun* the root of an Asian plant, used as a tonic, stimulant and aphrodisiac

Gipsy another spelling of **Gypsy**

giraffe *noun* an African animal with very long legs and neck

ⓘ Called a *camelopard* until the 17th century

gird *verb, formal* to bind round

girder *noun* a beam of iron, steel or wood used in building

girdle *noun* **1** a belt for the waist **2** a tight-fitting piece of underwear to slim the waist

girl *noun* a female child or young woman

girlfriend *noun* a female friend, especially in a romantic relationship

girlhood *noun* the state or time of being a girl

girlie *adjective* **1** girlish **2** pornographic: *girlie magazines*

girlish *adjective* of a woman's appearance or behaviour: attractively youthful, like that of a girl

giro (*pronounced* **jai**-roh) *noun* (*plural* **giros**) **1** a system by which payment may be made through banks, post offices, etc **2** (*also called*: **girocheque**) a form like a cheque by which such payment is made **3** *informal* social security paid by girocheque

girth *noun* **1** measurement round the middle **2** a strap tying a saddle on a horse

GIS *abbreviation, geography* geographic information system

gist (*pronounced* jist) *noun* the main points or ideas of a story, argument, etc: *give me the gist of what happened*

give *verb* (**giving, gave, given**) **1** to hand over freely or in exchange **2** to utter (a shout or cry) **3** to break, crack: *the bridge gave under the weight of the train* **4** to produce: *this lamp gives a good light* ♦ **giver** *noun* (meaning 1) **give away 1** to hand over (something) to someone without payment **2** to betray: *his guilty behaviour gave him away* • **give in** to yield • **give over** *informal* to stop (doing something) • **give rise to** to cause • **give up 1** to hand over **2** to yield **3** to stop, abandon (a habit etc) • **give way 1** to yield **2** to collapse **3** to let traffic crossing your path go before you ⊕ Comes from Old English *gefan*

giveaway *noun* (*plural* **giveaways**) something that you say or do which reveals a secret to other people

given *adjective* **1** stated or specified: *on a given day* **2** assumed to be true ► *noun* something accepted as true: *that he is wrong is a given*

glacé (*pronounced* glah-**sei**) *adjective* iced or sugared: *glacé cherries*

glacial *adjective* **1** of ice or glaciers **2** icy, cold: *glacial expression*

glacial budget *noun, geography* the amount by which a glacier grows or shrinks in a year

glacial trough *noun, geography* a U-shaped river valley, caused by erosion of its sides by a moving glacier (*also called*: **U-shaped valley**)

glaciation *noun, geography* the covering of masses of land with glaciers or ice sheets

glacier *noun, geography* a slow-moving river of ice in valleys between high mountains

glad *adjective* **1** pleased: *I'm glad you were able to come* **2** giving pleasure: *glad tidings* **3** (**glad to**) perfectly willing and happy to ♦ **gladly** *adverb* (meanings 1 and 3) ♦ **gladness** *noun* (meanings 1 and 2)

gladden *verb* to make glad

glade *noun* an open space in a wood

gladiator *noun, history* in ancient Rome, a man trained to fight with other men or with animals for the amusement of spectators ♦ **gladiatorial** *adjective*

glad rags *plural noun, informal* best clothes

glam *adjective, slang* glamorous

glamorous *adjective* **1** dressing and behaving in a way which people find fascinating and attractive **2** fashionable and extravagant

glamour *noun* fascination, charm, beauty, especially artificial

glance *noun* a quick look ► *verb* to take a quick look at • **glance off** to hit and fly off sideways

gland *noun* **1** an organ that produces a specific chemical substance (eg a hormone) for use inside the body **2** a cell or group of cells in a plant that secretes eg nectar or resin

glandular *adjective* of, or affecting, the glands

glandular fever *noun* an infectious disease with symptoms including a slight fever and an enlargement of the glands

glans *noun,(plural* **glandes)** *anatomy* an acorn-shaped part of the body

glare *noun* **1** an unpleasantly bright light **2** an angry or fierce look ► *verb* **1** to shine with an unpleasantly bright light **2** to look angrily

glaring *adjective* **1** dazzling **2** very clear, obvious: *glaring mistake*

glaringly *adverb* extremely, in a way that cannot be missed: *glaringly obvious*

glasnost *noun* a political policy of openness and forthrightness, originally in the Soviet Union in the 1980s

glass *noun* (*plural* **glasses**) **1** a hard transparent substance made from metal and other oxides **2** (**glasses**) spectacles **3** a drinking vessel made of glass **4** *old* a mirror ► *adjective* made of glass

glass ceiling *noun* a barrier to promotion at work experienced by some women

glasshouse *noun* a greenhouse

glassware *noun* goods made from glass

glassy *adjective* **1** of eyes: without expression **2** of surfaces, especially water: smooth and shiny with no ripples

glaucoma *noun, medicine* a condition of increased pressure in the eye that can eventually cause loss of sight

glaucous *adjective* **1** having a dull green or blue colour **2** *botany* having a blue-green waxy coating that can be rubbed off, eg from grapes ☺ Comes from Greek *glaukos* meaning 'bluish-green' or 'bluish-grey'

glaze *verb* **1** to cover with a thin coating of glass or other shiny stuff **2** to ice (a cake etc) **3** to put panes of glass in a window **4** of eyes: to become glassy ► *noun* **1** a shiny surface **2** sugar icing

glazier *noun* someone who sets glass in window frames

gleam *verb* **1** to glow **2** to flash ► *noun* **1** a beam of light **2** brightness

glean *verb* **1** to collect, gather **2** *old* to gather corn in handfuls after the reapers

glee *noun* **1** joy **2** a song in parts

gleeful *adjective* merry, usually in a mischievous way ♦ **gleefully** *adverb*

Gleichschaltung (*pronounced* **glaikh**-shal-toong) *noun, history* elimination of all opposition, and enforcement of strict conformity, in politics, culture, etc ☺ Comes from German *gleich* meaning 'same' + *schalten* meaning 'to bring into line'

glen *noun* in Scotland, a long narrow valley

gley *noun, geography* a bluish-grey sticky clay found under some types of very damp soil ♦ **gleying** *noun* the formation of gley

glib *adjective* **1** speaking smoothly and fluently (often insincerely and superficially) **2** quick and ready, but showing little thought: *glib reply* ♦ **glibly** *adverb*

glide *verb* **1** to move smoothly and easily: *she glided effortlessly across the ice* **2** to travel by glider ► *noun* the act of gliding

glider *noun* an aeroplane without an engine

glimmer *noun* **1** a faint light **2** a faint indication: *a glimmer of hope* ► *verb* to burn or shine faintly

glimpse *noun* a brief view ► *verb* to get a brief look at

glint *verb* to sparkle, gleam ► *noun* a sparkle, a gleam

glissando *noun* (*plural* **glissandos** *or* **glissandi**), *music* the sound effect produced by gliding the finger along the keyboard or strings of an instrument

glisten *verb* to sparkle

glitch *noun* (*plural* **glitches**), *informal* a sudden brief failure to function, especially in electronic equipment

glitter *verb* to sparkle ➤ *noun* **1** sparkling **2** shiny granules used for decorating paper etc

glittery *adjective* shiny, sparkly

glitz *noun* showiness, garishness ♦ **glitzy** *adjective*

> ⏲ Originally a Yiddish word meaning 'glitter'

glitzy *adjective* (**glitzier, glitziest**) extravagantly showy; flashy

gloaming *noun* twilight, dusk

gloat *verb* to look at or think about with malicious joy: *gloating over their rivals' defeat*

global *adjective* **1** of or affecting the whole world: *global warming* **2** applying generally: *global increase in earnings*

globalization or **globalisation** *noun* **1** expansion of a company or an industry all over the world **2** use and acceptance of the same goods or cultural and social values by people all over the world

global village *noun* the world perceived as a single community, largely because of mass communication

global warming *noun* an increase in the temperature of the earth's atmosphere, great enough to cause changes in the earth's climate

globe *noun* **1** the earth **2** a ball with a map of the world drawn on it **3** a ball, a sphere **4** a glass covering for a lamp

globin *noun, biology, chemistry* a soluble protein present in haemoglobin

globular *adjective* ball-shaped

globule *noun* **1** a droplet **2** a small ball-shaped piece

globulin *noun, biology, chemistry* a type of protein that is soluble in salt solutions but not in pure water

glockenspiel *noun* a musical instrument consisting of a series of graded metal bars that are struck with hammers

gloom *noun* dullness, darkness; sadness

gloomy *adjective* **1** sad, depressed **2** miserable, depressing **3** dimly lighted ♦ **gloomily** *adverb* ♦ **gloominess** *noun*

glorify *verb* (**glorifies, glorifying, glorified**) **1** to make glorious **2** to praise highly

glorious *adjective* **1** splendid **2** deserving great praise **3** delightful ♦ **gloriously** *adverb*

glory *noun* (*plural* **glories**) **1** fame, honour **2** great show, splendour ➤ *verb* to rejoice, take great pleasure (in)

gloss[1] *noun* brightness on the surface ➤ *verb* to make bright ● **gloss over** to try to hide (a fault etc) by treating it quickly or superficially

gloss[2] *noun* an explanatory note in a text, eg in a margin ➤ *verb* **1** to add an explanatory note of (something) **2** to add glosses to a text

glossary *noun* (*plural* **glossaries**) a list of words with their meanings

glossy *adjective* shiny, highly polished

glottis *noun* (*plural* **glottises** or **glottides** – pronounced **glaw**-ti-deez), *anatomy* the opening through which air passes from the throat to the windpipe

glove *noun* **1** a covering for the hand with a separate covering for each finger **2** a boxing glove

glow *verb* **1** to burn without a flame **2** to give out a steady light **3** to be flushed from heat, cold, etc **4** to be radiant with emotion: *glow with pride* ➤ *noun* **1** a glowing state **2** great heat **3** bright light

glower (pronounced **glow**-er) *verb* to stare (at) with a frown

glowering (pronounced **glow**-er-ing) *adjective* **1** scowling **2** threatening

glowing *adjective* **1** giving out a steady light **2** flushed **3** radiant **4** full of praise: *glowing report*

glow-worm *noun* a kind of beetle which glows in the dark

glucagon *noun, biology, chemistry* a hormone in the liver that breaks down glycogen and increases the level of glucose released into the blood

glucose *noun, biology, chemistry* a sugar found in plants and animals, which in animals is the main form in which energy is transported around the bloodstream

glue *noun* a substance for sticking things together ➤ *verb* to join with glue

gluey *adjective* sticky

glum *adjective* (**glummer, glummest**) sad, gloomy ♦ **glumly** *adverb*

gluon *noun, physics* a hypothetical particle with no mass, believed to hold quarks together

glut *verb* (**glutting, glutted**) **1** to feed greedily till full **2** to supply too much to (a market) ➤ *noun* an oversupply: *a glut of fish on the market*

gluten *noun* a sticky protein found in wheat and certain other cereals, which is responsible for coeliac disease

glutentous *adjective* made from or containing gluten

gluteus *noun, anatomy* one of the three large muscles in the human buttock ♦ **gluteal** *adjective*

glutinous *adjective* sticky, gluey

glutton *noun* **1** someone who eats too much **2** someone who is eager for anything: *a glutton for punishment*

gluttonous *adjective* **1** fond of overeating **2** eating greedily

gluttony *noun* greediness in eating

glycerine (*pronounced* **gli**-se-reen) *noun* a non-technical name for **glycerol**

glycerol (*pronounced* **gli**-se-rol) *noun, chemistry* a thick, colourless, soluble liquid used to sweeten foods and medicines ℗ Comes from Greek *glykeros* meaning 'sweet'

glycogen (*pronounced* **glaik**-o-jen) *noun, biology, chemistry* a branched chain of glucose molecules, the main form in which carbohydrate is stored in the liver and muscles in vertebrates
♦ **glycogenic** *adjective*

glycol (*pronounced* **glai**-kol) *noun, chemistry* a compound with two hydroxyl groups on adjacent carbon atoms, intermediate between glycerine and alcohol

glycolysis (*pronounced* glai-**kol**-i-sis) *noun, biology, chemistry* during respiration in cells: the breaking down of glucose, accompanied by the release of energy

GM *abbreviation* genetically modified, used to describe a plant or animal in which some of the genes have been changed using genetic engineering: *GM crops*

GMO *abbreviation* genetically modified organism, a plant or animal in which some of the genes have been changed using genetic engineering

GMT *abbreviation* Greenwich Mean Time

gnarled (*pronounced* narld) *adjective* knotty, twisted

gnash (*pronounced* nash) *verb* to grind (the teeth)

gnat (*pronounced* nat) *noun* a small blood-sucking fly, a midge

gnaw (*pronounced* naw) *verb* to bite at with a scraping action

gnome (*pronounced* nohm) *noun* a small, imaginary, human-like creature who lives underground, often guarding treasure

GNP *abbreviation* gross national product

gnu (*pronounced* noo or nyoo) *noun* a type of African antelope, with a large head, horns and a long mane (*also called:* **wildebeest**)

GNVQ *abbreviation* General National Vocational Qualification

go *verb* (**going, went, gone**) **1** to move: *I want to go home/when are you going to Paris?* **2** to leave: *time to go* **3** to lead: *that road goes north* **4** to become: *go mad* **5** to work: *the car is going at last* **6** to intend (to do): *I'm going to have a bath* **7** to be removed or taken: *the best seats have all gone now* **8** to be given, awarded, etc: *the first prize went to Janet* ➤ *noun* **1** *informal* an attempt, a try: *have a go* **2** *informal* busy activity: *it's all go around here* **3** energy, spirit • **from the word go** from the start • **go about** to try, set about • **go ahead** to proceed (with), begin on • **go**

along with to agree with • **go back on** to fail to keep (a promise etc) • **go for 1** to aim to get **2** to attack • **go off 1** to explode **2** to become rotten **3** to come to dislike • **go on 1** to continue **2** to talk too much • **go round** to be enough for everyone: *will the trifle go round?* • **go steady with** to go out with: *she's been going steady with John for nearly a year now* • **go under** to be ruined: *the restaurant finally went under last winter* • **on the go** very active ℗ Comes from Old English *gan* meaning 'to go'

goad *noun* **1** a sharp-pointed stick for driving animals **2** something used to urge action ➤ *verb* to urge on by annoying

go-ahead *adjective* eager to succeed ➤ *noun* permission to act

goal *noun* **1** the upright posts between which the ball is to be driven in football and other games **2** a score in football and other games **3** anything aimed at or wished for: *my goal is to pass this exam*

goalkeeper *noun, sport* in various sports: the player who guards the goal and tries to prevent the opposition from scoring

goalpost *noun* in various sports: each of two upright posts forming the goal • **move the goalposts** to change the accepted rules or aims of an activity during its course

goat *noun* an animal of the sheep family with horns and a long-haired coat

goatee *noun* a pointed beard on the front of the chin

gob *noun, slang* the mouth

gobble *verb* **1** to eat quickly **2** to make a noise like a turkey

go-between *noun* someone who helps two people to communicate with each other

goblet *noun* **1** a large cup without handles **2** a drinking glass with a stem

goblin *noun* a mischievous, ugly spirit in folklore

gobsmacked *adjective, slang* shocked, astonished

gobstopper *noun* a hard round sweet for sucking

god *noun* **1** a male supernatural being who is worshipped **2** (**God**) the creator and ruler of the world in the Christian, Jewish, etc religions

god-daughter *noun* a girl for whom a godmother or godfather is responsible

goddess *noun* a female supernatural being who is worshipped

godfather *noun* a man who agrees to see that a child is brought up according to the beliefs of the Christian Church

godly *adjective* (**godlier, godliest**) holy, pious

godmother *noun* a woman who agrees to see that a child is brought up according to the beliefs of the Christian Church

godparent *noun* someone who agrees to see that a child is brought up according to the beliefs of the Christian Church

godsend *noun* a very welcome piece of unexpected good fortune

godson *noun* a boy for whom a godmother or godfather is responsible

goggle-eyed *adjective* with staring eyes

goggles *plural noun* spectacles for protecting the eyes from dust, sparks, etc

goitre or *US* **goiter** *noun, medicine* an abnormal enlargement of the thyroid gland

go-kart *noun* a small low-powered racing car

gold *noun* 1 *chemistry* (symbol **Au**) a soft yellow precious metallic element, used for making jewellery, coins, etc 2 articles made from gold 3 riches ▸ *adjective* 1 made of gold 2 having the colour of gold

golden *adjective* 1 of or like gold 2 very fine

golden rule *noun* a guiding principle

golden wedding *noun* the 50th anniversary of a wedding

goldfinch *noun* a small colourful bird

goldfish *noun* a golden-yellow Chinese carp, often kept as a pet

gold-leaf *noun* gold beaten to a thin sheet

gold medal *noun* a medal given to a competitor who comes first

goldsmith *noun* a maker of gold articles

gold standard *noun* a monetary system in which the unit of currency is given a value relative to gold

golf *noun* a game in which a ball is struck with a club and aimed at a series of holes on a large open course

golf club *noun* 1 a club used in golf 2 a society of golf players 3 the place where they meet

golfer *noun* someone who plays golf

goloshes another spelling of **galoshes**

-gon *suffix, maths* forms nouns to do with two-dimensional figures with a specified number of angles: *polygon*

gonad *noun, biology* an organ in which eggs or sperm are produced, especially the ovary or testis

gondola *noun* 1 a canal boat used in Venice 2 a car suspended from an airship, cable railway, etc 3 a shelved display unit in a supermarket

gondolier *noun* a boatman who rows a gondola

gone past participle of **go**

gong *noun* a metal plate which makes a booming sound when struck, used to summon people to meals etc

gonorrhoea or *N Am* **gonorrhea** *noun, medicine* a sexually transmitted disease that causes inflammation and a discharge

good *adjective* 1 having desired or positive qualities: *a good butcher will bone it for you/a good restaurant* 2 having a positive effect: *fruit is good for you* 3 virtuous: *a good person* 4 kind: *she was good to me* 5 pleasant, enjoyable: *a good time* 6 substantial, sufficiently large: *a good income* ☉ Comes from Old English *god*

good afternoon *interjection* a common formal greeting used when meeting or leaving people in the afternoon

goodbye *interjection* what you say when leaving people

good-day *interjection* an old-fashioned greeting used when meeting or leaving people

good evening *interjection* a common formal greeting used when meeting or leaving people in the evening

good-for-nothing *adjective* useless, lazy

Good Friday *noun* a Christian festival on the Friday before Easter, in memory of Christ's crucifixion

goodly *adjective* 1 large 2 ample, plentiful

good morning *exclamation* a common formal greeting used when meeting or leaving people in the morning

good name *noun* good reputation

good-natured *adjective* kind, cheerful

goodness *noun* the quality of being good ▸ *interjection* an exclamation of surprise

good night *exclamation* a phrase used when leaving people at night

goods *plural noun* 1 personal belongings 2 things to be bought and sold

good taste *noun* good judgement for what is aesthetically pleasing or socially acceptable

goodwill *noun* 1 kind wishes 2 a good reputation in business

goofy *adjective, US* stupid, silly

goose *noun* (*plural* **geese**) a web-footed bird larger than a duck

gooseberry *noun* a sour-tasting, pale green berry

goosebumps or **goosepimples** *plural noun* small bumps on the skin caused by cold or fear

gopher *noun* 1 a small, burrowing rodent 2 *computing* a piece of software used to search for or index services on the Internet

gore[1] *noun* a mass of blood ▸ *verb* to pierce with horns, tusks, etc: *gored by an elephant*

gore[2] *noun* a triangular-shaped piece of cloth in a garment etc

Gore-Tex *noun, trademark* a fabric which is water-repellent, but which has tiny pores to allow air and water vapour to escape from inside

gorge *noun* 1 the throat 2 a narrow valley between hills ▸ *verb* (**gorging, gorged**) to eat greedily till full: *gorging himself on chocolate biscuits*

gorgeous *adjective* **1** beautiful, very attractive **2** showy, splendid **3** *informal* excellent, very enjoyable

gorilla *noun* the largest kind of ape

❗ Do not confuse with: **guerrilla**

🕐 The *Gorillai* were a tribe of hairy people in ancient times

gormless *adjective, Brit* stupid, senseless

gorse or **furze** *noun* a prickly bush with yellow flowers

gory *adjective* full of gore; bloody: *a very gory film*

gosling *noun* a young goose

go-slow *noun* a slowing of speed at work as a form of protest

gospel *noun* **1** the teaching of Christ **2** *informal* the absolute truth

gossamer *noun* **1** fine spider-threads floating in the air or lying on bushes **2** a very thin material

gossip *noun* **1** talk, not necessarily true, about other people's personal affairs etc **2** someone who listens to and passes on gossip ➤ *verb* (**gossiping, gossiped**) **1** to engage in gossip **2** to chatter

🕐 Originally *godsibb*, meaning 'godparent'

got past form of **get**

gouge (*pronounced* gowj) *noun* a chisel with a hollow blade for cutting grooves ➤ *verb* (**gouging, gouged**) to scoop (out)

goulash *noun* (*plural* **goulashes**) a stew of meat and vegetables, flavoured with paprika

gourd (*pronounced* goord) *noun* **1** a large fleshy fruit **2** the skin of a gourd used to carry water etc

gourmand (*pronounced* goor-**mond**) *noun* a glutton

gourmet (*pronounced* **goor**-mei) *noun* someone who loves good wines or food

gout *noun, medicine* a disease in which excess uric acid in the bloodstream is deposited in the joints and causes swelling, especially in the big toe ◆ **gouty** *adjective*

govern *verb* **1** to rule, control **2** to put into action the laws etc of a country 🕐 Comes from Latin *gubernare* meaning 'to steer a ship'

governess *noun* especially in the past, a woman employed to teach young children at their home

government *noun* **1** rule; control **2** the people who rule and administer the laws of a country ◆ **governmental** *adjective*

governor *noun* someone who rules a state or country etc

gown *noun* **1** a woman's formal dress **2** a loose robe worn by members of the clergy, lawyers, etc

GP *abbreviation* general practitioner, a doctor who treats most ordinary illnesses

GPRS *abbreviation* General Packet Radio Service, a system providing rapid access to the Internet from mobile phones

Graafian follicle *noun, anatomy* in the ovary of female mammals: one of the small sacs in which an egg cell develops

🕐 Named after Dutch anatomist Regnier de *Graaf* (1641–73) who discovered these

grab *verb* (**grabbing, grabbed**) **1** to seize or grasp suddenly: *grabbed me by the arm* **2** to secure possession of quickly: *grab a seat* **3** to get in a hurry: *grab a bite to eat* ➤ *noun* a sudden grasp or catch

grab-bag *noun* a miscellaneous collection: *grab-bag of ideas*

grace *noun* **1** beauty of form or movement **2** a short prayer at a meal **3** favour, mercy: *by God's grace* **4** (**Grace**) a title used in addressing or referring to a duke or archbishop: *Your Grace* ● **with bad grace** unwillingly ● **with good grace** willingly

graceful *adjective* **1** beautiful in appearance or movement **2** done in a neat way **3** polite ◆ **gracefully** *adverb*

grace note *noun, music* a short note played before the main note in a melody

gracious *adjective* kind, polite ➤ *interjection* expressing surprise or shock ◆ **graciously** *adverb*

gradation *noun* arrangement in order of rank, difficulty, etc

grade *noun* **1** a step or placing according to quality or rank; class **2** *US* a particular class or year in school: *in the sixth grade* ➤ *verb* to arrange in order, eg from easy to difficult ● **make the grade** to reach the necessary standard

gradient *noun* **1** a slope on a road, railway, etc **2** the amount of a slope, worked out by dividing the vertical distance by the horizontal distance **3** *maths* the slope of a line or a tangent to a curve at a particular point **4** *physics* the rate of change of a variable quantity over a certain distance

gradual *adjective* step by step; going slowly but steadily ◆ **gradually** *adverb*

graduate *verb* (*pronounced* **grad**-yoo-eit) **1** to divide into regular spaces **2** to pass university examinations and receive a degree ➤ *noun* (*pronounced* **grad**-yoo-at) someone who has passed university examinations and received a degree

graduation *noun* the act of getting a degree from a university, or the ceremony to celebrate this

graffiti *plural noun, sometimes used as singular* words or drawings scratched or painted on a wall etc

graft *verb* **1** to fix a shoot or twig of one plant on to another for growing **2** *medicine* to fix (skin) from one part of the body on to another part **3** *medicine* to transfer (a part of the body) from one person to another **4** to get illegal profit ➤ *noun* **1** living tissue (eg skin) which is grafted **2** a shoot grafted **3** hard work **4** profit gained by illegal or unfair means

Grail *noun* the plate or cup believed to have been used by Christ at the Last Supper

grain *noun* **1** a seed eg of wheat, oats **2** corn in general **3** a very small quantity **4** a very small measure of weight **5** the run of the lines of fibre in wood, leather, etc • **against the grain** against your natural feelings or instincts

gram or **gramme** *noun* (*abbrev* **g**) the basic unit of weight in the metric system

-gram or **-gramme** *suffix* forms words for things which are written, printed or drawn: *telegram/anagram* ☉ Comes from Greek *gramma* meaning 'letter'

grammar *noun* **1** the correct use of words in speaking or writing: *his grammar is very bad* **2** the rules applying to a particular language: *French grammar*

grammar school *noun* a kind of secondary school

grammatical *adjective* correct according to rules of grammar • **grammatically** *adverb*

gramme another spelling of **gram**

Gram-negative and **Gram-positive** *adjective, biology* staining deep red (negative) or purple (positive) under Gram's stain, because of differences in cell wall structure

gramophone *noun, trademark, old* a record-player

Gram's stain *noun, biology* a staining procedure used to distinguish between two major groups of bacteria

☉ After Danish physician Hans *Gram* (1883–1938), who devised the procedure

gran *noun, informal* a grandmother

granary *noun* (*plural* **granaries**) a storehouse for grain ➤ *adjective* of bread: containing whole grains of wheat

grand *adjective* great; noble; fine ☉ Comes from French *grand* meaning 'big'

grandchild *noun* a son's or daughter's child

grand-daughter *noun* a son's or daughter's daughter

grand duke *noun* a duke of specially high rank

grandeur (*pronounced* **grand**-yer) *noun* greatness

grandfather *noun* a father's or mother's father

grandiloquent (*pronounced* grahn-**dil**-i-kwent) *adjective, derogatory* spoken or written, in a pompous, self-important style ☉ Comes from Latin *grandis* meaning 'great' + *loqui* meaning 'to speak' • **grandiloquence** *noun*

grandiose *adjective* planned on a large scale

grand master *noun* a chess-player of the greatest ability

grandmother *noun* a father's or mother's mother

grandparent *noun* a grandmother or grandfather

grand piano *noun* a piano with a large flat top

grand prix (*pronounced* **grawn** pree) *noun* (*plural* **grands prix** – *pronounced* **grawn** pree) any of a series of races held annually in various countries to decide the motor-racing championship of the world

grandson *noun* a son's or daughter's son

grandstand *noun* rows of raised seats at a sports ground giving a good view

granite *noun* a hard rock of greyish or reddish colour

granny *noun* (*plural* **grannies**) *informal* a grandmother

grant *verb* **1** to give, allow (something asked for) **2** to admit as true ➤ *noun* money awarded for a special purpose: *a research grant*

granted or **granting** *conjunction* (often with **that**) even if, assuming: *granted that you are right* • **take for granted 1** to assume that something will happen without checking **2** to treat (someone) casually, without respect or kindness

Granthi (*pronounced* **grunt**-ee) *noun, Sikhism* the guardian of the Guru Granth Sahib and of a gurdwara

granular *adjective* made up of grains

granulated *adjective* broken into grains: *granulated sugar*

granule *noun* a tiny grain or part

grape *noun* the green or black smooth-skinned berry from which wine is made

grapefruit *noun* a sharp-tasting fruit like a large yellow orange

grapevine *noun* **1** a climbing plant that produces grapes **2** (**the grapevine**) the spreading of information through casual conversation

graph *noun* lines drawn on squared paper to show changes in quantity, eg in temperature or money spent • **graphical** *adjective*

-graph or **-graphy** *suffix* **1** of or relating to writing: *biography/autograph* **2** used to form words describing printed images or pictures: *photograph(y)* ☉ Comes from Greek *graphein* meaning 'to write'

grapheme *noun* a letter or sequence of letters

that represent a sound, eg *f* or *ph* which can represent the sound 'f'

graphic *adjective* **1** relating to writing, drawing or painting **2** vivid, well told **3** explicit: *graphic violence* ➤ *noun* a visual image, eg a painting, print, illustration or diagram ♦ **graphically** *adverb*

graphical user interface *noun, computing* (*abbrev* **GUI**) mouse-controlled icons and other images on a desktop display

graphics *singular noun* the art of drawing according to mathematical principles ➤ *plural noun* **1** the pictures in a magazine **2** the use of computers to display data in a pictorial form **3** pictures produced by computer

graphics card *noun, computing* a printed circuit board that stores visual data and conveys it to the screen

graphics tablet *noun, computing* an input device which digitizes the movements of a pen over it, so that a traced pattern appears on the screen

graphite *noun* a form of carbon used in making pencils

graphology *noun* **1** the study of handwriting **2** the study of the systems and conventions of writing ♦ **graphologic** or **graphological** *adjective* ♦ **graphologist** *noun*

grapple *verb*: **grapple with 1** to struggle with **2** to try to deal with (a problem etc)

grasp *verb* **1** to clasp and grip with the fingers or arms **2** to understand ➤ *noun* **1** a grip with the hand or arms **2** someone's power of understanding

grasping *adjective* greedy, mean

grass *noun* (*plural* **grasses**) **1** the plant covering fields of pasture **2** a kind of plant with long narrow leaves, eg wheat, reeds, bamboo **3** *slang* the drug marijuana

grasshopper *noun* a type of jumping insect

grassland *noun* an area of grass or grass-like plants

grass roots *plural noun, politics* ordinary people, as opposed to those in a position of power

grass snake *noun* a type of harmless snake

grassy *adjective* covered with grass

grate[1] *verb* **1** to rub food, eg cheese, against a rough surface in order to break it down into small pieces **2** to make a harsh, grinding sound **3** to irritate

grate[2] *noun* a framework of iron bars for holding a fire

grateful *adjective* **1** feeling thankful **2** showing or giving thanks ♦ **gratefully** *adverb*

grater *noun* an instrument with a rough surface for rubbing cheese or other food into small pieces

gratification *noun* pleasure; satisfaction

gratify *verb* (**gratifying, gratified**) to please; satisfy

grating *noun* a frame of iron bars

gratis *adverb* for nothing, without payment

gratitude *noun* thankfulness; desire to repay kindness

gratuitous *adjective* uncalled-for, done without good reason: *gratuitous violence* ♦ **gratuitously** *adverb*

gratuity *noun* (*plural* **gratuities**) a money gift in return for a service; a tip

grave *noun* a pit in which a dead person is buried ➤ *adjective* **1** serious, important: *grave error* **2** not cheerful, solemn ♦ **gravely** *adverb*

grave accent (*pronounced* grahv) *noun* a backward-leaning stroke (`) placed over letters in some languages to show their pronunciation

gravel *noun* small stones or pebbles

graven *adjective, old* carved: *graven images*

gravestone *noun* a stone placed to mark a grave

graveyard *noun* a place where the dead are buried, a cemetery

gravid *adjective, medicine* pregnant ☺ Comes from Latin *gravis* meaning 'heavy'

gravitate *verb* to move towards as if strongly attracted (to)

gravitation *noun, physics* **1** the force of attraction between any two objects in the universe on account of their mass **2** the process of being moved by this or another force ♦ **gravitational** *adjective*

gravitational field *noun, physics* the region of space in which one object exerts gravitation on another object

gravity *noun* **1** the force of attraction between the earth and any object in its gravitational field, which pulls the object towards the ground **2** gravitation **3** seriousness, importance: *gravity of the situation* **4** lack of levity, solemnity

gravity wave *noun, physics* a surface wave in a liquid controlled by gravity and not surface tension

gravy *noun* (*plural* **gravies**) a sauce made from the juices of meat that is cooking

gravy train *noun* a situation producing large, easy profits

gray US spelling of **grey**

graze *verb* **1** to feed on (growing grass) **2** to scrape the skin of **3** to touch lightly in passing ➤ *noun* **1** a scraping of the skin **2** a light touch

grazing *noun* grass land for animals to graze on

grease *noun* **1** thick animal fat **2** an oily substance ➤ *verb* to smear with grease, apply grease to

greasepaint *noun* theatrical make-up

greasy *adjective* **1** full of, or covered in, grease **2**

of skin: having a slightly moist appearance because the body releases a lot of natural oils into it **3** wet and slippery

great *adjective* **1** very large **2** powerful **3** very important, distinguished **4** very talented: *a great singer* **5** of high rank, noble **6** *informal* excellent, very good ♦ **greatness** *noun* (meanings 1, 2, 3, 4 and 5) ⊙ Comes from Old English

great circle *noun, maths* a circle on the surface of a sphere, whose centre is the centre of the sphere

Great Depression *noun, history* (**the Great Depression**) the period of worldwide economic depression from 1929 to 1934 (*also called*: **the Depression**)

great-grandchild *noun* the son or daughter of a grandson or grand-daughter

great-grandfather *noun* the father of a grandfather or grandmother

great-grandmother *noun* the mother of a grandfather or grandmother

Great Leap Forward *noun, history* a movement in China from 1958 to 1960, aimed at accelerating agricultural and industrial production

greatly *adverb* very much

grebe *noun* a freshwater diving bird

greed *noun* great and selfish desire for food, money, etc

greedy *adjective* full of greed ♦ **greedily** *adverb*

green *adjective* **1** of the colour of growing grass etc **2** inexperienced, naive **3** concerned with care of the environment: *the green movement* ➤ *noun* **1** the colour of growing grass **2** a piece of ground covered with grass **3** (**Green**) a member of the Green Party; an environmentalist **4** (**greens**) green vegetables for food

green belt *noun* open land or parkland surrounding a town or city

green card *noun* **1** an international insurance document for drivers **2** an official US work and residence permit issued to foreign nationals

greenery *noun* green plants

greenfield site *noun* a newly developed commercial or industrial site (*compare with*: **brownfield site**)

green fingers *noun*: **have green fingers** to be a skilful gardener

greenfly *noun* (*plural* **greenfly**) a bright green, small insect which attacks plants

greengage *noun* a kind of plum, green but sweet

greengrocer *noun* someone who sells fresh vegetables

greenhouse *noun* a building with large glass panes in which plants are grown

greenhouse effect *noun* (**the greenhouse effect**) the warming-up of the earth's surface due to the sun's heat being trapped in the atmosphere by carbon dioxide and other gases (**greenhouse gases**), the increased output of which causes the earth to warm more quickly (the **enhanced greenhouse effect**)

green light *noun* (**the green light**) permission to go ahead with a plan

green paper *noun, Brit politics* (often **Green Paper**) a written statement of the Government's proposed policy on a particular issue, which is put forward for discussion before a **white paper** is issued

Green Party *noun* a political party concerned with conserving natural resources and decentralizing political and economic power

Greenpeace *noun, history* an international environmental pressure group that campaigns against the dumping of toxic waste at sea, the testing of nuclear weapons, etc

green revolution *noun, geography* agricultural advances in developing countries, eg the introduction of new varieties of crop leading to an increase in food production

greet *verb* **1** to meet someone with kind words **2** to say hello etc to **3** to react to, respond to: *greeted the news with relief* **4** to become evident to

greeting *noun* **1** words of welcome or kindness **2** reaction, response

gregarious *adjective* **1** sociable, liking the company of others **2** living in flocks and herds

grenade *noun* a small bomb thrown by hand

⊙ From a French word for 'pomegranate', because of its shape

grew past tense of **grow**

grey or *US* **gray** *adjective* **1** of a colour between black and white **2** grey-haired, old **3** relating to the elderly: *the grey vote* ➤ *noun* **1** grey colour **2** a grey horse

grey area *noun* an indistinct situation or subject that often does not conform to existing rules or categories

greyhound *noun* a breed of fast-running dog

greying *adjective* **1** becoming grey: *greying hair* **2** aging: *greying population*

greying population see **aging population**

grey matter *noun* **1** *anatomy* the tissue of the brain and spinal cord that appears grey in colour **2** *informal* intelligence or common sense

grid *noun* **1** a grating of bars **2** a network of lines, eg for helping to find a place on a map **3** a network of wires carrying electricity over a wide area

griddle *noun* a hot iron plate used for baking or frying

gridiron *noun* **1** a frame of iron bars for cooking

food over a fire **2** *US* a football field

gridlock *noun* **1** a severe traffic jam in which no vehicles are able to move **2** a situation in which no progress is possible

grid reference *noun* a set of numbers or letters used to indicate a place on a grid

grief *noun* deep sorrow, especially after bereavement • **come to grief** to meet with misfortune

grief-stricken *adjective* crushed with sorrow

grievance *noun* a cause for complaining

grieve *verb* to feel grief or sorrow

grievous *adjective* **1** painful; serious **2** causing grief

griffin or **griffon** *noun* a mythological animal with the body and legs of a lion and the beak and wings of an eagle

grill *verb* **1** to cook directly under heat (provided by an electric or gas cooker) **2** to cook on a gridiron over a fire **3** to question closely ➤ *noun* **1** a frame of bars for grilling food on **2** grilled food **3** the part of a cooker used for grilling **4** a restaurant serving grilled food

grille *noun* a metal grating over a door, window, etc

grim *adjective* **1** stern, fierce-looking **2** terrible; very unpleasant: *a grim sight* **3** unyielding, stubborn: *grim determination* ♦ **grimly** *adverb*

grimace *noun* a twisting of the face in fun or pain ➤ *verb* to make a grimace

grime *noun* dirt

grimy *adjective* covered with a layer of ground-in dirt

grin *verb* (**grinning, grinned**) to smile broadly ➤ *noun* a broad smile • **grin and bear it** to suffer something without complaining

grind *verb* (**grinding, ground**) **1** to crush to powder **2** to sharpen by rubbing **3** to rub together: *grinding his teeth* ➤ *noun* hard or unpleasant work

grinder *noun* someone or something that grinds

grindstone *noun* a revolving stone for grinding or sharpening tools • **back to the grindstone** back to work • **keep your nose to the grindstone** to work hard without stopping

grip *noun* **1** a firm hold, a grasp: *these shoes have a good grip* **2** a way of holding or grasping; control: *a loose grip* **3** a handle or part for holding **4** a travelling bag, a holdall ➤ *verb* (**gripping, gripped**) to take a firm hold of

gripe *noun* **1** a sharp stomach pain **2** *informal* a complaint ➤ *verb* to complain

gripping *adjective* commanding attention, compelling: *a gripping thriller*

grisly *adjective* (**grislier, grisliest**) frightful, hideous ℗ Comes from Old English *grislic* which is related to *agrisan* meaning 'to terrify'

❗ Do not confuse with: **grizzly**

grist *noun* corn for grinding • **grist to the mill** something which brings profit or advantage

gristle *noun* a tough elastic substance in meat ♦ **gristly** *adjective*

grit *noun* **1** a mixture of rough sand and gravel, spread on icy surfaces **2** courage ➤ *verb* (**gritting, gritted**) **1** to apply grit to (an icy surface): *has the road been gritted?* **2** to clench: *grit your teeth*

gritty *adjective* (**grittier, grittiest**) **1** covered in grit or having a texture like grit **2** courageous **3** honest in the portrayal of harsh realities: *a gritty drama* ♦ **grittiness** *noun*

grizzled *adjective* grey; mixed with grey

grizzly *adjective* (**grizzlier, grizzliest**) grey in colour ➤ *noun* (*plural* **grizzlies**) *informal* a grizzly bear ℗ Comes from French *gris* meaning 'grey'

❗ Do not confuse with: **grisly**

grizzly bear *noun* a type of large bear of North America

groan *verb* **1** to moan in pain, disapproval, etc **2** to be full or loaded: *a table groaning with food* ➤ *noun* an act of groaning or the sound of groaning

grocer *noun* a dealer in certain kinds of food and household supplies

groceries *plural noun* food etc sold by grocers

groggy *adjective* (**groggier, groggiest**) weak and light-headed after being ill or beaten

(℗ Originally meaning 'drunk', from *grog*, a mixture of rum and water)

groin *noun* the part of the body where the inner thigh joins the torso

groom *noun* **1** a bridegroom **2** someone in charge of horses ➤ *verb* **1** to look after (a horse) **2** to make smart and tidy **3** to prepare someone for a particular job or role

groove *noun* a furrow, a long hollow ➤ *verb* to cut a groove (in)

grope *verb* **1** to search (for) by feeling around as if blind: *groping for his socks in the dark* **2** *informal* to touch (someone) sexually

gross *adjective* **1** coarse **2** very fat **3** great, obvious: *gross error* **4** of money: total, before any deductions for tax etc: *gross profit* **5** *US informal* disgusting, revolting ➤ *noun* **1** the whole taken together **2** twelve dozen

gross domestic product *noun* (*abbrev* **GDP**) the total value of all goods and services produced within a nation in one year

grossly *adverb* extremely

gross national product *noun* (*abbrev* **GNP**) the total value of all goods produced and all services provided by a nation in one year, ie **gross domestic product** plus the value of income from investments abroad

grossness noun coarseness

gross primary productivity or **gross primary production** noun (abbrev **GPP**) the total amount of energy produced by a plant (compare with: **net primary productivity**)

grotesque adjective very odd or unnatural-looking

grotto noun (plural **grottoes** or **grottos**) a cave

grotty adjective (**grottier, grottiest**) dirty or shabby

grouchy adjective (**grouchier, grouchiest**) bad-tempered, tending to grumble

ground[1] noun 1 the surface of the earth 2 (also: **grounds**) a good reason: ground for complaint 3 (**grounds**) lands surrounding a large house etc 4 art the background in a painting 5 (**grounds**) dregs: coffee grounds ➤ verb 1 of a ship: to strike the seabed and become stuck 2 to prevent (aeroplanes) from flying 3 to prevent (someone in your charge) from going out: that's it! You're grounded

ground[2] past form of **grind**

ground bass noun, music a short, constantly repeated bass part in a piece of music

groundbreaking adjective innovative: groundbreaking research

ground control noun the control and monitoring from the ground of the flight of aircraft or spacecraft

ground floor noun the storey of a building at street level

groundhog noun a woodchuck (a N American species of marmot)

grounding noun the first steps in learning something

groundless adjective without reason

groundnut same as **peanut**

ground state noun, physics the lowest energy state of an atom

groundswell noun 1 a high swell of the sea caused by a distant storm or earthquake 2 a rapidly growing indication of public or political feeling: a groundswell of discontent

groundwater noun, geography water which occurs in the rocks beneath the surface of the Earth and which can surface in springs

groundwater flow noun, geography the movement of water sideways through soil

groundwork noun the first stages of a task

group noun 1 a number of people or things together 2 a band of musicians or singers 3 chemistry in the periodic table: a vertical column showing a series of elements with similar chemical properties 4 chemistry two or more

bonded atoms that tend to act as a single unit in chemical reactions ➤ verb 1 to form or gather into a group 2 to classify ⊙ Comes from French groupe meaning 'group'

grouped data noun, statistics data grouped into classes that do not overlap

groupware noun, computing software that is designed to be used on several computers, workstations, etc at the same time

grouse[1] noun (plural **grouse**) a game bird hunted on moors and hills

grouse[2] noun (plural **grouses**) a grumble, a complaint ➤ verb to grumble, complain

grove noun a small group of trees

grovel verb (**grovelling, grovelled**) 1 to crawl or lie on the ground 2 to be overly humble

grow verb (**growing, grew, grown**) 1 to become bigger or stronger: the local population is growing 2 to become: grow old 3 to rear, cause to grow (plants, trees, etc): grow from seed • **grow out of 1** to become too big to wear (clothes that were the right size at first) 2 to lose a liking for something, or the habit of doing it, as you get older • **grow up 1** to become an adult 2 to begin to behave like an adult

growl verb to utter a deep sound like a dog ➤ noun an angry dog's deep sound

grown past participle of **grow**

growth noun 1 growing 2 increase: growth in market shares 3 something that grows 4 something abnormal that grows on the body

groyne noun a breakwater built to stop erosion and drifting of sand

grub noun 1 the form of an insect after being hatched from the egg, eg a caterpillar 2 informal food ➤ verb (**grubbing, grubbed**) to dig

grubby adjective (**grubbier, grubbiest**) dirty ♦ **grubbily** adverb ♦ **grubbiness** noun

grudge verb 1 to be unwilling to accept or allow: I don't grudge him his success 2 to give unwillingly or reluctantly ➤ noun a feeling of resentment: she bears a grudge against me

gruel noun a thin mixture of oatmeal boiled in water

gruelling adjective straining, exhausting

gruesome adjective horrible

⊙ Originally a Scots word, derived from grue meaning 'to be terrified'

gruff adjective 1 rough in manner 2 of a voice: deep and harsh

grumble verb to complain in a bad-tempered, discontented way ➤ noun a complaint

grumpy adjective (**grumpier, grumpiest**) cross, bad-tempered ♦ **grumpily** adverb

grunge noun, informal 1 grime, dirt 2 thrift-shop fashion or its designer equivalent 3 a style of rock music ♦ **grungy** adjective

grunt *verb* to make a sound like that of a pig ➤ *noun* a pig-like snort

guacamole (*pronounced* gwahk-a-**moh**-li) *noun* a traditional Mexican dish of mashed avocado mixed with spicy seasoning

guanine *noun, chemistry* an almost insoluble base found in nucleic acid

guarantee *noun* **1** a promise to do something **2** a statement by the maker that something will work well **3** money put down which will be forfeited if a promise is broken ➤ *verb* to give a guarantee

guarantor *noun* someone who promises to pay if another person fails to keep an agreement to pay

guard *verb* to keep safe from danger or attack ➤ *noun* **1** someone or a group whose duty it is to protect **2** a screen etc which protects from danger **3** someone in charge of a railway train or coach **4** *sport* a position of defence

guarded *adjective* careful, not revealing much: *guarded comments*

guardian *noun* **1** someone with the legal right to take care of an orphan **2** someone who protects or guards ♦ **guardianship** *noun*

guerrilla *noun* one of a small band which makes sudden attacks on a larger army but does not fight openly ➤ *adjective* of fighting: in which many small bands acting independently make sudden raids on an enemy: *guerrilla tactics* ⊕ Comes from Spanish *guerrilla* meaning 'little war'

> ❗ Do not confuse with: **gorilla**

guess *verb* **1** to say without sure knowledge: *I can only guess the price* **2** *US* to suppose: *I guess I'll go* ➤ *noun* (*plural* **guesses**) an estimate

guesstimate *noun, informal* a very rough estimate based on guesswork

guesswork *noun* guessing

guest *noun* a visitor received and entertained in another's house or in a hotel etc

guesthouse *noun* a private home offering accommodation to paying guests

guff *noun, informal* rubbish, nonsense

guffaw *verb* to laugh loudly ➤ *noun* a loud laugh

GUI (*pronounced* **goo**-i) *abbreviation, computing* graphical user interface

guidance *noun* help or advice towards doing something

guide *verb* **1** to show the way to, lead, direct **2** to influence ➤ *noun* **1** someone who shows tourists around **2** someone who leads travellers on a route unfamiliar to them **3** a guidebook **4** (**Guide**) a girl belonging to the Guides organization

guidebook *noun* a book with information for tourists about a place

guided missile *noun* an explosive rocket which after being fired can be guided to its target by radio waves

guide dog *noun* a dog trained to guide a blind person safely

guideline *noun* an indication of what future action is required or recommended: *government guidelines*

guild *noun* **1** an association for those working in a particular trade or profession **2** a society, a social club ⊕ Comes from Old English *gield* meaning 'payment' or 'idol'

> ❗ Do not confuse with: **gild**

guile *noun* cunning, deceit

guillotine *noun* **1** *history* an instrument with a falling blade used for executing by beheading **2** a machine with a blade for cutting paper **3** the limiting of discussion time in parliament by prearranging voting times ➤ *verb* **1** to behead with the guillotine **2** to cut (paper) with a guillotine **3** to use a parliamentary guillotine on

> ⊕ Named after Joseph *Guillotin*, a French doctor who recommended its use for executions during the French Revolution

guilt *noun* **1** a sense of shame **2** blame for wrongdoing, eg breaking the law

> ❗ Do not confuse with: **gilt**

guilty *adjective* **1** ashamed about something bad you have done **2** having done something wrong **3** officially judged to have committed a crime ♦ **guiltily** *adverb* (meaning 1)

guinea *noun* **1** an old British gold coin **2** a sum of money equal to £1.05, sometimes used in expressing prices, fees, etc

guinea fowl *noun* a bird resembling a pheasant, with white-spotted feathers

guinea pig *noun* **1** a rodent about the size of a rabbit **2** someone used as the subject of an experiment

guise *noun* appearance, dress, especially in disguise: *in the guise of a priest*

guitar *noun* a stringed musical instrument with frets and a waisted body ♦ **guitarist** *noun*

gulf *noun* **1** a large inlet of the sea **2** a wide difference or separation, eg between points of view

gull *noun* a seagull

gullet *noun* a passage by which food goes down into the stomach

gullible *adjective* easily tricked

gully *noun* (*plural* **gullies**) a channel worn by water

gullying *noun, geography* a type of erosion of cliffs caused by rain eroding soft rock and forming gullies that wash away surface material

gulp *verb* to swallow quickly and in large mouthfuls ➤ *noun* a sudden fast swallowing

gum *noun* **1** the firm flesh in which the teeth grow **2** sticky juice got from some trees and plants **3** a sticky substance used as glue **4** a flavoured gummy sweet, chewing gum ➤ *verb* (**gumming, gummed**) to stick with gum

gummy *adjective* (**gummier, gummiest**) **1** sticky **2** toothless

gumption *noun* good sense

gum tree *noun* a tree that gives gum or gum resin, especially the eucalyptus • **up a gum tree** in a mess

gun *noun* any weapon firing bullets or shells • **stick to your guns** to keep determinedly to your opinion

gunboat *noun* a small warship with heavy guns

gunfire *noun* the firing of guns

gung-ho *adjective* boisterously enthusiastic

⊙ Based on a Chinese phrase meaning 'work together'

gunpoint *noun*: **at gunpoint** threatening, or being threatened, with a gun

gunpowder *noun* an explosive in powder form

gunrunning *noun* the act of smuggling guns into a country ✦ **gunrunner** *noun*

gunwale or **gunnel** (*both pronounced* **gun**-el) *noun* the upper edge of a boat's side

Guomindang another spelling of **Kuomintang**

gurdwara *noun* a Sikh place of worship ⊙ Comes from Sanskrit *guru* meaning 'teacher' + *dvara* meaning 'door'

gurgle *verb* **1** of water: to make a bubbling sound **2** to make such a sound, eg in pleasure ➤ *noun*: *the baby's gurgles*

guru (*pronounced* goo-roo) *noun* **1** a Hindu spiritual teacher **2** a revered instructor, a mentor

Guru Granth Sahib (*pronounced* goo-roo grunt **sah**-eeb) *noun* the sacred scripture of the Sikh religion (*also called*: **Adi-Granth**) ⊙ Comes from Hindi *granth* meaning 'book'

gush *verb* **1** to flow out in a strong stream **2** to talk at length with exaggerated emotions: *gushing on about the wedding* ➤ *noun* (*plural* **gushes**) a strong or sudden flow: *gush of tears*

gusset *noun* a piece of material sewn into a seam join to strengthen or widen part of a garment

gust *noun* a sudden blast of wind

gusto *noun* enthusiasm • **with gusto** enthusiastically

gusty *adjective* (**gustier, gustiest**) windy

gut *noun* **1** the alimentary canal **2** *informal* the stomach or abdomen **3** (**guts**) the internal organs of a person or animal **4** animal intestines used as strings for musical instruments **5** (**guts**) spirit, courage ➤ *verb* (**gutting, gutted**) **1** to take out the inner parts of: *gut a fish* **2** to destroy completely, especially by fire: *gutted the building*

gutter *noun* a water channel on a roof, at the edge of a roadside, etc

gutter press *noun* that part of the press that specializes in sensational journalism

guttersnipe *noun, old* a poor child living in the streets

guttural *adjective* harsh in sound, as if formed in the throat

guy[1] *noun* **1** *Brit* an effigy of Guy Fawkes, traditionally burned on 5 November **2** *informal* a man

guy[2] *noun* a steadying rope for a tent etc

guzzle *verb* to eat or drink greedily

gym *noun, informal* **1** a gymnasium **2** gymnastics

gymkhana *noun* a meeting for horse-riding competitions

gymnasium *noun* (*plural* **gymnasiums** or **gymnasia**) a building or room equipped for physical exercises

gymnast *noun* someone who does gymnastics

gymnastic *adjective* relating to gymnastics

gymnastics *plural noun* exercises to strengthen the body

gymnosperm *noun, botany* a plant that produces seeds on cones, eg the conifer

gynaecology *noun* the treatment of disorders of the female reproductive system

gynoecium, gynaecium or *US* **gynecium** *noun, botany* the female reproductive parts of a flower ⊙ Comes from Greek *gynaikeion* meaning 'women's apartments'

gypsum (*pronounced* **jip**-sum) *noun* a soft mineral used to make cement, rubber and paper

Gypsy or **Gipsy** *noun* (*plural* **Gypsies** or **Gipsies**) a member of a wandering people; a Romany

⊙ Based on *Egyptian*, because of the belief that the Romanies came originally from Egypt

gyrate *verb* to whirl round ✦ **gyration** *noun* ✦ **gyratory** *adjective*

Hh

H *symbol, chemistry* hydrogen

haar *noun, Scottish & NE English dialect* a cold mist or fog, especially from the sea

habeas corpus (*pronounced* hai-bi-as **kaw**-pus) *noun, law* a request to produce a prisoner in person and give the reasons for their detention

haberdasher (*pronounced* **hab**-er-dash-er) *noun* someone who sells haberdashery

haberdashery *noun* materials for sewing, mending, etc

habit *noun* **1** something you are used to doing: *nasty habits* **2** someone's usual behaviour **3** the dress of a monk or nun • **make a habit of** to do regularly or frequently

habitable *adjective* fit to live in

habitat *noun* the natural home of an animal or plant

habitation *noun* a dwelling place

habitual *adjective* usual, formed by habit

habitually *adverb* usually, as a matter of habit

habituate *verb* to make accustomed
♦ **habitually** *adverb*

hack[1] *verb* **1** to cut or chop up roughly **2** *informal* to use a computer to get unauthorized access to files or other systems ➤ *noun* **1** a rough cut, a gash **2** a short, dry cough

hack[2] *noun* **1** a writer who does hard work for low pay **2** a riding horse kept for hire ➤ *verb* to ride on horseback, especially along ordinary roads

hacker *noun, informal* **1** a skilled computer operator **2** someone who breaks into government or commercial computer systems

hackles *plural noun* **1** the feathers on the neck of a farmyard cock **2** the hair on a dog's neck • **make someone's hackles rise** to make them angry

hackney cab or **hackney carriage** *noun* **1** *history* a horse-drawn carriage for public hire **2** a taxi

hackneyed *adjective* overused, not fresh or original: *hackneyed phrase*

hacksaw *noun* a saw for cutting metal

had past form of **have**

haddock *noun* (*plural* **haddock** or **haddocks**) a small edible N Atlantic fish

Hadith (*pronounced* **had**-ith) *noun* the collection of traditions about Muhammad

hadj another spelling of **hajj**

Hadley cell *noun, meteorology* the equatorial weather cycle of rising warm air that condenses to form clouds, resulting in heavy rainfall followed by cool dry air, which heats up and rises again

> ⏱ Named after George *Hadley* (1685–1768), English writer on science

hadron *noun, physics* one of a class of subatomic particles, comprising baryons and mesons, that interact strongly with other subatomic particles

haem or *US* **heme** *noun, biology, chemistry* an iron compound which combines with the protein globin to form haemoglobin

haemo- or *US* **hemo-** *prefix* of or relating to blood ⏱ Comes from Greek *haima* meaning 'blood'

haemocyanin or *US* **hemocyanin** *noun, biology* a blue pigment that carries oxygen and carbon dioxide in the circulation of molluscs and crustaceans

haemoglobin or *US* **hemoglobin** (*both pronounced* heem-o-**glohb**-in) *noun* the oxygen-carrying substance in red blood cells

haemophilia or *US* **hemophilia** (*both pronounced* heem-o-**fil**-i-a) *noun* a hereditary disease causing extreme bleeding when cut

haemophiliac or *US* **hemophiliac** (*both pronounced* heem-o-**fil**-i-ak) *noun* someone suffering from haemophilia

haemorrhage or *US* **hemorrhage** (*both pronounced* **hem**-o-rij) *noun* a large amount of bleeding

haemorrhoids or *US* **hemorrhoids** (*both pronounced* **hem**-o-roidz) *plural noun* an uncomfortable condition commonly known as 'piles', in which the veins around the anus become dilated

hafnium *noun, chemistry* (symbol **Hf**) a metallic element used in electrodes

> ⏱ From *Hafnia*, the Latin name for Copenhagen (where it was discovered)

haft *noun* a handle of a knife, sword, axe, etc

hag *noun* **1** *offensive* an ugly old woman **2** a witch

Haganah *noun, history* a Jewish underground militia, formed in Palestine in the 1920s, which went on to become the official Israeli army

haggard *adjective* gaunt and hollow-eyed, from tiredness

Ⓘ Originally a falconer's term for an untamed hawk

haggis *noun* (*plural* **haggises**) a Scottish dish made from chopped sheep's offal and oatmeal, seasoned and boiled in a bag traditionally made from the animal's stomach

haggle *verb* to argue determinedly over a price

ha-ha¹ or **haw-haw** *interjection* **1** a conventional way of representing the sound of laughter **2** expressing triumph, mockery, scorn, etc

ha-ha² or **haw-haw** *noun* a wall or a fence separating areas of land in a large garden or park, but placed in a ditch so as not to interrupt the view

Ⓘ Possibly from the supposed cry made when discovering one

haiku *noun* a Japanese form of poem written in three lines of 5, 7, and 5 syllables

hail¹ *verb* **1** to greet, welcome **2** to call to, attract the attention of ➤ *noun* **1** a call from a distance **2** greeting, welcome • **hail from** to come from, belong to

hail² *noun* **1** frozen raindrops **2** a falling mass: *a hail of bullets* ➤ *verb* **1** to shower with hail **2** to descend in a mass

hail-fellow-well-met *adjective* friendly and familiar, especially overly so

hailstone *noun* a piece of hail

hair *noun* a thread-like growth on the skin of an animal; the whole mass of these (as on the head) • **split hairs** to worry about unimportant details; nitpick

hair-breadth or **hair's-breadth** *noun* a very small distance

haircut *noun* **1** the cutting of someone's hair **2** the shape or style in which it is cut

hairdo *noun* (*plural* **hairdos**) *informal* a woman's haircut, especially after styling and setting

hairdresser *noun* someone who cuts, washes, styles, and colours hair

hairdryer or **hairdrier** *noun* an electrical device which blows hot air to dry hair

hairline *noun* **1** the line along the forehead where the hair begins to grow **2** a very fine line

hairpiece *noun* an attachment of hair added to a person's own hair to give extra length or volume

hairpin *noun* a thin flat U-shaped piece of wire for keeping the hair in place

hair-raising *adjective* terrifying

hairspray *noun* a fine spray to fix a hairstyle

hairstyle *noun* a way of cutting or wearing the hair

hairy *adjective* (**hairier, hairiest**) **1** covered

with hair **2** *informal* risky, dangerous
♦ **hairiness** *noun*

hajj or **hadj** (*pronounced* haj) *noun* (*plural* **hajjes** or **hadjes**) the annual Muslim pilgrimage to Mecca

hajji or **hadji** *noun* (*plural* **hajjis** or **hadjis**) a Muslim who has made the pilgrimage to Mecca

hake *noun* (*plural* **hake** or **hakes**) an edible seafish similar to a cod

Halachah, Halakah or **Halacha** *noun*, *Judaism* the legal element in the Talmud, forming the Jewish code of conduct Ⓘ Comes from a Hebrew word meaning 'law'

halal (*pronounced* hal-al) *noun* meat from animals that have been slaughtered according to Islamic law ➤ *adjective* from animals slaughtered in this way

halcyon (*pronounced* hal-si-on) *adjective*: **halcyon days** a time of peace and happiness

Ⓘ From the Greek word for 'kingfisher' in the phrase 'kingfisher days', a period of calm weather in mid-winter

hale *adjective*: **hale and hearty** healthy

half *noun* (*plural* **halves**) one of two equal parts ➤ *adjective* **1** being one of two equal parts: *a half bottle of wine* **2** not full or complete: *a half smile* ➤ *adverb* partly, to some extent

halfback *noun* **1** *football, hockey, etc* a player or position immediately behind the forwards and in front of the fullbacks **2** *rugby* either the stand-off half or the scrum half

half-baked *adjective informal* not properly thought out, incomplete

half-board *noun* a hotel charge for bed, breakfast, and another meal

half-breed or **half-caste** *noun, derogatory, offensive* someone with a father and mother of different races

half-brother *noun* a brother sharing only one parent

half-cock *noun*: **at half-cock** not completely ready, unprepared

half day *noun* a day in which someone attends school or work only in the morning or afternoon

half-hearted *adjective* not eager

half-life *noun, physics* the time in which the radioactivity of a substance falls to half its original value

half-mast *adverb* of a flag: hoisted halfway up the mast to show that someone important has died

half moon *noun* the moon when half is visible

half nelson *noun, wrestling* a hold in which a wrestler puts an arm under one of their opponent's arms from behind, and pushes on the back of their neck

halfpenny (*pronounced* heip-ni) *noun* (*plural*

halfpennies) an old coin worth half of an old penny

half-rhyme *noun* a rhyme in which the consonants, but not the vowel, of the last stressed syllable have the same sound, eg *hair* and *hour* (*also called*: **pararhyme**)

half-sister *noun* a sister sharing only one parent

half-term *noun* a short holiday halfway through a school or college term

half-time *noun* an interval halfway through a sports game

half volley *noun, sport* a stroke in which the ball is hit just after it bounces or as it bounces

halfway *adverb & adjective* at or to a point equally far from the beginning and the end

halfway house *noun* **1** *informal* something which is between two extremes, with some features of each **2** a home where former prisoners, psychiatric patients, etc stay temporarily to readjust to life outside prison, hospital, etc

halfwit *noun* an idiot, a fool

halfwitted *adjective* stupid, idiotic

halibut *noun* (*plural* **halibut** or **halibuts**) a large edible flatfish

halide *noun, chemistry* a compound formed by a halogen and a metal or a radical

halitosis *noun* unpleasant-smelling breath ☉ Comes from Latin *halitus* meaning 'breath'

hall *noun* **1** (*also called*: **hallway**) a passage at the entrance to a house **2** a large public room **3** a large country house

hallelujah or **halleluia** *interjection* expressing praise to God (*also*: **alleluia**)

hallmark *noun* **1** a mark put on gold and silver articles to show quality **2** a characteristic sign: *the hallmark of a good editor*

hallo another spelling of **hello**

hallowed *adjective, old* holy, sacred

Hallowe'en *noun* the evening of 31 October, traditionally a time when spirits are believed to be around

hallucinate (*pronounced* ha-**loo**-si-neit) *verb* to see something that is not actually there
♦ **hallucination** *noun*

hallucinatory *adjective* causing hallucinations, or like a hallucination

hallucinogen (*pronounced* ha-**loo**-sin-o-jen) *noun* a substance that causes hallucinations
♦ **hallucinogenic** *adjective*

hallway see **hall**

halo *noun* (*plural* **haloes** or **halos**) **1** a circle of light surrounding eg the sun or moon **2** in paintings etc: a ring of light around the head of a saint, angel, etc

halogen (*pronounced* **hal**-o-jen) *noun, chemistry* one of a group of elements that includes chlorine, bromine and iodine

halt¹ *verb* to come or bring to a stop ► *noun* **1** a stop, a standstill: *call a halt* **2** a stopping place

halt² *verb* **1** *old* to be lame, limp **2** to hesitate, be uncertain ► *adjective, old* lame

halter *noun* a head-rope for holding and leading a horse

halterneck *noun* a woman's top or dress held in place by a strap round the neck, leaving the shoulders and back bare

halting *adjective* hesitant, uncertain

halve *verb* to divide in two

halyard *noun* a rope for raising or lowering a sail or flag on a ship

ham¹ *noun* **1** the meat from a pig's thigh salted and dried **2** *informal* the back of the thigh

ham² *noun, informal* **1** an actor who overacts **2** an amateur radio operator ► *verb* (**hamming, hammed**) (*also*: **ham up**) to overact or exaggerate

hamburger *noun* a round cake of minced beef, cooked by frying or grilling

ham-fisted *adjective, informal* clumsy

hamlet *noun* a small village

hammer *noun* **1** a tool with a heavy metal head for beating metal, driving nails, etc **2** a striking piece in a clock, piano, pistol, etc **3** *sport* a metal ball on a long flexible steel chain, thrown in competitions ► *verb* **1** to drive or shape with a hammer **2** *informal* to defeat overwhelmingly
• **hammer and tongs** *informal* determinedly, violently

hammock *noun* a length of netting, canvas, etc hung up by the corners, and used as a bed

hamper¹ *verb* to hinder, impede

hamper² *noun* a large basket with a lid

hamster *noun* a small rodent with large cheek pouches, often kept as a pet

hamstring *noun* a tendon at the back of the knee ► *verb* (**hamstringing, hamstrung**) **1** to make lame by cutting the hamstring **2** to make ineffective or powerless

hand *noun* **1** the part of the human body at the end of the arm **2** a pointer, eg on a clock **3** help, aid: *Can you give me a hand?* **4** a measure (four inches, 10.16 centimetres) for the height of horses **5** a worker, a labourer **6** a style of handwriting **7** side, direction: *left-hand side* **8** *cards* a group of playing-cards dealt to someone **9** *informal* clapping, applause: *a big hand* ► *verb* to pass (something) with the hand • **at hand** near by • **change hands** to pass to another owner • **hand over** to give • **hand over fist** *informal* progressing quickly and steadily: *making money hand over fist* • **in hand 1** in your possession: *cash in hand* **2** in preparation, under control • **out of hand 1** out of control **2** at once: *to dismiss it out of hand* • **out of someone's hands** no longer their concern • **take in hand**

to take charge of • **try your hand at** to have a go at, attempt

handbag *noun* a small bag for personal belongings

handball *noun* **1** a game in which two or four players hit a small ball against a wall with their hands **2** the small hard rubber ball used in this game **3** *football* the offence a player other than a goalkeeper in their own penalty area commits if they touch the ball with their hand

handbook *noun* a small book giving information or directions

handbrake *noun* a brake on a motor vehicle, or the lever which operates it

handcuffs *plural noun* steel bands joined by a short chain, put round the wrists of prisoners

handful *noun* (*plural* **handfuls**) **1** as much as can be held in one hand **2** a small amount **3** *informal* a difficult and demanding child, pet, etc

handgun *noun* a gun that can be held and fired in one hand

handicap *noun* **1** something that makes an action more difficult **2** a disadvantage, such as having to run a greater distance, given to the best competitors in a race **3** a race in which handicaps are given **4** the number of strokes by which a golfer's average score exceeds par for a course **5** a physical or mental disability ➤ *verb* **1** to give a handicap to **2** to burden, impede

⊙ Originally a gambling game in which wagers were drawn by *hand* from a *cap*

handicapped *adjective* **1** having or given a handicap **2** physically or mentally disabled

handicraft *noun* skilled work done by hand, not machine

hand-in-hand *adjective* **1** holding hands **2** in partnership

handiwork *noun* **1** thing(s) made by hand **2** something done by a particular person etc: *the handiwork of a sick mind*

handkerchief *noun* (*plural* **handkerchiefs**) a small cloth for wiping the nose etc

handle *verb* **1** to touch, hold or use with the hand **2** to manage, cope with ➤ *noun* **1** the part of anything meant to be held in the hand **2** a way of understanding something: *trying to get a handle on something* **3** *slang* a person's name or title

handlebars *plural noun* a steering bar at the front of a bicycle with a handle at each end

handler *noun* **1** someone who trains and works with an animal, eg a police dog **2** someone who handles something: *baggage handler*

hand-me-down *noun informal* a second-hand piece of clothing, especially one that used to belong to another member of the family

handout *noun* a sheet or bundle of information

given out at a lecture etc

hand-picked *adjective* chosen carefully

handrail *noun* a narrow rail running alongside a stairway for support

handset *noun* a telephone mouthpiece and earpiece together in a single unit

handshake *noun* an act of shaking a person's hand, especially as a greeting or when concluding a deal

handsome *adjective* **1** good-looking **2** generous: *a handsome gift*

hands-on *adjective* **1** hand-operated **2** involving practical experience

handstand *noun* an act of balancing on the hands with the legs in the air

hand-to-hand *adjective* of fighting: at close quarters

hand-to-mouth *adjective* with barely enough to live on and nothing to spare

handwriting *noun* writing with pen or pencil ✦ **handwritten** *adjective*

handy *adjective* (**handier, handiest**) **1** useful or convenient to use **2** easily reached, near **3** clever with the hands ✦ **handily** *adverb* (meanings 1 and 2)

handyman *noun* (*plural* **handymen**) a man who does odd jobs around the house

hang *verb* (**hanging, hung** or **hanged**) **1** to fix or be fixed to a point off the ground **2** to be suspended in the air **3** to attach (wallpaper) to a wall **4** *informal* to damn or be damned: *Hang the expense* **5** (*past form* **hanged**) to put (a prisoner) to death by putting a rope round their neck and letting them fall • **get the hang of** *informal* to understand, learn how to use • **hang about** or **hang around** to remain near, loiter • **hang back** to hesitate • **hang down** to droop or fall downwards • **hang fire** to delay • **hang on 1** to depend on **2** *informal* to wait, linger • **hang out** *informal* to relax and enjoy yourself: *hang out at the cinema* ⊙ Comes from Old English *hangian*

hangar (*pronounced* hang-ar) *noun* a shed for aeroplanes ⊙ Comes from French *hangar* meaning 'a shed'

⚠ Do not confuse: **hangar** and **hanger**

hangdog *adjective* guilty-looking

hanger *noun* a frame on which a coat etc is hung ⊙ For origin, see **hang**

hanger-on *noun* (*plural* **hangers-on**) someone who stays near someone in the hope of gaining some advantage

hang-gliding *noun* a form of gliding by hanging in a harness under a large kite ✦ **hang-glider** *noun*

hanging *noun* an execution in which the prisoner is hanged

hanging valley *noun, geography* a tributary valley which enters a main valley at a much higher level because the main valley has become deeper as a result of glacial erosion

hangman *noun* (*plural* **hangmen**) an executioner who hangs people

hangnail *noun* a torn shred of skin beside a fingernail

hang-out *noun, informal* a place where you spend a lot of time

hangover *noun* **1** uncomfortable after-effects of being drunk **2** something remaining: *a hangover from the 1960s*

hank *noun* a coil or loop of string, rope, wool, etc

hanker *verb* to long for something: *hankering after a chocolate biscuit*

hankie or **hanky** *noun* (*plural* **hankies**) *informal* a handkerchief

Hanukkah (*pronounced* hah-nuw-ka) or **Chanukkah** *noun* the Jewish festival of lights held in mid-December

haphazard *adjective* depending on chance, without planning or system ♦ **haphazardly** *adverb*

hapless *adjective* unlucky

haploid *biology, adjective* of a cell or organism, eg a germ cell: having a single set of unpaired chromosomes (*compare with*: **diploid**) ➤ *noun* a haploid cell or organism

happen *verb* **1** to take place **2** to occur by chance **3** to chance to do: *Did you happen to see the news?*

happening *noun* an event

happy *adjective* (**happier, happiest**) **1** joyful **2** contented **3** fortunate, lucky: *a happy coincidence* **4** willing: *happy to help* ♦ **happily** *adverb* ♦ **happiness** *noun*

happy-go-lucky *adjective* easy-going, taking things as they come

hara-kiri (*pronounced* har-a-**kir**-i) *noun* a Japanese form of ritual suicide by slitting the stomach with a sword

haram (*pronounced* hah-**ram**) *adjective* forbidden by the laws of Islam

harangue (*pronounced* ha-**rang**) *noun* a loud aggressive speech ➤ *verb* to deliver a harangue

harass (*pronounced* **har**-as) *verb* to annoy persistently, pester ♦ **harassed** *adjective* ♦ **harassment** *noun*

harbinger (*pronounced* hah-bin-jer) *noun* someone or something that announces or predicts something to come ⊘ Comes from French *herbergere* meaning 'host'

harbour or *US* **harbor** *noun* **1** a place of shelter for ships **2** a shelter, a place of safety ➤ *verb* **1** to give shelter or refuge to **2** to store in the mind: *harbouring ill will*

hard *adjective* **1** solid, firm **2** not easily broken or put out of shape **3** not easy to do, understand, etc **4** not easy to please **5** not easy to bear **6** having no kind or gentle feelings **7** of water: containing many minerals and so not forming a good lather **8** of drugs: habit-forming ➤ *adverb* **1** with great effort or energy: *She works hard* **2** strongly, violently ♦ **hardness** *noun* **hard of hearing** rather deaf

hard-and-fast *adjective* strict, rigid

hardback *noun* a book bound in a hard cover (*compare with*: **paperback**)

hardboard *noun* light strong board made from compressed wood pulp

hard copy *noun, computing* printed output of information held in computer files

hardcore *adjective* of pornography etc: very explicit, graphic

hard disk *noun, computing* a rigid magnetic disk, normally sealed within a hard drive, used to store large amounts of data

hard drive *noun, computing* a disk drive that holds, reads data stored on and writes to a hard disk

hard-earned *adjective* having taken a great deal of hard work to achieve or acquire

harden *verb* to make hard

hard engineering *noun, geography* coast management that involves building new structures such as sea walls and groynes, which tends to be more expensive, more short-term, and more damaging to the environment (*contrasted with*: **soft engineering**)

hard-hearted *adjective* having no kind feelings

hard-hit *adjective* badly affected

hard labour *noun* tiring work given to prisoners as part of their punishment

hardline *adjective* refusing to change or compromise: *a hardline socialist*

hard lines *plural noun* (*also*: **hard luck**) bad luck

hardly *adverb* scarcely; only just; with difficulty

hard-nosed *adjective, informal* tough, unsentimental

hardship *noun* something difficult to bear

hard shoulder *noun* the surfaced strip on the outer edges of a motorway, used when stopping in an emergency

hard up *adjective, informal* short of money

hardware *noun* **1** ironmongery **2** *computing* the casing, processor, disk drives, etc of a computer, not the programs which it runs (*contrasted with*: **software**)

hard-wired *adjective, computing* of computers: having functions that are controlled by hardware and cannot be altered by software programs

hardwood *noun* the wood of certain trees including oak, ash, elm, etc

hardy *adjective* (**hardier, hardiest**) strong, robust, tough ♦ **hardiness** *noun*

hare *noun* a fast-running animal, like a large rabbit

harebell *noun* a wild plant with blue bell-shaped flowers (*also called* (*Scot*): **bluebell**)

hare-brained *adjective* mad, foolish

hare-lip *noun* a split in the upper lip at birth, often occurring with a cleft palate

harem (*pronounced* **hei**-rem *or* hah-**reem**) *noun* **1** the women's rooms in an Islamic house **2** a set of wives and concubines

haricot (*pronounced* **har**-i-koh) *noun* a small white dried bean, used as food

hark *interjection literary* listen! • **hark back to** to recall or refer to (a previous time, remark, etc)

harlequin (*pronounced* **hah**-li-kwin) *noun* a comic pantomime character wearing a multicoloured costume

harm *noun* hurt, damage > *verb* **1** to wound, damage **2** to do wrong to

harmful *adjective* having a bad or damaging effect on people or things

harmless *adjective* **1** safe, eg to eat, use, or touch **2** causing no annoyance or disturbance to anyone

harmonic *adjective, music* relating to harmony or harmonics > *noun* **1** a ringing sound produced by lightly touching a string being played **2** *physics* a component of a sound

harmonica *noun* a mouth organ

harmonic progression *noun, maths* a series of terms in which there is a constant difference between the reciprocals of the terms, eg $1, \frac{1}{2}, \frac{1}{3}, \frac{1}{4}$, …

harmonics *singular noun* the science of musical sounds and their properties

harmonious *adjective* **1** pleasant-sounding **2** peaceful, without disagreement

harmonize *or* **harmonise** *verb* **1** to bring into harmony **2** to agree, go well (with) **3** *music* to add the different parts to a melody **4** *music* to sing in harmony, eg with other singers ♦ **harmonization** *noun*

harmony *noun* (*plural* **harmonies**) **1** agreement of one part, colour, or sound with another **2** agreement between people: *living in harmony* **3** *music* a part intended to agree in sound with the melody

harness *noun* (*plural* **harnesses**) **1** the leather and other fittings for a workhorse **2** an arrangement of straps etc attaching something to the body: *parachute harness* > *verb* **1** to put a harness on a horse **2** to use as a resource: *harnessing the power of the wind* • **in harness** working, not on holiday or retired

harp *noun* a triangular, stringed musical instrument played upright by plucking with the fingers > *verb* to play the harp • **harp on about** to talk too much about

harper *or* **harpist** *noun* a harp player

harpoon *noun* a spear tied to rope, used for killing whales > *verb* to strike with a harpoon

harpsichord *noun* an early musical instrument with keys, played like a piano

harrow *noun* a frame with iron spikes for breaking up lumps of earth > *verb* **1** to drag a harrow over **2** to distress greatly

harrowing *adjective* very distressing

harry *verb* (**harries, harrying, harried**) **1** to plunder, lay waste **2** to harass, worry

harsh *adjective* rough, bitter; cruel ♦ **harshly** *adverb*

hart *noun* the stag or male deer, especially from the age of six years

harvest *noun* **1** the time of the year when ripened crops are gathered in **2** the crops gathered at this time > *verb* to gather in (a crop)

harvester *noun* **1** a farm worker who helps with the harvest **2** a combine harvester **3** a creature like a spider

harvest home *noun* a feast held after a harvest is gathered in

has *see* **have**

has-been *noun, informal* someone no longer important or popular

hash *noun* a dish of chopped meat etc • **make a hash of** *informal* to spoil completely

hashish *noun* the strongest form of the drug made from hemp (*see also* **cannabis**)

Hasid *or* **Hassid** *noun* a member of a number of devout Jewish sects existing at various times throughout history (*also called*: **Chassid**) ♦ **Hasidic** *adjective* ♦ **Hasidism** *noun*

hassium *noun, chemistry* (symbol **Hs**) an artificially manufactured element

hassle *informal, verb* to cause problems for > *noun* difficulty, trouble

hassock *noun* a thick cushion used as a footstool or for kneeling on

haste *noun* speed, hurry • **make haste** to hurry

hasten *verb* **1** to hurry (on) **2** to drive forward

hasty *adjective* (**hastier, hastiest**) hurried; done without thinking ♦ **hastily** *adverb*

hat *noun* a covering for the head • **keep something under your hat** to keep it secret

hatch[1] *noun* (*plural* **hatches**) a door or cover over an opening in a floor, wall, etc

hatch[2] *verb* **1** to produce (young) from eggs **2** to form and set working: *They hatched a plan*

hatch[3] *verb* to shade (part of a picture etc) with fine lines

hatchback *noun* a car with a sloping rear door which opens upwards

hatchery noun (plural **hatcheries**) a place for hatching eggs (especially of fish)

hatchet noun a small axe • **bury the hatchet** to put an end to a quarrel

hate verb to dislike very much ➤ noun great dislike

hate crime noun a crime motivated by hatred of the victim on the grounds of race, religion, etc

hateful adjective horrible, causing hatred

hatred noun extreme dislike

hatter noun someone who makes or sells hats

hat-trick noun **1** cricket the putting out of three batsmen by three balls in a row **2** football three goals scored by the same player **3** any action performed three times in a row

haughty adjective (**haughtier, haughtiest**) proud, looking on others with scorn ♦ **haughtily** adverb ♦ **haughtiness** noun

haul verb to drag, pull with force ➤ noun **1** a strong pull **2** informal a difficult or tiring job: a long haul **3** an amount gathered at one time: a haul of fish **4** a rich find, booty

haulage noun **1** the carrying of goods **2** money charged for this

haulier noun a transporter of goods

haunch noun (plural **haunches**) **1** the fleshy part of the hip **2** a leg and loin of meat, especially venison

haunt verb **1** to visit often **2** of a ghost: to inhabit, linger in (a place) ➤ noun a place often visited

haunted adjective inhabited by ghosts

haunting adjective of a memory, piece of music, etc: making a very strong and moving impression

haute couture (pronounced oht kuw-**tyoo**-er) noun the leading fashion designers or their products, collectively ☺ Comes from French, meaning 'high dressmaking'

haute cuisine (pronounced oht kwi-**zeen**) noun cookery, especially French cookery, of a very high standard ☺ Comes from French, meaning 'high cooking'

have verb (**has, having, had**) **1** used with another verb to show that an action is in the past and completed: We have decided to move house **2** to own, possess: Do you have a cat? **3** to hold, contain: The hotel has a swimming pool **4** to give birth to: have a baby **5** to suffer from: have a cold **6** to cause to be done: have your hair cut **7** to put up with: I won't have him being so rude • **have done with** to finish • **have it out** to settle by argument • **have someone on** informal to trick or tease them ☺ Comes from Old English habban

haven noun a place of safety

haversack noun a bag made of canvas etc with shoulder-straps, for carrying on the back

havoc noun great destruction • **play havoc with something** to cause a great deal of damage or confusion to it

haw noun a berry of the hawthorn tree

hawk[1] noun **1** a bird of prey like a falcon **2** politics someone who favours aggression rather than peaceful means of settling disputes (contrasted with: **dove**) ➤ verb to hunt birds with trained hawks

hawk[2] verb to carry (goods) round, usually from door to door, trying to sell them ♦ **hawker** noun

hawk[3] verb to clear the throat noisily

hawthorn noun a prickly tree with white flowers and small red berries

hay noun cut and dried grass, used as cattle food

hay fever noun an illness with effects like a bad cold, caused by pollen etc

haystack or **hayrick** noun hay built up into a mound

haywire adjective, informal **1** of things: out of order; not working properly **2** of people: crazy or erratic

hazard noun **1** chance **2** risk of harm or danger ➤ verb **1** to risk **2** to put forward (a guess) at the risk of being wrong

hazardous adjective dangerous, risky

haze noun a thin mist

hazel noun a nut-producing tree of the birch family ➤ adjective light greenish-brown in colour

hazelnut noun a light brown nut produced by the hazel tree

hazy adjective (**hazier, haziest**) **1** misty **2** not clear, vague ♦ **hazily** adverb ♦ **haziness** noun

H-bomb noun a hydrogen bomb

HCF or **hcf** abbreviation, maths highest common factor

HDI abbreviation, geography Human Development Index

He symbol, chemistry helium

he pronoun a male person or animal already spoken about (used only as the subject of a verb): he ate a banana

head noun **1** the uppermost part of the body, containing the brain, skull, etc **2** someone's mind: can't get that tune out of my head **3** a person in charge, a chief **4** informal a head teacher **5** the foam on top of a glass of beer, lager, etc **6** a device in hard disks, tape recorders, etc for recording or erasing material **7** (**heads**) the side of a coin showing the head of a monarch or leader ➤ verb **1** to lead **2** to go in front of **3** to go in the direction of: heading for home **4** to hit (a ball) with the head • **head off** to turn aside, deflect: head off an attack • **head over heels** completely, thoroughly: head over heels in love • **off your head** informal mad, crazy • **per head** per person

headache noun 1 a pain in the head 2 informal a worrying problem

headband noun a band worn round the head

headboard noun a board across the top end of a bed

headdress noun (plural **headdresses**) a covering for the head, especially a highly decorative one used in ceremonies

header noun 1 a headfirst dive 2 football a shot at goal striking the ball with the head 3 a heading for a chapter, article or page

headfirst adverb 1 with the head first: fall headfirst down the stairs 2 rashly, without thinking

headhunting noun 1 anthropology the practice in certain societies of taking the heads of dead enemies as trophies 2 the practice of trying to attract a person away from their present job to work for another company ♦ **headhunt** verb ♦ **headhunter** noun

heading noun words at the head of a chapter, paragraph, etc

headland noun a point of land running out into the sea, a cape

headlight noun a strong light on the front of a car etc

headline noun a line in large letters at the top of a newspaper page

headlong adjective & adverb headfirst

headmaster noun a **head teacher**

headmistress noun a **head teacher**

head-on adjective & adverb with the head or front first

headphones plural noun a listening device that fits over the ears

headquarters singular noun & plural noun place from which the chief officers of an army etc control their operations; the chief office (of a business etc)

headrest noun a support for the head in a vehicle etc

headscarf noun (plural **headscarves**) a scarf worn over the head and sometimes fastened under the chin

headset noun a pair of headphones, often with a microphone attached

head start noun a boost or advantage at the beginning of something

headstone noun a gravestone

headstrong adjective determined, stubborn

head teacher noun (sometimes **headmaster** or **headmistress**) the principal teacher of a school

headway noun progress: making headway with the backlog

headwind noun a wind blowing straight in your face

heady adjective (**headier, headiest**) exciting

heal verb to make or become healthy or sound; cure ♦ **healer** noun

health noun 1 someone's physical condition: How's your health? 2 good or natural physical condition • **your health!** (as a toast) a wish that someone may have good health

health centre noun a building where nurses and doctors hold clinics

health farm noun a place where people go to improve their health through diet and exercise

health food noun food considered to be beneficial to health

health service noun a public service providing medical care, usually without charge

health visitor noun a trained nurse who visits people in their homes

healthy adjective (**healthier, healthiest**) 1 in good health or condition 2 encouraging good health ♦ **healthily** adverb

heap noun 1 a pile of things thrown one on top of another 2 (usually **heaps**) informal a great many (of) ➢ verb to throw in a pile

hear verb (**hearing, heard**) 1 to receive (sounds) by the ear 2 to listen to 3 to be told, understand: I hear you want to speak to me • **hear! hear!** a cry to show agreement with a speaker • **will not hear of** will not allow: He wouldn't hear of her going there alone

hearing noun 1 the act or power of listening 2 an investigation and listening to evidence

hearing aid noun a small electronic device worn on or in the ear to help hearing

hearsay noun gossip, rumour

hearse noun a car for carrying a dead body to the grave etc

heart noun 1 the part of the body which acts as a blood pump 2 the inner or chief part of anything: the heart of the problem 3 courage: take heart 4 will, enthusiasm: His heart isn't in it 5 love, affection: with all my heart 6 a sign (♥) representing a heart, or often love 7 this sign used in one of the suits of playing-cards • **take to heart** to be deeply affected or upset by

heartache noun sorrow, grief

heart attack noun a sudden and painful interruption in the functioning of the heart

heartbeat noun 1 the pulsing of the heart 2 a single pulsing action of the heart

heartbreak noun great sorrow or grief ♦ **heartbreaking** adjective

heartbroken adjective very upset, very sad

heartburn noun a burning feeling in the chest after eating, indigestion

hearten verb to cheer on, encourage

heart failure noun the sudden stopping of the heart's beating

heartfelt adjective felt deeply, sincere: heartfelt thanks

hearth *noun* a fireplace

heartily *adverb* **1** cheerfully and with great enthusiasm **2** thoroughly, absolutely: *I'm heartily sick of his moaning*

heartless *adjective* cruel

heart rate *noun* the number of single heartbeats per minute

heart-rending *adjective* very moving, very upsetting

heartstrings *plural noun* inmost feelings of love: *His tale of woe really tugged at our heartstrings*

heart-throb *noun informal* someone, especially a male actor or singer, that many people find very attractive

heart-to-heart *noun* a frank, intimate discussion

heartwarming *adjective* pleasing; emotionally moving

hearty *adjective* (**heartier, heartiest**) **1** strong, healthy **2** of a meal: large, satisfying **3** eager, over-cheerful ♦ **heartily** *adverb*

heat *noun* **1** high temperature **2** anger **3** *sport* a round in a competition, race, etc ➤ *verb* to make or become hot • **in heat** of a female animal: ready for mating in the breeding season • **in the heat of the moment** without pausing to think

heat capacity *noun, physics* the ratio between the heat supplied to a substance and the resulting rise in temperature (*also called:* **specific heat capacity**)

heater *noun* an apparatus for heating a room, building, water in a tank, etc

heat exchanger *noun, physics* a device that transfers heat from one stream of fluid to another without allowing the two fluids to come into contact, eg a car radiator

heath *noun* **1** barren, open country **2** heather

heathen *noun* someone who does not believe in an established religion, especially someone who worships idols ➤ *adjective* of heathens, pagan

heather *noun* a plant with small purple, white, or pink flowers growing on moorland ➤ *adjective* of the colour of purple heather

heatstroke *noun* exhaustion, illness, or collapse caused by exposure to extreme heat (*also called:* **sunstroke**)

heat wave *noun* a period of hot weather

heave *verb* **1** to lift by force **2** to throw **3** to rise and fall **4** to produce, let out (especially a sigh)

heaven *noun* **1** (often **the heavens**) the sky **2** (often **Heaven**) the dwelling place of God; paradise **3** any place of great happiness

heavenly *adjective* **1** living in heaven **2** *informal* delightful

heavenly bodies *plural noun* the sun, moon, and stars

heavily *adverb* **1** with great force, in great amount: *It was raining heavily* **2** to a serious or great extent, intensely: *heavily in debt* **3** loudly and deeply: *He sighed heavily/breathing heavily* **4** in a thick, solid-looking way: *He was short, but heavily built* **5** in a slow, sleepy, or sad way: *'I can't help you,' he said heavily*

heavy *adjective* (**heavier, heaviest**) **1** of great weight **2** great in amount, force, etc: *heavy rainfall* **3** not easy to bear **4** slow; sleepy **5** loud and deep: *heavy breathing* **6** having a thick, solid appearance: *heavy eyebrows/a heavy oak table* ♦ **heaviness** *noun*

heavy-duty *adjective* designed to withstand very hard wear

heavy-handed *adjective* clumsy, awkward

heavy industry *noun* industries such as coalmining, steel-making, shipbuilding, etc using heavy equipment (*compare with:* **light industry**)

heavy metal *noun* a very loud repetitive form of rock music

heavyweight *noun* **1** a boxer in the highest weight category **2** *informal* someone very important or powerful

Hebrew *noun* an ancient language spoken in its modern form by Jews in Israel

heckle *verb* to shout insults at or ask awkward questions of (a public speaker) ♦ **heckler** *noun*

hectare *noun* 10 000 square metres

hectic *adjective* rushed; feverish

hecto- or **hect-** *prefix* forms words of measurement equal to one hundred times the basic unit: *hectare* (= 100 ares, each equivalent to 100 square metres) ⊙ Comes from Greek *hekaton* meaning 'one hundred'

hector *verb* to bully

> ⊙ After *Hector*, a fierce warrior who fought against the Greeks in the siege of Troy

hedge *noun* a fence of bushes, shrubs, etc ➤ *verb* **1** to make a hedge **2** to shut in with a hedge **3** to avoid giving a straight answer • **hedge your bets** to keep open two or more possible courses of action

hedgehog *noun* a small animal with prickly spines on its back

hedgerow *noun* a row of bushes forming a hedge

hedonism *noun* **1** the belief that pleasure is the highest good in life **2** the pursuit of pleasure ♦ **hedonist** *noun* ♦ **hedonistic** *adjective*

-hedron *suffix, maths* forms nouns to do with a geometric solid with a specified number of faces: *polyhedron*

heed *verb* to give attention to, listen to • **pay heed to** to take notice of

heedless *adjective* careless

heel[1] *noun* the back part of the foot ➤ *verb* **1** to hit (especially a ball) with the heel **2** to put a heel on (a shoe) • **take to your heels** or **show a clean pair of heels** to run away

heel[2] *verb* of a ship: to lean over

hefty *adjective* (**heftier, heftiest**) *informal* **1** powerful, muscular **2** heavy **3** large in amount: *a hefty sum of money*

hegemony (*pronounced* hi-**gem**-on-i or hi-**jem**-on-i) *noun* (*plural* **hegemonies**) authority or control, especially of one state over another ⊙ Comes from Greek *hegemonia* meaning 'leadership'

Hegira or **Hejira** (*pronounced* **hej**-i-ra) *noun* the flight of the prophet Muhammad from Mecca to Medina in 622 AD, marking the beginning of the Islamic era ⊙ Comes from Arabic *hejira* meaning 'flight'

heifer (*pronounced* **hef**-er) *noun* a young cow

height *noun* **1** the state of being high **2** distance from bottom to top **3** the highest point **4** (often **heights**) a high place

heighten *verb* to make higher, greater, stronger, etc

heinous (*pronounced* **hei**-nus) *adjective* extremely bad, atrocious: *heinous crime*

heir *noun* the legal inheritor of a title or property on the death of the owner

heir apparent *noun* (*plural* **heirs apparent**) someone expected to receive a title or property when the present holder dies

heiress *noun* (*plural* **heiresses**) a woman or girl who is the legal inheritor of a large amount of property or money

heirloom *noun* something that has been handed down in a family from generation to generation

heist (*pronounced* haist) *noun, US slang* a robbery

hejab another spelling of **hijab**

held past form of **hold**[1]

helicopter *noun* a flying machine kept in the air by propellers rotating on a vertical axis

⊙ A coinage based on Greek words meaning 'spiral wing'

helio- *prefix* of or relating to the sun: *heliograph/ heliotrope* (= a plant that turns its flowers towards the sun) */helium* (= a gas first discovered in the atmosphere of the sun) ⊙ Comes from Greek *helios* meaning 'the sun'

heliograph *noun* a means of signalling, using the sun's rays

heliotrope *noun* **1** a plant with small, sweet-smelling, lilac-blue flowers **2** a light purple colour

helium *noun, chemistry* (symbol **He**) a very light gas

helix (*pronounced* **hee**-liks) *noun* (*plural* **helices** – *pronounced* **hee**-li-seez – or **helixes**) **1** a screw-shaped coil **2** *maths* a curve that lies on the lateral surface of a cylinder or cone, and becomes a straight line if unrolled into a plane

hell *noun* **1** a place of punishment of the wicked after death **2** (often **Hell**) the dwelling place of the Devil **3** any place of great misery or pain

hellbent on *adjective, informal* determined to

hellish *adjective, informal* very bad, unpleasant, horrible, or difficult ♦ **hellishly** *adverb*

hello or **hallo** or **hullo** *noun* (*plural* **hellos** or **helloes** etc) a greeting used between people

hellraiser *noun slang* a boisterously debauched person

helm *noun* the wheel or handle by which a ship is steered

helmet *noun* an armoured or protective covering for the head

helmsman *noun* (*plural* **helmsmen**) the person who steers a ship

help *verb* **1** to aid, do something useful for **2** to give the means for doing something to **3** to stop yourself from (doing): *I can't help liking him* ➤ *noun* **1** aid, assistance **2** someone who assists ♦ **helper** *noun* **help yourself** serve yourself, take what you want ⊙ Comes from Old English *helpan*

helpful *adjective* useful, giving help ♦ **helpfully** *adverb*

helping *noun* a share, especially of food

helping verb *noun* an auxiliary verb

helpless *adjective* useless; powerless ♦ **helplessly** *adverb*

helpline *noun* a telephone service that people with a particular problem can call in order to contact counsellors who are qualified in that specific field: *victim support helpline*

helpmate *noun* a partner, especially a husband or wife

helter-skelter *adverb* in a great hurry, in confusion ➤ *noun* a spiral slide in a fairground etc

hem *noun* the border of a garment doubled down and stitched ➤ *verb* (**hemming, hemmed**) to put or form a hem on • **hem in** to surround

hemi- *prefix* half ⊙ Comes from Greek *hemi* meaning 'half'

hemisphere *noun* **1** a half of a sphere or ball-shape **2** half of the earth: *western hemisphere/ southern hemisphere*

hemispherical *adjective* like half a ball in shape

hemline *noun* the height of a hem on a dress or skirt

hemlock *noun* a poisonous plant with spotted leaves

hemo- US spelling of **haemo-**

hemp noun a plant used for making ropes, bags, sails, etc and the drug cannabis

hen noun **1** a female bird **2** a female domestic fowl

hence adverb **1** from this place or time: ten years hence **2** for this reason: hence, I am unable to go

henceforth or **henceforward** adverb from now on

henchman noun (plural **henchmen**) a follower; a servant

henna noun a reddish plant dye used for colouring the hair and decorating the skin

hen party or **hen night** noun a party for women only, especially to celebrate the imminent marriage of one of the group

henpecked adjective of a husband: dominated by his wife

heparin noun a chemical substance that prevents the clotting of the blood

hepatitis noun inflammation of the liver caused by one of several viruses

hepta- prefix seven ☉ Comes from Greek hepta meaning 'seven'

heptagon noun a seven-sided figure
♦ **heptagonal** adjective

heptane noun, chemistry a hydrocarbon that is the seventh member of the methane series

heptathlon noun an athletic contest for women comprising seven events (compare with: **decathlon**, **pentathlon**) ♦ **heptathlete** noun

her pronoun a female person already spoken about (used only as the object in a sentence): Have you seen her? ➤ adjective belonging to such a person: her house

herald noun **1** something that is a sign of future things **2** history someone who carried and read important notices ➤ verb **1** to announce loudly **2** to be a sign of

heraldic (pronounced hi-**ral**-dik) adjective of heraldry

heraldry noun the study of coats of arms, crests, etc

herb noun a plant used in the making of medicines or in cooking ☉ Comes from French herbe meaning 'grass'

herbaceous adjective **1** of a plant: with a stem which dies every year **2** of a flower-bed: filled with such plants

herbal adjective of or using herbs: herbal remedy

herbalism noun the study and use of plants in medicine ♦ **herbalist** noun

herbicide noun a chemical used to kill weeds

herbivore noun an animal which feeds on plants ♦ **herbivorous** adjective

Herculean adjective requiring tremendous strength or effort: a Herculean task

☉ After the Greek hero, Hercules, who was given twelve seemingly impossible tasks to do by the gods

herd noun **1** a group of animals of one kind **2** (**the herd**) most people ➤ verb to group together like a herd of animals

herdsman or **herdswoman** (plural **herdsmen** or **herdswomen**) **1** a keeper of cattle, sheep, etc **2** someone who tends cattle, sheep, etc

here adverb at, in, or to this place: He's here already/Come here!

hereabouts adverb approximately in this place

hereafter adverb, formal after this • **the hereafter** life after death

hereby adverb, formal by this means

hereditary adjective passed on from parents to children

heredity noun the passing on of physical qualities from parents to children

heresy (pronounced **he**-re-si) noun (plural **heresies**) an opinion which goes against the official (especially religious) view ♦ **heretic** (pronounced **he**-re-tik) noun ♦ **heretical** (pronounced he-**ret**-i-kal) adjective

heritage noun something passed on by or inherited from an earlier generation

hermaphrodite (pronounced her-**maf**-ro-dait) noun an animal which has the qualities of both male and female sexes

hermetically adverb: **hermetically sealed** closed completely and airtight

hermit noun someone who lives alone, often for religious reasons

hermitage noun the dwelling of a hermit

hermit crab noun a kind of crab which lives in the abandoned shell of a shellfish

hernia noun the bursting out of part of an internal organ through a weak spot in surrounding body tissue

hero noun (plural **heroes**) **1** someone much admired for their bravery **2** the chief male character in a story, film, etc

heroic adjective **1** brave as a hero **2** of heroes ♦ **heroically** adverb

heroin (pronounced **he**-roh-in) noun a very addictive drug derived from morphine

heroine (pronounced **he**-roh-in) noun **1** a woman much admired for her bravery **2** the chief female character in a story, film, etc

heroism (pronounced **he**-roh-izm) noun bravery

heron noun a large water bird, with long legs and neck

hero-worship noun an excessive fondness and admiration for someone ➤ verb to idealize or to have a great admiration for

herpes (*pronounced* **her**-peez) *noun* a name for various types of a skin disease caused by a virus

herring *noun* (*plural* **herring** or **herrings**) an edible sea fish with silvery colouring, which moves in large shoals

hers *pronoun* something belonging to a female person already spoken about: *The idea was hers*

herself *pronoun* **1** used reflexively: *She washed herself* **2** used for emphasis: *She herself won't be there but her brother will*

hertz *noun* (*plural* **hertz**; *symbol* **Hz**) the standard unit of frequency for radio waves etc

hesitant *adjective* undecided about whether to do something or not, because of anxiety or worry about the possible results ♦ **hesitancy** *noun*

hesitate *verb* **1** to pause because of uncertainty **2** to be unwilling (to do something): *I hesitate to ask* ♦ **hesitation** *noun*

hessian *noun* a type of coarse cloth

hetero- *prefix* forms words containing the idea of 'other' or 'different' ⊙ Comes from Greek *heteros* meaning 'other'

heterodox *adjective* heretical, having an opinion other than the accepted one (*contrasted with*: **orthodox**) ♦ **heterodoxy** *noun*

heterogamy *noun, genetics* reproduction from unlike reproductive cells ♦ **heterogamous** *adjective*

heterogeneous (*pronounced* het-e-ro-jeen-i-us) *adjective* composed of many different kinds (*contrasted with*: **homogeneous**) ♦ **heterogeneity** *noun*

heterogenesis *noun, biology* **1** alteration of generations **2** spontaneous generation ♦ **heterogenetic** *adjective*

heteromorphic *adjective, biology* **1** different in form from a given type **2** of insects: changing in form at various stages of life ♦ **heteromorphism** or **heteromorphy** *noun*

heterosexual *noun* someone who is sexually attracted to the opposite sex ➤ *adjective* sexually attracted to the opposite sex (*contrasted with*: **homosexual**) ♦ **heterosexuality** *noun*

heterotrophy *noun, biology* the dependence of some animals and plants on green plants, and organic compounds generally, as food ♦ **heterotroph** *noun* a heterotrophic organism ♦ **heterotrophic** *adjective*

heterozygote *noun, genetics* a zygote or individual that contains two different alleles for a particular gene, and which may therefore produce offspring that differ from the parent with respect to that gene ♦ **heterozygous** *adjective*

het up *adjective, informal* angry; agitated

hew *verb* (**hewing, hewed, hewn** or **hewed**) to cut or shape with an axe etc

hex[1] *noun* a spell to bring bad luck; a curse

hex[2] *noun* hexadecimal

hexa- *prefix* six ⊙ Comes from Greek *hex* meaning 'six'

hexadecimal *adjective, computing* relating to or being a number system with a base of 16

hexagon *noun* a six-sided figure ♦ **hexagonal** *adjective*

hexane *noun, chemistry* a hydrocarbon that is the sixth member of the methane series

hexose *noun, chemistry* a simple sugar with carbon atoms in each molecule

hey *interjection* expressing surprise or dismay or used to attract someone's attention

heyday *noun* the time of greatest strength, the prime

⊙ From an old English expression *heyda*, meaning 'hurrah'.

Hf *symbol, chemistry* hafnium

Hg *symbol, chemistry* mercury

HGV *abbreviation* heavy goods vehicle (now called **large goods vehicle**)

hi *interjection, informal* **1** hello **2** hey

hiatus (*pronounced* hai-ei-tus) *noun* (*plural* **hiatus** or **hiatuses**) a gap, a rift

hibernate *verb* of an animal: to pass the winter in a sleep-like state ♦ **hibernation** *noun* ♦ **hibernator** *noun*

hibiscus *noun* a tropical tree or shrub with large brightly coloured flowers ⊙ Comes from Greek *ibiskos* meaning 'marshmallow'

hiccup *noun* **1** a sharp gasp, caused by laughing, eating, drinking, etc **2** (**hiccups**) a fit of such gasping **3** *informal* a minor setback or difficulty ➤ *verb* to make a hiccuping sound

hick *noun, chiefly N Am derogatory* **1** someone from the country **2** any unsophisticated or ignorant person ⊙ A familiar form of *Richard*

hickory *noun* (*plural* **hickories**) a N American tree

hidden *adjective* **1** concealed, out of sight **2** unknown: *hidden meaning*

hide[1] *verb* (**hiding, hid, hidden**) to put or keep out of sight ➤ *noun* a concealed place from which to watch birds etc

hide[2] *noun* the skin of an animal

hideaway *noun* a refuge or retreat

hidebound *adjective, derogatory* not open to new ideas

hideous *adjective* **1** horrible, ghastly **2** very ugly

hideout *noun* a place where someone goes to hide or to get away from others

hiding *noun informal* a beating

hie (*pronounced* hai) *verb* (**hieing** or **hying, hied**) *old* to hurry, hasten

hierarchy (*pronounced* **hai**-e-rah-ki) *noun* (*plural* **hierarchies**) a number of people or things arranged in graded order ✦ **hierarchical** *adjective*

hieroglyphics (*pronounced* hai-e-ro-**glif**-iks) *plural noun* ancient Egyptian writing, in which pictures are used as letters

hi-fi *adjective short for* **high-fidelity** ➤ *noun, informal* high-quality equipment for reproducing recorded sound

higgledy-piggledy *adverb & adjective, informal* in a complete muddle

high *adjective* **1** raised far above **2** extending far upwards, tall **3** well up on any scale of measurement, rank, etc **4** great, large: *high hopes/high prices* **5** of sound: shrill, acute in pitch **6** of meat: beginning to go bad **7** overexcited **8** *informal* under the influence of drugs or alcohol ➤ *adverb* **1** far above in the air **2** well up on any scale **3** to a high degree ➤ *noun informal* a state of overexcitement, often produced by drugs or alcohol: *on a high* • **on your high horse** *informal* behaving with exaggerated pride or superiority ⓞ Comes from Old English *heah*

highbrow *adjective, often derogatory* intellectual, very literary (*contrasted with*: **lowbrow**)

high chair *noun* a tall chair with a small detachable table, for young children

high court *noun* **1** a supreme court **2** (**the High Court**) the supreme court for civil cases in England and Wales

Higher *noun* an examination in Scottish secondary schools, usually taken at the end of the 5th year

higher education *noun* education beyond secondary-school level, ie at university or college, usually studying for a degree

highest common factor *noun, maths* (*abbrev* **HCF** or **hcf**) the common factor of two or more numbers that has the highest value, eg the highest common factor of 10 and 25 is 5

high-fidelity *adjective* reproducing sound very clearly

high-five *noun* a greeting made by slapping together one another's raised palms

high-flier *noun* a highly ambitious and successful person

high-flown *adjective* of language or style: using words that sound too grand or pompous

high-handed *adjective* thoughtless, overbearing

high jinks *plural noun* lively games or play

high jump *noun* an athletics contest in which competitors jump over a high bar which is raised

after every jump • **for the high jump** *informal* expecting trouble or punishment

Highland Clearances *plural noun, history* the eviction of thousands of crofting families in the Scottish Highlands by landlords who wanted the land for sheep farming

Highlander *noun* someone who comes from the Highlands

Highland Games *noun* an event consisting of sports competitions, traditional dancing, etc, traditionally held in the Scottish Highlands

Highlands *noun* (**the Highlands**) a mountainous region, especially the north of Scotland

high-level language *noun, computing* a programming language using instructions that resemble non-programming language, rather than machine code (*compare with*: **low-level language**)

highlight *noun* **1** a bright spot or area in a picture **2** a lighter patch in the hair, often bleached or dyed **3** the most memorable part or experience: *the highlight of the week* ➤ *verb* to emphasize, make the focus of attention

highlighter *noun* a coloured felt-tip pen used to mark but not obscure lines of text

highly *adverb* **1** very: *highly delighted* **2** to or at a high level **3** in an approving way: *I've always thought highly of him*

highly-strung *adjective* nervous, easily excited

high-minded *adjective* having strong principles and high moral standards

Highness *noun* (*plural* **Highnesses**) a title of a monarch

high order goods *noun, economics, geography* expensive or luxury goods such as electrical goods, jewellery, etc that are not bought regularly (*contrasted with*: **low order goods**)

high priest or **high priestess** *noun* the chief priest or priestess of a cult

high-rise *adjective* of a building: having many storeys ➤ *noun* a building with many storeys

high road *noun* a main road

high school *noun* a secondary school

high seas *plural noun*: (**the high seas**) the open seas

high society *noun* the upper classes

high-spirited *adjective* bold, lively

high tea *noun* a cooked meal with bread, cakes, and tea, served in the late afternoon

high-tech or **hi-tech** *adjective* (*short for* **high-technology**) using advanced, especially electronic, equipment and devices

high tide or **high water** *noun* the time when the tide is farthest up the shore

high treason *noun* the crime of acting against

the safety of your own country

highway *noun* the public road

Highway Code *noun* a set of official rules for road users in Britain

highwayman *noun* (*plural* **highwaymen**), *history* a robber who attacked people on the public road

high wire *noun* a tightrope stretched high above the ground for performing

high yielding variety *noun, geography* (*abbrev* **HYV**) a genetically modified seed that produces more food per plant than other varieties

hijab or **hejab** *noun* a covering for a Muslim woman's head and face ⊙ Arabic

hijack *verb* to steal (a car, aeroplane, etc) while it is moving, forcing the driver or pilot to take a new route ➤ *noun* the action of hijacking a vehicle etc ◆ **hijacker** *noun*

hike *verb* **1** to travel on foot through countryside **2** to increase (prices) suddenly ➤ *noun* a country walk ◆ **hiker** *noun*

hilarious *adjective* extremely funny

hilarity *noun* great amusement and laughter

hill *noun* a mound of high land, less high than a mountain • **over the hill** *informal* past your best

hillock *noun* a small hill

hillwalking *noun* the activity of walking in hilly or mountainous country ◆ **hillwalker** *noun*

hilly *adjective* (**hillier, hilliest**) covered with hills

hilt *noun* the handle of a sword • **up to the hilt** thoroughly, completely

hilum *noun, botany* a scar on the seed of a plant indicating where it was attached to its stalk

him *pronoun* a male person already spoken about (used only as the object in a sentence): *I saw him yesterday/What did you say to him?*

himself *pronoun* **1** used reflexively: *He cut himself shaving* **2** used for emphasis: *He wrote it himself*

hind[1] *adjective* at the back: *hind legs*

hind[2] *noun* a female deer

hindbrain *noun* the lowest part of the brain, containing the cerebellum and the medulla oblongata

hinder *verb* to keep back, delay, prevent

Hindi *noun* one of the official languages of India ➤ *adjective* relating to this language

hindmost *adjective* farthest behind

hindrance *noun* something that hinders

hindsight *noun* realizing what should have been done after an event: *With hindsight, I shouldn't have said that*

Hinduism *noun* a religion whose followers believe people who die are born again in different bodies ◆ **Hindu** *noun & adjective*

hinge *noun* **1** a joint on which a door, lid, etc turns **2** *biology* the pivot from which a bivalve opens and closes ➤ *verb* **1** to move on a hinge **2** to depend (on): *Everything hinges on the weather*

hint *noun* **1** a remark which suggests a meaning without stating it clearly: *I'll give you a hint* **2** a slight impression, a suggestion: *a hint of panic in her voice* ➤ *verb* to suggest without stating clearly: *He hinted that he might be there*

hinterland *noun* an area lying inland from the coast

hip[1] *noun* the part of the side of the body just below the waist

hip[2] *noun* the fruit of the wild rose

hip[3] *adjective* (**hipper, hippest**) *informal* very fashionable, trendy

hip flask *noun* a small pocket flask for alcohol

hip-hop *noun* a popular culture movement which started in the US in the early 1980s and is associated with rap music, graffiti art, and baggy sports clothes

hippie *noun, informal* a member of a youth movement, which originated in the 1960s, rebelling against conventional society, dress codes, etc

hippo short for **hippopotamus**

Hippocratic oath (*pronounced* hip-o-**krat**-ik) *noun* an oath taken by a doctor agreeing to observe a code of medical ethics

hippodrome *noun* **1** an arena for horse-racing **2** a large theatre

hippopotamus *noun* (*plural* **hippopotami** – *pronounced* hip-o-**pot**-a-mai – or **hippopotamuses**) a large African mammal living in and near rivers (often shortened to **hippo**)

⊙ Based on a Greek word which translates as 'river horse'

hire *noun* money paid for work done, or for the use of something belonging to another person ➤ *verb* to give or get the use of by paying money

hire-purchase *noun* a way of buying an article by paying for it in instalments

hirsute (*pronounced* **her**-syoot) *adjective* hairy, shaggy

his *adjective* belonging to a male person already spoken about: *his book* ➤ *pronoun* something belonging to such a person: *That jacket is his*

Hispanic *adjective* **1** Spanish **2** Spanish-American

hiss *verb* to make a sound like a snake ➤ *noun* (*plural* **hisses**) such a sound, made to show anger or displeasure

histamine (*pronounced* **his**-ta-meen) *noun* *biochemistry* a chemical present in pollen etc which can cause an allergic reaction

histidine *noun, biochemistry* an amino acid that is a component of proteins

histogenesis or **histogeny** *noun, biology* the development and differentiation of tissues
♦ **histogenetic** or **histogenic** *adjective*
♦ **histogenetically** or **histogenically** *adverb*

histogram *noun, maths* a graph representing grouped data, with class intervals shown as segments on the x-axis, and the frequency in each class represented by the area of the rectangle at each segment

historian *noun* someone who studies or writes history

historic *adjective* important, likely to be remembered

⚠ Do not confuse: **historic** and **historical**

historical *adjective* **1** of history **2** true of something in the past

history *noun* (*plural* **histories**) **1** the study of the past **2** a description of past events, society, etc

histrionic *adjective, old* relating to stage-acting or actors

histrionics *plural noun* an exaggerated show of strong feeling

hit *verb* (**hitting, hit**) **1** to strike with a blow **2** to occur suddenly to: *It finally hit me* ➤ *noun* **1** a blow, a stroke **2** a shot which hits a target **3** a success **4** a successful song, recording, etc **5** *slang* a murder by criminals **6** *computing* an instance of a computer file, especially a website, being contacted: *50 hits to our website today*
• **hit it off with someone** to get on well with them • **hit on** or **hit upon** to come upon, discover • **hit the ceiling** or **hit the roof** to explode with anger • **hit the ground running** to react immediately and efficiently • **hit the nail on the head** to identify the important point, be exactly right

hit-and-miss *adjective, informal* haphazard, sometimes working and sometimes not

hit-and-run *adjective* of a driver: driving away after causing injury without reporting the accident

hitch *verb* **1** to fasten with a hook etc **2** to lift with a jerk **3** *informal* to hitch-hike ➤ *noun* (*plural* **hitches**) **1** a jerk **2** an unexpected stop or delay **3** a type of knot • **get hitched** *informal* to get married

hitch-hike *verb* to travel by getting free lifts from passing vehicles ♦ **hitch-hiker** *noun*

hi-tech another spelling of **high-tech**

hither *adverb, old* to this place • **hither and thither** back and forwards

hitherto *adverb* up till now

Hitler Youth *noun, history* an organization set up by Adolf Hitler in 1933, to instil Nazi principles in German youths ⊕ Comes from a translation of German *Hitler Jugend*

hit list *noun, informal* a list of targeted victims

hitman *noun* (*plural* **hitmen**) *slang* someone employed to kill or attack others

HIV *abbreviation* human immuno-deficiency virus, the virus which can cause AIDS

hive *noun* **1** a box or basket where bees live **2** a busy place: *hive of industry*

hives a non-technical name for **urticaria**

HIV-positive *adjective* carrying HIV

HM *abbreviation* Her or His Majesty

HMS *abbreviation* **1** Her or His Majesty's Service **2** Her or His Majesty's Ship

Ho *symbol, chemistry* holmium

hoard *noun* a hidden store of treasure, food, etc ➤ *verb* to store up secretly ⊕ Comes from Old English *hord* meaning 'treasure' or 'secret place'

⚠ Do not confuse with: **horde**

hoarding *noun* a fence of boards

hoarfrost *noun* white frost

hoarse *adjective* (**hoarser, hoarsest**) having a harsh voice, eg from a cold or cough

hoary *adjective* (**hoarier, hoariest**) **1** white with age **2** very old

hoax *noun* (*plural* **hoaxes**) a trick played to deceive ➤ *verb* to play a hoax on

hob *noun* **1** the top of a cooker, with rings for heating etc **2** a small shelf next to a fireplace for keeping pans etc hot

hobbit *noun* one of an imaginary race of people, half the size of humans and with hairy feet, who live below the ground ⊕ Created by J R R Tolkien in his novel *The Hobbit* (1937)

hobble *verb* **1** to walk with short unsteady steps **2** to tie the legs of (a horse etc) loosely **3** to impede, hamper

hobby *noun* (*plural* **hobbies**) a favourite way of passing your spare time

⊕ Originally *hobby-horse*, a horse used in morris dances and therefore for amusement or pleasure

hobby-horse *noun* **1** a toy wooden horse **2** a favourite subject of discussion

hobgoblin *noun* a mischievous fairy

hobnail *noun* a large nail used for horseshoes and in the soles of heavy boots

hobnob *verb* (**hobnobbing, hobnobbed**) to be on friendly terms (with); socialize (with)

hobo *noun* (*plural* **hobos** or **hoboes**) *US* a tramp

Hobson's choice *noun* the choice of having something as offered, or nothing at all

⊙ Named after *Hobson*, a Cambridge horsekeeper who reputedly gave customers the choice of the horse nearest the door or none at all

hock¹ *noun* a joint on the hind leg of an animal, below the knee

hock² *noun* a white German wine

hock³ *slang, verb* to pawn ➤ *noun*: **in hock** pawned

hockey *noun* an eleven-a-side ball-game played with clubs curved at one end

hod *noun* an open V-shaped box on a pole, used for carrying bricks, etc ⊙ Comes from French *hotte* meaning 'pannier'

Hodgkin's disease *noun* a disease in which the spleen, liver and lymph nodes become enlarged, and anaemia occurs

⊙ Named after Thomas *Hodgkin* (1798–1866), British physician

hoe *noun* a tool used for weeding, loosening earth, etc ➤ *verb* (**hoeing, hoed**) to dig, loosen, or weed (the ground) with a hoe

hog *noun, US* a pig ➤ *verb* (**hogging, hogged**) *informal* to take or use selfishly • **go the whole hog** to do something thoroughly

Hogmanay (*pronounced* hog-ma-**nei**) *noun* the name in Scotland for 31 December and the celebrations held that night

⊙ From an old French word *aguillanneuf*, a gift given at New Year

hogwash *noun, informal* nonsense, rubbish

hoi polloi *plural noun* the masses, the rabble

⊙ Taken from a Greek phrase for 'the people'

hoist *verb* to lift, raise ➤ *noun* a lift, an elevator for goods

hoity-toity *adjective* haughty, superior

hold¹ *verb* (**holding, held**) **1** to keep in your possession or power; have **2** to contain **3** to occupy (a position etc) **4** to think, believe **5** to put on, organize: *hold a meeting* **6** to apply: *That rule doesn't hold any longer* **7** to stop (shooting etc): *hold fire* **8** to wait on a telephone without hanging up for the person on the other end to return ➤ *noun* **1** grip, grasp **2** influence: *a hold over the others* • **hold forth** to speak at length • **hold good** to be true • **hold off** to delay or refrain from doing something • **hold on** *informal* to wait • **hold out** to refuse to give in • **hold over** to keep till later • **hold up 1** to support **2** to hinder **3** to attack and demand money from ⊙ Comes from Old English *haldan*

hold² *noun* a large space for carrying a ship's cargo

holdall *noun* a large carrying bag with a zip

holder *noun* **1** a container **2** someone who holds (a position etc)

holding *noun* an amount of land, shares, etc held

hold-up *noun* **1** an armed attempt at robbery **2** a delay, or something that causes it

hole *noun* **1** an opening in something solid **2** a pit, a burrow **3** *informal* a miserable place • **in a hole** *informal* in a difficult situation

hole in one *noun, golf* a single hit of the ball from the tee which results in it going straight into the hole

Holi *noun, Hinduism* the spring festival

holiday *noun* **1** a day when businesses etc are closed **2** a period away from work for rest

holidaymaker *noun* a person on holiday

holier-than-thou *adjective* superior and smug

holiness *noun* **1** the quality of being holy or sacred **2** (**Holiness**) a title used in addressing or referring to religious leaders such as the Pope: *Your Holiness/His Holiness the Dalai Lama*

holism (*pronounced* **hoh**-lizm) *noun* **1** the theory that a complex being or system is more than merely the sum of its parts **2** the treatment of a disease by taking social, psychological, etc factors into consideration, rather than just the ailment ◆ **holistic** *adjective* ◆ **holistically** *adverb*

hollandaise sauce (*pronounced* hol-an-**deiz**) *noun* a sauce made from egg yolks, butter, and lemon juice or vinegar

hollow *adjective* **1** having empty space inside, not solid **2** false, unreal: *hollow victory/hollow smile* ➤ *noun* **1** a sunken place **2** a dip in the land ➤ *verb* to scoop (out)

holly *noun* (*plural* **hollies**) an evergreen shrub with scarlet berries and prickly leaves

hollyhock *noun* a tall garden plant

holmium *noun, chemistry* (symbol **Ho**) a soft metallic element

⊙ From *Holmia*, the Latin name for Stockholm, where it is commonly found in minerals

holocaust *noun* **1** a great destruction (by fire) **2** *history* (**the Holocaust**) the mass killing of Jews by the Nazis in World War II

Holocene *adjective* of the most recent geological epoch, dating roughly from the last glaciation

hologram *noun* a 3-D image created by laser beams

holograph *noun* a document written entirely by one person

holster *noun* a case for a pistol

holy *adjective* (**holier, holiest**) **1** of or like God **2** religious, righteous **3** for religious use; sacred

Holy Land *noun Christianity,* (**the Holy Land**) Palestine, the scene of Christ's work in the New Testament

holy of holies *noun* any place or thing regarded as especially sacred

Holy Roman Empire *noun, history* the empire of Europe under a Christian emperor (**Holy Roman Emperor**) with the Pope's blessing, from 800–814 AD and 962–1806 AD

Holy Spirit *noun* (**the Holy Spirit**) the third person of the Christian trinity

holy war *noun* a war waged in the name of a religion

holy water *noun* water blessed for use in religious ceremonies

Holy Week *noun* in the Christian church, the week before Easter Sunday

homage *noun* a show of respect; an acknowledgement of debt: *paying homage to the pioneers of cinema*

home *noun* **1** the place where someone lives **2** the house of someone's family **3** a centre or place of origin: *Nashville is the home of country music* **4** a place where children, the elderly, etc live and are looked after ➤ *adjective* **1** of someone's house or family: *home comforts* **2** domestic, not foreign: *home affairs* ➤ *adverb* **1** towards home **2** to the full length: *drive the nail home* • **bring home to** to make (someone) realize ⊙ Comes from Old English *ham*

home economics *singular noun* the study of how to run a home

Home Guard *noun, history* (**the Home Guard**) a volunteer army formed to defend Britain from invasion during World War II

home help *noun* a person who is hired, often by the local authority, to help sick, aged, etc people with domestic chores

homeless *adjective* without a home and living, sleeping, etc in public places or in hostels ♦ **homelessness** *noun*

homely *adjective* (**homelier, homeliest**) **1** plain but pleasant **2** *US* plain, not attractive

home-made *adjective* made at home

homeo- or **homoeo-** (*both pronounced* hom-i-o or hoh-mi-o) *prefix* like, similar: *homeostasis/homoeopathy* ⊙ Comes from Greek *homoios* meaning 'similar'

homeopath or **homoeopath** (*pronounced* **hom**-i-o-path) *noun* a practitioner of homeopathy

homeopathic or **homoeopathic** (*pronounced* hom-i-o-**path**-ik) *adjective* of or using homeopathy (*contrasted with:* **allopathic**)

homeopathy or **homoeopathy** (*pronounced* hom-i-**op**-a-thi) *noun* the treatment of illness by small quantities of

substances that produce symptoms similar to those of the illness

homeostasis or **homoeostasis** (*pronounced* hom-i-**os**-ta-sis) *noun, biology* a tendency to maintain a stable condition despite changes in the environment ♦ **homeostatic** *adjective*

homeothermic or **homoeothermic** *same as* **warm-blooded**

home page *noun, computing* the first page that appears on a computer screen after a connection is made to the Internet, or the access page of a Web site

home rule *noun* government of a country etc by its own parliament

home run *noun, baseball* a hit that sends the ball out of the playing area and allows the batter to make a complete circuit of all four bases

Home Secretary *noun, Brit* the government minister who deals with domestic issues, eg law and order, immigration, etc

homesick *adjective* longing for home

homespun *adjective* **1** of character, advice, etc: artless, simple and straightforward **2** *old* of cloth: woven at home

homestead *noun* a farmhouse

home truth *noun* a frank statement of something true but unpleasant

homewards *adverb* towards home

homework *noun* work for school etc done at home

homi- *prefix* of or relating to men or people: *homicide* ⊙ Comes from Latin *homo* meaning 'man'

homicidal *adjective* likely to commit murder

homicide *noun* **1** the killing of a human being **2** someone who kills a person

homily *noun* (*plural* **homilies**) **1** a plain, practical sermon **2** a talk giving advice

homing instinct *noun, biology* the ability of several animal species to navigate their way home

homing pigeon *noun* a pigeon with a strong homing instinct, used in racing

homo- *prefix* **1** same: *homosexual/homonym* **2** of or relating to homosexuality: *homoerotic* ⊙ Comes from Greek *homos* meaning 'same'

homeopathy another spelling of **homeopathy**

homoeostasis another spelling of **homeostasis**

homoeothermic another spelling of **homeothermic**

homogeneous (*pronounced* hom-oh-**jee**-ni-us) *adjective* **1** of the same kind, or composed of parts of the same kind (*contrasted with:* **heterogeneous**) **2** *biology* having a similar structure owing to common origin

♦ **homogeneity** or (meaning 2) **homogeny**
noun

homogenize or **homogenise** (*pronounced*
ho-**moj**-e-naiz) *verb* to treat (milk) so that the
cream does not separate and rise to the surface
♦ **homogenization** *noun*

homograph *noun* a word which has the same
spelling as, but a different meaning from,
another, eg *keen* meaning 'eager' is a
homograph of *keen* meaning 'lament'

homologous *adjective* **1** having a similar
function or position **2** *biology* of plant or animal
structures: having a common origin, but having
evolved to perform different functions, eg an
arm and a wing (*compare with*: **analogous**) **3**
genetics of two chromosomes in a cell: pairing
during meiosis, and containing genes for the
same set of characteristics, but derived from
different parents **4** *chemistry* denoting a series of
compounds where each member has one more
of a chemical group in its molecule than the one
before

homonym *noun* a word which has the same
sound and perhaps the same spelling as, but a
different origin and meaning from, another, eg
mole (the animal) is a homonym of *mole* (a mark
on the skin)

homophobe *noun* a person with a hatred of
homosexuals ♦ **homophobia** *noun*
♦ **homophobic** *adjective*

homophone *noun* a word which has the same
sound as, but a different meaning from, another,
eg *pair* is a homophone of *pear*

homophonic *adjective* **1** sounding alike **2**
music relating to homophony

homophony (*pronounced* hom-**of**-o-ni) *noun*
musical composition in which one part carries
the melody, and the other parts add texture with
accompaniment (*compare with*: **polyphony**)

homo sapiens (*pronounced* hoh-moh **sap**-i-
enz) *noun* the name for modern man as a
species ⊙ Comes from Latin *homo* meaning
'man' + *sapiens* meaning 'wise'

homosexual *noun* someone who is sexually
attracted to the same sex ► *adjective* sexually
attracted to the same sex (*contrasted with*:
heterosexual) ♦ **homosexuality** *noun*

homozygote *noun, genetics* a zygote
produced by the union of two identical gametes

homozygous *adjective, genetics* of an
individual: having two identical DNA segments
for a particular gene, and producing offspring
that are identical to the parent with respect to
that gene

hone *verb* to sharpen (a knife etc)

honest *adjective* truthful; not inclined to steal,
cheat, etc

honestly *adverb* **1** truthfully **2** without cheating

or stealing etc **3** when you are trying to convince
someone of something: really **4** an expression of
annoyance: *Honestly, I don't know why I bother!*

honesty *noun* the quality of being honest,
truthful, or trustworthy

honey *noun* **1** a sweet, thick fluid made by bees
from the nectar of flowers **2** *informal*
sweetheart, dear

honeycomb *noun* a network of wax cells in
which bees store honey

honeymoon *noun* a holiday spent immediately
after marriage ► *verb* to spend a honeymoon

honeypot or **honeypot site** *noun,*
geography an area that attracts many visitors

honeysuckle *noun* a climbing shrub with
sweet-smelling flowers

honk *noun* a noise like the cry of the wild goose
or the sound of a motor horn ► *verb* to make this
sound

honorary *adjective* **1** done to give honour **2**
without payment

honour or *US* **honor** *noun* **1** respect for truth,
honesty, etc **2** fame, glory **3** reputation, good
name **4** a title of respect, especially to a judge:
Your Honour **5** a privilege **6** (**honours**)
recognition given for exceptional achievements
► *verb* **1** to give respect to **2** to give high rank to **3**
to pay when due: *honour a debt* ● **do the**
honours *informal* to perform a ceremonial task

honourable *adjective* worthy of honour
♦ **honourably** *adverb*

hood[1] *noun* **1** a covering for the head **2** a
protective cover for anything **3** *US* the bonnet of
a car

hood[2] *noun, slang* a hoodlum

hood[3] or **'hood** *noun, US informal* a shortened
form of **neighbourhood**

-hood *suffix* meaning 'the state of being':
childhood, likelihood

hoodwink *verb* to deceive

hoodlum *noun* a destructive or badly-behaved
youth

hoof *noun* (*plural* **hoofs** or **hooves**) the horny
part on the feet of certain animals (eg horses)
● **on the hoof** *informal* on the move, while
moving

hook *noun* **1** a bent piece of metal etc for
hanging things on **2** a piece of metal on the end
of a line for catching fish ► *verb* to hang or catch
with a hook ● **by hook or by crook** by one
means or another, whatever the cost

hookah or **hooka** *noun* a tobacco pipe in
which the smoke is drawn through water

hooked *adjective* **1** curved, bent **2** caught by a
hook **3** *informal* addicted (to), fascinated (by):
hooked on heroin

Hooke's law *noun, physics* the law that states
that, up to a certain limit, the extension

produced by stretching an elastic material is proportional to the force that is producing the extension

⊙ Named after Robert *Hooke* (1635–1703), English physicist

hooligan *noun* a wild, unruly person

hooliganism *noun* unruly behaviour

hoop *noun* a thin ring of wood or metal

hooray another spelling of **hurrah**

hoot *verb* **1** to sound (a siren, car horn, etc) **2** of an owl: to call, cry **3** to laugh loudly ➤ *noun* **1** the sound made by a car horn, siren, or owl **2** a shout of scorn or disgust **3** *informal* someone or something extremely funny

hooter *noun* **1** a siren or horn which makes a hooting sound **2** *slang* a large nose

Hoover *noun, trademark* a vacuum cleaner ➤ *verb* (**hoover**) to vacuum (a floor etc)

hop¹ *verb* (**hopping, hopped**) to leap on one leg ➤ *noun* a short jump on one leg

hop² *noun* a climbing plant with bitter-tasting fruits used in brewing beer

hope *noun* **1** the state of expecting or wishing something good to happen **2** something desired ➤ *verb* to expect or wish good to happen

hopeful *adjective* **1** confident or optimistic about something **2** promising, encouraging

hopefully *adverb* **1** with hope **2** used when expressing hopes: 'I hope that … '

hopeless *adjective* **1** without hope **2** *informal* very bad: *He is hopeless at maths* ♦ **hopelessly** *adverb*

hopscotch *noun* a hopping game over lines drawn on the ground

horde *noun* a large crowd or group ⊙ Comes from Turkish *ordu* meaning 'camp'

❗ Do not confuse with: **hoard**

horizon *noun* **1** the imaginary line formed where the earth meets the sky **2** the limit of someone's experience or understanding

horizontal *adjective* lying level or flat ♦ **horizontally** *adverb*

hormone *noun* a substance produced by certain glands of the body, which acts on a particular organ ♦ **hormonal** *adjective*

horn *noun* **1** a hard growth on the heads of certain animals, eg deer, sheep **2** something curved or sticking out like an animal's horn **3** part of a car which gives a warning sound **4** a brass wind instrument (originally made of horn)

horned *adjective* having horns

hornet *noun* a kind of large wasp • **stir up a hornet's nest** to cause a commotion or violent reaction

hornpipe *noun* a lively sailor's dance

horny *adjective* (**hornier, horniest**) hard like horn

horoscope *noun* a prediction of someone's future based on the position of the stars at their birth

horrendous *adjective, informal* awful, terrible

horrible *adjective* **1** causing horror, dread, or fear **2** *informal* unpleasant, detestable, or foul ♦ **horribly** *adverb*

horrid *adjective* hateful; very unpleasant

horrific *adjective* **1** terrifying **2** *informal* awful, very bad ♦ **horrifically** *adverb*

horrify *verb* (**horrifies, horrifying, horrified**) to frighten greatly, shock: *We were horrified by his behaviour* ♦ **horrifying** *adjective*

horror *noun* **1** great fear, terror **2** something which causes fear **3** *informal* an unruly or demanding child

horror-stricken or **horror-struck** *adjective* shocked, horrified, or dismayed

hors d'oeuvre (*pronounced* aw **dervr**) *noun* (*plural* **hors d'oeuvre** or **hors d'oeuvres**) a savoury appetizer served at the beginning of a meal to whet the appetite ⊙ Comes from French, meaning 'out of the work'

horse *noun* **1** a four-footed animal with hooves and a mane **2** a wooden frame for drying clothes on **3** a piece of gymnastic equipment for vaulting • **from the horse's mouth** directly from the source, first-hand • **horses for courses** people will do best in situations which suit them individually

horse-box *noun* (*plural* **horse-boxes**) a closed trailer pulled by a car or train, designed to carry horses

horse chestnut *noun* a tree which produces a shiny, inedible nut (a conker)

horsefly *noun* (*plural* **horseflies**) a large fly which bites

horse laugh *noun* a loud, harsh laugh

horseplay *noun* rough play, fooling around

horsepower *noun* (*abbrev* **hp**) a unit of mechanical power for car engines

horseradish *noun* (*plural* **horseradishes**) a plant with a sharp-tasting root which is used in sauces

horseshoe *noun* **1** a shoe for horses, made of a curved piece of iron **2** anything shaped like a horseshoe, especially as a symbol of good luck

horticulture *noun* the study and art of gardening ♦ **horticultural** *adjective*

hosanna *noun* an exclamation of praise to God

hose *noun* **1** (*plural* **hose**) an old-fashioned word meaning 'a covering for the legs or feet', eg stockings **2** (*plural* **hoses**) a rubber tube for carrying water

hosiery *noun* stockings, tights, etc

hospice *noun* a home providing special nursing care for incurable invalids

hospitable *adjective* showing kindness to guests or strangers ◆ **hospitably** *adverb*

hospital *noun* a building for the treatment of the sick and injured

hospitality *noun* the quality of being hospitable, or of being friendly and welcoming to guests and strangers, entertaining them with food or drink, or providing them with accommodation

hospitalize or **hospitalise** *verb* 1 to admit to hospital for treatment 2 to injure so badly that hospital treatment is necessary ◆ **hospitalization** *noun*

host¹ *noun* 1 someone who welcomes and entertains guests 2 an innkeeper or hotel-keeper 3 the person on a television or radio show who introduces guests and performers to the audience, or interviews them 4 *biology* the person or animal on which an insect or other organism is living or feeding as a parasite 5 the recipient of a skin graft or organ transplant 6 *computing* a computer in control of a multi-terminal computer system 7 *computing* a computer attached to a multi-computer network and able to provide access to a number of databases ➤ *verb* to be the host of (an event, programme, show, etc)

host² *noun* a very large number

hostage *noun* someone held prisoner by an enemy to make sure that an agreement will be kept to

hostel *noun* a building providing rooms for students etc

hostelling *noun* the use of youth hostels when on holiday ◆ **hosteller** *noun*

hostelry *noun* (*plural* **hostelries**) *old* an inn

hostess *noun* (*plural* **hostesses**) 1 a woman who welcomes and entertains guests 2 *old* an air hostess

hostile *adjective* 1 of an enemy 2 not friendly 3 showing dislike or opposition (to)

hostility *noun* 1 unfriendliness, dislike 2 (*plural* **hostilities**) acts of warfare

hot *adjective* (**hotter, hottest**) 1 very warm 2 spicy 3 *slang* sexually attractive or excited 4 *slang* radioactive 5 *slang* stolen 6 *slang* not safe • **hot on someone's heels** *informal* following them closely • **hot under the collar** *informal* indignant, enraged • **in hot water** *informal* in trouble • **sell like hot cakes** to sell very quickly

hot air *noun, informal* meaningless talk

hotbed *noun* a centre or breeding ground for anything: *a hotbed of rebellion*

hot-blooded *adjective* passionate, easily angered

hot cross bun *noun* a fruit bun with a pastry cross on top, customarily eaten on Good Friday

hot dog *noun* a hot sausage in a long roll

hotel *noun* a building with several rooms which people can pay to stay in for a number of nights

hotelier (*pronounced* hoh-**tel**-i-ei) *noun* someone who owns or manages a hotel

hotfoot *adverb, informal* in great haste

hotheaded *adjective* inclined to act rashly without thinking

hothouse *noun* a heated glasshouse for plants ➤ *verb* to give (a child) intensive schooling at an early age

hot key *noun, computing* a key which activates a program when pressed

hotline *noun* a direct telephone line between heads of government

hotplate *noun* 1 the flat top surface of a cooker on which food is cooked 2 a portable heated surface for keeping food or dishes hot

hotpot *noun* meat and vegetables, seasoned and covered with sliced potatoes, and cooked slowly in a sealed pot

hot potato *noun* a touchy subject

hot seat *noun, informal* an uncomfortable or difficult position

hot spot *noun* 1 an area of (too) high temperature in an engine etc 2 *geography* an area of the earth where there is isolated volcanic activity due to hot material rising up through the mantle 3 an area of potential political or military trouble 4 a popular place of entertainment 5 *computing* an area of a web page that activates a hyperlink when clicked on with a mouse

hot-water bottle *noun* a rubber container filled with hot water and used to warm a bed

hot-wire *verb, informal* to start (a vehicle engine) by touching electrical wires together

hound *noun* a dog used in hunting ➤ *verb* to hunt, pursue

hour *noun* 1 sixty minutes, the 24th part of a day 2 a time or occasion: *the hour of reckoning*

hourglass *noun* (*plural* **hourglasses**) an instrument which measures the hours by the running of sand from one glass into another

hourly *adjective* happening or done every hour ➤ *adverb* every hour

house *noun* (*pronounced* hows) 1 a building in which people live 2 a household 3 a business firm 4 a building where school boarders stay ➤ *verb* (*pronounced* howz) to provide a house for; accommodate • **like a house on fire** *informal* very successfully, extremely well • **on the house** free, complimentary ⊙ Comes from Old English *hus*

house arrest *noun* confinement under guard in a private house, hospital, etc

houseboat *noun* a river barge with a cabin for living in

housebound *adjective* confined to one's house because of illness, responsibility to young children, etc

housebreaker *noun* someone who breaks into a house to steal ♦ **housebreaking** *noun*

household *noun* the people who live together in a house

householder *noun* someone who owns or pays the rent of a house

household name or **household word** *noun* someone or something that is well known and often mentioned by people

house husband *noun* a man who looks after the house and family instead of having a paid job

housekeeper *noun* someone employed to look after the running of a house

housekeeping *noun* 1 the management of a household's domestic arrangements 2 money set aside to pay for this 3 *computing* operations carried out on a computer program or system ensuring that it functions efficiently

house music *noun* a style of dance music that features a strong beat and often incorporates edited fragments of other recordings

House of Commons *noun* the lower (elected) house of the British parliament (often shortened to **the Commons**)

House of Lords *noun* the upper (non-elected) house of the British parliament (often shortened to **the Lords**)

house-proud *adjective* proud of keeping your house clean and tidy

house-sit *verb* to look after someone's house by living in it while they are away

house-trained *adjective* of a pet: trained to go outdoors to pass urine and faeces

housewarming *noun* a party held when someone moves into a new house

housewife *noun* (*plural* **housewives**) a woman who looks after a house and her family

housework *noun* the work involved in keeping a house clean and tidy

housing *noun* 1 accommodation, eg houses, flats, etc 2 a casing for a machine etc

housing tenure *noun, geography* the right or agreement an occupant has to live in a house

hovel *noun* a small squalid dwelling

hover *verb* 1 to stay in the air in the same spot 2 to stay near, linger (about) 3 to be undecided or uncertain

hovercraft *noun* a craft able to travel over land or sea supported on a cushion of air

how *adverb* 1 in what manner: *How are they getting there?* 2 to what extent: *How old are you?/How cold is it outside?* 3 to a great extent: *How young he seems/How well you play* 4 by what means: *How do you switch this on?* 5 in what condition: *How is she?*

however *adverb* 1 no matter how 2 in spite of that

howitzer *noun* a short heavy gun which fires shells high in the air ℗ Comes from Czech *houfnice* meaning 'sling' or 'catapult'

howl *verb* 1 to make a long, loud sound like that of a dog or wolf 2 to yell in pain, anger, etc 3 to laugh loudly ➤ *noun* a howling sound

howler *noun, informal* a ridiculous mistake

HP or **hp** *abbreviation* 1 hire-purchase 2 horsepower

HQ *abbreviation* headquarters

HRT *abbreviation* hormone replacement therapy, a treatment to restore the balance of hormones in older women

Hs *symbol, chemistry* hassium

HTML *abbreviation, computing* hypertext markup language, the language used to create World Wide Web documents

http *abbreviation, computing* hypertext transfer protocol, by which documents are transferred over the Internet

hub *noun* 1 the centre part of a wheel through which the axle passes 2 a thriving centre of anything: *the hub of the entertainment industry* 3 *computing* a device on a server that connects networked workstations

hubbub *noun* a confused sound of many voices

℗ Originally meaning 'battle' or 'war cry', based on an Irish Gaelic word

hubris *noun* (*pronounced* **hjoo**-bris) arrogance or overconfidence, especially when likely to result in disaster ℗ Comes from Greek *hybris*

huddle *verb* to crowd together ➤ *noun* a close group

hue *noun* colour, shade

hue and cry *noun* a commotion, a fuss

huff *noun* a fit of bad temper and sulking

huffy *adjective* (**huffier, huffiest**) inclined to sulk; peevish

hug *verb* (**hugging, hugged**) 1 to hold tightly with the arms 2 to keep close to: *hugging the kerb* ➤ *noun* a tight embrace

huge *adjective* (**huger, hugest**) extremely big

hula or **hula-hula** *noun* a Hawaiian dance in which the dancer sways their hips and moves their arms gracefully

hula hoop *noun* a light hoop for spinning round the waist

hulk *noun* 1 an old ship unfit for use 2 something big and clumsy

hulking *adjective, informal* big and clumsy

hull *noun* the body or framework of a ship

hullabaloo *noun, informal* a noisy disturbance

hullo another spelling of **hello**

hum *verb* (**humming, hummed**) 1 to make a buzzing sound like that of bees 2 to sing with the

lips shut **3** *informal* of a place: to be noisily busy
➤ *noun* **1** the noise of bees **2** any buzzing,
droning sound

human *adjective* **1** relating to people as
opposed to animals or gods **2** having natural
qualities, feelings, etc ➤ *noun* a man, woman, or
child ✦ **humanly** *adverb*

human being *noun* a member of the human
race

Human Development Index *noun*,
geography (*abbrev* **HDI**) a scale used to measure
the development of a country by a number of
indicators, eg adult literacy, infant mortality, etc

humane *adjective* kind, showing mercy, gentle
✦ **humanely** *adverb*

humanism *noun* a set of ideas about or interest
in ethics and mankind, not including religious
belief ✦ **humanist** *noun*

humanitarian *adjective* kind to fellow human
beings

humanity *noun* **1** people in general **2** kindness,
gentleness

humanize or **humanise** *verb* **1** to make or
become human **2** to make more caring, more
thoughtful, etc ✦ **humanization** *noun*

humankind *noun* **1** the human species **2**
people generally

human race *noun* (**the human race**) all
people collectively

human resources *plural noun* **1** people
collectively in terms of their skills, training, etc in
the work place **2** the workforce of an
organization

human rights *plural noun* the rights every
person has to justice, freedom, etc

humble *adjective* (**humbler, humblest**) **1**
modest, meek **2** not of high rank, unimportant
➤ *verb* to make (someone) feel low and
unimportant

humble pie *noun*: **eat humble pie** to admit a
mistake openly

humbug *noun* **1** nonsense, rubbish **2** a kind of
hard minty sweet

humdrum *adjective* dull, not exciting

humerus *noun* (*plural* **humeri** – *pronounced*
hyoom-e-rai) *anatomy* the bone of the upper
arm

humid *adjective* of air etc: moist, damp

humidifier *noun* a device which controls the
amount of humidity in the air

humidity *noun* dampness

humiliate *verb* to make (someone) feel humble
or ashamed, hurt someone's pride
✦ **humiliating** *adjective* ✦ **humiliation** *noun*

humility *noun* humble state of mind, meekness

hummingbird *noun* a small brightly coloured
bird which beats its wings rapidly making a
humming noise

hummus or **hummous** or **houmus**
(*pronounced* **huw**-mus) *noun* a Middle-Eastern
dip made from chickpeas and oil, flavoured with
lemon juice and garlic ◔ Comes from Arabic,
meaning 'chickpeas'

humongous or **humungous** *adjective*,
informal enormous, huge

humorist *noun* a comedian, a comic writer

humorous *adjective* funny, amusing

humour or *US* **humor** *noun* **1** the ability to see
things as amusing or ridiculous **2** funniness; the
amusing side of anything: *failed to see the
humour of the situation* **3** state of mind; temper,
mood: *He is in good humour today* **4** *biology* a
type of fluid in the body: *aqueous humour*
➤ *verb* to please or gratify (someone) by doing
what they wish

hump *noun* **1** a lump, a mound **2** a lump on the
back

humpback *noun* **1** a back with a hump **2**
someone with a hump on their back ➤ *adjective*
of a bridge: rising and falling so as to form a
hump shape

humungous another spelling of **humongous**

humus (*pronounced* **hyoom**-us) *noun* soil
made of rotted leaves etc

hunch *noun* (*plural* **hunches**) a suspicion that
something is untrue or is going to happen etc
➤ *verb* to draw (your shoulders) up towards your
ears and forward towards your chest, giving your
body a rounded, stooping appearance

hunchback *noun* a humpback

hunchbacked *adjective* humpbacked

hundred *noun* the number 100 ➤ *adjective* 100
in number

Hundred Flowers Campaign *noun, history*
a campaign in China in 1956–7 which
encouraged freedom of expression in art and
literature, and in political debate

hundredth *adjective* the last of a series of one
hundred ➤ *noun* one of a hundred equal parts

hundredweight *noun* 112 pounds, 50.8
kilograms (*often written*: **cwt**)

hunger *noun* **1** a desire for food **2** a strong desire
for anything ➤ *verb* to long (for)

hunger strike *noun* a refusal to eat as a protest
✦ **hunger striker** *noun*

hungover *adjective* suffering from a hangover

hungry *adjective* (**hungrier, hungriest**)
wanting or needing food ✦ **hungrily** *adverb*

hunk *noun, informal* a muscular, sexually
attractive man

hunker *verb*: **hunker down** to squat

hunt *verb* **1** to chase (animals or birds) for food
or sport **2** to search (for) ➤ *noun* **1** chasing wild
animals **2** a search ✦ **hunter** *noun*

hunter-gatherer *noun* a member of a society
which lives by hunting animals from the land and

sea, and by gathering wild plants

huntsman or **huntswoman** noun (plural **huntsmen** or **huntswomen**) someone who hunts

hurdle noun **1** a light frame to be jumped over in a race **2** a difficulty which must be overcome ♦ **hurdler** noun ♦ **hurdling** noun

hurl verb to throw with force

hurling or **hurley** noun a traditional Irish game resembling hockey, played with curved broad-bladed sticks or **hurleys**

hurly-burly noun a great stir, uproar

hurrah or **hurray** interjection a shout of joy, approval, etc

hurricane noun a violent tropical windstorm originating in the Atlantic, with wind blowing at a speed of over 75 miles (120 kilometres) per hour (see also: **cyclone**, **typhoon**)

hurricane lamp noun a lamp specially made to keep alight in strong wind

hurried adjective done in a hurry ♦ **hurriedly** adverb

hurry verb (**hurries, hurrying, hurried**) **1** to act or move quickly **2** to make (someone) act quickly ➤ noun eagerness to act quickly, haste: in a hurry

hurt verb (**hurting, hurt**) **1** to cause pain or distress to **2** to injure physically, wound **3** to damage, spoil ➤ noun **1** pain, distress **2** damage

hurtful adjective causing pain, distress, or damage

hurtle verb to rush at great speed

husband noun a married man (the partner of a **wife**) ➤ verb to spend or use (eg money, strength) carefully

husbandry noun **1** farming **2** management **3** care with money, thrift

hush interjection be quiet! ➤ noun, informal silence, quiet ➤ verb to make quiet • **hush up** to stop (a scandal etc) becoming public

hush-hush adjective, informal top-secret

husk noun the dry thin covering of certain fruits and seeds

husky[1] adjective (**huskier, huskiest**) **1** of a voice: deep and rough **2** informal big and strong ♦ **huskily** adverb (meaning 1)

husky[2] noun (plural **huskies**) a Canadian sledge-dog

hussar (pronounced hu-**zah**) noun a light-armed horse soldier

hussy noun (plural **hussies**) a forward, cheeky girl

hustings plural noun political campaigning just before an election

hustle verb **1** to push rudely **2** to hurry

hut noun a small wooden building

hutch noun (plural **hutches**) a box in which pet rabbits are housed

hyacinth noun a sweet-smelling flower which grows from a bulb

hyaena another spelling of **hyena**

hybrid noun **1** an animal or plant bred from two different kinds, eg a mule, which is a hybrid from a horse and an ass **2** a word formed of parts from different languages

hybrid vigour noun, biology the increased vigour or size of a hybrid relative to its parents

hydra noun (plural **hydras** or **hydrae** - pronounced **hai**-dree) **1** a mythological many-headed snake that grew two heads for each one cut off **2** a sea creature that can divide and redivide itself

hydrant noun a connection to which a hose can be attached to draw water off the main water supply

hydrate verb, chemistry to combine a substance with water to produce a compound from which the water may be expelled without affecting the composition of the other substance

hydration noun, chemistry the attachment of water molecules to the ions of a solute as it is being dissolved in water

hydraulic adjective **1** carrying water **2** worked by water or other fluid

hydraulic action noun, geography the trapping of pressured air forced into cracks in rocks by the action of water (also called: **cavitation**)

hydro noun (plural **hydros**) a hotel with a swimming pool and gymnasium etc

hydro- or **hydr-** prefix water: hydroelectricity/ hydraulic ⊕ Comes from Greek hydor meaning 'water'

hydrocarbon noun a compound containing only carbon and hydrogen

hydrochloric acid noun a strong corrosive acid

hydroelectricity noun electricity obtained from water-power ♦ **hydroelectric** adjective

hydrofoil noun a boat with a device which raises it out of the water as it speeds up

hydrogen noun, chemistry (symbol **H**) the lightest gas, which with oxygen makes up water

hydrogenation noun, chemistry any chemical reaction where hydrogen is combined with another substance

hydrogen bomb noun an extremely powerful bomb using hydrogen

hydrogen bond noun, chemistry a weak chemical bond between an electronegative atom with a lone pair of electrons and covalently bonded hydrogen atoms

hydrogen peroxide noun an unstable colourless liquid used in rocket fuel and as a bleach

hydrograph noun, geography a graph showing

seasonal variations in level, force, etc of a body of water (*see also*: **falling limb, rising limb**)

hydrophilic *adjective, chemistry* denoting a substance that absorbs, attracts or has an affinity for water

hydrophobia *noun* **1** a fear of water, a symptom of rabies **2** rabies ◆ **hydrophobic** *adjective*

hydrophyte *noun, botany* a plant which grows in water or very moist conditions

hydroponics *singular noun* the technique of growing plants without using soil ◆ **hydroponic** *adjective*

hydrotherapy *noun, medicine* the treatment of diseases by the external use of water, especially through exercising in water

hydroxide *noun, chemistry* a compound containing one or more hydroxyl groups

hydroxyl *noun, chemistry* a radical group consisting of one oxygen atom and one hydrogen atom

hyena or **hyaena** *noun* a dog-like wild animal with a howl sounding like laughter

hygiene (*pronounced* **hai**-jeen) *noun* the maintaining of cleanliness as a means to health ◆ **hygienic** *adjective* ◆ **hygienically** *adverb*

hymen *noun, anatomy* a thin membrane partially covering the opening of the vagina, that is usually broken during the first instance of sexual intercourse

hymn *noun* a religious song of praise

hymnal (*pronounced* **him**-nal) or **hymnary** (*pronounced* **him**-na-ri) *noun* (*plural* **hymnals** or **hymnaries**) a book of hymns

hyp. *abbreviation, maths* hypotenuse

hype *informal, noun* extravagant advertisement or publicity ➤ *verb* to promote extravagantly

hyper *adjective, informal* of a person: overexcited

hyper- *prefix* to a greater extent than usual, excessive *hypersensitive* ⊙ Comes from Greek *hyper* meaning 'over'

hyperactive *adjective* of a child: abnormally active

hyperbola (*pronounced* **hai**-per-bo-la) *noun, maths* (*plural usually* **hyperbolas**) the curve produced when a **plane²** cuts through a cone so that the angle between the base of the cone and the plane is greater than the angle between the base and the sloping side of the cone ◆ **hyperbolic** or **hyperbolical** *adjective* ⊙ Comes from Greek *hyperbole*, from *hyper* meaning 'over' + *ballein* meaning 'to throw'

hyperbole (*pronounced* hai-**per**-bo-li) *noun* exaggeration ◆ **hyperbolic** or **hyperbolical** *adjective*

hyperglycaemia or **hyperglycemia** (*both pronounced* hai-per-glai-**see**-mi-a) *noun* an abnormally high amount of sugar in the blood (*compare with*: **hypoglycaemia**) ◆ **hyperglycaemic** or **hyperglycemic** *adjective*

hyperinflation *noun, economics* rapid inflation in which money loses its value

hyperlink *noun, computing* a piece of text a user can click on to take them to another file (*also called*: **link**)

hypermarket *noun* a large self-service store stocking a wide range of goods

hypermedia *noun, computing* a computer file and related software which identifies and links information in various media, such as text, graphics, and video clips

hypernym *noun* a general word whose meaning contains several specific words, eg *dance* is a hypernym of *waltz* and *reel* (*contrasted with*: **hyponym**)

hypersensitive *adjective* excessively sensitive ◆ **hypersensitivity** *noun*

hypertension *noun* abnormally high blood pressure (*compare with*: **hypotension**)

hypertext *noun, computing* electronic text containing cross-references which can be accessed by keystrokes etc

hypertonic *adjective, chemistry* of a solution: having a higher osmotic pressure than another solution with which it is being compared (*compare with*: **hypotonic**)

hypertrophy *biology* (*plural* **hypertrophies**), ➤ *noun* an abnormal increase in an organ's size resulting from overnourishment ➤ *verb* (**hypertrophies, hypertrophying, hypertrophied**) to subject or be subjected to hypertrophy ◆ **hypertrophic** *adjective*

hyperventilation *noun* a condition in which breathing becomes abnormally rapid, causing dizziness, a feeling of suffocation, and sometimes unconsciousness ◆ **hyperventilate** *verb*

hypha *noun* (*plural* **hyphae**), *biology* one of many thread-like filaments that form the mycelium of a fungus ◆ **hyphal** *adjective*

hyphen *noun* a short stroke (-) used to link or separate parts of a word or phrase: *touch-and-go/re-elect*

hyphenate *verb* to join (two or more words) with a hyphen ◆ **hyphenated** *adjective* ◆ **hyphenation** *noun*

hypnosis *noun* **1** a sleep-like state in which suggestions are obeyed **2** hypnotism

hypnotic *adjective* **1** of hypnosis or hypnotism **2** causing a sleep-like state

hypnotism *noun* the putting of someone into hypnosis ◆ **hypnotist** *noun*

hypnotize or **hypnotise** *verb* to put someone into hypnosis

hypo- *prefix* below, under *hypodermic/ hypothermia* ⊙ Comes from Greek *hypo* meaning 'under'

hypoallergenic *adjective* specially formulated to reduce the risk of allergy

hypochlorite *noun, chemistry* a salt of hypochlorous acid

hypochlorous acid *noun* a weak acid, used as a disinfectant and bleach

hypochondria *noun* over-anxiety about your own health

hypochondriac *noun* someone who is over-anxious about their health, and who is inclined to think they are ill when they are perfectly healthy ➤ *adjective* relating to or affected with hypochondria

hypocorism (*pronounced* hai-**pok**-o-rizm) *noun* a pet name ◆ **hypocoristic** *adjective*

hypocrite (*pronounced* **hip**-o-krit) *noun* someone who pretends to be something they are not, or to believe something they do not ◆ **hypocrisy** *noun* ◆ **hypocritical** *adjective*

hypodermic *adjective* used for injecting drugs just below the skin ➤ *noun* a hypodermic syringe

hypogeal, hypogean or **hypogeous** *adjective, botany* existing or growing underground

hypoglycaemia or **hypoglycemia** (*both pronounced* hai-po-glai-**see**-mi-a) *noun* an abnormally low amount of sugar in the blood (*compare with:* **hyperglycaemia**) ◆ **hypoglycaemic** or **hypoglycemic** *adjective*

hyponym *noun* one of a group of words whose meanings are included in a more general term, eg *guitar* and *piano* are hyponyms of *musical instrument* (*contrasted with:* **hypernym**)

hypostyle *adjective* of a roof: supported by pillars

hypotension *noun* abnormally low blood pressure (*compare with:* **hypertension**)

hypotenuse (*pronounced* hai-**pot**-e-nyooz) *noun, maths* (*abbrev* **hyp.**) the longest side of a right-angled triangle

hypothalamus *noun* (*plural* **hypothalami**) a part of the brain that is involved in the regulation of involuntary functions, eg body temperature

hypothermia *noun* an abnormally low body temperature caused by exposure to cold

hypothesis (*pronounced* hai-**poth**-e-sis) *noun* (*plural* **hypotheses**) **1** something taken as true for the sake of argument **2** a statement or theory to be proved or disproved by evidence or facts

hypothetical *adjective* supposed, based on an idea or a possibility rather than on facts ◆ **hypothetically** *adverb*

hypotonic *adjective, chemistry* of a solution: having a lower osmotic pressure than another solution with which it is being compared (*compare with:* **hypertonic**)

hysterectomy *noun* (*plural* **hysterectomies**) surgical removal of the womb

hysteresis *noun, physics* the delay or lag between the cause of an effect and the effect itself ⊙ Comes from Greek, meaning 'deficiency'

hysteria *noun* **1** a nervous excitement causing uncontrollable laughter, crying, etc **2** a nervous illness

⊙ Based on a Greek word for 'womb', because hysteria was originally thought to be caused by a disorder of the womb

hysterical *adjective* **1** suffering from a severe emotional disturbance, often as a result of shock **2** wild with panic, excitement, or anger **3** very funny ◆ **hysterically** *adverb*

hysterics *plural noun* a fit of hysteria • **in hysterics** *informal* laughing uncontrollably

HYV *abbreviation, geography* high yielding variety (of a plant)

Hz *symbol* hertz

I[1] *pronoun* the word used by a speaker or writer in mentioning themselves (as the subject of a verb): *you and I/I, myself*

ⓘ After a preposition, **me** should always be used:
✓ *between you and me*
✓ *between John and me*

I[2] *symbol, chemistry* iodine

iambic pentameter *noun, poetry* a verse form with lines each of five feet, each foot containing two syllables

iambus or **iamb** *noun* (*plural* **iambuses** or **iambi**) in verse: a metrical foot containing one short or unstressed syllable followed by one long or stressed one, the most common measure in English verse

Ibadat or **Ibadah** *noun, Islam* worship

ibex *noun* (*plural* **ibexes**) a wild mountain goat

ibid *adverb* in the same book, article, etc

ice *noun* **1** frozen water **2** ice-cream ➤ *verb* **1** to cover with icing **2** to freeze

ice age *noun* a long period when the earth was mostly covered with ice

iceberg *noun* a huge mass of floating ice

icebox *noun, US* refrigerator

icecap *noun, geography* a permanent covering of ice, as found at the North and South Poles

ice-cream *noun* a sweet creamy mixture, flavoured and frozen

ice floe *noun* a piece of floating ice

ice hockey *noun* hockey played with a rubber disc (called a **puck**) on an ice rink

ice lolly *noun* a portion of frozen, flavoured water or ice-cream on a stick

ice sheet *noun, geography* a layer of ice covering a whole region

ice-skate *noun* a skate for moving on ice

ice-skating *noun* the sport of moving about on ice wearing ice-skates

ice wedging another term for **freeze-thaw**

icicle *noun* a hanging, pointed piece of ice formed by the freezing of dropping water

icing *noun* powdered sugar, mixed with water or egg-white, spread on cakes or biscuits
• **icing on the cake** an agreeable extra detail, added to something which is already satisfactory

icing sugar *noun* very fine powdered sugar

icky *adjective* (**ickier, ickiest**) *informal* disgusting, repulsive

icon *noun* **1** (*also*: **ikon**) a painted or mosaic image of Christ or a saint **2** *computing* a small graphic image which is clicked to access a particular program or file

iconoclast *noun* someone who is opposed to traditional and cherished beliefs and attacks them ♦ **iconoclastic** *adjective*

icosahedron (*pronounced* ai-kos-a-**hee**-dron) *noun* (*plural* **icosahedrons** or **icosahedra**), *maths* a solid figure with 20 faces

ICT *abbreviation* information and communication technology

icy *adjective* (**icier, iciest**) **1** covered with ice **2** very cold **3** unfriendly ♦ **icily** *adverb*

ID *abbreviation* identification ➤ *noun* a means of identification, eg a driving licence: *show some ID*

I'd *short for* I would, I should *or* I had: *I'd sooner go than stay*

id *noun, psychoanalysis* the unconscious part of the personality, the source of instincts and dreams

-ide *suffix* used to describe a compound of an element with some other element: *oxide* (= a compound containing oxygen)/*chloride* (= a compound containing chlorine)

idea *noun* **1** a thought, a notion **2** a plan

ideal *adjective* **1** perfect **2** existing in imagination only (*contrasted with*: **real**) ➤ *noun* the highest and best; a standard of perfection

ideal gas *noun, physics* a hypothetical gas with molecules which are of negligible size and do not exert a force on one another

idealism *noun* the belief that perfection can be reached

idealist *noun* someone who thinks that perfection can be reached ♦ **idealistic** *adjective*

idealize or **idealise** *verb* to think of as perfect ♦ **idealization** *noun*

ideally *adverb* in ideal circumstances: *Ideally all children should have a place in nursery school*

identical *adjective* the same in all details ♦ **identically** *adverb*

identification *noun* **1** an official document, such as a passport or driving licence, that proves who you are **2** the process of finding out who someone is or what something is

identifier *noun* **1** someone or something that identifies **2** *computing* a name or label that identifies a program or a file

identify *verb* (**identifies, identifying, identified**) to claim to recognize, prove to be the same: *He identified the man as his attacker* ◆ **identifiable** *adjective* ● **identify with 1** to feel close to or involved with **2** to think of as the same, equate: *identifying money with happiness*

Identikit (picture) *noun trademark* a rough picture of a wanted person which police put together from descriptions

identity *noun* (*plural* **identities**) **1** who or what someone or something is **2** the state of being the same **3** *maths* an equation that is true for all possible values of the unknown variables **4** *maths* a member of a set that, when combined with another element or member of the set, is left unchanged. For example, the identity for the multiplication of numbers is 1 (*also called:* **identity element**)

ideological *adjective* **1** of or relating to an ideology **2** resulting from a clash between different ideologies

ideology *noun* (*plural* **ideologies**) a set of ideas, often political or philosophical

idiocy *noun* feeble-mindedness, foolishness

idiom *noun* a common expression whose meaning cannot be guessed from the individual words, eg 'I'm feeling *under the weather*' ◆ **idiomatic** *adjective* ◆ **idiomatically** *adverb*

idiosyncrasy *noun* (*plural* **idiosyncrasies**) a personal oddness of behaviour ◆ **idiosyncratic** *adjective*

idiot *noun* a stupid person; a fool

idiotic *adjective* extremely foolish, ridiculous ◆ **idiotically** *adverb*

idle *adjective* **1** not working: *machines lying idle* **2** lazy **3** meaningless, without a useful purpose: *idle chatter* ➤ *verb* **1** to spend time in doing nothing **2** of an engine: to run without doing any work ◆ **idly** *adverb* (adjective, meanings 2 and 3) ◎ Comes from Old English *idel* meaning 'empty' or 'worthless'

idler *noun* a person who wastes time or is reluctant to work

idol *noun* **1** an image worshipped as a god **2** someone much loved or honoured: *pop idols*

idolatry *noun* **1** the worship of an image as if it were a god **2** the excessive loving or honouring of someone or something ◆ **idolatrous** *adjective*

idolize or **idolise** *verb* to adore, worship

Id-ul-Adha or **Eid-ul-Adha** *noun* a Muslim festival celebrating Abraham's willingness to sacrifice his son

Id-ul-Fitr or **Eid-ul-Fitr** *noun* (also **Eid**) a Muslim festival celebrating the end of Ramadan

idyll *noun* **1** a poem on a pastoral theme **2** a time of pleasure and contentment

idyllic *adjective* very happy and content, blissful

ie *abbreviation* that is, that means (from Latin *id est*)

if *conjunction* **1** on condition that, supposing that: *If you go, I'll go* **2** whether: *Do you know if she'll be there?*

iffy *adjective* (**iffier, iffiest**) *informal* dubious, uncertain

ig- see **in-**

igloo *noun* an Inuit snow hut

igneous *adjective* **1** relating to fire **2** of rocks: formed by the cooling and hardening of magma or molten lava

ignite *verb* **1** to set on fire **2** to catch fire

ignition *noun* **1** the act of setting on fire or catching fire **2** the sparking part of a motor engine

ignoble *adjective* dishonourable; of low birth

ignominious *adjective* bringing disgrace or dishonour

ignominy (*pronounced* **ig**-nom-in-i) *noun* disgrace, dishonour

ignoramus (*pronounced* ig-no-**rei**-mus) *noun* an ignorant person

ignorant *adjective* **1** knowing little **2** (**ignorant of**) unaware of ◆ **ignorance** *noun*

ignore *verb* to take no notice of

iguana (*pronounced* ig-**wah**-na) *noun* a type of large lizard

ikon another spelling of **icon**

il- see **in-**

ileum *noun, anatomy* the lowest part of the small intestine

ilk *noun* type, kind or class

I'll *short for* I shall, I will

ill *adjective* **1** unwell, sick **2** evil, bad **3** unlucky ➤ *adverb* badly ➤ *noun* **1** evil **2** (**ills**) misfortunes, troubles

ill-advised *adjective* foolish; done or doing things with little thought or consideration

ill-at-ease *adjective* uncomfortable

illegal *adjective* against the law ◆ **illegality** *noun* (*plural* **illegalities**)

illegal immigrant *noun* an immigrant who has not been authorized to enter a country

illegible *adjective* impossible to read ◆ **illegibility** *noun* ◆ **illegibly** *adverb*

illegitimate *adjective* born of parents not married to each other

ill-fated *adjective* ending in or bringing bad luck or ruin

ill-feeling *noun* dislike, resentment

ill-gotten *adjective* obtained in a dishonest or unethical way

ill-humoured *adjective* bad-tempered

illiberal *adjective* **1** narrow-minded, prejudiced, intolerant **2** not generous

illicit *adjective* unlawful, forbidden ☉ Comes from Latin *il-* meaning 'not', and *licitus* meaning 'allowed'

! Do not confuse with: **elicit**

illiterate *adjective* not able to read or write
♦ **illiteracy** *noun*

ill-mannered *adjective* rude, uncouth

ill-natured *adjective* bad-tempered

illness *noun* disease, sickness

illogical *adjective* not logical, not showing sound reasoning ♦ **illogicality** *noun*
♦ **illogically** *adverb*

ill-starred *adjective* unlucky

ill-treat *verb* to treat badly

illuminate *verb* **1** to light up **2** to make more clear

illuminated *adjective* of a manuscript: decorated with ornamental lettering

illuminations *plural noun* a decorative display of lights

ill-use *verb* to treat badly

illusion *noun* **1** something which deceives the mind or eye **2** a mistaken belief ☉ Comes from Latin *illudere* meaning 'to make sport of'

! Do not confuse with: **allusion** and **delusion**

illusive *adjective* misleading, deceptive

! Do not confuse with: **allusive** and **elusive**. **Illusive** is related to the noun **illusion**.

illusory *adjective* mistaken or untrue, despite seeming believable

illustrate *verb* **1** to draw pictures for (a book etc) **2** to explain, show by example ♦ **illustrative** *adjective*

illustration *noun* **1** a picture in a book etc **2** an example which illustrates

illustrator *noun* someone who illustrates books etc

illustrious *adjective* famous, distinguished

ill-will *noun* dislike, resentment

I'm *short for* I am

im- see **in-**

image *noun* **1** a likeness made of someone or something **2** a striking likeness: *She is the image of her mother* **3** a picture in the mind **4** public reputation **5** *maths* the element of a set that is associated with an element in a different set when one set is a function or transformation of the other

imagery *noun* words that suggest images, used to make a piece of writing more vivid

imaginary *adjective* existing only in the imagination, not real ☉ Comes from Latin prefix

imagin-, a form of the word for 'image', and Latin suffix *-arius* meaning 'connected with'

! Do not confuse with: **imaginative**

imaginary number *noun, maths* the square root of a negative number

imagination *noun* the power of forming pictures in the mind of things not present or experienced

imaginative *adjective* **1** having a lively imagination **2** done with imagination: *an imaginative piece of writing* ☉ Comes from Latin prefix *imaginat-*, a form of a verb meaning 'to imagine', and French suffix *-ive* meaning 'tending to'

! Do not confuse with: **imaginary**

imagine *verb* **1** to form a picture in the mind, especially of something that does not exist **2** to think, suppose

imam *noun* **1** the person who leads the prayers in a mosque **2** (**Imam**) an Islamic leader

imbalance *noun* a lack of balance or proportion, inequality

imbecile *noun* a feeble-minded person; a fool ☉ Comes from Latin *imbecillus* meaning 'feeble' or 'fragile'

imbecility *noun* feeble-mindedness, stupidity

imbibe *verb, formal or literary* to drink (in)

imbroglio (*pronounced* im-**brohl**-yoh) *noun* a confused and complicated situation

imbue *verb* to fill or affect (with): *imbued her staff with enthusiasm*

imitate *verb* to try to be the same as, copy

imitation *noun* a copy ➤ *adjective* made to look like: *imitation leather*

imitator *noun* someone who copies, or tries to do the same things as, someone else

immaculate *adjective* spotless; very clean and neat ♦ **immaculately** *adverb*

immaterial *adjective* of little importance

immature *adjective* not mature ♦ **immaturity** *noun*

immediacy *noun* of paintings, photographs, writing, etc: a striking quality, giving the observer a strong sense of involvement

immediate *adjective* **1** happening straight away: *immediate reaction* **2** close: *immediate family* **3** direct: *my immediate successor*

immediately *adverb* without delay

immemorial *adjective* going further back in time than can be remembered

immense *adjective* very large ♦ **immensity** *noun*

immensely *adverb* greatly

immerse *verb* to plunge something into liquid so that it is completely covered • **immerse**

yourself in to give your whole attention to

immersion *noun* **1** the plunging of something into liquid so that it is completely covered **2** deep involvement in a certain subject or situation

immersion heater *noun* an electric water-heater inside a hot-water tank

immigrant *noun* **1** someone who immigrates or has immigrated **2** *biology* an animal or plant established in an area where it was previously not found

immigrate *verb* to come into a country and settle there ◆ **immigration** *noun* ◷ Comes from Latin *immigrare*, from *in* meaning 'into', and *migrare* meaning 'to remove'

! Do not confuse with: **emigrate**.
You **immigrate** to a new country where you plan to start living (the IM comes from the Latin meaning 'into'). You are **emigrating** when you leave your original or home country (the E comes from the Latin meaning 'from').

imminent *adjective* about to happen: *imminent danger* ◷ Comes from Latin *imminens* meaning 'overhanging'

! Do not confuse with: **eminent**

immiscible *adjective* of liquids: unable to be mixed together

immobile *adjective* **1** without moving **2** not easily moved ◆ **immobility** *noun*

immobilize or **immobilise** *verb* to put out of action

immobilizer or **immobiliser** *noun* a device that prevents a motor vehicle from being started without the proper key

immodest *adjective* **1** shameful, indecent **2** boastful and conceited ◆ **immodestly** *adverb* ◆ **immodesty** *noun*

immolate *verb* to offer or kill (something) as a sacrifice

immoral *adjective* **1** wrong, unscrupulous **2** sexually improper ◆ **immorality** *noun* ◆ **immorally** *adverb* ◷ Comes from prefix *im-* meaning 'not', and Latin *moralis* meaning 'moral'

! Do not confuse with: **amoral**.
An **immoral** person behaves badly in the full knowledge that what they are doing is wrong. An **amoral** person behaves badly because they do not understand the difference between right and wrong.

immortal *adjective* **1** living forever **2** famous forever

immortality *noun* unending life or fame

immortalize or **immortalise** *verb* to make immortal or famous forever

immovable *adjective* not able to be moved or changed ◆ **immovably** *adverb*

immune *adjective* **1** not likely to catch a particular disease: *immune to measles* **2** not able to be affected by: *She is immune to his charm* ◆ **immunity** *noun*

immune response *noun* the response of the body to a foreign substance, eg a virus

immune system *noun* the natural defensive system of an organism that identifies and neutralizes harmful matter within itself

immunize or **immunise** *verb* to make someone immune to (a disease), especially by inoculation ◆ **immunization** *noun*

immunoassay *noun, biology* a bioassay in which assessment is made by observing the reaction of suspected antigens with specific known antibodies

immunodeficiency *noun* weakened ability to produce antibodies

immunology *noun* the study of the human immune system

immunotherapy *noun* the treatment of disease, especially cancer, by antigens which stimulate the patient's natural immunity

immutable *adjective* **1** unable to be changed **2** not susceptible to change ◆ **immutability** *noun*

imp *noun* **1** a small malignant spirit **2** a mischievous child ◆ **impish** *adjective*

impact *noun* (*pronounced* im-pakt) **1** the blow of one thing striking another; a collision **2** strong effect: *made an impact on the audience* ➤ *verb* (*pronounced* im-pakt *or* im-**pakt**) to press firmly together • **impact on** to affect strongly

impact printer *noun* a device in which printed characters are formed by means of a hammer striking the ribbon, eg a dot matrix printer

impair *verb* to damage, weaken ◆ **impairment** *noun*

impala *noun* a large African antelope

impale *verb* to pierce through with a spear etc

impart *verb* to tell (information, news, etc) to others

impartial *adjective* not favouring one side over another; unbiased ◆ **impartiality** *noun* ◆ **impartially** *adverb*

impassable *adjective* of a road, path, etc: not able to be travelled along

impasse (*pronounced* am-pas) *noun* a situation from which there seems to be no way out

impassioned *adjective* moved by strong feeling

impassive *adjective* **1** not easily moved by strong feeling **2** showing no emotion: *His face was impassive* ◆ **impassively** *adverb*

impasto *noun, art* **1** applying paint thickly **2** thickly applied paint

impatient *adjective* **1** restlessly eager **2** irritable, short-tempered ◆ **impatience** *noun* ◆ **impatiently** *adverb*

impeach *verb* to accuse publicly of, or charge with, misconduct ♦ **impeachment** *noun*

impeccable *adjective* faultless, perfect ♦ **impeccably** *adverb*

impedance *noun* 1 (symbol **Z**) the resistance of an electric circuit or circuit component to the passage of an electric current, measured in ohms 2 anything that impedes

impede *verb* to hinder, keep back

impediment *noun* 1 a hindrance 2 a speech defect, eg a stutter or stammer

impel *verb* (**impelling, impelled**) 1 to urge 2 to drive on

impending *adjective* about to happen: *a feeling of impending doom*

impenetrable *adjective* 1 not allowing light etc through 2 incomprehensible, inscrutable

impenitent *adjective* not sorry for wrongdoing, unrepentant

imperative *adjective* 1 necessary, urgent 2 *grammar* of the mood of a verb: indicating a command, eg *look!* or *read this* ➤ *noun* 1 the imperative mood 2 the imperative form of a verb

imperceptible *adjective* so small as not to be noticed

imperfect *adjective* having a fault or flaw, not perfect ➤ *noun, grammar* (**the imperfect**) the tense used to describe continuing or incomplete actions or states in the past, eg *The sun **was** shining* and *the birds **were singing***

imperfection *noun* a fault or a flaw

imperfectly *adverb* not perfectly or thoroughly

imperial *adjective* 1 of an emperor or empire 2 commanding, superior

imperialism *noun* the policy of annexing the territory of, and ruling, other nations and people ♦ **imperialist** *adjective*: *imperialist policies*

imperial system *noun* the system of weights and measures using inches and feet, ounces and pounds, etc

imperious *adjective* having an air of authority, haughty

impermanence *noun* lack of permanence, transitoriness ♦ **impermanent** *adjective*

impermeable *adjective* not able to be passed through: *impermeable by water*

impersonal *adjective* 1 not influenced by personal feelings 2 not connected with any person ♦ **impersonally** *adverb*

impersonate *verb* to dress up as, or act the part of, someone ♦ **impersonation** *noun*

impersonator *noun* someone who impersonates others

impertinent *adjective* 1 cheeky, impudent 2 *old* not pertinent, irrelevant ♦ **impertinence** *noun* (meaning 1) ♦ **impertinently** *adverb* (meaning 1)

imperturbable *adjective* not easily worried, calm ♦ **imperturbably** *adverb*

impervious *adjective* (**impervious to**) not able to be affected by: *impervious to criticism*

impetigo (*pronounced* im-pit-**ai**-goh) *noun* a highly contagious skin disease

impetuous *adjective* rushing into action, rash ♦ **impetuosity** *noun*

impetus (*pronounced* **im**-pet-us) *noun* 1 moving force, motivation 2 impulse ⊙ Comes from Latin, literally meaning 'attack' or 'force'

impiety *noun* lack of respect for holy things

impinge *verb*: **impinge on** or **impinge upon** 1 to come in contact with 2 to trespass on, interfere with

impious (*pronounced* **im**-pai-us or im-pi-us)*adjective* lacking the proper respect, especially for holy things

implacable *adjective* not able to be soothed or calmed ♦ **implacably** *adverb*

implant *verb* (*pronounced* im-**plant**) to fix in, plant firmly ➤ *noun* (*pronounced* **im**-plant) an artificial organ, graft, etc inserted into the body: *breast implants* ♦ **implantation** *noun*

implement *noun* a tool ➤ *verb* to carry out, fulfil (eg a promise) ♦ **implementation** *noun*

implicate *verb* to bring in, involve: *The statement implicates you in the crime*

implication *noun* something meant though not actually said

implicit *adjective* 1 understood, meant though not actually said 2 unquestioning: *implicit obedience*

implicitly *adverb* without questioning or doubting: *trust someone implicitly*

implode *verb* to collapse inwards suddenly ♦ **implosion** *noun*

implore *verb* to beg, entreat

imply *verb* to suggest: *Her silence implies disapproval* ⊙ Comes from Latin *implicare* meaning 'to involve'

❗ Do not confuse with: **infer**.
Implying is an action of expression – you **imply** something by dropping subtle hints about it. **Inferring** is an action of understanding – you **infer** something by drawing conclusions from what you have seen or heard.

impolite *adjective* not polite, rude

imponderable *adjective* not able to be judged or evaluated

import *verb* (*pronounced* im-**pawt** or im-pawt) 1 to bring in (goods) from abroad for sale 2 to load a file, data, etc into a program ➤ *noun* (*pronounced* **im**-pawt) 1 the act of importing 2 something imported from abroad for sale 3 meaning, significance ♦ **importation** *noun*

important *adjective* worthy of attention; special ♦ **importance** *noun* ♦ **importantly** *adverb* ◷ Comes from Latin *importare* meaning 'to bring in'

importune *verb*: **importune someone** to keep asking them for something which they are unwilling to give

impose *verb* to place (a tax etc) on • **impose on** to take advantage of, inconvenience

imposing *adjective* impressive, commanding attention

imposition *noun* a burden, an inconvenience

impossible *adjective* **1** not able to be done or to happen **2** extremely difficult to deal with, intolerable ♦ **impossibility** *noun* (meaning 1) ♦ **impossibly** *adverb*

impostor or **imposter** *noun* someone who pretends to be someone else in order to deceive

imposture *noun* deceit consisting of pretending to be someone else

impotent (*pronounced* im-pot-ent) *adjective* **1** without power or effectiveness **2** of an adult male: unable to maintain an erection ♦ **impotence** *noun* ♦ **impotently** *adverb*

impound *verb* to seize possession of (something) by law: *goods impounded by Customs*

impoverish *verb* **1** to make financially poor **2** to lessen in quality: *an impoverished culture* ♦ **impoverishment** *noun*

impracticable *adjective* not able to be done ♦ **impracticability** *noun* ◷ Comes from prefix *im-* meaning 'not', and *practicable*

❗ Do not confuse: **impracticable** and **impractical**

impractical *adjective* lacking common sense ♦ **impracticality** *noun* ◷ Comes from prefix *im-* meaning 'not', and *practical*

imprecise *adjective* not precise, vague

impregnable *adjective* too strong to be taken by attack: *an impregnable fortress*

impregnate *verb* **1** to make pregnant **2** to saturate: *a tissue impregnated with perfume*

impresario (*pronounced* im-pre-**sah**-ree-oh) *noun* (*plural* **impresarios**) the organizer of an entertainment

impress *verb* **1** to arouse the interest or admiration of **2** to mark by pressing upon **3** to fix deeply in the mind

impression *noun* **1** someone's thoughts or feelings about something: *My impression is that it's likely to rain* **2** a deep or strong effect: *The film left a lasting impression on me* **3** a mark made by impressing **4** a quantity of copies of a book printed at one time

impressionable *adjective* easily influenced or affected

impressionism *noun* an artistic or literary style aiming to reproduce personal impressions of things or events

impressionist *noun* **1** a follower of impressionism **2** an entertainer who impersonates people

impressionistic *adjective* based on impressions or personal observation rather than definite facts or knowledge

impressive *adjective* having a strong effect on the mind

imprint *verb* (*pronounced* im-**print**) **1** to stamp, press **2** to fix in the mind ➤ *noun* (*pronounced* **im**-print) **1** the printer's or publisher's name etc on a book **2** a common title for a series of related books from one publisher

imprinting *noun, biology* the process by which animals learn the appearance, sound or smell of significant members of their own species, eg parents or suitable mates

imprison *verb* to shut up as in a prison ♦ **imprisonment** *noun*

improbable *adjective* not likely to happen ♦ **improbability** *noun*

impromptu *adjective* & *adverb* without preparation or rehearsal

improper *adjective* **1** not suitable; wrong **2** indecent

improper fraction *noun* a fraction in which the numerator is equal to or greater than the denominator, and so has a value equal to or greater than 1 (as $\frac{5}{4}$, $\frac{11}{8}$)

impropriety *noun* (*plural* **improprieties**) something improper

improve *verb* to make or become better ♦ **improvement** *noun*

improvident *adjective* giving no thought to future needs ♦ **improvidence** *noun*

improvise *verb* **1** to put together from available materials: *We improvised a stretcher* **2** to create (a tune, script, etc) spontaneously: *The actors had to improvise their lines* ♦ **improvisation** *noun*

impudent *adjective* cheeky, insolent ♦ **impudence** *noun* ♦ **impudently** *adverb*

impulse *noun* **1** a sudden force or push **2** a sudden urge resulting in sudden action **3** an electrical signal that sends information through the nervous system **4** *physics* the force produced when two objects briefly collide with each other

impulsive *adjective* acting on impulse, without taking time to consider ♦ **impulsively** *adverb*

impunity *noun* freedom from punishment, injury or loss

impure *adjective* mixed with other substances; not clean

impurity *noun* (*plural* **impurities**) **1** a small

amount of something which is present in, and spoils the quality of, another substance **2** the state of being impure

impute *verb* to think of as being caused, done, etc by someone: *imputing the blame to others* ♦ **imputation** *noun*

In *symbol, chemistry* indium

in *preposition* **1** showing position in space or time: *sitting in the garden/born in the 60s* **2** showing state, manner, etc: *in part/in cold blood* ➤ *adverb* **1** towards the inside, not out **2** in power **3** *informal* in fashion ➤ *adjective* **1** that is in, inside or coming in **2** *informal* fashionable • **be in for 1** to be trying to get (a prize etc) **2** to be about to receive (trouble, punishment)

in- *prefix* **1** (also **il-, im-, ir-, em-, en-**) into, on, towards: *inshore/illusion/impulse/embrace* (= to take in the arms)/*endure* **2** (also **ig-, il-, im-, ir-**) not: *inaccurate/ignoble* (= not noble)/*illiterate/improper/irregular* (= not regular)

inability *noun* (*plural* **inabilities**) lack of power, means, etc (to do something)

inaccessible *adjective* not able to be easily reached or obtained

inaccurate *adjective* **1** not correct **2** not exact ♦ **inaccuracy** *noun* (*plural* **inaccuracies**)

inaction *noun* lack of action

inactive *adjective* **1** not active **2** not working, doing nothing **3** *chemistry* of a substance: rarely or never taking part in chemical reactions

inactivity *noun* idleness; rest

inadequate *adjective* **1** not enough **2** unable to cope with a situation ♦ **inadequacy** *noun*

inadmissible *adjective* not allowable: *inadmissible evidence*

inadvertent *adjective* unintentional

inadvisable *adjective* not advisable, unwise

inalienable *adjective* not able to be removed or transferred: *inalienable rights*

inalterable *adjective* not able to be altered

inane *adjective* silly, foolish, mindless ⊙ Comes from Latin *inanus* meaning 'empty'

inanimate *adjective* without life

inanity *noun* (*plural* **inanities**) **1** an empty, meaningless remark **2** silliness, foolishness, mindlessness

inapplicable *adjective* not applicable

inappropriate *adjective* not suitable

inapt *adjective* unsuitable, unfit ⊙ Comes from prefix *in-* meaning 'not', + *apt*

❗ Do not confuse with: **inept**

inaptitude or **inaptness** *noun* unfitness, awkwardness

inarticulate *adjective* **1** unable to express yourself clearly **2** said indistinctly

inasmuch as *conjunction* because, since

inattentive *adjective* not paying attention ♦ **inattention** *noun*

inaudible *adjective* not loud enough to be heard

inaugural *adjective* relating to, or performed at, an inauguration

inaugurate *verb* to mark the beginning of (eg a presidency) with a ceremony ♦ **inauguration** *noun*

inauspicious *adjective* unlucky, unlikely to end in success

inborn *adjective* innate, natural: *inborn talent*

in-box *noun, computing* a file for storing incoming e-mail

inbred *adjective* **1** inborn **2** produced by inbreeding

inbreeding *noun* repeated mating and producing of offspring within the same family, or closely related individuals of a species

inbuilt *adjective* built in as part of: *cooker with inbuilt fan*

inc *abbreviation* **1** incorporated **2** inclusive **3** including

Inca *noun, history* **1** a member of a South American people of Peru, who had a complex civilization and empire **2** a king or emperor of the Incas ➤ *adjective* belonging or relating to this people

incalculable *adjective* not able to be counted or estimated

incandescent *adjective* **1** white-hot **2** *informal* extremely angry

incantation *noun* a spell

incapable *adjective* **1** unable (to do what is expected) **2** helpless (through drink etc)

incapacitate *verb* **1** to take away power, strength or rights **2** to disable

incapacity *noun* **1** inability **2** disability

incarcerate *verb* to imprison ♦ **incarceration** *noun*

incarnate *adjective* having human form: *the devil incarnate*

incarnation *noun* **1** a person whose appearance or behaviour are the perfect example of a particular quality, eg beauty or honour **2** of a spirit: appearance in a physical form **3** *Christianity* the belief that God took human form in Christ

incendiary *adjective* meant for setting (buildings etc) on fire: *an incendiary bomb*

incense *verb* (*pronounced* in-**sens**) to make angry ➤ *noun* (*pronounced* **in**-sens) a mixture of resins, gums, etc burned to give off fumes, especially in religious ceremonies

incentive *noun* something which encourages someone to do something

incentre *noun, maths* the centre of an inscribed circle or sphere

inception *noun* beginning

incessant *adjective* going on without pause

incest *noun* illegal sexual intercourse between close relatives

incestuous *adjective* 1 involving incest 2 done within a close-knit group

inch *noun* (*plural* **inches**) one twelfth of a foot (about 2.5 centimetres) ➤ *verb* to move very gradually

incidence *noun* 1 the frequency of something occurring 2 a falling of a ray of light etc

incident *noun* a happening ➤ *adjective* of a ray of light etc: falling on a surface

incidental *adjective* 1 happening in connection with something: *an incidental expense* 2 casual

incidentally *adverb* by the way

incinerate *verb* to burn to ashes
♦ **incineration** *noun*

incinerator *noun* an apparatus for burning rubbish etc

incipient *adjective* beginning to exist: *an incipient dislike*

incircle *noun, maths* a circle inscribed in a polygon

incise *verb* to cut into, engrave

incised stream *noun, geography* a stream that has cut a channel into the bed of a valley

incision *noun* 1 cutting into something 2 a cut, a gash

incisive *adjective* sharp, clear, firm

incisor *noun* a front tooth

incite *verb* to move to action; urge on
♦ **incitement** *noun*

incivility *noun* (*plural* **incivilities**) impoliteness

inclement *adjective* of weather: stormy
♦ **inclemency** *noun*

inclination *noun* 1 liking, tendency 2 a slope 3 *maths* a measurement in degrees of a slope from a plane (the **angle of inclination**)

incline *verb* (*pronounced* in-**klain**) 1 to lean, slope (towards) 2 to bend, bow 3 to have a liking for ➤ *noun* (*pronounced* **in**-klain) a slope

inclined *adjective* 1 talented or gifted 2 (**inclined to**) having a tendency, or a hesitant desire to

include *verb* to count in, along with others

inclusion *noun* the act of including something, or the fact that it is included

inclusive *adjective* including everything mentioned: *From Tuesday to Thursday inclusive is 3 days*

incognito (*pronounced* in-cog-**neet**-oh) *adjective & adverb* in disguise, with identity concealed ➤ *noun* (*plural* **incognitos**) a disguise

⊘ From Italian, literally meaning 'unknown'

incoherent *adjective* 1 unconnected, rambling 2 speaking in an unconnected, rambling way
♦ **incoherence** *noun*

incombustible *adjective* not able to be burned by fire

income *noun* 1 personal earnings 2 gain, profit

incoming *adjective* approaching, next

incommunicado (*pronounced* in-com-yoon-i-**kah**-doh) *adverb, adjective* not able or allowed to communicate with other people, especially when held in solitary confinement

incomparable *adjective* without equal

incompatible *adjective* 1 of statements: contradicting each other 2 of people: not suited, bound to disagree ♦ **incompatibility** *noun*

incompetent *adjective* 1 not good enough at doing a job 2 *geography* of rock: soft, and relatively likely to be eroded (*contrasted with*: **competent**) ♦ **incompetence** *noun*

incomplete *adjective* not finished

incomprehensible *adjective* not able to be understood, puzzling

incomprehension *noun* the state of not understanding something

inconceivable *adjective* not able to be imagined or believed

inconclusive *adjective* not leading to a definite decision or conclusion

incongruous *adjective* 1 not matching well 2 out of place, unsuitable ♦ **incongruity** (*plural* **incongruities**)

inconsequential *adjective* unimportant
♦ **inconsequence** *noun*

inconsiderable *adjective* slight, unimportant

inconsiderate *adjective* not thinking of others

inconsistent *adjective* not consistent, contradicting: *inconsistent statements*
♦ **inconsistency** *noun*

inconsolable *adjective* not able to be comforted

inconspicuous *adjective* not noticeable

inconstant *adjective* often changing
♦ **inconstancy** *noun*

incontinent *adjective* 1 unable to control the bladder or bowels 2 uncontrolled, unrestrained
♦ **incontinence** *noun*

incontrovertible *adjective* not to be doubted

inconvenience *noun* minor trouble or difficulty: *I don't want you to go to any inconvenience on my behalf*

inconvenient *adjective* causing awkwardness or difficulty

incorporate *verb* 1 to contain as parts of a whole: *The new complex incorporates a theatre, cinema and restaurant* 2 to include, take account of: *The new text incorporates the author's changes*

incorporated *adjective* (*abbrev* **inc**) formed into a company or society

incorrect *adjective* wrong

incorrigible *adjective* too bad to be put right or reformed

incorruptible *adjective* **1** not able to be bribed **2** not likely to decay

increase *verb* (*pronounced* in-**krees**) to grow, make greater or more numerous ➤ *noun* (*pronounced* **in**-krees) **1** growth **2** the amount added by growth

increasing function *noun*, *maths* any function that results in a variable which was previously lower in value than a second variable becoming higher in value than the second variable (*contrasted with*: **decreasing function**)

increasingly *adverb* more and more

incredible *adjective* impossible to believe
◆ **incredibility** *noun* ◷ Comes from Latin *incredibilis* meaning 'beyond belief'

> ❗ Do not confuse: **incredible** and **incredulous**. **Incredible** means unbelievable. **Incredulous** means unbelieving. You might, for example, be **incredulous** at (= unable to believe) another person's **incredible** (= unbelievable) stupidity.

incredibly *adverb* extremely, unbelievably

incredulity (*pronounced* in-kred-**yool**-it-i) *noun* disbelief

incredulous (*pronounced* in-**kred**-yul-us) *adjective* not believing what is said
◆ **incredulously** *adverb* ◷ Comes from Latin *incredulus* meaning 'unbelieving'

increment *noun* **1** an annual increase in a salary **2** *maths* a small positive or negative change in the value of a variable

incriminate *verb* to show that (someone) has taken part in a crime

incubate *verb* **1** of birds: to brood, hatch (eggs) **2** of germs: to remain inactive in an organism before the first signs of a disease appear **3** to encourage (bacteria, germs, etc) to grow, eg in a culture medium in a laboratory

incubation period *noun* the time that it takes for a disease to develop from infection to the first symptoms

incubator *noun* **1** a large heated box for hatching eggs **2** a hospital crib for rearing premature babies

incudes plural of **incus**

incumbent *adjective* resting on (someone) as a duty: *it is incumbent upon me to warn you* ➤ *noun* someone who holds an official position

incur *verb* (**incurring, incurred**) to bring (blame, debt, etc) upon yourself

incurable *adjective* unable to be cured

incurious *adjective* not curious, uninterested

incursion *noun* an invasion, a raid: *incursions across the border*

incus *noun* (*plural* **incudes**– *pronounced* **ink**-yoo-deez) a small, anvil-shaped bone in the ear ◷ from Latin meaning 'anvil'

indebted *adjective* having reason to be grateful: *We are indebted to you for your kindness*

indecent *adjective* offending against normal or usual standards of (especially sexual) behaviour
◆ **indecency** *noun*

indecent assault *noun* an assault involving indecency but not rape

indecipherable *adjective* **1** illegible **2** incomprehensible

indecision *noun* slowness in making up your mind, hesitation

indecisive *adjective* **1** not coming to a definite result **2** unable to make up your mind

indecorous *adjective* unseemly, inappropriate
◆ **indecorum** *noun*

indeed *adverb* **1** in fact: *She is indeed a splendid cook* **2** (used for emphasis) really: *Did he indeed?* ➤ *interjection* expressing surprise, disbelief, irony, etc

indefatigable *adjective* untiring

indefensible *adjective* **1** unable to be defended **2** inexcusable

indefinable *adjective* not able to be stated or described clearly

indefinite *adjective* **1** not fixed, uncertain: *indefinite about her plans* **2** without definite limits: *an indefinite period of leave*

indefinite article *noun*, *grammar* the name given to the adjectives *a* and *an*

indefinite integral see **integral**

indefinitely *adverb* for an indefinite period of time

indelible *adjective* unable to be rubbed out or removed ◆ **indelibly** *adverb*

indelicate *adjective* tending to embarrass or offend ◆ **indelicacy** *noun*

indemnify *verb* (**indemnifies, indemnifying, indemnified**) **1** to compensate for loss **2** to exempt (from)

indemnity *noun* **1** security from damage or loss **2** compensation for loss

indent *verb* to begin a new paragraph by going in from the margin • **indent for** to apply for (stores, equipment, etc)

indentation *noun* **1** a hollow, a dent **2** an inward curve in an outline, coastline, etc

indenture *noun* a written agreement ➤ *verb*, *law* to bind by a written agreement

independent *adjective* **1** free to think or act for yourself **2** not relying on someone else for support, guidance, etc **3** of a country: self-governing **4** *maths* of a variable: not depending on another for its value ♦ **independence** *noun*

independent event *noun, maths* an event the probability of which is not affected by other events (*compare with*: **dependent event**)

independent variable *noun, maths* a variable in an equation, the value of which determines that of another variable (the **dependent variable**)

in-depth *adjective* thorough; exhaustive: *an in-depth interview*

indescribable *adjective* not able to be described

indestructible *adjective* not able to be destroyed

indeterminate *adjective* **1** not fixed, indefinite **2** *maths* of an equation: having more than one variable and an infinite number of possible solutions

index *noun* (*plural* **indexes**) **1** an alphabetical list giving the page number of subjects mentioned in a book **2** an indication **3** (*plural* **indices**) *maths* another word for **exponent** (meaning 2) **4** a numerical scale showing changes in the cost of living, wages, etc **5** *computing* a file containing the location of items of data

---

⊙ Comes from a Latin word meaning 'pointer', which later took on the meaning 'forefinger'

---

index finger *noun* the forefinger

index laws *noun, maths* the rules for multiplying and dividing index numbers, eg $3^a \times 3^b = 3^{a+b}$

index-linked *adjective* of pensions etc: directly related to the cost-of-living index

index notation *noun, maths* notation using indices, eg so that $3 \times 3 \times 3 = 3^3$

Indian corn *noun* maize

Indian ink *noun* a very black ink used by artists

Indian National Congress *noun, history* a political organization, founded in India in 1885, which led the movement for independence from Britain

Indian summer *noun* a period of sun and warm weather in autumn

india-rubber *noun* a rubber eraser

indicate *verb* **1** to point out, show **2** to use an indicator on a car: *She indicated right*

indication *noun* a sign

indicative *adjective* **1** pointing out, being a sign of: *indicative of his attitude* **2** of the mood of a verb: used to state facts, describe events or ask questions ➤ *noun* **1** the indicative mood **2** the indicative form of a verb

indicator *noun* **1** something which indicates; a pointer **2** a flashing light on either side of a vehicle for signalling to other drivers **3** *chemistry* a substance that changes colour depending on the acidity or alkalinity of a solution, and that indicates when a chemical reaction is complete

indicator species *noun* a species whose presence or absence in an ecosystem indicates the levels of a particular environmental factor in the system, or signifies its overall health

indices plural of **index** (meaning 3)

indict (*pronounced* in-**dait**) *verb* to accuse formally of a crime

indictment (*pronounced* in-**dait**-ment) *noun* **1** a formal or written accusation **2** an act of indicting someone **3** something which shows or proves how bad something else is

indie (*pronounced* **in**-di) *informal, noun* an independent record, film or television company ➤ *adjective* of a band: using an independent company to record their music

indifferent *adjective* **1** neither very good nor very bad **2** (**indifferent to**) showing no interest in ♦ **indifference** *noun* (meaning 2)

indigenous *adjective* native to a country or area: *the indigenous population/indigenous flora and fauna*

indigent *adjective* poor, impoverished ♦ **indigence** *noun*

indigestible *adjective* difficult to digest

indigestion *noun* discomfort or pain in the abdomen or lower part of the chest caused by difficulty in digesting food

indignant *adjective* angry, especially because of wrong done to yourself or others ♦ **indignation** *noun*

indignity *noun* (*plural* **indignities**) **1** loss of dignity **2** insult

indigo *noun* a purplish-blue colour ➤ *adjective* purplish-blue

indirect *adjective* **1** not straight or direct **2** not affecting or affected directly

indirect object *noun, grammar* a noun, phrase or pronoun which is affected indirectly by the action of a verb, usually standing for the person or thing to whom something is given or for whom something is done, eg *the dog* in *Give the dog a bone* (*compare with*: **direct object**)

indirect question *noun, grammar* a question reported in indirect speech, as in *They're asking who you are*

indirect speech or **reported speech** *noun* speech reported not in the speaker's actual words, eg *They said that they'd leave the next day* rather than *They said, 'We'll leave tomorrow'* (*contrasted with*: **direct speech**)

indirect tax *noun* a tax on particular goods, paid by the customer in the form of a higher price

indiscipline *noun* lack of discipline ♦ **indisciplined** *adjective*

indiscreet *adjective* **1** rash, not cautious **2**

giving away too much information

indiscretion *noun* a rash or unwise remark or act, rash or unwise behaviour

indiscriminate *adjective* making no distinction between one person (or thing) and another: *indiscriminate killing*

indispensable *adjective* not able to be done without, necessary

indisposed *adjective* unwell ♦ **indisposition** *noun*

indisputable *adjective* not able to be denied

indistinct *adjective* not clear to someone's eye, ear or mind

indistinguishable *adjective* 1 difficult to make out 2 too alike to tell apart

indium *noun, chemistry* (symbol **In**) a soft metallic element

individual *adjective* 1 relating to a single person or thing 2 distinctive, unusual: *a very individual style of writing* ➤ *noun* a single person or thing

individualist *noun* someone with an independent or distinctive lifestyle
♦ **individualism** *noun* ♦ **individualistic** *adjective*

individuality *noun* 1 separate existence 2 the quality of standing out from others

indivisible *adjective* not able to be divided

indoctrinate *verb* to teach (a person or group) to accept and believe a particular set of ideas or beliefs without criticizing them
♦ **indoctrination** *noun*

indolent *adjective* lazy ♦ **indolence** *noun*

indomitable *adjective* unconquerable, unyielding

indoor *adjective* done, happening, belonging, etc inside a building

indoors *adverb* in or into a building etc

indubitable *adjective* not to be doubted
♦ **indubitably** *adverb*

induce *verb* 1 to persuade: *Nothing could induce her to stay* 2 to bring on, cause 3 *medicine* in childbirth: to start or speed up (labour) by artificial means 4 *biology* to cause (an embryonic cell) to become specialized

inducement *noun* something which encourages or persuades: *Money is an inducement to work*

induct *verb* to introduce, install

induction *noun* 1 the formal installation of someone in a new post 2 the production of electricity in something by placing it near an electric source 3 the magnetization of something by placing it near a magnetic field 4 the drawing of conclusions from particular cases
♦ **inductive** *adjective* (meaning 3)

induction coil *noun, physics* a transformer that can produce a high-voltage alternating current from a low-voltage direct current

induction course *noun* a course of introductory training that is given to familiarize someone in a new job

inductive *adjective* using particular cases to draw logical conclusions

indulge *verb* 1 to be inclined to give in to the wishes of; spoil: *She indulges that child too much* 2 to give way to, not restrain: *indulging his sweet tooth*

indulgence *noun* 1 the act of indulging 2 a pardon for a sin

indulgent *adjective* not strict, kind

industrial *adjective* 1 related to or used in trade or manufacture 2 of a country: having highly developed industry

industrial action *noun, Brit* action taken by workers as a protest, eg a strike

industrial estate *noun* an area in a town which is developed for industry and business (*also called:* **trading estate**)

industrial inertia *noun, economics, geography* the failure of an industry to move from an area even when the reasons for being there have gone

industrialism *noun* a social system in which industry (rather than agriculture) forms the basis of commerce and the economy

industrialist *noun* someone who owns a large industrial organization or is involved in its management at a senior level

industrialize or **industrialise** *verb* 1 of a country: to develop industry 2 to introduce industry to (a country, region, etc)
♦ **industrialization** *noun*

industrial relations *plural noun* relations between management and workers

industrious *adjective* hard-working

industry *noun* (*plural* **industries**) 1 the business of producing goods: *He works in industry* 2 a branch of trade or manufacture: *the clothing industry* 3 steady attention to work

inebriated *adjective* drunk

inedible *adjective* not eatable

ineffective *adjective* useless, having no effect

ineffectual *adjective* achieving nothing

inefficient *adjective* 1 not efficient, not capable 2 wasting time, energy, etc ♦ **inefficiency** *noun* (*plural* **inefficiencies**)

inelegant *adjective* not graceful ♦ **inelegance** *noun*

ineligible *adjective* not qualified or not suitable to be chosen

inept *adjective* clumsy, badly done
♦ **ineptitude** *noun* ⊙ Comes from Latin *ineptus* meaning 'useless'

⚠ Do not confuse with: **inapt**

inequality *noun* (*plural* **inequalities**) 1 lack of

equality, unfairness **2** unevenness **3** *maths* a statement that two values are not equal

inequity *noun* (*plural* **inequities**) lack of fairness or equality

inert *adjective* **1** not moving or able to move **2** disinclined to move or act; indolent **3** not lively **4** chemically inactive

inert gas see **noble gas**

inertia *noun* **1** lack of energy or the will to move or act; indolence **2** *physics* the resistance of an object to a change in its state of motion eg when you try to stop a moving object, or to set a stationary object in motion **3** see **industrial inertia**

inescapable *adjective* unable to be avoided

inessential *adjective* not essential, unnecessary

inestimable *adjective* too great to be estimated

inevitable *adjective* not able to be avoided; certain to happen ◆ **inevitability** *noun*

inexact *adjective* not exact, approximate

inexcusable *adjective* too bad to be excused or justified

inexhaustible *adjective* very plentiful; not likely to be used up

inexorable *adjective* not able to be persuaded; relentless

inexpensive *adjective* cheap in price

inexperience *noun* lack of (skilled) knowledge or experience ◆ **inexperienced** *adjective*

inexpert *adjective* unskilled, amateurish

inexplicable *adjective* not able to be explained

inexplicit *adjective* not clear

inexpressible *adjective* not able to be described in words

inextricable *adjective* not able to be disentangled

infallible *adjective* **1** never making an error **2** certain to produce the desired result: *infallible cure* ◆ **infallibility** *noun*

infamous *adjective* having a very bad reputation; notorious, disgraceful

infamy *noun* public disgrace, notoriety

infancy *noun* **1** early childhood, babyhood **2** the beginning of anything: *when psychiatry was in its infancy*

infant *noun* a baby

infanticide *noun* **1** the murder of a child **2** a child murderer

infantile *adjective* **1** of babies **2** childish

infant mortality rate *noun* the number of deaths in the first year of life per thousand inhabitants in a given area

infantry *noun* foot-soldiers

infarction *noun* the death of body tissue as a result of the blocking of its blood supply

infatuated *adjective* filled with foolish, intense love ◆ **infatuation** *noun*

infect *verb* **1** to contaminate (water, food, etc) with disease-causing pollutants **2** to pass on disease-causing micro-organisms to (a living organism) **3** to pass on, spread (eg enthusiasm) **4** *computing* to contaminate with a virus

infection *noun* **1** the invasion of a living organism by disease-causing micro-organisms **2** a disease caused by such a micro-organism, which can be spread to others **3** something that spreads widely and affects many people

infectious *adjective* **1** of a disease: caused by micro-organisms, and able to be transmitted by air, water, bodily fluids, etc (*compare with*: **contagious**) **2** likely to spread from person to person: *Her laugh is so infectious*

infelicitous *adjective* unfortunate, inappropriate: *an infelicitous remark*

infer *verb* (**inferring, inferred**) to reach a conclusion from facts or reasoning: *Am I to infer from what you say that you wish to resign?* ◷ Comes from Latin *inferre* meaning 'to bring in'

! **Infer** is sometimes used to mean 'imply' or 'suggest': *'Are you inferring that I'm a liar?'*, but this use is considered incorrect by some people.

inference *noun* a conclusion that you reach, based on information which you have been given

inferior *adjective* **1** lower in any way **2** not of best quality ► *noun* someone lower in rank etc ◆ **inferiority** *noun*

inferiority complex *noun* a constant feeling that you are less good in some way than other people

infernal *adjective* **1** belonging or relating to hell **2** *informal* annoying, blasted

inferno *noun* **1** hell **2** (*plural* **infernos**) a raging fire

infertile *adjective* **1** of soil: not producing much **2** not able to bear children or young ◆ **infertility** *noun*

infest *verb* to swarm over: *infested with lice* ◆ **infestation** *noun*

infidel *noun* someone who does not believe in a particular religion (especially Christianity or Islam)

infidelity *noun* unfaithfulness, disloyalty

infield *noun* **1** the land on a farm which is closest to the farm buildings **2** *cricket* the area of the field close to the wicket **3** *baseball* the diamond-shaped area of the pitch enclosed by the four bases **4** *cricket, baseball* the players who have positions in these areas (*compare with*: **outfield**) ◆ **infielder** *noun*

infighting *noun* rivalry or quarrelling between members of the same group

infiltrate *verb* **1** to enter (an organization etc) secretly to spy or cause damage **2** *geography* of precipitation: to filter into the ground through the pores of the soil **3** of a mineral dissolved in water: to become deposited among (the pores or grains of a rock) ♦ **infiltration** *noun*

infinite *adjective* **1** without end or limit **2** *maths* of a number, series, etc: having an unlimited number of elements, digits or terms

infinitely *adverb* very much: *Your work is infinitely better now*

infinitesimal *adjective* absolutely tiny

infinitive *noun, grammar* the form of a verb which expresses the action but not person, place or time, often written as *to* + the base form, eg *I hate to lose*

ⓘ If you put an adverb between *to* and the base form you get a **split infinitive**:
You have to quickly think of a number.
Although many people think this is incorrect, these days most tend to be more relaxed about its use.

infinity *noun* **1** space or time without end **2** *maths* (*symbol* ∞) a number that is larger than any finite value, that can be approached but never reached

infirm *adjective* feeble, weak

infirmary *noun* (*plural* **infirmaries**) a hospital

infirmity *noun* (*plural* **infirmities**) **1** a physical weakness **2** a character flaw

inflame *verb* **1** to make hot or red **2** to arouse passion in ♦ **inflamed** *adjective*

inflammable *adjective* **1** easily set on fire **2** easily excited

ⓘ Note that **inflammable** (meaning 1) and **flammable** are not opposites – they mean the same thing.

inflammation *noun* heat in a part of the body, with pain, redness and swelling

inflammatory *adjective* arousing passion (especially anger)

inflatable *adjective* able to be inflated for use ► *noun* an inflatable object

inflate *verb* **1** to blow up (a balloon, tyre, etc) **2** to puff up (with pride), exaggerate: *an inflated sense of her own importance* **3** to increase to a great extent

inflation *noun* **1** the act of inflating **2** an economic situation in which prices and wages keep forcing each other to increase

inflect *verb* **1** to change the tone of (your voice) **2** to vary the endings of (a word) to show tense, number, gender, etc

inflection *noun* **1** change in the tone of your voice **2** a change in the basic form of a word to show tense, number, etc **3** the new form of a word which has been changed in this way: *The inflections of the verb 'find' are: 'finds', 'finding' and 'found'* **4** *maths* a change in a curve from being convex to concave, or vice versa (at the **point of inflection** or **inflection point**) ♦ **inflectional** *adjective*

inflexible *adjective* **1** not yielding, unbending **2** unable to change or be changed ♦ **inflexibility** *noun*

inflict *verb* to bring down (blows, punishment, etc) on ♦ **infliction** *noun*

in-flight *adjective* happening or used during an air flight: *in-flight movie*

inflorescence *noun, botany* the complete head of a flowering plant

inflow *noun* a flowing in, influx

influence *noun* the power to affect other people or things ► *verb* to have power over ♦ **influential** *adjective*

influenza *noun* an infectious illness with fever, headache, muscle pains, etc

influx *noun* **1** a flowing in **2** the arrival of large numbers of people

info *noun, informal* information

inform *verb* **1** to give knowledge to **2** (**inform on** or **against**) to give incriminating evidence about someone to the authorities

informal *adjective* not formal; relaxed, friendly ♦ **informality** *noun*

informal sector *noun* the section of the working population that is unofficially employed, therefore not paying tax on earnings

informal settlement another term for a **shantytown**

informant *noun* someone who informs

information *noun* knowledge, news

information technology *noun* (*abbrev* **IT**) the development and use of computer systems and applications

informative *adjective* giving information

informer *noun* someone who gives information to the police or authorities

infra- *prefix* below, beneath: *infrasound* ⊙ Comes from Latin *infra* meaning 'below' or 'underneath'

infraction *noun, formal* a violation, a breaking of a law, rule, etc

infra-red *adjective* of rays of heat: with wavelengths longer than visible light

infrasound *noun* a sound whose frequency is too low to be heard by humans

infrastructure *noun* **1** inner structure, framework **2** a system of communications and services that supports industrial, commercial, military, etc operations

infrequent *adjective* rare, happening seldom

infringe *verb* to break (a rule or law)
♦ **infringement** *noun*

infuriate *verb* to drive into a rage

infuriating *adjective* extremely annoying

infuse *verb* of herbs, tea: to soak or be soaked in hot water to release flavour • **infuse someone with** to inspire or fill someone with (a positive feeling, desire, etc)

infusion *noun* **1** the act of infusing **2** a tea formed by steeping a herb etc in water

ingenious (*pronounced* in-**jeen**-i-us) *adjective* **1** skilful in inventing **2** cleverly thought out

! Do not confuse with: **ingenuous**.
It may help you remember which is which if you link the adjective **ingenuous** with the noun **ingénue** (= a naive young girl).

ingénue (*pronounced* an-szei-**noo**) *noun* a naive young girl

ingenuity *from* **ingenious** *noun* cleverness; quickness of ideas

ingenuous (*pronounced* in-**jen**-yoo-us) *adjective* frank; without cunning

! Do not confuse with: **ingenious**.

ingest *verb* to take (food, liquid, etc) into the body

ingot *noun* a block of metal (especially gold or silver) cast in a mould

ingrained *adjective* deeply fixed: *ingrained laziness/ingrained dirt*

ingratiate *verb* to work your way into someone's favour by flattery etc ♦ **ingratiating** *adjective*

ingratitude *noun* lack of gratitude or thankfulness

ingredient *noun* one of the things of which a mixture is made

ingrown *adjective* of a nail: growing into the flesh

inhabit *verb* to live in

inhabitant *noun* someone who lives permanently in a place

inhalant *noun* a medicine which is inhaled

inhalation *noun* **1** the act of inhaling **2** a medicine which is inhaled

inhale *verb* to breathe in

inhaler *noun* a small, portable device for breathing in medicine, steam, etc

inhere *verb* of character, a quality: to be an essential or permanent part

inherent *adjective* inborn, being a natural, essential or permanent part

inherit *verb* **1** to receive property, a title, etc as an heir **2** to get (a characteristic) from your parents etc: *She inherits her sense of humour from her father*

inheritance *noun* something received by will when someone dies

inheritor *noun* an heir

inhibit *verb* to hold back, prevent

inhibited *adjective* unable to express your feelings

inhibition *noun* a holding back of natural impulses etc, restraint

inhospitable *adjective* unwelcoming, unfriendly

in-house *adjective, adverb* within a particular company, organization, etc: *an in-house translator/working in-house*

inhuman *adjective* not human; brutal
♦ **inhumanity** *noun*

inhumane *adjective* cruel

inimical *adjective, formal* **1** tending to discourage, unfavourable **2** not friendly, in opposition ⊙ Comes from Latin *inimicalis*, from *inimicus* meaning 'enemy'

inimitable *adjective* impossible to imitate

iniquitous *adjective* unjust; wicked

iniquity *noun* (*plural* **iniquities**) wickedness; a sin

initial *adjective* of or at the beginning: *initial difficulties* ➤ *noun* the letter beginning a word, especially someone's name ➤ *verb* (**initialling, initialled**) to sign with the initials of your name

initially *adverb* at first: *Initially, I did not like her*

initiate *verb* **1** to begin, start: *initiate the reforms* **2** to give first lessons to **3** to make someone formally a member of a society etc ♦ **initiation** *noun* (meanings 1 and 3)

initiative *noun* **1** the right to take the first step **2** readiness to take a lead

inject *verb* **1** to force (a fluid etc) into the veins or muscles with a syringe **2** to put (eg enthusiasm) into ♦ **injection** *noun*

in-joke *noun* a joke only understood by a particular group

injudicious *adjective* unwise

injunction *noun* an official order or command

injure *verb* to harm, damage, wrong

injured *adjective* hurt; offended

injurious *adjective* causing injury or damage

injury *noun* (*plural* **injuries**) **1** hurt, damage, harm **2** a wrong

injustice *noun* **1** unfairness **2** a wrong

ink *noun* **1** a coloured liquid used in writing, printing, etc **2** a dark liquid ejected by some cephalopods, eg squid and octopus ➤ *verb* to mark with ink

inkjet printer *noun, computing* a printer which produces characters by spraying a fine jet of ink

inkling *noun* a hint or slight sign

inky *adjective* (**inkier, inkiest**) **1** of or covered in ink **2** very dark

inlaid past form of **inlay**

inland *adjective* **1** not beside the sea **2** happening inside a country ➤ *adverb* towards the inner part of a country

inland revenue *noun* taxes etc collected within a country

in-laws *plural noun, informal* relatives by marriage

inlay *noun* decoration made by fitting pieces of different shapes and colours into a background ➤ *verb* (**inlaying, inlaid**) to fit into a background as decoration ♦ **inlaid** *adjective*

inlet *noun* a small bay

inmate *noun* a resident, an occupant (especially of an institution): *the inmates of the prison*

inmost *adjective* the most inward, the farthest in

inn *noun* a public house or small hotel in the country

innards *plural noun* **1** internal parts **2** entrails

innate *adjective* inborn, natural

inner *adjective* **1** farther in **2** of feelings etc: hidden

inner city *noun* the central area of a city where it is densely populated and poor, with bad housing etc ➤ *adjective* of this area: *inner-city housing*

innermost *adjective* farthest in; most secret

innings *singular noun* **1** a team's turn for batting in cricket **2** a turn, a go at something

innkeeper *noun* someone who keeps an inn

innocent *adjective* **1** not guilty, blameless **2** having no experience of how unpleasant people, and life in general, can be, and therefore tending to trust everyone **3** harmless **4** (**innocent of**) lacking, without ♦ **innocence** *noun* (meanings 1 and 2)

innocuous *adjective* not harmful or offensive

innovate *verb* to make changes or introduce new ideas, methods, etc ♦ **innovative** or **innovatory** *adjective* ♦ **innovator** *noun* ⊙ Comes from Latin *innovare* meaning 'to renew'

innovation *noun* something new

innuendo *noun* (*plural* **innuendoes**) **1** an indirectly unpleasant or critical reference, eg about someone's character **2** a rude or dirty insinuation

innumerable *adjective* too many to be counted

innumerate *adjective* not understanding arithmetic or mathematics ♦ **innumeracy** *noun*

inoculate *verb, medicine* to produce a mild form of a disease (in a person or animal) so they produce antibodies against it ♦ **inoculation** *noun*

inoffensive *adjective* harmless, giving no offence

inoperable *adjective, medicine* of a disease or condition: not able to be treated by surgery

inoperative *adjective* not active, not working

inopportune *adjective* at a bad or inconvenient time

inordinate *adjective* going beyond the limit, unreasonably great

inorganic *adjective* **1** not of animal or vegetable origin **2** of a chemical compound: not containing carbon

in-patient *noun* a patient who stays in a hospital during their treatment (*contrasted with*: **out-patient**)

input *noun* **1** an amount (of energy, labour, etc) put into something **2** *computing* data fed into a computer (*contrasted with*: **output**) ➤ *adjective* concerned with input: *input device* ➤ *verb* to enter (data) into a computer

inquest *noun* a legal inquiry into a case of sudden death

inquire or **enquire** *verb* to ask

inquiring or **enquiring** *adjective* questioning, curious: *inquiring mind*

inquiry or **enquiry** *noun* (*plural* **inquiries** or **enquiries**) **1** a question; a search for information **2** an official investigation

inquisition *noun* a careful questioning or investigation

inquisitive *adjective* **1** very curious **2** fond of prying, nosy ♦ **inquisitively** *adverb*

inquisitor *noun* an official investigator

inroad *noun* a raid, an advance ● **make inroads into** to use up large amounts of: *The holiday made inroads into their savings*

insane *adjective* mad, not sane ♦ **insanity** *noun*

insanitary *adjective* not sanitary; encouraging the spread of disease

insatiable *adjective* not able to be satisfied: *insatiable appetite*

inscribe *verb* **1** to write or engrave (eg a name) on a book, monument, etc **2** *maths* to draw (a figure) inside another figure so that they touch at as many points as possible but do not intersect (*compare with*: **circumscribe**)

inscribed *adjective, maths* of a figure: enclosed by another figure

inscription *noun* the writing on a book, monument, etc

inscrutable *adjective* not able to be understood, mysterious

insect *noun* a small six-legged creature with wings and a body divided into sections

insecticide *noun* powder or liquid for killing insects

insectivore *noun* an animal or plant which feeds on insects ♦ **insectivorous** *adjective*

insecure *adjective* **1** not safe; not firm **2** lacking confidence, not feeling settled ✦ **insecurity** *noun*

inselberg *noun* (*plural* **inselberge**), *geography* a steep-sided hill rising from a plain, often found in the semi-arid regions of tropical countries ☉ Comes from German, from *Insel* meaning 'island' + *Berg* meaning 'mountain'

inseminate *verb* **1** to plant, introduce (into) **2** to impregnate, especially artificially ✦ **insemination** *noun*

insensible *adjective* **1** unconscious, unaware (of) **2** not having feeling

insensitive *adjective* **1** (**insensitive to**) not feeling: *insensitive to cold* **2** unsympathetic (to): *insensitive to her grief* **3** unappreciative, crass ✦ **insensitivity** *noun*

inseparable *adjective* not able to be separated or kept apart ✦ **inseparably** *adverb*

insert *verb* (*pronounced* in-**sert**) to put in or among ➤ *noun* (*pronounced* **in**-sert) **1** a special feature added to a television programme etc **2** a separate leaflet or pull-out section in a magazine etc ✦ **insertion** *noun*

in-service *adjective* happening as part of someone's work: *in-service training*

inset *noun* **1** an insert **2** a small picture, map, etc in a corner of a larger one

inshore *adjective & adverb* in or on the water but near or towards the shore

inside *noun* **1** the inner side, space or part **2** indoors ➤ *adjective* **1** being on or in the inside **2** indoor **3** coming from or done by someone within an organization: *inside information* ➤ *adverb* to, in or on the inside ➤ *preposition* to the inside of; within

inside out *adverb* **1** with the inside surface on the outside: *Your jumper's inside out* **2** thoroughly, completely: *He knows his subject inside out*

insider *noun* a member of an organization or group who has access to confidential information about it

insidious *adjective* **1** likely to trap those who are not careful, treacherous **2** of a disease: coming on gradually and unnoticed

insight *noun* the ability to gain a relatively rapid, clear understanding of a complex situation, problem, etc

insignia *plural noun* signs or badges showing that someone holds an office, award, etc

insignificant *adjective* of little importance ✦ **insignificance** *noun*

insincere *adjective* not sincere ✦ **insincerity** *noun*

insinuate *verb* **1** to hint (at a fault) indirectly **2** to put in gradually and secretly **3** to work yourself into (someone's favour etc)

insinuation *noun* a sly hint

insipid *adjective* **1** dull, without liveliness **2** tasteless, bland

insist *verb* **1** to urge something strongly: *insist on punctuality* **2** to refuse to give way, hold firmly to your intentions: *He insists on walking there* **3** to go on saying (that): *She insists that she saw a UFO*

insistent *adjective* **1** insisting on having or doing something **2** forcing you to pay attention ✦ **insistence** *noun* (meaning 1) ✦ **insistently** *adverb* (meaning 1)

in situ *adverb & adjective* in position, in place

insolation *noun* the amount of solar radiation on a surface

insolent *adjective* rude, impertinent, insulting ✦ **insolence** *noun*

insoluble *adjective* **1** not able to be dissolved **2** of a problem: not able to be solved ✦ **insolubility** *noun*

insolvent *adjective* not able to pay your debts, impoverished ✦ **insolvency** *noun*

insomnia *noun* sleeplessness

insomniac *noun* someone who suffers from insomnia

inspect *verb* **1** to look carefully into, examine **2** to look over (troops etc) ceremonially

inspection *noun* careful examination

inspector *noun* **1** an official who inspects **2** a police officer below a superintendent and above a sergeant in rank

inspectorate *noun* a body of inspectors

inspiration *noun* **1** something or someone that influences or encourages others **2** a brilliant idea **3** breathing in

inspirational *adjective* inspiring, brilliant

inspire *verb* **1** to encourage, rouse **2** to be the source of creative ideas **3** to breathe in

inspired *adjective* **1** seeming to be aided by higher powers **2** brilliantly good

instability *noun* lack of steadiness or stability

install or **instal** *verb* (**installs** or **instals, installing, installed**) **1** to place in position, ready for use: *Has the telephone been installed?* **2** to introduce formally to a new job etc ✦ **installation** *noun*

instalment *noun* **1** a part of a sum of money paid at fixed times until the whole amount is paid **2** one part of a serial story

instance *noun* an example, a particular case ➤ *verb* to mention as an example ● **at the instance of** at the request of ● **for instance** for example

instant *adjective* **1** immediate, urgent **2** able to be prepared almost immediately: *instant coffee* ➤ *noun* **1** a very short time, a moment **2** point or moment of time: *I need it this instant*

instantaneous *adjective* done or happening very quickly

instantly *adverb* immediately

instar *noun, biology* the form of an insect between two successive moults, before it has become fully mature

instead *adverb* in place of someone or something: *You can go instead* • **instead of** in place of

instep *noun* the arching, upper part of the foot

instigate *verb* to stir up, encourage

instigation *noun*: **at someone's instigation** following that person's instructions or wishes

instil or **instill** *verb* (**instils** or **instills, instilling, instilled**) to put in little by little (especially ideas into the mind)

instinct *noun* a natural feeling or knowledge which someone has without thinking and without being taught

instinctive *adjective* due to instinct

institute *verb* to set up, establish, start ➤ *noun* a society, organization, etc or the building it uses

institution *noun* **1** an organization, building, etc established for a particular purpose (especially care or education) **2** an established custom ♦ **institutional** *adjective*

institutionalize or **institutionalise** *verb* **1** to confine in an institution **2** to make an established custom of

institutionalized or **institutionalised** *adjective* of a person: unable to think and act as an individual, and overdependent on routine, as a result of living in an institution for too long

instruct *verb* **1** to teach **2** to direct, command ♦ **instructor** *noun*

instruction *noun* **1** teaching **2** a command **3** (**instructions**) rules showing how something is to be used

instructive *adjective* containing or giving information or knowledge

instrument *noun* **1** something used for a particular purpose, a tool **2** a device for producing musical sounds, eg a piano, a harp

instrumental *adjective* **1** helpful in bringing (something) about **2** written for or played by musical instruments, without voice accompaniment ➤ *noun* a piece of music written for or played by musical instruments, without voice accompaniment

instrumentalist *noun* someone who plays on a musical instrument

instrumentation *noun* **1** the particular way in which a piece of music is written or arranged to be played **2** the instruments used to play a particular piece of music

insubordinate *adjective* rebellious, disobedient ♦ **insubordination** *noun*

insufferable *adjective* too annoying, unpleasant, etc to be endured

insufficient *adjective* not enough ♦ **insufficiency** *noun*

insular *adjective* **1** of an island or islands **2** narrow-minded, prejudiced ♦ **insularity** *noun*

insulate *verb* **1** to cover with a material that will not let through electrical currents, heat, frost, etc **2** to cut off, isolate ♦ **insulation** *noun*

insulator *noun* a material that will not let through electrical currents, heat, etc

insulin *noun, medicine* a hormone which controls the concentration of sugar in the blood and is used in the treatment of diabetes

🕐 Based on the Latin word for 'island', because insulin is secreted by the *islets* of Langerhans

insult *verb* to treat with scorn or rudeness ➤ *noun* a rude or scornful remark

insulting *adjective* scornful, rude

insuperable *adjective* too difficult to be overcome or dealt with successfully

insurance *noun* **1** an agreement by which a company promises to pay a person, organization, etc money in the event of loss, theft, damage to property, injury or death **2** the protection this agreement provides **3** the sum of money which will be paid according to such an agreement

insure *verb* to arrange for payment of a sum of money on (something) if it should be lost, damaged, stolen, etc ♦ **insurer** *noun*

❗ Do not confuse with: **ensure**

insured *noun, law* the person whose life, health or property is covered by insurance

insurgent *adjective* rising up in rebellion ➤ *noun* a rebel ♦ **insurgency** *noun*

insurmountable *adjective* not able to be got over or dealt with

insurrection *noun* an act of rebellion against authority

intact *adjective* whole, unbroken

intake *noun* an amount of people or things taken in: *this year's intake of students*

intangible *adjective* **1** not able to be felt by touch **2** difficult to define or describe, not clear

integer *noun, maths* any positive or negative whole number or zero, as opposed to a fraction

integral *adjective* **1** of or essential to a whole: *an integral part of the machine* **2** made up of parts forming a whole **3** *maths* being or involving an integer ➤ *noun, maths* the sum of a large number of small quantities, either between definite limits (a **definite integral**) or without limits (an **indefinite integral**)

integral calculus *noun, maths* the branch of calculus concerned with finding integrals and applying them to find eg the solution of differential equations, the areas enclosed by curves, etc (*see also*: **integration**)

integrand *noun, maths* a function that is to be integrated

integrate *verb* **1** to fit parts together to form a whole **2** to enable (racial groups) to mix freely and live on equal terms **3** *maths* to use the process of integration to find the integral of (a function or variable) **4** *maths* to find the total or mean value of (a variable)

integrated circuit *noun* interconnected electronic components etched on to a tiny piece of a semiconductor such as silicon (*also called:* **chip**)

integration *noun* **1** the process of integrating **2** *maths* a method used in calculus of determining the sum of a large number of infinitely small quantities, ie finding the integral of a function or variable, used to calculate the area under a curve (*compare with:* **differentiation**)

integrity *noun* **1** honesty **2** wholeness, completeness

integument *noun, biology* a protective outer layer or coat

intellect *noun* **1** the thinking power of the mind **2** the capacity to use this **3** someone of great mental ability

intellectual *adjective* **1** involving or requiring intellect **2** having a highly developed ability to think, reason and understand ➤ *noun* someone of natural ability or with academic interests

intellectual property *noun, law* property, such as copyright, trademarks, etc, that is the product of creative work

intelligence *noun* **1** mental ability **2** information sent, news **3** the gathering of secret information about an enemy

intelligent *adjective* **1** clever, quick at understanding **2** of a machine, computer, etc: able to change its behaviour according to the situation

intelligentsia *noun* the intellectuals within a particular society

intelligible *adjective* able to be understood

intemperate *adjective* **1** going beyond reasonable limits, uncontrolled **2** tending to drink too much alcohol ♦ **intemperance** *noun*

intend *verb* to mean or plan (to do something)

intense *adjective* **1** very great **2** tending to feel emotions deeply ♦ **intensely** *adverb*

intensifier *noun, grammar* a word that adds emphasis to another word, eg *very* good, *extremely* difficult

intensify *verb* (**intensifies, intensifying, intensified**) to increase, make more concentrated

intensity *noun* (*plural* **intensities**) strength, eg of feeling, colour, energy, etc

intensive *adjective* very thorough, concentrated

intensive care *noun* a unit in a hospital where the condition of a patient who is critically ill is carefully monitored

intensive farming *noun, geography* a method of farming using large amounts of labour or capital to obtain the maximum yield from a limited area of land

intent *noun* purpose ➤ *adjective* **1** with all your concentration (on), attentive **2** determined (to)

intention *noun* **1** what someone means to do, an aim **2** meaning

intentional *adjective* done on purpose ♦ **intentionally** *adverb*

inter (*pronounced* in-**ter**) *verb* (**interring, interred**) to bury ⊙ Comes from Latin *in* meaning 'into', and *terra* meaning 'the earth'

inter- *prefix* between, among, together: *intermingle/interplanetary* ⊙ Comes from Latin *inter* meaning 'between', 'among' or 'mutually'

interact *verb* to act on one another ♦ **interaction** *noun*

interactive *adjective* allowing two-way communication, eg between a computer or television and its user

interactive whiteboard *noun* a display board which responds to input and on which computer output can be projected

interbreed *verb* (**interbreeding, interbred**) to breed within a single family, often in order to control the appearance of particular characteristics in the offspring

intercede *verb* to act as peacemaker between two people, nations, etc ♦ **intercession** *noun*

intercellular *adjective, biology* between cells

intercept *verb* **1** to stop or catch (a person, missile, etc) on their way from one place to another **2** to cut off, interrupt (a view, the light, etc) **3** *maths* to cut a line, plane, etc with another line, plane, etc that crosses it **4** *geography* of a plant, building, etc: to collect precipitation ➤ *noun, maths* the part of a line or plane that is cut off by another line or plane crossing it ♦ **interception** *noun*

interchange *verb* **1** to put each in the place of the other **2** to alternate ➤ *noun* **1** the act of interchanging **2** a junction of two or more major roads on separate levels

interchangeable *adjective* able to be used one for the other

intercom *noun* a telephone system within a building, aeroplane, etc

interconnect *verb* to join or link together ♦ **interconnection** *noun*

intercostal *noun* between the ribs

intercourse *noun* **1** communication **2** dealings between people etc **3** sexual intercourse

interdependent *adjective* depending on one another ♦ **interdependence** *noun*

interdict *noun* an order forbidding something

interest *noun* **1** special attention, curiosity **2** someone's personal concern or field of study **3** advantage, benefit **4** a sum paid for the loan of money ➤ *verb* to catch or hold the attention of

interested *adjective* having or taking an interest

interesting *adjective* holding the attention

interest rate *noun* a charge made for borrowing money, usually shown as a percentage of the amount borrowed

interface *noun, computing* **1** a connection between two parts of the same system **2** the connection between a computer and a user

interfere *verb* **1** (**interfere in**) to take part in what is not your business, meddle in **2** (**interfere with**) to get in the way of, hinder, have a harmful effect on: *interfering with her work* **3** *physics* of sound waves etc: to combine together to cause disturbance

interference *noun* **1** the act of interfering **2** *physics* the interaction between two or more waves of the same frequency **3** the spoiling of radio or television reception by another station or disturbance from traffic etc

interferon *noun* a protein that is capable of preventing a virus from multiplying

interim *noun* time between; the meantime ➤ *adjective* temporary

interior *adjective* **1** inner **2** inside a building **3** inland ➤ *noun* **1** the inside of anything **2** the inland part of a country

interior angle *noun, maths* an angle inside a polygon, at a vertex

interject *verb* **1** to make a sudden remark in a conversation **2** to exclaim

interjection *noun* a word or phrase of exclamation, eg *Ah!* or *Oh dear!*

interlock *verb* **1** to lock or clasp together **2** to fit into each other

interloper *noun* someone who enters without permission, an intruder

interlude *noun* **1** an interval **2** a short piece of music played between the parts of a play, film, etc

intermarry *verb* **1** to marry with members of another race etc **2** to marry with members of the same group, race, etc

intermediary *noun* (*plural* **intermediaries**) someone who mediates between two people, for example in trying to settle a quarrel

intermediate *adjective* in the middle; coming between two points, stages or extremes ➤ *noun* **1** an intermediate thing **2** a short-lived chemical compound formed during the middle of a series of chemical reactions

intermediate technology *noun* technology which combines basic materials with modern tools and methods, often appropriate for a developing country (*see also:* **appropriate technology**)

interment *noun* a burial

! Do not confuse with: **internment**

interminable *adjective* never-ending, boringly long

intermingle *verb* to mix together

intermission *noun* an interval, a pause

intermittent *adjective* stopping every now and then and starting again

intern *verb* (*pronounced* in-**tern**) to keep (someone from an enemy country) prisoner during a war ➤ *noun* (*pronounced* **in**-tern) *US* an advanced student or graduate who gains practical experience by working, eg in a hospital

internal *adjective* **1** of the inner part, especially of the body **2** inside, within a country, organization, etc: *internal affairs*

internal-combustion engine *noun* an engine that produces power by the burning of fuel and air within an enclosed space

internalize or **internalise** *verb* **1** to make (a characteristic, behaviour, etc) part of your personality **2** to keep (an emotion etc) inside yourself rather than express it

internal market *noun, business* a system where units within an organization behave as though they were in economic competition with each other

internal rhyme *noun* a rhyme occurring inside a line of verse

international *adjective* **1** happening between nations **2** concerning more than one nation **3** worldwide ➤ *noun* a sports match between teams of two countries

internee *noun* someone from an enemy country who is confined as a prisoner during a war

Internet *noun* an international computer network linking users through telephone lines

Internet service provider *noun* (*abbrev* **ISP**) a company or organization that provides access to the Internet

internment *noun* confinement within a country or prison, especially during a war ℭ Comes from French *interne* meaning 'internal'

! Do not confuse with: **interment**

internode *noun, botany* the part of a plant stem between two successive leaves or branches

interoperable *adjective, computing* of hardware or software systems: able to exchange and use information from different computer systems ✦ **interoperability** *noun*

interphase *noun, biology* the period between successive divisions by mitosis of a cell

interplanetary *adjective* between planets

interplay *noun* the action and influence of two or more things on each other

interpolate *verb* **1** to add words to a book or document **2** to interrupt someone speaking (with a comment etc) **3** *maths* to estimate (the value of a function) between values that are already known ♦ **interpolation** *noun*

interpose *verb* **1** to place or come between **2** to make (a remark etc) which interrupts someone

interpret *verb* **1** to explain the meaning of something **2** to translate **3** to bring out the meaning of (music, a part in a play, etc) in performance **4** to take the meaning of something to be ♦ **interpretation** *noun*

interpreter *noun* **1** someone who translates (on the spot) the words of a speaker into another language **2** *computing* a program that translates and executes a program written in a high-level language one line at a time

interquartile range *noun, statistics* the difference between the first and third quartile values of quantitative data, used as a measure of spread

interracial *adjective* between different races of people

interregnum *noun* the time between the end of one reign and the beginning of the next

interrogate *verb* **1** to examine by asking questions **2** *computing* to transmit a request to a device or program ♦ **interrogation** *noun* ♦ **interrogator** *noun*

interrogative *noun* a word used in asking a question, eg who? where? ► *adjective* questioning

interrupt *verb* **1** to stop (someone) while they are saying or doing something **2** to stop doing (something) **3** to get in the way of, cut off (a view etc) ♦ **interruption** *noun*

intersect *verb* **1** of lines: to meet and cross **2** *maths* to have a common point or points

intersection *noun* **1** the point where two lines cross **2** a crossroads **3** *maths* a point or points common to two or more figures **4** *maths* a set of members common to two or more sets

intersex *noun, biology* an individual with characteristics of both sexes

intersperse *verb* to scatter here and there in ♦ **interspersion** *noun*

intertropical convergence zone *noun, geography* (*abbrev* **ITCZ**) an area of converging trade winds near the equator

intertwine *verb* to twine or twist together

interval *noun* **1** a time or space between two things **2** a short pause in a programme etc **3** *maths* a set of real numbers or points between two given numbers or points

interval training *noun, athletics* alternate fast and slow running, done as training for long-distance races

intervene *verb* **1** to come or be between, or in the way **2** to join in (in order to stop) a fight or quarrel between other persons or nations ♦ **intervention** *noun*

interventionism *noun* the belief that the government of a country should interfere in the economic affairs of the country, or in the affairs of other countries ♦ **interventionist** *noun & adjective*

interview *noun* a formal meeting of one person with others to apply for a job, give information to the media etc ► *verb* **1** to ask questions etc of in an interview **2** to conduct an interview

interweave *verb* (**interwove, interwoven**) to weave or be woven together

intestate *adjective, law* of a person: not having made a valid will before their death

intestines *plural noun* the inside parts of the body, especially the bowels and passages leading to them ♦ **intestinal** *adjective*

intifada (*pronounced* in-ti-**fa**-da) *noun* the uprising in 1987 and continued resistance by Palestinians to Israeli occupation of the Gaza Strip and West Bank of the Jordan ⊙ Comes from Arabic meaning 'shaking off'

intimacy *noun* (*plural* **intimacies**) **1** close friendship **2** familiarity **3** sexual intercourse

intimate *adjective* (*pronounced* in-tim-at) **1** knowing a lot about, familiar (with) **2** of friends: very close **3** private, personal: *intimate details* **4** having a sexual relationship (with) ► *noun* (*pronounced* in-tim-at) a close friend ► *verb* (*pronounced* in-tim-eit) **1** to hint **2** to announce ♦ **intimately** *adverb*

intimation *noun* **1** a hint **2** announcement

intimidate *verb* to frighten or threaten into submission ♦ **intimidating** *adjective* ♦ **intimidation** *noun*

into *preposition* **1** to the inside: *into the room* **2** towards: *into the millennium* **3** to a different state: *a tadpole changes into a frog* **4** *maths* expressing the idea of division: *2 into 4 goes twice*

intolerable *adjective* too bad, painful, etc to be endured

intolerant *adjective* not willing to put up with (people of different ideas, religion, etc) ♦ **intolerance** *noun*

intonation *noun* the rise and fall of the voice

intone *verb* to speak in a singing manner, chant: *monks intoning a prayer*

intoxicant *noun* a strong alcoholic drink

intoxicate *verb* **1** to make drunk **2** to enthuse, excite

⊙ Literally, to affect with arrow-poison

intoxication *noun* drunkenness

intra- *prefix* within: *intramural* ☉ Comes from Latin *intra* meaning 'within'

intracellular *adjective, biology* within cells

intractable *adjective* difficult, stubborn
♦ **intractability** *noun*

intramural *adjective* **1** amongst the people in an institution, especially a school, college or university **2** within the scope of normal studies
♦ **intramurally** *adverb*

intranet *noun, computing* a restricted network of computers, eg in a company

intransigent *adjective* refusing to change or come to an agreement ♦ **intransigence** *noun*

intransitive *adjective, grammar* of a verb: not needing an object, eg to *go*, to *fall*

intravenous *adjective, medicine* located within or introduced into a vein

in-tray *noun* an office tray for letters and work still to be dealt with (*contrasted with*: **out-tray**)

intrepid *adjective* without fear, brave
♦ **intrepidity** *noun*

intricate *adjective* complicated, having many twists and turns ♦ **intricacy** *noun* (*plural* **intricacies**) ☉ Comes from Latin *intricare* meaning 'to perplex'

intrigue *noun* (*pronounced* in-treeg) **1** secret plotting or a secret plot **2** a secret love affair
➤ *verb* (*pronounced* in-**treeg**) (**intriguing, intrigued**) **1** to plot, scheme **2** to rouse the curiosity of, fascinate ♦ **intriguing** *adjective*

intrinsic *adjective* belonging to something as part of its nature

introduce *verb* **1** to bring in or put in **2** to present (someone) to another person by name **3** to announce or present (a television or radio programme) to an audience • **introduce somebody to** to cause someone to experience or discover something for the first time

introduction *noun* **1** the introducing of someone or something **2** an essay at the beginning of a book etc briefly explaining its contents

introductory *adjective* coming at the beginning

intron *noun, genetics* a segment of DNA in a gene that does not carry coded instructions for the manufacture of a protein

introspective *adjective* inward-looking, fond of examining your own thoughts and feelings
♦ **introspection** *noun*

introvert *noun* a person who tends to be uncommunicative and unsociable (*contrasted with*: **extrovert**)

intrude *verb* to thrust yourself into somewhere uninvited ♦ **intrusion** *noun*

intruder *noun* someone who breaks in or intrudes

intrusive *adjective* **1** tending to intrude **2** *geography* of rock: formed by the cooling and solidification of magma beneath the Earth's surface

intuition *noun* **1** ability to understand something without thinking it out **2** an instinctive feeling or belief

Inuit *noun* **1** the Eskimo people, especially those in Greenland, Canada and N Alaska **2** their language

inundate *verb* **1** to flood **2** to overwhelm: *inundated with work* ♦ **inundation** *noun*

inure *verb* to make accustomed (to something unpleasant): *inured to pain*

invade *verb* **1** to enter (a country etc) as an enemy to take possession **2** to interfere with (someone's rights, privacy, etc) ♦ **invader** *noun*
♦ **invasion** *noun*

invalid[1] (*pronounced* in-**val**-id) *adjective* **1** not legally effective **2** mistaken, incorrect or unacceptable: *invalid data* ♦ **invalidity** *noun*

invalid[2] (*pronounced* **in**-val-id) *noun* someone who is ill or disabled ➤ *adjective* **1** ill or disabled **2** suitable for people who are ill or disabled ➤ *verb* to make an invalid of • **invalid out** to discharge from the army as an invalid

invalidate *verb* to prove to be wrong, or make legally ineffective

invaluable *adjective* priceless, essential

invariable *adjective* unchanging

invariably *adverb* always

invariant *noun, maths* an expression or quantity that is not changed by a particular procedure ➤ *adjective* unchanging

invasion see **invade**

invective *noun* abusive words; scorn

inveigle *verb* (**inveigle into**) to coax, trick or persuade someone into doing something
♦ **inveiglement** *noun*

invent *verb* **1** to make or think up for the first time **2** to make up (a story, an excuse)
♦ **inventor** *noun*

invention *noun* something invented

inventive *adjective* good at inventing, resourceful

inventory *noun* (*plural* **inventories**) a detailed list of contents

inverse *adjective* opposite, reverse ➤ *noun* **1** the opposite **2** *maths* one of two numbers that cancel each other out in a mathematical operation, eg the inverse of 3 in addition is -3, because $3 + -3 = 0$ ♦ **inversely** *adverb*

inverse operation *noun, maths* an operation that undoes another and leaves the operand unchanged, eg addition and subtraction are inverse operations: $2 + 4 - 4 = 2$

inverse proportion or **inverse variation** *noun, maths* a link between two quantities such that as one gets larger the other gets smaller

inversion *noun* **1** a turning upside-down **2** a reversal

invert *verb* **1** to turn upside down **2** to reverse the order of

invertebrate *adjective* of an animal: not having a backbone ➤ *noun* an animal with no backbone, eg a worm or insect

inverted commas *plural noun* punctuation marks, which look like commas or commas upside down (' ' or " "), showing where direct speech begins and ends

invest *verb* **1** to put money in a firm, property, etc to make a profit **2** to devote (time, effort, etc) to something **3** to give a particular quality to **4** *old* to besiege

investigate *verb* to search into with care ✦ **investigator** *noun*

investigation *noun* a careful search

investiture *noun* a ceremony before taking on an important office

investment *noun* **1** money invested **2** something in which money is invested **3** *old* a siege

investor *noun* someone who invests

inveterate *adjective* **1** firmly fixed in a habit: *an inveterate gambler* **2** deep-rooted

invidious *adjective* likely to cause ill-will or envy

invigilate *verb* to supervise (an examination etc) ✦ **invigilator** *noun*

invigorate *verb* to strengthen, refresh ✦ **invigorating** *adjective*

invincible *adjective* not able to be defeated or overcome ✦ **invincibility** *noun*

inviolable *adjective* sacred, not to be disregarded or harmed ✦ **inviolability** *noun*

inviolate *adjective* not violated, free from harm etc

invisible *adjective* not able to be seen ✦ **invisibility** *noun*

invitation *noun* a request to do something

invite *verb* **1** to ask (someone) to do something, especially to come for a meal etc **2** to seem to ask for: *inviting punishment*

inviting *adjective* tempting, attractive

in vitro *adverb & adjective* taking place in an artificial environment such as a test tube (*contrasted with*: **in vivo**)

in vivo *adverb & adjective* taking place inside a living organism (*contrasted with*: **in vitro**)

invoice *noun* a letter sent with goods with details of price and quantity ➤ *verb* to send an invoice to (a customer)

invoke *verb* **1** to call upon in prayer **2** to ask for (eg help) ✦ **invocation** *noun*

involuntary *adjective* not done willingly or intentionally ✦ **involuntarily** *adverb*

involuntary muscle *noun, anatomy* a muscle that is not controlled consciously, such as the heart or stomach

involve *verb* **1** to have as a consequence, require **2** to take part (in), be concerned (in): *involved in publishing/involved in the scandal* ✦ **involvement** *noun*

involved *adjective* complicated

invulnerable *adjective* not vulnerable, not able to be hurt ✦ **invulnerability** *noun*

inward *adjective* **1** placed within **2** moving towards the inside **3** situated in the mind or soul ➤ *adverb* (*also* **inwards**) towards the inside

inwardly *adverb* **1** within **2** in your heart, privately

iodine *noun, chemistry* (symbol I) a liquid chemical used to kill germs

ion *noun* an electrically charged atom or group of atoms ✦ **ionic** *adjective*

ion exchange *noun* a chemical reaction in which ions which have the same charge are exchanged between a solution and a solid in contact with it

ionic bond *noun, chemistry* a chemical bond formed between ions with opposite charges

ionize *or* **ionise** *verb* to produce or make something produce ions ✦ **ionization** *noun*

ionizer *or* **ioniser** *noun* a device which sends out negative ions to improve the quality of the air

iota *noun* a little bit, a jot

> ⏱ After the smallest letter in the Greek alphabet

IOU *noun short for* I owe you, a note given as a receipt for money borrowed

IP address *abbreviation, computing* a number that identifies a computer on a network using TCP/IP

IQ *abbreviation* intelligence quotient, a measure of a person's intellectual ability

Ir *symbol, chemistry* iridium

ir- see **in-**

IRA *abbreviation* Irish Republican Army, an anti-British paramilitary guerrilla force

irascible *adjective* easily made angry ✦ **irascibility** *noun*

irate *adjective* angry

ire *noun, formal* anger

iridescent *adjective* **1** coloured like a rainbow **2** shimmering with changing colours ✦ **iridescence** *noun*

iridium *noun, chemistry* (symbol Ir) a silvery metallic element

iris *noun* (*plural* **irises**) **1** the coloured part of the eye around the pupil **2** a lily-like flower which grows from a bulb

irk *verb* to weary, annoy

irksome *adjective* tiresome

iron (*pronounced* **ai**-on *or Scottish* **ai**-ron) *noun* **1** a common metal, widely used to make tools etc **2** an iron instrument: *a branding iron* **3** a golf club (originally with an iron head) **4** an appliance for pressing clothes **5** (**irons**) a prisoner's chains ➤ *adjective* **1** made of iron **2** stern, resolute: *iron will* **3** of a rule: not to be broken ➤ *verb* to press (clothes) with an iron • **iron out** to smooth out (difficulties)

Iron Age *noun* human culture at the stage of using iron for tools etc

Iron Curtain *noun, history* a notional barrier between the West and the countries of the former Soviet bloc

ironic or **ironical** *adjective* **1** containing or expressing irony **2** of a person: frequently using irony • **ironically** *adverb*

ironmonger *noun* a shopkeeper selling household tools, gardening equipment, etc

ironmongery *noun* goods sold by an ironmonger

iron pyrites same as **pyrites**

irony *noun* (*plural* **ironies**) **1** a form of humour in which someone says the opposite of what is obviously true **2** an absurd contradiction or paradox: *The irony of it was that she would have given him the money if he hadn't stolen it*

irrational *adjective* **1** against logic or common sense **2** *maths* of a number: unable to be expressed as an integer or common fraction • **irrationality** *noun*

irregular *adjective* **1** uneven, variable **2** against the rules • **irregularity** *noun* (*plural* **irregularities**)

irrelevant *adjective* not having to do with what is being spoken about • **irrelevance** or **irrelevancy** *noun* (*plural* **irrelevancies**)

irreligious *adjective* **1** not having a religion **2** having hostility towards religion • **irreligion** *noun*

irreparable *adjective* not able to be repaired

irreplaceable *adjective* too good or rare to be replaced

irrepressible *adjective* not restrainable or controllable

irreproachable *adjective* not able to be criticized or blamed

irresistible *adjective* too strong or too charming to be resisted

irresolute *adjective* not able to make up your mind or keep to a decision

irrespective *adjective* taking no account of: *irrespective of the weather*

irresponsible *adjective* having no sense of responsibility, thoughtless

irreverent *adjective* having no respect, eg for holy things • **irreverence** *noun*

irreversible *adjective* not able to be changed

back to a previous state • **irreversibly** *adverb*

irrevocable (*pronounced* i-**rev**-ok-a-bl) *adjective* not to be changed

irrigate *verb* to supply (land) with water by channels etc, especially to enable crops to be grown in dry regions • **irrigation** *noun*

irritable *adjective* **1** cross, easily annoyed **2** *biology* capable of responding to an external stimulus such as heat or touch • **irritability** *noun*

irritant *noun* someone or something that causes annoyance or discomfort

irritate *verb* **1** to annoy **2** to cause discomfort to (the skin, eyes, etc) **3** *biology* to stimulate (something eg an organ) to respond in a characteristic way • **irritation** *noun*

ISA *abbreviation* Individual Savings Account

ISDN *abbreviation, computing* integrated services digital network, an advanced telecommunications network

-ish *suffix* **1** from that place: *English* **2** like: *girlish* **3** a little: *quietish*

Islam *noun* **1** the Muslim religion, based on the teachings of the prophet Muhammad **2** the followers of this religion as a group • **Islamic** *adjective* ⊕ Comes from Arabic, literally 'surrender' (to God)

Islamist *noun* **1** a person who studies Islam and Islamic law *etc* **2** a person in a political movement seeking to establish a traditional Islamic society

island *noun* **1** an area of land surrounded by water **2** an isolated place, a haven

islander *noun* an inhabitant of an island

isle *noun, formal* an island

islets of Langerhans *plural noun, biology* cells in the pancreas which control the level of glucose in the blood

⊕ Named after the German anatomist Paul Langerhans (1847–88)

-ism *suffix* **1** indicating a system, set of beliefs, etc: *socialism/Catholicism* **2** indicating prejudice against a particular group: *racism/sexism* ⊕ Comes from Greek suffix *-ismos*, used to form nouns of action from verbs

iso- *prefix* equal: *isobar/isotherm* ⊕ Comes from Greek *isos* meaning 'equal'

isobar *noun* a line on the map connecting places where atmospheric pressure is the same

isolate *verb* **1** to place or keep separate from other people or things **2** to consider (something) by itself: *isolate the problem* • **isolated** *adjective* • **isolation** *noun*

isolationism *noun* the political policy of avoiding as much as possible any dealings with other countries • **isolationist** *adjective*

isomer *noun* **1** a chemical substance with the

same molecular weight as another, but with its atoms in a different arrangement **2** an atomic nucleus with the same mass number as another, but with different properties ♦ **isomeric** *adjective*

isometric *adjective* **1** of equal size **2** to do with muscular contraction that does not shorten the muscle fibres and does not move a joint (*compare with*: **isotonic**) ♦ **isometry** *noun*

isomorphism *noun* **1** *biology* apparent similarity of form between individuals belonging to different races or species **2** *chemistry* the existence of two or more chemical compounds with the same crystal structure **3** *maths* a one-to-one correspondence between the elements of two or more sets and between their sums or products ♦ **isomorph** *noun* ♦ **isomorphic** or **isomorphous** *adjective*

isoprene *noun* a colourless liquid that is the basic unit of natural rubber, and can be used to form synthetic rubber

isosceles *adjective* of a triangle: with two sides and therefore two angles equal; an equilateral triangle is considered a special case of isosceles triangle

isostatic adjustment *noun, geography* changes in sea levels as a result of changes in land levels, caused by eg an earthquake (*compare with*: **eustatic adjustment**)

isotherm *noun* a line on the map connecting places which have the same temperature

isotonic *adjective* **1** *chemistry* of a solution: having the same osmotic pressure as another solution with which it is being compared **2** to do with muscular contraction that shortens the muscle fibres and moves a joint (*compare with*: **isometric**)

isotope *noun* an atom with the same atomic number as, but different mass number from, another

ISP *abbreviation, computing* Internet service provider

issue *verb* **1** to go or come out **2** to give out (orders etc) **3** to publish ➤ *noun* **1** a flowing out **2** something published **3** one number in a series of magazines etc **4** result, consequence **5** a matter being discussed **6** *formal* children: *He died without issue* • **take issue with** to disagree with

isthmus *noun* (*plural* **isthmuses**) a narrow strip of land, bounded by water on both sides, that joins two larger areas of land

IT *abbreviation* information technology, the development and use of computer systems and applications

it *pronoun* **1** the thing spoken of: *I meant to bring the book, but I left it at home* **2** used in sentences with no definite subject: *It snowed today* **3** used in phrases as a kind of object: *go it alone*

italicize or **italicise** *verb* to print in italics

italics *plural noun* a kind of type which *slopes to the right*

itch *noun* **1** an irritating feeling in the skin, made better by scratching **2** a strong desire ➤ *verb* **1** to have an itch **2** to be impatient (to do), long (to): *itching to open his presents* ♦ **itchy** *adjective* (**itchier, itchiest**)

ITCZ *abbreviation, geography* intertropical convergence zone

item *noun* a separate article in a list

itemize or **itemise** *verb* to list in items

iterate *verb* to say or do again, to repeat ♦ **iteration** *noun* ♦ **iterative** *adjective*

itinerant *adjective* travelling from place to place, especially on business ➤ *noun* someone who travels around, especially a tramp, pedlar, etc

itinerary *noun* (*plural* **itineraries**) a route or plan of a journey

-itis *suffix* used to describe diseases which involve inflammation: *tonsillitis* (= inflammation of the tonsils)/*bronchitis* (= inflammation of the windpipe) ◷ Comes from Greek suffix -*itis* meaning 'belonging to'

its *adjective* belonging to it: *Keep the hat in its box*

❗ Do not confuse: **its** and **it's**.
Its, meaning 'belonging to it', is spelt with no apostrophe ('). **It's** means 'it is' or 'it has'.

it's *short for* it is or it has

itself *pronoun* **1** used reflexively: *The cat licked itself* **2** used for emphasis or contrast: *After I've read the introduction, I'll begin the book itself*

ITV *abbreviation* Independent Television, a group of British television companies that broadcast programmes paid for by advertising

IUD *abbreviation* intrauterine device, a contraceptive device inserted into the womb to prevent implantation of the fertilized egg

IVF *abbreviation* in-vitro fertilization, the medical technique in which a woman's egg is fertilized in a test-tube then put back into her womb to develop

ivory *noun* (*plural* **ivories**) the hard white substance which forms the tusks of the elephant, walrus, etc

ivy *noun* (*plural* **ivies**) a creeping evergreen plant

Jj

J *symbol* joule

jab *verb* (**jabbing, jabbed**) **1** to prod (someone) **2** to strike with a quick punch ‣ *noun* **1** a prod **2** *informal* an injection: *flu jab*

jabber *verb* to talk rapidly and indistinctly

jack *noun* **1** a device with a lever for raising heavy weights **2** (*also called*: **knave**) the playing-card between ten and queen • **jack up 1** to raise with a jack **2** to raise (prices etc) steeply

jackal *noun* a dog-like wild animal

jackass *noun* **1** a male ass **2** *informal* an idiot

jackboots *plural noun* large boots reaching above the knee

jackdaw *noun* a type of small crow

jacket *noun* **1** a short coat **2** a loose paper cover for a book

jacket potato *noun* a baked potato

jack-in-the-box *noun* a doll fixed to a spring inside a box that leaps out when the lid is opened

jack-knife *noun* **1** a large folding knife **2** a dive forming a sharp angle and then straightening ‣ *verb* of a vehicle and its trailer: to swing together to form a sharp angle

jackpot *noun* a fund of prize money which increases until someone wins it

Jacobean *adjective, history* relating to the period when James VI of Scotland and I of England reigned (1603–1625)

Jacobin *noun, history* **1** a member of a radical political society in the French Revolution, so called from their meeting in the hall of a Jacobin convent **2** an extremist or radical in politics

⊙ Comes from Latin *Jacobus 'James'*, a name applied to Dominican friars of St Jacques, Paris

Jacobite *noun, history* a supporter of James VII of Scotland and II of England and his descendants

Jacuzzi (*pronounced* ja-**koo**-zi) *noun, trademark* a bath fitted with underwater jets that massage and invigorate the body

jade *noun* a hard green mineral substance used for ornaments

jaded *adjective* tired or bored

jagged *adjective* rough-edged, uneven

jaguar *noun* a S American animal similar to a leopard

jail *noun* a prison ‣ *verb* to put in prison

jailbird *noun* a convict or ex-convict

jailer *noun* someone in charge of a jail or prisoners

Jain *noun* a member of an Indian religion similar to Buddhism ♦ **Jainist** *noun & adjective*

jalopy or **jaloppy** *noun* (*plural* **jalopies** or **jaloppies**), *informal* a worn-out old car

jam *noun* **1** fruit boiled with sugar till it is set **2** a crush **3** a blockage caused by crowding **4** *informal* a difficult situation ‣ *verb* (**jamming, jammed**) **1** to press or squeeze tight **2** to crowd full **3** to stick and so be unable to move: *The back wheel has jammed* **4** to cause interference with another radio station's broadcast **5** *music* to play with other musicians in an improvised style

jamb *noun* the side post of a door

jamboree *noun* **1** a large, lively gathering **2** a rally of Scouts

jammy *adjective* (**jammier, jammiest**) **1** covered or filled with jam **2** *informal* lucky

jam-packed *adjective* packed tightly

jam session *noun* an informal gathering to play improvised music

jangle *verb* **1** to make a harsh ringing noise **2** to irritate

janitor *noun* **1** a caretaker **2** a doorkeeper ⊙ Comes from Latin *janua* meaning 'a door'

January *noun* the first month of the year

⊙ After *Janus*, a Roman god who had two faces, one looking into the new year, the other looking back to the old year

jape *noun, informal* a trick, a practical joke

jar *noun* a glass or earthenware bottle with a wide mouth ‣ *verb* (**jarring, jarred**) **1** to have a harsh, startling effect **2** to be discordant, not agree: *His ideas jarred with my attitude*

jargon *noun* special words used within a particular trade, profession, etc

jarring *adjective* harsh, startling

jasmine *noun* a shrub with white or yellow sweet-smelling flowers

jaundice *noun* a disease which causes the skin and eyes to turn yellow, caused by an excess of a bile pigment in the blood

jaundiced *adjective* **1** having jaundice **2** discontented, bitter

jaunt *noun* a short journey for pleasure

jaunty *adjective* cheerful ♦ **jauntily** *adverb*

Java *noun, trademark, computing* a

programming language, designed for the Internet

⊙ Named after *Java*, a strong Indonesian coffee the creators are said to have drunk

JavaScript *noun, trademark, computing* a programming language based on Java

javelin *noun* **1** a long spear for throwing **2** (**the javelin**) the event in athletics of throwing the javelin

jaw *noun* **1** either of the two bony structures that form the framework of the mouth and in which the teeth are set **2** the lower part of the face, including the mouth and chin **3** (**jaws**) an animal's mouth

jawbone *noun* the upper or lower bone of the jaw (*technical names*: **mandible** and **maxilla**)

jay *noun* a brightly coloured bird like a crow

jaywalking *noun* walking carelessly among traffic ♦ **jaywalker** *noun* ⊙ Originally US, from *jay* meaning 'fool'

jazz *noun* a style of music with a strong rhythm, based on African-American folk music • **jazz up** to make (something) more lively or colourful

jazzy *adjective* (**jazzier, jazziest**) **1** resembling or containing certain elements of jazz **2** colourful, flamboyant

JCB *noun* a type of mobile digger used in the construction industry

⊙ **JCB** is an abbreviation of *J C Bamford*, the manufacturer's name

jealous *adjective* **1** wanting to have what someone else has; envious **2** guarding closely (your possessions etc) ♦ **jealousy** *noun*

jeans *plural noun* denim trousers

Jeep *noun, trademark* a light four-wheel-drive, usually military, vehicle that can travel over rough country

jeer *verb* to make fun of, scoff ➤ *noun* a scoff

Jehovah *noun* the Hebrew God of the Old Testament

jejune (*pronounced* je-**joon**) *adjective* naive, inexperienced

⊙ From a Latin word meaning 'hungry' or 'fasting'

jejunum (*pronounced* je-**joo**-num) *noun* the part of the small intestine between the duodenum and the ileum

Jekyll and Hyde *noun* a person with two distinct personalities, one good, the other evil

⊙ After the character in *The Strange Case of Dr Jekyll and Mr Hyde*, a novel by Robert Louis Stevenson (1850–94)

jelly *noun* (*plural* **jellies**) **1** fruit juice boiled with

sugar till it becomes firm **2** a transparent wobbly food, often fruit-flavoured

jellyfish *noun* a sea animal with a jelly-like body

jemmy *noun* (*plural* **jemmies**) a small crowbar used by burglars for forcing open windows etc

jeopardize or **jeopardise** *verb* to put in danger or at risk

jeopardy *noun* danger of harm or loss: *His job was in jeopardy after the takeover*

⊙ Originally a gambling term, based on French *jeu parti* meaning 'even chance'

jeremiad *noun, formal* a long sad story

jerk *verb* to give a sudden sharp movement ➤ *noun* a sudden sharp movement

jerkin *noun* a type of short coat

jerky *adjective* (**jerkier, jerkiest**) moving or coming in jerks ♦ **jerkily** *adverb*

jerry-built *adjective* hastily and badly built

jersey *noun* (*plural* **jerseys**) a sweater, pullover

jest *noun* a joke ➤ *verb* to joke

jester *noun, history* a fool employed to amuse a royal court etc

jet *noun* **1** a hard black mineral, used for ornaments and jewellery **2** a spout of flame, air or liquid **3** a jet plane

jet-black *adjective* very black

jet engine *noun* an aircraft engine which generates forward thrust by ejecting a jet of gases

jet lag *noun* tiredness caused by the body's inability to cope with being in a new time zone

jet plane *noun* an aeroplane driven by jet propulsion

jet propulsion *noun* high-speed forward motion produced by sucking in air or liquid and forcing it out from behind

jetsam *noun* goods thrown overboard and washed ashore

jet set *noun* (**the jet set**) rich people who enjoy frequent expensive holidays ♦ **jet setter** *noun* ♦ **jet setting** *noun & adjective*

jet stream *noun* **1** *meteorology* a narrow band of high-speed, westerly winds more than 10,000m above the earth **2** the exhaust of a jet engine

jettison *verb* **1** to throw overboard **2** to abandon

jetty *noun* (*plural* **jetties**) a small pier

Jew *noun* **1** a person who practises Judaism **2** a member of the Hebrew race

jewel *noun* **1** a precious stone **2** someone or something highly valued

jewelled or *US* **jeweled** *adjective* set with jewels

jeweller or *US* **jeweler** *noun* someone who makes or sells articles made of precious jewels and metals

jewellery or US **jewelry** noun articles made of precious jewels and metals

Jewish adjective of the Jews

Jew's harp noun a small harp-shaped musical instrument played between the teeth

Jezebel noun a wicked, scheming woman

🕔 After the wicked Queen *Jezebel*, the wife of King Ahab in the Bible

jib noun **1** a three-cornered sail in front of a ship's foremast **2** the jutting-out arm of a crane • **jib at** (**jibbing, jibbed**) to refuse to do, object to

jibe or **gibe** verb to jeer, scoff ➤ noun a jeer

jiffy noun, informal a moment

Jiffy bag noun, trademark a padded envelope

jig noun **1** a lively dance or tune for this dance **2** a jerky movement **3** a device that holds a piece of work in position so tools can be used on it ➤ verb (**jigging, jigged**) **1** to dance a jig **2** to jump or jerk up and down

jigsaw or **jigsaw puzzle** noun a puzzle consisting of many different-shaped pieces that fit together to form a picture

jihad (pronounced jee-**had**) noun a holy war for the Muslim faith 🕔 Comes from Arabic, meaning 'a struggle'

jilt verb to cast aside (a lover)

Jim Crow Laws plural noun, history a name given to US state laws from the 1890s onwards which segregated blacks from whites in the south in schools, housing, public transport, etc

🕔 *Jim Crow* was a derogatory name for a black person, from a black minstrel song with the refrain 'Wheel about and turn about and jump Jim Crow'

jingle noun **1** a clinking sound like that of coins **2** a simple rhyme or tune, especially one used in an advertisement

jingoism (pronounced jing-goh-i-zm) noun chauvinism, narrow-minded nationalism ♦ **jingoistic** adjective

jinx noun someone or something thought to bring bad luck

🕔 Probably from the *Jynx* bird which was once invoked in spells and charms

JIT abbreviation, business just-in-time

jitterbug noun an energetic dance popular in the 1940s

jitters plural noun: **have the jitters** informal to be very nervous

jittery adjective very nervous, shaking with nerves

jive noun a style of fast dancing to jazz or rock-and-roll music

job noun **1** someone's regular paid work **2** a piece of work **3** a completed task: *made a good job of the decorating* **4** a function or responsibility: *It's your job to keep everything clean* **5** informal a problem; difficulty: *I had a job finding the place* **6** a crime, especially a burglary • **a good job** informal fortunate; lucky: *It's a good job I caught him* • **just the job** exactly what is required • **make the best of a bad job** to do your best in difficult circumstances

job centre noun a government office where information about available jobs is shown

jobless adjective having no paid employment, unemployed

job lot noun a mixed collection of objects sold as one item at an auction, etc

Jobseeker's Allowance noun, Brit an allowance paid to the unemployed

job-share noun the division of one job between two people, each working part-time ♦ **job-sharing** noun

jockey noun (plural **jockeys**) someone who rides in horse races, especially as a profession ➤ verb: **jockey for position** to try to gain something, especially against rivals, by manoeuvring

🕔 A diminutive of the name *Jock*, meaning 'lad'

jockstrap noun a genital support for men while playing sports

jocular adjective joking, merry ♦ **jocularity** noun ♦ **jocularly** adverb

jocund adjective merry, cheerful

jodhpurs plural noun riding breeches, fitting tightly from knee to ankle

joey noun (plural **joeys**) Aust, informal a young kangaroo

jog verb (**jogging, jogged**) **1** to nudge, push slightly **2** to run at a gentle pace, especially for exercise **3** (also **jog along** or **on**) to progress slowly and steadily • **jog someone's memory** to remind someone of something ➤ noun a gentle run ♦ **jogging** noun (meaning 2)

jogger noun someone who runs gently to keep fit

joggle verb to shake slightly

joie de vivre (pronounced szwah de **vee**-vre) noun enthusiasm for life; sparkle, spirit 🕔 From French, literally meaning 'joy of living'

join verb **1** to connect, fasten **2** to become a member of: *joined the swimming club* **3** to come into the company of: *Join me for lunch* **4** to meet: *The roads join at the town* **5** to take part in: *join the fun* ➤ noun the place where two or more things join

joiner noun someone who makes wooden fittings, furniture, etc

joint noun **1** the place where two or more things join **2** the place where two bones are joined, eg an elbow or knee **3** meat containing a bone **4**

slang a cannabis cigarette ➤ *adjective* **1** united: *a joint effort* **2** shared among more than one: *joint bank account*

jointly *adverb* together

joist *noun* the beam to which the boards of a floor or the beams of a ceiling are nailed

joke *noun* something said or done to cause laughter ➤ *verb* to make a joke, tease • **no joke** not something to laugh about or dismiss

joker *noun* **1** someone who jokes **2** an extra playing-card in a pack, with a picture of a jester on it

jollification *noun* noisy festivity or celebration

jolliness or **jollity** *noun* merriment

jolly *adjective* merry

jolt *verb* **1** to shake suddenly **2** to go forward with sudden jerks ➤ *noun* a sudden jerk

Jonah *noun* a person who brings bad luck

⊙ Named after *Jonah* in the Old Testament of the Bible, who almost brought disaster to the ship on which he was sailing

josh *informal, verb* to tease ➤ *noun* a bit of teasing, a joke

joss-stick *noun* a stick of gum which gives off a sweet smell when burned

jostle *verb* to push or knock against

jot *noun* a very small amount ➤ *verb* (**jotting, jotted**) (usually **jot down**) to write down hurriedly or briefly

jotter *noun* a book for taking notes

joule *noun* (symbol **J**) the standard unit of measurement of work, energy and heat

⊙ Named after British physicist James *Joule* (1818–89)

journal *noun* **1** a personal account of each day's events; a diary **2** a newspaper, a magazine

journalism *noun* the business of recording events for the media ✦ **journalist** *noun* ✦ **journalistic** *adjective*

journey *noun* (*plural* **journeys**) a distance travelled ➤ *verb* to travel

journeyman *noun* a craftsman qualified in a particular trade

joust *noun, history* the armed contest between two knights on horseback at a tournament ➤ *verb* to fight on horseback at a tournament

jovial *adjective* cheerful, good-humoured ✦ **joviality** *noun*

jowl *noun* the lower part of the jaw or cheek

joy *noun* gladness

joyful or **joyous** *adjective* full of joy

joyless *adjective* dismal

joyride *noun* a reckless trip for amusement in a stolen car ✦ **joyrider** *noun*

joystick *noun* a control lever for eg an aeroplane or a video game

JP *abbreviation* Justice of the Peace

JPEG (*pronounced* **jei**-peg) *abbreviation, computing* Joint Photographic Experts Group, a standard format for image files

Jr *abbreviation* Junior: *John Brown Jr*

jubilant *adjective* triumphant, full of rejoicing ✦ **jubilation** *noun*

jubilee *noun* celebrations of eg the anniversary of a coronation

⊙ From a Hebrew word for 'ram's horn', which was blown to announce the start of a celebratory Jewish year

Judaism *noun* the Jewish religion or way of life ✦ **Judaic** *adjective*

judder *noun* a strong vibration or jerky movement

judge *verb* **1** to make a decision on (a law case) after hearing all the evidence **2** to form an opinion **3** to decide the winners in a competition etc ➤ *noun* **1** an official who hears cases in the law-courts and decides on them according to the country's or state's laws **2** someone skilled in evaluating anything: *a good judge of character*

judgement or **judgment** *noun* **1** a decision in a law case **2** an opinion **3** good sense in forming opinions

judgemental or **judgmental** *adjective* **1** involving judgement **2** with a tendency to make moral judgements or criticize

judicial *adjective* of a judge or court of justice ✦ **judicially** *adverb*

judiciary *noun* the judges of a country or state

judicious *adjective* wise, sensible ✦ **judiciously** *adverb*

judo *noun* a Japanese form of wrestling for self-defence

jug *noun* a dish for liquids with a handle and a shaped lip for pouring

juggernaut *noun* a large articulated lorry

⊙ From a Hindi word for a large wagon used to carry the image of the god Krishna in religious processions

juggle *verb* **1** to toss a number of things (balls, clubs, etc) into the air and catch them in order **2** to keep several activities in progress at once **3** (usually **juggle with**) to adjust (facts or figures) to create a misleading impression ✦ **juggler** *noun* (meaning 1) ✦ **juggling** *noun* ⊙ Comes from French *jogler* meaning 'to act as jester'

jugular vein *noun* the large vein at the side of the neck that carries blood from the head to the heart

juice *noun* the liquid in fruits, vegetables, etc

juicy *adjective* **1** full of juice **2** *informal* sensational, scandalous: *juicy gossip*

jujitsu *noun* a Japanese martial art similar to judo

jukebox *noun* a coin-operated machine which plays records and CDs you select

July *noun* the seventh month of the year

🕐 Named in honour of the Roman general *Julius* Caesar

---

jumah *noun, Islam* Friday prayers to be attended by Muslim males

jumble *verb* to throw together without order, muddle ➤ *noun* **1** a confused mixture **2** second-hand goods to be sold in a jumble sale

jumble sale *noun* a sale of odds and ends, cast-off clothing, etc

jumbo *noun* (*plural* **jumbos**) **1** a child's name for an elephant **2** a jumbo jet ➤ *adjective* very large

jumbo jet *noun* a large jet aircraft

jump *verb* **1** to spring off the ground **2** to get over (something) by jumping **3** to make a sudden startled movement **4** to rise abruptly **5** to pass over without spending time on: *He jumped a few chapters* **6** *informal* of a car: to pass through (a red traffic light) ➤ *noun* **1** a leap **2** an obstacle to be jumped, eg a fence on a racecourse **3** a sudden rise in amount, cost or value **4** a sudden start • **jump at** to accept eagerly • **jump down someone's throat** *informal* to snap at them impatiently • **jump the gun 1** to get off your mark too soon in a race **2** to act prematurely • **jump the queue** to get ahead of your turn

jumped-up *adjective, derogatory* having an inflated view of one's own importance

jumper *noun* a sweater, a jersey

jump jet *noun* an aircraft that can take off and land vertically

jumpsuit *noun* a one-piece garment combining trousers and top

jumpy *adjective* (**jumpier, jumpiest**) easily startled

junction *noun* a place or point of joining, especially of roads or railway lines

juncture *noun* point: *It's too early to decide at this juncture*

June *noun* the sixth month of the year

🕐 After *Juno*, the queen of the Roman gods

---

jungle *noun* a dense growth of trees and plants in tropical areas

junior *adjective* **1** younger **2** in a lower class or rank **3** *Brit* relating to or for schoolchildren aged between 7 and 11: *junior schools* ➤ *noun* **1** a person of low or lower rank in a profession, organization, etc **2** *Brit* a pupil in a junior school **3** a person younger than the one in question: *She's three years his junior* 🕐 From Latin, literally meaning 'younger'

juniper *noun* an evergreen shrub with berries and prickly leaves

junk[1] *noun* worthless articles, rubbish

junk[2] *noun* a Chinese flat-bottomed sailing ship, high in the bow and stern

Junker (*pronounced* **yoongk**-er) *noun, history* one of a group of powerful German aristocrats who dominated the German army during World War I 🕐 Comes from German *jung* meaning 'young' + *Herr* meaning 'lord'

junket *noun* **1** a dish made of curdled milk sweetened and flavoured **2** a trip made by a government official and paid for out of public funds

junk food *noun* convenience food with little nutritional value

junkie or **junky** *noun* (*plural* **junkies**) **1** *slang* a drug addict **2** *informal* someone addicted to something: *a computer games junkie*

junk mail *noun* unsolicited mail, especially advertising material

junta (*pronounced* **hoon**-ta) *noun* a government of military officers formed after a coup d'état 🕐 Comes from Spanish, literally meaning 'meeting' or 'council'

Jurassic *adjective* of the geological period 210 million to 140 million years ago

juridicial *adjective* relating to the law or the administration of justice

jurisdiction *noun* **1** a legal authority or power **2** the district over which a judge, court, etc has power

jurisprudence *noun* the study or knowledge of law

jurist *noun* **1** an expert in law **2** *US* a lawyer

juror *noun* someone who serves on a jury

jury *noun* (*plural* **juries**) **1** a group of people selected to reach a decision on whether an accused person appearing in court is guilty or not **2** a group of judges for a competition, etc

juryman, jurywoman *noun* someone who serves on a jury

just[1] *adjective* **1** fair in judgement: *a just ruler* **2** correct, right: *a just result* ♦ **justly** *adverb*

just[2] *adverb* **1** exactly: *just right* **2** not long since: *only just arrived* **3** merely, only: *just a brief visit* **4** really, absolutely: *just beautiful* • **just about** almost: *I'm just about ready* • **just now** at this particular moment • **just so 1** yes indeed **2** neat and tidy • **just the same** nevertheless

justice *noun* **1** fairness in making judgements **2** what is right or rightly deserved **3** a judge

Justice of the Peace *noun* (*abbrev* **JP**) a citizen who acts as a judge for certain matters

justifiable *adjective* able to be justified or defended, having good grounds: *justifiable anger* ♦ **justifiably** *adverb*

justification *noun* **1** good reason **2** the arrangement of text so that it forms an even margin down the page

justify *verb* (**justifies, justifying, justified**) **1** to prove or show to be right or desirable **2** to make (text) form an even margin down the page

just-in-time *noun, business* (*abbrev* **JIT**) a method of stock control in which little or no stock is kept at the production site, and supplies are delivered just in time for use

jut *verb* (**jutting, jutted**) to stand or stick out

jute *noun* fibre from certain plants for making sacking, canvas, etc

juvenile *adjective* **1** young; of young people **2** childish ➤ *noun* a young person

juvenile delinquent *noun* a fairly old-fashioned term for a young person guilty of an offence such as vandalism ◆ **juvenile deliquency** *noun*

juxtapose *verb* to place side by side ◆ **juxtaposition** *noun*

K¹ *abbreviation* **1** kelvin **2** kilometre(s) **3** *computing* kilobyte(s)

K² *symbol* **1** kilo **2** *chemistry* potassium **3** thousand

k *symbol, chemistry, physics* constant

kabala or **kabbala** see **cabbala**

kaftan another spelling of **caftan**

kaiser (*pronounced* **kaiz**-er) *noun, history* a German emperor

Kalashnikov *noun* a type of submachine-gun manufactured in Russia

> ⊙ Named after its Russian inventor, M T Kalashnikov (born 1919)

kale *noun* a cabbage with open curled leaves

kaleidoscope *noun* a tube held to the eye and turned, so that loose, coloured shapes reflected in two mirrors change patterns

kaleidoscopic *adjective* **1** with changing colours **2** changing quickly

kalif *noun* a caliph

kamikaze *noun, history* a Japanese pilot trained to make a suicidal attack ➤ *adjective* suicidal, self-destructive ⊙ Comes from Japanese *kami* meaning 'divine' + *kaze* meaning 'wind'

kangaroo *noun* a large Australian animal with long hindlegs and great jumping power, the female carrying its young in a pouch on the front of her body

kangaroo court *noun* a court that has no legal status, composed of a group of people judging one of their number

kaolin (*pronounced* **kei**-oh-lin) *noun* a soft white clay used for making fine porcelain, bricks and cement, and in some medicines (*also called*: **china clay**)

> ⊙ Comes from Chinese *Gaoling*, literally 'high ridge', the name of a mountain in Northern China where it was mined

kaon *noun, physics* a type of meson (*also called*: **K-meson**)

kaput (*pronounced* ka-**poot**) *adjective, slang* broken, not working

karaoke (*pronounced* kar-i-**oh**-kei) *noun* an entertainment of singing well-known songs against pre-recorded backing music

karate (*pronounced* ka-**ra**-ti) *noun* a Japanese form of unarmed fighting using blows and kicks

karma *noun, Buddhism, Hinduism* **1** someone's destiny as determined by their actions in a previous life **2** the theory that everything has an inevitable result

karyotype *noun, biology* the number and shape of chromosomes in a cell nucleus

kayak *noun* **1** an Inuit sealskin canoe **2** a lightweight canoe for one person, manoeuvred with a single paddle

KB, Kb or **Kbit** *abbreviation, computing* kilobyte(s)

kbyte *abbreviation, computing* kilobyte

kcal *abbreviation* kilocalorie(s)

kebab *noun* small pieces of meat or vegetables cooked on a skewer

kedgeree *noun* a dish made with rice, fish and hard-boiled eggs

keek *verb, Scottish* to look, peep

keel *noun* **1** the piece of a ship's frame that lies lengthways along the bottom **2** *biology* in birds: the projecting bone to which the flight muscles are attached • **keel over** to overturn, fall over

keen¹ *adjective* **1** eager, enthusiastic **2** very sharp; bitingly cold ♦ **keenness** *noun*

keen² *verb* to wail in grief; lament ♦ **keening** *noun*

keenly *adverb* intensely, passionately, alertly

keep *verb* (**keeping, kept**) **1** to hold on to, not give or throw away **2** to look after, support **3** to store: *Keep everything in one place* **4** to fulfil (a promise) **5** to remain in a position or state: *keep to the left/keep warm* **6** (also **keep on**) to continue (doing something): *Keep taking the tablets* **7** of food: to stay in good condition **8** to celebrate: *keep Christmas* ➤ *noun* **1** food, board: *earn your keep* **2** a castle stronghold • **how are you keeping?** how are you? • **keep in with** to remain on good terms with • **keep out 1** to exclude **2** to stay outside • **keep up** to go on with, continue • **keep up with** to go as fast etc as ⊙ Comes from Old English *cepan*

keeper *noun* someone who looks after something: *zookeeper*

keeping *noun* care, charge • **in keeping with** suitable for or fitting in with

keepsake *noun* a gift in memory of an occasion etc

keg *noun* a small cask or barrel

kelp *noun* a type of large brown seaweed

kelvin *noun, physics* (abbreviation **K**) the standard unit of measure of thermodynamic or absolute temperature ⊙ Named after the British physicist Sir WilliamThomson, Lord *Kelvin* (1824–1907)

ken *noun* knowledge or understanding: *beyond the ken of the average person*

kendo *noun* a Japanese martial art using bamboo staves

kennel *noun* **1** a hut for a dog **2** (**kennels**) a place where dogs can be looked after

kenning *noun* a phrase used in Old English poetry to refer to something without saying its name, eg, 'mouse chaser' meaning 'cat'

kept past form of **keep**

keratin *noun, biology* a protein that forms the main component of hair, nails, claws, etc

kerb *noun* the edge of a pavement

❗ Do not confuse with: **curb**

kerchief *noun* a square of cloth used as a headscarf

kerfuffle, kefuffle or **carfuffle** (*pronounced* ka-**fu**-fl) *noun* commotion, fuss

kernel *noun* **1** a soft substance in the shell of a nut, or inside the stone of a fruit **2** the important part of anything

kerosene or **kerosine** *noun* paraffin oil obtained from shale or the distillation of petroleum

kestrel *noun* a type of small falcon which hovers

ketchup *noun* a flavouring sauce made from tomatoes etc

⊙ Originally spelt *catsup*, as it still is in US English; based on a Chinese word for 'fish brine'

ketone *noun, chemistry* any of a class of organic compounds derived from alcohols

ketone body *noun, biochemistry* any of three compounds that are produced in excessive amounts in the blood and urine of diabetics

kettle *noun* **1** a container with a spout for boiling water **2** a metal container for cooking something in liquid

kettledrum *noun* a drum made of a metal bowl covered with stretched skin etc

key *noun* **1** a device which is turned in a corresponding hole to lock or unlock, tighten, tune, etc **2** a lever pressed on a piano etc to produce a note **3** a button on a typewriter or computer keyboard which is pressed to type letters **4** the chief note of a piece of music **5** something which explains a mystery or deciphers a code **6** a book containing answers to exercises **7** *biology* a taxonomic system for distinguishing similar species ➤ *verb* to type on a typewriter or computer ➤ *adjective* important, essential

keyboard *noun* **1** the keys in a piano or organ arranged along a flat board **2** the keys of a

typewriter or computer **3** an electronic musical instrument with keys arranged as on a piano etc

keyed-up *adjective* excited

keyhole *noun* the hole in which a key of a door is placed

keyhole surgery *noun, medicine* surgery using miniature instruments, performed through tiny holes instead of large openings in the patient's flesh

keynote *noun* **1** the chief note of a piece of music **2** a central theme ➤ *adjective* **1** of a speech, lecture, etc: dealing with central principles **2** of fundamental importance

keypad *noun* a device with buttons that can be pushed to operate a television, telephone, etc

key signature *noun, music* the sharps and flats shown on the stave at the start of a piece of music, indicating the key in which it is to be played

keystone *noun* the stone at the highest point of an arch holding the rest in position

keystroke *noun* a single press of a key on a keyboard etc

kg *abbreviation* kilogram(s)

KGB *abbreviation, history* Committee of State Security (in Russian, *Komitet Gosudarstvennoi Bezopasnosti*), the former Soviet secret police

khaki *adjective* greenish-brown in colour ➤ *noun* **1** greenish-brown **2** cloth of this colour used for military uniforms

⊙ From an Urdu word meaning 'dusty'

khalifa or **khalifah** *noun* a caliph

Khalsa *noun* the baptized Sikh community

khan *noun* **1** a ruler or prince in central Asia **2** *history* a governor in ancient Persia ⊙ Related to Turkish *kagan* meaning 'ruler'

Khmer Rouge (*pronounced* k-mer roosz) *noun, history* a Communist guerrilla movement formerly active in Cambodia, and in government between 1975 and 1979

kHz *abbreviation* kilohertz, a unit of frequency equal to one thousand hertz

kibbutz (*pronounced* ki-**bootz**) *noun* (*plural* **kibbutzim**) a farming settlement in Israel in which all share the work

kibosh (*pronounced* **kai**-bosh) *verb, informal* to ruin or destroy

kick *verb* **1** to hit or strike out with the foot **2** *dancing, gymnastics, etc* to jerk (the leg) vigorously or swing it high **3** *rugby* to score (a drop goal) or make (a conversion) by kicking the ball between the posts **4** of a gun: to spring back violently when fired **5** *informal* to get rid of (a habit etc): *kick drugs* ➤ *noun* **1** a blow with the foot **2** *dancing, gymnastics, etc* a swing of the leg **3** the springing-back of a gun when fired **4** *informal* a thrill of excitement: *He gets a kick out* *of watching his son race* **5** power, pungency: *chilli with a kick* **6** *informal* the powerful effect of certain drugs or strong drink: *That fruit punch has quite a kick* • **for kicks** *informal* for fun

kickboxing *noun* a martial art involving kicking with bare feet and punching with gloved fists

kick-off *noun* the start (of a football game)

kick-start *noun* **1** (*also called*: **kick-starter**) a pedal on a motorcycle that is kicked downwards to start the engine **2** the starting of an engine with this pedal ➤ *verb* **1** to start (a motorcycle) using this pedal **2** to get something moving, to give an impulse to something

kid *noun* **1** *informal* a child **2** a young goat **3** the skin of a young goat ➤ *adjective* made of kid leather • **with kid gloves** very carefully or tactfully

kidnap *verb* (**kidnapping, kidnapped**) to carry (someone) off by force, often to demand payment for their return ✦ **kidnapper** *noun* ✦ **kidnapping** *noun*

kidney *noun* (*plural* **kidneys**), *anatomy* either of a pair of organs in the lower back which filter waste from the blood and produce urine

kidney bean *noun* a bean with a curved shape like a kidney

kill *verb* **1** to cause death to **2** to put an end to: *kill the rumours* ➤ *noun* **1** the act of killing **2** the animals killed by a hunter • **be in at the kill** to be there at the most exciting moment ✦ **killer** *noun*

killing *noun* the act of causing death • **make a killing** to make a lot of money quickly

killjoy *noun* someone who spoils the pleasure of others

kiln *noun* a large oven or furnace for baking pottery, bricks, etc or for drying grain, hops, etc

kilo *noun* (*plural* **kilos**, *abbrev* **K**) **1** a kilogram **2** a kilometre

kilo- *prefix* a thousand: *kilogram/kilometre* ⊙ Comes from Greek *chilioi* meaning 'a thousand'

kilobit *noun* (*abbrev* **Kbit**) a measure of computer data or memory, equal to 1024 bits

kilobyte *noun* (*abbrev* **KB, Kb** or **Kbyte**) a measure of computer data or memory, equal to 1024 bytes

kilocalorie *noun* a measure of energy equal to 1000 calories

kilogram or **kilogramme** *noun* (*abbrev* **kg**) the standard measure of weight, equal to 1000 grams

kilohertz *noun* (*plural* **kilohertz**; *symbol* **kHz**) a unit of frequency equal to 1000 hertz

kilojoule *noun* (*abbrev* **kJ**) a measure of energy, work and heat equal to 1000 joules

kilolitre *noun* (*abbrev* **kl**) a measure of volume equal to 1000 litres

kilometre *noun* (*abbrev* **km**) a measure of length equal to 1000 metres

kilovolt *noun* (*abbrev* **kV**) a measure of electric potential equal to 1000 volts

kilowatt *noun* (*abbrev* **kW**) a measure of electrical power equal to 1000 watts

kilt *noun* a pleated tartan skirt reaching to the knee, part of traditional Scottish dress

kilter *noun*: **out of kilter** out of sequence, off balance

kimono *noun* (*plural* **kimonos**) a loose Japanese robe, fastened with a sash

kin *noun* members of the same family, relations • **kith and kin** see **kith** • **next of kin** your nearest relative

kind[1] *noun* a sort, type • **in kind 1** in goods, not money: *paid in kind* **2** of repayment or retaliation: in the same form as the treatment received • **kind of** *informal* somewhat; slightly: *kind of old-fashioned* • **nothing of the kind** not at all; completely the reverse • **of a kind 1** of the same sort: *They're three of a kind* **2** denoting something not very satisfactory: *an explanation of a kind*

kind[2] *adjective* having good feelings towards others; generous, gentle ✦ **kindness** *noun*

kindergarten *noun* a nursery school

kind-hearted *adjective* kind

kindle *verb* **1** to light a fire **2** to catch fire **3** to stir up (feelings)

kindling *noun* material for starting a fire

kindly *adverb* in a kind way ➤ *adjective* kind, warm-hearted ✦ **kindliness** *noun*

kindred *noun* relatives, relations ➤ *adjective* of the same sort; related: *a kindred spirit*

kinematics *singular noun* the branch of physics concerned with the motion of objects, without consideration of the forces acting on them

kinesis *noun, biology* the movement of an organism or cell in response to a stimulus

kinetic *adjective* of or expressing motion: *kinetic energy/kinetic sculpture* (= sculpture which moves)

kinetic energy *noun* the energy a body has as a result of being in motion (*compare with*: **potential energy**)

kinetics *singular noun* **1** *physics* the scientific study of movement and force (also called: **dynamics**) **2** *chemistry* the scientific study of the rates of chemical reactions

kinetic theory *noun, physics* a theory which accounts for the physical properties of gases in terms of the motion of their molecules

king *noun* **1** the male ruler of a nation, especially one who has inherited the title **2** someone or something considered dominant: *king of the jungle* **3** a playing-card with a picture of a king **4** the most important chess piece, which must be protected from checkmate

kingcup *noun* the marsh marigold

kingdom *noun* **1** the area ruled by a king **2** any of the major divisions of the natural world, ie animal, plant or mineral

kingfisher *noun* a type of fish-eating bird with brightly coloured feathers

kingly *adjective* like a king; royal

kingpin *noun* the most important person in an organization

king-size *adjective* of a larger than usual size

kink *noun* **1** a bend or curl in a rope, hair, etc **2** an oddness in personality, especially a strange sexual preference

kinky *adjective* (**kinkier, kinkiest**) **1** twisted, contorted **2** interested in unusual sexual acts

kinsfolk *plural noun* relations, relatives

kinship *noun* **1** family relationship **2** a state of having common characteristics

kinsman, kinswoman *noun* a close relation

kiosk *noun* **1** a small stall for the sale of papers, sweets, etc **2** a telephone box

kip *noun, slang* a bed ➤ *verb* (**kipping, kipped**) to go to bed, sleep

kipper *noun* a smoked and dried herring

kirk *noun, Scottish* a church

kiss *verb* **1** to touch lovingly with the lips **2** to touch gently ➤ *noun* (*plural* **kisses**) a loving touch with the lips • **kiss of life** a mouth-to-mouth method of restoring breathing

kit *noun* an outfit of clothes, tools, etc necessary for a particular job

kitchen *noun* a room where food is cooked

kitchenette *noun* a small kitchen

kitchen garden *noun* a vegetable garden

kite *noun* **1** a light frame, covered with paper or other material, for flying in the air **2** a four-sided figure, with two pairs of equal sides that are not parallel **3** a kind of hawk

kith *noun*: **kith and kin** friends and relatives

kitsch *noun* sentimental or vulgar tastelessness in art, design, etc ➤ *adjective* tastelessly or vulgarly sentimental ⊙ Comes from German, from *kitschen* meaning 'to throw' (a work of art together)

kitten *noun* a young cat • **have kittens** *informal* to make a great fuss

kittenish *adjective* behaving like a kitten, playful

kitty¹ *noun* (*plural* **kitties**) a sum of money set aside for a purpose

kitty² *noun* (*plural* **kitties**) *informal* a cat or kitten

kiwi *noun* **1** a fast-running almost wingless bird of New Zealand **2** a kiwi fruit

kiwi fruit *noun* an edible fruit with a thin hairy skin and bright green flesh

kJ *abbreviation* kilojoule(s)

kl *abbreviation* kilolitre(s)

klaxon *noun* a loud electric horn used as a signal

> ⊙ Originally a tradename for a type of hooter on early cars

kleptomania *noun* an uncontrollable desire to steal ♦ **kleptomaniac** *noun & adjective*

km *abbreviation* kilometre(s)

K-meson another word for **kaon**

knack (*pronounced* nak) *noun* a special talent or ability: *a knack for saying the right thing*

knacker (*pronounced* **nak**-er) *noun* a buyer of old horses for slaughter ➤ *verb, informal* to exhaust, tire out

knapsack (*pronounced* **nap**-sak) *noun* a bag for food, clothes, etc slung on the back

knave (*pronounced* neiv) *noun* **1** a cheating rogue **2** in playing-cards, the jack

knavery (*pronounced* **neiv**-e-ri) *noun* dishonesty

knavish (*pronounced* **neiv**-ish) *adjective* cheating, wicked

knead (*pronounced* need) *verb* **1** to work (dough etc) by pressing with the fingers **2** to massage

knee (*pronounced* nee) *noun* the joint at the bend of the leg

kneecap (*pronounced* **nee**-kap) *noun* the flat round bone on the front of the knee joint ➤ *verb* to cause to suffer

knee-jerk *noun* an involuntary kick of the lower leg, caused by a reflex to a sharp tap just below the kneecap ➤ *adjective* said of a response or reaction: unthinking, predictable

kneel (*pronounced* neel) *verb* (**kneeling, knelt**) to go down on one or both knees

knell (*pronounced* nel) *noun* **1** the tolling of a bell for a death or funeral **2** a warning of a sad end or failure

knickerbockers (*pronounced* **nik**-e-bok-ez) *plural noun* loose breeches tucked in at the knee

> ⊙ Named after Diedrich *Knickerbocker*, a fictional Dutchman invented by US author Washington Irving in the 19th century

knickers (*pronounced* **nik**-ez) *plural noun* women's or girls' underpants

knick-knack (*pronounced* **nik**-nak) *noun* a small, ornamental article

knife (*pronounced* naif) *noun* (*plural* **knives**) a tool for cutting ➤ *verb* to stab • **at knife point** under threat of injury

knight (*pronounced* nait) *noun* **1** *history* a man of high social status, trained to use arms to serve a lord **2** *Brit* a rank, with the title *Sir*, awarded by the monarch or the government **3** a piece used in chess, shaped like a horse's head ➤ *verb* to raise to the rank of knight

knight errant *noun, history* a knight who

travelled in search of adventures

knighthood (*pronounced* **nait**-huwd) *noun* the rank of a knight

knightly (*pronounced* **nait**-li) *adjective* **1** to do with knights **2** gallant, courageous

knit (*pronounced* nit) *verb* (**knitting, knitted**) **1** to form a garment from yarn by making a series of knots using knitting needles **2** to join closely

knitting (*pronounced* **nit**-ing) *noun* **1** a garment, etc that is being knitted **2** the art of producing something knitted

knitting needles *plural noun* a pair of thin pointed rods used in knitting

knitwear *noun* woollen clothes produced by knitting

knob (*pronounced* nob) *noun* **1** a small rounded projection **2** a round door-handle

knock (*pronounced* nok) *verb* **1** to tap on something, especially a door, to have it opened **2** to strike, hit **3** *informal* to criticize ➤ *noun* **1** a sudden stroke **2** a tap (on a door) **3** *informal* a personal misfortune, setback, etc • **knock back** *informal* **1** to refuse or reject **2** to eat or drink greedily • **knock down 1** to demolish **2** *informal* to reduce in price • **knock off** *informal* **1** to stop work for the day **2** to plagiarize, copy illegally • **knock out** to hit (someone) hard enough to make them unconscious • **knock up 1** to put together hastily **2** to knock on someone's door to wake them up **3** *slang* to make pregnant

knock-back *noun* **1** a rejection or refusal **2** a financial setback

knocker (*pronounced* **nok**-er) *noun* a hinged weight on a door for knocking with

knock-kneed (*pronounced* nok-**need**) *adjective* having knees that touch in walking

knockout *noun* **1** *informal* someone or something stunning **2** a competition in which the defeated competitors are dropped after each round **3** *boxing etc* the act of knocking someone unconscious **4** *boxing etc* a blow that knocks someone unconscious ➤ *adjective* **1** of a competition: eliminating the losers in each round **2** of a punch etc: leaving the victim unconscious **3** *informal* excellent

knoll (*pronounced* nohl) *noun* a small rounded hill

knot (*pronounced* not) *noun* **1** a hard lump, eg one made by tying string, or found in wood at the join between trunk and branch **2** a tangle **3** a small gathering, a cluster of people **4** a measure of speed for ships (about 1.85 kilometre per hour) ➤ *verb* (**knotting, knotted**) to tie in a knot

knotted (*pronounced* **not**-id) *adjective* full of knots

knotty (*pronounced* **not**-i) *adjective* (**knottier, knottiest**) **1** having knots **2** difficult, complicated: *knotty problem*

know (*pronounced* noh) *verb* (**knowing, known, knew**) **1** to be aware or sure of **2** to have learnt or have an understanding of: *I know some French* **3** to be familiar with: *I know James well* **4** to identify or recognize: *I don't know this song* • **in the know** having information not known to most people • **you never know** *informal* it's not impossible ⊙ Comes from Old English *cnawan*

know-all or *N Am* **know-it-all** *noun* (*plural* **know-alls**), *derogatory* someone who seems, or claims, to know more than others

know-how *noun, informal* the ability or skill to do something

knowing (*pronounced* **noh**-ing) *adjective* **1** clever; cunning **2** of a glance, smile, etc: signifying secret awareness of something

knowingly (*pronounced* **noh**-ing-li) *adverb* **1** intentionally **2** in a way which shows you understand something which is secret or which has not been directly expressed

knowledge (*pronounced* **nol**-ij) *noun* **1** that which is known **2** information **3** ability, skill

knowledgeable (*pronounced* **nol**-ij-a-bl) *adjective* showing or having knowledge

knowledge base *noun, computing* a collection of specialist knowledge used in an expert system ♦ **knowledge-based** *adjective* of a software system: using a knowledge base

knuckle (*pronounced* **nu**-kl) *noun* a joint of the fingers • **knuckle down** to begin to work hard • **knuckle under** to give in, yield • **near the knuckle** *informal* bordering on the indecent

knuckleduster *noun* a metal covering worn on the knuckles as a weapon

KO or **k.o.** *abbreviation* **1** kick-off **2** knockout **3** knock out ➤ *noun* (*plural* **KO's** or **k.o.'s**), *informal* a knockout ➤ *verb* (**KO'd** or **k.o.'d, KO'ing** or **k.o.ing**), *informal* to knock someone out

koala *noun* an Australian tree-climbing animal resembling a small bear

kohl *noun* a black powder used as an eyeliner

kookaburra another word for **laughing jackass**

Koran, Qoran, Quran or **Qur'an** *noun* (*pronounced* kaw-**ran** or ko-**ran**) the sacred book of Islam

kosher (*pronounced* **ko**-sher) *adjective* **1** *Judaism* pure and clean according to Jewish law **2** *informal* acceptable, all right

kowtow *verb* (usually **kowtow to**) to treat with too much respect

⊙ Based on a Chinese phrase meaning to prostrate yourself before the emperor

kph *abbreviation* kilometres per hour

Kr *symbol, chemistry* krypton

kremlin *noun* (**the Kremlin**) the government of Russia, and of the former USSR ◷ Comes from Russian *kreml* meaning 'a citadel'

krill *noun* a small shrimplike creature eaten by whales etc

Krishna *noun, Hinduism* an important deity that is a form of Vishnu

krypton *noun, chemistry* (symbol **Kr**) an inert gas present in the air, used in fluorescent lighting

kudos (*pronounced* **kyood**-os) *noun* fame, glory

Ku Klux Klan *noun* a secret society of White Protestants in the southern USA, formed after the American Civil War, which in the 20th century used violence against Blacks, Jews and Catholics ◷ Comes from Greek *kyklos* meaning 'circle' + **clan**

kulak (*pronounced* **koo**-lak) *noun, history* a relatively wealthy, property-owning Russian peasant ◷ Comes from Russian meaning 'fist' or 'tight-fisted person'

Kulturkampf (*pronounced* kool-**toor**-kampf) *noun, history* a conflict in the German Empire between the Prussian state and the Roman Catholic Church, most intense between 1870 and 1878 ◷ Comes from German *kultur* meaning 'culture' + *kampf* meaning 'struggle' or 'fight'

kung-fu *noun* a Chinese form of self-defence

Kuomintang (*pronounced* **kwo**-min-tang) *noun* the Chinese nationalist people's party

kW *abbreviation* kilowatt(s)

Kwanzaa *noun* a seven-day holiday (from 26 December to 2 January) celebrating African-American life, history and culture

◷ From a Swahili term meaning 'first fruits'

kyrie (*pronounced* **kee**-ri-ei) *noun* **1** a prayer in the Roman Catholic mass following the opening anthem **2** a musical setting for this

Ll

L *symbol* the Roman numeral for 50

l *abbreviation* litre(s)

La *symbol, chemistry* lanthanum

la same as **lah**

lab *noun, informal* a laboratory

label *noun* a small written note fixed onto something listing its contents, price, etc ➤ *verb* (**labels, labelling, labelled**) **1** to fix a label to **2** to call by a certain name: *The media labelled him a 'love rat'*

labial (*pronounced* **lei**-bi-al) *adjective* of the lips

labile *noun, chemistry* of a chemical compound: readily altered by heat etc

labium (*pronounced* **lei**-bi-um) *noun* (*plural* **labia**) **1** a lip or something like a lip **2** one of the fleshy folds forming part of the human vulva

laboratory *noun* (*plural* **laboratories**) a scientist's workroom

laborious *adjective* requiring hard work; wearisome

labour or *US* **labor** *noun* **1** hard work **2** workers on a job **3** the process of childbirth ➤ *verb* **1** to work hard **2** to move slowly or with difficulty **3** to emphasize (a point) excessively

laboured *adjective* showing signs of effort

labourer *noun* someone who does heavy unskilled work

labour-intensive *adjective, economics, geography* of an industry: requiring a large resource of workers for the capital invested, as opposed to machinery etc (*compare with:* **capital-intensive**)

Labour Party *noun* one of the chief political parties of the UK, supporting greater social equality

labour-saving *adjective* of a device: reducing the amount of work or effort needed

labrador *noun* a large black or fawn-coloured dog

laburnum *noun* (*plural* **laburnums**) a tree with large clusters of yellow flowers and poisonous seeds

labyrinth (*pronounced* **lab**-ir-inth) *noun* **1** a maze **2** the complex arrangement of structures in the inner ear

lace *noun* **1** a cord for fastening shoes etc **2** decorative fabric made with fine thread ➤ *verb* **1** to fasten with a lace **2** to add alcohol to (a drink)

lacerate (*pronounced* **las**-e-reit) *verb* **1** to tear, rip **2** to wound ♦ **laceration** *noun*

lachrymal (*pronounced* **lak**-ri-mal) *adjective, formal* of tears

lachrymal gland *noun* a gland at the edge of the eye that produces tears

lachrymose (*pronounced* **lak**-ri-mohs) *adjective, formal* prone to crying

lack *verb* **1** to be missing: *What's lacking is a sense of adventure* **2** to be without: *She lacks intelligence* ➤ *noun* want, need

lackadaisical *adjective* bored, half-hearted

lackey *noun* (*plural* **lackeys**) **1** a manservant **2** someone who acts like a slave

lacklustre or *US* **lackluster** *adjective* dull, insipid

laconic *adjective* using few words to express meaning ♦ **laconically** *adverb*

lacquer *noun* a varnish ➤ *verb* to varnish

lacrosse *noun* a twelve-a-side ball game played with sticks having a shallow net at the end

lactate[1] *verb* to produce or secrete milk

lactate[2] *noun, chemistry* a salt or ester of lactic acid

lactation *noun* in female mammals: the controlled secretion of milk by the mammary glands

lactic *adjective* of milk

lactic acid *noun* an organic acid found in sour milk and in muscle tissue when not enough oxygen is available to break down carbohydrate, eg during exercise

lactose *noun* a sugar obtained by evaporating whey (*also called:* **milk sugar**)

lacy *adjective* (**lacier, laciest**) like, made of, or trimmed with lace

lad *noun* a boy, a youth

ladder *noun* **1** a set of rungs or steps between two supports, for climbing up or down **2** a run from a broken stitch, in a stocking etc

laden *adjective* loaded, burdened

la-di-da or **lah-di-dah** *adjective, informal* pretentiously snobbish

lading *noun* a load; cargo

ladle *noun* a large spoon for lifting liquid out of a container ➤ *verb* to lift with a ladle

lady *noun* (*plural* **ladies**) **1** a woman of good manners **2** a title for the wife of a knight, lord or baronet, or a daughter of a member of the aristocracy **3** (**the ladies**) a public lavatory for women

ladybird *noun* a small beetle, usually red with black spots

lady-in-waiting *noun* (*plural* **ladies-in-waiting**) a woman who attends a queen or princess

lady-killer *noun, informal* a man who is irresistibly attractive to women

ladylike *adjective* showing attributes, eg refinement and politeness, considered appropriate to a lady

ladyship *noun* used in talking to or about a titled lady: *your ladyship*

lag *verb* (**lagging, lagged**) 1 to move slowly and fall behind 2 to cover (a boiler or pipes) with a warm covering for insulation ➤ *noun* a delay

lager *noun* a light beer

laggard *noun* someone who lags behind ➤ *adjective* lagging behind

lagging *noun* material for covering pipes etc for insulation

lagoon *noun* a shallow stretch of water separated from the sea by low sandbanks, rocks, etc

lag time *noun, geography* the amount of time between peak rainfall and peak river discharge

lah or **la** *noun, music* in sol-fa notation: the sixth note of the major scale

lahar *noun, geography* a mudflow

laid past form of **lay**[1]

laid-back *adjective, informal* relaxed, easy-going

laid-up *adjective* ill in bed

lain past participle of **lie**[2]

lair (*pronounced* leir) *noun* the den of a wild beast ⊙ Comes from Old English *leger* meaning 'a couch'

⚠ Do not confuse with: **layer**

laird *noun* in Scotland, a landowner

laissez-faire (*pronounced* les-ei-**feir**) *noun* a general principle of not interfering

laity (*pronounced* **lei**-i-ti) *noun* ordinary people, not clergymen

lake *noun* a large stretch of water surrounded by land

lama *noun* a Buddhist priest, monk or spiritual leader of Tibet

lamb *noun* 1 a young sheep 2 the meat of this animal 3 a gentle person

lambast (*pronounced* lam-**bast**) *verb* to beat or reprimand severely

lame *adjective* 1 unable to walk, disabled 2 not good enough, not very convincing or impressive: *a lame excuse* ➤ *verb* to make lame ◆ **lamely** *adverb* (adjective, meaning 2)

lame duck *noun* an inefficient, useless person or organization

lamella *noun* (*plural* **lamellae**), *biology* 1 a thin sheet or plate of tissue, especially one of the layers that make up compact bone 2 any of the thin sheet-like membranes within the chloroplasts of plant cells 3 any of the vertical spore-bearing structures on the underside of the cap of a mushroom or toadstool

lament (*pronounced* la-**ment**) *verb* 1 to mourn, feel or express grief for 2 to regret ➤ *noun* 1 a show of grief 2 a mournful poem or piece of music ◆ **lamentation** *noun*

lamentable (*pronounced* **lam**-en-tab-l) *adjective* 1 pitiful: *a lamentable waste of young lives* 2 very bad: *a lamentable performance* ◆ **lamentably**

lamina *noun* (*plural* **laminae**), *biology* the flattened part of a leaf blade

laminate (*pronounced* **lam**-i-nit) *noun* a laminated sheet, material, etc

laminated *adjective* 1 made by putting layers together: *laminated glass* 2 covered with a thin sheet of protective material, eg transparent plastic film

Lammas *noun* 1 August, an old feast day celebrating the beginning of the harvest

lamp *noun* a device which gives out light, containing an electric bulb, candle, etc

lampoon *noun* a piece of ridicule or satire directed at someone ➤ *verb* to ridicule, satirize

lamppost *noun* a pillar supporting a street lamp

lamprey (*pronounced* **lamp**-ri) *noun* (*plural* **lampreys**) a type of fish like an eel

lampshade *noun* a shade placed over a lamp or light bulb to soften the light coming from it

LAN (*pronounced* lan) *abbreviation, computing* local area network, a computer network which operates over a small area, such as an office or group of offices

lance *noun* a long shaft of wood, with a spearhead ➤ *verb* to cut open (a boil etc) with a knife

lance-corporal *noun* a soldier with rank just below a corporal

lancet *noun* a sharp surgical instrument

land *noun* 1 the solid portion of the earth's surface 2 ground 3 soil 4 a part of a country ➤ *verb* 1 to arrive on land or on shore 2 to set (an aircraft, ship, etc) on land or on shore

landed *adjective* owning lands and estates: *landed gentry*

landfill *noun* 1 a site where rubbish is disposed of by burying it under layers of earth 2 the rubbish that is disposed of in this way

landform *noun* a natural feature on the earth's surface

landing *noun* 1 a coming ashore or to ground 2 a place for getting on shore 3 the level part of a staircase between the flights of steps

landlocked *adjective* almost or completely shut in by land

landlord or **landlady** *noun* (*plural* **landlords** or **landladies**) **1** the owner of land or accommodation for rent **2** the owner or manager of an inn etc

landlubber *noun* someone who works on land and knows little about the sea

landmark *noun* **1** an object on land that serves as a guide **2** an important event

landmass *noun* (*plural* **landmasses**) a large area of land not broken up by seas

land mine *noun* a bomb laid on or near the surface of the ground which explodes when someone passes over it

land reform *noun, geography* the redistribution of agricultural land to people without land

landscape *noun* **1** an area of land and the features it contains **2** a painting, photograph, etc of inland scenery **3** an orientation of a page, illustration, etc that is wider than it is tall or deep (*compare with*: **portrait**)

landscape gardening *noun* the art of laying out grounds so as to produce the effect of a picturesque landscape

landslide *noun* a mass of land that slips down from the side of a hill

landslide victory *noun* a win in an election in which a great mass of votes goes to one side

lane *noun* **1** a narrow street or passage **2** a part of the road, sea or air to which cars, ships, aircraft, etc must keep **3** a marked subdivision of a running track or swimming pool for one competitor **4** a division of a bowling alley

language *noun* **1** human speech **2** the speech of a particular people or nation

language laboratory *noun* a room equipped with audio equipment or computers, used for language learning

languid *adjective* lacking liveliness

languish *verb* **1** to grow weak, droop **2** to pine: *The dog was languishing for its master*
♦ **languishing** *adjective*

languor (*pronounced* **lang**-gor) *noun* a languid state, listlessness

laniard another spelling of **lanyard**

La Niña (*pronounced* la **nee**-nya) *noun, meteorology* unusually cool temperatures in the Eastern Pacific Ocean, which causes extreme weather conditions (*compare with*: **El Niño**)

⊕ A Spanish term meaning 'the little girl', modelled on *El Niño*

lank *adjective* **1** tall and thin **2** of hair: straight and limp

lanky *adjective* (**lankier, lankiest**) tall and thin

lanolin *noun* a fat extracted from sheep's wool

lantern *noun* a lamp or light contained in a transparent case, usually of glass

lantern-jawed *adjective* hollow-cheeked, long-jawed

lanthanide series *noun, chemistry* a group of 15 highly reactive metallic elements with atomic numbers from 57 (lanthanum) to 71 (lutetium), which have similar chemical properties and are difficult to separate

lanthanum *noun, chemistry* (symbol **La**) a silvery-white metallic element

lanyard or **laniard** *noun* **1** a short rope used for fastening rigging etc on a ship **2** a cord for hanging a whistle etc round the neck

lap *verb* (**lapping, lapped**) **1** to lick up with the tongue **2** to wash or flow against **3** to wrap round, surround **4** to get a lap ahead of other competitors in a race ➤ *noun* **1** the front part, from waist to knees, of someone seated **2** a fold **3** one round of a racetrack or competition course • **lap up** to accept (praise etc) greedily

lapdog *noun* a small pet dog

lapel *noun* the part of a coat joined to the collar and folded back on the chest

lapis lazuli (*pronounced* lap-is **laz**-yuw-lee) *noun* **1** *geology* a deep-blue mineral used as a gemstone **2** a bright-blue colour ⊕ Comes from Latin *lapis* meaning 'stone' + *lazuli* meaning 'azure'

lap of honour *noun* (*plural* **laps of honour**) a celebratory lap of a racecourse or sports ground by the winner or winners

lapse *verb* **1** to fall into bad habits **2** to cease, be no longer valid ➤ *noun* **1** a mistake, a failure **2** a period of time passing

lapse rate *noun, geography* rate of change in temperature in relation to atmospheric height

laptop *noun* a compact portable computer combining screen, keyboard, and processor in one unit (*also called*: **laptop computer**)

lapwing *noun* a type of bird of the plover family (*also called*: **peewit**)

larceny *noun* stealing, theft

larch *noun* (*plural* **larches**) a cone-bearing deciduous tree

lard *noun* the melted fat of a pig ➤ *verb* **1** to put strips of bacon in meat before cooking **2** to smear with lard

larder *noun* **1** a room or place where food is kept **2** a stock of food

large *adjective* great in size, amount, etc • **at large 1** at liberty, free **2** in general: *the public at large* ⊕ Comes from French *large* meaning 'broad' or 'wide'

large intestine *noun, anatomy* in mammals: the part of the alimentary canal comprising the caecum, colon and rectum

largely *adverb* mainly, to a great extent

largesse (*pronounced* lah-**szes**) *noun* a generous giving away of money etc

largo *music, adverb* in a slow and dignified manner ➤ *noun* (*plural* **largos**) a piece of music to be played in a slow and dignified manner ⓘ Comes from Italian, meaning 'broad'

lariat (*pronounced* **lar**-i-at) *noun* a lasso ⓘ Comes from Spanish *la reata* meaning 'the lasso'

lark *noun* **1** a general name for several kinds of singing bird **2** a piece of fun or mischief ➤ *verb* to fool about, behave mischievously

larkspur *noun* a plant with blue, white or pink flowers

larva *noun* (*plural* **larvae** – *pronounced* **lah**-vee) an insect in its first stage after coming out of the egg, a grub

laryngitis (*pronounced* lar-in-**jai**-tis) *noun* inflammation of the larynx

larynx (*pronounced* **lar**-ingks) *noun* (*plural* **larynxes** or **larynges** – *pronounced* la-**rin**-jeez)the upper part of the windpipe containing the vocal cords

lasagne (*pronounced* la-**zan**-ya) *plural noun* flat sheets of pasta ➤ *singular noun* (also **lasagna**) a baked dish made with this

lascivious (*pronounced* la-**siv**-i-us) *adjective* lustful; indecent, lewd

laser *noun* **1** a very narrow powerful beam of light, used for eg printing, optical scanning, surgical operations, etc **2** an instrument that concentrates light into such a beam

ⓘ An acronym of '*l*ight *a*mplification by *s*timulated *e*mission of *r*adiation'

laser printer *noun, computing* a type of high-quality printer which uses a laser beam to produce text, etc and transfers this to paper

lash *noun* (*plural* **lashes**) **1** a thong or cord of a whip **2** a stroke with a whip **3** an eyelash ➤ *verb* **1** to strike with a whip **2** to fasten tightly with a rope etc **3** to attack with bitter words • **lash out 1** to kick or swing out without thinking **2** to speak angrily **3** to spend extravagantly

lass *noun* (*plural* **lasses**) a girl

lassitude (*pronounced* **las**-i-tyood) *noun* lack of energy, weariness

lasso (*pronounced* la-**soo**)*noun* (*plural* **lassoes** or **lassos**) a long rope with a loop that tightens when the rope is pulled, used for catching wild horses etc ➤ *verb* (**lassos** or **lassoes, lassoing, lassoed**) to catch with a lasso

last *adjective* **1** coming after all the others: *last person to arrive* **2** the final one remaining: *last ticket* **3** most recent: *my last employer* ➤ *adverb* **1** after all others **2** most recently **3** lastly ➤ *verb* **1** to continue, go on **2** to remain in good condition ➤ *noun* a foot-shaped tool on which shoes are made or repaired • **at last** in the end • **on your last legs** completely worn out, about to collapse • **to the last** to the end

last-ditch *adjective* done as a last resort: *a last-ditch attempt*

lastly *adverb* finally

last-minute *adjective* made, done or given at the latest possible moment

last rites *plural noun* religious ceremonies performed for a person who is dying

last straw *noun* the last in a series of unpleasant events, which makes a situation unbearable

last word *noun* the final comment or decision about something

latch *noun* (*plural* **latches**) **1** a wooden or metal catch used to fasten a door **2** a light door-lock ➤ *verb* to fasten with a latch

latchkey *noun* a key to raise the latch of a door

latchkey child *noun* a child who regularly returns home to an empty house

late *adjective & adverb* **1** coming after the expected time: *His train was late* **2** far on in time: *It's getting late* **3** recent: *our late disagreement* **4** recently dead: *the late author* **5** recently, but no longer, holding an office or position: *the late chairman* • **of late** recently ♦ **lateness** *noun* (meanings 1 and 2)

lately *adverb* recently

latent *adjective* hidden, undeveloped as yet: *latent ability/latent hostility*

latent heat *noun, physics* the amount of heat energy required to change a solid to a liquid, or a liquid to a gas, without a change in temperature

lateral *adjective* of, at, to or from the side

lateral thinking *noun* thinking which seeks new ways of looking at a problem and does not merely proceed in logical stages

latex (*pronounced* **lei**-teks)*noun* the milky juice of plants, especially of the rubber tree

lath (*pronounced* lahth) *noun* a thin narrow strip of wood ⓘ Comes from Old English *lætt*

❗ Do not confuse: **lath** and **lathe**

lathe (*pronounced* leidh) *noun* a machine for turning and shaping articles of wood, metal, etc ⓘ Probably comes from Old Danish *lad* meaning 'a supporting framework'

lather *noun* **1** a foam or froth, eg from soap and water **2** *informal* a state of agitation: *She was in a lather about the broken window* ➤ *verb* to cover with lather

Latin *noun* the language of ancient Rome

latitude *noun* **1** *maths* the angle between the great circle of a sphere and a point on its surface (*compare with*: **longitude**) **2** *geography* the angle between the equator and a place on earth, measured in degrees (*compare with*: **longitude**) **3** freedom of action or choice

latrine (*pronounced* la-**treen**)*noun* a toilet in a camp, barracks, etc

latter *adjective* **1** (*contrasted with*: **former**) the last of two things mentioned: *Between working and sleeping, I prefer the latter* **2** recent

latter-day *adjective* of recent times

latterly *adverb* recently

lattice *noun* **1** a network of crossed wooden etc strips **2** a window constructed this way **3** *chemistry* the regular three-dimensional arrangement of atoms, ions or molecules that forms the structure of a crystalline solid

laud *verb, formal* to praise

laudable *adjective* worthy of being praised ♦ **laudably** *adverb*

laudanum (*pronounced* **lawd**-an-um) *noun* an alcoholic solution of opium, taken as a popular medicine in Victorian times

laudatory *adjective* expressing praise

laugh *verb* to make sounds with the voice in showing amusement, scorn, etc ➤ *noun* the sound of laughing

laughable *adjective* comical, ridiculous

laughing gas *noun* nitrous oxide, used as an anaesthetic

laughing jackass *noun* the Australian giant kingfisher (*also called*: **kookaburra**)

laughing stock *noun* an object of scornful laughter

laughter *noun* the act or noise of laughing

launch *verb* **1** to slide (a boat or ship) into water, especially on its first voyage **2** to fire off (a rocket etc) **3** to start off on a course **4** to put (a product) on the market with publicity **5** to throw, hurl ➤ *noun* (*plural* **launches**) **1** the act of launching **2** a large motor boat

launch pad *noun* the area for launching a spacecraft or missile

launder *verb* to wash and iron clothes etc

launderette *noun* a shop where customers may wash clothes etc in washing machines

laundry *noun* (*plural* **laundries**) **1** a place where clothes are washed **2** clothes to be washed

laureate (*pronounced* **law**-ri-it) *adjective* honoured for artistic or intellectual achievement: *poet laureate*

laurel *noun* **1** the bay tree, from which ceremonial wreaths were made in ancient times **2** (**laurels**) honours or victories gained ● **rest on your laurels** to be content with past successes and not try for any more

lava *noun* molten rock etc thrown out by a volcano, becoming solid as it cools

lavatory *noun* (*plural* **lavatories**) a toilet

lavender *noun* **1** a sweet-smelling plant with small pale-purple flowers **2** a pale purple colour

lavish *verb* to spend or give very freely

➤ *adjective* very generous

law *noun* **1** the official rules that apply in a country or state **2** one such rule **3** a scientific rule stating the conditions under which certain things always happen

law-abiding *adjective* obeying the law

law court *noun* a place where people accused of crimes are tried

lawful *adjective* allowed by law ♦ **lawfully** *adverb*

lawless *adjective* paying no attention to, and not observing, the laws

lawn[1] *noun* an area of smooth grass, eg as part of a garden

lawn[2] *noun* a kind of fine linen

lawnmower *noun* a machine for cutting grass

lawn tennis *noun* tennis played on a hard or grass court

lawrencium *noun, chemistry* (symbol **Lr**) a synthetic radioactive metallic element

⊙ Named after Ernest Orlando *Lawrence* (1901–58), US physicist

lawsuit *noun* a quarrel or dispute to be settled by a court of law

lawyer *noun* someone whose work it is to give advice in matters of law

lax *adjective* **1** not strict **2** careless, negligent ♦ **laxity** *noun*

laxative *noun* a medicine which loosens the bowels

lay[1] *verb* (**laying, laid**) **1** to place or set down: *lay the book on the table* **2** to put (eg a burden, duty) on (someone): *new laws laying a heavy burden of responsibility on teachers/try to lay the blame on someone else* **3** to beat down: *All the barley in the field had been laid flat by the storm* **4** to make to leave or subside: *lay a ghost* **5** to set in order, arrange: *lay a trap/lay the table* **6** of a hen: to produce eggs: *Young hens quite often lay double-yolkers* **7** to bet, wager: *He's sure to be late. I'd lay money on it* ● **lay about someone** to beat them all over ● **lay down 1** to assert: *laying down the law* **2** to store (eg wine) ● **lay off 1** to dismiss (workers) temporarily **2** *informal* to stop: *lay off arguing* ● **lay up** to store for future use ● **lay waste** to ruin, destroy

❗ Do not confuse with: **lie**.
It may help to remember that the verb **lay** always takes an object, while an object is not used with the verb **lie**.

lay[2] past tense of **lie**[2]

lay[3] *adjective* **1** not of the clergy **2** without special training in a particular subject: *a medical book aimed at the lay reader*

lay[4] *noun, old* a short poem or song

layabout *noun* a lazy idle person

lay-by *noun* (*plural* **lay-bys**) a parking area at the side of a road

layer *noun* a thickness forming a covering or level

! Do not confuse with: **lair**.
Layer comes from the verb 'to lay'

layered *adjective* having a number of distinct layers: *layered cake*

lay-figure *noun* a jointed model of a human figure used by artists

layman *noun* (*plural* **laymen**)a man without special training in a subject

layout *noun* the way something, eg a printed page, is arranged

laze *verb* to be lazy; idle

lazy *adjective* (**lazier, laziest**) not inclined to work; idle ◆ **lazily** *adverb*

lazybones *noun, informal* an idler

lb *abbreviation* pound(s) (in weight)

lbw *abbreviation, cricket* leg before wicket

LCD or **lcd** *abbreviation* **1** liquid crystal display, used in digital devices to display figures **2** *maths* lowest (or least) common denominator

LCM or **lcm** *abbreviation, maths* lowest (or least) common multiple

lea *noun, old* a meadow

leach *verb* to allow liquid to seep slowly through or out of something ⊙ Comes from Old English *leccan* meaning 'to water' or 'to moisten'

! Do not confuse with: **leech**

leaching *noun, geography* removal of nutrients from the soil, caused by the action of rainwater

lead¹ (*pronounced* leed) *verb* (**leads, leading, led**) **1** to show the way by going first **2** to direct, guide **3** to persuade **4** to live (a busy, quiet, etc life) **5** of a road: to go (to) ➤ *noun* **1** the first or front place **2** guidance, direction **3** a leash for a dog etc

lead² (*pronounced* led) *noun* **1** *chemistry* (symbol **Pb**) a soft bluish-grey metal **2** the part of a pencil that writes, which is actually made of graphite **3** a weight used for sounding depths at sea etc

leaden *adjective* **1** made of lead **2** lead-coloured **3** dull, heavy

leader *noun* **1** someone who leads or goes first; a chief **2** a column in a newspaper expressing the editor's opinions

leadership *noun* **1** the state of being a leader **2** the ability to lead

lead-free *adjective* of petrol: containing no lead

leading (*pronounced* led-ing)*noun* the vertical distance between the bottom of one line of type and the top of the next in a document

leading light *noun* someone who is very important in a particular field

leading question *noun* one asked in such a way as to suggest the desired answer

leaf *noun* (*plural* **leaves**) **1** a part of a plant growing from the side of a stem **2** a page of a book **3** a hinged flap on a table etc • **turn over a new leaf** to begin again and do better

leaflet *noun* a small printed sheet

leaf litter *noun, geography* fallen leaves on the ground, especially when regarded as part of an ecosystem

leafy *adjective* (**leafier, leafiest**) **1** of a plant or tree: having a lot of leaves **2** of a place: having a lot of trees and plants

league *noun* **1** a union of people, nations, etc for the benefit of each other **2** an association of clubs for games **3** *old* a measure of distance, approximately 3 miles (about 4.8 kilometres) • **in league with** allied with

League of Nations *noun, history* an international body, whose constitution was drawn up in 1919, formed to secure peace, settlement of disputes, and international co-operation, and replaced in 1945 by the United Nations

league table *noun* **1** a list where people or clubs are placed according to performance or points gained **2** any grouping where relative success is compared

leak *noun* **1** a hole through which liquid passes **2** an escape of gas or liquid **3** a release of secret information ➤ *verb* **1** to escape, pass out **2** to give (secret information) to the media etc

leakage *noun* a leaking

lean *verb* (**leaning, leaned** or **leant** – *pronounced* lent)**1** to slope over to one side **2** to rest (against) **3** to rely (on) ➤ *adjective* **1** thin **2** poor, scanty **3** of meat: not fat

leaning *noun* a liking for, or interest in, something

lean-to *noun* a shed etc built against another building or wall

leap *verb* (**leaps, leaping, leaped** or **leapt** – *pronounced* lept)**1** to move with jumps **2** to jump (over) ➤ *noun* a jump

leapfrog *noun* a game in which one player leaps over another's bent back

leap year *noun* a year which has 366 days (February having 29), occurring every fourth year

learn *verb* (**learns, learning, learnt** or **learned**) **1** to get to know (something) **2** to gain skill

learned (*pronounced* **ler**-nid) *adjective* having or showing great knowledge

learner *noun* someone who is learning something

learning *noun* knowledge

lease *noun* **1** an agreement giving the use of a house etc in return for payment of rent **2** the period of this agreement ➤ *verb* to let or rent

leasehold *noun* property or land held by lease

leash *noun* (*plural* **leashes**) a lead by which a dog etc is held ➤ *verb* to put (a dog etc) on a leash

least *adjective* the smallest amount of anything: *He had the least money* ➤ *adverb* (often **the least**) the smallest or lowest degree: *I like her least* • **at least** at any rate, anyway • **not in the least** not at all

leather *noun* the skin of an animal, prepared by tanning for use ➤ *verb* to beat

leathering *noun* a thrashing

leatherjacket *noun* the larva of the cranefly, which has a greyish-brown leathery skin

leathery *adjective* like leather; tough

leave¹ *verb* (**leaving, left**) **1** to allow to remain **2** to abandon, forsake **3** to depart (from) **4** to hand down to someone in a will **5** to give over to someone's responsibility, care, etc: *Leave the choice to her*

leave² *noun* **1** permission to do something (eg to be absent) **2** a holiday • **take your leave of 1** to part from **2** to say goodbye to

leaven (*pronounced* **lev**-en)*noun* yeast

leavened *adjective* raised with yeast

leaves plural of **leaf**

leavings *plural noun* things left over

Lebensraum (*pronounced* **lei**-benz-rowm) *noun* **1** (sometimes **lebensraum**) space in which to live and, if necessary, expand **2** *history* a Nazi concept involving the colonization of territory outside Germany that they claimed was necessary for economic growth ◐ Comes from German *Lebens* meaning 'of life' + *Raum* meaning 'space'

lecher *noun* a lustful man

lecherous *adjective* lustful in a sexual way ◆ **lechery** *noun*

lecithin (*pronounced* **les**-i-thin)*noun* an organic chemical compound that is a major component of cell membranes in animals and plants

lectern *noun* a stand for a book to be read from

lecture *noun* **1** a formal talk on a certain subject given to an audience **2** a scolding ➤ *verb* **1** to deliver a lecture **2** to scold

lecturer *noun* someone who lectures, especially to students

LED *abbreviation* light-emitting diode, a semiconductor that lights up when an electric current passes through it

led past form of **lead**¹

LEDC or **ELDC** *abbreviation, geography* Less Economically Developed Country or

Economically Less Developed Country

ledge *noun* **1** a shelf or projecting rim: *window-ledge* **2** an underwater ridge

ledger *noun* the accounts book of an office or shop

lee *noun* the side away from the wind, the sheltered side: *in the lee of the mountain*

leech *noun* (*plural* **leeches**) a kind of blood-sucking worm ◐ Comes from Old English *læce*

! Do not confuse with: **leach**

leek *noun* a long green and white vegetable of the onion family

leer *noun* a sly, sidelong or lustful look ➤ *verb* to look sideways or lustfully (at)

leeward *adjective & adverb* in the direction towards which the wind blows

leeway *noun* **1** a ship's drift off course **2** lost time, ground, etc: *a lot of leeway to make up* **3** room to manoeuvre, latitude

left¹ *adjective* on or of the side of the body that in most people has the less skilful hand (*contrasted with*: **right**) ➤ *adverb* on or towards the left side ➤ *noun* **1** the left side **2** a political grouping with left-wing ideas etc

left² past form of **leave**¹

left-click *verb, computing* to press and release the left-hand button on a computer mouse

left-field *adjective, informal* odd, eccentric

left-handed *adjective* **1** using the left hand rather than the right **2** awkward

left wing *noun* **1** the more radical or socialist members of a group or political party **2** *sport* the extreme left side of a pitch or team in a field game **3** (*also called*: **left-winger**) *sport* a member of a team who plays on the left side of the field ➤ *adjective* (**left-wing**) belonging or relating to the left wing ◆ **left-winger** *noun*

leg *noun* **1** one of the limbs by which humans and animals walk **2** a long slender support for a table etc **3** one stage in a journey, contest, etc

legacy *noun* (*plural* **legacies**) **1** something which is left by will **2** something left behind by the previous occupant of a house, job, etc

legal *adjective* **1** allowed by law, lawful **2** of law

legal aid *noun* legal advice provided free from public funds for those who cannot afford to pay

legalistic *adjective* sticking rigidly to the law or rules

legality *noun* (*plural* **legalities**) the state of being legal

legalize or **legalise** *verb* to make lawful

legal tender *noun* currency which, by law, must be accepted in payment of a debt

legate *noun* an ambassador, especially from the Pope

legato (*pronounced* le-**ga**-to) *adverb, music* smoothly, with each note running into the next without a break (*contrasted with*: **staccato**) ➤ *noun* (*plural* **legatos**) a piece of music to be played with each note running into the next ① Comes from Italian, meaning 'bound' or 'tied'

legend *noun* 1 a traditional story handed down, a myth 2 a caption

legendary *adjective* 1 of legend; famous 2 not to be believed

leggings *plural noun* 1 outer coverings for the lower legs 2 close-fitting trousers for women

leggy *adjective* (**leggier, leggiest**) having long legs

legible *adjective* able to be read easily ◆ **legibility** *noun*

legion *noun* 1 *history* a body of from three to six thousand Roman soldiers 2 a very great number

legionary *noun* (*plural* **legionaries**) a soldier of a legion

legionnaire *noun* a member of a legion

Legionnaires' disease *noun* a serious disease similar to pneumonia caused by a bacterium

① So called after an outbreak of the disease at an American *Legion* convention (for war veterans) in 1976

legislate *verb* to make laws ◆ **legislation** *noun*

legislative *adjective* law-making

legislator *noun* someone who makes laws

legislature *noun* the part of the government which has the powers of making laws

legitimate *adjective* 1 lawful 2 of a child: born of parents married to each other 3 correct, reasonable ◆ **legitimacy** *noun*

legitimize or **legitimise** *verb* 1 to make legitimate 2 to make (an argument) valid ◆ **legitimization** *noun*

legless *adjective, informal* drunk

Lego *noun, trademark* a construction toy consisting of small plastic bricks, windows, wheels, etc which can be fastened together ① Comes from Danish *leg godt* meaning 'play well'

legroom *noun* room to move the legs

legside *noun, cricket* the half of the field on the side where the batsman stands when waiting to receive the ball (*contrasted with*: **offside**)

legume (*pronounced* **leg**-yoom) *noun, botany* 1 any of a family of plants that produce a pod, eg pea, bean, lentil 2 the pod of such a plant, containing edible seeds 3 the edible seeds of these pods ◆ **leguminous** *adjective* ① Comes from Latin *legere* meaning 'to gather'

lei (*pronounced* lei) *noun* a Polynesian garland of flowers worn round the neck

leisure *noun* time free from work, spare time

leisure centre *noun* a centre providing a wide variety of leisure activities, especially sporting ones

leisured *adjective* not occupied with business

leisurely *adjective* unhurried: *leisurely pace*

leitmotiv (*pronounced* **lait**-moh-teef) *noun* 1 *music* a musical theme in an opera associated with a particular character etc 2 *literature* a recurring theme

lemma *noun, maths* 1 a proposition 2 a premise taken for granted

lemming *noun* 1 a small rat-like animal of the arctic regions, reputed to follow others of its kind over sea cliffs when migrating 2 someone who follows others unquestioningly

lemon *noun* 1 an oval fruit with pale yellow rind and sour juice 2 the tree that bears this fruit 3 a pale yellow colour ➤ *adjective* 1 pale yellow in colour 2 tasting of or flavoured with lemon ◆ **lemony** *adjective*

lemonade *noun* a soft drink flavoured with lemons

lemon curd or **lemon cheese** *noun* a thick creamy paste made from lemons, sugar, butter, and egg

lemur (*pronounced* **lee**-mer) *noun* a long-tailed animal related to the monkey but with a pointed nose

① From a Latin word meaning 'ghost', because the animal has a thin, pale face and appears at night

lend *verb* (**lending, lent**) 1 to give use of for a time 2 to give, add (a quality) to someone or something: *His presence lent an air of respectability to the occasion* • **lend itself to** to be suitable for, adapt easily to

length *noun* 1 extent from end to end in space or time 2 the quality of being long 3 a great extent 4 a piece of cloth etc 5 the longer measurement of a swimming pool, or this distance swum • **at length** 1 in detail 2 at last

lengthen *verb* to make or grow longer

lengthways or **lengthwise** *adverb* in the direction of the length: *Measure the picture lengthways*

lengthy (**lengthier, lengthiest**) *adjective* 1 long 2 tiresomely long

lenient (*pronounced* **lee**-ni-ent) *adjective* merciful, punishing only lightly ◆ **lenience** or **leniency** *noun*

lens *noun* (*plural* **lenses**) 1 a piece of glass curved on one or both sides, used in spectacles, cameras, etc 2 a contact lens 3 a part of the eye

Lent *noun* in the Christian church, a period of fasting before Easter lasting forty days

lent past form of **lend**

lentil *noun* the seed of a pod-bearing plant, used in soups etc

Leo *noun* 1 the fifth sign of the zodiac, represented by the lion 2 someone born under this sign, between 24 July and 23 August

leonine (*pronounced* **lee**-*o*-nain) *adjective* like a lion

leopard *noun* an animal of the cat family with a spotted skin

leopardess *noun* (*plural* **leopardesses**) a female leopard

leotard *noun* a tight-fitting, stretchy garment worn for dancing, gymnastics, etc

⊙ After Jules *Léotard*, a French trapeze artist who popularized it

leper *noun* 1 someone with leprosy 2 an outcast

lepidopterist *noun* someone who studies butterflies and moths

lepidopterology *noun* the study of butterflies and moths

lepidopterous *adjective* of the order of insects that contains butterflies and moths

leprechaun *noun* a creature in Irish folklore

leprosy *noun* a contagious skin disease causing thickening or numbness in the skin ♦ **leprous** *adjective*

lepton *noun, physics* any of various subatomic particles that only participate in weak interactions with other particles

lesbian *noun* a female homosexual ➤ *adjective* of a woman: homosexual

lesion *noun* 1 a wound 2 an abnormal change in the structure of an organ or tissue as a result of disease or injury

less *adjective* 1 not as much: *take less time* 2 smaller: *Think of a number less than 40* ➤ *adverb* not as much, to a smaller extent: *He goes less often than he should* ➤ *noun* a smaller amount: *He has less than I have* ➤ *preposition* minus: *5 less 2 equals 3*

ⓘ **Fewer** should be used with plurals:
There are fewer cars on the roads.
However, **less** should be used with amounts, and with measurements:
There are less than twelve hours to go.
People aged twenty or less.
Less should also be used with *than*:
Less than twenty of them made it back.

Less Economically Developed Country *noun, geography* (*abbrev* **LEDC**) a country with a low level of development, as measured by indicators such as income from trade (*contrasted with*: **More Economically Developed Country**)

lessen *verb* to make smaller

lesser *adjective* smaller

lesson *noun* 1 something which is learned or taught 2 a part of the Bible read in church 3 a period of teaching 4 an experience or example which one should take as a warning or

encouragement: *Let that be a lesson to you*

lest *conjunction* for fear that, in case

let *verb* (**letting, let**) 1 to allow 2 to grant use of (eg a house, shop, farm) in return for payment • **let down** to fail to act as expected, disappoint • **let off** to excuse, not punish • **let up** to become less

lethal (*pronounced* **lee**-thal) *adjective* causing death

lethargy (*pronounced* **leth**-ar-ji) *noun* a lack of energy or interest; sleepiness ♦ **lethargic** *adjective*

let's *short for* let us: *Let's go home*

letter *noun* 1 a mark expressing a sound 2 a written message 3 (**letters**) learning: *a woman of letters* • **to the letter** according to the exact meaning of the words: *following instructions to the letter*

letter bomb *noun* an envelope containing a device that is designed to explode when someone opens it

letter box *noun* 1 a slot in a door through which letters are delivered 2 a large box, with a slot in the front, for people to post letters (*also called*: **pillarbox, postbox**)

letterhead *noun* 1 a printed heading on notepaper giving a company's or a person's name, address, etc 2 a piece of notepaper with this kind of heading

lettering *noun* letters which have been drawn or painted, usually in a particular style

lettuce *noun* a kind of green plant whose leaves are used in a salad

leucocyte (*pronounced* **lyoo**-koh-sait) *noun* a white blood corpuscle

leukaemia *or US* **leukemia** (*pronounced* loo-**kee**-mi-a) *noun* a cancerous disease of the white blood cells in the body

levee (*pronounced* **lev**-i) *noun* (*plural* **levees**) 1 *geography* an artificial or natural embankment along a watercourse 2 a quay ⊙ Comes from French *levée* meaning 'raised'

level *noun* 1 a flat, smooth surface 2 a height, position, etc in comparison with some standard: *water level* 3 an instrument for showing whether a surface is level: *spirit level* 4 personal rank or degree of understanding: *a bit above my level* ➤ *adjective* 1 flat, even, smooth 2 horizontal ➤ *verb* (**levelling, levelled**) 1 to make flat, smooth or horizontal 2 to make equal 3 to aim (a gun etc) 4 to pull down (a building etc) 5 to direct (an accusation, criticism, etc) at

level crossing *noun* a place where a road crosses a railway track

level-headed *adjective* having good sense

level playing-field *noun* a position of equality from which to compete fairly

lever *noun* 1 a bar of metal, wood, etc used to

raise or shift something heavy **2** a handle for operating a machine **3** a method of gaining advantage

leverage *noun* **1** the use of a lever **2** power, influence

leveret (*pronounced* **lev**-e-rit) *noun* a young hare

levitate *verb* to float in the air

levitation *noun* the illusion of raising a heavy body in the air without support

levity *noun* lack of seriousness, frivolity

levy *verb* (**levies, levying, levied**) to collect (eg a tax, army conscripts) by order ➤ *noun* (*plural* **levies**) money, troops, etc collected by order

lewd *adjective* taking delight in indecent thoughts or acts ♦ **lewdness** *noun*

lexical *adjective* of words

lexicographer *noun* someone who compiles or edits a dictionary ♦ **lexicography** *noun*

lexicon *noun* **1** a dictionary **2** a glossary of terms

lexis *noun* **1** all the words of a language **2** the way a piece of writing is expressed in words

LGV *abbreviation* large goods vehicle

Li *symbol, chemistry* lithium

liability *noun* (*plural* **liabilities**) **1** legal responsibility **2** a debt **3** a disadvantage

liable *adjective* **1** legally responsible (for) **2** likely or apt (to do something or happen) **3** **liable to** likely to have, suffer from: *liable to colds*

liaise (*pronounced* lee-**eiz**) *verb* to make a connection (with), be in touch (with)

liaison (*pronounced* lee-**eiz**-on) *noun* **1** contact, communication **2** a sexual affair

liar *noun* someone who tells lies

lib *noun, informal* liberation: *women's lib*

libation (*pronounced* lai-**bei**-shon) *noun* wine poured to honour a god

Lib Dem *short for* Liberal Democrat

libel *noun* something written to hurt another's reputation ➤ *verb* (**libelling, libelled**) to write something libellous about

libellous *adjective* containing a written false statement which hurts a person's reputation

liberal *adjective* generous; broad-minded, tolerant ➤ *noun* (**Liberal**) a member of the former Liberal Party, which supported social and political reform ♦ **liberality** *noun*

Liberal Democrats *plural noun* one of the chief political parties of Great Britain, formed in 1988 from the Liberal Party and the Social Democratic Party, supporting democratic reform

liberate *verb* to set free ♦ **liberation** *noun*

liberated *adjective* **1** not bound by traditional ideas about sexuality and morality **2** freed from enemy occupation

liberation theology *noun* a Christian doctrine that began in the 1960s in Latin America, which emphasizes a commitment to liberation from social, political and economic oppression

libertine *noun* someone who lives a wicked, immoral life

liberty *noun* (*plural* **liberties**) **1** freedom, especially of speech or action **2** (**liberties**) rights, privileges • **take liberties** to behave rudely or impertinently

libidinous (*pronounced* li-**bid**-i-nus) *adjective* lustful; lewd

libido (*pronounced* li-**bee**-doh) *noun* sexual drive or urge

Libra *noun* **1** the fifth sign of the zodiac, represented by the balance **2** someone born under this sign, between 24 September and 22 October

librarian *noun* a person employed in or in charge of a library

library *noun* (*plural* **libraries**) **1** a collection of books, records, etc **2** a building or room housing these

libretto *noun* (*plural* **libretti** or **librettos**) *music* the words of an opera, musical show, etc

lice *plural of* **louse**

licence *noun* **1** a document giving permission to do something, eg to keep a television set, drive a car, etc **2** too great freedom of action

! Do not confuse: **licence** and **license**. **Licence/license** and **practice/practise** follow the same pattern: you spell the verbs with an S (licen**S**e, practi**S**e), and the nouns with a C (licen**C**e, practi**C**e.)

license *verb* to permit

licensee *noun* someone to whom a licence is given

licentiate (*pronounced* lai-**sen**-shi-it) *noun* someone who holds a certificate authorizing them to practise a profession

licentious *adjective* given to behaving immorally or improperly

lichee another spelling of **lychee**

lichen (*pronounced* **laik**-en) *noun* a large group of moss-like plants that grow on rocks etc

lick *verb* **1** to pass the tongue over **2** of flames: to reach up, touch ➤ *noun* **1** the act of licking **2** a tiny amount • **lick into shape** to make vigorous improvements on

licorice another spelling of **liquorice**

lid *noun* **1** a cover for a box, pot, etc **2** the cover of the eye

lido (*pronounced* **lee**-doh) *noun* **1** a bathing beach **2** an open-air swimming pool

lie¹ *noun* a false statement meant to deceive ➤ *verb* (**lying, lied**) to tell a lie

lie² *verb* (**lying, lay, lain**) **1** to rest in a flat position: *Lie flat on your back* **2** to be or remain in a state or position: *lie dormant* ➤ *noun* the position or situation in which something lies • **lie low** to keep quiet or hidden • **the lie of the land** the present state of affairs

! Do not confuse with: **lay**.
It may help to remember that an object is not used with the verb **lie**, while the verb **lay** always takes an object.

lie detector *noun* a machine used for telling whether someone is lying by measuring changes in their blood pressure, perspiration, pulse, etc, when they reply to questions

liege (*pronounced* leej) *noun* **1** a loyal subject **2** a lord or superior

lieu (*pronounced* lyoo or loo) *noun*: **in lieu of** instead of

lieutenant (*pronounced* lef-**ten**-ant or *US* loo-**ten**-ant) *noun* **1** an army officer below a captain **2** in the navy, an officer below a lieutenant-commander **3** a rank below a higher officer: *lieutenant-colonel*

⊙ From a French word meaning literally 'holding a place'

life *noun* (*plural* **lives**) **1** the period between birth and death **2** the state of being alive **3** liveliness **4** manner of living **5** the story of someone's life **6** living things: *animal life* ⊙ Comes from Old English *lif*

life-and-death *adjective* of a situation: extremely serious or critical

lifebelt *noun* a ring made of cork or filled with air for keeping someone afloat

lifeblood *noun* a source of necessary strength or life

lifeboat *noun* a boat for rescuing people in difficulties at sea

lifebuoy *noun* a float to support someone awaiting rescue at sea

lifecycle *noun* the various stages through which a living thing passes

life drawing *noun* drawing from a live human model

life expectancy *noun* the average length of time for which a person from a particular place might be expected to live

lifeguard *noun* an expert swimmer employed to save people in danger of drowning

life jacket *noun* a buoyant jacket for keeping someone afloat in water

lifeless *adjective* **1** dead **2** not lively, spiritless

lifelike *adjective* of a portrait etc: very like the person or thing represented

lifeline *noun* a vital means of communication

lifelong *adjective* lasting the length of a life

life sciences *plural noun* the branches of science concerned with the study of living

things, eg biochemistry and genetics

life-size *adjective* full size, as in life

lifespan *noun* the length of someone's life

lifestyle *noun* the way in which someone lives

life-support machine *noun* a device for keeping a person alive during severe illness, space travel, etc

lifetime *noun* the period during which someone is alive

lift *verb* **1** to raise, take up **2** *informal* to steal **3** of fog: to disappear, disperse ➤ *noun* **1** a moving platform carrying goods or people between floors in a large building **2** a ride in someone's car etc **3** a boost

lift-off *noun* the take-off of a rocket, spacecraft, etc

ligament *noun* a tough tissue that connects the bones of the body

ligand *noun, chemistry* an atom, molecule or ion attached to the central atom in certain compounds

ligature *noun* **1** something which binds **2** a printed character formed from two or more letters joined together, eg æ

light¹ *noun* **1** the brightness given by the sun, moon, lamps, etc that makes things visible **2** a source of light, eg a lamp **3** a flame on a cigarette lighter **4** a hint, clue, or help towards understanding: *shed a little light on the subject* ➤ *adjective* **1** bright **2** of a colour: pale **3** having light, not dark ➤ *verb* (**lighting, lit** or **lighted**) **1** to give light to **2** to set fire to • **bring to light** to reveal, cause to be noticed • **come to light** to be revealed or discovered • **in the light of** taking into consideration (information etc)

light² *adjective* **1** not heavy **2** easy to bear or do: *light work* **3** easy to digest **4** nimble **5** lively **6** not grave, cheerful **7** not serious: *light reading* **8** of rain etc: little in quantity

light³ *verb* (**lighting, lit** or **lighted**), *old*: **light on 1** to land, settle on **2** to come upon by chance

lighten *verb* **1** to make less heavy **2** to make or become brighter **3** of lightning: to flash

lightening (*pronounced* **lait**-en-ing) *noun* a making or becoming lighter or brighter

! Do not confuse with: **lightning**

lighter *noun* **1** a device with a flame etc for lighting **2** a large open boat used in unloading and loading ships

light-fingered *adjective* apt to steal

light-headed *adjective* dizzy

light-hearted *adjective* cheerful

lighthouse *noun* a tower-like building with a flashing light to warn or guide ships

light industry *noun* the production of smaller goods, eg knitwear, glass, electronics components, etc (*compare with*: **heavy industry**)

lighting *noun* **1** a means of providing light **2** the combination of lights used eg in a theatre or a nightclub

lightly *adverb* **1** gently **2** not seriously

lightning *noun* an electric flash in the clouds

❗ Do not confuse with: **lightening**

lightning conductor *noun* a metal rod on a building etc which conducts electricity down to earth

light pen *noun* **1** *computing* a light-sensitive pen-like device used to move images about on a computer screen by touching the screen with the device **2** a barcode reader shaped like a pen

lightweight *noun* a weight category in boxing ➤ *adjective* not serious enough to demand much concentration

light-year *noun* the distance light travels in a year (6 billion miles)

lignin *noun*, *botany* the substance that cements together the fibres within the cell walls of plants, making them woody and rigid

like¹ *adjective* the same as or similar to ➤ *adverb* in the same way as: *He sings like an angel* ➤ *noun* something or someone that is the equal of another: *You won't see her like again*

like² *verb* **1** to be pleased with **2** to be fond of ⊙ Comes from Old English *lician* meaning 'to please' or 'to be suitable'

likeable or **likable** *adjective* attractive, lovable

likelihood *noun* probability

likely *adjective* **1** probable **2** liable (to do something) ➤ *adverb* probably

liken *verb* to think of as similar, compare: *She likened the experience to a nightmare*

likeness (*plural* **likenesses**) *noun* **1** similarity, resemblance **2** a portrait, photograph, etc of someone

like terms *plural noun*, *maths* terms that can be added to or subtracted from each other, eg *x, 6x, -3x*, etc

likewise *adverb* **1** in the same way **2** also

liking *noun* **1** fondness **2** satisfaction: *to my liking*

lilac *noun* a small tree with hanging clusters of pale purple or white flowers ➤ *adjective* of pale purple colour

lilliputian *adjective* tiny, minuscule

⊙ After *Lilliput*, a country on a tiny scale in Jonathan Swift's 18th-century satirical novel, *Gulliver's Travels*

Lilo or **Li-lo** (*pronounced* **lai**-loh) *noun*, *trademark* a type of inflatable mattress, often used in a swimming pool

lilt *noun* a striking rhythm or swing ➤ *verb* to have this rhythm

lily *noun* (*plural* **lilies**) a tall plant grown from a bulb with large white or coloured flowers

lily-livered *adjective* cowardly

lily-of-the-valley *noun* (*plural* **lilies-of-the-valley**) a plant with small white bell-shaped flowers

limb *noun* **1** a leg or arm **2** a branch

limber *adjective* easily bent, supple • **limber up** to exercise so as to become supple

limbo¹ *noun*, *Christianity* the land bordering Hell, reserved for those unbaptized before death • **in limbo** forgotten, neglected

limbo² *noun* a W Indian dance in which the dancer passes under a low bar

lime¹ *noun* a white, lumpy powder of calcium oxide, used in making glass and cement (*also called*: **quicklime**)

lime² *noun* **1** a tree related to the lemon **2** the greenish-yellow fruit of this tree **3** the greenish-yellow colour of this fruit

lime³ *noun* a deciduous tree or shrub with clusters of sweet-smelling flowers (*also called*: **linden**)

limelight *noun* the glare of publicity • **in the limelight** attracting publicity or attention

limerick *noun* a type of humorous poetry in five-line verses

⊙ After *Limerick* in Ireland, the name of which was repeated in nonsense songs in an old Victorian parlour game

limescale *noun* a type of scale caused by calcium deposits

limestone *noun* white, grey, or black rock consisting mainly of calcium carbonate

limewater *noun* an alkaline solution of calcium hydroxide in water

limit *noun* **1** the farthest point or place **2** a boundary **3** the largest (or smallest) extent, degree, etc **4** a restriction **5** *maths* in calculus: a value that is approached increasingly closely, but never reached ➤ *verb* to set or keep to a limit

limitation *noun* **1** something which limits **2** a weak point, a flaw

limited edition *noun* an edition of a book, art print, etc of which only a certain number of copies are printed or made

limo *noun*, *informal* a limousine

limousine *noun* a large, luxurious car, especially one with a separate compartment for the driver

⊙ Named after a type of cloak worn in *Limousin* in France, because the car's roof was supposedly similar in shape

limp *adjective* **1** not stiff, floppy **2** weak ➤ *verb* **1**

to walk with an awkward or uneven step, often because one leg is weak or injured **2** of a damaged ship etc: to move with difficulty ‣ *noun* **1** the act of limping **2** a limping walk

limpet *noun* **1** a small cone-shaped shellfish which clings to rocks **2** someone who is difficult to get rid of

limpid *adjective* clear, transparent

linchpin *noun* **1** a pin-shaped rod used to keep a wheel on an axle **2** someone or something essential to a business, plan, etc

linctus (*pronounced* **lingk**-tus) *noun* a syrupy cough medicine ⊕ Comes from Latin, from *lingere* meaning 'to lick'

linden see **lime**³

line¹ *noun* **1** a cord, rope, etc **2** a long thin stroke or mark **3** a wrinkle **4** a row of people, printed words, etc **5** a service of ships or aircraft **6** a railway **7** a telephone connection **8** a short letter **9** a family from generation to generation **10** course, direction **11** a subject of interest, activity, etc **12** (**lines**) army trenches **13** (**lines**) a written school punishment exercise ‣ *verb* **1** to mark out with lines **2** (often **line up**) to place in a row or alongside of **3** to form lines along (a street) • **draw the line at** to refuse to allow or accept

line² *verb* to cover on the inside: *line a dress*

lineage (*pronounced* **lin**-i-ij) *noun* descent, traced back to your ancestors

lineal (*pronounced* **lin**-i-al)*adjective* directly descended through the father, grandfather, etc

linear (*pronounced* **lin**-i-ar) *adjective* **1** made of lines **2** in one dimension (length, breadth or height) only **3** capable of being represented on a graph by a straight line **4** *art* with perspective, shade, etc shown by the use of lines

linear equation *noun, maths* an equation in which none of the variables are raised above the power of one, and which can be shown by a straight line on a graph

line drawing *noun* a drawing in pen or pencil using lines only, not shading etc

line graph *noun* a chart or graph which uses horizontal or vertical lines to show amounts

linen *noun* **1** cloth made of flax **2** articles made of linen: *tablelinen/bedlinen*

line of best fit *noun, maths* a line on a scatter graph between values, showing the best estimate of a linear relationship between them

liner *noun* a ship or aeroplane working on a regular service

linesman or **lineswoman** *noun* (*plural* **linesmen** or **lineswomen**) an umpire at a boundary line

line-up *noun* **1** an arrangement of things or people in line **2** a list of people selected for a sports team **3** the artistes appearing in a show **4** an identity parade

linger *verb* **1** to stay for a long time or for longer than expected **2** to loiter, delay

lingerie (*pronounced* **lan**-sze-ri) *plural noun* women's underwear and nightclothes

lingo *noun* (*plural* **lingoes**) *informal* a language, a dialect

lingua franca (*pronounced* ling-gwa **frang**-ka) *noun* (*plural* **lingua francas**) a simplified form of a language, used as a means of communication amongst the speakers of different languages ⊕ Comes from Italian *lingua franca* meaning 'Frankish language'

linguist *noun* **1** someone skilled in languages **2** someone who studies language

linguistic *adjective* to do with language

linguistics *singular noun* the scientific study of languages and of language in general

liniment (*pronounced* **lin**-i-ment) *noun* an oil or ointment rubbed into the skin to cure stiffness in the muscles, joints, etc

lining *noun* a covering on the inside

link *noun* **1** a ring of a chain **2** a single part of a series **3** anything connecting two things **4** *computing* a hyperlink ‣ *verb* **1** to connect with a link **2** to join closely **3** to be connected

links *plural noun* **1** a stretch of flat or slightly hilly ground near the seashore **2** a golf course by the sea

linnet *noun* a small songbird of the finch family

lino *noun, informal* linoleum

lino-cut *noun* a design for printing cut into a block of linoleum

linoleum *noun, dated* a type of smooth, hard-wearing covering for floors

linseed *noun* flax seed

linseed oil *noun* oil from flax seed

lint *noun* **1** a soft woolly material for putting over wounds **2** fine pieces of fluff

lintel *noun* a timber or stone over a doorway or window

Linux (*pronounced* **lai**-nuks) *noun, computing* a computer operating system similar to Unix, but designed for use on personal computers

⊕ The name comes from *Linus* Torvalds (born 1969), the Finnish computer programmer who created the system

lion *noun* a powerful animal of the cat family, the male of which has a shaggy mane • **the lion's share** the largest share

lioness *noun* (*plural* **lionesses**)a female lion

lionize or **lionise** *verb* to treat as a celebrity or hero

lip *noun* **1** either of the two fleshy flaps in front of the teeth forming the rim of the mouth **2** the edge of a jug etc

lipid *noun, biology, chemistry* any of a group of organic compounds, mainly oils and fats, that occur naturally in living organisms, and are generally insoluble in water

liposuction (*pronounced* **lip**-oh-suk-shon) *noun* a surgical operation to remove unwanted body fat by sucking it out through an incision in the skin

lip-reading *noun* reading what someone says from the movement of their lips

lip-service *noun* saying one thing but believing another: *paying lip-service to the rules*

lipstick *noun* a stick of red, pink, etc colouring for the lips

liquefy *verb* (**liquefies, liquefying, liquefied**) to make or become liquid ◆ **liquefaction** *noun*

liqueur (*pronounced* lik-**yoor**) *noun* a strong alcoholic drink, strongly flavoured and sweet

❗ Do not confuse with: **liquor**

liquid *noun* a flowing, water-like substance ➤ *adjective* **1** flowing **2** looking like water **3** soft and clear **4** *business* of a company's assets: easy to convert into cash

liquidate *verb* **1** to close down, wind up the affairs of (a bankrupt business company) **2** *slang* to kill, murder ◆ **liquidation** *noun* ◆ **liquidator** *noun*

liquid crystal *noun* any organic compound that flows like a liquid but resembles a solid crystalline substance in its optical properties

liquid crystal display *noun* (*abbrev* **LCD**) in digital watches, calculators, etc: a display of numbers or letters produced by applying an electric field across a liquid crystal solution

liquidity *noun* **1** the state of being liquid **2** *business* the amount of liquid assets a company has **3** *business* a measure of how easily an asset can be turned into cash

liquidize or **liquidise** *verb* **1** to make liquid **2** to make into a purée

liquidizer or **liquidiser** *noun* a machine for liquidizing

liquor (*pronounced* **lik**-er) *noun* an alcoholic drink, especially a spirit (eg whisky)

❗ Do not confuse with: **liqueur**

liquorice or **licorice** *noun* **1** a plant with a sweet-tasting root **2** a black, sticky sweet flavoured with this root

lisp *verb* **1** to say *th* for *s* or *z* because of being unable to pronounce these letters correctly **2** to speak imperfectly, like a child ➤ *noun* a speech disorder of this kind

list¹ *noun* a series of names, numbers, prices, etc written down one after the other ➤ *verb* to write down in this way: *List your chosen subjects*

list² *verb* of a ship: to lean over to one side ➤ *noun* a slope to one side

list box *noun, computing* a pull-down box on screen containing a choice of options in a list

listed building *noun* one protected from being changed, knocked down, etc because it is of architectural or historical interest

listen *verb* to hear, pay attention to ◆ **listener** *noun*

listeria *noun* a bacterium found in certain foods which can damage the nervous system if not killed during cooking

listing *noun* **1** a list **2** a position in a list **3** *computing* a printout of a file or a program **4** (**listings**) a guide to entertainment, eg, on television or radio, or at the cinema, theatre, etc

listless *adjective* weary, without energy or interest

lit past form of **light¹** and **light³**

litany *noun* (*plural* **litanies**) **1** *Christianity* a series of prayers with a response which is repeated several times by the congregation **2** a long list or catalogue

litchi another spelling of **lychee**

liter US spelling of **litre**

literacy *noun* ability to read and write

literal *adjective* of a word or phrase: following the exact or most obvious meaning (*contrasted with*: **figurative**)

literally *adverb* exactly as stated, not just as a figure of speech: *He was literally blinded by the flash*

ⓘ It is generally considered wrong to use the word **literally** when something did not actually happen, as in *I literally laughed my head off*.

literary *adjective* **1** relating to books, authors, etc **2** knowledgeable about books

literate *adjective* **1** able to read and write **2** educated

literati (*pronounced* li-te-**rah**-tea) learned and scholarly people

literature *noun* **1** the books etc that are written in any language **2** anything in written form on a subject

lithe (*pronounced* laidh)*adjective* bending easily, supple, flexible

lithium (*pronounced* **lith**-i-um) *noun, chemistry* (symbol **Li**) a light metallic element used in batteries and alloys

lithograph (*pronounced* **lith**-oh-grahf) *noun* a picture made from a drawing done on stone or metal ◆ **lithography** *noun* printing done by this method

lithophyte *noun, botany* any plant that grows on rocks or stones

lithosphere *noun, geography* the rigid outer layer of the earth, consisting of the crust and the outermost layer of the mantle

litigation *noun* a law case ⓞ Comes from Latin *litigium* meaning 'quarrel'

litigious (*pronounced* li-**tij**-us) *adjective* **1** relating to litigation **2** inclined to taking legal action over arguments, problems, etc

litmus paper *noun* treated paper which changes colour when dipped in an acid or alkaline solution

litmus test *noun* **1** *chemistry* a test for relative acidity or alkalinity using litmus paper **2** anything which indicates underlying attitudes etc

litre or *US* **liter** *noun* (*abbrev* **l**) the basic unit for measuring liquids in the metric system

litter *noun* **1** an untidy mess of paper, rubbish, etc **2** a heap of straw as bedding for animals **3** absorbent material put in a tray for an indoor cat to urinate and defecate in **4** a number of animals born at one birth **5** a bed for carrying the sick and injured ➤ *verb* **1** to scatter rubbish carelessly about **2** to produce a litter of young

little *adjective* small in quantity or size ➤ *adverb* **1** (**a little**) to a small extent or degree **2** not much **3** not at all: *Little does she know* ➤ *pronoun* a small amount, distance, etc: *Have a little more/Move a little to the right* ◷ Comes from Old English *lytel*

littoral *adjective* on or near the shore of a sea or lake ➤ *noun* the shore or an area of land on a shore or coast

liturgy (*pronounced* **lit**-u-ji) *noun* (*plural* **liturgies**) the standard form of service of a church ◆ **liturgical** *adjective*

live¹ (*pronounced* liv) *verb* **1** to have life **2** to dwell **3** to pass your life in a certain way: *to live well* **4** to continue to be alive **5** to survive **6** to be lifelike or vivid • **live and let live** to allow others to live as they please • **live down** to live until (an embarrassment etc) is forgotten by others • **live on 1** to continue to live **2** to be supported by: *to live on benefits* • **live up to** to be as good as expected from ◷ Comes from Old English *lifian*

live² (*pronounced* laiv) *adjective* **1** having life, not dead **2** full of energy **3** of a television broadcast etc: seen as the event takes place, not recorded **4** charged with electricity and apt to give an electric shock **5** *computing* fully operational: *live data*

livelihood (*pronounced* **laiv**-li-huwd) *noun* someone's means of living, eg their daily work

livelong (*pronounced* **liv**-long or **laiv**-long) *adjective, old* whole: *the livelong day*

lively *adjective* full of life, high spirits ◆ **liveliness** *noun*

liven *verb* to make lively

liver *noun* a large gland in the body that carries out several important functions including purifying the blood

liver sausage or *US* **liverwurst** *noun* a sausage made from finely minced liver combined with either pork or veal

livery *noun* (*plural* **liveries**) the uniform of a manservant etc • **at livery** of a horse: being kept at a livery stable in exchange for payment by its owner

livery stable *noun* a stable where horses may be kept at livery or hired

lives plural of **life**

livestock (*pronounced* **laiv**-stok) *noun* farm animals

livewire (*pronounced* **laiv**-wair) *noun* a very lively, energetic person

livid *adjective* **1** of a bluish lead-like colour **2** very angry

living *adjective* **1** having life **2** active, lively **3** of a likeness: exact ➤ *noun* means of living

living room *noun* an informal sitting room

living wage *noun* a wage on which it is possible to live comfortably

lizard *noun* a four-footed reptile

llama *noun* a S American animal of the camel family without a hump

lo *interjection, old* look

load *verb* **1** to put (what is to be carried) on or in a vehicle etc: *Load the furniture into the van* **2** to put the ammunition in (a gun) **3** to put a film in (a camera) **4** *computing* to put (a disk, computer tape, etc) into a drive **5** *computing* to transfer (a program or data) into main memory, so that it may be used **6** to weight for some purpose: *loaded dice* ➤ *noun* **1** as much as can be carried at once **2** cargo **3** a heavy weight or task **4** the power carried by an electric circuit

loaded question *noun* one meant to trap someone into making a damaging admission

loaf *noun* (*plural* **loaves**) a shaped mass of bread ➤ *verb* to pass time idly or lazily

loafer *noun* **1** an idler **2** (**loafers**) casual shoes

loam *noun* a rich soil ◆ **loamy** *adjective*

loan *noun* something lent, especially a sum of money ➤ *verb* to lend

loan shark *noun, informal* someone who lends money at extremely high rates of interest

loath or **loth** (*pronounced* lohth) *adjective* unwilling (to)

❗ Do not confuse: **loath** and **loathe**. Remember that loaTHE has an ending common to a few other verbs, eg cloTHE and baTHE.

loathe (*pronounced* lohdh) *verb* to dislike greatly

loathing (*pronounced* **lohdh**-ing) *noun* great hate or disgust

loathsome (*pronounced* **lohdh**-som) *adjective* causing loathing or disgust, horrible

loaves plural of **loaf**

lob *noun* **1** *cricket* a slow, high ball bowled

underhand **2** *tennis* a ball high overhead dropping near the back of the court ▸ *verb* (**lobbing, lobbed**) **1** to send (a ball) in such a movement **2** *informal* to throw

lobby *noun* (*plural* **lobbies**) **1** a small entrance hall **2** a passage off which rooms open **3** a group of people who try to influence the government or another authority ▸ *verb* (**lobbies, lobbying, lobbied**) **1** to try to influence (public officials) **2** to conduct a campaign to influence public officials ♦ **lobbying** *noun*

lobe *noun* **1** the hanging-down part of an ear **2** a division of the brain, lungs, etc

lobelia *noun* a garden plant with red, white, purple, blue or yellow flowers

lobotomy (*plural* **lobotomies**) *noun* **1** the surgical operation of cutting into a lobe or gland **2** a surgical operation on the front lobes of the brain which has the effect of changing the patient's character

lobster *noun* a kind of shellfish with large claws, used for food

lobster pot *noun* a basket in which lobsters are caught

local *adjective* of or confined to a certain place ▸ *noun, informal* **1** the public house nearest someone's home **2** **locals** the people living in a particular place or area ① Comes from Latin *locus* meaning 'a place'

local anaesthetic *noun, medicine* an injection that anaesthetizes only a certain part of the body

local authority *noun* the elected local government body in an area

local colour *noun* details in a story which make it more interesting and realistic

locale *noun* scene, location

local government *noun* administration of the local affairs of a district by an elected council (*compare with*: **central government**)

locality *noun* (*plural* **localities**) a particular place and the area round about

localize or **localise** *verb* to confine to one area, keep from spreading

locate *verb* **1** to find **2** to set in a particular place: *a house located in the Highlands*

location *noun* **1** the act of locating **2** position, situation ● **on location** of filming etc: in natural surroundings, not in a studio

loch *noun, Scottish* **1** a lake **2** an arm of the sea

loci (*pronounced* loh-sai) plural of **locus**

lock¹ *noun* **1** a fastening for doors etc needing a key to open it **2** a part of a canal for raising or lowering boats **3** the part of a gun which explodes the charge **4** a tight hold ▸ *verb* **1** to fasten with a lock **2** to become fastened ● **lock, stock and barrel** completely ● **lock up** to shut in with a lock

lock² *noun* **1** a section of hair **2** (**locks**) hair

locker *noun* a small cupboard

locker-room *noun* a room for changing clothes and storing personal belongings

locket *noun* a little ornamental case, often containing a photograph, worn on a chain round the neck

lockjaw *noun* a form of tetanus which stiffens the jaw muscles

lockout *noun* the locking out of workers by their employer during industrial disputes

locksmith *noun* a person who makes locks

lock-up *noun* a lockable garage

locomotion *noun* movement from place to place

locomotive *noun* a railway engine ▸ *adjective* of or capable of locomotion

locum *noun* (*plural* **locums**) a doctor, dentist, etc taking another's place for a time

locus *noun* (*plural* **loci**) **1** a place, a locality **2** *maths* a set of values or points that make an equation or a set of conditions work **3** *genetics* the position of a particular gene on a chromosome

locust *noun* a large insect of the grasshopper family which destroys growing plants

locution *noun* **1** a style of speech **2** an expression, word or phrase

lode *noun* a vein containing metallic ore

lodestar *noun* the Pole Star

lodestone *noun* **1** a form of the mineral magnetite with magnetic properties **2** a magnet

lodge *noun* **1** a small house, often at the entrance to a larger building **2** a beaver's dwelling **3** a house occupied during the shooting or hunting season **4** a branch of a society ▸ *verb* **1** to live in rented rooms **2** to become fixed (in) **3** to put in a safe place **4** to make (a complaint, appeal, etc) officially

lodger *noun* someone who stays in rented rooms

lodging *noun* **1** a place to stay, sleep, etc **2** (**lodgings**) a room or rooms rented in someone else's house

loft *noun* **1** a room just under a roof **2** a gallery in a hall, church, etc

lofty (**loftier, loftiest**) *adjective* **1** of great height **2** noble, proud ♦ **loftily** *adverb* (meaning 2)

log *noun* **1** a thick, rough piece of wood, part of a felled tree **2** a device for measuring a ship's speed **3** a logbook **4** *computing* a record eg of all the files accessed, websites visited, etc over a certain period of time ▸ *verb* (**logging, logged**) to write down (events) in a logbook ● **log in** or **on** *computing* to start a session on a computer, usually by typing in a password ● **log out** or **off** *computing* to end a session on a computer, using a closing command

loganberry (*plural* **loganberries**) *noun* a kind of fruit like a large raspberry

logarithm *noun, maths* the power to which a real number, called the **base**, must be raised to give another number or variable, eg the logarithm of 100 to the base 10 is 2
♦ **logarithmic** *adjective*

logarithmic function *noun, maths* any function of the form $a = \log b$

logbook *noun* **1** an official record of a ship's or aeroplane's progress **2** a record of progress, attendance, etc **3** the registration documents of a motor vehicle

loggerhead *noun*: **at loggerheads** quarrelling

logic *noun* **1** the study of reasoning correctly **2** correctness of reasoning **3** the system underlying the design and operation of computers

logical *adjective* according to the rules of logic or sound reasoning ♦ **logically** *adverb*

logic circuit *noun, computing* an electronic circuit with two or more inputs and one output, and which performs a logical operation, eg *and*, *not*

logic gate *noun, computing* a part of a logic circuit, eg an AND gate, whose output is controlled by the combination of inputs it receives

logistics *singular or plural noun* **1** the organizing of everything needed for any large-scale operation **2** *business* the control and regulation of the flow of goods, materials, staff, etc **3** the moving and supplying of troops and military equipment ♦ **logistical** *adjective* ♦ **logistically** *adverb* ⊙ Comes from French *logistique*, from *loger* meaning 'to lodge'

Logo *noun, computing* a simple programming language with distinctive graphics

logo *noun* (*plural* **logos**) a symbol of a business firm etc consisting of a simple picture or lettering

-logy or **-ology** *suffix* **1** forms words describing the scientific or serious study of something: *biology/psychology* **2** forms terms related to words or discourse: *tautology* (= a form of repetition using two words or phrases that say the same thing)/*eulogy* ⊙ Comes from Greek *logos* meaning 'word' or 'reason'

loin *noun* **1** the back of an animal cut for food **2** (**loins**) the lower part of the body from the bottom rib to the pelvis

loincloth *noun* a piece of cloth worn round the hips, especially in India and south-east Asia

loiter *verb* **1** to proceed, move slowly **2** to linger **3** to stand around

loll *verb* **1** to lie lazily about **2** of the tongue: to hang down or out

lollipop *noun* a large boiled sweet on a stick

lollipop man or **lollipop woman** *noun, Brit* a person employed to stop cars to allow schoolchildren to cross the street, who carries a pole with a disc at the top

lollop *verb* (**lolloping, lolloped**) **1** to bound clumsily **2** to lounge, idle

lolly *noun* (*plural* **lollies**) **1** *informal* a lollipop **2** *slang* money

lone *adjective* alone; standing by itself

lonely (**lonelier, loneliest**) *adjective* **1** lone **2** lacking or needing companionship **3** of a place: having few people ♦ **loneliness** *noun*

loner *noun, sometimes derogatory* someone who prefers to live or work alone

lonesome *adjective* **1** lone **2** feeling lonely

long *adjective* **1** not short, measuring a lot from end to end **2** measuring a certain amount: *cut a strip 2cm long/the film is 3 hours long* **3** far-reaching **4** slow to do something ➤ *adverb* **1** for a great time **2** through the whole time: *all day long* ➤ *verb* to wish very much (for): *longing to see him again* • **before long** soon • **in the long run** in the end • **so long** *informal* goodbye ⊙ Adjective: comes from Old English *lang/long*; adverb: comes from Old English *lange/longe*; verb: comes from Old English *langian*

longevity (*pronounced* lon-**jev**-i-ti) *noun* great length of life

longhand *noun* writing in full (*contrasted with*: **shorthand**)

longing *noun* a strong desire

longitude (*pronounced* **lon**-ji-tyood or **long**-gi-tyood) *noun* **1** *maths* the angle between a point on a sphere and a given meridian (*compare with*: **latitude**) **2** *geography* the angle between a given place on earth and the Greenwich meridian, measured in degrees (*compare with*: **latitude**)

longitudinal (*pronounced* lon-ji-**tyood**-inal or long-gi-**tyood**-inal) *adjective* **1** relating to longitude **2** relating to length **3** lengthways ♦ **longitudinally** *adverb*

longitudinal wave *noun, physics* a wave in which particles are displaced in the same direction as that in which the wave is advancing, eg sound waves

long johns *plural noun, informal* men's long underpants reaching to the ankles

long jump *noun* an athletics contest in which competitors jump as far as possible along the ground from a running start

long profile *noun, geography* the course of a river, from its source to the mouth

long-range *adjective* **1** able to reach a great distance **2** looking a long way into the future

longship *noun* a narrow Viking sailing ship

longshore drift *noun, geography* the movement of material along the seashore by a current flowing parallel to the shoreline

long shot *noun, informal* **1** a guess, attempt, etc which is unlikely to be successful **2** a bet made with only a slim chance of winning • **not by a long shot** not by any means

long-sighted *adjective* able to see things at a distance but not those close at hand

long-standing *adjective* begun a long time ago, having lasted a long time

long-suffering *adjective* putting up with troubles without complaining

long-term *adjective* **1** extending over a long time **2** taking the future, not just the present, into account

long-wave *adjective* of radio: using wavelengths over 1000 metres (*compare with*: **short-wave**)

long-winded *adjective* using too many words

loo *noun, informal* a toilet

loofah *noun* the dried inner part of the fibrous fruit of a tropical plant, used as a rough sponge

look *verb* **1** to turn the eyes towards so as to see **2** to appear, seem: *You look tired/It looks as if I can go after all* **3** to face: *His room looks south* ➤ *noun* **1** the act of looking **2** the expression on someone's face **3** appearance **4** (**looks**) personal appearance • **look after** to take care of, take responsibility for • **look alive** *informal* to rouse yourself, get ready for action • **look down on** to think of as being inferior • **look for** to search for • **look forward to** to anticipate with pleasure • **look into** to investigate • **look on 1** to stand by and watch **2** to think of (as): *He looks on her as his mother* • **look out!** be careful! • **look over** to examine briefly • **look sharp** *informal* to be quick, hurry up ⊙ Comes from Old English *locian* meaning 'to look'

look-alike *noun* someone who looks physically like someone else

look-in *noun* a chance of doing something

looking-glass *noun, old* a mirror

lookout *noun* **1** (someone who keeps) a careful watch **2** a high place for watching from **3** concern, responsibility: *That's your lookout*

loom *noun* a machine for weaving cloth ➤ *verb* to appear indistinctly, often threateningly

loony *informal, noun* (*plural* **loonies**) a lunatic, an insane person ➤ *adjective* (**loonier, looniest**) mad, insane

loop *noun* **1** a doubled-over part in a piece of string etc **2** a U-shaped bend **3** *computing* a series of instructions in a program that is repeated until a certain condition is met • **loop the loop** to fly (an aircraft) upwards, back and down as if going round in a circle

loophole *noun* **1** a narrow slit in a wall **2** a way of avoiding a difficulty

loose (*pronounced* loos) *adjective* **1** not tight,

slack **2** not tied, free **3** not closely packed **4** vague, not exact **5** careless ➤ *verb* **1** to make loose, slacken **2** to untie • **break loose** to escape • **on the loose** free ◆ **loosely** *adverb* (adjective, meanings 1, 3, 4 and 5)

‼ Do not confuse with: **lose**

loose box *noun* a part of a stable or horse box where horses are kept untied

loose-leaf *adjective* having a cover that allows pages to be inserted or removed

loosen *verb* to make loose or looser

loot *noun* goods stolen or plundered ➤ *verb* to plunder, ransack

lop *verb* (**lopping, lopped**) to cut off the top or ends of

lope *verb* to run with a long stride

lop-eared *adjective* of an animal: having ears hanging down

lopsided *adjective* leaning to one side, not symmetrical

loquacious (*pronounced* lok-**wei**-shus) *adjective* talkative ◆ **loquacity** (*pronounced* lok-**was**-it-i) *noun*

lord *noun* **1** the owner of an estate **2** a title for a male member of the aristocracy, bishop, judge, etc **3** *old* a master, a ruler **4** (**the Lord**) God or Christ **5** (**the Lords**) the House of Lords • **lord it over someone** to act in a domineering manner towards them

Lord Chancellor *noun* the head of the English legal system

lordly *adjective* (**lordlier, lordliest**) **1** relating to a lord **2** noble, proud

lordship *noun* **1** power, rule **2** used in talking to or about a lord: *his lordship*

lore *noun* knowledge, beliefs, etc handed down through generations

lorelei (*pronounced* **lo**-rel-ai) *noun* a mythological siren in the Rhine who lured sailors to their death

lorgnette (*pronounced* lawn-**yet**) *noun* eyeglasses with a handle

lorry *noun* (*plural* **lorries**) a motor vehicle for carrying heavy loads

lose (*pronounced* looz) *verb* (**losing, lost**) **1** to cease to have, have no longer **2** to have (something) taken away from you **3** to put (something) where it cannot be found **4** to suffer the loss of (a close friend or relative) through death **5** to waste (time) **6** to miss (a train, a chance, etc) **7** to not win (a game)

‼ Do not confuse with: **loose**

loser *noun* **1** someone unlikely to succeed at anything **2** someone who loses a game or contest

loss *noun* (*plural* **losses**) **1** the act of losing **2** something which is lost **3** waste, harm, destruction **4** the death of a close friend or relative • **at a loss** uncertain what to do or say

loss leader *noun, business* something sold at a low price and at a loss to attract other custom

lost *adjective* **1** not able to be found **2** no longer possessed; thrown away **3** not won **4** ruined • **lost in** completely taken up by, engrossed in: *lost in thought*

lost cause *noun* an aim, ideal, person, etc that has no chance of success

lot *noun* **1** a large number or quantity **2** someone's fortune or fate **3** a separate portion • **draw lots** to decide who is to do something by drawing names out of a hat etc

loth another spelling of **loath**

lotion *noun* a liquid for treating or cleaning the skin or hair

lottery *noun* (*plural* **lotteries**) an event in which money or prizes are won through drawing lots

lotto *noun* **1** an old name for **bingo 2** a lottery

lotus *noun* (*plural* **lotuses**) **1** a kind of water-lily **2** a mythical tree whose fruit caused forgetfulness

lotus position *noun* in yoga: a seated position with the legs crossed and each foot resting on the opposite thigh

louche (*pronounced* loosh) *adjective* shady, disreputable

⊙ A French word, literally meaning 'squinting'

loud *adjective* **1** making a great sound; noisy **2** showy, over-bright ➤ *adverb* in a way that makes a great sound; noisily ◆ **loudly** *adverb* (adjective, meaning 1) ◆ **loudness** *noun* (adjective, meaning 1)

loudhailer *noun* a megaphone with microphone and amplifier

loudmouth *noun, informal* someone who talks offensively and too much

loudspeaker *noun* a device for converting electrical signals into sound

lounge *verb* **1** to lie back in a relaxed way **2** to move about lazily ➤ *noun* a sitting room

lounger *noun* **1** a lazy person **2** an extending chair or light couch for relaxing on

lounge suit *noun* a man's suit for everyday (but not casual) wear

lour another spelling of **lower²**

louse (*pronounced* lows) *noun* (*plural* **lice**) a small blood-sucking insect sometimes found on the bodies of animals and people

lousy (*pronounced* low-zi) *adjective* (**lousier, lousiest**) **1** swarming with lice **2** *informal* inferior, of poor quality

lout *noun* a clumsy or boorish man ◆ **loutish** *adjective*

louvre or *US* **louver** (*pronounced* loo-ver) *noun* a slat set at an angle

louvre door *noun* a slatted door allowing air and light to pass through

louvre window *noun* **1** a window covered with sloping slats **2** a window with narrow panes that can be set open at an angle

lovable or **loveable** *adjective* worthy of love

love *noun* **1** a great liking or affection **2** a loved person **3** *tennis* no score, zero ➤ *verb* to be very fond of; like very much • **in love (with) 1** feeling love and desire (for) **2** having a great liking (for): *in love with his own voice* • **make love to 1** to have sexual intercourse with **2** *old* to make sexual advances to, court

love affair *noun* a relationship between people in love but not married

lovebite *noun* a mark on the skin caused by the sucking bites of a lover

love-child *noun* (*plural* **love-children**), *old* an illegitimate child

lovelorn *adjective* sad because the love you feel for someone else is not returned

lovely *adjective* (**lovelier, loveliest**) beautiful; delightful ◆ **loveliness** *noun*

lovemaking *noun* **1** *old* courtship **2** sexual play and intercourse

lover *noun* **1** someone who loves another **2** an admirer, an enthusiast: *an art lover* **3** someone who is having a love affair

lovesick *adjective* languishing with love

loving *adjective* full of love ◆ **lovingly** *adverb*

low¹ *adjective* **1** not high; not lying or reaching far up **2** of a voice: not loud **3** cheap: *low air fares* **4** feeling sad, depressed **5** humble **6** mean, unworthy ➤ *adverb* **1** in or to a low position **2** not loudly **3** cheaply ➤ *noun* flattish country, without high hills • **keep a low profile** to not make your feelings or presence known

low² *verb* to make the noise of cattle; bellow, moo

lowbrow *adjective* designed to be popular, not intellectual (*contrasted with:* **highbrow**)

lowdown *informal, noun* (**the lowdown**) information ➤ *adjective* dishonest, despicable

lower¹ (*pronounced* loh-er) *adjective* less high ➤ *verb* **1** to make less high: *lower the price* **2** to let or come down: *lower the blinds*

lower² or **lour** (*pronounced* low-er) *verb* **1** of the sky: to become dark and cloudy **2** to frown ◆ **lowering** *adjective*

lower-case *adjective* of a letter: not a capital, eg *a* not *A* (*contrasted with:* **upper-case**)

⊙ So called because in the tray or case containing a typesetter's metal letters the capital letters were held in the top half and the uncapitalized small ones were kept in the bottom half

lowest common denominator or **least common denominator** *noun, maths* (*abbrev* **LCD** or **lcd**) the lowest common multiple of all the denominators in a group of fractions, eg the LCD of $\frac{1}{3}$ and $\frac{1}{4}$ is 12

lowest common multiple or **least common multiple** *noun, maths* (*abbrev* **LCM** or **lcm**) the smallest number into which every member of a group of numbers will divide exactly, eg the LCM of 2, 3, and 4 is 12

low-key *adjective* not elaborate, unpretentious

lowland *noun* land which is comparatively low-lying and flat (*also*: **lowlands**)

low-level language *noun, computing* a programming language using easily remembered words or letters, each translating into one machine code instruction (*compare with*: **high-level language**)

lowly *adjective* (**lowlier, lowliest**) low in rank, humble ♦ **lowliness** *noun*

low order goods *noun, economics, geography* convenience items such as food, toiletries, etc that are bought regularly (*contrasted with*: **high order goods**)

loyal *adjective* faithful, true ♦ **loyally** *adverb*

loyalist *noun* **1** someone loyal to their sovereign or country **2** (**Loyalist**) in Northern Ireland: a Protestant in favour of continuing parliamentary union with Great Britain

loyalty *noun* (*plural* **loyalties**) **1** faithful support of eg your friends **2** (**loyalties**) feelings of faithful friendship and support, especially for a particular person or thing

loyalty card *noun* a machine-readable plastic card issued by some retailers, enabling customers to collect credits to be exchanged for goods or cash

lozenge *noun* **1** a diamond-shaped figure **2** a small sweet for sucking

LP *noun, old* a long-playing record

L-plate *noun* a small square white sign with a red letter *L* on it which a learner driver must show on the back and front of a car

Lr *symbol, chemistry* lawrencium

LSD *abbreviation* **1** lysergic acid diethylamide, a hallucinogenic drug **2** pounds, shillings and pence (British coinage before decimalization)

Ltd *abbreviation* limited liability

Lu *symbol, chemistry* lutetium

lubricant *noun* something which lubricates; an oil

lubricate *verb* to apply oil etc to (something) to overcome friction and make movement easier ♦ **lubrication** *noun*

lucid *adjective* **1** easily understood **2** clear in mind; not confused ♦ **lucidity** *noun* ♦ **lucidly** *adverb*

Lucifer *noun* Satan, the Devil

luck *noun* **1** fortune, either good or bad **2** chance: *as luck would have it* **3** good fortune: *Have any luck?*

luckless *adjective* unfortunate, unhappy

lucky *adjective* (**luckier, luckiest**) **1** fortunate, having good luck **2** bringing good luck: *lucky charm* **3** happening as a result of good luck: *a lucky coincidence* ♦ **luckily** *adverb*

lucrative *adjective* profitable

lucre (*pronounced* **loo**-ker) *noun* gain; money

Luddite *noun* **1** *history* one of a group in the early 19th century who destroyed new machinery, especially in the textile industry, because they feared that many jobs would be lost **2** an opponent of technological innovation

⊙ Said to be named after Ned *Ludd*, an earlier opponent of machines for weaving stockings

ludicrous *adjective* ridiculous ♦ **ludicrously** *adverb* ♦ **ludicrousness** *noun*

ludo *noun* a game played with counters on a board

lug[1] *verb* (**lugging, lugged**) to pull or drag with effort

lug[2] *noun, informal* the ear

luge (*pronounced* loosz) *noun* a light toboggan ➤ *verb* to glide on such a sledge as a sport

luggage *noun* suitcases and other travelling baggage

lugger *noun* a small sailing vessel

lugubrious (*pronounced* lu-**goo**-bri-*us*) *adjective* mournful, dismal ♦ **lugubriously** *adverb*

lukewarm *adjective* **1** neither hot nor cold **2** not very keen, unenthusiastic

lull *verb* to soothe or calm ➤ *noun* a period of calm

lullaby (*pronounced* lul-a-bai) *noun* (*plural* **lullabies**) a song to lull children to sleep

lumbago (*pronounced* lum-**bei**-goh) *noun* a pain in the lower part of the back

lumbar *adjective* of or in the lower part of the back

lumbar puncture *noun, medicine* a method of diagnosing a disease which involves removing some spinal fluid through a needle inserted into the bottom of the spine

lumber *noun* **1** sawn-up timber **2** discarded old furniture etc ➤ *verb* to move about clumsily

lumberjack *noun* someone who fells, saws and shifts trees

lumen *noun* (*plural* **lumina** or **lumens**) **1** *physics* (symbol **lm**) the IS unit of luminous flux **2** *biology* in living organisms: the space enclosed by a vessel or tube, eg by a blood vessel or intestine

luminance *noun, physics* a measure of the brightness of a surface that is radiating or reflecting light, expressed in candelas per square metre

luminary *noun* (*plural* **luminaries**) **1** an expert or authority in a particular field **2** a famous or important member of a group

luminescent *adjective* giving out light ♦ **luminescence** *noun*

luminous *adjective* **1** giving light **2** shining; clear ♦ **luminosity** *noun*

luminous flux *noun, physics* a measure of the rate of flow of light energy

luminous intensity *noun, physics* the amount of light capable of causing illumination that is emitted from a source

lump *noun* **1** a small, solid mass of indefinite shape **2** a swelling **3** the whole taken together: *considered in a lump* **4** a heavy, dull person ➤ *verb* **1** to form into lumps **2** to treat as being alike: *lumped all of us together*

lumpectomy *noun* (*plural* **lumpectomies**) surgery to remove a lump in the breast

lumpish *adjective* heavy, dull

lump sum *noun* an amount of money given all at once

lumpy *adjective* (**lumpier, lumpiest**) full of lumps

lunacy *noun* madness, insanity

lunar *adjective* of the moon: *lunar eclipse*

lunate *adjective, biology* crescent-shaped

lunatic (*pronounced* **loo**-na-tik) *noun* someone who is insane or crazy ➤ *adjective* insane, mad

lunch *noun* (*plural* **lunches**) a midday meal ➤ *verb* to eat lunch

luncheon *noun, formal* lunch

luncheon voucher *noun* a voucher given by employers to workers to use towards paying for lunch at certain restaurants

lung *noun* either of the two bag-like organs which fill with and expel air in the course of breathing

lunge *noun* a sudden thrust or push ➤ *verb* to thrust or plunge forward suddenly

lupin (*pronounced* **loo**-pin) *noun* a type of garden plant with flowers on long spikes

lupine (*pronounced* **loo**-pain) *adjective* like a wolf

lupus (*pronounced* **loo**-pus) *noun* a skin disease causing ulcers and lesions

lurch *verb* to roll or pitch suddenly to one side; stagger ➤ *noun* (*plural* **lurches**) a pitch to one side • **leave in the lurch** to leave in a difficult position without help

lure *noun* something which entices; a bait ➤ *verb* to attract, entice away

lurid *adjective* **1** glaring, garish: *lurid book cover* **2** horrifying, sensational: *lurid story* **3** pale, ghostly

lurk *verb* **1** to keep out of sight; be hidden **2** to move or act secretly and slyly ♦ **lurker** *noun*

lurking *adjective* vague, hidden

luscious *adjective* sweet, delicious, juicy

lush *adjective* of grass etc: thick and plentiful

lust *noun* **1** a greedy desire for power, riches, etc **2** a strong sexual desire ➤ *verb* to have a strong desire (for)

luster US spelling of **lustre**

lustful *adjective* full of, or showing, strong sexual desire

lustre or US **luster** *noun* brightness, shine, gloss

ⓘ This is one of a large number of words which is spelled with an **-re** ending in British English, but with an **-er** in American English, eg *centre/center, calibre/caliber, metre/meter*.

lustrous *adjective* bright, shining

lusty *adjective* (**lustier, lustiest**) lively, strong ♦ **lustily** *adverb*

lute *noun* a stringed musical instrument with a pear-shaped, round-backed body and fretted fingerboard

lutein (*pronounced* **loo**-tee-in) *noun* a yellow pigment found in egg yolks

luteinizing hormone *noun, biology* a hormone secreted by the pituitary gland

lutetium *noun, chemistry* (symbol **Lu**) a very rare metallic element

🕒 From *Lutetia*, the Latin name for Paris (where it was discovered)

Lutheran *noun* a member of the Lutheran church, a major Protestant church founded by German theologian Martin Luther (1483–1546)

luxuriant *adjective* **1** thick with leaves, flowers, etc: *ornamental gardens full of luxuriant plants* **2** richly ornamented

❗ Do not confuse with: **luxurious**

luxuriate *verb* **1** to be luxuriant **2** to enjoy; take delight (in)

luxurious *adjective* full of luxuries; very comfortable: *a luxurious new home* ♦ **luxuriously** *adverb*

❗ Do not confuse with: **luxuriant**

luxury *noun* (*plural* **luxuries**) **1** something very pleasant or expensive but not necessary: *Having a car is a luxury* **2** the use or enjoyment of such things

LW *abbreviation* long-wave

lychee, lichee or **litchi** (*pronounced* lai-**chee**) *noun* a small fruit with sweet white juicy flesh enclosing a single seed

lychgate (*pronounced* **lich**-geit) *noun* a churchyard gate with a porch

Lycra *noun, trademark* a lightweight synthetic elastic fabric

lying see **lie**[1], **lie**[2]

lymph *noun* a colourless fluid in the body, containing mostly white blood cells
♦ **lymphatic** *adjective*

lymphatic system *noun, anatomy* the network of vessels that transports lymph around the body

lymph node or **lymph gland** *noun* in the lymphatic system: one of many small rounded structures, found in large clusters in the neck, armpit, and groin, that produce antibodies in immune responses

lymphocyte *noun* a type of white blood cell that attacks antigens

lymphoma *noun* (*plural* **lymphomas** or **lymphomata**) a tumour of the tissues in the lymphatic system

lynch *verb* to condemn and put to death without legal trial

⊙ Named after William *Lynch*, 19th-century Virginian planter who organized unofficial trials of suspected criminals

lynch mob *noun* a group of people who go out to lynch someone

lynx *noun* (*plural* **lynxes**) a wild animal of the cat family, noted for its keen sight

lyre *noun* an ancient stringed musical instrument, played like a harp

lyrebird *noun* an Australian bird with a lyre-shaped tail

lyric *noun* **1** a short poem, often expressing the poet's feelings **2** (**lyrics**) the words of a song ➤ *adjective* **1** of a lyric **2** full of joy

lyrical *adjective* **1** lyric **2** song-like **3** full of enthusiastic praise ♦ **lyrically** *adverb*

lyricism *noun* a song-like quality

lyricist *noun* someone who writes the words for songs

lysis *noun* (*plural* **lyses**), *biology* any process that destroys a living cell by disrupting the cell membrane and releasing the cell contents

-lysis *suffix* forms words containing the idea of splitting-up or breaking-down into smaller or simpler parts: *analysis* ⊙ Comes from Greek *lysis* meaning 'a loosening'

lysosome *noun, biology* a structure, found mainly in animal cells, containing enzymes which help destroy foreign particles and break down damaged cells

M *abbreviation* **1** Master **2** Monsieur **3** Motorway: *M6*

M *symbol* the Roman numeral for 1000

m¹ *abbreviation* **1** metre(s) **2** mile(s) **3** million(s)

m² *symbol* metre

MA *abbreviation* Master of Arts, a degree in a non-scientific subject such as a language

mac short for **mackintosh**

macabre (*pronounced* ma-**kah**-ber) *adjective* gruesome, horrible

macadamize or **macadamise** *verb* to surface (a road) with small, broken stones

⊙ Named after the 19th-century Scottish engineer John *McAdam* who invented the process

macaroni *noun* pasta shaped into short, hollow tubes

macaroon *noun* a sweet cake or biscuit made with ground almonds and sugar

macaw *noun* a long-tailed, brightly coloured parrot

mace¹ *noun* a heavy staff with an ornamental head, carried as a sign of office

mace² *noun* a spice made from the covering of a nutmeg

macerate (*pronounced* **mas**-e-reit) *verb* **1** to make into pulp by steeping **2** to emaciate

machete (*pronounced* ma-**shet**-i) *noun* a heavy knife used to cut through foliage etc

machinations (*pronounced* mak-i-**nei**-shonz or mash-i-**nei**-shonz) *plural noun* a crafty scheme, a plot

machine *noun* **1** a working arrangement of wheels, levers, etc **2** a (motor) bicycle **3** a political party organization ▸ *verb* to make, shape or sew with a machine

machine code *noun, computing* a system of symbols that can be understood by a computer

machine gun *noun* an automatic, rapid-firing gun

machine-readable *adjective, computing* of data, text, etc: in a form that can be directly processed by a computer

machinery *noun* **1** machines in general **2** the working parts of a machine **3** the combination of processes, systems or people that keep something working or produce a desired result: *the machinery of local government*

machine tool *noun* a stationary, power-driven machine used for cutting and shaping metal, wood or plastic

machinist *noun* **1** someone who operates a machine **2** someone who makes or repairs machines

machismo (*pronounced* ma-**kiz**-moh or ma-**chiz**-moh) *noun* overt or aggressive masculinity

Mach number (*pronounced* mahk or mak or mahkh) *noun* the ratio of the speed of an aircraft to the speed of sound (eg Mach 5 = 5 times the speed of sound)

macho (*pronounced* **mach**-oh) *adjective* overtly or aggressively masculine

mackerel *noun* an edible sea fish with wavy markings

mackintosh *noun* (*plural* **mackintoshes**) a waterproof overcoat

macro *noun, computing* a single instruction that prompts a computer to carry out a series of short instructions embedded in it

macro- *prefix* forms words for things which are long, large or great: *macromolecule* ⊙ Comes from Greek *makros* meaning 'long' or 'great'

macrobiotic *adjective* of diet: consisting of organic unprocessed food, especially vegetables, and originally intended to prolong life

macromolecule *noun, chemistry* a very large molecule, usually consisting of a large number of relatively simple units

macron *noun* a straight horizontal bar (⁻) placed over a letter to show that it is a long or stressed vowel ⊙ Comes from Greek *makros* meaning 'long'

mad *adjective* (**madder, maddest**) **1** mentally disturbed, insane **2** wildly foolish **3** furious with anger **4** (**mad about** or **on**) very keen or enthusiastic • **like mad** very quickly or energetically: *We had to work like mad to finish* ◆ **madness** *noun* (meanings 1 and 2)

madam *noun* a polite form of address to a woman

madcap *noun* a rash, hot-headed person ▸ *adjective* foolishly rash: *a madcap scheme*

mad cow disease see **BSE**

madden *verb* to make angry or mad

maddening *adjective* extremely annoying

made past form of **make**

madhouse *noun* **1** a place of confusion and noise **2** *old* an insane asylum

madly *adverb* **1** insanely **2** extremely: *madly in love*

madman or **madwoman** *noun* (*plural* **madmen** or **madwomen**) someone who is mad

Madonna *noun* the Virgin Mary as depicted in art

madrigal *noun* a part-song for several voices

maelstrom (*pronounced* **meil**-strom) *noun* **1** a whirlpool **2** any place of great confusion

maestro (*pronounced* **mais**-troh) *noun* (*plural* **maestros**) someone highly skilled in an art, especially music

mafia *noun* **1** (**the Mafia**) a secret criminal organization, originating in Sicily, that controls many illegal activities in Italy, the US and worldwide **2** any group that exerts a secret and powerful influence, especially using unscrupulous or ruthless criminal methods

magazine *noun* **1** a paperback periodical publication containing articles, stories and pictures **2** a storage place for military equipment **3** a place for extra cartridges in a rifle

⊙ The meaning of *magazine* as a periodical developed from the military use, being intended as a storehouse or treasury of information

magenta *noun* a reddish-purple colour ➤ *adjective* of this colour

maggot *noun* a small worm-like creature, the grub of a bluebottle etc

maggoty *adjective* full of maggots

magi plural of **magus**

magic *noun* **1** a process which supposedly uses supernatural forces, spells, etc to produce results which cannot be explained or which are remarkable **2** conjuring tricks **3** the quality of being wonderful or delightful ➤ *adjective* **1** using magic: *magic tricks* **2** used in magic: *a magic wand* **3** wonderful or mysterious

magical *adjective* **1** of or produced by magic **2** very wonderful or mysterious ♦ **magically** *adverb*

magical realism or **magic realism** *noun* a style of art, literature or cinema in which fantastic events or images are presented in a realistic context

magician *noun* someone skilled in magic

Maginot Line (*pronounced* **ma**-szi-noh) *noun, history* a line of defensive fortifications built by France along its border with Germany

⊙ Named after André *Maginot* (1877–1932), French Minister of Defence when construction began in 1929

magisterial *adjective* **1** of magistrates **2** having an air of authority

magistrate *noun* someone with the power to enforce the law, eg a justice of the peace

magistrate's court *noun* in England and Wales: a court of law dealing with minor criminal and civil cases

magma *noun* molten rock

Magna Carta *noun, history* the charter obtained by barons from King John of England in 1215, defining a body of law and custom the king should observe ⊙ Comes from Latin, meaning 'great charter'

magnanimity (*pronounced* mag-na-**nim**-it-i) *noun* generosity

magnanimous (*pronounced* mag-**nan**-im-us) *adjective* very generous ♦ **magnanimously** *adverb*

magnate *noun* someone with great power or wealth

magnesia *noun* a light, white powder, magnesium oxide

magnesium *noun, chemistry* (symbol **Mg**) a white metal which burns with an intense white light

magnet *noun* **1** a piece of iron, steel, etc which has the power to attract other pieces of metal **2** someone or something that attracts strongly

magnetic *adjective* **1** having the powers of a magnet **2** strongly attractive: *a magnetic personality*

magnetic field *noun* the area which is affected by a magnet

magnetic flux *noun, physics* a measure of the amount of magnetism, considering both the strength and extent of the magnetic field

magnetic north *noun* the direction in which the magnetized needle of a compass points, slightly east or west of true north

magnetic pole *noun* **1** either of two areas on a magnet where the magnetic field is strongest **2** *geography* the two points on the earth's surface (**North Pole** and **South Pole**) at either end of its axis

magnetic stripe *noun* a dark magnetic strip on the back of a credit card, identity card, etc containing information which can be read electronically

magnetic tape *noun* tape on which sound, pictures, computer material, etc can be recorded

magnetism *noun* **1** the properties of attraction possessed by a magnet **2** attraction, great charm

magnetite *noun* a shiny, black, magnetic iron ore

magnetize or **magnetise** *verb* **1** to make magnetic **2** to attract, influence ♦ **magnetization** *noun*

magneto (*pronounced* mag-**nee**-toh) *noun* (*plural* **magnetos**) a device producing electric sparks, used for lighting the fuel in some internal combustion engines, eg in a lawnmower

magnetron *noun* a device for generating microwaves

magnification *noun* 1 the process of making objects appear larger or closer, or the power that instruments such as microscopes and binoculars have to do this 2 a measure of how much larger or closer an object is made to appear than it is in reality

magnificent *adjective* 1 splendid in appearance or action 2 excellent, very fine ♦ **magnificence** *noun* ♦ **magnificently** *adverb*

magnify *verb* (**magnifies, magnifying, magnified**) 1 to make (something) appear larger by using special lenses 2 to exaggerate

magnifying glass *noun* a lens through which things appear larger

magnitude *noun* 1 size or extent 2 importance

magnolia *noun* a tree which produces large, white or purplish, sweet-scented flowers

magnox *noun, trademark* (sometimes **Magnox**) a material consisting of an aluminium alloy and a small amount of magnesium, used for fuel containers in some nuclear reactors ☉ From *magnesium no oxidation*

magnum *noun* a bottle of wine or champagne equal to two ordinary bottles

magnum opus *noun* a great work, a masterpiece

magpie *noun* a black-and-white bird of the crow family, known for its habit of collecting objects

☉ Originally *Magot pie*, a short form of the name 'Margaret' + *pie*, an old word for 'magpie'

magus (*pronounced* **mei**-gus) *noun* (*plural* **magi** *pronounced* **mei**-jai) an ancient Persian priest or astrologer • **the Magi** the three wise men who brought gifts to the infant Christ in the Bible

maharaja or **maharajah** *noun* an important Indian prince, especially the ruler of a state

maharishi *noun* a Hindu religious teacher or spiritual leader

Mahdi (*pronounced* **ma**-dee) *noun* (**the Mahdi**) 1 *Islam* the great leader of the faithful Muslims, who is to appear in the last days 2 *history* a title of various rebellious leaders

mah-jong *noun* a Chinese table game played with small painted bricks

☉ The name **mah-jong** means *sparrows* in Chinese, and is thought to refer to the chattering sound which the little bricks make while the game is being played

mahogany *noun* (*plural* **mahoganies**) 1 a tropical American hardwood tree 2 its hard

reddish-brown wood, often used for furniture

maid *noun* 1 a female servant 2 *old* an unmarried woman; a young girl

maiden *noun, old* an unmarried girl; a virgin ➤ *adjective* 1 unmarried: *a maiden aunt* 2 first, initial: *a maiden voyage*

maiden name *noun* the surname of a married woman before her marriage

maiden over *noun, cricket* an over in which no runs are made

mail¹ *noun* letters, parcels, etc carried by post ➤ *verb* to post

mail² *noun* body armour of steel rings or plates

mailbag *noun* 1 a bag in which mail is carried 2 the letters received by a TV programme, magazine, etc

mailbox *noun* 1 *esp N Am* a public or private letter box 2 *computing* a part of a computer's memory in which e-mail messages are stored

mailing list *noun* 1 a list of the names and addresses of people to whom an organization regularly sends information 2 *computing* a file containing a list of addresses to which an e-mail is to be sent

mail order *noun* a system of buying and selling goods by post ➤ *adjective* relating to, bought, sold, etc by mail order

mail shot *noun* 1 unsolicited advertising material sent by post 2 the sending out of a batch of this

maim *verb* to cripple, disable

main *adjective* chief, most important ➤ *noun, old* the ocean • **in the main** for the most part • **the mains** a supply of gas, water or electricity through a branching system of pipes or conductors

main clause *noun, grammar* a clause in a sentence that can make sense on its own, eg *'I liked the book* that you gave me for my birthday' (*compare with*: **subordinate clause**)

mainframe *noun, computing* a large, powerful computer to which several smaller computers can be linked

mainland *noun* a large piece of land off whose coast lie smaller islands

mainly *adverb* chiefly, mostly

mainstay *noun* the chief support

maintain *verb* 1 to keep (something) as it is 2 to continue to keep in good working order 3 to support (a family etc) 4 to state (an opinion) firmly

maintenance *noun* 1 the act of maintaining; upkeep, repair 2 means of support, especially money for food, clothing, etc

maisonette *noun* a flat within a house or block, especially one with two floors

maître d' (*pronounced* mei-tre-**dee**) *noun* (*plural* **maîtres d'** or **maître d's**) the manager or head waiter of a hotel or restaurant

maize *noun* a type of corn widely grown for food

majestic *adjective* stately, regal

majesty *noun* (*plural* **majesties**) **1** greatness of rank or manner **2** (**Majesty**) a title used in addressing or referring to a king or queen: *Your Majesty/a royal visit from Their Majesties*

major *adjective* great in size, importance, etc (*contrasted with*: **minor**) ➤ *noun* a senior army officer

majority *noun* (*plural* **majorities**) **1** the greater number or quantity **2** the difference in amount between the greater and the lesser number **3** the age when someone becomes legally an adult (18 in the UK)

make *verb* (**making, made**) **1** to form, construct **2** to cause to be: *He makes me mad at times* **3** to bring about: *make trouble* **4** to amount to: *2 and 2 make 4* **5** to earn: *She made £300 last week* **6** to force: *I made him do it* **7** to undergo (a journey etc) **8** to prepare (a meal etc): *I'll make some tea* ➤ *noun* **1** kind, shape, form **2** brand • **make believe** to pretend • **make good 1** to do well **2** to carry out (a promise) **3** to make up for (a loss) • **make light of** to treat as unimportant • **make much of** to fuss over, treat as important • **make nothing of 1** to be unable to understand, do, etc **2** to make light of • **make off** to run away • **make out 1** to see in the distance or indistinctly **2** to declare, prove **3** to write out (a bill, cheque, etc) • **make up 1** to form a whole: *Eleven players make up the side* **2** to put together, invent (a false story) **3** to put make-up on the face **4** to be friendly again after a quarrel • **make up for** to give or do something in return for damage done • **on the make** *informal* looking for personal gain ◷ Comes from Old English *macian*

make-believe *noun* fantasy

makeover *noun* a complete change in a person's style of dress, appearance, make-up, etc

maker *noun* the person or organization that has made something • **meet your maker** to die

makeshift *adjective* used for a time as a substitute for something better

make-up *noun* cosmetics

makings *plural noun*: **have the makings of** to have the ability to become a specified thing: *He has the makings of a great teacher*

maladjusted *adjective* of a person: unable to deal with everyday situations and relationships

maladministration *noun* bad or dishonest management, especially of public affairs

malady *noun* (*plural* **maladies**) illness, disease

malaise (*pronounced* ma-**leiz**) *noun* a feeling or general air of unease, depression or despondency

malapropism (*pronounced* **mal**-a-prop-izm) *noun* the use of a wrong word which sounds similar to the one intended, eg *contemptuous for contemporary*

◷ After Mrs *Malaprop* in Sheridan's play, *The Rivals* (1775), who habitually used the wrong word. One of the most famous is her exclamation: 'She's as headstrong as an allegory on the banks of the Nile.'

malaria *noun* a fever caused by the bite of a particular type of mosquito ✦ **malarial** *adjective*

◷ From an Italian phrase meaning 'bad air', malarial fever being originally thought to be caused by poisonous marsh gases

malarkey (*pronounced* ma-**lahr**-ki) *noun* nonsense; absurd behaviour or talk

male *adjective* of the sex that is able to father children or young; masculine ➤ *noun* a member of this sex

male chauvinist *noun* a man who believes in the superiority of men over women and acts in a prejudiced way towards them

malediction *noun* a curse; cursing ✦ **maledictory** *adjective*

malefactor *noun* an evildoer

malevolent *adjective* wishing ill to others; spiteful ✦ **malevolence** *noun* ✦ **malevolently** *adverb*

malformation *noun* faulty or wrong shape ✦ **malformed** *adjective*

malfunction *verb* to fail to work or operate properly ➤ *noun* failure to operate

malice *noun* ill will; spite

malicious *adjective* intending harm; spiteful ✦ **maliciously** *adverb*

malign (*pronounced* ma-**lain**) *verb* to say or write unpleasant things about someone, especially falsely or spitefully

malignant (*pronounced* ma-**lig**-nant) *adjective* **1** wishing harm to someone, spiteful **2** of a disease: likely to cause death (*contrasted with*: **benign**) ✦ **malignancy** *noun* ✦ **malignantly** *adverb*

malinger (*pronounced* ma-**ling**-ger) *verb* to pretend to be ill to avoid work etc ✦ **malingerer** *noun*

mall (*pronounced* mawl) *noun, originally US* a shopping centre

malleable (*pronounced* **mal**-i-a-bl) *adjective* **1** of metal: able to be beaten out by hammering **2** of people: easy to influence ✦ **malleability** *noun*

mallet *noun* a heavy wooden hammer

malleus (*pronounced* **mal**-i-us) *noun* (*plural*

mallei – *pronounced* **mal**-i-ai) a small, hammer-shaped bone in the ear ⏲ from Latin meaning 'hammer'

malnourished *adjective* ill or weak due to lack of sufficient or proper food

malnutrition *noun* lack of sufficient or proper food; undernourishment

malpractice *noun* **1** wrongdoing **2** professional misconduct

malt *noun* **1** barley or other grain prepared for making beer or whisky **2** a malt whisky

Malthusian (*pronounced* mal-**thyoo**-zi-an) *adjective* of the theory that the increase of population tends to outstrip that of the means of living and therefore sexual restraint should be exercised

⏲ After T R *Malthus* (1766–1834), the English economist who presented the theory

maltose (*pronounced* **mawl**-tohz) *noun, chemistry* a hard, white, crystalline sugar composed of two glucose molecules linked together

maltreat *verb* to treat roughly or unkindly ♦ **maltreatment** *noun*

mama or **mamma** (*both pronounced* ma-**mah**) *noun, informal* mother

mammal *noun* a member of the class of animals of which the female parent feeds the young with her own milk ♦ **mammalian** *adjective*

mammary *adjective, biology* of the female breasts or other milk-producing glands

mammary gland *noun, biology, anatomy* the milk-producing gland of a mammal, eg a woman's breast or a cow's udder

mammogram *noun* an X-ray taken of a woman's breast to detect early signs of cancer

mammoth *noun* a very large elephant, now extinct ➤ *adjective* enormous, huge: *mammoth savings*

man *noun* (*plural* **men**) **1** a grown-up human male **2** a human being **3** the human race **4** *informal* a husband **5** a piece in chess or draughts ➤ *verb* (**manning, manned**) to supply with workers, crew, etc: *man the boats* • **the man in the street** the ordinary person • **to a man** every single one ⏲ Comes from Old English *mann*

manacle *noun, formal* a handcuff ➤ *verb* to handcuff

manage *verb* **1** to have control or charge of **2** to deal with, cope: *can't manage on his own* **3** to succeed: *managed to finish on time*

manageable *adjective* easily managed or controlled

managed retreat *noun, geography* allowing parts of a coast to erode and flood naturally

management *noun* **1** those in charge of a business etc **2** the art of managing a business etc

manager *noun* someone in charge of a business etc ♦ **managerial** *adjective*

manageress *noun* a female manager of a shop etc

Manchester school *noun, history* the followers of John Bright (1811–89) and Richard Cobden (1804–65), advocates of free trade and of individual freedom of action

Mancunian (*pronounced* man-**kyoo**-ni-an) *noun* someone born or living in Manchester

mandala *noun, Buddhism, Hinduism* a pictorial symbol of the universe, usually a circle enclosing images of deities or geometric designs

mandarin *noun* **1** a small orange-like citrus fruit **2** *history* a senior Chinese official

mandate *noun* **1** a right or power to act on someone else's behalf **2** a command, especially one given from a superior to a subordinate **3** *history* (also **Mandate**) a territory administered by a country on behalf of the League of Nations, especially the former territories of the German and Ottoman empires after World War I (*also called*: **mandated territory**)

mandatory *adjective* compulsory

mandible *noun, anatomy* the jaw or lower jawbone

mandir *noun* a Hindu or Jain temple

mandolin or **mandoline** *noun* a round-backed stringed instrument similar to a lute

mane *noun* **1** long hair on the head and neck of a horse or male lion **2** a long or thick head of hair

maneuver US spelling of **manoeuvre**

manful *adjective* courageous and noble-minded ♦ **manfully** *adverb*

manganese *noun, chemistry* (symbol **Mn**) a hard, easily broken metal of a greyish-white colour

mange (*pronounced* meinj) *noun* a skin disease of dogs, cats, etc

mangel-wurzel (*pronounced* mang-gel-**wer**-zel) *noun* a kind of beetroot used as cattle food

manger (*pronounced* **meinj**-er) *noun* a box or trough holding dry food for horses and cattle

mangetout (*pronounced* **monj**-too) *noun* a variety of garden pea with an edible pod

mangle *noun* a machine for squeezing water out of clothes or for smoothing them ➤ *verb* **1** to squeeze (clothes) through a mangle **2** to crush, tear, damage badly

mango *noun* (*plural* **mangoes**) **1** the fruit of a tropical Indian tree, with juicy orange flesh **2** the tree which produces mangoes

mangrove *noun* a type of tree which grows in swamps in hot countries

mangy (*pronounced* **meinj**-ee) *adjective* (**mangier, mangiest**) **1** shabby, squalid **2** of an animal: suffering from mange

manhandle *verb* to handle roughly

manhole *noun* a hole (into a drain, sewer, etc) large enough to let a person through

manhood *noun* the state of being a man

man-hour *noun* a unit of work equal to the work done by one person in one hour

manhunt *noun* an intensive, often large-scale, organized search for someone such as a criminal or fugitive

mania (*pronounced* **mei**-ni-a) *noun* **1** a form of mental illness in which the sufferer is over-active, over-excited and unreasonably happy **2** extreme fondness or enthusiasm: *a mania for computer games*

maniac *noun* **1** a mad person **2** a very rash or over-enthusiastic person

manic (*pronounced* **man**-ik) *adjective* **1** suffering from mania **2** very energetic or excited

manicure *noun* **1** the care of hands and nails **2** professional treatment for the hands and nails ► *verb* to perform a manicure on

manicurist *noun* someone who performs manicures

manifest *adjective* easily seen or understood ► *verb* to show plainly

manifestation *noun* behaviour, actions or events which reveal or display something

Manifest Destiny *noun, history* the doctrine of US expansion throughout North America in the 19th century, encapsulating the idea that it was God's will

manifestly *adverb* obviously, clearly

manifesto *noun* (*plural* **manifestoes** or **manifestos**) a public announcement of intentions, eg by a political party

manifold *adjective* many and various

manioc *noun* tapioca

manipulate *verb* **1** to handle something, especially in a skilful way **2** to control or influence someone cleverly and unscrupulously, to your own advantage **3** to change something such as statistics, figures, etc to give a false picture of a situation ♦ **manipulation** *noun*

mankind *noun* the human race

manly *adjective* brave, strong ♦ **manliness** *noun*

manna *noun* an unexpected or delicious treat

⊙ The name given in the Bible to the food miraculously provided for the Israelites in the wilderness

mannequin *noun* **1** someone who models clothes for prospective buyers **2** a display dummy

manner *noun* **1** the way in which something is done **2** the way in which someone behaves **3** (**manners**) polite behaviour towards others • **all manner of** all kinds of

mannerism *noun* an odd and obvious habit or characteristic

mannerly *adjective* polite

mannish *adjective* of a woman: behaving or looking like a man

manoeuvre or *US* **maneuver** *noun* **1** a planned movement of troops, ships or aircraft **2** a trick, a cunning plan ► *verb* **1** to perform a manoeuvre **2** to manipulate

man-of-war *noun* a warship

manometer *noun* an instrument for measuring the difference in pressure between two fluids

manor *noun* **1** a large house, usually attached to a country estate **2** *history* the land belonging to a lord or squire ♦ **manorial** *adjective*

manpower *noun* the number of people available for work

manse *noun* the house of a minister in certain Christian churches, eg the Church of Scotland

manservant *noun* (*plural* **menservants**) a male servant

mansion *noun* a large house

manslaughter *noun* killing someone without deliberate intent

mantelpiece *noun* a shelf over a fireplace

mantis *noun* (*plural* **mantises** or **mantes** – *pronounced* **man**-teez) an insect of the cockroach family, with large spiny forelegs (*also called*: **praying mantis**)

mantissa *noun, maths* the part of a logarithm comprising the decimal point and the figures following it ⊙ Comes from Latin, meaning 'something added'

mantle *noun* **1** a cloak or loose outer garment **2** a covering: *a mantle of snow* **3** a thin, transparent shade around the flame of a gas or paraffin lamp **4** *geology* the part of the earth immediately beneath the crust, thought to consist of solid, heavy rock

mantra *noun, Hinduism, Buddhism* a word or phrase, chanted or repeated inwardly in meditation

manual *adjective* **1** of the hand or hands **2** worked by hand **3** working with the hands: *a manual worker* ► *noun* a handbook giving instructions on how to use something: *a car manual* ♦ **manually** *adverb* (adjective, meaning 2)

manufacture *verb* **1** to make (articles or materials) in large quantities, usually by machine **2** to invent or fabricate (an excuse etc) ► *noun* **1** the process of manufacturing **2** a manufactured article ♦ **manufacturer** *noun* ♦ **manufacturing** *adjective & noun*

manure *noun* a substance, especially animal dung, spread on soil to make it more fertile ► *verb* to treat with manure

manuscript *noun* **1** the prepared material for a

book etc before it is printed **2** a book or paper written by hand

Manx *adjective* of or relating to the Isle of Man

Manx cat *noun* a tailless breed of cat

many *adjective* a large number of: *Many people were present* ➤ *noun* a large number: *Many survived* • **many a** a large number of: *Many a voice was raised*

Maori *noun* a member of a race of people who were first to arrive in New Zealand

map *noun* a flat drawing of all or part of the earth's surface, showing geographical features ➤ *verb* (**mapping, mapped**) **1** to make a map of **2** *maths* to correspond single members of a set (the **domain**) with single members of another set (the **codomain**) • **map something out** to plan something

maple *noun* **1** a tree related to the sycamore, one variety of which produces sugar **2** its hard, light-coloured wood, used for furniture etc

mapping *noun, maths* a diagram showing the correspondence of single members of one set with those of another

mar *verb* (**marring, marred**) to spoil, deface

maracas *plural noun* a pair of filled gourds shaken as a percussion instrument

marathon *noun* a long-distance foot-race, usually covering 26 miles 385 yards

○ After the distance run by a Greek soldier from *Marathon* to Athens with news of the victory over the Persians in 490 BC

maraud *verb* to plunder, raid

marauder *noun* a plundering robber

marauding *adjective* roaming about with the intention of plundering or killing

marble *noun* **1** limestone that takes a high polish, used for sculpture, decorating buildings, etc **2** a small glass ball used in a children's game

March *noun* the third month of the year

○ After *Mars*, the Roman god of war

march¹ *verb* **1** to (cause to) walk in time with regular steps **2** to go on steadily ➤ *noun* (*plural* **marches**) **1** a marching movement **2** a piece of music for marching to **3** the distance covered by marching **4** a steady progression of events: *the march of time*

march² *noun* (*plural* **marches**) a boundary or border • **riding the marches** the traditional ceremony of riding around the boundaries of a town etc

marchioness (*pronounced* mahr-shon-**es**) *noun* (*plural* **marchionesses**) a woman who holds the rank of marquess or is the wife or widow of a marquess

Mardi Gras (*pronounced* mahr-di **grah**) *noun* a carnival held on Shrove Tuesday in certain countries

mare *noun* a female horse

margarine (*pronounced* **mahr**-ja-reen) *noun* an edible spread similar to butter, made mainly of vegetable fats

margin *noun* **1** an edge, a border **2** the blank edge on the page of a book **3** additional space or room; allowance: *a margin for error*

marginal *adjective* **1** of or in a margin **2** borderline, close to a limit **3** of a political constituency: without a clear majority for any one candidate or party **4** of little effect or importance: *a marginal improvement* ➤ *noun* a marginal political constituency

marginalize or **marginalise** *verb* to make less important or central

marginally *adverb* very slightly, to a very small degree

marigold *noun* a kind of plant with a yellow or orange flower

marijuana *noun* an illegal drug made from the plant hemp

marina *noun* a place with moorings for yachts, dinghies, etc

marinade *noun* a mixture of oil, wine, herbs, spices, etc in which food is soaked for flavour before it is cooked ➤ *verb* to marinate

marinate *verb* to steep in a marinade

marine *adjective* of the sea ➤ *noun* a soldier trained to serve on land or at sea

mariner (*pronounced* ma-rin-er) *noun, old* a sailor

marionette *noun* a puppet moved by strings

marital *adjective* of marriage

maritime *adjective* **1** of the sea or ships **2** lying near the sea **3** *geography* of climate: cool in summer and mild in winter, because of the nearness of the sea

marjoram *noun* a sweet-smelling herb used in cooking

mark *noun* **1** a sign that can be seen **2** a stain, spot, etc **3** a target aimed at **4** a trace **5** a point used to assess the merit of a piece of schoolwork etc **6** the starting-line in a race: *On your marks!* ➤ *verb* **1** to make a mark on; stain **2** to observe, watch **3** to stay close to (an opponent in football etc) **4** to award marks to (a piece of schoolwork etc) • **mark off** to separate, distinguish • **mark time 1** to move the feet up and down, as if marching, but without going forward **2** to keep things going without progressing • **up to the mark** coming up to the required standard

marked *adjective* easily noticed: *a marked improvement*

markedly *adverb* noticeably

marker *noun* **1** a pen with a thick point, used for

writing signs etc **2** something used to show a position

market noun **1** a public place for buying and selling **2** (a country, place, etc where there is) a need or demand (for certain types of goods): *the teenage market* ➤ *verb* to put on sale • **on the market** for sale

market forces *plural noun, business* the effect of supply and demand on the price and quantity of a product being traded

market garden *noun* an area of land in which fruit and vegetables are grown to be sold

marketing *noun* the act or practice of advertising and selling

market leader *noun, business* a company, or brand of goods, that outsells its competitors

marketplace *noun* **1** an area in a town etc where a market is held **2** the world of commerce

market research *noun, business* analysis of the habits, needs and preferences of customers, often in relation to a particular product

marksman or **markswoman** *noun* (*plural* **marksmen** or **markswomen**) someone who shoots well

marmalade *noun* a jam made from citrus fruit, especially oranges

marmoset *noun* a type of small monkey found in America

marmot *noun* a stout burrowing rodent

maroon¹ *noun* **1** a brownish-red colour **2** a firework used as a distress signal ➤ *adjective* brownish-red

maroon² *verb* **1** to abandon on an island etc without means of escape **2** to leave in a helpless or uncomfortable position

marquee (*pronounced* mahr-**kee**) *noun* a large tent used for large gatherings, eg a wedding reception or circus

marquess or **marquis** (*both pronounced* **mahr**-kwis) *noun* (*plural* **marquesses** or **marquises**) a nobleman below a duke in rank

marram *noun* a coarse grass that grows on sandy shores

marriage *noun* **1** the ceremony by which two people become husband and wife **2** a joining together: *a marriage of minds*

marriageable *adjective* suitable or old enough for marriage

marrow *noun* **1** the soft substance in the hollow part of bones **2** a long vegetable with a thick green or striped skin and soft white flesh

marry *verb* (**marries, marrying, married**) to join, or be joined, together in marriage

marsh *noun* (*plural* **marshes**) a piece of low-lying wet ground

marshal *noun* **1** a high-ranking officer in the army or air force **2** someone who directs processions etc **3** *US* a law-court official **4** *US* the

head of a police force ➤ *verb* (**marshalling, marshalled**) **1** to arrange (troops, facts, arguments, etc) in order **2** to show the way, conduct, lead

Marshall Aid *noun, history* US economic aid to Europe after World War II

⊙ Named after George *Marshall* (1880–1959), US Secretary of State who announced the aid

marsh-gas see **methane**

marshmallow *noun* **1** a spongy, jelly-like sweet made from sugar and egg-whites **2** a marsh plant with pink flowers, similar to the hollyhock

marsh marigold *noun* a marsh plant with yellow flowers (*also called*: **kingcup**)

marshy *adjective* (**marshier, marshiest**) wet underfoot; boggy

marsupial *noun* an animal which carries its young in a pouch, eg the kangaroo

marten *noun* an animal related to the weasel

martial *adjective* **1** of war or battle **2** warlike

martial art *noun* a combative sport or method of self-defence

martial law *noun* the government of a country by its army

Martian *noun* a potential or imaginary being from the planet Mars

martin *noun* a bird of the swallow family

martinet *noun* someone who keeps strict order; a disciplinarian

⊙ Named after Jean *Martinet*, a 17th-century French officer who invented a type of military drill

Martinmas *noun* 11 November, the feast of St Martin

martyr *noun* someone who suffers death or hardship for their beliefs ➤ *verb* to execute or make suffer for beliefs

martyrdom *noun* the death or suffering of a martyr

marvel *noun* something astonishing or wonderful ➤ *verb* (**marvelling, marvelled**) to feel amazement (at)

marvellous *adjective* **1** astonishing, extraordinary **2** *informal* excellent, very good

Marxist *noun* a follower of the theories of Karl Marx; a communist ♦ **Marxism** *noun*

marzipan *noun* a mixture of ground almonds, sugar, etc, used in cake-making and confectionery

mascara *noun* a cosmetic used to colour the eyelashes

mascot *noun* a person, animal or thing believed to bring good luck

masculine *adjective* **1** of the male sex **2** manly **3** *grammar* of the gender to which words denoting males belong ♦ **masculinity** *noun*

mash verb to beat or crush into a pulp ➤ noun (plural **mashes**) **1** mashed potato **2** a mixture of bran, meal, etc, used as animal food

masjid (pronounced **mus**-jid) noun a mosque

mask noun **1** a cover for the face for disguise or protection: an oxygen mask/a surgical mask/a Hallowe'en mask **2** a pretence, a disguise ➤ verb **1** to hide, disguise **2** to cover the face with a mask

masochism (pronounced **maz**-o-kizm) noun **1** the practice of deriving sexual pleasure from being dominated, treated cruelly or made to suffer in any way **2** a tendency to take pleasure in one's own suffering ♦ **masochist** noun ♦ **masochistic** adjective

ⓘ After Leopold von Sacher-Masoch, the 19th-century Austrian novelist who wrote about the practice

mason noun **1** someone who carves stone **2** a Freemason ♦ **masonic** adjective (meaning 2): a masonic lodge

masonry noun stonework

masquerade (pronounced mas-ke-**reid** or mahs-ke-**reid**) noun **1** a dance at which masks are worn **2** pretence ➤ verb to pretend to be someone else: masquerading as a journalist

Mass noun (plural **Masses**) **1** (in some Christian churches) the celebration commemorating Christ's last meal with his disciples **2** music for a Mass

mass noun (plural **masses**) **1** physics the amount of matter that an object contains **2** a lump or quantity gathered together **3** a large quantity **4** the main part or body **5** a measure of quantity of matter in an object ➤ adjective **1** of a mass **2** of or consisting of large numbers or quantities ➤ verb to form into a mass ● **the masses** ordinary people

massacre noun the merciless killing of a large number of people ➤ verb to kill (a large number) in a cruel way

massage (pronounced **mas**-ahsz) noun the rubbing of parts of the body to remove pain or tension ➤ verb to perform massage on

masseur (pronounced mas-**er**) noun someone who performs massage

masseuse (pronounced mas-**erz**) noun a female masseur

massif (pronounced mas-**eef**) noun, geography a mountainous plateau surrounded by lowland

massive adjective bulky, heavy, huge

massively adverb enormously, heavily

mass media plural noun means of communicating information to a large number of people, eg television, radio and the press

mass movement noun, geography downhill movements of soil, rocks, etc, caused by gravity

mass noun noun, grammar a noun which cannot be qualified in the singular by the indefinite article and cannot be used in the plural, eg furniture but not car (compare with: **countable noun**)

mass number noun, chemistry the total number of protons and neutrons in the nucleus of an atom (also called: **nucleon number**)

mass production noun production in large quantities of articles all exactly the same

mass spectrograph noun, chemistry, physics an instrument which uses a photographic plate to give precise measurements of the atomic mass units of different isotopes of an element

mass spectrometer noun, chemistry, physics an instrument which uses an electrical detector to give precise measurements of the atomic mass units of different isotopes of an element ♦ **mass spectrometry** noun

mast noun a long upright pole holding up the sails etc in a ship, or holding an aerial, flag, etc

mastectomy (plural **mastectomies**) noun the surgical removal of a woman's breast or breasts

master noun **1** someone who controls or commands **2** an owner of a dog etc **3** an employer **4** a male teacher **5** the commander of a merchant ship **6** someone who is very skilled in something, an expert **7** a degree at the level above a bachelor: Master of Arts **8** an original film, recording, etc from which copies are made ➤ adjective chief, controlling: a master switch ➤ verb **1** to overcome, defeat **2** to become able to do or use properly: I've finally mastered this computer program

masterful adjective strong-willed and expecting to be obeyed

master-key noun a key which is so made that it opens a number of different locks

masterly adjective showing the skill of an expert or master, clever

mastermind verb to plan, work out the details of (a scheme etc) ➤ noun the person responsible for devising a scheme or plan

master of ceremonies noun someone who directs the form and order of events at a public occasion; a compère

masterpiece noun the best example of someone's work, especially a very fine picture, book, piece of music, etc

mastery noun **1** victory (over) **2** control (of) **3** great skill (in)

masthead noun **1** the top of a ship's mast **2** journalism the title of a newspaper, its logo, price and place of publication, printed at the top of its front page

mastic noun **1** a gum resin from a Mediterranean tree, used as a varnish or glue **2** a waterproof, putty-like paste used as a filler in building work

masticate *verb, formal* to chew ♦ **mastication** *noun*

mastiff *noun* a breed of large, powerful dog

mastoid *anatomy, adjective* shaped like a nipple or breast ➤ *noun* the raised area of bone behind the ear ⊙ Comes from Greek *mastoeides* meaning 'like a breast'

masturbate *verb* to rub or stroke the sexual organs to a state of orgasm ♦ **masturbation** *noun*

mat *noun* **1** a piece of material (coarse plaited plant fibre, carpet, etc) for wiping shoes on, covering the floor, etc **2** a piece of material, wood, etc put under dishes on a table to protect the surface ➤ *adjective* another spelling of **matt**

matador *noun* the person who kills the bull in bullfights

match¹ *noun* (*plural* **matches**) a small stick of wood etc tipped with a substance which catches fire when rubbed against an abrasive surface

match² *noun* (*plural* **matches**) **1** a person or thing similar to or the same as another **2** a person or thing agreeing with or suiting another **3** an equal **4** someone suitable for marriage **5** a contest or game ➤ *verb* **1** to be of the same make, size, colour, etc **2** to set (two things, teams, etc) against each other **3** to hold your own with, be equal to

matchbox *noun* (*plural* **matchboxes**) a box for holding matches

matchless *adjective* having no equal

matchmaker *noun* someone who tries to arrange marriages or partnerships

matchstick *noun* a single match

mate *noun* **1** a friend, a companion **2** an assistant worker: *a plumber's mate* **3** a husband or wife **4** the sexual partner of an animal, bird, etc **5** a merchant ship's officer, next in rank to the captain ➤ *verb* **1** to marry **2** to bring or come together to breed

material *adjective* **1** made of matter, able to be seen and felt **2** not spiritual, concerned with physical comfort, money, etc: *a material outlook on life* **3** important, essential: *no material difference* ➤ *noun* **1** something out of which anything is, or may be, made **2** cloth, fabric

materialism *noun* **1** a tendency to attach too much importance to material things (eg physical comfort, money) **2** the belief that only things we can see or feel really exist or are important ♦ **materialist** *noun* ♦ **materialistic** *adjective*

materialize or **materialise** *verb* **1** to appear in bodily form **2** to happen, come about

materially *adverb* **1** to a large extent, greatly **2** relating to objects, possessions or physical comfort, rather than to emotional or spiritual wellbeing

maternal *adjective* **1** of a mother **2** like a mother, motherly **3** related through your mother: *her maternal grandmother* ♦ **maternally** *adverb*

maternity *noun* the state of being a mother, motherhood ➤ *adjective* of or for a woman having or about to have a baby: *maternity clothes*

math *noun, US informal* mathematics

mathematical *adjective* **1** of or done by mathematics **2** very exact

mathematician *noun* an expert in mathematics

mathematics *singular noun* the study of measurements, numbers and quantities

maths *singular noun, informal* mathematics

matinée (*pronounced* **mat**-in-ei) *noun* an afternoon performance in a theatre or cinema

matins *plural noun* the morning service in certain churches

matri- *prefix* mother: *matricide* ⊙ Comes from Latin *mater* meaning 'mother'

matriarch (*pronounced* **meit**-ri-ahrk) *noun* a woman who controls a family or community

matriarchal (*pronounced* meit-ri-**ahrk**-al) *adjective* of a family, community or social system: controlled by women ♦ **matriarchy** *noun*

matrices *plural of* **matrix**

matricide *noun* **1** the killing of your own mother **2** someone who kills their own mother

matriculate *verb* to admit, or be admitted, to a university ♦ **matriculation** *noun*

matrilineal *adjective* of family descent: progressing through the female line

matrimonial *adjective* relating to marriage

matrimony *noun, formal* marriage

matrix (*pronounced* **mei**-triks) *noun* (*plural* **matrices** – *pronounced* **mei**-tri-seez – or **matrixes**) **1** *maths* a rectangular table of data in rows and columns, used to show relationships between quantities etc **2** *biology* the substance in tissues such as bone and cartilage in which cells are embedded **3** *anatomy* the tissue beneath the root of a fingernail or toenail **4** a mould in which metals etc are shaped **5** a mass of rock in which gems etc are found

matron (*pronounced* **meit**-ron) *noun* **1** a married woman **2** a senior nurse in charge of a hospital **3** *old* a woman in charge of housekeeping or nursing in a school, hostel, etc

matronly (*pronounced* **meit**-ron-li) *adjective* **1** of a woman: dignified, staid **2** rather plump

matt or **mat** *adjective* having a dull surface; not shiny or glossy

matted *adjective* thickly tangled

matter *noun* **1** anything that takes up space, can be seen, felt, etc; material, substance **2** a subject written or spoken about **3** (**matters**) affairs, business **4** trouble, difficulty: *What is the matter?* **5** importance: *of no great matter* **6** *medicine* pus ▸ *verb* **1** to be of importance: *It doesn't matter* **2** *medicine* to give out pus • **a matter of course** something that is to be expected • **a matter of opinion** a subject on which different opinions are held • **as a matter of fact** in fact

matter-of-fact *adjective* keeping to the actual facts; unimaginative, uninteresting

matting *noun* material from which mats are made

mattress *noun* (*plural* **mattresses**) a thick layer of padding covered in cloth, usually as part of a bed

mature *adjective* **1** fully grown or developed **2** ripe, ready for use ▸ *verb* **1** to (cause to) become mature **2** of an insurance policy etc: to be due to be paid out ♦ **maturely** *adverb*

maturity *noun* ripeness

maudlin *adjective* silly, sentimental

⊙ From Mary *Magdalene* in the New Testament of the Bible, who was frequently depicted crying in paintings

maul *verb* to hurt badly by rough or savage treatment: *mauled by a lion*

Maundy Thursday *noun* the day before Good Friday in the Christian calendar

mausoleum *noun* a large or elaborate tomb

mauve *noun* a light bluish-purple colour ▸ *adjective* of this colour

maverick *noun* someone who refuses to conform; a determined individualist

⊙ After Samuel *Maverick*, a Texas rancher who never branded his cattle

maw *noun* **1** an animal's jaws or gullet **2** a wide or gaping cavity

mawkish *adjective* weak and sentimental

maxi- *prefix* very large or long: *maxi-skirt*

maxilla *noun* (*plural* **maxillae** – *pronounced* mak-**sil**-ee) **1** *anatomy* the upper jawbone **2** *biology* the chewing organ of an insect, just behind the mouth

maxim *noun* a general truth or rule about behaviour etc

maximum *adjective* greatest, most ▸ *noun* (*plural* **maximums** or **maxima**) **1** the greatest number or quantity **2** the highest point or degree **3** *maths* in co-ordinate geometry: the point at which the slope of a curve changes from positive to negative

May *noun* the fifth month of the year

⊙ After *Maia*, the Roman earth goddess

may *verb* (**may, might**) **1** used with another verb to express permission or possibility: *You*

may watch the film/I thought I might find him there **2** used to express a wish: *May your wishes come true*

maybe *adverb* perhaps

Mayday *noun* the first day of May

mayday *noun* an international distress signal

mayfly *noun* (*plural* **mayflies**) a short-lived insect that appears in May

mayhem *noun* widespread chaos or confusion

mayonnaise (*pronounced* mei-o-**neiz**) *noun* a sauce made of eggs, oil and vinegar or lemon juice

mayor *noun* the chief elected public official of a city or town

ⓘ Note: *mayor* is used for a woman mayor, never *mayoress*.

mayoress *noun* (*plural* **mayoresses**) a mayor's wife

maypole *noun* a decorated pole traditionally danced around on Mayday

maze *noun* **1** a series of winding paths in a park etc, planned to make exit difficult **2** something complicated and confusing: *a maze of regulations*

mazel tov (*pronounced* **maz**-il tov) *interjection* conveying congratulations or best wishes ⊙ Comes from Yiddish, from Hebrew *mazzal tobh* meaning 'good luck'

MB or **Mb** *abbreviation, computing* megabyte(s)

MBE *abbreviation* Member of the Order of the British Empire, a special honour in the UK, given for achievement

Mbit *abbreviation, computing* megabit(s)

mbyte *abbreviation, computing* megabyte

MC *abbreviation* **1** master of ceremonies **2** Military Cross, an honour given to officers in the British Army who have shown exceptional bravery

McCarthyism *noun* the policy of finding people suspected of having links with Communism and removing them from public employment

⊙ Named after the US Republican senator Joseph R *McCarthy* (1909–57), who headed a fierce campaign to hunt out suspected Communists in the USA in the early 1950s

MD *abbreviation* **1** Doctor of Medicine (from Latin *Medicinae Doctor*) **2** Managing Director

Md *symbol, chemistry* mendelevium

MDF *abbreviation* medium density fibreboard, a strong board used in furniture and house-building

ME *abbreviation* myalgic encephalomyelitis, a condition of chronic fatigue and muscle pain following a viral infection

me[1] *pronoun* the word used by a speaker or

writer in mentioning themselves: *She kissed me/ Give it to me*

ⓘ **Me** should always be used after a preposition, not **I**:
✓*between you and me*
✓*between John and me*

me² or **mi** *noun, music* in sol-fa notation: the third note of the major scale

mead *noun* an alcoholic drink made with honey

meadow *noun* a field of grass

meadowsweet *noun* a wild flower with sweet-smelling, cream-coloured flowers

meagre or *US* **meager** *adjective* **1** thin **2** poor in quality **3** scanty, not enough

meal¹ *noun* the food eaten at one time, eg breakfast or dinner

meal² *noun* grain ground to a coarse powder

mealy-mouthed *adjective* not frank and straightforward in speech

mean¹ *adjective* **1** not generous with money etc **2** unkind, selfish **3** lowly, humble ♦ **meanness** *noun*

mean² *noun, maths (also called:* **arithmetic mean***)* the average value of a set of numbers, equal to the sum of the numbers divided by the number in the set (*compare with:* **median, mode***)*

mean³ *verb* (**meaning, meant**) **1** to intend to express; indicate: *What do you mean?/When I say no, I mean no* **2** to intend: *How do you mean to do that?* ♦ **mean well** to have good intentions

meander (*pronounced* mee-**and**-er) *verb* **1** of a river: to flow in a winding course **2** to wander about slowly and aimlessly ➤ *noun* a bend in a winding river

☉ After *Maeander*, the ancient Roman name for the winding river Menderes in Turkey

meaning *noun* **1** what is intended to be expressed or conveyed **2** purpose, intention

meaningful *adjective* full of significance; expressive

meaningless *adjective* **1** pointless **2** having no meaning

means *noun* **1** *singular* an action or instrument by which something is brought about: *a means of transport* **2** *plural* money, property, etc: *a woman of means* ♦ **by all means 1** certainly, of course **2** in every way possible ♦ **by no means** certainly not; not at all

means test *noun* an official inquiry into someone's wealth or income to determine their eligibility for financial benefits from the state

meant past form of **mean³**

meantime *noun*: **in the meantime** meanwhile

meanwhile *adverb* in the time between two things happening

measles *singular noun* an infectious disease causing a fever, sore throat and red spots

measly *adjective* (**measlier, measliest**), *informal* mean, stingy

measure *noun* **1** size or amount (found by measuring) **2** an instrument or container for measuring **3** musical time **4** (**measures**) a plan of action: *measures to prevent crime* **5** a law brought before parliament to be considered ➤ *verb* **1** to find out size, quantity, etc by using some form of measure **2** to be of a certain length, amount, etc **3** to indicate the measurement of **4** to mark (off) or weigh (out) in portions ♦ **for good measure** as a bonus

measured *adjective* steady, unhurried

measurement *noun* **1** the act of measuring **2** the size, amount, etc found by measuring

meat *noun* animal flesh used as food

meatball *noun* a ball of minced meat

meaty *adjective* (**meatier, meatiest**) **1** full of meat; tasting of meat **2** of a book etc: full of information

Mecca *noun* **1** the birthplace of Muhammad **2** (*usually* **mecca**) a place of pilgrimage

mechanic *noun* a skilled worker with tools or machines

mechanical *adjective* **1** of machinery: *mechanical engineering* **2** worked by machinery **3** of an action etc: done without thinking ♦ **mechanically** *adverb*

mechanical weathering or **physical weathering** *noun, geography* the decomposition of rock caused by natural processes such as freeze-thaw, and not by chemical changes (*compare with:* **chemical weathering***)*

mechanics *noun* **1** *singular* the study and art of constructing machinery **2** *plural* the actual details of how something works: *The mechanics of the plan are beyond me*

mechanism *noun* **1** a piece of machinery **2** the way a piece of machinery works **3** an action by which a result is produced

mechanize or **mechanise** *verb* **1** to change (the manufacture of something, a procedure, etc) from a manual to a mechanical process **2** to supply (troops) with armoured vehicles ♦ **mechanization** *noun*

medal *noun* a metal disc stamped with a design, inscription, etc, made to commemorate an event or given as a prize

medallion *noun* a large medal or piece of jewellery like one

medallist *noun* someone who has gained a medal

MEDC or **EMDC** *abbreviation, geography* More Economically Developed Country or Economically More Developed Country

meddle *verb* **1** to concern yourself with things that are not your business **2** to interfere or tamper (with) ♦ **meddler** *noun*

meddlesome *adjective* fond of meddling

media *plural noun* (**the media**) television, newspapers, etc as a form of communication

mediaeval another spelling of **medieval**

median *noun*, *maths* **1** a straight line from an angle of a triangle to the centre of the opposite side **2** the middle value or point of a series of numbers, eg the median of 1, 5, 11 is 5 (*compare with:* **mean²**, **mode**) ➤ *adjective* mid, middle

mediate *verb* to act as a peacemaker (between) ♦ **mediation** *noun*

mediator *noun* someone who tries to make peace between people who are quarrelling

medic *noun*, *informal* a medical worker or student

medical *adjective* of doctors or their work ➤ *noun* a health check, a physical examination

medicate *verb* to give medicine to

medicated *adjective* including medicine or disinfectant

medication *noun* **1** medical treatment **2** a medicine

medicinal *adjective* **1** used in medicine **2** used as a medicine ♦ **medicinally** *adverb*

medicine *noun* **1** something given to a sick person to make them better **2** the science or practice of treating or preventing illnesses

medicine man *noun* a tribal healer or shaman

medieval or **mediaeval** *adjective* of or in the Middle Ages

mediocre *adjective* not very good, ordinary ♦ **mediocrity** *noun*

meditate *verb* **1** to think deeply and in quietness **2** to contemplate religious or spiritual matters **3** to consider, think about

meditation *noun* **1** deep, quiet thought **2** contemplation on a religious or spiritual theme

meditative *adjective* thinking deeply

Mediterranean *adjective* **1** relating to the area of the Mediterranean Sea **2** *geography* of climate: with mild winters and hot, dry summers

medium *noun* (*plural* **media** or **mediums**) **1** a means or substance through which an effect is produced **2** (*plural* **mediums**) someone through whom spirits (of dead people) are said to speak **3** *art* the material used as a means of expression, eg watercolours or clay **4** *computing* (*plural* **media**) any material on which data is recorded, eg magnetic disk **5** a **culture medium** ➤ *adjective* middle or average in size, quality, etc • **the media** see **media**

medley *noun* (*plural* **medleys**) **1** a mixture **2** a piece of music put together from a number of other pieces

medulla *noun* (*plural* **medullas** or **medullae** – pronounced me-**dul**-ee) the central part of an organ or tissue, when this is different in structure or function from the outer layer

medulla oblongata *noun* (*plural* **medulla oblongatae** or **medulla oblongatas**) the part of the brain that controls breathing, heartbeat, etc

meek *adjective* gentle, uncomplaining ♦ **meekly** *adverb*

meet¹ *verb* (**meeting, met**) **1** to come face to face (with) **2** to come together, join **3** to make the acquaintance of **4** to pay (bills etc) fully **5** to be suitable for, satisfy: *able to meet the demand* ➤ *noun* a gathering for a sports event

meet² *adjective, old* proper, suitable

meeting *noun* a gathering of people for a particular purpose

mega *adjective, slang* **1** huge **2** excellent, very good

mega- *prefix* **1** great, huge: *megaphone* **2** a million: *megaton* ⓞ Comes from Greek *megas* meaning 'big'

megabit *noun* (*abbrev* **Mbit**) a measure of computer data or memory, approximately 2^{20} (one million) bits

megabyte *noun* (*abbrev* **MB** or **Mb**) a measure of computer data or memory, roughly equivalent to a million bytes

megahertz *noun* (*plural* **megahertz**, symbol **MHz**) a unit of frequency equal to one million hertz

megalith *noun* a huge stone erected in prehistoric times

megalomania *noun* an exaggerated idea of your own importance or abilities

megalomaniac *noun* someone suffering from megalomania

megaphone *noun* a portable cone-shaped device with microphone and amplifier to increase sound

megastore *noun* a very large shop, especially one that is part of a large chain

megaton *adjective* of a bomb: having an explosive force equal to a million tons of TNT

meiosis (*pronounced* mai-**oh**-sis) *noun, biology* a type of cell division that halves the number of chromosomes in reproductive cells ♦ **meiotic** *adjective*

meitnerium (*pronounced* mait-**neer**-i-um) *noun, chemistry* (symbol **Mt**) an artificially manufactured radioactive element

ⓞ Named after Lise *Meitner* (1878–1968), Austrian physicist

mela *noun, Hinduism, Sikhism* a festival or fair

melancholy (*pronounced* **mel**-an-ko-li) *noun* lowness of spirits, sadness ➤ *adjective* sad, depressed ♦ **melancholic** *adjective*

melanin *noun* the dark pigment in human skin or hair

melanoma (*pronounced* me-la-**noh**-ma) *noun* (*plural* **melanomas** or **melanomata** – *pronounced* me-la-**noh**-ma-ta) a skin tumour which usually develops from a mole

mêlée (*pronounced* **mel**-ei) *noun* a confused fight between two groups of people

mellifluous *adjective* sweet-sounding

mellow *adjective* 1 of fruit: ripe, juicy, sweet 2 having become pleasant or agreeable with age 3 of light, colour, etc: soft, not harsh > *verb* to make or become mellow

melodic *adjective* of or relating to melody

melodious *adjective* pleasant sounding; tuneful

melodrama *noun* a type of play with a sensational or exaggerated plot

melodramatic *adjective* exaggerated, sensational, over-dramatic

melody *noun* (*plural* **melodies**) 1 a tune 2 pleasant music

melon *noun* a large, round fruit with soft, juicy flesh

melt *verb* 1 to make or become liquid, eg by heating 2 to disappear gradually: *The crowd melted away* 3 to make or become emotionally tender: *His heart melted at the sight*

meltdown *noun* 1 the process in which the radioactive fuel in a nuclear reactor overheats and melts through the insulation into the environment 2 a major disaster or failure

melting point *noun* the temperature at which a solid turns to liquid

member *noun* 1 someone who belongs to a group or society 2 a limb or organ of the body

Member of Parliament *noun* someone elected to the House of Commons (*short form* **MP**)

membership *noun* 1 the group of people who are members, or the number of members, of a club etc 2 the state of being a member

membrane *noun* 1 a thin skin or covering, especially as part of a human or animal body, plant, etc 2 *biology* a thin flexible layer of lipid and protein molecules that separates, connects or lines parts of a cell or organ (*see also:* **cell membrane**)

memento *noun* (*plural* **mementos**) something by which an event is remembered

memento mori (*pronounced* mi-**men**-toh **mawr**-ai or **mawr**-ee) *noun* (*plural* **memento mori**) an object used as a reminder of human mortality

memo *noun* (*plural* **memos**) short for **memorandum**

memoirs (*pronounced* **mem**-wahrz) *plural noun* a personal account of someone's life; an autobiography

memorabilia *plural noun* souvenirs of people or events

memorable *adjective* worthy of being remembered; famous ♦ **memorably** *adverb*

memorandum *noun* (*plural* **memoranda**) (*short form* **memo**) 1 a note which acts as a reminder 2 a written statement of something under discussion 3 a brief note sent to colleagues in an office etc

memorial *noun* a monument commemorating a historical event or person > *adjective* commemorating an event or person

memorize or **memorise** *verb* to learn by heart

memory *noun* (*plural* **memories**) 1 the power to remember 2 the mind's store of remembered things 3 something remembered: *childhood memories* 4 *computing* a store of information 5 what is remembered about someone: *Her memory lives on* ● **in memory of** in remembrance of, as a memorial of

menace *noun* 1 potential harm or danger 2 someone persistently threatening or annoying > *verb* to be a danger to; threaten

menacing *adjective* looking evil or threatening

menagerie (*pronounced* me-**naj**-e-ri) *noun* 1 a collection of wild animals 2 a place where these are kept

menarche (*pronounced* me-**nahr**-ki) *noun* the first instance of menstruation in puberty

mend *verb* to repair; make or grow better > *noun* a repaired part ● **on the mend** getting better, recovering

mendacious *adjective* not true; lying ♦ **mendaciously** *adverb* ♦ **mendacity** *noun*

mendelevium *noun, chemistry* (symbol **Md**) an artificially produced, radioactive metallic element

⊙ Named after Russian chemist Dmitri *Mendeleev* (1834–1907)

Mendelian *adjective, biology* relating to the principles of heredity put forward by Gregor J *Mendel* (1822–84), an Austrian monk and botanist

mendicant *noun* a beggar > *adjective* begging

menial (*pronounced* **meen**-i-al) *adjective* of work: unskilled, unchallenging

meninges (*pronounced* men-**in**-jeez) *plural noun* (*singular* **meninx** – *pronounced* **men**-ingks), *anatomy* the three membranes that cover the brain and spinal cord ♦ **meningeal** (*pronounced* men-**in**-ji-al) *adjective* ⊙ Comes from Latin, from Greek *meninx, meningos* meaning 'membrane'

meningitis *noun, medicine* inflammation of

the meninges, usually caused by bacterial or viral infection, the main symptoms being severe headache, fever, stiffness of the neck and aversion to light

meniscus noun (plural **meniscuses** or **menisci** – pronounced men-**is**-kai or men-**is**-ai) **1** the curved upper surface of a liquid in a partly filled narrow tube, caused by the effects of surface tension **2** anatomy any crescent-shaped structure

menopause noun the ending of menstruation in middle age ♦ **menopausal** adjective

menorah noun a candelabrum with seven branches regarded as a symbol of Judaism

menses (pronounced **men**-seez) plural noun the fluids discharged from the womb during menstruation

Menshevik noun, history a moderate socialist in revolutionary Russia (compare with: **Bolshevik**)

⊙ A Russian word based on menshye 'smaller'

menstrual adjective of menstruation

menstrual cycle noun in some primates including humans: a repeating cycle of reproductive changes happening about once in every 28 days in humans

menstruate verb to discharge blood and other fluids from the womb through the vagina during menstruation

menstruation noun the monthly discharge of blood from the womb of a woman of child-bearing age who is not pregnant

mensuration noun measuring and calculating length, area, volume, etc

mental adjective **1** of the mind **2** done, made, happening, etc in the mind: mental arithmetic **3** of illness: affecting the mind ♦ **mentally** adverb

mentality noun (plural **mentalities**) **1** mental power **2** type of mind; way of thinking

menthol noun a sharp-smelling substance obtained from peppermint oil

mention verb **1** to speak of briefly **2** to remark (that) ➤ noun a mentioning, a remark

mentor noun someone who gives advice as a tutor or supervisor

⊙ After Mentor, who guided Telemachus in his search for his father in Homer's poem The Odyssey

menu noun (plural **menus**) **1** (a card with) a list of dishes to be served at a meal **2** computing a list of options

menu bar noun, computing a bar in a window giving a list of options

menu-driven adjective, computing denoting an interactive program in which commands are displayed as options in a menu

MEP abbreviation Member of the European Parliament, a politician who represents a constituency in one of the member countries at the European Parliament

mercantile adjective of buying and selling; trading

Mercator's projection noun a map of the globe in the form of a rectangle evenly marked with lines of latitude and longitude

⊙ From a Latin translation of the surname of the German cartographer Gerhard Kremer (1512–94), which literally means 'shopkeeper'

mercenary adjective **1** working for money **2** influenced by the desire for money ➤ noun (plural **mercenaries**) a soldier paid by a foreign country to fight in its army

merchandise noun goods to be bought and sold

merchant noun someone who carries on a business in the buying and selling of goods, a trader ➤ adjective of trade

merchant bank noun a bank providing banking services for trade and business

merchant navy noun ships and crews employed in trading

merciful adjective **1** willing to forgive or be lenient **2** easing or relieving pain, trouble or difficulty

mercifully adverb fortunately, to one's great relief

merciless adjective showing no mercy; cruel ♦ **mercilessly** adverb

mercurial adjective of someone's personality: changeable, unpredictable

mercury noun, chemistry (symbol **Hg**) a heavy, silvery, liquid metallic element (also called: **quicksilver**)

mercy noun (plural **mercies**) **1** lenience or forgiveness towards an enemy etc; pity **2** a fortunate occurrence or kind act • **at someone's mercy** in their power

mere adjective nothing more than: mere nonsense

merely adverb only, simply

meretricious adjective, formal superficially attractive, flashy ⊙ Comes from Latin meretrix meaning 'a prostitute'

❗ Do not confuse with: **meritorious**

merge verb **1** to combine or join together **2** to blend, come together gradually

merger noun a joining together, eg of business companies

meridian (pronounced me-**rid**-i-an) noun **1** an imaginary line around a sphere passing through its poles, eg the prime meridian around the earth **2** the highest point of the sun's path **3** in Chinese medicine: a main energy channel in the body

meringue (*pronounced* me-**rang**) *noun* a baked cake or shell made of sugar and egg-white

merino *noun* (*plural* **merinos**) 1 a sheep with very fine soft wool 2 its wool, or a soft fabric made from it

merit *noun* 1 positive worth or value 2 a commendable quality ➤ *verb* to deserve

meritocracy (*pronounced* mer-i-**tawk**-ra-si) *noun* (*plural* **meritocracies**) a social system based on leadership by the most talented or intelligent people, rather than the wealthy or the aristocracy

meritorious *adjective, formal* deserving honour or reward ⊙ Comes from Latin *meritum* meaning 'an act deserving praise (or blame)'

⚠ Do not confuse with: **meretricious**

mermaid *noun* an imaginary sea creature with a woman's upper body and a fish's tail

merriment *noun* laughter and noise, hilarity

merry *adjective* (**merrier, merriest**) 1 full of fun; cheerful and lively 2 slightly drunk
♦ **merrily** *adverb* (meaning 1)

merry-go-round *noun, Brit* a fairground roundabout with wooden horses etc for riding on

merrymaking *noun* lively enjoyment
♦ **merrymaker** *noun*

mesh *noun* (*plural* **meshes**) 1 network, netting 2 the opening between the threads of a net ➤ *verb* of gears etc: to interconnect, engage

mesmeric *adjective* 1 hypnotic 2 commanding complete attention, fascinating

mesmerize or **mesmerise** *verb* 1 to hypnotize 2 to hold the attention of completely; fascinate

⊙ An earlier term than *hypnotize*, the word comes from the name of the 18th-century Austrian doctor, Franz Anton *Mesmer*, who claimed to be able to cure disease through the influence of his will on patients

mesomorph *noun* a person of muscular body build (*compare with*: **ectomorph, endomorph**) ♦ **mesomorphic** *adjective*

meson (*pronounced* **mee**-zon or **mes**-on) *noun, physics* any of a group of unstable, strongly interacting, elementary particles, with a mass between that of an electron and a proton

mesophyll *noun, botany* the tissue between the upper and lower surfaces of a plant leaf

Mesozoic *adjective* of the geological era 250 million to 65 million years ago

mess *noun* (*plural* **messes**) 1 an untidy or disgusting sight 2 disorder, confusion 3 a group of soldiers etc who take their meals together, or

the place where they eat • **mess up** to make untidy, dirty or muddled • **mess with** *US informal* to interfere with, fool with

message *noun* 1 a piece of news or information sent from one person to another 2 a lesson, a moral: *a children's story with a message* • **get the message** *informal* to understand, get the point

messaging *noun* the sending of text or picture messages by mobile phone

messenger *noun* someone who carries a message

messenger RNA *noun, biochemistry* a molecule of RNA that transports coded genetic instructions for the manufacture of proteins

Messiah *noun* 1 *Christianity* Jesus Christ 2 *Judaism* the saviour expected by the Jews 3 (**messiah**) a saviour, a deliverer

messy *adjective* (**messier, messiest**) 1 dirty 2 untidy, disordered ♦ **messily** *adverb*

met past form of **meet**[1]

metabolic *adjective* of metabolism

metabolism *noun, biology* 1 the combined chemical changes in the cells of a living organism that provide energy for living processes and activity 2 the conversion of nourishment into energy

metabolite *noun, biology* a substance involved in metabolism

metabolize or **metabolise** *verb, biology* to break down complex organic compounds into simpler molecules

metacarpus *noun, anatomy* the set of five bones in the hand between the wrist and the knuckles ♦ **metacarpal** *adjective*

metal *noun* any of a group of substances (eg gold, silver, iron, etc) able to conduct heat and electricity ➤ *adjective* made of metal

⚠ Do not confuse with: **mettle**

metalanguage *noun* a language or system of symbols used to discuss another language or symbolic system

metallic *adjective* 1 relating to or made of metal 2 shining like metal: *metallic thread*

metallic bond *noun, chemistry* a chemical bond that holds the atoms of a metal together

metalloid *noun, chemistry* a chemical element that has both metallic and non-metallic properties, eg silicon or arsenic

metallurgy *noun* the study of metals
♦ **metallurgic** or **metallurgical** *adjective*
♦ **metallurgist** *noun*

metamorphic *adjective* 1 to do with metamorphosis 2 of rocks: formed when other rocks undergo a change through heat and pressure

metamorphose (*pronounced* met-a-**mawr**-

fohz) *verb* to change completely in appearance or character

metamorphosis (*pronounced* met-a-**mawr**-fos-is) *noun* (*plural* **metamorphoses**) **1** a complete change in appearance or character; a transformation **2** *biology* a change of physical form that occurs during the growth of some creatures, eg from a tadpole into a frog

metaphor *noun* a way of describing something by suggesting that it is, or has the qualities of, something else, eg *The camel is the ship of the desert*

metaphorical *adjective* using a metaphor or metaphors

metaphorically *adverb* not in real terms, but as an imaginative way of describing something

metaphysics *noun* **1** the study of being and knowledge **2** any abstruse or abstract philosophy ♦ **metaphysical** *adjective*
♦ **metaphysician** *noun*

meta-tag *noun, computing* a tag on a web page outlining its subject etc, invisible to the user but which can be found by a browser making particular searches

metatarsus *noun, anatomy* the set of five bones in the foot between the ankle and the toes
♦ **metatarsal** *adjective*

mete *verb*: **mete out** to deal out (punishment etc)

meteor *noun* a small piece of matter moving rapidly through space, becoming bright as it enters the earth's atmosphere

meteoric *adjective* **1** of a meteor **2** extremely rapid: *her meteoric rise to fame*

meteorite *noun* a meteor which falls to the earth as a piece of rock

meteorologist *noun* someone who studies or forecasts the weather

meteorology *noun* the study of weather and climate ♦ **meteorological** *adjective*

meter¹ *noun* an instrument for measuring the amount of gas, electricity, etc used ➤ *verb* to measure with a meter

meter² US spelling of **metre**

-meter *suffix* forms words for measuring devices: *speedometer/barometer* ◔ Comes from Greek *metron* meaning 'measure'

meth *noun, slang* the drug methadone

methadone *noun* a synthetic drug similar to morphine, used as a painkiller and as a heroin substitute when treating addiction

methanal *noun, chemistry* formaldehyde

methane *noun* a colourless gas produced by rotting vegetable matter (*also called*: **marsh-gas**)

methanol *noun* a colourless, flammable, toxic liquid used as a solvent and antifreeze (*also called*: **wood spirit**)

method *noun* **1** a planned or regular way of doing something **2** orderly arrangement

methodical *adjective* orderly, done or acting according to some plan

Methodist *Christianity, noun* **1** a member of the Methodist Church, a Nonconformist Protestant denomination **2** a supporter of Methodism
➤ *adjective* relating to Methodism
♦ **Methodism** *noun*

meths *singular noun, informal* methylated spirits

methyl alcohol *noun* methanol

methylated spirits *noun* an alcohol with added violet dye, used as a solvent or fuel

methylene blue *noun, chemistry* a blue dye used as an indicator of acidity or alkalinity

methyl group *noun, chemistry* a group consisting of one carbon and three hydrogen atoms

meticulous *adjective* careful and accurate about small details ♦ **meticulously** *adverb*

métier (*pronounced* **mei**-ti-ei) *noun, formal* occupation, profession

metonymy *noun* (*plural* **metonymies**) the use of a word referring to an element of something to mean the thing itself, eg 'the crown' for 'the monarch' ◔ Comes from Greek *metonymia* meaning 'change of name' ♦ **metonymic** or **metonymical** *adjective*

metre or *US* **meter** *noun* **1** (symbol **m**) the standard unit of measurement of length **2** the arrangement of syllables in poetry, or of musical notes, in a regular rhythm ◔ Comes from Greek *metron* meaning 'measure'

ⓘ This is one of a large number of words which is spelled with an **-re** ending in British English, but with an **-er** in American English, eg *centre/center, calibre/caliber, lustre/luster*.

metric *adjective* **1** of the metric system **2** metrical

metrical *adjective* **1** of poetry: of or in metre **2** arranged in the form of verse

metrication *noun* the change-over of a country's units of measurements to the metric system

metric system *noun* the system of weights and measures based on tens, eg 1 metre = 10 decimetres = 100 centimetres etc (*compare with*: **avoirdupois**)

metro *noun* (*plural* **metros**) an urban railway system, often one that is mostly underground

metronome *noun, music* an instrument that keeps a regular beat, used for music practice

metropolis *noun* (*plural* **metropolises**) a large city, usually the capital city of a country
♦ **metropolitan** *adjective*

mettle *noun, formal* courage, pluck • **on your mettle** out to do your best

⚠ Do not confuse with: **metal**

mew *noun* a whining cry made by a cat etc
➤ *verb* to cry in this way

mews *singular* or *plural noun* buildings
(originally stables) built around a yard or in a lane

> ⏱ Originally a cage for hawks, *mews* took on its present meaning after royal stables were built in the 17th century on a site formerly used to house the King's hawks

mezzanine *noun* **1** a low storey between two main storeys **2** *US* a balcony in a theatre

Mg *symbol, chemistry* magnesium

mg *abbreviation* milligram(s)

MHz *abbreviation* megahertz, a unit of frequency equal to one million hertz

mi same as **me²**

MI5 *noun, informal* a British government agency which works to prevent other countries from getting information about the UK

MI6 *noun, informal* a British espionage and intelligence agency which sends people to other countries to get secret political and military information about them

miaow *noun* the sound made by a cat ➤ *verb* to make the sound of a cat

miasma (*pronounced* mai-**az**-ma) *noun* an unhealthy or depressing atmosphere

mica *noun* a mineral which glitters and divides easily into thin transparent layers

mice plural of **mouse**

Michaelmas (*pronounced* **mik**-el-mas) *noun* the festival of St Michael, 29 September

mickey *noun*: **take the mickey** *informal* to tease, make fun of someone

micro *noun, informal* (*plural* **micros**) **1** a microwave oven **2** a microcomputer

micro- *prefix* **1** very small: *microchip/microphone* (= an instrument which picks up and can amplify small sounds) **2** using a microscope: *microsurgery* ⏱ Comes from Greek *mikros* meaning 'small'

microbe *noun* a tiny living organism

microbiology *noun* the study of micro-organisms ◆ **microbiologist** *noun*

microchip *noun* a tiny piece of silicon designed to act as a complex electronic circuit

microclimate *noun* the climate of a small place within a larger area

microcomputer *noun* a small desktop computer containing a microprocessor

microcosm *noun* a version on a small scale: *a microcosm of society*

microelectronics *singular noun* the study of very small electronic devices

microfibre *noun* a synthetic, very closely woven fabric

microfiche (*pronounced* **maik**-roh-feesh) *noun* a sheet of microfilm suitable for filing

microfilm *noun* narrow photographic film on which books, newspapers, etc are recorded in miniaturized form ➤ *verb* to record on microfilm

microhabitat *noun, biology* a small area that has different environmental conditions from those of the surrounding area

microlight *noun* a very light, small-engined aircraft, like a powered hang-glider

micro-organism *noun* an organism that can only be seen through a microscope

microphone *noun* an instrument which picks up sound waves for broadcasting, recording or amplifying

microprocessor *noun* a computer processor consisting of one or more microchips

micropyle *noun, biology* in flowering plants: a small opening in the ovule through which pollination takes place

microscope *noun* a scientific instrument which magnifies very small objects placed under its lens

microscopic *adjective* tiny, minuscule

microsecond *noun* a millionth of a second

microsurgeon *noun* a surgeon who performs microsurgery

microsurgery *noun* delicate surgery carried out under a microscope

microwave *noun* **1** a microwave oven **2** a very short radio wave **3** a short electromagnetic wave used for cooking food and transmitting data

microwave oven *noun* an oven which cooks food by passing microwaves through it

mid- *prefix* placed or occurring in the middle: *mid-morning* ⏱ Comes from Old English *midd*

midday *noun* noon

midden *noun* a rubbish or dung heap

middle *noun* the point or part of anything equally distant from its ends or edges; the centre ➤ *adjective* **1** occurring in the middle or centre **2** coming between extreme positions etc: *trying to find a middle way* • **in the middle of** in the midst of doing, busy doing

middle-aged *adjective* between youth and old age

Middle Ages *noun* (**the Middle Ages**) the time roughly between AD 500 and AD 1500

middle class *noun* the class of people between the working and upper classes, usually thought of as being made up of educated people with professional or business careers

middle distance *noun* in a painting etc: the area between the foreground and the background ➤ *adjective* **1** of an athlete: competing in races over distances of 400, 800 and 1500 m **2** of a race: run over any of these distances

middle eight *noun, music* an eight-bar section occurring two thirds of the way through a pop song

Middle English *noun* the English language from about 1100 or 1150 AD up to about 1500

middle-of-the-road *adjective* bland, unadventurous

middle school *noun* a school for children from 8 or 9 to 12 or 13 years old

middling *adjective* **1** of middle size or quality **2** neither good nor bad; mediocre

midfield *noun, football* the middle area of the pitch, not near to the goal of either team ◆ **midfielder** *noun*

midge *noun* a small biting insect

midget *noun* an abnormally small person or thing ➤ *adjective* very small

midland *noun* the central, inland part of a country

midnight *noun* twelve o'clock at night ➤ *adjective* occurring at midnight

mid-ocean ridge *noun, geography* a major mountain range, largely below water, where two plates are moving apart

midriff *noun* the middle of the body, just below the ribs

midst *noun* the middle • **in our midst** among us

midsummer *noun* the time around 21 June, which is the summer solstice and the longest day in the year

midterm *noun* **1** the middle of an academic term, a term in political office, etc **2** the middle of a particular period of time, eg a pregnancy

midway *adverb* halfway

midweek *adjective & adverb* at the period of time in the middle of the week: *a match played midweek/a midweek fixture*

midwife *noun* (*plural* **midwives**) a nurse trained to assist women during childbirth ☉ Comes from Old English *mid* meaning 'with' + *wif* meaning 'woman'

midwifery (*pronounced* **mid**-wif-e-ri or mid-**waif**-ri) *noun* the practice or occupation of being a midwife

midwinter *noun* the time around 21 December, the winter solstice and shortest day in the year

mien (*pronounced* meen) *noun, formal* look, appearance, aspect

miffed *adjective* offended, upset or annoyed

might¹ *noun* power, strength

might² past tense of **may** ☉ Comes from Old English *mihte*

mightily *adverb* **1** extremely, greatly **2** with great strength or force

mighty *adjective* (**mightier, mightiest**) very

great or powerful ➤ *adverb, US informal* very ◆ **mightiness** *noun*

migraine (*pronounced* **mee**-grein or **mai**-grein) *noun* a severe form of headache

migrant *noun* **1** someone migrating, or recently migrated, from another country **2** a bird that migrates annually

migrate *verb* **1** to change your home or move to another area or country **2** of birds: to fly to a warmer region for the winter ◆ **migration** *noun*

migratory *adjective* **1** migrating **2** wandering

mike *noun, informal* a microphone

milch cow (*pronounced* milch or milsh) *noun* **1** a cow kept for milk production **2** a ready source of money

mild *adjective* **1** not harsh or severe; gentle **2** of flavour: not sharp or bitter **3** of weather: not cold **4** of an illness: not serious

mildew *noun* whitish patches on plants, fabric, etc caused by fungus

mildly *adverb* **1** in a mild or calm manner **2** slightly • **to put it mildly** expressing oneself much less strongly than one could, in a particular situation: *She was quite annoyed, to put it mildly*

mile *noun* a measure of length (1.61 kilometres or 1760 yards)

mileage *noun* **1** distance in miles **2** travel expenses (counted by the mile) **3** the amount of use or benefit you can get out of something: *He got a lot of mileage out of that story*

mileometer or **milometer** *noun* an instrument in a motor vehicle for recording the number of miles travelled

milestone *noun* **1** a stone beside the road showing the number of miles to a certain place **2** something which marks an important event

milieu (*pronounced* meel-**yer**) *noun* (*plural* **milieux** – *pronounced* meel-**yer** or meel-**yerz** – or **milieus**) surroundings

militant *adjective* **1** fighting, warlike **2** aggressive, favouring or taking part in forceful action ➤ *noun* someone who is militant

militarize or **militarise** *verb* **1** to provide (a country, group, etc) with a military force **2** to make something military in nature

military *adjective* of soldiers or warfare ➤ *noun* (**the military**) the army

militate *verb* **1** to fight or work (against): *Her age will certainly militate against her finding employment* **2** to act to your disadvantage ☉ Comes from Latin *militare* meaning 'to serve as a soldier'

⚠ Do not confuse with: **mitigate**.
It may be helpful to remember that the idea of fighting is contained in the word **MILITate** (in common with 'military' and 'militia') but not in **mitigate**.

militia *noun* a group of fighters, not regular soldiers, trained for emergencies

milk *noun* **1** a white liquid produced by female mammals as food for their young **2** this liquid, especially from cows, used as a drink ➤ *verb* **1** to draw milk from **2** to obtain (money, information, etc) from, especially dishonestly: *She milked the scandal for all it was worth*

milk float *noun* a vehicle that makes deliveries of milk to homes

milkmaid *noun, old* a woman who milks cows

milkman *noun* a man who sells or delivers milk

milk of magnesia *noun* magnesium carbonate, used as an antacid and laxative

milkshake *noun* a drink of milk and a flavouring whipped together

milk tooth *noun* a tooth from the first set of teeth in humans and other mammals

milky *adjective* (**milkier, milkiest**) **1** like milk, creamy **2** white

Milky Way *noun* (**the Milky Way**) a bright band of stars seen in the night sky

mill *noun* **1** a machine for grinding or crushing grain, coffee, etc **2** a building where grain is ground **3** a factory ➤ *verb* **1** to grind **2** to cut grooves round the edge of (a coin) **3** to move round aimlessly in a crowd

millennium *noun* (*plural* **millennia**) a period of a thousand years

miller *noun* someone who grinds grain

millet *noun* a type of grain used for food

milli- or **mill-** *prefix* thousand; a thousandth part of: *millimetre/millennium/millipede* (= an insect with many although not actually a thousand legs) ℗ Comes from Latin *mille* meaning 'thousand'

milligram or **milligramme** *noun* (*abbrev* **mg**) a thousandth of a gram

millilitre *noun* (*abbrev* **ml**) a thousandth of a litre

millimetre *noun* (*abbrev* **mm**) a thousandth of a metre

milliner *noun* someone who makes and sells women's hats

millinery *noun* the goods sold by a milliner

million *noun* a thousand thousands (1,000,000)

millionaire or **millionairess** *noun* someone who owns money and property worth over a million pounds, dollars, etc

millionth *adjective* the last of a series of a million ➤ *noun* one of a million equal parts

millipede *noun* a small crawling insect with a long body and many pairs of legs

millisecond *noun* (*abbrev* **ms**) a thousandth of a second

millrace *noun* the stream of water which turns a millwheel

millstone *noun* **1** one of two heavy stones used to grind grain **2** something felt as a burden or hindrance

millwheel *noun* a waterwheel which drives the machinery of a mill

mime *noun* **1** a theatrical art using body movements and facial expressions in place of speech **2** a play performed through mime ➤ *verb* **1** to perform a mime **2** to express through mime

mimic *verb* (**mimicking, mimicked**) **1** to imitate, especially in a mocking way **2** *biology* to resemble something closely, especially as a defence mechanism ➤ *noun* **1** someone who mimics **2** *biology* a plant or animal displaying mimicry ♦ **mimicry** *noun*

mimosa *noun* a tree producing bunches of yellow, scented flowers

min *abbreviation* minute

minaret *noun* a slender tower on a mosque

mince *verb* **1** to cut or chop into small pieces **2** to walk primly with short steps ➤ *noun* meat chopped finely • **not mince matters** to not try to soften an unpleasant fact or statement

mincemeat *noun* a chopped-up mixture of dried fruit, suet, etc • **make mincemeat of** to pulverize, destroy

mince pie *noun* a pie filled with mince or mincemeat

mincer *noun* a machine for mincing food

mind *noun* **1** consciousness, intelligence, understanding **2** intention: *I've a good mind to tell him so* **3** attention: *Keep your mind on your work* ➤ *verb* **1** to see to, look after: *mind the children* **2** to watch out for, be careful of: *Mind the step* **3** to object to: *Do you mind if I open the window?* • **change your mind** to change your opinion or intention • **in two minds** undecided • **make up your mind** to decide • **out of your mind** mad, crazy • **presence of mind** ability to act calmly and sensibly • **speak your mind** to speak frankly

mind-blowing *adjective* very surprising, shocking or exciting

mind-boggling *adjective, informal* too difficult, large, strange, etc to imagine or understand; impossible to take in

minder *noun* **1** someone who looks after a child etc **2** an aide or bodyguard to a public figure

mindful *adjective* (**mindful of**) paying attention to

mindless *adjective* foolish, unthinking; pointless

mine¹ *noun* **1** an underground pit or system of tunnels from which metals, coal, etc are dug **2** a heavy charge of explosive material ➤ *verb* **1** to dig or work a mine **2** to lay explosive mines in

mine² *pronoun* a thing or things belonging to me: *That drink is mine*

minefield *noun* an area covered with explosive mines

minelayer *noun* a ship which lays explosive mines

miner *noun* someone who works in a mine

mineral *noun* a natural substance mined from the earth, eg coal, metals, gems, etc ➤ *adjective* of or containing minerals

mineralogy *noun* the study of minerals ◆ **mineralogist** *noun*

mineral oil *noun* oil derived from minerals rather than from plant or animal sources

mineral water *noun* **1** water containing small amounts of minerals **2** *informal* carbonated water

minestrone (*pronounced* min-is-**troh**-ni) *noun* a thick Italian vegetable soup containing rice or pasta

minesweeper *noun* a ship which removes explosive mines

mingle *verb* to mix

mingy (*pronounced* **min**-ji) *adjective* (**mingier, mingiest**) *informal* stingy, mean

mini- *prefix* smaller than average; compact: *minibus/minicab*

> ⏱ The prefix **mini-** is an abbreviation of 'mini**ature'

miniature *noun* **1** a small-scale painting **2** a small bottle of spirits ➤ *adjective* on a small scale

minibus *noun* (*plural* **minibuses**) a type of small bus

minicab *noun* a taxi that is ordered by phone from a private company, not one that can be stopped in the street

minicomputer *noun* a powerful computer, larger than a microcomputer but smaller than a mainframe

minim *noun, music* a note (𝅗𝅥) equal to two crotchets, or half a semibreve, in length

minimal *adjective* very little indeed: *minimal fuss*

minimalism *noun* in music, art and design: the policy of using the minimum means, eg the fewest and simplest elements, to achieve the desired result ◆ **minimalist** *noun & adjective*

minimize or **minimise** *verb* **1** to make something seem small or unimportant **2** to make as small as possible

minimum *noun* (*plural* **minimums** or **minima**) the smallest possible quantity ➤ *adjective* the least possible

minimum wage *noun* the lowest wage per hour which can legally be paid for a particular type of work

minion *noun* a slave-like follower

miniscule another spelling of **minuscule**

> ⓘ The **miniscule** spelling is not yet standard.

minister *noun* **1** the head of a government department: *the minister of trade* **2** a member of the clergy **3** an agent, a representative ➤ *verb* (**minister to**) to help, supply the needs of

ministerial *adjective* of a minister

ministry *noun* (*plural* **ministries**) **1** a government department or its headquarters **2** the work of a member of the clergy

mink *noun* a small, weasel-like animal or its fur

minnow *noun* a type of very small river or pond fish

minor *adjective* **1** of less importance, size, etc **2** small, unimportant (*contrasted with:* **major**) ➤ *noun* someone not yet legally an adult (ie in the UK, under 18)

minority *noun* (*plural* **minorities**) **1** the smaller number or part **2** a group of people who are different in terms of race, religion, sexuality, etc from most of the people in a country or region **3** the state of being a minor

Minotaur *noun* (**the Minotaur**) a mythological creature with a bull's head

minster *noun* a large church or cathedral

minstrel *noun* **1** *history* a medieval travelling musician **2** a singer, an entertainer

mint¹ *noun* **1** a plant with strong-smelling leaves, used as flavouring **2** a sweet flavoured with mint or with a synthetic substitute for mint ◆ **minty** *adjective* (**mintier, mintiest**)

mint² *noun* **1** a place where coins are made **2** *informal* a large sum of money: *cost a mint* ➤ *verb* to make coins • **in mint condition** in perfect condition

minuet *noun* **1** a kind of slow, graceful dance, popular in the 17th and 18th centuries **2** the music for this

minus *preposition* **1** used to show subtraction, represented by the sign ($-$), eg *five minus two equals three* or $5 - 2 = 3$ **2** *informal* without: *I'm minus my car today* ➤ *adjective* of a quantity less than zero

minuscule (*pronounced* **min**-is-kyool) *noun* a small cursive script originally used by monks for manuscripts ➤ *adjective* **1** written in minuscule **2** tiny, minute

minute¹ (*pronounced* **min**-it) *noun* **1** a sixtieth part of an hour **2** *maths* in measuring an angle, the sixtieth part of a degree **3** a very short time **4** (**minutes**) notes taken of what is said at a meeting

minute² (*pronounced* mai-**nyoot**) *adjective* **1** very small **2** very exact

minx *noun* (*plural* **minxes**) a cheeky young girl

Miocene *adjective* of the geological epoch 25 million to 7 million years ago

miracle *noun* **1** a wonderful act beyond normal

human powers **2** a fortunate happening with no natural cause or explanation ♦ **miraculous** *adjective* ♦ **miraculously** *adverb*

mirage (*pronounced* mi-**rahsz** or **mi**-rahsz) *noun* an optical illusion, usually resembling a pool of water on the horizon in deserts, caused by the refraction of light by very hot air near the ground

mire *noun* deep mud ♦ **miry** *adjective*

mirror *noun* a reflective piece of glass which shows the image of someone looking into it ➤ *verb* **1** to reflect like a mirror **2** to copy exactly

mirth *noun* merriment, laughter ♦ **mirthful** *adjective*

mirthless *adjective* of a laugh or smile: not showing genuine amusement

mis- *prefix* wrong(ly), bad(ly): *mispronounce/ misapply* ⊕ Comes from Old English prefix *mis-* with the same meaning

misadventure *noun* **1** an unlucky happening **2** *law* an accident, with total absence of negligence or intent to commit crime: *death by misadventure*

misandry *noun* hatred of men

misanthropist *noun* someone who hates humanity ♦ **misanthropic** *adjective* ♦ **misanthropy** *noun*

misappropriate (*pronounced* mis-ap-**roh**-pri-eit) *verb* to put to a wrong use, eg use (someone else's money) for yourself

misbehave *verb* to behave badly ♦ **misbehaviour** *noun*

miscarriage *noun* **1** a going wrong, failure: *a miscarriage of justice* **2** the accidental loss of a foetus during pregnancy

miscarry *verb* (**miscarries, miscarrying, miscarried**) **1** to go wrong or astray **2** to be unsuccessful **3** to have a miscarriage in pregnancy

miscellaneous *adjective* assorted, made up of several kinds

miscellany *noun* (*plural* **miscellanies**) a mixture or collection of things, eg pieces of writing

mischance *noun* an unlucky accident

mischief *noun* **1** naughtiness **2** *old* harm, damage

mischievous *adjective* naughty, teasing; causing trouble ♦ **mischievously** *adverb*

miscible *adjective* of substances: able to be mixed together without separating

misconceive *verb* to misunderstand

misconception *noun* a wrong idea, a misunderstanding

misconduct *noun* bad or immoral behaviour

misconstruction *noun* a wrong interpretation

misconstrue *verb* to misunderstand

miscreant *noun* a wicked person

misdeed *noun* a bad deed; a crime

misdemeanour *noun* a minor offence

miser *noun* someone who hoards money and spends very little

miserable *adjective* **1** very unhappy; wretched **2** having a tendency to be bad-tempered and grumpy **3** depressing

miserly *adjective* stingy, mean

misery *noun* (*plural* **miseries**) **1** great unhappiness, pain, poverty, etc **2** a person who is always sad or bad-tempered • **put someone** or **something out of their misery 1** to relieve someone from their physical or mental suffering **2** to kill (an animal that is in pain)

misfire *verb* **1** of a gun: to fail to go off **2** of a plan: to go wrong

misfit *noun* **1** someone who cannot fit in happily in society etc **2** something that fits badly

misfortune *noun* **1** bad luck **2** an unlucky accident

misgiving *noun* fear or doubt, eg about the result of an action

misguided *adjective* acting from or showing mistaken ideas or bad judgement

mishandle *verb* to treat badly or roughly

mishap *noun* an unlucky accident, especially a minor one

mishear *verb* (**mishearing, misheard**) to hear incorrectly

mishmash *noun* a jumbled assortment or mixture

misinform *verb* to give someone incorrect or misleading information

misinterpret *verb* to interpret wrongly

misjudge *verb* to judge unfairly or wrongly

mislay *verb* (**mislaying, mislaid**) to put (something) aside and forget where it is; lose

mislead *verb* (**misleading, misled**) to give a false idea (to); deceive ♦ **misleading** *adjective*

mismanage *verb* to conduct or manage badly ♦ **mismanagement** *noun*

mismatch *noun* (*plural* **mismatches**) an unsuitable match

misnomer *noun* a wrong or unsuitable name

misogyny (*pronounced* mi-**so**-jin-i) *noun* hatred of women ♦ **misogynist** *noun*

misplace *verb* to put in the wrong place; mislay

misprint *noun* a mistake in printing

misquote *verb* to make a mistake in repeating something written or said

misrepresent *verb* to give a wrong idea of (someone's words, actions, etc)

Miss *noun* (*plural* **Misses**) **1** a form of address used before the surname of an unmarried woman **2** (**miss**) a young woman or girl

miss *verb* **1** to fail to hit, see, hear, understand, etc **2** to fail to arrive in time to catch (a bus, train, plane, etc) **3** to discover the loss or absence of **4**

to feel the lack of: *missing old friends* ➤ *noun* (*plural* **misses**) **1** the act of missing **2** a failure to hit a target **3** a loss • **miss out 1** to leave out **2** to be left out of something worthwhile or advantageous

missal *noun* a book containing the service for the Roman Catholic Mass

misshapen *adjective* abnormally or badly shaped

missile *noun* a weapon or other object that is thrown or fired

missing *adjective* lost

mission *noun* **1** a task that someone is sent to do **2** a group of representatives sent to another country **3** a group sent to spread a religion **4** the headquarters of such groups **5** someone's chosen task or purpose: *His only mission is to make money*

missionary *noun* (*plural* **missionaries**) someone sent abroad etc to spread a religion

mission statement *noun, business* a summary of the aims and principles of an organization

missive *noun, formal* something sent, eg a letter

misspell *verb* (**misspelling, misspelled** or **misspelt**) to spell wrongly ♦ **misspelling** *noun*

misspent *adjective* spent unwisely, wasted: *a misspent youth*

mist *noun* a cloud of moisture in the air; thin fog or drizzle • **mist up** or **mist over** to cover or become covered with condensation ♦ **misty** *adjective* (**mistier, mistiest**)

mistake *verb* (**mistaking, mistook, mistaken**) **1** to misunderstand, be wrong or make an error about **2** to take (one thing or person) for another: *He mistook the house in the dark* ➤ *noun* a wrong action or statement; an error

mistaken *adjective* making an error, unwise: *a mistaken belief*

Mister full form of **Mr**

mistletoe *noun* a plant with white berries, used as a Christmas decoration

mistook past tense of **mistake**

mistreat *verb* to treat badly; abuse

mistress *noun* (*plural* **mistresses**) **1** a female teacher **2** a female owner of a dog etc **3** a woman skilled in an art **4** a woman who is the lover though not the legal wife of a man

mistrust *noun* a lack of trust or confidence in ➤ *verb* to have no trust or confidence in

misunderstand *verb* to fail to understand someone or something properly

misunderstanding *noun* **1** a mistake about a meaning **2** a slight disagreement

misuse (*pronounced* mis-**yoos**) *noun* bad or wrong use ➤ (*pronounced* mis-**yooz**) *verb* **1** to use wrongly **2** to treat badly

mite *noun* **1** something very small, eg a tiny child **2** a very small spider **3** *history* a very small coin

mitigate *verb* to make (punishment, anger, etc) less great or severe: *Reasonable efforts must be made to mitigate the risks to society* ♦ **mitigation** *noun* ⓒ Comes from Latin *mitigare* meaning 'to make mild or soft'

! Do not confuse with: **militate**.
It may be helpful to remember that the idea of fighting is contained in the word **MILITate** (in common with 'military' and 'militia') but not in **mitigate**.

mitochondrion (*pronounced* mai-toh-**kon**-dri-on) *noun* (*plural* **mitochondria**), *biology* a structure in cells in which food is converted to energy

mitosis (*pronounced* mai-**toh**-sis) *noun, biology* a type of cell division that produces two cells, which occurs when tissue is growing or repairing itself

mitral valve (*pronounced* **mai**-tral) *noun, anatomy* the valve in the heart that allows blood to flow from the left atrium to the left ventricle

mitre *noun* **1** the pointed headdress worn by archbishops and bishops **2** a slanting joint between two pieces of wood

mitt or **mitten** *noun* a glove without separate divisions for the four fingers

mix *verb* **1** to unite or blend two or more things together **2** to have social contact with other people ➤ *noun* (*plural* **mixes**) a mixture, a blending • **mix up** to confuse, muddle

mixed *adjective* **1** jumbled together **2** confused, muddled **3** consisting of different kinds **4** for both sexes: *mixed doubles*

mixed blessing *noun* something that has both advantages and disadvantages

mixed metaphor *noun, grammar* a combination of two or more metaphors which produces an incongruous mental image, eg *He put his foot down with a heavy hand*

mixed number *noun, maths* a number consisting of an integer and a vulgar fraction, eg $2\frac{3}{4}$

mixed-up *adjective* confused, bewildered, emotionally unstable

mixer *noun* **1** a machine that mixes food **2** someone who mixes socially **3** a soft drink added to alcohol

mixture *noun* **1** a number of things mixed together **2** a medicine

mizzenmast *noun* the mast nearest the stern of a ship

ml *abbreviation* millilitre(s)

MLitt *abbreviation* Master of Letters or Literature, an advanced degree in literature (from Latin *Magister Litterarum*)

mm *abbreviation* millimetre(s)

MMR *abbreviation, medicine* measles, mumps and rubella, a vaccine given to protect children against these diseases

Mn *symbol, chemistry* manganese

mnemonic (*pronounced* ni-**mon**-ik) *noun* a rhyme etc which helps you to remember something

Mo *symbol, chemistry* molybdenum

moan *noun* a low sound of grief or pain ➤ *verb* to make this sound

moat *noun* a deep trench round a castle etc, often filled with water

mob *noun* a noisy crowd ➤ *verb* (**mobbing, mobbed**) to crowd round, or attack, in disorder: *mobbed by fans*

mobbed *adjective, informal* very busy, crowded

mobile *adjective* 1 able to move or be moved easily 2 not fixed, changing quickly ➤ *noun* 1 a decoration or toy hung so that it moves slightly in the air 2 *informal* a mobile phone

mobile dune *noun, geography* a growing sand dune on which marram grass gathers sand blown by the wind

mobile phone *noun* a small portable telephone, powered by a battery, that operates by means of a cellular radio system

mobility *noun* freedom or ease of movement, either in physical or career terms

mobilize or **mobilise** *verb* to gather (troops etc) together ready for active service ♦ **mobilization** *noun*

Möbius strip (*pronounced* **mer**-bi-us) *noun, maths* a one-sided surface made by twisting and joining together the ends of a rectangular strip

---

⊙ Named after August F *Möbius* (1790–1868), German mathematician

---

moccasin *noun* a soft leather shoe of the type originally worn by Native Americans

mocha (*pronounced* **mok**-a or **mohk**-a) *noun* 1 a fine coffee 2 coffee and chocolate mixed together 3 a deep brown colour

mock *verb* to laugh at, make fun of ➤ *adjective* false, pretended, imitation: *mock battle*

mockery *noun* 1 the act of mocking 2 a ridiculous imitation

MOD *abbreviation* Ministry of Defence

modal verb *noun, grammar* a verb which modifies the sense of a main verb, eg *can, may, must*, etc

mode *noun* 1 a manner of doing or acting 2 kind, sort; fashion 3 *computing* a method of operation in which a computer is running: *print mode* 4 *maths* the most frequent value in a set of numbers (*compare with*: **mean², median**)

model *noun* 1 a design or pattern to be copied 2 a small-scale copy of something: *a model*

railway 3 a living person who poses for an artist 4 someone employed to wear and display new clothes ➤ *adjective* 1 acting as a model 2 fit to be copied, perfect: *model behaviour* ➤ *verb* (**modelling, modelled**) 1 to make a model of 2 to plan, build or create something according to a particular pattern 3 to wear and display (clothes)

modem *noun, computing* a device that allows data to be transferred from one computer to another via telephone lines

moderate *verb* (*pronounced* **mod**-e-reit) 1 to make or become less great or severe 2 to control what is published, eg in an Internet newsgroup ➤ *adjective* (*pronounced* **mod**-e-rat) 1 keeping within reason, not going to extremes 2 of medium or average quality, ability, etc

moderately *adverb* slightly, quite, fairly

moderation *noun* 1 a lessening or calming down 2 the practice of not going to extremes

moderator *noun* 1 someone who settles disputes 2 someone who controls what is published, eg in an Internet newsgroup 3 *physics* a substance used for slowing down neutrons in nuclear reactors

modern *adjective* belonging to the present or to recent times; not old ♦ **modernity** *noun*

modernize or **modernise** *verb* to bring up to date ♦ **modernization** *noun*

modest *adjective* 1 not exaggerating achievements; not boastful 2 not very large: *modest salary* 3 behaving decently; not shocking ♦ **modesty** *noun*

modicum *noun* (*plural* **modicums**) a small amount

modifier *noun* 1 *grammar* a word or phrase that modifies or identifies the meaning of another word, eg *in the green hat* in the phrase *the man in the green hat*, and *vaguely* in the phrase *He was vaguely embarrassed* 2 *grammar* a noun that functions as an adjective, eg *mohair* in *mohair jumper* 3 a person or thing that modifies

modify *verb* (**modifies, modifying, modified**) 1 to make a slight change in: *modified my design* 2 to make less extreme: *modified his demands* ♦ **modification** *noun*

modish *adjective* fashionable, smart

modular *adjective* of or composed of modules

modulate *verb* 1 to vary or soften in tone or pitch 2 *music* to change key ♦ **modulation** *noun*

module *noun* 1 a set course forming a unit in an educational scheme 2 a separate, self-contained section of a spacecraft 3 *computing* a self-contained part of a program

modulus *noun* (*plural* **moduli** – *pronounced* mod-**yuw**-lai), *maths* the absolute value of a real number, whether positive or negative

mogul¹ *noun* 1 a powerful or influential person,

especially in a business or industry **2** (**Mogul**) *history* one of the Muslim rulers of India between the sixteenth and nineteenth centuries ▸ *adjective* relating to the Moguls or the Mogul Empire of India

mogul² *noun* a mound of hard snow forming an obstacle on a ski-slope

mohair *noun* **1** the long silky hair of an Angora goat **2** fabric made from this

moist *adjective* damp, very slightly wet

moisten *verb* to make slightly wet or damp

moisture *noun* slight wetness; water or other liquid in tiny drops in the atmosphere or on a surface

moisturize or **moisturise** *verb* **1** to add moisture to **2** to apply moisturizer to (the skin)

moisturizer or **moisturiser** *noun* a cosmetic cream that restores moisture to the skin

mol *symbol, chemistry* mole(s)

molar *noun* a back tooth used for grinding food

molasses *singular noun* a thick dark syrup left when sugar is refined

mole¹ *noun* **1** a small burrowing animal, with tiny eyes and soft fur **2** a spy who successfully infiltrates a rival organization

mole² *noun* a small dark spot on the skin, often raised

mole³ *noun, chemistry* (symbol **mol**) the standard unit of amount of a substance

molecular *adjective* to do with a molecule or molecules: *molecular formula/molecular weight*

molecule *noun* a group of two or more atoms linked together

molehill *noun* a small heap of earth created by a burrowing mole

molest *verb* **1** to annoy or torment **2** to injure or abuse sexually

mollify *verb* (**mollifies, mollifying, mollified**) to calm down; lessen the anger of

mollusc *noun* any of a group of boneless animals, usually with hard shells, eg shellfish and snails

mollycoddle *verb* to pamper, overprotect

molten *adjective* of metal etc: melted

molybdenum *noun, chemistry* (symbol **Mo**) a hard, silvery, metallic element ℗ Comes from Greek *molybdos* meaning 'lead'

moment *noun* **1** a very short space of time; an instant **2** importance, consequence **3** *physics* a measure of the turning effect produced by a force **4** *physics* the **moment of inertia**

momentary *adjective* lasting for a moment ♦ **momentarily** *adverb*

moment of inertia *noun, physics* (shortened to: **moment**) the idea that the turning force required to make a rotating object turn faster depends on the way the object's mass is distributed about the axis of rotation

momentous *adjective* of great importance: *a momentous discovery*

momentum *noun* (*plural* **momenta**) **1** the force that an object gains as it moves **2** continuous speed of progress: *The campaign is gaining momentum*

mon- see **mono-**

monarch *noun* a king, queen, emperor or empress

monarchist *noun* someone who believes in government by a monarch ♦ **monarchist** *noun*

monarchy *noun* (*plural* **monarchies**) **1** government by a monarch **2** an area governed by a monarch **3** the royal family

monastery *noun* (*plural* **monasteries**) a building housing a group of monks

monastic *adjective* of or like monasteries or monks

monasticism *noun* the way of life in a monastery

Monday *noun* the second day of the week

⊙ From an Old English word meaning 'day of the moon'

monetarism (*pronounced* **mun**-it-ar-izm) *noun* an economic policy based on control of a country's money supply

monetary (*pronounced* **mun**-i-tar-i) *adjective* of money or coinage

money *noun* **1** coins and banknotes used for payment **2** wealth

⊙ The Roman goddess Juno was known in ancient times as Juno *Moneta*, and it was in her temple in Rome that money was coined. This resulted in the word *moneta* being used first to mean 'a mint', and then the money which was made there

moneyed or **monied** *adjective* wealthy

money-spinner *noun* an idea, project, etc that brings in large sums of money

mongoose *noun* (*plural* **mongooses**) a small weasel-like animal which kills snakes

mongrel *noun* an animal of mixed breed

monied another spelling of **moneyed**

monitor *noun* **1** an instrument used to check the operation of a system or apparatus **2** a screen in a television studio showing the picture being transmitted **3** a computer screen **4** a school pupil given certain responsibilities **5** someone whose job is to monitor a situation, process, etc ▸ *verb* **1** to keep a check on **2** to listen to and report on foreign broadcasts etc

monk *noun* a member of a male religious group living secluded in a monastery

monkey *noun* (*plural* **monkeys**) **1** a long-tailed primate mammal **2** a mischievous child

• **monkey about** to fool about

monkey nut *noun* a peanut

monkey puzzle *noun* a pine tree with prickly spines along its branches

monkey wrench *noun* an adjustable spanner

monkfish *noun* (*plural* **monkfish** or **monkfishes**) a type of sea fish, used as food

mono *noun* (*plural* **monos**), *informal* a monophonic ringtone for a mobile phone

mono- or **mon-** *prefix* one, single: *monarch* (= a person who is the sole ruler of a country)/ *carbon monoxide* (= a gas with only one oxygen atom in its molecule) ⊙ Comes from Greek *monos* meaning 'single' or 'alone'

monochromatic *adjective, physics* of light: having only one wavelength

monochrome *adjective* **1** in one colour **2** black and white

monocle *noun* a single eyeglass

monoclonal *adjective, biology* of an antibody: of a type produced by any of various clones and used in the production of vaccines

monocotyledon (*pronounced* mo-noh-kot-i-**lee**-don) *noun, botany* a flowering plant with an embryo that has one cotyledon

monoculture *noun* **1** growing the same crop each year on a piece of land, rather than growing different crops in rotation **2** an area where there is one, shared culture, eg a single social or religious culture

monocyte *noun, biology* the largest type of white blood cell, with a single nucleus and clear cytoplasm

monoecious *adjective, biology* **1** of a plant: having separate male and female reproductive parts in the same plant **2** with the male and female sexual organs on the same individual or creature (*compare with:* **dioecious**)

monogamy *noun* having only one spouse or mate at a time ♦ **monogamous** *adjective*

monogram *noun* two or more letters, usually initials, made into a single design

monolith *noun* **1** an upright block of stone **2** something unmovable or intractable

monolithic *adjective* intractable, obstinate

monologue *noun* a long speech by one person

monomer *noun* a molecule that joins with others to form a polymer

monophonic *adjective* reproducing sound on one channel only, rather than splitting it into two

monoplane *noun* an aeroplane with a single pair of wings

monopolize or **monopolise** *verb* **1** to have exclusive rights to provide a particular service or product **2** to dominate, while excluding all others: *monopolizing the conversation*

monopoly *noun* (*plural* **monopolies**) **1** an exclusive right to make or sell something **2** complete unshared possession, control, etc

monorail *noun* a railway on which the trains run along a single rail

monosaccharide *noun, chemistry* a simple sugar that cannot be broken down into smaller units, eg glucose

monosodium glutamate *noun* a white crystalline chemical substance used to enhance the flavour of many processed savoury foods

monosyllable *noun* a word of one syllable ♦ **monosyllabic** *adjective*

monotheism *noun* the belief that there is only one God ♦ **monotheist** *noun* ♦ **monotheistic** *adjective*

monotone *noun* a single, unchanging tone

monotonous *adjective* **1** in a single tone **2** unchanging, dull ♦ **monotonously** *adverb*

monotony *noun* lack of variety

monounsaturated *adjective* of an oil or fat: containing only one double or triple bond per molecule (*compare with:* **polyunsaturated**)

monovalent *adjective, chemistry* of an atom: able to combine with one atom of hydrogen (*also:* **univalent**)

monoxide *noun, chemistry* a compound that contains one oxygen atom in each molecule

Monroe Doctrine *noun, history* a statement of US foreign policy proclaimed in 1823, announcing hostility to further European colonization, and non-interference with existing European colonies or affairs

⊙ Attributed to and named after then US President James *Monroe* (1758–1831), but in fact written by Secretary of State John Quincy Adams (1767–1848)

monsoon *noun* **1** a wind that blows around the area of the Indian Ocean and S Asia, from the north-east in winter (the **dry monsoon**) and from the south-west in summer (the **wet monsoon**) **2** in India: the rainy season caused by the south-west monsoon in summer

monster *noun* **1** something of unusual size or appearance **2** a huge terrifying creature **3** an evil person ➤ *adjective* huge

monstrosity *noun* (*plural* **monstrosities**) **1** something unnatural **2** something very ugly

monstrous *adjective* huge, horrible

montage (*pronounced* mon-**tahsz**) *noun* **1** a composite picture **2** a film made up of parts of other films

month *noun* a twelfth part of a year, approximately four weeks

monthly *adjective & adverb* happening once a month ➤ *noun* (*plural* **monthlies**) a magazine etc published once a month

monument *noun* a building, pillar, tomb, etc built in memory of someone or an event

monumental *adjective* **1** of or relating to a monument **2** huge, enormous
♦ **monumentally** *adverb* (meaning 2)

moo *noun* the sound made by a cow ➤ *verb* to make such a sound

mood¹ *noun* the state of a person's feelings or temper

mood² *noun, grammar* the form of a verb that shows whether it is expressing a command (**imperative**), a fact (**indicative**) or a possibility (**subjunctive**)

moody *adjective* (**moodier, moodiest**) **1** often changing in mood **2** ill-tempered, cross
♦ **moodily** *adverb* (meaning 2)

moon *noun* **1** the heavenly body which travels round the earth once each month and reflects light from the sun **2** a natural satellite of any planet: *the moons of Jupiter* ➤ *verb* **1** to wander (about) or spend time idly **2** to gaze dreamily (at) **3** to show one's naked bottom to someone as an insult

moonbeam *noun* a beam of light from the moon

moonlight *noun* the light of the moon ➤ *verb* to work secretly at a second job, usually avoiding paying tax on the money earned

moonshine *noun* **1** the shining of the moon **2** rubbish; foolish ideas or talk **3** alcoholic spirits which have been illegally distilled or smuggled

moor¹ *noun* a large stretch of open ground, often covered with heather

moor² *verb* to tie up or anchor (a ship etc)

moorhen *noun* a kind of water bird

moorings *plural noun* **1** the place where a ship is moored **2** the anchor, rope, etc holding a moored ship

moorland *noun* a stretch of moor

moose *noun* (*plural* **moose**) a large deer-like animal, found in N America

moot point *noun* a debatable point; a question with no obvious solution

mop *noun* **1** a pad of sponge or a bunch of short pieces of coarse yarn, fabric, etc on a handle for washing or cleaning **2** a thick head of hair ➤ *verb* (**mopping, mopped**) **1** to clean with a mop **2** to clean or wipe: *mopped his brow* • **mop up** to clean up

mope *verb* to be unhappy and gloomy

moped (*pronounced* **moh**-ped) *noun* a pedal bicycle with a motor

moquette *noun* fabric with a velvety pile and canvas backing, used for upholstery

moraine *noun, geography* a ridge of rocks and gravel left by a glacier

moral *adjective* **1** relating to the principles of right and wrong **2** considered by society to be good or proper: *moral behaviour* **3** based on conscience or a knowledge of what is right: a

moral obligation to help the poor ➤ *noun* **1** the lesson of a story **2** (**morals**) principles and standards of (especially sexual) behaviour

morale (*pronounced* mo-**rahl**) *noun* spirit and confidence

morality *noun* a system of moral standards based on principles of right and wrong

moralize or **moralise** *verb* **1** to write or speak, often critically, about moral standards **2** to draw a lesson from a story or event

moral support *noun* encouragement without active help

moral victory *noun* a failure that can really be seen as a success

morass *noun* (*plural* **morasses**) **1** a marsh or bog **2** a bewildering mass of something: *a morass of regulations*

moratorium *noun* (*plural* **moratoriums** or **moratoria**) an official suspension or temporary ban

morbid *adjective* **1** too concerned with gloomy, unpleasant things, especially death **2** diseased, unhealthy ♦ **morbidity** *noun* ♦ **morbidly** *adverb*

mordant *adjective* **1** sharply sarcastic or critical **2** of a chemical substance: corrosive

more *adjective* a greater number or amount of: *more money* ➤ *adverb* to a greater extent: *more beautiful/more than I can say* ➤ *noun* **1** a greater proportion or amount **2** a further or additional number: *There are more where this came from*

More Economically Developed Country *noun, geography* (*abbrev* **MEDC**) a country with a high level of development, as measured by indicators such as income from trade (*contrasted with*: **Less Economically Developed Country**)

moreish *adjective* of food etc: enjoyable, making you want more

morel (*pronounced* mawr-**el**) *noun* a type of edible fungus

moreover *adverb* besides

mores (*pronounced* **maw**-rez) *plural noun, formal* social customs that reflect the moral and social values of a particular society

morganatic *adjective* of a marriage: in which the woman has no claim to the title or property of her husband

⊙ From Latin, from early German *morgengabe* 'morning gift', a present given to a spouse on the morning after the wedding

morgue (*pronounced* mawrg) *noun* a place where dead bodies are laid, awaiting identification etc

MORI *abbreviation* Market and Opinion Research Institute, a British organization that carries out and publishes opinion polls

moribund *adjective* **1** dying **2** stagnant

morn *noun, poetic* morning

morning *noun* the part of the day before noon ➤ *adjective* of or in the morning

morning-after pill *noun* a contraceptive drug which can be taken within 72 hours of unprotected sexual intercourse by a woman wanting to prevent conception

morning star *noun* Venus when it rises before the sun

morocco *noun* a fine goatskin leather first brought from Morocco

moron *noun* **1** *informal* an idiot **2** *offensive* someone of low mental ability ♦ **moronic** *adjective*

morose *adjective* bad-tempered, gloomy ♦ **morosely** *adverb* ♦ **morosity** *noun*

morph *verb, computing* in computer animation: to change one image into another smoothly and gradually using computer graphics

morpheme *noun, linguistics* the smallest meaningful unit that a word can be divided into, eg *out, go* and *ing* forming the word *outgoing*

morphia *noun* morphine

morphine *noun* a drug which causes sleep or deadens pain

morphogenesis *noun, biology* the development of form and structure in a living organism

morphology *noun* **1** *linguistics* the study of forms and structures of words **2** *biology* the scientific study of the structure of plants and animals

morris dance *noun* a traditional English country dance in which male dancers carry sticks and wear bells

⊙ Originally a *Moorish* dance brought from Spain

morrow *noun, old* (**the morrow**) tomorrow, the day after

morse *noun* a signalling code in which each letter is represented by a particular set of dots and dashes (*also called:* **morse code**)

morsel *noun* a small piece, eg of food

mort- forms words related to death: *mortal/mortuary* ⊙ Comes from Latin *mort-*, a form of *mori* meaning 'to die'

mortal *adjective* **1** liable to die **2** causing death; deadly: *mortal injury* ➤ *noun* a human being

mortality *noun* (*plural* **mortalities**) **1** the state of being mortal **2** death **3** frequency of death; death-rate: *infant mortality*

mortally *adverb* **1** fatally: *mortally wounded* **2** very much, dreadfully: *mortally offended*

mortar *noun* **1** a heavy bowl for crushing and grinding substances with a pestle **2** a short gun for throwing shells **3** a mixture of lime, sand and water, used for fixing stones etc

mortarboard *noun* a university or college cap with a square flat top

mortgage (*pronounced* **mawr**-gij) *noun* a sum of money lent through a legal agreement for buying buildings, land, etc ➤ *verb* to offer (buildings etc) as security for money borrowed

mortice another spelling of **mortise**

mortician *noun, US* an undertaker

mortify *verb* (**mortifies, mortifying, mortified**) **1** to make someone feel ashamed or humble: *I was mortified by her behaviour* **2** of a limb, etc: to die ♦ **mortification** *noun* ♦ **mortifying** *adjective*

mortise or **mortice** *noun* a hole in a piece of wood made to receive the shaped end (**tenon**) of another piece

mortise lock or **mortice lock** *noun* a lock whose mechanism is sunk into the edge of a door

mortuary *noun* (*plural* **mortuaries**) a place where dead bodies are kept before burial or cremation

mosaic *noun* a picture or design made up of many small pieces of coloured glass, stone, etc

Moses basket *noun* a soft portable cot for babies

Moslem another spelling of **Muslim**

mosque *noun* an Islamic place of worship

mosquito *noun* (*plural* **mosquitoes** or **mosquitos**) a biting or blood-sucking insect, often carrying disease

moss *noun* (*plural* **mosses**) a very small flowerless plant, found in moist places

mossy *adjective* (**mossier, mossiest**) covered with moss

most *adjective* the greatest number or amount of: *Most children attend school regularly* ➤ *adverb* **1** very, extremely: *most grateful* **2** to the greatest extent: *the most severely injured/the most difficult* ➤ *noun* the greatest number or amount: *Most of the choir are here* • **at most** not more than • **for the most part** mostly

mostly *adverb* mainly, chiefly

MOT *noun* a compulsory annual check on behalf of the Ministry of Transport on vehicles over three years old

motel *noun* a hotel built to accommodate motorists

motet *noun* a short piece of religious music for several voices ⊙ Comes from French, diminutive of *mot* meaning 'word'

moth *noun* **1** a flying insect that resembles a butterfly, seen mostly at night **2** the cloth-eating grub of the clothes-moth

mothball *noun* a small ball of chemical used to protect clothes from moths ➤ *verb* (*also* **put in mothballs**) to put aside for later use etc

moth-eaten *adjective* **1** full of holes made by moths **2** tatty, shabby

mother *noun* **1** a female parent **2** (*also called*: **mother superior**) the female head of a convent ➤ *verb* **1** to be the mother of **2** to care for like a mother

motherboard *noun, computing* a printed circuit board into which other boards can be slotted

motherhood *noun* the state of being a mother

mother-in-law *noun* (*plural* **mothers-in-law**) the mother of your husband or wife

motherland *noun* the country of your birth

motherly *adjective* of or like a mother

mother-of-pearl *noun* a hard, shiny substance which forms a layer on the inside of certain shells, eg oysters (*also called*: **nacre**)

mother tongue *noun* a native language

motif (*pronounced* moh-**teef**) *noun* a distinctive feature or idea in a piece of music, a play, etc

⚠ Do not confuse with: **motive**

motile *adjective* of a living organism or structure: capable of independent spontaneous movement ✦ **motility** *noun*

motion *noun* **1** the act or state of moving **2** a single movement **3** a suggestion put before a meeting for discussion ➤ *verb* **1** to make a signal by a movement or gesture **2** to direct (someone) in this way: *The policeman motioned us forward*

motionless *adjective* not moving

motivate *verb* to cause (someone) to act in a certain way ✦ **motivation** *noun* a motivating force

motive *noun* the cause of someone's actions; a reason

⚠ Do not confuse with: **motif**

motley *adjective* made up of different colours or kinds

motocross *noun* the sport of motorcycle racing across rough terrain

motor *noun* **1** an engine which causes motion **2** a car ➤ *verb* to travel by motor vehicle ➤ *adjective* **1** giving or transmitting motion **2** of a nerve: transmitting impulses from the central nervous system to a muscle or gland

motorboat *noun* a boat with an engine

motorcade *noun* a procession of cars carrying a head of state etc

motorcycle or **motorbike** *noun* a bicycle with a petrol-driven engine ✦ **motorcyclist** or **motorbiker** *noun*

motorist *noun* someone who drives a car

motorize or **motorise** *verb* to supply with an engine

motor neurone *noun* a nerve cell that carries impulses from the spinal cord or the brain to another part of the body

motorway *noun* a road for fast-moving traffic, with separate carriageways for vehicles travelling in opposite directions

mottled *adjective* marked with spots or blotches

motto *noun* (*plural* **mottoes**) a phrase which acts as a guiding principle or rule

mould¹ or *N Am* **mold** *noun* a shape into which a liquid is poured to take on that shape when it cools or sets: *a jelly mould* ➤ *verb* **1** to form in a mould **2** to shape

mould² or *N Am* **mold** *noun* **1** a fluffy growth on stale food etc **2** soil containing rotted leaves etc

moulder or *N Am* **molder** *verb* to crumble away to dust

moulding *noun* a decorated border of moulded plaster round a ceiling etc

mouldy or *N Am* **moldy** *adjective* (**mouldier**, **mouldiest**) affected by mould; stale

moult *verb* of an animal: to shed its feathers, hair or skin

mound *noun* **1** a bank of earth or stones **2** a hill; a heap

mount *verb* **1** to go up, ascend **2** to climb on to (a horse, bicycle, etc) **3** to fix (a picture etc) on to a backing or support **4** to fix (a gemstone) in a casing **5** to organize (an exhibition) **6** to increase in level or intensity: *Tension is mounting* ➤ *noun* **1** a support or backing for display **2** a horse, bicycle, etc to ride on **3** in place names: a mountain: *Mount Everest*

mountain *noun* **1** a large hill **2** a large quantity

mountain ash same as **rowan**

mountain bike *noun* a sturdy bike with thick, deep-tread tyres and straight handlebars, designed for riding over hilly terrain

mountaineer *noun* a mountain climber

mountainous *adjective* **1** having many mountains **2** huge

mountebank *noun* a swindler or deceiver

⊙ Comes from Italian *montimbanco*, a word for a street pedlar who climbed on a mound or bench to sell his goods

mounted *adjective* on horseback: *mounted police*

Mounties *plural noun, informal* (**the Mounties**) the Canadian mounted police

mourn *verb* **1** to grieve for **2** to be sorrowful ✦ **mourner** *noun*

mournful *adjective* sad

mourning *noun* **1** grief felt or shown over a death **2** the period during which someone grieves **3** dark-coloured clothes traditionally worn by mourners

mouse *noun* (*plural* **mice**) **1** a small gnawing animal, found in houses and fields **2** a shy, timid, uninteresting person **3** *computing* a device moved by hand on a flat surface, causing corresponding cursor movements on a screen

mousemat or **mousepad** *noun* a small flat piece of material backed with foam rubber, used as a surface on which to move a computer mouse

mouseover see **rollover**

mousse (*pronounced* moos) *noun* **1** a frothy set dish made from eggs, cream, etc, that can be either sweet or savoury: *chocolate mousse/ salmon mousse* **2** a foamy substance used to style the hair

moustache or *US* **mustache** *noun* unshaved hair above a man's upper lip

mousy *adjective* (**mousier, mousiest**) **1** of a light-brown colour **2** shy, timid, uninteresting

mouth *noun* (*pronounced* mowth) **1** the opening in the head through which an animal or person eats and makes sounds **2** the point of a river where it flows into the sea **3** an opening, an entrance ➤ *verb* (*pronounced* mowdh) **1** to shape (words) without actually speaking **2** to speak pompously or insincerely

mouthful *noun* (*plural* **mouthfuls**) as much as fills the mouth

mouth organ *noun* a small wind instrument, moved across the lips

mouthpiece *noun* **1** the part of a musical instrument, tobacco-pipe, etc held in the mouth **2** someone who speaks for others

mouth-to-mouth *noun* a method of resuscitation involving someone breathing air directly into the mouth of the person to be revived in order to inflate their lungs

mouthwash *noun* (*plural* **mouthwashes**) an antiseptic liquid used for gargling or freshening the mouth

movable or **moveable** *adjective* able to be moved, changed, etc

move *verb* **1** to (cause to) change place or position **2** to change where you live, work, etc **3** to rouse or affect the feelings of **4** to rouse into action **5** *formal* to propose, suggest ➤ *noun* **1** an act of moving **2** an act of changing homes or premises **3** a step, an action **4** a shifting of a piece in a game of chess etc

movement *noun* **1** the act or manner of moving **2** a change of position **3** *music* a division of a piece of music **4** a group of people united in a common aim: *the peace movement* **5** an organized attempt to achieve an aim: *the movement to reform the divorce laws*

movie *noun* a cinema film • **the movies** the cinema

moving *adjective* **1** in motion **2** having an affect on the emotions ♦ **movingly** *adverb* (meaning 2)

moving average *noun, maths* the mean of successive sets with the same number of members

mow *verb* (**mowing, mowed, mown**) to cut (grass, hay, etc) with a scythe or machine • **mow someone down** or **mow something down** to destroy them in great numbers

mower *noun* a machine for mowing

mozzarella *noun* a soft, white, Italian curd cheese, used especially on top of pizza and in salads

MP *abbreviation* **1** Member of Parliament **2** Military Police

MPEG (*pronounced* **em**-peg) *abbreviation, computing* Moving Picture Experts Group, a standard compressed file format for audiovisual information

MPhil *abbreviation* Master of Philosophy, an advanced degree in philosophy or other subjects

MP3 *abbreviation, computing* MPEG-1 Layer 3, a compressed file format that allows fast downloading of audio data from the Internet

Mr *noun* (*short for* **Mister**) the form of address used before a man's surname

mRNA *abbreviation* messenger RNA

Mrs *noun* the form of address used before a married woman's surname

MRSA *abbreviation, medicine* methicillin-resistant Staphylococcus aureus, a bacterium that is resistant to most antibiotics

MS *abbreviation* **1** multiple sclerosis, a progressive disease of the central nervous system, resulting in paralysis **2** manuscript

Ms *noun* a form of address used before the surname of a married or unmarried woman

ms *abbreviation* millisecond(s)

MSc *abbreviation* Master of Science, an advanced degree in a subject such as biology or physics

MSG *abbreviation* monosodium glutamate

MSP *abbreviation* Member of the Scottish Parliament

Mt[1] *abbreviation* Mount(ain): *Mt Etna*

Mt[2] *symbol, chemistry* meitnerium

much *adjective* a great amount of ➤ *adverb* to or by a great extent: *much loved/much faster* ➤ *pronoun* **1** a great amount **2** something important: *made much of it* • **much the same** nearly the same

muck *noun* dung, dirt, filth

muck-raking *noun* looking for scandals to expose

mucky *adjective* (**muckier, muckiest**) dirty: *mucky hands*

mucous *adjective* like, covered by or producing mucus

! Do not confuse: **mucous** and **mucus**

mucous membrane *noun, anatomy* the moist, mucus-secreting lining of various internal cavities of the body

mucus *noun* slimy fluid secreted from the nose etc

mud *noun* wet, soft earth

muddle *verb* **1** to confuse, bewilder **2** to mix up **3** to make a mess of ➤ *noun* **1** a mess **2** a state of confusion

muddy *adjective* (**muddier, muddiest**) **1** covered with mud **2** unclear, confused ➤ *verb* to make or become muddy

mudflow *noun* a flow of mud down a slope

mudguard *noun* a shield or guard over wheels to catch mud splashes

muesli *noun* a mixture of grains, nuts and fruit eaten with milk

muezzin (*pronounced* moo-**ez**-in) *noun, Islam* the Muslim official who calls the faithful to prayer (*also called*: **mueddin**)

muff¹ *noun* a tube of warm fabric to cover and keep the hands warm

muff² *verb* to fail in an opportunity, eg to catch a ball

muffin *noun* **1** a round, flat, spongy cake, toasted and eaten hot with butter **2** a small, sweet cake made of flour or corn meal with fruit, nuts, chocolate, etc: *blueberry muffins*

muffle *verb* **1** to wrap up for warmth etc **2** to deaden (a sound)

muffler *noun* **1** a scarf **2** *US* a silencer for a car

mufti *noun* clothes worn by soldiers etc when off duty

mug¹ *noun* **1** a large, straight-sided cup **2** *informal* someone who is easily fooled **3** *informal* the face

mug² *verb* (**mugging, mugged**) to attack and rob (someone) in the street ◆ **mugger** *noun*

mug³ *verb*: **mug up** *informal* to study hard; swot up

muggy *adjective* (**muggier, muggiest**) of weather: warm and damp ◆ **mugginess** *noun*

mujaheddin, mujahedin or **mujahadeen** (*pronounced* moo-ja-he-**deen**) *plural noun* in Afghanistan, Iran and Pakistan: Muslim fundamentalist guerillas

mulberry *noun* (*plural* **mulberries**) **1** a tree on whose leaves silkworms are fed **2** its purple berry

mulch *noun* (*plural* **mulches**) loose straw etc laid down to protect plant roots ➤ *verb* to cover with mulch

mule¹ *noun* an animal bred from a female horse and a male donkey

mule² *noun* a backless slipper

mulish *adjective* stubborn

mulled *adjective* of wine etc: mixed with spices and served warm

mullet *noun* a small, edible sea fish

mull over *verb* to think over, ponder over

multi- *prefix* many ⊙ Comes from Latin *multus* meaning 'many'

multi-access *see* **multi-user**

multicellular *adjective* consisting of many cells: *multicellular organisms*

multicoloured *adjective* having many colours

multicultural *adjective* of a society, community, etc: made up of or involving several distinct racial or religious groups

multi-faith *adjective* of a society, institution, etc: made up of or involving several distinct religious groups

multifarious *adjective* of many kinds

multilateral *adjective* (*compare with*: **unilateral**) **1** involving or affecting several people, groups or nations: *a multilateral treaty* **2** many-sided ◆ **multilaterally** *adverb*

multimedia *adjective* of a computer: able to run various sound and visual applications

multimillionaire *noun* someone who has property worth several million pounds (or dollars)

multinational company *noun* a large business that has operations in several countries (*also called*: **transnational corporation**)

multiple *adjective* **1** affecting many parts: *multiple injuries* **2** involving many things of the same sort: *vehicles in a multiple crash* ➤ *noun, maths* a number or quantity which contains another number an exact number of times

multiple deprivation *noun* socioeconomic deprivation of more than one type, eg in the areas of housing, health, education, etc

multiple sclerosis *noun* (*abbrev* **MS**) a progressive nerve disease resulting in paralysis

multiplex *adjective* of a cinema: including several screens and theatres in one building

multiplicand *noun, maths* a number which is to be multiplied by another (the **multiplier**)

multiplication *noun* the act of multiplying ◆ **multiplicative** *adjective*

multiplicity *noun*: **a multiplicity of** a great number of

multiplier *noun* **1** *maths* the number by which another (the **multiplicand**) is to be multiplied **2** *economics, geography* a cause of social and economic improvement (**positive multiplier**) or decline (**negative multiplier**)

multiply *verb* (**multiplies, multiplying, multiplied**) **1** to increase **2** to increase a number by adding it to itself a certain number of times: *2 multiplied by 3 is 6*

multipurpose *adjective* having many uses

multiracial *adjective* consisting of or taking in many races

multistorey *adjective* of a building: having many floors ➤ *noun* (*plural* **multistoreys**), *informal* a car park that has several floors

multitasking *noun* **1** *computing* the action of running several processes simultaneously **2** of a person: doing several things at the same time

multitude *noun* a great number; a crowd

multitudinous *adjective* very many

multi-user *adjective, computing* of a system: consisting of several terminals linked to a main computer (*also*: **multi-access**)

multivalent *adjective, chemistry* of an atom: able to combine with more than one atom of hydrogen

multivitamin *noun* a pill containing several vitamins, taken to supplement the diet

mum¹ *noun, informal* mother

mum² *adjective* silent

mumble *verb* to speak indistinctly

mumin (*pronounced* **moo**-min) *noun, Islam* a practising Muslim

mummify *verb* (**mummifies, mummifying, mummified**) to make into a mummy (meaning 2)

mummy¹ *noun* (*plural* **mummies**), *informal* mother

mummy² *noun* (*plural* **mummies**) a dead body preserved by wrapping in bandages and treating with wax, spices, etc

mumps *singular noun* an infectious disease affecting glands at the side of the neck, causing swelling

munch *verb* to chew noisily

mundane *adjective* dull, ordinary

municipal *adjective* of or owned by a city or town

municipality *noun* (*plural* **municipalities**) a city or town; an area covered by local government

munificent *adjective* very generous ♦ **munificence** *noun*

munitions *plural noun* weapons and ammunition used in war

mural *adjective* of or on a wall ➤ *noun* a painting or design on a wall

murder *verb* to kill someone unlawfully and on purpose ➤ *noun* the act of murdering

murderer *noun* someone who commits murder

murderess *noun, old* a woman murderer

murderous *adjective* capable or guilty of murder; wicked

murky *adjective* (**murkier, murkiest**) dark, gloomy ♦ **murkiness** *noun*

murmur *noun* **1** a low, indistinct, continuous sound **2** a hushed speech or tone ➤ *verb* **1** to make a murmur **2** to complain, grumble

muscle *noun* **1** fleshy tissue which contracts and stretches to cause body movements **2** an area of this in the body **3** physical strength or power **4** power or influence of any kind: *financial muscle*

muscular *adjective* **1** of or relating to muscles **2** strong

muscular dystrophy *noun, medicine* a hereditary disease in which the muscles gradually deteriorate

Muse *noun* any of the nine goddesses of poetry, music, dancing, etc in classical mythology

muse *verb* to think (over) in a quiet, leisurely way

museum *noun* a building for housing and displaying objects of artistic, scientific or historic interest

mush *noun* (*plural* **mushes**) **1** something soft and pulpy **2** an overly sentimental film, song, etc

mushroom *noun* a fungus, usually umbrella-shaped, with some edible varieties ➤ *verb* to grow very quickly: *Buildings mushroomed all over town*

mushy *adjective* (**mushier, mushiest**) **1** soft and pulpy **2** overly sentimental

music *noun* **1** the art of arranging, combining, etc certain sounds able to be produced by the voice, or by instruments **2** an arrangement of such sounds or its written form **3** a sweet or pleasant sound

musical *adjective* **1** of music **2** sounding sweet or pleasant **3** having a talent for music ➤ *noun* a light play or film with a lot of songs and dancing in it ♦ **musically** *adverb*

musician *noun* **1** a specialist in music **2** someone who plays a musical instrument

musk *noun* a strong perfume, obtained from the male musk deer or artificially

musket *noun* an early rifle-like gun that was loaded through the barrel, once used by soldiers

musketeer *noun* a soldier armed with a musket

musky *adjective* (**muskier, muskiest**) smelling like musk

Muslim or **Moslem** *noun* a follower of the Islamic religion ➤ *adjective* Islamic

muslin *noun* a fine, soft cotton cloth

mussel *noun* an edible shellfish with two separate halves to its blue-black shell

must *verb* **1** used with another verb to express necessity: *I must finish this today* **2** expressing compulsion: *You must do as you're told* **3** expressing certainty or probability: *That must be the right answer* ➤ *noun* something that must be done; a necessity ⊙ Comes from Old English *moste*

mustache US spelling of **moustache**

mustang *noun* a North American wild horse

mustard *noun* **1** a plant with sharp-tasting seeds **2** a hot yellow paste made from its seeds, used as a condiment or seasoning

mustard gas *noun* **1** a highly poisonous gas used in chemical warfare in World War I **2** the colourless oily liquid of which it is a vapour

muster *verb* to gather up or together (eg troops, courage) • **pass muster** to be accepted as satisfactory

musty *adjective* (**mustier, mustiest**) smelling old and stale ✦ **mustiness** *noun*

mutable *adjective* changeable ✦ **mutability** *noun*

mutagen *noun, biology* an agent which increases the frequency of mutations in an organism

mutate *verb* **1** *biology* to undergo mutation **2** to change

mutation *noun* **1** *biology* a change in the genes or chromosomes of an organism which may result in a change in the appearance or behaviour of the organism **2** any change

mute *adjective* **1** not able to speak; dumb **2** silent **3** of a letter in a word: not pronounced ➤ *noun* **1** a mute person **2** a device that softens the sound of a musical instrument ➤ *verb* **1** to soften the sound of (a musical instrument) **2** to make silent

muted *adjective* **1** of a sound: made quieter, hushed: *muted criticism* **2** of a colour: not bright

mutilate *verb* **1** to inflict great physical damage on; maim **2** to damage greatly ✦ **mutilation** *noun*

mutineer *noun* someone who takes part in a mutiny

mutinous *adjective* rebellious; refusing to obey orders

mutiny *verb* (**mutinies, mutinying, mutinied**) **1** to rise against those in power **2** to refuse to obey the commands of military officers ➤ *noun* (*plural* **mutinies**) refusal to obey commands; rebellion

mutt *noun, slang* **1** a dog **2** an idiot

mutter *verb* to speak in a low voice; mumble

mutton *noun* meat from a sheep, used as food • **mutton dressed as lamb** *informal* an older woman dressed in a style more suitable for a young woman

mutual *adjective* **1** given by each to the other(s); reciprocal: *mutual help* **2** shared by two or more: *a mutual friend*

mutualism *noun, biology* a close association of two organisms of different species, with both gaining from the relationship (*compare with*: **commensalism, parasitism**)

mutually *adverb* of a relationship between two people or things: each to the other, in both directions

mutually exclusive *adjective* denoting events, things, etc that cannot happen or exist at the same time

Muzak *noun, trademark* recorded music played in shops etc

muzzle *noun* **1** an animal's nose and mouth **2** an arrangement of straps fastened over an animal's mouth to prevent it biting **3** the open end of a gun ➤ *verb* **1** to put a muzzle on (a dog etc) **2** to prevent from speaking freely

muzzy *adjective* (**muzzier, muzziest**) cloudy, confused

MW *abbreviation* medium-wave

my *adjective* belonging to me: *This is my book*

mycelium (*pronounced* mai-**see**-li-um) *noun* (*plural* **mycelia**), *biology* a mass or network of filaments that form a fungus

mycology *noun* the biological study of fungi ✦ **mycologist** *noun*

myelin *noun, biology* a soft white substance that forms a thin sheath around nerve cells

myelitis *noun, medicine* **1** inflammation of the spinal cord **2** inflammation of the bone marrow

myeloma (*pronounced* mai-e-**loh**-ma) *noun* (*plural* **myelomas** or **myelomata** – *pronounced* mai-e-**loh**-ma-ta), *medicine* a tumour of the bone marrow

myna or **mynah** *noun* a bird which can imitate human speech

myocardial infarction *noun, medicine* a heart attack

myocardium *noun* (*plural* **myocardia**) the muscular tissue of the heart

myoglobin *noun* a protein that stores oxygen in a muscle

myopia *noun* short-sightedness

myopic *adjective* short-sighted

myriad (*pronounced* **mi**-ri-ad) *noun* a very great number ➤ *adjective* very many, countless

myriapod *noun, zoology* an arthropod with many legs, eg the centipede or the millipede ⊙ Comes from Greek *myriopodos*, meaning 'many-footed'

myrrh *noun* a bitter-tasting resin used in medicines, perfumes, etc

myrtle *noun* a type of evergreen shrub

myself *pronoun* **1** used reflexively: *I can see myself in the mirror* **2** used for emphasis: *I wrote this myself*

mysterious *adjective* **1** puzzling, difficult to understand **2** secret, hidden, intriguing ✦ **mysteriously** *adverb*

mystery *noun* (*plural* **mysteries**) **1** something that cannot be or has not been explained; something puzzling **2** a deep secret

mystic *noun* someone who seeks knowledge of

sacred or mystical things by going into a state of spiritual ecstasy

mystical *adjective* having a secret or sacred meaning beyond ordinary human understanding

mysticism *noun* **1** the practice of communicating directly with God through prayer and meditation **2** the belief in the existence of a state of reality hidden from ordinary human understanding

mystify *verb* (**mystifies, mystifying, mystified**) **1** to puzzle greatly **2** to confuse, bewilder

mystique (*pronounced* mis-**teek**) *noun* a compelling atmosphere of mystery about someone or something

myth *noun* **1** a story about gods, heroes, etc of ancient times; a fable **2** something imagined or untrue: *a popular myth*

mythical *adjective* **1** of or relating to a myth **2** invented, imagined

mythological *adjective* of myth or mythology; mythical

mythology *noun* **1** the study of myths **2** a collection of myths

myxomatosis *noun* a contagious, usually fatal, disease of rabbits, transmitted by fleas

Nn

N¹ *abbreviation* **1** National **2** Nationalist **3** New **4** Norse **5** north **6** northern

N² *symbol* **1** *chess* Knight **2** *physics* newton **3** *chemistry* nitrogen

n¹ *noun, maths* an indefinite number ➤ *adjective* being an indefinite or large number

n² *abbreviation* **1** nano- **2** *physics* neutron

Na *symbol, chemistry* sodium ☉ Comes from Latin *natrium*

n/a *abbreviation* not applicable: used when filling in forms to show the question is not relevant to you

NAACP *abbreviation* in the USA: National Association for the Advancement of Colored People, a pressure group which aims to make Black people aware of their political rights

naan another spelling of **nan**

nab *verb* (**nabbing, nabbed**) *informal* **1** to snatch, seize **2** to arrest

nabob (*pronounced* **nei**-bob) *noun, informal* a wealthy influential person ☉ Comes from Hindi *nawwab*, plural of *na'ib* meaning 'deputy'

nachos (*pronounced* **nah**-chohz) *plural noun, cookery* tortilla chips topped with chillis, melted cheese, etc

nacre (*pronounced* **neik**-er) *noun* mother-of-pearl

nadir (*pronounced* **nei**-deer or **na**-deer) *noun* **1** the point of the heavens opposite the zenith **2** the lowest point of anything

naevus or *US* **nevus** (*both pronounced* **neev**-us) *noun* (*plural* **naevi** or **nevi** – *both pronounced* **neev**-ai) a birthmark ☉ Comes from Latin *naevus* meaning 'a mole on the body'

naff *adjective, slang* inferior, crass, tasteless

nag¹ *verb* (**nagging, nagged**) to find fault with constantly

nag² *noun* a horse

naiad (*pronounced* **nai**-ad) *noun* a mythological river nymph

nail *noun* **1** a horny covering protecting the tips of the fingers and toes **2** a thin, pointed piece of metal for fastening wood etc ➤ *verb* **1** to fasten with nails **2** to enclose in a box etc by means of nails **3** *informal* to catch, trap • **hit the nail on the head 1** to identify a problem exactly **2** to state something precisely

naive or **naïve** (*both pronounced* nai-**eev**) *adjective* **1** simple in thought, manner or speech **2** inexperienced and lacking knowledge of the world • **naiveté** or **naïveté** (*both pronounced* nai-**eev**-i-tei) *noun*

naked *adjective* **1** without clothes **2** having no covering **3** not hidden nor controlled: *naked aggression* • **nakedly** *adverb* (meaning 3)

namby-pamby *adjective* childish, feeble

☉ Originally a nickname of the 18th-century sentimental English poet, *Ambrose* Philips

name *noun* **1** a word by which a person, place or thing is known **2** fame, reputation: *making a name for himself* **3** an offensive description: *Don't call people names* **4** authority: *I arrest you in the name of the king* ➤ *verb* **1** to give a name to **2** to speak of by name, mention **3** to appoint: *She was named as the new head teacher*

nameless *adjective* without a name, not named

namely *adverb* that is to say

namesake *noun* someone with the same name as another person

nan or **naan** *noun* a flat, slightly leavened Indian and Pakistani bread

nanny *noun* (*plural* **nannies**) a children's nurse

nanny goat *noun* a female goat

nano- *prefix* **1** a thousand millionth: *nanosecond* **2** microscopic in size: *nanoplankton* ☉ Comes from Greek *nanos* meaning 'a dwarf'

nanotechnology *noun* the manufacture or measuring of tiny objects

nap¹ *noun* a short sleep ➤ *verb* (**napping, napped**) to take a short sleep • **caught napping** taken unawares

nap² *noun* a woolly or fluffy surface on cloth

nap³ *noun* a kind of card game

napalm (*pronounced* **nei**-pahm) *noun* petroleum jelly, used to make bombs

nape *noun* the back of the neck

naphtha *noun, chemistry* any of several flammable liquids distilled from coal or petroleum

naphthalene *noun, chemistry* a white crystalline hydrocarbon distilled from coal tar, used in mothballs and dyes

napkin *noun* a small piece of cloth or paper for wiping the lips at meals

nappy *noun* (*plural* **nappies**) a piece of cloth, or thick pad, put between a baby's legs to absorb urine and faeces

narcissism *noun* excessive admiration of yourself • **narcissistic** *adjective*

narcissus noun (plural **narcissi** – pronounced nahr-**sis**-ai – or **narcissuses**) a plant like a daffodil with a white, star-shaped flower

narcosis noun (plural **narcoses**), medicine drowsiness, unconsciousness, or other effects produced by a narcotic ⊕ Comes from Greek narkosis meaning 'numbing'

narcotic noun, medicine a type of drug that brings on sleep or stops pain

nark informal, noun a persistent complainer ➤ verb to grumble

narky adjective (**narkier, narkiest**), informal irritable, complaining

narrate verb to tell a story ♦ **narration** noun ♦ **narrator** noun

narrative noun a story ➤ adjective telling a story

narrow adjective 1 of small extent from side to side; not wide: a narrow road 2 with little to spare: a narrow escape 3 lacking wide interests or experience: narrow views ➤ verb to make or become narrow

narrowband adjective denoting telecommunications broadcasting across a narrow range of frequencies (compare with: **broadband**)

narrow-gauge adjective of a railway: having the distance between rails less than the standard gauge of 4 feet 8 inches or 1.435 metres (compare with: **broad-gauge**)

narrowly adverb closely; barely

narrow-minded adjective unwilling to accept or tolerate new ideas

narrows plural noun a narrow sea passage, a strait

narwhal noun a type of arctic whale ⊕ From Danish narhval

NASA abbreviation in the USA: National Aeronautics and Space Administration

nasal adjective 1 of the nose 2 sounded through the nose

nascent (pronounced **nei**-sent) adjective beginning to develop, in an early stage ♦ **nascency** noun

nastic movement noun, biology movement of a plant organ in response to an external stimulus, but not related to the direction of the stimulus

nasturtium noun a climbing plant with brightly coloured flowers

nasty adjective (**nastier, nastiest**) 1 very disagreeable or unpleasant 2 of a problem etc: difficult to deal with 3 of an injury: serious ♦ **nastily** adverb (meaning 1)

nat- forms words related to being born: natal/nature (= the basic qualities or features that a person or thing is born with) ⊕ Comes from Latin nat-, a form of nasci meaning 'to be born'

natal (pronounced **nei**-tal) adjective of birth

nation noun 1 the people living in the same country, or under the same government 2 a race of people: the Jewish nation

national adjective of, relating to or belonging to a nation or race ➤ noun someone belonging to a nation: a British national ♦ **nationally** adverb

national anthem noun a nation's official song or hymn

national call noun a long-distance, but not international, telephone call

national government noun administration of the affairs of a country by eg the Prime Minister and members of parliament in the UK

National Health Service noun, Brit (abbrev **NHS**) the system set up in 1948 to provide medical treatment for all UK residents free, or at a small charge, paid for mainly by public taxation

national insurance noun, Brit (abbrev **NI**) a system of state insurance to which employers and employees contribute, to provide for the sick, unemployed, etc

nationalism noun the desire to bring the people of a nation together under their own government ♦ **nationalist** noun & adjective ♦ **nationalistic** adjective

nationality noun (plural **nationalities**) 1 membership of a particular nation 2 the people belonging to a nation: women of many nationalities

nationalize or **nationalise** verb to place (industries etc) under the control of the government ♦ **nationalization** noun

national park noun an area of countryside owned by the nation and preserved

national service noun compulsory service in the armed forces

Nation of Islam noun a Black religious movement in the USA that claims Black Americans are descended from an ancient Muslim tribe (also called: **Black Muslims**)

nation state noun an independent state with a population that broadly shares descent, language and culture

nationwide adjective & adverb over the whole of a nation

native adjective 1 born in a person: native intelligence 2 of someone's birth: my native land ➤ noun 1 someone born in a certain place: a native of Scotland 2 an inhabitant of a country from earliest times before the discovery by explorers, settlers, etc

Native American noun a member of one of the peoples originating in America

Nativity noun: (**the Nativity**) the birth of Christ

NATO abbreviation North Atlantic Treaty Organization, an alliance of countries providing mutual military protection

natter *informal, verb* to chat busily ➤ *noun* an intensive chat

natty *adjective* (**nattier, nattiest**) trim, tidy, smart ✦ **nattily** *adverb*

natural *adjective* **1** of nature **2** produced by nature; not artificial **3** of a quality etc: present at birth, not learned afterwards **4** unpretentious, simple **5** of a result etc: expected, normal ➤ *noun* **1** someone with a natural ability **2** *music* a note which is neither a sharp nor a flat, shown by the sign (♮)

natural frequency *noun, physics* the frequency at which an object or system will vibrate freely, in the absence of external forces

natural gas *noun* gas suitable for burning, found in the earth or under the sea

natural history *noun* the study of animals and plants

natural increase *noun* the difference between the birth rate and the death rate in a given area, ie the birth rate per one thousand people minus the death rate per one thousand people

naturalist *noun* someone who studies animal and plant life

naturalize or **naturalise** *verb* to give the rights of a citizen to (someone born in another country)

natural language *noun* a language which has evolved naturally, and has not been artificially created

naturally *adverb* **1** by nature **2** simply **3** of course

natural number *noun, maths* the numbers 1, 2, 3, and so on, and sometimes including 0; a positive integer

natural philosophy *noun* physics

natural resources *plural noun* the natural wealth of a country in its forests, minerals, water, etc

natural selection *noun, biology* evolution by survival of the fittest, who pass their characteristics on to the next generation

nature *noun* **1** the things which make up the physical world, eg animals, trees, rivers, mountains, etc **2** the qualities which characterize someone or something: *a kindly nature*

-natured *adjective* (added to another word) having a certain temper or personality: *good-natured*

nature reserve *noun* an area of land kept to preserve the animals and plants in it

nature trail *noun* a path through the countryside with signposts showing natural features

naturism *noun* the belief in nudity practised openly ✦ **naturist** *noun*

naught *noun* nothing: *plans came to naught*

‼ Do not confuse with: **nought**

naughty *adjective* (**naughtier, naughtiest**) bad, misbehaving ✦ **naughtily** *adverb*

nausea *noun* a feeling of sickness

nauseate *verb* to make sick, fill with disgust ✦ **nauseating** *adjective* sickening

nauseous *adjective* **1** sickening; disgusting **2** feeling sick

nautical *adjective* of ships or sailors ⊙ Comes from Greek *nautes* meaning 'a sailor'

nautical mile *noun* a measure of distance traditionally used at sea, approximately 1.85 kilometres (6080 feet)

nautilus *noun* (*plural* **nautiluses** or **nautili** – *pronounced* **naw**-ti-lai) a small sea creature related to the octopus

naval *adjective* of the navy

nave *noun* the middle or main part of a church

navel *noun* the small hollow in the centre of the front of the belly

navigable *adjective* **1** able to be used by ships **2** able to be steered

navigate *verb* **1** to steer or pilot a ship, aircraft, etc on its course **2** to sail on, over or through **3** to move around the different parts of a website

navigation *noun* the art of navigating ✦ **navigational** *adjective* of or used in navigation

navigator *noun* someone who steers or sails a ship etc

navvy *noun* (*plural* **navvies**) a labourer working on roads etc

navy *noun* (*plural* **navies**) **1** a nation's fighting ships **2** the men and women serving on these

navy blue *noun & adjective* dark blue

nawab (*pronounced* na-**wahb**) *noun, history* a Muslim ruler or landowner in India ⊙ Comes from Hindi *nawwab*, plural of *na'ib* meaning 'deputy'

nay *adverb, old* no ➤ *noun* a person who is voting or has voted 'no'

Nazi (*pronounced* **naht**-si) *noun, history* a member of the German National Socialist Workers' Party, a fascist party ruling Germany in 1933–45 under Adolf Hitler ✦ **Nazism** *noun*

NB or **nb** *abbreviation* note well ⊙ Comes from Latin *nota bene*

Nb *symbol, chemistry* niobium

NCO *abbreviation* non-commissioned officer

Nd *symbol, chemistry* neodymium

NE *abbreviation* north-east; north-eastern

Ne *symbol, chemistry* neon

Neanderthal (*pronounced* ni-**an**-der-tal) *adjective* **1** of a primitive type of human living during the Stone Age **2** *informal* primitive or old-fashioned

neap tide *noun* a tidal pattern that occurs at the first and last quarters of the Moon, when there is least variation between high and low tides (*compare with*: **spring tide**)

near *adjective* **1** not far away in place or time **2** close in relationship, friendship, etc **3** barely avoiding or almost reaching (something): *a near disaster* ➤ *adverb* at or to a place or time not far away ➤ *preposition* close to ➤ *verb* to approach or come close to: *The building is nearing completion*

nearby *adverb* to or at a short distance: *Do you live nearby?*

nearly *adverb* **1** almost: *nearly four o'clock* **2** closely: *nearly related*

near miss *noun* **1** something not quite achieved, eg a shot that almost hits the target **2** something only just avoided, eg an air collision

nearside *adjective* of the side of a vehicle: furthest from the centre of the road (*contrasted with*: **offside**)

near-sighted *adjective* short-sighted

neat *adjective* **1** trim, tidy **2** skilfully done **3** of an alcoholic drink: not diluted with water etc
♦ **neaten** *verb*

nebula *noun* (*plural* **nebulae** – *pronounced* **neb**-yuw-lee) a shining cloud-like appearance in the night sky, produced by very distant stars or by a mass of gas and dust

nebulizer or **nebuliser** *noun* a device with a mouthpiece, used for administering a drug as a fine mist

nebulous *adjective* hazy, vague

necessarily (*pronounced* nes-e-sa-ri-li or nes-e-**se**-ri-li) *adverb* for certain, definitely, inevitably

necessary *adjective* not able to be done without ➤ *noun* (*plural* **necessaries**) something that cannot be done without, such as food, clothing, etc

necessitate *verb* to make necessary; force
♦ **necessity** *noun* (*plural* **necessities**) **1** something necessary **2** great need; want, poverty

neck *noun* **1** the part between the head and body **2** a narrow passage or area: *neck of a bottle/neck of land* • **neck and neck** running side by side, staying exactly equal

necklace *noun* a string of beads or precious stones etc worn round the neck

neckline *noun* the edge of an item of clothing at the neck

necktie *noun, US* a man's tie

necromancer *noun* someone who works with black magic ♦ **necromancy** *noun*

necrophilia *noun* sexual interest in dead bodies

necropolis (*pronounced* nik-**rop**-o-lis) *noun* (*plural* **necropolises**) a cemetery or burial site ℗ Comes from Greek *nekros* meaning 'corpse' + *polis* meaning 'city'

necrosis *noun* the death of living tissue or bone, especially where the blood supply has been interrupted

nectar *noun* **1** the sweet liquid collected from flowers by bees to make honey **2** the drink of the ancient Greek gods **3** a delicious drink

nectarine *noun* a kind of peach with a smooth skin

née (*pronounced* nei) *adjective* born (in stating a woman's surname before her marriage): *Mrs Janet Brown, née Phillips*

need *verb* **1** to be without, be in want of **2** to require ➤ *noun* **1** necessity, needfulness **2** difficulty, want, poverty ℗ Comes from Old English *ned, nied, nyd*

needful *adjective* necessary

needle *noun* **1** a small, sharp piece of steel used in sewing, with a small hole (**eye**) at the top for thread **2** a long, thin piece of metal, wood, etc used eg in knitting **3** a thin tube of steel attached to a hypodermic syringe etc **4** the moving pointer in a compass **5** the long, sharp-pointed leaf of a pine, fir, etc **6** a stylus on a record-player

needless *adjective* unnecessary

needlework *noun* sewing and embroidery

needy *adjective* (**needier, neediest**) poor

ne'er *adjective, formal* never

ne'er-do-well *noun* a lazy, worthless person

nefarious (*pronounced* ni-**feir**-i-us) *adjective* very wicked; villainous, shady

negate *verb* **1** to prove the opposite **2** to refuse to accept, reject (a proposal etc) ℗ Comes from Latin *negare* meaning 'to deny'

negative *adjective* **1** meaning or saying 'no', as an answer **2** of a person, attitude, etc: timid, lacking spirit or ideas **3** *maths* of a number: less than zero **4** *physics* having the kind of electrical charge produced by an excess of electrons **5** *biology* in a direction away from a stimulus (*contrasted with*: **positive**) ➤ *noun* **1** a word or statement by which something is denied **2** the photographic film from which prints are made, in which light objects appear dark and dark objects appear light

negative equity *noun* a situation where the value of a property falls below the value of the mortgage held on it

neglect *verb* **1** to treat carelessly **2** to fail to give proper attention to **3** to fail to do ➤ *noun* lack of care and attention

neglectful *adjective* careless, having a habit of not bothering to do things

negligée noun a women's loose dressing-gown made of thin material

negligent adjective careless, not paying enough attention ♦ **negligence** noun ♦ **negligently** adverb ◷ Comes from Latin negligens meaning 'neglecting'

❗ Do not confuse: **negligent** and **negligible**

negligible adjective not worth thinking about, very small: a negligible amount ◷ Comes from an old spelling of French négligeable meaning 'able to be neglected'

negotiable adjective able to be negotiated

negotiate verb **1** to discuss a subject (with) in order to reach agreement **2** to arrange (a treaty, payment, etc) **3** to get past (an obstacle or difficulty) ♦ **negotiation** noun ♦ **negotiator** noun (meanings 1 and 2)

Negro noun (plural **Negroes**), offensive a Black African, or Black person of African descent

neigh verb to cry like a horse ➤ noun a horse's cry

neighbour or US **neighbor** noun someone who lives near another

neighbourhood noun **1** a district: a poor neighbourhood **2** the surrounding district or area: in the neighbourhood of Paris • **in the neighbourhood of** approximately, nearly

neighbouring adjective near or next in position

neighbourly adjective friendly and helpful

neither adjective & pronoun not either: Neither bus goes that way/Neither can afford it ➤ conjunction (sometimes with **nor**) used to show alternatives in the negative: Neither Bill nor David knew the answer/She is neither eating nor sleeping

ⓘ **Neither** can be followed by a singular or plural verb, although a singular verb is usually regarded as more correct, eg Neither of us likes the idea very much.
Note that **neither** should be paired with **nor**, not with **or**, eg He possessed neither arms nor armour.

nematode noun a tiny, thin worm living in soil, water, plants and animals

nemesis noun (plural **nemeses**) fate, punishment that is bound to follow wrongdoing

◷ After Nemesis, who was the goddess of revenge in Greek mythology

neo- prefix new, recently, or a new or recent form of: neo-Nazi/neonatal ◷ Comes from Greek neos meaning 'new'

neoclassical adjective of an artistic or architectural style imitating the styles of the ancient classical world ♦ **neoclassicism** noun

neocolonialism noun the domination by powerful states of weaker states by means of economic pressure ♦ **neocolonialist** adjective & noun

neo-Darwinism noun, biology a later development of Darwinism, laying greater stress on natural selection

neodymium noun, chemistry (symbol **Nd**) a silvery metallic element, one of the lanthanide series ◷ Comes from didymium, a substance once thought to be an element

Neolithic adjective relating to the later Stone Age

neologism (pronounced nee-ol-o-jism) noun a new word or expression ♦ **neologistic** adjective

neon noun, chemistry (symbol **Ne**) an element in the form of a gas that glows red when electricity is passed through it ◷ From Greek neos meaning 'new'

neonate noun a newborn child ♦ **neonatal** adjective

neon lighting noun a form of lighting in which an electric current is passed through a small quantity of neon

neophyte noun **1** a new convert **2** a novice, a beginner

nephew noun the son of a brother or sister, or of a brother-in-law or sister-in-law

nephritis noun inflammation of a kidney ♦ **nephritic** adjective

nepotism noun the favouring of one's relatives or friends, especially in making official appointments ♦ **nepotist** noun ♦ **nepotistic** adjective ◷ Comes from Latin nepos meaning 'grandson' or 'nephew'

neptunium noun, chemistry (symbol **Np**) a metallic element obtained artificially in nuclear reactors during the production of plutonium ◷ Named after the planet Neptune

nerd noun, informal a socially inept, irritating person

nerve noun **1** anatomy one of the fibres which carry feeling from all parts of the body to the brain **2** courage, coolness **3** informal impudence, cheek ➤ verb to strengthen the nerve or will of

nerve cell noun, anatomy any of the cells in the nervous system (also called: **neurone** or **neuron**)

nerve-racking or **nerve-wracking** adjective causing nervousness or stress

nerves plural noun, informal nervousness or stress

nervous adjective **1** of the nerves: the nervous system **2** easily excited or frightened; timid **3** worried, frightened or uneasy ♦ **nervously**

adverb (meaning 3) ♦ **nervousness** *noun* (meanings 2 and 3)

nervous breakdown *noun* a mental illness attributed loosely to stress, with intense anxiety, low self-esteem and loss of concentration

nervous system *noun, anatomy* the brain, spinal cord and nerves of an animal or human being

nervy *adjective* (**nervier, nerviest**) excitable, jumpy

ness *noun* a headland ⊙ Comes from Anglo-Saxon *næs*

-ness *suffix* forming nouns denoting a state or condition: *happiness/unkindness*

nest *noun* 1 a structure in which birds (and some animals and insects) live and rear their young 2 a shelter, a den ➤ *verb* to build a nest and live in it

nest egg *noun, informal* a sum of money saved up for the future

nestle (*pronounced* **ne**-sl) *verb* 1 to lie close together as in a nest 2 to settle comfortably

nestling (*pronounced* **nest**-ling) *noun* a newly hatched bird

Net *noun, informal* (**the Net**) the Internet

net¹ *noun* 1 a loose arrangement of crossed and knotted cord, string or thread 2 a piece of this, used for catching fish, weaving over the hair, etc, or fitted to a frame to form a goal in some sports 3 fine meshed material, used to make curtains, petticoats, etc 4 *maths* a flat figure made up of polygons which fold and join to form a polyhedron ➤ *verb* (**netting, netted**) 1 to catch or cover with a net 2 to put (a ball) into a net

net² or **nett** *adjective* 1 of profit etc: remaining after expenses and taxes have been paid 2 of weight: not including packaging ➤ *verb* (**netting, netted**) to make by way of profit

netball *noun* a team game in which a ball is thrown into a high net

nether *adjective* lower

nethermost *adjective* lowest

netiquette *noun, computing* etiquette on the Internet, especially in e-mail

net primary productivity or **net primary production** *noun, botany* (*abbrev* **NPP**) the amount of energy produced by a plant minus the energy it uses for respiration (*compare with*: **gross primary productivity**)

nett another spelling of **net**

netting *noun* fabric of netted string, wire, etc

nettle *noun* a plant covered with hairs which sting sharply ➤ *verb* to make angry, provoke

nettle rash a non-technical name for **urticaria**

network *noun* 1 an arrangement of lines crossing one another 2 a widespread organization 3 a system of linked computers, radio stations, etc ➤ *verb* 1 to broadcast on a network 2 to link computer terminals etc to

operate interactively 3 *informal* to build relationships with a number of people

neur- or **neuro-** *prefix* of the nerves: *neuralgia* ⊙ Comes from Greek *neuron* meaning 'nerve'

neural *adjective* relating to the nerves or nervous system

neuralgia *noun* a pain in the nerves, especially in those of the head and face

neurology *noun, medicine* the study of the central nervous system, and the peripheral nerves ♦ **neurological** *adjective* ♦ **neurologist** *noun*

neurone or **neuron** see **nerve cell**

neurosis *noun* (*plural* **neuroses**) 1 a type of mental illness in which the patient suffers from extreme anxiety 2 *informal* an anxiety or obsession

neurotic *adjective* 1 suffering from neurosis 2 in a bad nervous state ➤ *noun* someone suffering from neurosis ♦ **neurotically** *adverb*

neuter *adjective* 1 *grammar* neither masculine nor feminine 2 of an animal: neither male nor female 3 of an animal: infertile, sterile ➤ *verb* to sterilize (an animal)

neutral *adjective* 1 taking no side in a quarrel or war 2 of a colour: not strong or definite 3 of a chemical substance: neither acid nor alkaline 4 *physics* with no positive or negative electrical charge ➤ *noun* 1 a person or a nation that takes no side in a war etc 2 the gear position used when a vehicle is not moving ♦ **neutrality** *noun* (adjective, meaning 1)

neutralize or **neutralise** *verb* 1 to make neutral 2 to make useless or harmless

neutrino (*pronounced* nyoo-**tree**-noh) *noun* (*plural* **neutrinos**), *physics* a subatomic particle with no electrical charge

neutron *noun, physics* an uncharged particle which forms part of the nucleus of an atom (*see also* **electron, proton**)

neutron bomb *noun* a nuclear bomb that kills people by intense radiation but leaves buildings intact

never *adverb* 1 not ever; at no time 2 under no circumstances

nevermore *adverb, formal or literary* never again

never-never *noun, informal* (**the never-never**) the hire-purchase system

nevertheless *adverb* in spite of that: *I hate opera, but I shall come with you nevertheless*

nevus US spelling of **naevus**

new *adjective* 1 recent; not seen or known before 2 not used or worn; fresh 3 of a person's present circumstances, and replacing something in their past: *She has a new boyfriend* ⊙ Comes from Old English *niwe, neowe*

newborn *adjective* just or very recently born

newcomer *noun* someone lately arrived

New Deal *noun* **1** *history* President Franklin D Roosevelt's policies for prosperity and social improvement in the USA after the Great Depression **2** (**new deal**) any new arrangements or conditions considered better than previous ones

New Economic Policy *noun, history* the Soviet economic programme from 1921 to 1928, which allowed some private ownership of business

newfangled *adjective* new and not thought very good

New Liberalism *noun, Brit history* the movement in the Liberal Party at the end of the 19th century towards policies of social reform and welfare

newly *adverb* (*used before past participles*) only recently: *a newly published book*

New Model Unions *plural noun, Brit history* trade unions for skilled workers which flourished during the mid-18th century, and which tended to avoid confrontation with employers

new moon *noun* **1** the moment when the moon is directly in line between the earth and sun and becomes invisible **2** the moon when it becomes visible again as a narrow crescent

news *singular noun* **1** report of a recent event or recent events **2** (**the news**) a report of news on radio, TV, the Internet, etc **3** new information: *Is there any news on Tom's health?*

news agency *noun* an agency that collects news stories and supplies them to newspapers etc

newsagent *noun* a shopkeeper who sells newspapers

newscast *noun* a radio or TV broadcast of news items ♦ **newscaster** *noun*

news conference see **press conference**

newsflash *noun* (*plural* **newsflashes**) a brief announcement of important news that interrupts a radio or TV broadcast

newsgroup *noun, computing* on the Internet, a group of individuals who share information, often on a particular subject

newsletter *noun* a sheet containing news, issued to members of an organization etc

newspaper *noun* a paper printed daily or weekly containing news

newspeak *noun, ironic* the ambiguous language used by politicians and other people who try to persuade

⊙ Comes from *Newspeak*, a form of English used as an official language in George Orwell's novel *Nineteen Eighty-Four*

newsprint *noun* **1** the paper on which

newspapers are printed **2** the ink used to print newspapers

newsreader *noun* a radio or television news announcer

newsworthy *adjective* interesting or important enough to be reported as news

newt *noun* a small lizard-like animal, living on land and in water

New Testament *noun* the part of the Bible concerned with the teachings of Christ and his earliest followers (*compare with*: **Old Testament**)

newton *noun, physics* (symbol **N**) the standard unit used to measure force

new town *noun* a town specially built to relieve overcrowding in nearby cities

next *adjective* nearest, closest in place, time, etc: *the next page* ➤ *adverb* in the nearest place or at the nearest time: *Do that sum next* ⊙ Comes from Old English *nehst* meaning 'nearest'

nexus *noun* (**nexus** or **nexuses**) **1** a connected series or group **2** a bond or link ⊙ From Latin *nectere* meaning 'to bind'

NHS *abbreviation, Brit* National Health Service

NI *abbreviation* **1** National Insurance **2** Northern Ireland

Ni *symbol, chemistry* nickel

niacin (*pronounced* **nai**-as-in) *noun* vitamin B₇ (*also called*: **nicotinic acid**)

nib *noun* a pen point

nibble *verb* to take little bites (of) ➤ *noun* a little bite

NIC *abbreviation* newly industrialized country

nice *adjective* **1** agreeable, pleasant **2** careful, precise, exact: *a nice distinction*

nicely *adverb* pleasantly; very well

nicety (*pronounced* **nais**-e-ti) *noun* (*plural* **niceties**) a small fine detail ● **to a nicety** with great exactness

niche (*pronounced* neesh) *noun* **1** a hollow in a wall for a statue, vase, etc **2** a suitable place in life: *She hasn't yet found her niche* **3** *business* a gap in a market for a type of product

nick *noun* **1** a little cut, a notch **2** *slang* prison, jail ➤ *verb* **1** to cut notches in **2** *slang* to steal

nickel *noun* **1** *chemistry* (symbol **Ni**) a greyish-white metallic element used for mixing with other metals and for plating **2** *US* a 5-cent coin ⊙ Comes from German *Kupfernickel* meaning 'copper devil', so called by miners mistaking it for copper

nickname *noun* an informal name used instead of someone's real name, eg for fun or as an insult

nicotine *noun* a poisonous substance contained in tobacco

⊙ Named after Jean *Nicot*, 16th-century French ambassador who sent tobacco samples back from Portugal

nictitating membrane *noun, biology* in some animals: a transparent membrane which can be drawn across the eye for protection

niece *noun* the daughter of a brother or sister, or of a brother-in-law or sister-in-law

niff *noun, slang* a bad smell

nifty *adjective* (**niftier, niftiest**), *slang* **1** fine, smart, neat **2** speedy, agile

niggardly *adjective* mean, stingy

niggle *verb* to irritate, rankle ➤ *noun* **1** an irritation **2** a minor criticism

niggling *adjective* **1** unimportant, trivial, fussy **2** of a worry or fear: small but always present

nigh *adjective, old* near • **nigh on** or **well nigh** nearly, almost

night *noun* **1** the period of darkness between sunset and sunrise **2** the end of the day, evening **3** darkness ➤ *adjective* **1** of or for night: *the night hours* **2** happening, active, etc at night: *the night shift* ☺ Comes from Old English *niht*

nightcap *noun* **1** a drink taken before going to bed **2** *old* a cap worn in bed at night

nightclub *noun* a club open from the evening until late at night for dancing, drinking, etc (*short form*: **club**)

nightdress (*plural* **nightdresses**) or **nightgown** *noun* a garment worn in bed

nightfall *noun* the beginning of night

nightingale *noun* a small bird, the male of which sings beautifully by night and day

nightly *adjective & adverb* **1** by night **2** every night

nightmare *noun* a frightening dream

☺ The *-mare* ending comes from an old English word meaning 'evil spirit', nightmares being thought to be caused by an evil spirit pressing on the body

night school *noun* educational classes held in the evening, especially for those who work during the day

night shift *noun* a session of work during the night

nightshirt *noun* a garment like a long shirt worn in bed

nihilism (*pronounced* **nai**-hil-izm or **ni**-hil-izm) *noun* **1** belief in nothing, extreme scepticism **2** anarchy; destructiveness ♦ **nihilist** *noun* ♦ **nihilistic** *adjective*

-nik *suffix sometimes derogatory* denoting someone involved with a cause, activity, etc: *peacenik*

nil *noun* nothing

nimble *adjective* quick and neat, agile ♦ **nimbly** *adverb*

nimbus *noun* (*plural* **nimbuses** or **nimbi** – *pronounced* **nim**-bai) a rain cloud

NIMBY or **Nimby** *abbreviation* not in my back yard: denoting an attitude of being willing to have something happen so long as it does not affect you or your locality ♦ **Nimbyism** *noun*

nincompoop *noun* a weak, foolish person

nine *noun* the number 9 ➤ *adjective* 9 in number

ninepins *singular noun* a game in which nine bottle-shaped objects are set up, and knocked down by a ball

nineteen *noun* the number 19 ➤ *adjective* 19 in number

nineteenth *adjective* the last of a series of nineteen ➤ *noun* one of nineteen equal parts

nineties *plural noun* (also **90s, 90's**) **1** the period of time between a person's ninetieth and one hundredth birthdays **2** the range of temperatures between ninety and one hundred degrees **3** the period between the ninetieth years of a century and a new century

ninetieth *adjective* the last of a series of ninety ➤ *noun* one of ninety equal parts

ninety *noun* the number 90 ➤ *adjective* 90 in number

ninja *noun, history* (*plural* **ninja** or **ninjas**) an assassin in feudal Japan, trained in martial arts

ninny *noun* (*plural* **ninnies**) a fool

ninth *adjective* the last of a series of nine ➤ *noun* one of nine equal parts

niobium (*pronounced* nai-**oh**-bi-um) *noun, chemistry* (symbol **Nb**) a relatively unreactive, soft, greyish-blue, metallic element ☺ Comes from *Niobe*, daughter of Tantalus in Greek mythology, because it was discovered in the mineral tantalite

nip *verb* (**nipping, nipped**) **1** to pinch, squeeze tightly **2** to be stingingly painful **3** to bite, cut (off) **4** to halt the growth of, damage (plants etc) **5** *informal* to go nimbly or quickly ➤ *noun* **1** a pinch **2** a sharp coldness in the weather: *a nip in the air* **3** a small amount: *a nip of whisky*

nipper *noun, informal* **1** a child, a youngster **2** (**nippers**) pincers, pliers

nipple *noun* the pointed part of the breast from which a baby sucks milk

nippy *adjective* (**nippier, nippiest**), *informal* **1** speedy, nimble **2** frosty, very cold

Nirvana *noun* **1** the state to which a Buddhist or Hindu aspires as the best attainable **2** (**nirvana**) a blissful state

nit *noun* **1** the egg of a louse or other small insect **2** *informal* an idiot, a nitwit

nit-picking *noun* petty criticism or fault-finding ♦ **nit-pick** *verb* ♦ **nit-picker** *noun*

nitrate *noun, chemistry* a substance formed from nitric acid

nitre *noun, chemistry* potassium nitrate ☺ Comes from French, ultimately from Greek *nitron* meaning 'sodium carbonate'

nitric *noun, chemistry* containing nitrogen

nitric acid noun, chemistry a strong acid containing nitrogen

nitride noun, chemistry a compound which contains nitrogen and a metallic element

nitrify verb (**nitrifies, nitrifying, nitrified**), biology, chemistry to convert or be converted into nitrates or nitrites through the action of bacteria ♦ **nitrification** noun

nitrite noun, chemistry a salt or ester of nitrous acid

nitro- prefix, chemistry containing nitrogen: nitrobenzene

nitrogen noun, chemistry (symbol **N**) a gas forming nearly four-fifths of ordinary air ♦ **nitrogenous** adjective ⏱ Comes from nitre + Greek -genes meaning 'born'

nitrogen cycle noun, chemistry a continuous exchange of nitrogen between organisms and the environment

nitrogen fixation noun (shortened to: **fixation**) the conversion of atmospheric nitrogen into nitrogen compounds, either naturally (in plants) or artificially (eg in industry)

nitroglycerine noun, chemistry a powerful kind of explosive

nitrous acid noun, chemistry a weak acid containing nitrogen

nitrous oxide noun, chemistry a colourless, odourless gas, used as an anaesthetic (also called: **laughing gas**)

nitwit noun a very stupid person

nivation noun, geography erosion caused by snow, eg freeze-thaw and the carrying of material by melting snow

nivation hollow noun, geography a depression caused by material being eroded by the action of snow

No¹, No. or **no** abbreviation number

No² symbol, chemistry nobelium

no adjective **1** not any: They have no money **2** not a: He is no cheat ➤ adverb not at all: The patient is no better ➤ interjection expressing a negative: Are you feeling better today? No ➤ noun (plural **noes**) **1** a refusal **2** a vote against ● **no way** informal under no circumstances, absolutely not

no-ball noun, cricket a bowled ball disallowed by the rules

nobble verb, slang **1** get hold of **2** persuade, coerce **3** seize, arrest

nobelium (pronounced noh-**bee**-li-um or noh-**bee**-li-um) noun, chemistry (symbol **No**) a radioactive element produced artificially ⏱ Named after the Nobel Institute, Stockholm

Nobel prize noun an annual international prize awarded for achievements in arts, science, politics, etc

noble adjective **1** great and good, fine **2** of aristocratic birth ➤ noun an aristocrat ♦ **nobility** noun **1** the aristocracy **2** goodness, greatness of mind or character ♦ **nobleman, noblewoman** noun ♦ **nobly** adverb

noble gas noun, chemistry one of the gases helium, neon, argon, krypton, xenon and radon, that do not react with other substances (also called: **inert gas**)

nobody pronoun not any person ➤ noun (plural **nobodies**) someone of no importance: just a nobody

nock noun a notch, especially on an arrow or a bow

nocturnal adjective happening or active at night

nocturne noun a piece of music intended to have an atmosphere of night-time

nod verb (**nodding, nodded**) **1** to bend the head forward quickly, often as a sign of agreement **2** to let the head drop in weariness ➤ noun an action of nodding ● **a nodding acquaintance with** a slight knowledge of ● **nod off** to fall asleep

node noun **1** botany the swollen part of a branch or twig where leaf-stalks join it **2** a swelling **3** maths the point where a curve crosses itself **4** physics the point of least movement in a vibrating body **5** computing a location where processing takes place, eg a computer on a network

nodule noun a small rounded lump or swelling

Noel or **Noël** (pronounced noh-**el**) noun Christmas

nog noun an alcoholic drink made with whipped eggs

no-go area noun an area to which access is not allowed

noise noun a sound, often one which is loud or harsh ➤ verb, old to spread (a rumour etc) ♦ **noiseless** adjective ♦ **noisy** adjective (**noisier, noisiest**) making a loud sound

noisome adjective **1** disgusting, stinking **2** harmful, poisonous

nomad noun **1** one of a group of people without a fixed home who wander with their animals in search of pasture **2** someone who wanders from place to place ♦ **nomadic** adjective

no-man's-land noun land owned by no one, especially that lying between two opposing armies

nom de plume noun (plural **noms de plume**) a pen name

nomenclature (pronounced no-**men**-kla-cher) noun **1** a system of naming **2** names

nominal adjective **1** in name only **2** very small: a nominal fee

nominate verb to propose (someone) for a post or for election; appoint ♦ **nomination** noun

nominative *grammar, noun* **1** the form or case of the subject of a verb in some languages **2** a noun etc in this case ➤ *adjective* belonging to or in this case ℗ Comes from Latin *nominativus*, from *nominare* meaning 'to name'

nominee *noun* someone whose name is put forward for a post

-nomy *suffix* forms words relating to different systems of regulation, or to the science and study of how these work: *astronomy/autonomy* (= the power or right of a country or person to regulate themselves) ℗ Comes from Greek *nomos* meaning 'law'

non- *prefix* not (used with many words to change their meaning to the opposite): *non-aggression/non-event/non-smoking* ℗ Comes from Latin *non* meaning 'not'

nonagenarian *noun* someone from ninety to ninety-nine years old

nonagon *noun* a nine-sided figure

nonce *noun*: **for the nonce** for the time being

℗ The phrase was originally *for then ones*, meaning 'for the once', but then it came to be understood as *for the nonce*

nonce-word *noun* a word coined for one particular occasion

nonchalant (*pronounced* **non**-sha-lant) *adjective* not easily roused or upset, cool ♦ **nonchalance** *noun* ♦ **nonchalantly** *adverb*

non-commissioned *adjective* belonging to the lower ranks of army officers, below second-lieutenant

non-committal *adjective* unwilling to express, or not expressing, an opinion

non compos mentis *adjective, often humorous* not of sound mind, insane ℗ From Latin, meaning 'not in command of one's mind'

nonconformist *noun* **1** someone who does not agree with accepted attitudes, modes of behaviour, etc **2** (**Nonconformist**) in England: a Protestant in a church separated from the Church of England ➤ *adjective* **1** not agreeing with accepted attitudes or behaviour **2** (**Nonconformist**) to do with Nonconformists ♦ **nonconformity** *noun*

non-contributory *adjective, Brit* of a pension scheme: paid for by the employer, without contributions from the employee

non-denominational *adjective* not linked with any particular religious denomination

nondescript *adjective* lacking anything noticeable or interesting

none *adverb* not at all: *none the worse* ➤ *pronoun* not one, not any

ⓘ When **none** refers to a number of individual people or things, it can be followed by a singular or a plural verb, depending on whether you are talking about the individuals or the group as a whole, for example *The hotel is half a mile from the beach and none of the rooms overlook the sea* or *None of us has time for much else but the work in hand.*

nonentity *noun* (*plural* **nonentities**) someone of no importance

non-existent *adjective* not existing, not real ♦ **non-existence** *noun*

non-fiction *noun* literature concerning factual characters or events

nonpareil (*pronounced* non-pa-**reil**) *adjective* having no equal; matchless ➤ *noun* a person or thing without equal ℗ From French, from *non-* meaning 'not' + *pareil* meaning 'equal'

nonplussed *adjective* taken aback, confused

non-renewable resource *noun* any naturally occurring substance, eg coal and oil, which forms over such a long period of time that it cannot be replaced

non-resident *noun & adjective* (someone) not living in a country or place ♦ **non-residence** *noun*

non-returnable *adjective* **1** of a bottle or other container: on which a returnable deposit is not paid and which will not be accepted after use by the vendor for recycling **2** of a deposit etc: that will not be returned in case of cancellation etc

nonsense *noun* **1** words that have no sense or meaning **2** foolishness ♦ **nonsensical** *adjective*

non sequitur (*pronounced* non **sek**-wi-tur) *noun* a remark unconnected with what has gone before

℗ A Latin phrase meaning literally 'it does not follow'

non-stop *adjective* going on without a stop

non-violence *noun* refraining from violence on principle ♦ **non-violent** *adjective*

noodle *noun* a long thin strip of pasta, eaten in soup or served with a sauce

nook *noun* **1** a corner **2** a small recess • **every nook and cranny** *informal* everywhere

noon *noun* twelve o'clock midday

no one or **no-one** *pronoun* not any person, nobody

noose *noun* a loop in a rope etc that tightens when pulled

nor *conjunction* (*often with* **neither**) used to show alternatives in the negative: *Neither James nor I can speak French*

Nordic *adjective* **1** relating to Finland or Scandinavia **2** of skiing: involving cross-country and jumping events

norm *noun* a pattern or standard to judge other things from

normal adjective **1** ordinary, usual according to a standard **2** maths perpendicular ♦ **normality** noun ♦ **normally** adverb

Norman noun **1** a person from Normandy, especially one who conquered England in 1066 **2** Norman French, the Normans' dialect of French ➤ adjective relating to the Normans or their language

normative adjective establishing a guiding standard or rules

Norse adjective **1** relating to ancient or medieval Scandinavia **2** relating to Norway ➤ noun **1** the Germanic group of languages of Scandinavia **2** the language used in medieval Norway and its colonies

north noun one of the four chief directions, that to the left of someone facing the rising sun ➤ adjective **1** in or to the north **2** of the wind: from the north ➤ adverb in, to or towards the north: We headed north

north-east noun the point of the compass midway between north and east

northerly adjective **1** of the wind: coming from the north **2** in or towards the north

northern adjective of the north

northern lights plural noun (**the northern lights**) the **aurora borealis**

North Pole noun the point on the Earth's surface that represents the northern end of its axis

northward or **northwards** adjective & adverb towards the north

north-west noun the point of the compass midway between north and west

nose noun **1** the part of the face by which people and animals smell and breathe **2** a jutting-out part, eg the front of an aeroplane ➤ verb **1** to track by smelling **2** informal to interfere in other people's affairs, pry (into) **3** to push a way through: The ship nosed through the ice

nosedive noun a headfirst dive, especially by an aeroplane ➤ verb to dive headfirst

nosegay noun, old a bunch of flowers

nosey or **nosy** adjective (**nosier, nosiest**) inquisitive, fond of prying ♦ **nosiness** noun

nosey parker or **nosy parker** noun, informal a nosy person, a busybody

nosh informal, noun food ◷ From Yiddish, from German nascheln meaning 'to nibble at something'

no-show noun someone expected who does not arrive

nostalgia noun **1** a longing for past times **2** a longing for home ♦ **nostalgic** adjective ♦ **nostalgically** adverb

nostril noun either of the two openings of the nose

nostrum noun **1** a cure-all **2** a pet solution or remedy ◷ From Latin, meaning 'our own (make or brand)'

not adverb expressing a negative, refusal or denial: I am not going/Give it to me, not to him/I did not break the window

notability noun (plural **notabilities**) a well-known person

notable adjective worth taking notice of; important, remarkable ➤ noun an important person ♦ **notably** adverb

notary noun (plural **notaries**) an official who sees that written documents are drawn up in a way required by law

notation noun **1** the showing of numbers, musical sounds, etc by signs: sol-fa notation/mathematical notation **2** a set of such signs

notch noun (plural **notches**) a small V-shaped cut ➤ verb to make a notch ♦ **notched** adjective

note noun **1** (often **notes**) a brief written record made for later reference **2** a short explanation **3** a short letter **4** a piece of paper used as money: £5 note **5** a single sound or the sign standing for it in music **6** a key on the piano etc ➤ verb **1** to make a note of **2** to notice • **of note** well-known, distinguished • **take note of** to notice particularly

notebook noun **1** a small book for taking notes **2** a small laptop computer

noted adjective well-known

notepaper noun writing paper

noteworthy adjective notable, remarkable

NOT gate noun, computing a circuit that reverses the input it receives (compare with: **AND gate, OR gate**)

nothing noun **1** no thing, not anything **2** nought, zero **3** something of no importance ➤ adverb not at all: He's nothing like his father

nothingness noun **1** non-existence **2** space, emptiness

notice noun **1** a public announcement **2** attention: The colour attracted my notice **3** a period of warning given before leaving, or before dismissing someone from, a job ➤ verb to see, observe, take note of • **at short notice** with little warning or time for preparation • **take notice** to pay attention

noticeable adjective easily noticed, standing out ♦ **noticeably** adverb

notifiable adjective that must be reported: a notifiable disease

notify verb (**notifies, notifying, notified**) **1** to inform **2** to give notice of ♦ **notification** noun

notion noun **1** an idea **2** a vague belief or opinion ◷ Comes from Latin notio meaning 'an idea'

notional adjective **1** existing in imagination only **2** hypothetical ♦ **notionally** adverb

notochord noun, zoology a flexible, rod-like

structure supporting the body in some more primitive animals

notorious *adjective* well known because of badness: *a notorious criminal* ◆ **notoriety** *noun*

not-out *adjective & adverb, cricket* at the end of the innings without having been put out

not proven *noun, Scots law* a verdict delivered when there is not enough evidence to convict the accused

notwithstanding *preposition* in spite of: *Notwithstanding his poverty, he refused all help*

nougat (*pronounced* **noo**-gah or **nug**-et) *noun* a sticky kind of sweet containing nuts etc

nought *noun* the figure 0, zero

! Do not confuse with: **naught**

noun *noun, grammar* the word used as the name of someone or something, eg *John* and *tickets* in the sentence *John bought the tickets*

nourish *verb* 1 to feed 2 to encourage the growth of

nourishing *adjective* giving the body what is necessary for health and growth

nourishment *noun* 1 food 2 an act of nourishing

nous (*pronounced* nows) *noun, informal* common sense ○ Comes from Greek meaning 'mind'

nouveau riche (*pronounced* noo-voh **reesh**) *noun* (*plural* **nouveaux riches** – *pronounced* noo-voh **reesh**) someone who has recently acquired wealth but not good taste

nova *noun* (*plural* **novae** – *pronounced* **noh**-vee – or **novas**) a star that suddenly increases in brightness for a time

novel (*pronounced* **nov**-el) *adjective* new and strange ➤ *noun* a book telling a long story

novelist (*pronounced* **nov**-el-ist) *noun* a writer of novels

novella (*pronounced* no-**vel**-a) *noun* a short story or short novel ○ Comes from Italian

novelty (*pronounced* **nov**-el-ti) *noun* (*plural* **novelties**) 1 something new and strange 2 newness 3 a small, cheap souvenir or toy

November *noun* the eleventh month of the year

○ From a Latin word meaning 'ninth', because November was originally the ninth month of the year, before January and February were added

novena (*pronounced* no-**vee**-na) *noun, RC Church* a series of prayers and services held over nine days ○ Comes from Latin *noveni* meaning 'nine each'

novice *noun* a beginner

now *adverb* 1 at the present time: *I can see him now* 2 immediately before the present time: *I*

thought of her just now 3 in the present circumstances: *I can't go now because my mother is ill* ➤ *conjunction* (often **now that**) because, since: *You can't go out now that it's raining* • **now and then** or **now and again** sometimes, from time to time

nowadays *adverb* in present times, these days

nowhere *adverb* not in, or to, any place

no-win *adjective* of a situation: in which you are bound to lose or fail

noxious *adjective* harmful: *noxious fumes* ○ Comes from Latin *noxius* meaning 'hurtful'

! Do not confuse with: **obnoxious**

nozzle *noun* a spout fitted to the end of a pipe, tube, etc

Np *symbol, chemistry* neptunium

NPP *abbreviation, botany* net primary productivity or net primary production

NSPCC *abbreviation* National Society for the Prevention of Cruelty to Children

nth *adjective* denoting an indefinite position in a sequence: *to the nth degree*

nuance (*pronounced* **nyoo**-ons) *noun* a slight difference in meaning or colour etc

nub *noun* 1 a small lump, a knob 2 (**the nub**) the central and most important point: *the nub of the argument*

nubile *adjective* of a young woman: attractive, and old enough to be sexually mature

nuclear *adjective* 1 of a nucleus, especially that of an atom 2 produced by the splitting of the nuclei of atoms

nuclear energy *noun* energy released or absorbed during reactions taking place in atomic nuclei

nuclear family *noun* a family unit made up of mother, father and children

nuclear fission *noun, physics* the spontaneous or induced disintegration of a heavy atomic nucleus into two or more lighter fragments, with a release of nuclear energy

nuclear fusion *noun, physics* the process in which a new, heavy atomic nucleus is produced when two lighter nuclei combine with each other, with a release of nuclear energy

nuclear missile *noun* a missile whose warhead is an atomic bomb

nuclear physics *singular noun* the study of atomic nuclei, especially relating to the generation of nuclear energy

nuclear power *noun* power, especially electricity, obtained from reactions by nuclear fission or nuclear fusion

nuclear reaction *noun, physics* a process of nuclear fusion or nuclear fission

nuclear reactor *noun, physics* apparatus for producing nuclear energy

nuclear waste *noun* radioactive waste material

nuclear winter *noun* a period without light, heat or growth, predicted as an after-effect of nuclear war

nuclease (*pronounced* **nyoo**-klee-eiz) *noun, biochemistry* any enzyme that catalyses the splitting of the chain of nucleotides comprising a nucleic acid

nucleate *verb* to form, or form something into, a nucleus ➤ *adjective* having a nucleus

nucleic acid *noun, biochemistry* a complex compound, either DNA or RNA, found in all living cells

nucleolus *noun* (*plural* **nucleoli** – *pronounced* nyoo-klee-**oh**-lai), *biology* a round body in the nucleus of most plant and animal cells, involved the production of protein

nucleon *noun, physics* a proton or neutron

nucleonics *singular noun* the study of the uses of radioactivity and nuclear energy

nucleon number same as **mass number**

nucleotide *noun, biochemistry* an organic compound forming part of a DNA or RNA molecule

nucleus *noun* (*plural* **nuclei** – *pronounced* nyoo-klee-ai) **1** *physics* the positively charged central part of an atom **2** *biology* the central part of a plant or animal cell, containing genetic material **3** *chemistry* a stable group of atoms in a molecule acting as a base for the formation of compounds **4** the central part round which something collects or from which it grows: *the nucleus of my book collection*

nuclide *noun, physics* one of two or more atoms that contain the same number of protons and the same number of neutrons in their nuclei

nude *adjective* without clothes, naked ➤ *noun* **1** an unclothed human figure **2** a painting or statue of such a figure • **in the nude** naked

nudge *noun* a gentle push, eg with the elbow or shoulder ➤ *verb: I nudged him*

nudist *noun* someone who is in favour of going without clothes in public ♦ **nudism** *noun*

nudity *noun* the state of being nude

nugatory (*pronounced* **nyoo**-ga-to-ri) *adjective, formal* **1** worthless, trifling **2** ineffective, futile **3** invalid ⊙ Comes from Latin *nugae* meaning 'trifles'

nugget *noun* a lump, especially of gold

nuisance *noun* someone or something annoying or troublesome

nuke *slang, verb* to attack with nuclear weapons ➤ *noun* a nuclear weapon

null *adjective* **1** having no legal force **2** *maths* of a set: having no members, empty • **null and void** having no legal force

null hypothesis *noun, maths* a hypothesis that

is taken to be true until it is disproved

nullify *verb* (**nullifies, nullifying, nullified**) **1** to make useless or of no effect **2** to declare to be null and void

numb *adjective* having lost the power to feel or move ➤ *verb* to make numb ♦ **numbness** *noun*

number *noun* **1** a word or figure showing how many, or showing a position in a series **2** a collection of people or things **3** a single issue of a newspaper or magazine **4** a popular song or piece of music ➤ *verb* **1** to count **2** to give numbers to **3** to amount to in number ⊙ Comes from French *nombre* meaning 'number'

numberless *adjective* more than can be counted

numerable *adjective* able to be numbered or counted

numeral *noun* a figure (eg 1, 2, etc) used to express a number

numerate (*pronounced* **nyom**-e-rat) *adjective* able to do arithmetic ♦ **numeracy** *noun*

numeration *noun* **1** the process of counting or numbering **2** a system of numbering

numerator *noun, maths* the number above the line in vulgar fractions, eg 2 in $\frac{2}{3}$ (*compare with:* **denominator**)

numerical or **numeric** *adjective* of, in, using or consisting of numbers

numerous *adjective* many

numinous *adjective* **1** mysterious, awe-inspiring **2** giving the sense of a deity's presence ⊙ Comes from Latin *numen* meaning 'deity'

numismatics *singular noun* the collection or study of coins ♦ **numismatist** *noun*

numskull *noun* a stupid person

nun *noun* a member of a female religious group living in a convent

nuncio *noun* (*plural* **nuncios**) an ambassador from the pope ⊙ Comes from Latin *nuntius* meaning 'messenger'

nunnery *noun* (*plural* **nunneries**) a house where a group of nuns live, a convent

nuptial *adjective* of marriage

nuptials *plural noun, formal* a wedding ceremony

nurse *noun* **1** someone who looks after sick or injured people, especially in a hospital **2** someone who looks after small children ➤ *verb* **1** to look after sick people etc **2** to give (a baby) milk from the breast **3** to hold or look after with care: *He nurses his tomato plants* **4** to encourage (feelings) in yourself: *nursing her wrath*

nursery *noun* (*plural* **nurseries**) **1** a room for young children **2** a place where young plants are reared **3** a nursery school

nursery school *noun* a school for very young children

nursery slopes *plural noun, skiing* lower, more

gentle slopes used for practice by beginners

nursing home *noun* a small private hospital, especially one for old people

nurture *verb* to bring up, rear; to nourish: *nurture tenderness* ➤ *noun* care, upbringing; food, nourishment

NUT *abbreviation* National Union of Teachers

nut *noun* **1** a fruit with a hard shell which contains a kernel **2** a small metal block with a hole in it for screwing on the end of a bolt

nutcrackers *plural noun* an instrument for cracking nuts open

nutmeg *noun* a hard, aromatic seed used as a spice in cooking

nutrient *noun* a substance which provides nourishment

nutrient cycle *noun* the circulation of nourishing substances among the organisms within an ecosystem

nutriment *noun* nourishment, food

nutrition *noun* **1** the process of taking in nutrients **2** nourishment, food **3** the study of the nourishment provided by food ♦ **nutritional** *adjective*

nutritious *adjective* valuable as food, nourishing

nutritive *adjective* **1** nourishing **2** relating to nutrition

nutshell *noun* the case containing the kernel of a nut • **in a nutshell** expressed very briefly

nutty *adjective* (**nuttier, nuttiest**) **1** containing, or having, the flavour of nuts **2** *informal* mad, insane

nuzzle *verb* **1** to press, rub or caress with the nose **2** to lie close to, snuggle, nestle

NVQ *abbreviation, Brit* National Vocational Qualification

NW *abbreviation* north-west; north-western

nylon *noun* **1** a synthetic material used to make fibres **2** (**nylons**) stockings made of nylon

-nym see -onym

nymph *noun* **1** a mythological female river or tree spirit **2** a beautiful girl **3** *biology* an insect not yet fully developed

nymphomania *noun* excessively strong sexual desire in women ♦ **nymphomaniac** *noun*

NZ *abbreviation* New Zealand

O¹ *noun, medicine* the name of a blood group

O² *symbol, chemistry* oxygen

o or **oh** *interjection* expressing surprise, admiration, pain, etc

oaf *noun* (*plural* **oafs**) a stupid or clumsy person ♦ **oafish** *adjective*

oak *noun* **1** a tree which produces acorns as fruit **2** its hard wood ♦ **oak** or **oaken** *adjective* made of oak

OAP *abbreviation* **1** Old Age Pension, money paid by the government to people who have retired **2** Old Age Pensioner, an elderly, retired person

oar *noun* a pole for rowing, with a flat blade at one end ➤ *verb* to row • **put your oar in** to interfere in

oarsman or **oarswoman** *noun* (*plural* **oarsman** or **oarswomen**) a person who rows

oasis *noun* (*plural* **oases** – *pronounced* oh-**ei**-seez) a place in a desert where water is found and trees etc grow

oat *noun* **1** a type of grassy plant **2** (**oats**) the grains of this plant, used as food

oatcake *noun* a thin, flat biscuit made of oatmeal

oath *noun* (*plural* **oaths** – *pronounced* ohdhz) **1** a solemn promise to speak the truth, keep your word, be loyal, etc **2** a swear-word

oatmeal *noun* **1** meal made by grinding oat grains **2** the pale yellowish-brown colour of this meal

OB *abbreviation* outside broadcast

obbligato (*pronounced* ob-li-**gah**-toh) *noun* (*plural* **obbligatos** or **obbligati** – *pronounced* ob-li-**gah**-tee), *music* an accompaniment that is an essential part of a piece of music

obdurate *adjective* **1** hard-hearted **2** stubborn ♦ **obduracy** *noun*

OBE *abbreviation* Officer of the Order of the British Empire, a special honour in the UK, given for work that has helped the country

obedience *noun* **1** the act of obeying **2** willingness to obey

obedient *adjective* obeying, ready to obey ♦ **obediently** *adverb*

obeisance (*pronounced* oh-**bei**-sans) *noun* a bow or curtsy showing respect

obelisk *noun* a tall four-sided pillar with a pointed top

obese *adjective* abnormally fat ♦ **obesity** *noun*

obey *verb* to do what you are told to do

obituary *noun* (*plural* **obituaries**) a notice in a newspaper etc of someone's death, sometimes with a brief biography

object *noun* (*pronounced* **ob**-jekt) **1** something that can be seen or felt **2** an aim, a purpose: *The object of the exercise is to make Internet access available to everyone* **3** *grammar* the word in a sentence which stands for the person or thing on which the action of the verb is done, eg *me* in the sentence *He hit me* **4** *maths* an element in the domain of a function, to be mapped onto the codomain **5** *computing* an entity that can be individually manipulated, eg a command button or picture ➤ *verb* (*pronounced* ob-**jekt**) (**object to**) to feel or show disapproval of something

object code *noun, computing* the translated version of source code, run from the operating system

objection *noun* **1** the act of objecting **2** a reason for objecting

objectionable *adjective* nasty, disagreeable

objective *adjective* not influenced by personal interests, fair (*contrasted with*: **subjective**) ➤ *noun* aim, purpose, goal ♦ **objectively** *adverb* ♦ **objectivity** *noun*

object lesson *noun* an instructive experience or event that provides a practical example of a principle or ideal

objector *noun* someone who objects to something

obligate *verb* **1** to bind someone by contract or by duty **2** to bind someone by gratitude: *I felt obligated to help after he had been so kind* ➤ *adjective, biology* of an organism: limited to specific functions and conditions

obligation *noun* **1** a promise or duty by which someone is bound: *under an obligation to help* **2** a debt of gratitude for a favour received

obligatory (*pronounced* ob-**lig**-at-o-ri) *adjective* required to be done with no exceptions by law, rule or custom

oblige *verb* **1** to force, compel: *We were obliged to go home* **2** to do a favour or service to: *Oblige me by shutting the door*

obliged *adjective* owing or feeling gratitude for a favour or service done

obliging *adjective* ready to help others

oblique *adjective* **1** slanting **2** *maths* of lines or planes: not at a right angle **3** *maths* of an angle:

not a right angle or multiple of a right angle **4** indirect, not straight or straightforward: *an oblique reference* ◆ **obliquely** *adverb*

obliterate *verb* **1** to blot out (writing etc), efface **2** to destroy completely ◆ **obliteration** *noun*

oblivion *noun* **1** forgetfulness, unconsciousness **2** the state of being forgotten

oblivious *adjective* unaware, unconscious, forgetful

oblong *noun* a rectangle which is longer than it is wide, eg ▭ ► *adjective* of this shape

obnoxious *adjective* offensive, causing dislike ◆ **obnoxiously** *adverb* ⊕ Comes from Latin *obnoxius* meaning 'liable to punishment' or 'guilty of'

❗ Do not confuse with: **noxious**

oboe *noun* (*plural* **oboes**) a high-pitched woodwind instrument

⊕ From a French word meaning literally 'high wood'

oboist *noun* someone who plays the oboe

obscene *adjective* **1** sexually indecent, lewd **2** disgusting, repellent

obscenity *noun* (*plural* **obscenities**) **1** the state or quality of being obscene: *the obscenity of war* **2** an obscene act or word: *The youths shouted obscenities at the police*

obscure *adjective* **1** dark **2** not clear or easily understood **3** unknown, not famous: *an obscure poet* ► *verb* **1** to darken **2** to make less clear

obscurity *noun* **1** the state of being difficult to see or understand **2** the state of being unknown or forgotten

obsequious *adjective* submissive and fawning

observance *noun* the act of obeying or keeping (a law, tradition, etc)

observant *adjective* good at noticing

observation *noun* **1** the act of seeing and noting; attention **2** a remark **3** a result obtained from an experiment

observatory *noun* (*plural* **observatories**) a place for making observations of the stars, weather, etc

observe *verb* **1** to notice **2** to watch with attention **3** to remark (that) **4** to obey (a law etc) **5** to keep, preserve: *observe a tradition* ◆ **observer** *noun*

obsess *verb* to fill the mind completely

obsession *noun* **1** a feeling or idea which someone cannot stop thinking about **2** the state of being obsessed ◆ **obsessional** *adjective*

obsessive *adjective* **1** forming an obsession **2** having or likely to have an obsession

obsidian *noun* a shiny black glass formed from volcanic lava

obsolescence *noun* being obsolescent

obsolescent *adjective* going out of date ⊕ Comes from Latin *obsolescere* meaning 'to go out of use, wear out'

obsolete *adjective* **1** gone out of use **2** *biology* of organs etc: no longer working or fully developed ⊕ Comes from Latin *obsoletus* meaning 'grown old, worn out, gone out of use'

❗ Do not confuse: **obsolete** and **obsolescent**

obstacle *noun* something which stands in the way and hinders

obstacle race *noun* a race in which obstacles have to be passed, climbed, etc

obstetric or **obstetrical** *adjective* of obstetrics

obstetrician *noun* a doctor trained in obstetrics

obstetrics *singular noun* the branch of medicine and surgery dealing with pregnancy and childbirth

obstinacy *noun* stubbornness

obstinate *adjective* **1** of a person: rigidly sticking to decisions or opinions and unwilling to be influenced by persuasion **2** difficult to deal with, defeat or remove: *obstinate stains*

obstreperous *adjective* noisy, unruly

obstruct *verb* **1** to block or close **2** to hold back or hinder ◆ **obstruction** *noun*

obstructive *adjective* causing or meant to cause an obstruction

obtain *verb* **1** to get, gain **2** to be in use, be valid: *That rule still obtains* ◆ **obtainable** *adjective* (meaning 1)

obtrude *verb* **1** to be or become too noticeable **2** to thrust (yourself or your opinions) forward when not wanted ◆ **obtrusion** *noun*

obtrusive *adjective* **1** too noticeable **2** pushy, impudent

obtuse *adjective* **1** *maths* of an angle: greater than 90° and less than 180° (*compare with*: **acute, reflex**) **2** blunt, not pointed **3** stupid, slow to understand

obverse *noun* the side of a coin showing the head or main design

obvious *adjective* easily seen or understood; plain, evident

obviously *adverb* in an obvious way; as is obvious, clearly

occasion *noun* **1** a particular time: *on that occasion* **2** a special event: *a great occasion* **3** a cause, a reason: *You had no occasion to get cross* **4** opportunity ► *verb* to cause

occasional *adjective* happening or used now and then ◆ **occasionally** *adverb*

Occident *noun* (**the Occident**) the West

occidental *adjective* from or relating to the Occident; western

occluded front *noun, meteorology* the final

stage in an atmospheric depression, when a cold front catches up with and overtakes a warm front, lifting the warm air mass off the ground (*also called*: **occlusion**)

occult *adjective* **1** secret, mysterious **2** supernatural ▸ *noun* (**the occult**) the knowledge and study of magical, mystical and supernatural things

occupancy *noun* (*plural* **occupancies**) the act, fact or period of occupying (a house, flat, etc)

occupant *noun* a person who occupies, has, or takes possession of something, not always the owner

occupation *noun* **1** the act of occupying or state of being occupied: *the students' occupation of the building* **2** an activity that occupies someone's attention or free time **3** someone's trade or job **4** the act of taking and keeping control of a foreign country with military forces: *the army's occupation of the city*

occupational therapy *noun* the treatment of a mental or physical disease or injury by a course of suitable activities

occupier *noun* someone who lives in a building, as a tenant or owner

occupy *verb* (**occupies, occupying, occupied**) **1** to live in **2** to keep busy **3** to take up, fill (space, time, etc) **4** to seize, capture (a town, country, etc)

occur *verb* (**occurring, occurred**) **1** to happen **2** to appear, be found • **occur to someone** to come into their mind: *That never occurred to me* ♦ **occurrence** *noun*

ocean *noun* **1** the expanse of salt water surrounding all the land masses of the earth **2** one of five main divisions of this, ie the Atlantic, Pacific, Indian, Arctic or Antarctic

oceanic *adjective* **1** relating to the ocean **2** *biology* formed or found in the ocean beyond a continental shelf

oceanic crust *noun, geography* that part of the earth's crust that is normally beneath ocean, consisting of sediments and basalt

ocean trench *noun, geography* a long narrow steep-sided depression in the floor of an ocean, especially one that runs parallel to a continent

ocelot *noun* a wild American cat like a small leopard

oche (*pronounced* ok-ee) *noun* the line on the floor behind which a darts player must stand to throw

ochre or *US* **ocher** (*pronounced* oh-ker) *noun* a fine pale-yellow or red clay, used for colouring

o'clock *adverb* used after a number from one to twelve: specifying the time, indicating the number of hours after midday or midnight

OCR *abbreviation, computing* optical character recognition, a computer's ability to read written or printed letters or numbers

octa- also **octo-, oct-** *prefix* eight: *octave/octopus/October* (which was the eighth month in the Roman calendar) ⊙ Comes from Latin and Greek *octo* meaning 'eight'

octagon *noun* an eight-sided figure

octagonal *adjective* having eight sides

octahedron (*pronounced* ok-ta-**hee**-dron) *noun* (*plural* **octahedrons** or **octahedra**) a solid figure with eight faces

octal *adjective, maths* containing or having the number 8 as a basis

octane *noun* a colourless liquid found in petroleum and used in petrol

octave *noun, music* a range of eight notes, eg from one C to the next C above or below it

octavo *noun* (*plural* **octavos**) a book folded to give eight leaves to each sheet of paper

octet *noun* a group of eight things which go together eg the first eight lines of a sonnet or a group of eight singers

octo- see **octa-**

October *noun* the tenth month of the year

⊙ From a Latin word meaning 'eighth', because October was originally the eighth month of the year, before January and February were added

octogenarian *noun* someone from eighty to eighty-nine years old

octopus *noun* (*plural* **octopuses**) a sea creature with eight arms

ocular *adjective* of or relating to the eye

oculist *noun* someone who specializes in diseases and defects of the eye

OD (*pronounced* oh-**dee**) *noun* (*plural* **ODs** or **OD's**) an overdose of drugs ▸ *verb* (**OD's, OD'd, OD'ing**) to take a drug overdose

odd *adjective* **1** of a number: leaving a remainder of one when divided by two, eg the numbers 3, 17, 31 (*contrasted with*: **even**) **2** unusual, strange **3** not one of a matching pair or group, left over: *an odd glove/wearing odd socks*

oddball *noun* a strange or eccentric person

oddity *noun* (*plural* **oddities**) **1** queerness, strangeness **2** a strange person or thing

odd jobs *plural noun* jobs of different kinds, done occasionally and not part of regular employment

oddments *plural noun* scraps left over from a larger quantity: *oddments of fabric*

odds *plural noun* **1** the chances of something happening: *The odds are he will win* **2** difference: *It makes no odds* • **at odds** quarrelling • **odds and ends** small objects of different kinds and with little value

odds-on *adjective* very likely to win, succeed or happen

ode *noun* a type of poem, often written to

someone or something: *ode to autumn*

Oder-Neisse Line (*pronounced* **oo**-der **nais**-*i*) *noun, history* the Polish-German border drawn by the World War II Allies in 1944–5, which gave a sizable amount of German territory to Poland

odious *adjective* hateful ✦ **odiously** *adverb*

odium *noun* strong dislike, hatred

odontology *noun* the study of the teeth ✦ **odontologist** *noun*

odour *noun* smell, either pleasant or unpleasant

odourless *adjective* without smell

odyssey *noun* (*plural* **odysseys**) a long, adventurous journey

oedema (*pronounced* i-**dee**-ma) *noun* (*plural* **oedemata** or **oedemas**) *medicine* an abnormal accumulation of fluid within body tissues, causing swelling

Oedipus complex (*pronounced* **ee**-di-p*u*s) *noun, psychiatry* the repressed sexual desire of a son for his mother

o'er *preposition & adverb, poetic* over

oesophagus (*pronounced* ee-**sof**-ag-*u*s) or *US* **esophagus** (*pronounced* i-**sof**-ag-*u*s) *noun* the narrow muscular tube through which food passes from the mouth to the stomach

oestrogen (*pronounced* **ees**-tro-jen) or *US* **estrogen** (*pronounced* **es**-tro-jen) *noun* a female sex hormone which regulates the menstrual cycle, prepares the body for pregnancy, etc

oestrus (*pronounced* **ees**-trus) or *US* **estrus** (*pronounced* **es**-trus) *noun* the period during which a female mammal is ready for conceiving; heat

of *preposition* **1** belonging to: *the house of my parents* **2** from (a place, person, etc): *within two miles of his home* **3** from among: *one of my pupils* **4** made from, made up of: *a house of bricks* **5** indicating an amount, a measurement, etc: *a gallon of petrol* **6** about, concerning: *talk of old friends* **7** with, containing: *a class of twenty children/a cup of coffee* **8** as a result of: *die of hunger* **9** indicating removal or taking away: *robbed her of her jewels* **10** indicating a connection between an action and its object: *the joining of the pieces* **11** indicating character, qualities, etc: *a man of good taste/It was good of you to come* **12** *US* (in telling the time) before, to: *ten of eight*

off *adverb* **1** away from a place, or from a particular state, position, etc: *He walked off muttering/Switch the light off* **2** entirely, completely: *Finish off your work* ➤ *adjective* **1** cancelled: *The holiday is off* **2** rotten, bad: *The meat is off* **3** not working, not on: *The control is in the off position* **4** not quite pure in colour: *off-white* ➤ *preposition* **1** not on, away from: *fell off the table* **2** taken away: *10% off the usual price* **3**

below the normal standard: *off his game* • **be off** to go away, leave quickly • **off and on** occasionally • **off the cuff** see **cuff** • **off the wall** see **wall**

offal *noun* some internal organs of an animal (heart, liver, etc), used as food

off-beat *adjective* not standard, eccentric

off-chance *noun* a slight chance • **on the off-chance** just in case

off-colour *adjective* not feeling well

offence or *US* **offense** *noun* **1** displeasure, hurt feelings **2** a crime, a sin • **take offence at** to be angry or feel hurt at

offend *verb* **1** to hurt the feelings of; insult, displease **2** to do wrong

offender *noun* a person who has committed an offence

offensive *noun* **1** the position of someone who attacks: *go on the offensive* **2** an attack ➤ *adjective* **1** insulting, disgusting **2** used for attack or assault: *an offensive weapon*

offer *verb* **1** to put forward (a gift, payment, etc) for acceptance or refusal **2** to lay (a choice, chance, etc) before **3** to say that you are willing to do something ➤ *noun* **1** an act of offering **2** a bid of money **3** something proposed • **under offer** of a property etc for sale: for which a buyer has made an offer, but the contracts are still to be signed

offering *noun* **1** a gift **2** a collection of money in church

offertory *noun* (*plural* **offertories**) **1** money collected during a church service **2** the offering of bread and wine to God during the Eucharist **3** a hymn sung while this is happening

offhand *adjective* **1** said or done without thinking or preparing **2** rude, curt ➤ *adverb* without preparation; impromptu: *I can't remember his name offhand*

office *noun* **1** a place where business is carried on **2** the people working in such a place **3** a duty, a job **4** a position of authority, especially in the government **5** (**offices**) services, helpful acts

officer *noun* **1** someone who carries out a public duty **2** someone holding a commission in the armed forces **3** a policeman or policewoman

official *adjective* **1** done or given out by those in power: *an official announcement/official action* **2** forming part of the tasks of a job or office: *official duties* **3** having full and proper authority ➤ *noun* someone who holds an office in the service of the government etc

! Do not confuse with: **officious**.
Official is a neutral adjective showing neither approval nor disapproval, and it is used most often with reference to position or authority rather than people's characters.

officially *adverb* **1** as an official, formally **2** as announced or said in public (though not necessarily truthfully)

officiate *verb* to perform a duty or service, especially as a clergyman at a wedding etc

officious *adjective* fond of interfering, especially in a pompous way ♦ **officiously** *adverb*

❗ Do not confuse with: **official**.
Officious is a negative adjective showing disapproval, and it is used to describe people and their characters.

offing *noun*: **in the offing** expected to happen soon, forthcoming

off-key *adjective & adverb* in the wrong key; out of tune

off-licence *noun* a shop selling alcohol which must not be drunk on the premises

off-line or **offline** *adjective & adverb, computing* **1** not under the control of the central processing unit **2** not switched on or connected (*compare with*: **on-line**)

offload *verb* **1** to unload **2** to get rid of (something) by passing it on to someone else

offpeak *adjective* not at the time of highest use or demand: *an offpeak travel card*

off-putting *adjective* unpleasant, distracting

off-road *adjective & adverb* **1** of vehicle use: not on public roads but on rough terrain **2** of a car, bike, etc: suitable for such use

offset *verb* to weigh against, make up for: *The cost was partly offset by a grant*

offshoot *noun* **1** a shoot growing out of the main stem **2** a small business, project, etc created out of a larger one: *an offshoot of an international firm*

offshore *adjective & adverb* **1** in or on the sea close to the coast **2** at a distance from the shore **3** from the shore: *offshore winds*

offside *adjective & adverb* **1** (*pronounced* of-**said**) *sport* illegally ahead of the ball, eg in football, in an illegal position between the ball and the opponent's goal (*contrasted with*: **onside**) **2** (*pronounced* **of**-said) of the side of a vehicle: nearest to the centre of the road (*contrasted with*: **nearside**): *the offside wing mirror* **3** (*pronounced* **of**-said) *cricket* the half of the field on the side opposite to where the batsman stands when waiting to receive the ball (*contrasted with*: **legside**)

off-site *adjective & adverb* working, happening, etc away from a working site

offspring *noun* **1** someone's child or children **2** the young of animals etc

offstage *adjective & adverb, theatre* not on the stage and not seen by the audience

off-the-peg *adjective* of clothes: ready to wear

off-the-shelf *adjective* **1** immediately available **2** ready to use

off-the-wall *adjective, informal* of humour, behaviour: outlandish

oft *adverb, poetic* often

often *adverb* many times

ogle *verb* to look at (someone or something) in an admiring or amorous way

ogre or **ogress** *noun* **1** a mythological giant that eats people **2** someone extremely frightening or threatening

oh another spelling of **o**

ohm *noun* (symbol Ω) the standard unit of electrical resistance

🕐 Named after Georg *Ohm* (1787–1854), German physicist

OHMS *abbreviation* On Her (or His) Majesty's Service, often printed on mail from government departments

Ohm's law *noun, physics* a law which states that the direct current flowing in an electrical circuit is directly proportional to the voltage applied to the circuit, and inversely proportional to the resistance of the circuit

-oholic *see* **-aholic**

-oid *suffix* forms technical terms containing the meaning 'like': *anthropoid/android* (= a humanlike robot)/*tabloid* (= originally a trademark for a medicine in tablet form) 🕐 Comes from Greek *eidos* meaning 'form'

oil *noun* **1** a greasy liquid obtained from plants (eg olive oil), from animals (eg whale oil), and from minerals (eg petroleum) **2** (**oils**) oil paints ➤ *verb* to smear with oil, put oil on or in

oilfield *noun* an area where mineral oil is found

oil paint *noun* paint made by mixing a colouring substance with oil

oil painting *noun* a picture painted in oil paints

oil rig *noun* a structure set up for drilling an oil well

oilskin *noun* **1** cloth made waterproof with oil **2** a heavy coat made of this

oil well *noun* a hole drilled into the earth's surface or into the seabed to extract petroleum

oily *adjective* (**oilier, oiliest**) **1** of or like oil **2** obsequious, too friendly or flattering

oink *noun* the noise of a pig ➤ *verb* to make this noise

ointment *noun* a greasy substance rubbed on the skin to soothe, heal, etc

OK or **okay** *interjection, adjective & adverb* all right ♦ **okay** *verb* (**okaying, okayed**) to mark or pass as being acceptable

🕐 The origin of this word is uncertain, but it probably comes from the initial letters of the phrase *oll korrect*, used as a playful way of spelling 'all correct'

okapi (*pronounced* oh-**kah**-pi) *noun* (*plural* **okapis** or **okapi**) an animal related to the giraffe, with a brown coat with black and white horizontal stripes on the hindquarters and upper legs

okra *noun* (a plant that produces) long green seed pods that are cooked and eaten in soups, stews, etc

old *adjective* **1** advanced in age, aged **2** having a certain age: *ten years old* **3** not new, having existed a long time: *an old joke* **4** belonging to the past **5** worn, worn-out **6** out-of-date, old-fashioned **7** of a person's past, replaced by something different in the present: *I preferred my old school to the one I'm at now* • **of old** from the past, from history ⊙ Comes from Old English *ald*

old age *noun* the later part of life

olden *adjective*: **the olden days** past times

Old English *noun* the English language from about 500 AD up to about 1100 or 1150 AD (*also called*: **Anglo-Saxon**)

old-fashioned *adjective* in a style from the past, out-of-date

old guard *noun* the conservative element in an organization etc

old hand *noun* someone with long experience in a job etc

old maid *noun* **1** *derogatory* a spinster **2** a game played by passing and matching playing-cards

Old Testament *noun* the first part of the Christian Bible, containing the Hebrew scriptures (*compare with*: **New Testament**)

old wives' tale *noun* an old superstition, belief or theory that is now considered foolish or unscientific

oleum *noun, chemistry* a solution of sulphur trioxide in sulphuric acid (*also called*: **fuming sulphuric acid**)

olfactory *adjective* of or used for smelling: *olfactory glands*

oligarch (*pronounced* **ol**-ig-ahrk) *noun* a member of an oligarchy

oligarchy (*pronounced* **ol**-ig-ahrk-i) *noun* **1** government by a small exclusive group **2** such a group **3** a state ruled by such a group
♦ **oligarchic** or **oligarchical** *adjective*

Oligocene *adjective* of the geological epoch 38 million to 25 million years ago

olive *noun* **1** a small, oval fruit with a hard stone, which is pressed to produce a cooking oil **2** the Mediterranean tree that bears this fruit
➤ *adjective* of a yellowish-green colour

olive branch *noun* a sign of a wish for peace

olive oil *noun* a pale-yellow oil obtained from olives, used in cooking and in soaps and ointments

-ology see **-logy**

Olympiad *noun* **1** in ancient Greece: a period of four years, the interval from one celebration of the Olympic games to another, used as a way of calculating time **2** a celebration of the Olympic Games **3** a regular international contest, especially in chess or bridge

Olympian *noun* **1** any of the ancient Greek gods thought to live on Mount Olympus in Greece **2** someone who competes in the Olympic Games **3** a godlike person ➤ *adjective* **1** relating to Mount Olympus or to the Greek gods **2** relating to the Olympic Games **3** godlike or condescending

Olympic *adjective* to do with the Olympic Games

Olympic Games *plural noun* **1** games celebrated every four years at Olympia in ancient Greece, that included athletic and artistic competitions **2** an international athletics competition held every four years (*also called*: **Olympics**)

Om see **Aum**

ombudsman *noun* an official appointed to look into complaints against government departments

⊙ From a Swedish word meaning 'administration man', introduced into English in the 1960s

omega (*pronounced* **oh**-mi-ga) *noun* the last letter of the Greek alphabet

omelette or **omelet** *noun* beaten eggs fried in a single layer in a pan

omen *noun* a sign of future events

ominous *adjective* suggesting future trouble
♦ **ominously** *adverb*

omission *noun* **1** something omitted **2** the act of omitting

omit *verb* (**omitting, omitted**) **1** to leave out **2** to fail to do

omni- *prefix* all: *omniscient* (= all-knowing)/ *omnipotent* (= all-powerful) ⊙ Comes from Latin *omnis* meaning 'all'

omnibus *noun* (*plural* **omnibuses**) **1** *old* a bus **2** a book containing several connected items

⊙ A Latin word meaning 'for all', because it originally referred to a vehicle which could seat a large number of people

omnibus edition *noun* a radio or TV programme made up of material from preceding editions of a series

omnipotence *noun* unlimited power

omnipotent (*pronounced* om-**ni**-po-tent) *adjective* **1** of God or a deity: having absolute, unlimited power **2** with very great power or influence ♦ **omnipotence** *noun*

omnipresent *adjective* especially of God or a deity: present everywhere at the same time ♦ **omnipresence** *noun*

omniscient (*pronounced* om-**ni**-si-ent) *adjective* **1** of God or a deity: having infinite knowledge **2** having very great knowledge ♦ **omniscience** *noun*

omnivore *noun* an organism that feeds on both plants and animals ♦ **omnivorous** *adjective*

on *preposition* **1** touching or fixed to the outer or upper side: *on the table* **2** supported by: *standing on one foot* **3** receiving, taking, etc: *suspended on half-pay/on antibiotics* **4** occurring in the course of a specified time: *on the following day* **5** about: *a book on Scottish history* **6** with: *Do you have your cheque book on you?* **7** next to, near: *a city on the Rhine* **8** indicating membership of: *on the committee* **9** in the process or state of: *on sale/on show* **10** by means of: *Can you play that on the piano?* **11** followed by: *disaster on disaster* ➤ *adverb* **1** so as to be touching or fixed to the outer or upper side: *Put your coat on* **2** onwards, further: *They carried on towards home* **3** at a further point: *later on* ➤ *adjective* **1** working, performing: *The television is on* **2** arranged, planned: *Do you have anything on this afternoon?* • **from now on** after this time, henceforth • **on and off** occasionally, intermittently • **on and on** continually • **you're on!** I agree, accept the challenge, etc

once *adverb* **1** at an earlier time in the past: *People once lived in caves* **2** for one time only: *I've been to Paris once in the last two years* ➤ *noun* one time only: *Do it just this once* ➤ *conjunction* when: *Once you've finished, you can go* • **all at once** suddenly • **at once 1** immediately: *Come here at once!* **2** (sometimes **all at once**) at the same time, together: *trying to do several things all at once* • **for once** on this one occasion: *For once, will you do the washing-up?* • **once and for all** for the last time • **once upon a time** at some time in the past

oncogene *noun* a gene that causes a normal cell to develop into a cancerous cell

oncology *noun* the diagnosis and treatment of cancer ♦ **oncologist** *noun*

oncoming *adjective* approaching from the front: *oncoming traffic*

one *noun* **1** the number 1 **2** a particular member of a group: *She's the one I want to meet* ➤ *pronoun* **1** a single person or thing: *one of my cats* **2** in formal or pompous English used instead of **you**, meaning anyone: *One must do what one can* ➤ *adjective* **1** 1 in number, a single: *We had only one reply* **2** identical, the same: *We are all of one mind* **3** some, an unnamed (time etc): *one day soon* • **one another** used when an action takes place between two or more people: *They*

looked at one another ⏱ Comes from Old English *an*

one-off *noun* something made or happening etc on one occasion only

onerous *adjective* heavy, hard to bear or do: *onerous task*

oneself *pronoun* **1** used reflexively: *wash oneself* **2** used for emphasis: *One prefers to feed the dogs oneself*

one-sided *adjective* with one person, side, etc having a great advantage over the other: *a one-sided match*

one-stop *adjective* of a shop etc: able to provide a full range of goods

one-to-one *adjective* in which someone is involved with only one other person: *one-to-one teaching*

one-track *adjective* **1** with a single track **2** of someone's mind: obsessed with one idea

one-way *adjective* for traffic moving in one direction only

ongoing *adjective* continuing: *ongoing talks*

onion *noun* a bulb vegetable with a strong taste and smell • **know your onions** *informal* to know your subject or job well

oniony *adjective* tasting of onions

on-line or **online** *adjective & adverb, computing* **1** under the control of a central processing unit **2** switched on or connected (*compare with*: **off-line**)

onlooker *noun* someone who watches an event, but does not take part in it

only *adverb* **1** not more than: *only two weeks left* **2** alone, solely: *Only you are invited* **3** not longer ago than: *I saw her only yesterday* **4** indicating an unavoidable result: *He'll only be offended if you ask* ➤ *adjective* single, solitary: *an only child* ➤ *conjunction, informal* but, except that: *I'd like to go, only I have to work* • **only too** extremely: *I'm only too pleased to help*

onomatopoeia (*pronounced* on-oh-mat-oh-**pee**-a) *noun* the forming of a word which sounds like the thing it refers to, eg *moo, swish* ♦ **onomatopoeic** *adjective*

onrush *noun* a rush forward

onscreen *adjective & adverb* (relating to information) displayed on a monitor or television screen

onset *noun* **1** beginning **2** an attack

onside see **offside**

onslaught *noun* a fierce attack

onstage *adjective & adverb* on the stage and visible to the audience

onto or **on to** *preposition* to a position on or in • **onto someone** *informal* aware of what they are doing

onus *noun* burden; responsibility

onward *adjective* going forward in place or

time: *the onward march of science* ♦ **onward** or **onwards** *adverb*: *We stumbled onward, close to exhaustion/from four o'clock onwards*

-onym (*pronounced* on-im) or **-nym** *suffix* forms terms containing the idea of 'word' or 'name': *synonym/pseudonym* ⊙ Comes from Greek *onyma* meaning 'a name'

onyx *noun* a precious stone with layers of different colours

oocyte (*pronounced* **oh**-*o*-sait) *noun, biology* a cell that gives rise to an ovum by two meiotic divisions

oodles *plural noun, informal* lots (of), many

oogamy (*pronounced* oh-**og**-a-mi) *noun, biology* sexual reproduction in which a large female gamete is fertilized by a smaller male gamete

oogenesis (*pronounced* oh-o-**jen**-i-sis) *noun, biology* the production and development of an ovum in the ovary

oospore (*pronounced* **oh**-*o*-spawr) *noun, biology* a fertilized ovum

ooze *verb* **1** to flow gently or slowly: *The mud oozed between her toes* **2** to exude: *He oozed charm* ➤ *noun* **1** soft mud **2** a gentle flow

opacity *noun* opaqueness

opal *noun* a bluish-white precious stone, with flecks of various colours

opalescent *noun* milky and iridescent

opaque *adjective* not able to be seen through ♦ **opaqueness** *noun*

OPEC *abbreviation* Organization of the Petroleum-Exporting Countries, an association that negotiates with oil companies on production, prices, etc

open *adjective* **1** not shut, allowing entry or exit **2** not enclosed or fenced **3** showing the inside or inner part; uncovered **4** not blocked **5** free for all to enter **6** honest, frank **7** of land: without many trees **8** *maths* of a set: not including the limits that define that set, eg the set rational numbers greater than 1 and less than 5 ➤ *verb* **1** to make open; unlock **2** to begin • **in the open 1** out-of-doors, in the open air **2** widely known, not secret • **open to** likely or willing to receive: *open to attack/open to suggestions* • **with open arms** warmly, enthusiastically: *She was welcomed with open arms*

open air *noun* (**the open air**) any place not indoors or underground

open-air *adjective* outside; in the open air: *an open-air swimming pool*

open-and-shut *adjective* easily proved, decided or solved: *an open-and-shut case*

open book *noun* someone who has no secrets and can be easily understood

open-cast *adjective* of a mine: excavating from the surface downwards

open day *noun* a day when people can visit an institution (eg a school) that is usually closed to them

open-ended *adjective* without definite limits: *an open-ended agreement*

opener *noun* **1** something that opens: *a tin opener* **2** an opening remark

open-heart *adjective* of surgery: performed on a heart which has been temporarily stopped, with blood being circulated by a heart-lung machine

opening *noun* **1** a hole, a gap **2** an opportunity **3** a vacant job **4** the beginning of something

openly *adverb* without trying to hide or conceal anything

open-minded *adjective* ready to consider or take up new ideas

open-plan *adjective* with large rooms, undivided by walls or partitions: *an open-plan office/an open-plan school*

open prison *noun* a prison where prisoners who are not dangerous or violent have more freedom of movement than in a normal prison

open skill *noun* a physical skill that can be affected by external forces, eg dribbling past defenders in a ball game

open-source *adjective, computing* **1** of software: with its basic code freely available **2** of programming: using open-source software that can be developed, tested, etc by many programmers working together

opera[1] *noun* **1** a play in which the characters sing accompanied by an orchestra **2** the score or libretto etc of such a work **3** operas as an art form ♦ **operatic** *adjective* **1** relating to or like opera **2** dramatic or overly theatrical ⊙ Comes from Latin *opus* meaning 'a work'

opera[2] plural of **opus**

operable *adjective* of a disease or injury: able to be treated by surgery

operand *noun* **1** *maths* a number on which a mathematical operation is carried out **2** *computing* data on which a computing operation is carried out

operate *verb* **1** to act, work **2** to bring about an effect **3** to perform an operation

operatic *adjective* of or for opera: *an operatic voice*

operating *adjective* of or for surgical operations

operating system (*abbrev* **OS**) *noun, computing* a program which manages all other software programs on a computer and the hardware devices linked to that computer, eg printer, scanner, disk drives, etc (*compare with*: **application**)

operating theatre or **operating room** *noun* the specially equipped room in a hospital where surgical operations are performed

operation *noun* 1 action 2 method or way of working 3 the cutting of a part of the human body to treat disease or repair damage 4 (**operations**) movements of armies, troops

operational *adjective* working

operative *adjective* 1 working, in action 2 of a rule etc: in force, having effect ➤ *noun* a worker in a factory etc

operator *noun* 1 someone who works a machine 2 someone who connects telephone calls 3 a mathematical symbol showing which operation is to be carried out, eg + for addition

operetta *noun* a play with light music, singing and often dancing

ophthalmia *noun* inflammation of the eye

ophthalmic *adjective* relating to the eye: *an ophthalmic surgeon*

ophthalmic optician *noun* an optician qualified both to examine the eyes and to prescribe glasses or contact lenses (*also called*: **optometrist**)

ophthalmologist *noun, medicine* a doctor who specializes in eye diseases, defects and injuries

ophthalmology *noun, medicine* the study, diagnosis and treatment of diseases and defects of the eye

opiate *noun* 1 a drug containing opium used to make someone sleep 2 anything that calms or dulls the mind or feelings

opinion *noun* 1 what someone thinks or believes 2 professional judgement or point of view: *He wanted another opinion on his son's condition* 3 judgement of the value of someone or something: *I have a low opinion of her*

opinionated *adjective* having and expressing strong opinions

opinion poll *noun* a survey of what people think of something

opium *noun* a drug made from the dried juice of a type of poppy

opossum *noun* a small American animal that carries its young in a pouch

opponent *noun* someone who opposes; an enemy, a rival

opportune *adjective* coming at the right or a convenient time: *I waited for an opportune moment to speak to her*

opportunist *noun* someone who takes advantage of a favourable situation ♦ **opportunism** *noun* ♦ **opportunistic** *adjective*

opportunity *noun* (*plural* **opportunities**) a chance (to do something)

opposable *adjective* of the thumb: able to face and touch the fingers on the same hand

oppose *verb* 1 to struggle against, resist 2 to

stand against, compete against

opposite *adjective* 1 facing, across from 2 lying on the other side (of) 3 *maths* of an angle in a triangle: facing the side that does not make up the angle 4 as different as possible: *I was trying to cheer her up but had the opposite effect* ➤ *preposition* 1 facing, across from: *He lives opposite the post office* 2 acting a role in a play, opera, etc in relation to another: *She played Ophelia opposite his Hamlet* ➤ *noun* something as different as possible (from something else): *Black is the opposite of white*

opposition *noun* 1 resistance 2 those who resist 3 (**the opposition**) the main political party that is against the governing party

oppress *verb* 1 to govern harshly like a tyrant 2 to treat cruelly 3 to distress, worry greatly ♦ **oppression** *noun*

oppressive *adjective* 1 oppressing 2 cruel, harsh 3 of weather: close, tiring

opt *verb* to choose; to decide between several options: *She opted to take the job/I opted for the red dress* • **opt out** to decide not to take part in something

optic or **optical** *adjective* relating to the eyes or sight

optical character recognition *noun, computing* (*abbrev* **OCR**) the scanning and identification of printed letters or numbers by a computer

optical disk *noun, computing* a disk that can be read from and often written to by a laser

optical fibre *noun* a thin, flexible strand of glass or plastic used to convey information, eg in the cables for telephones, cable television, etc

optical illusion *noun* an impression that something seen is different from what it is

optician *noun* someone who makes and sells spectacles

optic nerve *noun, anatomy* a nerve, responsible for sight, which transmits information from the retina in the eye to the visual cortex of the brain

optics *singular noun* the study of light and its practical application in devices and systems

optimal *adjective* very best, optimum

optimism *noun* the habit of taking a positive, hopeful view of things (*contrasted with*: **pessimism**) ♦ **optimist** *noun* ♦ **optimistic** *adjective* ♦ **optimistically** *adverb*

optimize or **optimise** *verb* to make the most of (a situation)

optimum *adjective* best, most favourable: *optimum conditions*

optimum population *noun, geography* the population that will fully use an area's natural resources, resulting in maximum production

option *noun* 1 choice; the right or power to

choose **2** something that is or may be chosen

optional *adjective* left to choice, not compulsory: *alloy wheels and other optional extras*

optometrist *noun* an **ophthalmic optician**

opulence *noun* wealth and luxury ♦ **opulent** *adjective*

opus (*pronounced* **oh**-pus) *noun* (*plural* **opera** – *pronounced* **op**-e-ra) an artistic work, especially a musical composition

or *conjunction* **1** used (often with **either**) to show alternatives: *Would you prefer tea or coffee?* **2** (often **or else**) because if not: *You'd better go or you'll miss your bus*

oracle *noun* **1** someone thought to be very wise or knowledgeable **2** a sacred place where a god is asked questions **3** someone through whom the answers to these questions are made known

oracular *adjective* **1** of or like an oracle **2** difficult to interpret; mysterious and ambiguous **3** prophetic

oral *adjective* **1** spoken, not written: *oral literature* **2** relating to the mouth: *oral hygiene* ➤ *noun* an oral examination or test ⏱ Comes from Latin *or-*, a form of *os* meaning 'mouth'

❗ Do not confuse with: **aural**.
Aural means 'relating to the ear'. It may help to think of the 'O' of 'oral' as looking like an open mouth.

orally *adverb* by mouth

orange *noun* **1** a juicy citrus fruit, with a thick reddish-yellow skin **2** the colour of this fruit ➤ *adjective* of this colour ♦ **orangey** *adjective*

orang-utan *noun* a large man-like ape, with long arms and long reddish hair

⏱ Based on a Malay phrase which translates as 'wild man'

oration *noun* a public speech, especially one in fine, formal language

orator *noun* a public speaker

oratorio *noun* (*plural* **oratorios**), *music* a sacred story set to music, performed by soloists, choir and often orchestra

oratory *noun* the art of speaking in public, rhetoric

orb *noun* anything in the shape of a ball, a sphere

orbit *noun* **1** the path of a planet round a sun, or of a moon or a space capsule round a planet **2** *chemistry* the path of an electron around the nucleus of an atom **3** range or area of influence: *within his orbit* **4** *anatomy* an eye socket ➤ *verb* to go round the earth etc in space

orbital *adjective* **1** relating to or going round in an orbit **2** of a road: forming a circle around a town ➤ *noun*, *chemistry* a region outside the nucleus of an atom or molecule where there is a

high probability of finding an electron

orchard *noun* a large garden of fruit trees

orchestra *noun* a group of musicians playing together under a conductor ♦ **orchestral** *adjective*

orchestrate *verb* **1** to arrange (a piece of music) for an orchestra **2** to organize (a situation, the elements of a plan, etc) so as to produce the best effect

orchid (*pronounced* **awr**-kid) *noun* a plant with unusually shaped, often brightly coloured, flowers

ordain *verb* **1** to declare something to be law **2** to admit (someone) as a member of the clergy: *He was ordained a priest in 1976*

ordeal *noun* **1** a hard trial or test **2** suffering, painful experience

order *noun* **1** an instruction to act made by someone in authority **2** a request or list of requests: *put an order in with the grocer* **3** an arrangement according to a system **4** an accepted way of doing things **5** a tidy or efficient state **6** peaceful conditions: *law and order* **7** rank, position, class **8** a society or brotherhood, eg of monks **9** any of the groups of animals or plants into which a class is divided and which in turn is subdivided into one or more families ➤ *verb* **1** to give an order to, tell to do **2** to put in an order for: *I've ordered another copy of the book* **3** to arrange • **in order 1** correct according to what is regularly done: *Is your passport in order?* **2** in a tidy arrangement • **in order to** for the purpose of: *In order to live you must eat* • **out of order 1** not working **2** not the correct way of doing things: *He shouldn't have said that. It was out of order* **3** not in a tidy arrangement: *The papers on his desk were all out of order*

orderly *adjective* **1** in proper order **2** well-behaved, quiet ➤ *noun* (*plural* **orderlies**) **1** a soldier who carries the orders and messages of an officer **2** a hospital attendant who does routine jobs

ordinal *adjective* of or in an order

ordinal number *noun* a number which shows order in a series, eg first, second, third (*compare with*: **cardinal number**)

ordinance *noun* a command; a law

ordinarily *adverb* usually, normally

ordinariness *noun* being ordinary

ordinary *adjective* **1** common, usual **2** normal; not exceptional • **out of the ordinary** unusual

ordinate *noun*, *maths* in Cartesian co-ordinates: the distance of a point from the horizontal or x-axis (*see also* **abscissa**) ⏱ Comes from Latin *ordinatus* meaning 'ordained'

ordination *noun* the act of ordaining someone as a member of the clergy

Ordnance Survey *noun* a government office which produces official detailed maps

Ordovician *adjective* of the geological period 505 million to 440 million years ago

ore *noun* a mineral from which a metal is obtained: *iron ore*

oregano (*pronounced* o-ri-**gah**-noh or *US* o-**reg**-an-oh) *noun* a Mediterranean herb used in cooking

organ *noun* **1** an internal part of the body, eg the liver **2** a large musical wind instrument with a keyboard **3** a means of spreading information, eg a newspaper: *an organ of conservatism*

organdie (*pronounced* **awr**-gan-di) *noun* a fine, thin, stiff muslin

organelle *noun, biology* in the cell of a living organism: any of various types of structure, each of which has a specialized function

organic *adjective* **1** of or produced by the bodily organs **2** of, or with the characteristics of, a living organism **3** made up of parts each with its separate function **4** (grown) without the use of artificial fertilizers etc: *organic farming/organic foods* **5** of a chemical compound: containing carbon atoms arranged in chains or rings
♦ **organically** *adverb*

organism *noun* any living thing

organist *noun* someone who plays the organ

organization or **organisation** *noun* **1** the act of organizing **2** a group of people working together for a purpose ♦ **organizational** *adjective*

organize or **organise** *verb* **1** to arrange, set up (an event etc) **2** to form into a whole
♦ **organizer** *noun*

organophosphate *noun, chemistry* any of a group of chemical insecticides

organza *noun* a very fine, stiff dress fabric made of silk or synthetic fibres

orgasm *noun* the climax of sexual excitement
♦ **orgasmic** *adjective*

OR gate *noun, computing* a circuit that gives out a signal when it receives either of two signals (*compare with:* **AND gate, NOT gate**)

orgy *noun* (*plural* **orgies**) a drunken or other unrestrained celebration

Orient *noun, old* (**the Orient**) the countries of the East

orient see **orientate**

oriental *adjective* eastern; from the East

orientate *verb* (also **orient**) **1** to find your position and sense of direction **2** to set or put facing a particular direction

orientation *noun* **1** the act or an instance of orientating or being orientated **2** a position relative to a fixed point

orienteering *noun* the sport of finding your

way across country with the help of map and compass

orifice *noun, formal* an opening

origami *noun* the Japanese art of folding paper to make figures shaped like animals, birds, etc

origin *noun* **1** the starting point **2** the place from which someone or something comes **3** cause **4** *maths* in co-ordinate geometry: the point on a graph where the horizontal x-axis and the vertical y-axis cross each other, which has a value of zero on both axes

original *adjective* **1** first in time **2** not copied: *an original painting* **3** able to think or do something new: *an original mind* ➤ *noun* **1** the earliest version **2** a model from which other things are made: *Send a copy and keep the original*
♦ **originality** *noun*

originally *adverb* **1** in or from the beginning: *His family is from Ireland originally* **2** in a new and different way: *She dresses very originally*

originate *verb* **1** to bring or come into being **2** to produce ♦ **originator** *noun*

ornament (*pronounced* **awr**-na-ment) *noun* **1** something added to give or enhance beauty **2** a small decorative object: *Christmas tree ornaments/a china ornament* ➤ *verb* (*pronounced* **awr**-na-ment) to adorn, decorate

ornamental *adjective* used for ornament; decorative

ornamentation *noun* decorating or the state of being decorated

ornate *adjective* richly decorated ♦ **ornately** *adverb*

ornithological *adjective* relating to or involving ornithology

ornithologist *noun* someone who studies or is an expert on birds

ornithology *noun* the scientific study of birds and their behaviour

orographic rainfall another term for **relief rainfall**

orphan *noun* a child who has lost both parents

orphanage *noun* a home for orphans

ortho- or **orth-** *prefix* forms words containing the idea of 'straightness' or 'correctness': *orthography* (= originally the art of spelling words correctly)/*orthopaedics* (= the correction of bone diseases and injuries) ⊙ Comes from Greek *orthos* meaning 'straight', 'upright' or 'correct'

orthocentre *noun, maths* the point of intersection of the three altitudes of a triangle

orthodontics (*pronounced* awrth-o-**don**-tiks) *singular noun, dentistry* the branch of dentistry concerned with preventing and correcting irregularities in the alignment of the teeth or jaws ♦ **orthodontist** *noun*

orthodox *adjective* **1** agreeing with the

prevailing or established religious, political, etc views (*contrasted with*: **heterodox**) **2** normal, generally practised and accepted **3** (usually **Orthodox**) belonging or relating to the Orthodox Church, a group of Christian churches led by the Patriarch of Constantinople **4** (usually **Orthodox**) belonging or relating to the branch of Judaism which keeps to strict interpretations of doctrine and scripture

orthodoxy *noun* **1** the state of being orthodox or of having orthodox beliefs **2** an orthodox belief or practice

orthogonal *adjective, maths* right-angled, perpendicular ♦ **orthogonally** *adverb*

orthographic or **orthographical** *adjective* relating to spelling

orthography *noun* an established system of spelling

orthopaedic or *US* **orthopedic** *adjective* relating to orthopaedics

orthopaedics or *US* **orthopedics** *singular noun* the branch of medicine which deals with bone diseases and injuries

Os *symbol, chemistry* osmium

oscillate *verb* **1** to swing to and fro like the pendulum of a clock **2** to keep changing your mind **3** of an electrical current: to vary regularly in strength or direction ♦ **oscillation** *noun*

⊙ From Latin *oscillum*, literally 'small face', referring to a mask of the god Bacchus which hung in Roman vineyards and swung to and fro in the wind

oscilloscope *noun* an instrument that measures changing electric voltages

-ose *suffix* used in the names of carbohydrates: *glucose*

osier (*pronounced* **oh**-zi-er) *noun* **1** a type of willow tree whose twigs are used for weaving baskets etc **2** a twig from this tree

-osis *suffix* **1** *medicine* forms terms for diseased conditions: *neurosis/thrombosis* **2** forms words describing different processes: *metamorphosis* (= the process of changing appearance or character)/*osmosis* (= a gradual process of absorption or assimilation) ⊙ Comes from Greek suffix *-osis*, used to form nouns from verbs

osmiridium *noun* an alloy of osmium and iridium, used to make pen nibs

osmium *noun, chemistry* (symbol **Os**) a very hard, bluish-white metal, the densest known element

osmoregulation *noun, biology* the process by which the water and salts within a living organism are kept at a constant level

osmosis *noun* **1** diffusion of liquids through a membrane **2** gradual absorption or assimilation ♦ **osmotic** *adjective*

osmotic pressure *noun, chemistry* the pressure that must be applied to prevent the diffusion of liquids through a membrane

osprey *noun* (*plural* **ospreys**) a type of eagle which eats fish

ossicle *noun, anatomy* a small bone

ossify *verb* (**ossifies, ossifying, ossified**) **1** to turn into or make something turn into bone **2** of opinions, habits, etc: to become rigid or inflexible ♦ **ossification** *noun* ⊙ Comes from French *ossifier*, from Latin *os* meaning 'bone' + *facere* meaning 'to make'

ostensible *adjective* of a reason etc: apparent, but not always real or true

ostentation *noun* pretentious display of wealth, knowledge, etc, especially to attract attention or admiration

ostentatious *adjective* showy, meant to catch the eye

osteomyelitis (*pronounced* ost-ee-oh-mai-e-**lai**-tis) *noun, medicine* inflammation of bone and bone marrow

osteopath (*pronounced* **ost**-ee-oh-path) *noun* someone who practises osteopathy

osteopathy (*pronounced* ost-ee-**op**-ath-i) *noun* a system of healing or treatment of bone and joint disorders, mainly involving manipulation and massage

osteoporosis *noun, medicine* a disease which makes bones porous and brittle, caused by lack of calcium

ostinato (*pronounced* ost-in-**ah**-toh) *noun* (*plural* **ostinatos**), *music* a short, repeated pattern in a piece of music

ostracism *noun* social exclusion

⊙ Based on *ostrakon*, a piece of pottery used in ancient Greece to cast votes to decide if someone was to be exiled

ostracize or **ostracise** *verb* to banish (someone) from the company of a group of people

ostrich *noun* (*plural* **ostriches**) a large African bird with showy plumage, which cannot fly but runs very fast

ostrich-like *adjective* avoiding facing up to difficulties (after the ostrich's supposed habit of burying its head in the sand when chased)

other *adjective* **1** the second of two: *Where is the other sock?* **2** remaining, not previously mentioned: *These are for the other children* **3** different, additional: *There must be some other reason* **4** (**every other**) every second: *I visit Gran every other day* **5** recently past: *the other day* ➤ *pronoun* **1** the second of two **2** those remaining, those not previously mentioned: *The others arrived the next day* **3** the previous one: *one after the other* • **other than** except: *no* hope other than to retreat • **someone or other** or **something or other** someone or something not named or specified: *There's always someone or other here*

otherwise *conjunction* or else: *Be quiet; otherwise leave* ➤ *adverb* **1** in a different way **2** in different circumstances: *I took the bus, otherwise I'd have been late*

-otomy *see* **-tomy**

OTT *abbreviation, informal* over-the-top, extravagant

otter *noun* a type of river animal living on fish

Ottoman *adjective, history* relating to the Turkish empire from the 14th to the 19th centuries

ottoman *noun* a low, cushioned seat without a back

ouch *interjection* expressing sudden sharp pain

ought *verb* **1** used with other verbs to indicate duty or need: *We ought to set an example/I ought to practise more* **2** to indicate what can be reasonably expected: *It's August; the weather ought to be fine*

Ouija (*pronounced* **wee**-ja) or **Ouija board** *noun, trademark* (sometimes **ouija**) a board with the letters of the alphabet printed round the edge, used in attempts to receive messages from the dead

⊙ The name is a combination of French *oui*, meaning 'yes', and German *ja*, also meaning 'yes'

ounce *noun* (*abbrev* **oz**) a unit of weight, equal to one-sixteenth of a pound (about 28.35 grams)

our *adjective* belonging to us: *our house*

ours *pronoun* something belonging to us: *The green car is ours*

ourselves *pronoun* **1** used reflexively: *We exhausted ourselves swimming* **2** used for emphasis: *We ourselves don't like it, but other people may*

oust *verb* **1** to drive out (from) **2** to drive out and take the place of: *She ousted him as leader of the party*

out *adverb* **1** into or towards the open air: *go out for a walk* **2** from inside: *take out a handkerchief* **3** not inside: *out of prison* **4** far from here: *out in the Far East* **5** not at home, not in the office, etc: *She's out at the moment* **6** aloud: *shouted out* **7** to or at an end: *Hear me out* **8** inaccurate: *The total was five pounds out* **9** *informal* on strike **10** published, released (for viewing, hire or purchase): *The video is out next week* **11** no longer hidden: *The secret is out* **12** openly admitting to being homosexual **13** dismissed from a game of cricket, baseball, etc **14** finished, having won at cards, etc **15** no longer in power or

office **16** no longer fashionable: *Flared jeans are out* **17** determined: *out to win*

out-and-out *adjective* complete, total, thorough: *an out-and-out liar*

outback *noun* the wild interior parts of Australia

outbid *verb* to offer a higher price than (somebody else)

outboard *adjective* on the outside of a ship or boat: *an outboard motor*

outbreak *noun* a beginning, a breaking out, eg of war or disease: *an oubreak of salmonella*

outbuilding *noun* a building that is separate from the main building

outburst *noun* an eruption, especially of strong or angry feelings

outcast *noun* someone driven away from friends and home

outclass *verb* **1** to be of a much better quality or class than (something else) **2** to defeat (a person, team, etc) easily

outcome *noun* result

outcrop *noun* the part of a rock formation that sticks out above the surface of the ground

outcry *noun* (*plural* **outcries**) a widespread show of anger, disapproval, etc

outdated *adjective* no longer useful or fashionable

outdo *verb* (**outdoing, outdid, outdone**) to do better than

outdoor *adjective* of, for or in the open air

outdoors *adverb* **1** outside the house **2** in or into the open air

outer *adjective* nearer the edge, surface, etc; further away

outermost *adjective* nearest the edge; furthest away

outfield *noun* **1** the outlying land on a farm **2** *cricket* the area of the pitch far from the part where the stumps etc are **3** *baseball* the area of the field beyond the diamond-shaped pitch where the bases are **4** *cricket, baseball* the players who have positions in these areas (*compare with*: **infield**) ♦ **outfielder** *noun*

outfit *noun* a set of clothes worn together, often for a special occasion etc

outfitter *noun* a seller of outfits, especially men's clothes

outfox *verb* to get the better of someone by being more cunning

outgoing *adjective* **1** of a person: friendly and sociable; extrovert **2** of a politician, official, etc: about to leave office: *the outgoing president*

outgoings *plural noun* money spent or being spent

outgrow *verb* (**outgrowing, outgrew, outgrown**) **1** to grow more than (someone or something) **2** to get too big or old for (clothes, toys, etc)

outgrowth noun something which grows out of something else

outhouse noun a shed

outing noun a trip, excursion

outlandish adjective looking or sounding very strange

outlaw noun someone put outside the protection of the law; a robber or bandit ➤ verb 1 to place beyond the protection of the law 2 to ban, forbid by law

outlay noun money paid out

outlet noun 1 a passage to the outside, eg for a water pipe 2 a means of expressing or getting rid of (a feeling, energy, etc) 3 a market for goods

outline noun 1 the outer line of a figure in a drawing etc 2 a sketch showing only the main lines 3 the main points etc, without the details: an outline of the plot 4 the most important features of something ➤ verb 1 to draw an outline of 2 to briefly describe the main features of

outlive verb to live longer than

outlook noun 1 a view from a window etc 2 what is thought likely to happen: the weather outlook 3 someone's mental attitude or point of view

outlying adjective far from the centre, distant

outnumber verb to be greater in number than: Their team outnumbered ours

out-of-date or **out of date** adjective 1 old-fashioned 2 no longer valid: This voucher is out of date/an out-of-date ticket

out-patient noun a patient who does not stay in a hospital while receiving treatment (contrasted with: **in-patient**)

outpost noun a military station in front of or far from the main army; an outlying settlement

output noun 1 the goods produced by a machine, factory, etc; the amount of work done by a person 2 data transferred from a computer to a disk, tape or output device such as a VDU or printer (contrasted with: **input**) ➤ adjective concerned with output: an output device ➤ verb to transfer (data) from a computer to a disk or tape, or to an output device

outrage noun 1 an act of great violence 2 an act which shocks or causes offence ➤ verb 1 to injure, hurt by violence 2 to insult, shock

outrageous adjective 1 violent, very wrong 2 not moderate, extravagant

outrank verb to have a higher rank than (someone)

outright adverb 1 completely 2 immediately: killed outright 3 openly, honestly: asked outright ➤ adjective 1 complete, thorough 2 clear: the outright winner 3 open, honest: outright contempt

outset noun start, beginning

outside noun the outer surface or place: the outside of the box ➤ adjective 1 in, on or of the outer surface or place: the outside seat 2 relating to leisure rather than your full-time job: outside interests 3 slight, remote: an outside chance of winning ➤ adverb out of doors; in or into the open air: Let's eat outside ➤ preposition beyond the range of, not within: outside the building/outside working hours • at the outside at the most: ten miles at the outside

outside broadcast noun a radio or television programme that is recorded or transmitted from somewhere other than in a studio

outsider noun 1 someone not included in a particular social group 2 a runner etc whom no one expects to win

outsize adjective of a very large size

outskirts plural noun the outer areas of a city etc

outsmart verb to outwit

outsource verb 1 to pay another company to do particular work 2 to buy in parts from another company rather than manufacture them

outspoken adjective bold and frank in speech

outstanding adjective 1 well-known 2 excellent 3 of a debt: unpaid

outstretched adjective reaching out

outstrip verb (outstripped, outstripping) 1 to go faster than (someone or something else) 2 to do better than (someone or something else)

outtake noun a section of film removed from the final version of a motion picture or TV programme

out-tray noun an office tray for letters and work already dealt with (contrasted with: **in-tray**)

outvote verb to defeat by a greater number of votes

outward adjective 1 towards or on the outside 2 of a journey: away from home, not towards it ➤ adverb (also **outwards**) towards the outside

outwardly adverb on the outside, in appearance: He was outwardly confident

outweigh verb to be more important than: The advantages outweigh the disadvantages

outwit verb (outwitting, outwitted) to defeat or get the better of (someone) by being clever or cunning

outwith preposition, Scottish outside of, beyond

ova plural of **ovum**

oval adjective having the shape of an egg, or, roughly, an ellipse ➤ noun an egg or elliptical shape

ovary noun (plural **ovaries**) 1 biology one of two organs in the female body in which eggs are formed 2 botany the part of the flower that contains the ovules

ovation noun an outburst of cheering, hand-clapping, etc

oven noun a covered place for baking; a small furnace

over preposition **1** higher than, above: *The number is over the door/She won over £200/We've lived here for over thirty years* **2** across: *going over the bridge* **3** on the other side of: *the house over the road* **4** on top of: *threw his coat over the body* **5** here and there on: *paper scattered over the carpet* **6** about: *They quarrelled over their money* **7** by means of: *over the telephone* **8** during, throughout: *over the years* **9** while doing, having, etc: *fell asleep over his dinner* ➤ adverb **1** above, higher up: *Two birds flew over* **2** across a distance: *He walked over and spoke* **3** downwards: *Did you fall over?* **4** above in number etc: *aged four and over* **5** as a remainder: *three left over* **6** through: *Read the passage over* ➤ adjective finished: *The sale is over* ➤ noun, cricket a fixed number of balls bowled from one end of the wicket • **over again** once more

over- prefix too much, to too great an extent: *overcook/over-excited*

overall noun **1** a garment worn over ordinary clothes to protect them against dirt **2** (**overalls**) hard-wearing trousers with a bib worn as work clothes ➤ adjective **1** from one end to the other: *overall length* **2** including everything: *overall cost* • **over all** altogether: *His work's quite good, over all*

overarm adjective of bowling etc: with the arm above the shoulder (*compare with:* **underarm**)

overawe verb to frighten or astonish into silence

overbalance verb to lose your balance and fall

overbank noun, geography a point in a river where it flows over its banks

overbearing adjective over-confident, domineering

overboard adverb out of a ship into the water: *Man overboard!*

overcast adjective of the sky: cloudy

overcharge verb **1** to charge (someone) too much money **2** to overload (something)

overcoat noun an outdoor coat worn over all other clothes

overcome verb to get the better of, defeat ➤ adjective helpless from exhaustion, emotion, etc

overdo verb **1** to do too much **2** to exaggerate: *They rather overdid the righteous indignation* **3** to cook (food) too long

overdose noun too great an amount (of medicine, a drug, etc) ➤ verb to give or take too much medicine etc

overdraft noun the amount of money overdrawn from a bank

overdraw verb to draw more money from the bank than you have in your account: *He's £500 overdrawn*

overdrive noun an additional high gear in a motor vehicle's gearbox, which saves fuel when travelling at high speeds • **go into overdrive** to operate at a faster or more active level than normal

overdue adjective **1** later than the stated or anticipated time: *Her baby is overdue* **2** of a bill etc: still unpaid although the time for payment has passed

overflow verb **1** to flow or spill over: *The river overflowed its banks/The crowd overflowed into the next room* **2** to be so full as to flow over ➤ noun **1** something that overflows **2** a pipe or channel for getting rid of excess water etc

overgrazing noun to allow more animals to graze on a piece of land than it can sustain, destroying vegetation

overgrown adjective **1** covered with plant growth **2** grown too large or beyond normal size: *Boston is just an overgrown farm town* **3** behaving, usually in a foolish way, like someone much younger: *Dad is just an overgrown teenager*

overhang verb to jut out over

overhaul verb to examine carefully and carry out repairs ➤ noun a thorough examination and repair

overhead adverb directly above: *The aeroplane flew overhead* ➤ adjective placed high above the ground: *overhead cables* ➤ noun (**overheads**) the regular expenses of a business etc, eg rent, rates, electricity

overhear verb to hear what you were not meant to hear

overjoyed adjective filled with great joy

overkill noun action, behaviour or treatment that is far in excess of what is required

overland adverb & adjective on or by land, not sea

overland flow another term for **run-off**

overlap verb **1** to extend over and partly cover: *The two pieces of cloth overlapped* **2** to cover a part of the same area or subject as another; partly coincide ➤ noun the amount by which something overlaps

overleaf adjective on the other side of a leaf of a book

overload verb to load or fill too much

overlook verb **1** to look down on from a higher point; have or give a view of: *The house overlooked the village* **2** to fail to see, miss **3** to pardon, not punish

overlord noun, history a lord with power over other lords

overly adverb too, excessively

overmuch adverb & noun too much

overnight adverb **1** during the night: staying overnight with a friend **2** in a very short time: His hair turned grey overnight ➤ adjective **1** for the night or for a night: an overnight bag/an overnight stop **2** got or made in a very short time: an overnight success

overpass noun a road going over above another road, railway, canal, etc

overpopulation noun more people in a given area than the natural resources of the area can sustain ◆ **overpopulated** adjective

overpower verb **1** to defeat through greater strength **2** to overwhelm, make helpless ◆ **overpowering** adjective **1** unable to be resisted **2** overwhelming, very strong: an overpowering smell

overproduction noun the production of more food, goods, etc than can be sold

overrate verb to value more highly than is deserved: Her books are overrated ◆ **overrated** adjective

overreach verb: **overreach yourself** to try to do or get more than you can and so fail

overreact verb to react too strongly ◆ **overreaction** noun

override verb **1** to ignore, set aside: overriding the committee's decisions **2** to take over control from: override the automatic alarm signal

overrule verb to go against or cancel an earlier judgement or request

overrun verb **1** to grow or spread over: overrun with weeds **2** to take possession of (a country)

overseas adjective & adverb abroad; beyond the sea

oversee verb to watch over, supervise

overseer noun a person who oversees workers, a supervisor

overshadow verb to lessen the importance of (someone or something) by doing better than them

oversight noun **1** something left out or forgotten by mistake **2** failure to notice

overstep verb to go further than (a set limit, rules, etc)

overt adjective not hidden or secret; openly done

overtake verb to catch up with and pass

over-the-counter adjective of drugs, medicines, etc: sold legally directly to the customer

overthrow verb to defeat

overtime noun **1** time spent working beyond the agreed normal hours **2** payment for this, usually at a higher rate

overtone noun an additional meaning or association, not directly stated

overture noun **1** a piece of music played as an introduction to an opera **2** a proposal intended to open discussions: overtures of peace

overturn noun **1** to turn over or upside down **2** to bring down (a government) **3** to overrule or cancel (a previous legal decision)

overview noun a brief general account of a subject, a summary

overweight adjective above an acceptable or healthy weight

overwhelm verb **1** to defeat completely **2** to load with too great an amount: overwhelmed with work **3** to overcome, make helpless: overwhelmed with grief

overwhelming adjective physically or mentally crushing; intensely powerful

overwork verb to work more than is good for you

overwrought adjective excessively nervous or excited, agitated

oviduct noun, anatomy a tube through which egg cells are carried to the uterus in mammals, eg the fallopian tube in humans

oviparous noun, biology of an animal: laying eggs that hatch outside the mother's body

ovipositor noun, biology an egg-laying organ

ovoid adjective egg-shaped ➤ noun an egg-shaped form or object

ovoviviparous noun, biology of an animal: producing eggs that hatch inside the mother's body

ovulate verb to release an egg cell from the ovary ◆ **ovulation** noun

ovule noun, botany in flowering plants: the structure that develops into a seed when fertilized

ovum noun (plural **ova**), biology an unfertilized female egg cell

owe verb **1** to be in debt to: I owe Peter three pounds **2** to have (a person or thing) to thank for: He owes his success to his family ● **owing to** because of

owl noun a bird of prey which comes out at night

owlet noun a young owl

own verb **1** to have as a possession **2** to admit, confess to be true ➤ adjective belonging to the person mentioned: Is this all your own work? ● **hold your own** to keep your place or position, not weaken ● **on your own 1** by your own efforts **2** alone

owner noun someone who possesses anything ◆ **ownership** noun

own goal noun a goal scored by mistake against your own side

ox noun (plural **oxen**) a male cow, usually castrated, used for pulling loads etc

oxalic acid noun, chemistry, botany a highly poisonous white crystalline solid that occurs in the leaves of some plants

oxbow lake noun, geography a shallow curved

lake found alongside a meandering river, formed when one of the bends has been cut off

Oxford Movement *noun, history* a religious movement in the mid-19th century which advocated the revival of authority and ceremony in the Church of England (*also called*: **Tractarianism**)

oxidant *noun, chemistry* an oxidizing agent

oxidation *noun, chemistry* a chemical reaction that involves the addition of oxygen to, or the removal of hydrogen from, a substance which loses electrons

oxide *noun* a compound of oxygen and another element

oxidize or **oxidise** *verb* **1** to combine with oxygen **2** *chemistry* to lose or cause (an atom or ion) to lose electrons **3** to become rusty ♦ **oxidization** *noun*

oxidizing agent or **oxidising agent** *noun, chemistry* any substance that oxidizes another substance in a chemical reaction

oxygen *noun, chemistry* (symbol **O**) a gas with no taste, colour or smell, forming part of the air and of water

⏱ Based on two Greek words, meaning 'producing acid'

oxygenate *verb* to supply (eg the blood) with oxygen ♦ **oxygenation** *noun*

oxygen debt *noun, biology* the depletion of the body's store of oxygen during strenuous exercise, replaced after the exercise stops

oxyhaemoglobin *noun, biochemistry* the red compound formed in blood by the combination of oxygen and haemoglobin as a result of respiration

oxymoron (*pronounced* ok-si-**maw**-ron) *noun* a figure of speech in which contradictory terms are used together, eg *cruel kindness, falsely true,* etc

oyster *noun* a type of shellfish, often eaten raw

oz *abbreviation* ounce(s)

ozone *noun* a form of oxygen, O_3

ozone depletion *noun, geography* damage to the ozone layer caused by compounds such as chlorofluorocarbons (or CFCs)

ozone-friendly *adjective* of products: not harmful to the ozone layer; free from chlorofluorocarbons that deplete the ozone layer

ozone layer *noun* a layer of the upper atmosphere where ozone is formed, which protects the earth from the sun's ultraviolet rays

Pp

P *symbol, chemistry* phosphorus

p *abbreviation* **1** page **2** pence

PA *abbreviation* **1** personal assistant **2** public-address system

Pa *symbol* **1** *chemistry* protactinium **2** *physics* pascal

pace *noun* **1** a step **2** rate of walking, running, etc ➤ *verb* **1** to measure by steps **2** to walk backwards and forwards

pacemaker *noun* **1** someone who sets the pace in a race **2** an electronic device used to correct weak or irregular heart rhythms

pachyderm (*pronounced* **pak**-id-erm) *noun* a thick-skinned animal such as an elephant

pacifist *noun* someone who is against war
♦ **pacifism** *noun*

pacify *verb* (**pacifies, pacifying, pacified**) **1** to make peaceful **2** to calm, soothe

pack *noun* **1** a bundle, especially one carried on the back **2** a set of playing-cards **3** a group of animals, especially dogs or wolves **4** a compact package, eg of equipment for a purpose: *a first-aid pack* ➤ *verb* **1** to place (clothes etc) in a case or trunk for a journey **2** to press or crowd together closely • **pack in** to cram in tightly • **send someone packing** to send them away forcefully

package *noun* **1** a bundle, a parcel **2** *computing* a group of related programs designed to perform a particular complex task ➤ *verb* **1** to put into a container **2** to wrap

package holiday or **package tour** *noun* a holiday or tour arranged by an organizer with all travel and accommodation included in the price

packaging *noun* the wrappers or containers in which goods are packed

packet *noun* **1** a small parcel **2** a container made of paper, cardboard, etc **3** *telecommunications* a block of coded data

packet switching *noun, telecommunications* transferring coded data over a network by breaking it down into small units and putting it together again at its destination

pack ice *noun* a mass of pieces of floating ice driven together by currents etc

packing *noun* **1** the act of putting things in cases, parcels, etc **2** material for wrapping goods to pack **3** something used to fill an empty space

pact *noun* **1** an agreement **2** a treaty, a contract

pad¹ *noun* **1** a soft cushion-like object to prevent jarring, rubbing etc **2** a bundle of sheets of paper fixed together **3** the paw of certain animals **4** a rocket-launching platform **5** *slang* the place where someone lives ➤ *verb* (**padding, padded**) **1** to stuff or protect with a soft material **2** (often **pad out**) to fill (something) up with unnecessary material

pad² *verb* (**padding, padded**) to walk making a dull, soft noise

padding *noun* **1** stuffing material **2** words included in a speech, book, etc just to fill space or time

paddle¹ *verb* to wade in shallow water

paddle² *noun* **1** a short, broad, spoon-shaped oar **2** one of the slats fitted round the edge of the wheels of a paddle steamer ➤ *verb* to move forward by the use of paddles; row

paddle steamer *noun* a steamer driven by two large wheels made up of paddles

paddock *noun* a small, closed-in field used for pasture

paddy field *noun* a small, enclosed field for keeping a horse in

padlock *noun* a removable lock with a hinged, U-shaped bar

padre (*pronounced* **pah**-drei) *noun* a chaplain in any of the armed services ⊕ from Portuguese, Spanish, and Italian, meaning 'father'

paean or *US* **pean** (*pronounced* **pee**-an) *noun* a song of praise or thanksgiving

paediatrician or *US* **pediatrician** *noun* a doctor who specializes in studying and treating children's illnesses

paediatrics or *US* **pediatrics** *singular noun* the treatment of children's diseases

paedo- (*pronounced* pee-doh) also **paed-** (*pronounced* peed), also **pedo-, ped-** *prefix* of or relating to children: *paedophile/pedagogical* (relating to the education of children) ⊕ Comes from Greek *paidos* meaning 'of a boy'

paedophile or *US* **pedophile** *noun* an adult who has sexual desire for children
♦ **paedophilia** *noun*

paella (*pronounced* pai-**el**-a) *noun, cookery* a Spanish rice dish of fish or chicken with vegetables and saffron

pagan *noun* **1** a person who is not a member of one of the major relations such as Christianity, Judaism or Islam **2** someone who does not believe in any religion; a heathen ➤ *adjective* to do with pagans or paganism ♦ **paganism** *noun*

page¹ *noun* one side of a blank, written, or printed sheet of paper

page² *noun* **1** a boy servant **2** a boy who carries the train of the bride's dress in a marriage service ➤ *verb* to contact someone using a pager

pageant (*pronounced* **paj**-ant) *noun* **1** a show or procession made up of scenes from history **2** an elaborate parade or display ♦ **pageantry** *noun* (meaning 2)

pager *noun* a small radio device that can be used to receive a signal, usually a beeping noise, from elsewhere

pagoda *noun* an Eastern temple, especially in China or India

paid past form of **pay**

pail *noun* an open vessel of tin, zinc, plastic, etc for carrying liquids; a bucket

pain *noun* **1** feeling caused by hurt to mind or body **2** threat of punishment: *under pain of death* **3** *derogatory informal* an irritating or troublesome person or thing **4** (**pains**) care: *takes great pains with his work* ➤ *verb* to cause suffering to, distress

pained *adjective* showing pain or distress: *a pained expression*

painful *adjective* **1** causing pain: *a painful injury* **2** affected by something which causes pain: *a painful finger* **3** causing distress: *a painful duty* **4** laborious: *painful progress* ♦ **painfully** *adverb*

painkiller *noun* a medicine taken to lessen pain

painless *adjective* without pain ♦ **painlessly** *adverb*

painstaking *adjective* very careful ♦ **painstakingly** *adverb*

paint *verb* **1** to apply colour to in the form of liquid or paste **2** to describe in words ➤ *noun* a liquid substance used for colouring and applied with a brush, a spray, etc

painter¹ *noun* **1** someone whose trade is painting **2** an artist who works in paint

painter² *noun* a rope used to fasten a boat

painting *noun* **1** the act or art of creating pictures with paint **2** a painted picture

pair *noun* **1** two of the same kind **2** a set of two ➤ *verb* **1** to join to form a pair **2** to go in twos **3** to mate

paisley pattern *noun* a design with a very ornate device which looks like a tree cone with a curving point, used mainly on fabrics

⊙ First used on shawls made in *Paisley*, Scotland

pajamas US for **pyjamas**

pal *noun, informal* a friend

palace *noun* the house of a king, queen, archbishop or aristocrat

⊙ From the *Palatine* Hill in Rome, where the Roman emperors lived

Palaeocene *adjective* of the geological epoch from 65 million to 54 million years ago

palaeolithic or **paleolithic** *adjective* relating to the early Stone Age when people used stone tools

palaeontology *noun* the study of extinct life forms by examining their fossilized remains ♦ **palaeontologist** *noun*

Palaeozoic *adjective* of the geological era from 580 million to 250 million years ago

palatable *adjective* **1** pleasant to the taste **2** acceptable, pleasing

palate (*pronounced* **pal**-at) *noun* **1** the roof of the mouth **2** the sense of taste ⊙ Comes from Latin *palatum* meaning 'the roof of the mouth'

⚠ Do not confuse with: **palette** and **pallet**

palatial (*pronounced* pa-**lei**-shal) *adjective* like a palace, magnificent

palaver (*pronounced* pa-**lah**-ver) *noun* an unnecessary fuss ⊙ Comes from Portuguese *palavra* meaning 'talk'

pale¹ *noun* a wooden stake used in making a fence to enclose ground

pale² *adjective* **1** light or whitish in colour **2** not bright ➤ *verb* to make or turn pale

palette (*pronounced* **pal**-et) *noun* a board or plate on which an artist mixes paints ⊙ Comes from Italian *paletta* meaning 'a small shovel'

⚠ Do not confuse with: **pallet** and **palate**

palindrome *noun* a word or phrase that reads the same backwards as forwards, eg 'level' ⊙ From Greek *palindromos*, meaning 'running back'

paling *noun* a row of wooden stakes forming a fence

palisade *noun* a fence of pointed wooden stakes

pall¹ (*pronounced* pawl) *noun* **1** the cloth over a coffin at a funeral **2** a dark covering or cloud: *a pall of smoke*

pall² (*pronounced* pawl) *verb* to become dull or uninteresting

palladium (*pronounced* pa-**lei**-di-um) *noun, chemistry* (symbol **Pd**) a soft, silvery-white metallic element

⊙ Named after the asteroid *Pallas*, discovered at about the same time (1802) as the element

pallbearer *noun* one of those carrying or walking beside the coffin at a funeral

pallet¹ (*pronounced* **pal**-et) *noun* a straw bed or mattress ⊙ Comes from French *paille* meaning 'straw'

pallet² (*pronounced* **pal**-et) *noun* a platform that can be lifted by a fork-lift truck for stacking goods ◑ Shares the same origin as 'palette'

❗ Do not confuse with: **palette** and **palate**

palliative (*pronounced* **pal**-i-a-tiv) *adjective* making less severe or harsh ➤ *noun* something which lessens pain, eg a drug

pallid *adjective* pale

pallor *noun* paleness

palm¹ *noun* the inner surface of the hand between the wrist and the base of the fingers • **palm off** to give with the intention of cheating: *That shopkeeper palmed off a foreign coin on me*

palm² *noun* a tall tree with broad fan-shaped leaves, which grows in hot countries

palmate (*pronounced* **pal**-meit) *adjective* **1** *botany* of a leaf: divided into lobes and resembling an open hand **2** *zoology* of an animal or bird: having webbed toes

palmist *noun* someone who tells fortunes by palmistry

palmistry *noun* the telling of fortunes from the lines and markings of the hand

Palm Sunday *noun, Christianity* the Sunday before Easter, commemorating Christ's entry into Jerusalem

palmtop *noun* a portable computer, usually small enough to be held in the hand (*also called*: **palmtop computer**)

palomino (*pronounced* pa-loh-**mee**-noh) *noun* (*plural* **palominos**) a golden or cream horse with a white or silver tail and mane

palpable *adjective* **1** *medicine* able to be touched or felt **2** easily noticed, obvious

palpate *verb, medicine* to examine by touch ◆ **palpation** *noun*

palpitate *verb* of the heart: to beat rapidly, throb

palpitations *plural noun* uncomfortable rapid beating of the heart

palsied (*pronounced* **pawl**-zid) *adjective* affected with palsy; paralysed

palsy (*pronounced* **pawl**-zi) *noun* a loss of power and feeling in the muscles

paltry (*pronounced* **pawl**-tri) *adjective* (**paltrier, paltriest**) of little value

pampas *plural noun* (*pronounced* **pam**-paz) or *singular noun* (*pronounced* **pam**-pas) (**the pampas**) the vast, treeless plains of South America

pampas grass *noun* a type of very tall, feathery grass

pamper *verb* to spoil (a child etc) by giving too much attention to

pamphlet *noun* a small book, stitched or stapled, often with a light paper cover

pan¹ *noun* **1** a broad, shallow pot used in cooking, a saucepan **2** a shallow dent in the ground **3** the bowl of a toilet

pan² *verb* (**panning, panned**) to move a television or film camera so as to follow an object or give a wide view • **pan out 1** to turn out (well or badly) **2** to come to an end

pan- *prefix* all, whole: *pandemonium/panoply* ◑ Comes from Greek *pan*, a form of *pas* meaning 'all'

panacea (*pronounced* pan-a-**see**-a) *noun* a cure for all things

panache (*pronounced* pa-**nash**) *noun* a sense of style, swagger

◑ Literally meaning 'a plume', from the use of feathers in flamboyant headgear

Pan-American *adjective* including all America or Americans, North and South

pancake *noun* a thin cake of flour, eggs, sugar and milk, fried in a pan or on a griddle

pancreas (*pronounced* **pang**-kri-as) *noun, anatomy* a gland behind the stomach producing fluids that aid digestion ◆ **pancreatic** *adjective*

pancreatic juice (*pronounced* pang-kri-**at**-ik) *noun, anatomy* an alkaline mixture of digestive enzymes secreted by the pancreas (*also called*: **pancreatin**)

panda *noun* **1** a large black-and-white bear-like animal found in Tibet etc **2** a raccoon-like animal found in the Himalayas

pandemic *adjective* of a disease etc: occurring over a wide area and affecting a large number of people

pandemonium *noun* a state of confusion and uproar

◑ The name of the capital of Hell in Milton's *Paradise Lost* (1667)

pander *noun* a pimp ➤ *verb* (**pander to**) to indulge, easily comply with

◑ After *Pandarus*, who acts as a go-between in the story of Troilus and Cressida

Pandora's box *noun* something which is the source of great or unexpected troubles

◑ After the story of *Pandora*, who disobeyed the Greek gods and opened a box containing all the troubles of the world

p & p *abbreviation* postage and packing

pane *noun* a sheet of glass

panegyric (*pronounced* pan-i-**jir**-ik) *noun* a speech praising someone, an achievement, etc

panel *noun* **1** a flat rectangular piece of wood such as is set into a door or wall **2** a group of people chosen to judge a contest, take part in a television quiz, etc

panel-beating *noun* the removal of dents

from the bodywork of a vehicle, using a soft-headed hammer ♦ **panel-beater** noun

panelling or US **paneling** noun **1** panels covering a wall or part of a wall, usually as decoration **2** material for making these

panellist or US **panelist** noun a member of a panel of people, especially in a panel game on TV or radio

pang noun a sudden sharp pain; a twinge

panic noun **1** a sudden and great fright **2** fear that spreads from person to person ➤ verb (**panicking, panicked**) **1** to throw into panic **2** to act wildly through fear

> ⊙ From a Greek word meaning 'fear of the god Pan'. Pan was said to roam about the woodland and scare people and animals

panicle noun, botany a branched stem, with flowers attached to the branches

pannier noun **1** a basket slung over a horse's back **2** a light container attached to a bicycle etc

panoply (pronounced **pan**-o-pli) noun (plural **panoplies**) **1** the ceremonial dress, equipment, etc associated with a particular event: the panoply of a military funeral **2** history a full suit of armour

panorama noun a wide view of a landscape, scene, etc

Pan-pipes plural noun a musical instrument made of reeds fastened in a row

pansy noun (plural **pansies**) a flower like the violet but larger

pant verb **1** to gasp for breath **2** to say breathlessly **3** to wish eagerly (for)

pantechnicon noun a large van for transporting furniture

panth (pronounced punth) noun, Sikhism the Sikh community

pantheism noun **1** the belief that all things in the physical universe are part of God **2** belief in many gods

pantheist noun a believer in pantheism

pantheistic or **pantheistical** adjective relating to pantheism or pantheists

panther noun **1** a large leopard **2** US a puma

panties plural noun thin, light knickers worn by women and children

pantile noun a roofing tile with an S-shaped cross-section

panto noun (plural **pantos**), informal pantomime

pantomime noun a Christmas play, with songs, jokes, etc, based on a popular fairy tale, eg Cinderella

pantry noun (plural **pantries**) a room for storing food

pants plural noun **1** underpants **2** women's short-legged knickers **3** US trousers

papacy (pronounced **pei**-pa-si) noun the position or power of the Pope

papal (pronounced **pei**-pal) adjective of, or relating to, the pope or the papacy

paparazzo (pronounced pa-pa-**rat**-soh) noun (plural **paparazzi** – pronounced pa-pa-**rat**-see) a press photographer who hounds celebrities etc

> ⊙ After the name of a photographer in Federico Fellini's film La Dolce Vita

papaya (pronounced pa-**pai**-a) noun a green-skinned edible fruit from S America (also called: **pawpaw**)

paper noun **1** a material made from rags, wood, etc used for writing or wrapping **2** a single sheet of this **3** a newspaper **4** an essay on a learned subject **5** a set of examination questions **6** (**papers**) documents proving someone's identity, nationality, etc ➤ verb to cover up (especially walls) with paper

paperback noun a book bound in a flexible paper cover (compare with: **hardback**)

paperchase noun a game in which one runner leaves a trail of paper so that others may track them

paper clip noun a metal clip formed from bent wire, for holding papers together

paper tiger noun someone who appears to be powerful but really is not

paperweight noun a heavy glass, metal, etc object used to keep papers in place

paperwork noun routine written work, eg keeping files, writing letters and reports, etc

papier-mâché (pronounced pap-yei-**mash**-ei) noun a substance consisting of paper pulp and some sticky liquid or glue, shaped into models, bowls, etc

papilla (pronounced pa-**pil**-a) noun (plural **papillae** – pronounced pa-**pil**-ee), anatomy, biology **1** a small nipple-like projection from the surface of a structure **2** a small elevation on the skin in which a nerve ends, such as those on the tongue **3** a protuberance at the base of a hair, feather, tooth, etc **4** a minute conical protuberance as on the surface of a petal ⊙ Comes from Latin, diminutive of papula meaning 'pimple' ♦ **papillary** adjective like or having papillae ♦ **papillate, papillated** or **papilliferous** adjective having papillae

paprika (pronounced **pa**-pri-ka or pa-**pree**-ka) noun a type of ground red pepper

papyrus (pronounced pa-**pai**-rus) noun (plural **papyri** – pronounced pa-**pai**-rai – or **papyruses**) **1** a reed used by the ancient Egyptians etc to make paper **2** a document written in papyrus

par noun **1** an accepted standard, value, etc **2** golf the number of strokes allowed for each hole if the play is perfect • **below par 1** not up to standard **2** not feeling very well • **on a par with** equal to or comparable with

parable *noun* a story (eg in the Bible) which teaches a moral lesson

parabola (*pronounced* pa-**rab**-*o*-la) *noun* **1** a curve **2** *maths* the intersection of a cone by a plane parallel to its sloping side

paracetamol (*pronounced* pa-ra-**set**-a-mol) *noun* a pain-relieving drug

parachute *noun* an umbrella-shaped device made of light material and rope which supports someone or something dropping slowly to the ground from an aeroplane ➤ *verb* to drop by parachute

parachutist *noun* someone dropped by parachute from an aeroplane

parade *noun* **1** an orderly arrangement of troops for inspection or exercise **2** a procession of people, vehicles, etc in celebration of some event ➤ *verb* **1** to arrange (troops) in order **2** to march in a procession **3** to display in an obvious way

paradigm (*pronounced* **par**-a-daim) *noun* an example, model or pattern ☉ Comes from Greek *paradeigma* meaning 'pattern'

paradise *noun* **1** heaven **2** a place or state of great happiness

paradox *noun* (*plural* **paradoxes**) a saying which seems to contradict itself but which may be true

paradoxical *adjective* combining two apparently contradictory elements: *It is paradoxical that many people are homeless when there are many empty houses* ◆ **paradoxically** *adverb*

paraffin *noun*, *Brit* a liquid obtained from petroleum or coal which is used as a fuel in aeroplanes, heaters, etc (*N Am & Aust name:* **kerosene**)

paraffin oil *noun* an oil obtained from the manufacture of paraffin, consisting of a mix of paraffin and other hydrocarbons

paraffin wax *noun*, *chemistry* a white, tasteless, odourless solid, obtained from the distillation of petroleum, used to make candles, polishes, wax crayons, etc

paragliding *noun* the sport of gliding supported by a modified type of parachute

paragon *noun* a model of perfection or excellence: *a paragon of good manners*

paragraph *noun* **1** a division of a piece of writing shown by beginning the first sentence on a new line **2** a short item in a newspaper

parakeet *noun* a small, brightly coloured parrot

parallax *noun*, *physics* an apparent change in the position of an object when viewed from two different positions

parallel *adjective* **1** of lines: going in the same direction and never meeting, always remaining equidistant **2** similar or alike in some way: *parallel cases* ➤ *noun* **1** *maths* a line or plane parallel with something else **2** something comparable in some way with something else **3** *geography* a line to mark latitude, drawn east and west across a map or round a globe at a set distance from the equator

parallel circuit *noun* an electrical circuit where a power source is directly connected to two or more components and the current is split between parallel paths (*compare with:* **series circuit**)

parallelogram *noun*, *maths* a four-sided figure, the opposite sides of which are parallel and equal in length

parallel port *noun*, *computing* a connection on a computer for a device such as a mouse or a scanner, and through which data can be sent and received using two or more wires simultaneously

paralyse or *US* **paralyze** *verb* **1** to affect with paralysis **2** to make helpless or ineffective **3** to bring to a halt

paralysis *noun* (*plural* **paralyses**) loss of the power to move and feel in part of the body

paralytic *adjective* **1** suffering from paralysis **2** *informal* helplessly drunk ➤ *noun* a paralysed person

paramedic *noun* someone helping doctors and nurses, eg a member of an ambulance crew

paramedical *adjective* denoting personnel or services that are supplementary to and support the work of the medical profession

parameter (*pronounced* pa-**ram**-i-ter) *noun* **1** *maths* a constant or variable that, when it is changed, affects the form of the expression in which it appears, for example in $y = ax + b$, a and b are parameters **2** (*often* **parameters**) the limiting factors which affect the way in which something can be done ☉ Comes from Greek *para* meaning 'beside' or 'beyond', and *metron* meaning 'measure'

❗ Do not confuse with: **perimeter**. Notice that words starting with **peri-** often relate to the idea of 'going around' and the **perimeter** of a figure or shape is the line that goes around it.

paramilitary *adjective* **1** on military lines and intended to supplement the military **2** organized illegally as a military force ➤ *noun* (*plural* **paramilitaries**) **1** a group organized in this way **2** a member of a such group

paramount *adjective* very greatest, supreme: *of paramount importance*

paranoia *noun* **1** a form of mental disorder characterized by delusions of grandeur, persecution, etc **2** intense, irrational fear or suspicion

paranoid *adjective* suffering from paranoia

paranormal *adjective* beyond what is normal in nature or scientific explanation ➤ *noun* (**the paranormal**) paranormal occurrences

parapet *noun* a low wall on a bridge or balcony to prevent people falling over the side

paraphernalia *plural noun* belongings; gear, equipment

> ⊙ Originally a woman's property which was not part of her dowry, and which therefore remained her own after marriage

paraphrase *verb* to express (a piece of writing) in other words ➤ *noun* an expression in different words

paraplegia (*pronounced* par-a-**plee**-ji-a) *noun, medicine* paralysis of the lower part of the body and legs

paraplegic *medicine, adjective* of paraplegia ➤ *noun* someone who suffers from paraplegia

pararhyme another word for **half-rhyme**

parasite *noun* **1** *biology* an animal or plant which gains food and protection from an organism of another species which is damaged in some way by it **2** *derogatory* a person living at the expense of another without being any use in return ◆ **parasitic** *adjective*

parasitism *noun, biology* a close association of two organisms of different species, with one gaining from the relationship, and the other usually damaged in some way by it (*compare with*: **commensalism, mutualism**) ◆ **parasitic** *adjective*

parasitology (*pronounced* par-a-sai-**tawl**-o-ji) *noun* the scientific study of parasites ◆ **parasitologist** *noun*

parasol *noun* a light umbrella used as a sunshade

parasympathetic nervous system *noun, biology* a division of the autonomic nervous system, which tends to slow down the heart rate, promote digestion and conserve energy (*compare with*: **sympathetic nervous system**)

paratrooper *noun* a soldier who is specially trained to drop from an aeroplane using a parachute

paratroops *plural noun* soldiers carried by air to be dropped by parachute into enemy country

parboil *verb* to partly cook (food) by boiling for a short time

parcel *noun* a wrapped and tied package to be sent by post ➤ *verb* (**parcelling, parcelled**):

parcel something out to divide it into portions • **parcel something up** to wrap it up as a package • **part and parcel** an absolutely necessary part

parch *verb* **1** to make hot and very dry **2** to make thirsty

parched *adjective* **1** very dry **2** very thirsty

parchment *noun* **1** the dried skin of a goat or sheep used for writing on **2** paper resembling this

pardon *verb* **1** to forgive **2** to free from punishment **3** to allow to go unpunished ➤ *noun* **1** forgiveness **2** the act of pardoning

pardonable *adjective* able to be forgiven

pare *verb* **1** to peel or cut off the edge or outer surface of **2** to make smaller gradually

parent *noun* **1** a father or mother **2** someone who acts as a father or mother to a child **3** an animal or plant that has produced offspring **4** a source or origin

parentage *noun* descent from parents or ancestors: *of Italian parentage*

parental *adjective* **1** of parents **2** with the manner or attitude of a parent **3** *biology* denoting the first generation that gives rise to all subsequent generations

parent company *noun* a business company that owns other smaller companies

parenthesis (*pronounced* pa-**ren**-the-sis) *noun* (*plural* **parentheses** – *pronounced* pa-**ren**-the-seez) **1** a word or group of words in a sentence forming an explanation or comment, often separated by brackets or dashes, eg he and his wife (*so he said*) were separated **2** (**parentheses**) brackets

parenthetical *adjective* **1** of the nature of a parenthesis **2** using parenthesis

parenthood *noun* the state of being a parent

par excellence (*pronounced* pahr ek-se-**lons**) *adverb* beyond compare ⊙ Comes from French, meaning 'as an example of excellence'

pariah (*pronounced* pa-**rai**-a) *noun* someone driven out from a community or group; an outcast

> ⊙ Originally a member of a low caste in southern India

parings *plural noun* small pieces cut away or peeled off

parish *noun* (*plural* **parishes**) a district with its own church and minister or priest

parishioner (*pronounced* pa-**rish**-on-er) *noun* a member of a parish

parity *noun* equality

parity check *noun, computing* the addition of a redundant bit to a word in order to detect simple bit errors

park *noun* **1** a public place for walking, with

grass and trees **2** an enclosed piece of land surrounding a country house ➤ *verb* to stop and leave (a car etc) in a place

parka *noun* a type of thick jacket with a hood

parkin or **perkin** *noun Scottish and Northern English* a moist, ginger-flavoured oatmeal cake made with treacle

Parkinson's disease *noun* a disease causing trembling in the hands etc and rigid muscles

parkland *noun* a grass area dotted with trees

parley *verb* (**parleys, parleying, parleyed**) to hold a conference, especially with an enemy ➤ *noun* (*plural* **parleys**) a meeting between enemies to settle terms of peace etc

parliament *noun* **1** the chief law-making council of a nation **2** (**Parliament**) *Brit* the House of Commons and the House of Lords

parliamentarian *noun* **1** someone who is skilled in the methods and practices of parliament **2** (**Parliamentarian**) a supporter of Parliament in opposition to Charles I during the English Civil War (*contrasted with*: **Royalist**) ➤ *adjective* relating to parliamentarians ♦ **parliamentarianism** or **parliamentarism** *noun*

parliamentary *adjective* **1** of, for or concerned with parliament: *a parliamentary candidate* **2** used in or suitable for parliament: *parliamentary procedures*

parlour or *US* **parlor** *noun* a sitting room in a house

parlourmaid or *US* **parlormaid** *noun* a woman or girl whose job is to wait at table

Parmesan (*pronounced* **pahr**-me-zan) *noun* a hard, dry Italian cheese made from skimmed milk, rennet and saffron

parochial (*pronounced* pa-**roh**-ki-al) *adjective* **1** relating to a parish **2** interested only in local affairs; narrow-minded ♦ **parochially** *adverb*

parody *noun* (*plural* **parodies**) an amusing imitation of someone's writing style, subject matter, etc ➤ *verb* (**parodies, parodying, parodied**) to make a parody of

parole (*pronounced* pa-**rohl**) *noun* the release of a prisoner before the end of a sentence on condition that they will have to return if they break the law ➤ *verb* to release on parole

⊙ From French *parole* meaning 'word' because prisoners are released on their word of honour

parotid gland (*pronounced* pa-**rot**-id) *noun, anatomy* one of a pair of glands in front of the ear, producing saliva

paroxysm *noun* a fit of pain, rage, laughter, etc ♦ **paroxysmal** *adjective*

parquet (*pronounced* **pahr**-kei) *noun* a floor covering of wooden blocks arranged in a pattern

parricide *noun* **1** the killing of one or both of your own parents **2** someone who kills their parents

parrot *noun* a bird with a hooked bill and often brightly coloured feathers

parrot-fashion *adverb* by unthinking repetition: *We learnt our tables parrot-fashion*

parry *verb* (**parries, parrying, parried**) to deflect, turn aside (a blow, question, etc)

parse *verb* to name the parts of speech of (words in a sentence) and say how the words are connected with each other

parsec *noun, astronomy* a unit of astronomical measurement equal to 3.26 light years or 3.09×10^{13} km

Parsee or **Parsi** *noun* a member of an Indian religious sect descended from the Persian Zoroastrians

parsimonious *adjective* too careful in spending money; stingy

parsimony (*pronounced* **pahr**-si-mo-ni) *noun* great care in spending money, meanness

parsley *noun* a bright-green, leafy herb, used in cookery

parsnip *noun* a plant with an edible, yellowish root shaped like a carrot

parson *noun* a member of the clergy, especially one in charge of a parish of the Church of England

parsonage *noun* a parson's house

part *noun* **1** a portion, a share **2** a piece forming part of a whole: *the various parts of a car engine* **3** a character taken by an actor in a play **4** a role in an action or event: *played a vital part in the campaign* **5** *music* the notes to be played or sung by a particular instrument or voice **6** (**parts**) talents: *a man of many parts* ➤ *verb* **1** to divide **2** to separate, send or go in different ways **3** to put or keep apart • **in good part** without being hurt or taking offence • **part with** to let go, be separated from • **take someone's part** to support them in an argument etc ⊙ Comes from Latin *pars* meaning 'a part', 'a section' or 'a share'

partake *verb* (**partaking, partook, partaken**): **partake of 1** to eat or drink some of **2** to take a part in

parthenogenesis (*pronounced* pahr-the-noh-**jen**-e-sis) *noun, biology* in some insects and plants: reproduction without fertilization by the male ♦ **parthenogenetic** *adjective*

partial *adjective* **1** in part only, not total or complete: *partial payment* **2** having a liking for (someone or something): *partial to cheese*

partial derivative *noun, maths* a derivative obtained by changing only one of the independent variables and holding the others constant

partial fractions *plural noun, maths* two or

more fractions, with denominators that cannot be factorized, into which a given fraction can be broken down

partiality noun (plural **partialities**) **1** the favouring of one thing more than another, bias **2** a particular liking (for something)

partially adverb not completely or wholly; not yet to the point of completion: The house is only partially built

participant or **participator** noun someone who takes part in anything

participate verb **1** to take part (in) **2** to have a share (in) ♦ **participation** noun

participatory adjective capable of being participated in or shared

participle noun, grammar **1** a form of a verb which can be used with other verbs to form tenses, eg 'he was eating' or 'she has arrived' **2** a form of verb used as an adjective, eg 'stolen jewels'

particle noun **1** a very small piece: a particle of sand **2** physics a tiny unit of matter such as a molecule, atom or electron **3** grammar a word which does not have any inflected forms, eg a preposition, conjunction or interjection **4** grammar an affix, such as un-, de-, -fy and -ly

particle accelerator noun, physics a device that is used to accelerate charged subatomic particles to a high velocity

particular adjective **1** relating to a single definite person, thing, etc considered separately from others: I want this particular colour **2** special: Take particular care of the china **3** fussy, difficult to please: particular about her food ➤ noun (**particulars**) the facts or details about someone or something ♦ **particularly** adverb

parting noun **1** the act of separating or dividing **2** a place of separation **3** a going away (from each other), a leave-taking **4** a line dividing hair on the head brushed in opposite directions

parting shot noun a final hostile remark made on departing

partisan (pronounced pahr-ti-**zan** or **pahr**-ti-zan) adjective giving strong support or loyalty to a particular cause, theory, etc, often without considering other points of view ➤ noun someone with partisan views

partition noun **1** a division **2** something which divides, eg a wall between rooms ➤ verb **1** to divide into parts **2** to divide by making a wall etc **3** maths to divide (a set) into subsets **4** maths to split (a number) into component parts, eg 24 into 12 + 12 or 14 + 10

partly adverb in part, or in some parts; not wholly or completely: The house is built partly of stone and partly of wood

partner noun **1** someone who shares the ownership of a business etc with another or

others **2** one of a pair in games, dancing, etc **3** a husband, wife, or lover **4** biology an animal or plant that take part in commensalism or symbiosis ➤ verb to be the partner of

partnership noun **1** a relationship in which two or more people or groups operate together as partners **2** the status of a partner: She was offered a partnership at the age of 30 **3** a business or other enterprise jointly owned or run by two or more people etc

part of speech noun (plural **parts of speech**) grammar any of the grammatical groups into which words are divided, eg noun, verb, adjective, preposition

partook past tense of **partake**

partridge noun (plural **partridge** or **partridges**) a bird with brown or grey feathers which is shot as game

part-song noun, music a song sung, usually unaccompanied, in parts in harmony

part-time adjective for only part of the working week: I went part-time in my job (compare with: **full-time**)

party noun (plural **parties**) **1** a gathering of guests: a birthday party/dinner party **2** a group of people travelling together: a party of tourists **3** a number of people with the same plans or ideas: a political party **4** someone taking part in, or approving, an action

party line noun **1** a shared telephone line **2** the official policy laid down by the leaders of a political party

PASCAL (pronounced pas-**kal**) noun, computing a high-level computer programming language used for general programming

⊙ Named after Blaise Pascal (1623–62), French philosopher and scientist, because he devised and built a calculating machine

pascal (pronounced pas-kal) noun (symbol **Pa**) the standard unit of pressure, equal to a force of one newton per square metre

⊙ Named after Blaise Pascal (1623–62), French philosopher and scientist

Pascal's triangle (pronounced pas-**kalz**) noun, statistics a group of numbers arranged to form a triangle in which each number is the sum of the two numbers to its right and left in the line above

pass verb **1** to go, move, travel, etc: He passed out of sight over the hill **2** to move on or along: Pass the salt **3** to go by: I saw the bus pass our house **4** to overtake **5** of parliament: to put (a law) into force **6** to be successful in (an examination) **7** to be declared healthy or in good condition after (an inspection) **8** to come to an end: The feeling of dizziness passed **9** to hand on, give: He passed the story on to his son **10** to spend (time): passing *a pleasant hour by the river* **11** to make, utter (eg a remark) **12** to discharge (urine or faeces) from the body ➤ *noun* **1** a narrow passage over or through a range of mountains **2** a ticket or card allowing someone to go somewhere **3** success in an examination **4** a sexual advance • **pass away** to die • **pass off** to present (a forgery etc) as genuine • **pass on 1** to go forward, proceed **2** to hand on **3** to die • **pass out** to faint • **pass up** to fail to take up (an opportunity)

❗ Do not confuse **passed**, which is a verb tense, with **past**.

passable *adjective* **1** fairly good **2** of a river etc: able to be crossed ◆ **passably** *adverb* (meaning 1)

passage *noun* **1** the act of passing: *the passage of time* **2** a journey in a ship **3** a corridor **4** a way through **5** a part of the text of a book

passageway *noun* a passage, a way through

passé (*pronounced* pas-ei) *adjective* old-fashioned ⊙ Comes from French, meaning 'passed'

passenger *noun* a traveller, not a member of the crew, in a train, ship, aeroplane, etc

passer-by *noun* (*plural* **passers-by**) someone who happens to pass by when something happens

passing *adjective* **1** going by: *a passing car* **2** not lasting long: *passing interest* **3** casual: *a passing remark* ➤ *noun* **1** the act of someone or something which passes **2** a going away, a coming to an end **3** death

passion *noun* **1** strong feeling, especially anger or love **2** (**the Passion**) the sufferings and death of Christ

passionate *adjective* **1** easily moved to passion **2** full of passion ◆ **passionately** *adverb*

passionfruit *noun* the edible, oblong fruit of a tropical plant

passive *adjective* **1** making no resistance **2** acted upon, not acting **3** *grammar* describing the form of a verb in which the subject undergoes, rather than performs, the action of the verb, eg 'The postman was bitten by the dog' (*compare with:* **active**) ◆ **passively** *adverb* ◆ **passivity** *noun*

passive resistance *noun* the use of non-violent means, eg fasting, peaceful demonstration, etc, as a protest

passive smoking *noun* the involuntary inhaling of smoke from tobacco smoked by others

Passover *noun* a Jewish festival celebrating the exodus of the Israelites from Egypt (*also:* **Pesach**)

passport *noun* a card or booklet which gives someone's name and description, needed to travel in another country

password *noun* **1** a secret word which allows those who know it to pass **2** *computing* a word typed into a computer to allow access to restricted data

past *noun* **1** (**the past**) the time gone by **2** someone's previous life or career **3** *grammar* the past tense ➤ *adjective* **1** of an earlier time: *past kindnesses* **2** just over, recently ended: *the past year* **3** gone, finished: *The time for argument is past* ➤ *preposition* **1** after: *It's past midday* **2** up to and beyond, further than: *Go past the traffic lights* ➤ *adverb* by: *She walked past, looking at no one*

❗ Do not confuse **passed**, which is a verb tense, with **past**.

pasta *noun* **1** a dough used in making spaghetti, macaroni, etc **2** the prepared shapes of this, eg spaghetti

paste *noun* **1** pastry dough **2** a gluey liquid for sticking paper etc together **3** any soft, kneadable mixture: *almond paste* **4** fine glass used to make imitation gems ➤ *verb* **1** to stick something with paste **2** *computing* to insert (text that has been cut or copied from another document etc)

pasteboard *noun* stiff board made from sheets of paper pasted together

pastel *adjective* of a colour: soft, pale ➤ *noun* **1** a chalk-like crayon used for drawing **2** a drawing made with this

pasteurize or **pasteurise** *verb* to heat food (especially milk) in order to kill harmful germs in it ◆ **pasteurization** *noun*

⊙ Named after Louis *Pasteur*, the 19th-century French chemist who invented the process

pastiche (*pronounced* pas-**teesh**) *noun* a humorous imitation, a parody

pastille (*pronounced* pas-til or pas-**teel**) *noun* a small sweet, sometimes sucked as a medicine

pastime *noun* a hobby, a spare-time interest

past master *noun* an expert: *She is a past master at quizzes*

pastor *noun* a member of the clergy

pastoral *adjective* **1** relating to country life **2** of a pastor or the work of the clergy

pastoralism or **pastoral farming** *noun, geography* a system of farming involving the rearing of livestock

past participle *noun, grammar* the form of a verb used after an auxiliary verb to indicate that something took place in the past, for instance *gone* in 'he has *gone*'

pastrami *noun* a smoked highly seasoned cut of beef ⊙ Comes from Yiddish *pastrame*

pastry *noun* (*plural* **pastries**) **1** a flour paste used to make the bases and crusts of pies, tarts, etc **2** a small cake

past tense *noun, grammar* the tense of a verb which indicates that something took place in the past

pasture *noun* ground covered with grass on which cattle graze

pasty[1] (*pronounced* **peis**-ti) *adjective* (**pastier, pastiest**) **1** like paste **2** pale

pasty[2] (*pronounced* **pas**-ti) *noun* (*plural* **pasties**) a pie containing meat and vegetables in a covering of pastry

pat *noun* **1** a light, quick blow or tap with the hand **2** a small lump of butter etc **3** a cake of animal dung ➤ *verb* (**patting, patted**) to strike gently, tap • **off pat** memorized thoroughly, ready to be said when necessary

patch *verb* to mend (clothes) by putting in a new piece of material to cover a hole ➤ *noun* (*plural* **patches**) **1** a piece of material sewn on to mend a hole **2** a small piece of ground **3** *computing* a set of instructions added to a program to correct an error • **patch up 1** to mend, especially hastily or clumsily **2** to settle (a quarrel)

patchwork *noun* fabric formed of small patches or pieces of material sewn together

patchy *adjective* (**patchier, patchiest**) uneven, mixed in quality ♦ **patchily** *adverb*

pate (*pronounced* peit) *noun, formal* the head: *a bald pate*

pâté or **paté** (*pronounced* **pa**-tei) *noun* a paste made of finely minced meat, fish or vegetables, flavoured with herbs, spices, etc

patella *noun* (*plural* **patellas** or **patellae** – *pronounced* pa-**tel**-ee), *anatomy* the kneecap

patent (*pronounced* **pei**-tent) *noun* an official written statement granting someone the sole right to make or sell something that they have invented ➤ *adjective* **1** protected from copying by a patent **2** open, easily seen ➤ *verb* to obtain a patent for

patent leather *noun* leather with a very glossy surface

patently *adverb* openly, clearly: *patently obvious*

paternal *adjective* **1** of a father **2** like a father, fatherly **3** on the father's side of the family: *my paternal grandfather*

paternalism *noun* governmental or managerial benevolence taken to the extreme of over-protectiveness and authoritarianism ♦ **paternalistic** *adjective*

paternity *noun* the state or fact of being a father

paternity leave *noun* leave of absence from work for a father after the birth of a child

path *noun* **1** a way made by people or animals walking on it, a track **2** the route to be taken by a person or vehicle: *in the lorry's path* **3** a course of action, a way of life

-path *suffix* **1** forms words describing people who are suffering from particular disorders **2** forms words describing people who provide therapy for particular disorders: *osteopath* (= someone who provides therapy for bone and muscle injuries) ⏲ Comes from Greek *patheia* meaning 'suffering'

pathetic *adjective* **1** causing pity **2** causing contempt; feeble, inadequate: *a pathetic attempt* ♦ **pathetically** *adverb*

pathname *noun, computing* a name that specifies the location of a particular file within a directory

patho- (*pronounced* path-oh) *prefix* of or relating to diseases or other disorders: *pathology* ⏲ Comes from Greek *patheia* meaning 'suffering'

pathogen *noun* a micro-organism, eg a bacterium or virus, that causes infection or disease

pathological *adjective* **1** relating to disease **2** *informal* compulsive, obsessive: *a pathological liar*

pathologist *noun* **1** a doctor who studies the causes and effects of disease **2** a doctor who makes post-mortem examinations

pathology *noun* the study of diseases

pathos (*pronounced* **pei**-thos) *noun* a quality that arouses pity

pathway *noun* a path

-pathy *suffix* forms words describing disorders and therapies: *osteopathy* ⏲ Comes from Greek *patheia* meaning 'suffering'

patience *noun* **1** the ability or willingness to be patient **2** (*also called:* **solitaire**) a card game played by one person

patient *adjective* suffering delay, discomfort, etc without complaint or anger ➤ *noun* someone under the care of a doctor etc ♦ **patiently** *adverb*

patio (*pronounced* **pat**-i-oh) *noun* (*plural* **patios**) a paved open yard attached to a house

patisserie (*pronounced* pa-**tees**-e-ree) *noun* **1** a shop or café selling fancy cakes, sweet pastries, etc in the continental style **2** such cakes

patri- *prefix* father: *patricide* ⏲ Comes from Latin *pater* meaning 'father'

patriarch (*pronounced* **pei**-tri-ahrk) *noun* **1** the male head of a family or tribe **2** a high-ranking bishop of the Orthodox Church

patriarchal (*pronounced* pei-tri-**ahrk**-kal) *adjective* ruled or controlled by men or patriarchs

patriarchy (*pronounced* **pei**-tri-ahr-ki) *noun* (*plural* **patriarchies**) a society in which a man is head of the family and descent is traced through the male line

patrician *adjective* aristocratic

patricide *noun* **1** the act of killing one's own father **2** someone who commits such a murder

patrimony *noun* (*plural* **patrimonies**) property handed down from a father or ancestors

patriot (*pronounced* **pat**-ri-ot or **peit**-ri-ot) *noun* someone who loves and is loyal to their country

patriotic *adjective* loyal or devoted to your country ♦ **patriotically** *adverb*

patriotism *noun* love of and loyalty to your country

patrol *verb* (**patrolling, patrolled**) to keep guard or watch by moving regularly around (an area etc) ➤ *noun* **1** the act of keeping guard in this way **2** the people keeping watch **3** a small group of Scouts or Guides

patrol car *noun* a police car used to patrol an area

patron (*pronounced* **pei**-tron) *noun* **1** someone who protects or supports (an artist, a form of art, etc) **2** a customer of a shop etc

patronage (*pronounced* **pat**-ro-nij) *noun* the support given by a patron

patronize or **patronise** (*pronounced* pat-ro-naiz) *verb* **1** to be a patron towards: *Patronize your local shops* **2** to treat (someone) as an inferior, look down on: *Don't patronize me*

patron saint *noun* a saint chosen as the protector of a country etc

patter[1] *verb* of rain, footsteps, etc: to make a quick tapping sound ➤ *noun* the sound of falling rain, of footsteps, etc

patter[2] *noun* **1** chatter; rapid talk, especially that used by salesmen to encourage people to buy their goods **2** the jargon of a particular group

pattern *noun* **1** an example suitable to be copied **2** a model or guide for making something **3** a decorative design **4** a sample: *a book of tweed patterns* **5** *maths* a systematic arrangement of numbers, shapes, etc

patterned *adjective* having a design, not self-coloured

patty *noun* (*plural* **patties**) a small, flat cake of chopped meat etc

paucity *noun, formal* smallness of number or quantity

paunch *noun* (*plural* **paunches**) a fat stomach

pauper *noun* a very poor person

pause *noun* **1** a short stop, an interval **2** a break or hesitation in speaking or writing **3** *music* a symbol (␣) showing the holding of a note or rest ➤ *verb* to stop for a short time

pave *verb* to lay (a street) with stone or concrete to form a level surface for walking on • **pave the way for** to prepare or make the way easy for

pavement *noun* a paved footway at the side of a road for pedestrians

pavilion *noun* **1** a building in a sports ground with facilities for changing clothes **2** a large ornamental building **3** a large tent

Pavlovian *adjective, psychology* of reactions, responses, etc: automatic, unthinking

○ From research by Russian physiologist, Ivan *Pavlov* (1849–1936), on conditioned reflexes

paw *noun* the foot of an animal ➤ *verb* **1** of an animal: to scrape with one of the front feet **2** to handle or touch roughly or rudely **3** to strike out wildly with the hand: *paw the air*

pawn *verb* to put (an article of some value) in someone's keeping in exchange for a sum of money which, when repaid, buys back the article ➤ *noun* **1** *chess* a small piece of the lowest rank **2** someone who lets themselves be used by another for some purpose • **in pawn** having been pawned

pawnbroker *noun* someone who lends money in exchange for pawned articles

pawnshop *noun* a pawnbroker's place of business

pawpaw another word for **papaya**

pay *verb* (**paying, paid**) **1** to give (money) in exchange for (goods etc): *I paid £30 for it* **2** to suffer the punishment (for) **3** to be advantageous or profitable: *It pays to be prepared* **4** to give (eg attention) ➤ *noun* money given or received for work; wages • **pay off 1** to pay in full and discharge (workers) owing to lack of work **2** to have good results: *His hard work paid off* • **pay out 1** to spend **2** to give out (a length of rope etc)

payable *adjective* requiring to be paid

PAYE *abbreviation* pay as you earn, a system by which income tax is deducted from a salary before it is given to the worker

payee *noun* someone to whom money is paid

payment *noun* **1** the act of paying **2** money paid for goods etc

payphone *noun* a coin- or card-operated public telephone

payroll *noun* a register of employees that lists the wage or salary due to each

pay TV or **pay television** *noun* TV programmes, video entertainment, etc distributed to an audience which pays for the programmes by subscribing to a cable TV or satellite TV network

Pb *symbol, chemistry* lead

PC *abbreviation* **1** police constable **2** personal computer **3** privy councillor **4** political correctness

pc *abbreviation* **1** personal computer **2** postcard **3** per cent

PCV *abbreviation* passenger carrying vehicle

Pd *symbol, chemistry* palladium

PDA *abbreviation* personal digital assistant, a

hand-held computer for managing personal information

PDF *abbreviation, computing* Portable Document Format, a file format that allows documents to keep their original appearance when viewed on a different operating system

PE *abbreviation* physical education

pea *noun* **1** a climbing plant which produces round, green seeds in pods **2** the seed itself, eaten as a vegetable

peace *noun* **1** quietness, calm **2** freedom from war or disturbance **3** a treaty bringing this about

peaceable *adjective* of a quiet nature, fond of peace

peaceful *adjective* quiet; calm ♦ **peacefully** *adverb*

peach *noun* (*plural* **peaches**) **1** a juicy, velvety-skinned fruit **2** the tree that bears it **3** an orangey-pink colour

peacock *noun* a large bird, the male of which has brightly coloured, patterned tail feathers

peahen *noun* a female peacock

peak *noun* **1** the pointed top of a mountain or hill **2** the highest point **3** the jutting-out part of the brim of a cap ➤ *verb* **1** to rise to a peak **2** to reach the highest point: *Prices peaked in July*

peaked *adjective* **1** pointed **2** of a cap: having a peak

peaky *adjective* (**peakier, peakiest**) looking pale and unhealthy

peal *noun* **1** a set of bells tuned to each other **2** the changes rung on such bells **3** a succession of loud sounds: *peals of laughter* ➤ *verb* to sound loudly

⚠ Do not confuse with: **peel**

pean US spelling of **paean**

peanut *noun* a type of nut similar to a pea in shape (*also called*: **groundnut, monkey nut**)

peanut butter *noun* a paste of ground roasted peanuts, spread on bread etc

pear *noun* **1** a fruit with sweet, juicy, white pulp, which is narrow at the top and widens at the bottom **2** the tree that produces this fruit

pearl *noun* **1** a gem formed in the shell of the oyster and several other shellfish **2** a valuable remark etc: *pearls of wisdom*

pearl barley *noun* seeds of barley ground into round, polished grains, used in soups and stews

pearly gates *noun, informal* (**the pearly gates**) the entrance to heaven

pear-shaped *adjective* narrow at the top and wider at the bottom ● **go pear-shaped** *informal* to go wrong

peasant *noun* someone who works and lives on the land, especially in an underdeveloped area

pea-shooter *noun* a short tube through which

you fire dried peas by blowing, used as a toy weapon

peat *noun* turf cut out of boggy places, dried and used as fuel

pebble *noun* a small, roundish stone

pebble dash *noun* a coating for outside walls with small stones set into the mortar

pebbly *adjective* (**pebblier, pebbliest**) **1** full of pebbles **2** rough, knobbly

pecan (*pronounced* pi-**kan** or **pee**-kan) *noun* **1** a N American tree, widely cultivated for its edible nut **2** the oblong reddish-brown edible nut produced by this tree

peccadillo *noun* (*plural* **peccadilloes** or **peccadillos**) a slight misdemeanour or wrong

peck *verb* **1** to strike with the beak **2** to pick up with the beak **3** to eat little, nibble (at) **4** to kiss quickly and briefly ➤ *noun* **1** a sharp blow with the beak **2** a brief kiss

peckish *adjective* slightly hungry

pecs *plural noun, informal* pectoral muscles

pectin *noun, biology, chemistry* a complex carbohydrate that cements plant cell walls ⓖ Comes from Greek *pektos* meaning 'congealed'

pectoral *adjective* of the breast or chest: *pectoral muscles*

pectoral fin *noun* in fish: one of a pair of fins situated just behind the gills, used to control direction and for slowing down

peculiar *adjective* strange, odd: *He is a very peculiar person* ● **peculiar to** belonging to one person or thing only: *a custom peculiar to England*

peculiarity *noun* (*plural* **peculiarities**) that which marks someone or something off from others in some way; something odd

peculiarly *adverb* in a peculiar way

pecuniary *adjective* of money

pedagogic (*pronounced* ped-a-**gog**-ik or ped-a-**goj**-ik) or **pedagogical** *adjective, old* of a teacher or education

pedagogue (*pronounced* **ped**-a-gog) *noun, old* a teacher

pedal *noun* **1** a lever worked by the foot on a bicycle, piano, harp, etc **2** a key worked by the foot on an organ ➤ *verb* (**pedalling, pedalled**) **1** to work the pedals of **2** to ride on a bicycle ➤ *adjective, zoology* relating to the foot or feet

pedant *noun* **1** someone who makes a great show of their knowledge **2** someone overly fussy about minor details

pedantic *adjective* over-concerned with correctness

pedantry *noun* **1** fussiness about unimportant details **2** a display of knowledge

pedate *adjective, biology* footed or foot-like

peddle *verb* to travel from door to door selling goods

pedestal *noun* the foot or support of a pillar, statue, etc

pedestrian *adjective* **1** going on foot **2** for those on foot **3** unexciting, dull: *a pedestrian account* ▸ *noun* someone who goes or travels on foot

pedestrian crossing *noun* a place where pedestrians may cross the road when the traffic stops

pedestrianize or **pedestrianise** *verb* to convert (a shopping street etc) into an area for pedestrians only ♦ **pedestrianization** *noun*

pedestrian precinct *noun* a shopping street or similar area from which traffic is excluded

pediatrics, pediatrician US spelling of **paediatrics, paediatrician**

pedicel *noun, biology* **1** the stalk of a single flower **2** the stalk of an animal organ, eg a crab's eye ◉ Comes from Latin *pedicelus*, diminutive of *pediculus* meaning 'a little foot'

pedicure *noun* a treatment for the feet, including treating corns, cutting nails, etc

pedigree *noun* **1** a list of someone's ancestors **2** the ancestry of a pure-bred animal **3** a distinguished descent or ancestry ▸ *adjective* of an animal: pure-bred, from a long line of ancestors of the same breed

◉ Literally 'crane's foot', because the lines of a family tree were thought to resemble the forked feet of the bird

pediment *noun* **1** *geography* a gently sloping surface, usually consisting of bare rock covered by a thin layer of sediment, formed by the erosion of cliffs or steep slopes **2** a triangular structure over the front of an ancient Greek building

pedlar *noun* someone who peddles, a hawker

pedo- see **paedo-**

pedometer (*pronounced* pi-**dom**-i-ter) *noun* a device that measures distance walked by recording the number of steps taken

pee *informal, verb* (**peeing, peed**) to urinate ▸ *noun* **1** the act of urinating **2** urine

peek *verb* to peep, glance, especially secretively ▸ *noun* a secret look

peel *verb* **1** to strip off the outer covering or skin of: *peel an apple* **2** of skin, paint, etc: to come off in small pieces **3** to lose skin in small flakes, eg as a result of sunburn ▸ *noun* skin, rind ◉ Comes from Latin *pelare* meaning 'to deprive of hair'

⚠ Do not confuse with: **peal**

peep¹ *verb* **1** to look through a narrow opening, round a corner, etc **2** to look slyly or quickly (at) **3** to begin to appear: *The sun peeped out* ▸ *noun* a quick look, a glimpse, often from hiding

peep² *noun* a high, small sound ▸ *verb* to make such a sound

peer¹ *noun* **1** someone's equal in rank, merit, or age **2** a nobleman of the rank of baron upwards **3** a member of the House of Lords

peer² *verb* to look at with half-closed eyes, as if with difficulty

peerage *noun* **1** a peer's title **2** the peers as a group

peer group *noun* people of similar age or rank, considered as a group

peerless *adjective* without any equal, better than all others

peer pressure *noun* compulsion to do the same things as others in your peer group

peer-to-peer *adjective, computing* (*abbrev* **P2P**) denoting a system which has no server, and in which all the computers can be used as workstations

peeve *verb, informal* to irritate

peeved *adjective, informal* annoyed

peevish *adjective* cross, bad-tempered, irritable

peewit *noun* the lapwing

peg *noun* **1** a pin or stake of wood, metal, etc **2** a hook fixed to a wall for hanging clothes etc ▸ *verb* (**pegging, pegged**) **1** to fasten with a peg **2** to fix (prices etc) at a certain level

pejorative (*pronounced* pe-**jor**-a-tiv) *adjective* showing disapproval, scorn, etc: *a pejorative remark*

Pekinese or **Pekingese** *noun* a breed of small dog with a long coat and flat face

pelagic *adjective, biology* denoting the living organisms that swim freely in surface waters, eg plankton and fish ♦ **pelagian** *noun & adjective* (*compare with:* **benthos**) ◉ Comes from Greek *pelagos* meaning 'sea'

pelican *noun* a large water bird with a pouched bill for storing fish

pelican crossing *noun* a street-crossing where the lights are operated by pedestrians

◉ Taken from the phrase '*pedestrian light controlled crossing*'

pellet *noun* **1** a small ball of shot etc **2** a small pill

pellicle *noun* **1** a thin skin or film **2** *biology* a protein covering which preserves the shape of single-cell organisms ◉ Comes from Latin *pellicula*, diminutive of *pellis* meaning 'skin' ♦ **pellicular** *adjective*

pell-mell *adverb* in great confusion; headlong

Pelmanism *noun* a card game in which cards are spread out face down and must be picked up in matching pairs

◉ Named after a form of memory training devised by the *Pelman* Institute

pelmet *noun* a strip of fabric or a narrow board at the top of a window to hide a curtain rail

pelt¹ *verb* **1** to throw (things) at **2** to run fast **3** of rain: to fall heavily ➤ *noun*: **at full pelt** at top speed

pelt² *noun* the untreated skin of an animal

pelvis *noun* (*plural* **pelvises** or **pelves** – *pronounced* **pel**-veez) **1** the frame of two hip-bones which is attached to the spine and the bones of the legs **2** the cavity formed by this ◆ **pelvic** *adjective*

pen¹ *noun* an instrument with a nib for writing in ink ➤ *verb* (**penning, penned**) to write (eg a letter)

pen² *noun* a small enclosure for sheep, cattle, etc ➤ *verb* (**penning, penned**) to enclose in a pen

pen³ *noun* a female swan

penalize or **penalise** (*pronounced* **pee**-na-laiz) *verb* **1** to punish **2** to put under a disadvantage

penal servitude *noun* imprisonment with hard labour as an added punishment

penalty *noun* (*plural* **penalties**) **1** punishment **2** a disadvantage put on a player or team for having broken a rule of a game

penance *noun* punishment willingly suffered by someone to make up for a wrong

pence a plural of **penny**

penchant (*pronounced* **pon**-shon) *noun* an inclination (for), a bias

pencil *noun* an instrument containing a length of graphite or other substance for writing, drawing, etc ➤ *verb* (**pencilling, pencilled**) to draw, mark, etc with a pencil • **pencil in** to note down a provisional arrangement in your diary, for later confirmation

pendant *noun* **1** an ornament hung from a necklace etc **2** a necklace with such an ornament

pendent *adjective* hanging

pending *adjective* awaiting a decision or attention: *This matter is pending* ➤ *preposition* awaiting, until the coming of: *pending confirmation*

pendulous *adjective* hanging down, drooping

pendulum *noun* **1** *physics* a weight, suspended from a fixed point, that swings freely back and forth through a small angle with simple harmonic motion **2** a swinging weight which drives the mechanism of a clock

penetrate *verb* **1** to pierce or pass into or through **2** to enter by force ◆ **penetration** *noun*

penetrating *adjective* **1** of a sound: piercing **2** keen, probing: *a penetrating question*

pen friend or **pen pal** *noun* someone you have never seen (usually living abroad) with whom you exchange letters

penguin *noun* a large sea bird of Antarctic regions, which cannot fly

penicillin *noun* a medicine obtained from

mould, which kills many bacteria

peninsula (*pronounced* pe-**nin**-sjuw-la) *noun* a piece of land almost surrounded by water ◆ **peninsular** *adjective*

penis *noun* (*plural* **penises** or **penes** – *pronounced* **pee**-neez) the part of the body which a male human or animal uses in sexual intercourse and for urinating

penitence *noun* being penitent and wishing to improve

penitent *adjective* sorry for your sins ➤ *noun* a penitent person

penitential *adjective* relating to penitence or penance

penitentiary *noun* (*plural* **penitentiaries**), *US* a prison

penknife *noun* (*plural* **penknives**) a pocket knife with folding blades

pen name *noun* a name adopted by a writer instead of their own name

pennant *noun* a long flag coming to a point at the end

penniless *adjective* having no money

penny *noun* (*plural* **pence** or **pennies**) **1** a coin worth $\frac{1}{100}$ of £1 **2** (*plural* **pence**) used to show an amount in pennies: *The newspaper costs forty-two pence* **3** (*plural* **pennies**) used for a number of coins: *I need five pennies for the coffee machine*

penny-pinching *adjective, derogatory* mean, stingy

pension *noun* a sum of money paid regularly to a retired person, a widow, someone wounded in war, etc ➤ *verb*: **pension off** to dismiss or allow to retire with a pension

pensionable *adjective* having or giving the right to a pension: *pensionable age*

pensioner *noun* someone who receives a pension

pensive *adjective* thoughtful ◆ **pensively** *adverb*

pent or **pent-up** *adjective* **1** shut up, not allowed to go free **2** of emotions: not freely expressed

penta- *prefix* five ⊙ Comes from Greek *pente* meaning 'five'

pentagon *noun* a flat figure with five sides ◆ **pentagonal** *adjective*

pentagram *noun* a star-shaped figure with five points and consisting of five lines

pentahedron (*pronounced* pen-ta-**heed**-ron) *noun* (*plural* **pentahedrons** or **pentahedra**), *maths* a solid figure with five faces ◆ **pentahedral** *adjective*

pentameter (*pronounced* pen-**tam**-e-ter) *noun* a line of verse with five metrical feet

pentane *noun, chemistry* a hydrocarbon of the alkane series with five carbon atoms

pentanoic acid noun, chemistry a colourless acid used in the perfume industry

pentathlon (pronounced pen-**tath**-lon) noun an athletic contest comprising five events (compare with: **decathlon**, **heptathlon**)
♦ **pentathlete** noun

pentatonic adjective, music of a scale: consisting of five notes, ie a major scale omitting the fourth and seventh

pentavalent adjective, chemistry having a valency of five

Pentecost noun **1** a Jewish festival held fifty days after Passover **2** a Christian festival held seven weeks after Easter

Pentecostalist Christianity, noun a member of the Pentecostal church, which puts emphasis on God's gifts through the Holy Spirit ➤ adjective relating to Pentecostalism ♦ **Pentecostalism** noun

penthouse noun a luxurious flat at the top of a building

Pentium noun, trademark a type of fast microprocessor used in personal computers

penultimate adjective last but one

penumbra noun (plural **penumbras** or **penumbrae** – pronounced pe-**num**-bree) a light shadow surrounding the main shadow of an eclipse

penurious adjective impoverished, penniless

penury noun poverty, want

peony (pronounced **pee**-o-ni) noun (plural **peonies**) a type of garden plant with large red, white or pink flowers

people plural noun **1** the men, women and children of a country or nation **2** persons generally ➤ verb **1** to fill with people **2** to inhabit, make up the population of ⓞ Comes from Latin populus meaning 'a people' or 'a nation'

pep informal, noun spirit, verve ➤ verb (**pepping, pepped**): **pep up** to invigorate, enliven

pepper noun **1** a plant whose berries are dried, powdered and used as seasoning **2** the spicy powder it produces **3** a hot-tasting hollow fruit containing many seeds, eaten raw, cooked or pickled ➤ verb to sprinkle with pepper
• **pepper with** to throw at or hit: peppered with bullets

peppercorn noun the dried berry of the pepper plant

pepper mill noun a device for grinding peppercorns over food

peppermint noun **1** a type of plant with a powerful taste and smell **2** a flavouring taken from this and used in sweets etc

pepperoni or **peperoni** (pronounced pe-pe-**roh**-ni) noun a hard, spicy beef and pork sausage

peppery adjective **1** containing much pepper **2** inclined to be hot-tempered

pep pill noun a pill containing a stimulating drug

pepsin noun, biology, chemistry a digestive enzyme

pep talk noun a talk meant to encourage or arouse enthusiasm

peptic adjective **1** of the digestive system **2** of the stomach: peptic ulcer **3** relating to the enzyme pepsin

peptide noun, biology, chemistry a molecule that is a relatively short chain of amino acids

per preposition **1** in, out of **2** for each: £2 per dozen **3** in each: six times per week

perambulator full form of **pram**

per annum adverb in each year ⓞ from Latin

per capita or **per head** adverb for each person ⓞ per capita from Latin meaning 'by heads'

perceive verb **1** to become aware of through the senses **2** to see **3** to understand

per cent or **percent** adverb (symbol **%**) out of every hundred: five per cent (= 5 out of every hundred)

percentage noun the number of parts per hundred, eg ½ expressed as a percentage = 50%

percentage error noun, maths error expressed as a percentage of the total amount

perceptible adjective able to be seen or understood ♦ **perceptibly** adverb

perception noun the ability to perceive; understanding

perceptive adjective able or quick to perceive or understand

perch¹ noun (plural **perches**) **1** a rod on which birds roost **2** a high seat or position ➤ verb to roost

perch² noun (plural **perches**) a type of freshwater fish

perchance adverb, old by chance; perhaps

percolate verb **1** of a liquid: to drip or drain through small holes in a porous material **2** to cause (a liquid) to do this **3** of news etc: to pass slowly down or through ♦ **percolation** noun

percolator noun a device for percolating: a coffee percolator

percussion noun **1** a striking of one object against another **2** musical instruments played by striking, eg drums, cymbals, etc

percussive adjective making the noise of percussion; loud, striking

perdition noun **1** utter loss or ruin **2** everlasting punishment

peregrinations (pronounced pe-ri-gri-**nei**-shonz) plural noun, literary wanderings

peregrine (pronounced **pe**-ri-grin) noun a type of falcon

peremptory (pronounced pi-**remp**-to-ri)

adjective **1** urgent **2** of a command: to be obeyed at once **3** domineering, dictatorial

perennial *adjective* **1** lasting through the year **2** everlasting, perpetual **3** of a plant: growing from year to year ➤ *noun* a perennial plant (*compare with*: **annual, biennial**)

perestroika (*pronounced* pe-ri-**stroi**-ka) *noun* reconstruction, restructuring of the state (originally in the former Soviet Union)

perfect *adjective* (*pronounced* **per**-fikt) **1** complete, finished **2** faultless **3** exact ➤ *verb* (*pronounced* per-**fekt**) **1** to make perfect **2** to finish

perfection *noun* **1** the state of being perfect **2** the highest state or degree

perfectionist *noun* someone who is satisfied only by perfection

perfectly *adverb* **1** in a perfect way **2** completely; quite: *a perfectly reasonable reaction*

perfect number *noun, maths* a number that is equal to the sum of all its factors, eg 6 (because $1+2+3=6$)

perfect tense *noun, grammar* a verb tense formed by *have* and the past participle, eg *He has failed* (**present perfect**), *He had failed* (**past perfect**), *He will have failed* (**future perfect**)

perfidious (*pronounced* per-**fid**-i-us) *adjective* treacherous, unfaithful

perfidy (*pronounced* **per**-fi-di) *noun* perfidious behaviour or an instance of this

perforate *verb* to make a hole or holes through

perforated *adjective* pierced with holes

perforce *adverb, old* of necessity, unavoidably

perform *verb* **1** to do, act **2** to act (a part) on the stage **3** to provide entertainment for an audience **4** to play (a piece of music)

performance *noun* **1** an entertainment in a theatre etc **2** the act of doing something **3** the level of success of a machine, car, etc

performance poetry *noun* poetry written to be read out in public

performer *noun* someone who acts or performs

perfume *noun* (*pronounced* **per**-fyoom) **1** smell, fragrance **2** a fragrant liquid put on the skin; scent ➤ *verb* (*pronounced* per-**fyoom** or **per**-fyoom) **1** to put scent on or in **2** to give a sweet smell to

perfumery *noun* (*plural* **perfumeries**) **1** a shop or factory where perfume is sold or made **2** perfumes

perfunctory *adjective* done carelessly or half-heartedly: *a perfunctory inspection*
♦ **perfunctorily** *adverb*

perfusion *noun* **1** *biology* the movement of a fluid through a tissue or organ **2** *medicine* the

injection of a fluid into a blood vessel ♦ **perfuse** *verb* ◎ Comes from Latin *perfusus* meaning 'poured over'

pergola (*pronounced* **per**-go-la) *noun* an arched framework constructed from slender branches ◎ from Italian

perhaps *adverb* it may be (that); possibly: *Perhaps she'll resign*

peri- *prefix* around: *perimeter* (= the outside line around a figure or shape)/*perinatal* (= around the time of birth) ◎ Comes from Greek *peri* meaning 'around'

perianth *noun, botany* the outer part of flower, usually consisting of petals and sepals

pericardium *noun* (*plural* **pericardia**), *anatomy* the sac that surrounds the heart

pericarp *noun, botany* the wall of a fruit

periglacial *adjective, geography* of or like a region bordering a glacier

peril *noun* a great danger • **at your peril** at your own risk

perilous *adjective* very dangerous
♦ **perilously** *adverb*

perimeter (*pronounced* pe-**rim**-i-ter) *noun* **1** the outside line enclosing a figure or shape **2** the outer edge of any area ◎ Comes from Greek *peri* meaning 'around', and *metron* meaning 'measure'

❗ Do not confuse with: **parameter**.
Notice that words starting with **peri-** often relate to the idea of 'going around' and the **perimeter** of a figure or shape is the line that goes around it.

perinatal (*pronounced* pe-ri-**nei**-tal) *adjective, medicine* relating to the period between the seventh month of pregnancy and the first week of the baby's life

perineum (*pronounced* pe-ri-**nee**-um) *noun* (*plural* **perinea**), *anatomy* the part of the body between the genitals and the anus

period *noun* **1** a stretch of time **2** a stage in the earth's development or in history **3** a full stop after a sentence **4** a time of menstruation **5** the interval of time before events recur in the same order **6** *maths, physics* the time required for a complete repeat of a wave or an event **7** *maths* the difference between two successive values of a variable for which a function has the same value **8** *chemistry* in the periodic table: any of the seven horizontal rows of elements

periodic *adjective* **1** of a period **2** happening at regular intervals, eg every month or year **3** happening every now and then: *a periodic clearing out of rubbish* **4** *chemistry* relating to the periodic table

periodical *adjective* issued or done at regular intervals; periodic ➤ *noun* a magazine which appears at regular intervals ♦ **periodically** adverb

periodic function noun, maths a function that repeats itself at constant intervals

periodic law noun, chemistry the law that the properties of the chemical elements tend to recur periodically with increasing atomic number

periodic table noun, chemistry a table in which chemical elements are arranged by atomic number and in groups with similar properties

peripatetic (pronounced pe-ri-pa-**tet**-ik) adjective moving from place to place; travelling

peripheral (pronounced pe-**rif**-e-ral) adjective **1** of or on a periphery; away from the centre **2** not essential, of little importance ➤ noun, computing a device in a computer system connected to and controlled by the central processing unit

peripheral nervous system noun the nerves and sense organs that send signals to the brain

periphery (pronounced pe-**rif**-e-ri) noun (plural **peripheries**) **1** the line surrounding something **2** an outer boundary or edge **3** geography the least economically important and often poorest part of a country or region (contrasted with: **core**)

periphrastic (pronounced pe-ri-**fras**-tik) adjective of speech: roundabout, using more words than necessary

periscope noun a tube with mirrors by which a viewer in a submarine etc is able to see objects on the surface

perish verb **1** to be destroyed, pass away completely; die **2** to decay, rot

perishable adjective liable to go bad quickly

peristalsis noun the involuntary muscle contractions in hollow tubular organs that force the contents forward, eg food in the intestine

peristyle noun a group of columns surrounding a building

peritoneum (pronounced pe-ri-to-**nee**-um) noun (plural **peritoneums** or **peritonea**) a membrane lining the abdominal cavity and covering the stomach ♦ **peritoneal** adjective

peritonitis noun inflammation of the peritoneum

periwinkle[1] noun a small shellfish, shaped like a small snail, eaten as food when boiled

periwinkle[2] noun a creeping evergreen plant with a small blue flower

perjure verb: **perjure yourself** to tell a lie when you have sworn to tell the truth, especially in a court of law

perjury noun (plural **perjuries**) the crime of lying while under oath in a court of law

perk[1] noun, informal something of value allowed in addition to payment for work

perk[2] verb: **perk up** to recover energy or spirits

perkin another word for **parkin**

perky adjective (**perkier, perkiest**) jaunty, in good spirits ♦ **perkily** adverb

Perl or **PERL** noun, computing a high-level programming language

⊙ An acronym of practical extraction and report language

perm noun short for **permanent wave** ➤ verb to give a permanent wave to (hair)

permaculture noun farming without using artificial fertilizers and with minimal weeding

permafrost noun, geology permanently frozen subsoil

permanence or **permanency** noun the state of continuing or remaining for a long time or for ever

permanent adjective lasting, not temporary ♦ **permanently** adverb

permanent magnet noun, physics a magnet that keeps its magnetic properties after the force which magnetized it has been removed

permanent wave noun a wave or curl put into the hair by a special process and usually lasting for some months

permeable adjective able to be permeated by liquids, gases, etc

permeate verb **1** to pass into through small holes, soak into **2** to fill every part of

Permian adjective of the geological period from 290 million to 250 million years ago

permissible adjective allowable

permission noun agreement or authorization to do something

permissive adjective **1** allowing something to be done **2** too tolerant ♦ **permissiveness** noun

permit verb (pronounced per-**mit**) (**permitting, permitted**) **1** to agree to an action, allow **2** to make possible ➤ noun (pronounced **per**-mit) a written order, allowing someone to do something: a fishing permit

permutation noun **1** any of several different ways in which things can be ordered or arranged **2** the act of changing the order of things **3** maths arranging a set of objects or numbers into groups ordered by their possible combinations (compare with: **combination** meaning 4) **4** maths any of the groups resulting from permutation

pernicious adjective destructive

pernickety adjective fussy about small details

peroration (pronounced pe-raw-**rei**-shon) noun **1** the closing part of a speech **2** a speech

peroxide *noun, chemistry* any of various strong oxidizing agents used in rocket fuels, disinfectants and bleaches

perpendicular *adjective* **1** standing upright, vertical **2** at right angles (to) ➤ *noun, maths* a line or plane at right angles to another line or plane

perpetrate *verb* to commit (a sin, error, etc)
♦ **perpetration** *noun* ◷ Comes from Latin *perpetrare* meaning 'to achieve'

❗ Do not confuse with: **perpetuate**

perpetrator *noun* a person who perpetrates; the one who is guilty

perpetual *adjective* everlasting, unending
♦ **perpetually** *adverb*

perpetuate *verb* to make last for ever or for a long time ◷ Comes from Latin *perpetuare* meaning 'to cause to continue uninterruptedly'

❗ Do not confuse with: **perpetrate**

perpetuity *noun*: **in perpetuity 1** for ever **2** for the length of someone's life

perplex *verb* **1** to puzzle, bewilder **2** to make more complicated

perplexity *noun* (*plural* **perplexities**) **1** a puzzled state of mind **2** something which puzzles

perquisite *noun, formal* a perk

per se (*pronounced* per **sei**) *adverb* in itself, essentially

persecute *verb* **1** to harass over a period of time **2** to cause to suffer, especially because of religious beliefs ♦ **persecution** *noun*
♦ **persecutor** *noun* ◷ Comes from Latin *persequi* meaning 'to follow persistently'

❗ Do not confuse with: **prosecute**

perseverance *noun* the act of persevering

persevere *verb* to keep trying to do a thing (in spite of difficulties)

persist *verb* **1** to hold fast to (eg an idea) **2** to continue to do something in spite of difficulties **3** to survive, last

persistence *noun* **1** persisting **2** being persistent

persistent *adjective* **1** obstinate, refusing to be discouraged **2** lasting, not dying out
♦ **persistently** *adverb*

person *noun* **1** a human being **2** someone's body: *jewels hidden on his person* **3** form, shape: *Trouble arrived in the person of Gordon* **4** *grammar* a form of a word when it relates to the person or thing speaking or writing (**first person**), being spoken or written to (**second person**), or being spoken or written about (**third person**) • **in person** personally, not represented by someone else

persona *noun* (*plural* **personas** or **personae** – *pronounced* per-**soh**-nee) the outward part of the personality presented to others

personable *adjective* good-looking

personage *noun* a well-known person

personal *adjective* **1** your own; private: *personal belongings* **2** of a remark: insulting, offensive to the person it is aimed at ◷ Comes from Latin *persona* meaning 'an actor's mask'

❗ Do not confuse with: **personnel**

personal assistant *noun* a secretary or administrator, especially one who helps a senior executive

personal column *noun* a newspaper column in which members of the public may place advertisements, enquiries, etc

personal computer *noun* (*abbrev* **PC**) a microcomputer designed for personal use

personality *noun* (*plural* **personalities**) **1** all of a person's characteristics as seen by others **2** a well-known person

personalize or **personalise** *verb* to mark (something) distinctively, eg with name, initials, etc, as the property of a particular person

personally *adverb* **1** speaking from your own point of view **2** by your own action, not using an agent or representative: *He thanked me personally*

personal organizer *noun* a small loose-leaf filing system containing a diary and an address book, maps, indexes, etc

personal pronoun *noun, grammar* any pronoun that represents a person or thing, eg *I, you, she, it, us*

personal stereo *noun* a small portable cassette player with earphones

persona non grata *noun* (*plural* **personae non gratae** – *pronounced* per-**soh**-nee non **grah**-tee) someone disliked or out of favour

personification *noun* **1** giving human qualities to things or ideas **2** in art or literature, representing an idea or quality as a person **3** a person or thing that is seen as a perfect example of a quality: *the personification of patience*

personify *verb* (**personifies, personifying, personified**) **1** to talk about things, ideas, etc as if they were living persons (eg 'Time marches on') **2** to typify, be a perfect example of

personnel (*pronounced* per-so-**nel**) *noun* the people employed in a firm etc

❗ Do not confuse with: **personal**.
Personnel is a noun coming from French company terminology, used to describe the 'person-assets' of a company (= the people who work for it) in contrast to its 'material-assets' (= all its non-human items of value).

perspective *noun* **1** a point of view **2** the giving of a sense of depth, distance, etc in a painting like that in real life • **in perspective 1** of an object in a painting etc: of a size in relation to other things that it would have in real life **2** of an event: in its true degree of importance when considered in relation to other events: *Keep things in perspective*

Perspex *noun, trademark* a transparent plastic which looks like glass

perspicacious *adjective* of clear or sharp understanding ♦ **perspicacity** *noun*

perspicuity *noun* clearness in expressing thoughts

perspiration *noun* sweat

perspire *verb* to sweat

persuade *verb* to bring someone to do or think something, by arguing with them or advising them

persuasion *noun* **1** the act of persuading **2** a firm belief, especially a religious belief

persuasive *adjective* having the power to convince

pert *adjective* saucy, cheeky

pertain *verb:* **pertain to** to belong to, have to do with: *duties pertaining to the job*

pertinacious *adjective* holding strongly to an idea, obstinate ♦ **pertinacity** *noun*

pertinent *adjective* connected with the subject spoken about, to the point

perturb *verb* to disturb greatly; to make anxious or uneasy ♦ **perturbation** *noun*

perusal *noun* perusing; careful reading

peruse *verb* to read (with care)

pervade *verb* to spread through: *Silence pervaded the room*

perverse *adjective* obstinate in holding to the wrong point of view; unreasonable

perverseness or **perversity** *noun* stubbornness

perversion *noun* **1** the act of perverting **2** an unnatural or perverted act

pervert *verb* (*pronounced* per-**vert**) **1** to turn away from what is normal or right: *pervert the course of justice* **2** to turn (someone) to crime or evil; corrupt ➤ *noun* (*pronounced* **per**-vert) someone who commits unnatural or perverted acts

Pesach (*pronounced* **pei**-sakh) *noun* Passover

pessimism *noun* the habit of thinking that things will always turn out badly (*contrasted with:* **optimism**) ♦ **pessimist** *noun* ♦ **pessimistic** *adjective* ♦ **pessimistically** *adverb*

pest *noun* **1** a troublesome person or thing **2** a creature that is harmful or destructive, eg a mosquito

pester *verb* to annoy continually

pesticide *noun* any substance which kills insect pests

pestilence *noun* a deadly, spreading disease

pestilent or **pestilential** *adjective* **1** very unhealthy **2** *informal* troublesome

pestle *noun* a tool for pounding things to powder in a **mortar**

pet¹ *noun* **1** a tame animal kept in the home, such as a cat **2** a favourite ➤ *adjective* **1** kept as a pet **2** favourite **3** chief: *my pet hate* ➤ *verb* (**petting, petted**) **1** to pat or stroke (an animal etc) **2** to fondle

pet² *noun* a fit of sulks

petal *noun* one of the leaf-like parts of a flower, often scented and brightly coloured

petard (*pronounced* pi-**tahrd**) *noun:* **hoist with your own petard** caught in a trap of your own making

peter *verb:* **peter out** to fade or dwindle away to nothing

petiole *noun* **1** *botany* the stalk attaching a leaf to the stem of a plant **2** *zoology* any stalk-like structure, eg the abdomen in wasps

petite (*pronounced* pe-**teet**) *adjective* small and neat in appearance

petition *noun* a request or note of protest signed by many people and sent to a government or authority ➤ *verb* to send a petition to

petitioner *noun* **1** a person who petitions **2** a person who applies for a divorce

petits pois (*pronounced* pet-i **pwah**) *plural noun* small, young, green peas ⊙ from French meaning 'little peas'

pet name *noun* a special name used as an endearment

petrel *noun* a small, long-winged sea bird

Petri dish (*pronounced* **peet**-ri or **pet**-ri) *noun* a shallow, circular container used for growing bacteria etc

petrifaction or **petrification** *noun* the process whereby something is turned into stone

petrify *verb* (**petrifies, petrifying, petrified**) **1** to turn into stone **2** to turn (someone) stiff with fear

petrochemical *noun* a chemical made from petroleum or natural gas

petrol *noun* petroleum when refined as fuel for use in cars etc

petroleum *noun* oil in its raw, unrefined form, extracted from natural wells below the earth's surface

petrol station *noun* a filling station

petticoat *noun* an underskirt worn by women

pettifogger *noun* **1** a lawyer who deals in trivial cases **2** someone who argues over trivial details ♦ **pettifogging** *noun & adjective*

pettish *adjective* sulky

petty *adjective* (**pettier, pettiest**) **1** of little importance, trivial **2** small-minded; spiteful ♦ **pettiness** *noun*

petty cash *noun* money paid or received in small sums

petty officer *noun* a rank of officer in the navy (equal to a non-commissioned officer in the army)

petulance *noun* being petulant

petulant *adjective* **1** cross, irritable **2** unreasonably impatient

petunia *noun* a S American flowering plant related to tobacco

pew *noun* a seat or bench in a church

pewter *noun* a mixture of tin and lead

PFI *abbreviation* Private Finance Initiative, a scheme for financing public works such as schools and hospitals

PG *abbreviation* parental guidance (denoting a film that is possibly not suitable for young children)

pH *noun, chemistry* a measure of the acidity or alkalinity of a solution

phage (*pronounced* **feij**) *noun, biology* short for **bacteriophage**

phagocyte (*pronounced* **fag**-o-sait) *noun, biology* a white blood corpuscle that surrounds and destroys bacteria

phalanx (*pronounced* **fa**-langks) *noun* (*plural* **phalanxes** or **phalanges** – *pronounced* fa-**lan**-jeez) **1** *history* a company of foot soldiers in an oblong-shaped formation **2** a group of supporters **3** *anatomy* in vertebrates: any of the bones of the digits

phallic *adjective* relating to or resembling a phallus

phallus *noun* (*plural* **phalluses** or **phalli** – *pronounced* **fal**-ai) (a representation of) a penis

phantasm *noun* a vision, an illusion

phantasmagoria *noun* a dream-like series of visions or hallucinations

phantom *noun* a ghost

Pharaoh (*pronounced* **fei**-roh) *noun, history* a ruler of ancient Egypt

Pharisee *noun* **1** a member of a strict ancient Jewish sect **2** *informal* a hypocritical person

pharmaceutical (*pronounced* fahr-ma-**syoo**-ti-kal) *adjective* relating to the making up of medicines and drugs

pharmacist *noun* someone who prepares and sells medicines

pharmacological *adjective* relating to or involving pharmacology

pharmacologist *noun* an expert in pharmacology

pharmacology *noun* the scientific study of drugs and their effects

pharmacy *noun* (*plural* **pharmacies**) **1** the art of preparing medicines **2** a chemist's shop

pharynx (*pronounced* **fahr**-ings) *noun* (*plural* **pharynxes** or **pharynges** – *pronounced* fa-**rin**-jeez), *anatomy* the back part of the throat linking the mouth and nasal passages with the windpipe ♦ **pharyngeal** *adjective*

phase *noun* **1** one in a series of changes in the shape or appearance of something (eg the moon) **2** a stage in the development of something (eg a war, a scheme, etc) **3** *physics* the stage that a periodically varying wave has reached at a specific moment ➤ *verb* (**phase in** or **out**) to introduce or end something in stages

phase difference *noun, physics* the amount by which a wave is ahead of or behind another of the same frequency

phatic *adjective* of spoken language: used for social reasons and to build relationships with other people rather than to communicate ideas or facts ⊙ Comes form Greek *phatos* meaning 'spoken'

PhD *abbreviation* Doctor of Philosophy, a higher university degree

pheasant *noun* a bird with brightly coloured feathers which is shot as game

phenobarbitone (*pronounced* fee-noh-**bahr**-bi-tohn) or **phenobarbital** *noun* a sedative drug used to treat epilepsy

phenol (*pronounced* **fee**-nol) *noun, chemistry* **1** a colourless, crystalline, toxic solid used in resins, solvents, explosives, drugs, dyes and perfumes (*also called:* **carbolic acid**) **2** any of a group of weakly acidic chemical compounds, many of which are used as antiseptics

phenolphthalein (*pronounced* fee-nol-**thei**-leen or fee-nol-**tha**-leen) *noun, chemistry* a dye which is colourless in acidic solutions and turns red in alkaline solutions, used as a pH indicator

phenomenal *adjective* very unusual, remarkable ♦ **phenomenally** *adverb*

phenomenon *noun* (*plural* **phenomena**) **1** an event (especially in nature) that is observed by the senses: *the phenomenon of lightning* **2** something remarkable or very unusual, a wonder

phenotype (*pronounced* **fee**-noh-taip) *noun, biology* **1** the physical appearance of an organism (as distinguished from its genetic make-up) **2** a group with the same physical characteristics

phenyl (*pronounced* **fee**-nil or **fee**-nail or **fe**-nil) *noun, chemistry* an organic radical found in benzene, phenol, etc

pheromone (*pronounced* **fe**-roh-mohn) *noun, zoology* a chemical substance secreted by an animal and which has a specific effect on other members of the same species

phial *noun* a small glass bottle

phil- see **philo-**

philander (*pronounced* fi-**lan**-der) *verb* to flirt, or have casual love affairs, with women

philanderer *noun* a womanizer

philanthropic (*pronounced* fil-an-**throp**-ik) *adjective* kind and generous

philanthropist *noun* someone who does good to others

philanthropy (*pronounced* fi-**lan**-thro-pi) *noun* love of mankind, often shown by giving money for the benefit of others

philatelist (*pronounced* fi-**lat**-e-list) *noun* a stamp-collector

philately (*pronounced* fi-**lat**-e-li) *noun* the study and collecting of stamps

philharmonic (*pronounced* fil-ahr-**mon**-ik) *adjective* (in names of orchestras etc) music-loving

philistine (*pronounced* **fil**-is-tain) *noun* someone ignorant of, or hostile to, culture and the arts

⊙ After a people of ancient Palestine, enemies of the Israelites

philo- or **phil-** *prefix* forms words related to the love of a particular thing: *philharmonic/ philosopher* (= a friend or lover of wisdom) ⊙ Comes from Greek *philos* meaning 'friend', and *phileein* meaning 'to love'

philologist *noun* a person who studies or is expert in philology

philology *noun* the study of words and their history

philosopher *noun* someone who studies philosophy

philosophical or **philosophic** *adjective* **1** of philosophy **2** calm, not easily upset

philosophize or **philosophise** *verb* **1** to form philosophical theories **2** to speculate in the way a philosopher does ◆ **philosophizer** *noun*

philosophy *noun* (*plural* **philosophies**) **1** the study of the nature of the universe, or of human behaviour **2** someone's personal view of life

philtre or *US* **philter** (*pronounced* **fil**-ter) *noun* a love potion

phlebitis *noun, medicine* inflammation of the wall of a vein, often causing a blood clot

phlegm (*pronounced* flem) *noun* **1** thick slimy matter that lines the air passages, brought up by coughing **2** coolness of temper, calmness

phlegmatic (*pronounced* fleg-**mat**-ik) *adjective* not easily excited

phloem (*pronounced* **floh**-em) *noun, botany* a tissue in some plants that conducts food from the leaves to other parts

-phobe *suffix* forms words describing people who suffer from particular phobias ⊙ Comes from Greek *phobos* meaning 'fear'

phobia *noun* an intense, often irrational, fear or dislike ⊙ Comes from Greek *phobos* meaning 'fear'

phoenix (*pronounced* **fee**-niks) *noun* (*plural* **phoenixes**) a mythological bird believed to burn itself and to rise again from its ashes

phon- *prefix* forms words relating to sound or speech: *phonetics* ⊙ Comes from Greek *phone* meaning 'sound' or 'voice'

phone *noun* short for **telephone**

phonecard *noun* a card that can be used instead of cash to operate certain public telephones

phoneme *noun, linguistics* the smallest meaningful unit of sound in a language

phonetic *adjective* **1** relating to the sounds of language **2** of a word: spelt according to sound, eg *flem* for 'phlegm'

phonetics *singular noun* **1** the study of the production and perception of speech sounds **2** a system of writing according to sound

phoney or **phony** *informal, adjective* (**phonier, phoniest**) fake, not genuine ➤ *noun* (*plural* **phoneys** or **phonies**) someone or something fake

phonology *noun* **1** the study of the sounds in any particular language **2** any particular system of speech sounds

phosgene (*pronounced* **fos**-jeen) *noun, chemistry* a poisonous gas, carbonyl chloride, used in the manufacture of pesticides and dyes

phosphate *noun, chemistry* a salt or ester containing phosphoric acid, used in a soil fertilizer, detergents, etc

phosphorescence *noun* faint glow of light in the dark

phosphorescent *adjective* glowing in the dark

phosphoric *adjective, chemistry* referring to or containing phosphorus in higher (pentavalent) valency

phosphoric acid *adjective, chemistry* a transparent, crystalline, water-soluble compound used in soft drinks, rust removers, and as a rustproof layer on iron and steel

phosphorous *adjective, chemistry* referring to or containing phosphorus in lower (trivalent) valency

phosphorus *noun, chemistry* (symbol **P**) a non-metallic element that exists as several different allotropes, including a solid that ignites spontaneously in air ⊙ Comes from Greek *phosphoros* meaning 'bringer of light'

photo *noun* (*plural* **photos**) *informal* a photograph

photo- *prefix* **1** of or relating to light: *photosensitive/photograph* **2** forms words relating to photography: *photocopy/*

photogenic ◷ Comes from Greek *photos* meaning 'of light'

photochemical smog *noun* smog caused by the reaction of pollutants emitted by motor vehicles with sunlight

photochemistry *noun, chemistry* the branch of chemistry concerned with the study of chemical reactions that only take place in the presence of light or ultraviolet radiation, or in which light is produced ◆ **photochemical** *adjective*

photocopier *noun* a machine that makes photocopies

photocopy *noun* (*plural* **photocopies**) a copy of a document made by a device which photographs and develops images ➤ *verb* (**photocopies, photocopying, photocopied**) to make a photocopy of

photoelectric effect *noun, physics* the emission of electrons from the surface of some materials as a result of irradiation with light

photo finish *noun* a race finish so close that the result must be decided by looking at a photograph taken at the finishing line

photofit *noun, trademark* a method of making identification pictures by combining photographs of individual features

photogenic (*pronounced* foh-toh-**jen**-ik) *adjective* **1** looking attractive in photographs **2** *biology* producing, or produced by, light

photograph *noun* a picture taken with a camera ➤ *verb* to take a picture of someone or something with a camera

photographer *noun* a person who takes photographs, especially professionally

photographic *adjective* **1** relating to photographs or photography **2** of memory: retaining images in exact detail ◆ **photographically** *adverb*

photography *noun* the art of taking pictures with a camera

photojournalism *noun* journalism using mainly photographs to convey the meaning of the article ◆ **photojournalist** *noun*

photolysis (*pronounced* foh-**to**-li-sis) *noun, chemistry* a reaction in which a chemical bond is broken as a result of exposure to light or ultraviolet radiation ◆ **photolytic** *adjective*

photon *noun* a particle of electromagnetic radiation, such as light, that behaves as a particle as well as a wave

photoreceptor *noun, biology* a cell or group of cells that is sensitive to and responds to light

photosensitive *adjective* affected by light

photosynthesis *noun* the manufacture by green plants of carbohydrates from carbon dioxide and water, using light for energy

◆ **photosynthesize** *verb* ◆ **photosynthetic** *adjective*

phototaxis *noun, biology* the movement of a cell or an organism towards or away from a light source ◆ **phototactic** *adjective*

phototropism (*pronounced* foh-toh-**troh**-pizm or foh-**to**-tro-pizm) *noun, botany* the growth of the roots or shoots of plants towards or away from a light source ◆ **phototropic** *adjective*

phrasal verb *noun, grammar* a phrase made up of a verb and an adverb or preposition, the meaning of which cannot be worked out from its separate parts, eg 'put up with'

phrase *noun* **1** *grammar* a group of words smaller than a clause, expressing a single idea, eg 'after dinner', 'on the water' **2** a short saying or expression **3** *music* a short group of bars forming a distinct unit ➤ *verb* to express in words: *He could have phrased it more tactfully*

phraseology (*pronounced* freiz-i-**ol**-o-ji) *noun* someone's personal choice of words and phrases

phrenology *noun* the study of the surface of the skull as a supposed sign of personality etc

phyllo another spelling of **filo**

phylum (*pronounced* **fai**-lum) *noun* (*plural* **phyla**), *biology* a division of natural objects below a kingdom and above a class

physical *adjective* **1** relating to the body: *physical strength/physical exercises* **2** relating to things that can be seen or felt ◆ **physically** *adverb*: *She is physically fit*

physical education *noun* instruction in sports, games and keeping fit (*short form*: **PE**)

physical weathering another term for **mechanical weathering**

physician *noun* a doctor specializing in medical rather than surgical treatment

physicist *noun* someone who specializes in physics

physics *singular noun* the science which includes the study of heat, light, sound, electricity, magnetism, etc

physio *noun* (*plural* **physios**) **1** physiotherapy **2** a physiotherapist

physio- *prefix* **1** of or relating to the body or the natural processes of life: *physiology* **2** forms words describing the treatment of disease by physical rather than medicinal means: *physiotherapy* ◷ Comes from Greek *physis* meaning 'nature'

physiognomy (*pronounced* fiz-i-**on**-o-mi) *noun* (*plural* **physiognomies**) the features or expression of the face

physiological *adjective* relating to or involving physiology

physiologist *noun* a person skilled in physiology

physiology *noun* the study of the way in which living bodies work, including blood circulation, food digestion, etc

physiotherapist *noun* a person skilled in treatment by physiotherapy

physiotherapy *noun* the treatment of disease by bodily exercise, massage, etc rather than by drugs

physique (*pronounced* fi-**zeek**) *noun* **1** the build of someone's body **2** bodily strength

pi (*pronounced* pai) *noun, maths* a number that is equal to the circumference of any circle divided by its diameter, approximately 3.142

pianist *noun* someone who plays the piano

piano *noun* (*plural* **pianos**) a large musical instrument played by striking keys

⊙ A shortened form of *pianoforte*, which was formed from the Italian words for 'soft' and 'loud'

piazza (*pronounced* pee-**at**-sa) *noun* a market-place or town square surrounded by buildings

piccolo *noun* (*plural* **piccolos**) a small, high-pitched flute

pick¹ *verb* **1** to choose **2** to pluck, gather (flowers, fruit, etc) **3** to peck, bite, nibble (at) **4** to poke, probe (teeth etc) **5** to open (a lock) with a tool other than a key ➤ *noun* **1** choice: *take your pick* **2** the best or best part • **pick a quarrel** to start a quarrel deliberately • **pick on 1** to single out for criticism etc **2** to nag at • **pick up 1** to lift up **2** to learn (a language, habit, etc) **3** to give (someone) a lift in a car **4** to find or get by chance **5** to improve, gain strength

pick² *noun* **1** a pickaxe **2** an instrument for picking, eg a toothpick

pickaxe *noun* a heavy tool for breaking ground, pointed at one end or both ends

picket *noun* **1** a pointed stake **2** a small sentry-post or guard **3** a number of workers on strike who prevent others from going into work ➤ *verb* (**picketing, picketed**) **1** to fasten (a horse etc) to a stake **2** to place a guard or a group of strikers at (a place)

picket line *noun* a line of people acting as pickets in an industrial dispute

pickle *noun* **1** a liquid in which food is preserved **2** vegetables preserved in vinegar **3** *informal* an awkward, unpleasant situation ➤ *verb* to preserve with salt, vinegar, etc

pickpocket *noun* someone who robs people's pockets or handbags

picky *adjective* (**pickier, pickiest**) choosy, fussy

picnic *noun* a meal eaten outdoors, often during an outing etc ➤ *verb* (**picnicking, picnicked**) to have a picnic ♦ **picnicker** *noun*

pictogram *noun* a chart or graph which uses pictures to show amounts, with one picture standing for a particular amount

pictorial *adjective* **1** having pictures **2** consisting of pictures **3** calling up pictures in the mind

picture *noun* **1** a painting or drawing **2** a portrait **3** a photograph **4** a film **5** a vivid description ➤ *verb* **1** to make a picture of **2** to see in the mind, imagine • **the pictures** the cinema

picturesque *adjective* such as would make a good or striking picture; pretty, colourful

pidgin *noun* a simplified and altered form of a language arising from its combination with a different language, used as a means of communication between speakers of different languages

⊙ **Pidgin** is a distorted form of the word 'business', originally used in China

❗ Do not confuse with: **pigeon**

pie *noun* meat, fruit, or other food baked in a casing or covering of pastry

piebald *adjective* white and black in patches

piece *noun* **1** a part or portion of anything **2** a single article or example: *a piece of paper* **3** an artistic work: *a piece of popular music* **4** a coin **5** a man in chess, draughts, etc ➤ *verb* to put (together)

pièce de résistance (*pronounced* pyes de rei-zees-**tons**) *noun* the best item or work

piecemeal *adverb* by pieces, little by little

piece of cake *noun* something easy to do

piecework *noun* work paid according to how much is done, not to the time spent on it

pie chart *noun* a circular diagram split into sections showing the different percentages into which a whole amount is divided

pied *adjective* with two or more colours in patches

pier *noun* **1** a platform stretching from the shore into the sea as a landing place for ships **2** a pillar supporting an arch, bridge, etc

pierce *verb* **1** to make a hole through **2** to force a way into **3** to move (the feelings) deeply

piercing *adjective* shrill, loud; sharp

piety (*pronounced* **pai**-i-ti) *noun* respect for holy things

piezoelectric effect (*pronounced* pai-ee-zoh-i-**lek**-trik) *noun, physics* **1** the generation of electricity (**piezoelectricity**) by stretching or compressing crystals such as quartz **2** the reverse effect in which electricity can produce slight physical distortion in crystals

piffle *noun, informal* nonsense

pig¹ *noun* **1** a farm animal, from whose flesh ham and bacon are made **2** an abusive term for someone greedy, dirty, selfish, or brutal

pig² *noun* an oblong, moulded piece of metal (eg pig-iron)

pigeon *noun* a bird of the dove family ⊙ Comes from Latin *pipire* meaning 'to cheep'

⚠ Do not confuse with: **pidgin**

pigeonhole *noun* a small division in a case or desk for papers etc ➤ *verb* **1** to lay aside **2** to classify, put into a category

pigeon-toed *adjective* of a person: standing and walking with their toes turned in

piggyback *noun* a ride on someone's back with your arms round their neck

piggy bank *noun* a china pig with a slit along its back to insert coins for saving

pigheaded *adjective* stubborn

pig-in-the-middle or **piggy-in-the-middle** *noun* **1** a game in which one person stands between two others and tries to catch the ball they are throwing to each other **2** any person helplessly caught between two contending parties

piglet *noun* a young pig

pigment *noun* **1** paint or other substance used for colouring **2** a substance in animals and plants that gives colour to the skin etc
♦ **pigmentation** *noun* (meaning 2)

pigmy another spelling of **pygmy**

pigsty or **piggery** *noun* (*plural* **pigsties** or **piggeries**) a place where pigs are kept

pigtail *noun* hair formed into a plait

pike¹ *noun* (*plural* **pike** or **pikes**) a freshwater fish

pike² *noun* a weapon like a spear, with a long shaft and a sharp head

pilau (*pronounced* pi-**low**) or **pilaf** or **pilaff** (*pronounced* pi-**laf**) *noun* an oriental dish of spiced rice with, or to accompany, chicken, fish, etc ⊙ from Persian *pilaw*

pilchard *noun* a small sea fish like a herring, often tinned

pile¹ *noun* **1** a number of things lying one on top of another, a heap **2** a great quantity **3** a large building **4** a nuclear reactor ➤ *verb* (often **pile up** or **pile something up**) to make or form a pile or heap

pile² *noun* a large stake or pillar driven into the earth as a foundation for a building, bridge, etc

pile³ *noun* the thick, soft surface on carpets and on cloth such as velvet

pile-driver *noun* a machine for driving piles into the ground

piles *plural noun* haemorrhoids

pile-up *noun* a vehicle collision in which following vehicles also crash, causing a number of collisions

pilfer *verb* to steal small things

pilgrim *noun* a traveller to a holy place

pilgrimage *noun* a journey to a holy place

pill *noun* **1** a tablet of medicine **2** (often **the pill**) a contraceptive in the form of a small tablet taken by mouth

pillage *verb* to seize goods and money, especially as loot in war ➤ *noun* the act of plundering in this way

pillar *noun* **1** an upright support for roofs, arches, etc **2** someone or something that gives support: *a pillar of the community*

pillarbox *noun* (*plural* **pillarboxes**) a tall box with a slot through which letters etc are posted

pillion *noun* **1** a seat for a passenger on a motorcycle **2** *old* a light saddle for a passenger on horseback, behind the main saddle

pillory *noun* (*plural* **pillories**) *history* a wooden frame fitted over the head and hands of wrongdoers as a punishment ➤ *verb* (**pillories, pillorying, pilloried**) to mock in public

pillow *noun* a soft cushion for the head ➤ *verb* to rest or support on a pillow

pillowcase or **pillowslip** *noun* a cover for a pillow

pilot *noun* **1** someone who steers a ship in or out of a harbour **2** someone who flies an aeroplane **3** a guide, a leader ➤ *adjective* of a scheme, programme, etc: as a test which may be modified before the final version: *a pilot project* ➤ *verb* (**piloting, piloted**) **1** to steer, guide **2** to give (a scheme, programme, etc) a first test

pilot light *noun* **1** a small gas-light from which larger jets are lit **2** an electric light showing that a current is switched on

pilot survey *noun, statistics* a test survey of a representative sample taken to see if any refinements to the final survey are needed

pi-meson another word for **pion**

pimiento (*pronounced* pim-i-**en**-toh) *noun* (*plural* **pimientos**) **1** a variety of sweet pepper with mild-flavoured red fruit **2** the fruit of this plant, eaten raw or cooked ⊙ from Spanish meaning 'paprika'

pimp *noun* a man who manages prostitutes and takes money from them

pimpernel (*pronounced* **pim**-per-nel) *noun* a plant of the primrose family, with small pink or scarlet flowers

pimple *noun* a small round infected swelling on the skin

pimpled or **pimply** *adjective* (**pimplier, pimpliest**) having pimples

PIN (*pronounced* pin) *abbreviation* personal identification number (for automatic teller machines etc)

pin *noun* **1** a short, pointed piece of metal with a small round head, used for fastening fabric **2** a wooden or metal peg **3** a skittle ➤ *verb* (**pinning, pinned**) **1** to fasten with a pin **2** to hold fast, pressed against something: *The bloodhound pinned him to the ground*

pinafore *noun* **1** an apron to protect the front of a dress **2** a sleeveless dress worn over a jersey, blouse, etc

pinball *noun* a game played on a slot-machine in which a ball runs down a sloping board between obstacles

pincers *plural noun* **1** a tool like pliers, but with sharp points for gripping, pulling out nails, etc **2** the claw of a crab or lobster

pinch *verb* **1** to squeeze (especially flesh) between the thumb and forefinger; nip **2** to grip tightly, hurt by tightness **3** *informal* to steal ➤ *noun* (*plural* **pinches**) **1** a squeeze, a nip **2** a small amount (eg of salt) • **at a pinch** if really necessary or urgent • **feel the pinch** to suffer from lack of money

pinchbeck *adjective* sham, in poor imitation

Ⓘ From Christopher *Pinchbeck*, a 17th-century watchmaker who invented a copper alloy to imitate gold

---

pinched *adjective* of a face: looking cold, pale or thin

pine[1] *noun* **1** an evergreen tree with needle-like leaves which produces cones **2** the soft wood of such a tree used for furniture etc

pine[2] *verb* **1** to waste away, lose strength **2** to long (for something)

pineal gland or **pineal body** (*pronounced* pin-i-al) *noun, anatomy* a small gland in the brain

pineapple *noun* a large tropical fruit with tough spiny skin, shaped like a pine cone

pine cone *noun* the seed case of the pine tree

pine nut or **pine kernel** *noun* the edible oily seed of various species of pine tree

ping *noun* a whistling sound such as that of a bullet ➤ *verb* to make a brief high-pitched sound

ping-pong *noun, trademark* table tennis

pinion[1] *noun* a bird's wing ➤ *verb* **1** to hold (someone) fast by binding or holding their arms **2** to cut or fasten the wings of (a bird)

pinion[2] *noun* a small, toothed wheel

pink[1] *noun* **1** a pale red colour **2** a sweet-scented garden flower like a carnation **3** a healthy or good state: *feeling in the pink*

pink[2] *verb* to cut (cloth etc) with pinking scissors

pink[3] *verb* of an engine: to make a faint clinking noise

pinkie *noun, Scot & N Amer informal* the little finger

pinking scissors or **pinking shears** *plural noun* scissors with blades which give cloth a zigzag edge

pinna *noun* **1** *anatomy* the part of the ear that projects from the head **2** *biology* in birds: a feather or wing

pinnacle *noun* **1** a slender spire or turret **2** a high pointed rock or mountain **3** the highest point

pinnate *adjective, botany* of a leaf: having pairs of leaflets in rows on either side of a central axis

pins and needles *plural noun* a tingling or prickling sensation in a limb etc as the flow of blood returns to it after being temporarily obstructed

pinstripe *noun* **1** a very narrow stripe in cloth **2** cloth with such stripes ◆ **pinstriped** *adjective*

pint *noun* a liquid measure equal to just over $\frac{1}{2}$ litre

pint-size or **pint-sized** *adjective, humorous* of a person: very small

pin-up *noun* **1** a picture of a famous person you admire that you pin on your wall **2** someone whose picture is pinned up in this way

pion (*pronounced* **pai**-on) *noun, physics* a type of meson involved in the forces holding protons and neutrons together (*also called*: **pi-meson**)

pioneer *noun* **1** an explorer **2** an inventor, or an early exponent of something: *pioneers of the cinema* ➤ *verb* to act as a pioneer

pious *adjective* respectful in religious matters

pip[1] *noun* a seed of a fruit

pip[2] *noun* a short beep as part of a time signal etc on the radio or telephone

pip[3] *noun* **1** a spot or symbol on dice or cards **2** a star on an army officer's tunic

pipe *noun* **1** a tube for carrying water, gas, etc **2** a tube with a bowl at the end, for smoking tobacco **3** (**pipes**) a musical instrument made of several small pipes joined together **4** (**pipes**) bagpipes ➤ *verb* **1** to play (notes, a tune) on a pipe or pipes **2** to whistle, chirp **3** to speak in a shrill, high voice **4** to convey (eg water) by pipe • **pipe down** *informal* to become silent, stop talking • **pipe up** to speak up, express an opinion

piped music *noun* light, popular, recorded music played continuously through loudspeakers in public places

pipe dream *noun* a delightful fantasy

pipeline *noun* a long line of pipes, eg to carry oil from an oilfield • **in the pipeline** in preparation, soon to become available

piper *noun* someone who plays a pipe, especially the bagpipes

pipette (*pronounced* pi-**pet**) *noun* a small glass tube used in laboratories

piping *adjective* high-pitched, shrill ➤ *noun* **1** a length of tubing **2** a system of pipes **3** a narrow ornamental cord for trimming clothes **4** a strip of decorative icing round a cake • **piping hot** very hot

pippin *noun* a kind of apple

pipsqueak *noun, informal* an insignificant, or very small, person

piquant (*pronounced* **peek**-ant) *adjective* **1** sharp-tasting, spicy **2** arousing interest
♦ **piquancy** *noun*

pique (*pronounced* peek) *noun* anger caused by wounded pride, spite, resentment, etc ➤ *verb* **1** to wound the pride of **2** to arouse (curiosity)

piracy *noun* **1** the activity of pirates **2** unauthorized publication or reproduction of copyright material

piranha (*pronounced* pi-**rah**-na) *noun* a S American river-fish, some types of which eat flesh

pirate *noun* **1** someone who robs ships at sea **2** someone who steals or plagiarizes another's work

piratical *adjective* **1** relating to pirates **2** practising piracy

pirouette *noun* a rapid whirling on the toes in dancing ➤ *verb* to twirl in a pirouette

Pisces *noun* **1** the twelfth sign of the zodiac, represented by the fishes **2** someone born under this sign, between 20 February and 20 March

pistachio (*pronounced* pi-**stash**-i-oh) *noun* (*plural* **pistachios**) a greenish nut, often used as a flavouring

pistil *noun* the female, seed-bearing part of a flower

pistol *noun* a small gun held in the hand

piston *noun* a round piece of metal that moves up and down inside a cylinder, eg in an engine

pit *noun* **1** a hole in the ground **2** a place from which coal and other minerals are dug **3** the ground floor of a theatre behind the stalls **4** (often **pits**) a place beside the racetrack for repairing and refuelling racing cars etc **5** *anatomy* a hollow or depression, eg the pit of the stomach (ie the hollow below the breastbone) ➤ *verb* (**pitting, pitted**) to set one thing or person against another: *pitting my wits against his*

pitch¹ *verb* **1** to fix a tent etc to the ground **2** to throw **3** to fall heavily; lurch: *pitch forward* **4** to set the level or key of a tune ➤ *noun* (*plural* **pitches**) **1** a throw **2** an attempt at selling or persuading: *a sales pitch* **3** the height or depth of a note **4** a peak, an extreme point: *reach fever pitch* **5** the field for certain sports **6** *cricket* the ground between wickets **7** the slope of a roof etc **8** the spot reserved for a street seller or street entertainer

pitch² *noun* a thick, dark substance obtained by boiling down tar

pitchblende *noun* a black mineral made up of uranium oxides

pitch-dark *adjective* very dark

pitched battle *noun* a battle on chosen ground between sides arranged in position beforehand

pitcher *noun* a kind of large jug

pitchfork *noun* a fork for lifting and throwing hay

piteous or **pitiable** *adjective* deserving pity; wretched

pitfall *noun* a trap, a possible danger

pith *noun* **1** the soft substance in the centre of plant stems **2** the white substance under the rind of an orange, lemon, etc **3** the important part of anything

pithy *adjective* (**pithier, pithiest**) **1** full of pith **2** full of meaning, to the point: *a pithy saying*

pitiable see **piteous**

pitiful *adjective* poor, wretched ♦ **pitifully** *adverb*

pitta *noun* a Middle-Eastern slightly leavened bread, usually in a hollow oval shape that can be filled with other foods ⊕ from modern Greek meaning 'cake' or 'pie'

pittance *noun* a very small wage or allowance

pitted *adjective* marked with small holes

pituitary gland *noun, physiology* a gland in the brain responsible for hormones affecting growth, reproduction and adrenaline production

pity *noun* (*plural* **pities**) **1** feeling for the sufferings of others, sympathy **2** a cause of grief **3** a regrettable fact ➤ *verb* (**pities, pitying, pitied**) to feel sorry for • **take pity on** to show pity for

pivot *noun* **1** the pin or centre on which anything turns **2** something or someone greatly depended on ➤ *verb* (**pivoting, pivoted**) **1** to turn on a pivot **2** to depend (on)

pivotal *adjective* **1** acting as a pivot **2** crucially important; critical

pixel *noun, electronics* the smallest element in an image on a TV or computer screen, consisting of a tiny dot

pixellated *adjective, electronics* of a picture: broken down into a number of small squares
♦ **pixellation** *noun*

pixie or **pixy** *noun* (*plural* **pixies**) a kind of fairy

pizza *noun* a flat piece of dough spread with tomato, cheese, etc and baked

pizzeria (*pronounced* peet-se-**ree**-a) *noun* a restaurant specializing in pizzas

pizzicato (*pronounced* pit-si-**kah**-toh) *adverb, music* played by plucking the strings rather than drawing a bow across them

placard *noun* a printed notice (as an advertisement etc) placed on a wall etc

placate *verb* to calm, make less angry, etc

place *noun* **1** a physical location; any area or building **2** a particular spot **3** an open space in a town: *a market place* **4** a seat in a theatre, train, at a table, etc **5** a position on a course, in a job, etc **6** rank ‣ *verb* **1** to put in a particular place **2** to find a place for **3** to give (an order for goods etc) **4** to remember who someone is: *I can't place him at all* • **in place 1** in the proper position **2** suitable • **in place of** instead of • **out of place 1** not in the proper position **2** unsuitable ⊙ Comes from Latin *platea* meaning 'a street'

placebo (*pronounced* pla-**see**-boh) *noun* (*plural* **placebos**), *medicine* a substance resembling a drug but with no medicinal ingredients

placed *adjective* **1** having a place **2** among the first three in a competition

placenta (*pronounced* pla-**sen**-ta) *noun*, *biology* a part of the womb that connects an unborn mammal to its mother, shed at birth

placid *adjective* calm, not easily disturbed

placidity *noun* being placid

plagiarism (*pronounced* **plei**-ja-rizm) *noun* plagiarizing

plagiarist *noun* a person who plagiarizes

plagiarize or **plagiarise** (*pronounced* **plei**-ja-raiz) *verb* to steal or borrow from the writings or ideas of someone else without permission

plague *noun* **1** *medicine* a fatal infectious disease carried by rat fleas **2** a great and troublesome quantity: *a plague of flies* ‣ *verb* to pester or annoy continually

plaice *noun* (*plural* **plaice**) a type of edible flatfish

plaid (*pronounced* plad) *noun* a long piece of cloth (especially tartan) worn over the shoulder

Plaid Cymru *noun* (*pronounced* plaid **kum**-ri) a Welsh nationalist political party in the UK ⊙ Comes from Welsh *plaid* meaning 'party' + *Cymru* meaning 'Wales'

plain *adjective* **1** flat, level **2** simple, ordinary **3** without ornament or decoration **4** clear, easy to see or understand **5** not good-looking, not attractive ‣ *noun* a level stretch of land

plain chocolate *noun* dark-coloured chocolate made without much milk

plain-clothes *adjective* of a police officer: wearing ordinary clothes, not uniform

plain flour *noun* flour that contains no raising agent

plain sailing *noun* **1** easy, unimpeded progress **2** *nautical* sailing in unobstructed waters

plain text *noun*, *computing* the format of most e-mail messages, using simple upper-case and lower-case letters

plaintiff *noun*, *law* someone who takes action against another in the law courts

plaintive *adjective* sad, sorrowful

plait (*pronounced* plat) *noun* **1** a length of hair arranged by intertwining three or more separate pieces **2** threads etc intertwined in this way ‣ *verb* to form into a plait

plan *noun* **1** a diagram of a building, town, etc as if seen from above **2** a scheme or arrangement to do something ‣ *verb* (**planning, planned**) **1** to make a sketch or plan of **2** to decide or arrange to do

Planck's constant *noun*, *physics* a constant equal to the energy of a quantum of light divided by its frequency

⊙ Named after Max *Planck* (1858–1957), German physicist

plane¹ *short for* **aeroplane**

plane² *noun* **1** *maths* a flat surface on which a line joining two points lies **2** a level surface **3** a standard (of achievement etc) ‣ *adjective* **1** flat, level **2** *maths* lying in one plane: *a plane figure/ plane shape* ‣ *verb* **1** to smooth with a plane **2** to glide over water etc

plane³ *noun* a carpentry tool for smoothing wood

plane⁴ *noun* a type of tree with broad leaves

plane angle *noun*, *maths* the angle formed by two lines in a polygon or other plane figure

plane of symmetry *noun*, *maths* the hypothetical line dividing a solid, either side of which are mirror images of each other

planet *noun* any of the bodies (eg the earth, Venus) which move round the sun or round another fixed star

planetarium *noun* (*plural* **planetaria** or **planetariums**) **1** a special projector by which the positions and movements of stars and planets can be projected on to a domed ceiling in order to simulate the appearance of the night sky **2** the building that houses such a projector

planetary *adjective* relating to, consisting of, or produced by planets

plank *noun* a long, flat piece of timber

plankton *noun* microscopic creatures floating in seas, lakes, etc

plant *noun* **1** a living growth, usually from the ground, and usually with a stem, a root and leaves **2** a factory or machinery ‣ *verb* **1** to put (something) into the ground so that it will grow **2** to put (an idea) into the mind **3** to put in position: *plant a bomb* **4** to set down firmly: *plant your feet on the floor* **5** *informal* to place (something) as false evidence

plantation *noun* **1** an area planted with trees **2** an estate for growing cotton, sugar, rubber, tobacco, etc **3** *old* a colony

planter *noun* the owner of a plantation

plaque *noun* **1** a decorative plate of metal, china, etc for fixing to a wall **2** *dentistry* a thin layer of food debris and bacteria which forms on the teeth and can cause decay

plasma noun **1** biology the liquid part of blood and certain other fluids **2** physics a gaseous discharge with a balanced number of electrical charges that occurs naturally in the atmosphere of stars

plasma membrane noun, biology a cell membrane

plaster noun **1** a mixture of lime, water and sand which sets hard, for covering walls etc **2** (also called: **plaster of Paris**) a fine mixture containing gypsum used for moulding, making casts for broken limbs, etc **3** a small dressing which can be stuck over a wound ▸ adjective made of plaster ▸ verb **1** to apply plaster to **2** to cover too thickly (with)

plasterboard noun a material consisting of hardened plaster faced on both sides with paper or thin board, used to form or line interior walls

plaster cast noun **1** a model of an object obtained by pouring a mixture of plaster of Paris and water into a mould formed from that object **2** a covering of plaster of Paris for a broken limb etc

plasterer noun someone whose trade is plastering walls

plastic adjective **1** easily moulded or shaped **2** made of plastic ▸ noun a chemically manufactured substance that can be moulded when soft, formed into fibres, etc

plastic bullet noun a solid plastic cylinder fired by the police to disperse riots etc

plastic explosive noun an explosive substance resembling putty that can be moulded by hand

Plasticine noun, trademark a soft clay-like substance used for modelling

plasticity noun the quality of being easily moulded

plastic surgery noun an operation to repair or replace damaged areas of skin, or to improve the appearance of a facial or other body feature

plate noun **1** a shallow dish for holding food **2** a flat piece of metal, glass, china, etc **3** gold and silver articles **4** a sheet of metal used in printing **5** a book illustration **6** the part of false teeth that fits to the mouth **7** same as **tectonic plate** ▸ verb to cover with a coating of metal

plateau (pronounced plat-oh) noun (plural **plateaus** or **plateaux** – pronounced plat-oh or plat-ohz) **1** a broad level stretch of high land **2** a steady, unchanging state: Prices have now reached a plateau

plate boundary noun, geography the point where two tectonic plates meet (see also: **conservative plate boundary, constructive plate boundary, destructive plate boundary**)

plate glass noun glass in thick sheets, used for shop windows, mirrors, etc

platelet noun, physiology a cell fragment in blood that is responsible for clotting around bleeding

plate tectonics singular noun the study of the earth's crust using the theory that it is composed of a small number of large plates of solid rock floating on the semi-molten mantle

platform noun **1** a raised level surface for passengers at a railway station **2** a raised floor for speakers, entertainers, etc **3** computing the hardware and software used by a computer system

plating noun a thin covering of metal

platinum noun, chemistry (symbol **Pt**) a silvery-white, precious, metallic element used to make jewellery, coins and surgical instruments

platitude noun a dull, ordinary remark made as if it were important

platonic adjective of a relationship: not sexual

⊙ After the Greek philosopher Plato, whose teachings were interpreted in the Middle Ages as advocating this sort of relationship

Platonic solid noun, maths any of the five solids whose faces are congruent regular polygons

platoon noun a section of a company of soldiers

platter noun a large, flat plate

platypus noun (plural **platypuses**) a small water animal of Australia that has webbed feet and a duck-like bill and lays eggs (also called: **duck-billed platypus**)

plaudits plural noun applause, praise

plausibility noun a plausible quality

plausible adjective **1** seeming to be truthful or honest **2** seeming probable or reasonable

play verb **1** to amuse yourself **2** to take part in a game **3** to gamble **4** to act (on a stage etc) **5** to perform on (a musical instrument) **6** to carry out (a trick) **7** to trifle or fiddle (with): Don't play with your food **8** to move over lightly: The firelight played on his face ▸ noun **1** amusement, recreation **2** gambling **3** a story for acting, a drama **4** a way of behaving: foul play **5** freedom of movement • **play at** to treat in a light-hearted, not serious way: He only plays at being a businessman • **play off** to set off (one person) against another to gain some advantage for yourself • **play on** to make use of (someone's feelings) to turn to your own advantage • **play the game** to act fairly and honestly ⊙ Comes from Old English verb plegian and noun plega

playa (pronounced plah-ya) noun, geography a basin which becomes a shallow lake after heavy rainfall and dries out again in hot weather

playboy noun a man of wealth, leisure and frivolous lifestyle

player noun 1 an actor 2 someone who plays a game, musical instrument, etc: a lute player

playful adjective 1 wanting to play: a playful kitten 2 fond of joking, not serious ♦ **playfully** adverb

playground noun an open area for playing at school, in a park, etc

playgroup noun a group of young children who play together supervised by adults

playing-card noun one of a pack of cards used in playing card games

playmate noun a friend with whom you play

play-off noun 1 a game to decide a tie 2 a game between the winners of other competitions

play on words noun a pun

playpen noun a collapsible frame which forms an enclosure where a baby may play safely

playschool noun a nursery school or playgroup

plaything noun 1 a toy 2 a person or thing treated as if they were a toy

playwright noun a writer of plays

PLC abbreviation public limited company

plea noun 1 an excuse 2 law an accused person's answer to a charge in a law court 3 an urgent request

plead verb 1 law to state your case in a law court 2 to give as an excuse • **plead guilty** or **not guilty** law to admit or deny guilt in a law court • **plead with** to beg earnestly

pleasant adjective giving pleasure; agreeable

pleasantry noun (plural **pleasantries**) a good-humoured joke

please verb 1 to give pleasure or delight to 2 to satisfy 3 to choose, like (to do): Do as you please ➤ interjection added for politeness to a command or request: Please keep off the grass • **if you please** please

pleasurable adjective delightful, pleasant

pleasure noun 1 enjoyment, joy, delight 2 what you wish: What is your pleasure? • **at your pleasure** when or if you please

pleat noun a fold in cloth, which has been pressed or stitched down ➤ verb to put pleats in

pleated adjective having pleats

pleb noun, informal someone of no taste or culture, a boor

plebeian (pronounced ple-**bee**-an) adjective 1 of the ordinary or common people 2 vulgar, lacking culture or taste

plebiscite (pronounced **pleb**-i-sait) noun a vote by everyone in an area on a special issue, for or against

plectrum noun (plural **plectrums** or **plectra**) a small piece of horn, metal, etc used for plucking the strings of a guitar

pledge noun 1 something handed over as security for a loan 2 a solemn promise ➤ verb 1 to give as security, pawn 2 to promise solemnly:

pledged himself to carry out the plan 3 to drink to the health of, toast

Pleistocene adjective of the geological epoch two million to ten thousand years ago

plenary (pronounced **plee**-na-ri) adjective full, complete

plentiful or **plenteous** adjective not scarce, abundant

plenty noun 1 a full supply, as much as is needed 2 a large number or quantity (of)

plethora (pronounced **pleth**-o-ra) noun too large a quantity of anything: a plethora of politicians

pleura (pronounced **ploo**-ra) noun (plural **pleurae** – pronounced **ploo**-ree), anatomy the membrane that covers the lungs and lines the chest cavity

pleurisy (pronounced **ploo**-ri-si) noun an illness in which the pleura become inflamed

plexus noun (plural **plexus** or **plexuses**), anatomy a network of nerves or blood vessels

pliable adjective 1 easily bent or folded 2 easily persuaded ♦ **pliability** noun

pliant adjective pliable

pliers plural noun a tool used for gripping, bending, and cutting wire etc

plight[1] noun a bad state or situation

plight[2] verb, old to promise solemnly, pledge

plimsoll noun, old a light, rubber-soled canvas shoe for sports

Plimsoll line noun a line on a ship's side marking where the water should reach when the ship has its maximum load

⊙ Named after Samuel Plimsoll (1826–98), the English politician who recommended it

plinth noun 1 the square slab at the foot of a column 2 the base or pedestal of a statue, vase, etc

Pliocene adjective of the geological epoch seven million to two million years ago

PLO abbreviation Palestine Liberation Organization, an organization of several Palestinian groups opposed to Israel

plod verb (**plodding, plodded**) 1 to travel slowly and steadily 2 to work on steadily

plodder noun a dull but hard-working person

ploidy noun (plural **ploidies**), biology the number of complete chromosome sets present in a cell or living organism

plonk[1] informal, noun a sound made by something dropping heavily ➤ verb to drop (something) heavily: plonked his bag on the floor

plonk[2] noun, informal cheap wine

plop noun the sound made by a small object falling into water ➤ verb (**plopping, plopped**) to make this sound

plot[1] *noun* **1** a plan for an illegal or malicious action **2** the story of a play, novel, etc ➤ *verb* (**plotting, plotted**) **1** to plan secretly **2** to make a chart, graph, etc of **3** to mark points on a graph using co-ordinates ◆ **plotter** *noun*

plot[2] *noun* a small piece of ground

plough or *US* **plow** (*both pronounced* plow) *noun* a farm tool for turning over the soil ➤ *verb* **1** to turn up the ground in furrows **2** *informal* to work through slowly: *ploughing through the ironing*

ploughman's lunch *noun* a cold meal of bread, cheese, pickle, and sometimes meat

ploughshare or *US* **plowshare** *noun* the blade of a plough

plover (*pronounced* **pluv**-er) *noun* any of several kinds of bird of shores and open country that nest on the ground

ploy *noun* a stratagem, dodge or manoeuvre to gain an advantage

pluck *verb* **1** to pull out or off **2** to pick (flowers, fruit, etc) **3** to strip off the feathers of (a bird) before cooking it **4** to shape (the eyebrows) by removing hairs from them ➤ *noun* courage, spirit ● **pluck up courage** to prepare yourself to face a danger or difficulty

plucking *noun, geography* a type of erosion caused by melt water from a glacier freezing to ice on rocks around it, and plucking pieces from the rock as the ice moves

plucky *adjective* (**pluckier, pluckiest**) *informal* brave, determined

plug *noun* **1** an object fitted into a hole to stop it up **2** a fitting on an appliance put into a socket to connect with an electric current **3** *informal* a brief advertisement ➤ *verb* (**plugging, plugged**) **1** to stop up with a plug **2** *informal* to advertise, publicize

plug-and-play *adjective, computing* of a piece of hardware: having an identifier that allows it to be installed automatically

plug-in *noun, computing* an additional piece of software that extends an existing one in specific ways

plum *noun* **1** a soft fruit, often dark red or purple, with a stone in the centre **2** the tree that produces this fruit ➤ *adjective* very good, very profitable etc: *a plum job*

plumage (*pronounced* **ploo**-mij) *noun* the feathers of a bird ⊙ Comes from French *plume* meaning 'feather'

plumb *noun* a lead weight hung on a string (**plumbline**), used to test if a wall has been built straight up, wallpaper hung straight, etc ➤ *adjective & adverb* standing straight up, vertical ➤ *verb* to test the depth of (the sea etc)

plumber *noun* someone who fits and mends water, gas, and sewage pipes

plumbing *noun* **1** the work of a plumber **2** the drainage and water systems of a building etc

plume *noun* **1** a feather, especially an ornamental one **2** something looking like a feather: *a plume of smoke*

plummet *noun* a weight of lead hung on a line, for taking depths at sea ➤ *verb* (**plummeting, plummeted**) to plunge

plump[1] *adjective* fat, rounded, well filled out ➤ *verb* **1** (often **plump up** or **plump out**) to grow fat, swell **2** to beat or shake (cushions etc) back into shape

plump[2] *verb* to sit or sink down heavily ● **plump for something** to choose, vote for it

plum pudding *noun* a rich pudding containing dried fruit

plunder *verb* to carry off goods by force, loot, rob ➤ *noun* goods seized by force

plunge *verb* **1** to dive (into water etc) **2** to rush or lurch forward **3** to thrust suddenly (into): *He plunged the knife into its neck* ➤ *noun* a thrust; a dive

plunger *noun* a rubber suction cup at the end of a long handle, used to clear blocked drains etc

plunging breaker *noun, geography* a steep wave that curls over and breaks suddenly and violently (*compare with*: **spilling wave**)

pluperfect *noun, grammar* a verb tense showing an action which took place before the main past actions being described, eg 'he *had* already *left* when you phoned'

plural *adjective* more than one ➤ *noun, grammar* the form which shows more than one, eg *mice* is the plural of *mouse* (*compare with*: **singular**)

pluralism *noun* the existence in a society of many cultural, religious, etc groups ◆ **pluralist** *noun & adjective*

plurality *noun* (*plural* **pluralities**) **1** the fact of being plural or more than one **2** a large number or variety **3** a majority that is not absolute, ie a winning number of votes that represents less than half of the votes cast

plus *preposition* used to show addition and represented by the sign (+): *Five plus two equals seven* ➤ *adjective* **1** of a quantity more than zero **2** *physics* electrically positive ➤ *adverb, informal* and a bit extra: *She earns £20,000 plus*

plus fours *plural noun* baggy trousers reaching to just below the knees

⊙ So called from the four additional inches of cloth needed for their length

plush *noun* cloth with a soft velvety surface on one side ➤ *adjective, informal* luxurious

plutocracy (*pronounced* ploo-**tawk**-ra-si) *noun* (*plural* **plutocracies**) **1** a social system based on leadership by the wealthy **2** a state governed by the wealthy **3** a group who have influence because of their wealth ☉ Comes from Greek *ploutos* meaning 'wealth'

plutocrat *noun* **1** a member of a plutocracy **2** someone who is powerful because of their wealth

plutonium *noun, chemistry* (symbol **Pu**) a highly poisonous, silvery-grey, radioactive metallic element, whose isotope plutonium-239 is used for nuclear weapons and some nuclear reactors

☉ Named after the planet *Pluto*

ply¹ *verb* (**plies, plying, plied**) **1** to work at steadily **2** to make regular journeys: *The ferry plies between Oban and Mull* **3** to use (a tool) energetically **4** to keep supplying with (food, questions to answer, etc)

ply² *noun*: **two-ply, three-ply, etc** having two, three, etc layers or strands

plyometrics *singular noun* a method of exercising that stretches the muscles quickly, eg jumping

plywood *noun* a board made up of thin sheets of wood glued together

PM *abbreviation* prime minister

Pm *symbol, chemistry* promethium

pm *abbreviation* after noon (from Latin *post meridiem*)

PMS *abbreviation* premenstrual syndrome

PMT *abbreviation* premenstrual tension

pneumatic (*pronounced* nyoo-**mat**-ik) *adjective* **1** filled with air **2** worked by air: *a pneumatic drill* ☉ Comes from Greek *pneuma* meaning 'breath'

pneumonia (*pronounced* nyoo-**moh**-ni-*a*) *noun* a disease in which the lungs become inflamed ☉ Comes from Greek *pneumon* meaning 'lung'

PO *abbreviation* **1** post office **2** postal order

Po *symbol, chemistry* polonium

poach¹ *verb* to cook gently in boiling water or stock

poach² *verb* to catch fish or hunt game illegally

poacher *noun* someone who hunts or fishes illegally

pocket *noun* **1** a small pouch or bag, especially as part of a garment **2** a personal supply of money: *well beyond my pocket* **3** a small isolated area: *a pocket of unemployment* ➤ *verb* (**pocketing, pocketed**) **1** to put in a pocket **2** *informal* to steal • **in** or **out of pocket** having gained or lost money on a deal etc

pocketbook *noun, US* a wallet

pocket knife *noun* a knife with folding blades

pocket money *noun* an allowance of money for personal spending

pockmark *noun* a scar or small hole in the skin left by disease

pod *noun* a long seedcase of the pea, bean, etc ➤ *verb* (**podding, podded**) **1** to remove from a pod **2** to form pods

podcasting *noun* a method of publishing sound files on the Internet, enabling people to create broadcasts without sophisticated equipment ♦ **podcast** *noun* ♦ **podcaster** *noun*

podgy *adjective* (**podgier, podgiest**) short and fat

podium *noun* (*plural* **podiums** or **podia**) a low pedestal, a platform

podsol *noun, geography* a type of soil, found under heath and coniferous forests in cold temperate regions, with a greyish upper layer from which minerals have been leached ☉ Comes from Russian *pod* meaning 'under' + *zola* meaning 'ash'

poem *noun* a piece of imaginative writing set out in lines which often have a regular rhythm or rhyme

poet *noun* someone who writes poetry

poetic *adjective* of or like poetry ♦ **poetically** *adverb*

poetic justice *noun* a fitting reward or punishment

poetic licence *noun* a departure from truth, logic, etc for the sake of effect

poet laureate *noun* (*plural* **poets laureate** or **poet laureates**) in the UK: an officially appointed court poet, commissioned to produce poems for state occasions

poetry *noun* **1** the art of writing poems **2** poems

po-faced *adjective* stupidly solemn, humourless

pogo stick *noun* a spring-mounted pole with a handlebar and foot rests, on which to bounce

pogrom (*pronounced* **po**-grom) *noun* an organized killing or massacre of a group of people

poignancy (*pronounced* **poi**-nyan-si) *noun* a poignant quality

poignant (*pronounced* **poi**-nyant) *adjective* **1** sharp, keen **2** very painful or moving; pathetic

point *noun* **1** a sharp end of anything **2** a headland **3** a dot: *decimal point* **4** a full stop in punctuation **5** an exact place or spot **6** an exact moment of time **7** the chief matter of an argument **8** the meaning of a joke **9** a mark in a competition **10** a purpose, an advantage: *There is no point in going* **11** a movable rail to direct a railway engine from one line to another **12** an electrical wall socket **13** a mark of character: *He has many good points* **14** *printing* a unit of measurement of type ➤ *verb* **1** to make pointed: *point your toes* **2** to direct, aim **3** to indicate with a gesture: *pointing to the building* **4** to fill (wall joints) with mortar ◷ Comes from French *point* meaning 'dot' or 'stitch', and *pointe* meaning 'sharp point'

point bar *noun, geography* a beach formed by material deposited by slow-flowing water on the inside of a meander in a river

point-blank *adjective* **1** of a shot: fired from very close range **2** of a question: direct

pointed *adjective* **1** having a point, sharp **2** of a remark: obviously aimed at someone

pointer *noun* **1** a rod for pointing **2** *informal* a suggestion or hint **3** a type of dog used to show where game has fallen after it has been shot

pointless *adjective* having no meaning or purpose

point of view *noun* (*plural* **points of view**) **1** someone's attitude towards something **2** the perspective from which a book is written, a film is shot, etc

poise *verb* **1** to balance, keep steady **2** to hover in the air ➤ *noun* **1** a state of balance **2** dignity, self-confidence

poised *adjective* **1** balanced, having poise **2** prepared, ready: *poised for action*

poison *noun* **1** a substance which, when taken into the body, kills or harms **2** anything harmful ➤ *verb* **1** to kill or harm with poison **2** to add poison to **3** to make bitter or bad: *poisoned her mind*

poisonous *adjective* **1** harmful because of containing poison **2** *informal* of a person, remark, etc: malicious

poison pen letter *noun* a malicious letter written anonymously

Poisson distribution (*pronounced* **pwah**-son) *noun, statistics* a distribution that is characterized by a small probability of a specific event occurring during a large number of observations

◷ Named after its discoverer, French mathematician S D *Poisson* (1742–1840)

poke *verb* **1** to push (eg a finger or stick) into something **2** to prod, thrust at **3** to search about inquisitively ➤ *noun* **1** a nudge, a prod **2** a prying search

poker[1] *noun* a rod for stirring up a fire

poker[2] *noun* a card game in which players bet on their chance of winning

poky *adjective* (**pokier, pokiest**) cramped and shabby

polar *adjective* **1** of the regions round the North or South Poles **2** of climate: very cold and dry **3** as different as possible: *polar opposites*

polar bear *noun* a type of large, white bear found in the Arctic

polar cell *noun, geography* a weather cycle in which air rises at the polar front (where colder

polar air meets warmer tropical air) and descends at the poles

polar co-ordinates *noun, maths* co-ordinates that identify a point by the length of a line from the origin to the point (a **radius vector**), and the angle it makes with the origin

polarity *noun* (*plural* **polarities**) **1** the state of having two opposite poles **2** *physics* the status, positive or negative, of the poles of a magnet, the terminals of an electrode, etc

polarization or **polarisation** *noun* **1** *chemistry* the separation of the positive and negative charges of the atoms or molecules of a substance **2** *physics* controlling the direction of the electric and magnetic fields of an electromagnetic wave

polarize or **polarise** *verb* **1** to give polarity to **2** to split into opposing sides **3** *physics* to control the direction of the electric and magnetic fields of an electromagnetic wave

Polaroid *noun, trademark* **1** a plastic through which light is seen less brightly, used in sunglasses **2** a camera that develops individual pictures in a few seconds

pole[1] *noun* **1** the north or south end of the earth's axis (**the North** or **South Pole**) **2** either of the opposing points of a magnet or electric battery

pole[2] *noun* a long, rounded rod or post

polecat *noun* **1** a large kind of weasel **2** *US* a skunk

polemic (*pronounced* po-**lem**-ik) *noun* **1** a controversial speech or piece of writing that fiercely attacks or defends an idea, etc **2** writing or public speaking of this sort ➤ *adjective* (also **polemical**) relating to or involving polemics or controversy ◷ Comes from Greek *polemikos* meaning 'relating to war'

polemics *singular noun* the art of verbal debate

Pole Star *noun* (**the Pole Star**) the star most directly above the North Pole

pole vault *noun* a sport in which an athlete jumps over a bar with the aid of a flexible pole ◆ **pole vaulter** *noun*

police *noun* the body of men and women whose work it is to see that laws are obeyed etc ➤ *verb* to keep law and order in (a place) by use of police

policeman *noun* (*plural* **policemen**) a male police officer

police officer *noun* a member of a police force

police state *noun* a state with a repressive government that operates through secret police to eliminate opposition

police station *noun* the headquarters of the police in a district

policewoman *noun* (*plural* **policewomen**) a female police officer

policy¹ *noun* (*plural* **policies**) an agreed course of action

policy² *noun* (*plural* **policies**) a written agreement with an insurance company

polio short for **poliomyelitis**

poliomyelitis (*pronounced* poh-li-oh-mai-e-lai-tis) *noun* a disease of the spinal cord, causing weakness or paralysis of the muscles

polish *verb* 1 to make smooth and shiny by rubbing 2 to improve (a piece of writing etc) 3 to make more polite ➤ *noun* (*plural* **polishes**) 1 a gloss on a surface 2 a substance used for polishing 3 fine manners, style, etc

politburo *noun* (*plural* **politburos**), *history* the supreme policy-making committee of a Communist state or party, especially that of the former Soviet Union

polite *adjective* having good manners, courteous ◆ **politely** *adverb* ◆ **politeness** *noun*

politic *adjective* wise, cautious

political *adjective* of government, politicians, or politics

political correctness *noun* the avoidance of expressions or actions which may appear to exclude or belittle people on the grounds of race, gender, disability, sexual orientation, etc ◆ **politically correct** *adjective*

political party *noun* an organized group of people with the same political aims

political prisoner *noun* someone imprisoned for their political beliefs, activities, etc, usually because they oppose the government

politician *noun* someone involved in politics, especially a member of parliament

politicize or **politicise** *verb* 1 to make aware of political issues 2 to give a political character to: *politicize an issue*

politics *singular noun* the art or study of government ➤ *singular* or *plural noun* 1 political affairs 2 political opinions

polka (*pronounced* pol-ka or pohl-ka) *noun* a lively dance or the music for it

polka dot *noun* any one of numerous regularly spaced dots forming a pattern on fabric etc

poll (*pronounced* pohl) *noun* 1 a counting of voters at an election 2 total number of votes 3 (*also called:* **opinion poll**) a test of public opinion by asking what people think of something ➤ *verb* 1 to cut or clip off (hair, branches, etc) 2 to receive (votes): *They polled 5000 votes*

pollard *noun* a tree with its top cut off to allow new growth ➤ *verb* to cut the top off (a tree)

pollen *noun* the fertilizing powder of flowers

pollinate *verb* to fertilize with pollen

pollination *noun* the transfer of pollen to achieve fertilization

polling booth *noun* an enclosed compartment at a polling station in which a voter can mark their ballot paper

polling station *noun* the building where people go to vote during an election

poll tax *noun* a fixed tax on each adult member of a population

pollutant *noun* something that pollutes

pollute *verb* 1 to make dirty or impure 2 to make (the environment) harmful to life

pollution *noun* 1 the act of polluting 2 dirt

polo *noun* a game like hockey played on horseback

polo neck *noun* 1 a close-fitting neck with a part turned over at the top 2 a jumper with a neck like this

polonium *noun, chemistry* (symbol **Po**) a rare radioactive metallic element

⊙ From *Polonia*, the Latin name for Poland, the native country of Marie Curie who discovered the element

polo shirt *noun* a short-sleeved open-necked casual shirt with a collar, usually made of a knitted cotton fabric

poltergeist (*pronounced* **pohl**-ter-gaist) *noun* a kind of ghost believed to move furniture and throw objects around a room ⊙ Comes from German, literally 'a ghost which makes a racket'

poly *noun* (*plural* **polys**), *informal* 1 a polyphonic ringtone for a mobile phone 2 a polytechnic

poly- *prefix* 1 many, much: *polyglot/polygon* 2 *chemistry* a polymer of: *polystyrene* (= a polymer of styrene)/*polythene* (= the name of a number of polymers of ethylene) ⊙ Comes from Greek *polys* meaning 'much'

polyamide *noun, chemistry* a polymer, eg nylon, formed by the linking of the amino group of one molecule with the carboxyl group of the next

polyanthus *noun* (*plural* **polyanthuses**) a hybrid plant which produces many flowers

polycarpous *adjective* of a tree: producing fruit year after year

polyester *noun* a synthetic material often used in clothing

polygamy (*pronounced* po-**lig**-a-mi) *noun* the fact of having more than one wife or husband at the same time (*compare with:* **bigamy, monogamy**) ◆ **polygamist** *noun* ◆ **polygamous** *adjective*

polyglot *adjective* speaking, or written in, many languages ➤ *noun* someone fluent in many languages

polygon *noun, maths* a plane figure with a number of angles and sides, usually more than three ◆ **polygonal** *adjective*

polygraph *noun* an instrument which

measures pulse rate etc, used as a lie-detector

polyhedron (*pronounced* pol-i-**hee**-dron) *noun* (*plural* **polyhedrons** or **polyhedra**), *maths* a solid figure with four or more faces, all of which are polygons ♦ **polyhedral** *adjective*

polymath *noun* someone with knowledge of a wide range of subjects

polymer *noun, chemistry* a large molecule made up of linked smaller molecules (**monomers**) forming a series of repeating units

polymerization or **polymerisation** *noun, chemistry* a chemical reaction in which two or more monomers are joined to form a polymer

polymorphism *noun* **1** *biology* the occurrence of a living organism in two or more different forms at different stages of its life cycle **2** *chemistry* the occurrence of a chemical substance in two or more different crystalline forms, eg diamond and graphite
♦ **polymorphic** or **polymorphous** *adjective*

polynomial *maths, adjective* of an expression: consisting of a sum of terms ➤ *noun* an expression consisting of a sum of terms

polyp *noun* (*pronounced* **pol**-ip) **1** a small sea animal with arms or tentacles **2** a small, usually benign, tumour

polypeptide *noun, chemistry* a peptide of in which many amino acids are linked to form a chain

polyphonic (*pronounced* pol-i-**fon**-ik) *adjective* **1** relating to polyphony **2** reproducing sound on a number of channels, rather than one or two

polyphony (*pronounced* po-**lif**-on-i) *noun* musical composition in parts, each with a separate melody (*compare with*: **homophony**)

polysaccharide *noun, biology, chemistry* a large carbohydrate molecule consisting of many monosaccharides linked to form long chains, eg starch, cellulose

polysemy (*pronounced* po-**lis**-em-i) *noun* the existence of more than one meaning for a single word ♦ **polysemous** *adjective*

polystyrene *noun* a tough thermoplastic material which resists moisture, used for packing, disposable cups, etc

polysyllabic *adjective* of a word: having three or more syllables

polysyllable *noun* a word of three or more syllables

polytechnic *noun* formerly, a college which taught technical and vocational subjects

polytheism *noun* the belief in more than one God ♦ **polytheist** *noun* ♦ **polytheistic** *adjective*

polythene *noun* a type of plastic that can be moulded when hot

polyunsaturated *adjective, chemistry* of a fat or oil: containing two or more double bonds per molecule (*compare with*: **monounsaturated**)

polyurethane (*pronounced* pol-i-**yoo**-ri-thein) *noun, chemistry* a polymer used to produce protective coatings, paints, plastics and foams

polyvinyl chloride *noun, chemistry* (*abbrev* **PVC**) a tough thermoplastic used in pipes, food packaging, waterproof clothing and electrical insulation

pomander (*pronounced* poh-**man**-der) *noun* **1** a perfumed ball composed of various aromatic substances **2** a perforated container for this or anything similarly performed

pomegranate (*pronounced* **pom**-i-gran-it) *noun* a fruit with a thick skin, many seeds and pulpy edible flesh ☉ Comes from Old French *pome grenate* meaning 'grainy apple'

pommel (*pronounced* **pu**-mel or **po**-mel) *noun* **1** the knob on the hilt of a sword **2** the high part of a saddle

pomp *noun* solemn and splendid ceremony, magnificence

pompous *adjective* self-important, excessively dignified ♦ **pomposity** *noun*

poncho *noun* (*plural* **ponchos**) a S American cloak made of a blanket with a hole for the head

pond *noun* a small lake or pool

ponder *verb* to think over, consider

ponderous *adjective* **1** weighty **2** clumsy **3** sounding very important

pong *informal, noun* a stink; a bad smell ➤ *verb* to smell bad ♦ **pongy** *adjective* (**pongier, pongiest**)

pons *noun* (*plural* **pontes** – *pronounced* **pon**-teez**), *anatomy* the mass of nerve fibres that connects and relays impulses between parts of the brain

pontiff *noun* **1** a Roman Catholic bishop **2** the Pope

pontifical *adjective* **1** of a pontiff **2** *derogatory* pompous in speech

pontificate *verb* to speak in a pompous manner

pontoon[1] *noun* a flat-bottomed boat used to support a temporary bridge (a **pontoon bridge**)

pontoon[2] *noun* a card game in which players try to collect 21 points

pony *noun* (*plural* **ponies**) a small horse

ponytail *noun* a hairstyle in which the hair is drawn back and gathered by a band

pony-trekking *noun* riding cross-country in small parties

poodle *noun* a breed of dog with curly hair often clipped in a fancy way

pool[1] *noun* **1** a small area of still water **2** a deep part of a river

pool² noun **1** a joint fund or stock (of money, typists, etc) **2** the money played for in a gambling game ➤ verb to put (money etc) into a joint fund

pools plural noun (**the pools**) organized betting on football match results (also called: **football pools**)

poop noun **1** a ship's stern, or back part **2** a high deck in the stern

poor adjective **1** having little money or property **2** not good: This work is poor **3** lacking (in): poor in sports facilities **4** deserving pity: Poor Tom has broken his leg ➤ plural noun (**the poor**) poor people in general

poorhouse noun, history an institution maintained at public expense, for housing the poor

poor law noun, history a law or set of laws concerned with supporting the poor

poorly adverb not well; badly ➤ adjective, informal in bad health, ill

POP abbreviation, computing **1** point of presence, a point of access to the Internet **2** post office protocol, the rules controlling the interaction between an e-mail client and server

pop¹ noun **1** a sharp quick noise, eg that made by a cork coming out of a bottle **2** informal a fizzy soft drink ➤ verb (**popping, popped**) **1** to make a pop **2** to move quickly, dash: pop in/pop along the road

pop² noun popular music ➤ adjective of music: popular

popadom or **popadum** noun a thin circle of dough fried in oil until crisp

popcorn noun **1** maize grains that puff up and burst open when heated **2** the edible puffed-up kernels of this grain

Pope or **pope** noun the bishop of Rome, head of the Roman Catholic Church

poplar noun a tall, narrow, quick-growing tree

poplin noun strong cotton cloth

poppy noun (plural **poppies**) a scarlet flower growing wild in fields etc, or any of various related species

populace noun the people of a country or area

popular adjective **1** of the people: the popular vote **2** liked by most people **3** widely held or believed: popular belief

popular front noun a left-wing group or alliance, especially one set up from the 1930s onwards to oppose fascism

popularity noun the state of being generally liked

popularize or **popularise** verb to make popular or widely known

popularly adverb in a popular way; in terms of most people: a popularly held belief

populate verb to fill (an area) with people
 ♦ **populated** adjective

population noun **1** the number of people living in a place **2** statistics a group that consists of all the possible values relevant to a study, from which samples are taken to determine the characteristics of the whole

population density noun, geography the number of people living in a given area, usually per square kilometre

population pyramid noun, geography a graph showing population structure, with age groups marked along a vertical axis, and horizontal bars to the right showing the number of females in that age group, and horizontal bars to the left showing the number of males

population structure noun, geography the number of males and females within each age group in a population

populous adjective full of people

pop-up adjective **1** of a picture book, greetings card, etc: having cut-out parts which stand upright as the page is opened **2** of appliances etc: having a mechanism which causes a component, or the item being prepared, to pop up **3** computing of a utility: appearing on the screen when an option is selected: a pop-up menu

porcelain noun a kind of fine china

porch noun (plural **porches**) a covered entrance to a building

porcupine noun a large rodent covered with sharp quills

pore¹ noun **1** a tiny hole **2** the hole of a sweat gland in the skin ◉ Comes from Greek poros meaning 'a passage'

pore² verb: **pore over** to study closely or eagerly

! Do not confuse with: **pour**

poriferan (pronounced po-**rif**-e-ran) noun, zoology a sponge

pork noun the flesh of the pig, prepared for eating

porn noun, informal pornography

pornographic adjective relating to pornography

pornography noun literature or art that is sexually explicit and often offensive

porosity noun being porous

porous adjective **1** having pores **2** allowing fluid to pass through

porpoise noun a blunt-nosed sea animal of the dolphin family

porridge noun a food made from oatmeal boiled in water or milk

porringer (pronounced por-in-jer) noun a small bowl for soup, porridge, etc

port¹ *noun* **1** a harbour **2** a town with a harbour

port² *noun* the left side of a ship as you face the front

port³ *noun, computing* a socket or plug for connecting a hardware device to a computer

port⁴ *noun* a strong, dark-red, sweet wine

portability *noun* the quality of being portable

portable *adjective* **1** able to be lifted and carried **2** *computing* of software: able to run on more than one platform ➤ *noun* a computer, telephone, etc that can be carried around

portal *noun, formal* a grand entrance or doorway

portcullis *noun* (*plural* **portcullises**), *history* a grating which is let down quickly to close a gateway

portend (*pronounced* pawr-**tend**) *verb* to give warning of, foretell

portent (*pronounced* **pawr**-tent) *noun* a warning sign

portentous (*pronounced* pawr-**ten**-tus) *adjective* **1** strange, wonderful **2** important, weighty

porter¹ *noun* a doorkeeper

porter² *noun* **1** someone employed to carry luggage, push hospital trolleys, etc **2** a kind of dark-brown beer

portfolio *noun* (*plural* **portfolios**) **1** a flat case for carrying papers, drawings, etc **2** *politics* the job of a government minister

porthole *noun* a small, round window in a ship's side

portico *noun* (*plural* **porticoes** or **porticos**) a row of columns in front of a building forming a porch or covered walk

portion *noun* **1** a part **2** a share, a helping ➤ *verb* to divide into parts

portly *adjective* (**portlier, portliest**) stout and dignified

portmanteau (*pronounced* pawrt-**man**-toh) *noun* (*plural* **portmanteaus** or **portmanteaux** – *pronounced* pawrt-**man**-tohz) a large leather travelling bag

portrait *noun* **1** a drawing, painting or photograph of a person **2** a description of a person, place, etc **3** *printing* an orientation of a page, illustration, etc that is taller than it is wide or deep (*compare with:* **landscape**)

portray *verb* **1** to make a painting or drawing of **2** to describe in words **3** to act the part of
◆ **portrayal** *noun*

Portuguese man-of-war *noun* (*plural* **Portuguese men-of-war**) a stinging jellyfish

pose *noun* **1** a position of the body: *a relaxed pose* **2** behaviour put on to impress others, a pretence ➤ *verb* **1** to position yourself for a photograph etc **2** to put forward (a problem, question, etc) **3** (**pose as**) to pretend or claim to be

poser¹ *noun* a difficult question

poser² *noun, derogatory* someone who poses to impress others

poseur (*pronounced* poh-**zer**) *noun, derogatory* someone who behaves in an affected way, especially to impress others

posh *adjective, informal* high-class; smart

> ⊙ The word probably comes from a Romany word meaning 'a smart person', although many people think it stands for *Port Out, Starboard Home*, which represented the most desirable position of cabins for European passengers on ships travelling to Asia and back

position *noun* **1** place, situation **2** manner of standing, sitting, etc; posture: *in a crouching position* **3** a rank or job: *a high position in a bank* ➤ *verb* to place

positive *adjective* **1** meaning or saying 'yes': *a positive answer* (*contrasted with:* **negative**) **2** not able to be doubted: *positive proof* **3** certain, convinced: *I am positive that she did it* **4** definite: *a positive improvement* **5** *maths* of a number: greater than zero **6** *physics* having an electrical charge produced by a deficiency of electrons **7** *grammar* of an adjective or adverb: of the first degree of comparison, not comparative or superlative, eg *big*, not *bigger* or *biggest*

positron *noun, physics* a subatomic particle with the same mass as an electron but with a positive electrical charge

posse (*pronounced* **pos**-i) *noun, US* a body of men enlisted by a sheriff to assist him

possess *verb* **1** to own, have **2** to take hold of your mind: *Anger possessed her*

possessed *adjective* **1** in the power of an evil spirit **2** obsessed

possession *noun* **1** the state of possessing or of being possessed **2** (**possessions**) someone's property or belongings

possessive *adjective* **1** *grammar* of an adjective or pronoun: showing possession, for example *my, mine, your, their*, etc **2** over-protective and jealous in attitude

possibility *noun* (*plural* **possibilities**) something that may happen or that may be done

possible *adjective* **1** able to happen or to be done **2** not unlikely ⊙ Comes from Latin *possibilis* meaning 'which may exist' or 'which may be done'

possibly *adverb* perhaps

possum *noun:* **play possum** *informal* to pretend to be asleep or dead

post¹ *noun* an upright pole or stake ➤ *verb* **1** to put up, stick up (a notice etc) **2** to put (information etc) on an Internet site

post² *noun* 1 a job: *a teaching post* 2 a place of duty: *The soldier remained at his post* 3 a settlement, a camp: *a military post/trading post* ➤ *verb* to send or station somewhere: *posted abroad*

post³ *noun* the service which delivers letters and other mail ➤ *verb* to put (a letter) in a postbox for collection

post- *prefix* after: *postgraduate/post-mortem* ⓘ Comes from Latin *post* meaning 'after' or 'behind'

postage *noun* money paid for sending a letter etc by post

postage stamp *noun* a small printed label to show that postage has been paid

postal *adjective* of or by post

postal order *noun* a document bought at a post office which can be exchanged for a stated amount of money

postbag *noun* 1 a mailbag 2 the letters received by a radio or TV programme, magazine, famous person, etc

postbox *noun* (*plural* **postboxes**) a box with an opening in which to post letters etc

postcard *noun* a card for sending a message by post

postcode *noun* a short series of letters and numbers, used for sorting mail by machine

post-date *verb* to mark (a cheque) with a date in the future, so that it cannot be cashed immediately

poster *noun* 1 a large notice or placard 2 a large printed picture

posterior *adjective* 1 coming after in time 2 at or nearer the back ➤ *noun* the buttocks

posterity *noun* 1 all future generations 2 someone's descendants

postern *noun*, *history* a back door or gate to a castle etc

postgraduate *adjective* of study etc: following on from a first university degree ➤ *noun* someone continuing to study after a first degree

post-haste *adverb* with great speed

posthumous (*pronounced* pos-tyuw-mus) *adjective* 1 of a book: published after the author's death 2 of a child: born after the father's death

postilion or **postillion** *noun*, *old* a carriage driver who rides on one of the horses

Post-it *noun*, *trademark* a small sticky label for writing messages on

postman or **postwoman** *noun* (*plural* **postmen** or **postwomen**) someone who delivers letters

postmark *noun* a date stamp put on a letter at a post office

postmaster or **postmistress** *noun* a person in charge of a post office

post-mortem *noun* an examination of a dead body to find out the cause of death

post office *noun* an office for receiving and sending off letters by post etc

post-operative *adjective*, *medicine* relating to the period immediately following a surgical operation

postpone *verb* to put off to a future time ◆ **postponement** *noun*

postscript *noun* an added remark at the end of a letter, after the sender's name

postulant *noun* someone applying to enter a religious order

postulate *verb* to assume or take for granted (that)

posture *noun* 1 the manner in which someone holds themselves in standing or walking 2 a position, a pose

postwar *adjective* relating to the time after a war

posy *noun* (*plural* **posies**) a small bunch of flowers

pot¹ *noun* 1 a deep vessel used in cooking, as a container or for growing plants 2 (**pots**) *informal* a great deal: *pots of money* ➤ *verb* (**potting, potted**) 1 to plant in a pot 2 to make articles of baked clay

pot² *noun slang* the drug marijuana

potash *noun* potassium carbonate, obtained from the ashes of wood

potassium *noun*, *chemistry* (symbol **K**) a soft, silvery-white, metallic element

potassium hydroxide *noun*, *chemistry* a corrosive, white, crystalline solid that dissolves to form a strong alkaline solution, used in the manufacture of soft soap and in batteries

potassium nitrate *noun*, *chemistry* a white or transparent, highly explosive, crystalline solid, used in the manufacture of fireworks, matches, gunpowder, fertilizers, etc (*also called:* **nitre, saltpetre**)

potato *noun* (*plural* **potatoes**) 1 a plant with round, starchy roots which are eaten as a vegetable 2 the vegetable itself

pot belly *noun*, *informal* a protruding stomach

potboiler *noun*, *derogatory* a book etc of little artistic value, produced simply to make money

potency *noun* (*plural* **potencies**) power, strength

potent *adjective* powerful, strong

potentate *noun* a powerful ruler

potential *adjective* that may develop, possible ➤ *noun* 1 the possibility of further development 2 *physics* the energy required to move a unit of mass, electric charge, etc from an infinite distance to a point where it is to be measured

potential difference *noun*, *physics* a measure of the work involved in moving a charge between two points in an electric field (*also called*: **voltage**)

potential energy *noun, physics* the energy that a body has because of its position or the positions of its atoms, rather than motion (*compare with*: **kinetic energy**)

potentiality *noun* (*plural* **potentialities**) a possibility

pothole *noun* **1** a deep cave **2** a hole worn in a road surface

potholer *noun* someone who explores caves ♦ **potholing** *noun*

potion *noun* a drink, often containing medicine or poison

pot luck *noun*: **take pot luck** to take whatever is available or offered

pot plant *noun* a household plant kept in a pot

potpourri (*pronounced* poh-**poo**-ri) *noun* **1** a scented mixture of dried petals etc **2** a mixture or medley

pot shot *noun* a casual or random shot

potted *adjective* **1** of meat: pressed down and preserved in a jar **2** condensed and simplified: *potted history*

potter¹ *noun* someone who makes articles of baked clay

potter² *verb* **1** to do small odd jobs **2** to dawdle

pottery *noun* (*plural* **potteries**) **1** articles made of baked clay **2** a place where such things are made **3** the art of making them

potting shed *noun* a shed where garden tools are kept, plants are put into pots, etc

potty¹ *adjective* (**pottier, pottiest**) *informal* mad, eccentric

potty² *noun* (*plural* **potties**) *informal* a child's chamberpot

potty-train *verb* to teach (a toddler) to use a potty or the toilet ♦ **potty-trained** *adjective*

pouch *noun* (*plural* **pouches**) **1** a pocket or small bag **2** a bag-like fold on the front of a kangaroo, for carrying its young

pouffe (*pronounced* poof) *noun* a low, stuffed seat without back or arms

poultice (*pronounced* **pohl**-tis) *noun* a wet dressing spread on a bandage and put on inflamed skin

poultry *noun* farmyard fowls, eg hens, ducks, geese, turkeys

pounce *verb*: **pounce on something** or **someone** to seize or attack them ➤ *noun* a sudden attack

pound¹ *noun* **1** the standard unit of money in Britain, shown by the sign (£), equal to 100 new pence **2** (*abbrev* **lb**) a measure of weight, equal to 16 ounces (about $\frac{1}{2}$ kilogram)

pound² *noun* an enclosure for animals

pound³ *verb* **1** to beat into powder **2** to beat heavily **3** to walk or run with heavy steps

pour *verb* **1** to flow in a stream: *The blood poured out* **2** to make flow: *pour the tea* **3** to rain heavily ⊙ Comes from Middle English *pouren*

❗ Do not confuse with: **pore**

pout *verb* to push out the lips sulkily to show displeasure ➤ *noun* a sulky look

poverty *noun* **1** the state of being poor **2** lack, want: *poverty of ideas*

poverty-stricken *adjective* suffering from poverty

POW *abbreviation* prisoner of war

powder *noun* **1** a substance made up of very fine particles **2** gunpowder **3** cosmetic face powder ➤ *verb* **1** to sprinkle or dab with powder **2** to grind down to powder

powdered *adjective* **1** in fine particles **2** covered with powder

powder room *noun* a women's cloakroom or toilet in a restaurant, hotel, etc

powdery *adjective* **1** covered with powder **2** like powder: *powdery snow*

power *noun* **1** strength, force **2** ability to do things **3** authority or legal right **4** a strong nation **5** someone in authority **6** the force used for driving machines: *electric power/steam power* **7** *maths* the product obtained by multiplying a number by itself a given number of times (eg $2 \times 2 \times 2$ or 2^3 is the third power of 2) **8** *physics* the rate of doing work or converting energy from one form into another

power-driven or **powered** *adjective* worked by electricity, not by hand

powerful *adjective* having great power, strength, vigour, authority, influence, force or effectiveness

powerless *adjective* without power or ability

power station *noun* a building where electricity is produced

power tool *noun* a hand-held tool worked by electrical power

pox *noun, medicine* any of various viral diseases that cause pimples containing pus: *chickenpox/smallpox*

pp *abbreviation* pages

PR *abbreviation* **1** public relations **2** proportional representation

Pr *symbol, chemistry* praseodymium

practicable *adjective* able to be used or done: *a plan that is practicable in reality* ⊙ Comes from an old spelling of French *praticable* meaning 'able to be put into practice'

❗ Do not confuse: **practicable** and **practical**

practical *adjective* **1** preferring action to thought **2** efficient **3** learned by practice, rather than from books: *practical knowledge* ⊙ Comes from an old spelling of French *pratique* meaning 'handy', + suffix *-al*

practical joke *noun* a joke consisting of action, not words; a trick played on someone

practically *adverb* 1 in a practical way 2 in effect, in reality 3 almost: *practically empty*

practice *noun* 1 habit: *It is my practice to get up early* 2 the actual doing of something: *I always intend to get up early but in practice I stay in bed* 3 repeated performance to improve skill: *piano practice/in practice for the race* 4 the business of a doctor, lawyer, etc

! Do not confuse: **practice** and **practise**. To help you remember 'ice' is a noun, 'ise' is not!

practise or *US* **practice** *verb* 1 to perform or exercise repeatedly to improve a skill: *She practises judo nightly* 2 to make a habit of: *practise self-control* 3 to follow (a profession): *practise dentistry*

practitioner *noun* someone engaged in a profession: *a medical practitioner*

pragmatic or **pragmatical** *adjective* practical; matter-of-fact; realistic

pragmatism *noun* a practical, matter-of-fact approach to dealing with problems etc ♦ **pragmatist** *noun*

Prague Spring *noun, history* the attempts in 1968 by Czechoslovakia's First Secretary, Alexander Dubček, to reform communism, which resulted in occupation by Soviet forces

prairie *noun* a stretch of level grassland in N America

praise *verb* 1 to speak highly of 2 to glorify (God) by singing hymns etc ➤ *noun* an expression of approval

praiseworthy *adjective* deserving to be praised

prajna (*pronounced* **prahj**-na) *noun, Buddhism* direct understanding of the truth

praline (*pronounced* **prah**-leen) *noun* a sweet consisting of nuts in caramelized sugar

pram *noun* a small wheeled carriage for a baby, pushed by hand (*short for* **perambulator**)

prance *verb* 1 to strut or swagger about 2 to dance about 3 of a horse: to spring from the hind legs

prank *noun* a trick played for mischief

praseodymium (*pronounced* prei-zi-oh-**dim**-i-um) *noun, chemistry* (symbol **Pr**) a soft, silvery, metallic element

prat *noun, informal* an idiot

prattle *verb* to talk or chatter meaninglessly ➤ *noun* meaningless talk

prawn *noun* a type of shellfish like the shrimp

pray *verb* 1 to speak to God 2 to ask earnestly, beg ◑ Comes from French *prier*, from Latin *precarius* meaning 'obtained by prayer'

! Do not confuse with: **prey**

prayer *noun* 1 a request, thanks, etc given to God 2 an earnest request for something

praying mantis see **mantis**

pre- *prefix* 1 before: *prehistoric* 2 to the highest degree: *pre-eminent* ◑ Comes from Latin *prae* meaning 'in front of' or 'before'

preach *verb* 1 to give a sermon 2 to teach, speak in favour of: *preach caution*

preacher *noun* a religious teacher

preamble *noun* something said as an introduction

prearrange *verb* to arrange beforehand

Precambrian *adjective* of the earliest geological aeon, when primitive life forms appeared on earth

precancerous *adjective, medicine* especially of cells: showing early indications of possible malignancy

precarious *adjective* uncertain, risky, dangerous

precaution *noun* care taken beforehand to avoid an accident etc ♦ **precautionary** *adjective*

precede *verb* to go before in time, rank, or importance ◑ Comes from Latin *praecedere* meaning 'to go before'

! Do not confuse with: **proceed**

precedence *noun* the right to go before; priority

precedent *noun* a past action which serves as an example or rule for the future

preceding *adjective* going before; previous

precept *noun* a guiding rule, a commandment

precinct *noun* 1 an area enclosed by the boundary walls of a building 2 (**precincts**) the area closely surrounding any place 3 *US* an administrative district

precious *adjective* 1 highly valued or valuable 2 over-fussy or precise

precipice *noun* a steep cliff

precipitate *verb* (*pronounced* pri-**sip**-it-eit) 1 to throw head foremost 2 to force into (hasty action etc) 3 to hasten (death, illness etc) 4 *chemistry* to cause something to form a suspension of small solid particles in a solution ➤ *adjective* (*pronounced* pri-**sip**-it-it) 1 headlong 2 hasty, rash ➤ *noun* (*pronounced* pri-**sip**-it-it) 1 *chemistry* a suspension of small solid particles in a solution 2 *meteorology* moisture deposited in the form of rain, snow, etc

precipitation *noun* 1 great hurry 2 *meteorology* water that falls from clouds in the atmosphere to the earth's surface in the form of rain, snow, etc 3 *chemistry* the formation of a precipitate

precipitous adjective very steep
précis (pronounced **prei**-see) noun (plural **précis** – pronounced **prei**-seez) a summary of a piece of writing
precise adjective **1** definite **2** exact, accurate ♦ **precisely** adverb ⓞ Comes from Latin praecisus meaning 'cut short'

❗ Do not confuse with: **concise**

precision noun **1** preciseness **2** exactness, accuracy
preclude verb to prevent, make impossible
preclusion noun precluding
precocious adjective of a child: unusually advanced or well-developed ♦ **precocity** noun
precognitive adjective knowing beforehand, foretelling
preconceive verb to form (ideas etc) before having actual knowledge or experience
preconception noun an idea formed without actual knowledge
precursor noun a person or thing which goes before; an early form of something: the precursor of jazz
predate verb to happen before in time
predator noun a bird or animal that kills others for food ♦ **predation** noun
predatory (pronounced **pred**-a-to-ri) adjective **1** of a predator **2** using other people for your own advantage
predecessor noun the previous holder of a job or office
predestine verb to destine beforehand, preordain ♦ **predestination** noun
predetermine verb to settle beforehand
predicament noun an unfortunate or difficult situation
predicate noun, grammar something said about the subject of a sentence, eg has green eyes in the sentence Anne has green eyes
predict verb to foretell, forecast
predictable adjective able to be foretold
prediction noun an act of predicting; something predicted
predilection (pronounced pree-di-**lek**-shon) noun a preference, a liking for something
predispose verb **1** to make (someone) in favour of something beforehand: We were predisposed to believe her **2** to make liable (to): predisposed to colds ♦ **predisposition** noun
predominance noun being predominant
predominant adjective **1** ruling **2** most noticeable or outstanding
predominantly adverb mostly, mainly: Her books are predominantly about life in Africa
predominate verb **1** to be the strongest or most numerous **2** to have control (over)

pre-eclampsia noun, medicine a toxic condition that can occur in late pregnancy and lead to eclampsia
pre-embryo noun, biology, medicine a human embryo in the first fourteen days after fertilization of an ovum
pre-eminence noun a pre-eminent quality or state: His pre-eminence in the field of family law
pre-eminent adjective outstanding, excelling all others ♦ **pre-eminently** adverb
pre-empt verb to block or stop by making a first move ♦ **pre-emptive** adjective
preen verb **1** of a bird: to arrange its feathers **2** to smarten your appearance in a conceited way
• **preen yourself** to show obvious pride in your achievements
prefab noun a prefabricated house
prefabricated adjective made of parts made beforehand, ready to be fitted together
preface (pronounced **pref**-is) noun an introduction to a book etc ➤ verb to precede or introduce (with)
prefect noun **1** the head of an administrative district in France etc **2** a senior pupil in some schools with certain powers
prefer verb (**preferring, preferred**) **1** to like better: I prefer tea to coffee **2** to put forward (a claim or request)
preferable (pronounced **pref**-ra-bl) adjective more desirable
preference noun **1** greater liking **2** something preferred: What is your preference?
preferential adjective giving preference
preferment noun promotion
prefix noun (plural **prefixes**) a syllable or element at the beginning of a word which adds to or alters its meaning, eg dis-, un-, re-, in dislike, unhappy, regain
pregnancy noun (plural **pregnancies**) the state of being pregnant or the time during which a female is pregnant
pregnant adjective **1** carrying a developing embryo in the womb **2** full of meaning: a pregnant pause
preheat verb to heat (an oven etc) before use
prehensile adjective able to grasp or hold: a prehensile tail
prehistoric adjective relating to the time before history was written down
prehistory noun the period before historical records
prejudge verb to decide (something) before hearing the facts of a case
prejudice noun **1** an unfair feeling for or against anything **2** an opinion formed without careful thought **3** harm, injury ➤ verb **1** to fill with prejudice **2** to do harm to, damage: His late arrival prejudiced his chances of success

prejudiced *adjective* showing prejudice

prejudicial *adjective* damaging, harmful

prelate (*pronounced* **prel**-it) *noun* a bishop or archbishop

preliminary *adjective* going before, preparatory: *preliminary investigation* ➤ *noun* (*plural* **preliminaries**) something that goes or is done before

prelude (*pronounced* **prel**-yood) *noun* **1** a piece of music played as an introduction to the main piece **2** a preceding event: *a prelude to war*

premarital *adjective* happening before marriage: *premarital sex*

premature *adjective* coming, born, etc before the right, proper or expected time

premeditate *verb* to think out beforehand, plan: *premeditated murder* ✦ **premeditation** *noun*

premenstrual *adjective* before menstruation

premenstrual tension or **premenstrual syndrome** *noun, medicine* (*abbrev* **PMT** and **PMS**) a condition associated with hormonal changes just before menstruation, characterized by fluid retention, depression and irritability

premier (*pronounced* **prem**-i-er) *adjective* first, leading, foremost ➤ *noun* a prime minister

❗ Do not confuse: **premier** and **première**

première (*pronounced* **prem**-i-eir) *noun* a first performance of a play, film, etc

premise or **premiss** *noun* (*plural* **premises** or **premisses**) something assumed from which a conclusion is drawn

premises *plural noun* a building and its grounds

premium (*pronounced* **pree**-mi-um) *noun* (*plural* **premiums**) **1** a reward **2** a payment on an insurance policy • **at a premium** very desirable and therefore difficult to obtain

premolar *noun* a tooth between the canine teeth and the molars

premonition *noun* a feeling that something is going to happen; a forewarning

prenatal *adjective* before birth, or before giving birth

preoccupation *noun* **1** being preoccupied **2** something that preoccupies: *She has a preoccupation with death*

preoccupied *adjective* deep in thought

preoccupy *verb* (**preoccupies**, **preoccupying**, **preoccupied**) to completely engross the attention of (someone)

preordain *verb* to determine beforehand

prep *noun, informal* preparation

prepaid past form of **prepay**

preparation *noun* **1** an act of preparing **2** study for a lesson **3** something prepared for use, eg a medicine

preparatory *adjective* acting as an introduction to or preparation for

preparatory school *noun* a private school educating children of primary-school age

prepare *verb* **1** to make or get ready **2** to train, equip

prepared *adjective* **1** ready **2** willing

prepay *verb* (**prepaying, prepaid**) to pay beforehand

prepayment *noun* payment in advance

preponderance *noun* greater amount or number: *a preponderance of young people in the audience*

preposition *noun, grammar* a word placed before a noun, pronoun, etc to show its relation to another word, eg 'through the door', 'in the town', 'written by me'

❗ Do not confuse with: **proposition**

prepossessing *adjective* pleasant, making a good impression

preposterous *adjective* very foolish, absurd ℗ Comes from Latin *praeposterous* meaning 'back to front'

prepotent (*pronounced* pree-**poh**-tent) *adjective* **1** more powerfully influential than others **2** *biology* of a parent: exceptionally likely to pass on hereditary characteristics to the next generation ✦ **prepotency** *noun*

prep school *noun* a preparatory school

prequel *noun* a book or film produced after one that has been a success, but with the story beginning before the start of the original story

pre-Raphaelite *noun* any of a group of 19th-century British artists who painted in a truthful, natural style

prerequisite *noun* something necessary before another thing can happen

prerogative *noun* a right enjoyed by someone because of their rank or position

Prerogative Court *noun, history* a court dealing with matters to do with wills and testaments

presbyter (*pronounced* **prez**-bi-ter) *noun, Christianity* a minister or elder in a Presbyterian church

Presbyterian *adjective* **1** of a church: managed by ministers and elders **2** belonging to such a church ➤ *noun* a member of a Presbyterian church

presbytery *noun* (*plural* **presbyteries**) **1** a body of presbyters **2** the house of a Roman Catholic priest

prescribe *verb* **1** to lay down as a rule **2** to order the use of (a medicine) ℗ Comes from Latin *praescribere* meaning 'to write before'

! Do not confuse with: **proscribe**.
It may help to remember that the **pre-** in **prescribe** means 'before', and that the whole verb refers to the process by which a doctor has to write down an order for medication before it can be obtained by a patient.

prescription *noun* **1** a doctor's written instructions for preparing a medicine **2** something prescribed

! Do not confuse with: **proscription**.
Prescription is related to the verb **prescribe**.

prescriptive *adjective* laying down rules
presence *noun* **1** the state of being present **2** someone's personal appearance, manner, etc • **in your presence** while you are present
presence of mind *noun* calmness; ability to act sensibly in an emergency, difficulty, etc
present¹ (*pronounced* **prez**-ent) *adjective* **1** here, in this place **2** happening or existing now: *present rates of pay/the present situation* ➤ *noun* **1** the time now **2** *grammar* the present tense
present² *noun* (*pronounced* **prez**-ent) a gift ➤ *verb* (*pronounced* pri-**zent**) **1** to hand over (a gift) formally **2** to offer, put forward **3** to introduce (someone) to another • **present yourself 1** to introduce yourself **2** to arrive
presentable *adjective* **1** fit to be seen or to appear in company **2** passable; satisfactory
presentation *noun* **1** the giving of a present **2** something presented **3** a formal talk or demonstration **4** a showing of a play etc
present-day *adjective* modern; contemporary
presenter *noun, broadcasting* someone who introduces a programme and provides a linking commentary between items
presentiment (*pronounced* pri-**zen**-ti-ment) *noun* a feeling that something is about to happen
presently *adverb* soon
present participle *noun, grammar* the form of a verb used after an auxiliary verb to indicate that something is taking place in the present, for instance *going* in 'I am *going*'
present tense *noun, grammar* the tense describing events happening now, eg 'we *are* on holiday'
preservation *noun* preserving or being preserved
preservative *noun* a substance added to food to prevent it from going bad
preserve *verb* **1** to keep safe from harm **2** to keep in existence, maintain **3** to treat (food) so that it will not go bad ➤ *noun* **1** a place where game animals, birds, etc are protected **2** jam
preset *verb* (*pronounced* pree-**set**) (**presetting, preset**) to adjust (a piece of

electronic equipment etc) so that it will operate at the required time ➤ *noun* (*pronounced* **pree**-set) a device or facility for presetting
preside *verb* to be in charge at a meeting etc
presidency *noun* (*plural* **presidencies**) the position of president or time of being president
president *noun* **1** the leading member of a society etc **2** the head of a republic
press *verb* **1** to push on, against or down **2** to urge, force **3** to iron (clothes etc) ➤ *noun* (*plural* **presses**) **1** a crowd **2** a printing machine **3** (**the press**) the news media, journalists
press conference or **news conference** *noun* an interview granted to reporters by a politician or other person in the news
pressgang *history, noun* a group of men employed to carry off people by force into the army or navy ➤ *verb* **1** to carry off in a pressgang **2** to force (someone) to do something: *pressganged into joining the committee*
pressing *adjective* requiring immediate action, insistent
press release *noun* an official statement given to the press by an organization etc
press-up *noun* an exercise performed by raising and lowering the body on the arms while face down
pressure *noun* **1** *physics* a measure of the force on or against a surface **2** strong persuasion, compulsion **3** stress, strain **4** urgency ➤ *verb* to try to persuade; to force or pressurize
pressure cooker *noun* a pan in which food is cooked quickly by steam under pressure
pressure group *noun* a group of people who try to influence public opinion and government policy on a particular issue
pressurize or **pressurise** *verb* **1** to fit (an aeroplane etc) with a device that maintains normal air pressure **2** to force (someone) to do something
prestige (*pronounced* pre-**steesz**) *noun* reputation, influence due to rank, success, etc
prestigious (*pronounced* pre-**stij**-us) *adjective* having or giving prestige
presto *music, adverb* in a very fast manner ➤ *noun* (*plural* **prestos**) a piece of music to be played in a very fast way ☉ Comes from Italian, meaning 'quick'
presumably *adverb* I suppose
presume *verb* **1** to take for granted, assume (that) **2** to be bold, especially without the proper right or knowledge: *I wouldn't presume to advise the experts* **3** (**presume on**) to take advantage of (someone's kindness etc)
presumption *noun* **1** something presumed, a strong likelihood **2** arrogant or impertinent behaviour
presumptuous *adjective* insolent or arrogant

presuppose *verb* to take for granted
  ♦ **presupposition** *noun*

pretence or *US* **pretense** *noun* **1** the act of pretending **2** a false claim

pretend *verb* **1** to make believe, fantasize **2** to make a false claim: *pretending to be ill*

pretender *noun* someone who lays claim to something (especially to the crown)

pretension *noun* **1** a claim (whether true or not) **2** self-importance

pretentious *adjective* self-important; showy, ostentatious

pretext *noun* an excuse

prettify *verb* (**prettifies, prettifying, prettified**) to attempt to make (something or someone) prettier by superficial ornamentation

pretty *adjective* (**prettier, prettiest**) pleasing or attractive to see, listen to, etc ► *adverb* fairly, quite: *pretty good* ♦ **prettiness** *noun*

pretzel *noun* a crisp salted biscuit in the shape of a knot

prevail *verb* **1** to win, succeed **2** to be most usual or common **3** (**prevail against** or **over**) to gain control over **4** (**prevail on**) to persuade (someone): *She prevailed on me to stay*

prevailing *adjective* **1** controlling **2** most common: *the prevailing mood*

prevailing wind *noun, meteorology* the most frequent wind direction in any particular region

prevalent (*pronounced* **prev**-a-lent) *adjective* common, widespread ♦ **prevalence** *noun*

prevaricate *verb* to avoid telling the truth
  ♦ **prevarication** *noun* ♦ **prevaricator** *noun*

prevent *verb* to hinder, stop happening
  ♦ **preventible** *adjective* ♦ **prevention** *noun* the act of preventing

preventive or **preventative** *adjective* of medicine: helping to prevent illness

preview *noun* a view of a performance, exhibition, etc before its official opening

previous *adjective* earlier; former; prior
  ♦ **previously** *adverb*

prey *noun* **1** an animal killed by others for food **2** a victim ► *verb*: **prey on someone** or **something 1** to seize and eat them: *preying on smaller birds* **2** to stalk and harass them ⊙ Comes from Latin *praeda* meaning 'booty'

! Do not confuse with: **pray**

price *noun* **1** the money for which something is bought or sold, the cost **2** something that must be given up in order to gain something: *the price of fame*

priceless *adjective* **1** very valuable **2** *informal* very funny

pricey or **pricy** *adjective* (**pricier, priciest**) *informal* expensive

prick *verb* **1** to pierce slightly **2** to give a sharp

pain to **3** to stick up (the ears) ► *noun* a pricking feeling on the skin

prickle *noun* a sharp point on a plant or animal
  ► *verb* **1** to be prickly **2** to feel prickly

prickly *adjective* (**pricklier, prickliest**) **1** full of prickles **2** stinging, pricking

pride *noun* **1** too great an opinion of yourself **2** pleasure in having done something well **3** dignity **4** a group of lions ► *verb*: **pride yourself on** to feel or show pride in

priest *noun* **1** a member of the clergy in the Roman Catholic, Orthodox and Anglican churches **2** an official in a non-Christian religion

priestess *noun* (*plural* **priestesses**) a female non-Christian priest

priesthood *noun* those who are priests

prig *noun* a smug, self-righteous person
  ♦ **priggish** *adjective*

prim *adjective* (**primmer, primmest**) unnecessarily formal and correct

prima ballerina *noun* the leading female dancer of a ballet company

prima donna *noun* **1** a leading female opera singer **2** a woman who is over-sensitive and temperamental

primaeval another spelling of **primeval**

primarily *adverb* **1** chiefly; mainly **2** in the first place; initially

primary *adjective* **1** first **2** most important, chief

primary cell or **primary battery** *noun, physics* a cell or battery that produces an electric current by chemical reactions that are not readily reversible (*also called*: **voltaic cell**)

primary colour *noun* one of the colours from which all others can be made, that is red, blue, and yellow

primary industry *noun, geography* an industry, eg coalmining, concerned with extracting raw materials (*compare with*: **secondary industry, tertiary industry**)

primary school *noun* a school for the early stages of education

primate *noun* **1** a member of the highest order of mammals, including humans, monkeys and apes, which has hands and grasping thumbs **2** an archbishop

prime *adjective* **1** first in time or importance **2** best quality, excellent **3** of a number: having only two factors, itself and 1, eg 3 (which has the factors 1 and 3 but no others) ► *noun* the time of greatest health and strength: *the prime of life* ► *verb* **1** to prepare the surface of for painting: *prime a canvas* **2** to prepare by supplying detailed information: *She was well primed before the meeting*

prime factor decomposition *noun, maths* expressing a number as the product of factors which are prime numbers

prime meridian *noun, geography* a meridian chosen to represent 0, usually that passing through Greenwich, UK, from which other lines of longitude are calculated (*also called:* **first meridian**)

prime minister *noun* the head of a government

prime mover *noun* the force that is most effective in setting something in motion

primer¹ *noun* a simple introductory book on a subject

primer² *noun* a substance for preparing a surface for painting

primeval or **primaeval** *adjective* **1** relating to the beginning of the world **2** primitive, instinctive

primitive *adjective* **1** belonging to very early times or the earliest stages of development **2** old-fashioned **3** not skilfully made, rough

primogeniture (*pronounced* prai-moh-**jen**-i-chur) *noun* **1** the fact of being born first **2** the rights of a first-born child

primordial (*pronounced* prai-**mawr**-di-al) *adjective* **1** existing from the beginning; formed earliest *primordial matter* **2** *biology* relating to an early stage in growth

primrose *noun* a pale-yellow spring flower common in woods and hedges

prince *noun* **1** the son of a king or queen **2** a ruler of certain states

princely *adjective* splendid, impressive: *a princely reward*

princess *noun* (*plural* **princesses**) **1** the daughter of a king or queen **2** the wife or daughter of a prince

principal *adjective* most important, chief ➤ *noun* **1** the head of a school or university **2** a leading part in a play etc **3** money in a bank on which interest is paid ⊙ Comes from Latin *principalis* meaning 'first'

⚠ Do not confuse: **principal** and **principle**. It may help to remember that the adjective **principAl** means 'first or most important', and it contains an A, the first letter of the alphabet.

principality *noun* (*plural* **principalities**) a state ruled by a prince

principally *adverb* chiefly, mostly

principle *noun* **1** a general truth or law **2** the theory on which the working of a machine is based **3** (**principles**) someone's personal rules of behaviour, sense of right and wrong, etc ⊙ Comes from Latin *principium* meaning 'beginning'

principled *adjective* holding high moral principles

print *verb* **1** to mark letters on paper with type **2** to write in capital letters **3** to publish in printed

form **4** to stamp patterns on (cloth etc) **5** to make a finished photograph ➤ *noun* **1** a mark made by pressure: *a footprint* **2** printed lettering **3** a photograph made from a negative **4** a printed reproduction of a painting etc **5** cloth printed with a design • **in print** of a book: published and available to buy ✦ **printing** *noun*

printed circuit *noun* an electronic circuit consisting of components connected by thin strips of conducting material printed onto a thin board of insulating material

printer *noun* **1** someone who prints books, newspapers, etc **2** *computing* a machine that prints, attached to a computer system

printout *noun, computing* the printed information produced by a computer

prion (*pronounced* **prai**-on) *noun, biology, chemistry* a protein that occurs in the brain

prior¹ *adjective* **1** earlier **2** previous (to)

prior² *noun* the head of a priory

prioritize or **prioritise** *verb* **1** to decide what must be done first **2** to make (something) a priority

priority *noun* (*plural* **priorities**) **1** first position **2** the right to be first: *Ambulances must have priority in traffic* **3** something that must be done first: *Our priority is to get him into hospital*

priory *noun* (*plural* **priories**) a building where a community of monks or nuns live

prise *verb* to force open or off with a lever: *prised off the lid*

⚠ Do not confuse with: **prize**

prism *noun* **1** a triangular glass tube that breaks light into different colours **2** *maths* a solid with two congruent, parallel polygons at either end (the **bases**) and with parallelograms as its other faces

prison *noun* **1** a building for holding criminals **2** a place where someone is confined against their will

prisoner *noun* someone held under arrest or locked up

prisoner of war *noun* (*plural* **prisoners of war**) someone captured by the enemy forces during war

pristine *adjective* in the original or unspoilt state

privacy (*pronounced* **pri**-va-si or **prai**-va-si) *noun* freedom from intrusion or observation; secrecy

private *adjective* **1** relating to an individual, not to the general public; personal **2** not open to the public **3** secret, not generally known ➤ *noun* the lowest rank of ordinary soldier (not an officer)

private detective *noun* a person hired to investigate crime, watch suspects, gather information, etc

private enterprise noun the management and financing of industry etc by private companies, not by the state

private eye noun, informal a private detective

privately adverb in a private way

private parts plural noun, euphemistic the external sexual organs

private sector noun that part of a country's economy consisting of privately owned businesses etc (compare with: **public sector**)

privation noun 1 want, poverty, hardship 2 taking away, loss

privatize or **privatise** verb to transfer from state to private ownership, denationalize ♦ **privatization** noun

privet (pronounced **pri**-vit) noun a type of shrub used for hedges

privilege noun a right available to one person or to only a few people

privileged adjective having privileges

privy adjective: **privy to** knowing about (something secret) ♦ **privy councillor** noun

privy council noun an appointed group of advisers to a king or queen ♦ **privy councillor** noun

prize noun 1 a reward 2 something won in a competition 3 something captured 4 something highly valued ➤ adjective very fine, worthy of a prize ➤ verb to value highly

! Do not confuse with: **prise**

pro short for **professional**

pro- prefix 1 before, forward, front: proactive, progenitor 2 in favour of: pro-devolution ⊙ Comes from Latin and Greek pro meaning 'before' or 'for'

proactive adjective actively initiating change, rather than merely reacting to events as they occur

probability noun (plural **probabilities**) 1 likelihood 2 something likely to happen 3 statistics an expression, usually as a fraction or a numeral, of the likelihood of a particular event occurring

probability theory noun, maths the branch of mathematics concerned with the likelihood of particular events occurring

probable adjective 1 likely to happen 2 likely to be true

probably adverb very likely

probation noun 1 a trial period in a new job etc 2 a system of releasing prisoners on condition that they commit no more offences and report regularly to the authorities

probationer noun someone who is training to be a member of a profession

probe noun 1 a long, thin instrument used to examine a wound 2 a thorough investigation 3 a spacecraft for exploring space ➤ verb 1 to examine very carefully 2 to investigate thoroughly to find out information

probity noun honesty, goodness of character

problem noun a question to be solved; a matter which is difficult to deal with

problematic or **problematical** adjective doubtful, uncertain

proboscis (pronounced pro-**boh**-sis or pro-**bos**-is or pro-**bos**-kis) noun (plural **proboscises**) 1 the long snout of the elephant or the tapir 2 the long, tubular mouth parts of some insects

procaryote another spelling of **prokaryote**

procedure noun 1 a method of doing business 2 a course of action

proceed verb 1 to go on with, continue 2 to begin (to do something) 3 to take legal action (against) ⊙ Comes from Latin procedere meaning 'to go forward'

! Do not confuse with: **precede**

proceeding noun 1 a step forward 2 (**proceedings**) a record of the meetings of a society, lectures at a conference, etc 3 a law action

proceeds (pronounced **proh**-seedz) plural noun profit made from a sale etc

process noun (plural **processes**) 1 a series of operations in manufacturing goods 2 a series of events producing change or development 3 a lawcourt case 4 anatomy a projection or outgrowth, especially on a bone • **in the process of** in the course of

procession noun a line of people or vehicles moving forward in order

processor noun 1 a machine or person that processes something 2 computing a central processing unit or microprocessor

pro-choice adjective supporting the right of a woman to have an abortion (compare with: **pro-life**)

proclaim verb to announce publicly, declare openly

proclamation noun an official announcement made to the public

procrastinate verb to put things off, delay doing something till a later time ♦ **procrastination** noun

procreate verb to produce (offspring), to reproduce ♦ **procreation** noun ♦ **procreative** adjective ♦ **procreator** noun

procure verb to obtain; to bring about

prod verb (**prodding, prodded**) to poke; urge on

prodigal adjective spending money recklessly, wasteful ♦ **prodigality** noun

prodigious *adjective* **1** strange, astonishing **2** enormous

prodigy *noun* (*plural* **prodigies**) **1** a wonder **2** someone astonishingly clever: *a child prodigy*

produce *verb* (*pronounced* proh-**dyoos**) **1** to bring into being **2** to bring about, cause **3** to prepare (a programme) for broadcasting on radio or television **4** to prepare (a play etc) for the stage **5** to make, manufacture ➤ *noun* (*pronounced* **prod**-yoos) food grown or produced on a farm or in a garden

producer *noun* **1** a person or thing that produces **2** someone who produces a play, television programme, etc **3** someone who exercises general control over, but does not actually make, a cinema film

product *noun* **1** something produced **2** a result **3** *maths* the number that results from the multiplication of two or more numbers

production *noun* **1** the act of producing; the process of producing or being produced: *The new model goes into production next year* **2** the quantity produced or rate of producing it: *an increase in oil production* **3** a particular presentation of a play, opera, ballet, etc: *a new production of 'The Marriage of Figaro'*

productive *adjective* fruitful, producing results

productivity *noun* the rate of work done

Prof *abbreviation* Professor

profane *adjective* **1** not sacred **2** treating holy things without respect

profanity (*pronounced* pro-**fan**-it-i) *noun* (*plural* **profanities**) **1** swearing **2** lack of respect for sacred things

profess *verb* **1** to declare (a belief etc) openly **2** to pretend, claim: *He professes to be an expert on football*

professed *adjective* **1** declared **2** pretended

profession *noun* **1** an occupation requiring special training, eg that of a doctor, lawyer, teacher, etc **2** an open declaration

professional *adjective* **1** of a profession **2** earning a living from a game or an art (*contrasted with*: **amateur**) **3** skilful, competent ➤ *noun* **1** someone who works in a profession **2** someone who earns money from a game or art

professionalism *noun* **1** a professional status **2** professional expertise or competence

professionally *adverb* in a professional way; in terms of your profession: *professionally qualified*

professor *noun* **1** a teacher of the highest rank in a university **2** *US* a university teacher ◆ **professorship** *noun*

proffer *verb* to offer

proficiency *noun* skill

proficient *adjective* skilled, expert

profile *noun* **1** an outline **2** a side view of a face, head, etc **3** a short description of someone's life, achievements, etc

profit *noun* **1** gain, benefit **2** money got by selling an article for a higher price than was paid for it ➤ *verb* (**profiting, profited**) to gain (from), benefit

profitable *adjective* bringing profit or gain

profiteer *noun* someone who makes large profits unfairly ➤ *verb* to make large profits unfairly

profligate (*pronounced* **prof**-li-git) *adjective* **1** living an immoral life **2** very extravagant ➤ *noun* a profligate person ◆ **profligacy** *noun*

profound *adjective* **1** very deep **2** deeply felt **3** showing great knowledge or understanding: *a profound comment*

profundity *noun* **1** being profound **2** depth

profuse *adjective* abundant, lavish, extravagant ◆ **profusely** *adverb* ◆ **profusion** *noun*

progenitor (*pronounced* pro-**jen**-i-tor) *noun* an ancestor

progeny (*pronounced* **proj**-e-ni) *plural noun* children

progesterone (*pronounced* pro-**jes**-te-rohn) *noun, biology* a female sex hormone that prepares the uterus for and maintains pregnancy

prognosis *noun* (*plural* **prognoses** – *pronounced* prog-**noh**-seez) a prediction of the course of a disease

prognosticate *verb* to foretell ◆ **prognostication** *noun*

program *computing, noun* a set of instructions telling a computer to carry out certain actions ➤ *verb* (**programming, programmed**) **1** to give instructions to **2** to prepare instructions to be carried out by a computer ◆ **programmable** *adjective* ◆ **programmer** *noun*

programme or *US* **program** *noun* **1** a booklet with details of an entertainment, ceremony, etc **2** a scheme, a plan **3** a TV or radio broadcast

programming language *noun, computing* any system of codes, symbols, rules, etc designed for writing computer programs

progress *noun* (*pronounced* **proh**-gres) **1** advance, forward movement **2** improvement ➤ *verb* (*pronounced* pro-**gres**) **1** to go forward **2** to improve

progression *noun* **1** the process of moving forwards or advancing in stages **2** *music* a succession of chords, the advance from one to the next being determined on a fixed pattern **3** *maths* a sequence of numbers, each of which bears a specific relationship to the preceding one, eg an arithmetic progression or a geometric progression

progressive *adjective* **1** going forward **2** favouring reforms ◆ **progressively** *adverb*

prohibit *verb* **1** to forbid **2** to prevent

prohibition noun 1 the act of forbidding, especially the forbidding by law of making and selling alcoholic drinks 2 history (**Prohibition**) the period between 1920 and 1933 when the manufacture and sale of alcoholic drinks was prohibited in the USA

prohibitive adjective 1 prohibiting 2 of price: too expensive, discouraging

project noun (pronounced proj-ekt) 1 a plan, a scheme 2 a task 3 a piece of study or research ➤ verb (pronounced proh-**jekt**) 1 to throw out or up 2 to jut out 3 to cast (an image, a light, etc) on to a surface 4 to plan, propose

projectile noun a missile

projection noun 1 an act of projecting 2 something projected 3 something which juts out 4 a mapping of points of a three-dimensional figure onto a plane

projectionist noun someone who operates a film projector

projector noun a machine for projecting pictures on a screen

prokaryote or **procaryote** (pronounced proh-**ka**-ri-oht) noun, biology an organism, including all bacteria, that has no distinct cell nucleus and has DNA that is not organized into chromosomes ♦ **prokaryotic** or **procaryotic** adjective

prolapse medicine, noun the slipping out of place or falling down of a body part ➤ verb of an organ of the body: to slip out of place

proletarian noun a member of the proletariat

proletariat (pronounced proh-le-**teir**-i-at) noun the ordinary working people

pro-life adjective opposing abortion, euthanasia and experimentation on human embryos (compare with: **pro-choice**)

proliferate verb 1 to grow or increase in number rapidly 2 biology to reproduce (cells etc) rapidly ♦ **proliferation** noun

prolific adjective producing a lot, fruitful

PROLOG or **Prolog** noun, computing a high-level programming language, often used in artificial intelligence

⊙ A contraction of programming in logic

prologue noun a preface or introduction to a play etc

prolong verb to make longer

prom noun, informal short for 1 promenade 2 promenade concert

promenade (pronounced prom-e-**nahd**) noun 1 a level roadway or walk, especially by the seaside 2 a walk, a stroll ➤ verb to walk for pleasure

promenade concert noun a concert, usually of classical music, at which a large part of the audience stands instead of being seated

promethium (pronounced proh-**mee**-thi-um) noun, chemistry (symbol **Pm**) a radioactive metallic element

prominent adjective 1 standing out, easily seen 2 famous, distinguished ♦ **prominence** noun

promiscuity noun indulgence in many casual sexual relationships

promiscuous adjective 1 having many casual sexual relationships 2 mixed in kind 3 not making distinctions between people or things

promise verb 1 to give your word (to do or not do something) 2 to show signs for the future: The weather promises to improve ➤ noun 1 a statement of something promised 2 a sign of something to come 3 a sign of future success: Her painting shows great promise

promising adjective showing signs of being successful

promo noun (plural **promos**), informal something which is used to publicize a product, especially a video for a pop single

promontory noun (plural **promontories**) a headland jutting out into the sea

promote verb 1 to raise to a higher rank 2 to help onwards, encourage 3 to advertise, encourage the sales of ♦ **promoter** noun

promotion noun 1 advancement in rank or honour 2 encouragement 3 advertising, or an effort to publicize and increase sales of a particular brand

promotional adjective relating to or involving promotion

prompt adjective 1 quick, immediate 2 punctual ➤ noun 1 something serving as a reminder 2 words supplied by a prompter to an actor 3 a prompter 4 computing a question, statement, etc which appears on a computer screen, indicating that it is ready for a command ➤ verb 1 to move to action 2 to supply words to (an actor who has forgotten their lines) ♦ **promptness** noun

prompter noun a person positioned offstage to prompt actors when they forget their lines

promptly adverb 1 without delay 2 punctually

promulgate (pronounced **prom**-ul-geit) verb to make widely known ♦ **promulgation** noun

pro-natalist policy noun a government policy, eg providing child care and other benefits, designed to encourage people to have children

prone adjective lying face downward ● **prone to** inclined to: prone to laziness

prong noun the spike of a fork

pronged adjective having prongs

pronoun noun, grammar a word used instead of a noun, eg I, you, who

pronounce verb 1 to speak (words, sounds) 2 to announce (an opinion), declare

pronounced *adjective* noticeable, marked

pronouncement *noun* a statement, an announcement

pronto *adverb, informal* quickly

pronunciation *noun* the way a word is said

proof *noun* **1** evidence that makes something clear beyond doubt **2** the standard strength of whisky etc **3** *printing* a copy of a printed sheet for correction before publication **4** *maths* a step-by-step process that proves the truth of a mathematical proposition ➤ *adjective* able to keep out or withstand: *proof against attack*

-proof *suffix* protected against: *waterproof*

proofread *verb* to read and correct printed page proofs of a text ♦ **proofreader** *noun*

prop¹ *noun* a support ➤ *verb* (**propping, propped**) to hold up, support

prop² *informal* short for **propeller**

prop³ *informal* short for **stage property** (= an item needed on stage for a play)

propaganda *noun* **1** the spreading of ideas to influence public opinion **2** material used for this, eg posters, leaflets

propagandist *noun* someone who spreads propaganda

propagate *verb* **1** to spread (ideas etc) **2** to produce (new plants) ♦ **propagation** *noun*

propagator *noun* **1** a person or thing that propagates **2** a heated box with a cover in which plants may be grown from cuttings or seeds

propane *noun* a colourless, odourless gas obtained from petroleum and used as fuel

propanoic acid (*pronounced* proh-pa-**noh**-ik) *noun, chemistry* a fatty acid used to control the growth of certain moulds

propanone another term for **acetone**

propel *verb* (**propelling, propelled**) to drive forward

propellant *noun* **1** an explosive for firing a rocket **2** the gas in an aerosol used to release the contents as a fine spray

propeller *noun* a shaft with revolving blades which drives forward a ship, aircraft, etc

propensity *noun* (*plural* **propensities**) a natural inclination: *a propensity for bumping into things*

proper *adjective* **1** right, correct: *the proper way to do it* **2** full, thorough: *a proper search* **3** prim, well-behaved **4** strictly so called; without things usually associated with it: *entering the city proper*

proper fraction *noun, maths* a fraction in which the numerator is less than the denominator, eg $\frac{1}{2}$ (compare with: **improper fraction**)

properly *adverb* **1** in the right way **2** thoroughly

proper noun or **proper name** *noun, grammar* a name for a particular person, place,

or thing, eg *Shakespeare, the Parthenon* (*contrasted with*: **common noun**)

property *noun* (*plural* **properties**) **1** something that is owned: *That book is my property* **2** possessions collectively **3** land or buildings **4** a quality: *the property of dissolving easily* **5** (**properties**) the furniture etc required by actors in a play

prophase *noun, biology* in mitosis and meiosis: the first stage of cell division, during which the chromosomes condense and separate

prophecy (*pronounced* **prof**-e-si) *noun* (*plural* **prophecies**) **1** foretelling the future **2** something prophesied

> ❗ Do not confuse: **prophecy** and **prophesy**. The spelling with the 'c' is the noun, the spelling with the 's' the verb. It may help to remember that this is a common pattern, seen also in such pairs as *practice/practise, licence/license,* and *advice/advise.*

prophesy (*pronounced* **prof**-e-sai) *verb* (**prophesies, prophesying, prophesied**) to foretell the future, predict

prophet *noun* **1** someone who claims to foretell events **2** someone who tells what they believe to be the will of God

prophetic *adjective* **1** foretelling the future **2** relating to prophets

propinquity *noun, formal* nearness

propitiate (*pronounced* proh-**pish**-i-eit) *verb* to calm the anger of

propitious (*pronounced* proh-**pish**-us) *adjective* favourable: *propitious circumstances*

proponent *noun* someone in favour of a thing

proportion *noun* **1** a part of a total amount: *A large proportion of income is taxed* **2** relation in size, number, etc compared with something else: *The proportion of girls to boys is small* **3** *maths* correspondence between the ratios of two pairs of quantities, eg 2 is to 8 as 3 is to 12 • **in** or **out of proportion** appropriate or inappropriate in size or degree when compared with other things

proportional or **proportionate** *adjective* **1** matching in number, size, etc **2** in proportion ➤ *noun, maths* a number or quantity shown in a proportion ♦ **proportionally** *adverb*

proportional representation *noun* (*abbrev* **PR**) an system of election in which the number of representatives each political party has in parliament, councils, etc is in proportion to the number of votes it receives

proposal *noun* **1** an act of proposing **2** anything proposed **3** an offer of marriage

propose *verb* **1** to put forward for consideration, suggest **2** to intend **3** to make an offer of marriage (to)

proposition *noun* **1** a proposal, a suggestion **2** a statement **3** a situation that must be dealt with: *a tough proposition*

Do not confuse with: **preposition**

propound *verb* to state, put forward for consideration

proprietor or **proprietress** *noun* (*plural* **proprietors** or **proprietresses**) an owner, especially of a hotel

propriety *noun* (*plural* **proprieties**) **1** fitness, suitability **2** correct behaviour, decency

propulsion *noun* an act of driving forward

pro rata (*pronounced* proh **rah**-ta) *adverb* in proportion ⏱ from Latin meaning 'for the rate'

prorogation *noun, formal* proroguing

prorogue (*pronounced* proh-**rohg**) *verb, formal* to discontinue meetings of (parliament etc) for a period

prosaic (*pronounced* proh-**zei**-ik) *adjective* dull, not interesting

pros and cons *plural noun* the arguments for and against anything

proscenium (*pronounced* proh-**see**-ni-um) *noun* (*plural* **prosceniums** or **proscenia**) the front part of a stage

proscribe *verb* to ban, prohibit ⏱ Comes from Latin *proscribere* meaning 'to publish in writing'.

Do not confuse with: **prescribe**.
It may help to remember that **PROscribe** and **PROhibit** share the same three first letters.

proscription *noun* proscribing or being proscribed

Do not confuse with: **prescription**.
Proscription is related to the verb **proscribe**.

proscriptive *adjective* tending to proscribe

prose *noun* **1** writing which is not in verse **2** ordinary written or spoken language

prosecute *verb* **1** to bring a case against someone in a court **2** *formal* to carry on (studies, an investigation, etc) ⏱ Comes from Latin *prosequi* meaning 'to accompany someone on their way forth'

Do not confuse with: **persecute**

prosecution *noun* **1** an act of prosecuting **2** *law* those bringing the case in a trial (*contrasted with*: **defence**)

proselyte (*pronounced* **pros**-e-lait) *noun* a convert

prosody (*pronounced* **pros**-o-di) *noun* the study of the rhythms and construction of poetry

prospect *noun* (*pronounced* **pros**-pekt) **1** a view, a scene **2** a future outlook or expectation: *the prospect of a free weekend/a job with good*

prospects ➤ *verb* (*pronounced* pros-**pekt**) to search for gold or other minerals

prospective *adjective* soon to be, likely to be: *the prospective election*

prospector *noun* someone who prospects for minerals

prospectus *noun* (*plural* **prospectuses**) a booklet giving information about a school, organization, etc

prosper *verb* to get on well, succeed

prosperity *noun* success, good fortune

prosperous *adjective* successful, wealthy

prostate *noun, anatomy* a gland around the base of a man's bladder which releases a fluid used in semen

prosthesis (*pronounced* pros-**thee**-sis) *noun* (*plural* **prostheses** – *pronounced* pros-**thee**-seez) *medicine* **1** an artificial substitute for a part of the body that is missing or not working properly, eg an artificial limb or a pacemaker **2** the fitting of such a part to the body
♦ **prosthetic** *adjective*

prostitute *noun* someone who offers sexual intercourse for payment ♦ **prostitution** *noun*

prostrate *adjective* (*pronounced* **pros**-treit) **1** lying flat face downwards **2** worn out, exhausted ➤ *verb* (*pronounced* pros-**treit**) **1** to lie on the ground as a sign of respect: *prostrated themselves before the emperor* **2** to exhaust, tire out completely

prostrated *adjective* worn out by grief, tiredness, etc

prostration *noun* the act of prostrating

protactinium *noun, chemistry* (symbol **Pa**) a white, highly toxic, radioactive metallic element

protagonist *noun* a chief character in a play etc

protease (*pronounced* **proh**-ti-eiz) *noun, biology, chemistry* an enzyme that catalyses the breakdown of proteins

protect *verb* to shield from danger, keep safe ♦ **protection** *noun*

protectionism *noun* the policy of protecting home industry from foreign competition, especially by charging high import duties ♦ **protectionist** *noun & adjective*

protective *adjective* giving protection; intended to protect

protector *noun* a guardian, a defender

protectorate *noun* a country which is partly governed and defended by another country

protégé or *feminine* **protégée** (*both pronounced* **proh**-te-szei) *noun* a pupil or employee who is taught or helped in their career by someone important or powerful

protein *noun* **1** any of thousands of different organic compounds, found in all living organisms, that have molecules consisting of long chains of amino acids **2** protein as found in meat, fish, eggs, etc, considered as an essential part of your diet

Proterozoic adjective of the geological era from which the oldest forms of life date

protest verb (pronounced proh-**test**) **1** to object strongly **2** to declare solemnly: protesting his innocence ➤ noun (pronounced **proh**-test) a strong objection

Protestant noun a member of one of the Christian churches that broke away from the Roman Catholic Church at the time of the Reformation

protestation noun **1** a solemn declaration **2** a protest

protist noun, biology any member of the kingdom of unicellular organisms **Protista**, including the protozoans, slime moulds, etc ⊙ Comes from Greek protistos meaning 'very first'

protocol noun **1** correct formal or diplomatic procedures **2** a first draft of a diplomatic document, eg with the terms of a treaty **3** computing the set of rules controlling the transmission of data between two computers

proton noun, physics a particle with a positive electrical charge, forming part of the nucleus of an atom (see also **electron, neutron**)

protoplasm noun, biology the mass of protein material of which cells are composed, consisting of the cytoplasm and usually a nucleus

prototype noun the original model from which something is copied

protozoan (pronounced proh-to-**zoh**-an) noun a member of the **Protozoa**, the simplest animals, consisting of single-celled organisms ✦ **protozoic** adjective

protract verb to lengthen in time

protractor noun, maths an instrument for drawing and measuring angles on paper

protrude verb to stick out, thrust forward ✦ **protrusion** noun

protuberance noun a swelling, a bulge ✦ **protuberant** adjective

proud adjective **1** thinking too highly of yourself, conceited **2** feeling pleased at an achievement etc **3** dignified, self-respecting: too proud to accept the money ➤ adverb: **do someone proud** to treat them grandly

prove verb **1** to show to be true or correct **2** to try out, test **3** to turn out (to be): His prediction proved correct **4** maths to formulate a step-by-step process that establishes the truth of a mathematical proposition

provenance (pronounced **prov**-e-nans) noun source, origin

provender noun food, especially for horses and cattle

proverb noun a well-known wise saying, eg 'nothing ventured, nothing gained'

proverbial adjective well-known, widely spoken of

provide verb to supply

provided or **providing** conjunction on condition that

providence noun **1** foresight; thrift **2** (**Providence**) God

provident adjective thinking of the future; thrifty

providential adjective fortunate, coming as if by divine help

province noun **1** a division of a country **2** the extent of someone's duties or knowledge **3** (**the provinces**) all parts of a country outside the capital

provincial adjective **1** of a province or provinces **2** derogatory narrow-minded, parochial

provision noun **1** an agreed arrangement **2** a rule or condition **3** (**provisions**) a supply of food

provisional adjective used for the time being; temporary

proviso (pronounced pro-**vai**-zoh) noun (plural **provisos**) a condition laid down beforehand

provocative (pronounced pro-**vok**-a-tiv) adjective **1** tending to rouse anger **2** likely to arouse sexual interest

provoke verb **1** to cause, result in **2** to rouse to anger or action: Don't let him provoke you ✦ **provocation** noun (meaning 2)

provoking adjective annoying

provost noun the mayor of a burgh in Scotland

prow noun the front part of a ship

prowess noun skill, ability

prowl verb to go about stealthily

proximal adjective, biology denoting the part of an organ or limb that is nearest to the point of attachment to the body (compare with: **distal**) ⊙ Comes from Latin proximus meaning 'nearest' ✦ **proximally** adverb

proximity noun nearness

proxy noun (plural **proxies**) someone who acts or votes on behalf of another

prude noun an over-modest, priggish person ✦ **prudery** noun ✦ **prudish** adjective

prudent adjective wise and cautious ✦ **prudence** noun ✦ **prudently** adverb

prune[1] verb **1** to trim (a tree) by cutting off unneeded twigs **2** to shorten, reduce

prune[2] noun a dried plum

prurient adjective excessively concerned with sexual matters ✦ **prurience** noun

pry verb (**pries, prying, pried**) to look closely into things that are not your business ✦ **prying** adjective

PS abbreviation postscript

psalm (pronounced sahm) noun a sacred song

psalmist (pronounced **sahm**-ist) noun a writer of psalms

psalter (*pronounced* **sawl**-ter) *noun* a book of psalms

p's and q's *plural noun* correct social manners

psephologist (*pronounced* se-**fol**-o-jist) *noun* someone who studies elections and voting trends

> ⊙ Based on a Greek word for 'pebble', because pebbles were used in ancient Greece to cast votes

pseud (*pronounced* syood or sood) *informal, adjective* pseudo ➤ *noun* a fraud

pseud- (*pronounced* syood or sood) or **pseudo-** *prefix* false *pseudonym* ⊙ Comes from Greek *pseudes* meaning 'false'

pseudo (*pronounced* **syood**-oh or **sood**-oh) *adjective, informal* false, fake, pretended: *His Spanish accent is pseudo*

pseudonym (*pronounced* **syoo**-do-nim or **soo**-do-nim) *noun* a false name used by eg an author

psittacosis (*pronounced* sit-a-**koh**-sis) *noun, medicine* a contagious bird disease that can be transmitted to humans as pneumonia

psoriasis (*pronounced* soh-**rai**-a-sis) *noun, medicine* a skin disease characterized by red patches covered with white scales

psych or **psyche** (*both pronounced* saik) *verb*: **psych out** *informal* to intimidate or undermine the confidence of (an opponent etc) • **psych up** to prepare mentally for a challenge etc

psych- see **psycho-**

psyche (*pronounced* **sai**-kei) *noun* the mind, soul or spirit, especially deep feelings and attitudes ⊙ Comes from Greek meaning 'breath' or 'life'

psychedelic (*pronounced* sai-ke-**del**-ik) *adjective* bright and multi-coloured

psychiatrist (*pronounced* sai-**kai**-a-trist) *noun* someone who treats mental illness

psychiatry (*pronounced* sai-**kai**-a-tri) *noun* the treatment of mental illness ♦ **psychiatric** (*pronounced* sai-ki-**at**-rik) *adjective*

psychic (*pronounced* **sai**-kik) or **psychical** *adjective* **1** relating to the mind **2** able to read other people's minds, or tell the future

psycho- (*pronounced* **sai**-koh) or **psych-** *prefix* relating to the mind *psychology/ psychoanalysis* ⊙ Comes from Greek *psyche* meaning 'soul'

psychoanalyse or *US* **psychoanalyze** *verb* to treat by psychoanalysis

psychoanalysis *noun* a method of treating mental illness by discussing with the patient its possible causes in their past ♦ **psychoanalyst** *noun*

psychological *adjective* of psychology or the mind

psychology *noun* the science which studies the human mind ♦ **psychologist** *noun*

psychopath *noun* **1** *technical* someone with a personality disorder, who is liable to behave antisocially or violently in getting their own way, without any feelings of remorse **2** *informal* someone who is dangerously unstable mentally or emotionally

psychosis *noun* (*plural* **psychoses** – *pronounced* sai-**koh**-seez) a mental illness

psychosomatic *adjective* of an illness: having a psychological cause

psychotherapy *noun* treatment of mental illness by psychoanalysis etc ♦ **psychotherapist** *noun*

psychotic *adjective* affected by mental illness, mad

PT *abbreviation, old* physical training

Pt *symbol, chemistry* platinum

PTA *abbreviation* parent teacher association

ptarmigan (*pronounced* **tahr**-mi-gan) *noun* a mountain-dwelling bird of the grouse family, which turns white in winter

pterodactyl (*pronounced* ter-oh-**dak**-til) *noun* an extinct flying reptile

PTO *abbreviation* please turn over

P2P *abbreviation, computing* peer-to-peer

ptyalin (*pronounced* **tai**-a-lin) *noun, biology, chemistry* an enzyme in the saliva that breaks down starch

Pu *symbol, chemistry* plutonium

pub short for **public house**

puberty (*pronounced* **pyoo**-bert-i) *noun* the time when the body becomes sexually mature and the reproductive organs become functional

pubes (*pronounced* **pyoo**-beez) *noun* (*plural* **pubes**) **1** *anatomy* the region of the lower abdomen, above the genitals **2** (*also treated informally as a plural noun pronounced* pyoobz) the hair that grows on this part from puberty onward

pubescence *noun* **1** the onset of puberty **2** *biology* a soft downy covering on plants and animals ♦ **pubescent** *adjective*

pubic (*pronounced* **pyoo**-bik) *adjective* relating to the pubis or pubes: *pubic hair*

pubis (*pronounced* **pyoo**-bis) *noun* (*plural* **pubises**), *anatomy* in most vertebrates: one of the two bones forming the lower front part of each side of the pelvis

public *adjective* **1** relating to or shared by the people of a community or nation in general: *public opinion/public library* **2** generally or widely known: *a public figure* ➤ *noun* (**the public**) people in general • **in public** in front of or among other people

public address system *noun* a system of microphones, amplifiers and loudspeakers used to enable an audience to hear voices, music, etc

publican *noun* the keeper of an inn or public house

publication *noun* **1** the act of making news etc public **2** the act of publishing a book, newspaper, etc **3** a published book, magazine, etc

public convenience *noun* a public toilet

public domain *noun*: **in the public domain** of a published work, computer program, etc: not subject to copyright and available to everyone

public house *noun* a building where alcoholic drinks are sold and consumed; a pub

publicity *noun* advertising; bringing to public notice or attention

publicize or **publicise** *verb* to make public, advertise

public relations *plural noun* the relations between a business etc and the public ➤ *singular noun* a department of a business etc dealing with this

public sector *noun* the part of a country's economy which consists of nationalized industries and of institutions and services run by the state or local authorities (*compare with*: **private sector**)

publish *verb* **1** to make generally known **2** to prepare and put out (a book etc) for sale

publisher *noun* someone who publishes books ✦ **publishing** *noun*

puce *adjective* of a brownish-purple colour

puck *noun* a thick disc of rubber that is struck in ice hockey

pucker *verb* to wrinkle ➤ *noun* a wrinkle, a fold

pudding *noun* **1** the sweet course of a meal **2** a sweet dish made with eggs, flour, milk, etc **3** a type of sausage: *mealy pudding*

puddle *noun* a small, often muddy, pool

puerile (*pronounced* **pyoor**-ail) *adjective* childish, silly ✦ **puerility** *noun* ⊙ Comes from Latin *puerilis* meaning 'childish'

puerperal (*pronounced* pyuw-**er**-pe-ral) *adjective, formal* relating to childbirth ⊙ Comes from Latin *puerpera* meaning 'a woman in labour'

puerperal fever *noun, medicine* fever and blood poisoning caused by infection during or following childbirth

puff *verb* **1** to blow out in small gusts **2** to breathe heavily, eg after running **3** to blow up, inflate **4** to swell (up or out) ➤ *noun* **1** a short, sudden gust of wind, breath, etc **2** a powder puff **3** a piece of advertising

puffin *noun* a type of sea bird, with a short, thick, brightly coloured beak

puff pastry *noun* a light, flaky kind of pastry

puffy *adjective* (**puffier, puffiest**) **1** swollen, flabby **2** breathing heavily

pug *noun* a breed of small dog with a snub nose

pugilism (*pronounced* **pyoo**-ji-lizm) *noun* boxing ✦ **pugilist** *noun* ⊙ Comes from Latin *pugil* meaning 'a boxer'

pugnacious *adjective* quarrelsome, fond of fighting ✦ **pugnacity** *noun* ⊙ Comes from Latin *pugnax* meaning 'warlike'

puja (*pronounced* **poo**-ja) *noun, Hinduism* worship, or an act of worship

puke *noun & verb, slang* (to) vomit

pukka *adjective, informal* **1** superior; high-quality **2** upper-class; well-bred **3** genuine ⊙ from Hindi *pakka* cooked, firm or ripe

pulchritude (*pronounced* **pul**-kri-tyood) *noun, formal* beauty ✦ **pulchritudinous** *adjective* ⊙ Comes from Latin *pulchritudo* meaning 'beauty'

pull *verb* **1** to move or try to move (something) towards yourself by force **2** to drag, tug **3** to stretch, strain: *pull a muscle* **4** to tear: *pull to pieces* ➤ *noun* **1** the act of pulling **2** a pulling force, eg of a magnet **3** a handle for pulling **4** *informal* advantage, influence • **pull out 1** to withdraw from a competition etc **2** of a driver or vehicle: to move into the centre of the road • **pull through** to get safely to the end of a difficult or dangerous experience • **pull yourself together** to regain self-control or self-possession • **pull up** to stop, halt

pull-down menu *noun, computing* a menu on a computer screen viewed by clicking on a button on the toolbar and keeping the mouse pressed down (*compare with*: **drop-down menu**)

pullet *noun* a young hen

pulley *noun* (*plural* **pulleys**) a grooved wheel fitted with a cord and set in a block, used for lifting weights etc

Pullman *noun* (*plural* **Pullmans**) luxurious or superior seating on a train, in a cinema, etc

⊙ Named after George M *Pullman*, an American who made the first luxury sleeping car for railways in the 19th century

pull-out *noun* a complete section that can be taken out of a newspaper etc

pullover *noun* a knitted garment for the top half of the body, a jersey

pulmonary (*pronounced* **pul**-mo-na-ri or **puwl**-mo-na-ri) *adjective* relating to the lungs

pulmonary vein *noun, anatomy* a vein that carries blood from the lungs to the heart

pulp *noun* **1** the soft fleshy part of a fruit **2** a soft mass of wood etc which is made into paper **3** any soft mass **4** the tissue in the cavity of a tooth ➤ *verb* to reduce to pulp ✦ **pulpy** *adjective* (**pulpier, pulpiest**)

pulpit *noun* an enclosed platform in a church for the minister or priest

pulsate *verb* to beat, throb

pulse *noun* **1** the regular beating or throbbing of the heart and arteries as blood flows through them **2** the rate of this beat, often used as an indicator of health ➤ *verb* to throb, pulsate

pulses *plural noun* beans, peas, lentils and other edible seeds of this family

pulverize or **pulverise** *verb* to make or crush into powder

puma *noun* an American wild animal like a large cat

pumice (*pronounced* **pum**-is) or **pumice stone** *noun* a piece of light solidified lava used for smoothing skin and for rubbing away stains

pummel *verb* (**pummelling, pummelled**) to beat with the fists

pump¹ *noun* **1** a machine used for making water rise from beneath the ground to the surface **2** a machine for drawing out or forcing in air, gas, etc: *a bicycle pump* ➤ *verb* **1** to raise or force with a pump **2** *informal* to draw out information from by clever questioning

pump² *noun* a kind of thin- or soft-soled shoe for dancing, gymnastics, etc

pumpernickel *noun* a dark, heavy, coarse rye bread, eaten especially in Germany ⊕ from German meaning 'lout'

pumpkin *noun* a large, roundish, thick-skinned, orange fruit, with stringy, edible flesh

pun *noun* a play upon words which sound similar but have different meanings, eg 'two *pears* make a *pair*' ➤ *verb* (**punning, punned**) to make a pun

punch¹ *verb* to hit with the fist ➤ *noun* (*plural* **punches**) a blow with the fist

punch² *noun* (*plural* **punches**) a tool for punching holes ➤ *verb* to make a hole in with a tool: *punch a ticket*

punch³ *noun* a drink made of spirits or wine, water, sugar, etc

punchbag *noun* **1** a stuffed leather bag hanging from the ceiling on a rope, used for boxing practice **2** someone who is used and abused, either physically and emotionally

punch-drunk *adjective* dizzy from being hit

punchline *noun* the words that give the main point to a joke

punchy *adjective* (**punchier, punchiest**) having a powerful effect, striking

punctilious *adjective* paying attention to details, especially in behaviour; fastidious

punctual *adjective* **1** on time, not late **2** strict in keeping the time of appointments
  ♦ **punctuality** *noun*

punctuate *verb* **1** to divide up sentences by commas, full stops, etc **2** to interrupt at intervals: *The silence was punctuated by occasional coughing*

punctuation *noun* the use of punctuation marks

punctuation mark *noun* any of the symbols used in punctuating sentences, eg full stop, comma, colon, question mark, etc

puncture *noun* **1** an act of pricking or piercing **2** a small hole made with a sharp point **3** a hole in a tyre ➤ *verb* to make a puncture in

pundit *noun* an expert

pungent *adjective* **1** sharp-tasting or sharp-smelling **2** of a remark: strongly sarcastic
  ♦ **pungency** *noun*

punish *verb* **1** to make (someone) suffer for a fault or crime **2** to inflict suffering on **3** to treat roughly or harshly

punishable *adjective* likely to bring punishment

punishment *noun* pain or constraints inflicted for a fault or crime

punitive (*pronounced* **pyoo**-ni-tiv) *adjective* inflicting punishment or suffering

punk *noun* **1** a type of loud and aggressive rock music **2** a young person who dresses in a shocking way and listens to punk music **3** *US* a useless person

punnet *noun* a small basket or container for soft fruit

punt *noun* a flat-bottomed boat with square ends ➤ *verb* to move (a punt) by pushing a pole against the bottom of a river

punter *noun* **1** a professional gambler **2** *informal* a customer, a client **3** *informal* an ordinary person

puny *adjective* (**punier, puniest**) little and weak

pup *noun* **1** a young dog **2** the young of certain other animals, eg a seal

pupa (*pronounced* **pyoo**-pa) *noun* (*plural* **pupae** – pronounced **pyoo**-pee), *zoology* the stage in the growth of an insect in which it changes from a larva to its mature form, eg from a caterpillar into a butterfly

pupate (*pronounced* pyoo-**peit**) *verb*, *zoology* to become a pupa

pupil¹ *noun* someone who is being taught by a teacher

pupil² *noun*, *anatomy* the dark round opening in the middle of the eye which varies in size to allow more or less light in

puppet *noun* **1** a doll which is moved by strings or wires **2** a doll that fits over the hand and is moved by the fingers **3** someone who acts exactly as they are told to

puppeteer *noun* someone who operates puppets

puppy *noun* (*plural* **puppies**) a young dog

puppy fat *noun* temporary fat in childhood or adolescence

puppy love *noun* immature love when very young

purchase *verb* to buy ➤ *noun* **1** the act of buying **2** something which is bought **3** the power to lift by using a lever etc **4** firm grip or hold

purchaser *noun* someone who buys

purdah *noun* the seclusion of Hindu or Islamic women from strangers, behind a screen or under a veil

pure *adjective* **1** clean, spotless **2** free from dust, dirt, etc **3** not mixed with other substances **4** free from faults or sin, innocent **5** utter, absolute, nothing but: *pure nonsense*

pure-bred *adjective* of unmixed race or blood

purée (*pronounced* **pyoor**-ei) *noun* food made into a pulp by being put through a sieve or liquidizing machine ➤ *verb* (**puréeing, puréed**) to make into a purée, pulp

purely *adverb* **1** in a pure way **2** wholly, entirely: *purely on merit* **3** merely, only: *purely for the sake of appearance*

purgative *noun* a medicine which clears waste matter out of the body ➤ *adjective* of a medicine: having this effect

purgatory *noun* **1** in the teaching of the Roman Catholic Church, a place where souls are made pure before entering heaven **2** *informal* a state of suffering for a time

purge *verb* **1** to make clean, purify **2** to clear (something) of anything unwanted ➤ *noun* **1** a removal of impurities **2** a removal of something unwanted

purify *verb* (**purifies, purifying, purified**) to make pure ♦ **purification** *noun*

Purim (*pronounced* **poor**-im, **pyoor**-im or **poo-reem**) *noun* the Jewish Feast of Lots, commemorating their rescue from a plot to have them massacred

purist *noun* someone who insists on correctness

puritan *noun* **1** someone of strict, often narrow-minded, morals **2** (**Puritan**) *history* a person who in the time of Elizabeth I and the Stuarts wished to abolish ceremony from the Church of England ♦ **puritanical** *adjective* ♦ **puritanism** *noun*

purity *noun* the state of being pure

purl *verb* to knit in stitches made with the wool in front of the work

purloin *verb* to steal

purple *noun* a dark colour formed by the mixture of blue and red

purport *noun* (*pronounced* **per**-pawrt) meaning ➤ *verb* (*pronounced* per-**pawrt**) **1** to mean **2** to seem, pretend: *She purports to be a film expert*

purpose (*pronounced* **per**-pohs) *noun* **1** aim, intention **2** use, function (of a tool etc) ➤ *verb* to intend • **on purpose** intentionally • **to the purpose** to the point

purposeful *adjective* determined ♦ **purposefully** *adverb*

⚠️ Do not confuse: **purposefully** and **purposely**

purposely *adverb* intentionally

purr *noun* the low, murmuring sound made by a cat when pleased ➤ *verb* of a cat: to make this sound

purse *noun* **1** a small bag for carrying money **2** *US* a handbag ➤ *verb* to close (the lips) tightly

purser *noun* the officer who looks after a ship's money

pursue *verb* **1** to follow after (in order to overtake or capture), chase **2** to be engaged in, carry on (studies, an enquiry, etc) **3** to follow (a route, path, etc)

pursuer *noun* someone who pursues

pursuit *noun* **1** the act of pursuing **2** an occupation or hobby

purvey *verb* (**purveys, purveying, purveyed**) to supply (food etc) as a business ♦ **purveyor** *noun*

pus *noun* a thick, yellowish liquid produced from infected wounds

push *verb* **1** to press hard against **2** to thrust (something) away with force, shove **3** to urge on **4** to make a big effort ➤ *noun* (*plural* **pushes**) **1** a thrust **2** effort **3** *informal* energy and determination

pushbike *noun, informal* a bicycle propelled by pedals alone

push button *noun* a button pressed to operate a machine etc

pushchair *noun* a folding chair on wheels for a young child

pushover *noun, informal* **1** someone who is easily defeated or outwitted **2** a task that is easily accomplished

pushy *adjective* (**pushier, pushiest**) aggressively assertive

pusillanimous (*pronounced* pyoo-si-**lan**-im-us) *adjective* cowardly ♦ **pusillanimity** *noun*

pussy or **puss** *noun* (*plural* **pussies** or **pusses**) *informal* a cat, a kitten

pussyfoot *verb* to act timidly or non-committally

pussy-willow *noun* an American willow tree with silky catkins

pustule *noun* a pus-filled pimple

put *verb* (**putting, put**) **1** to place, lay, set: *put the book on the table* **2** to bring to a certain position or state: *put the light on/put it out of your mind* **3** to express: *put the question more clearly* • **put about 1** to change course at sea **2** to spread (news) • **put by** to set aside, save up • **put down** to defeat • **put in for** to make a claim for, apply for • **put off 1** to delay **2** to turn (someone) away from their plan or intention • **put out 1** to extinguish (a fire, light, etc) **2** to annoy, embarrass • **put up 1** to build **2** to propose, suggest (a plan, candidate, etc) **3** to let (someone) stay in your house etc **4** to stay as a guest (in someone's house) • **put up with** to bear patiently, tolerate ⊕ Comes from Late Old English *putian*

putative (*pronounced* **pyoo**-ta-tiv) *adjective* supposed, commonly accepted ⊕ Comes from Latin *putare* meaning 'to suppose'

put-down *noun, informal* a snub or humiliation

putrefy (*pronounced* **pyoo**-tri-fai) *verb* (**putrefies, putrefying, putrefied**) to go bad, rot ♦ **putrefaction** *noun*

putrid (*pronounced* **pyoo**-trid) *adjective* rotten; stinking

putsch (*pronounced* puwch) *noun* (*plural* **putsches**) a sudden move to seize political power; a coup d'état

putt *verb, golf* to send (a ball) gently forward ♦ **putting** *noun*

putter *noun* a golf club used for putting

putty *noun* a cement made from ground chalk, used in putting glass in windows etc

puzzle *verb* **1** to present with a difficult problem, situation, etc **2** to be difficult (for someone) to understand: *Her moods puzzled him* ➤ *noun* **1** a difficulty which needs a lot of thought **2** a toy or riddle to test knowledge or skill: *a crossword puzzle/jigsaw puzzle* • **puzzle something out** to consider long and carefully in order to solve (a problem)

PVC *abbreviation* polyvinyl chloride

pygmy or **pigmy** *noun* (*plural* **pygmies** or **pigmies**) a member of one of the unusually short peoples of equatorial Africa

pyjamas or *US* **pajamas** *plural noun* a sleeping suit consisting of trousers and a top

pylon *noun* **1** a high steel tower supporting electric power cables **2** a guiding mark at an airfield

pylorus *noun* (*plural* **pylori** – *pronounced* pai-**law**-rai), *anatomy* the opening at the base of the stomach that digested food passes through

pyramid *noun* **1** *maths* a solid shape figure with a square or triangular base, with sloping sides which come to a point at the top **2** *history* a building of this shape, built on a square base, used as a tomb in ancient Egypt ♦ **pyramidal** *adjective*

pyramidal peak *noun, geography* a summit

with a sharp point formed by glacial erosion

pyre *noun* a pile of wood on which a dead body is burned

Pyrex *noun, trademark* a type of glassware that will withstand heat

pyridoxine (*pronounced* pi-ri-**dok**-seen) *noun* vitamin B_6

pyrite (*pronounced* **pai**-rait) *noun* a brassy yellow mineral, a form of the compound iron disulphide (*also called*: **iron pyrites, fool's gold**)

pyrites (*pronounced* pai-**rai**-teez) *noun* **1** pyrite **2** *chemistry* any of a large class of sulphides, especially copper or tin ⊕ Comes from Latin meaning 'fire-stone'

pyro- (*pronounced* pai-roh) *prefix* relating to fire, heat or fever ⊕ Comes from Greek *pyr* meaning 'fire'

pyroclastics or **pyroclastic flow** *noun, geography* ash and other debris ejected by a volcano

pyromania *noun* an obsessive fascination with fire

pyromaniac *noun* someone who gets pleasure from starting fires

pyrotechnics *plural noun* a display of fireworks

Pyrrhic victory (*pronounced* **pir**-ik) *noun* a victory gained at so great a cost that it is equal to a defeat

⊕ After the costly defeat of the Romans by *Pyrrhus*, king of Epirus, in 280 BC

pyruvic acid (*pronounced* pai-**roo**-vik) *noun, biology, chemistry* an acid that is a product of the breakdown of carbohydrates

Pythagoras' theorem *noun, maths* the theorem that in a right-angled triangle the square of the length of the hypotenuse is equal to the sum of the squares of the lengths of the other two sides

⊕ After the 6th-century Greek philosopher *Pythagoras* of Samos, to whom the theorem is attributed

Python *noun, computing* a scripting language

⊕ Named in honour of *Monty Python's Flying Circus*, an old British TV comedy show

python *noun* a large, non-poisonous snake which crushes its victims

Qq

QC *abbreviation* Queen's Counsel

QED or **qed** (*pronounced* kyoo ee **dee**) *abbreviation quod erat demonstrandum* (Latin), which was to be demonstrated (used to signify a statement or theory that has at that point been shown to be true or proved)

quack¹ *noun* the cry of a duck ➤ *verb* to make the noise of a duck

quack² *noun* someone who falsely claims to have medical knowledge or training

quad short for **1** quadruplet **2** quadrangle

quadrangle *noun* **1** *maths* a figure with four equal sides and angles **2** a four-sided courtyard surrounded by buildings in a school, college, etc (*short form*: **quad**)

quadrangular *adjective* having the shape of a quadrangle

quadrant *noun* **1** *maths* one quarter of the circumference of a circle **2** *maths* one quarter of the area of a circle, as bound by two perpendicular radii and the arc between them **3** *maths* one of the four areas into which a plane is divided by axes **4** an instrument used in astronomy, navigation, etc for measuring heights

quadraphonic or **quadrophonic** *adjective* said of sound recording or reproduction: using four loudspeakers that are fed by four separate channels

quadrate *noun* something that has a square or rectangular shape ➤ *verb* to make something square

quadratic *maths, noun* (*also called*: **quadratic equation**) an equation that involves the square of at least one of the variables, but no higher power ➤ *adjective* involving the square of a variable, but no higher power

quadratic function *noun, maths* a function that involves the square, but no higher power, of an unknown variable

quadri- or **quadru-** *prefix* four: *quadrilateral/ quadruped* ◷ Comes from Latin *quattuor* meaning 'four'

quadriceps *singular noun* (*plural* **quadricepses** or **quadriceps**) the large four-part muscle that runs down the front of the thigh

quadrilateral *noun* a four-sided figure or area ➤ *adjective* four-sided

quadrille (*pronounced* kwa-**dril**) *noun* a dance for four couples arranged to form a square

quadriplegia (*pronounced* kwod-ri-**plee**-ji-a) *noun, medicine* paralysis of both arms and both legs

quadriplegic *medicine, adjective* relating to quadriplegia ➤ *noun* someone suffering from quadriplegia

quadruped *noun* a four-footed animal

quadruple *adjective* **1** four times as much or many **2** made up of four parts ➤ *verb* to make or become four times greater: *quadrupled the price*

quadruplet *noun* one of four children born to the same mother at one birth (*short form*: **quad**)

quaff (*pronounced* kwahf or kwof) *verb* to drink up eagerly

quagmire *noun* wet, boggy ground

quail¹ *noun* a type of small bird like a partridge

quail² *verb* to shrink back in fear

quaint *adjective* pleasantly odd or old-fashioned

quake *verb* to shake, tremble with fear ➤ *noun, informal* an earthquake

Quaker *noun* a member of a Christian religious group opposed to violence and war, founded in the 17th century

◷ Originally a nickname given to the group because their founder, George Fox, told them to *quake* at the word of God

qualification *noun* **1** a certificate gained, examination passed, etc showing a level of achievement **2** a skill that makes someone suitable for a job **3** a qualifying statement

qualified *adjective* having the necessary qualifications for a job

qualify *verb* (**qualifies, qualifying, qualified**) **1** to be suitable for a job or position **2** to pass a test **3** to proceed to a later stage of a competition etc by doing well in an earlier round **4** to lessen the force of (a statement) by adding or changing words

qualitative *adjective* relating to quality rather than quantity (*contrasted with*: **quantitative**)

qualitative analysis *noun, chemistry* the identification of the different constituents, eg the elements, ions, groups, etc, present in a substance (*compare with*: **quantitative analysis**)

quality *noun* (*plural* **qualities**) **1** an outstanding feature of someone or thing: *Kindness is a* quality admired by all **2** degree of worth: *cloth of poor quality*

quality of life *noun* standard of living as measured by social and economic environment, access to amenities, etc

qualm (*pronounced* kwahm) *noun* doubt about whether something is right

quandary *noun* (*plural* **quandaries**) **1** a state of uncertainty **2** a situation in which it is difficult to decide what to do

quango (*pronounced* **kwang**-goh) *noun* (*plural* **quangos**) an official body, funded and appointed by the government, that supervises some national activity etc

> ⊕ An acronym of *quasi-autonomous non-governmental organization*

quantifiable *adjective* capable of being quantified

quantify *verb* (**quantifies, quantifying, quantified**) to measure or state the quantity of

quantitative *adjective* relating to quantity rather than quality (*contrasted with:* **qualitative**)

quantitative analysis *noun, chemistry* the measurement of the amounts of the different constituents present in a substance (*compare with:* **qualitative analysis**)

quantity *noun* (*plural* **quantities**) **1** amount: *a large quantity of paper* **2** a symbol which represents an amount: *X is the unknown quantity*

quantity surveyor *noun* a person whose job is to estimate the cost of the materials, labour, etc that a building project requires

quantum *noun* (*plural* **quanta**), *physics* the smallest amount of a physical property such as momentum, energy, charge, etc that can exist

quantum leap *noun* **1** *physics* a sudden change from one energy state in an atom or molecule to another **2** a huge, dramatic jump

quantum mechanics *singular noun, physics* a branch of mechanics based on the quantum theory, used in predicting the behaviour of elementary particles

quantum theory *noun, physics* the theory that matter and energy are made up of tiny units called **quanta** that behave both as particles and as waves

quarantine *noun* the isolation of people or animals who might be carrying an infectious disease ➤ *verb* to put in quarantine

quark (*pronounced* kwahrk) *noun, physics* any of six hypothetical subatomic particles thought to make up all protons, neutrons and other hadrons

> ⊕ A word invented by James Joyce in *Finnegans Wake* (1939)

quarrel *noun* an angry disagreement or argument ➤ *verb* (**quarrelling, quarrelled**) **1** to disagree violently or argue angrily (with) **2** to find fault (with)

quarrelsome *adjective* fond of quarrelling, inclined to quarrel

quarry¹ *noun* (*plural* **quarries**) a pit from which stone is taken for building ➤ *verb* (**quarries, quarrying, quarried**) to dig (stone etc) from a quarry

quarry² *noun* (*plural* **quarries**) **1** a hunted animal **2** someone or something eagerly looked for

quart *noun* an imperial measure of liquids, equal to 2 pints (1.136 litres)

quarter *noun* **1** one of four equal parts of something **2** a fourth part of a year, three months **3** a district of a town, city, etc: *the Spanish quarter* **4** a section of the public or society, certain people or a certain person: *No help came from any quarter* **5** (**quarters**) lodgings, accommodation **6** mercy shown to an enemy: *No quarter was given by either side* ➤ *verb* **1** to divide into four equal parts **2** to accommodate

quarterback *noun* in American football: the player who directs the attacking play

quarterdeck *noun* the upper deck of a ship between the stern and the mast nearest it

quarter-final *noun* a match in a competition immediately before a semi-final

quarterly *adjective* happening every three months ➤ *adverb* every three months ➤ *noun* (*plural* **quarterlies**) a magazine etc published every three months

quartet *noun* **1** a group of four players or singers **2** a piece of music written for such a group

quartic *noun, maths* (*also called:* **quartic equation**) an equation that involves a variable up to the power four, but no higher power

quartile *noun, statistics* in a frequency distribution: a value arising from the division of data into four equal parts, such that one quarter, one half, or three quarters of the numbers are contained within it (ie in the first, second and third quartiles respectively)

quarto *noun* (*plural* **quartos**) a book folded to give four leaves to each sheet of paper

quartz *noun* a hard substance often in crystal form, found in rocks

quartz crystal *noun* a transparent, colourless form of quartz used in optics and electronics

quartzite *noun* a sandstone consisting of grains of quartz cemented together by silica

quasar (*pronounced* **kwei**-zar) *noun* an extremely distant, star-like object in the sky

quash (*pronounced* kwosh) *verb* **1** to crush, put down (eg a rebellion) **2** to wipe out, annul (eg a judge's decision)

quasi- (*pronounced* **kwei**-zai) *prefix* **1** to some extent, but not completely: *quasi-historical* **2** seemingly, but not actually, so: *quasi-experts* ⊙ Comes from Latin *quasi* meaning 'as if'

Quaternary *adjective* of the geological period from two million years ago to the present day

quaternary *adjective* having four parts

quatrain *noun* a poetic stanza of four lines

quaver *verb* **1** to shake, tremble **2** to speak in a shaking voice ➤ *noun* **1** a trembling of the voice **2** *music* a note (♪) equal to half a crotchet in length

quay (*pronounced* kee) *noun* a solid landing place for loading and unloading boats

queasy *adjective* ➤ *verb* (**queasier, queasiest**) **1** feeling nauseous **2** easily shocked or disgusted ◆ **queasiness** *noun*

queen *noun* **1** a female monarch **2** the wife of a king **3** a playing-card with a picture of a queen **4** the most powerful piece in chess **5** an egg-laying female bee, ant or wasp

queen bee *noun* **1** an egg-laying female bee **2** a woman who is the centre of attention

queenly *adjective* of or like a queen

queen mother *noun* the mother of the reigning king or queen who was once herself queen

queer *adjective* **1** odd, strange **2** *informal* (*sometimes derogatory*) homosexual ➤ *noun, informal* (*sometimes derogatory*) a homosexual

quell *verb* **1** to crush (a rebellion etc) **2** to remove (fears, suspicions, etc)

quench *verb* **1** to drink and so satisfy (thirst) **2** to put out (eg a fire)

querulous *adjective* complaining

query *noun* (*plural* **queries**) **1** a question **2** a question mark ➤ *verb* (**queries, querying, queried**) to question (eg a statement)

quest *noun* a search

question *noun* **1** a sentence requiring an answer, eg 'where do you live?' **2** a subject, matter, etc: *the energy question/a question of ability* **3** a matter for dispute or doubt: *There's no question of him leaving* ➤ *verb* **1** to ask questions of (someone) **2** to express doubt about, query: *questioning my authority* • **out of the question** not even to be considered, unthinkable

questionable *adjective* doubtful

question mark *noun* a symbol (?) put after a question in writing

questionnaire *noun* a written list of questions to be answered by several people to provide information for a survey

queue *noun* **1** a line of people, vehicles, etc, especially when waiting for something **2** *computing* a list of items waiting to be processed ➤ *verb* **1** to stand in, or form, a queue

2 *computing* to line up items to be processed

quibble *verb* to avoid an important part of an argument by quarrelling over details ➤ *noun* a petty argument or complaint

quiche (*pronounced* keesh) *noun* an open pastry case filled with beaten eggs, cheese, etc and baked

quick *adjective* **1** done or happening in a short time **2** acting without delay, fast-moving: *a quick brain* ➤ *noun* a tender area of skin under the nails ➤ *adverb, informal* quickly • **the quick** *old* the living

quicken *verb* to speed up, become or make faster

quicklime see **lime**

quickly *adverb* without delay, rapidly

quicksand *noun* sand that sucks in anyone who stands on it

quicksilver *noun* mercury

quickstep *noun* a ballroom dance like a fast foxtrot

quick-tempered *adjective* easily made angry

quid *noun, slang* a pound (£1)

quiddity *noun* (*plural* **quiddities**) **1** the essence or nature of something **2** a quibble

quiescent (*pronounced* kwi-**es**-ent) *adjective* not active ◆ **quiescence** *noun*

quiet *adjective* **1** making little or no noise **2** calm: *a quiet life/quiet seas* ➤ *noun* **1** the state of being quiet **2** lack of noise, peace ➤ *verb* to make or become quiet ◆ **quietness** *noun*

⚠ Do not confuse with: **quite**

quieten *verb* to make or become quiet

quietly *adverb* in a quiet way; with little or no sound

quiff *noun* a tuft of hair brushed up and back from the forehead

quill *noun* **1** a large feather of a goose or other bird made into a pen **2** one of the sharp spines of a porcupine

quilt *noun* a bed cover filled with down, feathers, etc

quilted *adjective* made of two layers of material with padding between them

quin short for **quintuplet**

quince *noun* a pear-like fruit with a sharp taste, used to make jams etc

quinine *noun* a bitter drug from the bark of a S American tree, used to treat malaria

quint- *prefix* fifth ⊙ Comes from Latin *quintus* meaning 'fifth'

quintessence *noun* **1** the most important part of anything **2** the purest part or form of something

⊙ Literally 'fifth essence', sought after by medieval alchemists as the highest essence

quintessential *adjective* central, essential

quintet *noun* **1** a group of five players or singers **2** a piece of music written for such a group

quintic *noun, maths (also called:* **quintic equation**) an equation that involves a variable up to the power five, but no higher power

quintuplet *noun* one of five children born to a mother at the same time (*short form:* **quin**)

quip *noun* a witty remark or reply ➤ *verb* (**quipping, quipped**) to make a witty remark

quire *noun* twenty-four or twenty-five sheets of paper of the same size and quality

quirk *noun* **1** an odd feature of someone's behaviour **2** a trick, a sudden turn: *a quirk of fate* ♦ **quirky** *adjective* (**quirkier, quirkiest**)

quisling *noun* someone who collaborates with an enemy, especially a puppet ruler

> ◷ Named after the Norwegian puppet prime minister Vidkun *Quisling* (1887–1945), who collaborated with the Germans during their occupation of his country

quit *verb* (**quitting, quit** or **quitted**) **1** to give up, stop: *I'm going to quit smoking* **2** to leave, resign from (a job)

quite *adverb* **1** fairly, moderately: *quite good* **2** completely, entirely: *quite empty*

> ⚠ Do not confuse with: **quiet**

quits *adjective, informal* **1** on an equal footing **2** even, especially in relation to money borrowed and lent • **call it quits** to stop arguing, bargaining, etc and agree that the outcome is even: *Just give me a fiver and we'll call it quits*

quiver[1] *noun* a tremble, a shake ➤ *verb* to tremble, shake

quiver[2] *noun* a carrying case for arrows

quixotic (*pronounced* kwik-**sot**-ik) *adjective* having noble but foolish and unrealistic aims

> ◷ After Don *Quixote*, the knight in Cervantes's 16th-century Spanish romance

quiz *verb* (**quizzing, quizzed**) to question

➤ *noun* (*plural* **quizzes**) a competition to test knowledge

quizzical *adjective* of a look: as if asking a question, especially mockingly ♦ **quizzically** *adverb*

quoits (*pronounced* koits) *singular noun* a game in which heavy flat rings (**quoits**) are thrown on to small rods

quorate *adjective* of a meeting etc: attended by enough people to form a quorum

quorum *noun* the least number of people who must be present at a meeting before any business can be done

quota *noun* **1** a part or share to be given or received by each member of a group **2** the quantity of goods allowed by a government to be manufactured, exported, or imported

quotation *noun* **1** the act of repeating something said or written **2** the words repeated **3** a price stated

quotation marks *plural noun* marks (" " or ' ') used in writing to show that someone's words are being repeated exactly, eg *He said, 'I'm going out'* (*also called:* **inverted commas, speech marks**)

quote *verb* **1** to repeat the words of (someone) exactly as said or written **2** to give or state (a price for something) ➤ *noun* **1** a quotation **2** a price quoted **3** (**quotes**) quotation marks

quoth (*pronounced* kwohth) *verb, old* said

quotidian *adjective* **1** everyday, commonplace **2** daily ◷ Comes from Latin *quotidianus*, from *quotidie* meaning 'daily'

quotient (*pronounced* **kwoh**-shent) *noun, maths* the result obtained by dividing one number by another, eg 4 is the quotient when 12 is divided by 3

Qur'an or **Quran** *noun* (*pronounced* kuw-**ran**) the Koran, the sacred book of Islam

qwerty or **QWERTY** *adjective* said of an English language typewriter or other keyboard: arranged with the letters *q w e r t y* appearing in that order at the top left of the letter keys

Ra *symbol, chemistry* radium

rabbi (*pronounced* rab-ai) *noun* (*plural* **rabbis**) a Jewish priest or teacher of the law

rabbit *noun* a small, burrowing, long-eared animal

rabble *noun* a disorderly, noisy crowd

rabid (*pronounced* **rab**-id) *adjective* 1 of a dog: suffering from rabies 2 violently enthusiastic or extreme: *a rabid nationalist*

rabies (*pronounced* **rei**-beez) *noun* a disease transmitted by the bite of an infected animal, causing fear of water and madness (*also called*: **hydrophobia**)

raccoon or **racoon** *noun* a small, furry animal of N America with black eye patches

race[1] *noun* 1 a group of people with the same ancestors and physical characteristics, eg skin colour and height 2 descent: *of noble race*

race[2] *noun* a competition to find the fastest person, animal, vehicle, etc ➤ *verb* 1 to run fast 2 to take part in a race

racecourse or **racetrack** *noun* a course over which races are run

racehorse *noun* a horse bred and used for racing

raceme (*pronounced* ra-**seem** or **rah**-seem) *noun, botany* a cluster of individual flowers, each attached to a stem by a short stalk ⊕ Comes from Latin *racemus* meaning 'bunch of grapes'

race relations *plural noun* social relations between people of different races living in the same community

racial *adjective* of or according to race

racism or **racialism** *noun* 1 the belief that some races of people are superior to others 2 prejudice on the grounds of race ♦ **racist** or **racialist** *noun & adjective*

rack[1] *noun* 1 a framework for holding letters, plates, coats, etc 2 *history* an instrument for torturing victims by stretching their joints 3 a bar with teeth which fits into and moves a toothed wheel ➤ *verb*: **rack your brains** to think hard about something

rack[2] *noun*: **go to rack and ruin** to get into a state of neglect and decay

racket[1] or **racquet** *noun* a bat made up of a strong frame strung with gut or nylon for playing tennis, badminton, etc

racket[2] *noun, informal* 1 a great noise, a din 2 a dishonest way of making a profit

racketeer *noun* someone who makes money dishonestly

raconteur (*pronounced* ra-kon-**ter**) *noun* someone who tells amusing stories

racoon another spelling of **raccoon**

racquet another spelling of **racket**[1]

racy *adjective* (**racier, raciest**) of a story: full of action, and often involving sexual exploits

radar *noun* a method of detecting solid objects using radio waves which bounce back off the object and indicate its position on a screen

radian *noun, maths* (*abbrev* **rad**) the angle that is made at the centre of a circle by an arc whose length is equal to the radius of the circle, approximately 57°

radiance *noun* brightness, splendour

radiant *adjective* 1 sending out rays of light, heat, etc 2 showing joy and happiness: *a radiant smile*

radiate *verb* 1 to send out rays of light, heat, etc 2 to spread or send out from a centre

radiation *noun* 1 energy in the form of electromagnetic waves or photons, eg heat and light 2 emissions of particles that arise from radioactive decay

radiation sickness *noun* illness caused by exposure to high levels of radiation

radiator *noun* 1 a device (especially a series of connected hot-water pipes) which sends out heat 2 the part of a car which cools the engine

radical *adjective* 1 thorough: *a radical change* 2 basic, deep-seated: *radical differences* 3 proposing dramatic changes in the method of government ➤ *noun* 1 someone who has radical political views 2 *chemistry* in a molecule: a group of atoms that behaves like a single atom and passes unchanged into another compound ♦ **radicalism** *noun* ♦ **radically** *adverb*

radicchio (*pronounced* ra-**dee**-ki-oh) *noun* a variety of chicory with reddish or purplish leaves used in salads ⊕ from Italian meaning 'chicory'

radicle *noun* 1 *botany* the part of a plant embryo which develops into the root 2 *botany* a small root 3 *anatomy* the origin of a vein or nerve

radio *noun* (*plural* **radios**) 1 a device for sending and receiving signals by means of electromagnetic waves 2 the use of such waves to transmit and receive information such as television or radio programmes and computer data, without connecting wires 3 the business or profession of sound broadcasting ▸ *verb* (**radioing, radioed**) to send a message to (someone) by radio

radioactive *adjective* giving off particles or rays which are often dangerous but which can be used in medicine

radioactivity *noun, physics* (*also called:* **radioactive decay**) the spontaneous disintegration of the nuclei of certain heavy elements, eg radium and uranium, resulting in the emission of particles or radiation

radiobiology *noun* the branch of biology concerned with the effects of radiation on living things

radiocarbon dating same as **carbon dating**

radiochemistry *noun* the branch of chemistry concerned with the study of radioactive elements and their compounds

radio frequency *noun* a frequency of electromagnetic waves between 3 kilohertz and 300,000 megahertz, used for radio and television broadcasting

radiographer (*pronounced* rei-di-**og**-ra-fer) *noun, medicine* a technician involved in radiology, eg in taking X-rays or giving radiotherapy

radiography (*pronounced* rei-di-**og**-ra-fi) *noun, medicine* photography of the interior of the body by X-rays

radioisotope (*pronounced* rei-di-**oh**-**ai**-soh-tohp) *noun, physics* a radioactive isotope of a chemical element

radiologist (*pronounced* rei-di-**ol**-o-jist) *noun* a specialist in the use of X-rays

radiology (*pronounced* rei-di-**ol**-o-ji) *noun* **1** the study of X-rays, gamma rays and other radiation **2** the branch of medicine involving the use of X-rays and radium

radio telescope *noun* an apparatus used to study distant stars, galaxies, etc by detecting the radio waves they emit

radiotherapy *noun* the treatment of certain diseases by X-rays or radioactive substances

radio wave *noun, physics* an electromagnetic wave of radio frequency (3 kilohertz to 300,000 megahertz), widely used for communication

radish *noun* (*plural* **radishes**) a plant with a sharp-tasting root, eaten raw in salads

radium *noun, chemistry* (symbol **Ra**) a radioactive metallic element used in radiotherapy ⏴ Comes from Latin *radius* meaning 'ray'

radius *noun* (*plural* **radii** – *pronounced* **rei**-di-ai) **1** *maths* a straight line from the centre to the circumference of a circle **2** an area within a certain distance from a central point: *houses within a radius of 10km* **3** *anatomy* the shorter

bone of the forearm, nearest the thumb (*compare with*: **ulna**)

radon (*pronounced* **rei**-don) *noun, chemistry* (symbol **Rn**) a highly toxic, colourless, radioactive, gaseous element

RAF *abbreviation* Royal Air Force

raffia *noun* strips of fibre from the leaves of a palm tree, used in weaving mats etc

raffish *adjective* flashy, dashing

raffle *noun* a way of raising money by selling numbered tickets, one or more of which wins a prize ▸ *verb* to give as a prize in a raffle

raft *noun* a number of logs etc fastened together and used as a boat

rafter *noun* one of the sloping beams supporting a roof

rag[1] *noun* **1** a torn or worn piece of cloth **2** (**rags**) worn-out, shabby clothes **3** *informal* a newspaper ▸ *adjective* made of rags: *a rag doll*

rag[2] *verb* (**ragged, ragging**) to tease, play tricks on

raga *noun* **1** a traditional pattern of notes in Indian music, around which melodies can be created **2** a piece of music composed around this pattern ⏴ Comes from Sanskrit *raga* meaning 'colour' or 'musical tone'

ragamuffin *noun* a ragged, dirty child

rag doll *noun* a floppy doll made of scrap material

rage *noun* great anger, fury ▸ *verb* **1** to be violently angry **2** of a storm, battle, etc: to be violent • **all the rage** *informal* very fashionable or popular

ragged (*pronounced* **rag**-id) *adjective* **1** in torn, shabby clothes **2** torn and tattered

raglan *noun* a cardigan or coat with the sleeves in one piece with the shoulders

⏴ Named after Lord *Raglan*, British commander in the Crimean War

ragout (*pronounced* ra-**goo**) *noun* a highly seasoned stew of meat and vegetables

ragtime *noun* a style of jazz music with a highly syncopated melody

raid *noun* **1** a short, sudden attack **2** an unexpected visit by the police to catch a criminal, recover stolen goods, etc ▸ *verb* to make a raid on ◆ **raider** *noun*

rail[1] *noun* **1** a bar of metal used in fences **2** (**rails**) strips of steel which form the track on which trains and trams run **3** the railway: *I came here by rail*

rail[2] *verb*: **rail against** or **at something** or **someone** to complain about or criticize them angrily or bitterly

railing *noun* a fence or barrier of rails

railway or *US* **railroad** *noun* a track laid with steel rails on which trains run

raiment *noun, old* clothing

rain *noun* **1** water falling from the clouds in drops **2** a great number of things falling: *a rain of bullets* ‣ *verb* to pour or fall in drops: *It's raining today*

rainbow *noun* **1** the brilliant coloured bow or arch sometimes to be seen in the sky opposite the sun when rain is falling **2** (**Rainbow**) a member of the most junior branch of the Guides

rain check *noun, chiefly N Am* a ticket for future use, given to spectators when a game or sports meeting is cancelled or stopped due to bad weather • **take a rain check (on)** *informal* to promise to accept (an invitation) at a later date

raincoat *noun* a waterproof coat to keep out the rain

rainfall *noun* the amount of rain that falls in a certain time

rainforest *noun* a tropical forest with very heavy rainfall

rain splash or **rainsplash** *noun, geography* the washing away of tiny particles of rock and soil by the action of rain, a cause of erosion

rainy *adjective* (**rainier, rainiest**) **1** full of rain: *rainy skies* **2** showery, wet: *a rainy day*

raise *verb* **1** to lift up: *raise the flag* **2** to make higher: *raise the price* **3** to bring up (a subject) for consideration **4** to bring up (a child, family, etc) **5** to breed or grow (eg pigs, crops) **6** to collect, get together (a sum of money) **7** *maths* to increase (a quantity) to a given power, ie by multiplying it by itself a given number of times, eg 3 raised to the power of 4 is 81 ⊙ Comes from Old Norse *reisa* meaning 'to cause to rise'

❗ Do not confuse with: **raze**

raised beach *noun, geography* an old sea margin above the present water level

raisin *noun* a dried grape

Raj *noun, history* (**the Raj**) the time of British rule in India, 1858–1947

raja or **rajah** *noun, history* an Indian prince

rake¹ *noun* a tool, like a large comb with a long handle, for smoothing earth, gathering hay, etc ‣ *verb* **1** to draw a rake over **2** to scrape (together) **3** to aim gunfire at (eg a ship) from one end to the other

rake² *noun, old* someone who lives an immoral life

rakish *adjective* at a slanting, jaunty angle

rallentando *music, adjective & adverb* becoming gradually slower ‣ *noun* (*plural* **rallentandos** or **rallentandi** – (*pronounced* ra-len-**tan**-dee)) a piece of music that becomes gradually slower ⊙ Comes from Italian *rallentare* meaning 'to slow down'

Ralliement (*pronounced* ra-lee-mong) *noun, history* a political movement set up in 1890 in France, encouraging Roman Catholics to accept the Republic

rally *verb* (**rallies, rallying, rallied**) **1** to gather again: *rally troops* **2** to come together for a joint action or effort: *The club's supporters rallied to save it* **3** to recover from an illness ‣ *noun* (*plural* **rallies**) **1** a gathering **2** a political mass meeting **3** an improvement in health after an illness **4** *tennis* a long series of shots before a point is won or lost **5** a competition to test driving skills over an unknown route

RAM *abbreviation, computing* random access memory

ram *noun* **1** a male sheep **2** something heavy, especially as part of a machine, for ramming ‣ *verb* (**ramming, rammed**) **1** to press or push down hard **2** of a ship, car, etc: to run into and cause damage to

Rama *noun, Hinduism* an incarnation of Vishnu

Ramadan *noun* **1** the ninth month of the Islamic calendar, a period of fasting by day **2** the fast itself

ramble *verb* **1** to walk about for pleasure, especially in the countryside **2** to speak in an aimless or confused way ‣ *noun* a country walk for pleasure

rambler *noun* **1** someone who goes walking in the country for pleasure **2** a climbing rose or other plant

rambunctious *adjective* boisterous, exuberant

ramekin (*pronounced* **ram**-e-kin) *noun* **1** a baked mixture of cheese and eggs **2** a baking dish for a single portion

ramification *noun* **1** a branch or part of a subject, plot, etc **2** a consequence, usually indirect and one of several

ramp *noun* a sloping surface (eg of a road)

rampage *verb* to rush about angrily or violently ‣ *noun*: **on the rampage** rampaging

rampant *adjective* **1** widespread and uncontrolled **2** *heraldry* standing on the left hind leg: *a lion rampant*

rampart *noun* a mound or wall built as a defence

ram-raid *noun* a raid in which the front window of a shop is smashed with a vehicle and goods are stolen

ramrod *noun* **1** a rod for pushing the charge down a gun barrel **2** someone strict or inflexible in their views

ramshackle *adjective* badly made, falling to pieces

ran past tense of **run**

ranch *noun* (*plural* **ranches**) a large farm in North America for rearing cattle or horses

rancid *adjective* of butter: smelling or tasting off or bad

rancorous *adjective* resentful, bitter

rancour or *US* **rancor** *noun* ill-will, hatred

rand (*plural* **rand** or **rands**) the standard monetary unit used in South Africa and some neighbouring countries

R & B *abbreviation* rhythm and blues

random *adjective* done without any aim or plan; chance: *a random sample* ➤ *noun*: **at random** without any plan or purpose

random access *noun, computing* direct and immediate access to data stored on a disk or in the memory of a computer

random access memory *noun, computing* (*abbrev* **RAM**) a computer memory in which data can be directly located

random sample *noun, statistics* a sample chosen in such a way that each sample of the same size is equally likely to be chosen

random variable *noun, statistics* a variable which can take any one of a range of values which occur randomly

rang past tense of **ring**²

range *noun* **1** a line or row: *a range of mountains* **2** extent, number: *a wide range of goods* **3** a piece of ground with targets for shooting or archery practice **4** the distance which an object can be thrown, or across which a sound can be heard **5** the distance between the top and bottom notes of a singing voice **6** a large kitchen stove with a flat top **7** *maths* the set of values that a function or dependent variable may take **8** *statistics* the difference between the greatest and least values in a set of data ➤ *verb* **1** to set in a row or in order **2** to wander (over) **3** to stretch, extend

ranger *noun* a keeper who looks after a forest or park

Ranger Guide *noun* an older member of the Guide movement

rangy (*pronounced* **rein**-ji) *adjective* (**rangier**, **rangiest**) of a person: with long thin limbs and a slender body

rank¹ *noun* **1** a row or line (eg of soldiers) **2** class, order: *the upper ranks of society/the rank of captain* **3** (**the ranks**) ordinary soldiers, not officers ➤ *verb* **1** to place in order of importance, merit, etc **2** to have a place in an order: *Apes rank above dogs in intelligence* • **the rank and file 1** soldiers of the rank of private **2** ordinary people, the majority

rank² *adjective* **1** of a plant: growing too plentifully **2** having a strong, unpleasant taste or smell **3** absolute: *rank nonsense*

rankle *verb* to cause lasting annoyance, bitterness, etc

ransack *verb* to search thoroughly; plunder

ransom *noun* the price paid for the freeing of a captive ➤ *verb* to pay money to free (a captive)

• **hold to ransom 1** to keep (someone) prisoner until a ransom is paid **2** to blackmail into agreeing to demands

rant *verb* to talk foolishly and angrily for a long time ➤ *noun* a loud, angry speech

rap *noun* **1** a sharp blow or knock **2** *slang* a criminal charge **3** a fast, rhythmic monologue recited over a musical backing with a pronounced beat **4** a style of music accompanied by a rhythmic monologue **5** *informal* an informal talk or discussion ➤ *verb* (**rapping, rapped**) **1** (often **rap on**) to strike with a quick, sharp blow **2** to perform a rhythmic monologue to music with a pronounced beat **3** to criticize sharply • **rap out** to say (something) sharply

rapacious *adjective* greedy, eager to seize as much as possible ♦ **rapacity** *noun*

rape¹ *verb* to have sexual intercourse with (someone) against their will, usually by force ➤ *noun* **1** the act of raping **2** the act of seizing and carrying off by force

rape² *noun* a type of plant like the turnip whose seeds give oil

rapid *adjective* quick, fast: *a rapid rise to fame* ♦ **rapidity** *noun* ♦ **rapidness** *noun*

rapid eye movement *noun* (*abbrev* **REM**) quick movements of the eyes behind the closed eyelids during REM sleep

rapids *plural noun* a part in a river where the current flows swiftly

rapier (*pronounced* **rei**-pi-er) *noun* a type of light sword with a narrow blade

rapist *noun* someone who commits rape

rapport (*pronounced* ra-**pawr**) *noun* a good relationship, sympathy

rapt *adjective* having the mind fully occupied, engrossed: *rapt attention*

raptor *noun* a bird of prey ⊕ from Latin meaning 'plunderer'

rapture *noun* great delight

rapturous *adjective* experiencing or demonstrating rapture

rare¹ *adjective* seldom found, uncommon

rare² *adjective* of meat: lightly cooked

rare earth *noun, chemistry* **1** (also **rare-earth element**) any of the metallic elements in the lanthanide series **2** an oxide of an element in the lanthanide series

rarefy (*pronounced* **reir**-i-fai) *verb* (**rarefies, rarefying, rarefied**) to make thin or less dense

raring *adjective*: **raring to go** *informal* very keen to go, start, etc

rarity *noun* (*plural* **rarities**) **1** something uncommon **2** uncommonness

rascal *noun* a naughty or wicked person

rash¹ *adjective* acting, or done, without thought ♦ **rashness** *noun*

rash² *noun* (*plural* **rashes**) redness or outbreak of spots on the skin

rasher *noun* a thin slice (of bacon or ham)

rasp *noun* **1** a coarse file **2** a rough, grating sound ➤ *verb* **1** to rub with a file **2** to make a rough, grating noise **3** to say in a rough voice

raspberry *noun* (*plural* **raspberries**) **1** a type of soft red berry **2** the bush which bears this fruit **3** a sound expressing contempt, made by blowing through the lips

rasping *adjective* of a sound: rough and unpleasant

raster *noun* a set of scanning lines on a television or computer screen, seen as a rectangular patch of light on which the image is reproduced

rat *noun* **1** a gnawing animal, larger than a mouse **2** *informal* a despicable person ➤ *verb* (**ratting, ratted**) to hunt or kill rats • **rat on** *informal* to inform against

ratafia (*pronounced* rat-a-**fee**-a) *noun* **1** a liqueur flavoured with fruit kernels and almonds **2** an almond-flavoured biscuit or small cake

ratatouille (*pronounced* rat-a-**too**-i) *noun* a vegetable dish made with tomatoes, peppers, courgettes, aubergines, onions and garlic simmered in olive oil ⊙ from French, from *touiller* meaning 'to stir'

ratchet *noun* a toothed wheel, eg in a watch

rate *noun* **1** the frequency with which something happens or is done: *a high rate of road accidents* **2** speed: *speak at a tremendous rate* **3** level of cost, price, etc: *paid at a higher rate* **4** (**rates**) the sum of money to be paid by the owner of a shop etc to pay for local public services ➤ *verb* **1** to work out the value of for taxation etc **2** to value: *I don't rate his work very highly*

rather *adverb* **1** somewhat, fairly: *It's rather cold today* **2** more willingly: *I'd rather talk about it now than later* **3** more correctly speaking: *He agreed, or rather he didn't say no*

ratification *noun* ratifying or being ratified

ratify *verb* (**ratifies, ratifying, ratified**) to approve officially and formally: *ratified the treaty*

rating *noun* **1** a classification according to order, rank, or value **2** a sailor below the rank of an officer **3** a measure of a TV or radio programme's popularity based on its estimated audience

ratio *noun* (*plural* **ratios**) **1** the proportion of one thing to another: *a ratio of two parts flour to one of sugar* **2** *maths* the relative number of times two quantities can be divided by another quantity, eg 12 (2 × 6) and 18 (3 × 6) are in the ratio 2:3

ration *noun* **1** a measured amount of food given out at intervals **2** an allowance ➤ *verb* **1** to deal out (eg food) in measured amounts **2** to allow only a certain amount to (someone)

rational *adjective* **1** able to reason **2** sensible; based on reason: *rational arguments* **3** *maths* denoting a number that can be expressed as a fraction whose denominator is not zero, eg 1 or $\frac{1}{3}$
♦ **rationality** *noun* ♦ **rationally** *adverb*

rationale (*pronounced* rash-on-**ahl**) *noun* the underlying principle on which something is based

rationalize or **rationalise** *verb* **1** to think up a good reason for (an action or feeling) so as not to feel guilty about it **2** to make (an industry or organization) more efficient and profitable by reorganizing it to get rid of unnecessary costs and labour **3** *maths* to make (a number) rational, especially by expressing the denominator of a fraction so that it does not contain a root
♦ **rationalization** *noun*

rat race *noun, informal* a fierce, unending competition for success or wealth

rattan (*pronounced* ra-**tan**) *noun* **1** a climbing palm with very long thin tough stems **2** a cane made from the stem of this palm ⊙ Comes from Malay *rotan*

rattle *verb* **1** to give out short, sharp, repeated sounds: *The coins rattled in the tin* **2** *informal* to fluster or irritate ➤ *noun* **1** a sharp noise, quickly repeated several times **2** a toy or instrument which makes such a sound • **rattle off** to go through (a list of names etc) quickly

rattlesnake *noun* a poisonous snake with bony rings on its tail which rattle when shaken

ratty *adjective* (**rattier, rattiest**) irritable

raucous *adjective* hoarse, harsh: *a raucous voice*

raunchy *adjective* (**raunchier, raunchiest**) sexually suggestive, lewd ♦ **raunchily** *adverb*

ravage *verb* to cause destruction or damage to; plunder ➤ *plural noun* damaging effects: *the ravages of time*

rave *verb* **1** to talk wildly, as if mad **2** *informal* to talk very enthusiastically (about) ➤ *noun* a large party held in a warehouse etc with electronic music

raven *noun* a type of large, black bird of the crow family ➤ *adjective* of hair: black and glossy

ravenous (*pronounced* **rav**-en-us) *adjective* very hungry

ravine (*pronounced* ra-**veen**) *noun* a deep, narrow valley between hills

raving *adjective* mad, crazy

ravioli (*pronounced* ra-vi-**oh**-li) *singular or plural noun* small, square pasta cases with a savoury filling of meat, cheese, etc

ravish *verb* **1** to plunder **2** to rape **3** to delight

ravishing *adjective* lovely; very attractive

raw *adjective* **1** not cooked **2** not prepared, refined, or processed: *raw cotton/raw data* **3** of weather: cold **4** sore • **get a raw deal** *informal* to be treated unjustly

raw materials *plural noun* substances in their natural state, used in manufacturing

ray¹ *noun* **1** a line of light, heat, etc **2** a small degree or amount: *a ray of hope* **3** any of several lines going outwards from a centre

ray² *noun* a kind of flat-bodied fish

ray³ or **re** *noun, music* in sol-fa notation: the second note of the major scale

rayon *noun* a type of artificial silk

raze *verb* to destroy, knock flat (a town, house, etc) ◑ Comes from French *raser* meaning 'to shave'

❗ Do not confuse with: **raise**

razor *noun* a sharp-edged instrument for shaving

razzle-dazzle *noun, slang* **1** excitement, confusion, dazzling show, etc **2** a lively spree

razzmatazz *noun* showiness, glamorous or extravagant show

Rb *symbol, chemistry* rubidium

RC *abbreviation* Roman Catholic

RE *abbreviation* religious education

Re *symbol, chemistry* rhenium

re¹ *preposition* concerning, about

re² same as **ray**³

re- *prefix* **1** again, once more: *recreate/redo* **2** back: *reclaim/refund* ◑ Comes from Latin prefix *re-* with the same meaning

reach *verb* **1** to arrive at: *reach the summit/Your message never reached me* **2** to stretch out (the hand) so as to touch: *I couldn't reach the top shelf* **3** to extend ▸ *noun* (*plural* **reaches**) **1** a distance that can be travelled easily: *within reach of home* **2** the distance someone can stretch their arm **3** a straight part of a stream or river between bends

react *verb* **1** to act or behave in response to something done or said **2** *chemistry* to undergo a chemical change: *Metals react with sulphuric acid* **3** *physics* to exert an equal force in the opposite direction

reactant *noun, chemistry* a substance participating in a chemical reaction

reaction *noun* **1** behaviour as a result of action **2** an emotional response to something **3** a movement against a situation or belief: *a reaction against Victorian morality* **4** *medicine* an effect of a drug on the body or mind **5** *chemistry* a process in which the electrons surrounding the nuclei in the atoms of one or more elements or compounds react to form new products **6** *chemistry* chemical change **7** *physics* a change in an atomic nucleus, eg radioactive decay, nuclear fission, nuclear fusion **8** *physics* the force offered by a body that is equal in magnitude but opposite in direction to the force applied to it

reactionary *adjective* favouring a return to old ways, laws, etc ▸ *noun* (*plural* **reactionaries**) someone who holds reactionary views

read (*pronounced* reed) *verb* (**reading, read** – *pronounced* red) **1** to look at and understand, or say aloud written or printed words **2** to study a subject in a university or college: *reading law* **3** *computing* to retrieve (data) from a storage device

readable *adjective* **1** able to be read **2** quite interesting to read

reader *noun* **1** someone who reads books etc **2** someone who reads manuscripts for a publisher **3** a senior university lecturer **4** a reading book for children **5** *computing* a document reader

readership *noun* the total number of readers (of a newspaper, magazine, etc)

readily *adverb* easily; willingly

readiness *noun* **1** the state of being ready and prepared **2** willingness: *the readiness of the troops to fight*

readjust *verb* to alter to suit a new environment or new conditions ◆ **readjustment** *noun*

read-only memory *noun, computing* (*abbrev* **ROM**) memory with data that can be read, but not written to

read-out *noun* **1** *computing* data from a computer; output **2** data from a radio transmitter

read-write head *noun, computing* a head in a disk drive that can both retrieve and record data

ready *adjective* (**readier, readiest**) **1** prepared: *packed and ready to go* **2** willing: *always ready to help* **3** quick: *too ready to find fault* **4** available for use: *Your coat is ready for collection*

ready-made *adjective* of clothes: made for general sale, not made specially for one person

reafforest *verb* to replant trees in a (cleared area of land that was formerly forested)
◆ **reafforestation** *noun*

reagent (*pronounced* ree-**ei**-jent) *noun, computing* any substance involved in a chemical reaction (*compare with*: **agent**)

real *adjective* **1** actually existing, not imagined **2** not imitation, genuine: *real leather* **3** sincere: *a real love of music* ● **the real Mackay** or **the real McCoy** the genuine article, the real thing

real ale *noun* ale or beer which is allowed to continue to ferment and mature in the cask after brewing

realign (*pronounced* ree-a-**lain**) *verb* **1** to put back into alignment **2** to group together or divide in a new way: *The political map was realigned after the war* **3** to change position or grouping: *The MP realigned herself with the new party* ◆ **realignment** *noun*

realism *noun* the showing or viewing of things as they really are

realist *noun* someone who claims to see life as it really is

realistic *adjective* **1** lifelike **2** viewing things as they really are ♦ **realistically** *adverb*

reality *noun* (*plural* **realities**) that which is real and not imaginary; truth

reality TV *noun* a genre of television programme which presents members of the public as subjects

realize or **realise** *verb* **1** to come to understand, know: *I never realized you could sing* **2** to make real, accomplish: *realize an ambition* **3** to get (money) for: *realized £16,000 on the sale of the house* ♦ **realization** *noun*

really *adverb* **1** in fact **2** very: *really dark hair*

realm (*pronounced* relm) *noun* **1** a kingdom, a country **2** an area of activity or interest

real number *noun, maths* any rational or irrational number

real-time *adjective, computing* of a system etc: processing data as it is input or generated

ream *noun* **1** a measure for paper, 20 quires **2** (**reams**) *informal* a large quantity, especially of paper: *She wrote reams in her English exam*

reap *verb* **1** to cut and gather (corn etc) **2** to gain: *reap the benefits of hard work*

reaper *noun* **1** someone who reaps **2** a machine for reaping

rear¹ *noun* **1** the back part of anything **2** the last part of an army or fleet **3** *informal* the buttocks • **bring up the rear** to come or be last in a series

rear² *verb* **1** to bring up (children) **2** to breed (animals) **3** of an animal: to stand on its hindlegs

rear admiral *noun* a naval officer of the rank below vice-admiral

rearguard *noun* troops which protect the rear of an army • **rearguard action 1** military action by the rearguard **2** an effort to prevent or delay defeat, eg in an argument

reason *noun* **1** cause, excuse: *What is the reason for this noise?* **2** purpose: *What is your reason for visiting America?* **3** the power of the mind to form opinions, judge right and truth, etc **4** common sense ➤ *verb* to think out (opinions etc) • **reason with** to try to persuade by arguing

reasonable *adjective* **1** sensible **2** fair

reassurance *noun* something which reassures, or the feeling of being reassured

reassure *verb* to take away (someone's) doubts or fears

reassuring *adjective* that reassures

rebarbative *adjective, formal* repellent

rebate *noun* a part of a payment or tax which is given back to the payer

rebel *noun* (*pronounced* **reb**-el) someone who opposes or fights against those in power ➤ *verb* (*pronounced* ri-**bel**) (**rebelling, rebelled**) to

take up arms against or oppose those in power

rebellion *noun* **1** an open or armed fight against those in power **2** a refusal to obey

rebellious *adjective* rebelling or likely to rebel ♦ **rebelliousness** *noun*

rebirth *noun* **1** reincarnation **2** any revival, renaissance or renewal

reboot *verb, computing* to restart (a computer) using its start-up programs

reborn *adjective* **1** reincarnated **2** revived or spiritually renewed **3** converted to Christianity

rebound *verb* (*pronounced* ri-**bownd**) to bounce back: *The ball rebounded off the wall* ➤ *noun* (*pronounced* **ree**-bownd) **1** the act of rebounding **2** *informal* a reaction following an emotional situation or crisis: *on the rebound*

rebrand *verb, business* to market (a product) using a new brand name or image

rebuff *noun* a blunt refusal or rejection ➤ *verb* to reject bluntly

rebuke *verb* to scold, blame ➤ *noun* a scolding

rebut *verb* (**rebutting, rebutted**) to deny (what has been said)

rebuttal *noun* a rejection or contradiction

recalcitrance *noun* stubbornness; disobedience ♦ **recalcitrant** *adjective*

recall (*pronounced* ri-**kawl**) *verb* **1** to call back: *recalled to headquarters* **2** to remember ➤ *noun* (*pronounced* **ree**-kawl) **1** a signal or message to return **2** the act of recalling or remembering

recant *verb* **1** to take back what you have said **2** to reject publicly your beliefs ♦ **recantation** *noun*

recap *informal, noun* recapitulation ➤ *verb* (**recapping, recapped**) to recapitulate

recapitulate *verb* **1** to go over again quickly the chief points of anything (eg a discussion) **2** *biology* of an embryo: to repeat (stages in the evolutionary development of its species) during embryonic development

recapitulation *noun* **1** an act or instance of recapitulating or summing up **2** *biology* the repetition in the development of an embryo of stages in the evolutionary development of its species

recapture *verb* to capture (what has escaped or been lost)

recast *verb* (**recasting, recast**) to shape in a new form

recce (*pronounced* **rek**-i) *informal, noun* (*plural* **recces**) reconnaissance ➤ *verb* (**recceing, recced** or **recceed**) to reconnoitre

recede *verb* **1** to go back **2** to become more distant **3** to slope backwards **4** of hair: to stop growing above the forehead and at the temples

receding *adjective* **1** going or sloping backwards **2** becoming more distant **3** going bald above the forehead and at the temples

receipt (*pronounced* ri-**seet**) *noun* **1** the act of receiving (especially money or goods) **2** a written note saying that money has been received

receive *verb* **1** to have something given or brought to you: *receive a gift/receive a letter* **2** to meet and welcome: *receiving visitors* **3** to take (goods), knowing them to be stolen

Received Pronunciation *noun* an educated southern English pronunciation of English, regarded by many as the most socially acceptable

receiver *noun* **1** someone who receives stolen goods **2** a person appointed by a court to manage property under litigation, or take control of the business of someone who has gone bankrupt or who is certified insane **3** the part of a telephone through which words are heard and into which they are spoken **4** an apparatus through which television or radio broadcasts are received

receivership *noun* the status of a business that is under the control of an official receiver: *The business has gone into receivership*

recent *adjective* happening, done or made only a short time ago

recently *adverb* a short time ago

receptacle *noun* **1** an object to receive or hold things, a container **2** *botany* the top of a flower stalk, from which the flower parts grow

reception *noun* **1** a welcome: *a warm reception* **2** a formal party or social function to welcome guests, especially after a wedding **3** the quality of radio or television signals **4** an area or desk where visitors or clients are welcomed on arrival, eg in an office or hotel

receptionist *noun* someone employed in an office or hotel to answer the telephone etc

receptive *adjective* quick to take in or accept ideas etc

receptor *noun, biology* **1** a cell or group of cells that can detect stimuli, eg a sense organ **2** the area on the surface of a cell to which an antigen, drug or hormone can bind

recess *noun* (*plural* **recesses**) **1** part of a room set back from the rest, an alcove **2** the time during which parliament or the law courts do not work **3** (**recesses**) remote parts: *in the recesses of my memory*

recession *noun* **1** the act of moving back **2** a temporary fall in a country's or world business activities

recessive *adjective* **1** tending to recede **2** *biology* denoting a gene in a pair that produces a trait in an individual only when it is inherited from both parents (*compare with*: **dominant**)

recidivism (*pronounced* ri-**sid**-i-vizm) *noun* the habit of relapsing into crime ♦ **recidivist**

noun & adjective ⊙ Comes from Latin *recidivus*, from *recidere* meaning 'to fall back'

recipe (*pronounced* **re**-si-pi) *noun* instructions on how to prepare or cook a certain kind of food

recipient *noun* someone who receives something

reciprocal (*pronounced* ri-**sip**-ro-kal) *adjective* both given and received: *reciprocal affection* ➤ *noun, maths* one of a pair of numbers whose product is 1, eg 4 is the reciprocal of $\frac{1}{4}$

reciprocal function *noun, maths* a function that includes a reciprocal

reciprocate *verb* to feel or do the same in return: *I reciprocate his dislike of me*

recital (*pronounced* ri-**sai**-tal) *noun* **1** the act of reciting **2** a musical performance **3** the facts of a story told one after the other

recitation *noun* a poem etc recited

recitative (*pronounced* res-i-ta-**teev**) *noun, music* a narrative passage in an opera or oratorio, sung in a style resembling speech ⊙ Comes from Italian *recitativo*

recite *verb* to repeat aloud from memory

reckless *adjective* rash, careless ♦ **recklessly** *adverb*

reckon *verb* **1** to count **2** to consider, believe

reckoning *noun* **1** the settling of debts, grievances, etc **2** payment for sins **3** a bill **4** a sum, calculation

reclaim *verb* **1** to claim back **2** to win back (land from the sea) by draining, building banks, etc **3** to make (waste land) fit for use

reclamation *noun* reclaiming or being reclaimed

recline *verb* to lean or lie on your back or side

recluse *noun* someone who lives alone and avoids other people

reclusive *adjective* solitary

recognition *noun* the act of recognizing someone or something

recognizable or **recognisable** *adjective* capable of being recognized

recognize or **recognise** *verb* **1** to know from a previous meeting etc **2** to admit, acknowledge: *Everyone recognized his talent* **3** to show appreciation of: *They recognized her courage by giving her a medal*

recoil *verb* (*pronounced* ri-**koil**) **1** to shrink back in horror or fear **2** of a gun: to jump back after a shot is fired ➤ *noun* (*pronounced* **ree**-koil) **1** a shrinking back **2** the jumping back of a gun when it is fired

recollect *verb* to remember

recollection *noun* **1** the act or power of remembering **2** a memory, something remembered

recombinant DNA *noun, biology* material

produced by joining the DNA of different organisms

recombination *noun, biology* the rearrangement of genes when cells divide during reproduction, or through genetic engineering

recommend *verb* **1** to urge, advise: *I recommend that you take a long holiday* **2** to speak highly of

recommendation *noun* **1** the act of recommending **2** a point in favour of someone or something

recompense *verb* to pay money to or reward (a person) to make up for loss, inconvenience, etc ➤ *noun* payment in compensation

reconcile *verb* **1** to bring together in friendship, after a quarrel **2** to show that two statements, facts, etc do not contradict each other • **be reconciled to** or **reconcile yourself to** to agree to accept (an unwelcome fact or situation) patiently: *I became reconciled to her absence*

reconciliation *noun* the fact of being friendly with someone again, after an argument, dispute or conflict: *There seems little hope of reconciliation*

recondition *verb* to repair (an engine, piece of equipment, etc) to its original or a good working condition, eg by cleaning or replacing broken parts

reconnaissance (*pronounced* ri-**kon**-is-ans) *noun* a survey to obtain information, especially before a battle

reconnoitre (*pronounced* rek-o-**noi**-ter) *verb* to make a reconnaissance of

reconsider *verb* to consider (a decision, opinion, etc) again, especially for a possible change ♦ **reconsideration** *noun*

reconstitute *verb* **1** to put back into its original form: *reconstitute the milk* **2** to make up or form in a different way

reconstruct *verb* **1** to rebuild **2** to create an impression of (a past event etc) using what is known **3** to re-enact (a crime) ♦ **reconstruction** *noun*

record *verb* (*pronounced* ri-**kawd**) **1** to write down for future reference **2** to put (music, speech, etc) on tape or disc so that it can be listened to later **3** to show in writing (eg a vote) **4** to show, register: *The thermometer recorded 30°C yesterday* ➤ *noun* (*pronounced* **rek**-awd) **1** a written report of facts **2** a round, flat piece of plastic on which sounds are recorded for playing on a record player **3** *computing* a group of related fields forming a complete piece of information (eg a name and address) in a database **4** the best known performance: *John holds the school record for the mile* • **break** or **beat the record** to do better than any previous performance • **off the record** of a

remark etc: not to be made public

recorder *noun* **1** someone who records **2** a type of simple musical wind instrument **3** a judge in certain courts

recording *noun* **1** the act of recording **2** recorded music, speech, etc

record player *noun* a machine for playing records

recount *verb* **1** (*pronounced* ree-**kownt**) to count again **2** (*pronounced* ri-**kownt**) to tell (the story of) ➤ *noun* (*pronounced* **ree**-kownt) a second count, especially of votes in an election

recoup (*pronounced* ri-**koop**) *verb* to make good, recover (expenses, losses, etc) ℗ Comes from French *recouper* meaning 'to cut back'

⚠ Do not confuse with: **recuperate**

recourse *noun*: **have recourse to** to make use of in an emergency

recover *verb* **1** to get possession of again **2** to become well again after an illness

recoverable *adjective* able to be recovered

recovery *noun* (*plural* **recoveries**) **1** a return to health **2** the regaining of something lost etc

recreate or **re-create** *verb* to create something again; to reproduce

recreation (*pronounced* rek-ree-**ei**-shon) *noun* a sport, hobby, etc done in your spare time

recriminate *verb* to accuse your accuser in return

recrimination *noun* (usually **recriminations**) an accusation made by someone who is himself or herself accused of something

recruit *noun* a newly enlisted soldier, member, etc ➤ *verb* to enlist (someone) in an army, political party, etc ♦ **recruitment** *noun*

rectangle *noun* a four-sided figure with all its angles right angles and its opposite sides equal in length; an oblong

rectangular *adjective* of or like a rectangle

recti- or **rect-** *prefix* forms words containing the meaning 'straight' or 'correct': *rectilineal/ rectangle* ℗ Comes from Latin *rectus* meaning 'straight' or 'right'

rectifiable *adjective* capable of being rectified

rectifier *noun* **1** someone or something that rectifies **2** *chemistry* a piece of equipment for condensing hot vapour to liquid in distillation **3** *electricity* a device that converts alternating current into direct current

rectify *verb* (**rectifies, rectifying, rectified**) **1** to put right **2** *chemistry* to purify by repeated distillation **3** *electricity* to change alternating current into direct current

rectilineal or **rectilinear** *adjective* **1** in a straight line or lines **2** bounded by straight lines

rectitude *noun* honesty; correctness of behaviour

recto *noun, printing* the right-hand page of an open book (*compare with:* **verso**)

rector *noun* **1** a member of the Anglican clergy in charge of a parish **2** the head teacher of some Scottish secondary schools **3** a Scottish university official elected by the students

rectory *noun* (*plural* **rectories**) the house of an Anglican rector

rectum *noun* (*plural* **recta** or **rectums**), *anatomy* the lower part of the alimentary canal

recumbent *adjective* lying down

recuperate *verb* to recover strength or health ℗ Comes from Latin *recuperare* meaning 'to recover'

⚠ Do not confuse with: **recoup**

recuperation *noun* recovery

recur *verb* (**recurring, recurred**) to happen again

recurrent *adjective* happening often or regularly ♦ **recurrence** *noun*

recurring decimal *noun, maths* a decimal with an infinitely repeating digit or group of digits eg 0.9999 …

recursion *noun* **1** a return **2** *maths* the repeated application of a function to its own values to produce an infinite series of values ♦ **recursive** *adjective*

recycle *verb* **1** to remake into something different **2** to treat (material) by some process in order to use it again

red *adjective* (**redder, reddest**) **1** of the colour of blood **2** of hair: of a reddish-brown colour ➤ *noun* either of these colours • **see red** to become very angry

red alert *noun* a state of readiness to deal with an imminent emergency

red alga *noun* (*plural* **red algae**), *botany* an alga which contains a pigment giving it a pink or reddish colour

Red Army *noun, history* the official name of the army of the Soviet Union from 1918 to 1946

red card *noun, football* a piece of red card or plastic shown by the referee to a player to indicate that they are being sent off (*compare with:* **yellow card**)

red carpet *noun* **1** a strip of carpet put out for an important person to walk on **2** special treatment, as for a very important person

red deer *noun* a type of reddish-brown deer

redden *verb* to make or grow red

red dwarf *noun* a small cool star that is very faint

redeem *verb* **1** to buy back (eg articles from a pawnbroker) **2** to save from sin or condemnation **3** to free (yourself) from blame or debt **4** to exchange (tokens, vouchers, etc) for goods

redeemer *noun* a person who redeems • **the Redeemer** *Christianity* Jesus Christ

redeeming *adjective* making up for other faults: *a redeeming feature*

redemption *noun* **1** the act of redeeming or state of being redeemed **2** *Christianity* the freeing of humanity from sin by Christ ♦ **redemptive** *adjective*

redeploy *verb* to move (eg soldiers, workers) to a different place where they will be more useful

red giant *noun* a large cool luminous star thought to be in a late stage of its evolution

Red Guards *plural noun, history* young radical activists who spread the Cultural Revolution across China

red-handed *adverb* in the act of doing wrong: *caught red-handed*

redhead *noun* a person, especially a woman, with red hair

red herring *noun* something mentioned to lead a discussion away from the main subject; a false clue

℗ From a type of fish used by men who were being chased to put hunting dogs off their trail

red-letter *adjective* of a day: especially important or happy for some reason

℗ From the custom of marking saints' days in red on calendars

red light *noun* **1** a danger signal **2** a signal to stop

redo *verb* (**redoing, redid, redone**) **1** to do again or differently **2** *computing* to repeat a command, often by pressing a designated key

redolent (*pronounced* **red**-o-lent) *adjective* **1** sweet-smelling **2** smelling (of) **3** suggestive, making one think (of): *redolent of earlier times*

redouble *verb* to make twice as great: *redouble your efforts*

redoubtable *adjective* brave, bold

redox reaction (*pronounced* **ree**-doks) *noun, chemistry* a reaction in which one of the reacting substances is reduced and another is oxidized ℗ From *reduction + oxidation*

redress *verb* to set right, make up for (a wrong etc) ➤ *noun* something done or given to make up for a loss or wrong, compensation

Red Scare *noun, history* a period in US history (1919–20) marked by great distrust of radicals and foreigners

red shift *noun, astronomy* an increase in the wavelength of light as the source of light moves away from the observer

red tape *noun* unnecessary and troublesome rules about how things are to be done

℗ After the red tape which was once used to tie up official documents

reduce verb **1** to make smaller **2** to lessen **3** to bring to the point of by force of circumstances: reduced to begging in the streets **4** to bring to a lower rank or state **5** to change into other terms: reduce pounds to pence **6** cookery to thicken (a sauce) by slowly boiling off the excess liquid **7** chemistry to cause (a substance) to gain hydrogen or lose oxygen **8** chemistry to cause (an atom or ion) to gain electrons

reducible adjective capable of being reduced

reducing agent noun, chemistry a substance that brings about reduction in another substance and which is simultaneously oxidized

reductase noun, biology, chemistry an enzyme which brings about the reduction of organic compounds

reduction noun **1** an act or instance of reducing; the state of being reduced **2** the amount by which something is reduced **3** a reduced copy of a picture, document, etc **4** chemistry a reaction in which an atom or ion is reduced

redundancy noun (plural **redundancies**) **1** being redundant, or an instance of this **2** a dismissal or a person dismissed because they are no longer needed

redundant adjective **1** more than is needed **2** of a worker: no longer needed because of the lack of a suitable job

reed noun **1** a tall, stiff grass growing in moist or marshy places **2** a part (originally made of reed) of certain wind instruments which vibrates when the instrument is played

reedy adjective (**reedier, reediest**) **1** full of reeds **2** like a reed **3** sounding like a reed instrument: a reedy voice

reef noun a chain of rocks lying at or near the surface of the sea

reefer noun a short coat, as worn by sailors

reef knot noun a square, very secure knot

reek noun **1** a strong, unpleasant smell **2** Scottish smoke ➤ verb **1** Scottish to send out smoke **2** to smell strongly

reel noun **1** a cylinder of plastic, metal or wood on which thread, film, fishing lines, etc may be wound **2** a length of cinema film **3** a lively Scottish or Irish dance ➤ verb **1** to wind on a reel **2** to stagger • **reel in** to draw, pull in (a fish on a line) • **reel off** to repeat or recite quickly, without pausing

re-entry noun (plural **re-entries**) the return of a spacecraft to the earth's atmosphere

ref abbreviation **1** referee **2** reference

refectory noun (plural **refectories**) a communal dining hall for monks, students, etc

refer verb (**referring, referred**): **refer to 1** to mention **2** to turn to for information **3** to relate to, apply to **4** to direct to for information,

consideration, etc: I refer you to the managing director

referee noun **1** someone to whom a matter is taken for settlement **2** a judge in a sports match **3** someone willing to provide a note about someone's character, work record, etc

reference noun **1** the act of referring **2** a mention **3** a note about a person's character, work, etc

reference book noun a book to be consulted for information, eg an encyclopedia

referendum noun (plural **referenda** or **referendums**) a vote about some important matter by the people of a country, rather than by their representatives in government

referral noun the sending of a patient by a GP to a specialist for treatment

refill noun (pronounced ree-fil) a new filling for something which becomes empty ➤ verb (pronounced ree-**fil**) to fill again

refine verb **1** to purify **2** to improve, make more exact, etc

refined adjective **1** purified **2** polite in manners, free of vulgarity

refinement noun **1** good manners, taste, learning **2** an improvement

refinery noun (plural **refineries**) a place where sugar, oil, etc is refined

refit verb (**refitting, refitted**) to repair damages (especially to a ship) and re-equip ➤ noun the process or an instance of refitting

reflect verb **1** to throw back (light or heat): reflecting the sun's heat **2** to give an image of: reflected in the mirror **3** (**reflect on**) to throw blame on (someone): Her behaviour reflects on her mother **4** (**reflect on**) to think (something) over carefully

reflection noun **1** the change in direction of a wave, eg a ray of light, when it strikes a smooth surface **2** the act of throwing back **3** the image of someone etc reflected in a mirror **4** maths a transformation of a plane around an axis of symmetry in the plane, so that it produces a mirror image on the other side (compare with: **enlargement, rotation, translation**) **5** a reason for blame or unfavourable criticism: Their appalling behaviour is a reflection on their parents

reflective adjective thoughtful

reflector noun something (eg a piece of shiny metal) which throws back light

reflex noun (plural **reflexes**) **1** physiology an automatic response to a stimulus, eg jerking the leg when the kneecap is struck **2** a conditioned rather than considered response to a situation **3** reflected light, sound, heat, etc **4** a reflected image ➤ adjective **1** done as an automatic response, unthinking **2** bent or turned backwards **3** reflected **4** *maths* of an angle: greater than 180° degrees (*compare with*: **acute, obtuse**)

reflex arc *noun, physiology* the unit of the nervous system by which an impulse produces a reflex action

reflexive *adjective, physiology* relating to a reflex ➤ *noun, grammar* a reflexive pronoun or verb

reflexive pronoun *noun, grammar* a pronoun that turns the action of a verb back on the subject, eg *himself* in *He cut himself*

reflexive verb *noun, grammar* a verb which has a reflexive pronoun as its object, eg *cut* in *He cut himself*

reflexology *noun* the massaging of various points on the soles of the feet, the hands and the head as a form of therapy ♦ **reflexologist** *noun*

reflux *chemistry, noun* (*plural* **refluxes**) **1** the boiling of a liquid in a container attached to a condenser, so that the vapour produced condenses and flows back into the container **2** the condensed vapour involved in this process ➤ *verb* to boil or be boiled under reflux ⊕ Comes from Latin, from *fluxus* meaning 'flow'

reform *verb* **1** to improve, remove faults from **2** to improve (a law, institution, etc) by making changes to it **3** to give up bad habits, evil, etc ➤ *noun* **1** improvement in behaviour or morals **2** an improvement, correction of a fault: *reforms to the voting system*

reformation (*pronounced* ref-or-**mei**-shon) *noun* a change for the better • **the Reformation** the religious movement in the Christian Church in the 16th century from which Protestant churches arose

reformer *noun* someone who wishes to bring about improvements

refract *verb, physics* to change the direction of (a wave of light, sound, etc)

refraction *noun, physics* **1** the bending of a wave, eg a light or sound wave, as it passes from one medium to another of different density **2** the amount by which the direction of a wave changes

refractive index *noun, physics* the ratio of the speed of electromagnetic radiation, especially light, in air or a vacuum to its speed in another medium

refractory *adjective* **1** unruly, not easily controlled **2** of a disease: resistant to treatment **3** of a material: resistant to high temperatures

refrain¹ *noun* a chorus coming at the end of each verse of a song

refrain² *verb* to keep yourself back (from doing something): *Please refrain from smoking*

refresh *verb* **1** to give new strength, power or life to **2** *computing* to update (a screen display) with

data • **refresh your memory** to go over facts again so that they are clear in your mind

refresher course *noun* a course of study intended to keep up or increase existing knowledge of a subject

refreshing *adjective* **1** bringing back strength **2** cooling **3** pleasing because of being different or unexpected: *His attitude was refreshing* ♦ **refreshingly** *adverb*

refreshments *plural noun* food and drink

refrigerant *noun* a liquid used in the cooling mechanism of a refrigerator ➤ *adjective* cooling

refrigerate *verb* to make or keep cold or frozen, especially food to prevent it from going bad

refrigeration *noun* the process whereby a cabinet or room and its contents are kept at a low temperature, especially in order to prevent food from going bad

refrigerator *noun* a storage machine which keeps food cold and so prevents it from going bad

refuel *verb* (**refuelling, refuelled**) to supply with, or take in, fresh fuel

refuge *noun* a place of safety (from attack, danger etc)

refugee *noun* someone who seeks shelter from persecution in another country

refund *verb* (*pronounced* ri-**fund**) to pay back ➤ *noun* (*pronounced* **ree**-fund) a payment returned, eg for unsatisfactory goods

refurbish *verb* **1** to renovate **2** to redecorate or brighten (something) up ♦ **refurbishment** *noun*

refusal *noun* **1** an act of refusing **2** the option of accepting or refusing something: *I promised to give him first refusal on my car* (= offered to sell it to him before advertising it generally)

refuse¹ (*pronounced* ri-**fyooz**) *verb* **1** to say that you will not do something: *He refused to leave the room* **2** to withhold, not give (eg permission)

refuse² (*pronounced* **ref**-yoos) *noun* something which is thrown aside as worthless, rubbish

refutation *noun* **1** refuting **2** an argument etc that refutes

refute *verb* to prove wrong (something that has been said or written)

regain *verb* **1** to win back again **2** to get back to: *regain the shore*

regal *adjective* kingly or queenly; royal

regale (*pronounced* ri-**geil**) *verb* to entertain lavishly

regalia *plural noun* symbols of royalty, eg a crown and sceptre

regard *verb* **1** to look upon, consider: *I regard you as a nuisance* **2** to look at carefully **3** to pay attention to ➤ *noun* **1** concern **2** affection **3**

respect **4** (**regards**) good wishes • **with regard to** or **in regard to** concerning

regarding *preposition* concerning, to do with: *a reply regarding his application*

regardless *adverb* not thinking or caring about costs, problems, dangers, etc; in spite of everything: *carry on regardless* • **regardless of** paying no care or attention to

regatta *noun* a meeting for yacht or boat races

⊙ From the name of a gondola race held on the Grand Canal in Venice

regency *noun* (*plural* **regencies**) **1** rule by a regent **2** the period of a regent's rule **3** *Brit history* (**the Regency**) the period during which the Prince of Wales (later George IV) was regent, 1811–1820

regenerate *verb* **1** to make new or good again **2** to grow new tissue or an organ to replace (a damaged part) **3** of a damaged part of the body: to be replaced by new tissue ♦ **regeneration** *noun*

regent *noun* someone who governs in place of a king or queen

reggae *noun* a strongly rhythmic type of music, originally from the West Indies

regicide (*pronounced* rej-i-said) *noun* **1** the killing of a monarch **2** someone who kills a monarch

regime or **régime** (*both pronounced* rei-**szeem**) *noun* a method or system of government or administration, or the government or administration itself

regiment *noun* (*pronounced* **rej**-i-ment) a body of soldiers, commanded by a colonel ➤ *verb* (*pronounced* **rej**-i-ment) to organize or control too strictly

regimental *adjective* of a regiment

regimentation *noun* too strict control

region *noun* **1** an area, a district **2** an area of the body near a specified part: *the abdominal region* **3** *maths* a subset of points on a plane or in space, any two of which can be joined by a line that is still inside the region • **in the region of** somewhere near: *in the region of £100*

regional *adjective* of a region

register *noun* **1** a written list (eg of attendances at school, of those eligible to vote, etc) **2** the distance between the highest and lowest notes of a voice or instrument **3** *computing* a device for storing small amounts of data ➤ *verb* **1** to write down in a register **2** to record, cast (a vote etc) **3** to show, record: *A thermometer registers temperature*

registered letter *noun* a letter insured against loss by the post office

registrar *noun* a public official who keeps a register of births, deaths and marriages

registration *noun* **1** an act or the process of registering **2** something registered

registry *noun* (*plural* **registries**) an office where a register is kept

registry office *noun* an office where records of births, deaths and marriages are kept and where marriages may be performed

regolith *noun, geography* loose material on the earth's surface, including fragments of rock, soil, etc

regress *verb* to go back to an earlier state ♦ **regression** *noun*

regression line *noun, statistics* a line drawn through the points on a scatter graph to summarize the relationship between the variables

regret *verb* (**regretting, regretted**) **1** to be sorry about: *I regret any inconvenience you have suffered* **2** to be sorry (to have to say something): *we regret to inform you* ➤ *noun* sorrow for anything

regretful *adjective* feeling or showing regret ♦ **regretfully** *adverb*

regrettable *adjective* to be regretted, unwelcome ♦ **regrettably** *adverb*

regular *adjective* **1** done according to rule or habit; usual **2** arranged in order; even: *regular teeth* **3** happening at certain fixed times **4** *maths* of a polygon: with all its sides and angles equal **5** *maths* of a tessellation: using only one type of regular polygon, eg squares or equilateral triangles ➤ *noun* **1** a soldier of the regular army **2** *informal* a frequent customer, especially of a pub, shop, etc

regular army *noun* the part of the army which is kept always in training, even in times of peace

regularity *noun* being regular

regularly *adverb* in a regular way or at a regular time

regulate *verb* **1** to control or adjust (the amount of available heat, sound, etc) **2** to control or adjust (a machine) so that it functions correctly **3** to adjust to a certain order or rate

regulation *noun* a rule, an order

regulator *noun* someone or something that regulates

regurgitate (*pronounced* ri-**ger**-ji-teit) *verb* to bring back into the mouth after swallowing ♦ **regurgitation** *noun*

rehabilitate *verb* **1** to give back rights, powers or health to **2** to train or accustom (a disabled person etc) to live a normal life ♦ **rehabilitation** *noun*

rehash *informal, verb* to express in different words, make or do again without any noticeable improvement ➤ *noun* something done again without any real improvement

rehearsal *noun* **1** a private practice of a play,

concert, etc before performance in public **2** a practice for a future event or action

rehearse *verb* **1** to practise beforehand **2** to recount (facts, events, etc) in order

Reichstag (*pronounced* **raikh**-stag) *noun, history* the lower house of the parliament of Germany, dominated by the Nazi Party during the Third Reich

reign *noun* **1** rule **2** the time during which a king, queen, etc rules ▸ *verb* **1** to rule **2** to prevail: *Silence reigned at last*

reimburse *verb* to pay (someone) an amount to cover expenses

reimbursement *noun* **1** reimbursing **2** repayment

rein *noun* **1** one of two straps attached to a bridle for guiding a horse **2** (**reins**) a simple device for controlling a very young child when walking ▸ *verb* to control with reins

reincarnation *noun* the rebirth of the soul in another body after death

reindeer *noun* (*plural* **reindeer**) a type of deer found in the far North

reinforce *verb* to strengthen (eg an army with men, concrete with iron)

reinforcement *noun* **1** the act of reinforcing **2** something which strengthens or assists **3** (**reinforcements**) additional troops

reinstate *verb* to put back in a former position

reinstatement *noun* **1** reinstating **2** re-establishment

reiterate *verb* to repeat several times
♦ **reiteration** *noun*

reject *verb* (*pronounced* ri-**jekt**) **1** to throw away, cast aside **2** to refuse to take: *She rejected his offer of help* **3** to turn down (eg an application, request) ▸ *noun* (*pronounced* **ree**-jekt) something discarded or refused

rejection *noun* **1** rejecting or being rejected **2** something that is rejected

rejig *verb* (**rejigging, rejigged**) to rearrange, especially in an unexpected way

rejoice *verb* to feel or show joy

rejoicing *noun* **1** being joyful **2** festivities, celebrations, merrymaking

rejoin[1] (*pronounced* ri-**join**) *verb* to say in reply, especially abruptly or wittily

rejoin[2] (*pronounced* ree-**join**) *verb* to join again

rejoinder (*pronounced* ri-**join**-der) *noun* an answer to a reply

rejuvenate *verb* to make young again
♦ **rejuvenation** *noun*

relapse *verb* to fall back (eg into ill health, bad habits) ▸ *noun* a falling back

relate *verb* **1** to show a connection between (two or more things) **2** to tell (a story)

related *adjective* **1** (often **related to someone**)

of the same family (as): *I'm related to him/We are not related* **2** connected

relation *noun* **1** someone who is of the same family, either by birth or marriage **2** a connection between two or more things

relationship *noun* **1** a connection between things or people **2** an emotional or sexual partnership or affair: *He isn't married, but he's in a steady relationship*

relative *noun* someone who is of the same family, either by birth or marriage ▸ *adjective* **1** comparative: *relative merits* **2** in proportion to: *salary relative to experience*

relative atomic mass *noun, chemistry* (sometimes shortened to **atomic mass**) the ratio of the average mass of one atom of an element to that of one twelfth of the mass of carbon-12, expressed in atomic mass units (*formerly called:* **atomic weight**)

relative clause *noun, grammar* a type of subordinate clause that refers to a word or phrase immediately before it and is joined to it by a word such as *which, who* or *whose*, eg *whose cat was lost* in *the man whose cat was lost*

relative error *noun, maths* error expressed as a ratio to the total amount

relative frequency *noun, statistics* the ratio of an actual number of events to the number of possible events, used to estimate probability

relatively *adverb* more or less: *relatively happy*

relative pronoun *noun, grammar* a pronoun, such as *which, who* or *whose*, that refers back to a word or phrase immediately before it and attaches a subordinate clause to it, as in *the children who are playing*

relativity *noun* **1** the state of being relative **2** (*also:* **special theory of relativity**) Einstein's theory that the mass of a body varies with its speed, based on the fundamental assumptions that all motion is relative and that the speed of light relative to an observer is constant **3** (*also:* **general theory of relativity**) this same theory extended to include gravitation and accelerated motion

relax *verb* **1** to become or make less tense **2** to slacken (eg your grip or control) **3** to make (laws or rules) less severe

relaxation *noun* **1** a slackening **2** rest from work, leisure

relay *verb* (**relaying, relayed**) to receive and pass on (eg a message, a television programme) ▸ *noun* **1** a fresh set of people to replace others at a job etc **2** a relay race **3** *telecommunications* a device for amplifying weak signals and passing them to another link **4** *electronics* a device that switches parts of a circuit on and off in response to a small change in current • **in relays** in groups which take over from one another in series

relay race noun a race in which members of each team take over from each other, each running a set distance

release verb 1 to set free 2 to let go: released his hand 3 to allow (news etc) to be made public 4 to offer (a record, book, etc) for sale, performance, etc 5 to move (a catch, brake, etc) so it no longer prevents something from operating ➤ noun 1 the act of releasing or state of being released, from captivity, duty, etc 2 the act of making a record, book, etc available for sale, performance, etc 3 something made available for sale, performance, etc 4 an item of news which is made public 5 a handle or catch which releases part of a mechanism

relegate verb 1 to put down (to a lower position, group etc) 2 to leave (a task etc) to someone else ✦ **relegation** noun

relent verb to treat someone less severely or strictly

relentless adjective 1 without pity 2 refusing to be turned from a purpose ✦ **relentlessly** adverb

relevant adjective having to do with what is being spoken about ✦ **relevance** noun

reliable adjective able to be trusted or counted on ✦ **reliability** noun

reliant adjective relying on or having confidence in ✦ **reliance** noun

relic noun something left over from a past time; an antiquity

relief noun 1 a lessening of pain or anxiety 2 release from a post or duty 3 people taking over someone's duty etc 4 help given to those in need: famine relief 5 the act of freeing (a town etc) from a siege 6 art a way of carving or moulding in which the design stands out from its background

relief map noun a map in which variations in the height of the land are shown by shading

relief rainfall or **orographic rainfall** noun, meteorology rainfall caused by moist air being forced upwards by contact with high land and then cooling and condensing (compare with: convectional rainfall, frontal rainfall)

relieve verb 1 to lessen (pain or anxiety) 2 to take over a duty from (someone else) 3 to come to the help of (a town etc under attack)

religion noun 1 belief in, or worship of, a god 2 a particular system of belief or worship, such as Christianity or Islam

religious adjective 1 of or relating to religion: religious beliefs 2 following the rules of worship of a particular religion very closely 3 conscientious ✦ **religiously** adverb

relinquish verb to give up, abandon: relinquish control

relish verb 1 to enjoy 2 to like the taste of ➤ noun (plural **relishes**) 1 enjoyment 2 flavour 3

something which adds flavour

relocate verb to move to another position, residence, etc

reluctance noun unwillingness; lack of enthusiasm

reluctant adjective unwilling ✦ **reluctantly** adverb

rely verb (**relies, relying, relied**) to have full trust in, depend (on)

REM abbreviation rapid eye movement

remain verb 1 to stay, not leave 2 to be left: Only two tins of soup remained 3 to be still the same: The problem remains unsolved

remainder noun 1 something which is left behind after removal of the rest 2 maths the number left after subtraction or division

remains plural noun 1 that which is left 2 a dead body

remake noun (pronounced **ree**-meik) a second making of a film etc ➤ verb (pronounced ree-**meik**) (**remaking, remade**) to make again

remand verb to put (someone) back in prison until more evidence is found ➤ noun: **on remand** having been remanded

remark verb 1 to say 2 to comment (on) 3 to notice ➤ noun something said

remarkable adjective deserving notice, unusual ✦ **remarkably** adverb: She prepared it remarkably quickly

remarry verb (**remarries, remarrying, remarried**) to marry again ✦ **remarriage** noun

remaster verb to make a new **master** (noun meaning 8) of (a piece of recorded music)

remedial (pronounced ri-**mee**-di-al) adjective 1 remedying 2 formerly relating to the teaching of children with learning difficulties

remedy noun (plural **remedies**) a cure for an illness, evil. etc ➤ verb (**remedies, remedying, remedied**) 1 to cure 2 to put right

remember verb 1 to keep in mind 2 to recall after having forgotten 3 to send your best wishes (to): Remember me to your mother 4 to reward, give a present to: He remembered her in his will

remembrance noun 1 the act of remembering 2 memory 3 something given to remind someone of a person or event, a keepsake 4 (**remembrances**) a friendly greeting

remind verb 1 to bring (something) back to a person's mind: Remind me to post that letter 2 to cause (someone) to think about (someone or something) by resemblance: She reminds me of her sister

reminder noun something which reminds

reminisce (pronounced rem-i-**nis**) verb to think and talk about things remembered from the past

reminiscence (pronounced rem-i-**nis**-ens) noun 1 something remembered from the past 2 (**reminiscences**) memories, especially told or written

reminiscent (*pronounced* rem-i-**nis**-ent) *adjective* **1** reminding (of): *reminiscent of Paris* **2** in a mood to remember and think about past events etc

remiss *adjective* careless, unthinking

remission *noun* **1** a shortening of a prison sentence **2** a lessening of a disease or illness

remit *verb* (*pronounced* ri-**mit**) (**remitting, remitted**) **1** to pardon, excuse (a crime etc) **2** to wipe out, cancel (a debt etc) **3** to lessen, become less intense **4** to send (money) **5** to hand over (eg a prisoner to a higher court) ➤ *noun* (*pronounced* **ree**-mit) the authority given to a person or group in dealing with a matter

remittance *noun* **1** the sending of money in payment **2** the money sent

remix *music, verb* (*pronounced* ree-**miks**) to mix (a recording) again, changing the balance of the different parts, etc ➤ *noun* (*pronounced* **ree**-miks) a remixed recording

remnant *noun* a small piece or number left over

remonstrate *verb* to protest (about)

remorse *noun* regret about something done in the past

remorseful *adjective* full of remorse, sorrowful

remorseless *adjective* having no remorse; cruel

remote *adjective* **1** far away in time or place **2** isolated, far from other people **3** slight: *a remote chance* ➤ *noun* a remote control device, eg for a television set

remote access *noun, computing* access to a computer from a terminal at another site

remote control *noun* **1** the control of devices from a distance, using electrical signals or radio waves **2** a battery-operated device for transmitting such waves

remote sensor *noun* a device which scans the earth and other planets from space in order to collect data about them to transmit to a central computer ◆ **remote sensing** *noun*

removal *noun* the act of removing, especially of moving furniture to a new home

remove *verb* **1** to take (something) from its place **2** to dismiss from a job **3** to take off (clothes etc) **4** to get rid of: *remove a stain* ➤ *noun* a stage away (from): *one remove from anarchy* ◆ **remover** *noun*

removed *adjective* **1** distant (from) **2** of cousins: separated by a generation: *my first cousin once removed* (my cousin's child)

REM sleep *noun* a phase of restless sleep accompanied by rapid eye movement and dreaming

remunerate *verb* to pay (someone) for something done

remuneration *noun* pay, salary

remunerative *adjective* profitable

renaissance (*pronounced* ri-**nei**-sans) *noun* **1** a rebirth **2** a period of cultural revival and growth **3** (**the Renaissance**) the cultural revival and transition from the Middle Ages to modern times

renal (*pronounced* **ree**-nal) *adjective* of the kidneys

rend *verb* (**rending, rent**) *old* to tear (apart), divide

render *verb* **1** to give (eg thanks) **2** to translate into another language **3** to perform (music etc) **4** to cause to be: *His words rendered me speechless* **5** to melt (fat), especially to clarify it

rendezvous (*pronounced* **ron**-dei-voo) *noun* (*plural* **rendezvous** – *pronounced* **ron**-dei-vooz**) **1** a meeting place fixed beforehand **2** an arranged meeting

rendition *noun* **1** a performance of a piece of music, a dramatic role, etc **2** a translation

renegade (*pronounced* **ren**-i-geid) *noun* someone who deserts their own side, religion, or beliefs

renege or **renegue** (*pronounced* ri-**neig**) *verb* to go back (on): *He reneged on his promise to take us to the theatre* ☉ Comes from Latin *negare* meaning 'to deny'

renew *verb* **1** to make as if new again **2** to begin again: *renew your efforts* **3** to make valid for a further period (eg a driving licence) **4** to replace: *renew the water in the tank* ◆ **renewable** *adjective*

renewal *noun* renewing or being renewed: *My contract is due for renewal*

rennet *noun* a substance used in curdling milk for making cheeses etc, especially an extract from the stomachs of calves containing rennin

rennin *noun, biology, chemistry* an enzyme found in gastric juice that causes milk to curdle

renounce *verb* to give up publicly or formally

renovate *verb* to make (something) like new again, mend ◆ **renovation** *noun*

renown *noun* fame

renowned *adjective* famous

rent¹ *noun* payment made for the use of property or land ➤ *verb* **1** to pay rent for (a house etc) **2** (*also* **rent out**) to receive rent for (a house etc)

rent² *old, noun* a tear, a split ➤ *verb* past form of rend

rental *noun* money paid as rent

renunciation *noun* an act of renouncing: *their renunciation of trade links with Japan*

reorganize or **reorganise** *verb* to put in a different order ◆ **reorganization** *noun*

rep *noun, short for* **1** representative: *a sales rep* **2** repertory

repair¹ *verb* **1** to mend **2** to make up for (a wrong) ➤ *noun* **1** state, condition: *in bad repair* **2** mending: *in need of repair* **3** a mend, a patch

repair² *verb, old* to go, move: *repair to the drawing room*

reparation *noun* compensation for a wrong

repartee *noun* **1** an exchange of witty remarks **2** skill in witty conversation

repast (*pronounced* ri-**pahst**) *noun, old* a meal

repatriate *verb* to send (someone) back to their own country ♦ **repatriation** *noun*

repay *verb* (**repaying, repaid**) **1** to pay back **2** to give or do something in return: *He repaid her kindness with a gift*

repayment *noun* repaying

repeal *verb* to do away with, cancel (especially a law) ➤ *noun* the cancellation of a law etc

repeat *verb* **1** to say or do over again **2** to say from memory **3** to pass on (someone's words) ➤ *noun* a musical passage, television programme etc played or shown for a second time

repeatedly *adverb* again and again

repeater *noun* **1** someone or something that repeats **2** a clock or watch that strikes the last hour or quarter hour when required **3** a gun that can be fired several times without reloading **4** a device for automatically re-transmitting a telegraphic message **5** a device for amplifying the signal in a telephone circuit or a cable

repel *verb* (**repelling, repelled**) **1** to drive back or away **2** to disgust

repellent *adjective* disgusting ➤ *noun* something that repels: *insect repellent*

repent *verb* to be sorry for your actions • **repent of something** to regret it

repentant *adjective* feeling or showing sorrow and regret for your actions ♦ **repentance** *noun*

repercussion *noun* an indirect or resultant effect of something which has happened

repertoire (*pronounced* **rep**-er-twah) *noun* **1** the range of works performed by a musician, theatre company etc **2** the range of skills, techniques, talents, etc that someone or something has

repertory *noun* (*plural* **repertories**) **1** repertoire **2** acting in repertory theatres collectively

repertory company *noun* a group of actors which performs a series of plays at one theatre

repertory theatre *noun* a theatre with a permanent company which performs a series of plays

repetition *noun* **1** the act of repeating or being repeated **2** a thing which is repeated ♦ **repetitious** *adjective*

repetitive *adjective* repeating too often, predictable

rephrase *verb* to express (something) in different words

replace *verb* **1** to put (something) back where it was **2** to put in place of another ♦ **replacement** *noun*

replacement level *noun, geography* the birth rate required for the number of people in a population to remain the same

replay *noun* (*pronounced* **ree**-plei) **1** a repeat of a contest or game, because there was no winner the first time **2** the playing again of a recording, piece of film, etc ➤ *verb* (*pronounced* ree-**plei**) to play (a game, recording, etc) again

replenish *verb* to refill (a stock, supply)

replete *adjective* full

replica *noun* an exact copy of a work of art, etc

replicate *verb* (*pronounced* **re**-pli-keit) **1** to make a replica of something **2** to repeat (a scientific experiment) **3** of DNA, a molecule, etc: to make a replica of itself through cell division ➤ *adjective* (*pronounced* **re**-pli-kat) **1** *biology* of a leaf, insect's wing, etc: folded back **2** of a scientific experiment: being a repeat ♦ **replication** *noun*

reply *verb* (**replies, replying, replied**) to speak or act in answer to something ➤ *noun* (*plural* **replies**) an answer

report *verb* **1** to pass on news **2** to give a description of (an event) **3** to give information about events for a newspaper **4** to make a formal complaint against ➤ *noun* **1** a statement of facts **2** an account, a description **3** a news article **4** a rumour **5** a written description of a school pupil's work **6** a loud, explosive noise

reported speech see **indirect speech**

reporter *noun* a news journalist

repose¹ *formal, noun* sleep, rest ➤ *verb* to rest

repose² *verb, formal* to place (eg trust in a person)

repository *noun* (*plural* **repositories**) a storage place for safe keeping

repossess *verb* to take back (goods, property), especially because of non-payment

reprehensible *adjective* deserving blame

represent *verb* **1** to speak or act on behalf of others: *representing the tenants' association* **2** to stand for, be a symbol of: *Each letter represents a sound* **3** to claim to be **4** to explain, point out **5** to present an image of or portray, especially through painting or sculpture

representation *noun* **1** an image, a picture **2** (**representations**) a strong claim or appeal

representative *adjective* **1** typical, characteristic: *a representative specimen* **2** standing or acting for others ➤ *noun* **1** someone who acts or speaks on behalf of others **2** (*short* *form* **rep**) a travelling salesperson for a company

repress *verb* **1** to keep down by force **2** to keep under control

repression *noun* **1** the strict controlling of people, not allowing them to do things such as vote in elections or attend religious worship **2** *psychology* the deliberate exclusion of an unpleasant or unacceptable thought, memory or wish from conscious thought

repressive *adjective* severe; harsh

reprieve *verb* **1** to pardon (a criminal) **2** to relieve from trouble or difficulty ➤ *noun* a pardon, a relief

reprimand *verb* to scold severely, censure ➤ *noun* scolding, censure

reprint *verb* (*pronounced* ree-**print**) to print more copies of (a book etc) ➤ *noun* (*pronounced* **ree**-print) another printing of a book

reprisal *noun* a return of wrong for wrong, a repayment in kind

reprise (*pronounced* ri-**preez**) *music, noun* the repeating of a passage or theme ➤ *verb* to repeat (an earlier passage or theme) ℗ Comes from French *reprendre* meaning 'to take back'

reproach *verb* to scold, blame ➤ *noun* (*plural* **reproaches**) **1** blame, discredit **2** a cause of blame or censure • **beyond reproach** too good to be criticized

reproachful *adjective* expressing or full of reproach

reprobate (*pronounced* **rep**-roh-beit) *noun* someone of evil or immoral habits ➤ *adjective* immoral

reproduce *verb* **1** to produce a copy of **2** to produce (offspring)

reproduction *noun* **1** a copy or imitation (especially of a work of art) **2** the act or process of producing (offspring)

reproductive *adjective* involving, or required for, reproduction

reproductive system *noun, biology* the system of organs involved with reproduction, which includes the uterus in human females and the testes in human males

reproof *noun* a scolding, criticism for a fault

reprove *verb* to scold, blame

reproving *adjective* disapproving

reptile *noun* a scaly, cold-blooded animal, such as a snake, lizard, etc

reptilian (*pronounced* rep-**til**-i-an) *adjective* of or like reptiles

republic *noun* (a state with) a form of government without a monarch, in which power is in the hands of elected representatives

republican *adjective* **1** of or favouring a republic **2** (**Republican**) *US* belonging to the Republican Party ➤ *noun* **1** someone who

believes in a republican form of government **2** (**Republican**) *US* a supporter of the Republican Party **3** (**Republican**) in Northern Ireland: someone who advocates union with the Republic of Ireland ◆ **republicanism** *noun* (meaning 1)

Republican Party *noun* the more conservative of the two chief political parties in the USA (*compare with*: **Democratic Party**)

repudiate (*pronounced* ri-**pyoo**-di-eit) *verb* to refuse to acknowledge or accept: *repudiate a suggestion* ◆ **repudiation** *noun*

repugnance *noun* aversion, disgust

repugnant *adjective* hateful, distasteful

repulse *verb* **1** to drive back **2** to reject, snub

repulsion *noun* **1** disgust **2** *physics* a force that drives two objects apart

repulsive *adjective* causing disgust, loathsome

reputable (*pronounced* **rep**-yuw-ta-bl) *adjective* having a good reputation, well thought of

reputation *noun* **1** opinion held by people in general of a particular person **2** good name

repute *noun* reputation

reputed *adjective* **1** considered, thought (to be something): *reputed to be dangerous* **2** supposed: *the reputed author of the book*

reputedly *adverb* in the opinion of most people

request *verb* to ask for ➤ *noun* **1** an asking for something **2** something asked for

requiem (*pronounced* **rek**-wi-em) *noun* a hymn or mass sung for the dead

---

℗ A Latin word meaning literally 'rest', the first word in former church services for the dead

---

require *verb* **1** to need **2** to demand, order

requirement *noun* **1** something needed **2** a demand

requisite (*pronounced* **rek**-wi-zit) *adjective* required; necessary ➤ *noun* something needed or necessary

requisition *noun* a formal request for supplies, eg for a school or army ➤ *verb* to put in a formal request for

requite *verb* **1** to repay, give back in return **2** to avenge (one action) by another

rerun *verb* (*pronounced* ree-**run**) (**rerunning, reran, rerun**) to run again ➤ *noun* (*pronounced* **ree**-run) a repeated television programme

resat past form of **resit**

re-scale or **rescale** *verb* to form (something) on a different, usually smaller, scale

rescind (*pronounced* ri-**sind**) *verb* to cancel or revoke (an order, law, custom, etc) ℗ Comes from Latin *rescindere* meaning 'to cut off'

rescue *verb* **1** to save from danger **2** to free from capture ➤ *noun* an act of saving from danger or capture ◆ **rescuer** *noun*

research noun (plural **researches**) close and careful scientific study to try to find out new facts: *cancer research* ➤ verb to study carefully ♦ **researcher** noun

resemblance noun likeness

resemble verb to look like or be like: *He doesn't resemble his sister*

resent verb to feel injured, annoyed, or insulted by

resentful adjective full of or caused by resentment

resentment noun annoyance, bitterness

reservation noun 1 the act of reserving, booking 2 an exception or condition: *She agreed to the plan, but with certain reservations* 3 doubt, objection: *I had reservations about their friendship* 4 an area of land set aside by treaty for Native American people in the United States

reserve verb 1 to set aside for future use 2 to book, have kept for you (eg a seat, a table) ➤ noun 1 something reserved 2 (**reserves**) troops outside the regular army kept ready to help those already fighting 3 a piece of land set apart for some reason: *a nature reserve* 4 shyness, reluctance to speak or act openly

reserved adjective 1 shy, reluctant to speak openly 2 kept back for a particular person or purpose

reservist noun a member of the military reserves

reservoir (pronounced **rez**-er-vwah) noun 1 an artificial lake where water is kept in store 2 biology part of an animal or plant where fluid is retained

reshuffle politics, verb (pronounced ree-**shuf**-l) to rearrange ministerial posts within (a government cabinet) ➤ noun (pronounced **ree**-shuf-l) a rearrangement of a cabinet

reside verb 1 formal to live, stay (in) 2 of authority etc: to be placed (in)

residence noun 1 formal the building where someone lives 2 living, or time of living, in a place

resident noun someone who lives in a particular place: *a resident of Dublin* ➤ adjective 1 living in (a place) 2 living in a place of work: *the resident caretaker*

residential adjective 1 of an area: containing houses rather than shops, offices, etc 2 providing accommodation: *a residential course*

residual adjective remaining; left over ➤ noun 1 something that is left over 2 statistics the difference between the measured value of a quantity and its theoretical value

residue noun something that is left over

resign verb to give up (a job, position, etc) • **resign yourself to** to accept (a situation) patiently and calmly

resignation noun 1 the act of resigning 2 a letter to say you are resigning 3 patient, calm acceptance of a situation

resigned adjective patient, not actively complaining

resilient adjective 1 able to recover easily from misfortune, hurt, etc 2 of an object: readily recovering its original shape after being bent, twisted, etc ♦ **resilience** noun

resin (pronounced **rez**-in) noun 1 a sticky substance produced by certain plants (eg firs, pines) 2 chemistry a semisolid or solid mixture of organic compounds with no definite melting point and a tendency to crystallize

resinous adjective like or containing resin

resist verb 1 to struggle against, oppose 2 to stop yourself from (doing something)

resistance noun 1 the act of resisting 2 the ability to withstand something damaging 3 an organized opposition, especially to an occupying force 4 electricity (symbol **R**) a measure of how much a material or an electrical device opposes the flow of an electric current through it 5 physics a measure of how much a material opposes the flow of heat through it 6 a resistor

resistant adjective able to resist or remain unaffected or undamaged by something

resistor noun a device that controls current in an electric circuit by providing resistance

resit verb (pronounced ree-**sit**) (**resitting, resat**) to sit (an examination) again ➤ noun (pronounced **ree**-sit) a retaking of an examination

resolute adjective determined, with mind made up ♦ **resolutely** adverb

resolution noun 1 determination of mind or purpose 2 a firm decision (to do something) 3 a proposal put before a meeting 4 a decision expressed by a public meeting 5 the ability of a television screen, photographic film, etc to reproduce an image in fine detail

resolve verb 1 to decide firmly (to do something) 2 to solve (a difficulty) 3 to break up into parts ➤ noun a firm purpose

resonance noun 1 the quality of being resonant 2 sound produced by something vibrating in sympathy with another thing vibrating nearby 3 a ringing quality of the human voice 4 physics a rapid increase in the amplitude of the wave in a vibrating system, when a constant force is applied at intervals that match the frequency of the wave

resonant adjective 1 echoing, resounding 2 producing echoing sounds: *resonant walls* 3 with a ringing quality: *a resonant voice*

resonate verb to echo

resort verb: (**resort to**) 1 to begin to use 2 to

turn to in a difficulty: *resorting to bribery* ➤ *noun* a popular holiday destination • **in the last resort** when all else fails

resound (*pronounced* ri-**zound**) *verb* **1** to sound loudly **2** to echo

resounding *adjective* **1** echoing **2** thorough: *a resounding victory*

resourceful *adjective* good at finding ways out of difficulties

resources *plural noun* **1** a source of supplying what is required **2** the natural sources of wealth in a country etc **3** money or other property **4** an ability to handle situations skilfully and cleverly

respect *verb* **1** to feel a high regard for **2** to treat with consideration: *respect his wishes* ➤ *noun* **1** high regard, esteem **2** consideration **3** a detail, a way: *alike in some respects* **4** (**respects**) good wishes • **in respect of** or **with respect to** with reference to, concerning

respectable *adjective* **1** worthy of respect **2** having a good reputation **3** considerable, fairly good: *a respectable score* ♦ **respectability** *noun*

respectful *adjective* showing respect ♦ **respectfully** *adverb*

respecting *preposition* about; concerning; with regard to

respective *adjective* belonging to each (person or thing mentioned) separately: *My brother and his friends went to their respective homes* (that is, each went to their own home)

respectively *adverb* in the order given: *James, Andrew and Ian were first, second and third respectively*

respiration *noun* **1** the act of respiring or breathing **2** *biology, chemistry* the process by which organisms take in oxygen and give out carbon dioxide **3** *biology, chemistry* the process by which glucose and other food substances are broken down to release energy in the form of ATP

respirator *noun* **1** a mask worn over the mouth and nose to purify the air taken in **2** *medicine* a device to help people breathe when they are too ill to do so naturally

respiratory system (*pronounced* **res**-pir-a-to-ri) *noun* the system of organs in which gas exchange takes place, which includes the lungs and windpipe in humans

respire *verb* **1** to breathe **2** *biology, chemistry* to release energy from the breakdown of organic compounds

respite (*pronounced* **res**-pait) *noun* a pause, a rest: *no respite from work*

resplendent *adjective* very bright or splendid in appearance

respond *verb* **1** to answer **2** to react in response to: *I waved but he didn't respond* **3** to show a positive reaction to: *responding to treatment*

response *noun* **1** a reply **2** an action, feeling etc in answer to another **3** an answer made by the congregation during a church service

responsibility *noun* (*plural* **responsibilities**) **1** something or someone for which one is responsible **2** the state of being responsible or having important duties for which you are responsible

responsible *adjective* **1** involving making important decisions etc: *a responsible post* **2** trustworthy • **responsible for 1** being the cause of: *responsible for this mess* **2** liable to be blamed for: *responsible for the conduct of his staff*

responsive *adjective* quick to react, to show sympathy, etc

rest[1] *noun* **1** a break in work **2** a sleep **3** *music* a pause in playing or singing for a given number of beats **4** a support, a prop: *a book rest* ➤ *verb* **1** to stop working for a time **2** to be still **3** to sleep **4** to depend (on), be based on: *The case rests on your evidence* **5** to stop, develop no further: *I can't let the matter rest there* **6** to lean or place on a support • **rest with** to be the responsibility of: *The choice rests with you*

rest[2] *noun*: **the rest 1** what is left, the remainder **2** the others, those not mentioned: *I went home but the rest went to the cinema*

restaurant *noun* a place where meals may be bought and eaten

restaurateur (*pronounced* res-taw-ra-**ter**) *noun* the owner or manager of a restaurant

restful *adjective* **1** relaxing **2** relaxed

resting potential *noun, biology* the difference in electrical potential across the membrane of a nerve cell that is not conducting an impulse (*compare with:* **action potential**)

restitution *noun* **1** the return of what has been lost or taken away **2** compensation for harm or injury done

restive *adjective* restless, impatient

restless *adjective* **1** unable to keep still **2** agitated ♦ **restlessly** *adverb* ♦ **restlessness** *noun*

restoration *noun* **1** the act of giving back something lost or stolen **2** a model or reconstruction (eg of a ruin)

restorative *adjective* curing, giving strength

restore *verb* **1** to put or give back **2** to repair (a building, a painting, etc) so that it looks as it used to **3** to cure (a person)

restrain *verb* **1** to hold back (from) **2** to keep under control ♦ **restrained** *adjective* **1** able to control your emotions **2** showing restraint, not excessive

restraint *noun* **1** the act of restraining **2** self-control **3** a tie or bond used to restrain

restrict *verb* **1** to limit, keep within certain bounds: *restricted space for parking* **2** to open only to certain people: *restricted area*

restriction *noun* **1** an act or instance of restricting **2** a regulation or rule which restricts or limits

restrictive *adjective* restricting

rest room *noun, US* a room with lavatories and washbasins, eg in a shop, theatre, factory, etc

result *noun* **1** a consequence of something already done or said **2** the answer to a sum **3** a score in a game ➤ *verb*: **result from** to be the result or effect of • **result in** to have as a result: *result in a draw*

resultant *adjective* happening as a result ➤ *noun, maths, physics* a vector that is the sum of two or more vectors, eg a single force which is the result of two or more forces acting on an object

resume *verb* **1** to begin again after an interruption: *resume a discussion* **2** to take again: *He resumed his seat*

résumé (*pronounced* **rez**-yoo-mei) *noun* **1** a summary **2** *US* a curriculum vitae

resumption *noun* the act of resuming

resurgence *noun* the act of returning to life, to a state of activity, etc after a period of decline

resurgent *adjective* rising again, becoming prominent again

resurrect *verb* to bring back to life or into use

resurrection *noun* **1** a rising from the dead **2** (**the Resurrection**) *Christianity* the rising of Christ from the dead **3** the act of bringing back into use

resuscitate (*pronounced* ri-**sus**-i-teit) *verb* to bring back to consciousness, revive ◆ **resuscitation** *noun*

retail *verb* **1** (*pronounced* **ree**-teil) to sell goods to someone who is going to use them, rather than to another seller (*compare with*: **wholesale**) **2** (*pronounced* ree-**teil**) to tell (eg a story) fully and in detail ➤ *noun* (*pronounced* **ree**-teil) the sale of goods to the actual user

retailer *noun* a shopkeeper, a trader

retain *verb* **1** to keep possession of **2** to keep (something) in mind **3** to reserve (someone's services) by paying a fee in advance **4** to hold back, keep in place

retainer *noun* **1** a fee for services paid in advance **2** *old* a servant (to a family)

retake *verb* (*pronounced* ree-**teik**) (**retaking, retook, retaken**) **1** to take or capture again **2** to sit (an examination) again ➤ *noun* (*pronounced* **ree**-teik) **1** an examination that someone sits again **2** the filming of part of a film again

retaliate *verb* to return an insult, injury, etc with a similar one, hit back ◆ **retaliation** *noun*

retard *verb* **1** to keep back, hinder **2** to make slow or late

retardation *noun* retarding or being retarded

retarded *adjective* slow in mental or physical growth

retch *verb* to make the actions and sound of vomiting, without actually vomiting

retention *noun* **1** the act of holding in or keeping **2** the act of retaining the services of (eg a lawyer)

retentive *adjective* able to hold or retain well: *a retentive memory*

rethink *verb* (*pronounced* ree-**thingk**) to think about (a plan etc) again, usually to reach a different conclusion ➤ *noun* (*pronounced* **ree**-thingk) an act of rethinking

reticent *adjective* unwilling to speak openly and freely, reserved ◆ **reticence** *noun*

reticulum (*pronounced* ri-**tik**-yuw-lum) *noun* (*plural* **reticula**), *biology* **1** a fine network, especially of fibres, vessels, etc **2** the second stomach of a ruminant

retina (*pronounced* **ret**-i-na) *noun* (*plural* **retinas** or **retinae** – *pronounced* **ret**-i-nee) the light-sensitive tissue at the back of the eye that relays nerve impulses to the brain, which interprets them as vision

retinol *noun* vitamin A

retinue *noun* the attendants of someone important

retire *verb* **1** to give up work permanently, usually because of age **2** *formal* to go to bed **3** to draw back, retreat

retired *adjective* **1** having given up work **2** out-of-the-way, quiet

retirement *noun* **1** the act of retiring from work **2** someone's life after they have given up work

retiring *adjective* shy, avoiding being noticed

retook past tense of **retake**

retort[1] *verb* to make a quick and witty reply ➤ *noun* a quick, witty reply

retort[2] *noun* a bottle of thin glass used for distilling liquids

retouch *verb* to improve or repair (a photograph, painting, etc) by making small alterations

retrace *verb* to go over again: *retrace your steps*

retract *verb* **1** to take back (something said or given) **2** to draw back, pull in: *The cat retracted its claws*

retractable *adjective* able to be retracted

retraction *noun* a retracting (especially of something one has said, agreed or promised)

retractor *noun, anatomy* a muscle that retracts or pulls in a part of the body

retreat *verb* **1** to draw back, withdraw **2** to go away ➤ *noun* **1** a movement backwards corresponding to the advance of an enemy **2** a withdrawal **3** a quiet, peaceful place

retrenchment *noun* economizing in spending

retribution *noun* punishment

retrieve *verb* **1** to get back, recover (something lost) **2** to search for and fetch

retriever *noun* a breed of dog trained to find and fetch shot birds

retro *adjective* recreating a style of the past for effect

retro- *prefix* forms words containing the meaning 'backwards' or 'behind' ⊙ Comes from Latin *retro* meaning 'back' or 'behind'

retroflex *adjective* bent backwards

retrograde *adjective* **1** going backwards **2** going from a better to a worse stage

retrospect *noun*: **in retrospect** considering or looking back on the past

retrospective *adjective* **1** looking back on past events **2** of a law: applying to the past as well as the present and the future ➤ *noun* a retrospective exhibition etc

retrovirus *noun, biology* a virus with genetic material consisting of RNA which is copied into DNA to allow integration into the host cell's DNA ♦ **retroviral** *adjective*

retry *verb* (**retries, retrying, retried**) to submit (someone) to a further court trial: *The suspect was retried when new evidence came to light* ♦ **retrial** *noun*

return *verb* **1** to go or come back **2** to give, send, pay etc back **3** to elect to parliament ➤ *noun* **1** the act of returning **2** a profit: *the return on your investment* **3** a statement of income for calculating income tax **4** the enter key on a computer keyboard • **by return** sent by the first post back

returning officer *noun* an official in charge of running an election in a constituency, counting the votes and declaring the result

return ticket *noun* a ticket which covers a journey both to and from a place

reunify *verb* (**reunifies, reunifying, reunified**) to unify (especially a country that had been divided) again ♦ **reunification** *noun*

reunion *noun* a meeting of people who have been apart for some time

reunite *verb* to join after having been separated

Rev or **Revd** *abbreviation* Reverend

rev *informal, noun* a revolution of an engine ➤ *verb* (often **rev up**) (**revving, revved**) to increase the speed of (an engine)

revamp *verb* to renovate, renew the appearance of

reveal *verb* **1** to make known **2** to show

reveille (*pronounced* ri-**val**-i) *noun* a bugle call at daybreak to waken soldiers

revel *verb* (**revelling, revelled**) **1** to take great

delight (in) **2** to celebrate ➤ *noun* (**revels**) festivities

revelation *noun* **1** the act of revealing **2** something unexpected which is made known **3** (**Revelation**) Apocalypse, the last book of the New Testament

revelry *noun* (*plural* **revelries**) noisy lively enjoyment, festivities or merrymaking ♦ **reveller** or *US* **reveler** *noun*

revenge *noun* **1** harm done to someone in return for harm they themselves have committed **2** the desire to do such harm ➤ *verb* to inflict punishment in return for harm done: *revenging his father's murder* • **revenge yourself** to take revenge: *He revenged himself on his enemies* ♦ **revengeful** *adjective*

revenue *noun* **1** money received as payment **2** a country's total income

reverberate *verb* to echo and re-echo, resound ♦ **reverberation** *noun*

revere *verb* to look upon with great respect

reverence *noun* great respect

reverend *adjective* **1** worthy of respect **2** (**Reverend**) a title given to a member of the clergy (*short form* **Rev** or **Revd**) ⊙ Comes from Latin *reverendus* meaning 'who must be respected'

! Do not confuse: **reverend** and **reverent**

reverent or **reverential** *adjective* showing respect ⊙ Comes from Latin *reverent-*, a form of *reverens* meaning 'respecting'

reverie (*pronounced* **rev**-e-ri) *noun* a daydream

reversal *noun* the act of reversing or being reversed

reverse *verb* **1** to turn upside down or the other way round **2** to move backwards **3** to undo (a decision, policy, etc) ➤ *noun* **1** the opposite (of) **2** the other side (of a coin etc) **3** a defeat

reversible *adjective* **1** able to be reversed: *a reversible decision* **2** of clothes: able to be worn with either side out

reversible reaction *noun, chemistry* **1** a reaction occurring in both directions at the same time, so products are converted back to reactants while reactants are being converted to products **2** a reaction that can be made to proceed in one direction or the other by altering the conditions

revert *verb* **1** to go back to an earlier topic **2** to return to a former state **3** *biology* to return to an earlier, usually less advanced, type ♦ **reversion** *noun*

revetment *noun, geography* a wall to hold back solid material, such as earth

review *verb* **1** to give an opinion or criticism of (an artistic work) **2** to consider again: *review the* facts **3** to inspect (eg troops) ➤ *noun* **1** a critical opinion of a book etc **2** a magazine consisting of reviews **3** a second look, a reconsideration **4** an inspection of troops etc

! Do not confuse with: **revue**

reviewer *noun* someone who reviews, a critic

revile *verb* to say harsh things about

revise *verb* **1** to correct faults in and make improvements **2** to study notes etc in preparation for an examination **3** to change (eg an opinion)

revision *noun* **1** the act of revising **2** a revised version of a book etc

revisionism *noun, politics* the policy of changing previously established political ideas, doctrines, etc ✦ **revisionist** *noun & adjective*

revitalize or **revitalise** *verb* to give new life or energy to

revival *noun* **1** a return to life, use, etc **2** a fresh show of interest: *a religious revival*

revive *verb* to bring or come back to life, use or fame

revoke *verb* **1** to cancel (a decision etc) **2** to fail to follow suit in a card game

revolt *verb* **1** to rise up (against), rebel **2** to feel disgust (at) **3** to disgust ➤ *noun* a rising, a rebellion

revolting *adjective* causing disgust

revolution *noun* **1** a full turn round a centre **2** the act of turning round a centre **3** a general uprising against those in power **4** a complete change in ideas, way of doing things, etc

revolutionary *adjective* **1** relating to a revolution **2** bringing about great changes **3** turning ➤ *noun* (*plural* **revolutionaries**) someone who is involved in, or is in favour of, revolution

revolutionize or **revolutionise** *verb* to bring about a complete change in

revolve *verb* to roll or turn round • **revolve around** or **revolve about** to have as a centre, focus, or main point

revolver *noun* a kind of pistol

revue *noun* a light theatre show, with short topical plays or sketches

! Do not confuse with: **review**

revulsion *noun* **1** disgust **2** a sudden change of feeling, especially from love to hate

reward *noun* **1** something given in return for work done or for good behaviour etc **2** a sum of money offered for helping to find a criminal, lost property, etc ➤ *verb* **1** to give a reward to **2** to give a reward for (a service)

rewarding *adjective* giving pleasure or satisfaction

rewind *verb* (**rewinding, rewound**) to wind back (a spool, tape, film, etc) to the beginning

rewire *verb* to fit (a house etc) with new electrical wiring

reword *verb* to express something in different words ✦ **rewording** *noun*

rework *verb* **1** to alter something in order to use it again **2** to revise or rewrite something ✦ **reworking** *noun*

rewritable *adjective, computing* of data: capable of being recorded in the area from which it has been read

rewrite *verb* (*pronounced* ree-**rait**) (**rewriting, rewrote, rewritten**) **1** to write again or in different words **2** *computing* to retain (data) in an area of store by recording it in the place from which it has been read ➤ *noun* (*pronounced* **ree**-rait) something rewritten

Rf *symbol, chemistry* rutherfordium

Rg *symbol, chemistry* roentgenium

Rh *abbreviation* rhesus

Rh *symbol, chemistry* rhodium

rhapsodize or **rhapsodise** *verb* to talk or write enthusiastically (about)

rhapsody *noun* (*plural* **rhapsodies**) music or poetry which expresses strong feeling • **go into rhapsodies over** to show wild enthusiasm for

rhenium (*pronounced* **ree**-ni-um) *noun, chemistry* (symbol **Re**) a rare, silvery-white metallic element

⊙ Named after the River *Rhine* in Germany

rheostat (*pronounced* **ree**-oh-stat) *noun, electricity* a resistor that enables the resistance in an electric circuit to be increased or decreased

rhesus factor (*pronounced* **ree**-sus) *noun* a substance present in most people's blood

⊙ After the *rhesus monkey*, an animal used in medical research, in which this substance was discovered

rhesus-negative *adjective* having blood which does not contain the rhesus factor

rhesus-positive *adjective* having blood which contains the rhesus factor

rhetoric (*pronounced* **ret**-or-ik) *noun* **1** the art of good speaking or writing **2** language which is too showy, consisting of unnecessarily long or difficult words etc

rhetorical (*pronounced* ri-**tor**-i-kal) *adjective* **1** relating to or using rhetoric **2** of language: over-elaborate

rhetorical question *noun* a question that is asked for effect and does not need an answer

rheumatic *adjective* relating to or caused by rheumatism

rheumatoid arthritis *noun* a disease causing swollen and painful joints

rheumatism *noun* a disease which causes stiffness and pain in the joints

rhinestone *noun* an artificial paste diamond

rhino *noun* (*plural* **rhinos**) short for rhinoceros

rhino- or **rhin-** *prefix* of or relating to the nose ⊙ Comes from Greek *rhis* meaning 'nose'

rhinoceros *noun* (*plural* **rhinoceros** or **rhinoceroses**) a large, thick-skinned animal, with a horn (or two) on its nose (often shortened to **rhino**)

rhinoplasty *noun* (*plural* **rhinoplasties**) plastic surgery on the nose

rhizome (*pronounced* **raiz**-ohm) *noun, botany* a thick, horizontal, underground stem which produces roots and leafy shoots (*also called:* **rootstock**)

rhodium *noun, chemistry* (symbol **Rh**) a hard, silvery-white metallic element

⊙ Comes from Greek *rhodon* meaning 'rose', because of its rose-coloured salts

rhododendron *noun* a flowering shrub with thick evergreen leaves and large flowers

rhomboid *noun, maths* a quadrilateral where only the opposite sides and angles are equal

rhombus *noun* (*plural* **rhombuses** or **rhombi** – *pronounced* **rom**-bai), *maths* a geometrical figure with four equal straight sides

rhubarb *noun* a plant with long, red-skinned, edible stalks

rhyme *noun* **1** a similarity in sounds between words or their endings, eg *humble* and *crumble*, or *convention* and *prevention* **2** a word which sounds like another **3** a short poem ➤ *verb* (sometimes **rhyme with**) to sound like, be rhymes: *'Harp' rhymes with 'carp'*

rhyme scheme *noun* the particular pattern of rhymes in a poem or stanza

rhyming couplet *noun* two consecutive lines of verse which rhyme and often have the same metre

rhyming slang *noun* slang, especially Cockney slang, where one word is replaced by a phrase that rhymes with it, eg *'butcher's hook'* for *'look'*

rhythm *noun* **1** a regular, repeated pattern of sounds or beats in music or poetry **2** a regularly repeated pattern of movements

rhythm and blues *singular noun* a type of music combining the styles of rock-and-roll and the blues

rhythmic or **rhythmical** *adjective* of or with rhythm ♦ **rhythmically** *adverb*

ria (*pronounced* **ree**-a) *noun, geography* a long, narrow, coastal inlet that gradually decreases in depth and width from its mouth inland ⊙ Comes from Spanish *ría* meaning 'river mouth'

rib *noun* **1** *anatomy* any of the bones which curve round and forward from the backbone, enclosing the heart and lungs **2** a spar of wood in the framework of a boat, curving up from the keel **3** a ridged knitting pattern ♦ **ribbing** *adverb*

ribald (*pronounced* **rib**-ald) *adjective* of a joke etc: coarse, vulgar

ribbed *adjective* arranged in ridges and furrows

ribbon *noun* a narrow strip of silk or other material, used for decoration, tying hair, etc

ribbon lake *noun, geography* a long, narrow lake in a depression carved into land by a glacier

ribcage *noun* the chest wall, formed by the ribs

riboflavin (*pronounced* rai-boh-**flei**-vin) *noun* vitamin B_2

ribonucleic acid see **RNA**

ribosome (*pronounced* **rai**-bo-sohm) *noun, biology* in the cytoplasm of a living cell: any of many small particles composed of RNA and protein that are the site of protein manufacture

rice *noun* (the seeds of) a plant, grown for food in well-watered ground in tropical countries

rice paper *noun* a thin, edible, paper-like material often put under baking to prevent it sticking

rich *adjective* **1** having a lot of money or valuables, wealthy **2** valuable: *a rich reward* **3** of food: containing a lot of fat, eggs, etc **4** of material: heavily decorated or textured, lavish **5** of a colour: deep in tone • **rich in** having a lot of: *rich in natural resources*

riches *plural noun* wealth

richly *adverb* **1** in a rich or elaborate way: *richly decorated* **2** fully and suitably: *richly deserved*

richness *noun* being rich

Richter scale (*pronounced* **rikh**-ter) *noun* a scale for measuring the intensity of earthquakes

rickets *singular noun* a children's disease caused by lack of calcium, with softening and bending of the bones

rickety *adjective* **1** suffering from rickets **2** unsteady: *a rickety table*

rickshaw *noun* a two-wheeled carriage pulled by a man, used in Japan etc

ricochet (*pronounced* **rik**-o-shei) *verb* (**ricocheting, ricocheted**) of a bullet: to rebound at an angle from a surface

ricotta *noun* a soft, white, unsalted, Italian curd cheese

rid *verb* (**ridding, rid**) to free from, clear of: *rid the city of rats* • **get rid of** to free yourself of

riddance *noun*: **good riddance to** I am happy to have got rid of

riddle[1] *noun* **1** a puzzle in the form of a question which describes something in a misleading way **2** something difficult to understand

riddle[2] *noun* a tray with holes for separating large objects from smaller ones ➤ *verb*: **riddled**

with covered with small holes made by: *riddled with woodworm*

ride *verb* (**riding, rode, ridden**) **1** to travel on a horse or bicycle, or in a vehicle **2** to travel on and control (a horse) **3** of a ship: to float at anchor ► *noun* **1** a journey on horseback, bicycle, etc **2** a path through a wood, for riding horses • **ride up** of a skirt etc: to work itself up out of position

rider *noun* **1** someone who rides **2** something added to what has already been said

ridge *noun* **1** a raised part between furrows **2** a long crest on high ground

ridicule *verb* to laugh at, mock ► *noun* mockery

ridiculous *adjective* deserving to be laughed at, very silly ♦ **ridiculously** *adverb*

rife *adjective* very common: *Disease was rife in the country*

riff *noun* a short, repeated pattern in a piece of pop music

riff-raff *noun* worthless people

rifle[1] *verb* **1** to search through and rob **2** to steal

rifle[2] *noun* a long gun fired from the shoulder

rift *noun* **1** a crack or gap left by splitting **2** a disagreement between friends

rift valley *noun, geography* a long valley formed when part of the earth's crust subsides between two faults

rig *verb* (**rigging, rigged**) to fix (an election result) illegally or dishonestly ► *noun* **1** *nautical* the arrangement of sails, rope and masts on a ship **2** an oil rig • **rig someone out** to clothe or dress them • **rig up 1** to fit (a ship) with sails and ropes **2** to make or build hastily

rigging *noun* ship's spars, ropes, etc

right *adjective* **1** on or belonging to the side of the body which in most people has the more skilful hand (*contrasted with*: **left**) **2** correct, true **3** just, good **4** straight **5** *maths* right-angled ► *adverb* **1** to or on the right side **2** correctly **3** straight **4** all the way: *right along the pier and back* ► *noun* **1** something good which ought to be done **2** something you are entitled to: *a right to a fair trial* **3** the right-hand side, direction, etc **4** the conservative side in politics ► *verb* to mend, set in order • **by right** because you have the right • **in your own right** not because of anyone else, independently

right angle *noun, maths* an angle of 90° ♦ **right-angled** *adjective*

right-angled triangle *noun, maths* a triangle with one right angle

right-click *verb, computing* to press and release the right-hand button on a computer mouse

righteous (*pronounced* **raich**-*us*) *adjective* living a good life; just ♦ **righteousness** *noun*

rightful *adjective* by right, proper: *the rightful owner* ♦ **rightfully** *adverb*

right-handed *adjective* using the right hand more easily than the left

right-hand man or **right-hand woman** *noun* a valuable and trusted assistant

right of way *noun* a road or path over private land along which people may go as a right

right wing *noun* **1** the more conservative members of a group or political party **2** *sport* the extreme right side of a pitch or team in a field game **3** *sport* (*also called*: **right-winger**) a member of a team who plays on the right side of the field ► *adjective* (**right-wing**) belonging or relating to the right wing ♦ **right-winger** *noun*

rigid *adjective* **1** not easily bent, stiff **2** strict

rigidity *noun* a rigid state or quality

rigmarole *noun* a long, rambling speech

⊙ Originally *ragman roll*, a Scots term for a long list or catalogue

rigor mortis *noun* stiffening of the body after death

rigorous *adjective* very strict ♦ **rigorously** *adverb*

rigour or *US* **rigor** *noun* strictness; harshness

rile *verb* to anger or annoy

rill *noun* a small stream

rim *noun* an edge or border, eg the top edge of a cup

rind (*pronounced* raind) *noun* a thick, firm covering, eg fruit peel, bacon skin, the outer covering of cheese

ring[1] *noun* **1** a small hoop worn on the finger, on the ear, etc **2** a hollow circle **3** an enclosed space for boxing, circus performances, etc **4** *maths* the area between two concentric circles **5** *chemistry* a closed chain of atoms in a molecule **6** a small group of people formed for business or criminal purposes: *a drug ring* ► *verb* (**ringing, ringed**) **1** to encircle, go round **2** to mark (a bird etc) by putting on a ring

ring[2] *verb* (**ringing, rang, rung**) **1** to make the sound of a bell **2** to strike (a bell etc) **3** to telephone ► *noun* **1** the sound of a bell being struck **2** a telephone call

ring binder *noun* a loose-leaf binder with metal rings which can be opened to add or take out pages

ringleader *noun* someone who takes the lead in mischief etc

ringlet *noun* a long curl of hair

ring main *noun, electricity* a domestic electrical supply system in which power points are connected to the mains in a closed circuit (**ring circuit**)

ringmaster *noun* someone who is in charge of the performance in a circus ring

ring pull *noun* a metal ring on a can etc, which, when pulled, breaks a seal

ring road *noun* a road that circles a town etc, avoiding the centre

ringtone *noun* a sound or tune made by a mobile phone when ringing

ringworm *noun, medicine* a fungal infection causing small, red, itchy, circular patches eg on the scalp or groin, or between the toes (**athlete's foot**)

rink *noun* **1** a sheet of ice, often artificial, for skating or curling **2** a building containing this

rinse *verb* **1** to wash lightly to remove soap etc **2** to clean (a cup, your mouth, etc) by swilling with water ➤ *noun* **1** the act of rinsing **2** liquid colour for the hair

riot *noun* **1** a noisy disturbance by a crowd **2** a striking display: *a riot of colour* **3** *informal* a hilarious event ➤ *verb* to take part in a riot
♦ **rioter** *noun*

riotous *adjective* noisy, uncontrolled
♦ **riotously** *adverb*

RIP *abbreviation* may he or she rest in peace

rip *verb* (**ripping, ripped**) **1** to tear apart or off **2** to come apart ➤ *noun* a tear • **let rip** to express yourself fully, without restraint

ripcord *noun* a cord which releases a parachute from its pack when pulled

ripe *adjective* **1** of fruit etc: ready to be picked or eaten **2** fully developed, mature ♦ **ripeness** *noun*

ripen *verb* to make or become ripe

rip-off *noun, slang* a cheat, a swindle ·

riposte (*pronounced* ri-**post**) *noun* a quick return or reply

ripple *noun* **1** a little wave or movement on the surface of water **2** a soft sound etc that rises and falls quickly and gently: *a ripple of laughter* ➤ *verb* **1** to mark with ripples, or form ripples in (a surface, material, etc) **2** to form ripples or move with an undulating motion

ripple tank *noun, physics* a shallow tank of water, used to demonstrate the behaviour of waves

rip rap *noun, geography* loose broken stones, used to form foundations or for building revetments and embankments

RISC *abbreviation, computing* reduced instruction set computer, a computer with fewer inbuilt instructions to enable faster processing

rise *verb* (**rising, rose, risen**) **1** to get up from bed **2** to stand up **3** to move upwards **4** of a river: to have its source (in): *The Rhone rises in the Alps* **5** to rebel (against) ➤ *noun* **1** a slope upwards **2** an increase in wages, prices etc • **give rise to** to cause

risible (*pronounced* **riz**-i-bl) *adjective* laughable

rising *noun* **1** an act of rising **2** a rebellion

rising limb *noun, geography* plotting on a

hydrograph showing an increase in river discharge (*contrasted with*: **falling limb**)

risk *noun* a chance of loss or injury; a danger
➤ *verb* **1** to take the chance of: *risk death* **2** to take the chance of losing: *risk your life or health*

risky *adjective* (**riskier, riskiest**) possibly resulting in loss or injury

Risorgimento (*pronounced* ri-sawr-ji-**men**-toh) *noun, history* the liberation and unification of Italy in the 19th century ⊙ Comes from Italian meaning 'renewal' or 'renaissance'

risotto (*pronounced* ri-**zo**-toh) *noun* (*plural* **risottos**) an Italian dish of rice cooked in stock with meat or seafood, onions, tomatoes, etc

risqué (*pronounced* **ris**-kei) *adjective* of a story, joke, etc: rather rude, but usually not offensive

rissole *noun* a fried cake or ball of minced meat, fish, etc

rite *noun* a solemn ceremony, especially a religious one

rite of passage *noun* (*plural* **rites of passage**) an event or ceremony which marks a person's change from one status to another in their society

ritual *noun* a traditional way of carrying out religious worship etc ➤ *adjective* relating to a rite or ceremony ♦ **ritually** *adverb*

ritualistic *adjective* done in a set, unchanging way ♦ **ritualistically** *adverb*

rival *noun* someone who tries to equal or beat another ➤ *verb* (**rivalling, rivalled**) to try to equal

rivalry *noun* (*plural* **rivalries**) the state of being a rival or rivals

riven (*pronounced* **riv**-en) *adjective, old* split

river *noun* a large stream of water flowing across land

riverbed *noun* the land at the bottom of a river

river cliff *noun, geography* a steep cliff on the outside of a meander in a river, formed from the erosion of the river bank by fast flowing water

river regime *noun, geography* seasonal changes in the volume of a river

river terrace *noun, geography* a flat terrace formed on either side of a river valley

rivet *noun* a bolt for fastening plates of metal together ➤ *verb* (**riveting, riveted**) **1** to fasten with a rivet **2** to fix firmly (someone's attention etc): *riveted to the spot*

riveting *noun* the joining of pieces of metal, etc by rivets ➤ *adjective* fascinating; enthralling

rivulet (*pronounced* **riv**-yuw-lit) *noun* a small stream

rms *abbreviation, maths* root mean square

Rn *symbol, chemistry* radon

RNA *abbreviation, biology* ribonucleic acid, a substance present in living cells, where it plays an important part in the production of proteins

roach noun (plural **roaches**) a type of freshwater fish

road noun 1 a hard, level surface for vehicles and people 2 a way of getting to (somewhere), a route 3 (**roads**) a place where ships may lie at anchor (also called: **roadstead**)

road hog noun, informal a reckless or selfish driver

roadie noun, informal a person who helps move and organize the instruments and equipment for a rock or pop group or artist, especially on tour

road map noun 1 a map of the road network in a particular area 2 a plan for achieving a goal in a series of stages

road movie noun a film showing the travels of a character or characters

road rage noun anger directed at other road users by a driver

road show noun 1 a touring group of theatrical or musical performers or a show given by such a group 2 a touring radio or TV presenter and their team, equipment, etc 3 a live broadcast in front of an audience, presented by such a presenter from one of the venues on the tour

roadstead see **road**

roadway noun the part of a road used by cars etc

roadworks plural noun the building or repairing of a road

roadworthy adjective (of a vehicle) fit to be used on the road

roam verb to wander about

roan noun a horse with a dark coat spotted with grey or white

roar verb 1 to give a loud, deep sound 2 to laugh loudly 3 to say (something) loudly ➤ noun a loud, deep sound or laugh

roast verb to cook or be cooked in an oven or over a fire ➤ adjective roasted: roast beef ➤ noun 1 meat roasted 2 meat for roasting

rob verb (**robbing, robbed**) to steal from

robber noun a person who robs; a thief

robbery noun (plural **robberies**) the act of stealing

robe noun 1 a long, loose garment 2 US a dressing-gown 3 (**robes**) the official dress of a judge etc ➤ verb, formal to dress

robin noun a type of small bird, known by its red breast

robot noun 1 a mechanical man or woman 2 a machine that can do the work of a person

⊙ A word invented by Karl Capek, a Czech playwright, based on a Czech word meaning 'work'

robotic adjective relating to or characteristic of robots

robotics singular noun the branch of engineering concerned with the design, construction and use of industrial robots

robust adjective strong, healthy ♦ **robustly** adverb

rock¹ noun 1 a large lump of stone 2 a hard sweet made in sticks

rock² verb to sway backwards and forwards or from side to side ➤ noun music with a heavy beat and simple melody (also called: **rock music**)

rock-and-roll or **rock'n'roll** noun a simpler, earlier form of rock music

rock cake noun a small cake with a rough, rock-like surface

rocker noun a curved support on which a chair, cradle, etc rocks

rockery noun (plural **rockeries**) a collection of stones amongst which small plants are grown

rocket¹ noun 1 a tube containing inflammable materials, used for launching a spacecraft, for signalling, and as a firework 2 a spacecraft ➤ verb (**rocketing, rocketed**) to move upwards rapidly: Prices are rocketing

rocket² noun a Mediterranean salad plant

rocking chair noun a chair which rocks backwards and forwards on rockers

rocking horse noun a toy horse which rocks backwards and forwards on rockers

rocky¹ adjective (**rockier, rockiest**) full of rocks

rocky² adjective (**rockier, rockiest**) inclined to rock, unsteady

rod noun 1 a long, thin stick 2 a fishing rod 3 an old measure of distance, about 5 metres 4 anatomy a type of cell in the retina of the eye that detects light intensity

rode past tense of **ride**

rodent noun a gnawing animal, such as a rat, beaver etc

rodeo noun (plural **rodeos**) 1 a round-up of cattle for marking 2 a show of riding by cowboys

roe noun 1 the eggs of fishes 2 (also called: **roe deer**) a small kind of deer

roentgenium (pronounced ront-**jeen**-i-um) noun, chemistry (symbol **Rg**) an artificially produced metallic element

⊙ Named after German physicist Wilhelm Conrad Röntgen (1845–1923), discoverer of X-rays

rogue noun a dishonest or mischievous person, a rascal

roguery noun (plural **rogueries**) dishonesty; mischief

roguish adjective characteristic of a rogue; mischievous, dishonest

role or **rôle** noun a part played by an actor

role model noun someone whose character, behaviour, etc is taken as a good example to follow

role-play or **role-playing** *noun* assuming and performing imaginary roles, as a method of training, therapy, etc

roll *verb* **1** to move along by turning over like a wheel **2** of a ship: to rock from side to side **3** of thunder etc: to rumble **4** to wrap round and round: *roll up a carpet* **5** to flatten with a roller: *roll the lawn* ➤ *noun* **1** a sheet of paper, length of cloth etc rolled into a cylinder **2** a very small loaf of bread **3** a rocking movement **4** a list of names **5** a long, rumbling sound ● **be rolling in** *informal* to have large amounts of (especially money) ● **on a roll** *informal* going through a period of continuous success ● **roll on ...** may a specified event etc come soon: *Roll on the holidays* ● **roll out** to introduce (a new product, service, etc) to the public ● **roll up 1** *informal* to arrive **2** to come in large numbers

roll-call *noun* the calling of names from a list

roller *noun* **1** a cylindrical tool for flattening **2** a tube over which hair is rolled and styled **3** a small, solid wheel **4** a long, heavy wave on the sea

Rollerblades *plural noun, trademark* rollerskates with the wheels in a single line

rollercoaster *noun* a raised railway with sharp curves and steep inclines and descents, ridden on for pleasure and excitement at funfairs and theme parks

rollerskates *plural noun* skates with wheels at each corner of the shoe ◆ **rollerskate** *verb*

rollicking *adjective* noisy and full of fun

rolling pin *noun* a roller for flattening dough

rolling stock *noun* the stock of engines, carriages etc that run on a railway

rollneck *adjective* of a garment: with a high neck which is folded over on itself

rollover *noun* **1** in the UK National Lottery: a jackpot prize which, having not been won in one week, is added to the jackpot for the following week **2** (*also called*: **mouseover**) *computing* an message or image that is displayed when the cursor rests over a point on the screen

roly-poly *adjective* round and podgy ➤ *noun* (*plural* **roly-polies**) suet pastry spread with jam and rolled up, then baked or steamed

ROM *abbreviation, computing* read-only memory

Roman *adjective* **1** of Rome (especially ancient Rome) or its people **2** of the Roman Catholic Church

Roman Catholic Church *noun* the Church whose head is the Pope, the Bishop of Rome

romance *noun* **1** a story about heroic events not likely to happen in real life **2** a love story **3** a love affair ➤ *verb* **1** to try to win the love of **2** to write or tell imaginative stories

Roman Empire *noun, history* the ancient empire of Rome, divided in the 4th century into the Eastern and Western empires

Roman numeral *noun* any of the figures in the number system developed by the ancient Romans, eg I, V, X, etc

romantic *adjective* **1** of romance **2** full of feeling and imagination **3** relating to love
◆ **romantically** *adverb*

romanticism *noun* (often **Romanticism**) the late 18th- and early 19th-century movement in art, literature and music, characterized by an emphasis on feelings and emotions

romanticize or **romanticise** *verb* **1** to make romantic **2** to describe, think of or interpret in an idealized and sometimes misleading way **3** to indulge in romantic ideas or act in a romantic way

Romany *noun* (*plural* **Romanies**) **1** a gypsy **2** the gypsy language

romp *verb* **1** to play in a lively way **2** to move quickly and easily ➤ *noun* a lively game

rompers *plural noun* a short suit for a baby

rondo *noun* (*plural* **rondos**) a musical composition with a recurring section

rood *noun, old* **1** a measure of area, equal to a quarter of an acre **2** a cross carrying an image of Christ

roof *noun* (*plural* **roofs**) **1** the top covering of a building, car, etc **2** the upper part of the mouth ➤ *verb* to cover with a roof

roof rack *noun* a frame attached to the roof of a car for carrying luggage etc

rook *noun* **1** a kind of crow **2** *chess* a castle

rookery *noun* (*plural* **rookeries**) **1** a nesting place of rooks **2** a breeding place of penguins or seals

rookie or **rooky** *noun* (*plural* **rookies**), *informal* a new recruit, especially in the police or the army

room *noun* **1** an inside compartment in a house **2** space: *room for everybody* **3** (**rooms**) lodgings

roomy *adjective* (**roomier, roomiest**) having plenty of space

roost *noun* a perch on which a bird rests at night ➤ *verb* to sit or sleep on a roost

rooster *noun* a farmyard cock

root[1] *noun* **1** the underground part of a plant, which anchors the plant in the soil and absorbs water and nutrients **2** one of the branches of the larger root **3** the base of anything, eg a tooth or fingernail **4** a cause, a source **5** a word from which other words have developed **6** *maths* a factor of a quantity that, when multiplied by itself a specified number of times, produces that quantity, eg 2 is the square root of 4 and the cube root of 8 **7** *maths* a value of an unknown variable for which an equation is true ➤ *verb* **1** to form roots and begin to grow **2** to be fixed • **root out** or **root up 1** to tear up by the roots **2** to get rid of completely • **take root 1** to form roots and grow firmly **2** to become firmly fixed

root² *verb* **1** of an animal: to turn up ground in a search for food **2** to search (about)

root³ *verb*: (**root for**) to cheer on, encourage or back

root canal *noun* the passage through which the nerves and blood vessels of a tooth enter the pulp

root directory *noun, computing* the highest level of directory, which contains all the others

rooted *adjective* firmly planted

root hair *noun* a hair-like growth from a plant root that absorbs water and minerals from soil

root mean square *noun, maths* (*abbrev* **rms**) the square root of the sum of the squares of a set of quantities divided by the total number of quantities in the set, eg the root mean square of 1, 2 and 3 is the square root of $(1^2 + 2^2 + 3^2)/3$

rootstock *noun, botany* an underground plant stem that bears buds; a rhizome

rope *noun* **1** a thick cord, made by twisting strands together **2** anything resembling a thick cord ➤ *verb* **1** to fasten or catch with a rope **2** to enclose, mark off with a rope

ropy *adjective* (**ropier, ropiest**) **1** like ropes, stringy **2** *informal* bad, not well

rosary *noun* (*plural* **rosaries**) **1** a set of prayers **2** a string of beads used in saying prayers **3** a rose garden

rose¹ past tense of **rise**

rose² *noun* **1** a type of flower, often scented, usually growing on a prickly bush **2** a deep pink colour

rosé (*pronounced* **roh**-zei) *noun* a pink-coloured wine produced by removing the skins of red grapes during fermentation

rosehip *noun* the fruit of the rose

rosemary *noun* an evergreen, sweet-smelling shrub, used as a cooking herb

rosette *noun* **1** a badge shaped like a rose, made of ribbons **2** *botany* a cluster of leaves growing from a central point

rosewood *noun* a dark Brazilian or Indian wood, which smells of roses when cut

Rosh Hashanah or **Rosh Hashana** (*both pronounced* rosh-ha-**shah**-na) *noun* the Jewish festival of New Year ① Comes from Hebrew, literally 'head of the year'

roster *noun* a list showing a repeated order of duties etc

rostrum *noun* (*plural* **rostrums** or **rostra**) a platform for public speaking

rosy *adjective* (**rosier, rosiest**) **1** red, pink **2** (of the future etc) bright, hopeful

rot *verb* (**rotting, rotted**) to go bad, decay

➤ *noun* **1** decay **2** *informal* nonsense

rota *noun* a list of duties etc to be repeated in a set order

rotary *adjective* turning round like a wheel

rotate *verb* **1** to turn round like a wheel **2** to go through a repeating series of changes

rotation *noun* **1** an act of rotating or state of being rotated **2** one complete turn around an axis **3** *maths* a transformation of a plane with a rotating movement around an axis (*compare with*: **enlargement, reflection, translation**) **4** a regular and recurring sequence **5** (*also called*: **crop rotation**) the growing of different crops in a field, usually in an ordered sequence, to help keep the land fertile

rotational symmetry *noun, maths* symmetry involving rotation around a fixed axis, so that a figure fits exactly onto itself in different positions

rotator *noun* **1** a device that rotates or makes something else rotate **2** *anatomy* a muscle that enables a limb etc to rotate

rote *noun*: **by rote** off by heart, automatically

rotisserie *noun* **1** a cooking apparatus with a spit on which meat etc is cooked by direct heat **2** a shop or restaurant that sells meat cooked in this way ① Comes from French *rôtir* meaning 'to roast'

rotor *noun* a turning part of a motor, dynamo, etc

rotten *adjective* **1** decayed, bad **2** *informal* worthless, disgraceful

rotter *noun, informal* a very bad, worthless person

rotund *adjective* **1** round **2** plump

rotunda *noun* a round domed building or hall

rotundity *noun* roundness

rouble or **ruble** (*both pronounced* **roo**-bl) *noun* the standard unit of Russian coinage

rouge (*pronounced* roosz) *noun* a powder or cream used to add colour to the cheeks

rough *adjective* **1** not smooth **2** uneven **3** coarse, harsh **4** boisterous, wild **5** not exact: *a rough guess* **6** stormy ➤ *noun* **1** a hooligan, a bully **2** rough ground • **rough and ready** not fine or carefully made, but effective • **rough out** to sketch or shape roughly

roughage *noun* bran or fibre in food

roughcast *noun* plaster mixed with fine gravel, for coating outside walls ➤ *verb* to cover with roughcast

rough diamond *noun* **1** an uncut and unpolished diamond **2** *informal* a good-natured person with unrefined manners

roughen *verb* to make rough

roughhouse *informal, noun* a disturbance or brawl ➤ *verb* **1** to create a disturbance; to brawl **2** to maltreat

roughly *adverb* **1** in a rough way **2** approximately

roughneck *noun, informal* **1** a worker on an oil rig, especially an unskilled labourer **2** a rough and rowdy person

roulette *noun* a gambling game, played with a ball which is placed on a wheel

round *adjective* **1** shaped like a circle **2** plump **3** even, exact: *a round dozen* **4** of a number: without any fractions ➤ *adverb & preposition* **1** on all sides (of), around: *look round the room* **2** in a circle (about): *The earth moves round the sun* **3** from one (person, place, etc) to another: *The news went round* ➤ *noun* **1** a circle, something round in shape **2** a single bullet or shell **3** a burst of firing, cheering etc **4** a song in which the singers take up the tune in turn **5** a usual route: *a postman's round* **6** a series of regular activities **7** each stage of a contest ➤ *verb* **1** to make or become round **2** of a ship: to go round (eg a headland) • **round down** to lower (a number) to an approximate or convenient figure • **round on** to make a sudden attack on • **round up 1** to gather or drive together **2** to raise (a number) to an approximate or convenient figure

roundabout *noun* **1** a revolving machine for children to ride on in a park etc **2** a meeting place of roads, where traffic must move in a circle ➤ *adjective* not straight or direct: *a roundabout route*

roundel *noun* **1** a small circular window or design **2** a round identification disc on the wing of a military aircraft ℗ Comes from French *rondel* meaning 'a little circle'

roundelay *noun, music* a simple song with a repeated refrain

rounders *singular noun* a ball game played with a bat in which players run around a series of stations

Roundhead *noun* a supporter of Parliament during the English Civil War (*compare with*: **Cavalier**)

℗ Because of the short-cut hair favoured by these soldiers

roundly *adverb* boldly, plainly: *He was roundly defeated*

round robin *noun* **1** a petition in which the names are written in a circle to conceal the first one **2** *sport* a tournament in which every competitor plays each of the others

round trip *noun* a journey to a place and back

round-up *noun* **1** a gathering together of animals, eg cattle **2** a gathering together of people wanted by the police **3** a summary of facts

roundworm *noun* a tiny parasitic worm with an unsegmented body

rouse *verb* **1** to awaken **2** to stir up, excite

rousing *adjective* stirring, exciting

rout *noun* a complete defeat ➤ *verb* to defeat utterly

route (*pronounced* root) *noun* the course to be followed, a way of getting to somewhere ➤ *verb* to fix the route of

router (*pronounced* root-er) *noun, computing* a device used for communication between two networks which can operate on different protocols

routine *noun* a fixed, unchanging order of doing things ➤ *adjective* regular, usual: *routine enquiries*

roux (*pronounced* roo) *noun* (*plural* **roux** – *pronounced* rooz), *cookery* a cooked mixture of flour and fat, used to thicken sauces

rove *verb* to wander or roam

rover *noun* **1** a wanderer; an unsettled person **2** *history* a pirate

Rover Scout *noun* an older member of the Scout Association

row[1] (*pronounced* roh) *noun* a line of people or things

row[2] (*pronounced* roh) *verb* to drive (a boat) by oars ➤ *noun* a trip in a rowing boat

row[3] (*pronounced* row) *noun* **1** a noisy quarrel **2** a noise **3** *informal* a scolding

rowan (*pronounced* roh-an or row-an) *noun* a tree with clusters of bright red berries (*also called*: **mountain ash**)

rowdy *adjective* (**rowdier, rowdiest**) noisy, disorderly

rower *noun* someone who rows a boat

rowing boat *noun* a boat rowed by oars

royal *adjective* **1** relating to a king or queen **2** splendid, magnificent: *a royal welcome*

royal assent *noun* in the UK: the formal permission given by the sovereign for an act of parliament to become law

royal blue *noun* a deep, bright blue

royal icing *noun* stiff cake icing made with egg-white

royalist or **Royalist** *noun* **1** a supporter of monarchy **2** a supporter of Charles I during the English Civil War (*contrasted with*: **Parliamentarian**) ➤ *adjective* relating to royalists ♦ **royalism** *noun*

royal jelly *noun* a jelly secreted by worker bees to feed developing larvae

royalty *noun* (*plural* **royalties**) **1** the state of being royal **2** royal people as a whole **3** a sum paid to the author of a book for each copy sold

RP *abbreviation* Received Pronunciation

rpm *abbreviation* revolutions per minute

RSA *abbreviation* **1** Royal Society of Arts **2** Royal Scottish Academy

RSI *abbreviation, medicine* repetitive strain injury

RSPB *abbreviation* Royal Society for the Protection of Birds

RSPCA *abbreviation* Royal Society for the Prevention of Cruelty to Animals

RSVP *abbreviation* please reply ⓘ Comes from French *répondez, s'il vous plaît*

RTF *abbreviation, computing* Rich Text Format, a standard format for text files

Ru *symbol, chemistry* ruthenium

rub *verb* (**rubbing, rubbed**) **1** to move one thing against the surface of another **2** to clean, polish (something) ➤ *noun* **1** the act of rubbing **2** a wipe • **rub in** to work into (a surface) by rubbing **2** to keep reminding someone of (something unpleasant) • **rub out** or **away** to remove (a mark)

rubato (*pronounced* roo-**bah**-toh) *music, adverb* with a modified or distorted tempo ➤ *noun* (**rubatos** or **rubati** – *pronounced* roo-**bah**-tee) a piece of music to be played in this way ⓘ Comes from Italian, literally 'robbed', from *rubare* meaning 'to steal'

rubber[1] *noun* **1** a tough elastic substance made from plant juices **2** a piece of rubber used for erasing pencil marks

rubber[2] *noun* an odd number (three or five) of games in cards, cricket, etc

rubber bullet *noun* a hard rubber pellet fired by police in riot control

rubberneck *verb, slang* to stare inquisitively or stupidly, eg at an accident

rubber stamp *noun* an instrument with rubber figures or letters for stamping dates etc on paper

rubber-stamp *verb* to authorize, approve

rubbish *noun* **1** waste material, litter **2** nonsense

rubble *noun* small, rough stones, bricks etc left from a building

rubella (*pronounced* roo-**bel**-a) *noun* a mild infectious disease causing pink spots and a sore throat (*also called*: **German measles**)

Rubicon *noun*: **cross the Rubicon** to take a decisive step

⓪ After Julius Caesar's bringing an army across the river *Rubicon*, which committed him to a civil war against the rulers of Rome

rubicund (*pronounced* **roo**-bi-kund) *adjective* red or rosy-faced

rubidium *noun, chemistry* (symbol **Rb**) a silvery-white, highly reactive metallic element ⓘ Comes from Latin *rubidus* meaning 'red'

ruble another spelling of **rouble**

rubric (*pronounced* **roo**-brik) *noun* **1** a heading **2** a guiding rule

⓪ From a Latin word for red ink, originally an entry in a Biblical text written in red ink

ruby *noun* (*plural* **rubies**) a type of red precious stone

ruck *noun* a wrinkle, a crease

rucksack *noun* a bag carried on the back by walkers, climbers, etc

ruckus *noun, US* an uproar, a rumpus

ructions *plural noun* a row, a disturbance

rudder *noun* a device fixed to the stern of a boat, or tail of an aeroplane, for steering

ruddy *adjective* (**ruddier, ruddiest**) **1** red **2** of the face: rosy, in good health

rude *adjective* **1** showing bad manners, not polite **2** roughly made: *a rude shelter* **3** rough, not refined **4** startling and sudden: *a rude awakening* **5** coarse, vulgar, lewd ♦ **rudely** *adverb* ♦ **rudeness** *noun*

rudiment *noun* **1** (**rudiments**) the fundamental facts or rules of a subject **2** *biology* an organ or part that no longer has a function and does not develop fully, eg mammary glands in male mammals

rudimentary *adjective* in an early stage of development

rue[1] *verb* (**ruing** or **rueing, rued**) to be sorry for, regret

rue[2] *noun* a shrub with bitter-tasting leaves

rueful *adjective* sorrowful, regretful ♦ **ruefully** *adverb*

ruff *noun* **1** in the past, a pleated frill worn round the neck **2** a band of feathers round a bird's neck

ruffian *noun* a rough, brutal person

ruffle *verb* **1** to make unsmooth, crumple (eg hair, a bird's feathers) **2** to annoy, offend

rug *noun* **1** a floor mat **2** a blanket

rugby or **Rugby** *noun* a form of football using an oval ball which can be handled

⓪ Named after *Rugby* School in Warwickshire, where the game was supposedly invented

rugged (*pronounced* **rug**-id) *adjective* **1** having a rough, uneven appearance **2** strong, robust **3** stern, harsh ♦ **ruggedly** *adverb* ♦ **ruggedness** *noun*

ruin *noun* **1** complete loss of money etc **2** a downfall **3** (often **ruins**) the broken-down remains of a building ➤ *verb* **1** to destroy **2** to spoil completely: *ruin your chances* **3** to make very poor

ruination *noun* the act of ruining or state of being ruined

ruined *adjective* in ruins, destroyed

ruinous *adjective* **1** ruined **2** likely to cause ruin

rule *noun* **1** government: *under military rule* **2** a regulation: *school rules* **3** what usually happens **4** a guiding principle **5** *maths* a procedure **6** a measuring ruler ➤ *verb* **1** to govern, be in power **2** to decide (that) **3** to draw (a line) **4** to mark with lines • **as a rule** usually • **rule out** to leave out, not consider

ruler *noun* **1** someone who rules **2** a marked tool for measuring length and drawing straight lines

ruling *adjective* governing; most important ▷ *noun* a decision, a rule

rum¹ *noun* an alcoholic spirit made from sugar cane

rum² *adjective, informal* strange, odd

rumba *noun* **1** a lively Afro-Cuban dance **2** a popular ballroom dance derived from this **3** the music for this dance, with a stressed second beat

rumble *verb* to make a low rolling noise like that of thunder etc ▷ *noun* a low rolling noise

rumen (*pronounced* **roo**-men) *noun* (*plural* **rumens** or **rumina** – *pronounced* **roo**-mi-na), *biology* the largest stomach chamber of a ruminant, in which food is stored before being regurgitated

ruminant *noun* an animal, such as a cow, that chews the cud

ruminate *verb* **1** to chew the cud **2** to be deep in thought

rumination *noun* deep thought

rummage *verb* to turn things over in search ▷ *noun* a thorough search

rummy *noun* a card game played with hands of seven cards

rumour or *US* **rumor** *noun* **1** general talk **2** a story passed from person to person which may not be true ▷ *verb* **1** to spread a rumour of **2** to tell widely

rump *noun* **1** the hind part of an animal **2** the meat from this part

rumple *verb* **1** to make untidy **2** to crease

rumpus *noun, informal* an uproar, a clamour

run *verb* (**running, ran, run**) **1** to move swiftly, hurry **2** to race **3** to travel: *The train runs every day* **4** of water: to flow **5** to follow a certain route: *the main road running between Glasgow and Edinburgh* **6** of a machine: to work **7** to spread (rapidly): *This colour is running* **8** to continue, extend: *The programme runs for two hours* **9** to operate (machinery etc) **10** to organize, conduct (a business etc) **11** to compete with other candidates in an election **12** *computing* to execute (a program) ▷ *noun* **1** a trip **2** a distance run **3** a spell of running **4** a continuous period: *a run of good luck* **5** a ladder in a stocking etc **6** free use of: *the run of the house* **7** a single score in cricket **8** an enclosure for hens etc • **run a risk** to take a chance of loss, failure, etc • **run down 1** to knock (someone) down **2** to speak ill of • **run into 1** to bump into, collide with **2** to meet accidentally • **run out of** to become short of • **run over** to knock down or pass over with a car

runaway *noun* a person that runs away ▷ *adjective* of an animal or vehicle: out of control and moving very fast

run-down *adjective* in poor health or condition

rune *noun* a letter of an early alphabet used in ancient writings and modern future-telling

rung¹ *noun* a step of a ladder

rung² past participle of **ring²**

runic (*pronounced* **roo**-nik) *adjective* written in runes

runner *noun* **1** someone who runs **2** a messenger **3** a plant stem that grows along the surface of the ground **4** a blade of a skate or sledge • **do a runner** *slang* to leave without paying a bill

runner bean *noun* **1** a climbing plant which produces long, green, edible beans **2** the bean this plant produces

runner-up *noun* (*plural* **runners-up**) someone who comes second in a race or competition

running *noun* **1** the act of moving fast **2** management, control ▷ *adjective* **1** for use in running: *running shoes* **2** giving out fluid: *a running sore* **3** carried on continuously: *a running commentary* ▷ *adverb* one after another: *three days running* • **in** (or **out of**) **the running** having (or not having) a chance of success

runny *adjective* (**runnier, runniest**) **1** running with liquid: *a runny egg* **2** too watery **3** of the nose: discharging mucus

run-off *noun, geography* rainwater which drains into rivers (*also called*: **overland flow**)

run-of-the-mill *adjective* ordinary

runt *noun* **1** the smallest animal in a litter **2** an undersized and weak person

runway *noun* a path for aircraft to take off from or land on

rupee (*pronounced* roo-**pee**) *noun* the standard currency of India, Pakistan, and Sri Lanka

rupture *noun* **1** a breaking, eg of a friendship **2** a tear in a part of the body ▷ *verb* to break, burst

rural *adjective* of the country (*contrasted with*: **urban**)

rural-urban fringe *noun, geography* an area where a city or town meets the countryside

ruse (*pronounced* rooz) *noun* a trick, a cunning plan

rush¹ *verb* **1** to move quickly, hurry **2** to make (someone) hurry **3** to take (a fort etc) by a sudden attack ▷ *noun* (*plural* **rushes**) **1** a quick forward movement **2** a hurry

rush² *noun* (*plural* **rushes**) a tall grasslike plant growing near water

rush hour *noun* the period at the beginning or end of a working day when traffic is at its busiest

rusk *noun* a hard, dry biscuit like toast, especially as a baby food

russet *adjective* reddish-brown ➤ *noun* a type of apple of russet colour

Russian roulette *noun* an act of daring, especially that of spinning the cylinder of a revolver which is loaded with just one bullet, pointing the revolver at your own head and pulling the trigger

rust *noun* **1** a reddish-brown coating on metal, caused by air and moisture **2** the colour of rust; reddish-brown ➤ *verb* to form rust

rustic *adjective* **1** relating to the country **2** roughly made **3** simple, unsophisticated ➤ *noun* someone who lives in the country

rusticate *verb* to live in the country

rusticity (*pronounced* rus-**tis**-i-ti) *noun* **1** country living **2** simplicity

rustle (*pronounced* **ru**-sl) *verb* **1** of silk etc: to make a soft, whispering sound **2** to steal (cattle) ➤ *noun* a soft, whispering sound • **rustle up** *informal* to prepare quickly: *rustle up a meal*

rustler *noun* someone who steals cattle

rustproof *adjective* **1** tending not to rust **2** preventing rusting ➤ *verb* to make rustproof

rusty *adjective* (**rustier, rustiest**) **1** covered with rust **2** *informal* showing lack of practice: *My French is rusty*

rut *noun* a deep track made by a wheel etc • **in a rut** having a dull, routine way of life

ruthenium (*pronounced* roo-**thee**-ni-um) *noun, chemistry* (symbol **Ru**) a brittle, silvery-white metallic element that occurs in some platinum ores

⊙ From *Ruthenia*, the Latin name for Russia, because it was discovered in ore in that country

rutherfordium (*pronounced* ru-dher-**fawr**-di-um) *noun, chemistry* (symbol **Rf**) an artificially produced radioactive metallic element

⊙ Named after Ernest Rutherford (1871–1937), New Zealand-born British physicist

ruthless (*pronounced* **rooth**-lis) *adjective* without pity, cruel ♦ **ruthlessly** *adverb* ♦ **ruthlessness** *noun*

rutted *adjective* full of ruts

rye *noun* a kind of grain

rye bread *noun* a bread made from rye flour

rye grass *noun* a grass grown for cattle-feeding

Ss

S¹ *abbreviation* **1** south **2** southern
S² *symbol* **1** *chemistry* sulphur **2** siemens
s *symbol* second(s)
Sabbath *noun* the day of the week regularly set aside for religious services and rest (among Muslims, Friday; Jews, Saturday; and Christians, Sunday)
sabbatical *noun* a period of paid leave from work
sable *noun* a small weasel-like animal with dark brown or blackish fur ➤ *adjective* black or dark brown in colour
sabotage (*pronounced* **sab**-ot-ahsz) *noun* deliberate destruction of machinery, an organization, etc by enemies or dissatisfied workers ➤ *verb* to destroy or damage deliberately

> ⊙ From a French word meaning 'clog', popularly supposed to refer to a form of protest in which workers put their clogs into machines in order to stop them working

saboteur (*pronounced* sab-ot-**er**) *noun* someone who carries out sabotage: *hunt saboteurs*
sabre *noun*, *history* a curved sword used by cavalry
sac *noun*, *biology* any bag-like part in a plant or animal, especially containing liquid
saccharide *noun*, *chemistry* any carbohydrate consisting of one or more simple sugars
saccharin or **saccharine** *noun* a very sweet substance used as a sugar substitute
sachet (*pronounced* **sash**-ei) *noun* **1** a small sealed packet containing powder or liquid, eg shampoo **2** a small bag containing pot pourri, used to perfume drawers etc
sack¹ *noun* **1** a large bag of coarse cloth for holding flour etc **2** the amount a sack holds **3** (**the sack**) *informal* dismissal from your job ➤ *verb*, *informal* to dismiss from a job • **get the sack** *informal* to be dismissed from your job
sack² *noun* the plundering of a captured town ➤ *verb* to plunder
sackcloth *noun* **1** coarse cloth for making sacks **2** a garment made of this, worn as a sign of repentance
sacking *noun* sackcloth
sacral (*pronounced* **seik**-ral) *adjective* of the

sacrum ⊙ Comes from Latin *sacrum* meaning 'a sacred object' + suffix *-al*

> ❗ Do not confuse with: **sacred**

sacrament *noun* **1** a religious ceremony, eg baptism or marriage, regarded as a channel to and from God or as a sign of grace **2** Holy Communion or the bread and wine consumed at Holy Communion
sacred *adjective* **1** holy **2** dedicated to some purpose or person: *sacred to her memory* **3** religious: *sacred music* ⊙ Comes from Middle English *sacre* meaning 'make holy', combined with the suffix *-ed* to give the sense of 'made holy'

> ❗ Do not confuse with: **sacral**

sacrifice *noun* **1** the offering of an animal killed on an altar to a god **2** an animal etc offered to a god **3** the giving up of something for the benefit of another person or to gain something more important **4** something given up for this purpose ➤ *verb* **1** to offer (an animal etc) as a sacrifice to a god **2** to give up (something) for someone or something else
sacrificial *adjective* of or for sacrifice
sacrilege (*pronounced* **sak**-re-lij) *noun* the use of something holy in a blasphemous way
  ♦ **sacrilegious** *adjective*
sacrosanct *adjective* **1** very sacred **2** not to be harmed or touched
sacrum (*pronounced* **seik**-rum) *noun* a triangular bone forming part of the human pelvis
SAD *abbreviation*, *psychology* seasonal affective disorder, an illness in which people feel tired and depressed during the months when there is little sunlight
sad *adjective* (**sadder, saddest**) **1** sorrowful, unhappy **2** showing sorrow **3** causing sorrow: *sad story* **4** *informal* pitiful, feeble
sadden *verb* to make or become sad
saddle *noun* **1** a seat for a rider on the back of a horse or bicycle **2** a cut or joint of meat from the back of an animal ➤ *verb* to put a saddle on (an animal) • **saddle with** to burden with: *saddled with debts*
saddler *noun* a maker of saddles and harnesses
sadhana *noun*, *Hinduism* practices carried out repeatedly to achieve spiritual perfection

sadhu (*pronounced* sa-**doo**) *noun* a Hindu holy man

sadism (*pronounced* **seid**-i-zm) *noun* taking pleasure in cruelty to others

⊙ **Sadism** is a word which was invented to describe the particular type of sexual cruelty which the 18th-century French author Marquis de Sade wrote about in his novels

sadist (*pronounced* **seid**-ist) *noun* someone who gets pleasure from inflicting pain and suffering on others

sadistic (*pronounced* sa-**dis**-tik) *adjective* getting, or seeming to get, pleasure from inflicting pain and suffering on others

sado-masochism *noun* the practice of deriving sexual pleasure from inflicting pain on another person and having pain inflicted on yourself by another person

SAE or **sae** *abbreviation* stamped addressed envelope

safari *noun* an expedition for observing or hunting wild animals

safari park *noun* an enclosed area where wild animals are kept outdoors and on view to visitors

safe *adjective* 1 unharmed 2 free from harm or danger 3 reliable, trustworthy ▸ *noun* 1 a lockable box for keeping money and valuables 2 a storage place for meat etc • **safe and sound** unharmed

safe-deposit or **safety-deposit** *noun* a vault, eg in a bank, where valuables can be locked away

safeguard *noun* anything that gives protection or security ▸ *verb* to protect

safekeeping *noun* care and protection

safe sex *noun* sexual intercourse or activity in which the transmission of disease or viruses such as HIV is protected against, eg by using a condom

safety *noun* freedom from harm or danger ▸ *adjective* giving protection or safety: *safety harness*

safety belt *noun* a seat belt

safety catch *noun* a catch to protect against something, eg the accidental firing of a gun

safety curtain *noun* a fireproof curtain between the stage and audience in a theatre

safety pin *noun* a curved pin in the shape of a clasp, with a guard covering its point

saffron *noun* a type of crocus whose stigmas are dried and used to dye food yellow and flavour it

sag *verb* (**sagging, sagged**) to droop or sink in the middle

saga *noun* 1 an ancient story about heroes etc 2 a novel or series of novels about several generations of a family 3 a long detailed story

sagacious *adjective* very wise, quick at understanding ♦ **sagaciously** *adverb*

sagacity *noun* wisdom, good judgement

sage *noun* 1 a type of herb with grey-green leaves which are used for flavouring 2 a wise man ▸ *adjective* wise ♦ **sagely** *adverb*

Sagittarius *noun* 1 the ninth sign of the zodiac, represented by the archer 2 someone born under this sign, between 23 November and 22 December

sago *noun* a white starchy substance obtained from a palm-tree, often used in puddings

said *adjective* mentioned before: *the said shopkeeper* ▸ *verb* past form of **say**

sail *noun* 1 a sheet of canvas spread out to catch the wind and drive forward a ship or boat 2 a journey in a ship or boat 3 an arm of a windmill ▸ *verb* 1 to travel in a ship or boat (with or without sails) 2 to navigate or steer a ship or boat 3 to begin a sea voyage 4 to glide along easily • **set sail** to set out on a sea voyage

sailboard *noun* a surfboard fitted with a mast and sail

sailor *noun* 1 someone who sails 2 a member of a ship's crew

saint *noun* 1 a very good or holy person 2 (*abbrev* **St**) a title conferred after death on a holy person by the Roman Catholic Church

Saint Bernard or **St Bernard** *noun* a breed of large dog, famous for its use in mountain rescues

⊙ From the use of such dogs by monks to rescue snowbound travellers in the *Saint Bernard* passes in the Alps

sainted *adjective* very holy or very good

saintly *adjective* (**saintlier, saintliest**) 1 relating to a saint or the saints 2 very good or holy

sake *noun* 1 cause, purpose: *for the sake of making money* 2 benefit, advantage: *for my sake*

Sakti (*pronounced* **shak**-tee) or **Shakti** *noun, Hinduism* power, personified by a female deity

sal *noun, chemistry* a salt

salaam *noun* a low bow with the right palm on the forehead, a form of Eastern greeting ▸ *verb* to perform this greeting

salacious (*pronounced* sa-**lei**-shus) *adjective* 1 lecherous or lustful 2 concerned with sex, especially crudely or obscenely ♦ **salaciousness** *noun*

salad *noun* a dish of raw vegetables, eg lettuce, tomatoes, etc

salah *noun, Islam* prescribed worship performed five times a day

salamander *noun* a kind of small lizard-like animal

salami *noun* a type of highly seasoned sausage, usually eaten cold and thinly sliced

salary *noun* (*plural* **salaries**) fixed wages regularly paid for work

○ Based on a Latin word for 'salt', from the money given to Roman soldiers to buy salt

salat *noun* the prayers said by Muslims five times daily

sale *noun* **1** the exchange of anything for money **2** a selling of goods at reduced prices **3** an auction

salesman, saleswoman or **salesperson** *noun* someone who sells or shows goods to customers

salicylic acid (*pronounced* sal-*i*-**sil**-ik) *noun, chemistry* a white crystalline solid that is used in the manufacture of aspirin, dyes, etc

salient *adjective* **1** pointing outwards: *salient angle* **2** outstanding, chief: *salient points of the speech*

saline *adjective* containing salt, salty: *saline solution*

salinization or **salination** *noun, geography* the situation of soil becoming too salty, eg because of flooding by sea water

saliva *noun* the liquid that forms in the mouth to help digestion; spittle

salivary *adjective* of or producing saliva: *salivary gland*

salivate *verb* **1** to produce saliva **2** to anticipate keenly

sallow *adjective* (**sallower, sallowest**) of complexion: pale, yellowish

sally *noun* (*plural* **sallies**) **1** a sudden rush forward **2** a trip, an excursion **3** a witty remark or retort ➤ *verb* (**sallies, sallying, sallied**) to rush out suddenly • **sally forth** to go out, emerge

salmon (*pronounced* **sam**-on) *noun* a large fish with yellowish-pink flesh

salmonella (*pronounced* **sal**-mon-el-*a*) *noun* a bacterium which causes food poisoning

salon *noun* **1** a shop in which hairdressing etc is done **2** a large room for receiving important guests **3** a gathering of such people

saloon *noun* **1** a passengers' dining-room in a ship **2** any car with an enclosed compartment **3** a public house, a bar

salsa *noun* **1** a type of Latin-American music containing elements of jazz and rock, or a dance to this music **2** a spicy Mexican dip made from tomatoes, onions and chillies

SALT *abbreviation* Strategic Arms Limitation Talks or Treaty

salt *noun* **1** a substance used for seasoning, either mined from the earth or obtained from sea water **2** a chemical compound that is formed when an acid reacts with a base **3** *informal* a sailor ➤ *adjective* **1** containing salt: *salt water* **2** tasting of salt **3** preserved in salt: *salt herring*

➤ *verb* **1** to sprinkle with salt **2** to preserve with salt

saltation *noun* **1** *geography* the movement of sand and stones on a river bed, transported by water **2** *biology* a sudden change in appearance in a species from one generation to another

salt cellar *noun* a small container for salt

salt marsh *noun, geography* an area of land which is usually, or liable to be, flooded with salt water

saltpetre see **potassium nitrate**

salt water *noun* sea water, as characterized by the presence of salt ➤ *adjective* (**saltwater**) of or found in sea water: *saltwater fish*

salty *adjective* (**saltier, saltiest**) **1** tasting of salt **2** piquant, racy

salubrious *adjective* **1** health-giving **2** pleasant, respectable: *not a very salubrious neighbourhood*

salutary *adjective* **1** giving health or safety **2** beneficial, useful: *salutary lesson*

salutation *noun* an act of greeting

salute *verb* **1** to greet with words, an embrace, etc **2** *military* to raise the hand to the forehead to show respect to **3** to honour someone by a firing of guns etc ➤ *noun* an act or way of saluting

salvage *noun* **1** goods saved from destruction or waste **2** the act of saving a ship's cargo, goods from a fire, etc **3** payment made for this act ➤ *verb* to save from loss or ruin

salvation *noun* **1** an act, means or cause of saving: *The arrival of the police was his salvation* **2** the saving of humanity from sin

salve *noun* an ointment for healing or soothing ➤ *verb* to soothe (pride, conscience, etc)

salver *noun* a small tray, often of silver

salvo *noun* (*plural* **salvos** or **salvoes**) a great burst of gunfire, clapping, etc

Samaritan *noun* **1** (*full form*: **Good Samaritan**) a kind, considerate or helpful person **2** a voluntary worker with **the Samaritans**, a group offering counselling by telephone for people in distress

samarium *noun, chemistry* (symbol **Sm**) a soft silvery metallic element

○ So called because it was discovered in the mineral *samarskite*, which was itself named in honour of a Russian mine official called Colonel von *Samarski*

same *adjective* **1** exactly alike, identical: *We both had the same feeling* **2** not different, unchanged: *He still looks the same* **3** mentioned before: *The same person came again* ➤ *pronoun* the thing just mentioned • **all the same** or **just the same** in spite of that • **at the same time** still, nevertheless ○ Comes from Old Norse *same*

sameness *noun* lack of change or variety

samey *adjective, informal* boringly similar or unchanging

samosa *noun* a small, deep-fried triangular pastry, originally from India, filled with spicy meat or vegetables

samovar *noun* a Russian tea-urn

sampan *noun* a kind of small boat used in Far Eastern countries

sample *noun* a small part extracted to represent the whole ➤ *verb* **1** to test a sample of: *sample a cake* **2** *music* to mix (a short extract) from one recording into a different backing track

sampler *noun* **1** someone who takes samples **2** a piece of needlework etc showing skill in different techniques

sampling *noun* a group of people, things, numbers, etc selected to represent a whole

samsara *noun* **1** *Hinduism* the world, where the soul passes into other states **2** *Buddhism* the never-ending cycle of birth, death and rebirth

samurai (*pronounced* **sam**-u-rai) *noun* (*plural* **samurai**) an aristocratic Japanese warrior

sanatorium *noun* (*plural* **sanatoriums** or **sanatoria**) **1** a hospital, especially for people suffering from respiratory diseases **2** a sick-room in a school etc

sanctify *verb* (**sanctifies, sanctifying, sanctified**) to make holy or sacred ♦ **sanctification** *noun*

sanctimonious *adjective* self-righteous, priggish

sanction *noun* **1** permission, approval **2** a penalty for breaking a law or rule **3** (**sanctions**) measures applied to force another country etc to stop a course of action ➤ *verb* **1** to authorize or confirm formally **2** to permit

sanctity *noun* holiness; sacredness

sanctuary *noun* (*plural* **sanctuaries**) **1** a sacred place **2** the most sacred part of a temple or church **3** a place of safety from arrest or violence **4** a protected reserve for birds or animals

sanctum *noun*: **inner sanctum** a very sacred or private room etc

sand *noun* **1** a mass of tiny particles of crushed rocks etc **2** (**sands**) a stretch of sand on the seashore ➤ *verb* **1** to sprinkle with sand **2** to add sand to **3** to smooth or polish with sandpaper

sandal *noun* a shoe with straps to hold the sole onto the foot

sandalwood *noun* a fragrant E Indian wood

sandbag *noun* a bag filled with sand, used as a protective barrier against floods or gunfire

sand bank *noun* a bank of sand in a river, river mouth, etc

sand dune *noun* a ridge of sand blown up by the wind

sandpaper *noun* paper with a layer of sand glued to it for smoothing and polishing

sandpit *noun* an enclosure filled with sand for children to play in

sandshoe *noun* a light shoe with a canvas upper and rubber sole

sandstone *noun* a soft rock made of layers of sand pressed together

sandwich *noun* (*plural* **sandwiches**) two slices of bread, or a split roll, stuffed with a filling ➤ *verb* to fit between two other objects

⊙ After the 18th-century Earl of *Sandwich*, said to have invented it to allow him to gamble without interruption for meals

sandy *adjective* (**sandier, sandiest**) **1** covered with sand **2** like sand **3** of hair: yellowish-red in colour

sane *adjective* **1** of sound mind, not mad **2** sensible ♦ **sanely** *adverb*

sang past tense of **sing**

sangfroid (*pronounced* sawng-**frwa**) *noun* calmness and composure ⊙ Comes from French, literally meaning 'cold blood'

sangha (*pronounced* **sung**-ga) *noun* **1** the Buddhist community **2** the Buddhist monastic order

sangui- *prefix* of or relating to blood ⊙ Comes from Latin *sanguis* meaning 'blood'

sanguinary *adjective* bloodthirsty, bloody ⊙ Comes from Latin *sanguinarius* meaning 'for blood' or 'bloodthirsty'

❗ Do not confuse: **sanguinary** and **sanguine**

sanguine *adjective* **1** hopeful, cheerful **2** of a complexion: red, ruddy ⊙ Comes from Latin *sanguineus* meaning 'blood-stained'

sanitary *adjective* **1** promoting good health, especially by having good drainage and sewage disposal **2** free from dirt, infection, etc

sanitation *noun* arrangements for protecting health, especially drainage and sewage disposal

sanitize or **sanitise** *verb* **1** to make hygienic or sanitary **2** to make less controversial or more acceptable by removing things that might be offensive etc

sanity *noun* **1** soundness of mind **2** mental health **3** good sense or judgement

sank past tense of **sink**

sansculotte (*pronounced* sans kyoo-**lot**) *noun,* **1** *history* a nickname for an extreme republican during the French Revolution **2** an extremist or violent revolutionary

⊙ So named because French revolutionaries wore pantaloons instead of knee-breeches (*culottes*)

sanserif (*pronounced* san-**ser**-if) *noun* a printing font having characters without serifs

Sanskrit *noun* the ancient literary language of India

sap *noun* **1** the juice in plants, trees, etc that contains vital sugars and other nutrients **2** *informal* a weakling, a fool ➤ *verb* (**sapping, sapped**) to weaken (someone's strength etc)

sapling *noun* a young tree

saponification *noun, chemistry* a process by which fats are converted into soap ◷ Comes from Latin *sapo* meaning 'soap'

sapphire *noun* a precious stone of a deep blue colour

Saracen *noun, history* an Islamic opponent of the Crusaders; a Moor

sarcasm *noun* **1** scornful humour, characterized by the use of a mocking tone to say the exact opposite of what you really think **2** a hurtful remark made in scorn

sarcastic *adjective* **1** of a remark: containing sarcasm **2** often using sarcasm, scornful ✦ **sarcastically** *adverb*

sarcoma *noun* (*plural* **sarcomas** or **sarcomata**) a cancerous growth in the connective tissue of the body ◷ Comes from Greek *sarkoma* meaning 'fleshy growth'

sarcophagus *noun* a stone coffin

sardine *noun* a young pilchard, often tinned in oil • **like sardines** crowded closely together

sardonic *adjective* bitter, mocking, scornful

sargasso *noun* (*plural* **sargassos** or **sargassoes**) a brown seaweed that floats in large masses ◷ Comes from Portuguese *sargaço*

sari *noun* a long cloth wrapped round the waist and brought over the shoulder, traditionally worn by Indian women

sarong *noun* a skirt traditionally worn by Malay men and women

SARS (*pronounced* sars) *abbreviation, medicine* Severe Acute Respiratory Syndrome, a contagious lung infection which causes fever, a cough and breathing difficulties

sartorial *adjective* relating to dress or clothes: *sartorial elegance*

sash[1] *noun* (*plural* **sashes**) a decorative band worn round the waist or over the shoulder

sash[2] *noun* (*plural* **sashes**) a sliding frame for window panes

sashay *verb* to walk or move in a gliding or showy way ➤ *noun* an excursion or trip ◷ From an alteration of French *chassé*

sashimi *noun* a Japanese dish of thinly sliced raw fish ◷ Comes from Japanese *sashi* meaning 'pierce' + *mi* meaning 'flesh'

sat past form of **sit**

Satan *noun* the Devil

Satanic *adjective* of Satan, devilish

satanism *noun* devil worship

satchel *noun* a small bag for carrying schoolbooks etc

sate *verb, old* to satisfy fully; give more than enough to

satellite *noun* **1** a moon orbiting a larger planet **2** a man-made object launched into space to orbit a planet **3** a state controlled by a more powerful neighbour

satellite dish *noun* a saucer-shaped aerial for receiving satellite television signals

satellite television *noun* the broadcasting of television programmes via satellite

satiate *verb* to satisfy fully; to give more than enough to

satiety *noun* the state of being satisfied fully or to excess

satin *noun* a closely woven silk with a glossy surface

satire *noun* **1** a piece of writing etc which makes fun of particular people or events **2** ridicule, scorn

satirical *adjective* containing or using satire to attack or criticize someone or something

satirist *noun* a writer of satire

satirize or **satirise** *verb* **1** to write satire **2** to ridicule or criticize using satire ✦ **satirization** *noun*

satisfaction *noun* **1** the act of satisfying or being satisfied **2** a feeling of pleasure or comfort **3** something that satisfies **4** compensation for damage etc

satisfactory *adjective* **1** satisfying **2** fulfilling the necessary requirements ✦ **satisfactorily** *adverb*: *He completed the test satisfactorily*

satisfy *verb* (**satisfies, satisfying, satisfied**) **1** to give enough (of something) to **2** to please, make content **3** to give enough to lessen or quieten: *satisfied her curiosity* **4** to convince: *satisfied that he was innocent* **5** to fulfil: *satisfy all our requirements*

SATs *abbreviation, Brit* standard assessment tasks

satsuma *noun* a small seedless orange

saturate *verb* **1** to soak or immerse in water **2** to cover or fill completely (with): *saturated with information* **3** *chemistry* to add a substance to (a solution) until no more of it can be dissolved

saturated *adjective* **1** soaked in water **2** *chemistry* of a compound: containing no double bonds between its carbon atoms and therefore unable to combine with atoms of other substances (*contrasted with*: **unsaturated**) **3** *chemistry* of a solution: unable to dissolve any more of a solute (*contrasted with*: **unsaturated**)

saturated fat *noun* a fat that can raise the amount of cholesterol in the blood

saturation *noun* saturating or being saturated: *The market has reached saturation point*

Saturday *noun* the seventh day of the week

⊕ After *Saturn*, an old Roman god of the harvest

saturnine *adjective* gloomy, sullen

satyr (*pronounced* **sat**-er) *noun* a mythological creature, half man, half goat, living in the woods

sauce *noun* **1** a liquid seasoning added to food to improve flavour **2** *informal* cheek, impudence

saucepan *noun* a deep-sided cooking pan, usually with a long handle

saucer *noun* a small, shallow dish for placing under a cup

saucy *adjective* (**saucier, sauciest**) **1** impudent, cheeky **2** referring to sex, usually in an amusing way: *saucy postcards*

sauna *noun* a room filled with steam to induce sweating

saunter *verb* to stroll about without hurrying ➤ *noun* a leisurely stroll

sausage *noun* minced meat seasoned and stuffed into a tube of animal gut etc

sauté (*pronounced* soh-**tei**) *verb* (**sautéed, sautéing** or **sautéeing**) to fry lightly ➤ *adjective* fried in this way: *sauté potatoes*

savage *adjective* **1** wild, untamed **2** fierce and cruel **3** uncivilized **4** very angry ➤ *noun* **1** an uncivilized person **2** someone fierce or cruel ➤ *verb* to attack very fiercely ♦ **savagely** *adverb*

savagery *noun* extreme cruelty or fierceness

savanna or **savannah** *noun, geography* a grassy, treeless plain

savant or *feminine* **savante** (*pronounced* sav-ant) *noun* a wise and knowledgeable person ⊕ Comes from French, from *savoir* meaning 'to know'

save *verb* **1** to bring out of danger, rescue **2** to protect from harm, damage or loss **3** to keep from spending or using: *saving money/saves time* **4** to put money aside for the future **5** *computing* to transfer (data etc) onto a disk or tape for storage ➤ *preposition* except (for): *All the CDs were damaged save this one* ● **save up** to put money aside for future use

saveloy (*pronounced* **sav**-e-loi) *noun* (*plural* **saveloys**) a seasoned sausage, originally made from brains ⊕ Comes from French *cervelat*, from Latin *cerebellum*, a diminutive of *cerebrum* meaning 'the brain'

savings *plural noun* money put aside for the future

saviour *noun* **1** someone who saves others from harm or evil **2** (**Saviour**) *Christianity* Jesus Christ

savoir-faire (*pronounced* sav-war-**feir**) *noun* instinctively knowing what to do and how to do it; expertise

savour *noun* **1** characteristic taste or flavour **2** an interesting quality ➤ *verb* **1** to taste or smell of **2**

to taste with enjoyment **3** to have a trace or suggestion (of): *His reaction savours of jealousy* **4** to experience

savoury *adjective* **1** having a pleasant taste or smell **2** salt or sharp in flavour; not sweet ➤ *noun* (*plural* **savouries**) a savoury dish or snack

savoy *noun* a type of dark green winter cabbage

savvy *slang, verb* (**savvies, savvying, savvied**) to know or understand ➤ *noun* **1** general ability or common sense **2** skill; know-how ➤ *adjective* (**savvier, savviest**) knowledgeable or shrewd ⊕ Comes from Spanish *saber* meaning 'to know'

saw[1] *noun* **1** a tool with a toothed edge for cutting wood etc **2** *old* a wise saying ➤ *verb* (**sawing, sawed, sawn**) to cut with a saw

saw[2] past tense of **see**

sawdust *noun* a dust of fine fragments of wood, made in sawing

sawm *noun, Islam* fasting and abstinence

sawmill *noun* a factory where wood is sawn up

sax *noun* (*plural* **saxes**), *informal* a saxophone

Saxon *noun, history* one of a Germanic people who invaded southern Britain in the 5th and 6th centuries

saxophone *noun* a wind instrument with a curved metal tube and keys for the fingers

⊕ After Belgian Adolfe *Sax*, who invented it in the 19th century

saxophonist *noun* a player of the saxophone

say *verb* (**saying, said**) **1** to speak, utter: *Why don't you say 'Yes'?* **2** to express in words, state: *They said they knew him* **3** to indicate: *The clock says 6 o'clock* ➤ *noun* **1** the right to speak: *no say in the matter* **2** the opportunity to speak: *I've had my say* ♦ **I say!** *interjection* **1** expressing surprise or protest **2** used to try to attract attention ● **that is to say** in other words ⊕ Comes from Old English *secgan*

saying *noun* something often said; a proverb

Sb *symbol, chemistry* antimony

Sc *symbol, chemistry* scandium

scab *noun* **1** a crust formed over a sore **2** any of several diseases of animals or plants **3** *informal* a blackleg

scabbard *noun* the sheath in which the blade of a sword is kept

scabby *adjective* (**scabbier, scabbiest**) **1** covered in scabs **2** *informal* disgusting, revolting

scabies *noun* an itchy skin disease

scaffold *noun* a platform on which people are put to death by hanging

scaffolding *noun* a framework of poles and platforms used by people doing repairs on a building etc

scalar *noun, maths* a quantity, eg mass, length or speed, that has magnitude but not direction (*compare with:* **vector**)

scalar multiple *noun, maths* (also **scalar multiple of a vector**) the result of multiplying a non-zero vector by a scalar

scald *verb* **1** to burn with hot liquid or steam **2** to heat (milk etc) to just below boiling point ➤ *noun* a burn caused by hot liquid or steam

scale¹*noun* **1** a set of regularly spaced marks for measurement on a thermometer etc **2** a series or system of increasing values: *salary scale* **3** *music* a group of notes going up or down in order **4** the ratio of a representation of something to its actual size: *drawn to the scale 1:50,000* **5** the size of a business etc: *manufacture on a small scale* ➤ *verb* to climb up

scale²*noun* **1** a small thin flake on the skin of a fish or snake **2** *another word for* **limescale** ➤ *verb* **1** to remove the scales from (eg a fish) **2** to remove in thin layers

scale³*noun* (*usually* **scales**) a weighing machine

scale factor *noun, maths* the ratio of the lengths of corresponding edges in a figure to a similar figure

scalene *adjective* **1** of a triangle: having each side of a different length **2** of a cone or cylinder: having its axis oblique to the base

scallop *noun* a shellfish with a pair of hinged fan-shaped shells

scalloped *adjective* of an edge: cut into curves or notches

scallywag *noun* a rascal

scalp *noun* **1** the outer covering of the skull **2** the skin and hair on top of the head ➤ *verb* to cut the scalp from

scalpel *noun* a small, thin-bladed knife, used in surgery

scaly *adjective* (**scalier, scaliest**) having scales; flaky

scam *slang, noun* a trick or swindle ➤ *verb* (**scammed, scamming**) to trick or swindle

scamp *noun* a rascal

scamper *verb* **1** to run about playfully **2** to run off in haste

scampi *plural noun* large prawns cooked for eating

scan *verb* (**scanning, scanned**) **1** to examine carefully **2** *informal* to read quickly, skim over **3** to pass an X-ray, ultrasonic wave, etc over **4** to count the beats in a line of poetry **5** of poetry: to have the correct number of beats: *This line doesn't scan* ➤ *noun* an act of scanning

scandal *noun* **1** something disgraceful or shocking **2** talk or gossip about people's (supposed) misdeeds

scandalize or **scandalise** *verb* to shock, horrify

scandalmonger *noun* someone who spreads gossip or scandal

scandalous *adjective* **1** shameful, disgraceful **2** containing scandal ◆ **scandalously** *adverb*

scandium *noun, chemistry* (symbol **Sc**) a soft silvery-white metallic element

scanner *noun* a machine which scans, eg a device for scanning and recording graphic images so that they can be edited or viewed on a computer

scansion *noun* scanning of poetry

scant *adjective* not plentiful, hardly enough: *pay scant attention*

scanty *adjective* (**scantier, scantiest**) little or not enough in amount: *scanty clothing* ◆ **scantily** *adverb*

scapegoat *noun* someone who bears the blame for the wrongdoing of others

ⓘ Literally 'escape goat', after an ancient Jewish ritual of transferring the people's sins to a goat which was afterwards let free in the wilderness

scapula *noun* (*plural* **scapulas** or **scapulae** – pronounced **skap**-yoo-lee) *anatomy* the shoulderblade

scar *noun* **1** the mark left by a wound or sore **2** a mark, a blemish ➤ *verb* (**scarring, scarred**) to mark with a scar

scarab *noun* a beetle regarded as sacred by the ancient Egyptians

scarce *adjective* **1** not plentiful, not enough **2** rare, seldom found ● **make yourself scarce** to go, run away

scarcely *adverb* **1** only just, barely: *could scarcely hear* **2** surely not: *You can scarcely expect me to eat that*

scarcity *noun* (*plural* **scarcities**) want, shortage

scare *verb* **1** to drive away with fear **2** to startle, frighten ➤ *noun* a sudden fright or alarm

scarecrow *noun* a figure set up to scare birds away from crops

scaremonger *noun* someone who causes alarm by spreading rumours of disaster ◆ **scaremongering** *noun*

scarey another spelling of **scary**

scarf *noun* (*plural* **scarves** or **scarfs**) a length of fabric worn round the neck, shoulders or head

scarlet *noun* a bright red colour ➤ *adjective* bright red

scarlet fever *noun* an infectious illness, causing a rash, fever and a sore throat

scarp another word for **escarpment**

scarper *verb, slang* to run away

SCART *noun, electronics* a plug with 21 pins, used to connect parts of a video or audio system

ⓘ An acronym of French *S*yndicat des *C*onstructeurs des *A*ppareils *R*adiorécepteurs et *T*éléviseurs, the name of the European syndicate that developed it

scary or **scarey** *adjective* (**scarier, scariest**) frightening

scathing *adjective* cruel, hurtful: *scathing remark*

scatter *verb* **1** to throw loosely about; sprinkle **2** to spread widely **3** to run away in all directions

scatterbrain *noun* someone who frequently forgets things

scatter diagram or **scatter graph** *noun, statistics* a graph showing the distribution of measurements of two random variable quantities, showing them as paired values plotted as points against a set of axes

scattered *adjective* thrown or spread about widely

scattering *noun* **1** a small amount thinly spread or scattered **2** *physics* the deflection of photons or particles as a result of collisions with other particles

scatty *adjective* (**scattier, scattiest**), *Brit informal* mentally disorganized

scavenge *verb* to search among waste for usable items

scavenger *noun* an animal which feeds on dead flesh

scenario (*pronounced* si-**nah**-ri-oh) *noun* **1** a scene-by-scene outline of a play, film, etc **2** any hypothetical situation or sequence of events: *a worst-case scenario* ◑ Comes from Italian *scenario* meaning 'scenery'

⚠ Do not confuse with: **scene**

scene *noun* **1** the place where something happens: *scene of the accident* **2** a view, a landscape **3** a division of a play or opera **4** an area of activity: *the music scene* **5** a show of bad temper: *Don't make a scene* ◑ Comes from Latin *scaena* meaning 'the scene presented' or 'the stage'

⚠ Do not confuse with: **scenario**

scenery *noun* **1** the painted background on a theatre stage **2** the general appearance of a stretch of country

scenic *adjective* **1** of scenery **2** picturesque

scent *verb* **1** to discover by the smell **2** to have a suspicion of, sense: *scent danger* **3** to give a pleasant smell to: *Roses scented the air* ➤ *noun* **1** perfume **2** an odour, a smell **3** the trail of smell used to track an animal etc

sceptic (*pronounced* **skep**-tik) *noun* someone who doubts what they are told ◑ Comes from Greek *skeptikos* meaning 'thoughtful'

⚠ Do not confuse with: **septic**

sceptical (*pronounced* **skep**-tik-al) *adjective*

unwilling to believe, doubtful ♦ **sceptically** *adverb*

⚠ Do not confuse with: **cynical**.
A **sceptical** person is cautious about accepting something to be true, a **cynical** person is suspicious of apparently good things.

scepticism (*pronounced* **skep**-ti-sizm) *noun* a doubting state or attitude

sceptre (*pronounced* **sep**-ter) *noun* an ornamental rod carried by a monarch on ceremonial occasions

schedule (*pronounced* **shed**-yool or **sked**-yool) *noun* **1** the time set for doing something: *I'm two weeks behind schedule* **2** a written statement of details **3** a form for filling in information ➤ *verb* **1** to form into a schedule **2** to plan, arrange

schema (*pronounced* **skeem**-a) *noun* (*plural* **schemata**) **1** a scheme or plan **2** an outline of a theory etc

schematic *adjective* according to a plan

scheme (*pronounced* skeem) *noun* **1** a plan, a systematic arrangement **2** a dishonest or crafty plan ➤ *verb* to make schemes, plot

scheming *adjective* crafty, cunning

scherzo (*pronounced* **sker**-tsoh) *noun, music* (*plural* **scherzos**) a lively movement in triple time

schism (*pronounced* **si**-zm or **ski**-zm) *noun* a breaking away from the main group

schizo- (*pronounced* **skit**-so) *prefix* forms words containing the idea of a split or division: *schizophrenia* (= literally, 'a split mind') ◑ Comes from Greek *schizein* meaning 'to split'

schizophrenia (*pronounced* skit-sof-**ree**-ni-a) *noun* a mental illness involving a distorted perception of reality ♦ **schizophrenic** *noun & adjective*

schmaltz (*pronounced* shmawltz or smahltz) *noun, informal* excessive sentimentality, especially in music or art ♦ **schmaltzy** *adjective* ◑ Comes from Yiddish, from German *Schmalz* meaning 'cooking fat'

scholar *noun* **1** someone of great learning **2** someone who has been awarded a scholarship **3** a pupil, a student

scholarly *adjective* showing or having knowledge, high intelligence and a love of accuracy ♦ **scholarliness** *noun*

scholarship *noun* **1** learning **2** a sum of money given to help a clever student to carry on further studies

scholastic *adjective* of schools or scholars

school *noun* **1** a place for teaching, especially children **2** a group of artists etc who share the same ideas **3** a large number of fish, whales, etc

➤ *verb* **1** to educate in a school **2** to train by practice

schoolboy *noun* a boy attending school

schoolchild *noun* (*plural* **schoolchildren**) a child attending school

schoolgirl *noun* a girl attending school

schooling *noun* **1** education in a school **2** training

schoolmaster or **schoolmistress** *noun* a teacher at a school

schooner *noun* **1** a two-masted sailing ship **2** a large sherry glass **3** *US & Aust* a large beer glass

sci- *prefix* forms words containing the concept of knowledge: *science/prescient* (= having foreknowledge) ⊕ Comes from Latin *scire* meaning 'to know', and *scientia* meaning 'knowledge'

sciatic (*pronounced* sai-**at**-ik) *adjective* relating to the hip

sciatica (*pronounced* sai-**at**-ik-a) *noun* severe pain in the upper part of the leg

science *noun* **1** knowledge obtained by observation and experiment **2** a branch of this knowledge, eg chemistry, physics, biology, etc **3** these sciences considered together

science fiction *noun* stories dealing with future life on earth, space travel, other planets, etc

science park *noun* an industrial research centre, usually attached to a university

scientific *adjective* **1** of or relating to science **2** done according to the methods of science
♦ **scientifically** *adverb*

scientist *noun* someone who studies one or more branches of science

sci fi *abbreviation* science fiction

scimitar *noun* a sword with a short curved blade

scintillate *verb* **1** to sparkle **2** to show brilliant wit etc

scintillation *noun*, *physics* the emission of a flash of light when alpha, beta or gamma rays strike certain phosphorescent substances

scion (*pronounced* **sai**-on) *noun* **1** a young member of a family **2** a descendant **3** a cutting for grafting onto another plant

scissors *plural noun* a cutting instrument with two hinged blades

sclerosis *noun*, *medicine* abnormal hardening or thickening of a body part ⊕ Comes from Greek *sklerosis* meaning 'a hardening'

scoff *verb* to express scorn ● **scoff at someone** or **something** to make fun of, mock them

scold *verb* to tell off; blame or rebuke with angry words ➤ *noun* a bad-tempered person

scolding *noun* a telling-off

scoliosis (*pronounced* sko-li-**oh**-sis) *noun*, *medicine* abnormal curving of the spine

scone *noun* a small plain cake made with flour, milk and a little fat

scoop *noun* **1** a type of rounded spoon used for handling or serving food: *an ice-cream scoop* **2** the amount such a spoon holds: *two scoops of ice cream* **3** a hollow instrument used for lifting loose material, water, etc **4** an exclusive news story ➤ *verb* to lift or dig out with a scoop

scooter *noun* **1** a two-wheeled toy vehicle pushed along by foot **2** a low-powered motorcycle

scope *noun* **1** opportunity or room to do something: *scope for improvement* **2** extent, range: *outside the scope of this dictionary*

-scope *suffix* forms words describing devices which make things visible, or which allow examination of something which cannot be seen : *telescope/stethoscope* ⊕ Comes from Greek *skopeein* meaning 'to view'

scorch *verb* **1** to burn slightly, singe **2** to dry up with heat

scorching *adjective* **1** burning, singeing **2** very hot **3** harsh, severe: *scorching criticism*

score *noun* **1** a gash, a notch **2** an account, a debt: *settle old scores* **3** the total number of points gained in a game **4** a written piece of music showing separate parts for voices and instruments **5** a set of twenty **6** (**scores**) a great many: *scores of people* **7** a reason, account: *Don't worry on that score* ➤ *verb* **1** to mark with lines or notches **2** to gain (points) **3** to keep a note of points gained in a game ● **score out** to cross out

scorn *verb* **1** to look down on, despise **2** to refuse (help etc) because of pride ➤ *noun* mocking contempt

scornful *adjective* full of scorn ♦ **scornfully** *adverb*

Scorpio *noun* **1** the eighth sign of the zodiac, represented by the scorpion **2** someone born under this sign, between 23 October and 22 November

scorpion *noun* a spider-like creature with a poisonous sting in its tail

scotch *verb* to stamp out, suppress.

scot-free *adjective* unhurt; unpunished

scoundrel *noun* a rascal

scour *verb* **1** to clean by hard rubbing; scrub **2** to search thoroughly: *Police are scouring the area*

scourge *noun* **1** a whip **2** a cause of great suffering ➤ *verb* **1** to whip, lash **2** to afflict, cause to suffer

Scouse *noun*, *Brit* **1** (also **Scouser**) a native or inhabitant of Liverpool **2** the dialect of Liverpool

scout *noun* **1** a guide or spy sent ahead to bring back information **2** (**Scout**) a member of the Scout Association

scowl *verb* to wrinkle the brows in displeasure or anger ➤ *noun* a frown

Scrabble *noun, trademark* a word-building game

scrabble *verb* to scratch or grope about

scraggy *adjective* (**scraggier, scraggiest**) **1** long and thin **2** uneven, rugged

scram *interjection* go away!

scramble *verb* **1** to struggle to seize something before others **2** to wriggle along on hands and knees **3** to mix or toss together: *scrambled eggs* **4** to jumble up (a message) to make it unintelligible without decoding: *a scrambled TV channel* **5** of military aircraft or crew: to take off immediately in response to an emergency ➤ *noun* **1** a rush and struggle to get something **2** a motorcycle race over rough country

scrap *noun* **1** a small piece, a fragment **2** a picture for pasting in a scrapbook **3** *informal* a fight **4** parts of a car etc no longer required: *sold as scrap* **5** (**scraps**) small pieces, odds and ends ➤ *verb* (**scrapping, scrapped**) **1** to abandon as useless **2** *informal* to fight, quarrel

scrapbook *noun* a blank book in which to stick pictures etc

scrape *verb* **1** to rub and mark with something sharp **2** to drag or rub against or across a surface with a harsh grating sound ➤ *noun* **1** an act of scraping **2** a mark or sound made by scraping **3** *informal* a difficult situation • **scrape through** to only just avoid failure • **scrape something up** or **together** to collect (money etc) with difficulty

scrapheap *noun* a heap of old metal etc, a rubbish heap • **on the scrapheap** no longer needed

scrapie *noun* a disease of sheep

scrap metal *noun* metal for melting and re-using

scrappy *adjective* (**scrappier, scrappiest**) made up of odd scraps, not well put together ♦ **scrappily** *adverb*

scratch *verb* **1** to draw a sharp point across the surface of **2** to mark by doing this **3** to tear or dig with claws, nails, etc **4** to rub with the nails to relieve or stop itching **5** to withdraw from a competition ➤ *noun* (*plural* **scratches**) **1** a mark or sound made by scratching **2** a slight wound ➤ *adjective* **1** *golf* too good to be allowed a handicap **2** of a team: made up of players hastily got together ♦ **scratchy** *adjective* (**scratchier, scratchiest**) • **start from scratch** to start from nothing, right at the beginning • **up to scratch** satisfactory

scrawl *verb* to write or draw untidily or hastily ➤ *noun* **1** untidy, hasty or bad writing **2** something scrawled

scrawny *adjective* (**scrawnier, scrawniest**) thin, skinny

scream *verb* to utter a shrill, piercing cry as in fear etc; shriek ➤ *noun* a shrill cry

scree *noun* a sloping mass of loose stones at the base of a cliff or on the face of a mountain, caused by weathering of rock

screech *verb* to utter a harsh, shrill and sudden cry ➤ *noun* a harsh shrill cry

screed *noun* a long boring speech or letter

screen *noun* **1** a flat covered framework to shelter from view or protect from heat, cold, etc **2** something that shelters from wind, danger, difficulties, etc **3** the surface on which cinema films are projected **4** the surface on which a television picture, or computer data, appears ➤ *verb* **1** to shelter, hide **2** to make a film of **3** to show on a screen **4** to sift, sieve **5** to sort out (the good from the bad) by testing **6** to conduct examinations on someone to test for disease • **screen off** to hide behind, or separate by, a screen

screenplay *noun* the written text for a film, with dialogue and descriptions of characters and setting

screen printing *noun* a stencil technique in which coloured ink is forced through a fine silk or nylon mesh

screen saver *noun* an animated image displayed on a computer screen when the computer is not in use

screen test *noun* a filmed audition to see whether an actor is suitable for a particular film role

screenwriter *noun* someone who writes screenplays

screw *noun* **1** a nail with a slotted head and a winding groove or ridge (called the **thread**) on its surface **2** a kind of propeller (a **screw-propeller**) with spiral blades, used in ships and aircraft **3** a turn or twist (of a screw etc) ➤ *verb* **1** to fasten or tighten with a screw **2** to fix (eg a lid) in place with a twisting movement **3** to twist, turn round (your head etc) **4** to twist up, crumple, pucker

screwball *slang, chiefly N Am, esp US, noun* a crazy person; an eccentric ➤ *adjective* crazy; eccentric

screwdriver *noun* a tool for turning screws

screwed-up *adjective, informal* of a person: very anxious, nervous or psychologically disturbed

scribble *verb* **1** to write carelessly **2** to make untidy or meaningless marks with a pencil etc ➤ *noun* **1** careless writing **2** meaningless marks, a doodle

scribe *noun, history* **1** a clerk who copied out manuscripts **2** a Jewish teacher of law

scrimp *verb* to be sparing or stingy with money: *scrimping and saving for a holiday*

script *noun* **1** the text of a play, talk, etc **2** a piece of handwriting **3** print that looks like handwriting **4** a set of characters used for writing **5** *computing* a list of commands, written for an interpreter, to be executed by a computer ➤ *verb* to write the script of (a play, film, etc) ⊕ Comes from Latin *scriptum*, from *scribere* meaning 'to write'

scripting language *noun, computing* a high-level programming language that uses an interpreter to execute commands

scripture *noun* **1** sacred writings **2** (**Scripture**) the Christian Bible

scrofula *noun medicine* the former name for tuberculosis of the lymph nodes, especially of the neck ♦ **scrofulous** *adjective*

scroll *noun* **1** a piece of paper rolled up **2** an ornament shaped like this ➤ *verb, computing* to move text up or down on a screen to see more of a document

scroll bar *noun* a strip at the side of a computer screen, where you can click to scroll down or up

scrotum *noun* (*plural* **scrota** or **scrotums**) the bag of skin enclosing the testicles

scrounge *verb, slang* **1** to cadge **2** to get by begging ➤ *noun* an attempt to beg or cadge: *on the scrounge*

scrounger *noun, slang* a person who scrounges

scrub *verb* (**scrubbing, scrubbed**) to rub hard in order to clean ➤ *noun* countryside covered with low bushes

scruff *noun* the back of the neck

scruffy *adjective* (**scruffier, scruffiest**) untidy

scrum *noun, rugby* a struggle for the ball by the forwards of the opposing sides bunched together

scrumptious *adjective, informal* delicious

scrunch *verb* to crumple

scrunchie *noun* a fabric band to tie back the hair

scruple *noun* doubt over what is right or wrong that makes someone reluctant to do something ➤ *verb* to hesitate because of a scruple

scrupulous *adjective* careful over the smallest details

scrutinize or **scrutinise** *verb* to examine very closely

scrutiny *noun* (*plural* **scrutinies**) careful examination, a close look

SCSI (*pronounced* **skuh**-zi) *abbreviation, computing* Small Computer Systems Interface, a system that allows communication between a computer and several devices (eg hard disks)

scuba *noun* breathing apparatus used by skin-divers

⊕ An acronym of 'self-contained underwater breathing apparatus'

scuba diving *noun* swimming underwater using a device consisting of a breathing tube attached to a cylinder of air

scud *verb* (**scudding, scudded**) to move or sweep along quickly: *scudding clouds*

scuffle *noun* a confused fight

scull *noun* a short oar ➤ *verb* **1** to move (a boat) with a pair of these or with one oar worked at the back of the boat **2** to move in water by using the hands as paddles

scullery *noun* (*plural* **sculleries**) a room next to a kitchen for rough cleaning work

sculpt *verb* to carve or model

sculptor or **sculptress** *noun* an artist who carves or models figures in wood, stone, clay, etc

sculpture *noun* **1** the art of the sculptor or sculptress **2** a piece of their work

scum *noun* **1** foam that rises to the surface of liquids **2** the most worthless part of anything: *the scum of the earth*

scupper *noun* a hole in the side of a ship to drain water from the deck ➤ *verb* to put an end to, ruin: *scupper his chances*

scurf *noun* small flakes of dead skin (especially on the scalp)

scurrilous *adjective* insulting, abusive: *a scurrilous attack*

scurry *verb* (**scurries, scurrying, scurried**) to hurry along, scamper

scurvy *noun* a type of disease caused by a lack of fresh fruit and vegetables

scuttle *noun* **1** a fireside container for coal **2** an opening with a lid in a ship's deck or side ➤ *verb* **1** to make a hole in (a ship) in order to sink it **2** to hurry along, scamper

scythe (*pronounced* saidh) *noun* a large curved blade, on a long handle, for cutting grass etc by hand ➤ *verb* to cut with a scythe

SDI *abbreviation* Strategic Defense Initiative, a proposal made by US President Ronald Reagan in 1983 for developing defensive weapons based in space

SDLP *abbreviation* Social Democratic and Labour Party, a moderate Republican political party in Northern Ireland

SE *abbreviation* south-east; south-eastern

Se *symbol, chemistry* selenium

sea *noun* **1** the mass of salt water covering most of the earth's surface **2** a great stretch of water of less size than an ocean **3** a great expanse or number: *a sea of faces* • **at sea 1** on the sea **2** completely puzzled

sea anemone *noun* a type of small plant-like animal found on rocks at the seashore

sea arch *noun, geography* an arch of rock

formed at the meeting of two caves that have been eroded into rock by the sea

seabed *noun* the land at the bottom of the sea

seabird *noun* any bird that lives near the sea

seaboard *noun* land along the edge of the sea

seaborgium *noun, chemistry* (symbol **Sg**) an artificially manufactured radioactive chemical element

⊙ Named after Glenn *Seaborg* (1912–99), US atomic scientist

seafarer *noun* a traveller by sea, a sailor

seafaring *adjective* travelling by or working at sea

seafish *noun* a fish that lives in salt water

sea-floor spreading *noun, geography* the forming of new crust on the sea floor when tectonic plates under the sea move apart, and the gap fills with magma which then cools

seafood *noun* shellfish and other edible marine fish

seafront *noun* a promenade with its buildings facing the sea

seagull *noun* a type of web-footed sea bird

seahorse *noun* a type of small fish with a horse-like head and neck

seal[1] *noun* a four-flippered sea animal living partly on land

seal[2] *noun* 1 a piece of wax with a design pressed into it, attached to a document to show that it is legal or official 2 an engraved metal stamp for marking wax in this way 3 a piece of wax used to keep a parcel closed 4 anything that closes tightly or the state of being closed tightly: *an airtight seal* 5 a piece of sticky paper with a picture on it: *a Christmas seal* ➤ *verb* 1 to mark or fasten with a seal 2 to close up completely 3 to make (legally) binding and definite: *seal a bargain*

sealant *noun* any material used for sealing a gap to prevent water leaking etc

sea level *noun* the level of the surface of the sea

sealing wax *noun* a quickly hardening, waxy substance for sealing letters, documents, etc

sea lion *noun* a large kind of seal, the male of which has a mane

sealskin *noun* the prepared fur of the seal, used to make garments

seam *noun* 1 the line formed when you sew together two pieces of cloth 2 a line or layer of metal, coal, etc in the earth

seaman *noun* (*plural* **seamen**) a sailor, especially a member of a ship's crew who is not an officer

seamanship *noun* the art of steering and looking after ships at sea

seamstress *noun* a woman who sews for a living

seamy *adjective* (**seamier, seamiest**) sordid; disreputable • **the seamy side** the more unpleasant side (eg of life)

Seanad or **Seanad Eireann** (*pronounced* shan-adh **e**-ran) the upper house of parliament in the Republic of Ireland ⊙ Irish Gaelic, literally meaning 'senate'

séance (*pronounced* **sei**-ons) *noun* a meeting of people to receive messages from the spirits of the dead

seaplane *noun* an aeroplane which can take off from and land on the water

sear *verb* 1 to scorch, burn 2 to hurt severely

search *verb* 1 to look over in order to find something 2 (**search for something**) to look for it ➤ *noun* (*plural* **searches**) 1 an act of searching 2 an attempt to find

search engine *noun* on the Internet, a program that compares search requests against items in its index and returns search results to the user

searching *adjective* examining closely and carefully: *searching question*

searchlight *noun* a strong beam of light used for picking out objects at night

seascape *noun* a picture of a scene at sea

seashell *noun* the shell of a marine invertebrate, especially a mollusc

seashore *noun* the land next to the sea

seasick *adjective* made ill by the rocking movement of a ship

seaside *noun* the land beside the sea, especially a holiday resort

season *noun* 1 one of the four divisions of the year (spring, summer, autumn, winter) 2 the proper time for anything 3 a time associated with a particular activity: *football season* ➤ *verb* 1 to add (salt etc) to improve the flavour of (food) 2 to dry (wood) till it is ready for use

seasonable *adjective* 1 happening at the proper time 2 of weather: suitable for the season

seasonal *adjective* 1 of the seasons or a season 2 of work etc: taking place in one particular season only

seasoned *adjective* 1 of food: flavoured 2 of wood: ready to be used 3 trained, experienced: *a seasoned traveller*

seasoning *noun* something (eg salt, pepper) added to food to give it more taste

season ticket *noun* a ticket that can be used repeatedly for a certain period of time

sea stack *noun, geography* a pillar of rock rising from the sea, formed by the collapse of a sea arch

seat *noun* 1 a piece of furniture for sitting on 2 the part of a chair on which you sit 3 the buttocks 4 a mansion 5 a place in parliament, on a council, etc 6 the centre of some activity: *the seat of* *government* ➤ *verb* **1** to make to sit down **2** to have seats for (a certain number): *The room seats forty*

seat belt *noun* a belt fixed to a seat in a car etc to prevent an occupant from being thrown violently forward in the event of a crash

sea urchin *noun* a type of small sea creature with a spiny shell

sea wall *noun, geography* a wall built to keep out the sea and prevent erosion of land

seaward *adjective & adverb* towards the sea

seaweed *noun* any of many kinds of plants growing in the sea

seaworthy *adjective* in a good enough condition to go to sea

sebaceous glands *plural noun, biology* in mammals: tiny glands in the skin that protect the skin and hair by the secretion of sebum

sebum (*pronounced* see-bum) *noun, biology* the oily substance secreted by the sebaceous glands that lubricates and protects the hair and skin

sec *abbreviation, maths* secant

secant *noun, maths* (*abbrev* **sec**) for an angle in a right-angled triangle: a function that is the ratio of the length of the hypotenuse to the length of the side adjacent to the angle

secateurs *plural noun* a tool like scissors, for trimming bushes etc

secede *verb* to break away from a group, society, etc

secession *noun* **1** seceding **2** a group of seceders

seclude *verb* to keep (yourself) apart from people's notice or company

secluded *adjective* of a place: private and quiet

seclusion *noun* the state of being secluded; peacefulness and privacy

second *adjective* **1** next after the first in time, place, etc **2** other, alternate: *every second week* **3** another of the same kind as: *They thought him a second Mozart* ➤ *noun* **1** someone or something that is second **2** an attendant to someone who boxes or fights a duel **3** (symbol **s**) the standard unit of measure of time, the 60th part of a minute **4** the 60th part of a degree (in measuring angles) **5** an article not quite perfectly made: *These gloves are seconds* ➤ *verb* **1** to support, back up **2** (*pronounced* se-**kond**) to transfer temporarily to a special job ℗ Comes from Latin *secundus* meaning 'following'

secondary *adjective* second in position or importance

secondary cell *noun, physics* a battery or cell that can be charged before use by passing an electric current through it, and which can then be recharged

secondary industry *noun, geography* an industry concerned with processing raw materials and producing goods (*compare with*: **primary industry, tertiary industry**)

secondary school *noun* a school between primary school and university etc

secondary sexual characteristics *plural noun, biology* features other than reproductive organs that distinguish males from females after puberty, eg beard growth

second cousin *noun* a child of the cousin of either parent

second-degree *adjective* **1** *medicine* denoting the second of the three degrees of burning, with blistering but not permanent damage to the skin **2** *N Am law* denoting the least serious of the two levels of murder, ie with intent but not premeditation

second-hand *adjective* not new; having been used by another: *second-hand clothes*

secondly *adverb* in the second place

second nature *noun* a firmly fixed habit: *Organizing people is second nature to her*

second person *noun, grammar* a class into which pronouns and verb forms fall, denoting the person or people the speaker or writer is addressing, eg *you* ♦ **second-person** *adjective*

second-rate *adjective* not of the best quality, inferior

second sight *noun* the supposed power to see into the future or see things happening elsewhere

second thoughts *noun* **1** doubts: *They're having second thoughts about getting married* **2** a reconsideration leading to a different decision: *On second thoughts I think I'll stay*

second wind *noun* **1** the recovery of normal breathing after exertion **2** a burst of renewed energy or enthusiasm

secrecy *noun* the state of being secret, mystery

secret *adjective* **1** hidden from, or not known by, others **2** secretive ➤ *noun* a fact, plan, etc that is not told or known

secretarial *adjective* of a secretary or their work

secretariat *noun* the administrative department of a council or organization

secretary *noun* (*plural* **secretaries**) **1** someone employed to write letters, keep records, etc in an office **2** someone elected to deal with the written business of a club etc

℗ Comes from the Latin word *secretarius*, meaning 'a person spoken to in confidence'

Secretary of State *noun* **1** a government minister in charge of an administrative department **2** *US* the person in charge of foreign affairs

secrete *verb* **1** to hide, conceal in a secret place **2**

of a part of the body: to form, store up and release (a fluid)

secretion *noun* **1** a substance secreted **2** the process of secreting

secretive *adjective* inclined to hide or conceal your feelings, activities, etc

secret police *noun* a police force operating in secret to suppress opposition to the government

secret service *noun* a government department dealing with spying

sect *noun* a group of people who hold certain views, especially in religious matters

sectarian *adjective* **1** of a sect **2** loyal to a sect **3** narrow-minded **4** of a crime, especially a murder: committed as a result of hatred between rival religious groups

section *noun* **1** an act or process of cutting **2** a part, a division: *a section of the community* **3** *biology* a thin slice of a specimen for examination under a microscope **4** the view of the inside of anything when it is cut right through or across: *a section of a plant* **5** *maths* the surface formed when a plane cuts through a solid ➤ *verb* **1** to cut through something **2** to order the admission of (a mentally ill person) to a psychiatric hospital

sector *noun* **1** a part, a section **2** *maths* a three-sided part of a circle whose sides are two radii and a part of the circumference

secular *adjective* **1** of worldly, not spiritual or religious things **2** of music etc: not sacred or religious

secularism *noun* the belief that society's values should not be influenced by religion ✦ **secularist** *noun*

secure *adjective* **1** safe, free from danger or fear **2** confident: *secure in the knowledge that she had no rivals* **3** firmly fixed or fastened: *The lock is secure* ➤ *verb* **1** to make safe, firm or established: *secure your position* **2** to seize, get hold of: *secure the diamonds* **3** to fasten: *secure the lock*

security *noun* **1** safety **2** (**securities**) property or goods which a lender may keep until the loan is paid back

security of tenure *noun, geography* the right of a tenant to stay on a piece of land, in accommodation, etc in the long term

sedan *noun* **1** (*also called:* **sedan chair**) an enclosed chair for one person, carried on two poles by two bearers **2** *US* a saloon car

sedate *adjective* calm, serious, dignified

sedation *noun* the use of sedatives to calm a patient

sedative *adjective* calming, soothing ➤ *noun* a medicine with this effect

sedentary *adjective* of a job etc: involving a lot of sitting

sedge *noun* a type of coarse grass growing in swamps and rivers

sediment *noun* **1** the grains or solid parts which settle at the bottom of a liquid **2** sand, rocks, etc carried and deposited by wind, water or ice

sedimentary *adjective* of rocks: formed when sediment becomes tightly compacted

sedimentation *noun* **1** *chemistry* the settling of solid particles from a suspension **2** the formation of sedimentary rock

sedition *noun* the stirring up of rebellion against the government ✦ **seditious** *adjective*

seduce *verb* **1** to tempt (someone) away from right or moral behaviour **2** to persuade (someone) to have sexual intercourse **3** to attract ✦ **seducer** *noun* ✦ **seduction** *noun*

seductive *adjective* attractive, tempting

sedulous *adjective* diligent, painstaking

see *verb* (**seeing, saw, seen**) **1** to have sight **2** to be aware of, notice by means of the eye: *He can see us coming* **3** to form a picture of in the mind **4** to understand: *I see what you mean* **5** to find out: *I'll see what is happening* **6** to make sure: *See that he finishes his homework* **7** to accompany: *I'll see you home* **8** to meet: *I'll see you at the usual time* ➤ *noun* the district over which a bishop or archbishop has authority • **seeing that**, since, because • **see through 1** to take part in to the end **2** to not be deceived by (a person, trick, etc) • **see to** to take charge of (the preparation of): *see to a meal* ☉ Comes from Old English *seon*

seed *noun* **1** the part of a tree, plant, etc from which a new plant may grow **2** a seed-like part of a grain or a nut **3** the beginning from which anything grows: *the seeds of rebellion* **4** a seeded player in a tournament **5** *old* children, descendants **6** *chemistry* a single crystal introduced to a concentrated solution to induce crystallization ➤ *verb* **1** of a plant: to produce seed **2** to sow **3** to remove the seeds from (eg a fruit) **4** to arrange (good players) in a tournament so that they do not compete against each other till the later rounds **5** *chemistry* to introduce a single crystal to induce the formation of more crystals in (a solution) • **go to seed** or **run to seed 1** of a plant: to develop seeds **2** of a person, area, etc: to deteriorate, become run down

seedcase or **seedbox** *noun* a part of a plant in which the seeds are enclosed

seedling *noun* a young plant just sprung from a seed

seedy *adjective* (**seedier, seediest**) **1** full of seeds **2** shabby **3** sickly, not very well

seek *verb* (**seeking, sought**) **1** to look or search for **2** to try (to do something): *seek to establish proof* **3** to try to get (advice etc)

seem *verb* **1** to appear to be: *He seems kind* **2** to appear: *She seems to like it*

seeming adjective apparent but not actual or real: a seeming success ♦ **seemingly** adverb

seemly adjective (**seemlier, seemliest**) suitable; decent

seen past participle of **see**

seep verb to flow slowly through a small opening, leak

seer noun a prophet

seersucker noun a lightweight ribbed cotton fabric

seesaw noun 1 a plank balanced across a stand so that one end of it goes up when the other goes down 2 an up-and-down movement like that of a seesaw ➤ verb 1 to go up and down on a seesaw 2 to move with a seesaw-like movement

seethe verb 1 to boil 2 to be very angry

seething adjective 1 boiling 2 furious

see-through adjective able to be seen through

segment noun 1 a part cut off 2 maths a part of a circle or ellipse cut off by a straight line intersecting it 3 maths a part of a sphere cut off by a plane intersecting it 4 biology in certain animals, eg some worms: one of a number of repeating units of which the body is composed

segmentation noun 1 the act or process of dividing into segments 2 biology the cell divisions in an ovum immediately after fertilization

segregate verb to separate (someone or a group) from others ♦ **segregation** noun

seismic (pronounced **saiz**-mik) adjective of earthquakes

seismograph (pronounced **saiz**-mo-grahf) noun an instrument that records earthquake shocks

seismology (pronounced saiz-**mol**-oji) noun the scientific study of earthquakes ☉ Comes from Greek seismos meaning 'earthquake'

seize verb 1 to take suddenly by force: The army has seized the town 2 to overcome: seized by panic 3 (**seize up**) of machinery: to become stuck, break down

seizure noun 1 sudden capture 2 a sudden attack of illness, rage, etc

seldom adverb not often, rarely: You seldom see an owl during the day

select verb to pick out from several according to your preference, choose ➤ adjective 1 picked out, chosen 2 very good 3 exclusive, allowing only certain people in

selection noun 1 the act of choosing 2 things chosen 3 a number of things from which to choose 4 biology the process by which some individuals have more offspring than others

selective adjective 1 selecting carefully 2 of weedkiller: harmless to garden plants

selector noun someone who chooses (eg members for a national team)

selenium noun, chemistry (symbol **Se**) a non-metallic element that is a semiconductor, used in electronic devices

self noun (plural **selves**) 1 someone's own person 2 someone's personality, character

self-assured adjective trusting in your own power or ability, confident ♦ **self-assurance** noun

self-catering adjective of a holiday, accommodation, etc: providing facilities for guests to prepare their own meals

self-centred adjective concerned with your own affairs, selfish

self-coloured or US **self-colored** adjective 1 having the same colour all over 2 having its natural colour, undyed

self-confident adjective believing in your own powers or abilities ♦ **self-confidence** noun

self-conscious adjective too aware of your faults etc and therefore embarrassed in the company of others

self-contained adjective 1 of a house: complete in itself, not sharing any part with other houses 2 of a person: self-reliant

self-control noun control over yourself, your feelings, etc

self-defence noun the defence of your own person, property, etc

self-denial noun doing without something, especially in order to give to others

self-effacing adjective keeping yourself from being noticed, modest

self-employed adjective working for yourself rather than as an employee

self-esteem noun respect for yourself; conceit

self-evident adjective clear enough to need no proof

self-explanatory adjective easily understood or obvious

self-expression noun expressing your own personality in your activities

self-government noun government by the members of a nation, organization, etc without any outside control ♦ **self-governing** adjective

self-help noun solving one's own problems rather than relying on assistance from others

self-image noun your own idea or perception of yourself

self-important adjective having a mistakenly high sense of your importance

self-indulgent adjective too ready to satisfy your own inclinations and desires

self-interest noun a selfish desire to consider only your own interests or advantage

selfish adjective caring only for your own pleasure or advantage ♦ **selfishly** adverb

selfless adjective thinking of others before yourself, unselfish

self-made *adjective* owing success etc to your own efforts: *a self-made man*

self-pollination *noun, biology* in flowering plants: the transfer of pollen from the anther of the stamen to the stigma of the same flower

self-portrait *noun* an artist's portrait of themselves

self-possessed *adjective* calm in mind or manner, quietly confident

self-raising flour *noun* flour already containing an ingredient to make it rise

self-reliant *adjective* trusting in your own abilities etc ◆ **self-reliance** *noun*

self-respect *noun* respect for yourself and concern for your own character and reputation

self-righteous *adjective* thinking highly of your own goodness and virtue

self-sacrifice *noun* the act of giving up your own life, possessions, etc in order to do good to others

selfsame *adjective* the very same

self-satisfied *adjective* pleased, smug, satisfied with yourself

self-service *adjective* of a restaurant: where customers serve themselves and pay at a checkout

self-styled *adjective* called or considered so only by yourself: *a self-styled superstar*

self-sufficient *adjective* needing no help or support from anyone else

self-willed *adjective* determined to have your own way, obstinate

sell *verb* (**selling, sold**) **1** to give or hand over for money **2** to have or keep for sale: *He sells newspapers* **3** (**sell for**) to be sold for, cost: *This book sells for £20*

sell-by date *noun* a date stamped on a manufacturer's label indicating when food is no longer fit to be sold

seller *noun* someone who sells

Sellotape *noun, trademark* transparent adhesive tape, especially for use on paper

sell-out *noun* **1** an event for which all the tickets have been sold **2** *informal* a betrayal

selvage *noun* the firm edge of a piece of cloth, that does not fray

semantic *adjective* relating to the meaning of words etc

semantics *singular noun* the branch of linguistics that deals with meaning

semaphore *noun* a form of signalling using the arms to form different positions for each letter

semblance *noun* an outward, often false, appearance: *a semblance of listening*

semen *noun* the liquid that carries sperm

semester *noun* a term at a university etc that lasts for half a year ⊙ Comes from Latin *semestris* meaning 'six-monthly'

semi- *prefix* **1** half: *semicircle* **2** *informal* partly ⊙ Comes from Latin prefix *semi-* meaning 'half'

semibreve *noun, music* a whole-note (○), equal to four crotchets in length

semicircle *noun* half of a circle ◆ **semicircular** *adjective*

semicolon *noun* the punctuation mark (;) indicating a pause stronger than a pause marked by a comma

semiconductor *noun* a substance, eg silicon, which can conduct electricity less easily than a conductor

semi-detached *adjective* of a house: joined to another house on one side but not on the other

semi-final *noun* the stage or match of a contest immediately before the final

seminal *adjective* influential, important

seminar *noun* a group of students working on, or meeting to discuss, a particular subject

seminary *noun* (*plural* **seminaries**) a school or college

semiotics *singular noun* the study of signs, signals and symbols, especially in language and communication ◆ **semiotic** *adjective* ⊙ Comes from Greek *semeiotikos*, from *semeion* meaning 'sign'

semi-permeable *adjective, biology* **1** only allowing certain liquids or gases to pass through **2** only allowing certain molecules to pass through

semi-precious *adjective* of a stone: having some value, but not considered a gem

semiquaver *noun* a musical note equal to half a quaver or one-sixteenth of a semibreve

semisolid *adjective* of a substance: with a consistency between liquid and solid

Semitic *adjective* Jewish

semitone *noun, music* **1** half a tone **2** the interval between notes on a keyboard instrument

semolina *noun* the hard particles of wheat sifted from flour, used for puddings etc

senate *noun* **1** the upper house of parliament in the USA, Australia, etc **2** the governing council of some universities **3** *history* the law-making body in ancient Rome

senator *noun* a member of a senate

send *verb* (**sending, sent**) **1** to make (someone) go **2** to have (something) carried or delivered to a place • **send for** to order to be brought

sender *noun* a person who sends something, especially by post

send-off *noun* a display of good wishes from people gathered to say goodbye to someone who is leaving

send-up *noun, Brit informal* a parody or satire

senescence *noun, biology* the changes in a living organism as it ages ◆ **senescent** *adjective*

senile *adjective* **1** of old age **2** showing the mental feebleness of old age

senility *noun* **1** old age **2** mental deterioration in old age

senior *adjective* older in age or higher in rank ➤ *noun* someone older or in a senior position

senior citizen *noun* an elderly person

seniority *noun* the state of being senior

senna *noun* the dried leaves of certain plants, used as a laxative

sensation *noun* **1** a feeling through any of the five senses **2** a vague effect: *a floating sensation* **3** a state of excitement: *causing a sensation*

sensational *adjective* causing great excitement, horror, etc

sensationalism *noun* the practice of deliberately setting out to cause widespread excitement, shock, etc ◆ **sensationalist** *noun*

sense *noun* **1** one of the five powers by which humans feel or notice (hearing, taste, sight, smell, touch) **2** a feeling: *a sense of loss* **3** an ability to understand or appreciate: *a sense of humour* **4** (**senses**) right mind, common sense: *to take leave of your senses* **5** wisdom, ability to act in a reasonable way **6** ability to be understood: *Your sentence does not make sense* **7** meaning: *To what sense of this word are you referring?* ➤ *verb* to feel, realize: *sense disapproval*

senseless *adjective* stunned, unconscious; foolish

sense organ *noun* an organ, eg the eye, nose or mouth, that is sensitive to a stimulus such as sound or touch

sensibility *noun* (*plural* **sensibilities**) ability to feel, sensitivity

sensible *adjective* **1** wise **2** able to be felt or noticed **3** (**sensible of**) aware of

sensitive *adjective* **1** feeling, especially strongly or painfully **2** strongly affected by light, movements, etc **3** of a person: easily upset or offended **4** of documents etc: not for public discussion as they contain secret information, eg concerning national security **5** *biology* responding to a stimulus **6** of scientific instruments: reacting to extremely small changes

sensitivity *noun* the quality or condition of being sensitive

sensitize or **sensitise** *verb* to make sensitive (especially to light)

sensor *noun* a device that detects a physical change and turns it into an electrical signal

sensory *adjective* of the senses

sensory nerve *adjective* a nerve carrying impulses from the sense organs to the brain

sensual *adjective* **1** driven by, or affecting, the senses rather than the mind: *Discover the sensual pleasures of aromatherapy* **2** indulging too much in bodily pleasures

⚠ Do not confuse: sensual and sensuous

sensuality *noun* **1** the quality of being sensual **2** indulgence in physical pleasures

sensuous *adjective* pleasing to the senses, particularly by being beautiful or luxurious: *car designs favouring smooth edges and sensuous curves*

sent past form of **send**

sentence *noun* **1** a number of words which together make a grammatically complete statement, usually containing a verb **2** a judgement announced by a judge or court ➤ *verb* to condemn to a particular punishment

sentiment *noun* **1** a thought expressed in words **2** a show of feeling or emotion, often excessive

sentimental *adjective* having or showing too much feeling or emotion ◆ **sentimentality** *noun*

sentimentalize or **sentimentalise** *verb* **1** to behave sentimentally **2** to make, or treat as, sentimental

sentry *noun* (*plural* **sentries**) a soldier posted to guard an entrance

sepal *noun* one of the green leaves beneath the petals of a flower

separable *adjective* able to be separated

separate *verb* (pronounced **sep**-a-reit) **1** to set or keep apart **2** to divide into parts **3** to disconnect **4** to go different ways: *They separated at the station* **5** of a couple: to live apart by choice ➤ *adjective* (pronounced **sep**-a-rat) **1** placed, kept, etc apart **2** divided **3** not connected **4** different ◆ **separation** *noun* ◆ **separator** *noun*

separatism *noun* **1** a tendency to separate or to be separate **2** support for separation **3** the practices and principles of separatists

separatist *noun* someone who withdraws or urges separation from an established church, state, etc

Sephardim *plural noun* the Spanish and Portuguese Jews (as distinguished from the Ashkenazim, the Polish and German Jews) ◆ **Sephardi** ➤ *noun* a member of the Sephardim ➤ *adjective* of the Sephardim

sepia (pronounced **see**-pi-a) *noun* a brown colour

sept- *prefix* seven: *septet/September* (which was the seventh month in the Roman calendar) ⊕ Comes from Latin *septem* meaning 'seven'

September *noun* the ninth month of the year

⊕ From a Latin word meaning 'seventh', because September was originally the seventh month of the year, before January and February were added

septet *noun* a group of seven musicians etc

septic *adjective* of a wound: full of germs that are poisoning the blood ℗ Comes from Greek *sepein* meaning 'to putrefy'

❗ Do not confuse with: **sceptic**

septicaemia (*pronounced* sep-ti-**see**-mi-a) *noun, medicine* blood poisoning

septuagenarian (*pronounced* sep-tyoo-a-ji-**neir**-ri-an) *noun* someone from seventy to seventy-nine years old

septum *noun, anatomy, biology* any partition between holes, eg between the nostrils

septuplet *noun* any of seven children or animals born at one birth

sepulchral (*pronounced* sip-**ul**-kral) *adjective* 1 of sepulchres 2 dismal, gloomy

sepulchre (*pronounced* **sep**-ul-ker) *noun* a tomb

sequel *noun* 1 a result, a consequence 2 a story that is a continuation of an earlier story

sequence *noun* 1 the order (of events) in time 2 a number of things following in order, a connected series 3 *maths* a set of values or quantities where each one is greater or smaller than the last by a fixed amount 4 *music* the repetition of a melody in higher or lower parts of the scale

sequencing *noun, biochemistry* the process of determining the order of amino acids in a protein or the order of nucleotides in DNA or RNA

sequential *adjective* in a particular order or sequence

sequestrate *verb* to keep apart, isolate

sequin *noun* a small round sparkling ornament sewn on a dress etc

seraph *noun* (*plural* **seraphs** or **seraphim**) an angel of the highest rank

seraphic *adjective* like an angel

serenade *noun* music played or sung in the open air at night, especially under a woman's window ➤ *verb* to sing or play a serenade (to)

serendipitous *adjective* discovered by luck or chance

serendipity *noun* happy chance, luck

℗ After a fairy story called *The Princess of Serendip*, in which the heroes were always making lucky discoveries. *Serendip* was an old name for Sri Lanka

serene *adjective* 1 calm 2 not worried, happy, peaceful

serenity *noun* calmness, peacefulness

serf *noun, history* a slave bought and sold with the land on which he worked ♦ **serfdom** *noun*

serge *noun* a strong type of cloth

sergeant *noun* 1 an army rank above corporal 2 a rank in the police force above a constable

sergeant-major *noun* an army rank above sergeant

serial *noun* a story which is published, broadcast or televised in instalments

serialize or **serialise** *verb* to publish or broadcast (a story, television programme, etc) in instalments

serial number *noun* the individual identification number on each of a series of identical products

serial port *noun, computing* a connection on a computer for a device such as a mouse or a scanner, and through which data can only be sent one bit at a time

series *noun* (*plural* **series**) 1 a number of things following each other in order 2 a set of things of the same kind: *a series of books on art* 3 a regularly broadcast TV or radio programme with the same characters or a similar subject 4 *maths* the sum obtained when each member of a sequence of numbers is added to the previous ones

series circuit *noun* an electrical circuit where a power source is connected to two or more components one after the other (*compare with*: **parallel circuit**)

serif *noun* 1 a short line or stroke on the end of a printed character 2 a printing font having characters with serifs

serious *adjective* 1 grave, thoughtful: *serious expression on her face* 2 not joking, in earnest: *serious remark* 3 important, needing careful thought: *a serious matter* 4 likely to have dangerous results: *serious accident* ♦ **seriously** *adverb*

sermon *noun* a serious talk, especially one given in church

serology *noun* the scientific study of blood serum ♦ **serologist** *noun*

serotonin *noun* a hormone that acts as a neurotransmitter and affects mood

serpent *noun, old* a snake

serpentine *adjective* like a serpent; winding, full of twists

serrated *adjective* having notches or teeth like a saw: *a serrated edge*

serried *adjective* closely grouped together: *serried ranks*

serum *noun* 1 a yellowish fluid in blood, which contains specific antibodies and can be used for vaccination 2 the watery part of a plant fluid

servant *noun* 1 someone paid to work for another, especially in helping to run a house 2 a government employee: *civil servant/public servant*

serve *verb* 1 to work for and obey 2 to attend or wait upon at table 3 to give out food, goods, etc: *Are you being served?* 4 to be able to be used (as): *The cave will serve as a shelter* **5** to be suitable for: *serve a purpose* **6** to carry out duties as a member of the armed forces **7** to undergo (a sentence in prison etc) **8** *tennis* to throw up the ball and hit it with the racket to start play • **serve someone right** to be deserved by them

server *noun, computing* a computer that manages data, processes e-mail, provides printing facilities, etc for several smaller computers on a network

service *noun* **1** an act of serving **2** the duty required of a servant or other employee **3** a performance of (public) worship **4** use: *bring the new machine into service* **5** time spent in the armed forces **6** (**services**) the armed forces **7** (**services**) help: *services to refugees* **8** a regular supply: *bus service* **9** (**services**) public supply of water, gas, electricity, etc **10** a set of dishes: *dinner service* **11** a regular check on a car, machine, etc to keep it in good working order: *The car's due for a service* ➤ *verb* to keep (a car, machine, etc) in good working order by regular checks and repairs • **active service** service in battle • **at your service** ready to help or be of use

serviceable *adjective* useful; lasting a long time: *serviceable clothes*

service industry *noun* an industry concerned with providing services rather than manufacturing products (*also called*: **tertiary industry**)

service station *noun* a petrol station providing facilities such as a shop, car-washing, etc

serviette *noun* a table napkin

servile *adjective* slave-like; showing lack of spirit: *a servile attitude to his employer*

servility *noun* being servile

servitude *noun* slavery; the state of being under strict control

servomechanism *noun* a control system in which a small input power controls a larger output power

sesame (*pronounced* **ses**-am-i) *noun* a SE Asian plant whose seeds produce an edible oil

session *noun* **1** a meeting of a court, council, etc **2** the period of the year when classes are held in a school etc **3** a period of time spent on a particular activity

sestet *noun* a group of six musicians etc

set *verb* (**setting, set**) **1** to place or put **2** to fix in the proper place (eg broken bones) **3** to arrange (a table for a meal, jewels in a necklace, etc) **4** to fix (a date, a price, etc) **5** to fix hair (in waves or curls) **6** to adjust (a clock, a machine, etc) so that it is ready to work or perform some function **7** to give (a task etc): *set him three problems* **8** to put in a certain state or condition: *set free* **9** of a jelly etc: to become firm or solid **10** to compose

music for: *He set the poem to music* **11** of the sun: to go out of sight below the horizon ➤ *adjective* **1** fixed or arranged beforehand; ready: *all set* **2** fixed, stiff: *a set expression on his face* ➤ *noun* **1** a group of people **2** a number of things of a similar kind, or used together: *set of carving tools* **3** *maths* a group of objects or elements with something in common **4** an apparatus: *a television set* **5** scenery made ready for a play etc **6** pose, position: *the set of his head* **7** a series of six or more games in tennis **8** a fixing of hair in waves or curls **9** (*also called*: **sett**) a badger's burrow **10** (*also called*: **sett**) a street paving-block • **set about 1** to begin (doing something) **2** to attack • **set in** to begin: *Winter has set in* • **set off** or **out** or **forth** to start (on a journey etc) • **set on** or **upon** to attack • **set to 1** to start working **2** to start fighting • **set up 1** to establish (something) **2** to put (someone) into a position of security: *The inheritance has set him up for life* **3** *slang* to trick (someone) into taking blame or facing embarrassment ⊙ Comes from Old English verb *settan* and noun *set* meaning 'a seat'

set-aside *noun, economics, geography* the policy of taking agricultural land out of production, as in the EU scheme to reduce grain surpluses in which farmers are paid compensation for leaving land uncultivated

setback *noun* a movement in the wrong direction, a failure

set piece *noun* **1** a prepared musical or literary performance **2** *sport* a practised sequence of passes, movements, etc taken at free kick etc

set square *noun* a triangular drawing instrument, with one right angle

sett *noun* another spelling of **set** (meanings 9 and 10)

settee *noun* a sofa

setter *noun* a dog trained to point out game in hunting

setting *noun* **1** the act of someone or something that sets **2** an arrangement **3** a background: *against a setting of hills and lochs*

settle *verb* **1** to place in a position or at rest **2** to come to rest: *A butterfly settled on his arm* **3** to agree over (a matter): *settle the price* **4** (sometimes **settle down**) to become calm or quiet **5** (sometimes **settle down**) to make your home in a place **6** to pay (a bill) **7** to fix, decide (on) **8** to bring (a quarrel etc) to an end **9** to sink to the bottom ➤ *noun* a long high-backed bench

settlement *noun* **1** the act of settling **2** a decision, an agreement **3** payment of a bill **4** money given to a woman on her marriage **5** a number of people who have come to live in a country

settler *noun* someone who goes to live in a new area or country

set-to *noun* **1** *informal* a fight or argument **2** a fierce contest

set-up *noun* **1** *informal* an arrangement or set of arrangements **2** *slang* a trick to make a person unjustly blamed, accused or embarrassed

seven *noun* the number 7 ➤ *adjective* 7 in number

seventeen *noun* the number 17 ➤ *adjective* 17 in number

seventeenth *adjective* the last of a series of seventeen ➤ *noun* one of seventeen equal parts

seventh *adjective* the last of a series of seven ➤ *noun* one of seven equal parts

seventies *plural noun* (also **70s, 70's**) **1** the period of time between seventieth and eightieth birthdays **2** the range of temperatures between seventy and eighty degrees **3** the period of time between the seventieth and eightieth years of a century

seventieth *adjective* the last of a series of seventy ➤ *noun* one of seventy equal parts

seventy *noun* the number 70 ➤ *adjective* 70 in number

sever *verb* **1** to cut apart or away, break off **2** to separate, part

several *adjective* **1** more than one or two, but not many **2** various **3** different: *going their several ways* ➤ *pronoun* more than one or two people, things, etc, but not a great many

severance *noun* **1** severing or being severed **2** separation

severe *adjective* **1** serious: *a severe illness* **2** harsh, strict **3** very plain and simple, not fancy: *a severe haircut*

severity *noun* strictness, harshness

sew *verb* (**sewing, sewed, sewn**) **1** to join together with a needle and thread **2** to make or mend in this way

sewage *noun* water and waste matter

sewer *noun* an underground drain for carrying off water and waste matter

sewerage *noun* **1** a system or network of sewers **2** drainage of sewage and surface water using sewers

sex *noun* **1** either of the two classes (male or female) into which animals are divided according to the part they play in producing children or young **2** sexual intercourse

sex- *prefix* six ✆ Comes from Latin *sex* meaning 'six'

sexagenarian *noun* someone from sixty to sixty-nine years old

sex chromosome *noun* an X- or Y-chromosome, that in combination determines the sex of an individual

sex hormone *noun* a hormone that regulates sexual development and is needed for reproduction

sexism *noun* discrimination against someone on the grounds of their sex

sexist *noun* someone who treats the opposite sex unfairly or thinks that they are inferior ➤ *adjective* relating to or characteristic of sexism: *a sexist attitude*

sextant *noun* an instrument used for calculating distances by means of measuring angles, eg the distance between two stars

sextet *noun* a group of six musicians etc

sexton *noun* someone who has various responsibilities in a church, eg bell-ringing, grave-digging, etc

sextuplet *noun* any of six children or animals born at the same birth

sexual *adjective* **1** of sex or gender **2** relating to sexual intercourse ✦ **sexually** *adverb*

sexual intercourse *noun* physical union between a man and a woman involving the insertion of the penis into the vagina

sexuality *noun* the way in which a person expresses, or their ability to experience, sexual feelings

sexually transmitted disease *noun* (*abbrev* STD) any disease that is transmitted by sexual intercourse

sexual reproduction *noun* reproduction by the union of male and female reproductive cells

sexy *adjective* (**sexier, sexiest**) sexually attractive or sexually exciting

SF *abbreviation* science fiction

Sg *symbol, chemistry* seaborgium

Shabbat *noun, Judaism* the Sabbath, beginning at sunset on Friday and ending at nightfall on Saturday

shabby *adjective* (**shabbier, shabbiest**) **1** worn-looking **2** poorly dressed **3** of behaviour: mean, unfair ✦ **shabbily** *adverb*

shack *noun* a roughly built hut

shackle *verb* **1** to fasten with a chain **2** to hold back, prevent, hinder

shackles *plural noun* chains fastening a prisoner's legs or arms

shade *noun* **1** slight darkness caused by cutting off some light **2** a place not in full sunlight **3** a screen from the heat or light **4** (**shades**) *informal* sunglasses **5** the deepness or a variation of a colour **6** the dark parts in a picture **7** a very small amount or difference: *a shade larger* **8** *literary* a ghost ➤ *verb* **1** to shelter from the sun or light **2** to make parts of a picture darker **3** to change gradually, eg from one colour into another

shading *noun* the marking of the darker places in a picture

shadow *noun* **1** shade caused by some object coming in the way of a light **2** the dark shape of that object on the ground **3** a dark part in a picture **4** a very small amount: *a shadow of doubt* ➤ *verb* **1** to shade, darken **2** to follow someone about, sometimes secretly, and watch them closely

shadow-boxing *noun* boxing against an imaginary opponent as training

shadow cabinet *noun* leading members of the opposition in parliament

shady *adjective* (**shadier, shadiest**) **1** sheltered from light or heat **2** *informal* dishonest, underhand: *a shady character*

shaft *noun* **1** a long, straight handle or part of anything **2** the rod on which the head of an axe, arrow, etc is fixed **3** an arrow **4** a revolving rod which turns a machine or engine **5** the pole of a cart to which the horses are tied **6** the deep, narrow passageway leading to a mine **7** a deep vertical hole for a lift **8** a ray (of light)

shag¹ *noun* **1** a ragged mass of hair or something similar **2** in a carpet: long, thick fibres **3** a kind of shredded tobacco **4** a species of cormorant

shag² *taboo slang, verb* (**shagging, shagged**) to have sexual intercourse with someone ➤ *noun* an act of sexual intercourse

shaggy *adjective* (**shaggier, shaggiest**) rough, hairy or woolly

shahada (*pronounced* sha-**ha**-da) *noun, Islam* a declaration of Islamic faith

shake *verb* (**shaking, shook, shaken**) **1** to move backwards and forwards or up and down with quick, jerky movements **2** to make or be made unsteady **3** to shock, disturb: *His parting words shook me* ➤ *noun* **1** the act of shaking or trembling **2** a shock **3** a drink mixed by shaking or stirring quickly: *milk shake*

shaky *adjective* (**shakier, shakiest**) unsteady; trembling ♦ **shakily** *adverb*

shale *noun* a kind of rock from which oil can be obtained

shall *verb* **1** used to form future tenses of other verbs when the subject is *I* or *we*: *I shall tell you later* **2** used for emphasis, or to express a promise, when the subject is *you, he, she, it* or *they*: *You shall go if I say you must*/*You shall go if you want to* (*see also*: **should**)

shallot *noun* a kind of small onion

shallow *adjective* **1** not deep **2** not capable of thinking or feeling deeply ➤ *noun* (often **shallows**) a place where the water is not deep

sham *noun* something which is not what it appears to be, a pretence ➤ *adjective* false, imitation, pretended: *a sham fight* ➤ *verb* (**shamming, shammed**) to pretend, feign: *shamming sleep*

shaman (*pronounced* **shah**-man or **shei**-man) *noun* a tribal healer or medicine man

shamble *verb* to walk in a shuffling or awkward manner

shambles *singular noun, informal* a mess, confused disorder

> ⊘ Originally meaning a place where animals were slaughtered

shambolic *adjective, slang* chaotic, messy

shame *noun* **1** an uncomfortable feeling caused by realization of guilt or failure **2** disgrace, dishonour **3** bad luck, a pity: *It's a shame that you can't go* ➤ *verb* **1** to make to feel shame or ashamed **2** (**shame into**) to cause (someone to do something) by making them ashamed: *They shamed him into paying his share* • **put to shame** to cause to feel ashamed

shamefaced *adjective* showing shame or embarrassment

shameful *adjective* disgraceful

shameless *adjective* feeling or showing no shame

shammy another spelling of **chamois**

shampoo *verb* to wash (the hair, carpet) ➤ *noun* **1** an act of shampooing **2** a soapy liquid used for cleaning the hair **3** a similar liquid used for cleaning carpets or upholstery

shamrock *noun* a plant like clover with leaves divided in three

shandy *noun* (*plural* **shandies**) a mixture of beer with lemonade or ginger beer

shank *noun* **1** the part of the leg between the knee and the foot **2** a long straight part (of a tool etc)

shanks's pony *noun* walking, on foot

shan't *short for* shall not

shanty *noun* (*plural* **shanties**) **1** a roughly made hut **2** a sailors' song

shantytown *noun, geography* a town or area where the people are poor and have built makeshift houses

shape *noun* **1** the form or outline of anything **2** a mould for a jelly etc **3** a jelly etc turned out of a mould **4** condition: *in good shape* **5** a geometric figure ➤ *verb* **1** to make into a certain form **2** to model, mould **3** to develop (in a particular way): *Our plans are shaping well*

shapeless *adjective* having no shape or regular form

shapely *adjective* having an attractive shape

shape poem *noun* a poem written or printed so that it forms on the page a shape that represents its subject

share *noun* **1** one part of something that is divided among several people **2** one of the parts into which the money of a business firm is divided ➤ *verb* **1** to divide out among a number of people **2** to allow others to use (your possessions etc) **3** to have or use in common with someone else: *We share a liking for music*

shareholder *noun* someone who owns shares in a business company

shareware *noun, computing* software available to the public on a free trial, often for a limited time

sharia or **shariah** *noun, Islam* the body of Islamic religious law

shark *noun* **1** a large, flesh-eating fish **2** *informal* a swindler

sharp *adjective* **1** cutting, piercing **2** having a thin edge or fine point **3** hurting, stinging, biting: *sharp wind/sharp words* **4** alert, quick-witted **5** sensitive, perceptive, able to pick up faint signals: *sharp eyes* **6** severe, inclined to scold **7** *music* of a note: raised half a tone in pitch **8** of a voice: shrill **9** of an outline: clear ➤ *adverb* punctually: *Come at ten o'clock sharp* ➤ *noun, music* a sign (♯) showing that a note is to be raised half a tone • **look sharp** to hurry

sharpen *verb* to make or grow sharp

sharpener *noun* an instrument for sharpening: *pencil sharpener*

sharper *noun* a cheat, especially at cards

sharp practice *noun* cheating

shatter *verb* to break in pieces; to upset, ruin (hopes, health, etc)

shave *verb* **1** to cut away hair with a razor **2** to scrape away the surface of (wood etc) **3** to touch lightly, or just avoid touching, in passing ➤ *noun* **1** the act of shaving **2** a narrow escape: *a close shave*

shaven *adjective* shaved

shaver *noun* an electric device for shaving

shavings *plural noun* very thin slices of wood etc

Shavuot, Shavuoth or **Shabuoth** (*pronounced* shahv-**oo**-oth or shahv-**oo**-ot) *noun, Judaism* the Jewish Feast of Weeks, commemorating the giving of the law to Moses

shawl *noun* a loose covering for the shoulders

she *pronoun* a woman, girl or female animal etc already spoken about (used only as the subject of a verb): *When the girl saw us, she waved*

sheaf *noun* (*plural* **sheaves**) a bundle (eg of corn, papers) tied together

shear *verb* (**shearing, sheared, shorn**) **1** to clip, cut (especially wool from a sheep) **2** to cut through, cut off ➤ *noun* **1** the act of shearing **2** *physics* a force acting parallel to a plane rather than at right angles to it ⊙ Comes from Old English *sceran*, from a Germanic base meaning 'cut', 'divide', 'shear' or 'shave'

⚠ Do not confuse with: **sheer**

shears *plural noun* large scissors

sheath *noun* **1** a case for a sword or dagger **2** a long close-fitting covering **3** a condom **4** *biology*

any protective or encasing structure in an animal or plant

sheathe *verb* to put into a sheath

shed *noun* **1** a building for storage or shelter: *coalshed/bicycle shed* **2** an outhouse ➤ *verb* (**shedding, shed**) **1** to throw or cast off (leaves, a skin, clothing) **2** to pour out (tears, blood) **3** to give out (light etc)

sheen *noun* brightness, gloss

sheep *noun* **1** an animal whose flesh is used as food and whose fleece is used for wool **2** a very meek person who lacks confidence

sheep-dip *noun* a liquid for disinfecting sheep

sheepdog *noun* a dog trained to look after sheep

sheepish *adjective* shy; embarrassed, shamefaced

sheepshank *noun* a kind of knot, used for shortening a rope

sheepskin *noun* **1** the skin of a sheep **2** a kind of leather made from this

sheer *adjective* **1** very steep: *sheer drop from the cliff* **2** pure, not mixed: *sheer delight/sheer nonsense* **3** of cloth: very thin or fine ➤ *adverb* straight up and down, very steeply: *rock face rising sheer* ➤ *verb* to turn aside from a straight line, swerve ⊙ Adjective and adverb: come perhaps from the Old English equivalent of Old Norse *skærr* meaning 'bright'; verb: formed from a combination of Late German or Dutch *scheren* meaning 'to cut', and an alternative spelling of English *shear*

⚠ Do not confuse with: **shear**

sheet *noun* **1** a large piece of linen, cotton, nylon, etc used to cover the mattress of a bed **2** a large thin piece of metal, glass, ice, etc **3** a piece of paper **4** a sail **5** the rope fastened to the lower corner of a sail

sheikh (*pronounced* sheik or sheek) *noun* an Arab chief

shelf *noun* (*plural* **shelves**) **1** a board fixed on a wall, for laying things on **2** a flat layer of rock, a ledge **3** a sandbank

shell *noun* **1** a hard outer covering (of a shellfish, egg, nut, etc) **2** a husk or pod (eg of peas) **3** a metal case filled with explosive fired from a gun **4** a framework, eg of a building not yet completed or burnt out: *Only the shell of the warehouse was left* **5** *chemistry* one of a series of concentric spheres representing the possible orbits of electrons around the nucleus of an atom ➤ *verb* **1** to take the shell from (a nut, egg, peas, etc) **2** to fire shells at

shellac *noun* **1** a resin produced by certain tropical insects **2** a solution of this in alcohol, used as a varnish ➤ *verb* (**shellacking, shellacked**) to coat with shellac

shellfish *noun* a water creature covered with a shell, eg an oyster, limpet or mussel

shellshock *noun* a psychological disorder caused by prolonged exposure to military combat conditions

shelter *noun* 1 a building which acts as a protection from harm, rain, wind, etc 2 the state of being protected from any of these ➤ *verb* 1 to give protection to 2 to put in a place of safety or protection 3 to go to, or stay in, a place of safety • **take shelter** to go to a place of safety

sheltered *adjective* 1 protected from the effects of weather 2 protected from the harsh realities of the world: *a sheltered life*

shelve *verb* 1 to put up shelves in 2 to put aside (a problem etc) for later consideration 3 of land: to slope gently

shema (*pronounced* she-**ma**) *noun, Judaism* a prayer that is a declaration of religious faith

shenanigans *plural noun* foolish or underhand behaviour

shepherd *noun* a man who looks after sheep ➤ *verb* to watch over carefully, guide

shepherdess *noun* a woman who looks after sheep

shepherd's pie *noun* a dish of minced meat covered with mashed potatoes

sherbet *noun* 1 a fizzy drink 2 powder for making this

sheriff *noun* 1 the chief representative of a monarch in a county, whose duties include keeping the peace 2 in Scotland, the chief judge of a county 3 *US* the chief law-enforcement officer of a county

sheriff court *noun* in Scotland: a court dealing with civil actions and all but the most serious crimes

sherry *noun* (*plural* **sherries**) a strong kind of wine, often drunk before a meal

Shia or **Shiah** (*pronounced* shee-a) *noun* (*plural* **Shias** or **Shiahs**) 1 the branch of Islam which regards Ali, Muhammad's cousin and son-in-law, as his true successor as leader of Islam (*compare with*: **Sunni**) 2 a member of this branch of Islam ☉ Comes from Arabic, meaning 'sect'

shiatsu or **shiatzu** *noun, medical* a Japanese technique of healing massage involving the application of pressure to parts of the body distant from the affected area

shibboleth *noun* a word or attribute which identifies members of a group

☉ Originally a word giving membership to a group, after a Biblical story in which its correct pronunciation was used as a password

shied past form of **shy**

shield *noun* 1 anything that protects from harm

2 a broad piece of metal carried by a soldier etc as a defence against weapons 3 a shield-shaped trophy won in a competition 4 a shield-shaped plaque bearing a coat-of-arms ➤ *verb* to protect, defend, shelter

shift *verb* 1 to move, change the position of: *shift the furniture/trying to shift the blame* 2 to change position or direction: *The wind shifted* 3 to get rid of ➤ *noun* 1 a change: *shift of emphasis* 2 a change of position, transfer 3 a group of workers on duty at the same time 4 a specified period of work or duty: *day shift/night shift* 5 a loose-fitting lightweight dress • **shift for yourself** to manage to get on by your own efforts

shiftless *adjective* 1 having no motivation or initiative 2 inefficient

shifty *adjective* (**shiftier, shiftiest**) not to be trusted, looking dishonest

Shiite (*pronounced* **shee**-ait) *noun* a Muslim who is an adherent of Shia ➤ *adjective* relating to Shia ♦ **Shiism** *noun*

shilling *noun* a silver-coloured coin used before decimal currency, worth $\frac{1}{20}$ of £1

shillyshally *verb* (**shillyshallies, shillyshallying, shillyshallied**) to hesitate in making up your mind, waver

shimmer *verb* to shine with a quivering or unsteady light: *The lake shimmered in the moonlight* ➤ *noun* a quivering light

shin *noun* the front part of the leg below the knee • **shin up** to climb: *shin up a drainpipe*

shindig *noun* a lively party or celebration

shindy *noun* (*plural* **shindies**), *informal* a noise, uproar

shine *verb* (**shining, shone**) 1 to give out or reflect light 2 to be bright 3 to polish (shoes etc) 4 to be very good at: *He shines at arithmetic* ➤ *noun* 1 brightness 2 an act of polishing

shingle *noun* coarse gravel or rounded stones on the shores of rivers or of the sea

shingles *singular noun, medicine* an infectious disease causing a painful rash

shining *adjective* 1 very bright and clear 2 admired, distinguished: *a shining example*

shiny *adjective* (**shinier, shiniest**) glossy, polished

ship *noun* a large vessel for journeys across water ➤ *verb* (**shipping, shipped**) 1 to take onto a ship 2 to send by ship 3 to go by ship

-ship *suffix* 1 a state or condition: *friendship* 2 a skill: *craftsmanship*

shipment *noun* 1 an act of putting on board ship 2 a load of goods sent by ship

shipping *noun* 1 ships as traffic: *a gale warning to shipping* 2 the commercial transport of goods and freight, especially by ship

shipshape *adjective* in good order, neat, trim

shipwreck *noun* **1** the sinking or destruction of a ship (especially by accident) **2** a wrecked ship **3** ruin

shipyard *noun* the yard in which ships are built or repaired

shire *noun* a county

shirk *verb* to avoid or evade (doing your duty etc)

shirker *noun* a person who avoids work or responsibilities

shirt *noun* **1** a garment worn by men on the upper part of the body, having a collar, sleeves and buttons down the front **2** a similar garment for a woman

shirty *adjective* (**shirtier, shirtiest**), *informal* ill-tempered or irritable; annoyed

shit *taboo slang, noun* **1** excrement **2** an act of defecating **3** rubbish, nonsense **4** a despicable person ➤ *verb* (**shitting, shitted** or **shat**) to defecate

Shiva see **Siva**

shiver *verb* to tremble with cold or fear ➤ *noun* **1** the act of shivering **2** a small broken piece: *shivers of glass*

shoal *noun* **1** a group of fishes, moving and feeding together **2** a shallow place, a sandbank

shock *noun* **1** a sudden forceful blow **2** a feeling of fright, horror, dismay, etc **3** *medicine* a state of extreme physical collapse occurring as a result of severe burns, drug overdose, etc **4** the effect on the body of an electric current passing through it **5** an earthquake **6** a bushy mass (of hair) ➤ *verb* **1** to give a shock to **2** to upset or horrify

shock absorber *noun* a device in an aircraft, car, etc for lessening the impact or force of bumps

shocking *adjective* causing horror or dismay; disgusting

shock wave *noun* **1** *physics* a very intense sound wave caused by a violent explosion or by something moving faster than the speed of sound **2** a feeling of shock that spreads through a community after a disturbing event

shod *adjective* wearing shoes ➤ *verb* past form of **shoe**

shoddy *adjective* (**shoddier, shoddiest**) **1** of poor material or quality: *shoddy goods* **2** mean, low: *a shoddy trick*

shoe *noun* **1** a stiff outer covering for the foot, not reaching above the ankle **2** a rim of iron nailed to the hoof of a horse ➤ *verb* (**shoeing, shod**) to put shoes on (a horse)

shoehorn *noun* a curved piece of plastic, metal, etc for making a shoe slip easily over your heel

shoelace *noun* a cord or string used for fastening a shoe

shoemaker *noun* someone who makes and mends shoes

shoestring *noun, US* a shoelace • **on a shoestring** with very little money

shone past form of **shine**

shoo *interjection* used to scare away birds, animals, etc ➤ *verb* (**shooing, shooed**) to drive or scare away

shook past tense of **shake**

shoot *verb* (**shooting, shot**) **1** to send a bullet from a gun, or an arrow from a bow **2** to hit or kill with an arrow, bullet, etc **3** to let fly swiftly and with force **4** to kick for a goal **5** of a plant: to grow new buds **6** to photograph, film **7** to move very swiftly or suddenly **8** to slide (a bolt) ➤ *noun* **1** a new sprout on a plant **2** an expedition to shoot game **3** land where game is shot

shooting star *noun, informal* a meteor

shop *noun* **1** a place where goods are sold **2** a workshop ➤ *verb* (**shopping, shopped**) **1** to visit shops and buy goods **2** *slang* to betray (someone) to the police • **talk shop** *informal* to talk about work when off duty

shopkeeper *noun* someone who owns and keeps a shop

shoplifter *noun* someone who steals goods from a shop ♦ **shoplifting** *noun*

shopper *noun* someone who shops, a customer

shopping *noun* **1** visiting shops to buy goods **2** goods bought

shop steward *noun* a worker elected by the other workers as their representative

shore *noun* the land bordering on a sea or lake ➤ *verb* to prop (up), support: *shoring up an unprofitable organization*

shoreline *noun* the line formed where land meets water

shorn past participle of **shear**

short *adjective* **1** not long: *short skirt* **2** not tall **3** brief, not lasting long: *short talk* **4** not enough, less than it should be: *I'm £5 short* **5** rude, sharp, abrupt **6** of pastry: crisp and crumbling easily ➤ *adverb* **1** suddenly, abruptly: *stop short* **2** not as far as intended: *The shot fell short* ➤ *noun* **1** a short film **2** a short circuit **3** a drink of an alcoholic spirit **4** (**shorts**) short trousers ➤ *verb* to short-circuit • **in short** in a few words • **short of 1** not having enough of: *short of money* **2** less than, not as much or as far as: *5 miles short of Inverness/£5 short of the price* **3** without going as far as: *He didn't know how to get the money, short of stealing it*

shortage *noun* a lack

shortbread *noun* a thick biscuit made of butter and flour etc

short-change *verb* **1** to give (a customer) less than the correct amount of change, by accident or intentionally **2** *informal* to treat dishonestly

short circuit *noun* the missing out of a major part of an intended electric circuit, sometimes causing blowing of fuses

short-circuit *verb* **1** of an electrical appliance: to have a short circuit **2** to bypass (a difficulty etc)

shortcoming *noun* a fault, a defect

short cut *noun* a short way of going somewhere or doing something

shorten *verb* to make less in length

shortfall *noun* **1** a failure to reach a desired or expected level **2** the amount or margin by which something is deficient: *a shortfall of several thousand pounds*

shorthand *noun* a method of writing quickly using strokes and dots to show sounds (*contrasted with*: **longhand**)

short-handed *adjective* understaffed

short list *noun* a list of candidates selected from the total number of applicants or contestants

short-lived *adjective* living or lasting only a short time

shortly *adverb* **1** soon **2** curtly, abruptly **3** briefly

short-sighted *adjective* **1** seeing clearly only things which are near **2** taking no account of what may happen in the future

short-tempered *adjective* easily made angry

short-term *adjective* intended to last only a short time

short-wave *adjective* of a radio wave: using wavelengths between 10 and 100 metres (*compare with*: **long-wave**)

shot *noun* **1** something which is shot or fired **2** small lead bullets, used in cartridges **3** a single act of shooting **4** the sound of a gun being fired **5** the distance covered by a bullet, arrow, etc **6** a marksman **7** a throw or turn in a game **8** an attempt at doing something, guessing, etc **9** a photograph **10** a scene in a motion picture ➤ *adjective* **1** of silk: showing changing colours **2** streaked or mixed with (a colour etc) ➤ *verb* past form of **shoot** • **a shot in the dark** a guess

shotgun *noun* a light type of gun which fires shot

should *verb* **1** the form of the verb **shall** used to express a condition: *I should go if I had time* **2** used to mean 'ought to': *You should know that already*

shoulder *noun* **1** the part of the body between the neck and upper arm **2** the upper part of an animal's foreleg **3** a hump, a ridge: *the shoulder of the hill* ➤ *verb* **1** to carry on the shoulders **2** to bear the full weight of (a burden etc) **3** to push with the shoulder

shoulderblade *noun* the broad flat bone of the shoulder

shout *noun* **1** a loud cry or call **2** a loud burst (of laughter etc) ➤ *verb* to make a loud cry

shove *verb* to push roughly, thrust, push aside ➤ *noun* a rough push

shovel *noun* a spade-like tool used for lifting coal, gravel, etc ➤ *verb* to lift or move with a shovel

show *verb* (**showing, showed, shown**) **1** to allow, or cause, to be seen: *Show me your new dress* **2** to be able to be seen: *Your underskirt is showing* **3** to exhibit, display (an art collection etc) **4** to point out (the way etc) **5** to direct, guide: *Show her to a seat* **6** to make clear, demonstrate: *That shows that I was right* ➤ *noun* **1** the act of showing **2** a display, an exhibition: *an art show* **3** a performance, an entertainment • **show off 1** to show or display (something) **2** to try to impress others with your talents etc • **show up 1** to make to stand out clearly **2** to expose, make obvious (especially someone's faults)

show business *noun* the entertainment industry, especially light entertainment in film, theatre and television

showdown *noun, informal* a confrontation to settle a long-running dispute

shower *noun* **1** a short fall of rain **2** a large quantity: *a shower of questions* **3** a room or cubicle fitted with an apparatus that sprays water for bathing under while standing up **4** the apparatus that sprays water for this **5** *US* a party at which gifts are given to someone about to be married, have a baby, etc ➤ *verb* **1** to pour (something) down on **2** to bathe under a shower

showerproof *adjective* of material, a coat, etc: able to withstand light rain

showery *adjective* raining from time to time

showjumping *noun* a competitive sport in which riders on horseback take turns to jump a variety of obstacles as well and as quickly as possible ♦ **showjumper** *noun*

shown past participle of **show**

show-off *noun, informal* someone who shows off to attract attention

showroom *noun* a room where goods are laid out for people to see

showy *adjective* (**showier, showiest**) bright, gaudy; (too) obvious, striking

shrank past tense of **shrink**

shrapnel *noun* **1** a shell containing bullets etc which scatter on explosion **2** splinters of metal, a bomb, etc

⊙ After Henry *Shrapnel*, 18th-century British general who invented the shell

shred *noun* **1** a long narrow piece, cut or torn off **2** a scrap, a very small amount: *not a shred of evidence* ➤ *verb* (**shredding, shredded**) to cut or tear into shreds

shrew *noun* **1** a small mouse-like type of animal

with a long nose **2** a quarrelsome or scolding woman

shrewd *adjective* clever, cunning

shrewish *adjective* quarrelsome, ill-tempered

shriek *verb* to make a shrill scream or laugh
➤ *noun* a shrill scream or laugh

shrift *noun*: **give someone short shrift** to dismiss them quickly

⊙ Originally a short confession made before being executed

shrill *adjective* of a sound or voice: high in tone, piercing ♦ **shrilly** *adverb*

shrimp *noun* **1** a small, long-tailed edible shellfish **2** *informal* a small person

shrine *noun* a holy or sacred place

shrink *verb* (**shrinking, shrank, shrunk**) **1** to make or become smaller **2** to draw back in fear and disgust (from) ➤ *noun, informal* a psychiatrist

shrinkage *noun* the amount by which something grows smaller

shrinking violet *noun, informal* a shy hesitant person

shrink-wrap *verb* to wrap (goods) in clear plastic film that is then shrunk to fit tightly
➤ *noun* such clear plastic film

shrive *verb* (**shriving, shrove, shriven**) *old* **1** to hear a confession **2** to confess

shrivel *verb* (**shrivelling, shrivelled**) to dry up, wrinkle, wither

shroud *noun* **1** a cloth covering a dead body **2** something which covers: *a shroud of mist* ➤ *verb* to wrap up, cover

Shrove Tuesday *noun* sometimes called Pancake Day: the day before Ash Wednesday

shrub *noun* a small bush or plant

shrubbery *noun* (*plural* **shrubberies**) a place where shrubs grow

shrug *verb* (**shrugging, shrugged**) to show doubt, lack of interest, etc by drawing up the shoulders ➤ *noun* a movement of the shoulders to show doubt, lack of interest, etc ● **shrug off** to dismiss, treat as being unimportant

shrunk past participle of **shrink**

shrunken *adjective* shrunk

shudder *verb* to tremble from fear, cold, disgust
➤ *noun* a trembling

shuffle *verb* **1** to mix, rearrange (eg playing-cards) **2** to move by dragging or sliding the feet along the ground without lifting them **3** to move (the feet) in this way ➤ *noun* **1** a rearranging **2** a dragging movement of the feet

shun *verb* (**shunning, shunned**) to avoid, keep clear of

shunt *verb* to move (railway trains, engines, etc) onto a side track

shut *verb* (**shutting, shut**) **1** to move (a door,

window, lid, etc) so that it covers an opening **2** to close, lock (a building etc) **3** to become closed: *The door shut with a bang* **4** to confine, restrain in a building, etc: *Shut the dog in his kennel*
● **shut down** to close (a factory etc) ● **shut up 1** to close completely **2** *informal* to stop speaking or making other noise

shutter *noun* **1** a cover for a window **2** a cover which closes over a camera lens as it takes a picture

shuttle *noun* the part of a weaving loom which carries the cross thread from side to side
➤ *adjective* of a transport service: going to and fro between two places

shuttlecock *noun* a rounded cork stuck with feathers, used in the game of badminton

shy *adjective* **1** of a wild animal: easily frightened, timid **2** lacking confidence in the presence of others **3** not wanting to attract attention ➤ *verb* (**shies, shying, shied**) **1** of a horse etc: to jump or turn suddenly aside in fear **2** (**shy away**) to shrink from or recoil, showing reluctance
➤ *noun* a try, an attempt ♦ **shyly** *adverb* **fight shy of** to avoid, keep away from

Si *symbol, chemistry* silicon

Siamese cat *noun* a fawn-coloured domestic cat

Siamese twins *plural noun* an old name for conjoined twins

sibilant *adjective* of a sound: hissing

sibling *noun* a brother or sister

sibyl *noun* a prophetess

sick *adjective* **1** wanting to vomit **2** vomiting **3** not well, ill **4** (**sick of**) tired of someone or something ● **be sick** to vomit

sick bed or **sick room** *noun* a bed or room for people to rest in when ill

sicken *verb* to make or become sick

sickening *adjective* **1** causing sickness **2** disgusting, revolting

sickle *noun* a hooked knife for cutting or reaping grain, hay, etc

sick leave *noun* time off work for illness

sickle-cell anaemia *noun, medicine* a hereditary disorder in which the red blood cells are destroyed by the body's defence system

sickly *adjective* (**sicklier, sickliest**) **1** unhealthy **2** feeble

sickness *noun* **1** an illness: *a mysterious sickness* **2** vomiting or nausea: *Have you been having any sickness or diarrhoea?*

side *noun* **1** an edge, border or boundary line **2** a surface that is not the top, bottom, front or back **3** either surface of a piece of paper, cloth, etc **4** the right or left part of the body **5** a division, a part: *the north side of the town* **6** an aspect, point of view: *all sides of the problem* **7** a slope (of a hill) **8** a team or party which is opposing another

> *adjective* **1** on or towards the side: *side door* **2** indirect, additional but less important: *side issue*
> *verb* (**side with**) to support (one person, group, etc against another) • **take sides** to choose to support (a party, person) against another

sideboard *noun* a piece of furniture in a dining room for holding dishes etc

sideburns *plural noun* the lines of short hair growing in front of a man's ears

---

⊙ Changed from *Burnside*, the name of a US army general who had extensive hair growth here

---

sidecar *noun* a small car for a passenger, attached to a motorcycle

side effect *noun* an additional (often bad) effect of a drug

sidekick *noun, informal* **1** a close or special friend **2** a working partner or deputy

sideline *noun* an extra bit of business outside regular work

sidelong *adjective & adverb* from or to the side: *sidelong glance*

sidereal (*pronounced* sai-**dee**-ri-al) *adjective* relating to the stars

sideshow *noun* a less important show that is part of a larger one

sidestep *verb* to avoid by stepping to one side

sidetrack *verb* to turn (someone) away from what they were going to do or say

sidewalk *noun, US* a pavement

sideways *adverb* **1** with the side foremost **2** towards the side

siding *noun* a short line of rails on which trucks are shunted off the main line

sidle *verb* **1** to go or move sideways **2** to move stealthily, sneak

siege (*pronounced* seej) *noun* **1** an attempt to capture a town etc by keeping it surrounded by an armed force **2** a constant attempt to gain control • **lay siege to** to besiege

siemens *noun* (symbol **S**) the standard unit of electrical conductance

sienna *noun* a reddish-brown, or yellowish-brown, pigment used in paints

sierra *noun* a range of mountains with jagged peaks

siesta *noun* a short sleep or rest taken in the afternoon

sieve (*pronounced* siv) *noun* a container with a mesh used to separate liquids from solids, or fine pieces from coarse pieces, etc > *verb* to put through a sieve

sift *verb* **1** to separate by passing through a sieve: *sift the flour* **2** to consider and examine closely: *sifting all the evidence*

sigh *noun* a long, deep-sounding breath, showing tiredness, longing, etc > *verb* to give out a sigh

sight *noun* **1** the act or power of seeing **2** a view, a glimpse: *catch sight of her* **3** (often **sights**) something worth seeing: *the sights of London* **4** something or someone unusual, ridiculous, shocking, etc: *She's quite a sight in that hat* **5** a guide on a gun for taking aim > *verb* **1** to get a view of, see suddenly **2** to look at through the sight of a gun ⊙ Comes from Old English *sihth* meaning 'vision' or 'appearance'

! Do not confuse with: **site** and **cite**

sight-reading *noun* playing or singing from music that has not been seen previously

sightseeing *noun* visiting the chief buildings, monuments, etc of a place ♦ **sightseer** *noun*

sign *noun* **1** a mark with a special meaning, a symbol **2** a gesture (eg a nod, wave of the hand) to show your meaning **3** an advertisement or notice giving information **4** something which shows what is happening or is going to happen: *signs of irritation/a sign of good weather* > *verb* **1** to write your name on (a document, cheque, etc) **2** to make a sign or gesture to **3** to show (your meaning) by a sign or gesture • **sign off 1** to bring a broadcast to an end **2** to stop work etc • **sign on** or **up** to enter your name on a list for work, the army, etc

signal *noun* **1** a gesture, light or sound giving a command, warning, etc: *air-raid signal* **2** something used for this purpose: *railway signals* **3** the wave of sound received or sent out by a radio etc set > *verb* (**signalling, signalled**) **1** to make signals (to) **2** to send (information) by signal > *adjective* remarkable: *a signal success*

signalman *noun* someone who works railway signals, or who sends signals

signal-to-noise ratio *noun, physics* the ratio of the power of a desired electrical signal to the power of the unwanted background noise, usually expressed in decibels

signatory *noun* (*plural* **signatories**) someone who has signed an agreement etc

signature *noun* **1** a signed name **2** an act of signing **3** *music* the flats or sharps at the beginning of a piece which show its key, or figures showing its timing

signature tune *noun* a tune used to identify a particular radio or television series etc, played at the beginning or end of the programme

signet *noun* a small seal, usually bearing someone's initials ⊙ Comes from Medieval Latin *signetum* meaning 'a small seal'

! Do not confuse with: **cygnet**

signet ring *noun* a ring imprinted with a signet
significance *noun* **1** meaning **2** importance

significance test *noun, statistics* a test used to demonstrate the probability that observed patterns cannot be explained by chance

significant *adjective* meaning much; important: *no significant change*
♦ **significantly** *adverb*

signify *verb* (**signifies, signifying, signified**) **1** to mean, be a sign of **2** to show, make known by a gesture: *signifying disapproval* **3** to have meaning or importance

sign language *noun* communication, especially with the deaf, using gestures to represent words and ideas

signpost *noun* a post with a sign, especially one showing direction and distances to certain places

Sikhism *noun* a religion whose followers observe the teachings of its ten gurus ♦ **Sikh** *noun & adjective* ⊙ Comes from Hindi meaning 'disciple'

silage *noun* green fodder preserved in a silo

silence *noun* **1** absence of sound or speech **2** a time of quietness ➤ *verb* to cause to be silent

silencer *noun* a device (on a car engine, gun, etc) for making it less noisy

silent *adjective* **1** free from noise **2** not speaking
♦ **silently** *adverb*

silhouette *noun* **1** an outline drawing of someone, often in profile, filled in with black **2** a dark outline seen against the light

⊙ After the 18th-century French finance minister, Etienne de *Silhouette*, possibly because of his notorious stinginess

silica *noun* a hard white or colourless solid that occurs naturally as quartz, sand and flint

silicate *noun* any of various chemical compounds containing silicon, oxygen and one or more metals

silicon *noun, chemistry* (symbol **Si**) a non-metallic element used as a semiconductor to make silicon chips for computer circuits etc

❗ Do not confuse with: **silicone**

silicon carbide *noun* another name for **carborundum**

silicon chip *noun, computers* a tiny, very thin piece of silicon on which all the components of an integrated circuit are arranged

silicone *noun* a synthetic polymer used in paints, adhesives and surgical breast implants

❗ Do not confuse with: **silicon**

silicosis *noun, medicine* a lung disease caused by prolonged inhalation of dust

silk *noun* **1** very fine, soft fibres spun by silkworms **2** thread or cloth made from this ➤ *adjective* **1** made of silk **2** soft, smooth

silken *adjective* **1** made of silk **2** smooth like silk

silkworm *noun* the caterpillar of certain moths which spins silk

silky *adjective* (**silkier, silkiest**) like silk

sill *noun* a ledge of wood, stone, etc below a window or a door

silly *adjective* (**sillier, silliest**) foolish, not sensible

silo *noun* (*plural* **silos**) **1** a tower for storing grain etc **2** a pit or airtight chamber for holding silage **3** an underground chamber built to contain a guided missile

silt *noun* sand or mud left behind by flowing water • **silt up** to become blocked by mud

Silurian *adjective* **1** of the geological period 440 million to 410 million years ago

silver *noun* **1** *chemistry* (symbol **Ag**) a white precious metal, able to take on a high polish **2** money made of silver or of a metal alloy resembling it **3** objects (especially cutlery) made of, or plated with, silver ➤ *adjective* **1** made of, or looking like, silver **2** whitish-grey in colour ➤ *verb* **1** to cover with silver **2** to become like silver

silver medal *noun* a medal given to a competitor who comes second

silver nitrate *noun* a light-sensitive chemical compound, used in photographic film

silversmith *noun* someone who makes or sells articles of silver

silver wedding *noun* the 25th anniversary of a wedding

silvery *adjective* **1** like silver **2** of sound: ringing and musical

SIM card *noun* a removable electronic card inside a mobile phone that stores information about the user

⊙ An acronym of Subscriber *I*dentification *M*odule

simian *adjective* ape-like

simil- or **simul-** *prefix* forms words containing the notion 'like': *simile/simulate* ⊙ Comes from Latin *similis* meaning 'like'

similar *adjective* **1** alike, almost the same **2** *maths* exactly corresponding in shape, but not necessarily in size

similarity *noun* (*plural* **similarities**) **1** being similar, likeness **2** resemblance

similarly *adverb* **1** in the same, or a similar, way **2** likewise, also

simile *noun* an expression using 'like' or 'as', in which one thing is likened to another that is well-known for a particular quality (eg 'as black as night', 'to swim like a fish')

similitude *noun, formal* similarity; resemblance

simmer *verb* to cook gently just below boiling point

simper *verb* 1 to smile in a silly manner 2 to say with a simper ➤ *noun* a silly smile

simple *adjective* 1 easy, not difficult or complicated 2 plain, not fancy: *simple hairstyle* 3 ordinary: *simple, everyday objects* 4 of humble rank: *a simple peasant* 5 mere, nothing but: *the simple truth* 6 too trusting, easily cheated 7 foolish, half-witted

simple fraction *noun, maths* a vulgar fraction

simple harmonic motion *noun, physics* continuous and repetitive motion whereby a body oscillates in such a way that it ranges an equal distance on either side of a central point, and its acceleration towards the point is proportional to its distance from it, as with a pendulum

simple interest *noun* interest calculated only on the original sum borrowed (*compare with:* **compound interest**)

simple sentence *noun, grammar* a sentence that has only one verb and only one subject (*compare with:* **compound sentence, complex sentence**)

simpleton *noun* a foolish person

simplicity *noun* the state of being simple

simplification *noun* 1 an act of making simpler 2 a simple form of anything

simplify *verb* (**simplifies, simplifying, simplified**) 1 to make simpler 2 *maths* to reduce (a fraction or an equation) to its simplest form

simplistic *adjective* unrealistically straightforward or uncomplicated ♦ **simplistically** *adverb*

simply *adverb* 1 in a simple manner 2 only, merely: *I do it simply for the money* 3 completely, absolutely: *simply beautiful*

simulacrum (*pronounced* sim-yoo-**lei**-krum) *noun* (*plural* **simulacra**) a resemblance, an image

simulate *verb* 1 to pretend, feign: *She simulated illness* 2 to have the appearance of, look like

simulated *adjective* 1 pretended 2 having the appearance of: *simulated leather*

simulation *noun* 1 the act of simulating something or the methods used to simulate something 2 something that has been created artificially to reproduce a real event or real set of conditions

simulator *noun* a device that simulates a system or set of conditions, especially for training purposes: *flight simulator*

simultaneous *adjective* happening, or done, at the same time ♦ **simultaneously** *adverb*

simultaneous equations *plural noun* two or more equations which are satisfied when their variables are given the same values, with the number of variables the same as the number of equations

sin¹ *noun* 1 a wicked act, especially one which breaks religious laws 2 wrongdoing 3 *informal* a shame, pity ➤ *verb* (**sinning, sinned**) to commit a sin, do wrong ● **original sin** the supposed sinful nature of all human beings since the time of Adam

sin² *abbreviation, maths* sine

since *adverb* 1 (often **ever since**) from that time onwards: *I have avoided him ever since* 2 at a later time: *We have since become friends* 3 ago: *long since* ➤ *prep* from the time of: *since his arrival* ➤ *conjunction* 1 after the time when: *I have been at home since I returned from Italy* 2 because: *Since you are going, I will go too*

sincere *adjective* (**sincerer, sincerest**) 1 honest in word and deed, meaning what you say or do, true: *a sincere friend* 2 truly felt: *a sincere desire* ♦ **sincerely** *adverb*

sincerity *noun* the state or quality of being truthful and genuine in what you believe and say

sine *noun, maths* (*abbrev* **sin**) for an angle in a right-angled triangle: a function that is the length of the side opposite the angle divided by the length of the hypotenuse

sinecure (*pronounced* **sin**-ik-yoor) *noun* a job for which someone receives money but has little or no work to do ☉ Comes from Latin *sine* meaning 'without', and *cura* meaning 'care'

sine rule *noun, maths* a rule for calculating the sines and angles of a triangle

sinew *noun* 1 a tough cord that joins a muscle to a bone 2 (**sinews**) equipment and resources necessary for something: *sinews of war*

sine wave *noun, maths* a wave resembling that obtained by plotting a graph of the size of an angle against the value of its sine

sinewy *adjective* having strong sinews, tough

sinful *adjective* wicked

sing *verb* (**singing, sang, sung**) 1 to make musical sounds with your voice 2 to utter (words, a song, etc) by doing this

singe *verb* to burn slightly on the surface, scorch ➤ *noun* a surface burn

singer *noun* someone who sings or whose voice has been specially trained for singing

single *adjective* 1 one only 2 not double 3 not married 4 for one person: *a single bed* 5 between two people: *single combat* 6 for one direction of a journey: *a single ticket* ● **single out** to pick out, treat differently in some way

single-handed *adjective* working etc by yourself

single-minded *adjective* having one aim only

singlet *noun* a vest, an undershirt

singly *adverb* one by one, separately

sing-song *noun* a gathering of people singing

informally together ➤ *adjective* of a speaking voice etc: having a fluctuating rhythm

singular *adjective* **1** *grammar* the opposite of **plural**, showing one person, thing, etc **2** exceptional: *singular success* **3** unusual, strange: *a singular sight*

singularly *adverb* strangely, exceptionally: *singularly ugly*

sinister *adjective* suggesting evil, evil-looking

sink *verb* (**sank, sunk**) **1** to go down below the surface of the water etc **2** to go down or become less: *My hopes sank* **3** of a very ill person: to become weaker **4** to lower yourself (into): *sink into a chair* **5** to make by digging (a well etc) **6** to push (your teeth etc) deep into (something) **7** to invest (money etc) in a business ➤ *noun* a basin in a kitchen, bathroom, etc with a water supply connected to it and a drain for carrying off dirty water etc

sinner *noun* a person who has committed a sin or sins

Sinn Fein *noun* (*pronounced* shin fein) a Republican political movement and party in Ireland ⊙ Comes from Irish Gaelic, meaning literally 'we ourselves'

Sino- *prefix* relating to China or the Chinese ⊙ Comes from Greek *Sinai* meaning 'Chinese'

sinuous *adjective* bending in and out, winding

sinus (*pronounced* **sai**-nus) *noun* (*plural* **sinuses**) an air cavity in the head connected with the nose

sinusitis *noun* inflammation of (one of) the sinuses

sip *verb* (**sipping, sipped**) to drink in very small quantities ➤ *noun* a taste of a drink, a swallow

siphon or **syphon** *noun* **1** a bent tube for drawing off liquids from one container into another **2** a glass bottle, for soda water etc, containing such a tube ➤ *verb* to draw (off) through a siphon • **siphon off** to take (part of something) away gradually: *He siphoned off some of the club's funds*

sir *noun* **1** a polite form of address used to a man **2** (**Sir**) the title of a knight or baronet

sire *noun* **1** a male parent, especially of a horse **2** *old* a title used in speaking to a king ➤ *verb* of an animal: to be the male parent of

siren *noun* **1** an instrument that gives out a loud hooting noise as a warning or signal **2** (**Siren**) a mythical sea nymph whose singing enchanted sailors and tempted them into danger **3** an attractive but dangerous woman

sirloin *noun* the upper part of the loin of beef

sirocco *noun* a hot dry wind blowing from N Africa to the Mediterranean coast

sirrah *noun, old* sir

sisal *noun* a fibre from a W Indian plant, used for making ropes

sister *noun* **1** a female born of the same parents as yourself **2** a senior nurse, often in charge of a hospital ward **3** a nun ➤ *adjective* **1** closely related **2** of similar design or structure: *a sister ship*

sisterhood *noun* **1** the state of being a sister **2** a religious community of women

sister-in-law *noun* **1** the sister of your husband or wife **2** the wife of your brother or of your brother-in-law

sisterly *adjective* like a sister

sit *verb* (**sitting, sat**) **1** to rest on the buttocks, be seated **2** of a bird: to perch **3** to rest on eggs in order to hatch them **4** to be an official member: *sit in parliament/sit on a committee* **5** of a court etc: to meet officially **6** to pose for a photographer, painter, etc **7** to take (an examination etc) • **sit tight** to be unwilling to move • **sit up 1** to sit with your back straight **2** to stay up instead of going to bed

sitcom *noun* a television comedy series with the same characters and a running theme

site *noun* a place where a building, town, etc is or is to be placed ➤ *verb* to select a place for (a building etc) ⊙ Comes from Latin *situs* meaning 'situation'

❗ Do not confuse with: **sight** and **cite**

sit-in *noun* the occupation of a public building as a form of protest

sitter *noun* **1** someone who poses for a portrait etc **2** a babysitter **3** a bird sitting on eggs

sitting *noun* the state or time of sitting ➤ *adjective* **1** seated **2** for sitting in or on **3** in office: *sitting member of parliament* **4** in possession: *sitting tenant*

sitting-room *noun* a room chiefly for sitting in

situation *noun* **1** the place where anything stands: *a pleasant situation on the bank of the river* **2** a job, employment: *situations vacant* **3** a state of affairs, circumstances: *in an awkward situation*

sit-up *noun* a physical exercise in which the upper body is raised up from a lying position, often with the hands behind the head

Siva or **Shiva** (*pronounced* **shee**-va) *noun, Hinduism* the third god of the Trimurti, the destroyer and reproducer

six *noun* the number 6 ➤ *adjective* 6 in number • **at sixes and sevens** in confusion

six-pack *noun* **1** a pack containing six items sold as one unit, especially six cans of beer **2** *informal* a set of well-defined abdominal muscles

sixpence *noun* a silver-coloured coin used before decimal currency, worth $\frac{1}{40}$ of £1

sixteen *noun* the number 16 ➤ *adjective* 16 in number

sixteenth *adjective* the last of a series of sixteen

➤ *noun* one of sixteen equal parts

sixth *adjective* the last of a series of six ➤ *noun* one of six equal parts

sixth form *noun* the stage in which school subjects are taught to a level that prepares for higher education ♦ **sixth-former** *noun*

sixth-form college *noun* a school which provides the sixth-form education for the pupils of an area

sixth sense *noun* an ability to perceive things beyond the powers of the five senses

sixties *plural noun* (also **60s, 60's**) **1** the period of time between sixtieth and seventieth birthdays **2** the range of temperatures between sixty and seventy degrees **3** the period of time between the sixtieth and seventieth years of a century

sixtieth *adjective* the last of a series of sixty ➤ *noun* one of sixty equal parts

sixty *noun* the number 60 ➤ *adjective* 60 in number

size *noun* **1** space taken up by anything **2** measurements, dimensions **3** largeness **4** a class into which shoes and clothes are grouped according to size: *She takes size 4 in shoes* **5** a weak kind of glue used, eg in wallpapering • **size up** to form an opinion of a person, situation, etc

sizeable or **sizable** *adjective* fairly large

sizzle *verb* **1** to make a hissing sound **2** to fry, scorch

skate *noun* **1** a steel blade attached to a boot for gliding on ice **2** a boot with such a blade attached, for ice-skating **3** a rollerskate **4** a type of large flatfish ➤ *verb* to move on skates ♦ **skater** *noun*

skateboard *noun* a narrow board on four rollerskate wheels ♦ **skateboarding** *noun*

skein (*pronounced* skein) *noun* a coil of thread or yarn, loosely tied in a knot

skeletal *adjective* of or like a skeleton

skeleton *noun* **1** the bony framework of an animal or person, without the flesh **2** any framework or outline ➤ *adjective* of staff etc: reduced to a very small or minimum number • **skeleton in the cupboard** a hidden sorrow or shame

skeleton bob or **bobsleigh** *noun* a small flat sledge on which a person races headfirst

skeleton key *noun* a key from which the inner part has been cut away so that it can open many different locks

skerry *noun* (*plural* **skerries**) a reef of rock

sketch *noun* (*plural* **sketches**) **1** a rough plan or drawing **2** a short or rough account **3** any of several short pieces of comedy presented as a programme ➤ *verb* **1** to draw roughly **2** to give the chief points of **3** to draw in pencil or ink

sketchy *adjective* (**sketchier, sketchiest**) **1** roughly done **2** not thorough, incomplete: *My knowledge of geography is rather sketchy*

skew *adjective & adverb* **1** off the straight, slanting **2** *statistics* of a curve in the graph of a distribution: not symmetrical about the arithmetic mean ➤ *verb* to set at a slant

skewer *noun* a long pin of wood or metal for holding meat, eg kebabs, together while grilling, roasting, etc ➤ *verb* to fix with a skewer or with something sharp

skewness *noun, statistics* a measure of the degree of asymmetry of a curve about the arithmetic mean of a distribution

ski *noun* (*plural* **skis**) one of a pair of long narrow strips of wood or metal that are attached to boots for gliding over snow ➤ *verb* (**skiing, skied** or **ski'd**) to move or travel on skis

skid *noun* **1** a slide sideways: *The car went into a skid* **2** a wedge put under a wheel to check it on a steep slope **3** (**skids**) logs etc on which things can be moved by sliding ➤ *verb* (**skidding, skidded**) **1** of a wheel: to slide along without turning **2** to slip sideways • **on the skids** on the way down • **put the skids under** to hurry along

ski-jump *noun* **1** a steep, snow-covered track ending in a platform from which a skier jumps **2** a jump made by a skier from such a platform ♦ **ski-jumping** *noun*

skilful *adjective* having or showing skill ♦ **skilfully** *adverb*

skill *noun* cleverness at doing a thing, either from practice or as a natural gift

skilled *adjective* **1** having skill, especially through training **2** of a job: requiring skill

skim *verb* (**skimming, skimmed**) **1** to remove cream, scum, etc from the surface of (something) **2** to move lightly and quickly over (a surface) **3** to read quickly, missing parts

skimmed *adjective* of milk: with some of the fat removed

skimp *verb* **1** to give (someone) hardly enough **2** to do (a job) imperfectly **3** to spend too little money (on): *skimping on clothes*

skimpy *adjective* (**skimpier, skimpiest**) **1** too small **2** of clothes: too short or tight

skin *noun* **1** the natural outer covering of an animal or person **2** a thin outer layer on a fruit **3** a thin film that forms on a liquid ➤ *verb* (**skinning, skinned**) to strip the skin from • **by the skin of your teeth** very narrowly

skin-deep *adjective* as deep as the skin only, on the surface

skin-diver *noun* a diver who wears simple equipment

⏱ Originally someone who dived naked in search of pearls

skinflint *noun* a very mean person

skinny *adjective* (**skinnier, skinniest**) very thin

skint *adjective, Brit informal* broke, without much money

skip *verb* (**skipping, skipped**) **1** to go along with a rhythmic step and hop **2** to jump over a turning rope **3** to leap, especially lightly or joyfully **4** to leave out (parts of a book, a meal, etc) ➤ *noun* **1** an act of skipping **2** the captain of a side at bowls etc **3** a large metal container for collecting and transporting refuse

skipper *noun* the captain of a ship, aeroplane or team ➤ *verb* to act as captain for (a ship, team, etc)

skipping rope *noun* a rope used in skipping

skirmish *noun* (*plural* **skirmishes**) **1** a fight between small parties of soldiers or planes **2** a short sharp contest or disagreement ➤ *verb* to fight briefly or informally

skirt *noun* **1** a garment, worn by women, that hangs from the waist **2** the lower part of a dress **3** (**skirts**) the outer edge or border ➤ *verb* to pass along, or lie along, the edge of

skirting or **skirting-board** *noun* the narrow board next to the floor round the walls of a room (*also called:* **wainscot**)

skit *noun* a piece of writing, a short play, etc that makes fun of a person or event

skittish *adjective* frivolous, light-headed

skittle *noun* **1** a bottle-shaped object used as a target in bowling, a ninepin **2** (**skittles**) a game in which skittles are knocked over by a ball

skive *verb, informal* (often **skive off**) to avoid doing a duty ♦ **skiver** *noun*

skivvy *informal, noun* (*plural* **skivvies**) a domestic servant, a cleaner ➤ *verb* (**skivvies, skivvying, skivvied**) to work like a skivvy

skulduggery or *US* **skullduggery** *noun* trickery, underhand practices

skulk *verb* **1** to wait about, stay hidden **2** to move stealthily away, sneak

skull *noun* **1** the bony case which encloses the brain **2** the head • **skull and crossbones** the sign on a pirate's flag

skullcap *noun* a cap which fits closely to the head

skunk *noun* **1** a small American animal which defends itself by giving off a bad smell **2** *informal* a contemptible person

sky *noun* (*plural* **skies**) **1** the upper atmosphere, the heavens **2** the weather, the climate

sky-diving *noun* jumping with a parachute as a sport

skylark *noun* the common lark which sings while hovering far overhead

skylight *noun* a window in a roof or ceiling

skyline *noun* the horizon

skyscraper *noun* a high building of very many storeys

slab *noun* a thick flat slice or piece of anything: *stone slab/cut a slab of cake*

slack *adjective* **1** not firmly stretched **2** not firmly in position **3** not strict **4** lazy and careless **5** not busy: *slack holiday season* ➤ *noun* **1** the loose part of a rope **2** small coal and coal-dust **3** (**slacks**) loose, casual trousers ➤ *verb* **1** to do less work than you should, be lazy **2** to slacken

slacken *verb* **1** to make or become looser **2** to make or become less active, less busy, etc

slag *noun* waste left from metal-smelting ➤ *verb* (**slagging, slagged**) *slang* to criticize, make fun of cruelly: *She's always slagging him off*

slain past participle of **slay**

slake *verb* **1** to quench, satisfy (thirst, longing, etc) **2** to put out (fire) **3** to mix (lime) with water

slalom *noun* **1** a downhill, zigzag ski run among posts or trees **2** an obstacle race in canoes

slam *verb* (**slamming, slammed**) **1** to shut (a door, lid, etc) with a loud noise **2** to put down with a loud noise: *slammed the book on the table* ➤ *noun* **1** the act of slamming **2** (*also* **grand slam**) a winning of every trick in cards or every contest in a competition etc

slander *noun* an untrue statement (in England, a spoken one) aimed at harming someone's reputation ➤ *verb* to speak slander against (someone)

slanderous *adjective* of a statement: untrue and therefore unfairly damaging someone's reputation

slang *noun* **1** popular words and phrases that are used in informal, everyday speech or writing **2** the special language of a particular group: *Cockney rhyming slang*

slant *verb* **1** to slope **2** to lie or move diagonally or in a sloping position **3** to give or present (facts or information) in a distorted way that suits your own purpose ➤ *noun* **1** a slope **2** a diagonal direction **3** a point of view

slap *noun* a blow with the palm of the hand or anything flat ➤ *verb* (**slapping, slapped**) to give a slap to

slapdash *adjective* hasty, careless

slapstick *adjective* of comedy: boisterous, funny in a very obvious way ➤ *noun* comedy in this style

---

⊙ After the name of a theatrical device which made a loud noise when an actor was hit with it

---

slash *verb* **1** to make long cuts in **2** to strike at violently ➤ *noun* (*plural* **slashes**) **1** a long cut **2** a sweeping blow

slat *noun* a thin strip of wood, metal or other material ♦ **slatted** *adjective*

slate *noun* an easily split blue-grey rock, used for

roofing, or at one time for writing upon
> *adjective* **1** made of slate **2** slate-coloured
> *verb* **1** to cover with slate **2** to say or write harsh things to or about: *The play was slated*

slattern *noun, old* a woman of untidy appearance or habits

slaughter *noun* **1** the killing of animals, especially for food **2** cruel killing of large numbers of people > *verb* **1** to kill (an animal) for food **2** to kill brutally

slaughterhouse *noun* a place where animals are killed in order to be sold for food

slave *noun* **1** someone forced to work for a master and owner **2** someone who serves another devotedly **3** someone who works very hard **4** someone who is addicted to something: *a slave to fashion* > *verb* to work like a slave

slaver *noun* saliva running from the mouth
> *verb* to let saliva run out of the mouth

slavery *noun* **1** the state of being a slave **2** the system of owning slaves

Slavic *adjective* relating to a group of E European people or their languages, including Russian, Polish, etc

slavish *adjective* thinking or acting exactly according to rules or instructions

slay *verb* (**slaying, slew, slain**) *formal* to kill

sleaze *noun, informal* corrupt or illicit practices, especially in public life

sleazy *adjective* (**sleazier, sleaziest**) squalid, disreputable ♦ **sleaziness** *noun*

sled or **sledge** *noun* a vehicle with runners, made for sliding upon snow > *verb* to ride on a sledge

sledgehammer *noun* a large, heavy hammer

sleek *adjective* **1** smooth, glossy **2** of an animal: well-fed and well-cared for **3** elegant, well-groomed

sleep *verb* (**sleeping, slept**) to rest with your eyes closed in a state of natural unconsciousness > *noun* **1** the state of sleeping **2** a spell of sleeping ● **go to sleep 1** to pass into the state of being asleep **2** of a limb: to become numb, tingle ● **put to sleep 1** to make to go to sleep, make unconscious **2** to put (an animal) to death painlessly, eg by an injection of a drug ● **sleep with** *informal* to have sexual intercourse with

sleeper *noun* **1** someone who sleeps **2** a beam of wood or metal supporting railway lines **3** a sleeping car or sleeping berth on a railway train

sleeping bag *noun* a large warm bag for sleeping in, used by campers etc

sleeping policeman *noun, informal* a low hump in the surface of a road, intended to slow down traffic

sleepless *adjective* unable to sleep, without sleep

sleepwalker *noun* someone who walks etc while asleep

sleepy *adjective* (**sleepier, sleepiest**) **1** drowsy, wanting to sleep **2** looking as if needing sleep **3** quiet, not bustling: *sleepy town* ♦ **sleepily** *adverb*

sleet *noun* rain mixed with snow or hail

sleeve *noun* **1** the part of a garment which covers the arm **2** a cover for a gramophone record **3** a cover for an arm-like piece of machinery

sleeveless *adjective* without sleeves

sleigh *noun* a large horse-drawn sledge

sleight of hand *noun* skill and quickness of hand movement in performing card tricks etc

slender *adjective* **1** thin, narrow **2** slim **3** small in amount: *by a slender margin*

sleuth *noun* someone who tracks down criminals, a detective

slew past tense of **slay**

slice *noun* **1** a thin, broad piece of something: *slice of toast* **2** a broad-bladed utensil for serving fish etc > *verb* **1** to cut into slices **2** to cut through **3** to cut (off from etc) **4** *golf* to hit (a ball) in such a way that it curves away to the right

slick *adjective* **1** smart, clever, often too much so **2** smooth > *noun* a thin layer of spilt oil

slide *verb* (**sliding, slid**) **1** to move smoothly over a surface **2** to slip **3** to pass quietly or secretly > *noun* **1** an act of sliding **2** a smooth, slippery slope or track **3** a chute **4** a groove or rail on which a thing slides **5** a fastening for the hair **6** a picture for showing on a screen **7** a piece of glass on which to place objects to be examined under a microscope

slide rule *noun* an instrument used for calculating, made up of one ruler sliding against another

slight *adjective* **1** of little amount or importance: *slight breeze/slight quarrel* **2** small, slender > *verb* to treat as unimportant, insult by ignoring > *noun* an insult, an offence

slightly *adverb* a little: *slightly annoyed*

slim *adjective* (**slimmer, slimmest**) **1** slender, thin **2** small, slight: *slim chance* > *verb* (**slimming, slimmed**) **1** to make slender **2** to use means (such as eating less) to become slender

slime *noun* sticky, half-liquid material, especially thin, slippery mud

slime mould *noun, biology* any of a class of very simple plants or fungi consisting of a mass of protoplasm, and living on dead or decaying plant matter

slimy *adjective* (**slimier, slimiest**) **1** covered with slime **2** *informal* of a person: too attentive or flattering ♦ **sliminess** *noun*

sling *noun* **1** a bandage hanging from the neck or shoulders to support an injured arm **2** a strap with a string attached to each end, for flinging stones **3** a net of ropes etc for hoisting and carrying heavy objects ➤ verb (**slinging, slung**) **1** to throw with a sling **2** to move or swing by means of a sling **3** informal to throw

slink verb (**slinking, slunk**) to sneak away, move stealthily

slip verb (**slipping, slipped**) **1** to slide accidentally and lose footing or balance: slip on the ice **2** to fall out of place, or out of your control: The plate slipped from my grasp **3** to move quickly and easily **4** to move quietly, quickly and secretly **5** to escape from: slip your mind ➤ noun **1** the act of slipping **2** an error, a slight mistake **3** a cutting from a plant **4** a strip or narrow piece of anything (eg paper) **5** a slim, slight person: a slip of a girl **6** a slipway **7** a thin undergarment worn under a dress, an underskirt **8** a cover for a pillow **9** cricket a fielding position near to the wicketkeeper on the offside • **slip up** to make a mistake

slipknot noun a knot made with a loop so that it can slip

slipped disc noun a dislocation of one of the circular plates of cartilage between any of the vertebrae

slipper noun a soft, loose indoor shoe

slippery adjective **1** causing skidding or slipping **2** not trustworthy ♦ **slipperiness** noun

slip road noun a road by which vehicles join or leave a motorway

slipshod adjective untidy, careless

slipstream noun the stream of air driven back by an aircraft propeller etc

slip-up noun a mistake

slipway noun a smooth slope on which a ship is built

slit verb (**slitting, slit**) **1** to make a long narrow cut in **2** to cut into strips ➤ noun a long narrow cut or opening

slither verb **1** to slide or slip about (eg on mud) **2** to move with a gliding motion

slithery adjective slippery

sliver noun a thin strip or slice

slobber verb to let saliva dribble from the mouth, slaver

sloe noun a small black fruit used to flavour gin

slog verb (**slogging, slogged**) to work or plod on steadily, especially against difficulty ➤ noun a difficult spell of work

slogan noun an easily remembered and frequently repeated phrase, used in advertising etc ⊙ Comes from Scottish Gaelic sluagh-ghairm meaning 'war cry'

sloop noun a one-masted sailing ship

slop verb (**slopping, slopped**) **1** to flow over, spill **2** to splash ➤ noun **1** spilt liquid **2** (**slops**) dirty water **3** (**slops**) thin, tasteless food

slope noun **1** a position or direction that is neither level nor upright, a slant **2** a surface with one end higher than the other, eg a hillside ➤ verb to be in a slanting, sloping position

sloppy adjective (**sloppier, sloppiest**) **1** wet, muddy **2** watery, liquid: This mixture is too sloppy **3** careless, untidy: sloppy work **4** silly, sentimental **5** of clothes: baggy

slosh verb **1** to splash **2** informal to hit

slot noun **1** a small, narrow opening, eg to insert coins **2** a position ➤ verb (**slotting, slotted**) **1** to make a slot in **2** (sometimes **slot into**) to find a position or place for

sloth noun **1** laziness **2** a slow-moving S American animal that lives in trees

slothful adjective lazy

slot machine noun a vending machine worked by putting a coin in a slot

slouch noun a hunched-up body position ➤ verb to walk with shoulders rounded and head hanging

slough¹ (pronounced slow) noun a bog, a marsh

slough² (pronounced sluf) noun the cast-off skin of a snake ➤ verb **1** to cast off (eg a skin) **2** of skin: to come (off)

slovenly adjective untidy, careless, dirty

slow adjective **1** not fast **2** not hasty or hurrying **3** of a clock: behind in time **4** not quick in learning, dull ➤ verb (often **slow down**) to make or become slower ♦ **slowly** adverb

slowcoach noun someone who moves, works, etc slowly

slow motion noun **1** in film or television: a speed of movement that is much slower than real life **2** slower than normal real-life movement ➤ adjective (**slow-motion**) slower than actual motion: a slow-motion clip

slow neutron noun, physics a neutron with a relatively low energy content, used to initiate various nuclear reactions

sludge noun soft, slimy mud

slug noun **1** a snail-like animal with no shell **2** a small piece of metal used as a bullet **3** a heavy blow

sluggard noun someone who has slow and lazy habits

sluggish adjective moving slowly

sluice noun **1** (also called: **sluicegate**) a sliding gate for controlling a flow of water in an artificial channel **2** the stream which flows through this ➤ verb to clean out with a strong flow of water

slum noun **1** an overcrowded part of a town where the houses are dirty and unhealthy **2** a house in a slum

slumber verb to sleep ➤ noun sleep

slump verb **1** to fall or sink suddenly and heavily

2 to lose value suddenly ➤ *noun* a sudden fall in values, prices, etc

slung past form of **sling**

slunk past form of **slink**

slur *verb* (**slurring, slurred**) **1** to pronounce indistinctly **2** to damage (a reputation etc), speak evil of ➤ *noun* **1** a blot or stain (on someone's reputation) **2** a criticism, an insult

slurp *verb* to drink or gulp noisily ➤ *noun* a noisy gulp

slurry *noun* **1** thin, liquid cement **2** liquid waste

slush *noun* **1** watery mud **2** melting snow **3** something very sentimental **4** sentimentality

slushy *adjective* **1** covered with, or like, slush **2** *informal* sentimental

slut *noun, derogatory* **1** a woman who regularly engages in casual sex **2** a prostitute **3** a dirty, untidy woman

sly *adjective* cunning; wily; deceitful ♦ **slyly** *adverb* **on the sly** secretly, surreptitiously

Sm *symbol, chemistry* samarium

smack *verb* **1** to strike smartly, slap **2** to have a trace or suggestion (of): *This smacks of treason* ➤ *noun* **1** an act of smacking **2** the sound made by smacking **3** a boisterous kiss **4** a taste, a flavour **5** a trace, a suggestion **6** a small fishing vessel **7** *slang* the drug heroin ➤ *adverb* with sudden violence: *run smack into the door*

small *adjective* **1** little, not big or much **2** not important: *a small matter* **3** not having a large or successful business: *a small businessman* **4** of a voice: soft ➤ *noun* the most slender or narrow part: *the small of the back* ➤ *adverb* into small pieces: *cut up small*

small beer *noun* something trivial or unimportant

small claims *plural noun, law* claims for small amounts of money, dealt with through a simpler legal procedure than larger claims

smallholding *noun* a small farm

small hours *plural noun* the hours just after midnight

small intestine *noun, anatomy* in mammals: the part of the alimentary canal comprising the duodenum, jejunum and ileum

small-minded *adjective* having narrow opinions, ungenerous

smallpox *noun* a serious infectious illness, causing fever, vomiting and a rash of large pimples that often leave scars (**pocks**)

small print *noun* additional details of a contract etc, often printed very small, especially when containing unattractive conditions

small talk *noun* polite conversation about nothing very important

smarmy *adjective* (**smarmier, smarmiest**) nauseatingly smooth or charming

smart *adjective* **1** clever and quick in thought or action **2** well-dressed **3** brisk **4** sharp, stinging ➤ *noun* a sharp, stinging pain ➤ *verb* **1** to feel a sharp, stinging pain **2** to feel annoyed, resentful, etc after being insulted

smart card *noun* a plastic card fitted with a microprocessor and used in commercial transactions, telecommunications, etc

smarten *verb* **1** to make or become smart **2** (**smarten up**) to brighten

smash *verb* **1** to break into pieces, shatter **2** to strike with force: *smash a ball with a racket* **3** to crash (into etc): *The car smashed into the wall* ➤ *noun* (*plural* **smashes**) **1** an act of smashing **2** a crash, a collision (of vehicles) **3** the ruin of a business etc

smashing *adjective, informal* excellent

smattering *noun* a very slight knowledge of a subject: *a smattering of Italian*

smear *verb* **1** to spread (something sticky or oily): *smear paste on the wall* **2** to spread, smudge with (something sticky etc): *smear the wall with paste* **3** to become smeared **4** to slander, insult ➤ *noun* **1** a smudge of something sticky **2** *medicine* a test in which cells are taken from the neck of a woman's womb to check whether she has cancer

smell *noun* **1** the sense or power of being aware of things through your nose **2** an act of using this sense **3** something sensed through the nose, a scent ➤ *verb* (**smelling, smelt** or **smelled**) **1** to notice by the sense of smell: *I smell gas* **2** to use your sense of smell on: *Smell this fish* **3** to give off a smell: *The dustbin smells* • **smell out** to find out by prying or inquiring closely

smelling-salts *plural noun* strong-smelling chemicals in a bottle, used to revive people who are fainting

smelly *adjective* (**smellier, smelliest**) having a bad smell

smelt *verb* **1** to melt (ore) in order to separate the metal from other material **2** past form of **smell**

smile *verb* **1** to show pleasure by drawing up the corners of the lips **2** (sometimes **smile on**) to be favourable to: *Fortune smiled on him* ➤ *noun* an act of smiling

smiley *noun, computing* a symbol created from characters on a keyboard, eg :-) intended to look like a smiling face, used in e-mails and text messages

smirch *verb* to stain, soil ➤ *noun* a stain

smirk *verb* to smile in a self-satisfied or foolish manner ➤ *noun* a self-satisfied smile

smite *verb* (**smiting, smote, smitten**) to strike, hit hard

smith *noun* a worker in metals; a blacksmith

smithereens *plural noun* fragments

smithy *noun* (*plural* **smithies**) the workshop of a smith

smitten past participle of **smite** ➤ *adjective* affected (by); strongly attracted (by)

smock *noun* a loose shirt-like garment, sometimes worn over other clothes as a protection

smog *noun* thick, smoky fog

smoke *noun* **1** the cloud-like gases and particles of soot given off by anything burning **2** an act of smoking (a cigarette etc) ➤ *verb* **1** to give off smoke **2** to inhale and exhale tobacco smoke from a cigarette, pipe, etc **3** to cure or preserve (ham, fish, etc) by applying smoke **4** to darken (eg glass) by applying smoke

smokeless *adjective* **1** burning without smoke **2** where the emission of smoke is prohibited: *a smokeless zone*

smoker *noun* **1** someone who smokes **2** a railway compartment in which smoking is allowed

smokescreen *noun* anything (originally smoke) meant to confuse or mislead

smoky *adjective* (**smokier, smokiest**) **1** full of smoke **2** tasting of smoke

smooch *verb, informal* to kiss, pet

smooth *adjective* **1** not rough **2** having an even surface **3** without lumps: *a smooth sauce* **4** hairless **5** without breaks, stops or jolts: *smooth journey* **6** too agreeable in manner ➤ *verb* **1** to make smooth **2** to calm, soothe **3** to free from difficulty

smoothie *noun* a thick drink made with puréed fruit

smooth muscle *noun* muscle, eg in the walls of the intestines, that slowly contracts and relaxes and is not controlled consciously

smote past tense of **smite**

smother *verb* **1** to kill by keeping air from, eg by covering over the nose and mouth **2** to die by this means **3** to cover up, conceal (feelings etc) **4** to put down, suppress (a rebellion etc)

smoulder *verb* **1** to burn slowly without bursting into flame **2** to exist in a hidden state **3** to show otherwise hidden emotion, eg anger, hate: *Her eyes smouldered with hate*

SMS *abbreviation* short message service, a service for sending text messages

smudge *noun* a smear ➤ *verb* to make dirty with spots or smears

smug *adjective* (**smugger, smuggest**) well-satisfied, too obviously pleased with yourself

smuggle *verb* **1** to take (goods) into, or out of, a country without paying the required taxes **2** to send or take secretly

smuggler *noun* someone who smuggles goods

smut *noun* **1** a spot of dirt or soot **2** vulgar or indecent talk etc

smutty *adjective* (**smuttier, smuttiest**) **1** dirty, grimy **2** indecent, vulgar

Sn *symbol, chemistry* tin

snack *noun* a light, hasty meal

snaffle *verb, slang* to steal

snag *noun* a difficulty, an obstacle ➤ *verb* (**snagging, snagged**) to catch or tear on something sharp

snail *noun* **1** a soft-bodied, small, crawling animal with a shell **2** someone who is very slow

snail mail *noun, computing informal* the ordinary postal service, as opposed to e-mail

snake *noun* **1** a legless reptile with a long body, which moves along the ground with a winding movement **2** anything snake-like in form or movement **3** a cunning, deceitful person
• **snake in the grass** *informal* a treacherous person

snap *verb* (**snapping, snapped**) **1** to make a sudden bite **2** to break or shut suddenly with a sharp noise **3** to cause (the fingers) to make a sharp noise **4** to speak sharply **5** to take a photograph of ➤ *noun* **1** the noise made by snapping **2** a sudden spell (eg of cold weather) **3** a card game in which players try to match cards **4** a photograph • **snap up** to eat up or grab something eagerly

snapdragon *noun* a garden plant whose flower, when pinched, opens and shuts like a mouth

snappy *adjective* (**snappier, snappiest**) **1** quick: *Make it snappy* **2** irritable, inclined to speak sharply ♦ **snappily** *adverb*

snapshot *noun* a quickly taken photograph

snare *noun* **1** a noose or loop that draws tight when pulled, for catching an animal **2** a trap **3** a hidden danger or temptation ➤ *verb* to catch in or with a snare

snarl *verb* **1** to growl, showing the teeth **2** to speak in a furious, spiteful tone **3** to become tangled: *snarled up in the net* ➤ *noun* **1** a growl, a furious noise **2** a tangle, a knot **3** a muddled or confused state

snatch *verb* **1** to seize or grab suddenly **2** to take quickly when you have time: *snatch an hour's sleep* ➤ *noun* (*plural* **snatches**) **1** an attempt to seize **2** a small piece or quantity: *a snatch of music*

snazzy *adjective* (**snazzier, snazziest**) *informal* fashionably and often flashily smart ♦ **snazzily** *adverb*

sneak *verb* **1** to creep or move in a stealthy, secretive way **2** to tell tales, tell on others ➤ *noun* **1** someone who tells tales **2** a deceitful, underhand person

sneakers *plural noun, esp US* sports shoes; soft-soled shoes

sneaky *adjective* (**sneakier, sneakiest**) underhand, deceitful ♦ **sneakily** *adverb*

sneer *verb* to show contempt by a scornful

expression, words, etc ➤ *noun* a scornful expression or remark

sneeze *verb* to make a sudden, unintentional and violent blowing noise through the nose and mouth ➤ *noun* an involuntary blow through the nose

snicker *verb* 1 to snigger 2 of a horse: to neigh

snide *adjective* mean, malicious: *snide remark*

sniff *verb* 1 to draw in air through the nose with a slight noise, eg when having a cold, or showing disapproval 2 to smell (a scent etc) 3 (**sniff at**) to treat something with scorn or suspicion ➤ *noun* a quick drawing in of air through the nose

sniffle *noun* a light sniff, a snuffle ➤ *verb* to sniff lightly

snigger *verb* to laugh in a quiet, sly manner ➤ *noun* a quiet, sly laugh

snip *verb* (**snipping, snipped**) to cut off sharply, especially with a single cut ➤ *noun* 1 a cut with scissors 2 a small piece snipped off 3 *informal* a bargain: *a snip at the price*

snipe *noun* a bird with a long straight beak, found in marshy places ➤ *verb* **snipe at** 1 to shoot at someone from a place of hiding 2 to attack someone with critical remarks

sniper *noun* someone who shoots at a single person from cover

snippet *noun* a little piece, especially of information or gossip

snitch *noun* (*plural* **snitches**), *informal* an informer, a tell-tale ➤ *verb* to inform (on)

snivel *verb* (**snivelling, snivelled**) 1 to have a running nose, eg because of a cold 2 to whine or complain tearfully ➤ *noun* 1 a running nose 2 a whine

snob *noun* someone who looks down on those in a lower social class

⏃ Originally a slang term for 'shoemaker' which changed its meaning to someone of low social class, and later to someone who enjoys showing off their wealth and social standing

snobbery *noun* the behaviour that is typical of a snob or snobs

snobbish *adjective* admiring things associated with the higher social classes and despising things associated with the lower classes

snog *slang*, *verb* (**snogging, snogged**) to kiss and cuddle ➤ *noun* a kiss and cuddle

snooker *noun* a game like billiards, using 22 coloured balls

snoop *verb* to spy or pry in a sneaking secretive way ➤ *noun* someone who pries

snooty *adjective* (**snootier, snootiest**) haughty, snobbish

snooze *verb* to sleep lightly, doze ➤ *noun* a light sleep

snore *verb* to make a snorting noise in your sleep

while breathing ➤ *noun* a snorting sound made in sleep

snorkel *noun* 1 a tube with one end above the water, to enable an underwater swimmer to breathe 2 a similar device for bringing air into a submarine

snort *verb* 1 to force air noisily through the nostrils 2 to make such a noise to express disapproval, anger, laughter, etc ➤ *noun* a loud noise made through the nostrils

snot *noun* mucus of the nose

snotty *adjective* (**snottier, snottiest**) *informal* haughty or standoffish ◆ **snottily** *adverb* ◆ **snottiness** *noun*

snout *noun* the projecting nose and mouth of an animal, eg of a pig

snow *noun* 1 frozen water vapour which falls in light white flakes 2 *slang* the drug cocaine ➤ *verb* to fall down in, or like, flakes of snow • **snowed under** overwhelmed with work etc

snowball *noun* a ball made of snow pressed hard together ➤ *verb* 1 to throw snowballs 2 to grow increasingly quickly: *Unemployment has snowballed recently*

snowboard *noun* a single board used as a ski on snow ➤ *verb* to ski on a snowboard ◆ **snowboarding** *noun*

snowdrift *noun* a bank of snow blown together by the wind

snowdrop *noun* a small white flower growing from a bulb in early spring

snowfall *noun* 1 a fall of snow 2 an amount of fallen snow in a given time: *annual snowfall*

snowflake *noun* a flake of snow

snowman *noun* (*plural* **snowmen**) a figure shaped like a human being, made of snow

snowmobile *noun* a motorized vehicle, on skis or tracks, designed for travelling on snow

snowplough *noun* a large vehicle for clearing snow from roads etc

snowshoe *noun* a long broad frame with a mesh, one of a pair for walking on snow

snowy *adjective* (**snowier, snowiest**) 1 covered with snow 2 white 3 pure

SNP *abbreviation* Scottish National Party, a UK political party supporting independence for Scotland

snub *verb* (**snubbing, snubbed**) to treat or speak to in an abrupt, scornful way; insult ➤ *noun* an act of snubbing ➤ *adjective* of a nose: short and turned up at the end

snuff¹ *noun* powdered tobacco for drawing up into the nose

snuff² *verb* to put out or trim the wick of (a candle) • **snuff it** *slang* to die

snuffbox *noun* (*plural* **snuffboxes**) a box for holding snuff

snuffle *verb* to make a sniffing noise through the

nose, eg because of a cold ▹ *noun* a sniffling through the nose

snug *adjective* (**snugger, snuggest**) **1** lying close and warm **2** cosy, comfortable **3** closely fitting; neat and trim

snuggle *verb* **1** to curl up comfortably **2** to draw close to for warmth, affection, etc

so¹ *adverb* **1** as shown, eg by a hand gesture: *so high* **2** to such an extent, to a great extent: *so heavy/you look so happy* **3** in this or that way: *Point your toes so* **4** correct: *Is that so?* **5** (used in contradicting) indeed: *It's not true. It is so* **6** *informal* used to add vehemence to a statement: *I am so not going to his stupid party!*
▹ *conjunction* therefore: *You don't need it, so don't buy it* • **so as to** in order to • **so far** up to this or that point • **so forth** more of the same sort of thing: *pots, pans, and so forth* • **so much for** that is the end of: *So much for that idea!* • **so that** with the purpose or result that • **so what?** what difference does it make? does it matter?

so² same as **soh**

soak *verb* **1** to let stand in a liquid until wet through **2** to drench (with) • **soak something up** to suck it up, absorb it

soaking *adjective* wet through ▹ *noun* a wetting, drenching ▹ *adverb*: **soaking wet** thoroughly wet, drenched

so-and-so *noun* (*plural* **so-and-sos**) *informal* **1** this or that person or thing **2** *euphemistic* used instead of a stronger insult: *She's a real so-and-so, saying that to you!*

soap *noun* **1** a mixture containing oils or fats and other substances, used in washing **2** *informal* a soap opera ▹ *verb* to use soap on

soapbox *noun* (*plural* **soapboxes**) **1** a small box for holding soap **2** a makeshift platform for standing on when speaking to a crowd out of doors

soap opera *noun* a television series about a group of characters and their daily lives

⊙ So called because when these shows first started they were sponsored by soap companies and advertisements for soap were broadcast with them

soapsuds *plural noun* soapy water worked into a froth

soapy *adjective* (**soapier, soapiest**) **1** like soap **2** full of soap **3** *informal* like a soap opera

soar *verb* **1** to fly high into the air **2** of prices: to rise high and quickly

sob *verb* (**sobbing, sobbed**) to weep noisily ▹ *noun* a noisy weeping

sober *adjective* **1** not drunk **2** serious, staid **3** not florid, not elaborate ▹ *verb* (sometimes **sober up**) to make or become sober ♦ **soberly** *adverb*

soberness or **sobriety** (*pronounced* soh-**brai**-i-ti) *noun* the state of being sober

sobriquet (*pronounced* **soh**-bri-kei) or **soubriquet** *noun* a nickname

⊙ From a French phrase meaning literally an affectionate chuck under the chin

sob story *noun* (*plural* **sob stories**) a story told to arouse sympathy

so-called *adjective* called by such a name, often mistakenly: *a so-called expert*

soccer *noun* football

sociable *adjective* fond of the company of others, friendly ♦ **sociability** *noun*

social *adjective* **1** relating to society, or to a community: *social history* **2** living in communities: *social insects* **3** of companionship: *social gathering* **4** of rank or level in society: *social class* ♦ **socially** *adverb*

social climber *noun, often derogatory* someone who seeks to gain higher social status

social Darwinism *noun* the belief that people will come into conflict and that only the strongest will survive

social exclusion *noun* being deprived of the usual benefits of living in a society, such as employment, education, etc

social housing *noun, geography* flats or houses rented from a local authority or owned by a community, rather than owned by the tenants

socialism *noun* the belief that a country's wealth should belong to the people as a whole, not to private owners

socialist *noun* someone who believes in socialism ▹ *adjective* relating to or characteristic of socialism

socialite *noun* someone who mixes with people of high social status

socialize or **socialise** *verb* **1** to meet with people on an informal, friendly basis **2** to mingle or circulate among guests at a party

social science *noun* the scientific study of human society and behaviour, including the fields of sociology, economics, history, etc (the **social sciences**)

social security *noun* the system, paid for by taxes, of providing insurance against old age, illness, unemployment, etc

social services *plural noun* services provided by local or national government for the general welfare of people in society, eg housing, education, and health

social work *noun* work which deals with the care of the people in a community, especially of the poor or underprivileged ♦ **social worker** *noun*

society *noun* (*plural* **societies**) **1** humanity considered as a whole **2** a community of people **3** a social club, an association **4** the class of people who are wealthy, fashionable, etc **5** *formal* company, companionship: *I enjoy his society*

socio- *prefix* of or relating to society or social behaviour ⊙ Comes from Latin *socius* meaning 'a companion'

socioeconomic *adjective* relating to social and economic aspects of something together

socioeconomic group *noun, geography* a group of people who have similar levels of education, types of job, income, etc

sociological *adjective* dealing or concerned with social questions and problems of human society

sociologist *noun* someone who studies the structure and organization of human societies and human behaviour in society

sociology *noun* the study of human society

sociopath *noun* someone who hates the company of others ♦ **sociopathic** *adjective*

sock¹ *noun* a short stocking

sock² *informal, verb* to hit with a powerful blow ➤ *noun* a powerful blow

socket *noun* **1** a hole or set of holes into which something is fitted: *an electric socket* **2** *anatomy* a hollow structure into which another part fits

sod *noun* a piece of earth with grass growing on it, a turf

soda *noun* **1** the name of several substances formed from sodium, eg bicarbonate of soda **2** *informal* soda water

soda lime *noun, chemistry* a mixture of sodium or potassium hydroxide and calcium oxide

soda water *noun* water through which gas has been passed, making it fizzy

sodden *adjective* soaked through and through

sodium *noun, chemistry* (symbol **Na**) a metallic element from which many substances are formed, including common salt

sodium bicarbonate *noun* a powder used as a raising agent in baking (*also called*: **baking soda**)

sodium carbonate *noun, chemistry* a white powder or crystalline solid, used as a water softener and food additive and in various chemical processes

sodium chloride *noun, chemistry* common salt

sodium hydroxide *noun, chemistry* a white crystalline solid that dissolves in water to form a highly corrosive alkaline solution (*also called*: **caustic soda**)

sofa *noun* a kind of long, stuffed seat with back and arms

sofa bed *noun* a sofa incorporating a fold-away bed

soft *adjective* **1** easily put out of shape when pressed **2** not hard or firm **3** not loud **4** of a

colour: not bright or glaring **5** not strict enough **6** lacking strength or courage **7** lacking common sense, weak in the mind **8** of a drink: not alcoholic **9** of water: containing little calcium etc

softball *noun* a game similar to baseball, played with a larger, softer ball which is pitched underarm

soften (*pronounced* sof-en) *verb* to make or grow soft • **soften someone up** *informal* to prepare them for an unwelcome or difficult request

softener *noun* a substance added to another to increase its softness, pliability, etc, such as fabric softener

soft engineering *noun, geography* coast management that employs techniques such as beach nourishment, which tends to be less expensive, more long-term, and more sustainable (*contrasted with*: **hard engineering**)

soft-hearted *adjective* kind and generous

softly *adverb* gently, quietly

soft option *noun* the easiest of two or more alternative courses of action

soft-spoken *adjective* having a soft voice, and usually a mild manner

soft spot *noun, informal* a special liking or affection: *She has a soft spot for him*

software *noun, computing* programs etc as opposed to the machines (*contrasted with*: **hardware**)

softwood *noun* the wood of certain trees, eg pine, and including some woods that are in fact very hard

softy or **softie** *noun* (*plural* **softies**), *informal* **1** a weakly sentimental or soft-hearted person **2** someone not able to endure rough treatment

soggy *adjective* (**soggier, soggiest**) **1** soaked **2** soft and wet

soh or **so** *noun, music* in sol-fa notation: the fifth note of the major scale

soil¹ *noun* **1** the upper layer of the earth in which plants grow **2** loose earth; dirt

soil² *verb* to make dirty

soil erosion *noun, geography* the wearing away of the topsoil from an area of land

soil profile *noun, geography* a cross section through a soil, showing the characteristics of the layers between the surface and the bedrock

soil structure *noun, geography* the way granules in a particular soil fit together, which affects its stability

soil texture *noun, geography* the texture of a particular soil as determined by its mineral composition, ie predominantly sand, silt or clay

sojourn (*pronounced* soj-ern) *formal, verb* to stay for a time ➤ *noun* a short stay

solace (*pronounced* sol-is) *noun* something

which makes pain or sorrow easier to bear, comfort ➤ *verb* to comfort

solar *adjective* **1** relating to the sun **2** influenced by the sun **3** powered by energy from the sun's rays

solar battery *noun* a battery consisting of a number of solar cells

solar cell *noun* an electric cell that converts light into electrical energy

solar energy *noun* **1** energy produced by the sun **2** energy derived from the sun's radiation, eg in a solar cell

solarium *noun* (**solariums** or **solaria**) **1** a room equipped with sunbeds **2** a room designed to allow exposure to sunlight

solar plexus *noun* (*plural* **solar plexuses**), *anatomy* an area in the abdomen in which there is a concentration of nerves radiating from a central point

solar system *noun* the sun with the planets (including the earth) going round it

sold past form of **sell**

solder *noun* melted metal used for joining metal surfaces ➤ *verb* to join (with solder)

soldering-iron *noun* an electric tool for soldering joints

soldier *noun* someone in military service, especially someone who is not an officer

sole¹ *noun* **1** the underside of the foot **2** the underside of a shoe etc ➤ *verb* to put a sole on (a shoe etc)

sole² *adjective* **1** only: *the sole survivor* **2** belonging to one person or group only: *the sole right*

sole³ *noun* (*plural* **sole** or **soles**) an edible flatfish with a slender brown body

solecism (*pronounced* **sol**-i-sizm) *noun* **1** a mistake in the use of language **2** anything that is absurd or incongruous **3** an instance of bad or incorrect behaviour ☉ Comes from Greek *soloikos* meaning 'speaking incorrectly'

solely *adverb* only, alone

solemn (*pronounced* **sol**-em) *adjective* **1** serious, earnest **2** of an occasion: celebrated with special ceremonies ♦ **solemnity** (*pronounced* so-**lem**-ni-ti) *noun* ♦ **solemnly** *adverb*

solemnize or **solemnise** (*pronounced* **sol**-em-naiz) *verb* to carry out (a wedding etc) with religious ceremonies

solenoid *noun*, *physics* a wire that is magnetized when an electric current passes through it

sol-fa *noun*, *music* a system of syllables (do, ray, me, etc) to be sung to the notes of a scale (*also called*: **tonic sol-fa**)

solicit *verb* (**soliciting**, **solicited**) **1** *formal* to ask earnestly for: *solicit advice* **2** *formal* to ask

(someone for something) **3** to offer yourself as a prostitute

solicitor *noun* a lawyer who advises people about legal matters

solicitous *adjective* **1** anxious **2** considerate, careful ♦ **solicitously** *adverb*

solicitude *noun* care or anxiety about someone or something

solid *adjective* **1** fixed in shape, not in the form of gas or liquid **2** in three dimensions, with length, breadth, and height **3** not hollow **4** firm, strongly made **5** made or formed completely of one substance: *solid silver* **6** reliable, sound: *solid business* **7** *informal* without a break: *We waited for four solid hours* ➤ *noun* **1** a substance that is solid **2** a figure that has three dimensions ♦ **solidly** *adverb*

Solidarity *noun*, *history* a committee set up in 1980 in Communist Poland, running an independent trade union that became a force for political reform

solidarity *noun* mutual support and unity of interests, aims, and actions

solidify *verb* (**solidifies, solidifying, solidified**) to make or become firm or solid ♦ **solidification** *noun*

solidity *noun* the state of being solid

solid-state *adjective*, *electronics* denoting an electronic device that functions by the movement of electrons through solids

solifluxion or **solifluction** *noun*, *geography* the slow movement of soil or scree down a slope resulting from alternate freezing and thawing

soliloquize or **soliloquise** *verb* to speak to yourself, especially on the stage

soliloquy *noun* (*plural* **soliloquies**) a speech made by an actor etc to themselves

solitaire *noun* a card game for one player (*also called*: **patience**)

solitary *adjective* **1** lone, alone **2** single: *Not a solitary crumb remained* ➤ *noun*, *informal* solitary confinement

solitary confinement *noun* imprisonment in a cell by yourself

solitude *noun* the state of being alone; lack of company

solo *noun* (*plural* **solos**) a musical piece for one singer or player ➤ *adjective* performed by one person alone: *solo flight*

soloist *noun* someone who plays or sings a solo

solstice *noun* the time of longest daylight (**summer solstice** about 21 June in the northern hemisphere, 21 December in the southern hemisphere) or longest dark (**winter solstice** about 21 December in the northern hemisphere, 21 June in the southern hemisphere)

solubility *noun* the ability of a substance to dissolve

soluble *adjective* **1** able to be dissolved or made liquid **2** of a problem etc: able to be solved

solute *noun, chemistry* a substance that is dissolved in a liquid

solution *noun* **1** a mixture in which one substance is dissolved in another **2** *geography* (*also called*: **corrosion**) the dissolving of rock by chemicals in a sea or river **3** the act of solving a problem etc **4** an answer to a problem, puzzle, etc

solution set *noun, maths* the set of all the values that solve an equation

solvation *noun, chemistry* the interaction of molecules of a solvent with ions or molecules of a solute

solve *verb* **1** to clear up or explain (a mystery) **2** to discover the answer or solution to

solvency *noun* the state of being able to pay all debts

solvent *adjective* able to pay all debts ➤ *noun, chemistry* anything that dissolves another substance

soma *noun, biology* the body of a plant or animal excluding the germ cells

somatic *adjective, biology* **1** relating to the body, as opposed to the mind **2** relating to the body, as opposed to reproduction: *somatic cells*

somatotrophin *noun, biology* a growth hormone

sombre or US **somber** *adjective* gloomy, dark, dismal

sombrero *noun* (*plural* **sombreros**) a broad-brimmed Mexican hat

some *adjective* **1** several **2** a few: *some oranges, but not many* **3** a little: *some bread, but not much* **4** certain: *Some people are rich* ➤ *pronoun* **1** a number or part out of a quantity: *Please try some* **2** certain people: *Some won't be happy*

somebody or **someone** *pronoun* an unknown or unnamed person: *somebody I'd never seen before* ➤ *noun* an important person: *He really is somebody now*

somehow *adverb* in some way or other

somersault *noun* a forward or backward roll in which the heels go over the head ➤ *verb* to perform a somersault

something *pronoun* **1** a thing not known or not stated **2** a thing of importance **3** a slight amount, a degree: *He has something of his father's looks*

sometime *adverb* at a time not known or stated definitely

sometimes *adverb* at times, now and then

somewhat *adverb* rather: *somewhat boring*

somewhere *adverb* in some place

-somn- of or relating to sleep: *somnambulist/ insomnia* ⊕ Comes from Latin *somnus* meaning 'sleep'

somnambulist *noun* a sleepwalker
♦ **somnambulism** *noun*

somnolent *adjective, formal* sleepy; causing sleepiness ♦ **somnolence** *noun*

son *noun* a male child

sonar *noun* a system using reflected sound waves to locate underwater objects

sonata *noun* a piece of classical music with three or more movements, usually for one instrument

song *noun* **1** a piece of music to be sung **2** singing • **going for a song** *informal* at a bargain price

songbird *noun* a bird which sings

songster or **songstress** *noun* (*plural* **songsters** or **songstresses**), *old* a talented singer

sonic *adjective* of sound waves

sonic boom or **sonic bang** *noun* a loud boom that is heard when an aircraft reaches supersonic speed

son-in-law *noun* (*plural* **sons-in-law**) a daughter's husband

sonnet *noun* a type of poem in fourteen lines

sonorous *adjective* giving a clear, loud sound

soon *adverb* **1** in a short time from now or from the time mentioned: *He will come soon* **2** early: *too soon to tell* **3 as soon** as readily, as willingly: *I would as soon stand as sit*

sooner *adverb* more willingly, rather: *I would sooner stand than sit* • **sooner or later** at some time in the future

soot *noun* the black powder left by smoke

soothe *verb* **1** to calm or comfort (a person, feelings, etc) **2** to help or ease (a pain etc)

soothing *adjective* **1** comforting, calming **2** helping to relieve pain ♦ **soothingly** *adverb*

soothsayer *noun* someone who predicts the future

sooty *adjective* (**sootier, sootiest**) like, or covered with, soot

sop *noun* **1** bread dipped in soup etc **2** a bribe given to keep someone quiet ➤ *verb* (**sopping, sopped**) to soak (up)

soph- *prefix* forms words connected with the idea of wisdom ⊕ Comes from Greek *sophos* meaning 'wise', and *sophia* meaning 'wisdom'

sophism *noun* a convincing but false argument or explanation

sophist *noun* a person who uses clever arguments that are fundamentally unsound
♦ **sophistic** *adjective* ♦ **sophistry** *noun*

sophisticated *adjective* **1** of a person: full of experience, accustomed to an elegant, cultured way of life **2** of ways of thought, machinery, etc: highly developed, complicated, elaborate
♦ **sophistication** *noun*

sophomore *noun, US* a second-year college student

soporific *adjective* causing sleep ➤ *noun* a drug which causes sleep

sopping *adjective* wet through

soppy *adjective* (**soppier, soppiest**) *informal* overly sentimental ♦ **soppily** *adverb* ♦ **soppiness** *noun*

soprano *noun* (*plural* **sopranos**), *music* **1** the female singing voice of the highest pitch **2** a singer with such a voice

sorbet (*pronounced* **sawr**-bei) *noun* a water ice ℗ from French

sorcerer or *feminine* **sorceress** *noun* someone who works magic spells; a witch or wizard

sorcery *noun* magic, witchcraft

sordid *adjective* **1** dirty, filthy **2** mean, selfish **3** contemptible ♦ **sordidly** *adverb* ♦ **sordidness** *noun*

sore *adjective* (**sorer, sorest**) painful ➤ *noun* a painful, inflamed spot on the skin

sorely *adverb* very greatly: *sorely in need*

sorority *noun* (*plural* **sororities**) in North America, a society of female college students (*compare with*: **fraternity**)

sorrel *noun* a type of plant with sour-tasting leaves

sorrow *noun* sadness caused by a loss, disappointment, etc ➤ *verb* to be sad

sorrowful *adjective* full of sadness ♦ **sorrowfully** *adverb*

sorry *adjective* (**sorrier, sorriest**) **1** feeling regret for something you have done: *I'm sorry I mentioned it* **2** feeling sympathy or pity (for): *sorry for you* **3** miserable: *in a sorry state*

sort *noun* a kind of (person or thing): *the sort of sweets I like* ➤ *verb* to separate things, putting each in its place: *sort letters* • **a sort of** used of something which is like something else, but not exactly: *He wore a sort of crown* • **of a sort** or **of sorts** of a kind, usually inadequate: *a party of sorts* • **out of sorts** *informal* not feeling very well

sortie (*pronounced* **saw**-ti) *noun* **1** a sudden attack made by the defenders of a place on those who are trying to capture it **2** an operational flight made by one military aircraft

SOS *noun* **1** a code signal calling for help **2** *informal* any call for help

so-so *adjective, informal* not particularly good

sotto voce (*pronounced* sot-oh **voh**-chi) *adverb* in a low voice, so as not to be overheard

soubriquet see **sobriquet**

sought past form of **seek**

sought after *adjective* popular, much in demand

souk, suk or **sukh** *noun* a market or marketplace in Muslim countries ℗ Comes from Arabic *suq* meaning market place

soul *noun* **1** the spirit, the part of someone which is not the body **2** *informal* a person: *a dear old soul* **3** a perfect example (of): *the soul of kindness*

soulful *adjective* full of feeling ♦ **soulfully** *adverb*

soul mate *noun* someone who shares the same feelings, thoughts, tastes, etc as someone else

sound[1] *noun* **1** anything that can be heard, a noise **2** a distance from which something may be heard: *within the sound of Bow Bells* ➤ *verb* **1** to strike you as being: *That sounds awful* **2** to make a noise with: *sound a horn* **3** to examine by listening carefully to: *sound a patient's chest* • **sound like** to resemble in sound: *that sounds like Henry's voice*

sound[2] *adjective* **1** healthy, strong **2** of sleep: deep **3** thorough: *a sound beating* **4** reliable: *sound opinions*

sound[3] *verb* **1** to measure (the depths of water) **2** to try to find out the opinion of: *I'll sound him out tomorrow*

sound[4] *noun* a narrow passage of water

sound barrier *noun* a sudden increase in drag experienced by aircraft flying close to the speed of sound

soundbite *noun* a short statement extracted from a longer speech and quoted on TV or radio or in the press

soundcard *noun, computing* a printed circuit board added to a computer to provide or enhance sound effects

sound effects *plural noun* artificially produced sounds used in film, broadcasting, etc

soundproof *adjective* built or made so that sound cannot pass in or out ➤ *verb* to make soundproof

soundtrack *noun* the strip on a film where the speech and music are recorded

soup *noun* a liquid food made from meat, vegetables, etc

soupçon (*pronounced* **soop**-son) *noun, often humorous* the slightest amount; a dash ℗ Comes from French meaning 'suspicion'

soup kitchen *noun* a place where free or cheap food is supplied to people in need

sour *adjective* **1** having an acid or bitter taste, often as a stage in going bad: *sour milk* **2** bad-tempered ➤ *verb* to make sour

source *noun* **1** the place, thing, or person that something begins or develops from **2** a spring, especially one from which a river flows **3** a person, a book, or other document that can be used to provide information, evidence, etc

source code *noun, computing* a code written by a programmer that usually has to be translated by a compiler before it can be run

sour cream *noun* cream that has been deliberately made sour by the addition of lactic acid bacteria

sour grapes *plural noun* a hostile attitude towards something or someone, motivated by envy, bitterness, resentment, etc

sourpuss *noun, informal* a sullen or miserable person

souse *verb* to soak (eg herrings) in salted water

south *noun* one of the four chief directions, that to the left of someone facing the setting sun ➤ *adjective* **1** in or to the south **2** of the wind: from the south ➤ *adverb* in, to or towards the south: *We headed south*

south-east *noun* the point of the compass midway between south and east

southerly *adjective* **1** of the wind: coming from or facing the south **2** in or towards the south

southern *adjective* of the south

southern lights *plural noun* (**the southern lights**) the **aurora australis**

southpaw *noun, informal* someone whose left hand is more dominant than their right, especially a boxer

South Pole *noun* the point on the Earth's surface that represents the southern end of its axis

southward or **southwards** *adjective & adverb* towards the south

south-west *noun* the point of the compass midway between south and west

souvenir *noun* something bought or given as a reminder of a person, place, or occasion

sou'wester *noun* a kind of waterproof hat

sovereign *noun* **1** a king or queen **2** an old British gold coin worth £1 ➤ *adjective* **1** supreme, highest: *sovereign lord* **2** having its own government: *sovereign state*

sovereignty *noun* highest power

soviet *noun* **1** *history* one of the councils that made up the local and national governments of the former Soviet Union **2** (**Soviet**) a citizen or inhabitant of the former Soviet Union ➤ *adjective* (**Soviet**) relating to the former Soviet Union

sow¹ (*pronounced* sow) *noun* a female pig

sow² (*pronounced* soh) *verb* (**sowing, sowed, sown**) **1** to scatter (seeds) so that they may grow **2** to cover (an area) with seeds ♦ **sower** *noun*

soya bean or **soy bean** *noun* a kind of bean, rich in protein, used as a substitute for meat

soya sauce or **soy sauce** *noun* a sauce made from soya beans, used in Chinese cooking

spa *noun* a place where people go to drink or bathe in the water from a natural spring

○ After the town of *Spa* in Belgium, which was famous for its healthy spring water

space *noun* **1** a gap, an empty place **2** the distance between objects **3** an uncovered part on a sheet of paper **4** length of time: *in the space of a day* **5** the empty region in which all stars, planets, etc are situated ➤ *verb* to put things apart from each other, leaving room between them

space bar *noun* the long key below the character keys on a keyboard, for inserting a space in the text

spacecraft *noun* a machine for travelling in space

spaceman or **spacewoman** *noun* (*plural* **spacemen** or **spacewomen**) a traveller in space

spaceship *noun* a manned spacecraft

space suit *noun* a sealed suit designed for space travel

space walk *noun* an instance of manoeuvring by an astronaut outside his or her spacecraft while in space

spacial another spelling of **spatial**

spacious *adjective* having plenty of room

spade¹ *noun* a tool with a broad blade for digging in the earth • **call a spade a spade** to say plainly and clearly what you mean

spade² *noun* one of the four suits of playing-cards with a black spade-shaped symbol

spadix (*pronounced* **spei**-diks) *noun* (*plural* **spadices**), *botany* a fleshy spike of flowers ○ Comes from Greek, meaning 'a torn-off palm branch'

spaghetti *noun* a type of pasta made into long sticks

spaghetti western *noun* a film set in the American wild west, with an international cast and an Italian director

spake *verb, old* spoke

Spam *noun, trademark* a type of tinned processed cold meat, mainly pork, with added spices

spam *computing, noun* electronic junk mail ➤ *verb* (**spamming, spammed**) to send out electronic junk mail

span *noun* **1** the distance between the tips of the little finger and the thumb when the hand is spread out (about 23 centimetres, 9 inches) **2** the full time anything lasts **3** an arch of a bridge ➤ *verb* (**spanning, spanned**) to stretch across: *The bridge spans the river*

spangle *noun* a thin sparkling piece of metal used as an ornament ➤ *verb* to sprinkle with spangles etc

spaniel *noun* a breed of dog with large, hanging ears

spank *verb* to strike with the flat of the hand

➤ *noun* a slap with the hand, especially on the buttocks

spanking¹ *noun* a beating with the hand

spanking² *adjective, informal* fast: *a spanking pace*

spanner *noun* a tool used to tighten or loosen nuts, screws, etc

spar¹ *noun* a long piece of wood or metal used as a ship's mast or its crosspiece

spar² *verb* (**sparring, sparred**) **1** to fight with the fists **2** to engage in an argument

spare *verb* **1** to do without: *I can't spare you today* **2** to afford, set aside: *I can't spare the time to do it* **3** to treat with mercy, hold back from injuring **4** to avoid causing (trouble etc) to ➤ *adjective* **1** extra, not yet in use: *spare tyre* **2** thin, small: *spare but strong* ➤ *noun* another of the same kind (eg a tyre, part of a machine) kept for emergencies • **to spare** over and above what is needed

spare rib *noun* a cut of pork that consists of ribs with very little meat on them

spare tyre *noun* **1** an extra tyre for a motor vehicle, bicycle, etc **2** *informal* a roll of fat just above someone's waist

sparing *adjective* careful, economical

spark¹ *noun* **1** a small red-hot part thrown off from something burning **2** a trace: *a spark of humanity* ➤ *verb* to make sparks

spark² *noun, often ironic* a lively or intelligent person: *What bright spark left the oven on?*

sparkle *noun* **1** a little spark **2** brightness, liveliness **3** bubbles, as in wine ➤ *verb* **1** to shine in a glittering way **2** to be lively or witty **3** to bubble ♦ **sparkly** *adjective*

sparkler *noun* **1** a small hand-held firework that produces showers of silvery sparks **2** *informal* a diamond or other impressive jewel

sparkling *adjective* **1** glittering **2** witty **3** of a drink: bubbling, fizzy

spark plug or **sparking-plug** *noun* a device in a car engine that produces a spark to set on fire explosive gases

sparrow *noun* a type of small dull-coloured bird

sparse *adjective* **1** thinly scattered **2** not much, not enough ♦ **sparsely** *adverb* ♦ **sparseness** *noun*

Spartacist *noun, history* **1** a follower of Spartacus, leader of the slaves that revolted against Rome 73–71 BC **2** a member of an extreme German communist group that staged an unsuccessful uprising in Berlin in 1919

spartan *adjective* of conditions etc: hard, without luxury

spasm *noun* **1** a sudden involuntary jerk of the muscles **2** a strong, short burst (eg of anger, work)

spasmodic *adjective* **1** occurring in spasms **2** coming now and again, not regularly ♦ **spasmodically** *adverb*

spastic *adjective* suffering from cerebral palsy

spat past form of **spit¹**

spate *noun* **1** flood: *The river is in spate* **2** a sudden rush: *a spate of new books*

spatial or **spacial** *adjective* of or relating to space

spats *plural noun, history* cloth coverings over the tops of shoes which reach just above the ankles

spatter *verb* to splash (eg with mud)

spatula (*pronounced* **spat**-uw-la) *noun* a tool with a broad, blunt blade

spawn *noun* a mass of eggs of fish, frogs, etc ➤ *verb* **1** of fish etc: to lay eggs **2** to cause, produce: *The film's success spawned several sequels*

spay *verb* to remove the ovaries of (a female animal)

speak *verb* (**speaking, spoke, spoken**) **1** to say words, talk **2** to hold a conversation (with): *I spoke to Jack about the holidays* **3** to make a speech **4** to be able to talk (a certain language) • **speak your mind** to give your opinion openly • **speak up 1** to speak more loudly or clearly **2** to give your opinion openly

speakeasy *noun* (*plural* **speakeasies**), *informal* an illicit bar where alcohol was sold during Prohibition in the USA

speaker *noun* **1** someone who speaks, especially giving formal speeches **2** (**the Speaker**) a person in charge of debates in a parliament **3** a device attached to a radio etc which converts audio signals into sound

spear¹ *noun* a long weapon, with an iron or steel point ➤ *verb* to pierce with a spear

spear² *noun* a long, pointed shoot or leaf (especially of grass)

spearhead *noun* **1** the leading member of an attacking force **2** the tip of a spear ➤ *verb* to lead (a movement, campaign, attack, etc)

spearmint *noun* **1** a plant of the mint family with sweet-smelling leaves and spikes of purple flowers **2** the sweet-smelling oil obtained from its leaves and used as a flavouring in confectionery, toothpaste, etc

special *adjective* **1** not ordinary, exceptional: *special occasion/special friend* **2** put on for a particular purpose: *special train* **3** belonging to one person or thing and not to others: *special skills/special tool for drilling holes in tiles*

special effects *plural noun* techniques, including computer-generated imagery, lighting, manipulation of film or sound, etc used to contribute to the illusion in films, TV programmes, etc

specialist *noun* someone who studies one branch of a subject or field: *heart specialist*

speciality *noun* (*plural* **specialities**) something for which a person is well-known

specialize or **specialise** *verb* to work in, or study, a particular job, subject, etc
♦ **specialization** *noun*

specialized or **specialised** *adjective* of knowledge: obtained by specializing

specially *adverb* for a special purpose: *specially written for younger children*

! Do not confuse with: **especially**

speciation *noun, biology* the evolution of new species from an existing one

specie (*pronounced* **spee**-shi) *noun* gold and silver coins

species *noun* (*plural* **species**) **1** a related group of plants or animals, a division of a genus, the members of which are capable of breeding and producing fertile offspring **2** a kind (of anything)

specific *adjective* giving all the details clearly; particular, exactly stated: *a specific purpose*

specifically *adverb* **1** particularly or for the purpose stated and no other: *designed specifically for the elderly* **2** exactly and clearly: *I specifically told you not to leave the gate open*

specification *noun* **1** the act of specifying **2** a full description of details (eg in a plan or contract)

specify *verb* (**specifies, specifying, specified**) **1** to set down or say clearly (what is wanted) **2** to make particular mention of

specimen *noun* something used as a sample of a group or kind of anything, especially for study or for putting in a collection

specious (*pronounced* **spee**-shus) *adjective* looking or seeming good but really not so good

speck *noun* **1** a small spot **2** a tiny piece (eg of dust)

speckle *noun* a spot on a different-coloured background

speckled *adjective* dotted with speckles

specs *plural noun, informal* spectacles

-spect- or **-spec-** forms words connected with looking or seeing: *spectacle/inspect* (= to look into) ⏱ Comes from Latin *specere* meaning 'to look at'

spectacle *noun* a striking or wonderful sight

spectacles *plural noun* glasses which someone wears to improve eyesight

spectacular *adjective* **1** very impressive to see or watch: *spectacular scenery* **2** remarkable or dramatic: *a spectacular success* ➤ *noun* a spectacular show with lavish costumes, sets, and music ♦ **spectacularly** *adverb* (meaning 2): *The value of the shares has increased spectacularly*

spectate *verb* to look on rather than participate

spectator *noun* someone who watches an event, eg a football match

spectral *adjective* ghostly

spectre or *US* **specter** *noun* **1** a ghost **2** the threat of something unpleasant: *The spectre of famine was never far away*

spectrometer *noun, physics* an instrument used for measuring wavelength or energy distribution in a beam of radiation (*see also:* **mass spectrometer**) ♦ **spectrometry** *noun*

spectroscope *noun, chemistry* a device that is used to produce, observe and analyse the spectrum of a chemical compound

spectrum *noun* (*plural* **spectra** or **spectrums**) **1** *physics* the band of colours as seen in a rainbow, formed when white light is dispersed through a prism **2** *physics* a band or series of lines representing the wavelengths or frequencies of electromagnetic radiation **3** the range or extent of anything: *the whole spectrum of human emotions*

speculate *verb* **1** to guess **2** to wonder (about) **3** to buy goods, shares, etc in order to sell them again at a profit ♦ **speculation** *noun*

speculative *adjective* speculating

speculator *noun* a person who buys things in the hope of making a profit when they sell them, without knowing for sure what the future selling price will be: *a property speculator*

sped past form of **speed**

speech *noun* (*plural* **speeches**) **1** the power of making sounds which have meaning for other people **2** a way of speaking: *His speech is always clear* **3** (*plural* **speeches**) a formal talk given to an audience

speechless *adjective* so surprised, shocked, etc that you cannot speak

speech marks same as **quotation marks**

speech therapy *noun* the treatment of people with speech, language, and voice disorders ♦ **speech therapist** *noun*

speed *noun* **1** quickness of, or rate of, movement or action **2** *slang* the drug amphetamine ➤ *verb* (**speeding, sped** or **speeded**) **1** (*past form* **sped**) to (cause to) move along quickly, hurry **2** (*past form* **speeded**) to drive very fast in a car etc (especially faster than is allowed by law)
• **up to speed** fully competent at a new job etc

speedboat *noun* a motor boat capable of high speeds

speed camera *noun* a roadside camera triggered by vehicles that exceed the speed limit (*short form:* **speed cam**)

speeding *noun* driving at (an illegally) high speed

speed limit *noun* the greatest speed a vehicle may legally travel at on a particular road

speed of light *noun, physics* the constant and universal speed, 299,792,458 metres per second, at which electromagnetic waves travel through a vacuum

speedometer *noun* an instrument that shows how fast you are travelling

speedway *noun* a motorcycle racing track

speedwell *noun* a type of small plant with blue flowers

speedy *adjective* (**speedier, speediest**) fast; prompt; without delay ♦ **speedily** *adverb*

speleology (*pronounced* spee-li-**ol**-o-ji) *noun* the study or exploration of caves

spell[1] *verb* (**spelling, spelt** or **spelled**) **1** to give or write correctly the letters which make up (a word) **2** to mean, imply: *This defeat spells disaster for us all* • **spell out** to say (something) very frankly or clearly

spell[2] *noun* **1** words which, when spoken, are supposed to have magic power **2** magic or other powerful influence: *Many men fell under the spell of her beauty* • **under someone's spell** captivated by their influence

spell[3] *noun* **1** a (short) space of time: *a spell of dry weather* **2** a turn (at work, rest, play)

spellbind *verb* (**spellbinding, spellbound**) to captivate, enchant or fascinate ♦ **spellbinding** *adjective* ♦ **spellbound** *adjective*

spellcheck or **spellchecker** *noun* a computer program that checks the accuracy of spelling ♦ **spell-check** *verb* to run a spellcheck over (a document)

spelling *noun* **1** the ability to spell words **2** a way a word is spelt: *an American spelling*

spelling bee *noun* a spelling competition

spelt past form of **spell**[1]

spelunking *noun* the sport or activity of exploring caves; potholing ♦ **spelunker** *noun* ⊕ Comes from Latin *spelunca*, from Greek *spelynx* meaning 'a cave'

spend *verb* (**spending, spent**) **1** to use (money) for buying **2** to use (energy etc) **3** to pass (time): *I spent a week there* **4** to use up energy, force: *The storm spent itself and the sun shone*

spendthrift *noun* someone who spends money freely and carelessly

spent *adjective* exhausted; having lost force or power: *a spent bullet*

sperm *noun, biology* **1** the male sex cell that fertilizes the female egg; a spermatozoon **2** the fluid in a male carrying these cells; semen

spermatogenesis *noun, biology* the formation and development of sperm in the testes ♦ **spermatogenetic** *adjective*

spermatophyte or **spermophyte** *noun, botany* any seed-bearing plant

spermatozoid *noun, botany* in certain plants: a mature male sex cell

spermatozoon (*pronounced* sper-ma-toh-**zoh**-on) *noun* (*plural* **spermatozoa** – *pronounced* sper-ma-toh-**zoh**-a), *biology* a male sex cell contained in semen

spermicide *noun* a substance which kills spermatozoa

sperm whale *noun* a kind of whale from the head of which **spermaceti**, a waxy substance, is obtained

spew *verb* **1** to vomit **2** to pour or cause to pour or stream out

sphere *noun* **1** a ball or similar perfectly round object **2** a position or level in society: *He moves in the highest spheres* **3** range (of influence or action)

sphere of influence *noun* **1** the range or extent over which a place or person is dominant **2** *geography* the area from which a particular place will draw people to use its services, facilities, etc

spherical (*pronounced* **sfe**-ri-kal) *adjective* having the shape of a sphere

spheroid (*pronounced* **sfee**-roid) *noun, maths* a figure that is almost a sphere

sphincter (*pronounced* **sfingk**-ter) *noun, anatomy* a ring of muscle that can contract the entrance to a cavity in the body ⊕ Comes from Greek *sphingein* meaning 'to hold tight'

Sphinx *noun* **1** a mythological monster with the head of a woman and the body of a lioness **2** the large stone model of the Sphinx in Egypt **3** (**sphinx**) someone whose real thoughts you cannot guess ♦ **sphinxlike** *adjective*

spice *noun* **1** any substance used for flavouring, eg pepper, nutmeg **2** anything that adds liveliness, interest ➤ *verb* to flavour with spice • **spice something up** to add interest or enjoyment to it

spick-and-span *adjective* neat, clean, and tidy

spicy *adjective* (**spicier, spiciest**) **1** full of spices **2** *informal* lively and sometimes slightly indecent: *a spicy tale* ♦ **spiciness** *noun*

spider *noun* **1** a kind of small, insect-like creature with eight legs, that spins a web **2** *computing* a program that performs automatic searches on the Internet

spidery *adjective* **1** like a spider **2** of handwriting: having fine, sprawling strokes

spiel (*pronounced* speel or shpeel) *noun, informal* a (long or often repeated) story or speech ⊕ Comes from German *spielen* meaning 'to play'

spike[1] *noun* **1** a pointed piece of rod (of wood, metal, etc) **2** a type of large nail **3** (**spikes**) a pair of running-shoes with spiked soles ➤ *verb* **1** to pierce with a spike **2** to make useless **3** *informal* to add an alcoholic drink to (a soft drink)

spike² *noun* **1** an ear of corn **2** a pointed head of flowers, as in the hyacinth

spiky *adjective* (**spikier, spikiest**) having spikes or a sharp point

spill¹ *verb* (**spilling, spilt** or **spilled**) to (allow liquid to) run out or overflow ▸ *noun informal* a fall • **spill the beans** *informal* to give away a secret, especially unintentionally

spill² *noun* a thin strip of wood or twisted paper for lighting a candle, a pipe, etc

spillage *noun* an act of spilling or what is spilt

spilling wave *noun, geography* a wave in which water curls and spills down the front, and which breaks gradually (*compare with*: **plunging breaker**)

spin *verb* (**spinning, spun**) **1** to draw out (cotton, wood, silk, etc) and twist into threads **2** to (cause to) whirl round quickly **3** to travel quickly, especially on wheels **4** to produce a fine thread as a spider does ▸ *noun* **1** a whirling motion **2** *informal* a ride (especially on wheels) **3** of information, a news report, etc: a favourable bias: *The PR department will put a spin on it* • **spin a yarn** to tell a long story • **spin out** to make to last a long or longer time

spina bifida (*pronounced* **spai**-na **bif**-i-da) *noun* a birth defect which leaves part of the spinal cord exposed

spinach *noun* a type of plant whose leaves are eaten as a vegetable

spinal see **spine**

spinal cord *noun* a cord of nerve cells in the spine

spindle *noun* **1** the pin from which the thread is twisted in spinning wool or cotton **2** a pin on which anything turns round

spindly *adjective* (**spindlier, spindliest**) *informal* long and thin

spin doctor *noun, informal* someone, especially in politics, who tries to influence public opinion by putting a favourable bias on information presented to the public

spindrier *noun* a machine for taking water out of clothes by whirling them round

spindrift *noun* the spray blown from the tops of waves

spine *noun* **1** the line of linked bones running down the back in animals and humans, the backbone **2** the narrow middle section of the cover of a book which hides the part where the pages are glued or stitched **3** a stiff, pointed spike which is part of an animal's body (eg a porcupine) **4** a thorn ♦ **spinal** *adjective*

spine-chiller *noun* a frightening story, thought, etc ♦ **spine-chilling** *adjective*

spineless *adjective, informal* having no spine; weak

spinet *noun* a kind of small harpsichord

spinnaker *noun* a large triangular sail set at the front of a yacht

spinneret *noun* in spiders, silkworms, etc: a small tubular organ that produces silky thread

spinney *noun* (*plural* **spinneys**) a small clump of trees

spinning wheel *noun* a machine for spinning thread, consisting of a wheel which drives spindles

spin-off *noun* **1** a side-effect, especially one that is beneficial **2** something that comes about because of the success of an earlier product or idea, eg a television series derived from a successful film

spinster *noun* a woman who is not married ♦ **spinsterhood** *noun* ♦ **spinsterish** *adjective*

spiny *adjective* (**spinier, spiniest**) covered with spines

spiracle *noun* (**spiracles**), *zoology* **1** an opening on the side of an insect's body for breathing **2** the breathing hole in whales etc ⏱ Comes from Latin *spirare* meaning 'to breathe'

spiral *adjective* **1** coiled round like a spring **2** winding round and round, getting further and further away from the centre ▸ *noun* **1** anything with a spiral shape **2** a spiral movement **3** an increase which gets ever more rapid ▸ *verb* (**spiralling, spiralled**) **1** to move in a spiral **2** to increase ever more rapidly

spire *noun* a tall, sharp-pointed tower (especially on the roof of a church)

spirit *noun* **1** the soul **2** a being without a body, a ghost: *an evil spirit* **3** liveliness, boldness: *he acted with spirit* **4** a feeling or attitude: *a spirit of kindness* **5** the intended meaning: *the spirit of the laws* **6** a distilled liquid, especially alcohol **7** (**spirits**) strong alcoholic drinks in general (eg whisky) **8** (**spirits**) state of mind, mood: *in high spirits* ▸ *verb* (**spiriting, spirited**) (*especially* **spirit away**) to remove, as if by magic

spirited *adjective* lively

spirit level *noun* a flat bar into which is set a liquid-filled glass tube with a large air bubble, used for testing that horizontal or vertical surfaces are level

spiritual *adjective* having to do with the soul or with ghosts ▸ *noun* an emotional, religious song of a kind originally developed by the African American slaves ♦ **spiritually** *adverb*

spiritualism *noun* the belief that living people can communicate with the souls of dead people ♦ **spiritualist** *noun*

spit¹ *noun* the liquid which forms in a person's mouth ▸ *verb* (**spitting, spat**) **1** to throw liquid out from the mouth **2** to rain slightly

spit² *noun* **1** a metal bar on which meat is roasted **2** *geography* a long stretch of sand running into the sea from the mainland ▸ *verb* (**spitting,**

spitted) to pierce with something sharp

spite noun the wish to hurt (especially feelings) ➤ verb to annoy out of spite • **in spite of 1** taking no notice of: *He left in spite of his father's command* **2** although something has happened or is a fact: *The ground was dry in spite of all the rain*

spiteful adjective motivated by spite; malicious ♦ **spitefully** adverb

spitting image noun, informal an exact likeness

spittle noun spit

spittoon noun a kind of dish into which you may spit

splash verb **1** to spatter with water, mud, etc **2** to move or fall with a splash or splashes ➤ noun (plural **splashes**) **1** the sound made by, or the scattering of liquid caused by, something hitting water etc **2** a mark made by splashing (eg on your clothes) **3** a bright patch: *a splash of colour* • **make a splash** to attract a lot of attention • **splash out** informal to spend a lot of money (on)

splat noun the sound made by a soft wet object striking a surface ➤ adverb with this sound: *She gave him a custard pie splat in the face* ➤ verb (**splatting, splatted**) to hit, fall, land, etc with a splat

splatter verb **1** (often **splatter with**) to make dirty with lots of small scattered drops **2** to publicize, especially in a sensational way: *The news was splattered over every front page* ➤ noun **1** a splashing sound **2** a splash or spattering of colour, mud, etc

splay verb to turn out at an angle

spleen noun **1** a spongy, blood-filled organ inside the body, near the stomach **2** bad temper

splendid adjective **1** magnificent, brilliant **2** informal excellent ♦ **splendidly** adverb

splendour or US **splendor** noun the state or quality of being very grand and beautiful in appearance or style

splenetic adjective **1** of or relating to the spleen **2** bad-tempered; spiteful ♦ **splenetically** adverb

splice verb to join (two ends of a rope) by twining the threads together ➤ noun a joint so made

spliff noun, slang a cannabis cigarette

splint noun a piece of wood etc tied to a broken limb to keep it in a fixed position

splinter noun a sharp, thin, broken piece of wood, glass, etc ➤ verb to split into splinters

splinter group noun a small group formed by individuals who have broken away from the main group, especially because of some disagreement over policy, principles, etc

split verb (**splitting, split**) **1** to cut or break lengthways **2** to crack, break **3** to divide into pieces or groups etc ➤ noun **1** a crack, a break **2** (**the splits**) the feat of going down on the floor with one leg stretched forward and the other back • **split your sides** informal to laugh heartily

split infinitive noun, grammar an infinitive that has an adverb or other word coming in between the word *to* and the verb, as in *to boldly go* etc

ⓘ Although many people think the split infinitive is incorrect, these days most tend to be more relaxed about its use.

split personality noun, psychology a condition in which two or more distinct personalities coexist in a single person

split second noun a fraction of a second

splitting adjective of a headache: severe, intense

splutter verb **1** to make spitting noises **2** to speak hastily and unclearly

spoil verb (**spoiling, spoiled** or **spoilt**) **1** to make useless; damage, ruin **2** to give in to the wishes of (a child etc) and so ruin its character **3** of food: to become bad or useless **4** (past form **spoiled**) to rob, plunder ➤ noun (often **spoils**) plunder • **spoiling for** eager for (especially a fight)

spoiler noun **1** a flap on an aircraft wing which increases drag and so reduces the air speed on descent **2** a fixed horizontal structure on a car which puts pressure on the wheels and so increases its roadholding capacity **3** a preview of how a film etc ends, spoiling the dramatic effect **4** someone or something that spoils

spoilsport noun, informal someone who refuses to join in other people's fun

spoke¹ past tense of **speak**

spoke² noun one of the ribs or bars from the centre to the rim of a wheel

spoken past participle of **speak**

spokesman or **spokeswoman** noun (plural **spokesmen** or **spokeswomen**) someone who speaks on behalf of others

spoliation noun plundering

spondee noun a metrical foot of two long or stressed syllables ♦ **spondaic** adjective

sponge noun **1** a sea animal which consists of a large cluster of cells supported by a soft, elastic skeleton **2** its skeleton, which can soak up water and is used for washing **3** an artificial object like this used for washing **4** a light cake or pudding ➤ verb **1** to wipe with a sponge **2** informal to live off money etc given by others

sponger noun, informal someone who lives at others' expense

spongy adjective (**spongier, spongiest**) soft and springy, like a sponge

sponsor *noun* **1** someone who takes responsibility for introducing something, a promoter **2** someone who promises to pay a sum of money if another person completes a set task (eg a walk, swim, etc) **3** a business firm which pays for a radio or television programme and advertises its products during it ➤ *verb* to act as a sponsor to

sponsorship *noun* the act of sponsoring

spontaneity (*pronounced* spon-ta-**nei**-i-ti) *noun* being spontaneous

spontaneous *adjective* **1** not planned beforehand **2** natural, not forced ✦ **spontaneously** *adverb*

spontaneous combustion *noun* an instance of a body catching fire as a result of heat that is generated within it, as opposed to heat applied from outside

spontaneous generation *noun, biology* the theory, now discredited, that living matter can arise spontaneously from non-living matter (*compare with*: **biogenesis**)

spoof *informal, noun* **1** a satirical imitation; a parody **2** a trick played as a joke, a hoax ➤ *verb* **1** to parody **2** to play a hoax

spook *informal, noun* a ghost ➤ *verb* **1** to frighten or startle **2** to make (someone) feel nervous or uneasy

spooky *adjective* (**spookier, spookiest**) *informal* frightening or uncanny ✦ **spookily** *adverb* ✦ **spookiness** *noun*

spool *noun* a reel for thread, film, etc

spoon *noun* a piece of metal etc with a hollow bowl at one end, used for lifting food to the mouth ➤ *verb* to lift with a spoon

spoonerism *noun* a mistake in speaking in which the first sounds of words change position, as in *every crook and nanny* for *every nook and cranny*

⊙ After the Reverend William *Spooner*, who was famous for making this sort of mistake

spoonfeed *verb* (**spoonfeeding, spoonfed**) **1** to feed with a spoon **2** to teach without encouraging independent thought

spoor *noun* the footmarks or trail left by an animal

sporadic *adjective* happening here and there, or now and again ✦ **sporadically** *adverb*: *Fighting broke out sporadically*

spore *noun* the seed of certain plants (eg ferns, fungi)

sporran *noun* a small pouch worn hanging in front of a kilt

sport *noun* **1** games such as football, tennis, skiing, etc in general **2** any one game of this type **3** *informal* a good-natured, obliging person **4** *biology* an animal or plant that as a result of a mutation is very different from others of its species ➤ *verb* **1** to have fun, play **2** to wear: *sporting a pink tie*

sporting *adjective* **1** fond of sport **2** believing in fair play, good-natured

sporting chance *noun* a reasonably good chance

sports car *noun* a small, fast car with only two seats

sportsman or **sportswoman** *noun* (*plural* **sportsmen** or **sportswomen**) **1** someone who plays sports **2** someone who shows fair play in sports ✦ **sportsmanship** *noun*

sportsmanlike *adjective* fair, sporting

sportswear *noun* clothes designed for sport or for wearing casually

sporty *adjective* (**sportier, sportiest**) **1** of a person: fond of or good at sport **2** of clothes: casual; suitable for wearing when playing a sport **3** of a car: looking, performing, or handling like a sports car ✦ **sportiness** *noun*

spot *noun* **1** a small mark or stain (of mud, paint, etc) **2** a small amount, especially of liquid **3** a round mark as part of a pattern on material etc **4** a pimple **5** a place ➤ *verb* (**spotting, spotted**) **1** to mark with spots **2** to catch sight of • **in a spot** *informal* in trouble • **on the spot 1** in the place where someone is most needed **2** right away, immediately **3** in an embarrassing or difficult position

spot check *noun* an inspection made at random and without warning ➤ *verb* (**spot-check**) to carry out a random check

spotless *adjective* very clean ✦ **spotlessly** *adverb*

spotlight *noun* a bright light that is shone on an actor on the stage ➤ *verb* (**spotlighting, spotlit** or **spotlighted**) **1** to show up clearly **2** to draw attention to • **be in the spotlight** to have the attention of others, the media, etc focused on you

spot-on *adjective, informal* very accurate

spotted or **spotty** *adjective* (**spottier, spottiest**) covered with spots

spouse *noun* a husband or wife

spout *noun* **1** the part of a kettle, teapot, etc through which liquid is poured out **2** a strong jet of liquid ➤ *verb* to pour or spurt out

sprain *noun* a painful twisting (eg of an ankle) ➤ *verb* to twist painfully

sprang past tense of **spring**

sprat *noun* a small fish similar to a herring

sprawl *verb* **1** to sit, lie, or fall with the limbs spread out widely **2** of a town etc: to spread out in an untidy, irregular way

spray¹ *noun* **1** a fine mist of liquid like that made by a waterfall **2** a device with many small holes (eg on a watering-can or shower) for producing spray **3** a liquid for spraying ➤ *verb* to cover with a mist or fine jets of liquid

spray² *noun* **1** a shoot spreading out in flowers **2** a small bouquet of flowers

spread *verb* (**spreading, spread**) **1** to put more widely or thinly over an area: *Spread the butter on the bread* **2** to cover: *Spread the bread with jam* **3** to open out (eg your arms, a map) **4** to scatter or distribute over a wide area, length of time, etc ➤ *noun* **1** the act of spreading **2** the extent or range (of something) **3** a food which is spread on bread: *sandwich spread* **4** *informal* a large meal laid out on a table • **spread your wings** to attempt to broaden your experience

spread-eagled *adjective* with limbs spread out

spreadsheet *noun, computing* a computer program with which data can be viewed on screen and manipulated to make calculations etc

spree *noun* a careless spell of some activity: *a spending spree*

sprig *noun* a small twig or shoot

sprightly *adjective* (**sprightlier, sprightliest**) lively, brisk ♦ **sprightliness** *noun*

spring *verb* (**springing, sprang, sprung**) **1** to jump, leap **2** to move swiftly **3** to set off (a trap etc) **4** to give, reveal unexpectedly: *She sprang the news on me* **5** to come (from): *Her bravery springs from her love of adventure* ➤ *noun* **1** a leap **2** a coil of wire used in a mattress **3** the ability to stretch and spring back **4** bounce, energy **5** a small stream flowing out from the ground **6** the season of the year following winter, when plants begin to grow again • **spring a leak** to begin to leak • **spring back** to return suddenly to an earlier position when released • **spring up** to appear suddenly

springboard *noun* **1** a springy board from which swimmers may dive into a swimming pool **2** anything that serves to get things moving: *a springboard to success*

springbok *noun* (*plural* **springbok** or **springboks**) a type of deer found in S Africa

spring-cleaning *noun* a thorough cleaning of a house, especially in the spring ♦ **spring-clean** *noun & verb*

spring onion *noun* an onion picked when it is just a tiny white bulb with long thin green shoots, usually eaten raw in salads

spring roll *noun* a type of deep-fried folded Chinese pancake with a variety of savoury fillings

spring tide *noun* a tidal pattern that occurs when the Moon is full or new, and tides are at their highest and lowest (*compare with*: **neap tide**)

springy *adjective* (**springier, springiest**) able to spring back into its former position etc, elastic

sprinkle *verb* to scatter or cover in small drops or pieces

sprinkler *noun* something which sprinkles water

sprinkling *noun* a few, a small amount: *We had a sprinkling of snow in the night*

sprint *verb* to run at full speed ➤ *noun* **1** *athletics* a race at high speed over a short distance **2** a burst of speed at the end of a long race, eg in athletics, cycling, etc **3** a fast run ♦ **sprinter** *noun*

sprite *noun* **1** a supernatural spirit **2** *computing* an icon which can be moved about a screen

spritzer *noun* a drink of white wine and soda water ⊕ from German *spritzen* meaning 'to spray'

sprocket *noun* one of a set of teeth on the rim of a wheel

sprout *verb* **1** to begin to grow **2** to put out new shoots ➤ *noun* **1** a young bud **2** (**sprouts**) Brussels sprouts

spruce¹ *noun* a kind of fir tree

spruce² *adjective* (**sprucer, sprucest**) neat, smart

sprung past participle of **spring**

spry *adjective* (**spryer, spryest**) lively, active

spud *noun, informal* a potato

spume *noun* froth, foam ♦ **spumy** *adjective*

spun past form of **spin**

spur *noun* **1** a sharp point worn by a horse-rider on the heel and used to urge on a horse **2** a claw-like point at the back of a bird's leg **3** anything that urges someone on **4** a ridge of high land that projects out into a valley **5** a small line of mountains running off from a larger range ➤ *verb* (**spurring, spurred**) **1** to use spurs on (a horse) **2** to urge (on) • **on the spur of the moment** without thinking beforehand

spurious (*pronounced* **spyoo**-ri-us) *adjective* not genuine, false

spurn *verb* to cast aside, reject with scorn

spurt *verb* to pour out in a sudden stream ➤ *noun* **1** a sudden stream pouring or squirting out **2** a sudden increase of effort: *put a spurt on*

sputnik (*pronounced* **spuwt**-nik) *noun* a Russian artificial satellite

sputter *verb* to make a noise as of spitting and throw out moisture in drops

sputum (*pronounced* **spyuw**-tum) *noun* a mixture of saliva and mucus

spy *noun* (*plural* **spies**) someone who secretly collects (and reports) information about another person, country, firm, etc ➤ *verb* (**spies, spying, spied**) to catch sight of • **spy on someone** to watch them secretly

spyware *noun, computing* software that gathers information about a computer user and transmits it to another user

SQL *abbreviation, computing* structured query language, a programming language used to retrieve information from databases

squabble *verb* to quarrel noisily ➤ *noun* a noisy quarrel

squad *noun* **1** a group of soldiers, workmen, etc doing a particular job **2** a group of people

squaddie *noun, informal* a private, an ordinary soldier

squadron *noun* a division of a regiment, section of a fleet, or group of military aircraft

squalid *adjective* **1** very dirty, filthy **2** contemptible

squall[1] *noun* a sudden violent storm

squall[2] *noun* a squeal, a scream

squally *adjective* (**squallier, squalliest**) gusty; stormy

squalor *noun* dirty or squalid living conditions

squander *verb* to waste (money, goods, strength, etc)

square *noun* **1** a figure with four equal sides and four right angles, of this shape: □ **2** an open space enclosed by buildings in a town **3** *maths* the answer when a number is multiplied by itself (eg the square of 3 is 9) ➤ *adjective* **1** shaped like a square **2** in area: *one metre square* **3** equal in scores in a game **4** of two or more people: not owing one another anything **5** straight, level ➤ *verb* **1** to make like a square **2** to straighten (the shoulders) **3** to multiply a number by itself **4** to fit, agree: *That doesn't square with what you said earlier* ➤ *adverb* **1** in a straight or level position **2** directly; exactly: *hit square on the nose*
• **square metre** etc an area equal to that of a square each side of which is one metre etc long
• **square up** or **square something up** to settle a debt

square deal *noun* fair treatment

square meal *noun* a large, satisfying meal

square number *noun, maths* a number that is the square of an integer

square root *noun, maths* the number which, multiplied by itself, gives a certain other number (eg 3 is the square root of 9)

squash[1] *verb* **1** to crush flat or to a pulp **2** to put down, defeat (rebellion etc) ➤ *noun* **1** a crushing or crowding **2** a mass of people crowded together **3** a drink made from the juice of crushed fruit **4** a game with rackets and a rubber ball played in a walled court

squash[2] *noun, US* **1** any of various trailing plants with marrow-like gourds **2** the fruit of any of these plants which can be cooked and used as a vegetable

squat *verb* (**squatting, squatted**) **1** to sit down on the heels **2** to settle without permission in property which you do not pay rent for ➤ *adjective* short and thick

squatter *noun* someone who squats in a building, on land, etc

squatter settlement another term for a **shantytown**

squaw *noun, offensive* **1** a Native American woman or wife **2** a woman

squawk *verb* to give a harsh cry ➤ *noun* a harsh cry

squeak *verb* to give a short, high-pitched sound ➤ *noun* a high-pitched sound

squeaky *adjective* (**squeakier, squeakiest**) **1** high-pitched: *a squeaky voice* **2** tending to squeak: *a squeaky floorboard*

squeaky clean *adjective, informal* **1** spotlessly clean **2** virtuous, above reproach or criticism, but often with an implication that this impression is superficial

squeal *verb* **1** to give a loud, shrill cry **2** *informal* to inform on

squeamish *adjective* **1** easily sickened or shocked **2** feeling sick

squeegee *noun* a sponge for washing windows etc

squeeze *verb* **1** to press together **2** to grasp tightly **3** to force out (liquid or juice from) by pressing **4** to force a way: *squeezed through the hole in the wall* ➤ *noun* **1** a squeezing or pressing **2** a few drops got by squeezing: *a squeeze of lemon juice* **3** a crowd of people crushed together ◆ **squeezy** *adjective*

squelch *noun* (*plural* **squelches**) a sound made, eg by walking through marshy ground ➤ *verb* to make this sound

squib *noun* a type of small firework

squid *noun* a sea animal with tentacles, related to the cuttlefish

squidgy *adjective* (**squidgier, squidgiest**) soft, pliant and sometimes soggy

squiggle *noun* a curly or wavy mark ◆ **squiggly** *adjective*

squint *verb* **1** to screw up the eyes in looking at something **2** to have the eyes looking in different directions ➤ *noun* **1** a fault in eyesight which causes squinting **2** *informal* a quick, close glance ➤ *adjective, informal* not being properly straight or centred

squire *noun, history* **1** a country landowner **2** a knight's servant

squirm *verb* to wriggle or twist the body, especially in pain or embarrassment

squirrel *noun* a small gnawing animal, either reddish-brown or grey, with a bushy tail

squirt *verb* to shoot out (a narrow jet of liquid) ➤ *noun* **1** a narrow jet of liquid **2** a small, insignificant person, especially one who behaves arrogantly

Sr *symbol, chemistry* strontium

SS *abbreviation* Schutzstaffel, Hitler's bodyguard

of elite police which later formed military units in Nazi Germany and ran the concentration camps ⊙ Comes from German and literally means 'protection squad'

St *abbreviation* **1** saint **2** street **3** strait

stab *verb* (**stabbing, stabbed**) **1** to wound or pierce with a pointed weapon **2** to poke (at) ➤ *noun* **1** the act of stabbing **2** a wound made by stabbing **3** a sharp pain • **have a stab at** to make an attempt at • **stab someone in the back** to betray someone while posing as their friend or ally

stability *noun* steadiness

stabilize or **stabilise** *verb* to make steady

stabilizer or **stabiliser** *noun* either of the two small wheels fitted to the back of a child's bicycle to give it stability while they are learning to ride

stable[1] *adjective* **1** firm, steady **2** regular or constant; under control: *The patient's condition is stable* **3** of a person or their personality: not fickle, moody, impulsive, etc

stable[2] *noun* a building for keeping horses ➤ *verb* to put or keep (horses) in a stable

staccato (*pronounced* sta-**kah**-toh) *adjective* of sounds: sharp and separate, like the sound of tapping ➤ *adverb, music* with each note sounded separately and clearly (*contrasted with:* **legato**) ➤ *noun* (*plural* **staccatos**) a piece of music to be played with each note sounded separately ⊙ Comes from Italian *distaccare* meaning 'to separate'

stack *noun* **1** a large pile (of straw, hay, wood, etc) **2** (**stacks**) *informal* a large amount: *stacks of money* ➤ *verb* **1** to pile in a stack **2** to fill: *They stacked the fridge with goodies* • **stacker** *noun*

stadium *noun* (*plural* **stadiums** or **stadia**) a large sports ground or racecourse with seats for spectators

staff *noun* **1** a stick or pole carried in the hand **2** *music* a stave **3** workers employed in a business, school, etc **4** a group of army officers who assist a commanding officer ➤ *verb* to supply (a school etc) with staff

staff nurse *noun* a qualified nurse of the rank below sister

stag *noun* a male deer

stage *noun* **1** a platform for performing or acting on **2** a step in development: *the first stage of the plan* **3** a landing place (eg for boats) **4** a part of a journey **5** a stopping place on a journey ➤ *verb* **1** to prepare and put on a performance of (a play etc) **2** to arrange (an event, eg an exhibition) • **on the stage** in the theatre-world • **the stage** the theatre; the job of working as an actor

stagecoach *noun* (*plural* **stagecoaches**) *history* a coach running every day with passengers

stage door *noun* the back or side entrance to a theatre that is for the use of the performers

stage fright *noun* an actor's fear when acting in public, especially for the first time

stagehand *noun* someone employed to move scenery and props in a theatre

stage-manage *verb* **1** to supervise the arrangement of scenery and props for a play **2** to arrange for something to happen in a certain way, in order to create a particular effect ◆ **stage-management** *noun* ◆ **stage manager** *noun*

stage name *noun* a name used by an actor, performer, etc

stage-struck *adjective* having an overwhelming desire to become an actor

stage whisper *noun* a loud whisper

stagger *verb* **1** to walk unsteadily, totter **2** to astonish **3** to arrange (people's hours of work etc) so that they do not begin or end together

staggered *adjective* of two or more things: arranged to begin and end at different times

staggering *adjective* astonishing

staging *noun* **1** scaffolding **2** putting on the stage

stagnant *adjective* of water: standing still, not flowing and therefore not pure

stagnate *verb* **1** of water: to remain still and so become impure **2** to remain for a long time in the same situation and so become bored, inactive, etc

stagnation *noun* **1** stagnating **2** being stagnant

stag night or **stag party** *noun* (*plural* **stag nights** or **stag parties**) a party for men only, held shortly before one of them gets married

staid *adjective* set in your ways, sedate

stain *verb* **1** to give a different colour to (wood etc) **2** to mark or make dirty by accident ➤ *noun* **1** a liquid which dyes or colours something **2** a mark which is not easily removed **3** something shameful in someone's character or reputation

stained glass *noun* decorative coloured glass cut in shapes and leaded together

stainless steel *noun* a mixture of steel and chromium which does not rust

stair *noun* **1** one or all of a number of steps one after the other **2** (**stairs**) a series or flight of steps

staircase *noun* a stretch of stairs with rails on one or both sides (*also called:* **stairway**)

stairwell *noun* the vertical shaft containing a staircase

stake[1] *noun* **1** a strong stick pointed at one end **2** *history* a post to which people were tied to be burned ➤ *verb* to mark the limits or boundaries (of a field etc) with stakes • **stake a claim** to establish ownership or right (to something)

stake[2] *noun* money put down as a bet ➤ *verb* **1** to bet (money) **2** to risk • **at stake 1** to be won or lost **2** in great danger: *His life is at stake* • **have a**

stake in to be concerned in (because you have something to gain or lose)

stakeholder *noun* someone with an interest or concern in a business or enterprise ➤ *adjective* of a society etc: with everyone having an interest in it and wishing to contribute to its success ♦ **stakeholding** *adjective*

stalactite *noun* a spike of limestone hanging from the roof of a cave, formed by the dripping of water containing lime

stalagmite *noun* a spike of limestone, like a stalactite, rising from the floor of a cave

stale *adjective* (**staler, stalest**) **1** of food: no longer fresh **2** no longer interesting because heard, done, etc too often before **3** not able to do your best (because of overworking, boredom, etc)

stalemate *noun* **1** *chess* a position in which a player cannot move without putting their king in danger **2** a position in an argument in which neither side can win

stalk[1] *noun* **1** the stem of a plant, or of a leaf or flower **2** any slender connecting part

stalk[2] *verb* **1** to hunt, follow, or approach stealthily **2** to walk stiffly or proudly ♦ **stalking** *noun*

stall[1] *noun* **1** a division for one animal in a cowshed etc **2** a table on which things are laid out for sale **3** an open-fronted shop **4** a seat in a church (especially for choir or clergy) **5** (**stalls**) theatre seats on the ground floor ➤ *verb* **1** of a car engine: to come to a halt without the driver intending it to do so **2** of an aircraft: to lose flying speed and so fall out of control

stall[2] *verb, informal* to avoid action or decision for the time being

stallion *noun* a male horse, especially one kept for breeding purposes

stalwart *adjective* brave, stout-hearted ➤ *noun* a loyal supporter

stamen *noun* (*plural* **stamens** or **stamina**), *botany* the male reproductive part of a flowering plant, consisting of a thread-like spike carrying a chamber which produces pollen

stamina *noun* strength, power to keep going during physical or mental exertion

stammer *verb* **1** to have difficulty in saying the first letter of words in speaking **2** to stumble over words ➤ *noun* a speech difficulty of this kind

stamp *verb* **1** to bring (the foot) down firmly on the ground **2** to stick a (postage stamp) on **3** to mark with a design cut into a mould and inked **4** to fix or mark deeply: *forever stamped in my memory* ➤ *noun* **1** the act of stamping **2** a design etc made by stamping **3** a cut or moulded design for stamping **4** kind, sort: *of a different stamp* **5** a postage stamp • **stamp out 1** to put out (a fire) by stamping **2** to suppress, crush

stampede *noun* **1** a wild rush of frightened animals **2** a sudden, wild rush of people ➤ *verb* to rush wildly

stance *noun* **1** point of view or attitude to something **2** someone's manner of standing

stanchion (*pronounced* **stan**-shon) *noun* an upright iron bar used as a support (eg in windows, ships)

stand *verb* (**standing, stood**) **1** to be on your feet (not lying or sitting down) **2** to rise to your feet **3** of an object: to (cause to) be in a particular place: *It stood by the door/stood the case in the corner* **4** to bear: *I cannot stand this heat* **5** *old* to treat (someone) to: *stand you tea* **6** to remain: *This law still stands* **7** to be a candidate (for): *She stood for parliament* **8** to be short (for): *PO stands for Post Office* ➤ *noun* **1** something on which anything is placed **2** an object made to hold, or for hanging, things: *a hat-stand* **3** lines of raised seats from which people may watch games etc **4** an effort made to support, defend, resist, etc: *a stand against violence* **5** *US* a witness box in a law court • **stand by** to be ready or available to be used or help in an emergency etc • **stand down** to withdraw (from a contest) or resign (from a job) • **stand fast** to refuse to give in • **stand in (for)** to take another's place, job, etc for a time • **stand out** to stick out, be noticeable • **stand to reason** to be likely or reasonable • **stand up for** to defend strongly • **stand up to** to face or oppose bravely

stand-alone *noun & adjective, computing* (of) a system, device, etc that can operate unconnected to any other

standard *noun* **1** a level against which things may be judged **2** a level of excellence aimed at: *artistic standards* **3** a large flag etc on a pole ➤ *adjective* **1** normal, usual: *standard charge* **2** ordinary, without extras: *standard model*

standard deviation *noun, statistics* the square root of the mean of the squared deviations of a number of observations from their mean

Standard English *noun* the variety of English thought of as being spoken by educated people, generally accepted as the correct form and understood by most people

standard error *noun, statistics* the standard deviation divided by the root of the total number of observations

standard form or **standard index form** *noun, maths* expressing numbers as the product of a number between one and ten and a power of ten, eg the standard form of 5,000,000 is 5×10^6

standardize or **standardise** *verb* to make all of one kind or size ♦ **standardization** *noun*

standard lamp *noun* a kind of tall lamp which

stands on the floor of a room etc

standard of living *noun* a measure of the relative wealth and comfort in which people live

standby *noun* **1** something that is kept ready for use, especially in an emergency **2** (*usually* **standby ticket**) a ticket for a journey by air that is offered at a reduced price because you must wait until just before the flight takes off to see if there is a seat available

stand-in *noun* a deputy or substitute

standing *noun* social position or reputation ➤ *adjective* **1** on your feet **2** placed on end **3** not moving **4** lasting, permanent: *a standing joke*

standing order *noun* an instruction from an account-holder to a bank to make fixed payments from the account to a third party at regular intervals

standing wave *noun, physics* a wave that results from interference between waves of the same wavelength that are travelling in opposite directions (*also called:* **stationary wave**)

stand-off *noun* a stalemate

standoffish *adjective* unfriendly ◆ **standoffishness** *noun*

standpoint *noun* the position from which you look at something (eg a question, problem), point of view

standstill *noun* a complete stop

stand-up *adjective* **1** of a verbal or physical fight: earnest; passionate; fervent **2** of a comedian: performing solo in front of a live audience

stank past tense of **stink**

stannic *adjective, chemistry* of a compound: containing tin in its tetravalent state (*compare with:* **stannous**) ⊙ Comes from Latin *stannum* meaning 'tin'

stannous *adjective, chemistry* of a compound: containing tin in its divalent state (*compare with:* **stannic**)

stanza *noun* a group of lines making up a part of a poem, a verse

stapes (*pronounced* **stei**-peez) *noun* (*plural* **stapes**) a small, stirrup-shaped bone in the ear ⊙ from Latin meaning 'stirrup'

staphylococcus *noun* (*plural* **staphylococci**) *biology* a bacterium found in clusters on the skin and mucous membranes, some species of which can cause disease

staple¹ *noun* **1** a U-shaped iron nail **2** a piece of wire driven through sheets of paper to fasten them together ➤ *verb* to fasten with a staple

staple² *adjective* chief, main: *staple foods* ➤ *noun* **1** the main item in a country's production, a person's diet, etc **2** a fibre of wool, cotton, etc

stapler *noun* a hand-held device for attaching staples

star *noun* **1** any of the bodies in the sky appearing as points of light **2** any of the fixed bodies which are really distant suns, not the planets **3** an object, shape, or figure with a number of pointed rays (often five) **4** a leading actor or actress or other well-known performer ➤ *adjective* for or of a star (in a film etc) ➤ *verb* (**starring, starred**) **1** to act the chief part (in a film or play) **2** of a film or play: to have as its star: *a new film starring Orlando Bloom*

starboard *noun* the right side of a ship, as you look towards the bow (or front) ➤ *adjective* relating the right side of a ship

starch *noun* (*plural* **starches**) **1** a carbohydrate found in all green plants, serving as an energy store **2** a white powder form of this substance (found in flour, potatoes, bread, biscuits, etc) **3** a form of this used for stiffening clothes ➤ *verb* to stiffen with starch

starchy *adjective* (**starchier, starchiest**) **1** of food: containing starch **2** stiff and unfriendly ◆ **starchiness** *noun*

stardom *noun* the state of being a leading performer

stare *verb* to look with a fixed gaze ➤ *noun* a fixed gaze

starfish *noun* (*plural* **starfish** or **starfishes**) a type of small sea creature with five points or arms

stargaze *verb* **1** to study the stars **2** *informal* to daydream ◆ **stargazer** *noun* ◆ **stargazing** *noun & adjective*

stark *adjective* **1** barren, bare **2** harsh, severe **3** sheer: *stark idiocy* ➤ *adverb* completely: *stark naked*

starlet *noun* a young film actress who is thought to have the potential to become a star

starling *noun* a common bird with dark, glossy feathers

starry *adjective* (**starrier, starriest**) full of stars; shining like stars

starry-eyed *adjective* naively idealistic or optimistic

Stars and Stripes *singular noun* the flag of the United States of America

start *verb* **1** to begin (an action): *He started to walk home* **2** to get (a machine etc) working: *She started the car* **3** to jump or jerk (eg in surprise) ➤ *noun* **1** the act of starting (eg on a task, journey) **2** a sudden movement of the body **3** a sudden shock: *You gave me a start* **4** in a race etc the advantage of beginning before, or farther forward than, others, or the amount of this: *a start of five metres*

starter *noun* **1** an official who gives the signal for a race to begin **2** any of the competitors that assemble for the start of a race **3** (*also:* **starter motor**) an electric motor that is used to start the engine of a motor vehicle **4** the first course of a meal • **for starters** *informal* in the first place

startle *verb* to give a shock or fright to

startling *adjective* that startles, surprising ♦ **startlingly** *adverb*

starvation *noun* a potentially fatal form of malnutrition caused by eating insufficient quantities of food over a long period, or by total lack of food

starve *verb* **1** to die for want of food **2** to suffer greatly from hunger **3** *informal* to be very hungry **4** to deprive (of something needed or wanted badly): *starved of company here* ♦ **starving** *adjective*

state *noun* **1** the condition (of something): *the bad state of the roads* **2** the people of a country under a government **3** *US* an area and its people with its own laws forming part of the whole country **4** a government and its officials **5** great show, pomp: *The queen drove by in state* ➤ *adjective* **1** of the government **2** national and ceremonial: *state occasions* **3** *US* of a certain state of America: *The state capital of Texas is Austin* ➤ *verb* to tell, say, or write (especially clearly and fully)

stately *adjective* (**statelier, stateliest**) noble-looking; dignified ♦ **stateliness** *noun*

stately home *noun* a large, grand old house

statement *noun* **1** that which is said or written **2** a record of finances, especially one sent by a bank to an account-holder detailing the transactions within a particular period

state-of-the-art *adjective* most up-to-date

state school *noun* a school that is government funded and where the education is free

statesman *noun* (*plural* **statesmen**) an experienced and distinguished politician

statesmanlike *adjective* diplomatic

static *adjective* not moving ➤ *noun* **1** atmospheric disturbances causing poor reception of radio or television programmes **2** (*also called*: **static electricity**) electricity on the surface of objects which will not conduct it, eg hair, nylons, etc

station *noun* **1** a building with a ticket office, waiting rooms, etc where trains, buses, or coaches stop to pick up or set down passengers **2** a place which is the centre for work or duty of any kind: *fire station/police station* **3** a radio or TV channel **4** rank, position: *lowly station* ➤ *verb* **1** to assign to a position or place **2** to take up a position: *stationed himself by the door*

stationary *adjective* standing still, not moving ⏱ Comes from Latin *stationarius* meaning 'belonging to a military station'

❗ Do not confuse: **stationary** and **stationery**. Remember that a stationER's shop sells stationERy.

stationary wave another term for **standing wave**

stationer *noun* someone who sells writing paper, envelopes, pens, etc

⏱ In Medieval Latin, a *stationarius* was a tradesman, usually a bookseller, who did not travel from place to place, but had a regular station or a permanent shop

stationery *noun* writing paper, envelopes, pens, etc ⏱ For origin, see **stationer**

statistic *noun* a piece of information or data: *He became just another statistic amongst drug-related deaths*

statistical *adjective* of or shown by statistics: *The report includes a lot of statistical information* ♦ **statistically** *adverb*: *Statistically, a man is unlikely to live as long as a woman*

statistician *noun* someone who produces or studies statistics

statistics *plural noun* numerical data, interpreted and set out in order: *statistics of road accidents for last year* ➤ *singular noun* the branch of mathematics concerned with interpreting numerical data, especially in so far as conclusions can be drawn from a sample of a population

statue *noun* a likeness of someone or an animal carved in stone, metal, etc

statuesque (*pronounced* stat-chuw-**esk**) *adjective* like a statue in dignity etc

statuette *noun* a small statue

stature *noun* **1** height **2** importance, reputation

status *noun* position, rank (of a person) in the eyes of others

status quo *noun* the state of affairs now existing, or existing before a certain time or event

status symbol *noun* a possession which is thought to show the high status of the owner (eg a powerful car)

statute *noun* an official law passed by the government of a country

statutory *adjective* according to law

staunch *adjective* firm, loyal; trustworthy

stave *noun* **1** *music* a set of spaced lines on which music is written **2** one of the strips making the side of a barrel ➤ *verb* (**staving, stove** or **staved**): **stave something in** to crush it in • **stave something off** to keep it away, delay it

stay[1] *verb* **1** to continue to be: *stayed calm/stay here while I go for help* **2** to live (for a time): *staying in a hotel* **3** *old* to stop ➤ *noun* time spent in a place • **stay put** to remain in the same place

stay[2] *noun* a rope running from the side of a ship to the masthead

stay-at-home *informal, adjective* preferring the peaceful routine of domestic life to a busy and varied social life ➤ *noun* a stay-at-home person

stays *plural noun old* a corset stiffened with strips of bone or metal

St Bernard see **Saint Bernard**

stead *noun* place: *She went in my stead* • **stand you in good stead** to turn out to be helpful to you: *His German stood him in good stead*

steadfast *adjective* **1** steady, fixed **2** faithful, loyal ◆ **steadfastly** *adverb*

steading *noun* farm buildings

steady *adjective* (**steadier, steadiest**) **1** firm, not moving or changing **2** not easily upset or put off **3** even, regular, unchanging: *moving at a steady pace* ➤ *verb* (**steadies, steadying, steadied**) to make or become steady ◆ **steadily** *adverb*

steak *noun* a thick slice of meat, especially fine-quality beef, or fish, for cooking

steal *verb* (**stealing, stole, stolen**) **1** to take (something not belonging to you) without permission **2** to move quietly **3** to take quickly or secretly: *stole a look at him*

stealth *noun* a secret way of doing, acting, etc

stealthy *adjective* (**stealthier, stealthiest**) of movement: slow, quiet and secretive ◆ **stealthily** *adverb*

steam *noun* **1** vapour from hot liquid, especially from boiling water **2** power produced by steam: *in the days of steam* ➤ *verb* **1** to give off steam **2** to cook by steam **3** to open or loosen by putting into steam: *steam open the envelope* **4** to move or travel by steam • **steam up** of glass: to become covered with condensed steam in the form of small drops of water

steam engine *noun* an engine (especially a railway engine) worked by steam

steamer *noun* **1** a ship driven by steam **2** a pot with two layers in which food in the top layer is cooked by the action of steam from water heated in the bottom layer

steamroller *noun* a steam-driven engine with large and very heavy wheels, used for flattening the surfaces of roads ➤ *verb, informal* to make (someone) do something, using force or forceful persuasion to overcome their resistance: *He steamrollered us into helping with the decorating*

steamship *noun* a steamer

steamy *adjective* (**steamier, steamiest**) **1** full of steam: *steamy atmosphere* **2** *informal* passionate, erotic

stearate *noun, chemistry* a salt or ester of stearic acid

stearic acid *noun, chemistry* a colourless fatty acid, commonly found in animal fats

steed *noun, old* a horse

steel *noun* **1** a very hard mixture of iron and carbon **2** a bar of steel for sharpening knife blades • **of steel** hard, strong: *a grip of steel* • **steel yourself** to get up courage (to do something)

steel band *noun* a group, originating in the W Indies, who play music on oil drums which have been specially beaten so that striking different areas produces different notes

steel wool *noun* thin strands of steel in a woolly mass, used for scrubbing

steely *adjective* (**steelier, steeliest**) hard, cold, strong etc like steel: *a steely gaze*

steep[1] *adjective* **1** of a slope: rising nearly straight up **2** *informal* of a price: too great

steep[2] *verb* to soak in a liquid • **be steeped in something** to be very familiar with something (eg a subject of knowledge): *steeped in French literature*

steeple *noun* a tower of a church etc rising to a point, a spire

steeplechase *noun* **1** a horse race round a course with hurdles, usually in the form of man-made hedges **2** a track running race where athletes have to jump hurdles and, usually, a water jump

steeplejack *noun* someone who climbs steeples or other high buildings to make repairs

steer[1] *verb* **1** to control the course of (a car, ship, discussion, etc) **2** to follow (a course) • **steer clear of** to keep away from

steer[2] *noun* a young ox raised for its beef

steering *noun* the parts of a ship, car, etc which have to do with controlling its course

steering wheel *noun* the wheel in a car used by the driver to steer it

stele (*pronounced* **stee**-le) *noun* an ancient stone pillar or upright slab

stellar *adjective* of the stars

stem[1] *noun* **1** the part of a plant from which the leaves and flowers grow **2** the thin support of a wine glass ➤ *verb* (**stemming, stemmed**) to start, spring (from): *Hate stems from envy*

stem[2] *verb* (**stemming, stemmed**) to stop, halt: *stem the bleeding*

stem-and-leaf diagram *noun, statistics* a type of diagram representing grouped data, in which class intervals are shown on a vertical line (the **stem**) with observations given beside each class interval on a horizontal line (a **leaf**)

stem cell *noun* an undifferentiated cell that can develop into a cell with a specific function

stem flow another term for **drip and stem flow**

stench *noun* (*plural* **stenches**) a strong unpleasant smell

stencil *noun* **1** a sheet of metal, cardboard, etc with a pattern cut out **2** the drawing or design made by rubbing ink or brushing paint etc over a cut-out pattern ➤ *verb* (**stencilling, stencilled**) to make a design or copy in one of these ways

stentorian *adjective, literary* **1** of the voice: loud **2** loud-voiced

> ⏱ After *Stentor*, a loud-voiced Greek herald in Homer's poem *The Iliad*

step *noun* **1** a movement of the leg in walking, running, etc **2** the distance covered by this **3** a particular movement of the feet, as in dancing: **4** the sound made by the foot in walking etc: *heard a step outside* **5** a single stair or a rung on a ladder **6** one of a series of moves in a plan, career, etc: *Take the first step* **7** a way of walking: *springy step* **8** (**steps**) a flight of stairs **9** (**steps**) a stepladder ➤ *verb* (**stepping, stepped**) **1** to take a step **2** to walk, move: *Step this way, please* ● **in step 1** of two or more people walking: with the same foot going forward at the same time **2** acting etc in agreement (with) ● **out of step** not in step (with) ● **step up** to increase (eg production) ● **take steps** to begin to do something for a certain purpose

step- *prefix* related as the result of a second marriage *stepfather/stepdaughter* ⏱ Comes from Old English prefix *steop-* meaning 'orphan'

stepladder *noun* a ladder with a support on which it rests

steppe *noun* a dry, grassy treeless plain in SE Europe and Asia

stepping-stone *noun* **1** a stone rising above water or mud, used to cross on **2** anything that helps you to advance

stereo *adjective, short for* **stereophonic** ➤ *noun* (*plural* **stereos**) stereophonic equipment, especially a record-player and/or tape recorder, with amplifier and loudspeakers

stereo- *prefix* solid, three-dimensional: *stereophonic* (= with sounds coming from different directions in three-dimensional space)/*stereotype* (= a solid metal plate for printing) ⏱ Comes from Greek *stereos* meaning 'solid'

stereochemistry *noun, chemistry* the study of the three-dimensional arrangement of atoms within molecules

stereoisomer *noun, chemistry* a chemical substance that has the same composition, molecular weight and structure as another, but a different spatial arrangement of atoms

stereophonic *adjective* of sound: giving a lifelike effect, with different instruments, voices, etc coming from different directions

stereotype *noun* **1** a fixed and generalized idea of what characterizes someone or something **2** a characteristic type of person ➤ *verb* to attribute generalized and fixed characteristics to someone or something

> ⏱ Originally a printing term for a fixed block of type

stereotyped or **stereotypical** *adjective* fixed, not changing: *stereotyped ideas* ♦ **stereotypically** *adverb*

sterile *adjective* **1** unable to have children or reproduce **2** producing no ideas etc: *sterile imagination* **3** free from germs

sterility *noun* the state of being sterile

sterilization or **sterilisation** *noun* **1** a surgical operation that is performed on humans or animals so that offspring can no longer be produced **2** the treatment of food etc in order to destroy germs

sterilize or **sterilise** *verb* **1** to make sterile **2** to free from germs by boiling etc

sterling *noun* British money, when used in international trading: *one pound sterling* ➤ *adjective* **1** of silver: of a certain standard of purity **2** worthy, good: *sterling qualities*

> ⏱ So called after the image of a small star that was impressed on medieval silver pennies

stern¹ *adjective* **1** looking or sounding angry, or displeased **2** severe, strict, harsh: *stern prison sentence* ♦ **sternly** *adverb* ♦ **sternness** *noun*

stern² *noun* the back part of a ship

sternness *noun* the state or quality of being stern

sternum *noun* (*plural* **sternums** or **sterna**) *anatomy* the broad vertical bone in the chest which the ribs and collarbone are attached to (*also called*: **breastbone**) ⏱ Comes from Greek *sternon* meaning 'chest'

steroid *noun* **1** any of a number of substances, including certain hormones, with a complex molecular structure **2** a class of drug containing such a compound (*see also* **anabolic steroids**)

sterol *noun, biology, chemistry* a colourless steroid alcohol (eg cholesterol) found in plants, animals and fungi

stertorous *adjective, formal* making a snoring noise ⏱ Comes from Latin *stertere* meaning 'to snore'

stethoscope *noun* an instrument by means of which a doctor listens to someone's heartbeats, breathing, etc

Stetson *noun trademark* a man's broad-brimmed felt hat with a high crown indented at the top, worn especially by cowboys

stevedore (*pronounced* stee-va-daw) *noun* someone employed to load and unload ships

stew *verb* to cook by boiling slowly ➤ *noun* **1** a dish of stewed food, often containing meat and vegetables **2** *informal* a state of worry; a flap

steward *noun* **1** a flight attendant on an aircraft **2** someone who shows people to their seats at a meeting etc **3** an official at a race meeting etc **4** someone who manages an estate or farm for someone else ♦ **stewardship** noun **1** the position or job of a steward **2** management or care (of something)

stewardess noun (plural **stewardesses**) a female flight attendant (formerly called: **air hostess**)

stick¹ noun **1** a long thin piece of wood; a branch or twig from a tree **2** a piece of wood shaped for a special purpose: hockey-stick/drumstick **3** a long piece (eg of rhubarb)

stick² verb (**sticking, stuck**) **1** to push or thrust (something): Stick the knife in your belt **2** to fix with glue etc: I'll stick the pieces back together **3** to be or become caught, fixed or held back: stuck in the ditch **4** to hold fast to, keep to (eg a decision) ● **stick out 1** to project or protrude **2** to be obvious or noticeable; to stand out **3** to endure ● **stick up for** to speak in defence of

sticker noun a label, small poster, etc with an adhesive back

sticking-plaster noun a kind of tape with a sticky surface, used to protect slight cuts etc

stick insect noun a long, thin, tropical insect with legs that look like twigs

stick-in-the-mud noun someone who is against new ideas, change, etc

stickleback noun a type of small river-fish with prickles on its back

stickler noun someone who attaches great importance to a particular (often small) matter: stickler for punctuality

sticky adjective (**stickier, stickiest**) **1** clinging closely (like glue, treacle, etc) **2** covered with something sticky **3** informal difficult: a sticky problem ♦ **stickiness** noun

stiff adjective **1** not easily bent or moved **2** of a mixture, dough, etc: thick, not easily stirred **3** cold and distant in manner **4** hard, difficult: stiff examination **5** severe: stiff penalty **6** strong: stiff drink ♦ **stiffly** adverb

stiffen verb to make or become stiff

stifle verb **1** to suffocate **2** to put out (flames) **3** to keep back (tears, a yawn, etc)

stifling adjective very hot and stuffy ♦ **stiflingly** adverb

stigma noun **1** (plural **stigmata**) a mark of disgrace **2** (plural **stigmas**) in a flower: the sticky surface that receives pollen

stigmata plural noun Christianity marks said to have appeared on the bodies of certain holy people, thought to resemble Christ's crucifixion wounds

stigmatize or **stigmatise** verb to mark, describe as something bad: stigmatized for life

stile noun a step or set of steps for climbing over a wall or fence

stiletto noun (plural **stilettos**) **1** a dagger, or a type of instrument, with a narrow blade **2** (a shoe with) a stiletto heel

stiletto heel noun a high, thin heel on a shoe

still¹ adjective **1** not moving **2** calm, without wind; quiet **3** of drinks: not fizzy ➤ verb to make calm or quiet ➤ adverb **1** up to the present time or the time spoken of: It was still there **2** even so, nevertheless: It's difficult but we must still try **3** even: still more people ♦ **stillness** noun

still² noun an apparatus for distilling spirits (eg whisky)

stillborn adjective of a child: dead at birth ♦ **stillbirth** noun

still life noun (plural **still lifes**) a picture of something that is not living (as a bowl of fruit etc)

stilted adjective stiff, not natural

stilts plural noun **1** long poles with footrests on which someone may walk clear of the ground **2** tall poles (eg to support a house built above water)

stimulant noun something which makes a part of the body more active or which makes you feel livelier

stimulate verb **1** to make more active **2** to encourage **3** to excite ♦ **stimulating** adjective ♦ **stimulation** noun

stimulus (pronounced **stim**-yuw-lus) noun (plural **stimuli** – pronounced **stim**-yuw-lai) **1** something that brings on a reaction in a living thing **2** something that rouses (someone etc) to action or greater effort

sting noun **1** the part of some animals and plants (eg the wasp, the nettle) which can prick the skin and cause pain or irritation **2** the act of piercing with a sting **3** the wound, swelling, or pain caused by a sting ➤ verb (**stinging, stung**) **1** to pierce with a sting or cause pain like that of a sting **2** to be painful, smart: made his eyes sting **3** to hurt the feelings of: stung by his words

stingray noun a ray with a long whip-like tail tipped with spikes which can cause severe wounds

stingy (pronounced **stin**-ji) adjective (**stingier, stingiest**) mean, not generous ♦ **stinginess** noun

stink noun a bad smell ➤ verb (**stinking, stank** or **stunk, stunk**) **1** to give out a bad smell **2** informal to be contemptibly bad or unpleasant ● **kick up a stink** informal to cause trouble, especially disagreeably and in public

stint verb to allow (someone) very little: Don't stint on the sauce ➤ noun **1** limit: praise without stint **2** a fixed amount of work: my daily stint

stipend (pronounced **stai**-pend) noun pay, salary, especially of a parish minister

stipple verb to paint or mark with tiny dots from a brush

stipulate *verb* to state as a condition (of doing something)

stipulation *noun* something stipulated, a condition

stir *verb* (**stirring, stirred**) **1** to set (liquid) in motion, especially with a spoon etc moved circularly **2** to move slightly: *He stirred in his sleep* **3** to arouse (a person, a feeling, etc) ➤ *noun* disturbance, fuss • **stir up** to rouse, cause (eg trouble)

stir-fry *verb* (**stir-fries, stir-frying, stir-fried**) to cook (chopped meat, vegetables, etc) lightly by brisk frying in a wok or large frying pan on a high heat with a little oil ➤ *noun* (*plural* **stir-fries**) a dish of food that has been cooked in this way

stirrer *noun* **1** someone or something that stirs **2** *informal* someone who deliberately goes about making trouble

stirring *adjective* exciting or lively

stirrup *noun* a metal loop hung from a horse's saddle as a support for the rider's foot

stitch *noun* (*plural* **stitches**) **1** the loop made in a thread, wool, etc by a needle in sewing or knitting **2** a sharp, sudden pain in your side ➤ *verb* to put stitches in, sew

stoat *noun* a type of small fierce animal similar to a weasel, sometimes called an ermine when in its fur turns white in winter

stochastic (*pronounced* stoh-**kas**-tik) *adjective, statistics* random ♦ **stochastically** *adverb*

stock *noun* **1** family, race: *of ancient stock* **2** goods in a shop, warehouse, etc **3** the capital of a business company divided into shares **4** livestock **5** liquid (used for soup) obtained by boiling meat, bones, etc **6** a type of scented garden flower of the wallflower family **7** the handle of a whip, rifle, etc **8** (**stocks**) *history* a wooden frame, with holes for the ankles and wrists, in which criminals etc were fastened as a punishment **9** (**stocks**) the wooden framework upon which a ship is supported when being built ➤ *verb* **1** to keep a supply of (for sale) **2** to supply (a farm with animals etc) ➤ *adjective* **1** usual, known by everyone: *a stock joke* **2** usually stocked (by a shop etc) • **take stock of** to form an opinion or estimation about (a situation etc)

stockade *noun* a fence of strong posts set up round an area or building for defence

stockbroker *noun* someone who buys and sells shares in business companies on behalf of others

stock car *noun* a car that has been strengthened to take part in races where colliding is allowed

stock exchange *noun* **1** a place where stocks and shares are bought and sold **2** an association of people who do this

stocking *noun* a close-fitting covering in a knitted fabric (wool, nylon, etc) for the leg and foot

stock market *noun* the stock exchange; dealings in stocks and shares

stockpile *noun* a store, a reserve supply ➤ *verb* to build up a store of

stock-still *adjective* perfectly still

stocktaking *noun* a regular check of the goods in a shop or warehouse

stocky *adjective* (**stockier, stockiest**) short and stout ♦ **stockily** *adverb* ♦ **stockiness** *noun*

stodgy *adjective* (**stodgier, stodgiest**) **1** of food: heavy, not easily digested **2** of a person, book, etc: dull ♦ **stodginess** *noun*

stoic (*pronounced* **stoh**-ik) *noun* someone who bears pain, hardship, etc without showing any sign of feeling it

stoical *adjective* accepting pain, hardship, etc without showing any sign of feeling it

stoicism (*pronounced* **stoh**-i-sizm) *noun* the bearing of pain etc patiently

stoke *verb* to put coal, wood, or other fuel on (a fire)

stole¹ *noun* a length of silk, linen, or fur worn over the shoulders

stole² and **stolen** see **steal**

stolid *adjective* of a person etc: dull; not easily excited ♦ **stolidity** *noun* ♦ **stolidly** *adverb*

stoma *noun* (*plural* **stomata**) **1** *biology* a pore on the stems and leaves of plants for water loss and exchange of gases with the atmosphere **2** *biology* a small opening in the surface of a living organism **3** *medicine* an artificial opening in the body for the excretion of waste

stomach *noun* **1** the bag-like part of the body into which the food passes when swallowed **2** desire or courage (for something): *no stomach for a fight* ➤ *verb, informal* to put up with, bear: *can't stomach her rudeness*

stomach pump *noun* an apparatus with a long tube which is inserted down the throat and into the stomach, used medically for sucking out the contents of the stomach, especially in cases of drug overdosing

stomp *verb* to stamp the feet, especially noisily

stone *noun* **1** the material of which rocks are composed **2** a (small) loose piece of this **3** a piece of this shaped for a certain purpose: *tombstone* **4** a precious stone (eg a diamond) **5** the hard shell around the seed of some fruits (eg peach, cherry) **6** (*plural* **stone**) a measure of weight (14 pounds, 6.35 kilograms) **7** a piece of hard material that forms in the kidney, bladder, etc, causing pain ➤ *verb* **1** to throw stones at **2** to take the stones out of fruit ➤ *adjective* made of stone • **a stone's throw** a very short distance

- **leave no stone unturned** to do everything possible

Stone Age noun human culture before the use of metal

stone-cold adjective very cold

stone-dead adjective completely dead

stone-deaf adjective completely deaf

stoneground adjective of flour: produced by grinding between millstones

stonewall verb to hold up progress, especially in parliament, intentionally

stonewashed adjective of jeans, denim, etc: having a faded appearance because of the abrasive action of the small pieces of pumice stone that they have been washed with

stonework noun a structure or part of a building made from stone

stony adjective (**stonier, stoniest**) **1** like stone **2** covered with stones **3** hard, cold in manner: stony look

stood past form of **stand**

stooge noun someone who is used by another to do a (usually humble or unpleasant) job

stool noun **1** a seat without a back **2** a piece of faeces

stoop verb **1** to bend the body forwards and downwards **2** to be low or wicked enough (to do a certain thing): I wouldn't stoop to stealing ➤ noun **1** the act of stooping **2** a forward bend of the body

stop verb (**stopping, stopped**) **1** to bring to a halt: stop the car **2** to prevent from doing: stop him from working **3** to put an end to: Stop this nonsense **4** to come to an end: The rain has stopped ➤ noun **1** the state of being stopped **2** a place where something stops **3** a full stop **4** a knob on an organ which brings certain pipes into use • **stop something up** to block (a hole etc)

stopcock noun a tap for controlling the flow of liquid through a pipe

stopgap noun something which is used in an emergency until something better is found

stoppage noun **1** something which blocks up (eg a tube or a passage in the body) **2** a halt (eg in work in a factory)

stopper noun something that stops up an opening (especially in the neck of a bottle, jar, etc)

stop press noun a space in a newspaper for news put in at the last minute

stopwatch noun (plural **stopwatches**) a watch that can be stopped and started, used in timing races

storage noun **1** the act of storing **2** the state of being stored: Our furniture is in storage

storage device noun, computing any piece of equipment, eg a magnetic disk, that data can be stored on

store noun **1** a supply (eg of goods) from which things are taken when needed **2** a place where goods are kept **3** a shop **4** a collected amount or number **5** computing a computer's memory ➤ verb **1** to put aside for future use **2** computing to put something into a computer's memory • **in store for** awaiting: trouble in store for us • **set (great) store by** to value highly

store card noun a credit card that is issued by a department store for exclusive use in that store or any of its branches

storehouse noun a building where goods are kept; a warehouse

storey or US **story** noun (plural **storeys** or US **stories**) all that part of a building on the same floor

! Do not confuse with: **story**

stork noun a wading bird with a long bill, long neck, and long legs

storm noun **1** a sudden burst of bad weather (especially with heavy rain, lightning, thunder, high wind) **2** a violent outbreak (eg of anger) ➤ verb **1** to be in a fury **2** to rain, blow, etc violently **3** to attack (a stronghold etc) violently • **go down a storm** to be popular or well received • **storm in a teacup** informal a great fuss over nothing

stormy adjective (**stormier, stormiest**) **1** affected by storms or high winds **2** of a person, circumstances, etc: characterized by violence, emotion, tantrums, etc: a stormy relationship

story[1] noun (plural **stories**) an account of an event or events, real or imaginary

! Do not confuse with: **storey**

story[2] US for **storey**

storyboard noun a series of sketches, photos, etc that shows the order of the camera shots etc in the shooting of a film

storyline noun the plot of a novel, play, or film

stout adjective **1** fat, stocky **2** brave, reliable: stout resistance **3** strong: stout walking-stick ➤ noun a strong, dark-coloured beer ♦ **stoutly** adverb ♦ **stoutness** noun

stout-hearted adjective brave, reliable

stove[1] noun an apparatus using coal, gas, or electricity, etc, used for heating, cooking, etc

stove[2] a past form of **stave**

stow (pronounced stoh) verb **1** to pack or put away **2** to fill, pack

stowaway noun someone who hides in a ship, aeroplane, etc, in order to travel without paying a fare

straddle verb **1** to stand or walk with legs apart **2** to sit with one leg on each side of (eg a chair or horse)

strafe *verb* to attack someone or something with heavy machine-gun fire from a low-flying aircraft ⊕ Comes from German *strafen* meaning 'to punish'

straggle *verb* **1** to wander from the line of a march etc **2** to lag behind **3** to grow or spread beyond the intended limits: *His long beard straggled over his chest*

straggler *noun* a person or animal that wanders or lags behind

straggly *adjective* (**stragglier, straggliest**) spread out untidily

straight *adjective* **1** not bent or curved: *a straight line* **2** direct, frank, honest: *a straight answer* **3** in the proper position or order: *Your tie isn't straight* **4** of a hanging picture etc: placed level with ceiling or floor **5** of a drink: without anything added: *a straight vodka* **6** expressionless: *He kept a straight face* ➤ *adverb* **1** by the shortest way, directly: *straight across the desert* **2** at once, without delay: *I came straight here after work* **3** fairly, frankly: *She's not playing straight with you* ➤ *noun*: (**the straight**) the straight part of a racecourse etc • **straight away** immediately ⊕ Comes from Old English *streht*

straighten *verb* to make straight

straightener *noun* **1** something that straightens **2** (**straighteners**) a heated device for straightening hair

straightforward *adjective* **1** without any difficulties **2** honest, frank

straight man *noun* a comedian's stooge

strain¹ *verb* **1** to hurt (a muscle or other part of the body) by overworking or misusing it **2** to work or use to the fullest: *He strained his ears to hear the whisper* **3** to make a great effort: *She strained to reach the rope* **4** to stretch too far, to the point of breaking (a person's patience etc) **5** to separate liquid from a mixture of liquids and solids by passing it through a sieve **6** *physics* a measure of the change of an object when it is subjected to stress ➤ *noun* **1** the act of straining **2** a hurt to a muscle etc caused by straining it **3** (the effect of) too much work, worry, etc: *suffering from strain* **4** too great a demand: *a strain on my patience* **5** manner: *They grumbled on in the same strain for hours* **6** a tune

strain² *noun* **1** a kind, breed: *a strain of fowls* **2** a streak: *a strain of selfishness*

strained *adjective* **1** not natural, done with effort: *a strained conversation* **2** unfriendly: *strained relations*

strainer *noun* a sieve

strait *noun* **1** a narrow strip of sea between two pieces of land **2** (**straits**) difficulties, hardships:

dire straits ⊕ Comes from Latin *strictus* meaning 'straight' or 'narrow'

straitened *adjective* poor and needy

straitjacket *noun* a jacket with long sleeves tied behind to prevent a violent or disturbed person from using their arms

straitlaced *adjective* strict in attitude and behaviour

strand¹ *noun* a length of something soft and fine (eg hair, thread)

strand² *noun, old* the shore of a sea or lake

stranded *adjective* **1** of a ship: run aground on the shore **2** left helpless without money or friends

strange *adjective* (**stranger, strangest**) **1** unusual, odd: *a strange look on his face* **2** not known, seen, heard, etc, before, unfamiliar: *The method was strange to me* **3** not accustomed (to) **4** foreign: *a strange country* ♦ **strangely** *adverb* ♦ **strangeness** *noun*

stranger *noun* **1** someone who is unknown to you **2** a visitor • **a stranger to** someone who is quite unfamiliar with: *a stranger to hard work*

strangle *verb* **1** to kill by gripping or squeezing the throat tightly **2** to keep in, prevent oneself from giving (eg a scream, a sigh) **3** to stop the growth of ♦ **strangulation** *noun*

stranglehold *noun* a tight control over something which prevents it from escaping, growing, etc

strap *noun* a narrow strip of leather, cloth, etc, used to hold things in place or together etc ➤ *verb* (**strapping, strapped**) **1** to bind or fasten with a strap etc **2** to beat with a strap

strapping *adjective* tall and strong: *strapping young man*

stratagem *noun* a cunning act, meant to deceive and outwit an enemy

strategic (*pronounced* stra-**tee**-jik) *adjective* **1** of strategy **2** done according to a strategy: *a strategic retreat* **3** giving an advantage: *a strategic position* ♦ **strategically** *adverb*

strategist (*pronounced* **strat**-i-jist) *noun* someone who plans military operations

strategy *noun* (*plural* **strategies**) the art of guiding, forming, or carrying out a plan

stratification *noun* **1** the formation of strata **2** having strata

stratified sampling *noun, statistics* taking random samples from different groups (**strata**) of a population, with the size of each sample proportional to the size of each group ♦ **stratified sample** *noun*

stratify *verb* (**stratifies, stratified, stratifying**) **1** to deposit (rock) in layers or strata **2** to classify or arrange things into different grades, levels or classes ⊙ Comes from Latin *stratum* meaning 'something laid down' + *facere* meaning 'to make'

strato *adjective, geography* of a volcano: composite

stratocumulus *noun* (*plural* **stratocumuli**), *meteorology* a cloud that occurs as a large globular or rolled mass

stratosphere *noun* the layer of the earth's atmosphere between 10 and 60 kilometres above the earth

stratum (*pronounced* **strah**-tum) *noun* (*plural* **strata** – *pronounced* **strah**-ta) **1** a layer of rock or soil **2** a level of society

stratus *noun* (*plural* **strati**), *meteorology* a wide horizontal sheet of low grey layered cloud

straw *noun* **1** the stalk on which corn grows **2** a paper or plastic tube for sucking up a drink

strawberry *noun* (*plural* **strawberries**) a type of small, juicy, red fruit or the low creeping plant which bears it

strawberry blonde *noun* a woman with reddish blond hair

strawberry mark *noun* a reddish birthmark

straw poll or **straw vote** *noun* an unofficial vote taken among a small number of people to get an idea of the general opinion on an issue

stray *verb* **1** to wander **2** to lose your way, become separated (from companions etc) ➤ *adjective* **1** wandering, lost **2** happening etc here and there: *a stray example* ➤ *noun* a wandering animal which has been abandoned or lost

streak *noun* **1** a line or stripe different in colour from that which surrounds it **2** a smear of dirt, polish, etc **3** a flash (eg of lightning) **4** a trace of some quality in one's character: *a streak of selfishness* **5** *informal* a naked dash through a public place ➤ *verb* **1** to mark with streaks **2** *informal* to move very fast **3** *informal* to make a naked dash through a public place ♦ **streaker** *noun*

streaked *adjective* having streaks

streaky *adjective* (**streakier, streakiest**) marked with streaks ♦ **streakiness** *noun*

stream *noun* **1** a flow (of water, air, light, etc) **2** a small river, a brook **3** any steady flow of people or things: *a stream of traffic* ➤ *verb* to flow or pour out

streamer *noun* **1** a long strip, usually of paper, used for decorating rooms etc (especially at Christmas) **2** a narrow flag blowing in the wind

streamline *verb* **1** to shape (a vehicle etc) so that it may cut through the air or water as easily as possible **2** to make more efficient: *We've streamlined our methods of paying* ♦ **streamlined** *adjective*

street *noun* a road lined with houses etc

• **streets ahead of** *informal* much better etc than • **up someone's street** *informal* relating to their interests or abilities

street value *noun* the price something, such as illegal drugs, is likely to go for when it is sold to the person who will use it

streetwise *adjective, informal* **1** experienced in and well able to survive the ruthlessness of modern urban life, especially in areas such as drugs, crime, etc **2** cynical

strength *noun* **1** the state of being strong **2** an available number or force (of soldiers, volunteers, etc) **3** an area of high performance or particular ability: *Her greatest strength is her ability to listen to people* • **on the strength of** encouraged by or counting on

strengthen *verb* to make, or become, strong or stronger

strenuous *adjective* performed with or needing great effort: *The plans met strenuous resistance/Squash is a strenuous game* ♦ **strenuously** *adverb*

stress *noun* (*plural* **stresses**) **1** force, pressure, pull, etc of one thing on another **2** physical or nervous pressure or strain: *the stress of modern life* **3** emphasis, importance **4** extra weight laid on a part of a word (as in **but**ter) **5** *physics* the force exerted per unit area on a object causing it to change its dimensions ➤ *verb* to put stress, pressure, emphasis, or strain on

stressed-out *adjective* debilitated by emotional, nervous, or mental tension

stressful *adjective* causing stress: *a stressful job*

stretch *verb* **1** to draw out to greater length, or too far, or from one point to another: *Don't stretch that elastic too far/Stretch a rope from post to post* **2** to be able to be drawn out to a greater length or width: *that material stretches* **3** to (cause to) exert (yourself): *The work stretched him to the full* **4** to hold (out) **5** to make (something, eg words, the law) appear to mean more than it does ➤ *noun* (*plural* **stretches**) **1** the act of stretching **2** the state of being stretched **3** a length in distance or time: *a stretch of bad road* **4** *slang* a term of imprisonment • **at a stretch** continuously: *working three hours at a stretch* • **at full stretch** at the limit, using all resources ♦ **stretchy** *adjective* (**stretchier, stretchiest**)

stretcher *noun* a light folding bed with handles for carrying the sick or wounded

stretch limo *noun, informal* an elongated and very luxurious car (*full form*: **stretch limousine**)

strew *verb* (**strewing, strewed, strewn** or **strewed**) **1** to scatter: *papers strewn over the floor* **2** to cover, sprinkle (with): *The floor was strewn with papers*

striated *adjective* streaked

striated muscle *noun, anatomy* a type of voluntary muscle composed of fibres that appear as dark and light layers

stricken *adjective* 1 wounded 2 deeply affected (eg by illness) 3 struck

strict *adjective* 1 insisting on exact obedience to rules 2 exact: *the strict meaning of a word* 3 allowing no exception: *strict orders* 4 rather severe ♦ **strictly** *adverb* ♦ **strictness** *noun*

stricture *noun* criticism, blame

stride *verb* (**striding, strode, stridden**) 1 to walk with long steps 2 to take a long step 3 to walk over, along, etc ➤ *noun* 1 a long step 2 the distance covered by a step 3 a step forward • **make strides** to make significant progress • **take something in your stride** to manage to do it easily

strident *adjective* 1 of a sound: harsh, grating 2 forceful; assertive: *Their demands for reform became more and more strident* ♦ **stridency** *noun* ♦ **stridently** *adverb*

strife *noun* quarrelling; fighting

strike *verb* (**striking, struck**) 1 to hit with force 2 to give, deliver (a blow) 3 to knock: *to strike your head on the beam* 4 to attack: *The enemy struck at dawn* 5 to light (a match) 6 to make (a musical note) sound 7 of a clock: to sound (eg at ten o'clock with ten chimes) 8 (often **strike something off** *or* **out**) to cross it out, cancel it 9 to hit or discover suddenly: *strike oil* 10 to take a course: *He struck out across the fields* 11 to stop working (in support of a claim for more pay etc) 12 to give (someone) the impression of being: *Did he strike you as lazy?* 13 to affect, impress: *I am struck by her beauty* 14 to make (an agreement etc) • **strike camp** to take down tents • **strike home** 1 of a blow: to hit the point aimed at 2 of a remark: to have the intended effect • **strike up** 1 to begin to play or sing (a tune) 2 to begin (a friendship, conversation, etc)

striker *noun* 1 someone participating in a strike 2 in football, a player whose main role is to score goals

striking *adjective* 1 noticeable: *a striking resemblance* 2 impressive ♦ **strikingly** *adverb*

Strimmer *noun, trademark* an electrical garden tool for trimming long grass by means of a plastic or metal cord revolving at high speed

string *noun* 1 a long narrow cord for binding, tying, etc, made of threads twisted together 2 a piece of wire or gut producing a note on a musical instrument 3 (**strings**) the stringed instruments in an orchestra 4 a line of objects threaded together: *string of pearls* 5 a number of things coming one after another: *string of abuse* 6 *computing* a group of characters that a computer can handle as a single unit ➤ *verb* (**stringing, strung**) 1 to put on a string 2 to stretch out in a line • **string along** to give false

expectations to, deceive • **string someone up** *informal* to hang them

stringed *adjective* having strings

stringent *adjective* strictly enforced: *stringent rules* ♦ **stringency** *noun*

string quartet *noun* 1 a musical group that is made up of two violins, a cello and a viola 2 a piece of music for such a group

stringy *adjective* (**stringier, stringiest**) 1 like string 2 of meat: tough and fibrous

strip¹ *verb* (**stripping, stripped**) 1 to pull (off) in strips 2 to remove the clothes from 3 (*also*: **strip off**) *informal* to take your clothes off 4 to deprive: *stripped of his disguise* 5 to make bare or empty: *strip the bed*

strip² *noun* 1 a long narrow piece (eg of paper) 2 to remove (eg leaves, fruit) from

strip cartoon *noun* a line of drawings which tell a story

stripe *noun* a band of colour different from the background on which it lies ➤ *verb* to make stripes on

stripling *noun, literary* a growing youth

stripper *noun* 1 *informal* a striptease artiste 2 a substance or appliance for removing paint, varnish, etc

striptease *noun* an act in which a performer strips naked

stripy *or* **striped** *adjective* (**stripier, stripiest**) patterned with stripes

strive *verb* (**striving, strove, striven** – pronounced *striv*-en) 1 to try hard 2 to fight

strobe *noun* a light which produces a flickering beam

strode past tense of **stride**

stroke *noun* 1 the act of striking 2 a blow (eg with a sword, whip) 3 something unexpected: *a stroke of good luck* 4 one movement (of a pen, an oar) 5 one chime of a clock 6 one complete movement of the arms and legs in swimming 7 a particular style of swimming: *breast stroke* 8 a way of striking the ball (eg in tennis, cricket) 9 an achievement 10 *medicine* a sudden interruption of the blood supply to the brain, causing paralysis ➤ *verb* to rub gently, especially as a sign of affection • **at a stroke** in a single action or effort

stroll *verb* to walk slowly in a leisurely way ➤ *noun* a leisurely walk; an amble

stroma *noun* (*plural* **stromata**), *anatomy* the supporting framework of a body part, organ, blood corpuscle or cell ⊙ Comes from Latin, meaning 'a bed covering'

strong *adjective* 1 not easily worn away: *strong cloth* 2 not easily defeated etc 3 forceful, not easily resisted: *strong wind* 4 very healthy and robust, with great muscular strength 5 forceful, commanding respect or obedience 6 of a smell, colour, etc: striking, very noticeable **7** of a feeling: intense: *strong dislike* **8** in number: *a workforce 500 strong*

stronghold *noun* a place built to withstand attack, a fortress

strongly *adverb* **1** in a strong way **2** to a strong degree: *strongly flavoured*

strong point *noun* something in which a person excels

strongroom *noun* a room that is difficult to get into and where valuables, prisoners, etc can be held

strontium *noun, chemistry* (symbol **Sr**) a soft silvery-white highly reactive metallic element

○ Named after *Strontian*, the place in Scotland where it was discovered

strop[1] *noun* a strip of leather on which a razor is sharpened ➤ *verb* (**stropping, stropped**) to sharpen (a razor)

strop[2] *noun, informal* a bad temper: *She went off in a strop*

stroppy *adjective* (**stroppier, stroppiest**) *informal* quarrelsome, disobedient, rowdy ♦ **stroppily** *adverb*

strove past tense of **strive**

struck past form of **strike**

structural *adjective* of or relating to structure, or a basic structure or framework ♦ **structurally** *adverb*

structural formula *noun, chemistry* a formula that shows the exact arrangement of the atoms within a molecule of a chemical compound

structure *noun* **1** a building; a framework **2** the way the parts of anything are arranged: *the structure of the story*

strudel (*pronounced* stroo-del) *noun* a baked roll of thin pastry with a filling of fruit, usually apple ○ Comes from German meaning 'whirlpool', from the way the pastry is rolled

struggle *verb* **1** to try hard (to do something) **2** to twist and fight to escape **3** to fight (with or against someone) **4** to move with difficulty: *struggling through the mud* ➤ *noun* **1** a great effort **2** a fight

strum *verb* (**strumming, strummed**) to play (a guitar etc) in a relaxed way

strung past form of **string** • **highly strung** easily excited or agitated

strut *verb* (**strutting, strutted**) to walk in a proud manner ➤ *noun* **1** a proud way of walking **2** a bar etc which supports something

strychnine (*pronounced* strik-neen) *noun* a bitter, poisonous drug

stub *noun* a small stump (eg of a pencil, cigarette) ➤ *verb* (**stubbing, stubbed**) **1** to put out (eg a cigarette) by pressure against

something **2** to knock (your toe) painfully against something

stubble *noun* **1** the short ends of the stalks of corn left after it is cut **2** a short growth of beard

stubborn *adjective* **1** unwilling to give way, obstinate **2** of resistance etc: strong, determined **3** difficult to manage or deal with ♦ **stubbornly** *adverb* ♦ **stubbornness** *noun*

stubby *adjective* (**stubbier, stubbiest**) short, thick, and strong: *stubby fingers*

stucco *noun* (*plural* **stuccos**) **1** a kind of plaster used for covering walls, moulding ornaments, etc **2** work done in stucco

stuck past form of **stick**[2]

stuck-up *adjective, informal* snobbish; conceited

stud[1] *noun* **1** a nail with a large head **2** a decorative knob on a surface **3** a button with two heads for fastening a collar ➤ *verb* (**studding, studded**) **1** to cover or fit with studs **2** to sprinkle thickly (with): *The meadow is studded with flowers*

stud[2] *noun* **1** a collection of horses kept for breeding **2** *informal* a man regarded as having great sexual energy and prowess

student *noun* someone who studies, especially at college, university, etc

studied *adjective* **1** done on purpose, intentional: *a studied insult* **2** too careful, not natural: *a studied smile*

studio *noun* (*plural* **studios**) **1** the workshop of an artist or photographer **2** a building or place in which cinema films are made **3** a room from which television or radio programmes are broadcast

studious *adjective* **1** studying carefully and much **2** careful: *his studious avoidance of quarrels* ♦ **studiously** *adverb*

study *verb* (**studies, studying, studied**) **1** to gain knowledge of (a subject) by reading, experiment, etc **2** to look carefully at **3** to consider carefully (eg a problem) ➤ *noun* (*plural* **studies**) **1** the gaining of knowledge of a subject: *the study of history* **2** a room where someone reads and writes **3** a piece of music which is meant to develop the skill of the player **4** a work of art done as an exercise, or to try out ideas for a later work

stuff *noun* **1** the material of which anything is made **2** cloth, fabric **3** substance or material of any kind: *What is that stuff all over the wall?* ➤ *verb* **1** to pack full **2** to fill the skin of (a dead animal) to preserve it **3** to fill (a chicken, a pepper, etc) with stuffing before cooking • **get stuffed** *slang* get lost, go away

stuffed shirt *noun* an inflexible, old-fashioned person

stuffing *noun* **1** feathers, scraps of material, etc

used to stuff a cushion, chair, etc **2** breadcrumbs, onions, etc packed inside a fowl or other meat and cooked with it

stuffy adjective (**stuffier, stuffiest**) **1** full of stale air, badly ventilated **2** informal dull, having old-fashioned ideas ♦ **stuffily** adverb ♦ **stuffiness** noun

stultify verb (**stultifies, stultifying, stultified**) to dull the mind, make stupid

stumble verb **1** to trip in walking **2** to walk unsteadily, as if blind **3** to make mistakes or hesitate in speaking ► noun the act of stumbling • **stumble on something** to find it by chance

stumbling block noun a difficulty in the way of a plan or of progress

stump noun **1** the part of a tree, leg, tooth, etc left after the main part has been cut away **2** cricket one of the three wooden stakes which make up a wicket ► verb **1** cricket to put out (a batsman) by touching the stumps with the ball **2** to puzzle completely **3** to walk stiffly or heavily • **stump up** informal to pay up

stumpy adjective (**stumpier, stumpiest**) short and thick

stun verb (**stunning, stunned**) **1** to knock senseless (by a blow etc) **2** informal to surprise or shock very greatly: stunned by the news

stung past form of **sting**

stunk past form of **stink**

stunner noun informal someone or something that is extraordinarily beautiful, attractive, etc

stunning adjective, informal **1** extraordinarily beautiful, attractive, etc **2** extremely impressive ♦ **stunningly** adverb

stunt¹ verb to stop the growth of

stunt² noun **1** a daring trick **2** something done to attract attention: a publicity stunt

stunted adjective small and badly shaped

stup- prefix forms words related to the idea of being knocked senseless ℗ Comes from Latin stupere meaning 'to be stunned'

stupefaction noun **1** the state of being stupefied; numbness **2** astonishment

stupefy verb (**stupefies, stupefying, stupefied**) **1** to make stupid, deaden the feelings of **2** to astonish

stupendous adjective wonderful, amazing (eg because of size and power) ♦ **stupendously** adverb

stupid adjective **1** foolish: a stupid thing to do **2** dull, slow at learning **3** stupefied (eg from lack of sleep) ♦ **stupidity** noun

stupor noun the state of being only partly conscious

sturdy adjective (**sturdier, sturdiest**) strong, well built; healthy ♦ **sturdily** adverb ♦ **sturiness** noun

sturgeon noun a type of large fish from which caviare is obtained

stutter verb to speak in a halting, jerky way; stammer ► noun a stammer

sty¹ noun (plural **sties**) a pen in which pigs are kept

sty² or **stye** noun (plural **sties** or **styes**) an inflamed swelling on the eyelid

Stygian adjective, literary dark and gloomy

> ℗ After the River Styx in Hades, the underworld of Greek mythology

style noun **1** manner of acting, writing, speaking, etc **2** fashion: in the style of the late 19th century **3** an air of elegance **4** botany the part of a flower that connects the stigma to the ovary ► verb **1** to design, shape, etc in a particular way **2** to call, name: styling himself 'Lord John' • **in style** with no expense or effort spared

stylesheet noun, computing a set of specifications used as a template for documents or web pages

stylish adjective smart, elegant, fashionable ♦ **stylishly** adverb ♦ **stylishness** noun

stylist noun **1** a trained hairdresser **2** a writer, artist, etc who pays a lot of attention to style

stylistic adjective relating to artistic or literary style: stylistic analysis ♦ **stylistically** adverb

stylized or **stylised** adjective elaborate, especially creating an impression of unnaturalness

stylus noun (plural **styluses**) a needle for a record-player

stymie (pronounced **stai**-mi) verb to block, impede

> ℗ Originally a golfing term for an opponent's ball in the way of your own

suave (pronounced swahv) adjective (**suaver, suavest**) of a person: superficially polite and sophisticated, smooth

sub- prefix **1** under, below **2** less than **3** lower in rank or importance ℗ Comes from Latin sub meaning 'under' or 'near'

sub-aerial processes noun, geography those physical processes that occur on land on or near the earth's surface and above water, eg weathering, mass movement

subaltern (pronounced **sub**-al-tern) noun an officer in the army under the rank of captain

subatomic particle noun, physics one of the units, eg protons, neutrons, and electrons, from which atoms are made

subclavian adjective, anatomy below the clavicle

subconscious noun the contents of the mind of which someone is not themselves aware ► adjective of the subconscious, not conscious

or aware: *a subconscious desire for fame*
♦ **subconsciously** *adverb*

subcontinent *noun* a large part of a continent that is distinctive in some way, eg by its shape, culture, etc: *the Indian subcontinent*

subcontract *verb* to give a contract for (work forming part of a larger contract) to another company

subculture *noun* **1** an identifiable group within a larger culture or group **2** *biology* of bacteria etc: a culture that is derived from another

subcutaneous (*pronounced* sub-kyuw-**tei**-ni-*us*) *adjective* beneath the skin

subdirectory *noun* (*plural* **subdirectories**), *computing* a directory contained within another

subdivide *verb* to divide into smaller parts

subdivision *noun* a part made by subdividing

subduction *noun, geography* the process of one part of the earth's crust moving underneath another

subdue *verb* **1** to conquer (an enemy etc) **2** to keep under control (eg a desire) **3** to make less bright (eg a colour, a light) **4** to make quieter: *He seemed subdued after the fight* ♦ **subdued** *adjective*

subedit *verb* to select and prepare material for printing in a newspaper or magazine
♦ **subeditor** *noun*

subglacial *adjective, geography* at the base or bottom of a glacier

subheading *noun* a heading below the main heading in a document

subject *adjective* (*pronounced* **sub**-jikt) under the power of another: *a subject nation* ➤ *noun* (*pronounced* **sub**-jikt) **1** someone under the power of another: *the king's subjects* **2** a member of a nation with a monarchy: *a British subject* **3** something or someone spoken about, studied, etc **4** *grammar* the word in a sentence or clause which stands for the person or thing doing the action of the verb (eg *cat* is the subject in 'the *cat* drank the milk') ➤ *verb* (*pronounced* sub-**jekt**) (*often* **subject someone to something**) to force them to submit to it
• **subject to something 1** liable to suffer from it (eg colds) **2** depending on it: *subject to your approval*

subjection *noun* the act of subjecting or the state of being subjected

subjective *adjective* based on personal feelings, thoughts, etc, not impartial (*contrasted with*: **objective**) ♦ **subjectively** *adverb*
♦ **subjectivity** *noun*

subjugate *verb* to bring under your power; make obedient

subjunctive *grammar, adjective* of the mood a verb: indicating possibility etc, eg 'were' in: *If I*

were you ➤ *noun* **1** the subjunctive mood **2** a subjunctive form of a verb

sublet *verb* (**subletting, sublet**) to let out (rented property) to another person, eg while the original tenant is away

sublimation *noun* changing from a solid to a gas, or a gas to a solid, without becoming a liquid

sublime *adjective* very noble, great, or grand ➤ *verb* of a substance: to change from a solid to a gas, or a gas to a solid, without becoming a liquid

subliminal *adjective* working below the level of consciousness: *subliminal messages*

submachine-gun *noun* a light machine-gun fired from the hip or shoulder

submarine *noun* a type of ship which can travel under water ➤ *adjective* under the surface of the sea

submerge *verb* to cover with water; sink

submersible *noun* a boat that can operate under water

submersion or **submergence** *noun* submerging or being submerged

submission *noun* **1** the act of submitting **2** readiness to yield, meekness **3** an idea, statement, etc offered for consideration

submissive *adjective* meek, yielding easily
♦ **submissively** *adverb* ♦ **submissiveness** *noun*

submit *verb* (**submitting, submitted**) **1** to give in, yield **2** to place (a matter) before someone for making a judgement

submucosa *noun, anatomy* the layer of tissue below a mucous membrane ♦ **submucosal** or **submucous** *adjective*

subordinate *adjective* (*pronounced* su-**baw**-di-nit) (*often* **subordinate to someone**) lower in rank or importance ➤ *noun* (*pronounced* su-**baw**-di-nit) someone who is subordinate ➤ *verb* (*pronounced* su-**baw**-di-neit): **subordinate one person** or **subordinate something to another** to consider them as being of less importance ♦ **subordination** *noun*

subordinate clause *noun, grammar* (*also called*: **dependent clause**) a clause in a sentence that adds information to a main clause and depends on it to make sense, eg 'I liked the book *that you gave me for my birthday*' (*compare with*: **main clause**)

suborn *verb* to persuade (someone) to do something illegal, especially by bribery

subplot *noun* a minor storyline parallel to the main plot in a novel, film, play, opera, etc

subpoena (*pronounced* su-**pee**-na) *noun* (*plural* **subpoenas**) an order for someone to appear in court ➤ *verb* (**subpoenaing,**

subpoenaed or **subpoena'd**) to order to appear in court

subroutine *noun, computing* a self-contained part of a program which performs a specific task and can be called up at any time while the main program is running

subscribe *verb* **1** to make a contribution (especially of money) towards a charity **2** to promise to take and pay for a number of issues of a magazine etc • **subscribe to something** to agree with (an idea, statement, etc)

subscription *noun* a payment for eg a club membership fee or a number of issues of a magazine for a given period

subsequent *adjective* following, coming after

> ! Do not confuse with: **consequent**. **Consequent** means happening after something, **subsequent** means happening after something, but not necessarily as a result of it.

subservient *adjective* weak-willed, ready to do as you are told ♦ **subservience** *noun*

subset *noun, maths* a set that is part of a larger set, eg set X is a subset of set Y if all the members of set X can be included in set Y

subside *verb* **1** to settle down, sink lower **2** of noise etc: to get less and less

subsidence (*pronounced* **sub**-si-dens) *noun* the sinking of land, buildings, etc to a lower level

subsidiarity *noun* **1** the state of being subsidiary **2** the concept of a central governing body permitting its member states or branches to make their own decisions on certain local issues

subsidiary *adjective* **1** acting as a help **2** of less importance **3** of a company: controlled by another company ➤ *noun* (*plural* **subsidiaries**) **1** a subsidiary person or thing **2** a company controlled by another, larger, company or organization

subsidize or **subsidise** *verb* to give money as a help

subsidy *noun* (*plural* **subsidies**) money paid by a government or organization etc to help an industry

subsist *verb* to live (on a kind of food etc)

subsistence *noun* **1** existence **2** means or necessities for survival

subsistence farming *noun* farming producing enough only to meet the needs of the farmer

subsoil *noun* the layer of the earth just below the surface soil

subspecies *noun, biology* a subdivision of a species which because of geographical isolation displays some differences from others in the species

substance *noun* **1** a material that can be seen and felt: *Glue is a sticky substance* **2** general meaning (of a talk, essay, etc) **3** thickness, solidity **4** wealth, property: *a woman of substance*

substance abuse *noun* the inappropriate use of substances such as alcohol, solvents, drugs, etc, often leading to harmful effects

substantial *adjective* **1** solid, strong **2** large: *a substantial building* **3** able to be seen and felt **4** in the main, but not in detail: *substantial agreement*

substantially *adverb* for the most part: *substantially the same*

substantiate *verb* to give proof of, or evidence for ♦ **substantiation** *noun*

substitute *verb*: **substitute something** or **substitute one thing for another** to put one thing in place or instead of another ➤ *noun* someone or thing used instead of another

substitution *noun* **1** the process of substituting or being substituted **2** something which is substituted

substrate *noun, biology* **1** the material that a living organism grows on or is attached to **2** the substance on which an enzyme acts

substructure *noun* the part of a building or other construction that supports it

subsume *verb* **1** to include (an example, idea, etc) as part of a larger, more general group, category, rule, etc **2** to take over (something)

subsystem *noun* a single system that is part of a larger, more complex system

subtend *verb, maths* to be opposite and bounding (an angle or chord)

subterfuge *noun* a cunning trick to get out of difficulty etc

subterranean *adjective* found under the ground

subtext *noun* **1** an implied message in a play, film, book, picture, etc **2** anything implied but not stated in ordinary speech or writing

subtitle *noun* **1** a second additional title of a book etc **2** a translation of a foreign-language film, appearing at the bottom of the screen

subtle (*pronounced* **sut**-l) *adjective* **1** not straightforwardly or obviously stated or displayed **2** difficult to describe or explain: *a subtle difference* ♦ **subtlety** *noun* (*plural* **subtleties**) ♦ **subtly** *adverb*

subtotal *noun* a total of one set of figures within a larger group

subtract *verb* **1** to take away (a part from) **2** to take away (one number from another) ♦ **subtraction** *noun*

suburb *noun* a residential area on the outskirts of a town ♦ **suburban** *adjective*

suburbia *noun* the suburbs

subversive *adjective* likely to overthrow

(government, discipline, etc) ♦ **subversiveness** noun

subway noun **1** an underground crossing for pedestrians etc **2** Scot & US an underground railway

succeed verb **1** to manage to do what you have been trying to do: She succeeded in getting the grades she needed **2** to get on well **3** to take the place of, follow **4** (often **succeed to**) to follow in order (to the throne etc)

success noun (plural **successes**) **1** the achievement of something you have been trying to do **2** someone who succeeds **3** something that turns out well

successful adjective **1** having achieved what was aimed at **2** having achieved wealth, importance, etc **3** turning out as planned ♦ **successfully** adverb

succession noun **1** the act of following after **2** the right of becoming the next holder of a throne etc **3** a number of things coming one after the other: a succession of failures **4** geography the changes of species etc in an ecosystem over a period of time • **in succession** one after another

successive adjective following one after the other

successor noun someone who comes after, follows in a post, etc ♦ **successively** adverb

succinct adjective in a few words, brief, concise: a succinct reply ♦ **succinctly** adverb

succour or US **succor** (pronounced **suk**-or) formal, noun help in time of distress ➤ verb to help in time of distress

succulent adjective **1** juicy **2** botany of a plant: having thick, juicy leaves or stems ➤ noun, botany a plant with thick fleshy leaves or stems which allow it to store water in dry conditions ♦ **succulence** noun

succumb (pronounced su-**kum**) verb to yield (to): succumbed to temptation

such adjective **1** of a kind previously mentioned: Such things are difficult to find **2** similar: doctors, nurses, and such people **3** so great: His excitement was such that he shouted out loud **4** used for emphasis: It's such a disappointment! ➤ pronoun thing, people, etc of a kind already mentioned: Such as these are not to be trusted • **as such** by itself • **such as** of the same kind as

such-and-such adjective & pronoun any given (person or thing): such-and-such a book

suck verb **1** to draw into the mouth **2** to draw milk from with the mouth **3** to hold in the mouth and lick hard (eg a sweet) **4** (often **suck up** or **in**) to draw in, absorb **5** US slang to be contemptible or contemptibly bad: That movie sucks! ➤ noun **1** a sucking action **2** the act of sucking

sucker noun **1** something that sucks **2** informal someone easily fooled **3** (usually **sucker for**) informal someone who finds a thing or person irresistible: a sucker for chocolate ice cream **4** a pad (of rubber etc) which can stick to a surface **5** zoology a part of an animal's body by which it sticks to objects **6** botany a side shoot rising from the stem or root of a plant

suckle verb of a woman or female animal: to give milk from the breast or teat

suckling noun a baby or young animal which still sucks its mother's milk

sucrose noun a white soluble crystalline sugar found in most plants ⊕ Comes from French sucre meaning 'sugar'

suction noun **1** the act of sucking **2** the process of reducing the air pressure, and so producing a vacuum, on the surface or between surfaces

sudden adjective happening all at once without being expected: a sudden attack ♦ **suddenly** adverb ♦ **suddenness** noun **all of a sudden** without any warning; unexpectedly

sudden infant death syndrome noun, medicine (abbrev **SIDS**) the sudden unexpected death, often at night, of an apparently healthy baby (non-technical name: **cot death**)

Sudoku or **Su Doku** (pronounced soo-**doh**-koo) noun a type of puzzle in which numbers are entered into a square grid so that no number is repeated in any row, column or internal square ⊕ Comes from Japanese su meaning 'number' + doku meaning 'singular '

suds plural noun frothy, soapy water

sue verb (**suing, sued**) to start a law case against

suede (pronounced sweid) noun a soft leather, where the flesh side is brushed so that it has a velvety finish

suet noun a kind of hard animal fat used for making pastry etc

suffer verb **1** to feel pain or punishment **2** to bear, endure **3** old to allow **4** to go through, undergo (a change etc)

sufferance noun: **on sufferance** allowed or tolerated but not really wanted

suffering noun pain or distress

suffice verb to be enough, or good enough

sufficient adjective enough ♦ **sufficiency** noun ♦ **sufficiently** adverb

suffix noun (plural **suffixes**) a small part added to the end of a word to make another word, such as -ness to good to make goodness, -ly to quick to make quickly, etc

suffocate verb **1** to kill by preventing the breathing of **2** to die from lack of air **3** to feel unable to breathe freely: suffocating in this heat ♦ **suffocation** noun

suffrage noun **1** a vote **2** the right to vote

suffragette (pronounced suf-ra-**jet**) noun, history a woman who campaigned militantly in

Britain in the early years of the 20th century for women to have the same voting rights as men

suffuse *verb* to spread over: *The sky was suffused with red*

sugar *noun* a sweet substance obtained mostly from sugar cane and sugar beet ➤ *verb* to mix or sprinkle with sugar

sugar beet *noun* a vegetable whose root yields sugar

sugarcane *noun* a tall grass from whose juice sugar is obtained

sugar daddy *noun* (*plural* **sugar daddies**) an older man who lavishes money on a younger woman in exchange for companionship and, often, sex

sugary *adjective* **1** tasting of sugar **2** too sweet **3** *informal* exaggeratedly or insincerely pleasant or affectionate

suggest *verb* **1** to put forward, propose (an idea etc) **2** to put into the mind, hint

suggestible *adjective* easily influenced by suggestions

suggestion *noun* **1** an act of suggesting **2** an idea put forward **3** a slight trace: *a suggestion of anger in her voice*

suggestive *adjective* **1** that suggests something particular, especially sexually improper: *suggestive remarks* **2** giving the idea (of): *suggestive of mental illness*

suicidal *adjective* **1** of or considering suicide **2** likely to cause your death or ruin: *suicidal action*

suicide *noun* **1** the taking of your own life **2** someone who kills themselves

suit *noun* **1** a set of clothes to be worn together **2** a case in a law court **3** *old* a request for permission to court a woman **4** one of the four divisions (spades, hearts, diamonds, clubs) of playing-cards ➤ *verb* **1** to be convenient or suitable for: *The climate suits me* **2** to look well on: *That dress suits you* • **follow suit** **1** to play a card of the same suit as the previous one **2** to do just as someone else has done • **suit to** to make fitting or suitable for: *suited his words to the occasion*

suitable *adjective* **1** fitting the purpose **2** just what is wanted, convenient ♦ **suitability** *noun* ♦ **suitably** *adverb*

suitcase *noun* a travelling case for carrying clothes etc

suite (*pronounced* sweet) *noun* **1** a number of things in a set, eg rooms, furniture, pieces of music **2** a group of attendants for an important person

suitor *noun*, *old* a man who tries to gain the love of a woman

suk or **sukh** see souk

Sukkoth (*pronounced* **suw**-koht) *noun* a Jewish harvest festival commemorating the period

when the Israelites lived in tents during the exodus from Egypt ☉ Comes from Hebrew meaning 'tents' or 'huts'

sulk *verb* to keep silent because of being displeased ➤ *noun* (*also*: **the sulks**) a fit of sulking

sulky *adjective* (**sulkier, sulkiest**) sulking; inclined to sulk ♦ **sulkiness** *noun*

sullen *adjective* angry and silent, sulky ♦ **sullenly** *adverb* ♦ **sullenness** *noun*

sully *verb* (**sullies, sullying, sullied**) to make less pure, dirty

sulphate or *US* **sulfate** *noun* a compound made from sulphuric acid which contains the group SO_4

sulphide or *US* **sulfide** *noun*, *chemistry* a compound that contains sulphur and another element

sulphite or *US* **sulfite** *noun*, *chemistry* a salt or ester of sulphurous acid

sulphonamide or *US* **sulfonamide** *noun*, *medicine* a type of drug containing such a compound that destroys bacteria, now largely replaced by antibiotics

sulphur or *US* **sulfur** *noun*, *chemistry* a yellow substance found in the ground which gives off a choking smell when burnt, used in matches, gunpowder, etc

sulphur dioxide *noun*, *chemistry* a colourless, pungent-smelling, toxic gas

sulphuric acid or *US* **sulfuric acid** *noun*, *chemistry* a powerful acid much used in industry

sulphurous or *US* **sulfurous** *adjective* **1** relating to, like, or containing sulphur **2** having a yellow colour like sulphur **3** *chemistry* denoting a compound with sulphur in the tetravalent state

sulphurous acid or *US* **sulfurous acid** *noun*, *chemistry* a weak acidic solution containing sulphur

sultan *noun* **1** *history* the head of the Turkish Ottoman empire **2** an Islamic ruler

sultana *noun* **1** a sultan's wife **2** a light-coloured raisin

sultry *adjective* (**sultrier, sultriest**) **1** of weather: very hot and close **2** passionate, steamy

sum *noun* **1** the amount made by two or more things added together **2** a quantity of money **3** a problem in arithmetic **4** the general meaning (of something said or written) ➤ *verb* (**summing, summed**): **sum up** to give the main points of (a discussion, evidence in a trial, etc)

summarize or **summarise** *verb* to state briefly, make a summary of

summary *noun* (*plural* **summaries**) a shortened form (of a story, statement, etc) giving only the main points ➤ *adjective* **1** short, brief **2** done without wasting time or words

♦ **summarily** adverb: He was summarily dismissed

summer noun the warmest season of the year, following spring ➤ adjective relating to summer

summerhouse noun a small house in a garden for sitting in ♦ **summery** adjective

summer solstice see **solstice**

summit noun 1 the highest point of a hill etc 2 a summit conference

summit conference noun a conference between heads of governments

summon verb to order (someone) to come to you, appear in a court of law, etc • **summon up** to gather up (courage, strength, etc)

summons noun (plural **summonses**) an order to appear in court

sumo noun a Japanese form of wrestling

sump noun 1 part of a motor-engine which contains the oil 2 a small drainage pit

sumptuous adjective costly, splendid
♦ **sumptuously** adverb ♦ **sumptuousness** noun

sun noun 1 the round body in the sky which gives light and heat to the earth 2 sunshine ➤ verb (**sunning, sunned**): **sun yourself** to lie in the sunshine, sunbathe

sunbathe verb to lie or sit in the sun to acquire a suntan

sunbeam noun a ray of light from the sun

sunbed noun a device that has sun-lamps fitted above and often beneath a transparent screen and which someone can lie on to tan artificially the whole body

sunblock noun a lotion, cream, etc which completely or almost completely protects the skin from the harmful effects of the sun's rays

sunburn noun a burning or redness caused by over-exposure to the sun

sunburned or **sunburnt** adjective affected by sunburn

sundae (pronounced **sun**-dei) noun a sweet dish of ice-cream served with fruit, syrup, etc

Sunday noun the first day of the week

⊙ From an Old English word meaning 'day of the sun'

Sunday school noun a class held on Sundays for the religious instruction of children

sunder verb, old to separate, part

sundial noun an instrument for telling the time from the shadow of a rod on its surface cast by the sun

sun-dried adjective dried by exposure to the sun rather than by artificial heating and therefore retaining more flavour: sun-dried tomatoes

sundries plural noun odds and ends

sundry adjective several, various: sundry articles for sale

sunflower noun a large yellow flower with petals like rays of the sun

sung past participle of **sing**

sunglasses plural noun spectacles with tinted lenses that shield the eyes from sunlight

sunk adjective 1 on a lower level than the surroundings; sunken 2 informal defeated, done for

sunken adjective 1 that has been sunk 2 of cheeks etc: hollow

sun-lamp noun an electric lamp that emits rays similar to natural sunlight, which is used therapeutically and for artificially tanning the skin

sunlight noun the light from the sun

sunlit adjective lighted up by the sun

Sunni noun (plural **Sunni** or **Sunnis**) 1 the more orthodox of the two main branches of the Islamic religion (compare with: **Shia**) 2 a member of this branch of Islam ♦ **Sunnism** noun ⊙ Comes from Arabic sunnah meaning 'rule'

sunny adjective (**sunnier, sunniest**) 1 full of sunshine 2 cheerful: sunny nature

sunrise noun the rising of the sun in the morning ♦ **sunnily** adverb

sunrise industry noun any relatively new and rapidly expanding industry, especially involving computing, electronics, etc

sunroof noun a transparent panel that can be opened in the roof of a car

sunscreen noun a preparation that protects the skin by blocking out some or most of the sun's harmful rays

sunset noun the setting of the sun in the evening

sunshine noun bright sunlight

sunspot noun 1 a relatively dark patch on the Sun's surface with an intense magnetic field 2 informal a holiday resort renowned for its sunny weather

sunstroke noun an illness caused by over-exposure to hot sunshine

suntan noun a browning of the skin caused by exposure to the sun

sup verb (**supping, supped**) to eat or drink in small mouthfuls

super adjective, informal extremely good

super- prefix above, beyond, very, too: superannuate (= make someone retire because they are 'beyond the years')/superhuman (= beyond what a normal person is capable of) ⊙ Comes from Latin super meaning 'above'

superannuate verb to make (someone) retire from their job because of old age

superannuation noun a pension given to someone retired

superb adjective magnificent, very fine, excellent: a superb view ♦ **superbly** adverb

supercilious *adjective* looking down on others, haughty ♦ **superciliously** *adverb*

> ⓞ Based on a Latin word meaning 'eyebrow', from the habit of raising the eyebrows to show scorn or superiority

superconductivity *noun, physics* the property of having no electrical resistance, displayed by many metals and alloys at temperatures close to absolute zero
♦ **superconductive** *adjective*
♦ **superconductivity** *noun*

superconductor *noun* a metal or alloy that at a low temperature can conduct electricity with almost no resistance

superficial *adjective* **1** of a wound: affecting the surface of the skin only, not deep **2** not thorough or detailed: *superficial interest* **3** apparent at first glance, not actual: *superficial likeness* **4** of a person: not capable of deep thoughts or feelings ♦ **superficiality** *noun* ♦ **superficially** *adverb* ⓞ Comes from Latin *superficies* meaning 'surface'

> ⚠ Do not confuse: **superficial** and **superfluous**

superfluity (*pronounced* soo-per-**floo**-it-i) *noun* **1** being superfluous **2** a thing that is superfluous

superfluous (*pronounced* soo-**per**-floo-us) *adjective* beyond what is enough or necessary ⓞ Comes from Latin *superfluus* meaning 'overflowing'

> ⚠ Do not confuse: **superficial** and **superfluous**

superglue *noun* a type of quick-acting extra-strong adhesive ➤ *verb* to bond with superglue

superhero *noun* (*plural* **superheroes**) a character in a film, cartoon, comic, etc that has extraordinary powers, especially for saving the world from disaster

superhuman *adjective* **1** divine, godly **2** greater than would be expected of an ordinary person: *superhuman effort*

superimpose *verb* to lay or place (one thing on another)

superintend *verb* to be in charge or control, manage

superintendent *noun* **1** someone who is in charge of an institution, building, etc **2** a police officer above a chief inspector

superior *adjective* **1** higher in place or rank **2** better or greater than others: *superior forces/superior goods* **3** having an air of being better than others ➤ *noun* someone better than, or higher in rank than, others

superiority *noun* **1** a superior state **2** pre-eminence **3** advantage

superlative *adjective* **1** better than, or going beyond, all others: *superlative skill* **2** *grammar* an adjective or adverb of the highest degree of comparison, not positive or comparative, eg kind*est*, *worst*, *most* quickly

supermarket *noun* a large self-service store selling food etc

supermodel *noun* an extremely highly paid, usually female, fashion model

supernatural *adjective* not happening in the ordinary course of nature, miraculous ➤ *noun*: **the supernatural** the world of unexplained phenomena

supernova (*pronounced* soo-per-**noh**-va) *noun* (*plural* **supernovas** or **supernovae** – *pronounced* soo-per-**noh**-vee) an exploding star surrounded by a bright cloud of gas

superoxide *noun, chemistry* **1** a chemical compound that contains the negatively charged O_2 ion **2** an oxide that reacts with hydrogen ions to form hydrogen peroxide and oxygen

superphosphate *noun, chemistry* a type of fertilizer, made by treating calcium phosphate with an acid

superpower *noun* a nation that has outstanding political, economic, or military influence, especially the USA or the former USSR

supersede *verb* **1** to take the place of: *She superseded her brother as head teacher* **2** to replace (something with something else)

supersonic *adjective* faster than the speed of sound: *supersonic flight*

superstar *noun* an internationally famous celebrity, especially from the world of film, popular music, or sport ♦ **superstardom** *noun*

superstition *noun* **1** belief in magic and in things which cannot be explained by reason **2** an example of such belief (eg not walking under ladders)

superstitious *adjective* having superstitions

superstore *noun* **1** a very large supermarket which often sells clothes, etc as well as food and household goods **2** a very large store that sells a specified type of goods such as DIY products, electrical products, furniture, etc

supervene *verb* to come after or in addition
♦ **supervention** *noun*

supervise *verb* to be in charge of work and see that it is properly done

supervision *noun* the act of supervising; control, inspection

supervisor *noun* a person who is responsible for making sure that other people's work is done correctly

supine (*pronounced* **soo**-pain) *adjective* **1** lying on the back **2** not showing any interest or energy

supper *noun* a meal taken in the evening

supplant *verb* to take the place of: *The baby*

supplanted the dog in her affections

supple *adjective* **1** bending easily, flexible **2** of an object: bending easily without breaking
♦ **supply** (*pronounced* **sup**-li) *adverb*

supplement *noun* (*pronounced* **sup**-li-ment) **1** something added to supply a need or lack **2** a special section added to the main part of a newspaper or magazine **3** *maths* the amount by which an angle or arc is less than 180 degrees
➤ *verb* (*pronounced* **sup**-li-ment) to make or be an addition to: *Her earnings supplemented his income*

supplementary *adjective* added to supply a need; additional

supplementary angles *plural noun, maths* a pair of angles the sum of which is 180 degrees

suppliant (*pronounced* **sup**-li-ant) *adjective* asking earnestly and humbly ➤ *noun* someone who asks in this way

supplicate *verb* to ask earnestly, beg

supplication *noun* a humble, earnest request

supply *verb* (**supplies, supplying, supplied**) **1** to provide (what is wanted or needed) **2** to provide (someone with something) ➤ *noun* (*plural* **supplies**) **1** an act of supplying **2** something supplied **3** a stock or store **4** (**supplies**) a stock of essentials, eg food, equipment, money, etc ➤ *adjective* of a teacher: filling another's place or position for a time

support *verb* **1** to hold up, take part of the weight of **2** to help, encourage **3** to supply with a means of living: *support a family* **4** to bear, put up with: *I can't support lies* **5** to perform before (the main item in a concert, show, etc) **6** *computing* of a computer, an operating system, etc: to allow for the use of (a specified language, program, etc) ➤ *noun* **1** an act of supporting **2** something that supports **3** a band, singer, etc that accompanies or comes on before the main attraction ♦ **supporting** *adjective*

supporter *noun* someone who supports (eg a football club)

suppose *verb* **1** to take as true, assume for the sake of argument: *suppose that we have £100 to spend* **2** to believe, think probable: *I suppose you know* **3** used to give a polite order: *suppose you leave now* • **be supposed to** to be required or expected to (do) • **supposing** in the event that: *supposing it rains*

supposed *adjective* believed (often mistakenly) to be so: *her supposed generosity*

supposedly (*pronounced* su-**poh**-zid-li) *adverb* according to what is supposed

supposition *noun* **1** the act of supposing **2** something supposed

suppository *noun* (*plural* **suppositories**), *medicine* a solid preparation of medicine that dissolves when it is inserted into the rectum or vagina

suppress *verb* **1** to crush, put down (a rebellion etc) **2** to keep back (a yawn, a piece of news, etc)
♦ **suppression** *noun*

supra- *prefix* above ⊙ Comes from Latin *supra* meaning 'above'

supremacist (*pronounced* soo-**prem**-a-sist) *noun* someone who believes in the supremacy of their own race etc: *white supremacist*

supremacy (*pronounced* soo-**prem**-a-si) *noun* highest power or authority

supreme *adjective* **1** highest, most powerful: *supreme ruler* **2** greatest: *supreme courage*
♦ **supremely** *adverb*

Supreme Court *noun* **1** in the USA: the highest Federal court, with jurisdiction over all lower courts **2** the highest court in a number of nations and states

supremo (*pronounced* soo-**pree**-moh) *noun* (*plural* **supremos**), *informal* **1** a supreme head or leader **2** a boss ⊙ Comes from Spanish *generalísimo supremo* meaning 'supreme general'

sura or **surah** *noun* a chapter of the Koran ⊙ Comes from Arabic, meaning 'step'

surcharge *noun* an extra charge or tax

surd *noun, maths* an irrational number, especially shown as the root of a natural number

sure *adjective* (**surer, surest**) **1** having no doubt: *I'm sure that I can come* **2** certain (to do, happen, etc): *He is sure to be there* **3** reliable, dependable: *a sure method* • **be sure** to see to it that: *Be sure that he does it* • **make sure** to act so that, or check that, something is sure • **sure of yourself** confident • **to be sure 1** certainly! **2** undoubtedly: *To be sure, you are correct*

sure-footed *adjective, informal* unlikely to slip or stumble

surely *adverb* **1** certainly, without doubt **2** sometimes expressing a little doubt: *Surely you won't tell him?* **3** without hesitation, mistake, etc

surety (*pronounced* **shoor**-i-ti) *noun* (*plural* **sureties**) **1** someone who promises that another person will do something (especially appear in court) **2** a pledge, a guarantee

surf *noun* **1** the foam made by the breaking of waves **2** an act or instance of surfing ➤ *verb* **1** to stand or lie on a surfboard, try to catch the crest of a wave, and ride it to the shore **2** *computing* to browse through (the Internet) randomly

surface *noun* the outside or top part of anything (eg of the earth, of a road, etc) ➤ *verb* **1** to come up to the surface of water etc **2** to put a (smooth) surface on ➤ *adjective* **1** on the surface **2** travelling on the surface of land or water: *surface mail*

surface-active *adjective, chemistry* of a

substance such as a detergent: capable of affecting the wetting or surface tension properties of a liquid

surface tension noun, physics the film-like tension on the surface of a liquid that is caused by the cohesion of its particles, which has the effect of minimizing its surface area

surfactant noun, chemistry a soluble substance that reduces the surface tension of a liquid

surfboard noun a long, narrow board on which someone can ride over the surf

surfeit noun too much of anything

surfer noun someone who surfs

surfing noun the sport of riding on a surfboard

surge verb 1 to move (forward) like waves 2 to rise suddenly or excessively ➤ noun 1 the swelling of a large wave 2 a swelling or rising movement like this 3 a sudden rise or increase (of pain etc)

surgeon noun a doctor who performs operations, often cutting the body open to examine or remove a diseased part

surgery noun (plural **surgeries**) 1 treatment of diseases etc by operation 2 a doctor's or dentist's consulting room 3 a time when a professional person such as an MP, lawyer, etc can be consulted, usually free of charge

surgical adjective of, for use in, or by means of surgery: a surgical operation/a surgical mask/surgical equipment ♦ **surgically** adverb: The lump will have to be surgically removed

surgical spirit noun methylated spirit which is used for cleaning wounds and sterilizing medical equipment

surly adjective (**surlier, surliest**) gruff, rude, ill-mannered ♦ **surliness** noun

surmise verb to suppose, guess ➤ noun a supposition

surmount verb 1 to overcome (a difficulty etc) 2 to climb over, get over

surmountable adjective capable of being overcome or dealt with successfully

surname noun a person's last name or family name

surpass verb to go beyond, be more or better than: His work surpassed my expectations

surplice (pronounced ser-plis) noun a loose white gown worn by members of the clergy ℗ Comes from Late Latin superpellicium meaning 'an overgarment'

⚠ Do not confuse: **surplice** and **surplus**

surplus (pronounced ser-plus) noun the amount left over after what is needed has been used up ➤ adjective left over, extra ℗ Comes from French prefix sur- meaning 'over', and plus meaning 'more'

surprise noun 1 the feeling caused by an unexpected happening 2 an unexpected happening ➤ verb 1 to cause someone to feel surprise 2 to come upon (someone) suddenly and without warning ♦ **surprising** adjective ♦ **surprisingly** adverb **take by surprise** to come upon, or capture, without warning

surprised adjective experiencing feelings of surprise

surreal adjective dreamlike, using images from the subconscious

surrealism noun the use of surreal images in art

surrealist noun an adherent of surrealism ➤ adjective relating to or characteristic of surrealism: a surrealist painting

surrender verb 1 to give up, give in, yield: surrender to the enemy 2 to hand over: She surrendered the note to the teacher ➤ noun an act of surrender, especially in a war

surreptitious adjective done in a secret, underhand way ♦ **surreptitiously** adverb

surrogate adjective used or acting as a substitute for another person or thing: a surrogate mother ➤ noun a substitute ♦ **surrogacy** noun

surround verb 1 to be all round (someone or something) 2 to enclose, put round ➤ noun a border ♦ **surrounding** adjective

surroundings plural noun 1 the country lying round a place 2 the people and places with which you have to deal in daily life

surveillance noun a close watch or constant guard

survey verb (pronounced ser-vei) (**surveying, surveyed**) 1 to look over 2 to inspect, examine 3 to make careful measurements of (a piece of land etc) ➤ noun (pronounced ser-vei) (plural **surveys**) 1 a general view 2 a detailed examination or inspection 3 a piece of writing giving results of this 4 a careful measuring of land etc 5 a map made with the measurements obtained ♦ **surveying** noun

surveyor noun someone who makes surveys of land, buildings, etc

survival noun 1 the state of surviving 2 a custom, relic, etc that remains from earlier times

survive verb 1 to remain alive, continue to exist (after an event etc) 2 to live longer than: He survived his wife ♦ **surviving** adjective

survivor noun someone who remains alive: the only survivor of the crash

susceptibility noun (plural **susceptibilities**) 1 the state or degree of being susceptible to something 2 (**susceptibilities**) strong feelings or sensibilities

susceptible adjective easily affected or moved ● **susceptible to something** liable to be affected by it: susceptible to colds

sushi (pronounced soo-shi) noun a Japanese

dish of small rolls of cold boiled rice topped with egg, raw fish, or vegetables ⊕ from Japanese meaning 'it is sour'

suspect *verb* (*pronounced* sus-**pekt**) **1** to be inclined to think (someone) guilty: *I suspect her of the crime* **2** to distrust, have doubts about: *I suspected his air of frankness* **3** to guess: *I suspect that we're wrong* ➤ *noun* (*pronounced* **sus**-pekt) someone thought to be guilty of a crime etc ➤ *adjective* (*pronounced* **sus**-pekt) arousing doubt, suspected

suspend *verb* **1** to hang **2** to keep from falling or sinking: *particles suspended in a liquid* **3** to stop for a time: *suspend business* **4** to take away a job, privilege, etc from for a time: *They suspended the student from classes*

suspended animation *noun* a state in which a body's main functions are temporarily slowed down to a minimum, eg in hibernation

suspended sentence *noun* a judicial sentence that is put off for a set time providing the offender behaves well throughout the period

suspender *noun* **1** an elastic strap to keep up socks or stockings **2** (**suspenders**) *US* braces

suspense *noun* **1** a state of being undecided **2** a state of uncertainty or worry

suspension *noun* **1** the act of suspending **2** the state of being suspended **3** *chemistry* a mixture in which particles larger than those in a colloid or a solution are dispersed through a liquid **4** *geography* the carrying of small particles of sediment in rivers

suspension bridge *noun* a bridge which is suspended from cables hanging from towers

suspicion *noun* **1** a feeling of doubt or mistrust **2** an opinion, a guess

suspicious *adjective* **1** inclined to suspect or distrust **2** arousing suspicion ◆ **suspiciously** *adverb*

sustain *verb* **1** to hold up, support **2** to bear (an attack etc) without giving way **3** to suffer (an injury etc) **4** to give strength to: *The food will sustain you* **5** to keep up, keep going: *sustain a conversation* ◆ **sustainable** *adjective*

sustainable development *noun* the development and use of resources over the long term, to prevent damage to the environment

sustenance *noun* food, nourishment

sutra (*pronounced* **soot**-ra) or **sutta** *noun* **1** *Hinduism* a book of sayings on rituals, philosophy, etc **2** *Buddhism* a group of writings including the sermons of Buddha ⊕ Comes from Sanskrit, meaning 'thread' or 'rule'

suture (*pronounced* **soo**-choor) *noun* a stitch that joins the edges of a wound, surgical incision, etc together ➤ *verb* to sew up (a wound, surgical incision, etc)

suzerain *noun* **1** a feudal lord **2** a supreme ruler

svelte *adjective* slender, trim

SW *abbreviation* south-west; south-western

swab *noun* **1** a mop for cleaning a ship's deck **2** a piece of cotton wool used for cleaning, absorbing blood, etc ➤ *verb* (**swabbing, swabbed**) to clean with a swab

swaddle *verb* to wrap up (a young baby) tightly

swaddling clothes *noun, history* strips of cloth used to wrap up a young baby

swag *noun* **1** *slang* stolen goods **2** *Aust* a bundle of possessions

swagger *verb* **1** to walk proudly, swinging the arms and body **2** to boast ➤ *noun* a proud walk or attitude ◆ **swaggering** *adjective*

swallow[1] *verb* **1** to pass (food or drink) down the throat into the stomach **2** to receive (an insult etc) without objection **3** to keep back (tears, a laugh, etc) ➤ *noun* an act of swallowing
 • **swallow something up** to make it disappear

swallow[2] *noun* a bird with pointed wings and a forked tail

swam past tense of **swim**

swami (*pronounced* **swah**-mi) *noun* (*plural* **swamis** or **swamies**) a title for a Hindu male religious teacher ⊕ Comes from Hindi *svami* meaning 'lord or master'

swamp *noun* wet, marshy ground ➤ *verb* **1** to fill (a boat) with water **2** to overwhelm: *swamped with work* ◆ **swampy** *adjective*

swan *noun* a large, stately water bird, with white feathers and a long neck ➤ *verb* (**swanning, swanned**): **swan off** *informal* to wander off aimlessly or gracefully

swank *verb, informal* to show off

swanky *adjective* (**swankier, swankiest**) *informal* flashy, flamboyant, elaborate, fashionable, etc

swan song *noun* the last work of a musician, writer, etc

swap or **swop** *verb* (**swapping** or **swopping, swapped** or **swopped**) to give one thing in exchange for another: *swap addresses* ➤ *noun* an exchange or trading

swarm[1] *noun* **1** a large number of insects flying or moving together **2** a dense moving crowd ➤ *verb* **1** of insects: to gather together in great numbers **2** to move in crowds **3** to be crowded (with): *swarming with tourists*

swarm[2] *verb* to climb (up a wall etc)

swarthy *adjective* (**swarthier, swarthiest**) dark-skinned ◆ **swarthiness** *noun*

swash *noun,* a forward current, such as one caused by an incoming wave (*contrasted with:* **backwash**)

swashbuckler *noun* **1** a daring and flamboyant adventurer **2** a film, novel, etc which portrays exciting scenes of adventure, usually in a romanticized historical setting, and which usually features scenes of flamboyant swordsmanship ♦ **swashbuckling** *adjective*

swastika (*pronounced* **swos**-ti-ka) *noun* **1** an ancient design of a cross with four bent arms **2** this design taken up as a symbol of Nazism

swat *verb* (**swatting, swatted**) to squash (a fly etc) ➤ *noun* an instrument for squashing insects

swath (*pronounced* swoth) or **swathe** (*pronounced* sweidh) *noun* **1** a line of corn or grass cut by a scythe **2** a strip

swathe[1] *verb* to wrap round with clothes or bandages

swathe[2] another spelling of **swath**

sway *verb* **1** to swing or rock to and fro **2** to bend in one direction or to one side **3** to influence: *sway opinion* ➤ *noun* **1** a swaying movement **2** rule, power: *hold sway over*

swear *verb* (**swearing, swore, sworn**) **1** to promise or declare solemnly **2** to vow **3** to curse, using the name of God or other sacred things without respect **4** to make (someone) take an oath: *swear someone to secrecy* • **swear by** to rely on, have complete faith in

swear-word *noun* a word used in swearing or cursing

sweat *noun* moisture secreted by the skin, perspiration ➤ *verb* **1** to give out sweat **2** *informal* to work hard

sweatband *noun* a strip of elasticated fabric worn around the wrist or head to absorb sweat when playing sports

sweater *noun* a jersey, a pullover

sweatshirt *noun* a long-sleeved jersey of a thick soft cotton fabric, usually fleecy on the inside

sweatshop *noun* a workshop or factory with cheap labour, long hours and poor conditions

sweaty *adjective* (**sweatier, sweatiest**) wet, or stained, with sweat

swede *noun* a kind of large yellow turnip

sweep *verb* (**sweeping, swept**) **1** to clean (a floor etc) with a brush or broom **2** (often **sweep up** or **sweep something up**) to gather up (dust etc) by sweeping **3** to carry (away, along, off) with a long brushing movement **4** to travel over quickly, move with speed: *a new fad which is sweeping the country* **5** to move quickly in a proud manner (eg from a room) **6** to clear (something) of something: *Sweep the sea of enemy mines* **7** to curve widely or stretch far ➤ *noun* **1** a sweeping movement **2** a curve, a stretch **3** *informal* a chimney-sweep **4** *informal* a sweepstake

sweeper *noun* **1** a device for sweeping **2** *football* a player positioned behind the defenders

sweeping *adjective* **1** that sweeps **2** of a victory etc: great, overwhelming **3** of a statement etc: too general, allowing no exceptions, rash

sweepstake *noun* a gambling system in which those who take part stake money which goes to the holder of the winning ticket

sweet *adjective* **1** having the taste of sugar, not salty, sour or bitter **2** pleasing to the taste **3** pleasant to hear or smell **4** kindly, agreeable, charming ➤ *noun* **1** a small piece of sweet substance, eg chocolate, toffee, etc **2** something sweet served towards the end of a meal, a pudding

sweet-and-sour *adjective* cooked in a sauce that includes both sugar and vinegar or lemon juice ➤ *noun* a sweet-and-sour dish

sweetbreads *plural noun* an animal's pancreas used for food

sweetcorn *noun* maize

sweeten *verb* to make or become sweet

sweetener *noun* **1** an artificial substance used to sweeten food or drinks **2** *informal* a bribe

sweetheart *noun* a lover

sweetly *adverb* in a sweet way: *singing sweetly*

sweetmeat *noun, old* a sweet, a confection

sweetness *noun* a sweet quality • **sweetness and light** *informal* mildness, pleasantness, and reasonableness

sweet nothings *plural noun* the endearments that people in love say to each other

sweet pea *noun* a sweet-smelling climbing flower grown in gardens

sweet potato *noun* **1** a plant with trailing or climbing stems and large purple funnel-shaped flowers **2** the swollen edible root of this plant, which has sweet-tasting flesh surrounded by a red or purplish skin, cooked and eaten as a vegetable

sweet talk *informal, noun* flattery, persuasion ➤ *verb* (**sweet-talk**) to coax or persuade, eg with flattering words

sweet tooth *noun* a liking for sweet-tasting things

swell *verb* (**swelling, swelled, swollen** or **swelled**) **1** to grow in size or volume **2** of the sea: to rise into waves ➤ *noun* **1** an increase in size or volume **2** large, heaving waves **3** a gradual rise in the height of the ground **4** *old* a dandy ➤ *adjective, US informal* fine, splendid

swelling *noun* a swollen part of the body, a lump

swelter *verb* to be too hot

sweltering *adjective* very hot

swept past form of **sweep**

swerve *verb* to turn quickly to one side ➤ *noun* a quick turn aside

swift *adjective* moving quickly; rapid ➤ *noun* a bird rather like the swallow ♦ **swiftly** *adverb* ♦ **swiftness** *noun*

swig *informal, noun* a mouthful of liquid, a large

drink ➤ verb (**swigging, swigged**) to gulp down

swill verb 1 to wash out 2 informal to drink a great deal ➤ noun 1 partly liquid food given to pigs 2 informal a big drink

swim verb (**swimming, swam, swum**) 1 to move on or in water, using arms, legs, fins, etc 2 to cross by swimming: swim the Channel 3 to move with a gliding motion 4 to be dizzy 5 to be covered (with liquid): meat swimming in grease ➤ noun an act of swimming ✦ **swimming** noun

swim bladder noun, biology a structure inside a fish that can be filled with air and control its buoyancy in the water (also called: **air bladder**)

swimmer noun someone or something that swims: He's not a very strong swimmer

swimming costume or **swimsuit** noun a brief close-fitting garment for swimming in

swimmingly adverb, informal smoothly, easily, successfully: The meeting went swimmingly

swimming pool noun a large water-filled tank for swimming, diving in, etc

swindle verb 1 to cheat, defraud 2 to get (money etc from someone) by cheating ➤ noun a fraud, a deception ✦ **swindler** noun

swine noun 1 (plural **swine**) old a pig 2 (plural **swines**) informal a contemptible person

swineherd noun, old someone who looks after pigs

swing verb (**swinging, swung**) 1 to move to and fro, sway 2 to turn or whirl round 3 to walk quickly, moving the arms to and fro ➤ noun 1 a swinging movement 2 a seat for swinging, hung on ropes etc from a support • **in full swing** going on busily • **the swing of things** the usual routine or pace of activity: get back into the swing of things after a month off work ◷ Comes from Old English swingan

swingeing (pronounced swin-jing) adjective very great: swingeing cuts in taxation ◷ Comes from Old English swengan meaning 'to shake'

! Do not confuse with: **swinging**

swipe verb 1 to strike with a sweeping blow 2 informal to steal 3 to pass (a swipe card) through a device that electronically interprets the information encoded on the card ➤ noun a sweeping blow

swirl verb to sweep along with a whirling motion ➤ noun a whirling movement

swish verb 1 to strike or brush against with a rustling sound 2 to move making such a noise: swishing out of the room in her long dress ➤ noun (plural **swishes**) a rustling sound or movement

Swiss roll noun a cylindrical cake made by rolling up a thin slab of sponge spread with jam or cream

switch noun (plural **switches**) 1 a small lever or handle, eg for turning an electric current on and off 2 an act of switching 3 a change: a switch of loyalty 4 a thin stick ➤ verb 1 to strike with a switch 2 to turn (off or on) by means of a switch 3 to change, turn: switch jobs/hastily switching the conversation

switchback noun a road or railway with steep slopes or sharp turns

switchblade noun a flick-knife

switchboard noun a board with equipment for making telephone connections

swivel noun a joint that turns on a pin or pivot ➤ verb (**swivelling, swivelled**) to turn on a swivel, pivot

swollen adjective increased in size by swelling ➤ verb, past participle of **swell**

swoon old, verb to faint ➤ noun a fainting fit • **swoon over** to go into raptures of adoration about

swoop verb to come down with a sweep, like a bird of prey ➤ noun a sudden downward rush • **at one fell swoop** all at one time, at a stroke

swop another spelling of **swap**

sword noun a type of weapon with a long blade for cutting or piercing

swordfish noun (plural **swordfish** or **swordfishes**) a large type of fish with a long pointed upper jaw like a sword

swordsman noun (plural **swordsmen**) someone who is skilled in the use of a sword ✦ **swordsmanship** noun

swore past tense of **swear**

sworn past participle of **swear** adjective holding steadily to an attitude etc: The two rivals became sworn enemies

swot informal, verb (**swotting, swotted**) to study hard ➤ noun someone who studies hard

sybaritic (pronounced sib-a-**rit**-ik) adjective 1 luxurious 2 fond of luxury

◷ After the ancient city of Sybaris, which was famous for the luxurious lifestyle of its people

sycamore noun a name given to several different types of tree, the maple, plane, and a kind of fig tree

sycophant (pronounced **sik**o-fant) noun someone who flatters others in order to gain favour or personal advantage ✦ **sycophancy** noun ✦ **sycophantic** adjective

syl- see **syn-**

syllabic adjective to do with syllables, or the division of words into syllables

syllabify verb (**syllabifies, syllabified, syllabifying**) to divide (a word) into syllables ✦ **syllabification** noun

syllable noun a word or part of a word spoken

with one breath (*cheese* has one syllable, *but-ter* two, *mar-gar-ine* three)

syllabus *noun* (*plural* **syllabuses** or **syllabi** – *pronounced* **sil**-a-bai) a programme or list of lectures, classes, etc

syllogism *noun* a combination of two propositions which lead to a third conclusion, as in *All dogs are animals, foxhounds are dogs, therefore foxhounds are animals*

sylph *noun* a type of fairy supposed to inhabit the air

sym- see **syn-**

symbiont *noun, biology* either of two organisms in a symbiotic relationship

symbiosis *noun* (*plural* **symbioses**) **1** *biology* a close association between two organisms of different species, to the benefit of one or both (*see also*: **commensalism, mutualism, parasitism**) **2** a mutually beneficial or dependent relationship between two people or groups ♦ **symbiotic** *adjective*

symbol *noun* **1** something that stands for or represents another thing, eg the red cross, which stands for first aid **2** a character used as a short form of something, eg the signs + meaning 'plus', and O meaning 'oxygen'

symbolic or **symbolical** *adjective* standing as a symbol of ♦ **symbolically** *adverb*

symbolism *noun* the use of symbols to express ideas in art and literature

symbolize or **symbolise** *verb* to be a symbol of

symmetrical *adjective* having symmetry; not lopsided in appearance ♦ **symmetrically** *adverb*: *coloured squares arranged symmetrically*

symmetry *noun* (*contrasted with*: **asymmetry**) **1** the equality in size, shape and position of two halves on either side of a dividing line: *spoiling the symmetry of the building* **2** *maths* the quality of being unchanged by reflection or rotation

sympathetic *adjective* feeling or showing sympathy ♦ **sympathetically** *adverb*
sympathetic to or **towards** inclined to be in favour of: *sympathetic to the scheme*

sympathetic nervous system *noun, biology* a division of the autonomic nervous system, which tends to increase the heart rate and prepare the body for action (*compare with*: **parasympathetic nervous system**)

sympathize or **sympathise** *verb*:
sympathize with to express or feel sympathy for

sympathy *noun* (*plural* **sympathies**) **1** a feeling of pity or sorrow for someone in trouble **2** agreement with, or understanding of, the feelings, attitudes, etc of others

symphonic *adjective* of music: suitable for performance by a symphony orchestra

symphonic poem *noun* a large orchestral composition with the movements run together

symphony *noun* (*plural* **symphonies**) a long piece of music written for an orchestra of many different instruments

symphony orchestra *noun* a large orchestra capable of playing large-scale orchestral music

symptom *noun* an outward sign indicating the presence of a disease etc: *symptoms of measles*

symptomatic *adjective* serving as a symptom
♦ **symptomatically** *adverb*

syn- also **sym-, syl-** *prefix* with, together: *synthesis/sympathize* (= have so much pity for someone that you feel sorrow with them)/ *syllable* (= sounds pronounced together in one breath) ◑ Comes from Greek *syn* meaning 'with'

synagogue *noun* a Jewish place of worship

synapse *noun, biology* a tiny gap across which nerve impulses are transmitted between neurones ◔ Comes from Greek *synapsis* meaning 'contact' or 'junction'

synapsis *noun* (*plural* **synapses**), *biology* the pairing of paternal and maternal chromosomes during meiosis

synch or **sync** (*pronounced* singk) *informal, noun* synchronization, especially of sound and picture in film and television ➤ *verb* to synchronize

synchronize or **synchronise** *verb* **1** to cause to happen at the same time **2** to set to the same time: *synchronize watches* ♦ **synchronization** *noun*

syncopate *verb, music* to change (the beat) by accenting beats not usually accented

syncopation *noun* **1** syncopating **2** the beat produced by syncopating

syndicate *noun* a number of persons who join together to manage some piece of business

syndrome *noun* a pattern of behaviour, events, etc characteristic of some problem or condition

synergy (*pronounced* sin-er-ji) *noun* an increased effectiveness achieved by a number of people working together rather than on their own ◑ Comes from Greek *synergia* meaning 'co-operation'

synod (*pronounced* sin-od) *noun* a meeting of members of the clergy

synonym *noun* a word which has the same, or nearly the same, meaning as another, eg 'ass' and 'donkey', or 'brave' and 'courageous'

synonymous *adjective*: **synonymous with** having the same meaning as

synopsis *noun* (*plural* **synopses**) a short summary of the main points of a book, speech, etc

synoptic *adjective* **1** summarizing the main points **2** denoting the gospels of Matthew, Mark and Luke in the New Testament of the Bible

synovia *noun* a transparent liquid which lubricates a joint (*also called*: **synovial fluid**)

synovial membrane *noun, anatomy* a membrane of connective tissue that secretes synovia

synovitis *noun, medicine* inflammation of a synovial membrane

syntactic or **syntactical** *adjective* relating or belonging to syntax

syntax *noun* **1** rules for the correct combination of words to form sentences **2** *computing* rules for combining the elements of a programming language

synthesis *noun* **1** the act of making a whole by putting together its separate parts **2** *chemistry* the making of a substance by combining chemical elements

synthesize or **synthesise** *verb* to make (eg a drug) by synthesis

synthesizer or **synthesiser** *noun, music* a computerized instrument which creates electronic musical sounds

synthetic *adjective* **1** made artificially to look like a natural product: *synthetic leather* **2** not natural, pretended: *synthetic charm*
♦ **synthetically** *adverb*

syphilis *noun, medicine* a serious sexually transmitted disease caused by bacterial infection and characterized by painless ulcers on the genitals, fever, and a faint red rash
♦ **syphilitic** *adjective*

syphon another spelling of **siphon**

syringe *noun* a tubular instrument with a needle and plunger, used to extract blood, inject drugs, etc ▸ *verb* to clean out with a syringe: *had his ears syringed*

syrup *noun* **1** a thick sticky liquid made by boiling water or fruit juice with sugar **2** a purified form of treacle ♦ **syrupy** *adjective*

system *noun* **1** an arrangement of several parts which work together: *railway system/solar system* **2** a way of organizing: *democratic system of government* **3** a regular method of doing something **4** the body, or its parts, considered as a whole: *My system is run down* ⊕ Comes from Greek *sy-* meaning 'together', and the root of *histanai* meaning 'to set'

systematic *adjective* following a system; methodical ♦ **systematically** *adverb*

systematics *singular noun* the scientific study of the classification of living things into a hierarchy of groups and their relationships with each other

systemic *noun, biology* relating to a whole organism or to the whole body

systems analysis *noun* **1** analysis of all the activities of an organization in order to plan more efficient methods **2** *computing* analysis of a human task in business, industry, etc to see if and how it can be computerized ♦ **systems analyst** *noun*

Tt

t *abbreviation* ton(s) or tonne(s)

Ta *symbol, chemistry* tantalum

tab¹ *noun* **1** a small tag or flap attached to something **2** a running total, a tally

tab² *noun* a key on a typewriter or word processor which sets the position of the margins and columns in a table (also called **tabulator**)

tabard *noun* a short sleeveless tunic

tabby (*plural* **tabbies**) or **tabby-cat** *noun* (*plural* **tabby-cats**) a striped (usually female) cat

tabernacle *noun* **1** a place of worship for some nonconformist Christian denominations **2** in Roman Catholic and Eastern Orthodox churches: a small cupboard in which consecrated bread and wine are kept

tabla *noun* a pair of small drums played with the hands in Indian music

table *noun* **1** a flat-topped piece of furniture, supported by legs **2** (*also called*: **tableland**) an area of high land, a plateau **3** facts or figures set out in columns: *multiplication tables* ➤ *verb* **1** to make into a list or table **2** to put forward for discussion: *table a motion*

tableau *noun* (*plural* **tableaux**) a striking group or scene

tablecloth *noun* a cloth for covering a table

tableland *noun* a broad high plain or a plateau

tablespoon *noun* **1** a large size of spoon, used eg for serving food **2** (*abbrev* **tbsp**) the amount a tablespoon will hold (approximately 15ml), used as a measure in cookery (*also called*: **tablespoonful**)

tablespoonful *noun* (*plural* **tablespoonfuls**) the amount held in a tablespoon

tablet *noun* **1** a small flat plate on which to write, paint, etc **2** a small flat piece, eg of soap or chocolate **3** a pill

table tennis *noun* a form of tennis played across a table with small bats and a light ball

tabloid *noun* a small-sized newspaper giving news in shortened, often simplified form and an informal sensationalist style (*compare with*: **broadsheet**) ➤ *adjective* relating to this type of newspaper or this style of journalism: *tabloid television*

> ⏱ Originally a trademark for a medicine in tablet form, and then, by association, the name for a small-sized newspaper giving information in concentrated form

taboo *adjective* forbidden by common consent; not approved by social custom ➤ *noun* a taboo subject or behaviour

tabular *adjective* set in the form of a table

tabulate *verb* to set out (information etc) in columns or rows

tabulator see **tab²**

tachograph *noun* an instrument showing a vehicle's mileage, number of stops, etc

tachometer *noun* a device that measures engine speed in revolutions per minute

tacit (*pronounced* **tas**-it) *adjective* understood but not spoken aloud, silent: *tacit agreement*

taciturn (*pronounced* **tas**-it-ern) *adjective* not inclined to talk

taciturnity (*pronounced* tas-it-**ern**-it-i) *noun* an unwillingness to talk

tack *noun* **1** a short sharp nail with a broad head **2** a sideways movement allowing a yacht etc to sail against the wind **3** a direction, a course **4** a rough stitch to keep material in place while sewing ➤ *verb* **1** to fasten with tacks **2** to sew with tacks **3** of a yacht etc: to move from side to side across the face of the wind • **change tack** to change course or direction • **on the wrong tack** following the wrong train of thought

tackle *verb* **1** to come to grips with, deal with **2** in football etc: to try to stop, or take the ball from, another player ➤ *noun* **1** the ropes and rigging of a ship **2** equipment, gear: *fishing tackle* **3** ropes and pulleys for raising heavy weights **4** an act of tackling

tacky¹ *adjective* (**tackier, tackiest**) slightly sticky

tacky² *adjective* (**tackier, tackiest**) *informal* shabby; vulgar, in bad taste

taco *noun* a rolled or folded tortilla with a savoury filling

tact *noun* skill in dealing with people so as to avoid giving offence

tactful *adjective* using tact; avoiding giving offence ♦ **tactfully** *adverb*

tactical *adjective* **1** involving clever and successful planning **2** diplomatic, politic: *tactical withdrawal*

tactics *plural noun* **1** a way of acting in order to gain an advantage or achieve something **2** the art of coordinating military forces in action

tactile *adjective* of or perceived through touch

tactless *adjective* giving offence through lack of

thought ♦ **tactlessly** adverb

tad noun, informal a small amount, a bit

tadpole noun a young frog or toad in its first stage of life

tae kwon do (pronounced tei kwon **doh**) noun a Korean martial art similar to karate

taffeta noun a stiff glossy fabric made mainly of silk

tag noun 1 a label: price tag 2 computing a marker giving summarized information which applies to the text following it 3 a familiar saying or quotation 4 (also called: **tig**) a chasing game played by children ➤ verb (**tagging, tagged**) to put a tag or tags on • **tag on to** or **tag after** to follow closely and continually

tagliatelle (pronounced tal-ya-**tel**-i) plural noun pasta in long narrow ribbons

t'ai chi (pronounced tai **chee**) noun a Chinese system of exercise and self-defence stressing the importance of balance and coordination

taiga (pronounced **tai**-ga) noun, geography the large area of predominantly coniferous forest located south of the arctic tundra regions (also called: **boreal forest**)

tail noun 1 an appendage sticking out from the end of the spine on an animal, bird or fish 2 an appendage on the rear of a machine etc: tail of an aeroplane 3 the stalk on a piece of fruit 4 (**tails**) the side of a coin opposite to the head 5 (**tails**) a tail-coat ➤ verb 1 to follow closely 2 to remove the tails from (fruit etc) • **tail off** to become less, fewer or worse • **turn tail** to run away

tailback noun a long queue of traffic stretching back from an accident or roadworks

tailcoat noun a coat with a divided tail, part of a man's evening dress

tail-end noun the very end of a procession etc

tailgate noun the rear door which opens upwards on a hatchback vehicle ➤ verb, informal to drive dangerously close behind (another vehicle)

tailor noun someone who cuts out and makes clothes ➤ verb 1 to make and fit (clothes) 2 to make to fit the circumstances, adapt: tailored to your needs

tailor-made adjective 1 of clothes: made to fit a particular person 2 exactly suited to requirements: a tailor-made solution

tailspin noun 1 a downward spiral dive of an aeroplane 2 informal a state of great agitation

taint verb 1 to spoil by contact with something bad or rotten 2 to corrupt ➤ noun a trace of decay or evil

take verb (**taking, took, taken**) 1 to lay hold of, grasp 2 to choose: Take a card! 3 to accept, agree to have: Do you take credit cards?/Please take a biscuit 4 to have room for: My car only takes four people 5 to eat, swallow 6 to get or have regularly: doesn't take sugar 7 to capture (a fort etc) 8 (also: **take away**) to subtract: Take two from eight 9 to lead, carry, drive: take the children to school 10 to use, make use of: take care! 11 to require: It'll take too much time 12 to travel by: took the afternoon train 13 to experience, feel: takes great pride in his work 14 to photograph: took some shots inside the house 15 to understand: took what I said the wrong way 16 of a plant: to root successfully 17 to become popular, please • **take account of** to consider, remember • **take advantage of** 1 to make use of (an opportunity) 2 to treat or use unfairly • **take after** to be like in appearance or behaviour • **take care of** to look after • **take down** to write, note down • **take for** to believe (mistakenly) to be: I took him for his brother • **take heed** to pay careful attention • **take ill** to become ill • **take in** 1 to include 2 to receive 3 to understand: didn't take in what you said 4 to make smaller: take in a dress 5 to cheat, deceive • **take leave of** to say goodbye to • **take someone's life** to kill them • **taken with** attracted to • **take off** 1 to remove (clothes etc) 2 to imitate for comic effect 3 of an aircraft: to leave the ground • **take on** 1 to undertake (work etc) 2 to accept (as an opponent): take you on at tennis • **take over** to take control of • **take part in** to share or help in • **take place** to happen • **take to** 1 to like or be attracted to by: I took to him straightaway 2 to begin to do or use regularly: took to rising early • **take up** 1 to lift, raise 2 to occupy (space, time, etc) 3 to begin to learn, show interest in: take up playing the harp ◑ Comes from Late Old English tacan meaning 'to touch' or 'to take'

takeaway noun 1 a meal prepared and bought in a restaurant or shop but taken away and eaten somewhere else 2 a restaurant or shop providing such meals

take-off noun 1 the act of an aircraft leaving the ground 2 an act of imitating or mimicking

takeover noun the act of taking control of something, especially a company by buying the majority of its shares

taking adjective pleasing, attractive ➤ noun 1 an act of taking 2 (**takings**) money received from things sold

tala noun a rhythmic pattern found in Indian music

talc noun 1 a soft mineral, soapy to the touch 2 informal talcum powder

talcum noun a fine powder made from talc, used for sprinkling on the body (also called: **talcum powder**)

tale noun 1 a story 2 an untrue story, a lie • **tell tales** to give away information about the misdeeds of others

talent *noun* **1** a special ability or skill: *a talent for music* **2** an old measure of weight for gold or silver

talented *adjective* skilled, gifted

talisman *noun* (*plural* **talismans**) an object believed to have magic powers; a charm

talk *verb* **1** to speak **2** to gossip **3** to give information ➤ *noun* **1** conversation **2** gossip **3** the subject of conversation: *The talk is of revolution* **4** a discussion or lecture: *gave a talk on stained glass* • **talk over** to discuss • **talk round 1** to discuss without coming to the main point **2** to persuade: *talked him round to her point of view*

talkative *adjective* inclined to chatter

tall *adjective* **1** high or higher than average **2** hard to believe: *tall story*

tallith *noun* (*plural* **talliths** or **tallithim**) a shawl worn by Jewish men for prayer

tall order *noun* a request to do something awkward or unreasonable

tallow *noun* animal fat melted down to make soap, candles, etc

tally *noun* (*plural* **tallies**) **1** an account **2** a ticket, a label **3** *old* a notched stick for keeping a score ➤ *verb* (**tallies, tallying, tallied**) **1** to agree (with): *His story doesn't tally with yours* **2** to count by making a mark for each object

Talmud *noun* the fundamental body of Jewish law

talon *noun* a hooked claw

talus *noun* (*plural* **taluses**), *geography* a scree formed from frost-shattered rocks ⊕ Comes from French, originally from Latin *talutium* meaning 'a slope'

tambourine *noun* a small one-sided drum with tinkling metal discs set into the sides

tame *adjective* **1** of an animal: not wild, used to living with humans **2** dull, not exciting ➤ *verb* to make tame, subdue

tammy *noun* (*plural* **tammies**) a tam-o'-shanter

tam-o'-shanter *noun* a flat round Scottish cap with no brim and a bobble in the middle

⊕ Named after the hero of a poem by Scottish poet Robert Burns (1759–96)

tamp *verb* **1** to fill up (a hole containing explosive) before setting off the explosion **2** to pack (tobacco in a pipe or cigarette) into a tighter mass

tamper *verb*: **tamper with** to meddle with so as to damage or alter: *Someone had tampered with the brakes*

tampon *noun* a plug of cotton-wool inserted into the vagina to absorb blood during menstruation

tan¹ *verb* (**tanning, tanned**) **1** to make (animal skin) into leather by treating with tannin **2** to

make or become brown, eg by exposure to the sun ➤ *noun* **1** a yellowish-brown colour **2** a suntan

tan² *abbreviation, maths* tangent

tandem *noun* a long bicycle with two seats and two sets of pedals one behind the other ➤ *adverb* one behind the other • **in tandem** together, in conjunction

tandoori *noun* a style of Indian cookery in which food is baked over charcoal in a clay oven

tang *noun* a strong taste, flavour or smell: *the tang of the sea air*

tangent *noun* **1** *maths* a straight line which touches a circle or curve without crossing it **2** *maths* (*abbrev* **tan**) of an angle in a right-angled triangle: a function that is the length of the side opposite the angle to the length of the side adjacent to it • **go off at a tangent** to go off suddenly in another direction or line of thought

tangerine *noun* a small type of orange

⊕ Originally meaning 'from Tangiers', from where the fruit was exported in the 19th century

tangible *adjective* **1** able to be felt by touching **2** real, definite: *tangible profits* ✦ **tangibly** *adverb*

tangle *verb* **1** to twist together in knots **2** to make or become difficult or confusing ➤ *noun* **1** a twisted mass of knots **2** a confused situation

tango *noun* (*plural* **tangos**) a ballroom dance with long steps and pauses, originally from South America

tangram *noun* a puzzle made from a square cut into 7 pieces that will fit together in various ways

tank *noun* **1** a large container for water, petrol, etc **2** a heavy armoured vehicle which moves on caterpillar wheels

tanka *noun* a Japanese form of poem like a haiku, but with two extra lines of 7 syllables

tankard *noun* a large drinking mug

tanker *noun* **1** a ship or large lorry for carrying liquids, eg oil **2** an aircraft carrying fuel

tanner *noun* someone who works at tanning leather

tannery *noun* (*plural* **tanneries**) a place where leather is made

tannin *noun* a bitter-tasting substance found in tea, red wine, etc, also used in tanning and dyeing

tantalize or **tantalise** *verb* to torment by offering something and keeping it out of reach

tantalizing or **tantalising** *adjective* teasing; tormenting: *Tantalizing smells were coming from the kitchen*

tantalum *noun, chemistry* (symbol **Ta**) a hard bluish-grey metallic element

tantamount *adjective*: **tantamount to**

coming to the same thing as, equivalent to: *tantamount to stealing*

tantrum *noun* a fit of rage or bad temper

tap *noun* **1** a light touch or knock **2** a device with a valve for controlling the flow of liquid, gas, etc ▸ *verb* (**tapping, tapped**) **1** to knock or strike lightly **2** to draw on, start using **3** to attach a listening device secretly to (a telephone) • **on tap** ready, available for use

tapas *plural noun* savoury snacks, originally Spanish in style

tapdance *noun* a dance done with special shoes that make a tapping sound ▸ *verb* to perform a tapdance ♦ **tapdancing** *noun & adjective*

tape *noun* **1** a narrow band or strip used for tying **2** a piece of string over the finishing line on a racetrack **3** a tape measure **4** a strip of magnetic material for recording sound, pictures or data ▸ *verb* **1** to fasten with tape **2** to record on tape • **have someone taped** to have a good understanding of their character or worth

tape measure *noun* a narrow strip of paper, plastic, etc used for measuring distance

taper *noun* **1** a long, thin kind of candle **2** a long waxed wick used for lighting oil lamps etc ▸ *verb* to make or become thinner at one end

tape recorder *noun* a kind of instrument for recording sound etc on magnetic tape

tapering *adjective* becoming gradually thinner at one end

tapestry *noun* (*plural* **tapestries**) a cloth with designs or figures woven into it, used to decorate walls or cover furniture

tapeworm *noun* a type of long worm sometimes found in the intestines of humans and animals

tapioca *noun* a starchy food obtained from the root of the cassava plant

tapir *noun* a kind of wild animal something like a large pig

taproot *noun, botany* a long straight main root in some plants (eg carrot)

tar *noun* **1** a thick, black, sticky substance derived from wood or coal, used in making roads etc **2** *informal* a sailor ▸ *verb* (**tarring, tarred**) to smear with tar • **tarred with the same brush (as)** having the same faults (as)

taramasalata (*pronounced* ta-ra-ma-sal-**ah**-ta) *noun* a creamy pink pâté made from smoked fish roe, olive oil and garlic

tarantula *noun* a type of large, poisonous spider

tardiness *noun* being late or delayed

tardy *adjective* (**tardier, tardiest**) slow; late

target *noun* **1** a mark to aim at in shooting, darts, etc **2** a result or sum that is aimed at: *a target of £3000* **3** someone at whom unfriendly remarks are aimed: *the target of her criticism* **4** another word for **codomain** ▸ *verb* to direct or aim at

target audience *noun* the group of people a publication, advertisement, etc is aimed at

tariff *noun* **1** a list of prices **2** a list of taxes payable on goods brought into a country **3** a tax charged on particular goods

tarmac *noun* the surface of a road or airport runway, made of tarmacadam ▸ *verb* to surface with tarmacadam

tarmacadam *noun* a mixture of small stones and tar used to make road surfaces etc

tarn *noun* a small mountain lake

tarnish *verb* **1** of metal: to (cause to) become dull or discoloured **2** to spoil (a reputation etc)

tarot (*pronounced* **ta**-roh) *noun* a system of fortune-telling using special cards divided into suits

tarpaulin *noun* **1** strong waterproof cloth **2** a sheet of this material

tarragon *noun* a herb used in cooking

tarry[1] (*pronounced* **ta**-ri) *verb* (**tarries, tarrying, tarried**) **1** to stay behind, linger **2** to be slow or late

tarry[2] (*pronounced* **tah**-ri) *adjective* like or covered with tar; sticky

tarsus *noun* **1** *anatomy* the seven bones forming the upper part of the foot and ankle **2** *biology* in insects: the extremity of a limb, usually a five-jointed foot ♦ **tarsal** *adjective*

tart *noun* a pie containing fruit, vegetables, etc ▸ *adjective* sharp, sour

tartan *noun* **1** fabric patterned with squares of different colours, traditionally used by Scottish Highland clans **2** one of these patterns: *Macdonald tartan* ▸ *adjective* with a pattern of tartan

tartar *noun* **1** a substance that gathers on the teeth **2** a difficult or demanding person **3** a substance that forms inside wine casks • **cream of tartar** a white powder obtained from the tartar from wine casks, used in baking

tartaric acid *noun, chemistry* an organic acid that occurs naturally in many fruits

tartar sauce or **tartare sauce** *noun* mayonnaise with chopped pickles, capers, etc, often served with fish

tartrazine *noun* a yellow powder used as an artificial colouring in foods, drugs and cosmetics

task *noun* a set piece of work to be done • **take to task** to scold, find fault with

taskbar *noun, computing* an area on a computer screen displaying details of all programs currently running

task force *noun* a group of people gathered together with the purpose of performing a special or specific task

taskmaster *noun* someone who sets and

supervises work, especially strictly: *a hard taskmaster*

tassel *noun* a hanging bunch of threads, used to decorate a hat, curtain, etc

taste *verb* 1 to try by eating or drinking a sample 2 to eat or drink some of: *Taste this soup* 3 to recognize (a flavour): *Can you taste the chilli in it?* 4 to have a particular flavour: *tasting of garlic* 5 to experience: *taste success* ➤ *noun* 1 the act or sense of tasting 2 a flavour 3 a small quantity of something 4 a liking: *taste for literature* 5 ability to judge what is suitable in behaviour, dress, etc, or what is fine or beautiful

taste bud *noun* one of the sensory organs on the surface of the tongue which identifies salt, sweet, sour (acid) and bitter

tasteful *adjective* showing good taste and judgement ♦ **tastefully** *adverb* ♦ **tastefulness** *noun*

tasteless *adjective* 1 without flavour 2 not tasteful; vulgar ♦ **tastelessly** *adverb*

tasty *adjective* (**tastier, tastiest**) having a good flavour

tattered *adjective* ragged

tatters *plural noun* torn, ragged pieces

tattie *noun, Scottish* a potato

tattle *noun* gossip ➤ *verb* to chat or gossip

tattoo *noun* 1 a coloured design on the skin, made by pricking with needles 2 a drumbeat 3 an outdoor military display with music etc ➤ *verb* (**tattooing, tattooed**) to prick coloured designs into the skin

⊙ From a Dutch term meaning to shut off beer taps at closing time, later applied to a military drumbeat at the end of the day

tattooed *adjective* marked with tattoos

tatty *adjective* (**tattier, tattiest**) shabby, tawdry

taught past form of **teach**

taunt *verb* to tease or jeer at unkindly ➤ *noun* a jeer

⊙ Originally a phrase *taunt for taunt*, based on the French *tant pour tant* meaning 'tit for tat'

Taurus *noun* 1 the second sign of the zodiac, represented by the bull 2 someone born under this sign, between 21 April and 20 May

taut *adjective* 1 pulled tight 2 tense, strained

tauten *verb* to make or become tight

tautology *noun* a form of repetition in which the same thing is said in different ways, eg 'he looked *anxious* and *worried*'

tavern *noun, old* a public house, an inn

tawdry *adjective* (**tawdrier, tawdriest**) cheap-looking and gaudy

⊙ From *St Audrey's lace*, once used to make cheap lace neckties

tawny *adjective* (**tawnier, tawniest**) yellowish-brown

tax *noun* (*plural* **taxes**) 1 a charge made by the government on income, certain types of goods, etc 2 a strain, a burden: *severe tax on my patience* ➤ *verb* 1 to make to pay a tax 2 to put a strain on: *taxing her strength* • **tax with** to accuse of

taxation *noun* 1 the act or system of taxing 2 taxes

taxi *noun* (*plural* **taxis**) a vehicle which may be hired, with a driver (*also called:* **taxi-cab**) ➤ *verb* (**taxiing, taxied**) 1 to travel in a taxi 2 of an aeroplane: to travel on the runway before or after take-off

taxidermist *noun* someone who prepares and stuffs the skins of dead animals

taxidermy *noun* the art of preparing and stuffing the skins of animals to make them lifelike

taxis *noun, biology* the movement of a single cell in response to a stimulus

taxonomy *noun, biology* describing, naming and classifying organisms on the basis of the similarity of their features and structures etc ♦ **taxonomic** *adjective*

taxpayer *noun* someone who pays taxes

TB *abbreviation* tuberculosis, an infectious disease of humans and animals, characterized by the formation of swellings, especially in the lungs

Tb *symbol, chemistry* terbium

tbsp *abbreviation* tablespoon or tablespoonful

Tc *symbol, chemistry* technetium

TCP/IP *abbreviation, computing* Transmission Control Protocol/Internet Protocol, rules controlling how data is sent on the Internet

Te *symbol, chemistry* tellurium

te or **ti** *noun, music* in sol-fa notation: the seventh note of the major scale

tea *noun* 1 a plant grown in India, China, etc, or its dried and prepared leaves 2 a drink made by infusing its dried leaves 3 a hot drink, an infusion: *beef tea/camomile tea* 4 an afternoon or early evening meal: *What's for tea?*

teabag *noun* a small sachet of tea to which boiling water is added

teacake *noun* a light, flat bun

teach *verb* (**teaching, taught**) 1 to give (someone) skill or knowledge 2 to give knowledge of, or training in (a subject): *She teaches French* 3 to be a teacher: *decide to teach*

teacher *noun* someone employed to teach others in a school, or in a particular subject: *guitar teacher*

tea chest *noun* a tall box of thin wood used to pack tea for export, often used as a packing case when empty

teaching *noun* 1 the work of a teacher 2

guidance, instruction **3** (**teachings**) beliefs or rules of conduct that are preached or taught

teacup *noun* a medium-sized cup for drinking tea

teak *noun* **1** a hardwood tree from the East Indies **2** its very hard wood **3** a type of African tree

teal *noun* **1** a small water bird like a duck **2** a dark greenish-blue colour

team *noun* **1** a group of people working together **2** a side in a game: *a football team* **3** two or more animals working together: *team of oxen* • **team up with** to join together with, join forces with ⓈComes from Old English *team* meaning 'child-bearing', 'brood' or 'team'

⚠ Do not confuse with: **teem**

teamwork *noun* co-operation between those who are working together on a task

teapot *noun* a pot with a spout, for making and pouring tea

tear¹ (*pronounced* teer) *noun* **1** a drop of liquid from the eye **2** (**tears**) grief • **in tears** weeping

tear² (*pronounced* teir) *verb* (**tearing, tore, torn**) **1** to pull with force: *tear apart/tear down* **2** to make a hole or split in (material etc) **3** to hurt deeply **4** *informal* to rush: *tearing off down the road* ➤ *noun* a hole or split made by tearing

tearaway *noun, informal* an undisciplined young person

tearful *adjective* **1** inclined to weep **2** in tears, crying ♦ **tearfully** *adverb*

tear gas *noun* gas which causes the eyes to stream with tears

tease *verb* **1** to annoy, irritate on purpose **2** to pretend to upset or annoy for fun: *I'm only teasing* **3** to untangle (wool etc) with a comb **4** to sort out (a problem or puzzle) ➤ *noun* someone who teases

teasel *noun* a type of prickly plant

teaser *noun* a problem, a puzzle

teaspoon *noun* **1** a small spoon used for tea etc **2** (*abbrev* **tsp**) the amount a teaspoon will hold (approximately 5ml), used as a measure in cookery (*also called*: **teaspoonful**)

teat *noun* **1** the part of an animal through which milk passes to its young **2** a rubber object shaped like this attached to a baby's feeding bottle

tea towel *noun* a cloth for drying dishes

techn- see **techno-**

technetium *noun, chemistry* (symbol **Tc**) a radioactive metallic element

technical *adjective* **1** relating to a particular art or skill, especially a mechanical or industrial one: *What is the technical term for this?/a technical expert* **2** according to strict laws or rules: *technical defeat*

technical drawing *noun* the drawing of plans, machinery, etc for business and industry

technicality *noun* (*plural* **technicalities**) a technical detail or point

technically *adverb* according to the rules, strictly speaking

technician *noun* someone trained in the practical side of an art, or who does the practical work in a laboratory etc

technique *noun* the way in which a process is carried out; a method

techno *noun* a style of popular music which uses electronic effects

techno- or **techn-** *prefix* **1** forms words relating to the art or craft involved in doing something: *technical* **2** of or relating to technology ⓈComes from Greek *techne* meaning 'skill'

technological *adjective* relating to or involving technology ♦ **technologically** *adverb*: *a technologically advanced country*

technologist *noun* a person skilled in technology and its applications

technology *noun* **1** science applied to practical (especially industrial) purposes **2** the practical skills of a particular civilization, period, etc

technophobe *noun* someone who dislikes and tries to avoid using technology

tectonic *adjective* **1** to do with building **2** relating to the earth's crust and the movements that change it

tectonic plate *noun* one of the rigid sections forming the earth's crust (*often shortened to*: **plate**)

tectonics *singular noun* the study of the earth's crust and the forces that change it (*see also*: **plate tectonics**)

teddy¹ *noun* (*plural* **teddies**) a stuffed toy bear (*full form*: **teddy bear**)

Ⓢ Named after the American President *Teddy* Roosevelt (1868–1919), who was well-known as a bear hunter

teddy² *noun* (*plural* **teddies**) a one-piece woman's undergarment

tedious *adjective* long and tiresome ♦ **tediously** *adverb*

tedium *noun* boredom: *the endless tedium of dinner with his boring relations*

tee *noun* **1** the square of level ground from which a golf ball is driven **2** the peg or heap of sand on which the ball is placed for driving • **tee up** to place (a ball) on a tee

teem *verb* **1** to be full: *teeming with people* **2** to rain heavily ⓈMeaning 1: comes from Old English *tieman*, related to the word *team*; meaning 2: comes from Old Norse *tema* meaning 'to empty'

⚠ Do not confuse with: **team**

teenage *adjective* suitable for, or typical of, those in their teens

teenager *noun* someone in their teens

teens *plural noun* the years of age from thirteen to nineteen

teeny *adjective* (**teenier, teeniest**) *informal* tiny, minute

tee-shirt or **T-shirt** *noun* a short-sleeved top pulled on over the head

teeter *verb* 1 to wobble 2 to hesitate

teeth plural of **tooth**

teethe *verb* of a baby: to grow its first teeth
♦ **teething** *noun*

teething troubles or **teething problems** *plural noun* problems in the early stages of a project, with a new piece of machinery, etc

teetotal *adjective* never drinking alcohol

teetotaller *noun* a person who never drinks alcohol

Teflon *noun, trademark* a non-stick coating used eg on cooking pans

tele- *prefix* at a distance: *television/telegram* (= a message sent over a long distance) ⊙ Comes from Greek *tele* meaning 'far'

telebanking *noun* a system which enables banking transactions to be carried out over the telephone

telecommunications *singular noun* the sending of information over a distance by telephone, radio, television, etc

telecommuting *noun* the use of telecommunications, eg via a computer network such as the Internet, to work outside the normal office or workplace

teleconferencing *noun* the system by which people in different places can meet through video, audio and computer links

telecottage *noun* an office building in a rural area equipped with computers etc

telegram *noun* a message sent by telegraph

telegraph *noun* an instrument for sending messages to a place at a distance using electrical impulses ➤ *verb* to send (a message) by telegraph

telegraphic *adjective* 1 of a telegraph 2 short, brief, concise

telekinesis *noun* the supposed ability to move objects from a distance using willpower and no physical contact

telemetry *noun* receiving and sending data by means of electrical or radio signals ♦ **telemetric** *adjective*

telepathic *adjective* relating to or involving telepathy

telepathy *noun* the supposed ability of people to communicate without using sight, hearing, etc

telephone *noun* (short form **phone**) an instrument for speaking over distances, which uses an electric current travelling along a wire, or radio waves ➤ *verb* to send (a message) by telephone

telephonist *noun* an operator on a telephone switchboard

telephoto *adjective* of a lens: used to photograph enlarged images of distant objects

teleprinter *noun* a typewriter which receives and prints out messages sent by telegraph

telesales *noun* the selling of goods or services by telephone

telescope *noun* a tubular instrument fitted with lenses which magnify distant objects ➤ *verb* 1 to push or fit together so that one thing slides inside another 2 to force together, compress
♦ **telescopic** *adjective*: *a telescopic umbrella*

teletext *noun* news and general information transmitted by television companies, viewable only on special television sets

televise *verb* to broadcast on television: *Are they televising the football match?*

television *noun* 1 the reproduction on a small screen of pictures sent from a distance 2 an apparatus for receiving these pictures

teleworking *noun* working at home, communicating with the office by telephone, computer link, etc ♦ **teleworker** *noun*

telex *noun* 1 the sending of messages by means of teleprinters 2 a message sent in this way

tell *verb* (**telling, told**) 1 to say or express in words: *She's telling the truth* 2 to give the facts of (a story) 3 to inform, give information: *Can you tell me when it's 9 o'clock?* 4 to order, command: *Tell him to go away!* 5 to make out, distinguish: *I can't tell one wine from the other* 6 to give away a secret: *promise not to tell* 7 to be effective, produce results: *Training will tell in the end* • **all told** altogether, counting all • **tell off** *informal* to scold • **tell on** 1 to have an effect on 2 to give information about: *Your sister told on you*

teller *noun* 1 a bank clerk who receives and pays out money 2 someone who counts votes at an election

telling *adjective* having a marked effect: *telling remark*

tell-tale *noun* someone who spreads gossip about others ➤ *adjective* revealing: *tell-tale signs of illness*

tellurium *noun, chemistry* (symbol **Te**) a brittle silvery-white element

telly *noun* (*plural* **tellies**), *informal* (a) television

telophase *noun, biology* the final stage of cell division, resulting in the production of two daughter nuclei

temerity *noun* rashness, boldness

temp *abbreviation* 1 temperature 2 temporary ➤ *noun, informal* a temporarily employed worker ▸ *verb, informal* to work as a temp

temper *noun* **1** habitual state of mind: *of an even temper* **2** a passing mood: *in a good temper* **3** a tendency to get angry easily: *has a bit of a temper* **4** a fit of anger: *flew into a temper* **5** the amount of hardness in metal, glass, etc ▸ *verb* **1** to bring (metal) to the right degree of hardness by heating and cooling **2** to make less severe • **lose your temper** to show anger

temperament *noun* someone's nature as it affects the way they feel and act; disposition

temperamental *adjective* **1** of temperament **2** excitable, emotional

temperance *noun* the habit of not drinking much (or any) alcohol

temperate *adjective* **1** moderate in temper, eating or drinking, etc **2** of climate: neither very hot nor very cold **3** located between the tropics and the polar circles, where the climate is temperate

temperature *noun* **1** degree of heat or cold: *today's temperature* **2** a body heat higher than normal: *has got a temperature*

temperature inversion *noun* an increase in air temperature corresponding to increasing height in the troposphere, so that the lowest temperatures are closer to the ground

temperature range *noun* a measure of how much temperature can vary in a given area, gained by subtracting the minimum from the maximum recorded temperature

tempest *noun* a storm, with strong winds

tempestuous *adjective* **1** very stormy and windy **2** passionate, violently emotional

template *noun* **1** a thin plate cut in a design for drawing round **2** any model from which others are produced, eg a document **3** *biology* the coded instructions in a molecule for the formation of a new molecule of the same type

temple¹ *noun* a building used for public worship; a church

temple² *noun* a small flat area on each side of the forehead

tempo *noun* (*plural* **tempos** or **tempi**) **1** the speed at which music is played **2** the speed or rate of an activity

temporary *adjective* lasting only for a time, not permanent

temporize or **temporise** *verb* to avoid or delay taking action in order to gain time

tempt *verb* **1** to try to persuade or entice **2** to attract **3** to make inclined (to): *tempted to phone him*

temptation *noun* **1** the act of tempting **2** the feeling of being tempted **3** something which tempts

tempting *adjective* attractive

ten *noun* the number 10 ▸ *adjective* 10 in number

tenable *adjective* able to be defended; justifiable

tenacious *adjective* **1** keeping a firm hold or grip **2** obstinate, persistent, determined ♦ **tenaciously** *adverb*

tenacity *noun* persistence, determination

tenancy *noun* (*plural* **tenancies**) **1** the holding of a house, farm, etc by a tenant **2** the period of this holding

tenant *noun* someone who pays rent for the use of a house, land, etc

tend *verb* **1** to be likely or inclined to do something: *These flowers tend to wilt* **2** to move or slope in a certain direction **3** to take care of, look after

tendency *noun* (*plural* **tendencies**) a leaning or inclination (towards): *tendency to daydream*

tender *adjective* **1** soft, not hard or tough **2** easily hurt or damaged **3** hurting when touched **4** loving, gentle ▸ *verb* **1** to offer (a resignation etc) formally **2** to make a formal offer for a job ▸ *noun* **1** an offer to take on work, supply goods, etc for a fixed price **2** a small boat that carries stores for a large one **3** a truck for coal and water attached to a steam engine • **legal tender** coins or notes which must be accepted when offered • **of tender years** very young

tenderize or **tenderise** *verb* to make (meat) tender by pounding, marinating, etc

tendinitis or **tendonitis** *noun, medicine* inflammation of a tendon

tendon *noun* a tough cord joining a muscle to a bone

tendril *noun* **1** a thin curling stem of a climbing plant which attaches itself to a support **2** a curling strand of hair etc

tenement *noun* a large block of flats

tenet *noun* a belief, opinion

tenner *noun, informal* a ten-pound note; ten pounds

tennis *noun* a game for two or four players using rackets to hit a ball to each other over a net

tennis court *noun* a place made level and prepared for tennis

tenon *noun* a projecting part at the end of a piece of wood made to fit a **mortise** to form a strong joint

tenor *noun* **1** *music* a male singing voice between baritone and alto **2** *music* a singer with such a voice **3** the general course: *the even tenor of country life* **4** general meaning: *the tenor of the speech*

tenpin bowling *noun* a game like skittles played by bowling a ball at ten pins standing at the end of a bowling lane

tense¹ *noun, grammar* the form of a verb that

shows time of action, eg *'I was'* (**past tense**), *'I am'* (**present tense**), *'I shall be'* (**future tense**)

tense² *adjective* **1** tightly stretched **2** nervous, strained: *feeling tense/tense with excitement*

tensile *adjective* **1** able to be stretched **2** relating to stretching or tension

tensile strength *noun, physics* a measure of the ability of a material to resist tension, equal to the minimum stress needed to break it

tension *noun* **1** the state of being stretched **2** strain, anxiety **3** *physics* a force which causes a body to be stretched or elongated **4** *physics* electromotive force

tent *noun* a movable shelter of canvas or other material, supported by poles and pegged to the ground

tentacle *noun* a long thin flexible part of an animal used to feel or grasp, eg the arm of an octopus

tentative *adjective* **1** experimental, initial: *a tentative offer* **2** uncertain, hesitating: *tentative smile* ♦ **tentatively** *adverb*

tenterhooks *plural noun*: **on tenterhooks** uncertain and very anxious about what will happen

tenth *adjective* the last of ten items ➤ *noun* one of ten equal parts

tenuous *adjective* slight, weak: *tenuous connection*

tenure *noun* **1** the holding of property or a position of employment **2** the period, or terms or conditions, of this

tepee *noun* a traditional Native American tent made of animal skins

tepid *adjective* lukewarm

tequila (*pronounced* te-**kee**-la) *noun* a Mexican alcoholic drink obtained from the agave plant

teratoid *adjective, biology* resembling a monster

teratology *noun* the study of biological malformations or abnormal growths
♦ **teratological** *adjective* ♦ **teratologist** *noun*

terbium *noun, chemistry* (symbol **Tb**) a silvery metallic element

tercentenary (*pronounced* ter-sen-**tee**-nari) *noun* the three-hundredth year after an event, eg someone's birth

term *noun* **1** a length of time: *term of imprisonment* **2** a division of an academic or school year: *autumn term* **3** a word, an expression: *dictionary of computing terms* **4** (**terms**) the rules or conditions of an agreement: *What are their terms?* **5** (**terms**) fixed charges **6** (**terms**) footing, relationship: *on good terms with his neighbours* ➤ *verb* to name, call • **come to terms** to reach an agreement or understanding • **come to terms with** to

accept, be able to live with • **in terms of** from the point of view of

termagant *noun* a bad-tempered, noisy woman

terminal *adjective* **1** of or growing at the end: *terminal bud* **2** of an illness: fatal, incurable ➤ *noun* **1** an end **2** a point of connection in an electric circuit **3** a computer monitor connected to a network **4** a terminus **5** an airport building containing arrival and departure areas **6** a bus station in a town centre running a service to a nearby airport

terminal moraine *noun, geography* rocks and gravel left by a glacier at the point where the glacier melts

terminate *verb* to bring or come to an end

termination *noun* an act of ending or the state of being brought to an end

terminology *noun* the special words or expressions used in a particular art, science, etc

terminus *noun* (*plural* **termini** or **terminuses**) **1** the end **2** an end point on a railway, bus route, etc

termite *noun* a pale-coloured wood-eating insect, like an ant

tern *noun* a type of sea bird like a small gull

ternary form *noun, music* a musical form in which the first section is repeated after the second

-terr- of or relating to the earth or land: *terrestrial/subterranean* (= under the earth) ⊕ Comes from Latin *terra* meaning 'the earth' or 'land'

terrace *noun* **1** a raised level bank of earth **2** a raised flat place **3** a connected row of houses **4** (**terraces**) open areas rising in tiers around a sports ground, where spectators stand ➤ *verb* to form into a terrace or terraces

terracotta *noun* **1** a brownish-red mixture of clay and sand used for tiles, pottery, etc **2** a brownish-red colour

terra firma *noun* dry land as opposed to water or air; solid ground ⊕ Comes from Latin, meaning 'firm land'

terrain *noun* an area of land considered in terms of its physical features: *The terrain is a bit rocky*

terrapin *noun* a small turtle living in ponds or rivers

terrazzo *noun* a hard, shiny covering for concrete floors, eg in railway stations, consisting of marble chips set in cement and then polished

terrestrial *adjective* of or living on the earth

terrible *adjective* **1** causing great fear: *terrible sight* **2** causing great hardship or distress: *terrible disaster* **3** *informal* very bad: *a terrible writer*

terribly *adverb, informal* **1** badly: *sang terribly* **2** extremely: *terribly tired*

terrier *noun* a breed of small dog

terrific *adjective* **1** powerful, dreadful **2** huge, amazing **3** *informal* marvellous, enjoyable, etc: *a terrific party*

terrify *verb* (**terrifies, terrifying, terrified**) to frighten greatly

territorial *adjective* **1** of, belonging to a territory **2** of animals, birds: likely to establish and defend their own territory

territory *noun* (*plural* **territories**) **1** an area of land, a region **2** land under the control of a ruler or state **3** an area allocated to a salesman etc **4** a field of activity or interest

terror *noun* **1** very great fear **2** something which causes great fear **3** *informal* an uncontrollable child

terrorism *noun* the organized use of violence or intimidation for political or other ends

terrorist *noun* someone who practises terrorism

terrorize or **terrorise** *verb* to frighten very greatly

terry *noun* an absorbent fabric with tiny loops, used especially for towels ➤ *adjective* made of this fabric: *terry nappies*

terse *adjective* using few words; curt, brusque ◆ **tersely** *adverb*

tertiary *adjective* **1** third in position or order **2** denoting the extraction of petroleum by high-pressure pumping into rock structures **3** (**Tertiary**) of the geological period 65 million to 2 million years ago

tertiary education *noun* education at university or college level

tertiary industry *noun, geography* an industry concerned with providing services rather than production or extraction (*compare with*: **primary industry, secondary industry**)

tessellate *verb* of identical shapes: to fit together exactly, leaving no spaces between them ◆ **tessellation** *noun*

test *noun* **1** a short examination **2** something done to check soundness, reliability, etc: *ran tests on the new model* **3** a means of finding the presence of: *test for radioactivity* **4** an event that shows up a good or bad quality: *a test of courage* ➤ *verb* to carry out tests on

testa *noun* (*plural* **testae**), *biology* the hard outer covering of a seed

testament *noun* **1** a written statement of someone's wishes **2** a will ● **Old Testament** and **New Testament** the two main divisions of the Christian Bible

testator *noun* the writer of a will

testicle *noun* one of two sperm-producing glands enclosed in the male scrotum

testify *verb* (**testifies, testifying, testified**) **1** to give evidence in a law court **2** to make a solemn declaration of **3** (**testify to**) to show, give evidence of: *testifies to his ignorance*

testimonial *noun* **1** a personal statement about someone's character, abilities, etc **2** a gift given in thanks for services given

testimony *noun* (*plural* **testimonies**) **1** the statement made by someone who testifies **2** evidence

testis *noun* (*plural* **testes**) a testicle

test match *noun cricket* one of a series of five-day matches between two countries

testosterone *noun* the chief male sex hormone, secreted by the testicles

test pilot *noun* a pilot who tests new aircraft

test tube *noun* a glass tube closed at one end, used in chemical tests

testy *adjective* (**testier, testiest**) easily angered, irritable ◆ **testily** *adverb* ◆ **testiness** *noun*

tetanus *noun* a disease, caused especially by an infected wound, that can cause stiffening and spasms in the jaw muscles

tetchy *adjective* (**tetchier, tetchiest**) irritable, testy ◆ **tetchily** *adverb*

tête-à-tête (*pronounced* tet-a-**tet**) *noun* a private conversation between two people ⊙ Comes from French meaning literally 'head to head'

tether *noun* a rope or chain for tying an animal to restrict its movement ➤ *verb* **1** to tie with a tether **2** to limit the freedom of

tetrachloromethane *noun, chemistry* a toxic colourless pungent liquid, formerly used as a solvent, a dry-cleaning reagent and in certain types of fire-extinguisher

tetrahedron *noun* a solid body with four faces, all of which are polygons

tetrameter (*pronounced* tet-**ram**-et-er) *noun, poetry* a line of verse with four metrical feet

tetravalent *adjective, chemistry* of an atom: able to combine with four atoms of hydrogen

text *noun* **1** the main written part of a book, not the pictures, notes, etc **2** words or a piece of writing displayed on a computer screen **3** a printed or written version of a speech, play, etc **4** a Biblical passage used as the basis for a sermon **5** the subject matter of a speech, essay, etc **6** a text message ➤ *verb* to send a text message

textbook *noun* a book used for teaching, giving the main facts about a subject

textile *adjective* of weaving; woven ➤ *noun* a woven cloth or fabric

text message *noun* a short message typed into and sent by a mobile phone ◆ **text messaging** *noun*

textual *adjective* of or in a text

texture *noun* **1** the quality of cloth resulting from weaving: *loose texture* **2** the quality of a substance in terms of how it looks or feels: *rough*

texture/lumpy texture **3** the effect of the number of different sounds in a piece of music

Th symbol, chemistry thorium

thalamus noun (plural **thalami**), anatomy either of two egg-shaped masses of grey matter in the brain that relay sensory nerve impulses ☉ Comes from Greek thalamos meaning 'inner room'

thalidomide noun a drug formerly used as a sedative but withdrawn because it was found to cause malformation of the fetus if taken by pregnant women

thallium noun, chemistry (symbol **Tl**) a soft bluish-white metallic element

thallus noun (plural **thalluses** or **thalli**) in fungi, lichens and seaweeds: a flattened and sometimes branched structure that is not differentiated into stems, leaves and roots
♦ **thalloid** adjective

than conjunction & preposition used in comparisons: easier than I expected/better than usual

thane noun, history a noble who held land from the crown

thank verb to express gratitude to (someone) for a favour, gift, etc ● **thank you** or **thanks** a polite expression used to thank someone (see also **thanks**)

thankful adjective grateful; relieved and glad
♦ **thankfully** adverb: Thankfully, no-one was badly injured in the crash

thankless adjective neither worthwhile nor appreciated: thankless task

thanks plural noun gratitude; appreciation: You'll get no thanks for it ● **thanks to 1** with the help of: We arrived on time, thanks to our friends **2** owing to: We were late, thanks to our car breaking down

thanksgiving noun **1** a church service giving thanks to God **2** (**Thanksgiving**) US the fourth Thursday of November, a national holiday commemorating the first harvest of the Puritan settlers

that adjective & pronoun (plural **those**) used to point out a thing or person etc (contrasted with: **this**): that woman over there/Don't say that ➤ relative pronoun: the colours that he chose/ the man that I spoke to ➤ adverb to such an extent or degree: Why were you that late? ➤ conjunction **1** used in reporting speech: She said that she was there **2** used to connect clauses: I heard that you were ill

thatch noun straw etc used to make the roof of a house ➤ verb to cover with thatch

thaw verb **1** to melt **2** of frozen food: to defrost, become unfrozen **3** to become friendly ➤ noun **1** the melting of ice and snow by heat **2** a change in the weather that causes this

the adjective **1** referring to a particular person or thing: the boy in the park/I like the jacket you're wearing **2** referring to all or any of a general group: The horse is of great use to man

theatre or US **theater** noun **1** a place for the public performance of plays etc **2** a room in a hospital for surgical operations **3** the acting profession

theatrical adjective **1** of theatres or acting **2** over-dramatic, overdone

theatricality noun a theatrical quality

thee pronoun, old you as the object of a sentence

theft noun stealing

their adjective belonging to them: their car

❗ Do not confuse with: **there**.
Remember that the 'y' in the pronoun 'they' turns into an 'i' in **their** and that **there** is spelt the same as 'here' except for the first letter.

theirs pronoun belonging to them: The red car is theirs

them pronoun **1** people or things already spoken about (as the object of a verb): We've seen them **2** those: one of them over in the corner **3** used to avoid giving the gender of the person being referred to: If anyone phones, ask them to leave their number

theme noun **1** the subject of a discussion, essay, story, etc **2** music a main melody which is often repeated

theme park noun a large amusement park in which all the rides and attractions are based on a particular theme, eg outer space

theme song or **theme tune** noun a tune that is played at the beginning and end of a film, television series, etc

themselves pronoun **1** used reflexively: They tired themselves out walking **2** used for emphasis: They'll have to do it by themselves

then adverb **1** at that time: I didn't know you then **2** after that: And then where did you go? ➤ conjunction in that case, therefore: If you're busy, then don't come

thence adverb, old from that time or place

thenceforth adverb from that time onwards

theo- prefix forms words relating to God or gods: theology ☉ Comes from Greek theos meaning 'God' or 'a god'

theocracy noun government of a state according to religious laws

theocratic adjective relating to or involving theocracy

theologian noun someone who studies theology

theological adjective relating to or involving theology

theology noun the study of God and religion

theorem *noun* a proposition derived from premises, the truth of which can be established by a proof

theoretical *adjective* of theory, not experience or practice ♦ **theoretically** *adverb*: *It is theoretically possible to travel from Glasgow to Edinburgh in under one hour*

theorize or **theorise** *verb* to form theories

theory *noun* (*plural* **theories**) **1** an explanation that has not been proved or tested **2** the underlying ideas in an art, science, etc, compared to practice or performance

therapeutic *adjective* **1** of therapy **2** healing, curing

therapist *noun* someone who gives therapeutic treatment: *speech therapist*

therapy *noun* (*plural* **therapies**) treatment of disease or disorders

there *adverb* at, in or to that place: *What did you do there?* ➤ *pronoun* used (with *be*) as a subject of a sentence or clause when the real subject follows the verb: *There is nobody at home*

❗ Do not confuse with: **their**.
Remember that **there** is spelt the same as 'here' except for the first letter and that the 'y' in the pronoun 'they' turns into an 'i' in **their**.

thereabouts *adverb* approximately
thereafter *adverb* after that
thereby *adverb* by that means
therefore *adverb* for this or that reason
thereof *adverb* of that
thereupon *adverb* **1** because of this or that **2** immediately

therm *noun* a unit of heat used in measuring gas
thermal *adjective* **1** of heat **2** of hot springs

thermal imaging *noun* the visualization of people, things, etc in the dark by detecting and processing the infrared energy they emit

thermistor *noun, physics* a device with an electrical resistance that decreases as its temperature rises, used in electronic circuits for measuring or controlling temperature ⏱ A contraction of *thermal resistor*

thermo- or **therm-** *prefix* forms words relating to heat or temperature ⏱ Comes from Greek *therme* meaning 'heat', and *thermos* meaning 'hot'

thermocouple *noun* a device for measuring temperature, consisting of two different metallic conductors welded together at their ends

thermodynamics *singular noun* the science of the relation between heat and other forms of energy, especially mechanical energy

thermometer *noun* an instrument for measuring temperature

thermonuclear *adjective* relating to the fusion of nuclei at high temperatures

thermopile *noun, physics* a device consisting of several **thermocouple**s connected together, used to measure the intensity of thermal radiation

thermoplastic *noun, chemistry* a polymer that can be repeatedly softened and hardened, without any appreciable change in its properties, by heating and cooling it ➤ *adjective* having the properties of a thermoplastic

Thermos *noun, trademark* a kind of vacuum flask

thermostat *noun* a device for automatically controlling temperature in a room

thesaurus (*pronounced* the-**sor**-us) *noun* (*plural* **thesauri** or **thesauruses**) **1** a reference book listing words and their synonyms **2** a dictionary or encyclopedia

these see **this**

thesis *noun* (*plural* **theses**) **1** a long piece of written work on a topic, often part of a university degree **2** a statement of a point of view

thespian *noun, formal* an actor

⏱ Named after *Thespis*, founder of ancient Greek tragedy

they *pronoun* **1** some people or things already mentioned (used only as the subject of a verb): *They followed the others* **2** used to avoid giving the gender of the person being referred to: *Anyone can come if they like*

they'd *short for* they would
they'll *short for* they will
they're *short for* they are
they've *short for* they have

thiamine *noun* vitamin B_1

thick *adjective* **1** not thin, of reasonable width: *a thick slice/two metres thick* **2** of a mixture: containing solid matter, stiff: *a thick soup* **3** dense, difficult to see or pass through: *thick fog/thick woods* **4** of speech: not clear **5** *informal* stupid **6** *informal* very friendly ➤ *noun* the thickest, most crowded or active part: *in the thick of the fight*

thicken *verb* to make or become thick

thicket *noun* a group of close-set trees and bushes

thickness *noun* **1** the quality of being thick **2** the distance between opposite sides **3** a layer

thickset *adjective* **1** closely set or planted **2** having a thick sturdy body

thick-skinned *adjective* not sensitive or easily hurt

thief *noun* (*plural* **thieves**) someone who steals

thieve *verb* to steal

thieving *noun* stealing ➤ *adjective* that thieves

thievish *adjective* inclined to stealing

thigh *noun* the thick, fleshy part of the leg between the knee and the hip

thimble *noun* a small cap worn over a fingertip, used to push a needle while sewing

thin *adjective* (**thinner, thinnest**) **1** not very wide between its two sides: *thin paper/thin slice* **2** slim, not fat **3** not dense or crowded: *thin population* **4** poor in quality: *thin wine* **5** of a voice: weak, not resonating **6** of a mixture: not stiff, watery: *a thin soup* ➤ *verb* (**thinning, thinned**) to make or become thin or thinner ♦ **thinness** *noun*

thine *adjective, old* belonging to you (used before words beginning with a vowel or a vowel sound): *thine enemies* ➤ *pronoun, old* something belonging to you: *My heart is thine*

thing *noun* **1** an object that is not living **2** *informal* a person: *a nice old thing* **3** (**things**) belongings **4** an individual object, quality, idea, etc that may be referred to: *Several things must be taken into consideration* ℗ Comes from Old English and Old Norse *thing* meaning 'parliament' or 'object'

think *verb* (**thinking, thought**) **1** to work things out, reason **2** to form ideas in the mind **3** to believe, judge or consider: *I think that we should go* **4** (**think of doing something**) to intend to do it: *She is thinking of resigning* • **think better of** to change your mind about • **think highly of** or **think much of** to have a good opinion of • **think nothing of 1** to have a poor opinion of **2** to consider as easy • **think out** to work out in the mind ℗ Comes from Old English *thencan*

think tank *noun* a group of people who give expert advice and come up with ideas

thinner *noun* a liquid that is added to paint or varnish to dilute it

third *adjective* the last of a series of three ➤ *noun* one of three equal parts

third-class *adjective* of the class or rank next (especially in quality) after second

third degree *noun* prolonged and intensive interrogation ➤ *adjective* (**third-degree**), *medicine* denoting the most severe type of burn, in which there is damage to the lower layers of skin tissue

third party *noun, law* someone who is indirectly involved in a legal action or contract ➤ *adjective* (**third-party**) of insurance: covering damage done by or injury done to someone other than the insured person

third person *noun, grammar* a class into which pronouns and verb forms fall, denoting a person or people who are neither the speaker or writer nor those the speaker or narrator is addressing (eg *she* and *them*) ♦ **third-person** *adjective*

Third Reich (*pronounced* raikh) *noun, history* Germany as an empire under the dictatorship of the Nazi regime from 1933 to 1945

Third World see **Developing World**

thirst *noun* **1** a dry feeling in the mouth caused by lack of fluid **2** an eager desire (for): *thirst for knowledge* ➤ *verb* **1** to feel thirsty **2** (**thirst for something**) to desire it eagerly

thirsty *adjective* (**thirstier, thirstiest**) **1** needing or wanting to drink **2** of earth: parched, dry **3** eager (for)

thirteen *noun* the number 13 ➤ *adjective* 13 in number

thirteenth *adjective* the last of a series of thirteen ➤ *noun* one of thirteen equal parts

thirties *plural noun* (also **30s, 30's**) **1** the period of time between thirtieth and fortieth birthdays **2** the range of temperatures between thirty and forty degrees **3** the period of time between the thirtieth and fortieth years of a century

thirtieth *adjective* the last of a series of thirty ➤ *noun* one of thirty equal parts

thirty *noun* the number 30 ➤ *adjective* 30 in number

this *adjective & pronoun* (*plural* **these**) **1** used to point out someone or something, especially one nearby (*contrasted with:* **that**): *Look at this letter/Take this instead* **2** to such an extent or degree: *this early*

thistle *noun* a prickly plant with purple flowers

thistledown *noun* the feathery bristles of the seeds of the thistle

thither *adverb* to that place

-thon see **-athon**

thong *noun* **1** a thin strap of leather to fasten anything **2** the lash of a whip **3** a skimpy undergarment with a very narrow piece of material that goes between the buttocks

thorax *noun* (*plural* **thoraxes** or **thoraces**) **1** the chest in the human or animal body **2** the middle section of an insect's body

thorium *noun, chemistry* (symbol **Th**) a radioactive metallic element used in X-ray tubes and in some nuclear reactors

℗ Named after *Thor*, Norse god of thunder

thorn *noun* **1** a sharp prickle sticking out from the stem of a plant **2** a bush with thorns, especially the hawthorn • **thorn in the flesh** a cause of constant irritation

thorny *adjective* (**thornier, thorniest**) **1** full of thorns; prickly **2** difficult, causing arguments: *a thorny problem*

thorough *adjective* **1** complete, absolute: *a thorough muddle* **2** very careful, attending to every detail: *a thorough search*

thoroughbred *noun* an animal of pure breed

thoroughfare *noun* **1** a public street **2** a passage or way through: *no thoroughfare*

thoroughly *adverb* **1** completely, absolutely: *I*

thoroughly agree **2** very carefully: *The product has been tested thoroughly*

those see **that**

thou *pronoun, old* you (as the subject of a sentence)

though *conjunction* although: *Though he disliked it, he ate it all* ➤ *adverb, informal* however: *I wish I'd never said it, though*

thought *noun* **1** the act of thinking **2** something which you think, an idea **3** an opinion **4** consideration: *after much thought* ➤ *verb* past form of **think** ⊙ Noun: comes from Old English *thoht/gethoht*, past participle of *thencan* meaning 'to think'; verb past form: comes from Old English *thohte*, past tense of *thencan* meaning 'to think'

thoughtful *adjective* **1** full of thought **2** thinking of others, considerate

thoughtless *adjective* showing lack of thought; inconsiderate

thousand *noun* the number 1000 ➤ *adjective* 1000 in number

thousandth *adjective* the last of a series of a thousand ➤ *noun* one of a thousand equal parts

thrall (*pronounced* thrawl) *noun* **1** someone who is in the power of another; a slave **2** (also **thraldom** or **thralldom**) the state of being in the power of another person or thing: *held in thrall by her beauty* ⊙ Comes from Anglo-Saxon *thræl*

thrash *verb* **1** to beat severely **2** to move or toss violently (about) **3** to thresh (grain) • **thrash out** to discuss (a problem etc) thoroughly

thrashing *noun* a flogging, a beating

thread *noun* **1** a very thin strand of cotton, wool, silk, etc, often twisted and drawn out **2** the ridge which goes in a spiral round a screw **3** a connected series of details in correct order in a story ➤ *verb* **1** to put a thread through a needle etc **2** to make (your way) in a narrow space

threadbare *adjective* of clothes: worn thin

threadworm *noun* a parasitic worm which lives in the large intestine of humans

threat *noun* **1** a warning that you intend to hurt or punish someone **2** a warning of something bad that may come: *a threat of war* **3** something likely to cause harm: *a threat to our plans*

threaten *verb* **1** to make a threat: *threatened to kill himself* **2** to suggest the approach of something unpleasant **3** to be a danger to

three *noun* the number 3 ➤ *adjective* 3 in number ⊙ Comes from Old English *threo*

3-D short for **three-dimensional**

three-dimensional *adjective* having height, width and depth (*short form* **3-D**)

threefold *adjective & adverb* (by) three times as much

three-point turn *noun* a manoeuvre, usually

in three movements, in which a driver turns a vehicle around to face in the opposite direction

thresh *verb* to beat out (grain) from straw

threshold *noun* **1** a piece of wood or stone under the door of a building **2** a doorway **3** an entry or beginning: *on the threshold of a new era* **4** *biology* the minimum of a stimulus (eg pain) that produces a response **5** *physics* the minimum value of a quantity that is needed for a specified effect

threw past tense of **throw**

thrice *adverb* three times

thrift *noun* careful management of money in order to save

thrifty *adjective* (**thriftier, thriftiest**) careful about spending

thrill *noun* **1** an excited feeling **2** quivering, vibration ➤ *verb* **1** to feel excitement **2** to make excited

thriller *noun* an exciting story, often about crime and detection

thrilling *adjective* very exciting

thrive *verb* **1** to grow strong and healthy **2** to get on well, be successful

throat *noun* **1** the back part of the mouth **2** the front part of the neck

throaty *adjective* (**throatier, throatiest**) of a voice: deep and hoarse

throb *verb* (**throbbing, throbbed**) **1** of a pulse etc: to beat, especially more strongly than normal **2** to beat or vibrate rhythmically and regularly

throes *plural noun* great suffering or struggle • **in the throes of** in the middle of (a struggle, doing a task, etc)

thrombosis *noun, medicine* damage to the lining of a blood vessel, and the forming of a clot

thrombus *noun* (*plural* **thrombi** – *pronounced* **throm**-bai), *medicine* a blood clot which forms in an artery or vein, blocking circulation and potentially causing a stroke

throne *noun* **1** the seat of a monarch or bishop **2** a monarch or their power

throng *noun* a crowd ➤ *verb* **1** to move in a crowd **2** to crowd, fill (a place): *Revellers thronged the streets*

throttle *noun* the part of an engine through which steam or petrol can be turned on or off ➤ *verb* to choke by gripping the throat

through *preposition* **1** entering from one direction and going out in the other: *through the tunnel* **2** from end to end, or side to side, of: *all through the performance* **3** by way of: *related through his grandmother* **4** as a result of: *through his expertise* **5** *US* from (one date) to (another) inclusive: *Monday through Friday is five days* ➤ *adverb* into and out, from beginning to end: *all the way through the tunnel* ➤ *adjective* **1** without break or change: *through train* **2** *informal* finished: *Are you through with the newspaper?* **3** of a telephone call: connected: *I couldn't get through this morning*

through-and-through *adverb* completely, entirely: *a gentleman through-and-through*

through flow *noun, geography* sideways movement of water through soil, towards a river

throughout *preposition* **1** in all parts of: *throughout Europe* **2** from start to finish of: *throughout the journey*

throw *verb* (**throwing, threw, thrown**) **1** to send through the air with force **2** of a horse: to make (a rider) fall to the ground **3** to shape (pottery) on a wheel **4** to give (a party) **5** to have or suffer: *throw a fit* ➤ *noun* **1** the act of throwing **2** the distance a thing is thrown: *within a stone's throw of the house* **3** a decorative fabric covering a sofa, chair, etc • **throw away 1** to get rid of **2** to fail to take advantage of • **throw in 1** to include something as part of a deal at no extra cost **2** *sport* to return (the ball) to play by throwing it from the sideline

throwaway *adjective* **1** meant to be thrown away after use **2** of a remark: said casually or carelessly

throwback *noun* a reversion to an earlier form

throw-in *noun, sport* in football, basketball, etc: an act of throwing the ball back into play from a sideline

thrush *noun* **1** (*plural* **thrushes**) a type of singing bird with a speckled breast **2** an infection which can affect the mouth, throat or vagina

thrust *verb* (**thrusting, thrust**) **1** to push with force **2** to make a sudden push forward with a pointed weapon • **thrust something on** or **upon someone** to force someone to accept something ➤ *noun* **1** a stab **2** the force produced by an engine that propels an aircraft or rocket forward

thud *noun* a dull, hollow sound like that made by a heavy body falling ➤ *verb* (**thudding, thudded**) to move or fall with such a sound

thug *noun* a violent, brutal person

thulium *noun, chemistry* (symbol **Tm**) a silvery-white metallic element that is used as a source of X-rays

⊙ From Latin *Thule*, a region thought to be the most northerly in the world

thumb *noun* the short, thick finger on the side of the hand ➤ *verb* to turn over (the pages of a book) with the thumb or fingers • **rule of thumb** a rough-and-ready practical method • **thumbs down** or **thumbs up** a sign showing disapproval, or approval, of something • **under someone's thumb** under their control

thumbnail *noun* **1** the nail on the thumb **2**

(usually **thumbnail sketch**) a brief and concise outline or sketch **3** *computing* a miniature version of a graphic image

thumbscrew *noun, history* an instrument of torture which worked by squashing the thumbs

thump *noun* a heavy blow ➤ *verb* **1** to beat heavily **2** to move or fall with a dull, heavy noise

thunder *noun* **1** the deep, rumbling sound heard after a flash of lightning **2** any loud, rumbling noise ➤ *verb* **1** to produce the sound of, or a sound like, thunder **2** to shout out angrily

thunderbolt *noun* **1** a flash of lightning followed by thunder **2** a very great and sudden surprise

thunderclap *noun* a sudden roar of thunder

thunderous *adjective* **1** like thunder, very loud: *thunderous applause* **2** very angry

thunderstruck *adjective* overcome by surprise

thundery *adjective* of weather: sultry, bringing thunder

Thursday *noun* the fifth day of the week

⊙ After *Thor*, the Norse god of thunder

thus *adverb* **1** in this or that manner: *Thread the shuttle thus* **2** to this degree or extent: *thus far* **3** because of this, therefore: *Thus, we must go on*

thwart *verb* **1** to hinder (someone) from carrying out a plan, intention, etc **2** to prevent (an attempt etc) ➤ *noun* a seat for a rower that lies across a boat

thy *adjective, old* belonging to you: *thy wife and children*

thyme *noun* a small sweet-smelling herb used for seasoning food

thymus *noun* (*plural* **thymuses** or **thymi**), *anatomy* (*full form:* **thymus gland**) a gland just above the heart, which plays an important role in the development of the immune response

thyroid *noun, anatomy* (*full form:* **thyroid gland**) a large gland in the neck which secretes hormones controlling growth and metabolic rate

⊙ Based on a Greek word meaning 'door-shaped', because of the shape of the cartilage in the front of the throat

Ti *symbol, chemistry* titanium

ti same as **te**

tiara *noun* a jewelled ornament for the head like a crown

tibia *noun* the innermost of the two bones in the human leg between the knee and ankle

tic *noun* a twitching motion of certain muscles, especially of the face

tick[1] *noun* **1** a mark (✓) used to show something is correct or to mark off items on a list **2** a small quick noise, made regularly by a clock or watch **3**

informal a moment: *I'll just be a tick* ➤ *verb* **1** to mark with a tick **2** of a clock etc: to produce regular ticks

tick² *noun* a tiny blood-sucking animal

ticker *noun, slang* the heart

ticket *noun* **1** a card entitling the holder to admittance to a show, travel on public transport, etc **2** a notice that a traffic offence has been committed **3** a label on an item showing price, size, etc • **just the ticket** exactly what is required

ticking *noun* **1** the noise made by a clock etc **2** a strong coarse cotton fabric used to cover mattresses etc

tickle *verb* **1** to excite the surface nerves of a part of the body by touching lightly **2** to please or amuse

ticklish *adjective* **1** sensitive to tickling **2** not easy to deal with: *ticklish problem*

tickly *adjective* (**ticklier, tickliest**) ticklish

tidal *adjective* of the tide

tidal wave *noun* an enormous wave in the sea often caused by an earthquake etc

tiddler *noun, informal* **1** a small fish **2** a small person or thing

tiddly *adjective* (**tiddlier, tiddliest**) *Brit informal* slightly drunk

tiddlywinks *singular noun* a game in which small plastic discs (**tiddlywinks**) are flipped into a cup

tide *noun* **1** the rise and fall of the sea which happens regularly twice each day **2** *old* time, season: *Christmastide* • **tide over** to help to get over a difficulty for a time: *He lent me £50 to tide me over till pay day*

tidemark *noun* **1** a mark showing the highest level that the tide has reached or usually reaches **2** *Brit informal* a mark left on a bath which shows how high it was filled **3** *Brit informal* a dirty mark on the skin which shows the limit of washing

tidings *plural noun* news

tidy *adjective* (**tidier, tidiest**) **1** in good order, neat **2** *informal* fairly big: *a tidy sum of money* ➤ *verb* (**tidies, tidying, tidied**) to make neat ♦ **tidily** *adverb*

tie *verb* (**ties, tying, tied**) **1** to fasten with a cord, string, etc **2** to knot or put a bow in (string, shoelaces, etc) **3** to join, unite **4** to limit, restrict: *tied to a tight schedule* **5** to score the same number of points (in a game etc), draw ➤ *noun* **1** a band of fabric worn round the neck, especially by men, tied with a knot or bow at the front **2** something that connects: *ties of friendship* **3** something that restricts or limits **4** an equal score in a competition **5** a game or match to be played

tie-break or **tie-breaker** *noun* an extra

question or part of a tied contest to decide a winner

tie-dye *noun* a technique of dyeing fabrics in which some parts of the fabric are tied tightly to stop them absorbing the dye, producing a swirly pattern ➤ *verb* to dye like this

tie-in *noun* a product that is put on sale at the same time as something else happens, eg a computer game to coincide with the release of a film

tier (*pronounced* teer) *noun* a row of seats in a theatre etc, with others above or below it

tiff *noun* a slight quarrel

tig another name for **tag**

tiger *noun* a large animal of the cat family with a tawny coat striped with black

tight *adjective* **1** packed closely **2** firmly stretched, not loose **3** fitting too closely: *These jeans are a bit tight* **4** *informal* mean with money **5** *informal* drunk

tighten *verb* to make or become tight or tighter

tight-fisted *adjective* stingy

tight-knit or **tightly-knit** *adjective* closely organized or united: *a tight-knit community*

tight-lipped *adjective* uncommunicative

tightrope *noun* a tightly stretched rope on which acrobats perform

tights *plural noun* a close-fitting garment covering the feet, legs and body as far as the waist

tigress *noun* a female tiger

tilde (*pronounced* til-da) *noun* a mark (˜) placed over *n* in Spanish to show that it is pronounced *ny* (eg in Señor) and over *a* and *o* in Portuguese to show that they are nasalized

tile *noun* a piece of baked clay, linoleum, etc used in covering floors or roofs ➤ *verb* to cover with tiles

till¹ *noun* a container or drawer for money in a shop ➤ *verb* to cultivate (land); plough

till² see **until**

tiller *noun* the handle of a boat's rudder

tilt *verb* **1** to fall into, or place in, a sloping position **2** to joust (**tilt at**) to attack someone on horseback, using a lance ➤ *noun* **1** a slant **2** a thrust, a jab • **at full tilt** with full speed and force

timber *noun* **1** wood for building etc **2** trees suitable for this **3** a wooden beam in a house or ship

timbre (*pronounced* **tim**-ber or **tam**-ber) *noun* the quality of a musical sound or voice

time *noun* **1** the hour of the day **2** the period at which something happens **3** (often **times**) a particular period: *in modern times* **4** opportunity: *no time to listen* **5** a suitable or right moment: *Now is the time to ask* **6** one of a number of occasions: *He won four times* **7**

(**times**) multiplied by: *two times four* **8** the rhythm or rate of performance of a piece of music ➤ *adjective* **1** of or to do with time **2** arranged to go off at a particular time: *a time bomb* ➤ *verb* **1** to measure the minutes, seconds, etc taken to do anything **2** to choose the time for (well, badly, etc): *time your entrance well* • **at times** occasionally • **do time** *slang* to serve a prison sentence • **in time** early enough • **on time** punctual • **the time being** the present time: *You'll have to use your old football boots for the time being* ⊙ Comes from Old English *tima*

time bomb *noun* a bomb that has been set to explode at a particular time

time capsule *noun* a box containing objects from the current age, buried or preserved for discovery in the future

time-consuming *adjective* taking up a lot of time

time-honoured *adjective* respected because it has lasted a long time

timeless *adjective* **1** not belonging to any particular time **2** never ending: *timeless beauty*

timely *adjective* (**timelier, timeliest**) coming at the right moment: *a timely reminder*

time out *noun, chiefly N Am* **1** a brief pause or period of rest **2** *sport* a short break during a game for discussion of tactics, rest, etc

timer *noun* a device like a clock that switches an appliance on or off at preset times, or that makes a sound when a set amount of time has passed

timescale *noun* the time envisaged for the completion of a project

time series *noun, statistics* a set of observations taken at regularly spaced intervals over a period of time

time-sharing *noun* **1** a system of using a computer so that it can deal with several programs at the same time **2** a scheme by which someone buys the right to use a holiday home for a specified period each year

time signature *noun, music* a sign consisting of two numbers one above the other showing the rhythm a piece of music is to be played in

timetable *noun* a list showing times of classes, arrivals or departures of trains, etc

timid *adjective* easily frightened; shy

timidity *noun* nervousness, shyness

timidly *adverb* shyly

timing *noun* the coordination of when actions or events happen to achieve the best possible effect

timorous *adjective* very timid

timpani or **tympani** *plural noun* kettledrums

tin *noun* **1** *chemistry* (symbol **Sn**) soft silvery-white metallic element used as a thin protective coating for steel **2** a box or can made of **tinplate**,

thin steel covered with tin or other metal ➤ *verb* (**tinning, tinned**) **1** to cover with tin **2** to pack (food etc) in tins

tincture *noun* **1** a slight tinge of colour **2** a characteristic quality **3** a medicine mixed in alcohol

tinder *noun* dry material easily set alight by a spark

tine *noun* a spike of a fork or of a deer's antler

tinfoil *noun* a very thin sheet of tin, aluminium, etc used for wrapping food

tinge *verb* to tint, colour slightly • **tinge with** to add a trace or hint of (a quality, feeling, etc) to ➤ *noun* a slight amount; a hint: *tinge of pink/ tinge of sadness*

tingle *verb* **1** to feel a sharp prickling sensation **2** to feel a thrill of excitement ➤ *noun* a sharp prickle

tinker *noun* a mender of kettles, pans, etc ➤ *verb* **1** to work clumsily or unskilfully **2** to meddle (with)

tinkle *verb* to (cause to) make a light, ringing sound; clink, jingle ➤ *noun* a light, ringing sound

tinnitus (*pronounced* tin-i-tus) *noun, medicine* an abnormal ringing, buzzing or whistling noise in the ears, not caused by any external sound

tinny *adjective* (**tinnier, tinniest**) **1** like tin **2** of a sound: thin, high-pitched

tinplate *noun* thin iron or steel coated with tin ➤ *verb* to coat with tinplate

tinsel *noun* a sparkling, glittering material used for decoration

tint *noun* a variety or shade of a colour ➤ *verb* to give slight colour to

tiny *adjective* (**tinier, tiniest**) very small

tip *noun* **1** the top or point of something thin or tapering **2** a piece of useful information **3** a small gift of money to a waiter etc **4** a rubbish dump **5** a light stroke, a tap ➤ *verb* (**tipping, tipped**) **1** to slant **2** to put or form a tip on **3** (also **tip off**) to give a hint to **4** to give a small gift of money **5** *Brit* to dump (rubbish) **6** to strike lightly • **tip out** or **into** to empty out or into • **tip over** to overturn

Tipp-Ex *noun, trademark* correcting fluid for covering over mistakes in typing or writing

tipple *verb, informal* to drink small amounts of alcohol regularly ➤ *noun* an alcoholic drink

tippler *noun* someone who regularly drinks alcohol

tipsiness *noun* being slightly drunk

tipsy *adjective* (**tipsier, tipsiest**) rather drunk

tiptoe *verb* to walk on your toes in order to go very quietly • **on tiptoe** standing or walking on your toes

tirade *noun* a long, bitter, scolding speech

tire[1] *verb* **1** to make or become weary **2** (**tire of**) to lose patience with or interest in

tire[2] US spelling of **tyre**

tired *adjective* **1** weary **2** (**tired of**) bored with

tireless *adjective* **1** never becoming weary **2** never resting

tiresome *adjective* **1** making weary **2** long and dull **3** annoying: *a tiresome child*

tiring *adjective* causing tiredness or weariness: *a tiring journey*

tiro or **tyro** *noun* (*plural* **tiros** or **tyros**) a beginner

tissue *noun* **1** the substance of which body organs are made: *muscle tissue* **2** a mass, a network (of lies, nonsense, etc) **3** a paper handkerchief **4** finely woven cloth

tissue culture *noun, biology* **1** the growth of plant or animal cells, tissues or organs under controlled conditions **2** the tissue grown

tissue paper *noun* thin, soft paper used for wrapping

tit *noun* **1** a type of small bird: *blue tit/great tit* **2** a teat **3** *slang* a woman's breast • **tit for tat** blow for blow, the repayment of an injury with another injury

titanic *adjective* huge, enormous

titanium *noun, chemistry* (symbol **Ti**) a silvery-white metallic element used to make alloys for aircraft and missile parts

titbit *noun* a tasty piece of food etc

tithe (*pronounced* taidh) *noun, history* a tax paid to the church, a tenth part of someone's income or produce

titillate *verb* to gently stimulate or arouse (often sexually) ⊙ Comes from Latin *titillare* meaning 'to tickle'

⚠ Do not confuse: **titillate** and **titivate**

titivate *verb* to make smarter; improve in appearance

⊙ It is thought that **titivate** was created by taking 'tidy' and reforming it on the model of the verb 'cultivate'

title *noun* **1** the name of a book, poem, etc **2** a word in front of a name to show rank or office (eg *Sir, Lady, Major*), or in addressing anyone formally (eg *Mr, Mrs, Ms*) **3** right or claim to money, an estate, etc

titled *adjective* having a title which shows noble rank

title deed *noun* a document that proves a right to ownership (of a house etc)

title role *noun* the part in a play which is the same as the title eg *Hamlet*

titrate *verb, chemistry* to determine the concentration of (a chemical substance in a solution) by titration

titration *noun, chemistry* a technique to find the concentration of a substance in a solution by adding measures of another substance that is known to react with it, until the reaction reaches a known end point

titre *noun* **1** *chemistry* the concentration of a solution as determined by titration with a solution of known concentration **2** *biology* the concentration of a virus present in a suspension **3** the concentration of an antibody in a sample of serum

titter *verb* to giggle ➤ *noun* a giggle

tizzy *noun* (*plural* **tizzies**) a state of confusion, a flap

T-junction *noun* a junction where one road meets another at right angles but does not cross it

Tl *symbol, chemistry* thallium

TLC *abbreviation, informal* tender loving care

Tm *symbol, chemistry* thulium

TNC *abbreviation* transnational corporation

TNT *abbreviation* trinitrotoluene, a high explosive

to *preposition* **1** showing the place or direction aimed for: *going to the cinema/emigrating to New Zealand* **2** showing the indirect object in a phrase, sentence, etc: *show it to me* **3** used before a verb to indicate the infinitive: *To err is human* **4** showing that one thing belongs with another in some way: *key to the door* **5** compared with: *nothing to what happened before* **6** about, concerning: *What did he say to that?* **7** showing a ratio, proportion, etc: *odds are six to one against* **8** showing the purpose or result of an action: *Tear it to pieces* ➤ *adverb* almost closed: *pull the door to* • **to and fro** backwards and forwards

toad *noun* a type of amphibian like a frog

toad-in-the-hole *noun, Brit* a dish of sausages cooked in batter

toadstool *noun* a mushroom-like fungus, often poisonous

toady *verb* (**toadies, toadying, toadied**) to give way to someone's wishes, or flatter them, to gain favour ➤ *noun* (*plural* **toadies**) someone who acts in this way

toast *verb* **1** to brown (bread) by heating at a fire or grill **2** to drink to the success or health of (someone) **3** to warm (your feet etc) at a fire ➤ *noun* **1** bread toasted **2** the person to whom a toast is drunk **3** the drinking of a toast

toaster *noun* an electric machine for toasting bread

toastie *noun, informal* a toasted sandwich

toastmaster, toastmistress *noun* a man or woman who announces the toasts to be drunk at a ceremonial dinner

toast rack *noun* a stand with partitions for slices of toast

tobacco *noun* a type of plant whose dried leaves are used for smoking

tobacconist noun someone who sells tobacco, cigarettes, etc

toboggan noun a long, light sledge ➤ verb to go in a toboggan

toccata noun a piece of music for a keyboard instrument intended to show off the performer's skill ① Comes from Italian, from toccare meaning 'to touch'

tocopherol noun vitamin E

today adverb & noun 1 (on) this day 2 (at) the present time

toddle verb to walk unsteadily, with short steps

toddler noun a young child just able to walk

toddy noun (plural toddies) a hot drink of whisky and honey

to-do noun (plural to-dos) a bustle, commotion

toe noun 1 one of the five finger-like parts of the foot 2 the front part of an animal's foot 3 the front part of a shoe, golf club, etc • **on your toes** alert, ready for action • **toe the line** to do as you are told

toffee noun a kind of sweet made of sugar and butter

toffee-nosed adjective, informal snobbish, conceited

tofu noun a curd made from soya beans and used as a meat substitute

tog noun a unit for measuring the warmth of fabrics, clothes and quilts, etc

toga noun, history the loose outer garment worn by a citizen of ancient Rome

together adverb 1 with each other, in place or time: We must stay together/Three buses arrived together 2 so as to be in contact, joined or united: Glue the pages together 3 by joint action: Together we can afford it ➤ adjective, informal of a person: well-organized, competent

toggle noun 1 a cylindrical fastening that is passed through a loop, eg for a coat 2 computing a keyboard command which allows the user to switch between one mode and another ➤ verb, computing to switch quickly between two modes

toil verb 1 to work hard and for a long time 2 to walk, move, etc with effort ➤ noun hard work

toilet noun 1 a receptacle for waste matter from the body, with a water-supply for flushing this away 2 a room containing this 3 old the act of washing yourself, doing your hair, etc

toiletries plural noun soaps, cosmetics, etc

toilet water noun a lightly perfumed, spirit-based liquid for the skin

token noun 1 a mark, a sign: a token of my friendship 2 a stamped piece of plastic etc, or a voucher, for use in place of money: bus token/book token ➤ adjective done for show only, insincere: token gesture

tokenism noun the practice of doing only the minimum in a particular area, as a pretence that one is committed to it, eg employing one black person in a company to avoid charges of racism

told past form of **tell**

tolerable adjective 1 bearable, endurable 2 fairly good: tolerable player ♦ **tolerably** adverb

tolerance noun 1 accepting and being fair to people with different beliefs, manners, etc from your own 2 ability to resist the effects of a drug etc 3 biology lack of reactivity to an antigen that usually causes an immune response 4 biology the ability of a plant or animal to survive extreme conditions, eg drought

tolerant adjective 1 fair towards other people and accepting their right to have different political and religious beliefs 2 able to resist the effects of a drug etc

tolerate verb 1 to bear, endure; put up with 2 to allow

toleration noun 1 the act of tolerating 2 the practice of allowing people to practise religions which are different from the established religion of the country

toll[1] noun 1 a tax charged for crossing a bridge, using a road, etc 2 loss, damage • **take toll** to cause damage or loss

toll[2] verb 1 to sound (a large bell) slowly, as for a funeral 2 of a bell: to be sounded slowly

tollgate noun a gate or barrier across a road or bridge that is only lifted when travellers have paid the toll

toluene noun, chemistry a toxic, colourless flammable liquid used as an industrial solvent and in the manufacture of TNT

tomahawk noun, history a Native American light axe used as a weapon and tool

tomato noun (plural tomatoes) a juicy red-skinned fruit, used in salads, sauces, etc

tomb noun 1 a grave 2 a burial vault or chamber

tombola noun a kind of lottery in which winning tickets are drawn from a revolving drum

tombolo (pronounced tom-bo-lo) noun (plural tombolos), geography a bar of sand or gravel connecting an island with another or with the mainland

tomboy noun a high-spirited active girl who enjoys the rough, boisterous activities which people tend to associate with boys

tombstone noun a stone placed over a grave in memory of the dead person

tomcat noun a male cat

tome noun a large heavy book

tomfoolery noun stupid or foolish behaviour; nonsense

tomorrow adverb & noun 1 (on) the day after today 2 (in) the future: the children of tomorrow

tomtom noun a type of drum beaten with the hands

-tomy also **-ectomy, -otomy** *suffix* forms words relating to the surgical operation of cutting into an organ of the body: *vasectomy/ lobotomy* ⊙ Comes from Greek *tome* meaning 'a cutting'

ton *noun* 1 a measure of weight equal to 2240 pounds, about 1016 kilograms 2 a unit (100 cubic feet) of space in a ship • **metric ton** or **metric tonne** 1000 kilograms

tonality *noun* (*plural* **tonalities**) 1 *music* the organization of all of the notes and chords of a piece of music in relation to a single tonic 2 the colour scheme and tones used in a painting ♦ **tonal** *adjective*

tone *noun* 1 sound 2 quality of sound: *harsh tone* 3 *music* one of the larger intervals in a scale, eg between C and D 4 the quality of a voice expressing the mood of the speaker: *a gentle tone* 5 the general character or style of a piece of writing 6 a shade of colour 7 the harmony or general effect of colours in something 8 muscle firmness or strength ➤ *verb* 1 to give tone to 2 (sometimes **tone in**) to blend, fit in well • **tone down** to make or become softer • **tone up** to give strength to (muscles etc)

tone-deaf *adjective* unable to distinguish between notes of different pitch ♦ **tone-deafness** *noun*

tone poem *noun* a piece of music not divided into movements and which is based on a story or theme

toner *noun* 1 something that tones 2 a lotion for toning the skin 3 a fine, coloured powder used in printers and photocopiers

tongs *plural noun* an instrument for lifting and grasping coals, sugar lumps, etc

tongue *noun* 1 the fleshy organ inside the mouth, used in tasting, speaking, and swallowing 2 a flap in a shoe 3 a long, thin strip of land 4 the tongue of an animal served as food 5 a language: *his mother tongue*

tongue-tied *adjective* not able to speak freely

tongue-twister *noun* a phrase, sentence, etc not easy to say quickly, eg 'she sells sea shells'

tonic *noun* 1 a medicine which gives strength and energy 2 *music* the keynote of a scale 3 tonic water ➤ *adjective* 1 of tones or sounds 2 of a tonic

tonic sol-fa same as **sol-fa**

tonic water *noun* aerated water with quinine

tonight *adverb & noun* (on) the night of the present day

tonnage *noun* the space available in a ship, measured in tons

tonne *noun* a metric ton

tonsil *noun* one of a pair of soft, fleshy lumps at the back of the throat that produce lymphocytes

tonsillitis *noun* inflammation and painfulness of the tonsils

tonsure *noun* 1 the act of shaving the crown of the head, especially of someone about to become a monk 2 a (part of a) head shaved in this way

too *adverb* 1 to a greater extent, in a greater quantity, etc than is wanted: *too hot to go outside/too many people in the room* 2 (with a negative) very, particularly: *not feeling too well* (ie not feeling very well) 3 also, as well: *I'm feeling quite cold, too*

took past tense of **take**

tool *noun* an instrument for doing work, especially by hand

toolbar *noun, computing* a bar with a list of features and functions which appears at the top of a computer screen

toot *noun* the sound of a car horn etc

tooth *noun* (*plural* **teeth**) 1 any of the hard, bony objects projecting from the gums, arranged in two rows in the mouth 2 any of the points on a saw, cogwheel, comb, etc • **fight tooth and nail** to fight fiercely, determinedly

toothache *noun* pain in a tooth

toothbrush *noun* a brush for cleaning the teeth

toothpaste *noun* paste for cleaning the teeth

toothpick *noun* a small sharp instrument for picking out food from between the teeth

top *noun* 1 the highest part of anything 2 the upper surface 3 the highest place or rank 4 a lid 5 a garment that covers the upper part of the body: *a sleeveless top* 6 a circus tent 7 a kind of spinning toy ➤ *adjective* highest, chief ➤ *verb* (**topping, topped**) 1 to cover on the top 2 to rise above 3 to do better than 4 to reach the top of 5 to take off the top of

topaz *noun* a type of precious stone, of various colours

top dog *noun informal* a winner or leader

top hat *noun* a man's tall silk hat

top-heavy *adjective* having the upper part too heavy for the lower

topiary *noun* the art of trimming bushes, hedges, etc into decorative shapes

topic *noun* a subject spoken or written about

topical *adjective* of current interest, concerned with present events

topic sentence *noun* a sentence conveying the main idea contained in a paragraph of text

topless *adjective* 1 having no top 2 of clothing: having no upper part, leaving the breasts exposed 3 of a woman: with her breasts exposed

topmost *adjective* highest, uppermost

topographical *adjective* relating to or involving topography

topography *noun* the description of the

features of the land in a certain region

topology *noun* **1** *maths* the branch of geometry concerned with the properties of a figure that remain unchanged even when the figure is distorted by bending, stretching or twisting, etc **2** *computing* the interconnection and organization of computers within a network ♦ **topological** *adjective*

topping *noun* something that forms a covering or garnish for food: *a topping of whipped cream*

topple *verb* to become unsteady and fall

top-secret *adjective* (of information etc) very secret

topside *noun* a lean cut of beef from the rump

topsoil *noun* the rich uppermost layer of soil where most plant roots develop

topspin *noun, sport* a spin given to a ball to make it travel higher, further or faster

topsyturvy *adjective & adverb* turned upside down

tor *noun* a hill or rocky height ☉ Comes from Old English *torr*

Torah *noun, Judaism* the book of the law of Moses

torch *noun* (*plural* **torches**) **1** a small hand-held light with a switch and electric battery **2** a flaming piece of wood or coarse rope carried as a light in processions ➤ *verb, slang* to set fire to deliberately

tore past tense of **tear**¹

toreador *noun* a bullfighter mounted on horseback

torment *verb* **1** to treat cruelly and make suffer **2** to worry greatly **3** to tease ➤ *noun* **1** great pain, suffering **2** a cause of these

tormentor *noun* a person who torments

torn past participle of **tear**¹

tornado *noun* (*plural* **tornadoes**) a violent whirling windstorm characterized by a long, funnel-shaped column of air

torpedo *noun* (*plural* **torpedoes**) a large cigar-shaped type of missile fired by ships, planes, etc ➤ *verb* (**torpedoing, torpedoed**) to hit or sink (a ship) with a torpedo

torpid *adjective* slow, dull, stupid

torpor or **torpidity** *noun* the state of being torpid; dullness

torque *noun, physics* force multiplied by the perpendicular distance from a point about which it causes rotation

torrent *noun* **1** a rushing stream **2** a heavy downpour of rain **3** a violent flow of words etc: *torrent of abuse*

torrential *adjective* like a torrent; rushing violently

torrid *adjective* **1** parched by heat; very hot **2** very passionate: *torrid love affair*

torsion *noun* twisting; a twist

torso *noun* (*plural* **torsos**) the body, excluding the head and limbs

tortilla *noun* **1** a type of flat Mexican bread **2** a Spanish omelette

tortoise *noun* a four-footed, slow-moving kind of reptile, covered with a hard shell

tortoiseshell *noun* the shell of a kind of sea turtle, used in making ornamental articles ➤ *adjective* **1** made of this shell **2** mottled brown, yellow and black: *a tortoiseshell cat*

tortuous *adjective* winding, roundabout, not straightforward

torture *verb* **1** to treat someone cruelly as a punishment or to force them to confess something **2** to cause to suffer ➤ *noun* **1** the act of torturing **2** great suffering

torus *noun* **1** *physics* a circular ring with a D-shaped cross-section used to contain plasma in nuclear fission reactors **2** *maths* a solid curved surface with a hole in it, resembling a doughnut, obtained by rotating a circle about an axis lying in the same plane as the circle **3** *botany* the receptacle of a flower ♦ **toric** *adjective* ☉ Comes from Latin, meaning 'bulge' or 'swelling'

Tory *noun* (*plural* **Tories**) a member of the British Conservative Party

☉ Originally one of a group of Irish Catholics thrown off their land who waged guerrilla war on British settlers, later applied to any royalist supporter

toss *verb* **1** to throw up in the air **2** to throw up (a coin) to see which side falls uppermost **3** to turn restlessly from side to side **4** of a ship: to be thrown about by rough water • **toss off** to produce quickly • **toss up** to toss a coin

toss-up *noun* an equal choice or chance

tot¹ *noun* **1** a little child **2** a small amount of alcoholic spirits

tot² *verb*: **tot up** to add up

total *adjective* **1** whole: *total number* **2** complete: *total wreck* ➤ *noun* **1** the entire amount **2** the sum of amounts added together ➤ *verb* (**totalling, totalled**) **1** to add up **2** to amount to **3** *informal* to damage irreparably; wreck: *She totalled her dad's car*

totalitarianism *noun* government by a single party that demands obedience and allows no rivals ♦ **totalitarian** *noun & adjective*

totally *adverb* completely

totem *noun* an image of an animal or plant used as the badge or sign of a Native American tribe

totem pole *noun* a pole on which totems are carved and painted

totter *verb* **1** to shake as if about to fall **2** to stagger

toucan *noun* a type of S American bird with a heavy curved beak

touch *verb* **1** to feel (with the hand) **2** to come or be in contact (with): *A leaf touched his cheek* **3** to move, affect the feelings of: *The story touched those who heard it* **4** to mark slightly with colour: *touched with gold* **5** to reach the standard of: *I can't touch him at chess* **6** to have anything to do with: *I wouldn't touch a job like that* **7** to eat or drink: *He won't touch meat* **8** to concern (someone) **9** *informal* to persuade (someone) to lend you money: *I touched him for £10* ➤ *noun* **1** the act of touching **2** the physical sense of touch **3** a small quantity or degree: *a touch of salt* **4** of an artist, pianist, etc: skill or style **5** *football* the ground beyond the edges of the pitch marked off by **touchlines** • **in (or out of) touch with 1** in (or not in) communication or contact with **2** aware (or unaware) of • **touch down** of an aircraft: to land • **touch off** to cause to happen • **touch on** to mention briefly • **touch up** to improve (a drawing, photograph, etc) by making details clearer or correcting faults

touch-and-go *adjective* very uncertain: *It's touch-and-go whether we'll get it done on time*

touchdown *noun* an act or the process of an aircraft or spacecraft making contact with the ground when landing

touché (*pronounced* too-**shei**) *interjection* acknowledging a point scored in a game or argument

touched *adjective* **1** feeling sympathy, quiet pleasure, etc **2** *informal* slightly mad

touching *preposition* about, concerning ➤ *adjective* causing feelings of sympathy or pity, moving

touchline *noun, sport* either of the two lines that mark the side boundaries of the pitch, eg in football or rugby

touch pad *noun, computing* a small input device, used eg with a laptop, operated by touching different areas on its surface

touchpaper *noun* paper used for lighting fireworks or firing gunpowder

touch screen *noun, computing* a type of computer screen that doubles as an input device, operated by pressing it with a finger

touchstone *noun* a test or standard of measurement of quality etc

touch-type *verb* to use a typewriter without looking at the keyboard

touchy *adjective* (**touchier, touchiest**) **1** easily offended **2** needing to be handled with care and tact: *a touchy subject* ♦ **touchily** *adverb* (meaning 1)

tough *adjective* **1** strong, not easily broken **2** of meat etc: hard to chew **3** of strong character, able to stand hardship or strain **4** difficult to cope with or overcome: *tough opposition* **5** rough and violent: *a tough area* ➤ *noun* a rough, violent person • **tough luck 1** expressing sympathy when something has not gone well **2** expressing scorn: *Tough luck! You should have thought of that*

toughen *verb* to (cause to) become tough

toupee (*pronounced* **too**-pei) *noun* a small wig or hairpiece worn by a man to cover a bald patch

tour *noun* **1** a journey in which you visit various places; a pleasure trip **2** a journey with frequent stops for professional engagements, eg by a theatre company, rock band, etc ➤ *verb* to make a tour (of)

tourism *noun* **1** the practice of travelling to and visiting places for pleasure **2** the industry that is involved in offering services for tourists

tourist *noun* someone who travels for pleasure and visits places of interest

touristy *adjective, derogatory* appealing to, frequented by or full of tourists

tournament *noun* **1** a competition involving many contests and players **2** *history* a meeting at which knights fought together on horseback

tourniquet (*pronounced* **toorn**-ik-ei) *noun* a bandage tied tightly round a limb to prevent loss of blood from a wound

tousled *adjective* of hair: untidy, tangled

tout *verb* to go about looking for support, votes, buyers, etc ➤ *noun* **1** someone who does this **2** someone who gives tips to people who bet on horse races

tow (*pronounced* toh) *verb* to pull (a car etc) with a rope attached to another vehicle ➤ *noun* **1** the act of towing **2** the rope used for towing • **in tow** accompanying as a companion or escort • **on tow** being towed

towards or **toward** *preposition* **1** moving in the direction of (a place, person, etc): *walking towards the house* **2** to (a person, thing, etc): *his attitude towards his son* **3** as a help or contribution to: *I gave £5 towards the cost* **4** near, about (a time etc): *towards four o'clock*

towel *noun* a cloth for drying or wiping (eg the skin after washing) ➤ *verb* (**towelling, towelled**) to rub dry with a towel • **throw in the towel** to give up a fight or struggle

towelling *noun* a cotton cloth often used for making towels

tower *noun* **1** a high narrow building **2** a high narrow part of a castle etc ➤ *verb* to rise high (over, above)

towering *adjective* **1** rising high **2** violent: *a towering rage*

town *noun* a place, larger than a village, which includes many buildings, houses, shops, etc

town crier *noun, history* someone who made public announcements in a town

town hall *noun* the building where the official business of a town is done

town planning *noun* the planning and design of the future development of a town ◆ **town planner** *noun*

township *noun* an urban area in South Africa that was formerly set aside for non-white citizens

towpath *noun* a path alongside a canal originally used by horses which tow barges

-tox- also **-toxi-**, **-toxico-** of or relating to poison: *toxaemia* (= blood poisoning)/ *intoxication* ⊕ Comes from Greek *toxikon pharmacon* meaning 'poison for the bow', from *toxon* meaning 'bow'

toxaemia *noun* poisoning

toxic *adjective* **1** poisonous **2** caused by poison

toxicology *noun* the scientific study of poisons

toxin *noun* a naturally occurring poison

toxoid *noun* a toxin that has been treated so that it is no longer poisonous, but still stimulates the production of antibodies

toy *noun* **1** an object for a child to play with **2** an object for amusement only ● **toy with** to play or trifle with

toyboy *noun, informal* a woman's much younger male lover

trace *noun* **1** a mark or sign left behind **2** a footprint **3** a small amount **4** a line drawn by an instrument recording a change (eg in temperature) **5** (**traces**) the straps by which a horse pulls a cart etc along ➤ *verb* **1** to follow the tracks or course of **2** to copy (a drawing etc) on transparent paper placed over it

traceable *adjective* able to be traced (to)

trace element *noun* **1** a chemical element that is only found in very small amounts **2** a chemical element that living organisms require only in very small amounts

tracery *noun* decorated stonework holding the glass in some church windows

trachea (*pronounced* tra-ki-a) *noun* (*plural* **tracheae** – *pronounced* tra-ki-ai) **1** *anatomy* the windpipe **2** in insects: any of the openings on the surface of the body where air is absorbed **3** *botany* any fluid-conducting vessel in the woody tissue of plants

tracheotomy (*pronounced* trak-i-**awt**-o-mi) *noun* a surgical procedure making a hole in the front of the neck into the windpipe, as an alternative airway for breathing

tracing *noun* a traced copy

tracing paper *noun* semi-transparent paper used for tracing drawings etc

track *noun* **1** a mark left **2** (**tracks**) footprints **3** a path or rough road **4** a racecourse for runners, cyclists, etc **5** a railway line **6** an individual song, etc on an album, CD, cassette, etc **7** an area on the surface of a magnetic disk where data can be stored **8** an endless band on which wheels of a tank etc travel ➤ *verb* **1** to follow (an animal) by its footprints and other marks left **2** to follow and plot the course of (a spacecraft, satellite, etc) by radar **3** of a film camera or its operator: to follow a moving subject and keep it in focus ● **keep** or **lose track of** to keep or fail to keep aware of the whereabouts or progress of ● **make tracks for** to set off towards ● **track down** to search for (someone or something) until caught or found

track and field *noun* the branch of athletics that is made up of all the running, jumping and throwing events

trackball or **trackerball** *noun, computing* a ball that can be rotated with the palm to move a cursor on a screen

track record *noun, informal* someone's performance, achievements, etc in the past

tracksuit *noun* a loose suit worn while jogging, before and after an athletic performance, etc

tract *noun* **1** a stretch of land **2** a short pamphlet, especially on a religious subject **3** a system made up of connected parts of the body: *the digestive tract*

-tract- forms words related to the action of pulling or drawing: *tractable* (= easily pulled along)/*subtract* (= to draw away) ⊕ Comes from Latin *trahere* meaning 'to draw', and *tractare* meaning 'to drag about' or 'to deal with'

tractable *adjective* easily made to do what is wanted

traction *noun* **1** the act of pulling or dragging **2** the state of being pulled **3** *geography* the rolling of large rocks along a river bed

traction engine *noun* a road steam engine

tractor *noun* a motor vehicle for pulling loads, ploughs, etc

trade *noun* **1** the buying and selling of goods **2** someone's occupation, craft, job: *a carpenter by trade* ➤ *verb* **1** to buy and sell **2** to have business dealings (with) **3** to deal (in) **4** to exchange, swap ● **trade in** to give as part-payment for something else (eg an old car for a new one) ● **trade on** to take advantage of, often unfairly

trademark *noun* a registered mark or name put on goods to show that they are made by a certain company

tradename *noun* **1** a name given to a product, or a group of products, by the trade producing them **2** a name that a company or individual does business under

trader *noun* someone who buys and sells

tradesman *noun* **1** a shopkeeper **2** a workman in a skilled trade

trade union *noun* a group of workers of the same trade who join together to bargain with employers for fair wages etc

trade unionist *noun* a member of a trade union

trade wind *noun* a wind which blows towards the equator from the north-east and south-east, and is deflected westwards by the rotation of the earth

trading estate another term for an **industrial estate**

tradition *noun* 1 the handing-down of customs, beliefs, stories, etc from generation to generation 2 a custom, belief, etc handed down in this way

traditional *adjective* of customs: having existed for a long time without changing: *the traditional English breakfast*

traditionalist *noun* someone who believes in maintaining traditions

traffic *noun* 1 the cars, buses, boats, etc which use roads or waterways 2 trade 3 dishonest dealings (eg in drugs) ➤ *verb* (**trafficking, trafficked**) 1 to trade 2 to deal (in)

traffic calming *noun* the intentional curbing of the speed of road vehicles by having humps, narrowed passing places, etc on roads

traffic lights *plural noun* a system of red, amber and green lights for controlling traffic at road junctions or street crossings

traffic warden *noun, Brit* someone whose job is to control the flow of traffic and the parking of vehicles in towns

tragedian *noun* 1 an actor who specializes in tragic roles 2 a person who writes tragedies

tragedy *noun* (*plural* **tragedies**) 1 a very sad event 2 a play about unhappy events and with a sad ending (*contrasted with*: **comedy**)

tragic *adjective* 1 very sad 2 to do with or in the style of tragedy ♦ **tragically** *adverb*: *He was tragically killed in an accident*

tragicomedy *noun* (*plural* **tragicomedies**) a play, film, event, etc that includes a mixture of both tragedy and comedy ♦ **tragicomic** or **tragicomical** *adjective*

trail *verb* 1 to draw along, in or through: *trailing his foot through the water* 2 to hang down (from) or be dragged loosely behind 3 to hunt (animals) by following footprints etc 4 to walk wearily 5 of a plant: to grow over the ground or a wall ➤ *noun* 1 an animal's track 2 a pathway through a wild region: *a nature trail* 3 something left stretching behind: *a trail of dust*

trailblazer *noun* 1 someone who makes inroads into new territory 2 someone who makes innovations in a particular field

trailer *noun* 1 a vehicle pulled behind a car 2 a short film advertising a longer film or TV programme to be shown at a later date

train *noun* 1 a railway engine with carriages or trucks 2 a part of a dress which trails behind the wearer 3 the attendants who follow an important person 4 a line (of thought, events, etc) 5 a line of animals carrying people or baggage ➤ *verb* 1 to prepare yourself by practice or exercise for a sporting event, job, etc 2 to educate 3 to exercise (animals or people) in preparation for a race etc 4 to tame and teach (an animal) 5 (**train on** or **at**) to aim, point (a gun, telescope, etc) at (something) 6 to make (a tree or plant) grow in a certain direction

trainee *noun* someone who is being trained

trainer *noun* someone who trains people or animals for a sport, circus, etc

training *noun* 1 preparation for a sport 2 experience or learning of the practical side of a job

traipse *verb* to walk or trudge along aimlessly or wearily

trait *noun* a point that stands out in a person's character: *Patience is one of his good traits*

traitor *noun* 1 someone who goes over to the enemy's side, or gives away secrets to the enemy 2 someone who betrays trust

traitorous *adjective* like a traitor; treacherous

trajectory *noun* (*plural* **trajectories**) 1 *physics* the curved path of an object moving through the air or through space 2 *maths* a curve that passes through a set of given points at a constant angle ☉ Comes from Latin *trajectorius* meaning 'casting over'

tram *noun* a long vehicle running on rails and driven by electric power for carrying passengers (*also called*: **tramcar**)

tramline *noun* 1 a rail of a tramway 2 (**tramlines**) *tennis* the parallel lines marked at the sides of the court

trammel *noun* something that hinders movement ➤ *verb* (**trammelling, trammelled**) to hinder

tramp *verb* 1 to walk with heavy footsteps 2 to walk along, over, etc: *tramping the streets in search of a job* ➤ *noun* 1 someone with no fixed home and no job, who lives by begging 2 a journey made on foot 3 the sound of marching feet 4 a small cargo-boat with no fixed route

trample *verb* 1 to tread under foot, stamp on 2 (*usually* **trample on**) to treat roughly or unfeelingly 3 to tread heavily

trampoline *noun* a bed-like framework holding a sheet of elastic material for bouncing on, used by gymnasts etc

tramway *noun* a system of tracks on which trams run

trance *noun* a sleep-like or half-conscious state

tranquil *adjective* quiet, peaceful

tranquillity *noun* the state of being quiet, calm and peaceful: *She loved the tranquillity of the valley*

tranquillize, tranquillise or *US*

tranquilize *verb* to make calm, especially by administering a drug

tranquillizer, tranquilliser or *US* **tranquilizer** *noun* a drug to calm the nerves or make you sleep

trans- *prefix* across, through: *transatlantic/translate* (= to carry across into a different language) ⏲ Comes from Latin *trans* meaning 'across' or 'beyond'

transact *verb* to do (a piece of business)

transactinide *adjective, chemistry* referring to radioactive elements with atomic numbers higher than the actinide series ➤ *noun* a transactinide element

transaction *noun* a piece of business, a deal

transatlantic *adjective* **1** crossing the Atlantic Ocean: *transatlantic yacht race* **2** across or over the Atlantic: *transatlantic friends*

transceiver *noun* a piece of radio equipment that can transmit and receive signals

transcend *verb* **1** to be, or rise, above **2** to be, or do, better than

transcendental *adjective* **1** going beyond usual human knowledge and experience **2** supernatural or mystical **3** vague or abstract

transcribe *verb* **1** to copy from one book into another or from one form of writing (eg shorthand) into another **2** to adapt (a piece of music) for a particular instrument

transcript *noun* a written copy

transcription *noun* **1** the act of transcribing **2** a written copy

transducer *noun* any device that converts energy from one form to another, eg electrical energy into sound waves

transect *verb* to cut across (something)

transept *noun* the part of a church with a cross-shaped floor plan which lies across the main part

transfer *verb* (**transferring, transferred**) **1** to remove to another place **2** to hand over to another person **3** *Brit* of a professional footballer: to change clubs ➤ *noun* **1** the act of transferring **2** a design or picture which can be transferred from one surface to another

transferable *adjective* able to be transferred

transference *noun* the act of moving or transferring something from one person, place or group to another: *the transference of power from central to local government*

transfer RNA *noun, biology* (*abbrev* **tRNA**) a small RNA molecule that links a specific amino acid with messenger RNA so it can be used in protein synthesis

transfiguration *noun* a change in appearance, especially to something more beautiful, glorious, or exalted

transfigure *verb* to change (greatly and for the better) the form or appearance of

transfix *verb* **1** to make unable to move or act (eg because of surprise): *transfixed by the sight* **2** to pierce through (as with a sword)

transform *verb* to change in shape or appearance completely and often dramatically

transformation *noun* **1** transforming or being transformed **2** *maths* an operation, eg a mapping, that involves moving all the points of a figure on a plane

transformer *noun* an apparatus for changing electrical energy from one voltage to another

transform plate boundary another term for **conservative plate boundary**

transfuse *verb* **1** to pass (liquid) from one thing to another **2** to transfer (blood of one person) to the body of another

transfusion *noun* (*in full* **blood transfusion**) the introduction of blood into a person's body by allowing it to drip through a needle inserted in a vein

transgress *verb* to break a rule, law, etc

transgression *noun* the act of breaking a rule, law, etc; a sin

transience *noun* a transient quality

transient *adjective* not lasting, passing

transistor *noun* **1** a small semiconductor device, made up of a crystal enclosed in plastic or metal, which controls the flow of an electrical current **2** a portable radio set using these

transit *noun* **1** the carrying or movement of goods, passengers, etc from place to place **2** the passing of a planet between the sun and the earth

transition *noun* a change from one form, place, appearance, etc to another

transitional *adjective* involving transition; temporary: *The country will pass through a transitional period between constitutions*

transition element *noun, chemistry* in the periodic table: any of a group of metallic elements, eg copper, cobalt, iron, etc, that tend to show variable valency (*also called:* **transition metal**)

transitive *adjective, grammar* of a verb: having an object, eg the verb '*hit*' in 'he *hit* the ball'

transitory *adjective* lasting only for a short time

translate *verb* to turn (something said or written) into another language

translation *noun* **1** the act of translating **2** something translated **3** *maths* a transformation with a sliding movement but no turning (*compare with:* **enlargement**, **reflection**, **rotation**) **4** *genetics* in living cells: the organization of amino acids into a sequence to form proteins

translator *noun* **1** someone who translates **2** *computing* a program that converts source code into machine code

transliterate *verb* to write (a word) in the letters of another alphabet

translucence *noun* a translucent quality

translucent *adjective* allowing light to pass through, but not transparent

transmigrate *verb* of a soul: to pass into another body at death

transmission *noun* **1** the act of transmitting **2** a radio or television broadcast

transmit *verb* (**transmitting, transmitted**) **1** to pass on (a message, news, heat) **2** to send out signals which are received as programmes

transmitter *noun* an instrument for transmitting (especially radio signals)

transmogrify *verb* (**transmogrifies, transmogrifying, transmogrified**), *humorous* to transform, especially in appearance and often in a bizarre way
♦ **transmogrification** *noun*

transmutation *noun* **1** the act or the process of transmuting; a change of form **2** *physics* the changing of one element into another

transmute *verb* to change the form, substance or nature of ⓒ Comes from Latin *transmutare* meaning 'to change condition'

transnational corporation *noun* (*abbrev* **TNC**) a large business that has operations in several countries (*also called:* **multinational company**)

transom *noun* a beam across a window or the top of a door

transparency *noun* (*plural* **transparencies**) **1** the state of being transparent **2** a photograph printed on transparent material and viewed by shining light through it

transparent *adjective* **1** able to be seen through **2** easily seen to be true or false: *a transparent excuse*

transpire *verb* **1** of a secret: to become known **2** to happen: *Tell me what transpired* **3** of a plant: to absorb moisture through the roots and let out water vapour through the surface of leaves
♦ **transpiration** *noun*

transplant *verb* **1** to lift and plant (a growing plant) in another place **2** to remove (skin) and graft it on another part of the same body **3** to remove (an organ) and graft it in another person or animal ➤ *noun* **1** the act of transplanting **2** a transplanted organ, plant, etc

transplantation *noun* the transfer of an organ or tissue from one person to another, or from one part of the body to another

transponder *noun* a radio and radar device that receives a signal and then sends out its own signal in response ⓒ Comes from *trans*mit + res*pond*

transport *verb* **1** to carry from one place to another **2** to overcome with strong feeling:

transported with delight **3** *history* to send (a prisoner) to a prison in a different country ➤ *noun* **1** the act of transporting **2** any means of carrying persons or goods: *rail transport* **3** strong feeling: *transports of joy*

transportation *noun* **1** the act of transporting **2** means of transport **3** *history* punishment of prisoners by sending them to a prison in a different country **4** *geography* the collection and deposition of material by rivers

transporter *noun* a vehicle that carries other vehicles, heavy objects, etc

transpose *verb* **1** to cause (two things) to change places **2** to change (a piece of music) from one key to another

transposition *noun* **1** transposing or being transposed **2** something transposed

transubstantiation *noun* **1** the act or process of changing, or changing something, into something else **2** *Christianity* in the Roman Catholic and Eastern Orthodox churches: the conversion of bread and wine into the body and blood of Christ

transuranic *adjective, chemistry* of an element: having an atomic number greater than that of uranium, ie 93 or higher

transversal *noun, maths* a line that cuts a set of other lines

transverse *adjective* lying, placed, etc across: *transverse beams in the roof*

transverse wave *noun, physics* a wave where the disturbance of the medium occurs at right angles to the direction of propagation

transvestite *noun* someone who likes to wear clothes intended for the opposite sex

trap *noun* **1** a device for catching animals etc **2** a plan or trick for taking someone by surprise **3** a bend in a pipe which is kept full of water, for preventing the escape of air or gas **4** a carriage with two wheels ➤ *verb* (**trapping, trapped**) to catch in a trap, or in such a way that escape is not possible

trapdoor *noun* a door in a floor or ceiling

trapeze *noun* a swing used in performing gymnastic exercises or feats

trapezium *noun* a figure with four sides, two of which are parallel

trapezoid *noun* a figure with four sides, none of which are parallel

trapper *noun* someone who makes a living by catching animals for their skins and fur

trappings *plural noun* **1** clothes or ornaments suitable for a particular person or occasion **2** ornaments put on horses

trash *noun* **1** something of little worth, rubbish **2** a worthless or contemptible person or people: *white trash* ➤ *verb, informal* to wreck: *trashed their hotel room*

trashy *adjective* (**trashier, trashiest**) worthless

trauma *noun* **1** injury to the body **2** a very violent or distressing experience which has a lasting effect **3** a condition (of a person) caused by such an experience

traumatic *adjective* very upsetting, unpleasant or frightening: *Moving to a new house can be traumatic*

travail *noun, old* hard work

travel *verb* (**travelling, travelled**) **1** to go on a journey **2** to move **3** to go along, across **4** to visit foreign countries ➤ *noun* the act of travelling

traveller *noun* **1** someone who travels **2** a travelling representative of a business firm who tries to obtain orders for his firm's products

traverse *verb* to go across, pass through ➤ *noun* **1** something that crosses or lies across **2** a movement across a rock face etc by a climber **3** a zigzag track of a ship

travesty *noun* (*plural* **travesties**) a poor or ridiculous imitation: *a travesty of justice*

trawl *verb* to fish by dragging a trawl along the bottom of the sea ➤ *noun* a wide-mouthed, bag-shaped net

trawler *noun* a boat used for trawling

tray *noun* a flat piece of wood, metal, etc with a low edge, for carrying dishes

treacherous *adjective* **1** likely to betray **2** dangerous: *treacherous road conditions*
♦ **treacherously** *adverb*

treachery *noun* (*plural* **treacheries**) the act of betraying those who have trusted you

treacle *noun* a thick, dark syrup produced from sugar when it is being refined

tread *verb* (**treading, trod, trodden**) **1** to walk on or along **2** (**tread on**) to put your foot on (something) **3** to crush, trample under foot: *treading mud into the carpet* ➤ *noun* **1** a step **2** a way of walking **3** the part of a tyre which touches the ground **4** the horizontal part of a stair
• **tread on someone's toes 1** to offend or upset them **2** to encroach on their field of influence etc • **tread water** to keep yourself afloat in an upright position by moving your arms and legs

treadle *noun* part of a machine which is worked by the foot

treadmill *noun* **1** *history* a mill turned by the weight of people who were made to walk on steps fixed round a big wheel **2** a similar piece of equipment used for exercising **3** any tiring, routine work

treason *noun* disloyalty to your own country or its government, eg by giving away its secrets to an enemy

treasonable *adjective* consisting of, or involving, treason

treasure *noun* **1** a store of money, gold, jewels, etc **2** anything of great value or highly prized ➤ *verb* **1** to value greatly **2** to keep carefully because of its personal value: *She treasures the mirror her mother left her*

treasurer *noun* someone who has charge of the money of a club

treasure-trove *noun* treasure or money found hidden, the owner of which is unknown

treasury *noun* (*plural* **treasuries**) **1** (**Treasury**) the part of a government which has charge of the country's money **2** a store of valued items, eg a book containing popular poems

treat *verb* **1** to deal with, handle, act towards: *I was treated very well in prison* **2** to try to cure (someone) of a disease **3** to try to cure (a disease) **4** to write or speak about **5** to buy (someone) a meal, drink, etc **6** to try to arrange (a peace treaty etc) with ➤ *noun* something special (eg an outing) that gives much pleasure: *They went to the theatre as a treat*

treatise *noun* a long detailed essay etc on some subject

treatment *noun* **1** the act of treating (eg a disease) **2** remedy, medicine: *a new treatment for cancer* **3** the way in which someone or something is dealt with: *rough treatment*

treaty *noun* (*plural* **treaties**) an agreement made between countries

treble *adjective* **1** three times or three times normal: *wood of treble thickness* **2** high in pitch: *treble note* ➤ *verb* to become three times as great ➤ *noun* **1** the highest part in singing **2** a child who sings the treble part of a song

treble clef *noun, music* a sign (𝄞) at the beginning of a written piece of music placing the note G on the second line of the stave

tree *noun* **1** the largest kind of plant with a thick, firm wooden stem, and branches some distance from the ground **2** anything like a tree in shape

tree diagram *noun, statistics* a diagram in which the probabilities of different possible outcomes are presented as branches

trefoil *noun* a three-part leaf or decoration

trek *noun* **1** a long or wearisome journey **2** *old* a journey by wagon ➤ *verb* (**trekking, trekked**) **1** to make a long hard journey **2** *old* to make a journey by wagon

trellis *noun* (*plural* **trellises**) a network of strips for holding up growing plants

tremble *verb* **1** to shake with cold, fear, weakness **2** to feel fear (for another person's safety etc) ➤ *noun* **1** the act of trembling **2** a fit of trembling

tremendous *adjective* **1** very great or strong **2** *informal* very good, excellent

tremendously *adverb, informal* very

tremolo *noun* (*plural* **tremolos**), *music* a trembling effect produced by the quick succession of the same note

tremor noun **1** a shaking or quivering: *a tremor in his voice* **2** a small earthquake

tremulous adjective **1** shaking **2** showing fear: *a tremulous voice*

trench noun (plural **trenches**) a long narrow ditch dug in the ground (eg by soldiers as a protection against enemy fire) ▶ verb to dig a trench in

trenchant adjective **1** going deep, hurting: *a trenchant remark* **2** of a policy etc: effective, vigorous: *trenchant reforms*

trenchcoat noun a kind of waterproof overcoat with a belt

trend noun a general direction: *the trend of events*

trendsetter noun someone who starts off a fashion

trendy adjective (**trendier, trendiest**) informal **1** of clothes, clubs, music, etc: fashionable **2** of a person: following the latest fashions

trepidation noun fear, nervousness

trespass verb **1** to go illegally on private land etc **2** (**trespass on**) to intrude upon (someone's time, privacy, etc) **3** to sin ▶ noun (plural **trespasses**) the act of trespassing

trespasser noun someone who trespasses

tress noun (plural **tresses**) **1** a lock of hair **2** (**tresses**) hair, especially long

trestle noun a wooden support with legs, used for holding up a table, platform, etc

tri- prefix three: *triangle/tricycle* ⊕ Comes from Latin *tres* and Greek *treis*, both meaning 'three'

triad noun **1** music a chord of three notes played together **2** (also **Triad**) a Chinese secret society that is involved in crime in a foreign country

trial noun **1** the act of testing or trying (eg something new) **2** a test **3** the judging (of a prisoner) in a court of law **4** suffering ● **on trial 1** being tried (especially in a court of law) **2** for the purpose of trying out: *goods sent on trial* **3** being tested: *I'm still on trial with the company* ● **trial and error** the trying of various methods or choices until the right one is found

triangle noun **1** a figure with three sides and three angles: △ **2** a triangular metal musical instrument, played by striking with a small rod

triangular adjective having the shape of a triangle

triangular number noun, maths **1** a number that can be shown as a triangular array of dots with the number of dots in each line decreasing by 1 **2** a number in the series 0, 1, 3, 6, 10, 15, etc, which is formed by adding 1 to the first number in the series, 2 to the second number in the series, and so on

Triassic adjective of the geological period 250 million to 210 million years ago

triathlon noun a sporting contest consisting of three events, often swimming, running and cycling

triatomic adjective, chemistry having three atoms in the molecule

tribal adjective belonging to or done by a tribe or tribes: *tribal warfare*

tribe noun **1** a people who are all descended from the same ancestor **2** a group of families, especially of a wandering people ruled by a chief **3** biology a subdivision of a family of plants and animals, made up of several related genera

tribesman or **tribeswoman** noun someone who belongs to a particular tribe

tribulation noun great hardship or sorrow

tribunal noun **1** a group of people appointed to give judgement, especially on an appeal **2** a court of justice

tribune noun, history a high official elected by the people in ancient Rome

tributary noun (plural **tributaries**) **1** a stream that flows into a river or other stream **2** someone who gives money as a tribute

tribute noun **1** an expression, in word or deed, of praise, thanks, admiration, etc: *a warm tribute to his courage* **2** money paid regularly by one nation or ruler to another in return for protection or peace

trice noun: **in a trice** in a very short time

triceps singular noun, anatomy a muscle at the back of the arm that straightens the elbow

trichology (pronounced tri-**kawl**-o-ji) noun the branch of medicine that deals with the hair and its diseases ◆ **trichologist** noun

trick noun **1** a cunning or skilful action to puzzle, amuse, etc **2** something said or done to cheat or deceive someone **3** in card games, the cards picked up by the winner when each player has played a card **4** a deceptive appearance; an illusion: *a trick of the light* ▶ adjective meant to deceive: *trick photography* ▶ verb to cheat by some quick or cunning action

trickery noun cheating

trickle verb **1** to flow in small amounts **2** to arrive or leave slowly and gradually: *Replies are trickling in* ▶ noun a slow, gradual flow

trick or treat noun, esp US the children's practice of dressing up on Hallowe'en to call at people's houses for a small gift, otherwise they threaten to play a trick on them

trickster noun someone who deceives by tricks

tricky adjective (**trickier, trickiest**) not easy to do

tricolour adjective with three colours ▶ noun a three-coloured flag, especially that of France or of Ireland

tricycle noun a three-wheeled bicycle

trident noun a three-pronged spear

tried past form of **try**

triennial *adjective* **1** lasting for three years **2** happening every third year

tries see **try**

trifle *noun* **1** anything of little value **2** a small amount **3** a pudding of whipped cream, sponge cake, sherry, etc **4** (**a trifle**) slightly: *a trifle upset* ➤ *verb* **trifle with 1** to treat (someone) without sufficient respect: *in no mood to be trifled with* **2** to amuse yourself in an idle way (with): *He trifled with her affections*

trifling *adjective* very small in value or amount

trigger *noun* a small lever on a gun which, when pulled with the finger, causes the bullet to be fired ➤ *verb* (often **trigger off**) to start, be the cause of, an important event, chain of events, etc

triglyceride *noun, chemistry* a compound of a glycerol molecule combined with three acid radicals, found in most fats and oils

trigonometric or **trigonometrical** *adjective* relating to or involving trigonometry

trigonometric function *noun, maths* a function of an angle that is defined by the relationship between the angles and sides in a right-angled triangle, eg sine, cosine, tangent, secant, cosecant, cotangent

trigonometry *noun* the branch of mathematics which has to do chiefly with the relationship between the sides and angles of triangles

trilateral *adjective* **1** having three sides **2** affecting two sides, parties, etc: *a trilateral agreement* ◆ **trilaterally** *adverb*

trilby *noun* a man's hat with an indented crown and narrow brim

---

⊙ So called because a hat of this shape was worn by an actress in the original stage version of George du Maurier's novel, *Trilby* (1894)

---

trill *verb* to sing, play or utter in a quivering or bird-like way ➤ *noun* a trilled sound; in music, a rapid repeating of two notes several times

trillion *noun* **1** a million million millions **2** (originally *US*) a million millions

trilobite (*pronounced* **trai**-lo-bait) *noun* **1** *zoology* an extinct marine arthropod with an exoskeleton that was divided into three lobes **2** the fossilized remains of this animal

trilogy *noun* (*plural* **trilogies**) a group of three related plays, novels, etc by the same author, meant to be seen or read as a whole

trim *verb* (**trimming, trimmed**) **1** to clip the edges or ends of: *trim the hedge* **2** to arrange (sails, cargo) so that a boat is ready for sailing **3** to decorate (eg a hat) ➤ *noun* **1** the act of trimming **2** dress: *hunting trim* ➤ *adjective* (**trimmer, trimmest**) tidy, in good order, neat • **in good trim 1** in good order **2** fit

trimer (*pronounced* **trai**-mer) *noun, chemistry* a substance whose molecules are formed from three molecules of a monomer

trimester *noun* **1** a period of three months, eg one of the three periods of human gestation **2** a term at university that lasts for three months ⊙ Comes from Latin *trimestris* meaning 'lasting three months'

trimming *noun* **1** a decoration added to a dress, cake, etc **2** a piece of cloth, hair, etc cut off while trimming **3** (**trimmings**) the usual accompaniments of a particular meal or dish: *roast turkey with all the trimmings*

Trimurti *noun* (sometimes **trimurti**) the Hindu gods, Brahma, Siva and Vishnu, representing creation, preservation and destruction ⊙ Comes from Sanskrit *tri* meaning 'three' + *murti* meaning 'shape'

trinity *noun* **1** a group of three **2** *Christianity* the union of Father, Son and Holy Ghost in one God

trinket *noun* a small ornament (especially one of little value)

trio *noun* (*plural* **trios**) **1** three people or things **2** *music* a piece of music for three singers or players

trioxide *noun, chemistry* an oxide that contains three atoms of oxygen

trip *verb* (**tripping, tripped**) **1** (often **trip up**) to stumble, fall over **2** to move with short, light steps **3** (**trip up**) to make a mistake ➤ *noun* **1** a journey for pleasure or business **2** a light short step **3** a hallucinatory experience, especially one brought on by taking a drug, eg LSD: *a bad trip*

tripartite *adjective* **1** in or having three parts **2** of an agreement: between three countries

tripe *noun* **1** part of the stomach of the cow or sheep used as food **2** *informal* rubbish, nonsense

triple *adjective* **1** made up of three **2** three times as large (as something else) ➤ *verb* to make or become three times as large

Triple Alliance *noun, history* an alliance between Germany, Austria and Italy that was in place from 1882 to 1915 (*compare with*: **Triple Entente**)

Triple Entente (*pronounced* on-**tont**) *noun, history* a friendly understanding between Britain, France, and Russia (the **Entente powers**) that developed into a military alliance in 1914 with the outbreak of World War I (*compare with*: **Triple Alliance**)

triple jump *noun* an athletic event that consists of doing a hop, a skip and a jump ◆ **triple jumper** *noun*

triple point *noun, physics* the temperature and pressure at which solid, liquid and gas forms of a substance can coexist

triplet *noun* **1** one of three children or animals born of the same mother at one time **2** three rhyming lines in a poem **3** *music* a group of three notes played in the time of two

triplicate *noun*: **in triplicate** in three copies

triploid *biology, adjective* of an organism or cell: with three times the haploid number of chromosomes ➤ *noun* a triploid organism or cell

tripod *noun* a three-legged stand (especially for a camera)

tripper *noun* someone who goes on a short pleasure trip

triptych (*pronounced* **trip**-tik) *noun* three painted panels forming a whole work of art

trisect *verb* to cut into three

trisection *noun* trisecting, dividing into three parts

trite *adjective* of a remark: used so often that it has little force or meaning

tritium (*pronounced* **tri**-ti-um) *noun, chemistry* (symbol ^{3}**H** or **T**) a radioactive isotope of hydrogen that has two neutrons as well as one proton in its nucleus

triumph *noun* **1** a great success or victory **2** celebration after a success: *ride in triumph through the streets* ➤ *verb* **1** to win a victory **2** to rejoice openly because of a victory

triumphal *adjective* used in celebrating a triumph

triumphant *adjective* victorious; showing joy because of, or celebrating, triumph
   ♦ **triumphantly** *adverb*

triumvirate (*pronounced* trai-**uhm**-vir-at) *noun* a group of three people who share an official position, power, etc equally

⊙ The name given in ancient Rome to the coalition between Caesar, Pompey and Crassus in 60 BC (the 'first triumvirate') and of Caesar, Antony and Lepidus from 43 BC (the 'second triumvirate')

trivalent *adjective, chemistry* able to combine with three atoms of hydrogen

trivet *noun* a metal tripod for resting a teapot or kettle on

trivia *plural noun* unimportant matters or details

trivial *adjective* of very little importance

triviality *noun* (*plural* **trivialities**) **1** something unimportant **2** trivialness

trivialize or **trivialise** *verb* to make or treat as unimportant, worthless, etc

trivialness *noun* the state of being trivial

trochee (*pronounced* **troh**-kee) *noun* a metrical foot of one long or stressed syllable followed by one short or unstressed one
   ♦ **trochaic** *adjective*

trochoid *noun, maths* the curve traced by a point on the radius, but not on the circumference, of a circle as the circle rolls along

a straight line (*compare with*: **cycloid**)
   ♦ **trochoidal** *adjective*

trod past tense of **tread**

trodden past participle of **tread**

troglodyte *noun* a cave-dweller

trojan *noun, computing* a computer program which contains hidden instructions that can lead to data being destroyed, but which, unlike a virus, does not replicate itself

⊙ After the mythological *Trojan* horse, a huge hollow wooden horse that the Greeks used to get into Troy

troll *noun* a mythological creature, giant or dwarf, who lives in a cave

trolley *noun* (*plural* **trolleys**) **1** a small cart (eg as used by porters at railway stations) **2** a supermarket basket on wheels **3** a hospital bed on wheels for transporting patients **4** a table on wheels, used for serving tea etc

trolleybus *noun* a bus which gets its power from overhead wires

trombone *noun* a brass wind instrument with a sliding tube which changes the notes

trompe l'œil (*pronounced* tromp-**loi**) *noun* (*plural* **trompe l'œils**) a painting or decoration that gives a convincing illusion of reality

troop *noun* **1** a collection of people or animals **2** (**troops**) soldiers **3** a unit in cavalry etc ➤ *verb* **1** to gather in numbers **2** to move as a group: *They all trooped out* • **troop the colours** to carry a regiment's flag past the lined-up soldiers of the regiment

trooper *noun* **1** a private soldier, especially one in a cavalry unit **2** *US* a policeman mounted on a horse or motorcycle

trophic level *noun, biology, geography* a division of an ecosystem containing all organisms whose food is obtained from plants by the same number of steps ⊙ Comes from Greek *trophe* meaning 'food'

trophy *noun* (*plural* **trophies**) **1** something taken from an enemy and kept in memory of the victory **2** a prize such as a silver cup won in a sports competition etc ➤ *adjective* of someone's spouse, partner, etc: raising their status in the eyes of other people: *a trophy wife*

tropic *noun* **1** either of two imaginary circles running round the earth at about 23° north (**tropic of Cancer**) or south (**tropic of Capricorn**) of the equator **2** (**tropics**) the hot regions between these circles ➤ *adjective* of the tropics

tropical *adjective* **1** relating to or originating in the tropics: *tropical fish/tropical fruit* **2** of climate: very hot and wet **3** located between the tropics of Cancer and Capricorn

tropism *noun, biology* change in the direction

of growth of a plant or movement of an animal in response to light, heat, gravity, etc

troposphere noun, geography the lowest layer of the atmosphere in which temperature falls as height increases

trot verb (**trotting, trotted**) 1 of a horse: to run with short, high steps 2 of a person: to run slowly with short steps 3 to make (a horse) trot ► noun the pace of a horse or person when trotting

trotters plural noun the feet of pigs or sheep, especially when used as food

troubadour noun, history a medieval travelling singer-musician, especially in S France and N Italy

trouble verb 1 to cause worry or sorrow to 2 to cause inconvenience to 3 to make an effort, bother (to): I didn't trouble to ring him ► noun 1 worry, uneasiness 2 difficulty; disturbance 3 something which causes worry, difficulty, etc 4 illness, weakness or mechanical failure: heart trouble/engine trouble 5 care and effort put into doing something

troublemaker noun someone who continually causes trouble, worry, etc to others

troubleshooter noun someone whose job is to solve difficulties (eg in a firm's business activities) ♦ **troubleshoot** verb

troublesome adjective causing difficulty or inconvenience

trough noun 1 a long, open container for holding animals' food and water 2 an area of low atmospheric pressure 3 a dip between two sea waves

trounce verb 1 to punish or beat severely 2 to defeat heavily

troupe (pronounced troop) noun a company of actors, dancers, etc

trouser adjective of a pair of trousers: trouser leg

trousers plural noun an outer garment for the lower part of the body which covers each leg separately

trousseau (pronounced troos-oh) noun (plural **trousseaux** or **trousseaus** – both pronounced troos-ohz) the clothes, linen, etc a bride used to collect for her married life

trout noun (plural **trout** or **trouts**) a freshwater or sea fish, used as food

trowel noun 1 a small hand-held spade used in gardening 2 a similar tool with a flat blade, used for spreading mortar

troy weight noun a system of weights for weighing gold, gems, etc

truancy noun the practice of being absent from school without permission

truant noun someone who stays away from school etc without permission • **play truant** to stay away from school, work, etc without permission

truce noun a rest from fighting or quarrelling agreed to by both sides

truck noun 1 a wagon for carrying goods on a railway 2 a strong lorry for carrying heavy loads • **have no truck with** to refuse to have dealings with

trucker noun, US a lorry driver

truculence noun 1 being truculent 2 truculent behaviour

truculent adjective fierce and threatening, aggressive

trudge verb to walk with heavy steps, as if tired

true adjective 1 of a story etc: telling of something which really happened 2 correct, not invented or wrong: It's true that the earth is round 3 accurate 4 faithful: a true friend 5 real, properly so called: The spider is not a true insect 6 rightful: the true heir 7 in the correct or intended position

true north noun the direction of the north pole (rather than the direction of magnetic north)

truffle noun 1 a round fungus found underground and much valued as a flavouring for food 2 a type of chocolate sweet with a centre made from cream, butter, chocolate and often a flavouring such as rum

truism noun a statement which is so clearly true that it is not worth making

truly adverb 1 really: Is that truly what he said? 2 genuinely; honestly: I'm truly sorry 3 completely, utterly: a truly classless society

Truman Doctrine noun, history a US foreign policy after World War II, announced by President Harry S Truman, promising military and economic aid to countries threatened by communism

trump noun 1 a suit having a higher value than cards of other suits 2 a card of this suit ► verb to play a card which is a trump • **trump up** to make up, invent • **turn up trumps** to play your part well when things are difficult

trump card noun 1 a card which is a trump 2 something kept in reserve as a means of winning an argument etc

trumped-up adjective of evidence, charges, etc: invented or made up

trumpery noun (plural **trumperies**) something showy but worthless

trumpet noun 1 a brass musical instrument with a clear, high-pitched tone 2 the cry of an elephant ► verb 1 to announce (eg news) so that all may hear 2 to blow a trumpet 3 of elephants: to make a long, loud cry

truncate adjective 1 to cut off at the top or end 2 to shorten ♦ **truncated** adjective ♦ **truncation** noun

truncated spur noun, geography a spur that

has been cut off by glacial erosion of a river valley

truncheon *noun* a short heavy staff or baton such as that used by police officers

trundle *verb* to wheel or roll along

trunk *noun* **1** the main stem of a tree **2** the body (not counting the head, arms or legs) of a person or animal **3** the long nose of an elephant **4** a large box or chest for clothes etc **5** *US* the luggage compartment of a car **6** (**trunks**) short pants worn by boys and men for swimming

trunk road *noun* a main road

truss *noun* (*plural* **trusses**) **1** a bundle (eg of hay, straw) **2** a system of beams to support a bridge **3** a bandage or belt worn to support a hernia ➤ *verb* **1** to bind, tie tightly (up) **2** (often **truss up**) to prepare (a bird ready for cooking) by tying up the legs and wings

trust *noun* **1** belief in the power, truth or goodness of a thing or person **2** something (eg a task or an item of value) handed over to someone in the belief that they will do it, guard it, etc **3** charge, keeping: *The child was put in my trust* **4** arrangement by which something (eg money) is given to someone for use in a particular way **5** a number of business firms working closely together ➤ *verb* **1** to have faith or confidence (in) **2** to give (someone something) in the belief that they will use it well etc: *I can't trust your sister with my tennis racket* **3** to feel confident (that): *I trust that you can find your way here* • **take on trust** to believe without checking or testing

trustee *noun* **1** someone who manages money or property for someone else **2** a member of a group of people managing the affairs of a company or institution

trustful or **trusting** *adjective* ready to trust, not suspicious

trust fund *noun* money or property that is held in trust, eg until the owner is older

trustworthy *adjective* able to be trusted or depended on

trusty *adjective* (**trustier, trustiest**) able to be trusted or depended on; loyal

truth *noun* **1** the state of being true **2** a true statement **3** the facts

truthful *adjective* **1** telling the truth, not lying **2** of a statement: true ♦ **truthfully** *adverb*

try *verb* (**tries, trying, tried**) **1** to attempt, make an effort (to do something) **2** to test by using: *Try this new soap* **3** to test severely, strain: *You're trying my patience* **4** to attempt to use, open, etc: *I tried the door but it was locked* **5** to judge (a prisoner) in a court of law ➤ *noun* (*plural* **tries**) **1** an effort, an attempt **2** in rugby: an act of scoring by carrying the ball over the opponent's goal line and putting it down • **try on** to put on

(clothing) to see if it fits etc • **try out** to test by using

trying *adjective* hard to bear; testing

tryst (*pronounced* trist) *noun, old or literary* **1** an arrangement to meet someone, especially a lover **2** the meeting itself **3** the place where such a meeting takes place ⊙ Comes from French *triste* meaning 'a hunter's waiting-place'

tsar or **tzar** or **czar** (*pronounced* zar) *noun, history* the emperor of Russia before the Revolution

tsarina or **tzarina** or **czarina** (*pronounced* za-**ree**-na) *noun, history* **1** the wife of a tsar **2** an empress of Russia before the Revolution

tsetse or **tsetse fly** (*pronounced* **tset**-si) *noun* an African biting fly which spreads dangerous diseases

T-shirt another spelling of **tee-shirt**

tsp *abbreviation* teaspoon or teaspoonful

tsunami *noun* a very large wave caused by an underwater earthquake or volcanic eruption

tub *noun* **1** a round wooden container used for washing etc **2** a bath **3** a plastic container for ice-cream etc

tuba *noun* a large brass musical instrument giving a low note

tubby *adjective* (**tubbier, tubbiest**) fat and round

tube *noun* **1** a hollow, cylindrical object through which liquid may pass **2** an organ of this kind in humans, animals, etc **3** a container from which something may be squeezed **4** an underground railway system, especially the one in London, or one of its trains **5** a cathode ray tube

tuber *noun* the swollen underground stem of a plant (eg a potato), where food is stored

tuberculosis *noun* an infectious disease affecting the lungs

tubing *noun* a length or lengths of tube

tubular *adjective* shaped like a tube

TUC *abbreviation* Trades Union Congress

tuck *noun* **1** a fold stitched in a piece of cloth **2** *informal* sweets, cakes, etc ➤ *verb* **1** to gather (cloth) together into a fold **2** to fold or push (into or under a place): *tucked the envelope in her pocket* • **tuck in** *informal* to eat with enjoyment or greedily • **tuck someone in** or **up** to push bedclothes closely round (someone in bed)

tuck shop *noun* a shop in a school where sweets, cakes, etc are sold

Tuesday *noun* the third day of the week

⊙ After *Tiw*, the Norse god of war and the sky

tuft *noun* a bunch or clump of grass, hair, etc

tug *verb* (**tugging, tugged**) **1** to pull hard **2** to pull along ➤ *noun* **1** a strong pull **2** a tugboat

tugboat *noun* a small but powerful ship used for towing larger ones

tug-of-war noun a contest in which two teams, holding the ends of a strong rope, pull against each other

tuition noun 1 teaching 2 private coaching or teaching

tulip noun a type of plant with cup-shaped flowers grown from a bulb

⊙ Based on a Persian word for 'turban', because of the similarity in shape

tulle (pronounced tyool) noun a kind of cloth made of thin silk or rayon net

tumble verb 1 to fall or come down suddenly and violently 2 to roll, toss (about) 3 to do acrobatic tricks 4 to throw into disorder ➤ noun 1 a fall 2 a confused state • **tumble to something** to understand it suddenly

tumbledown adjective falling to pieces

tumble-dryer or **tumble-drier** noun an electrical appliance that dries wet laundry by tumbling it around in a current of warm air

tumbler noun 1 a large drinking glass 2 an acrobat

tumbrel or **tumbril** noun, history a two-wheeled cart of the kind used to take victims to the guillotine during the French Revolution

tummy noun (plural **tummies**), informal the stomach

tumour noun an abnormal growth on or in the body

tumult noun 1 a great noise made by a crowd 2 excitement, agitation

tumultuous adjective with great noise or confusion: a tumultuous welcome

tumulus noun (plural **tumuli**) an ancient burial mound ⊙ Comes from Latin, from tumere meaning 'to swell'

tun noun a large cask, especially for wine

tuna noun (plural **tuna** or **tunas**) a large sea fish, used as food (also called: **tunny**)

tundra noun a level treeless plain in Arctic regions

tune noun 1 notes put together to form a melody 2 the music of a song ➤ verb 1 to put (a musical instrument) in tune 2 to adjust a radio set to a particular station 3 (sometimes **tune up**) to improve the working of an engine • **change your tune** to change your opinions, attitudes, etc • **in tune 1** of a musical instrument: having each note adjusted to agree with the others or with the notes of other instruments 2 of a voice: agreeing with the notes of other voices or instruments 3 in agreement (with): in tune with public opinion • **to the tune of** to the sum of: out of pocket to the tune of £300

tuneful adjective having a pleasant or recognizable tune ♦ **tunefully** adverb

tungsten noun, chemistry (symbol **W**) a very hard metallic element used in the manufacture of filaments of electric light bulbs, TV sets, etc

tunic noun 1 a soldier's or police officer's jacket 2 history a loose garment reaching to the knees, worn in ancient Greece and Rome 3 a similar modern garment: gym tunic

tuning fork noun a steel fork which, when struck, gives a note of a certain pitch

tunnel noun an underground passage (eg for a railway train) ➤ verb (**tunnelling, tunnelled**) 1 to make a tunnel 2 of an animal: to burrow

tunnel vision noun 1 a medical condition in which you cannot see objects on the periphery of your field of vision 2 informal the inability or unwillingness to consider other opinions or viewpoints

tunny same as **tuna**

turban noun 1 a long piece of cloth wound round the head, worn by some Muslim and Sikh men 2 a kind of hat resembling this

turbid adjective of liquid: muddy, clouded

turbine noun an engine with curved blades, turned by the action of water, steam, hot air, etc

turbo- prefix using a turbine engine ⊙ Comes from Latin turbo meaning 'a spinning-top'

turbojet noun 1 (full form: **turbojet engine**) a gas turbine that uses exhaust gases to propel an aircraft 2 an aircraft powered by this kind of engine

turbot noun a type of large flat sea fish, used as food

turbulence noun irregular movement of air currents, especially when affecting the flight of aircraft

turbulent adjective 1 disturbed, in a restless state 2 likely to cause a disturbance or riot

turd noun a lump of dung

tureen noun a large dish for holding soup at table

turf noun 1 grass and the soil below it 2 (**the turf**) the world of horse-racing ➤ verb to cover with turf • **turf out** informal to throw out

turf accountant noun, Brit a bookmaker

turgid adjective 1 swollen 2 of language: sounding grand but meaning little, pompous

turkey noun (plural **turkeys**) a large farmyard bird, used as food

Turkish bath noun a type of hot air or steam bath in which someone is made to sweat heavily, is massaged and then slowly cooled

turmeric noun a yellow aromatic spice used in curries

turmoil noun a state of wild, confused movement or disorder

turn verb 1 to go round: wheels turning 2 to face or go in the opposite direction: turned and walked away 3 to change direction: The road turns sharply to the left 4 to direct (eg attention)

5 (**turn on**) to move, swing, etc on: *The door turns on its hinges* **6** of milk: to go sour **7** to become: *His hair turned white* **8** of leaves: to change colour **9** to shape in a lathe **10** to pass (the age of): *She must have turned 40* ➤ *noun* **1** the act of turning **2** a point where someone may change direction, eg a road junction: *Take the first turn on the left* **3** a bend (eg in a road) **4** a spell of duty: *your turn to wash the dishes* **5** an act (eg in a circus or show) **6** a short stroll: *a turn along the beach* **7** a fit of dizziness, shock, etc **8** requirement: *This will serve our turn* • **by turns** or **in turn** one after another in a regular order • **do someone a good (or bad) turn** to act helpfully (or unhelpfully) towards someone • **to a turn** exactly, perfectly: *cooked to a turn* • **turn against** to become hostile to • **turn down 1** to say no to, refuse (eg an offer, a request) **2** to reduce, lessen (heat, volume of sound, etc) • **turn someone's head** to fill them with pride or conceit • **turn in 1** to go to bed **2** to hand over to those in authority: *The bank robber turned himself in* • **turn off 1** to stop the flow of (a tap) **2** to switch off the power for (a television etc) • **turn on 1** to set running (eg water from a tap) **2** to switch on power for (a television etc) **3** to depend (on): *The whole argument turns on a single point* **4** to become angry with (someone) unexpectedly: *She suddenly turned on me* **5** *slang* to arouse sexually • **turn out 1** to make to leave, drive out **2** to make, produce **3** to empty: *turn out your pockets* **4** of a crowd: to come out, gather for a special purpose: *Thousands turned out to welcome him* **5** to switch off (a light) **6** to prove (to be): *He turned out to be right* • **turn to 1** to set to work **2** to go to for help etc • **turn up 1** to appear, arrive **2** to be found **3** to increase (eg heat, volume of sound, etc) ✆ Comes from Latin *tornare* meaning 'to turn in a lathe'

turnabout *noun* **1** an act of turning to face the opposite way **2** a complete change of direction, opinion, policy, etc

turnaround *noun* **1** the processing of something, eg through a manufacturing procedure **2** a turnabout

turncoat *noun* someone who betrays their party, principles, etc

turning *noun* **1** the act of turning **2** a point where one road etc joins another **3** the act of shaping in a lathe

turning-point *noun* **1** a crucial point of change **2** *maths* a maximum or minimum point on a graph

turnip *noun* a plant with a large round root used as a vegetable

turn-off *noun* **1** a road that branches off from a main road **2** *informal* someone or something that causes disgust or revulsion

turn-on *noun, informal* someone or something that causes excitement or interest, especially of a sexual nature

turn-out *noun* the number of people who attend an event, vote in an election, etc: *a high turn-out*

turnover *noun* **1** rate of change or replacement (eg of workers in a firm etc) **2** the total amount of sales made by a firm during a certain time **3** *biology* the formation, wearing away and replacement of body parts

turnpike *noun* **1** *history* a gate across a road which opened when the user paid a toll **2** *US* a road on which a toll is paid

turnstile *noun* a gate which turns, allowing only one person to pass at a time

turntable *noun* **1** a revolving platform for turning a railway engine round **2** the revolving part of a record-player on which the record rests

turn-up *noun, Brit* the bottom of a trouser-leg folded back on itself • **a turn-up for the books** an unexpected and usually pleasant surprise

turpentine *noun* an oil from certain trees used for mixing paints, cleaning paint brushes, etc

turpitude *noun* wickedness

turquoise *noun* **1** a greenish-blue precious stone **2** its greenish-blue colour ➤ *adjective* greenish-blue in colour

✆ Literally 'Turkish stone', because first found in Turkestan

turret *noun* **1** a small tower on a castle or other building **2** a structure for supporting guns on a warship

turreted *adjective* having turrets

turtle *noun* **1** a kind of large tortoise which lives in water **2** *computing* a type of cursor that is moved around in on-screen drawing • **turn turtle** of a boat etc: to turn upside down, capsize

turtledove *noun* a type of dove noted for its sweet, soft song

turtle-neck *noun* **1** a round close-fitting neckline **2** a jumper etc that has this kind of neckline

tusk *noun* a large tooth (one of a pair) sticking out from the mouth of certain animals (eg an elephant, a walrus)

tussle *noun* a struggle ➤ *verb* to struggle, compete

tussock *noun* a tuft of grass

tutor *noun* **1** a teacher of students in a university etc **2** a teacher employed privately to teach individual pupils ➤ *verb* to teach

tutorial *adjective* relating to a tutor ➤ *noun* a meeting for study or discussion between tutor and students

tutti-frutti (*pronounced* too-tee **froo**-tee)

noun an ice cream that contains mixed fruits ⊕ Comes from Italian, meaning 'all fruits'

tutu noun a ballet dancer's short, stiff, spreading skirt

tuxedo noun (plural **tuxedos** or **tuxedoes**) US a dinner-jacket

TV abbreviation television

twaddle noun, informal nonsense

twain noun, old two • **in twain** old in two, apart

twang noun **1** a tone of voice in which the words seem to come through the nose **2** a sound like that of a tightly stretched string being plucked ▸ verb to make such a sound

tweak verb to pull with a sudden jerk, twitch ▸ noun a sudden jerk or pull

twee adjective, Brit informal affectedly pretty, cute, sentimental, etc ◆ **tweeness** noun ⊕ Comes from tweet, a childish pronunciation of sweet

tweed noun **1** a woollen cloth with a rough surface **2** (**tweeds**) clothes made of this cloth ▸ adjective made of tweed

tweet noun a melodious chirping sound made by a small bird ▸ verb to chirp melodiously

tweezers plural noun small pincers for pulling out hairs, holding small things, etc

twelfth adjective the last of a series of twelve ▸ noun one of twelve equal parts

twelve noun the number 12 ▸ adjective 12 in number

twenties plural noun (also **20s, 20's**) **1** the period of time between twentieth and thirtieth birthdays **2** the range of temperatures between twenty and thirty degrees **3** the period of time between the twentieth and thirtieth years of a century

twentieth adjective the last of a series of twenty ▸ noun one of twenty equal parts

twenty noun the number 20 ▸ adjective 20 in number

twice adverb two times

twiddle verb to play with, twirl idly • **twiddle your thumbs 1** to turn your thumbs around one another **2** to have nothing to do

twig noun a small branch of a tree

twilight noun **1** the faint light between sunset and night, or before sunrise **2** the time just before or after the peak of something: the twilight of the dictatorship

twill noun a kind of strong cloth with a ridged appearance

twin noun **1** one of two children or animals born of the same mother at the same birth **2** one of two things exactly the same ▸ adjective **1** born at the same birth **2** very like another **3** made up of two parts or things which are alike

twine noun a strong kind of string made of twisted threads ▸ verb **1** to wind or twist together **2** to wind (about or around something)

twinge noun a sudden, sharp pain

twinkle verb **1** of a star etc: to shine with light which seems to vary in brightness **2** of eyes: to shine with amusement etc ◆ **twinkle** or **twinkling** noun the act or state of twinkling • **in a twinkling** in an instant

twirl verb **1** to turn or spin round quickly and lightly **2** to turn round and round with the fingers: twirling a baton ▸ noun a spin round and round

twist verb **1** to wind (threads) together **2** to wind round or about something **3** to make (eg a rope) into a coil **4** to bend out of shape **5** to bend or wrench painfully (eg your ankle) **6** to make (eg facts) appear to have a meaning which is really false ▸ noun **1** the act of twisting **2** a painful wrench **3** something twisted: a twist of tissue paper

twister noun, informal **1** Brit a dishonest and unreliable person **2** US a tornado

twit noun, informal a fool or idiot

twitch verb **1** to pull with a sudden light jerk **2** to jerk slightly and suddenly: A muscle in his face twitched ▸ noun **1** a sudden jerk **2** a muscle spasm

twitchy adjective (**twitchier, twitchiest**) **1** informal nervous, anxious or restless: getting a bit twitchy about the interview **2** characterized by twitching: a twitchy eye

twitter noun **1** high, rapidly repeated sounds, as are made by small birds **2** slight nervous excitement ▸ verb **1** of a bird: to make a series of high quivering notes **2** of a person: to talk continuously

two noun the number 2 ▸ adjective 2 in number ⊕ Comes from Old English twa meaning 'two'

two-dimensional adjective having height and width, but not depth (short form **2-D**)

two-faced adjective deceitful, insincere

twofold adjective & adverb (by) twice as much

two-time verb to have a love affair with two people at the same time

tycoon noun a business man of great wealth and power

⊕ Based on a Japanese title for a warlord

tympani another spelling of **timpani**

tympanic membrane (pronounced tim-pan-ik) noun, anatomy the membrane separating the middle ear from the outer ear; the eardrum

tympanum (pronounced **tim**-pa-num) noun (plural **tympana** or **tympanums**), anatomy **1** the cavity of the middle ear **2** the tympanic membrane ⊕ Comes from Greek tympanon meaning 'a drum'

type noun **1** kind **2** an example which has all the

usual characteristics of its kind **3** a small metal block with a raised letter or sign, used for printing **4** a set of these **5** printed lettering ➤ *verb* **1** to print with a typewriter **2** to use a typewriter **3** to identify or classify as a particular type

typecast *verb* to give (an actor) parts very similar in character

typeface *noun* a set of printed letters and characters in a particular style

typescript *noun* a typed script for a play etc

typeset *verb* (**typeset, typesetting**) to arrange (type) or set (a page) in type ready for printing

typewriter *noun* a machine with keys which, when struck, print letters on a sheet of paper

typhoid *noun* an infectious disease caused by germs in infected food or drinking water

typhoon *noun* a violent tropical windstorm originating in the Pacific (*see also*: **hurricane, tornado**)

typhus *noun* a dangerous fever carried by lice and characterized by fever, severe headache and a rash

typical *adjective* having or showing the usual characteristics: *a typical Irishman/typical of her* to be late ♦ **typically** *adverb*

typify *verb* (**typifies, typifying, typified**) to be a good example of: *typifying the English abroad*

typist *noun* someone who works with a typewriter and does other secretarial or clerical tasks

typo *noun, informal* a typographical error

typographical *adjective* relating to or involving printing or typography

typography *noun* the use of type for printing

tyrannical or **tyrannous** *adjective* like a tyrant, cruel

tyrannize or **tyrannise** *verb* to act as a tyrant; rule over harshly

tyranny *noun* (*plural* **tyrannies**) the rule of a tyrant

tyrant *noun* a ruler who governs cruelly and unjustly

tyre or *US* **tire** *noun* a thick rubber cover round a motor or cycle wheel

tyro another spelling of **tiro**

tzar another spelling of **tsar**

tzarina another spelling of **tsarina**

Uu

U¹ *abbreviation* universal (denoting a film that is suitable for everyone)

U² *symbol, chemistry* uranium

ubiquitous (*pronounced* yoo-**bik**-wit-*us*) *adjective* **1** being everywhere at once **2** found everywhere

ubiquity (*pronounced* yoo-**bik**-wit-i) *noun* existence everywhere

U-boat *noun* a German submarine, used especially in World Wars I and II ⊙ Comes from German *U-boot*, short for *Unterseeboot*, literally meaning 'undersea-boat'

udder *noun* a bag-like part of a cow, goat, etc with teats which supply milk

UFO (*pronounced* yoo-ef-**oh** or **yoo**-foh) *abbreviation* unidentified flying object

ugliness *noun* being ugly

ugly *adjective* (**uglier, ugliest**) **1** unpleasant to look at or hear: *ugly sound* **2** threatening, dangerous: *gave me an ugly look* • **ugly duckling** an unattractive or unappreciated person who later turns into a beauty, success, etc

UHF *abbreviation* ultra high frequency

UHT *abbreviation* **1** ultra-heat treated **2** ultra high temperature

ukulele or **ukelele** (*pronounced* yook-e-**lei**-li) *noun* a small, stringed musical instrument played like a banjo

⊙ A Hawaiian word meaning literally 'jumping flea'

ulcer *noun* an open sore on the skin or the mucous membrane inside the body

ulcerated *adjective* having an ulcer or ulcers

ulcerous *adjective* affected with ulcers

ulna *noun, anatomy* the thinner and longer of the two bones of the human forearm (*compare with*: **radius**)

Ulster Unionist Party *noun* a Protestant loyalist party of Northern Ireland

ulterior *adjective* beyond what is admitted or seen: *ulterior motive*

ultimate *adjective* last, final

ultimately *adverb* finally, in the end

ultimatum *noun* a final demand sent with a threat to break off discussion, declare war, etc if it is not met

ultra- *prefix* **1** very: *ultra-careful* **2** beyond: *ultramicroscopic* ⊙ Comes from Latin *ultra* meaning 'beyond'

ultramarine *adjective* of a deep blue colour

ultrasound *noun* **1** a sound whose frequency is too high to be heard by humans **2** the use of ultrasound waves to produce images of the inside of the body, to detect flaws in metals and to clean industrial tools ♦ **ultrasonic** *adjective*

ultrasound scan *noun* a medical examination of an internal part of the body, especially a fetus, by passing ultrasound waves through it to produce an image on a screen

ultraviolet *adjective* having rays of slightly shorter wavelength than visible light

umbel *noun, botany* a cluster of flowers with stalks of equal length arising from the same point on the main stem ⊙ Comes from Latin *umbella* meaning 'sunshade'

umber *noun* a mineral substance used to produce a brown paint

umbilical *adjective* of the navel

umbilical cord *noun* a tube connecting an unborn mammal to its mother through the placenta

umbilicus *noun* (*plural* **umbilici** or **umbilicuses**) **1** *anatomy* the navel **2** *biology* a small depression or hole similar to a navel, eg at the base of a shell

umbra *noun* the shadow cast by the earth or the moon during an eclipse

umbrage *noun* a feeling of offence or hurt: *took umbrage at my suggestion*

umbrella *noun* an object carried to provide shelter from rain, made up of a circular fabric canopy on a light, collapsible framework of ribs fitted around a central stick ➤ *adjective* to do with something that covers or protects a number of things: *an umbrella organization*

⊙ Literally 'little shadow' and originally used to refer to a sunshade

umlaut (*pronounced* **oom**-lowt) *noun* a character (¨) placed over a letter to modify its pronunciation

umma or **ummah** *noun, Islam* the body of Muslim believers considered as one community ⊙ Comes from Arabic meaning 'people', 'community'

umpire *noun* **1** a sports official who sees that a game is played according to the rules **2** a judge asked to settle a dispute ➤ *verb* to act as an umpire

umpteen *adjective* many, lots

⏱ Originally *umpty*, a signaller's slang term for a dash in Morse code

UN *abbreviation* United Nations

un- *prefix* **1** not: *unequal* **2** (with verbs) used to show the reversal of an action: *unfasten* ⏱ Comes from Old English prefixes *un-* meaning 'not' and *on-* meaning 'against'

unabashed *adjective* shameless, blatant

unable *adjective* lacking enough strength, power, skill, etc

unaccountable *adjective* not able to be explained ♦ **unaccountably** *adverb*: *She was feeling unaccountably depressed*

unaccustomed *adjective* not used (to)

unadulterated *adjective* pure, not mixed with anything else

unanimity (*pronounced* yoo-na-**nim**-it-i) *noun* unanimous agreement

unanimous (*pronounced* yoo-**nan**-im-u-s) *adjective* **1** all of the same opinion: *We were unanimous* **2** agreed to by all: *a unanimous decision* ♦ **unanimously** *adverb*: *He was elected unanimously*

unannounced *adjective* not announced; unexpected or without warning: *Our visitors arrived anannounced*

unapproachable *adjective* unfriendly and stiff in manner

unarmed *adjective* not armed

unassuming *adjective* modest

unattached *adjective* **1** not attached **2** single, not married or having a partner

unaware *adjective* not knowing, ignorant (of): *unaware of the danger*

unawares *adverb* **1** unexpectedly or without warning: *He caught me unawares* **2** unintentionally

unbalanced *adjective* mad; lacking balance: *unbalanced view*

unbearable *adjective* too painful or bad to be endured

unbeatable *adjective* not able to be beaten or surpassed: *unbeatable value for money*

unbeknown or **unbeknownst** *adverb* (usually **unbeknown** or **unbeknownst to**) without someone's knowledge

unbeliever *noun* someone who does not follow a certain religion

unbending *adjective* severe

unbounded *adjective* not limited, very great: *unbounded enthusiasm*

unbridled *adjective* not kept under control: *unbridled fury*

unburden *verb*: **unburden yourself** to tell your secrets or problems to someone else

uncalled *adjective*: **uncalled for** quite unnecessary: *Your remarks were uncalled for*

uncanny *adjective* strange, mysterious ♦ **uncannily** *adverb*

uncared *adjective*: **uncared for** not looked after properly

unceremonious *adjective* informal, offhand ♦ **unceremoniously** *adverb*: *bundled him unceremoniously into a taxi*

uncertain *adjective* **1** not certain, doubtful **2** not definitely known **3** of weather: changeable

uncharted *adjective* **1** not shown on a map or chart **2** little known

uncle *noun* **1** the brother of your father or mother **2** the husband of your father's or mother's sister

unclean *adjective* dirty, impure

Uncle Sam *noun, informal* the United States, its government or its people

⏱ Perhaps a humorous interpretation of the letters *US*

uncoil *verb* to unwind

uncomfortable *adjective* not comfortable

uncommon *adjective* not common, strange

uncommonly *adverb* very: *uncommonly talented*

uncompromising *adjective* not willing to give in or make concessions to others

unconcerned *adjective* **1** not anxious or troubled **2** not interested; indifferent

unconditional *adjective* with no conditions attached; absolute: *our unconditional support*

unconscious *adjective* **1** senseless, stunned (eg by an accident) **2** not aware (of) **3** not recognized by the person concerned: *unconscious prejudice against women* ➤ *noun* (**the unconscious**) the deepest level of the mind

unconstitutional *adjective* not allowed by or in keeping with a nation's constitution

uncouth *adjective* **1** clumsy, awkward **2** rude

uncover *verb* **1** to remove a cover from **2** to disclose: *uncover a plot*

unction *noun* anointing; anointment

unctuous *adjective* oily, ingratiating

undaunted *adjective* fearless; not discouraged

undecided *adjective* not yet decided

undeniable *adjective* not able to be denied, clearly true

under *preposition* **1** directly below or beneath: *under the table* **2** less than: *costing under £5* **3** within the authority or command of: *under General Montgomery* **4** going through, suffering: *under attack* **5** having, using: *under a false name* **6** in accordance with: *under our agreement* ➤ *adverb* in or to a lower position, condition, etc • **go under 1** to sink beneath the surface of water **2** to go bankrupt, go out of business • **under way** in motion, started

---

(○ **under** is an Old English word)

---

under- *prefix* **1** below, beneath: *underachieve/ underarm* **2** lower in position or rank: *underdog/ underling* **3** too little: *underdeveloped/ underrate*

underachieve *verb* to achieve less than your potential

under-age *adjective* **1** of a person: below an age required by law, too young: *I can't serve you: you're under-age* **2** of an activity etc: carried on by someone who is under-age: *under-age drinking*

underarm *adverb* of bowling etc: with the arm kept below the shoulder (*compare with*: **overarm**)

undercarriage *noun* the wheels of an aeroplane and their supports

underclothes *plural noun* clothes worn next to the skin under other clothes

undercover *adjective* acting or done in secret: *an undercover agent* (= a spy)

undercurrent *noun* **1** a flow or movement under the surface **2** a half-hidden feeling or tendency: *an undercurrent of despair in her voice*

undercut *verb* to sell at a lower price than someone else

underdeveloped *adjective* **1** not fully grown **2** of a country: lacking modern agricultural and industrial systems, and with a low standard of living

underdog *noun* the weaker side, or the loser in any conflict or fight

underdone *adjective* of food: not quite cooked

underestimate *verb* to estimate at less than the real worth, value, etc

underfloor *adjective* situated, operating, etc beneath the floor: *underfloor heating*

underfoot *adjective* under the feet

undergarment *noun* any garment worn under other clothes

undergo *verb* **1** to suffer, endure **2** to receive (eg as medical treatment)

undergraduate *noun* a university student who has not yet passed final examinations

underground *adjective* **1** below the surface of the ground **2** secret, covert ➤ *noun* **1** a railway which runs in a tunnel beneath the surface of the ground **2** a secret paramilitary organization fighting a government or occupying force **3** any artistic movement that tries to challenge or overturn established views and practices

undergrowth *noun* shrubs or low plants growing amongst trees

underhand *adjective* sly, deceitful

underlay *noun* a type of rubber matting laid under a carpet for protection

underlie *verb* to be the hidden cause or source of

underline *verb* **1** to draw a line under **2** to stress the importance of, emphasize

underling *noun* someone of lower rank

underlying *adjective* **1** lying under or beneath **2** fundamental, basic: *the underlying causes*

undermine *verb* to do damage to, weaken gradually (health, authority, etc)

underneath *adverb & preposition* in a lower position (than), beneath: *Look underneath the table/wearing a jacket underneath his coat*

undernourished *adjective* not well nourished
 ♦ **undernourishment** *noun*

underpants *plural noun* underwear covering the buttocks and upper legs

underpass *noun* a road passing under another one

underpay *verb* to pay too little

underpin *verb* to support from beneath, prop up

underpopulation *noun, geography* fewer people in a given area than can fully exploit the natural resources of the area

underprivileged *adjective* not having normal living standards or rights

underrate *verb* to think too little of, underestimate

underscore *verb* **1** to draw a line under something **2** to emphasize something ➤ *noun* a line inserted or drawn under a piece of text (_), often used in e-mail addresses

undersell *verb* **1** to sell for less than the true value **2** to sell for less than someone else

undersigned *noun*: (**the undersigned**) the people whose names are written at the end of a letter or statement

undersized *adjective* smaller than the usual or required size

underskirt *noun* a thin skirt worn under another skirt

understand *verb* **1** to see the meaning of **2** to appreciate the reasons for: *I don't understand your behaviour* **3** to have a thorough knowledge of: *Do you understand economics?* **4** to have the impression that: *I understood that you weren't coming* **5** to take for granted as part of an agreement

understandable *adjective* **1** reasonable, natural or normal: *He reacted with understandable fury* **2** capable of being understood: *His speech was barely understandable*

understanding *noun* **1** the ability to see the full meaning of something **2** someone's interpretation of information received **3** an agreement **4** condition: *on the understanding* that we both pay half **5** appreciation of other people's feelings, difficulties, etc ▸ *adjective* able to understand other people's feelings, sympathetic

understate *verb* to represent something as being less important or smaller than it really is

understated *adjective* of style, appearance, etc: effective because simple, not showy or overdone

understatement *noun* a statement which does not give the whole truth, making less of certain details than is actually the case

understudy *noun* (*plural* **understudies**) an actor who learns the part of another actor and is able to take their place if necessary

undertake *verb* **1** to promise (to do something) **2** to take upon yourself (a task, duty, etc): *I undertook responsibility for the food*

undertaker *noun* someone whose job is to organize funerals

undertaking *noun* **1** something which is being attempted or done **2** a promise **3** the business of an undertaker

under-the-counter *adjective* hidden from customers' sight; illegal

undertone *noun* **1** a soft voice **2** a partly hidden meaning, feeling, etc: *an undertone of discontent*

undertow *noun* a current below the surface of the water which moves in a direction opposite to the surface movement

undervalue *verb* to value (something) below its real worth

underwater *adjective* under the surface of the water

underwear *noun* underclothes

underweight *adjective* under the usual or required weight

underworld *noun* **1** the criminal world or level of society **2** the place where spirits go after death

underwrite *verb* **1** to accept for insurance **2** to accept responsibility or liability for

underwriter *noun* someone who insures ships

undesirable *adjective* not wanted; objectionable in some way

undeveloped *adjective* not developed

undies *plural noun, informal* items of underwear, especially women's bras, pants, etc

undivided *adjective* not split, complete, total: *undivided attention*

undo *verb* **1** to unfasten (a coat, parcel, etc) **2** to cancel the effect of, reverse: *undoing all the good I did* **3** *old* to ruin, dishonour (especially a reputation): *Alas, I am undone*

undoing *noun* ruin, dishonour

undoubted *adjective* not to be doubted

undoubtedly *adverb* without doubt, certainly

undreamt-of *adjective* more, better, etc than could have been imagined: *undreamt-of success*

undress *verb* to take your clothes off

undue *adjective* too much, more than is necessary: *undue expense*

undulate *verb* **1** to move as waves do **2** to have a rolling, wavelike appearance ♦ **undulating** *adjective* ♦ **undulation** *noun*

unduly *adverb* excessively; unreasonably: *unduly worried*

undying *adjective* unending, never fading: *undying love*

unearned income *noun* income, eg dividends and interest earned on savings etc, that is not payment for work done

unearth *verb* to bring or dig out from the earth, or from a place of hiding

unearthly *adjective* **1** strange, as if not of this world **2** *informal* absurd, especially absurdly early: *at this unearthly hour*

unease *noun* discomfort or apprehension: *feelings of unease*

uneasy *adjective* anxious, worried ♦ **uneasily** *adverb* ♦ **uneasiness** *noun*

unemployed *adjective* **1** without a job **2** not in use ▸ *noun* (**the unemployed**) unemployed people as a group

unemployment *noun* **1** the state of being unemployed **2** the total number of unemployed people in a country

unenviable *adjective* not arousing envy: *unenviable task*

unequal *adjective* **1** not equal; unfair: *unequal distribution* **2** lacking enough strength or skill: *unequal to the job*

unequalled *adjective* without an equal, unique

unequivocal (*pronounced* un-i-**kwiv**-ok-al) *adjective* clear, not ambiguous: *unequivocal orders*

unerring *adjective* always right, never making a mistake: *unerring judgement*

uneven *adjective* **1** not smooth or level **2** not all of the same quality etc: *This work is very uneven*

unexceptionable *adjective* not causing objections or criticism

❗ Do not confuse: **unexceptionable** and **unexceptional**

unexceptional *adjective* not exceptional, ordinary

unexpected *adjective* not expected, sudden

unfailing *adjective* never failing, never likely to fail: *unfailing accuracy*

unfair *adjective* not just

unfaithful *adjective* **1** not true to your marriage vows **2** failing to keep promises

unfamiliar *adjective* **1** not (already or previously) known, experienced, etc **2** strange; unusual **3** (usually **unfamiliar with**) of a person: not familiar with or aware of with something ♦ **unfamiliarity** noun

unfasten verb to loosen, undo (eg a buttoned coat)

unfathomable adjective not understandable, not clear

unfavourable adjective not helpful: unfavourable conditions for sailing

unfeeling adjective harsh, hard-hearted

unfettered adjective not restrained

unfit adjective **1** not suitable **2** not good enough, or not in a suitable state (to, for): unfit for drinking/unfit to travel **3** not in good physical condition: I'm so unfit

unfold verb **1** to spread out **2** to give details of (a story, plan) **3** of details of a plot etc: to become known: as the story unfolds

unforced adjective **1** not compelled or brought about by something else: unforced error **2** natural

unforgettable adjective unlikely to ever be forgotten; memorable

unfortunate adjective **1** unlucky **2** regrettable: unfortunate turn of phrase ♦ **unfortunately** adverb

unfounded adjective not based on fact; untrue: Her fears proved unfounded

unfurl verb to unfold (eg a flag)

ungainly adjective clumsy, awkward

ungodly adjective **1** wicked or sinful **2** informal outrageous, especially outrageously early: at an ungodly hour

ungracious adjective rude, not polite

ungrateful adjective not showing thanks for kindness

unguarded adjective **1** without protection **2** thoughtless, careless: unguarded remark

unguent (pronounced **ung**-gwent) noun ointment

ungulate chiefly zoology, adjective **1** hoof-shaped **2** of a mammal: hoofed ➤ noun a hoofed mammal ⓘ Comes from Latin ungula meaning 'hoof' or 'claw'

unhappy adjective **1** miserable, sad **2** unfortunate ♦ **unhappily** adverb

unhealthy adjective **1** not well, ill **2** harmful to health: unhealthy climate **3** showing signs of not being well: unhealthy complexion

unheard-of adjective very unusual, unprecedented

unhinged adjective mad, crazy

unholy adjective **1** evil **2** outrageous

uni noun, informal university

uni- prefix one, a single: unilateral/unit ⓘ Comes from Latin unus meaning 'one'

unicameral adjective of a legislative body: made up of only one chamber ⓘ Comes from Latin camera meaning 'a chamber'

unicellular adjective, biology having or consisting of a single cell

unicorn noun a mythological animal like a horse, but with one straight horn on its forehead

unicycle noun a cycle consisting of a single wheel with a seat and pedals attached, used by acrobats in circus performances etc ♦ **unicyclist** noun

unification noun the act of unifying or the state of being unified

uniform adjective the same in all parts or times, never varying ➤ noun the form of clothes worn by people in the armed forces, children at a particular school, etc

uniformity noun sameness: the uniformity of modern architecture

unify verb (**unifies, unifying, unified**) to combine into one

unilateral adjective (compare with: **multilateral**) **1** involving or affecting one person or group out of several: unilateral disarmament **2** one-sided ♦ **unilaterally** adverb

unilateralism noun unilateral policy, especially the abandoning of nuclear weapons by one country, without waiting for others to do likewise ♦ **unilateralist** noun & adjective

uninhibited adjective not inhibited, unrestrained

uninitiated adjective not knowing, ignorant

uninstall or **uninstal** verb (**uninstalls** or **uninstals, uninstalling, uninstalled**) to take out of position or use: Uninstall the program from your computer when you're finished

uninterested adjective not interested

⚠ Do not confuse with: **disinterested**. It is generally a negative thing to be **uninterested** (= bored). It is generally a positive thing to be **disinterested** (= fair), especially if you are trying to make an unbiased decision.

uninterrupted adjective **1** continuing without a break **2** of a view: not blocked by anything

union noun **1** the act of joining together **2** partnership; marriage **3** countries or states joined together **4** a trade union **5** maths a set made up of all the members of two or more smaller sets, but no others

unionist noun **1** a member of a trade union **2** (**Unionist**) someone who supports the union of the countries comprising the United Kingdom ♦ **unionism** noun

Union Jack or **Union flag** noun the flag of the United Kingdom

unique adjective without a like or equal: a unique sense of timing

! Do not confuse with: **rare**.
You can talk about something being **rare**, quite **rare**, very **rare**, etc. It would be incorrect, however, to describe something as 'very **unique**', since things either are or are not **unique** – there are no levels of this quality.

unisex adjective suitable for either men or women: a unisex hair salon

unisexual adjective **1** relating to one sex only **2** botany, zoology with either male or female reproductive organs ◆ **unisexuality** noun

unison noun **1** agreement, accord **2** exact sameness of musical pitch • **in unison** all together

unit noun **1** a single thing, person or group, especially when considered as part of a larger whole: army unit/storage unit/kitchen unit **2** a fixed amount or length used as a standard by which others are measured (eg metres, litres, centimetres, etc) **3** any whole number less than ten **4** a standard measure used to calculate alcohol intake

unitary adjective **1** forming a unit, not divided **2** using or based on units

unit circle noun, maths a circle in which the radius is considered to be one unit

unite verb **1** to join together; become one **2** to act together

united adjective **1** in agreement about something: united in their opposition **2** joined together: a united Ireland

United Nations singular noun or plural noun (abbrev **UN**) an association of states formed in 1945 to promote peace and international co-operation

unit fraction noun, maths a fraction whose numerator is 1 and whose denominator is an integer that is not 0, eg $\frac{1}{5}$

unit trust noun an investment scheme in which clients' money is invested in various companies, with the combined shares purchased divided into units that are allocated to each client according to how much they invested

unit vector noun, maths a vector with the magnitude 1

unity noun **1** complete agreement **2** the state of being one or a whole **3** the number one or numeral 1

univalent same as **monovalent**

univalve zoology, adjective of a mollusc: with a shell that is in one piece, lacking a hinge as in a bivalve ➤ noun a mollusc whose shell is composed of a single piece

universal adjective **1** relating to the universe **2** relating to, or coming from, all people: universal criticism ◆ **universally** adverb (meaning 2): universally acclaimed

universal indicator noun, chemistry a mixture of several chemical indicators, used to measure the pH of a solution

universe noun all known things, including the earth and planets

university noun (plural **universities**) a college which teaches a wide range of subjects to a high level, and which awards degrees to students who pass its examinations

UNIX or **Unix** (pronounced **yoo**-niks) noun, computing trademark a type of operating system designed to handle large file transfers and allow multi-user access

unkempt adjective untidy

unkind adjective not kind; harsh, cruel

unknown adjective **1** not known; unfamiliar **2** not at all famous ➤ noun a person who is not famous **2** (**the unknown**) things that are unexplained, undiscovered, etc • **unknown quantity** a person or thing whose nature or influence is not known or cannot be predicted

unleaded adjective of petrol: not containing lead compounds

unleash verb **1** to set free (a dog etc) **2** to let loose (eg anger)

unleavened (pronounced un-**lev**-end) adjective of bread: not made to rise with yeast

unless conjunction if not, except in a case where: Unless he's here soon, I'm going (= if he's not here soon)

unlike adjective different, not similar ➤ preposition **1** different from **2** not characteristic of: It was unlike her not to phone

unlikely adjective **1** not probable: It's unlikely that it will rain today **2** probably not true: an unlikely tale

unload verb **1** to take (the load) from: unloading the truck/unloaded the packages **2** to remove the charge from a gun

unlock verb **1** to undo the lock of (a door, suitcase, etc) **2** to release or reveal (emotions etc)

unlucky adjective **1** not lucky or fortunate **2** unsuccessful ◆ **unluckily** adverb

unmanly adjective weak, cowardly

unmask verb **1** to take a covering off **2** to show the true character of **3** to bring to light (a plot etc)

unmentionable adjective not fit to be spoken of, scandalous, indecent

unmistakable or **unmistakeable** adjective very clear; impossible to confuse with any other: unmistakable handwriting

unmitigated adjective complete, absolute: unmitigated disaster

unmoved adjective not affected, unsympathetic: unmoved by my pleas

unnatural adjective not natural, perverted

unnecessary *adjective* not necessary; avoidable

unnerve *verb* to disconcert, perturb

unobtrusive *adjective* not obvious or conspicuous; modest

unofficial *adjective* **1** not officially authorized or confirmed **2** not formal in character **3** of a strike: not called by the strikers' trade union
♦ **unofficially** *adverb*

unpack *verb* to open (a piece of luggage) and remove the contents

unpalatable *adjective* **1** not pleasing to the taste **2** not pleasant to have to face up to: *unpalatable facts*

unparalleled *adjective* not having an equal, unprecedented: *unparalleled success*

unpick *verb* to take out sewing stitches from

unpleasant *adjective* not pleasant, nasty

unprecedented *adjective* never having happened before

unprepossessing *adjective* not attractive

unprincipled *adjective* without (moral) principles

unprintable *adjective* not suitable to be printed; obscene

unprofessional *adjective* not in accordance with the rules governing, or standards expected from, members of a particular profession: *unprofessional conduct*

unquestionable *adjective* undoubted, certain

unravel *verb* (**unravelling, unravelled**) **1** to unwind, take the knots out of **2** to solve (a problem or mystery)

unreal *adjective* **1** not real, imaginary **2** *informal* amazing, incredible

unremitting *adjective* never stopping, unending: *unremitting rain*

unrequited *adjective* of love: not given in return, one-sided

unrest *noun* a state of trouble or discontent, especially among a group of people

unrivalled *adjective* without an equal

unruffled *adjective* **1** of a surface: smooth or still **2** of a person: not agitated or flustered

unruly *adjective* **1** badly behaved **2** not obeying laws or rules ♦ **unruliness** *noun*

unsaid *adjective* not said, expressed, spoken, etc, especially when it should have been

unsaturated *adjective, chemistry* (contrasted with: **saturated**) **1** of a compound: containing at least one double or triple bond between its carbon atoms, and therefore able to combine with atoms of other substances **2** of a solution: not containing the maximum amount of a solute that can be dissolved in it

unsaturated fat *noun* a fat that contains a high proportion of unsaturated fatty acids

unsavoury *adjective* very unpleasant, causing a feeling of disgust: *a rather unsavoury character*

unscathed *adjective* not harmed

unscrew *verb* to loosen (something screwed in)

unscrupulous *adjective* having no scruples or principles

unseat *verb* **1** to remove from a political seat **2** to throw from the saddle (of a horse)

unseeded *adjective sport* of a team or competitor: not placed among the top teams or competitors in the first rounds of a tournament

unseemly *adjective* unsuitable, improper: *unseemly haste*

unseen *adjective* not seen • **sight unseen** (bought etc) without having been seen, at the buyer's risk

unselfish *adjective* **1** showing concern for others **2** generous

unsettle *verb* to disturb, upset

unsettled *adjective* **1** disturbed **2** of weather: changeable **3** of a bill: unpaid

unsettling *adjective* disturbing, upsetting

unsightly *adjective* ugly

unsociable *adjective* not willing to mix with other people

unsolicited *adjective* not requested: *unsolicited advice*

unsophisticated *adjective* **1** simple, uncomplicated **2** naive, inexperienced

unsound *adjective* **1** incorrect, unfounded **2** not sane: *of unsound mind*

unspeakable *adjective* too bad to describe in words: *unspeakable rudeness*

unsteady *adjective* **1** not secure or firm **2** not regular or constant **3** of movement: unsure

unstinting *adjective* unrestrained, generous: *unstinting in his praise*

unstoppable *adjective* not able to be stopped

unstuck *adjective* loosened or released from being stuck • **come unstuck** *informal* of a person, plan, etc: to go wrong

unsung *adjective* not celebrated, neglected: *an unsung Scots poet*

unsuspecting *adjective* not aware of coming danger

unswerving *adjective* solid, unwavering

untenable *adjective* of an argument, opinion, etc: not able to be defended or justified: *The government's position is untenable*

unthinkable *adjective* **1** very unlikely **2** too bad to be thought of

unthinking *adjective* **1** inconsiderate; thoughtless **2** careless ♦ **unthinkingly** *adverb*

untidy *adjective* not neat or well-organized

untie *verb* **1** to release from bonds **2** to loosen (a knot)

until *preposition* up to the time of: *Can you wait until Tuesday?* ► *conjunction* up to the time that: *Keep walking until you come to the corner*

untimely *adjective* **1** happening too soon: *untimely arrival* **2** not suitable to the occasion: *untimely remark*

unto *preposition, old* to

untold *adjective* **1** not yet told: *the untold story* **2** too great to be counted or measured: *untold riches*

untoward *adjective* **1** unlucky, unfortunate **2** inconvenient

untrue *adjective* **1** not true, false **2** unfaithful

untruth *noun* a lie

untruthful *adjective* lying or dishonest

unusual *adjective* **1** not usual **2** rare, remarkable

unusually *adverb* to an unusual degree: *unusually cold for the time of year*

unvarnished *adjective* **1** not varnished **2** plain, straightforward: *the unvarnished truth*

unveil *verb* **1** to remove a veil from **2** to remove a cover from (a memorial, statue, etc) **3** to bring to light, reveal: *unveiled plans to raise the school-leaving age*

unwaged *adjective* unemployed

unwarranted *adjective* uncalled for, unnecessary

unwary *adjective* careless or incautious; not aware of possible danger ♦ **unwarily** *adverb* ♦ **unwariness** *noun*

unwashed *adjective* not washed; not clean • **the great unwashed** *informal, jocular* the lower classes; the masses

unwell *adjective* not in good health

unwieldy *adjective* not easily moved or handled ♦ **unwieldiness** *noun*

unwind *verb* **1** to wind off from a ball or reel **2** to relax

unwise *adjective* ill-advised, foolish

unwitting *adjective* **1** unintended: *unwitting insult* **2** unaware ♦ **unwittingly** *adverb*: *You have unwittingly caused a lot of trouble*

unwonted *adjective* unaccustomed, not usual: *unwonted cheerfulness*

unworthy *adjective* **1** not worthy **2** low, worthless, despicable **3** (**unworthy of something**) not deserving it: *unworthy of attention* **4** below someone's usual standard, out of character: *That remark is unworthy of you*

unwrap *verb* to remove the wrapping from something

unwritten *adjective* **1** not recorded in writing or print **2** of a rule or law: not formalized, but traditionally followed

unzip *verb* **1** to unfasten (a garment, bag, etc) by undoing a zip **2** of a garment, bag, etc: to open or come apart by means of a zip **3** *computing* to convert (compressed data) into a less compressed form

up *adverb* **1** towards or in a higher or more northerly position: *They live up in the Highlands*

2 completely, so as to finish: *Drink up your tea* **3** to a larger size: *blow up a balloon* **4** out of bed: *I got up late* **5** as far as: *He came up to me and shook hands* **6** towards a bigger city etc, not necessarily one further north: *going up to London from Manchester* ➤ *preposition* **1** towards or in the higher part of: *climbed up the ladder* **2** along: *walking up the road* ➤ *adjective* **1** ascending, going up: *the up escalator* **2** out of bed: *Is Tom up yet?* **3** ahead in score: *2 goals up* **4** better off, richer: *£50 up on the deal* **5** risen: *The sun is up* **6** of a given length of time: ended: *Your time is up* **7** *informal* wrong: *What's up with her today?* • **on the up and up** progressing steadily, getting better all the time • **up and about 1** awake **2** out of bed after an illness • **up front 1** at the front **2** of money: paid in advance **3** candidly, openly • **ups and downs** times of good and bad luck • **up to 1** until: *up to the present* **2** capable of: *Are you up to the job?* **3** dependent on, falling as a duty to: *It's up to you to decide* **4** doing: *up to his tricks again* • **up to date 1** to the present time **2** containing recent facts etc **3** aware of recent developments

up-and-coming *adjective* likely to succeed

upbeat *adjective, informal* cheerful, optimistic

upbraid *verb* to scold

upbringing *noun* the rearing of, or the training given to, a child

upcoming *adjective, informal* forthcoming; approaching

update *verb* **1** to bring up to date **2** to add new information ➤ *noun* **1** the act of updating **2** new information: *an update on yesterday's report*

up-end *verb* to turn upside down

upfront or **up-front** *adjective* **1** candid, frank **2** foremost

upgrade *verb* **1** to raise to a more important position **2** to improve the quality of ➤ *noun, computing* a newer version of a software program

upheaval *noun* a violent disturbance or change

uphill *adjective* **1** going upwards **2** difficult: *uphill struggle* ➤ *adverb* upwards

uphold *verb* **1** to defend, give support to **2** to maintain, keep going (eg a tradition)

upholster *verb* to fit (furniture) with springs, stuffing, covers, etc

upholstery *noun* **1** covers, cushions, etc **2** the skill of upholstering

upkeep *noun* **1** the act of keeping (eg a house or car) in a good state of repair **2** the cost of this

upland *noun* **1** high ground **2** (**uplands**) a hilly or mountainous region

uplift *verb* to raise the spirits of, cheer up

uplighter or **uplight** *noun* a type of lamp or wall light designed to throw light upwards

upload *verb, computing* to send (data, files, etc)

from your computer to another by means of a modem and telephone line

up-market *adjective* of high quality or price, luxury

upon *preposition* **1** on the top of: *upon the table* **2** at or after the time of: *upon completion of the task*

upper *adjective* higher, further up ➤ *noun* **1** the part of a shoe etc above the sole **2** *slang* the drug amphetamine • **upper hand** advantage; dominance, control

upper-case *adjective* of a letter: capital, eg *A* not *a* (*contrasted with*: **lower-case**)

> ℗ So called because in the tray or case containing a typesetter's metal letters the capital letters were held in the top half and the uncapitalized small ones were kept in the bottom half

upper-class *adjective* belonging to the highest social class, aristocratic

upper hand *noun* (**the upper hand**) a position of advantage or control

uppermost *adjective* highest, furthest up

uppity *adjective, informal* self-important; arrogant

upright *adjective* **1** standing up, vertical **2** honest, moral ➤ *noun* an upright post, piano, etc

uprising *noun* a revolt against a government etc

uproar *noun* a noisy disturbance

uproarious *adjective* very noisy

uproot *verb* **1** to tear up by the roots **2** to leave your home and go to live in another place

upset *verb* (*pronounced* up-**set**) (**upsetting, upset**) **1** to make unhappy, angry, worried, etc **2** to overturn **3** to disturb, put out of order **4** to ruin (plans etc) ➤ *adjective* (*pronounced* up-**set**) distressed, unhappy, etc; ill ➤ *noun* (*pronounced* **up**-set) **1** distress, unhappiness, worry, etc **2** something that causes distress

upshot (*pronounced* **up**-shot) *noun* the result or end of a matter: *What was the upshot of all this?*

upside-down *adjective & adverb* **1** with the top part underneath **2** in confusion: *turned the room upside-down looking for his camera*

upstage *adverb* away from the footlights on a theatre stage ➤ *adjective, informal* haughty, proud ➤ *verb* to divert attention from (someone) to yourself

upstairs *adverb* in or to the upper storey of a house etc ➤ *noun* the upper storey or storeys of a house ➤ *adjective* in the upper storey or storeys: *upstairs bedroom*

upstanding *adjective* **1** honest, respectable **2** strong and healthy **3** *old* standing up

upstart (*pronounced* **up**-staht) *noun* someone who has risen quickly from a low to a high

position in society, work, etc

upstream *adverb* higher up a river or stream, towards the source

upsurge (*pronounced* **up**-serj) *noun* a rising, a swelling up

uptake (*pronounced* **up**-teik) *noun*: **quick on the uptake** quick to understand

upthrust *noun* **1** an upward thrust or push **2** the action or an instance of thrusting up by volcanic action **3** *physics* the upward force exerted by a liquid that makes an object float

uptight *adjective* nervous, tense

up-to-date *adjective* **1** modern, in touch with recent ideas etc **2** belonging to the present time **3** containing all recent facts etc: *an up-to-date account*

upturn *noun* a positive change, an improvement

upward *adjective* moving up, ascending
♦ **upwards** *adverb* from lower to higher, up
• **upwards of** more than

upwardly mobile *adjective* moving to a higher social status

uranium (*pronounced* yoo-**rei**-ni-um) *noun, chemistry* a dense radioactive metallic element, chiefly used to produce nuclear energy

> ℗ Named after the planet *Uranus*

-urb- of or relating to a town or city: *urban/ urbane* (= cultured and sophisticated like a city-dweller)/*suburb* ℗ Comes from Latin *urbs* meaning 'a city'

urban *adjective* relating to a town or city (*contrasted with*: **rural**)

urban climate *noun, geography* the climate in a town or city relative to the surrounding rural areas

urbane *adjective* polite in a smooth way

urban heat island *noun, geography* a town or city that is warmer than surrounding rural areas, due to eg the storing of heat by tarmacadam, central heating in buildings, more cloud cover, etc

urbanity *noun* **1** smoothness of manner **2** (*plural* **urbanities**) urbane actions

urbanize or **urbanise** *verb* to make (an area or areas) less rural and more like a town
♦ **urbanization** *noun*

urban regeneration *noun, geography* the revitalizing of a town or city by improving jobs, the environment, housing, etc

urchin *noun* a dirty, ragged child

> ℗ Originally meaning 'hedgehog', the prickly sense of which survives in *sea urchin*

Urdu *noun* the official literary language of Pakistan, also spoken in Bangladesh and among Muslims in India

urea *noun, biology, chemistry* a compound formed in the liver of mammals and excreted in the urine, and manufactured synthetically for use in plastics, drugs and fertilizers

ureter (*pronounced* yoo-**ree**-ter) *noun, anatomy* one of the two tubes carrying urine from the kidneys to the bladder

urethra (*pronounced* yoo-**reeth**-ra) *noun, anatomy* the tube leading from the bladder down which urine travels on its way out of the body

urethritis (*pronounced* yoo-reeth-**rai**-tis) *noun, medicine* inflammation of the urethra

urge *verb* **1** to drive (on) **2** to try to persuade: *urging me to go home* **3** to advise, recommend: *urge caution* ➤ *noun* a strong desire or impulse

urgency *noun* an urgent state or condition

urgent *adjective* **1** requiring immediate attention **2** asking for immediate action
♦ **urgently** *adverb*

uric *adjective* relating to, present in, or derived from, urine

uric acid *noun, biology, chemistry* an organic acid present in urine and blood

urinal *noun* a sanitary fitting attached to a wall, designed for men to urinate into

urinary *adjective* of or relating to urine or the passing of urine

urinate *verb* to pass urine from the bladder

urine *noun* the waste liquid passed out of the body of animals and humans from the bladder

urinogenital or **urogenital** *adjective* relating to or affecting both the urinary and genital functions

URL *abbreviation, computing* Uniform Resource Locator, the system of addresses for the World Wide Web

urn *noun* **1** a vase for the ashes of the dead **2** a metal drum with a tap, used for heating water for tea or coffee

urticaria *noun, medicine* an allergic skin reaction with raised red or white itchy patches (*non-technical names:* **nettle rash**, **hives**)

US or **USA** *abbreviation* United States of America

us *pronoun* used by a speaker or writer in referring to themselves together with other people (as the object in a sentence): *When would you like us to come?*

usable *adjective* able to be used ♦ **usability** *noun*

usage *noun* **1** the act or manner of using: *a guide to correct usage of the product* **2** the established way of using a word etc **3** custom, habit **4** treatment: *rough usage*

use *verb* **1** to put to some purpose: *use a knife to open it* **2** to bring into action: *use your common sense* **3** to consume, take something as fuel **4** (often **use up**) to spend, exhaust (eg patience, energy) **5** to treat: *He used his wife cruelly* ➤ *noun* **1** the act of using **2** value or suitability for a purpose: *no use to anybody* **3** the fact of being used: *It's in use at the moment* **4** custom ● **no use** useless ● **used to 1** accustomed to **2** was or were in the habit of (doing something): *We used to go there every year* ⊙ Comes from Latin *uti* meaning 'to use', and *usus* meaning 'a using'

used *adjective* **1** employed, put to a purpose **2** not new: *used cars*

useful *adjective* serving a purpose; helpful
♦ **usefully** *adverb*

useless *adjective* having no use or effect

user *noun* **1** someone who uses anything (especially a computer) **2** someone who regularly takes a specified drug: *a heroin user*

user-friendly *adjective* easily understood, easy to use

username or **user ID** *noun, computing* in e-mail addresses, the name or alias of an individual, usually appearing before the @ sign

U-shaped valley another term for a **glacial trough**

usher *noun* **1** someone who shows people to their seats in a theatre, at a wedding, etc **2** an official in a court of law who guards the door and keeps order ➤ *verb*: **usher in** or **out** to lead or convey (someone) into or out of a room, building, etc

usherette *noun* a woman who shows people to their seats in a theatre or cinema

USSR *abbreviation, history* Union of Soviet Socialist Republics

usual *adjective* **1** done or happening most often: *usual method* **2** customary: *with his usual cheerfulness* **3** ordinary ➤ *noun* a customary event, order, etc

usually *adverb* on most occasions

usurer (*pronounced* **yooz**-yu-rer) *noun* a money-lender who demands an excessively high rate of interest

usurp (*pronounced* yoo-**zerp**) *verb* to take possession of (eg a throne) by force ♦ **usurper** *noun*

usury (*pronounced* **yooz**-yu-ri) *noun* the lending of money with an excessively high rate of interest

utensil *noun* an instrument or container used in the home (eg a ladle, knife, pan)

uterus *noun* (*plural* **uteri** – *pronounced* **yoo**-te-rai) the womb ♦ **uterine** *adjective*

utilitarian *adjective* **1** intended to be useful rather than beautiful **2** of, or characterized by, utilitarianism ➤ *noun* a believer in utilitarianism

utilitarianism *noun* the belief that an action is morally right if it benefits the majority of people

utility *noun* (*plural* **utilities**) **1** usefulness **2** a public service supplying water, gas, etc **3** *computing* a program designed to carry out a small routine function

utility room *noun* a room in a private house where the washing machine, dryer, etc are kept

utilize or **utilise** *verb* to make use of
♦ **utilization** *noun*

utmost *adjective* **1** the greatest possible: *utmost care* **2** furthest ● **do your utmost** to make the greatest possible effort

utopia (*pronounced* yoo-**toh**-pi-a) *noun* a perfect place, a paradise

> ⏱ Literally 'no place', coined by Thomas More for his fictional book *Utopia* (1516)

utopian (*pronounced* yoo-**toh**-pi-an) *adjective* unrealistically ideal

utter[1] *verb* to produce with the voice (words, a scream, etc)

utter[2] *adjective* complete, total: *utter darkness*

utterance *noun* something said

utterly *adverb* completely, absolutely

uttermost *adjective* most complete, utmost

U-turn *noun* a complete change in direction, policy, etc

UV *abbreviation* ultraviolet

UVA *abbreviation* ultraviolet A, a type of ultraviolet radiation

uvula (*pronounced* **yoo**-vyoo-la) *noun* (*plural* **uvulas** or **uvulae** – *pronounced* **yoo**-vyoo-lee), *anatomy* the small fleshy part that hangs over the back of the tongue at the entrance to the throat ⏱ Comes from Latin, literally 'small grape', from Latin *uva* meaning 'grape'

uxorious *adjective* excessively fond of your wife ⏱ Comes from Latin *uxor* meaning 'wife'

Vv

V *symbol* **1** *chemistry* vanadium **2** volt(s) **3** the Roman numeral for 5

v *abbreviation* **1** versus **2** very

-vac- forms words containing the idea 'empty': *vacant/evacuate* ⊙ Comes from Latin *vacare* meaning 'to be empty', and *vacuus* meaning 'empty'

vacancy *noun* (*plural* **vacancies**) **1** a job that has not been filled **2** a room not already booked in a hotel etc

vacant *adjective* **1** empty, not occupied **2** of an expression: showing no interest or intelligence ♦ **vacantly** *adverb* (meaning 2): *stare vacantly into space*

vacate *verb* to leave empty, cease to occupy

vacation *noun* **1** the act of vacating **2** a holiday

vaccinate *verb* to give a vaccine to, eg by injection into the skin

vaccination *noun* the act or process of injecting someone with a vaccine

vaccine *noun* a substance made from the germs that cause a disease, given to people and animals to try to prevent them catching that disease: *flu vaccine*

vacillate *verb* to move from one opinion to another; waver

vacuole *noun, biology* a small cavity in the cytoplasm of a cell, containing air, fluid, etc

vacuous *adjective* **1** empty **2** empty-headed, stupid ♦ **vacuously** *adverb*

vacuum *noun* a space from which all, or almost all, the air has been removed

vacuum cleaner *noun* a machine which cleans carpets etc by sucking up dust

vacuum flask *noun* a container with double walls enclosing a vacuum, for keeping liquids hot or cold

vagabond *noun* **1** someone with no permanent home; a wanderer **2** a rascal, a rogue

vagaries *plural noun* strange, unexpected behaviour: *vagaries of human nature*

vagina *noun, anatomy* the passage connecting a woman's genitals to her womb

vaginal *adjective* of or to do with the vagina

vaginitis *noun, medicine* inflammation of the vagina

vagrancy *noun* the state of being a tramp

vagrant *adjective* unsettled, wandering ➤ *noun* a wanderer or tramp, with no settled home

vague *adjective* **1** not clear; not definite: *vague idea/vague shape* **2** not practical or efficient; forgetful ♦ **vaguely** *adverb*

vain *adjective* **1** conceited, self-important **2** useless: *vain attempt* **3** empty, meaningless: *vain promises* • **in vain** without success: *He tried in vain to start the engine* ♦ **vainly** *adverb*

vainglory *noun, literary* extreme boastfulness; excessive pride ♦ **vainglorious** *adjective*

Vaisakhi same as **Baisakhi**

valance *noun* a decorative frill round the edge of a bed

vale *noun, literary* a valley

valediction *noun, formal* a farewell

valedictory *adjective, formal* saying farewell: *valedictory speech*

valence *noun, chemistry* **1** a chemical bond **2** *US* valency

valency or *US* **valence** *noun, chemistry* the number of hydrogen atoms that an atom or group can combine with to form a compound (eg in water (H_2O), oxygen has a valency of two)

valentine *noun* **1** a greetings card sent on St Valentine's Day, 14 February **2** a sweetheart, a lover

valerian *noun* a flowering plant or the sedative drug derived from its root

valet (*pronounced* **val**-et or **val**-ei) *noun* a manservant ➤ *verb* **1** to work as a valet **2** (*pronounced* **val**-et) to clean out (a car) as a service

valetudinarian (*pronounced* val-i-tyood-i-**neir**-ri-an) *noun* someone who is over-anxious about their health

valiant *adjective* brave ♦ **valiantly** *adverb*

valid *adjective* **1** sound, acceptable: *valid reason for not going* **2** legally in force: *valid passport*

validate *verb* **1** to make (a document etc) valid with a mark, stamp, etc **2** to confirm that (something) is true or sound **3** *computing* to check (a file) has been input according to certain rules ♦ **validation** *noun*

validity *noun* **1** the state of being valid or acceptable for use **2** soundness of an argument or proposition

valise (*pronounced* va-**leez**) *noun, now chiefly N Am, esp US* a small overnight case or bag ⊙ Comes from French, meaning 'suitcase'

valley *noun* (*plural* **valleys**) low land between hills, often with a river flowing through it

valorous *adjective* brave, courageous

valour *noun* courage, bravery

valuable *adjective* of great value or usefulness

valuables *plural noun* articles of worth

valuation *noun* 1 the act of valuing 2 an estimated price or value

value *noun* 1 worth; price 2 purchasing power (of a coin etc) 3 importance 4 usefulness 5 *maths* a number or quantity put as equal to an expression: *The value of x is 8* ▸ *verb* 1 to put a price on 2 to think highly of: *I'd value your opinion*

value-added tax *noun* a government tax raised on the selling-price of an article, or charged on certain services

value judgement *noun* an assessment of worth based on personal opinion rather than fact

valueless *adjective* worthless

valuer or **valuator** *noun* someone trained to estimate the value of property

valvate *adjective* 1 with a valve or valves 2 *biology* using valves 3 *biology* meeting at the edges without overlapping

valve *noun* 1 a device allowing air, steam or liquid to flow in one direction only 2 *anatomy* a small flap of tissue controlling the flow of blood in the body 3 an electronic component found in older television sets, radios, etc

vamp¹ *noun, informal* a woman who flaunts her sexual charm, especially to exploit men

vamp² *noun* the upper part of a boot or shoe

vampire *noun* a dead person supposed to rise at night and suck the blood of the living

vampire bat *noun* a South American bat that sucks blood

van¹ *noun* 1 a commercial road vehicle with a large space at the rear, lighter than a lorry 2 *Brit* a railway carriage in which luggage and parcels are transported

van² *short for* **vanguard**

vanadium *noun, chemistry* (symbol **V**) a silvery metallic element

⊙ After *Vanadis*, a name of the Norse goddess Freyja

vandal *noun* someone who pointlessly destroys or damages public buildings, private property, etc

⊙ After the *Vandals*, a German tribe who invaded and destroyed Rome in the 5th century

vandalism *noun* the activity of a vandal

vandalize or **vandalise** *verb* to damage by vandalism

Van de Graaff generator *noun, physics* a very high-voltage electrostatic generator, using a high-speed belt to accumulate charge in a large metal globe

⊙ Named after Robert J *Van de Graaff* (1901–67), US physicist

van der Waals' force (*pronounced* van de walz) *noun, physics* any of the weak attractive forces between atoms or molecules

⊙ Named after Johannes Diderik *van der Waals* (1837–1923), Dutch physicist

vane *noun* 1 a weathervane 2 the blade of a windmill, propeller, etc

vanguard *noun* 1 the leading group in a movement etc 2 the part of an army going in front of the main body

vanilla *noun* a sweet-scented flavouring obtained from the pods of a type of orchid

vanish *verb* 1 to go out of sight 2 to fade away to nothing

vanity *noun* (*plural* **vanities**) 1 conceit 2 worthlessness 3 something vain and worthless

vanity unit *noun* a unit made up of a washbasin set into a flat top with a cupboard underneath

vanquish *verb* to defeat

vantage point *noun* a position giving an advantage or a clear view

vapid *adjective* dull, uninteresting

vaporize or **vaporise** *verb* to change into vapour

vaporizer or **vaporiser** *noun* a device which sprays liquid very finely

vapour *noun* 1 the air-like or gas-like state of a substance that is usually liquid or solid: *water vapour* 2 tiny drops of liquid forming mist or smoke in the air

vapour pressure *noun, physics* the pressure exerted by the atoms or molecules of a vapour with its liquid or solid form

variable *adjective* changeable; that may be varied ▸ *noun* 1 something that can vary eg in value 2 *maths* a symbol for which one or more values can be substituted (*compare with:* **constant**)

variance *noun* 1 a state of differing or disagreement 2 *statistics* the square of the **standard deviation** (ie the mean of the squared deviations of a number of observations from their mean) • **at variance** in disagreement or conflict

variant *noun* a different form or version ▸ *adjective* in a different form

variation *noun* 1 a varying, a change 2 the extent of a difference or change: *variations in temperature* 3 *music* a repetition, in a slightly different form, of a main theme 4 *biology* differences between members of the same plant or animal species, due to environmental differences or genetic make-up

varicose vein noun a swollen or enlarged vein, usually on the leg

varied adjective having variety, diverse

variegated adjective of leaves or flowers: marked with different colours; multicoloured

variety noun (plural **varieties**) **1** the quality of being of many kinds, or of being different **2** a mixed collection: a variety of books **3** a sort, a type: a variety of potato **4** mixed theatrical entertainment including songs, comedy, etc

varifocals plural noun a pair of glasses with lenses of various focal lengths to allow a wide range of focusing distances (compare with: **bifocals**)

various adjective **1** of different kinds: various shades of green **2** several: various attempts

variously adverb in different ways or at different times: variously described as fascinating and dull

varna noun, Hinduism any of the four main divisions of Hindu society, within which there are castes

varnish noun a sticky liquid which gives a glossy surface to paper, wood, etc ➤ verb **1** to cover with varnish **2** to cover up (faults)

vary verb (**varies, varying, varied**) **1** to make, be or become different **2** to make changes in (a routine etc) **3** to differ, disagree

vas noun (plural **vasa**), biology a vessel, tube or duct that carries liquid ◷ Comes from Latin vas meaning 'vessel'

vascular adjective, biology **1** relating to the blood vessels of animals or sap-conducting tissues of plants **2** made up of, or having, such vessels

vascular tissue adjective, biology tissue within which water and nutrients are carried from one part of a living organism to another, eg blood vessels

vas deferens noun (plural **vasa deferentia**), anatomy the duct from each testicle that carries sperm to the penis ◷ Comes from Latin deferre meaning 'to carry away'

vase (pronounced vahz or US veiz) noun a jar of pottery, glass, etc used as an ornament or for holding cut flowers

vasectomy noun (plural **vasectomies**), medicine a surgical operation involving the tying and cutting of the **vas deferens** as a method of sterilization

Vaseline noun, trademark a type of ointment made from petroleum

vassal noun, history a tenant who held land from an overlord in return for certain services

vast adjective of very great size or amount

vastly adverb greatly or to a considerable extent: vastly different

vastness noun immensity

VAT or **vat** abbreviation value-added tax; a tax on goods and services

vat noun a large tub or tank, used eg for fermenting liquors and dyeing

Vatican noun (**the Vatican**) **1** a collection of buildings in Rome, including the official residence of the pope **2** the authority of the pope

vaudeville noun theatrical entertainment of dances and songs, usually comic

vault noun **1** an arched roof **2** an underground room, a cellar **3** a fortified room used for storing valuables, eg in a bank **4** an act of vaulting, especially over a piece of gymnastic equipment like a wooden box ➤ verb to leap, supporting your weight on your hands, or on a pole

vaunt verb to boast

VB abbreviation, computing Visual Basic

VCR abbreviation video cassette recorder

VD abbreviation venereal disease

VDU abbreviation visual display unit

veal noun the flesh of a calf, used as food

vector noun **1** maths a description of horizontal and vertical motion, shown in a pair of brackets with the horizontal value above the vertical value **2** maths a quantity, eg velocity or change of position, that has both magnitude and direction (compare with: **scalar**) **3** biology something, eg an insect, that can transfer a pathogen without catching the disease itself **4** biology in genetic engineering: a vehicle used to transfer DNA from one organism to another

Veda noun one, or all, of four ancient books of the Hindus

veer verb **1** to change direction or course **2** to change mood, opinions, etc

veg (pronounced vedj) verb (**vegges, vegging, vegged**), informal: **veg out** to relax, laze about

vegan (pronounced vee-gan) noun a vegetarian who does not eat or use any animal products

vegetable noun a plant, especially one grown for food ➤ adjective **1** of plants **2** made from or consisting of plants: vegetable dye/vegetable oil

vegetable oil noun any of various oils obtained from plants, used especially in cooking and cosmetics

vegetarian noun someone who eats no meat, only vegetable or dairy foods ➤ adjective consisting of, or eating, only vegetable or dairy foods

vegetate verb **1** to grow as a plant does **2** to lead a dull, aimless life: sitting at home vegetating

vegetation noun **1** plants in general **2** the plants growing in a particular area

vegetative adjective **1** referring to plants **2** biology denoting asexual reproduction in plants or animals such as bulbs or yeasts

veggie or **vegie** (pronounced vedj-i) noun,

informal **1** a vegetarian **2** a vegetable

vehemence *noun* strong and forceful feeling

vehement *adjective* emphatic and forceful in expressing opinions etc ♦ **vehemently** *adverb*

vehicle *noun* **1** a means of transport used on land, especially one with wheels: *motor vehicle* **2** a means of conveying information, eg television or newspapers

veil *noun* **1** a piece of cloth or netting worn to shade or hide the face **2** something that hides or covers up: *a veil of secrecy* ➤ *verb* **1** to cover with a veil **2** to hide ♦ **veiled** *adjective*: *veiled threats* **take the veil** to become a nun

vein *noun* **1** a blood vessel that carries the blood back to the heart **2** a small rib of a leaf **3** a thin layer of mineral in a rock **4** a streak in wood, stone, etc **5** a mood or personal characteristic: *a vein of cheerfulness*

Velcro *noun, trademark* a fastening material consisting of one surface of tiny hooks, and another of tiny loops

veldt (*pronounced* velt) *noun, S African* open grassland, with few or no trees

vellum *noun* **1** a fine parchment used for bookbinding, made from the skins of calves, kids or lambs **2** paper made in imitation of this

velocity *noun* rate or speed of movement

velour (*pronounced* ve-**loor**) *noun* a fabric with a soft, velvet-like surface

velvet *noun* a fabric made from silk etc, with a thick, soft surface ➤ *adjective* **1** made of velvet **2** soft or smooth as velvet; silky

velvety *adjective* soft, like velvet

vena cava (*pronounced* **vee**-na **ka**-va) *noun* (*plural* **venae cavae** – *pronounced* **vee**-nee **ka**-vee), *anatomy* either of the two large veins that carry deoxygenated blood to the right atrium of the heart ⊕ Comes from Latin, meaning 'hollow vein'

venal (*pronounced* **vee**-nal) *adjective* **1** willing to be bribed: *The majority of the councillors are venal and corrupt* **2** done for a bribe; unworthy ⊕ Comes from Latin *venalis* meaning 'for sale'

! Do not confuse with: **venial**.
Venal is related to the verb 'vend', since they both contain the concept of selling (from Latin *venum*). **Venial** comes from the Latin *venia* (= forgiveness) and means 'forgivable'.

vend *verb* to sell ⊕ Comes from Latin *vendere* meaning 'to sell'

vendetta *noun* a bitter, long-lasting quarrel or feud

vending machine *noun* a machine with sweets, drinks, etc for sale, operated by putting coins in a slot

vendor *noun* someone who sells

veneer *verb* **1** to cover a piece of wood with another thin piece of finer quality **2** to give a good appearance to what is really bad ➤ *noun* **1** a thin surface layer of fine wood **2** a false outward show hiding some bad quality: *a veneer of good manners*

venerable *adjective* worthy of respect because of age or wisdom

venerate *verb* to respect or honour greatly

veneration *noun* **1** the act of venerating **2** great respect

venereal disease (*pronounced* vi-**neer**-ri-al) *noun* a disease contracted through sexual intercourse

Venetian blind *noun* a window blind formed of horizontal slats of metal or plastic hung on tapes, that can be tilted to let in or shut out light

vengeance *noun* punishment given or harm done in return for wrong or injury, revenge
● **with a vengeance** with unexpected force or enthusiasm

vengeful *adjective* seeking revenge
♦ **vengefully** *adverb*

venial (*pronounced* **vee**-ni-al) *adjective* of a sin: not very bad, pardonable (*compare with*: **cardinal**) ⊕ Comes from Latin *venialis* meaning 'pardonable'

! Do not confuse with: **venal**.
Venial comes from the Latin *venia* (= forgiveness). **Venal** literally means 'willing to be bought' and is related to the verb 'vend', since they both contain the concept of selling (from the Latin *venum*).

venison *noun* the flesh of a deer, used as food

Venn diagram *noun, maths* a diagram showing the relationship between sets using overlapping circles and other figures

venom *noun* **1** poison **2** hatred, spite

venomous *adjective* **1** poisonous **2** spiteful
♦ **venomously** *adverb* (meaning 2)

vent *noun* **1** a small opening **2** a hole to allow air or smoke to pass through **3** an outlet: *a vent for his feelings* **4** a slit in a garment, especially upwards from the hem in a jacket, skirt, etc **5** *biology* the anus of a bird or small animal ➤ *verb* to express (strong emotion) in some way: *vented his frustration on her* ● **give vent to** to express, let out

ventilate *verb* **1** to allow fresh air to pass through (a room etc) **2** to supply air to (the lungs) **3** to talk about, discuss

ventilation *noun* circulation of fresh air: *This room has poor ventilation*

ventilator *noun* **1** a device that circulates or draws in fresh air **2** a machine that supplies air to the lungs of someone who cannot breathe on their own

ventral *adjective* of the lower surface of an

animal, or something like a leaf or wing: *ventral fin* (compare with: **dorsal**)

ventricle *noun, anatomy* in mammals: either of the two lower chambers of the heart

ventriloquism *noun* the art of speaking in a way that makes the sound appear to come from elsewhere, especially a puppet's mouth

ventriloquist *noun* someone who can speak without appearing to move their lips and can project their voice on to a puppet etc

⊙ Literally 'stomach speaker' and originally meaning someone possessed by a talking evil spirit

venture *noun* an undertaking which involves some risk: *business venture* ➤ *verb* **1** to risk, dare **2** to do or say something at the risk of causing annoyance or opposition: *may I venture to suggest*

venture capital *noun* money supplied by individual investors or businesses for a new business enterprise

venturesome *adjective* **1** prepared to take risks; enterprising **2** involving danger; risky

venue *noun* the scene of an event, eg a sports contest or conference

venule *noun, biology* **1** a branch of a vein in an insect's wing **2** any of the small blood vessels that join up to form veins

ver- see **veri-**

veracious *adjective* truthful ⊙ Comes from Latin *verax* meaning 'truthful'

❗ Do not confuse with: **voracious**

veracity *noun* truthfulness

veranda or **verandah** *noun* a kind of terrace with a roof supported by pillars, extending along the side of a house

verb *noun* a word that tells what someone or something does in a sentence, eg 'I *sing*'/'He *had* no idea'

-verb- forms words concerned with words: *verbose/proverb* (= well-known wise words) ⊙ Comes from Latin *verbum* meaning 'a word'

verbal *adjective* **1** of words **2** spoken, not written: *verbal agreement* **3** of verbs

verbalize or **verbalise** *verb* to express (thoughts, ideas, etc) in words

verbatim *adjective* in the exact words, word for word: *a verbatim account*

verbose *adjective* using more words than necessary

verbosity *noun* the practice of using or condition of containing too many words

verdant *adjective* green with grass or leaves

verdict *noun* **1** the judge's decision at the end of a trial **2** someone's personal opinion on a matter

verdigris *noun* the greenish rust of copper, brass or bronze

verdure *noun* green vegetation

verge *noun* **1** the grassy border along the edge of a road etc **2** edge, brink: *on the verge of a mental breakdown* • **verge on** to be close to: *verging on the absurd*

verger *noun* a church caretaker, or church official

veri- or **ver-** *prefix* forms words containing the concept of truth: *verify/veracity* ⊙ Comes from Latin *verus* meaning 'true'

verifiable *adjective* able to be verified

verify *verb* (**verifies, verifying, verified**) to prove, show to be true, confirm ♦ **verification** *noun*

verily *adverb, old* truly, really

verisimilitude *noun* realism, closeness to real life

veritable *adjective* **1** true **2** real, genuine

verity *noun* truth

vermicelli *noun* **1** a type of food like spaghetti but in much thinner strands **2** tiny splinters of chocolate used for decorating cakes and puddings ⊙ Comes from Italian meaning 'little worms'

vermiform appendix same as **appendix**

vermilion *noun* a bright red colour

vermin *plural noun* animals or insects that are considered pests, eg rats, mice, fleas, etc

verminous *adjective* full of vermin

vermouth (*pronounced* ver-mooth) *noun* an alcoholic drink made of wine flavoured with aromatic herbs

vernacular *noun* the ordinary spoken language of a country or district ➤ *adjective* in the vernacular

vernal *adjective* of the season of spring

verruca (*pronounced* ve-**roo**-ka) *noun* (*plural* **verrucas** or **verrucae** – *pronounced* ve-**roo**-see) a wart, especially on the foot

-vers- see **-vert-**

versatile *adjective* **1** able to turn easily from one subject or task to another **2** useful in many different ways

versatility *noun* the ability to be adaptable

verse *noun* **1** a number of lines of poetry forming a planned unit **2** poetry as opposed to prose **3** a short division of a chapter of the Bible • **versed in** skilled or experienced in: *well versed in the classics*

version *noun* **1** an account from one point of view **2** a form: *another version of the same tune* **3** a translation

verso *noun* the left-hand page of an open book (*compare with*: **recto**)

versus *preposition* against (*short form* **v**)

-vert- or **-vers-** forms words related to the

action of turning: *vertigo* (= a turning or whirling around)/*aversion* (= a turning away from) ⊙ Comes from Latin *vertere* meaning 'to turn'

vertebra *noun* (*plural* **vertebrae**) one of the segments that forms the spine

vertebrate *noun* an animal with a backbone ➤ *adjective* having a backbone, or relating to an animal with a backbone ◆ **vertebral** *adjective*

vertex *noun* (*plural* **vertices**) **1** the top or summit **2** *maths* the point opposite the base of a figure, eg the tip of a cone or pyramid **3** *maths* a point where two sides meet in a polygon, or where three or more surfaces meet in a polyhedron, and form an angle

vertical *adjective* **1** standing upright **2** straight up and down ◆ **vertically** *adverb*

vertically opposite angles or **vertical angles** *plural noun, maths* a pair of opposite, equal angles formed by intersecting lines

vertigo *noun* giddiness, dizziness

verve *noun* lively spirit, enthusiasm

very *adverb* **1** to a great extent or degree: *seem very happy/walk very quietly* **2** exactly: *the very same* ➤ *adjective* **1** same, identical: *The very people who claimed to support him voted against him* **2** ideal, exactly what is wanted: *the very man for the job* **3** actual: *in the very act of stealing* **4** mere: *the very thought of blood*

Vesak or **Wesak** (*pronounced* ves-ak) *noun* the most widely celebrated Buddhist festival, held in May to commemorate the birth, enlightenment and death of Buddha

vesicle *noun* **1** *biology* a small sac or cavity in the cytoplasm of a cell **2** *biology* a small blister on the skin containing serum **3** a cavity formed by trapped gas bubbles when molten lava solidifies

vespers *singular noun* a church service in the evening

vessel *noun* **1** a ship **2** a container for liquid **3** a tube carrying fluids in the body: *blood vessels*

vest *noun* **1** an undergarment for the top half of the body **2** *US* a waistcoat • **vest in** to give or bestow legally or officially: *by the power vested in me*

vested interest *noun* an interest a person has in the fortunes of a particular system or institution because that person is directly affected or closely associated, especially financially

vestibule *noun* an entrance hall; a lobby

vestige *noun* **1** a trace, an indication of something's existence **2** *biology* a small functionless part in an animal or plant, which was a fully developed organ in its ancestors

vestigial *adjective* surviving only as a trace of former existence: *vestigial wings*

vestment *noun* a ceremonial garment, worn eg by a religious officer during a service

vestry *noun* (*plural* **vestries**) a room in a church in which vestments are kept

vet[1] *noun, informal* **1** a veterinary surgeon **2** *N Am* a veteran

vet[2] *verb* (**vetting, vetted**) to examine, check for suitability or reliability

vetch *noun* a plant of the pea family

veteran *adjective* old, experienced ➤ *noun* **1** someone who has given long service **2** an old soldier **3** *US* anyone who has served in the armed forces

veteran car *noun* a very old car, specifically one made before 1905 (*compare with*: **vintage car**)

veterinary *adjective* relating to the treatment of animal diseases

veterinary surgeon *noun* a doctor who treats animals

veto (*pronounced* vee-toh) *noun* (*plural* **vetoes**) **1** the power to forbid or block (a proposal) **2** an act of forbidding or blocking ➤ *verb* (**vetoing, vetoed**) to forbid, block

⊙ Latin for 'I forbid', a phrase originally used by people's tribunes in the Roman Senate when objecting to proposals

vex *verb* to annoy; cause trouble to

vexation *noun* **1** the state of being vexed **2** something that vexes

vexatious *adjective* causing trouble or annoyance

VHF *abbreviation* very high frequency; a range of radio waves that produce good quality sound

via *preposition* by way of: *travelling to Paris via London*

viable *adjective* **1** of a plan etc: having a chance of success; practicable: *viable proposition* **2** of a fetus or baby: able to survive independently outside the womb ◆ **viability** *noun*

viaduct *noun* a long bridge taking a railway or road over a river etc

viands *plural noun, old* food

vibrant *adjective* full of energy; lively, sparkling

vibrate *verb* **1** to shake, tremble **2** to swing to and fro rapidly **3** of sound: to resound, ring ◆ **vibration** *noun*

vibrato (*pronounced* vee-**bra**-to) *noun* (*plural* **vibratos**), *music* a faint trembling effect in singing or the playing of string and wind instruments, achieved by vibrating the throat muscles or the fingers ⊙ Comes from Italian

vibrator *noun* a battery-powered vibrating device, used to get sexual pleasure

vicar *noun* an Anglican member of the clergy who is in charge of a parish

vicarage *noun* the house of a vicar

vicarious *adjective* **1** in place or on behalf of another person **2** not experienced personally but imagined through the experience of others: *vicarious thrill*

vice *noun* **1** a bad habit, a serious fault **2** wickedness, immorality **3** a tool with two jaws for gripping objects firmly

vice- *prefix* second in rank to *vice-chancellor/ vice-president* ◔ Comes from Latin *vicis* meaning 'a turn'

viceroy (*pronounced* **vais**-roi) *noun* a male governor of a province or colony ruling with the authority of a monarch or government
♦ **viceroyalty** or **viceroyship** *noun* ◔ Comes from French, from *roi* meaning 'king'

vice squad *noun* a branch of the police force that investigates crimes relating to immorality, eg prostitution or drug dealing

vice versa *adverb* the other way round: *I needed his help and vice versa* (= he needed mine)

vicinity *noun* (*plural* **vicinities**) **1** nearness **2** neighbourhood

vicious *adjective* wicked; spiteful ♦ **viciously** *adverb*

ⓘ If you have trouble spelling the '-sh-' sound in **vicious**, remember the single 'c' in the related word 'vice'.

vicious circle *noun* a bad situation whose results cause it to get worse

vicissitude (*pronounced* vi-**sis**-it-yood) *noun* **1** change from one state to another **2** (**vicissitudes**) changes of luck, ups and downs

victim *noun* **1** someone who is killed or harmed, intentionally or by accident: *victim of a brutal attack/victim of the financial situation* **2** an animal for sacrifice

victimize or **victimise** *verb* to single someone out for hostile, unfair or vindictive treatment

victor *noun* a winner of a contest etc

Victorian *adjective* **1** relating to or characteristic of Queen Victoria or the period of her reign (1837–1901) **2** of attitudes or values: strict, prudish or conventional **3** of attitudes or values: bigoted or hypocritical ➤ *noun* **1** someone who lived during Victoria's reign **2** someone with Victorian attitudes

victorious *adjective* successful in a battle or other contest

victory *noun* (*plural* **victories**) success in any battle, struggle or contest

victuals (*pronounced* **vit**-alz) *plural noun, old* food

video *adjective* **1** relating to the recording and broadcasting of TV pictures and sound **2** relating to recording by video ➤ *noun* (*plural* **videos**) **1** a videocassette recorder **2** a recording on videotape **3** *US* television ➤ *verb* (**videoing,**

videoed) to make a recording by video

video camera *noun* a portable camera that records images onto videotape

videocassette *noun* a cassette containing videotape

videocassette recorder *noun* a tape recorder using videocassettes for recording and playing back TV programmes

videoconference *noun* a discussion between people in different locations using electronically linked telephones and video screens
♦ **videoconferencing** *noun*

video game *noun* any electronically operated game involving the manipulation of images produced by a computer program on a visual display unit such as a computer or TV screen

videophone *noun* a device like a telephone that transmits pictures as well as sound

videotape *noun* magnetic tape for carrying pictures and sound

vie *verb* (**vying, vied**): **vie with** to compete with, try to outdo

Viet Cong or **Vietcong** *noun, history* a member of the South Vietnamese communist guerrilla army in the Vietnam war (1964–1975)

view *noun* **1** a range or field of sight: *a good view* **2** a scene **3** an opinion ➤ *verb* **1** to look at **2** to watch (television) **3** to consider **4** to inspect or examine: *view the house that's up for sale* • **in view 1** in sight **2** in your mind as an aim • **in view of** taking into consideration • **on view** on show; ready for inspecting • **with a view to** with the purpose or intention of

viewdata *noun* a system by which computerized information can be displayed on a TV screen

viewfinder *noun* a device on a camera that shows the area covered by the lens

viewing *noun* an act or opportunity of seeing or inspecting something, eg a property for sale

viewpoint *noun* **1** a place from which a scene is viewed **2** (*also*: **point of view**) a personal opinion

vigil *noun* a time of watching or of keeping awake at night, often before a religious festival

vigilance *noun* watchfulness, alertness

vigilant *adjective* watchful, alert

vigilante (*pronounced* vij-i-**lan**-tei) *noun* a private citizen who assumes the task of keeping order in a community

vignette (*pronounced* veen-**yet**) *noun* **1** a decorative design on a book's title page, traditionally of vine leaves **2** a photographic portrait with the background deliberately faded **3** a short essay, especially one describing a person's character ◔ Comes from French, meaning 'little vine'

vigorous *adjective* strong, healthy; forceful:

vigorous defence ♦ **vigorously** *adverb*: *vigorously denied the charge*

vigour *noun* strength of body or mind; energy

Viking *noun, history* a Norse invader of Western Europe between the 8th and 11th centuries

vile *adjective* **1** very bad **2** disgusting, revolting ♦ **vilely** *adverb*

vilify *verb* (**vilifies, vilifying, vilified**) to say bad things about

villa *noun* a house in the country, at the sea, etc used for holidays

village *noun* a collection of houses, not big enough to be called a town

villager *noun* someone who lives in a village

villain *noun* a scoundrel, a rascal

villainous *adjective* wicked

villainy *noun* (*plural* **villainies**) wickedness

villein *noun, history* a serf

villus *noun* (*plural* **villi**) **1** *anatomy* one of many tiny projections that line the inside of the small intestine **2** *botany* a long soft hair ♦ **villiform** *adjective* ♦ **villous** *adjective* ℗ Comes from Latin, meaning 'shaggy hair'

vim *noun, informal* energy; liveliness

vinaigrette (*pronounced* vin-ei-**gret**) *noun* a salad dressing made by mixing oil, vinegar and seasonings

vindaloo *noun* a hot Indian curry

vindicate *verb* **1** to clear from blame **2** to justify

vindictive *adjective* revengeful; spiteful

vine *noun* **1** a grapevine **2** any climbing or trailing plant

vinegar *noun* a sour-tasting liquid made from wine, beer, etc, used for seasoning or pickling

vineyard (*pronounced* **vin**-yad) *noun* an area planted with grapevines

vintage *noun* **1** the gathering of ripe grapes **2** the grapes gathered **3** wine of a particular year, especially when of very high quality **4** time of origin or manufacture ➤ *adjective* **1** of a vintage **2** of wine of a particular year **3** very characteristic of an author, style, etc: *vintage Monty Python*

vintage car *noun* an old car, specifically one built between 1919 and 1930 (*compare with*: **veteran car**)

vinyl *noun* **1** any of a group of light, tough plastics: *vinyl flooring/vinyl paint* **2** *informal* plastic records as distinct from CDs and cassettes: *Have you got it on vinyl?*

viola (*pronounced* vi-**oh**-la) *noun* **1** a stringed instrument like a large violin **2** a member of the family of plants which include violets and pansies

violate *verb* **1** to break (a law, a treaty, etc) **2** to harm sexually, especially rape **3** to treat with disrespect **4** to disturb, interrupt ♦ **violator** *noun*

violation *noun* the act or process of violating

violence *noun* great roughness and force

violent *adjective* **1** acting with great force: *violent storm* **2** caused by or characterized by violence: *violent death/a violent film* **3** uncontrollable: *violent temper*

violently *adverb* **1** in a violent or aggressive way **2** extremely; severely; ardently: *violently opposed to our involvement*

violet *noun* a kind of small bluish-purple flower

violin *noun* a musical instrument with four strings, held under the chin and played with a bow

violinist *noun* someone who plays the violin

violoncello see **cello**

VIP *abbreviation* very important person

viper *noun* **1** an adder **2** a vicious or treacherous person

virago (*pronounced* vir-**ah**-goh) *noun* (*plural* **viragos**) a noisy, bad-tempered woman

viral *adjective* of or relating to a virus

virgin *noun* someone who has had no sexual intercourse ♦ **virginity** *noun* **the Virgin Birth** *Christianity* the doctrine that the Virgin Mary conceived Christ by the power of the Holy Spirit • **the Virgin Mary** the mother of Christ

virginal[1] *adjective* of or like a virgin; chaste

virginal[2] or **virginals** *noun* an early type of musical instrument, with a keyboard

Virgo *noun* **1** the sixth sign of the zodiac, represented by the virgin **2** someone born under this sign, between 24 August and 23 September

virile *adjective* manly; strong, vigorous

virility *noun* manhood; manliness; strength, vigour

virtual *adjective* **1** in effect, though not in strict fact: *Traffic is at a virtual standstill* **2** *computing* any system that behaves or functions in the same way as a real person or thing

virtually *adverb* almost, nearly: *The war is virtually over*

virtual reality *noun* a computer-created environment that the person operating the computer is able to be a part of

virtue *noun* **1** goodness of character and behaviour **2** a good quality, eg honesty, generosity, etc **3** a good point: *One virtue of plastic crockery is that it doesn't break* • **by virtue of** because of

virtuosity *noun* brilliance of technique

virtuoso *noun* (*plural* **virtuosos**) a highly skilled artist, especially a musician

virtuous *adjective* good, just, honest ♦ **virtuously** *adverb*

virulence *noun* **1** causing extreme harm; poisonousness **2** bitter hostility

virulent *adjective* **1** full of poison **2** bitter, spiteful **3** of a disease: dangerous

virus *noun* (*plural* **viruses**) **1** a germ that is smaller than any bacteria, and causes diseases such as mumps, chickenpox, etc **2** a self-replicating program that attaches to a computer system and spreads to other systems, and which can destroy data stored on the hard disk

visa *noun* a permit given by the authorities of a country to allow someone to stay for a time in that country

visage (*pronounced* **viz**-ij) *noun, old* the face

viscera (*pronounced* **vis**-e-ra) *plural noun* the internal organs of the body

visceral (*pronounced* **vis**-e-ral) *adjective* **1** belonging or relating to the viscera **2** belonging or relating to basic human instincts as opposed to the intellect

viscose *noun* **1** cellulose in a viscous state, able to be made into thread **2** rayon made from such thread

viscosity *noun* the resistance of a fluid to flow, eg treacle has a higher viscosity than water

viscount (*pronounced* **vai**-kownt) *noun* a title of nobility next below an earl

viscountess (*pronounced* **vai**-kownt-es) *noun* a title of nobility next below a countess

viscous (*pronounced* **vis**-kus) *adjective* of a liquid: sticky, not flowing easily

vishnu *noun, Hinduism* the second god of the Trimurti, beloved to appear in many incarnations

visibility *noun* **1** the clearness with which objects may be seen **2** the extent or range of vision as affected by fog, rain, etc

visible *adjective* able to be seen ♦ **visibly** *adverb*: *visibly upset*

visible spectrum *noun, physics* the range of wavelengths of electromagnetic radiation that can be seen by the human eye, ie visible light

vision *noun* **1** the act or power of seeing **2** something seen in the imagination **3** a strange, supernatural sight: *a vision of the Virgin Mary* **4** the ability to foresee likely future events: *a man of great vision*

visionary *adjective* seen in imagination only, not real ▸ *noun* (*plural* **visionaries**) someone who dreams up imaginative plans

visit *verb* **1** to go to see; call on **2** to stay with as a guest ▸ *noun* **1** a call at a person's house or at a place of interest etc **2** a short stay

visitation *noun* **1** a visit of an important official **2** a great misfortune, seen as a punishment from God

visitor *noun* someone who makes a visit

visor (*pronounced* **vai**-zor) *noun* **1** a part of a helmet covering the face **2** a movable shade on a car's windscreen **3** a peak on a cap for shading the eyes

vista *noun* a view, especially one seen through a long, narrow opening

visual *adjective* relating to, or received through, sight: *visual aids*

visual aid *noun* a picture, film, etc used as an aid to teaching or presenting information

Visual Basic *noun, computing* (*abbrev* **VB**) a form of the programming language BASIC, widely used in creating graphics and software

visual display unit *noun* a device like a television set, on which data from a computer's memory can be displayed

visualize or **visualise** *verb* to form a clear picture of in the mind ♦ **visualization** *noun*

vital *adjective* **1** of the greatest importance: *vital information* **2** necessary to life **3** of life: *vital signs* **4** vigorous, energetic: *a vital personality*

vital capacity *noun* the amount of air that can be expelled from the lungs after taking the deepest breath possible

vitality *noun* life; liveliness; strength; ability to go on living

vitalize or **vitalise** *verb* to give life or vigour to

vitally *adverb* essentially; urgently: *It is vitally important to keep copies of all documents*

vitamin *noun* one of a group of substances necessary for health, occurring in different natural foods

vitamin A *noun* a vitamin found in liver, fish oils, dairy products and egg yolk, required for growth and especially the functioning of the retina (*also called*: **retinol**)

vitamin B complex *noun* any of a group of closely related, but distinctly different, water-soluble substances, found in yeast, liver and wheat germ, and referred to either by B numbers, eg vitamin B_1, vitamin B_2, or by specific names, eg thiamine, riboflavin

vitamin B_1 *noun* a member of the vitamin B complex found in yeast, wheat germ, peas, beans and green vegetables (*also called*: **thiamine**)

vitamin B_7 *noun* a member of the vitamin B complex found in liver, yeast extracts, cereals, peas and beans, which is essential for human nutrition (*also called*: **nicotinic acid, niacin**)

vitamin B_6 *noun* any of three organic compounds in the vitamin B complex found in milk, eggs, liver, cereal grains, yeast and fresh vegetables, required for the metabolism of amino acids (*also called*: **pyridoxine**)

vitamin B_{12} *noun* three active forms of the vitamin B complex found in eggs, milk and liver, and needed for the metabolism of fatty acids, DNA synthesis and the formation of red blood cells (*also called*: **cyanocobalamin**)

vitamin B_2 *noun* a member of the vitamin B complex, found in yeast, liver and green vegetables, which is required for growth in children (*also called*: **riboflavin**)

vitamin C *noun* a compound found in fresh fruits, especially citrus fruits and blackcurrants, potatoes and green vegetables, required for the maintenance of healthy bones, cartilage and teeth (*also called*: **ascorbic acid**)

vitamin D *noun* a complex of vitamins found in fish liver oils, egg yolk and milk, required for adequate amounts of calcium and phosphates in the bones and teeth

vitamin E *noun* any of various related organic compounds found in wholemeal flour, wheat germ and green vegetables, which may be required for maintenance of cell membranes (*also called*: **tocopherol**)

vitamin H *noun* biotin

vitamin K *noun* either of two organic compounds (vitamins K_1 and K_2) found in green leafy vegetables, and also manufactured in the intestines, required for blood clotting

vitamin P *noun* bioflavonoid

vitiate (*pronounced* **vish**-i-eit) *verb* to spoil, damage

vitreous *adjective* of or like glass

vitreous humour *noun* a gelatinous liquid between the lens and the retina of the eye

vitriol *noun* 1 sulphuric acid 2 bitter or hateful criticism

vitriolic *adjective* biting, scathing

vituperation *noun* abusive criticism or language

viva¹ (*pronounced* **vee**-va) *interjection* long live (someone or something named): *viva Rodriguez!* ◑ Comes from Spanish and Italian, meaning 'live'

viva² (*pronounced* **vai**-va) *noun* an oral examination, usually for an academic qualification (*full form*: **viva voce**) ◑ Comes from Latin *viva voce* meaning 'by the living voice'

vivace (*pronounced* vee-**va**-tche) *music, adverb* in a lively manner ➤ *noun* (*plural* **vivaces**) a piece of music to be played in this way ◑ Comes from Italian

vivacious *adjective* lively, sprightly
 ♦ **vivaciously** *adverb*

vivacity *noun* liveliness, spark

-vivi- or **-viv-** forms words related to living, or to things which are alive: *vivisection/survive* ◑ Comes from Latin *vivere* meaning 'to live', and *vivus* meaning 'alive'

vivid *adjective* 1 lifelike 2 brilliant, striking

vividly *adverb* brightly, clearly, intensely: *I remember my grandmother vividly*

viviparous *adjective* of an animal: giving birth to live young, as in most mammals, as opposed to laying eggs etc ◑ Comes from Latin *vivus* meaning 'alive' + *parere* meaning 'to produce'

vivisection *noun* the carrying out of experiments on living animals

vixen *noun* 1 a female fox 2 an ill-tempered woman

vizier *noun, history* a minister of state in some Muslim countries

vocabulary *noun* (*plural* **vocabularies**) 1 the range of words used by an individual or group 2 the words of a particular language 3 a list of words in alphabetical order, with their meanings

vocal *adjective* 1 of the voice 2 expressing your opinions loudly and fully

vocal cords *noun, anatomy* in mammals: the two folds of tissue in the larynx that vibrate and produce sound when air is expelled from the lungs

vocalist *noun* a singer

vocation *noun* 1 an occupation or profession to which someone feels called to dedicate themselves 2 a strong inclination or desire to follow a particular course of action or work ◑ Comes from Latin *vocare* meaning 'to call'

vocational *adjective* relating to, or in preparation for, a trade or occupation: *vocational subjects of study*

vociferous *adjective* loud in speech, noisy

vodka *noun* an alcoholic spirit made from grain or potatoes

vogue *noun* the fashion of the moment; popularity • **in vogue** in fashion

voice *noun* 1 the sound produced from the mouth in speech or song 2 the power of speech: *I've lost my voice* 3 ability to sing: *has a lovely voice* 4 an opinion ➤ *verb* to express (an opinion)

voice box *noun, informal* the larynx

voice mail or **voicemail** *noun* a telephone-answering system by which telephone messages can be stored to be picked up later

voice-over *noun* the voice of, or words spoken by, an unseen narrator in a film, TV advertisement, etc

voice recognition *noun* the ability of a computer or other machine to receive and interpret spoken language and commands

void *adjective* 1 empty, vacant 2 not valid ➤ *noun* an empty space • **void of** lacking completely

voile (*pronounced* voyl) *noun* any very thin semi-transparent fabric

volatile *adjective* 1 of a liquid: quickly turning into vapour 2 of a person: changeable in mood or behaviour, fickle 3 *computing* of memory: not keeping data after the power supply is cut off

vol-au-vent (*pronounced* vol-oh-vong) *noun* a small round puff pastry case with a savoury filling

volcanic *adjective* 1 relating to volcanoes 2 caused or produced by heat within the earth

volcano *noun* (*plural* **volcanoes**) a mountain

with an opening through which molten rock, ashes, etc are periodically thrown up from inside the earth

⊙ Named after *Vulcan*, the Roman god of fire

vole *noun* any of a group of small rodents, including the water rat

volition *noun* an act of will or choice: *He did it of his own volition*

volley *noun* (*plural* **volleys**) **1** a number of shots fired or missiles thrown at the same time **2** an outburst of abuse or criticism **3** *tennis* a return of a ball before it bounces on the ground ► *verb* **1** to shoot or throw in a volley **2** to return (a ball) before it bounces on the ground

volleyball *noun, sport* a game for two teams of six players, in which a large ball is sent back and forth over a high net with the hands

volt *noun* the standard unit of measure of electric potential

⊙ Named after the Italian physicist Alessandro *Volta* (1745–1827)

voltage *noun* electromotive force or potential difference, measured in volts

voltaic cell same as **primary cell**

volte-face (*pronounced* volt fas) *noun* (*plural* **volte-face**) a sudden and complete change of opinion ⊙ Comes from French

voltmeter *noun* an instrument that measures electromotive force in volts

volubility *noun* the act or process of speaking insistently, fluently or at great length

voluble *adjective* speaking with a great flow of words

volume *noun* **1** a book, often one of a series **2** the amount of space taken up by anything **3** amount: *volume of trade* **4** loudness or fullness of sound

volumetric analysis *noun, chemistry* a method of chemical analysis in which the concentration of a solution of known volume is determined

voluminous *adjective* bulky, of great volume

voluntary *adjective* **1** done or acting by choice, not under compulsion **2** working without payment ► *noun* (*plural* **voluntaries**) a piece of organ music of the organist's choice played at a church service

voluntary muscle *noun, anatomy* a muscle that is controlled consciously, such as the biceps or triceps

volunteer *noun* someone who offers to do something of their own accord, often for no payment ► *verb* **1** to act as a volunteer **2** to give (information, an opinion, etc) unasked

voluptuous *adjective* **1** full of, or too fond of, the pleasures of life **2** of a woman: sexually

attractive with a full, curvaceous figure

vomit *verb* to throw up the contents of the stomach through the mouth ► *noun* the matter thrown up by vomiting

voodoo *noun* witchcraft of a type originally practised by the black peoples of the West Indies and the southern US

voracious *adjective* very greedy, difficult to satisfy: *voracious appetite/voracious reader*
⊙ Comes from Latin *vorax* meaning 'devouring'

❗ Do not confuse with: **veracious**

voracity *noun* extreme greed or eagerness

-vore also **-vorous** *suffix* forms technical terms concerned with the eating habits of an animal or person: *carnivore* (= flesh-eating)/*herbivore* (= grass-eating) ⊙ Comes from Latin *vorare* meaning 'to devour'

vortex *noun* (*plural* **vortices** or **vortexes**) **1** a whirlpool **2** a whirlwind

vote *verb* **1** to give your support to (a particular candidate, a proposal, etc) in a ballot or show of hands **2** to decide by voting ► *noun* **1** an expression of opinion or support by voting **2** the right to vote

voter *noun* someone who votes

vouch *verb*: **vouch for something** to say that you are sure of it or can guarantee it: *I can vouch for his courage*

voucher *noun* a paper which can be exchanged for money or goods

vouchsafe *verb* to give or grant (a reply, privilege, etc)

vow *noun* a solemn promise or declaration, especially one made to God ► *verb* **1** to make a vow **2** to threaten (revenge etc)

vowel *noun* **1** a sound made by the voice that does not require the use of the tongue, teeth or lips **2** the letters *a, e, i, o, u* (or various combinations of them), and sometimes *y*, which represent those sounds

vox pop *noun, Brit* **1** popular opinion, public opinion **2** brief street interviews with members of the public on radio or TV ⊙ Shortened from Latin *vox populi* meaning 'the voice of the people'

voyage *noun* a journey, usually by sea ► *verb* to make a journey

voyeur *noun* someone who derives gratification from secretly watching the sexual activities of others ◆ **voyeurism** *noun*

vulcanite *noun* hard black vulcanized rubber

vulcanize or **vulcanise** *verb* to treat rubber with sulphur so as to harden it and increase its elasticity ◆ **vulcanization** *noun*

⊙ From *Vulcanus*, the Roman god of fire

vulgar *adjective* **1** coarse, ill-mannered **2** indecent **3** of the common people

vulgar fraction *noun, maths* a fraction not written as a decimal, eg $\frac{1}{3}$, $\frac{4}{5}$ (*also called:* **common fraction**, **simple fraction**)

vulgarity *noun* coarseness in speech or behaviour

vulgarize or **vulgarise** *verb* **1** to make vulgar or unrefined **2** to make (something) common or popular, and so spoil it

vulgarly *adverb* in a vulgar or coarse way

vulnerability *noun* a state of being vulnerable or easily harmed

vulnerable *adjective* **1** exposed to, or in danger of, attack **2** liable to be hurt physically or emotionally ⊙ Comes from Latin *vulnus* meaning 'a wound'

vulture *noun* a large bird that feeds mainly on the flesh of dead animals

vulva *noun* the two pairs of labia surrounding the opening to the vagina; the external female genitals

W¹ *abbreviation* west; western

W² *symbol* **1** *chemistry* tungsten (formerly called wolfram) **2** watt(s)

wacky or **whacky** *adjective* (**wackier, wackiest** or **whackier, whackiest**), *informal* mad or crazy, eccentric ♦ **wackily** *adverb* ♦ **wackiness** *noun*

⏲ Comes from a dialect word meaning 'left-handed' and 'fool'

wad *noun* **1** a lump of loose material (eg wool, cloth, paper) pressed together **2** a bunch of banknotes

wadding *noun* soft material (eg cotton wool) used for packing or padding

waddle *verb* to walk with short, unsteady steps, moving from side to side as a duck does ➤ *noun* the act of waddling

wade *verb* **1** to walk through deep water or mud **2** to get through with difficulty: *still wading through this book*

wader *noun* **1** a long-legged bird that wades in search of food **2** (**waders**) high waterproof boots worn by anglers for wading

wafer *noun* **1** a very thin, light type of biscuit **2** a very thin slice of anything

waffle¹ *noun* a light, crisp cake made from batter

waffle² *noun* pointless, long-drawn-out talk ➤ *verb* to talk long and meaninglessly

waft *verb* to carry or drift lightly through the air or over water

wag *verb* (**wagging, wagged**) to move from side to side or up and down ➤ *noun* **1** an act of wagging **2** someone who is always joking

wage *verb* to carry on (a war etc) ➤ *noun* (often **wages**) payment for work

wager *noun* a bet ➤ *verb* to bet

waggle *verb* to move from side to side in an unsteady manner ➤ *noun* an unsteady movement from side to side

wagon or **waggon** *noun* **1** a four-wheeled vehicle for carrying loads **2** an open railway carriage for goods

waif *noun* an uncared-for or homeless child or animal • **waifs and strays** homeless children or animals

wail *verb* to cry or moan in sorrow ➤ *noun* a sorrowful cry

wain *noun, old* a wagon

wainscot *noun* a skirting-board

waist *noun* the narrow part of the body, between the ribs and the hips

waistcoat *noun* a short, sleeveless jacket, often worn under an outer jacket

waistline *noun* **1** a line thought of as marking the waist **2** the level where the bodice and skirt of a dress meet **3** the measurement of a waist

wait *verb* **1** to put off or delay action **2** **wait for** to remain in expectation or readiness for: *waiting for the bus to come* **3** to be employed as a waiter or waitress ➤ *noun* a delay • **lie in wait** to keep hidden in order to surprise someone • **wait on 1** to serve (someone) at table **2** to act as a servant to

waiter *noun* a man whose job it is to serve people at table in a restaurant

waiting list *noun* a list of people waiting for something in order of priority

waiting room *noun* a room in which to wait at a railway station, clinic, etc

waitress *noun* a woman whose job it is to serve people at table in a restaurant

waive *verb* to give up (a claim or right) ⏲ Comes from Old French *guesver* meaning 'to abandon'

❗ Do not confuse with: **wave**

waiver *noun* **1** the act of waiving **2** a document indicating this

❗ Do not confuse with: **waver**

wake¹ *verb* (often **wake up**) (**waking, woke** or **waked, woken**) to stop sleeping ➤ *noun* a night of watching beside a dead body

wake² *noun* a streak of foamy water left in the track of a ship • **in the wake of** immediately behind or after

wakeful *adjective* not sleeping, unable to sleep

waken *verb* to wake, arouse or be aroused

waking *adjective* being or becoming awake

walk *verb* **1** to move along on foot **2** to travel along (streets etc) on foot ➤ *noun* **1** an act of walking **2** a manner of walking **3** a distance to be walked over: *a short walk from here* **4** a place for walking: *a covered walk* • **walk of life** someone's rank or occupation • **walk the plank** to be put to death by pirates by being made to walk off the end of a plank over a ship's side

walkabout *noun* **1** a stroll through a crowd of ordinary people by a member of the royal family or a politician etc **2** *Aust* a walk alone in the bush by an Australian Aboriginal • **go walkabout 1** *Aust* to walk alone in the bush **2** *informal* to become lost or mislaid

walkie-talkie *noun* a portable radio set for sending and receiving messages

walking stick *noun* a stick used for support when walking

Walkman *noun, trademark* a personal stereo

walkover *noun* an easy victory

wall *noun* **1** a structure built of stone, brick, etc used to separate or enclose **2** the side of a building or room **3** *biology* an outer covering, eg of a cell **4** *biology* the side of a hollow organ or cavity ➤ *verb*: **wall in** or **off** etc to enclose or separate with a wall • **off the wall** unusual, eccentric

wallaby *noun* (*plural* **wallabies**) a small kind of kangaroo

wallet *noun* a small folding case for holding banknotes, credit cards, etc

wallflower *noun* **1** a sweet-smelling spring flower **2** someone who is continually without a partner at a dance etc

wallop *informal, verb* to beat, hit ➤ *noun*

wallow *verb* **1** to roll about with enjoyment in water, mud, etc **2** to revel or luxuriate (in admiration etc) **3** to indulge excessively (in self-pity etc)

wallpaper *noun* **1** paper used in house decorating for covering walls **2** a background pattern on a computer screen ➤ *verb* to cover with wallpaper

Wall Street *noun* a street in New York, the chief financial centre in the United States

walnut *noun* **1** a tree whose wood is used for making furniture **2** the nut it produces

walrus *noun* (*plural* **walruses**) a large sea animal, like a seal, with two long tusks

⊙ A Dutch word meaning literally 'whale horse'

waltz *noun* (*plural* **waltzes**) **1** a ballroom dance for couples, with a circling movement **2** music for this dance, with three beats to each bar ➤ *verb* to dance a waltz

WAN *abbreviation, computing* wide area network, a computer network that operates over a wide area, not just in a single place

wan (*pronounced* won) *adjective* pale and sickly looking

wand *noun* **1** a long slender rod used by a conjuror, magician, etc **2** a device like a pen that reads bar codes

wander *verb* **1** to roam about with no definite purpose; roam **2** to go astray **3** to be mentally confused because of illness etc

wanderer *noun* a person or animal that wanders

wanderlust *noun* a keen desire for travel

wane *verb* **1** to become smaller (*contrasted with*: **wax²**) **2** to lose power, importance, etc • **on the wane** becoming less

wangle *verb* to get or achieve through craftiness, skilful planning, etc

want *verb* **1** to wish for **2** to need, lack ➤ *noun* **1** poverty **2** scarcity, lack ⊙ Comes from Old Norse *vant* meaning 'lacking', and *vanta* meaning 'to lack'

wanted *adjective* looked for, especially by the police

wanting *adjective* **1** absent, missing; without **2** not good enough: *He tried, but was found wanting* **3** (**wanting in**) lacking: *wanting in good taste*

wanton (*pronounced* **won**-ton) *adjective* thoughtless, pointless, without motive: *wanton cruelty*

WAP *abbreviation* Wireless Application Protocol, technology which allows Internet access from a mobile phone (**WAP phone**)

war *noun* an armed struggle, especially between nations ➤ *verb* (**warring, warred**) to fight in a war, make war

warble *verb* to sing like a bird, trill

warbler *noun* a type of songbird

War Communism *noun, history* strict communist policies introduced in Russia during the Civil War (1918–21)

war crime *noun* a crime committed during, and in connection with, a war, eg ill-treatment of prisoners or killing of civilians ♦ **war criminal** *noun*

ward *verb*: **ward off** to keep off, defend yourself against (a blow etc) ➤ *noun* **1** a hospital room containing a number of beds **2** one of the parts into which a town is divided for voting **3** someone who is in the care of a guardian

warden *noun* **1** someone who guards a game reserve **2** someone in charge of a hostel or college

warder *noun* a prison guard

wardrobe *noun* **1** a cupboard for clothes **2** someone's personal supply of clothes

-ware *suffix* manufactured material: *earthenware/glassware*

warehouse *noun* a building where goods are stored

wares *plural noun* goods for sale ⊙ Comes from Old English *waru*

warfare *noun* the carrying on of war

warhead *noun* the part of a missile containing the explosive

warlike *adjective* **1** fond of war **2** threatening war

warlord *noun* a powerful military leader

warm *adjective* **1** fairly hot **2** of clothes: keeping the wearer warm **3** of a person: friendly, loving ➤ *verb* to make or become warm • **warm up** to exercise the body gently in preparation for more strenuous exercise

warm-blooded *adjective* of an animal: having a body temperature that is relatively constant regardless of changes in the surrounding environment

warm front *noun, geography* the leading edge of a mass of warm air advancing against a mass of cold air

warm-hearted *adjective* kind, generous

warmonger *noun* someone who tries to start war, or who generates enthusiasm for it

warmth *noun* **1** pleasant or comfortable heat, or the condition or quality of being warm **2** affection, friendliness or enthusiasm: *We were immediately won over by her warmth and friendliness*

warm-up *noun* the act of gently exercising the body in preparation for more strenuous exercise

warn *verb* **1** to tell (someone) beforehand about possible danger, misfortune, etc: *I warned him about the icy roads* **2** to advise against: *I warned him not to be late*

warning *noun* a remark, notice, etc that warns

warp *verb* **1** to become twisted out of shape **2** to distort, make unsound: *His previous experiences had warped his judgement* ➤ *noun* the threads stretched lengthwise on a loom, which are crossed by the weft

warpaint *noun* **1** paint put on the face and body by primitive peoples when going to war **2** *informal* a woman's make-up

warpath *noun*: **on the warpath** in a fighting or angry mood

warrant (*pronounced* **wor**-ant) *noun* a certificate granting someone a right or authority: *search warrant* ➤ *verb* to justify, be a good enough reason for: *The crime does not warrant such punishment* • **I warrant you** or **I'll warrant** you may be sure, I assure you

warranty *noun* (*plural* **warranties**) an assurance of the quality of goods being sold, and a promise to carry out any initial repairs

warren *noun* **1** a collection of rabbit burrows **2** a building with many rooms and passages; a maze

warrior *noun* a great fighter

Warsaw Pact *noun, history* a military alliance of East European countries formed in 1955 and disbanded in 1991

warship *noun* a ship armed with guns etc

wart *noun* a small hard growth on the skin

warthog *noun* a large wild African pig, with wart-like lumps on its face and curving tusks

wary *adjective* cautious, on guard ♦ **warily** *adverb* ♦ **wariness** *noun*

was a past form of **be**

wash *verb* **1** to clean with water, soap, etc **2** to clean yourself with water etc **3** of water: to flow over or against **4** to sweep (away, along, etc) by force of water ➤ *noun* (*plural* **washes**) **1** a washing **2** a streak of foamy water left behind by a moving boat **3** a liquid with which anything is washed **4** a thin coat of paint etc • **wash up** to wash the dishes • **wash your hands of** to give up all responsibility for

washbasin, washbowl or **washhand basin** *noun* a basin or sink to wash your face and hands etc in

washed-out *adjective* **1** *informal* of a person: worn out and pale **2** of the colour in a fabric: faded by, or as if by, washing

washed-up *informal, adjective* **1** of a person: exhausted, lacking in energy **2** with no more resources left

washer *noun* **1** someone or something that washes **2** a flat ring of metal, rubber, etc for keeping joints tight

washing *noun* **1** the act of cleaning by water **2** clothes to be washed

washing machine *noun* an electric machine for washing clothes

washing powder or **washing liquid** *noun* a powdered or liquid detergent for washing clothes

washing-up *noun* dishes to be washed

washout *noun* **1** *informal* a flop or failure **2** *informal* a useless person **3** an event cancelled because of rain

wasp *noun* a stinging, winged insect, with a slender, yellow and black striped body

wassail *verb, old* **1** to have a sociable drinking session **2** to sing carols from house to house at Christmas

wastage *noun* **1** an amount wasted **2** loss through decay or squandering

waste *adjective* **1** thrown away, rejected as useless: *waste paper* **2** of land: uncultivated, barren and desolate ➤ *verb* **1** to spend (money, time, energy) extravagantly, without result or profit **2** to decay or wear away gradually ➤ *noun* **1** extravagant use, squandering **2** rubbish, waste material **3** matter excreted from the body; urine or faeces **4** a stretch of barren or devastated land

wasteful *adjective* causing waste, extravagant

wasteland *noun* a desolate and barren place

wastepaper basket *noun* a basket for paper rubbish

wastepipe *noun* a pipe for carrying away dirty water or semi-liquid waste

waster or **wastrel** *noun* an idle, good-for-nothing person

watch verb **1** to look at, observe closely **2** (often **watch over**) to look after, mind **3** old to keep awake ➤ noun (plural **watches**) **1** the act of keeping guard **2** someone who keeps, or those who keep, guard **3** a sailor's period of duty on deck **4** a small clock worn on the wrist or kept in a pocket

watchdog noun **1** a dog which guards a building **2** an organization which monitors business practices etc

watchful adjective alert, cautious
♦ **watchfully** adverb

watchman noun a man who guards a building etc at night

watchword noun a motto, a slogan

water noun **1** a colourless odourless tasteless liquid that freezes to form ice at 0°C and boils to form steam at 100°C **2** an expanse of this liquid in a lake, river, etc **3** a fluid produced by the body, eg urine, sweat, etc ➤ verb **1** to supply with water **2** to dilute or mix with water **3** of the mouth: to fill with saliva **4** of the eyes: to fill with tears ⊕ Comes from Old English wæter

water butt noun a large barrel for rain water

water chestnut noun the tuber of an Asian plant, used as a vegetable in Chinese and Japanese cookery

water closet noun a toilet, a lavatory (short form WC)

watercolour noun **1** a paint which is mixed with water, not oil **2** a painting done with this paint

watercourse noun **1** a stream, river or canal **2** the bed or channel along which any of these flow

watercress noun a plant which grows beside streams, with hot-tasting leaves which are eaten in salads

water cycle noun the process by which water is distributed throughout the earth and its atmosphere

watered-down adjective **1** very diluted **2** reduced in force or impact

waterfall noun a place where a river falls from a height, often over a ledge of rock

waterfront noun the buildings or part of a town along the edge of a river, lake or sea

Watergate noun, history a political scandal in the USA involving an attempted break-in at the Democratic Party headquarters in the Watergate building, Washington DC, in 1972 by agents employed by President Richard Nixon's re-election organization

waterhole noun (also **watering hole**) a pool or spring in a dried-up area, where animals can drink

waterlily noun (plural **waterlilies**) a plant which grows in ponds etc, with flat floating leaves and large flowers

waterlogged adjective **1** filled with water **2** soaked with water

water main noun a large underground pipe that carries a public water supply

watermark noun a faint design on paper, visible only when it is held up to the light

watermelon noun a large melon with red juicy flesh and a thick, green rind

watermill noun a mill driven by water

water polo noun a ball game played in a pool between teams of swimmers

waterproof adjective not allowing water to pass through ➤ noun an overcoat made of waterproof material

water rat noun a kind of vole

watershed noun **1** a high ridge separating two river valleys **2** a crucial point or dividing line between two periods, conditions, etc: adult TV shows broadcast after the 9pm watershed

water-skiing noun the sport of being towed very fast on skis behind a motorboat

water table noun, geography the level below which porous rocks are saturated with water

watertight adjective so closely fitted that water cannot leak through

water tower noun a tower that supports an elevated water tank

water vapour noun water in the form of a gas, especially where evaporation has occurred at a temperature below boiling point

waterway noun a channel along which ships can sail

waterwheel noun a wheel moved by water

waterwings plural noun a pair of inflatable armbands used by people learning to swim

waterworks plural noun **1** a place which purifies and stores a town's water supply **2** euphemistic the urinary system **3** informal tears

watery adjective **1** full of water **2** too liquid, textureless

watt (pronounced wot) noun (symbol **W**) the standard unit of electric power, equal to the power that produces energy at the rate of one joule per second

⊕ After James Watt (1736–1819), the British engineer who developed the commercial steam engine

wattage noun (pronounced wot) electric power measured in watts

wattle noun (pronounced **wot**-l) **1** interwoven twigs and branches used for fences etc **2** an Australian acacia tree **3** a fleshy part hanging from the neck of a turkey

wave noun **1** a moving ridge on the surface of the water **2** a hand gesture for attracting attention, or saying hello or goodbye **3** *physics* a regularly repeated disturbance or displacement in a medium eg water or air **4** a circles of disturbance moving outwards from the site of a shock such as an earthquake **5** a ridge or curve of hair **6** a rush of an emotion (eg despair, enthusiasm, etc) ➤ *verb* **1** to make a wave with the hand **2** to move to and fro, flutter: *flags waving in the wind* **3** to curl, curve ℗ Comes from Old English *wafian* meaning 'to wave'

! Do not confuse with: **waive**

wavecut platform *noun, geography* a level or slightly sloped ridge of rock on a shore, worn smooth by abrasion from rocks carried by the sea

wavelength *noun* **1** the distance from the highest or lowest point on a wave or vibration to the next similar point **2** *radio* the length of the radio wave used by a particular broadcasting station • **on the same wavelength** speaking or thinking in a similar way

waver *verb* **1** to be unsteady, wobble **2** to be uncertain or undecided ℗ Comes from Old Norse *vafra* meaning 'to flicker'

! Do not confuse with: **waiver**

wave refraction *noun, geography* the changing of direction of waves approaching the coast, caused by variations in the water's depth

wavy *adjective* (**wavier, waviest**) having waves

wax¹ *noun* **1** a sticky solid or semi-solid substance, either natural or synthetic, that is easily moulded when warm **2** beeswax **3** sealing wax **4** a brown, fatty substance secreted in the ear ➤ *adjective* made of wax ➤ *verb* to rub with wax

wax² *verb* to grow, increase (*contrasted with*: **wane**)

waxen *adjective* **1** of or like wax **2** pale

wax paper *noun* paper covered with a thin layer of wax to make it waterproof

waxwork *noun* **1** a lifelike model, especially of a famous person, made of wax **2** an object modelled from wax **3** (**waxworks**) a museum displaying wax models of famous people

waxy *adjective* (**waxier, waxiest**) of, or like, wax

way *noun* **1** an opening, a passage: *the way out* **2** a road, path **3** room to go forward or pass: *block the way* **4** direction: *he went that way* **5** correct route: *do you know the way?* **6** distance: *a long way* **7** position: *wrong way up* **8** condition: *in a bad way* **9** means, method: *There must be a way to do this* **10** manner: *in a clumsy way/his way of doing things* **11** someone's own wishes or choice: *He always gets his own way* • **by the way** incidentally, in passing • **by way of 1**

travelling through **2** as if, with the purpose of: *by way of a favour* • **in the way** blocking progress • **make your way** to go • **no way** *informal* under no circumstances ℗ Comes from Old English *weg*

wayfarer *noun, old* a traveller on foot
  ♦ **wayfaring** *noun*

waylay *verb* (**waylaying, waylaid**) to wait for and stop (someone)

-ways *suffix* in the direction of: *lengthways/ sideways*

ways and means *plural noun* **1** methods and resources for doing something **2** methods for obtaining funds for a government

wayside *noun* the edge of a road or path
  ➤ *adjective* located by the side of a road

wayward *adjective* wilful, following your own way

WC *abbreviation* water closet

we *pronoun* used by a speaker or writer in mentioning themselves together with other people (as the subject of a verb): *We are having a party this weekend*

weak *adjective* **1** not strong, feeble **2** lacking determination, easily persuaded **3** not able to support a great weight: *weak bridge* **4** lacking full flavour: *weak tea* **5** of an argument: unsound or unconvincing **6** faint: *a weak signal*

weaken *verb* to make or become weak

weakling *noun* a person or animal that is lacking in strength

weakly *adverb* in a weak way ➤ *adjective* (**weaklier, weakliest**) lacking strength, sickly

weakness *noun* (*plural* **weaknesses**) **1** lack of strength **2** a fault **3** a special fondness (for): *a weakness for chocolate*

weal *noun* a raised mark on the skin caused by a blow from a whip

wealth *noun* **1** riches **2** a large quantity: *wealth of information*

wealthy *adjective* (**wealthier, wealthiest**) rich

wean¹ (*pronounced* ween) *verb* **1** to make (a child or young animal) used to food other than the mother's milk **2** **wean from** or **off** to make (someone or something) gradually give up (a bad habit etc)

wean² (*pronounced* wein) *noun, Scottish* a child

weapon *noun* **1** an instrument used for fighting, eg a sword, gun, etc **2** any means of attack

weaponry *noun* (*plural* **weaponries**) weapons collectively

wear *verb* (**wearing, wore, worn**) **1** to be dressed in, have on the body **2** to arrange in a particular way: *she wears her hair long* **3** to have (a beard, moustache) on the face **4** to damage or weaken by use, rubbing etc **5** to be damaged in this way **6** to last: *wear well* ➤ *noun* **1** use by wearing: *for my own wear* **2** damage by use **3** ability to last **4** clothes etc: *school wear* • **wear and tear** damage by ordinary use • **wear off** to disappear gradually • **wear on** to become later: *the afternoon wore on* • **wear out 1** to make or become unfit for further use **2** to exhaust

wearable *adjective* fit to be worn

wearer *noun* a person who wears something: *wearers of contact lenses*

wearing *adjective* tiring, exhausting

wearisome *adjective* causing tiredness, boredom or impatience

weary *adjective* (**wearier, weariest**) **1** tired, having used up your strength or patience **2** (**weary of**) tired of, bored with **3** tiring, boring ➤ *verb* (**wearies, wearying, wearied**) to make or become tired, bored or impatient

weasel *noun* a small wild animal with a long and slender body, that lives on mice, birds, etc

weather *noun* the state of the atmosphere, eg heat, coldness, cloudiness, etc ➤ *verb* **1** *geography* to dry or wear away (rock etc) through exposure to the air, water, etc **2** to come safely through (a storm, difficulty, etc)

weatherbeaten *adjective* showing signs of having been out in all weathers

weather hazards *plural noun, geography* extreme weather conditions, eg hurricanes, that can cause danger to life and damage to the surroundings

weathering *noun, geography* the action of wind, water, etc in altering the form, colour, texture or composition of rocks

weatherproof *adjective* designed or treated so as to keep out wind and rain ➤ *verb* to make something weatherproof

weathervane *noun* a flat piece of metal that swings in the wind to show its direction

weave¹ *verb* (**weaving, wove, woven**) **1** to pass threads over and under each other on a loom etc to form cloth **2** to plait cane etc for basket-making **3** to put together (a story, plan, etc)

weave² *verb* (**weaving, weaved**) to move in and out between objects, or move from side to side: *weaving through the traffic*

weaver *noun* someone who weaves

Web *noun*: **the Web** the World Wide Web

web *noun* **1** the net made by a spider, a cobweb **2** the skin between the toes of ducks, swans, frogs, etc **3** something woven

web browser *noun, computing* a computer program used for searching and managing data from the World Wide Web

webcam *noun* a small digital video camera attached to a computer that can be used to send images across the Internet

webcast *noun* a programme broadcast live over the Internet ➤ *verb* to broadcast over the Internet

web crawler *noun, computing* a computer program that takes information from sites on the World Wide Web to create entries for a search engine's index

web designer *noun, computing* someone who creates and maintains websites

web-footed or **web-toed** *adjective* having webbed feet or toes

weblog *noun* a document containing personal comments, often in the form of a journal, posted on the Internet (*short form*: **blog**)

webmaster *noun* a person who creates, manages or maintains a website

web page *noun* one of the linked pages or files that make up a Web site

website or **web site** *noun* a linked collection of Web pages or files with a home page from which the other pages can be accessed

wed *verb* (**wedding, wed**) to marry

we'd *short for* **1** we would; we should **2** we had

wedding *noun* **1** marriage **2** a marriage ceremony

wedge *noun* **1** a piece of wood, metal, etc thick at one end with a thin edge at the other, used in splitting wood, forcing two surfaces apart, etc **2** anything shaped like a wedge ➤ *verb* **1** to fix or become fixed with a wedge **2** to push or squeeze (in): *wedged in amongst the crowd*

wedlock *noun* the state of being married

Wednesday *noun* the fourth day of the week

🕓 After *Woden*, the Germanic god of war and wisdom

wee *adjective, Scot* small, tiny

weed *noun* **1** a useless, troublesome plant **2** a weak, worthless person **3** (**weeds**) a widow's mourning clothes ➤ *verb* to clear (a garden etc) of weeds

weedy *adjective* (**weedier, weediest**) **1** full of weeds **2** like a weed **3** thin and puny

week *noun* **1** the space of seven days from Sunday to Saturday **2** the working days of the week, not Saturday and Sunday 🕓 Comes from Old English *wice*

weekday *noun* any day except Saturday and Sunday

weekend *noun* Saturday and Sunday

weekly *adjective* happening, or done, once a week ➤ *adverb* once a week ➤ *noun* (*plural* **weeklies**) a newspaper, magazine, etc coming out once a week

weep *verb* (**weeping, wept**) **1** to shed tears **2** to ooze, drip: *a weeping wound*

weeping willow *noun* a willow tree with drooping branches

weepy or **weepie** *adjective* (**weepier,**

weepiest) **1** tearful **2** of a film or novel etc: causing you to weep; poignant ➤ *noun* (*plural* **weepies**), *informal* a film or novel etc of this kind ◆ **weepiness** *noun*

weevil *noun* a small beetle that destroys grain, flour, etc

weft *noun* the threads on a loom which cross the warp

weigh *verb* **1** to find out how heavy (something) is by putting it on a scale etc **2** to have a certain heaviness: *weighing 10 kilograms* **3** to raise (a ship's anchor) **4** of burdens etc: to be heavy or troublesome **5** to consider (a matter, a point) carefully **6** to consider (something) important ● **weigh in** to test your weight before a boxing match ● **weigh out** to measure out a quantity by weighing it on a scale

weighbridge *noun* a large scale for weighing vehicles

weight *noun* **1** the amount that anything weighs **2** *physics* the force put on an object by the pull of gravity **3** a piece of metal weighing a certain amount: *a 100 gram weight* **4** a load, a burden **5** importance: *attach weight to the story* ➤ *verb* to make heavy by adding or attaching a weight

weightless *adjective* **1** weighing nothing or almost nothing **2** not affected by gravity, so able to float about ◆ **weightlessness** *noun*

weightlifting *noun* a sport in which competitors lift, or attempt to lift, a barbell which is made increasingly heavier ◆ **weightlifter** *noun*

weight training *noun* muscle-strengthening exercises performed using weights and pulleys

weighty *adjective* (**weightier, weightiest**) **1** heavy **2** important

Weimar Republic (*pronounced* **vai**-mar) *noun, history* the federal republic in Germany that was founded in 1919 and lasted until 1933

weir *noun* a dam across a stream

weird *adjective* **1** odd, strange **2** mysterious, supernatural

weirdo *noun* (*plural* **weirdos** or **weirdoes**), *derogatory informal* someone who behaves or dresses bizarrely or oddly

welcome *verb* **1** to receive with warmth or pleasure **2** to accept gladly: *I welcome the challenge* ➤ *noun* a welcoming, a warm reception ➤ *adjective* received with pleasure ● **welcome to** permitted to do or take: *You're welcome to those chocolates* ● **you're welcome!** used in reply to an expression of thanks

weld *verb* **1** to join (pieces of metal) by pressure, with or without heating **2** to join closely ➤ *noun* a joint made by welding ◆ **welder** *noun* ◆ **welding** *noun*

welfare *noun* comfort, good health

welfare state *noun* a country with a health service, insurance against unemployment, pensions for those who cannot work etc

well¹ *adjective* in good health ➤ *adverb* (**better, best**) **1** in a good and correct manner: *write well* **2** thoroughly: *well beaten* **3** successfully: *do well* **4** conveniently: *it fits in well with my plans* ➤ *interjection* expressing surprise, or used in explaining, narrating, etc: *Well! What a shock!* ● **as well as** in addition to ● **it is as well** or **it is just as well** it is a good thing, it is lucky ● **well off** rich

well² *noun* **1** a spring of water **2** a shaft in the earth to extract water, oil, etc **3** an enclosed space round which a staircase winds ➤ *verb* (often **well up**) to rise up and gush: *tears welled up in her eyes*

we'll *short for* we will; we shall

well-adjusted *adjective* emotionally and psychologically healthy

well-advised *adjective* wise

well-appointed *adjective* of a house etc: well furnished or equipped

well-behaved *adjective* with good manners

wellbeing *noun* welfare; contentment

well-born *adjective* descended from an aristocratic family

well-bred *adjective* **1** having good manners, showing good breeding **2** of animals: of good stock

well connected *adjective* having influential or aristocratic friends and relations

well-disposed *adjective*: **well-disposed to** inclined to favour

well-founded *adjective* **1** built on secure foundations **2** of suspicions etc: justified, based on good grounds: *a well-founded belief*

well-grounded *adjective* **1** of an argument etc: soundly based in fact **2** (usually **well grounded in**) having had a good basic education or training

well-heeled *adjective, informal* prosperous, wealthy

well-informed *adjective* having or showing knowledge

wellingtons *plural noun* high rubber boots covering the lower part of the legs

---

🕐 After the Duke of *Wellington* (1769–1852), British general and statesman who wore boots like this

---

well-known *adjective* **1** celebrated, famous **2** familiar

well-meaning *adjective* having good intentions

well-meant *adjective* rightly, kindly intended

well-nigh *adverb* almost, nearly

well-off *adjective* rich

well-read *adjective* having read many good books

well-rounded *adjective* 1 having had a broadly based and balanced education 2 well constructed and complete 3 pleasantly plump

well-spoken *adjective* having a fluent and refined way of speaking

wellspring *noun* 1 a spring or fountain 2 any rich source: *a wellspring of good ideas*

well-to-do *adjective* rich

well versed *adjective* thoroughly trained, knowledgeable: *He is well versed in law*

well-wisher *noun* someone who wishes someone success

well worn *adjective* 1 much worn or used; showing signs of wear: *a well-worn pullover* 2 of an expression etc: over-familiar from frequent use

welsh or **welch** *verb* 1 (usually **welsh on**) to fail to pay (debts) or fulfil (duties) 2 (usually **welsh on**) to fail to keep one's promise to (someone) 3 to cheat in such a way

welt *noun* 1 a firm edging or band, eg on the wrist or waist of a garment 2 a weal

welter *verb* to roll about, wallow ➤ *noun* 1 great disorder or confusion 2 a muddled mass, a jumble: *a welter of information*

Weltpolitik (*pronounced* **velt**-pol-i-teek) *noun* a policy of taking a more forceful part in world affairs ⊙ Comes from German *Welt* meaning 'world' + *politik* meaning 'politics' or 'policy'

wench *noun* (*plural* **wenches**), *old* a young woman, a girl

wend *verb*: **wend your way** to make your way slowly

went past tense of **go**

wept past form of **weep**

were a past form of **be** (plural)

we're *short for* we are

werewolf *noun* a mythical creature which changes periodically from a human into a wolf

west *noun* the direction in which the sun sets, one of the four main points of the compass ➤ *adjective* 1 in or to the west 2 of the wind: from the west ➤ *adverb* in, to or towards the west: *move out west*

westerly *adjective* 1 of the wind: coming from or facing the west 2 in or towards the west

western *adjective* of the west ➤ *noun* a film or story about life among the early settlers in the western United States

westward *adjective & adverb* towards the west

westwards *adverb* towards the west

wet *adjective* 1 soaked or covered with water or other liquid 2 rainy: *a wet day* ➤ *noun* 1 water 2 rain ➤ *verb* (**wetting, wet** or **wetted**) to make wet

wet blanket *noun* a dreary person who spoils the enjoyment of others

wetland *noun, geography* (often **wetlands**) a region of marshy land

wet nurse *noun* a woman employed to breastfeed another's baby

wet suit *noun* a suit that allows water to pass through but retains body heat

whack *noun* a loud, violent slap or blow ➤ *verb* to slap or hit violently

whale *noun* a very large mammal living in the sea ➤ *verb* to catch whales

whaler *noun* a ship engaged in catching whales

wharf *noun* (*plural* **wharfs** or **wharves**) a landing stage for loading and unloading ships

what *adjective & pronoun* used to indicate something about which a question is being asked: *What day is this?/What are you doing?* ➤ *adjective* any that: *Give me what money you have* ➤ *conjunction* anything that: *I'll take what you can give me* ➤ *adjective, adverb & pronoun* used for emphasis in exclamations: *What terrible ties he wears!/What rubbish!* • **what about?** used in asking whether the listener would like something: *What about a glass of milk?* • **what if?** what will or would happen if: *What if he comes back?* • **what with** because of: *What with all this noise, I can't hear myself think*

whatever *adjective & pronoun* 1 anything (that): *Show me whatever you have* 2 no matter what: *whatever happens*

whatsoever *adjective* at all: *nothing whatsoever to do with me*

wheat *noun* a grain from which the flour used for bread etc is made

wheaten *adjective* 1 made of wheat 2 wholemeal

wheatgerm *noun* the vitamin-rich embryo of wheat

wheedle *verb* to beg or coax, often by flattery

wheel *noun* 1 a circular frame or disc turning on an axle, used for transporting things 2 a steering wheel of a car etc ➤ *verb* 1 to move or push on wheels 2 to turn like a wheel or in a wide curve 3 to turn round suddenly: *wheeled round in surprise*

wheelbarrow *noun* a handcart with one wheel in front, two handles and legs behind

wheelchair *noun* a chair on wheels for an invalid

wheelhouse *noun* the shelter in which a ship's steering wheel is placed

wheeze *verb* to breathe with difficulty, making a whistling or croaking sound ➤ *noun* 1 the sound of difficult breathing 2 *informal* a joke

whelk *noun* a type of small shellfish, used as food

whelp *noun* 1 a puppy 2 *old* a young lion ➤ *verb*

of a lion, dog, etc: to give birth to young

when adverb at what time: When did you arrive? ➤ adverb & conjunction the time at which: I know when you left/I fell when I was coming in ➤ relative pronoun at which: at the time when I saw him ➤ conjunction seeing that, since: Why walk when you have a car?

whence old, adverb from what place: Whence did you come? ➤ conjunction to the place from which: He's gone back whence he came

whenever adverb & conjunction **1** at any given time: Come whenever you're ready **2** at every time: I go whenever I get the chance

where adverb & conjunction to or in what place: Where are you going?/I wonder where we are ➤ relative pronoun & conjunction (in the place) in which, (to the place) to which: Go where he tells you to go/It's still where it was

whereabouts adverb & conjunction near or in what place: Whereabouts is it?/I don't know whereabouts it is ➤ noun the place where someone or something is: I don't know her whereabouts

whereas conjunction **1** when in fact: They thought I was lying, whereas I was telling the truth **2** but, on the other hand: He's tall, whereas I'm short

whereby adverb & conjunction by which: the method by which you achieve your aims

whereupon adverb & conjunction at or after which time, event, etc

wherever adverb to what place: Wherever did you go? ➤ conjunction to any place: Wherever you may go

wherewithal noun **1** the means of doing something **2** money

whet verb (**whetting, whetted**) **1** to sharpen (a knife etc) by rubbing **2** to make (desire, appetite, etc) keener

whether conjunction **1** either if: whether you come or not **2** if: I don't know whether it's possible

whetstone noun a stone on which to sharpen blades

whey noun the watery part of milk, separated from the **curd** in making cheese

which adjective & pronoun **1** used to refer to a particular person or thing from a group: Which colour do you like best? **2** the one that: Show me which dress you would like ➤ relative pronoun referring to the person or thing just named: I bought the chair which you are sitting on
  • **which is which** which is one and which is the other: They are twins and I can't tell which is which

whichever adjective & pronoun any (one), no matter which: I'll take whichever you don't want/I saw trees whichever way I turned

whiff noun a sudden puff or scent: whiff of perfume

Whig noun, history a member of one of the main British political parties that emerged 1679–80, originally campaigning for the exclusion of the Catholic James, the Duke of York from the throne ◆ **Whiggery** or **Whiggism** noun & adjective

⊙ Probably from whiggamore, the name for a 17th century Scottish Presbyterian rebel

while or **whilst** conjunction **1** during the time that: while I'm at the office **2** although: While I sympathize, I can't really help ➤ noun a space of time ➤ verb: **while away** to pass (time) without boredom: He whiled away the time by reading

whim noun a sudden thought or desire

whimper verb to cry with a low, whining voice ➤ noun a low, whining cry

whimsical adjective **1** full of whims, fanciful **2** humorous

whimsy or **whimsey** noun (**whimsies** or **whimseys**) **1** quaint or fanciful humour **2** a whim

whine verb **1** to make a high-pitched, complaining cry **2** to complain unnecessarily ➤ noun an unnecessary complaint

whinge verb (**whingeing** or **whinging, whinged**) to whine, complain peevishly ➤ noun a peevish complaint

whinny verb (**whinnies, whinnying, whinnied**) of a horse: to neigh ➤ noun (plural **whinnies**) a neighing sound

whip noun **1** a lash with a handle, for punishing, urging on animals, etc **2** a member of a party in parliament who sees that all the party's members attend to give their vote when needed ➤ verb (**whipping, whipped**) **1** to hit or drive with a lash **2** to beat (eggs, cream, etc) into a froth **3** to snatch (away, off, out, up, etc): whipped out a revolver **4** to move fast, like a whip

whiplash noun **1** the springy end of a whip **2** the lash of a whip **3** (also **whiplash injury**) a neck injury caused by the sudden jerking back of the head and neck

whippet noun a breed of racing dog, like a small greyhound

whipping noun a beating with a whip

whip-round noun, informal a collection of money hastily made among a group of people

whir or **whirr** noun a sound of fast, continuous whirling ➤ verb (**whirring, whirred**) to move or whirl with a buzzing noise

whirl verb **1** to turn round quickly **2** to carry (off, away, etc) quickly ➤ noun **1** a fast circling movement **2** great excitement, confusion: in a whirl over the wedding arrangements

whirlpool *noun* a place in a river or sea where the current moves in a circle

whirlwind *noun* a violent current of wind with a whirling motion

whisk *verb* **1** to move quickly and lightly, sweep: *Their car whisked past* **2** to beat or whip (a mixture) ➤ *noun* **1** a quick sweeping movement **2** a kitchen utensil for beating eggs or mixtures **3** a small bunch of twigs etc used as a brush

whisker *noun* **1** a long bristle on the upper lip of a cat etc **2** (**whiskers**) hair on the sides of a man's face, sideburns

whisky or *Irish & US* **whiskey** *noun* (*plural* **whiskies** or **whiskeys**) an alcoholic spirit made from grain

⊙ Based on Scottish Gaelic *uisge beatha*, meaning 'water of life'

whisper *verb* **1** to speak very softly, using the breath only, not the voice **2** to make a soft, rustling sound ➤ *noun* a soft sound made with the breath

whist *noun* a type of card game for four players

whistle *verb* **1** to make a high-pitched sound by forcing breath through the lips or teeth **2** to make such a sound with an instrument **3** to move with such a sound, like a bullet ➤ *noun* **1** the sound made by whistling **2** any instrument for whistling

whistle-stop *adjective* of a tour: very rapid, with a number of brief stops

⊙ Originally denoting a place at which a train only stopped if signalled to by a whistle

whit *noun* a tiny bit: *not a whit better*

White *adjective* **1** of people: belonging to one of the pale-skinned races **2** belonging to or relating to White people ➤ *noun* a white-skinned person

white *adjective* **1** of the colour of pure snow **2** pale or light-coloured: *white wine* **3** of tea or coffee: containing milk ➤ *noun* **1** the colour of pure snow **2** the light part of the eyeball **3** the part of an egg surrounding the yolk ♦ **whitish** *adjective*

whitebait *noun* the young of herring or sprats

whiteboard *noun* a board, used for teaching or presentations, with a white plastic surface for writing on using felt-tipped pens

white-collar *adjective* referring to workers in clerical or other professions rather than manual labour (*compare with*: **blue-collar**)

white elephant *noun* something useless and costly or troublesome to maintain

⊙ From a story that the King of Siam gave white elephants as gifts to rude courtiers. The elephants cost a lot of money to look after, but could not be disposed of or put to work because they were thought to be sacred

white goods *noun* **1** large kitchen appliances such as washing machines, refrigerators, etc **2** household linen

white-hot *adjective* having reached a degree of heat at which metals glow with a white light (hotter than **red-hot**)

white lie *noun* a lie told to avoid hurting someone's feelings

white light *noun* light, such as that of the sun, that contains all the wavelengths in the visible range of the spectrum

white matter *noun, anatomy* pale tissue in the brain and spinal cord

whiten *verb* to make or become white or whiter

whiteness *noun* a white state or quality

white noise *noun* sound waves containing a large number of frequencies of roughly equal intensity

white paper *noun, Brit politics* (often **White Paper**) a government policy statement printed on white paper, issued to inform parliament how it intends to change the law (*compare with*: **green paper**)

white spirit *noun* a colourless liquid distilled from petroleum, used as a solvent and thinner for paints

whitewash *noun* **1** a mixture of ground chalk and water, or lime and water, for whitening walls etc **2** an attempt to cover up faults **3** *informal* a total defeat in a game, sporting contest, etc ➤ *verb* **1** to put whitewash on **2** to cover up the faults of, give a good appearance to **3** *informal* to beat (an opponent) in a game that he or she fails to score at all

whither *adverb & conjunction, old* to what place?

whiting *noun* a small type of fish related to the cod

Whitsun *noun* the week beginning with the seventh Sunday after Easter

whittle *verb* **1** to pare or cut (wood etc) with a knife **2** (often **whittle away** or **down**) to make gradually less: *whittled away his savings*

whizz or **whiz** *verb* (**whizzing, whizzed**) **1** to move with a hissing sound, like an arrow **2** to move very fast ➤ *noun* someone remarkably good at something

whizz kid or **whiz kid** *noun* someone who achieves rapid success while relatively young

WHO *abbreviation* World Health Organization, a United Nations agency monitoring people's health around the world

who *pronoun* used to refer to someone or some people unknown or unnamed (only as the subject of a verb): *Who is that woman in the green hat?* ➤ *relative pronoun* referring to the person or people just named: *Do you know who those people are?*

whoa *interjection* a command to stop, especially to a horse

whodunit or **whodunnit** *noun, informal* a detective novel or play etc ◷ Comes from *who done it?*, a non-standard form of *who did it?*

whoever *pronoun* any person or people

whole *adjective* **1** complete **2** all, with nothing or no one missing **3** not broken **4** in good health ➤ *noun* the entire thing • **on the whole** when everything is taken into account

wholefood *noun* unprocessed food produced without the aid of artificial fertilizers

wholehearted *adjective* enthusiastic, generous

wholemeal *noun* flour made from the entire wheat grain

whole number *noun, maths* a number without fractions, ie positive integer or zero

wholesale *noun* the sale of goods in large quantities to a shop from which they can be bought in small quantities by ordinary buyers (*compare with*: *retail*) ➤ *adjective* **1** buying or selling in large quantities **2** on a large scale: *wholesale killing*

wholesaler *noun* a person who buys goods on a large scale and sells them in smaller quantities to shopkeepers for sale to the public

wholesome *adjective* **1** giving health, healthy: *wholesome food* **2** spiritually or morally beneficial: *wholesome ideas*

who'll *short for* who will; who shall

wholly *adverb* entirely, altogether

whom *pronoun* **1** used to refer to someone or some people unknown or unnamed (only as the object of a sentence): *Whom did you see?/To whom am I speaking?* **2** which person: *Do you know to whom I gave it?* ➤ *relative pronoun* referring to the person or people just named: *the person whom I liked best*

whoop *noun* a loud cry, rising in pitch ➤ *verb* to give a whoop

whooping cough *noun* an infectious disease in which violent bouts of coughing are followed by a whoop as the breath is drawn in

whorl *noun* **1** *botany* the petals of a flower; a corolla **2** *zoology* one complete coil in the spiral shell of a mollusc, the number of which indicates the shell's age **3** a type of fingerprint in which there is a spiral arrangement of the ridges ◷ Comes from Anglo-Saxon *hwyrfel*

who's *short for* who is; who has

! Do not confuse: **who's** and **whose**

whose *adjective & pronoun* belonging to whom?: *Whose handwriting is this?* ➤ *relative pronoun* of whom: *the man whose wife I know*

why *adverb & pronoun* for which reason?: *Why did you not stay?* • **the whys and**

wherefores all the reasons, details

wick *noun* the twisted threads in a candle or lamp which draw up the oil or grease to the flame

wicked *adjective* **1** evil, sinful **2** mischievous, spiteful ♦ **wickedly** *adverb* ♦ **wickedness** *noun*

wicker *adjective* of a chair: made of woven willow twigs

wicket *noun* **1** a small gate or door, especially in or beside a larger one **2** *cricket* the set of three stumps, or one of these, at which the ball is bowled **3** *cricket* the ground between the bowler and the batsman

wicketkeeper *noun, cricket* the player who stands behind the batsman and whose job is to stop balls missed by the batsman

wide *adjective* **1** broad, not narrow **2** stretching far: *a wide grin* **3** general, big: *a wide selection* **4** measuring a certain amount from side to side: *5 centimetres wide* ➤ *adverb* **1** off the target: *the shots went wide* **2** (often **wide apart**) far apart: *hold your arms wide* • **wide of the mark** off the target, inaccurate

wide awake *adjective* fully awake; alert

wideband *adjective* another name for **broadband**

wide-eyed *adjective* with eyes wide open in surprise etc

widely *adverb* **1** over a wide area; among many: *widely believed* **2** far apart: *widely set eyes/ widely different ideas*

widen *verb* to make or become wide

wideness *noun* a wide state or quality

wide open *adjective* opened to the full extent

widespread *adjective* spread over a large area or among many people: *a widespread belief*

widow *noun* a woman whose husband is dead ♦ **widowhood** *noun*

widower *noun* a man whose wife is dead

width *noun* **1** measurement across, from side to side **2** large extent

wield *verb* **1** to swing or handle (a cricket bat, sword, etc) **2** to use (power, authority, etc)

wife *noun* (*plural* **wives**) **1** a married woman **2** the woman to whom a man is married

Wi-Fi (*pronounced* **wai**-fai) *noun, trademark* a method of transmitting data between computers without wires, using high-frequency radio waves

◷ A shortening of *wireless fidelity*, modelled on **hi-fi**

wig *noun* an artificial covering of hair for the head

wiggle *verb* to move from side to side with jerky or twisting movements ➤ *noun* a jerky movement from side to side

wiggly *adjective* (**wigglier, wiggliest**) wriggly, wavy: *She drew a wiggly line*

wigwam *noun, history* a conical tent of skins made by some Native Americans

wild *adjective* **1** of an animal: not tamed **2** of a plant: not cultivated in a garden **3** uncivilized **4** unruly, uncontrolled **5** of weather: stormy **6** frantic, mad: *wild with anxiety* **7** of a guess etc: rash, inaccurate ➤ *noun* (usually **wilds**) an uncultivated or uncivilized region

wild boar *noun* a wild type of pig

wild card *noun* **1** someone allowed to compete in a sports event, despite lacking the usual qualifications **2** *computing* a symbol, eg an asterisk, used to represent any character or set of characters

wildcat *noun* (often **wild cat**) a wild type of European cat ➤ *adjective* **1** of an industrial strike: not called by a trade union **2** of a business scheme: financially unsound or risky

wildebeest (*pronounced* **wild**-i-beest) *noun* (*plural* **wildebeest** or **wildebeests**) a gnu ⊕ Comes from Afrikaans, from Dutch *wilde* meaning 'wild' + *beest* meaning 'ox'

wilderness *noun* a wild, uncultivated or desolate region

wildfire *noun*: **spread like wildfire** of a disease or rumour etc: to spread rapidly and widely

wild-goose chase *noun* a troublesome and useless errand

wildlife *noun* wild animals, birds, etc in their natural habitats

Wild West *noun, history* (**the Wild West**) the west of the USA during the days of its first settlers in the 19th century, before the establishment of law and order

wile *noun* **1** a crafty trick **2** (**wiles**) charming personal ways

wilful *adjective* **1** fond of having one's own way: *a wilful child* **2** intentional: *wilful damage*

will¹ *verb* **1** (*past form* **would**) used to form future tenses of other verbs when the subject is **he, she, it, you** or **they**: *You will see me there* **2** *informal* often used for the same purpose when the subject is **I** or **we**: *I will tell you later* **3** used for emphasis, or to express a promise, when the subject is **I** or **we**: *I will do it if possible* (*see also* **shall, would**) ⊕ Comes from Old English *wyllan* meaning 'to wish' or 'to be willing'

will² *noun* **1** the power to choose or decide **2** wish or desire: *against my will* **3** determination: *the will to win* **4** feeling towards someone: *bore him ill will* **5** a written statement about what is to be done with your property after your death ➤ *verb* **1** to try to influence someone by exercising your will: *He willed her to win* **2** to hand down (property etc) by will ● **at will** as or

when you choose ● **with a will** eagerly ⊕ Comes from Old English *willa* meaning 'will' or 'determination'

willing *adjective* ready to do what is asked; eager

will-o'-the-wisp *noun* a pale light sometimes seen by night over marshy places

willow *noun* **1** a tree with long slender branches **2** its wood, used in cricket bats

willowy *adjective* especially of a woman: slender and graceful

willpower *noun* the determination and self-discipline needed to accomplish something

willy-nilly *adverb* **1** whether you wish or not **2** notwithstanding other people's feelings

⊕ From the phrase *will I, nill I*, meaning 'whether I want or don't want'

wilt *verb* **1** of a flower or plant: to droop **2** to lose strength

wily *adjective* (**wilier, wiliest**) cunning

wimp *noun, informal* an ineffectual person

wimple *noun* a veil folded around the head, neck and cheeks, worn as part of a nun's dress ⊕ Comes from Old English *wimpel* meaning 'neck-covering'

win *verb* (**winning, won**) **1** to come first in a contest **2** to gain by luck or in a contest: *I won a teddy bear* **3** to gain (the love of someone etc) by effort **4** (often **win over**) to gain the support or friendship of ➤ *noun* an act of winning; a victory

wince *verb* to shrink or start back in pain etc, flinch: *Her singing made me wince*

winch *noun* (*plural* **winches**) **1** a handle or crank for turning a wheel **2** a machine for lifting things, worked by winding a rope round a revolving cylinder **3** (usually **winch up**) to lift up with a winch

wind¹ (*pronounced* wind) *noun* **1** the movement of air across the earth's surface **2** a current of air **3** breath **4** the scent of an animal, predator, etc carried by the wind **5** air or gas in the stomach **6** the wind instruments in an orchestra ➤ *verb* to put out of breath ● **get the wind up** *informal* to become afraid ● **get wind of** *informal* to hear about in an indirect way

wind² (*pronounced* waind) *verb* (**winding, wound**) **1** to turn, twist or coil **2** (sometimes **wind up**) to screw up the spring of (a watch, clockwork toy, etc) **3** to wrap closely ● **wind up 1** to bring or come to an end: *wind up a meeting* **2** *informal* to annoy, tease ● **wind your way** to make your way circuitously

wind chill *noun, meteorology* the cooling effect of the wind on air temperature

winder *noun* a key etc for winding a clock

windfall *noun* **1** a fruit blown from a tree **2** an unexpected gain, eg a sum of money

wind farm *noun* a group of wind-driven turbines generating electricity

winding *adjective* curving, twisting

wind instrument *noun* a musical instrument sounded by blowing into it

windlass *noun* a machine for lifting up or hauling a winch

windmill *noun* a mill driven by sails which are moved by the wind, used for pumping water, grinding grain, etc

window *noun* **1** an opening in a wall, protected by glass, which lets in light and air **2** *computing* a rectangular section of a screen which can be used independently of the rest of the screen

Windows *singular noun, trademark* a type of computer operating system

window-shopping *noun* looking at goods in shop windows as an alternative to buying them ♦ **window-shop** *verb* (**window-shopping, window-shopped**)

windowsill or **window ledge** *noun* the ledge that runs along the bottom of a window

windpipe *noun* the air tube leading from the throat to the lungs (*also called*: **trachea**)

windscreen or *esp US* **windshield** *noun* a pane of glass in front of the driver of a car etc

windsock or **wind cone** *noun* a cone of fabric flying from a mast, eg at an airport, which shows the direction and speed of the wind

windsurfer *noun* **1** a board with a sail for riding the waves **2** someone who takes part in windsurfing

windsurfing *noun* the sport of riding the waves on a sailboard or windsurfer

windswept *adjective* exposed to strong winds and showing the effects of it: *windswept hair*

wind-up *noun* **1** the taunting or teasing of someone, eg by playing a practical joke **2** the ending of something, eg a film

windward *adjective & adverb* in the direction from which the wind blows

windy *adjective* (**windier, windiest**) **1** of weather: with a strong wind blowing **2** of a place: exposed to strong winds

wine *noun* **1** an alcoholic drink made from the fermented juice of grapes or other fruit **2** a rich dark red colour

wing *noun* **1** one of the arm-like limbs of a bird, bat or insect by means of which it flies **2** one of the two projections on the sides of an aeroplane **3** a part of a house built out to the side **4** the side of a stage, where actors wait to enter **5** *football etc* a player positioned at the edge of the field **6** a section of a political party: *the left wing* ➤ *verb* **1** to wound (a bird) in the wing **2** to soar • **on the wing** flying, in motion • **under someone's wing** under the protection or care of someone

winged *adjective* **1** having wings **2** swift

wing mirror *noun* a rear-view mirror attached to the side of a motor vehicle

wingspan *noun* the distance from tip to tip of the wings of an aircraft, or of the outstretched wings of a bird

wink *verb* **1** to open and close an eye quickly **2** to give a hint by winking **3** of lights etc: to flicker, twinkle ➤ *noun* **1** an act of winking **2** a hint given by winking • **forty winks** a short sleep

winkle *noun* a small edible shellfish (*also called*: **periwinkle**) • **winkle out** to force out gradually

winner *noun* **1** someone or something that wins a contest or race **2** an idea or suggestion that is likely to be popular or successful

winning *adjective* **1** victorious, successful **2** charming, attractive: *winning smile*

winnings *plural noun* money etc that has been won

winnow *verb* to separate chaff from grain by blowing a current of air through it

winsome *adjective* charming

winter *noun* the coldest season of the year, following autumn ➤ *adjective* relating to winter

winter solstice see **solstice**

winter sports *plural noun* sports on snow or ice, eg skiing, tobogganing, etc

wintry *adjective* **1** cold, frosty **2** cheerless, unfriendly: *a wintry look*

wipe *verb* **1** to clean or dry by rubbing **2** (**wipe away, out, off** or **up**) to clear away by wiping ➤ *noun* the act of cleaning by rubbing • **wipe out** to totally destroy

wiper *noun* one of a pair of moving parts which wipe the windscreen of a car

wire *noun* **1** a thread-like length of metal **2** a length of this enclosed in insulating material, used for carrying an electric current **3** the metal thread connecting points by telephone etc **4** *informal* a telegram ➤ *adjective* made of wire ➤ *verb* **1** to bind or fasten with wire **2** *informal* to send a telegram **3** (sometimes **wire up**) to supply (a building, equipment, etc) with wires for carrying an electric current

wireless *adjective* of communication: by radio waves ➤ *noun, old* a radio set

wiring *noun* the arrangement of wires that connects the components of electric circuits into an system, eg the mains wiring of a house

wiry *adjective* **1** made of wire **2** of a person: thin but strong

wisdom *noun* the quality of being wise

wisdom tooth *plural noun* one of four large back teeth which appear after childhood

wise *adjective* **1** very knowledgeable **2** judging rightly; sensible

-wise *suffix* **1** in the manner or way of: *crabwise* **2**

wish verb 1 to feel or express a desire: I wish he'd leave 2 (often **wish for**) to long for, desire: she wished for peace and quiet 3 to hope for on behalf of (someone): wish someone luck ➤ noun (plural **wishes**) 1 desire, longing 2 a thing desired or wanted: her great wish was to live abroad 3 an expression of desire: make a wish 4 (**wishes**) expression of hope for another's happiness, good fortune, etc: best wishes
• **wish someone well** to feel goodwill towards them

wishbone noun a forked bone in the breast of fowls

wishful adjective wishing, eager • **wishful thinking** basing your belief on (false) hopes rather than known facts

wishy-washy adjective 1 of liquid: thin and weak 2 feeble, not energetic or lively 3 lacking colour

wisp noun a small tuft or strand: a wisp of hair

wispy adjective (**wispier, wispiest**) wisp-like; light and fine in texture: wispy white clouds

wisteria noun a climbing shrub with lilac, violet or white flowers in long clusters

wistful adjective thoughtful and rather sad: a wistful glance ✦ **wistfully** adverb

wit noun 1 (often **wits**) intelligence, common sense 2 the ability to express ideas neatly and funnily 3 someone who can do this • **at your wits' end** unable to solve your difficulties, desperate • **keep your wits about you** to keep alert • **to wit** namely, that is to say

witch noun (plural **witches**) 1 a woman with magic power obtained through evil spirits 2 an ugly old woman

witchcraft noun magic performed by a witch

witch doctor noun someone believed to have magical powers to cure illnesses etc

witch hunt noun the persecution of a person or people with particular political etc views, claiming they are dangerous to society

with preposition 1 in the company of: I was walking with my father 2 by means of: cut it with a knife 3 in the same direction as: drifting with the current 4 against: fighting with his brother 5 on the same side as: I'm with Tommy on this one 6 having: a man with a limp 7 in the keeping of: leave the keys with me

withdraw verb (**withdrawing, withdrew, withdrawn**) 1 to go back or away 2 to take away, remove: withdraw cash/withdraw troops 3 to take back (an insult etc) ✦ **withdrawal** noun

withdrawn adjective 1 of a person: unwilling to communicate with others, unsociable 2 of a place: lonely, isolated

wither verb 1 to fade, dry up or decay 2 to make to feel very unimportant or embarrassed: She withered him with a look

withering adjective 1 drying up, dying 2 of a remark etc: scornful, sarcastic

withhold verb (**withholding, withheld**) to keep back, refuse to give

within preposition inside the limits of: keep within the law ➤ adverb on the inside

without preposition 1 in the absence of: We went without you 2 not having: without a penny 3 old outside the limits of: without the terms of the agreement ➤ adverb, old 1 on the outside 2 out-of-doors

withstand verb (**withstanding, withstood**) to oppose or resist successfully

witness noun (plural **witnesses**) 1 someone who sees or has direct knowledge of a thing 2 someone who gives evidence in a law court 3 proof, evidence ➤ verb 1 to see, be present at 2 to sign your name to confirm the authenticity of (someone else's signature) 3 to give or be evidence • **bear witness** to give or be evidence of: bear witness to his character

-witted adjective (added to another word) having wits (of a certain kind): slow-witted/quick-witted

witter verb (usually **witter on**) to talk or mutter ceaselessly and ineffectually

witticism noun a witty remark

wittingly adverb knowingly

witty adjective (**wittier, wittiest**) clever and amusing

wizard noun a man believed to have the power of magic

wizardry noun magic

wizened adjective dried up, shrivelled: a wizened old man

WMD abbreviation weapon(s) of mass destruction

woad noun 1 a blue dye 2 the plant from which it is obtained

wobble verb to rock unsteadily from side to side ➤ noun an unsteady rocking

wobbly adjective (**wobblier, wobbliest**) unsteady, rocking

woe noun 1 grief, misery 2 a cause of sorrow, a trouble

woebegone adjective dismal, sad-looking

woeful adjective sorrowful; pitiful ✦ **woefully** adverb

woggle noun a ring through which Cubs and Scouts etc thread their neckerchiefs

wok noun an Asian cooking-pan shaped like a large bowl

wolf noun (plural **wolves**) a wild animal like a dog that hunts in packs ➤ verb (usually **wolf down**) to eat greedily: wolfing down his food • **cry wolf** to give a false alarm • **keep the wolf from the door** to keep away hunger or want

wolfhound *noun* any of several large breeds of domestic dog, formerly used for hunting wolves

wolfram an old name for **tungsten**

woman *noun* (*plural* **women**) **1** an adult human female **2** human females in general **3** a domestic help ☉ Comes from Old English *wif* meaning 'a woman', and *man* meaning 'man' or 'human being'

womanhood *noun* the state of being a woman

womanish *adjective* behaving or looking like a woman

womanize or **womanise** *verb, derogatory informal* of a man: to pursue and have casual affairs with women ♦ **womanizer** *noun*

womankind or **womenkind** *noun* women generally

womanly *adjective* like, or suitable for, a woman

womb *noun* the part of a female mammal's body in which the young develop and stay till birth

wombat *noun* a small, beaver-like Australian animal, with a pouch

women plural of **woman**

won past form of **win**

wonder *noun* **1** the feeling produced by something unexpected or extraordinary; surprise, awe **2** something strange, amazing or miraculous ➤ *verb* **1** to be curious or in doubt: *I wonder what will happen/I wonder whether to go or not* **2** to feel surprise or amazement (at, that): *I wonder at you sometimes!*

wonderful *adjective* **1** excellent **2** arousing wonder; strange, marvellous

wonderment *noun, old* amazement

wondrous *adjective, old* wonderful

wonky *adjective* (**wonkier, wonkiest**), *Brit informal* **1** unsound, unsteady or wobbly **2** crooked or uneven

wont (*pronounced* wohnt) *formal or old, adjective* accustomed (to do something) ➤ *noun* habit: *as is his wont*

won't *short for* will not

woo *verb* (**wooing, wooed**) **1** to try to win the love of (someone) **2** to try to gain (eg success)

wood *noun* **1** a group of growing trees **2** the hard tissue beneath the bark of a tree, especially when cut for use

woodchuck *noun* a N American species of marmot

woodcut *noun* **1** a picture engraved on wood **2** a print made from this engraving

woodcutter *noun* someone who fells trees, cuts up wood, etc

wooded *adjective* covered with trees

wooden *adjective* **1** made of wood **2** dull, stiff, not lively: *a wooden speech* ♦ **woodenly** *adverb*

wooden spoon *noun* a booby prize

☉ From the wooden spoon presented to the person who came bottom in the mathematics examinations list at Cambridge University

woodland *noun* land covered with trees

woodlouse *noun* (*plural* **woodlice**) a small beetle-like creature with a jointed shell, found under stones etc

woodpecker *noun* a bird that pecks holes in the bark of trees with its beak, in search of insects

wood pulp *noun* wood fibres that have been pulped for making paper

wood spirit *same as* **methanol**

woodwind *noun* a family of wind instruments made of wood or metal, eg the flute or clarinet

woodwork *noun* **1** the making of wooden articles **2** the wooden parts of a house, room, etc

woodworm *noun* the larva of a beetle that bores holes in wood and destroys it

woody *adjective* (**woodier, woodiest**) **1** like wood **2** wooded

wooer *noun* someone who woos

woof *noun* the sound of, or an imitation of, a dog's bark ➤ *verb* to bark

wool *noun* **1** the soft hair of sheep and other animals **2** yarn or cloth made of wool

woollen *adjective* made of wool ➤ *noun* a knitted garment made of wool

woolly *adjective* (**woollier, woolliest**) **1** made of, or like, wool **2** vague, hazy: *a woolly argument* ➤ *noun* (*plural* **woollies**) a knitted woollen garment

woozy *adjective* (**woozier, wooziest**), *informal* **1** dazed; having blurred senses, due to drink or drugs etc **2** confused; dizzy ♦ **wooziness** *noun*

word *noun* **1** a written or spoken sign representing a thing or an idea **2** (**words**) talk, remarks: *kind words* **3** news: *word of his death* **4** a promise: *break your word* ➤ *verb* to choose words for: *He worded his refusal carefully* • **have words** *informal* to quarrel • **in a word** in short, to sum up • **take someone at their word** to treat what they say as true • **take someone's word for something** to trust that what they say is true • **word for word** in the exact words

wording *noun* choice or arrangement of words

word processor *noun* an electronic machine or computer program which can store, edit and print out text

word wrapping or **word wrap** *noun, computing* in word-processing: a facility that automatically puts a word that is too long to fit into the end of a line onto the start of the following line

wordy *adjective* (**wordier, wordiest**) using too many words

wore past tense of **wear**

work *noun* **1** a physical or mental effort to achieve or make something **2** a job, employment: *out of work* **3** a task: *I've got work to do* **4** anything made or done **5** something produced by art, eg a book, musical composition, painting, etc **6** manner of working, workmanship: *poor work* **7** (**works**) a factory **8** (**works**) a mechanism (eg of a watch) **9** (**works**) deeds: *good works* **10** *physics* the transfer of energy when force is exerted on a body to move it, measured in joules ➤ *verb* **1** to be engaged in physical or mental work **2** to be employed **3** to run or operate smoothly and efficiently **4** of a plan etc: to be successful **5** to manage, control: *work the land/work a machine/work magic* **6** to get into a position slowly and gradually: *The screw worked loose* • **work out 1** to solve **2** to discover as a result of deep thought **3** of a situation: to turn out all right in the end **4** to perform a set of physical exercises • **work up** to arouse, excite: *working himself up into a fury* ⊙ Comes from Old English *weorc*

workable *adjective* able to be done, practical

workaday *adjective* **1** ordinary or commonplace **2** suitable for a work day; practical

workaholic *noun, informal* someone addicted to work

workbench *noun* a table at which a mechanic or craftsman etc works

worker *noun* someone who works at a job

workforce *noun* **1** the number of workers in a particular industry, factory, etc **2** the total number of workers potentially available

workhorse *noun* **1** a horse used for labour rather than for recreation or sport **2** a person or machine etc depended upon to do hard work

workhouse *noun, history* an institution where the poor were housed and given work to do

working *adjective* **1** operating properly, not broken **2** having a job

working capital *noun, business* the money available to a business to cover its immediate costs

working class *noun* the social class including manual workers

working day or **working hours** *noun* the hours each day that someone spends at work, on duty, etc

working party *noun* a group of people appointed to investigate and report on something

workload *noun* the amount of work to be done by a person or machine, especially in a certain amount of time

workman *noun* (*plural* **workmen**) someone who works with their hands

workmanlike *adjective* done with skill

workmanship *noun* **1** the skill of a workman **2** the degree of expertise in making something: *satisfactory workmanship*

workout *noun* a session of physical exercise or training

workplace *noun* an office, factory, etc where people work

workroom *noun* a room for working in

workshop *noun* a room or building where manufacturing, craftwork, etc is done

workstation *noun* **1** a computer terminal, usually comprising a keyboard, screen and processor **2** a position at which a particular job is done in a production line

worktable *noun* a table on which work is done

work-to-rule *noun* a form of industrial action in which workers strictly observe all working regulations so that work slows down

world *noun* **1** the earth and all things on it **2** the people of the world **3** any planet or star **4** the universe **5** a state of existence: *the next world* **6** a particular area of life or activity: *the insect world/the world of fashion* **7** a great deal: *a world of good* ⊙ Comes from Old English *weorold* meaning 'age or life of man'

worldly *adjective* (**worldlier, worldliest**) concerned with material things such as money, possessions, etc, not the soul or spirit

worldly-wise *adjective* knowledgeable about life; having the wisdom of those experienced in the ways of the world

worldweary *adjective* tired of the world; bored with life ♦ **worldweariness** *noun*

worldwide *adjective* extending throughout the world ➤ *adverb* throughout the world

World Wide Web *noun* a vast collection of linked documents and stored information located on computers all around the world, which can be accessed via the Internet

WORM *abbreviation, computing* write once read many times, a CD system that allows the user to write data to it only once, but read it as often as they wish

worm *noun* **1** a small creeping animal without a backbone, often living in soil **2** *informal* a low, contemptible person **3** something spiral-shaped, eg the thread of a screw **4** (**worms**) the condition of having parasitic worms in the intestines **5** *computing* an unauthorized program designed to sabotage a system by reproducing itself throughout a network ➤ *verb* **1** to move gradually and stealthily (in or into) **2** (also **worm out**) to draw out (information) bit by bit **3** to rid (an animal) of worms

wormwood *noun* a plant with a bitter taste

worn *adjective* **1** damaged by use **2** tired, worn-out

worn-out *adjective* tired, exhausted

worried *adjective* in an unhappy and unrelaxed state, as a result of thinking about something bad which is happening, or which you fear may happen

worry *verb* (**worries, worrying, worried**) **1** to annoy **2** to make troubled and anxious **3** to be troubled and anxious **4** of a dog: to shake or tear (something) with its teeth ➤ *noun* (*plural* **worries**) **1** uneasiness, anxiety **2** a cause of unease or anxiety

worse *adjective* **1** bad or evil to a greater degree **2** more ill ➤ *adverb* badly to a greater degree, more severely: *It's snowing worse than ever* • **worse off** in a worse position, less wealthy, etc

worsen *verb* to make or become worse

worship *noun* **1** a religious ceremony or service **2** deep reverence, adoration **3** a title used in addressing a mayor, magistrate, etc ➤ *verb* (**worshipping, worshipped**) **1** to pay honour to (a god) **2** to adore or admire deeply

worshipful *adjective* **1** full of reverence **2** worthy of honour

worst *adjective* bad or evil to the greatest degree ➤ *adverb* badly to the greatest degree ➤ *verb* (**worsting, worsted**) to beat, defeat • **at worst** under the least favourable circumstances • **if the worst comes to the worst** if the worst possible circumstances occur

worsted (*pronounced* **woors**-tid) *noun* **1** a type of fine woollen yarn **2** a strong cloth made of this

worth *noun* **1** value; price **2** importance **3** excellence of character etc ➤ *adjective* **1** equal in value to: *jewellery worth a thousand pounds* **2** deserving of: *worth considering* • **worth your while** worth the trouble spent

worthless *adjective* of no merit or value ♦ **worthlessness** *noun*

worthwhile *adjective* deserving time and effort

worthy *adjective* (**worthier, worthiest**) **1** (often **worthy of**) deserving, suitable **2** of good character ➤ *noun* (*plural* **worthies**) a highly respected person: *local worthy*

would *verb* **1** the form of the verb **will** used to express a condition: *He would go if he could* **2** used for emphasis: *I tell you I would do it if possible* **3** old expressing a wish: *I would that he were gone* ⊕ Comes from Old English *wolde* which is the past tense of *wyllan* meaning 'to wish'

would-be *adjective* trying to be or pretending to be: *would-be actor*

wound (*pronounced* woond) *noun* **1** a cut or injury caused by a weapon, in an accident, etc **2** a hurt to someone's feelings ➤ *verb* **1** to make a cut or injury in **2** to hurt the feelings of

wounded (*pronounced* **woond**-ed) *adjective* having a wound, injured, hurt

WPC *abbreviation* Woman Police Constable

wrack *noun* **1** seaweed thrown on to the shore **2** destruction or devastation

wraith (*pronounced* reith) *noun* an apparition of a living person, often as a warning of death

wrangle (*pronounced* **rang**-gl) *verb* to quarrel noisily ➤ *noun* a noisy quarrel

wrap *verb* (**wrapping, wrapped**) **1** to fold or roll round: *Wrap the foil around the turkey* **2** (also **wrap up**) to cover by folding or winding something round: *Wrap it in tissue paper* **3** (also **wrap round**) *computing* of text on a screen: to start a new line automatically as soon as the last character space on the previous line is filled ➤ *noun* **1** a cloak or shawl **2** a snack made from a tortilla rolled around a filling

wrapper *noun* a loose paper cover, eg round a book or sweet

wrath (*pronounced* roth or rawth or rath) *noun* violent anger

wrathful (*pronounced* **roth**-fuwl or **rawth**-fuwl or **rath**-fuwl) *adjective* very angry

wreak (*pronounced* reek) *verb* **1** to carry out: *wreak vengeance* **2** to cause: *wreak havoc*

wreath (*pronounced* reeth) *noun* **1** a ring of flowers or leaves **2** a curling wisp of smoke, mist, etc

wreathe (*pronounced* reedh) *verb* to encircle

wreck *noun* **1** destruction, especially of a ship by the sea **2** the remains of anything destroyed, especially a ship **3** someone whose health or nerves are in bad condition ➤ *verb* to destroy

wreckage (*pronounced* **rek**-ij) *noun* the remains of something wrecked

wren *noun* a very small type of bird

wrench *verb* **1** to pull with a violent, often twisting, motion **2** to sprain (your ankle etc) ➤ *noun* (*plural* **wrenches**) **1** a violent twist **2** a tool for gripping and turning nuts, bolts, etc **3** sadness caused by parting from someone or something

wrest *verb, formal* to twist or take by force

wrestle (*pronounced* **re**-sl) *verb* **1** to fight with someone, trying to bring them to the ground **2** (also **wrestle with**) to struggle with or think deeply about (a problem etc)

wrestler (*pronounced* **res**-ler) *noun* someone who wrestles as a sport

wrestling (*pronounced* **res**-ling) *noun* the sport in which two people fight to throw each other to the ground

wretch *noun* (*plural* **wretches**) **1** a miserable, pitiable person: *a poor wretch* **2** a worthless or contemptible person

wretched (*pronounced* **rech**-id) *adjective* **1** very miserable **2** worthless, very bad
♦ **wretchedly** *adverb* ♦ **wretchedness** *noun*

wriggle *verb* **1** to twist to and fro **2** to move by doing this, as a worm does **3** (**wriggle out of**) to escape or evade (a difficulty etc) ♦ **wriggly** *adjective* (**wrigglier, wriggliest**)

-wright (*pronounced* rait) *suffix* a maker: shipwright/playwright ☉ Comes from Old English *wyrht* meaning 'a work'

wring *verb* (**wringing, wrung**) **1** to twist or squeeze (especially water out of wet clothes) **2** to clasp and unclasp (your hands) in grief, anxiety, etc **3** to cause pain to: *the story wrung everybody's heart* **4** to force out (eg a promise)

wringer *noun* a machine for forcing water from wet clothes

wrinkle *noun* a small crease or fold on the skin or other surface ➤ *verb* to make or become wrinkled

wrinkly *adjective* (**wrinklier, wrinkliest**) having wrinkles

wrist *noun* the joint by which the hand is joined to the arm

writ *noun* a formal document giving an order (especially to appear in a law court)

write (*pronounced* rait) *verb* (**writing, wrote, written**) **1** to form letters with a pen, pencil, etc **2** to put into writing: *write your name* **3** to compose (a letter, a book, etc) **4** to send a letter (to) **5** *computing* to copy (a data file) • **write down** to record in writing • **write off 1** to damage a vehicle beyond repair (in a crash) **2** to cancel (a debt) **3** to dismiss as unimportant etc: *wrote off our chances of winning* • **write to** *computing* to record data onto (a magnetic disk) • **write up** to make a written record or review of

write-off *noun* something that is written off, especially a motor vehicle involved in an accident

writer (*pronounced* **rai**-ter) *noun* someone who writes, an author

write-up *noun* a written account, especially a review in a newspaper or magazine

writhe (*pronounced* raidh) *verb* to twist or roll about, eg in pain

writing (*pronounced* **rai**-ting) *noun* **1** written or printed words **2** handwriting **3** a written text **4** the art or activity of literary composition **5** a form of script: *Chinese writing*

written *adjective* expressed in writing: *written confirmation* ➤ *verb* past participle of **write**

wrong *adjective* **1** not correct: *the wrong answer* **2** mistaken: *You are wrong if you think that* **3** unsuitable: *the wrong weather for camping/quite the wrong dress for the occasion* **4** not right or just: *It was wrong to punish him* **5** evil ➤ *noun* **1** whatever is not right or just **2** an injury done to another ➤ *verb* to do wrong to, harm ♦ **wrongly** *adverb* • **go wrong 1** to fail to work properly **2** to make a mistake or mistakes • **in the wrong** guilty of injustice or error

wrongdoer (*pronounced* **rong**-doo-er) *noun* someone who does wrong

wrongdoing (*pronounced* **rong**-doo-ing) *noun* immoral or illegal behaviour or actions

wrongfoot *verb* **1** *tennis etc* to catch (one's opponent) off balance by making an unpredictable shot in a different direction from which they are moving **2** to place (an opponent in a dispute etc) at a disadvantage or disconcert them

wrongful *adjective* not lawful or just: *wrongful criminal convictions*

wrote past tense of **write**

wrought (*pronounced* rawt) *adjective, old* made, manufactured ➤ *verb, old* past form of **work**

wrought iron (*pronounced* rawt **ai**-ron) *noun* iron hammered, rather than cast, into shape

wrung past form of **wring**

wry (*pronounced* rai) *adjective* **1** slightly mocking or bitter: *wry remark* **2** twisted or turned to one side ♦ **wryly** *adverb*

wuss (*pronounced* woos) *noun chiefly N Am slang* a weakling, a feeble person ♦ **wussy** *adjective* (**wussier, wussiest**)

WWW or **www** *abbreviation* World Wide Web

WYSIWYG *abbreviation, computing* what you see (on the screen) is what you get (in the printout)

X¹ or **x** *noun* an unknown or unnamed person

X² *symbol* **1** *maths* (usually **x**) an unknown quantity; the first of a pair or group of unknown quantities (*see also*: **Y, Z**) **2** the Roman numeral for 10 **3** *old* denoting a film that is suitable for adults only (now replaced by '18' in the UK) **4** a mark used to symbolize a kiss **5** a mark used to indicate an error

x-axis *noun, maths* the horizontal axis in a graph, along which the x-coordinate is plotted

X-chromosome *noun* the sex chromosome when present and paired with another X-chromosome determines the female sex in most animals

Xe *symbol, chemistry* xenon

xenon *noun, chemistry* (symbol **Xe**) an element, one of the noble gases, used in fluorescent lights and lasers ☉ Comes from Greek *xenos* meaning 'stranger'

xenophobia (*pronounced* zen-o-**foh**-bi-a or zeen-o-**foh**-bi-a) *noun* hatred of foreigners or strangers ♦ **xenophobe** *noun* ☉ Comes from Greek *xenos* meaning 'stranger'

xenotransplantation (*pronounced* zen-o- or zeen-o-) *noun* the transplantation of an animal organ into an animal of a different species

xerophyte (*pronounced* **zee**-ro-fait) *noun* a desert plant, eg a cactus, adapted to grow in conditions where water is scarce

Xerox (*pronounced* **zeer**-roks) *noun, trademark* **1** a photographic process used for copying documents **2** a copy made in this way ➤ *verb* to copy by Xerox

x-intercept *noun, maths* the point at which a line cuts the x-axis

Xmas (*pronounced* **eks**-mas or **kris**-mas) *noun, informal* Christmas

XML *abbreviation, computing* extensible markup language, text formatting instructions designed to aid data searching and the formatting of results

X-ray *noun* **1** an electromagnetic ray that can pass through material impenetrable by light, and produce a photographic image of the object through which it has passed **2** a shadow picture produced by X-rays on photographic film ➤ *verb* to take a photographic image of with X-rays

X-ray diffraction *noun, chemistry* the characteristic pattern produced when X-rays are passed through a crystal structure, used to determine atomic structure within crystals

xylem *noun* (*pronounced* **zai**-lem) a tissue in some plants that conducts water from the roots to the leaves

xylophone *noun* a musical instrument consisting of a series of graded wooden bars which are struck with hammers ♦ **xylophonist** *noun*

Yy

Y *symbol* **1** *chemistry* yttrium **2** *maths* (usually **y**) the second of a pair or group of unknown quantities (*see also*: X^2, **Z**)

yacht (*pronounced* yawt) *noun* a boat or small ship, with sails and sometimes with an engine, for racing or cruising ⊙ Comes from Dutch *jachtschip* meaning 'chasing ship'

yachting *noun* sailing in yachts, especially as a sport

yachtsman, yachtswoman *noun* someone who sails a yacht

yahoo¹ *noun, informal* a lout or ruffian

> ⊙ Named after the brutish characters that looked like humans in Jonathan Swift's *Gulliver's Travels* (1726)

yahoo² *interjection* expressing happiness, excitement, etc

yak *noun* a Tibetan long-haired ox

Yale lock *noun, trademark* a type of lock operated by a flat key with a notched upper edge

yam *noun* a tropical root vegetable, similar to a potato

Yank or **Yankee** *noun, Brit informal* an American

> ⊙ Originally a nickname for Dutch settlers in New England in the 18th century, possibly because of the Dutch forename *Jan*

yank *verb, informal* to tug or pull with a violent jerk ➤ *noun* a violent tug

yap *verb* (**yapping, yapped**) to bark sharply

yard *noun* **1** a measure of length (0.9144 metres, or 3 feet) **2** a long beam on a mast for spreading sails **3** an enclosed space used for a particular purpose: *railway yard/shipbuilding yard* **4** *US* a garden

yardstick *noun* **1** a yard-long measuring stick **2** any standard for comparison

yarmulka or **yarmulke** (*pronounced* yar-mul-ka) *noun* (**yarmulkas** or **yarmulkes**) a skullcap worn by Jewish men on ceremonial occasions, and at all times by orthodox Jews ⊙ Comes from Yiddish

yarn *noun* **1** wool, cotton, etc spun into thread **2** one of several threads forming a rope **3** a long, often improbable, story

yarrow *noun* a strong-smelling plant with flat clusters of white flowers

yashmak *noun* a veil covering the lower half of the face, worn by Muslim women

yawl *noun* a small rowing boat or fishing boat

yawn *verb* **1** to take a deep breath unintentionally with an open mouth, because of boredom or sleepiness **2** of a hole: to be wide open, gape ➤ *noun* an open-mouthed deep breath

y-axis *noun, maths* the vertical axis in a graph, along which the y-coordinate is plotted

Yb *symbol, chemistry* ytterbium

Y-chromosome *noun* the sex chromosome when present and paired with an X-chromosome determines the male sex in most animals

ye *pronoun, old* you

yea (*pronounced* yei) *interjection, old* yes ➤ *noun* a person who is voting or has voted 'yes'

year *noun* **1** the time taken by the earth to go once round the sun, about 365 days **2** the period 1 January to 31 December **3** a period of twelve months starting at any point **4** (**years**) age: *wise for her years* ⊙ Comes from Old English *gear*

yearbook *noun* a book of information published every year, usually reviewing events of the previous year

yearling *noun* a year-old animal

yearly *adjective* happening every year, or once a year

yearn (*pronounced* yern) *verb* **1** to long (for, to do something etc) **2** to feel pity or tenderness (for)

yearning (*pronounced* **yern**-ing) *noun* an eager longing

yeast *noun* a substance which causes fermentation, used to make bread dough rise and in brewing

yell *verb* to give a loud, shrill cry; scream ➤ *noun* a loud, shrill cry

yellow *noun* the colour of gold, egg-yolks, etc ➤ *adjective* of this colour ➤ *verb* to become yellow, due to ageing

yellow card *noun, football* a piece of yellow card or plastic shown as a warning by the referee to a player who has seriously violated the rules (*compare with*: **red card**)

yellow fever *noun, medicine* a serious viral disease of tropical regions, transmitted by mosquito bite

yelp *verb* to give a sharp bark or cry ➤ *noun* a sharp bark or cry

yen[1] *noun* the standard unit of Japanese currency

yen[2] *noun, informal* a strong desire, longing: *a yen to return to Scotland*

yeoman (*pronounced* **yoh**-man) *noun, history* a farmer with his own land •**Yeomen of the Guard** the company acting as bodyguard to the British king or queen on certain occasions

yeomanry (*pronounced* **yoh**-man-ri) *noun, history* **1** farmers **2** a troop of cavalrymen serving voluntarily in the British army

yes *interjection* expressing agreement or consent ➤ *noun* **1** an expression of agreement or consent **2** a vote in favour

yes-man *noun, derogatory* someone who always agrees with the opinions and suggestions of a superior, employer, etc

yesterday *noun* **1** the day before today **2** the past ➤ *adverb*: *I bought it yesterday*

yesteryear *noun, literary* the past in general

yet *adverb* **1** by now, by this time: *have you seen that film yet?* **2** still, before the matter is finished: *we may win yet* ➤ *conjunction* but, nevertheless: *I am defeated, yet I shall not surrender* • **yet another** and another one still • **yet more** still more

Yeti *noun* (**the Yeti**) a large animal believed to exist in the Himalayas (*also called*: **the Abominable Snowman**)

yew *noun* **1** a tree with dark green leaves and red berries **2** its wood

Y-fronts *plural noun* men's or boys' underpants with a Y-shaped front seam

YHA *abbreviation* Youth Hostels Association

Yiddish *noun* a language spoken by many Jews, based on German, with elements from **Hebrew** and other languages ⓒ Comes from German *jüdisch* meaning 'Jewish'

yield *verb* **1** to give in, surrender **2** to give way to pressure or persuasion **3** to produce (a crop, results, etc) ➤ *noun* an amount produced; a crop

yielding *adjective* giving way easily

yin and yang *noun* in traditional Chinese philosophy, medicine, etc: the negative, feminine, dark, cold and passive force (**yin**), and the opposite but complementary positive, masculine, light, warm and active force (**yang**) ⓒ Comes from Chinese *yin* meaning 'dark', and *yang* meaning 'bright'

y-intercept *noun, maths* the point at which a line cuts the y-axis

YMCA *abbreviation* Young Men's Christian Association, a charity providing accommodation, originally for young men and boys ➤ *noun* a hostel run by the YMCA

yob or **yobbo** *noun* (*plural* **yobboes** or **yobbos**) a lout, a hooligan

yodel *verb* (**yodelling, yodelled**) to sing in a style involving frequent changes between an ordinary and a very high-pitched voice • **yodeller** *noun*

yoga *noun* a Hindu system of philosophy and meditation, often involving special physical exercises

yogurt or **yoghurt** *noun* a semi-liquid food product made from fermented milk

yoke *noun* **1** a wooden frame joining oxen when pulling a plough or cart **2** a pair of oxen or horses **3** something that joins together **4** a frame placed across the shoulders for carrying pails etc ➤ *verb* **1** to put a yoke on **2** to join together

❗ Do not confuse with: **yolk**

yokel (*pronounced* **yoh**-kel) *noun, derogatory* an unsophisticated country person; a rustic

yolk *noun* the yellow part of an egg

❗ Do not confuse with: **yoke**

Yom Kippur *noun* the Day of Atonement, a Jewish fast day

yonder *old, adverb* in that place (at a distance but within sight) ➤ *adjective* that (object) over there: *by yonder tree*

yore *noun*: **of yore** *old* formerly, in times past

you *pronoun* the person(s) spoken or written to, used as the singular or plural subject or object of a verb: *What did you say?/Are you both free tomorrow?*

you'd *short for* **1** you would; you should **2** you had

you'll *short for* you will; you shall

young *adjective* **1** in the early part of life, mental or physical growth, etc **2** in the early stages: *The night is young* ➤ *noun* **1** the offspring of animals **2** (**the young**) young people ⓒ Comes from Old English *geong*

youngster *noun* a young person

your *adjective* belonging to you: *it's your life*

❗ Do not confuse: **your** and **you're**

you're *short for* you are

yours *pronoun* belonging to you: *Is this pen yours?* •**Yours, Yours faithfully, Yours sincerely, Yours truly** expressions used before a signature at the end of a letter

yourself *pronoun* (*plural* **yourselves**) **1** used reflexively: *don't trouble yourself* **2** used for emphasis: *you yourself can't go*

youth *noun* **1** the state of being young **2** the early part of life **3** a young person **4** young people in general

youth club *noun* a place or organization providing leisure activities for young people

youth court *noun, Brit* a court at which people aged under 16 are tried

youthful *adjective* **1** young **2** fresh and vigorous

youthful population *noun, geography* a population where there is a high proportion of young people

youth hostel *noun* a hostel where hikers etc may spend the night

you've *short for* you have

yo-yo *noun* a toy consisting of a reel which spins up and down on a string ➤ *verb* (**yo-yoing, yo-yoed**) to rise and fall or fluctuate repeatedly

ytterbium *noun, chemistry* (symbol **Yb**) a soft metallic element of the lanthanide series, used in lasers and in alloys

> ⏱ Named after *Ytterby*, a quarry in Sweden where it was discovered

yttrium *noun, chemistry* (symbol **Y**) a silvery-grey metallic element used to make superconductors and magnets ⏱ See *ytterbium*

yuck or **yuk** *informal, interjection* expressing disgust ◆ **yucky** or **yukky** *adjective* (**yuckier, yuckiest** or **yukkier, yukkiest**)

Yule *noun, old* Christmas

Yuletide *noun, old* Christmas time

yuppie or **yuppy** *noun* (*plural* **yuppies**), *derogatory informal* an ambitious young professional person working in a city job

> ⏱ Acronym of young urban professional, or young upwardly mobile professional

YWCA *abbreviation* Young Women's Christian Association, a charity providing accommodation for young women and girls ➤ *noun* a hostel run by the YWCA

Zz

Z *symbol* **1** *maths* (usually **z**) the third of a group of unknown quantities (*see also*: **X²,Y**) **2** *physics* impedance

zakat or **zakah** *noun, Islam* a tax payable by Muslims on certain kinds of property, to raise money for charity

zany *adjective* (**zanier, zaniest**), *informal* crazy, madcap

🕐 After the name of a clownish character in Italian comic drama

zap *verb* (**zapping, zapped**) **1** to strike, shoot, etc suddenly **2** to move rapidly; zip

zeal *noun* enthusiasm, keenness

zealot (*pronounced* **zel**-ot) *noun* a fanatical enthusiast

zealous (*pronounced* **zel**-us) *adjective* full of zeal ♦ **zealously** *adverb*

zebra *noun* a striped African animal of the horse family

zebra crossing *noun* a pedestrian street crossing, painted in black and white stripes

zeitgeist (*pronounced* **zait**-gaist) *noun* the attitudes of a particular time period: *the zeitgeist of Britain today*

Zen or **Zen Buddhism** *noun* a school of Buddhism stressing enlightenment through meditation and a simple way of life

zenith *noun* **1** the point of the heavens exactly overhead **2** the highest point, the peak

zephyr (*pronounced* **zef**-er) *noun, formal* a soft, gentle breeze

zeppelin or **Zeppelin** *noun* a cigar-shaped airship

🕐 Originally designed by the German Count Ferdinand von *Zeppelin* (1838–1917) in 1900

zero *noun* **1** nothing or the sign for it (0) **2** the point (marked 0) from which a scale (eg on a thermometer) begins

zero hour *noun* the exact time fixed for some action

zero option *noun, politics* a proposal to limit or abandon the deployment of nuclear missiles if the opposing side does likewise

zero population growth *noun, geography* a state in which the population of a country or area remains static, with births and immigration roughly equalling deaths plus emigration (*also called*: **zero growth**)

zero-rated *adjective* of goods: having no value-added tax

zero tolerance *noun* a policy of not allowing something to happen at all, especially a political or social wrong

zest *noun* **1** relish, keen enjoyment **2** orange or lemon peel

zestful *adjective* keen; full of enjoyment ♦ **zestfully** *adverb*

zigzag *adjective* having sharp bends or angles ► *verb* (**zigzagging, zigzagged**) move in a zigzag direction

zilch *noun, informal* nothing

zimmer *noun, trademark* a hand-held metal frame used to give support in walking

zinc *noun, chemistry* a bluish-white metallic element used in dry batteries and as a coating to galvanize steel

Zionism *noun* the movement which worked for the establishment of a national homeland in Palestine for Jews and now supports the state of Israel ♦ **Zionist** *noun & adjective*

🕐 From *Zion*, the name of one of the hills in Jerusalem, and often used to refer to Jerusalem itself

zip *noun* **1** a fastening device for clothes, bags, etc, consisting of two rows of metal or nylon teeth which interlock when a sliding tab is pulled between them **2** a whizzing sound, eg made by a fast-flying object **3** *informal* energy, vigour ► *verb* (**zipping, zipped**) **1** to fasten with a zip **2** to whiz, fly past at speed **3** *computing* to compress the data in a computer file, so that it takes up less memory

zip code *noun* in the US: a post code

Zip disk *noun, computing, trademark* a floppy disk with a very high capacity on which data is stored in compressed form

Zip drive *noun, computing, trademark* a specialized hard drive used to compress data

zirconium *noun, chemistry* (symbol **Zr**) a silvery-grey metallic element, used as a coating for fuel rods in nuclear reactors

zit *noun, slang* a pimple

zither *noun* a flat, stringed musical instrument, played with the fingers

Zn *symbol, chemistry* zinc

zodiac *noun* an imaginary strip in space, divided into twelve equal parts • **signs of the zodiac**

the divisions of the zodiac used in astrology, each named after a group of stars

> ⏱ From Greek, meaning literally 'circle of animals'

Zollverein (*pronounced* **tsol**-fer-ain) *noun, history* a union of the German states, officially formed in 1834, enabling them to act as one state in trading with other countries ⏱ Comes from German *Zoll* meaning 'duty' + *Verein* meaning 'union'

zombie *noun* **1** a corpse reanimated by witchcraft **2** a very slow or stupid person

> ⏱ After the name of a voodoo snake god

zone *noun* **1** any of the five main bands into which the earth's surface is divided according to temperature: *temperate zone* **2** a section of a place marked off for a particular purpose: *no-parking zone/smokeless zone* ➤ *verb* to divide into zones

zoo *noun* a place where wild animals are kept and shown to the public

zoo- *prefix* of or relating to animals ⏱ Comes from Greek *zoion* meaning 'animal'

zoological *adjective* **1** relating to animals **2** relating to zoos; containing a zoo: *zoological gardens*

zoological garden *noun, formal* a zoo

zoologist *noun* someone who studies animal life

zoology *noun* the science of animal life

zoom *verb* **1** to move quickly with a loud, low buzzing noise **2** to make such a noise **3** of an aircraft: to climb sharply at high speed for a short time **4** to use a zoom lens on a camera

zoom lens *noun* a lens used in photography which makes a distant object appear gradually nearer without the camera being moved

zoophyte (*pronounced* **zo**-e-fait) *noun, zoology* any of various invertebrate animals which resemble plants, such as sponges, corals and sea anemones

zooplankton (*pronounced* **zo**-eplangk-ton) *noun, zoology* drifting or floating microscopic animals

Zoroastrianism *noun* an ancient religion founded in Persia by Zoroaster (c.630–c.553 BC), which teaches the continuous opposition of good and evil

Zr *symbol, chemistry* zirconium

zucchini (*pronounced* zoo-**kee**-nee) *noun* (*plural* **zucchini** or **zucchinis**), *esp N Am & Aust* a courgette ⏱ Comes from Italian

Zulu (*pronounced* **zoo**-loo) *noun* (*plural* **Zulu** or **Zulus**) **1** a Bantu people of S Africa **2** their language

zygote (*pronounced* **zai**-goht) *noun, biology* the cell formed when two gametes are joined, especially an egg cell fertilized by a male gamete ♦ **zygotic** *adjective*

WORKING WITH ENGLISH
A Guide for Students

Essay writing

I. PLANNING YOUR ESSAY

An essay is a piece of writing that sets out to analyse a particular situation or idea, or to put across a particular point of view, supported by evidence. An essay often has to be written in a set number of words, and the ability to say everything you want to in the number of words allowed is one of the skills of a good essay writer.

- Essays take time and involve careful thought and planning. Begin by reading the title or question carefully in order to find out what it is that you are meant to be writing about – not just in terms of the subject matter, but also in terms of how to deal with it. It is important to do this before getting started on anything else, as it will give you a clear sense of direction from the outset.
- Make sure you actually answer the question you are being asked, rather than another question that you happen to know more about or are more interested in. Also, avoid just writing down everything you know about the topic in the hope that the relevant material will be in there somewhere.

Essay titles

An essay usually begins with a title. Titles come in one of two kinds:

1   a title that allows you to choose a topic of your own, either completely freely, or from a range of options. In this case, make sure you choose something that interests you – this may sound obvious, but it is easier to write well about something when the subject motivates you to do the work.

2   a title that gives you specific instructions about what to deal with, and how to deal with it. In this case, make sure that you answer the question or deal with the issue effectively.

Essay titles are usually carefully written, and often contain a 'key verb' or 'key phrase' that suggests what is required and what your approach should be. In fact, essays can be separated into five categories, according to the key verb in the essay title:

1 describing
2 analysing
3 comparing and contrasting
4 arguing
5 explaining

Describing

These essays are probably the most straightforward to deal with, as all you need to do is select and present relevant information in a logical order. Key verbs in the title will be:

- *state/describe/give an account of* – asking you to present a detailed description
- *outline/trace* – asking you to present the main features
- *summarize* – asking you to present briefly the main features
- *illustrate* – asking you to present the main features and give relevant examples

Analysing

These essays not only require relevant knowledge, but also the ability to separate a topic into different parts and examine each one. Key verbs in the title will be:

- *analyse/examine/investigate* – asking you to separate and look closely at the main features
- *assess/evaluate/say how far/say to what extent* – asking you to present your opinions or reactions, supported by evidence
- *define* – asking you to give a detailed explanation
- *explore* – asking you to look at the subject from different points of view

Comparing and contrasting

This asks you to look at what you regard as the most important similarities and differences between two or more things. Usually, the differences are more striking or important than the similarities. If this is the case deal briefly with the similarities first, then go on to examine the differences one by one in more detail.

Sometimes you can reach a conclusion about which option is preferable, on other occasions you might not. Either way, make it clear what you have decided.

Arguing

This kind of title often presents you with a controversial statement, for example *'All art is quite useless.'* Discuss. You can then either take a balanced view, weighing up the arguments for and against, or else argue a particular point of view forcefully.

Whichever of these approaches you decide on, it is important to show that you are aware of both sides of the issue and can deal with arguments against your own point of view.

Explaining

As in essays that ask you to describe or outline something, in these essays you need to display your factual knowledge. However, in addition to showing your own understanding, you might also need to show what you know about how something developed.

These titles tend to begin an open question such as *What?*, *Why?* or *How?*

Developing your ideas

Titles sometimes seem rather intimidating when you first see them. It might be hard to know where to begin with a topic such as *'The First World War was a mistake.'* *Discuss.* If this seems difficult, try to think of it as a question (*In what way could the First World War be seen as a mistake?*). The subject then becomes easier to grasp. It can also generate further questions, for example, *Who might see the First World War as a mistake?* or *Who might be to blame for this mistake?*

If you have been given a topic such as *Is photography an art form?*, try asking yourself a series of questions. You can begin by examining the words that are used in the title:

- What exactly is an art form?
- What different kinds of photography are there?
- Can any or all of these be regarded as art forms?
- Why/why not?

Questions like these will lead to answers, which can give you ideas and might offer you a structure for what you are going to say.

Organizing your ideas

The planning stage requires special care. You may have a number of different ideas that do not fit together easily into a coherent structure. You may have to sift through your ideas and decide which ones are essential to the essay and which can be left out:

- **Which of your ideas are linked?** You can show their relationship by joining them with arrows or by numbering them in your notes.
- **Which ideas seem most important?** Emphasize them by underlining, circling or highlighting them.
- **Are there any good arguments that can be made against your main points?** Add these to the plan.
- **Is each idea relevant to the essay title?** If it is not, remove it.
- **Does any point seem trivial or uninteresting?** If it does, delete it, and only keep what is important or interesting.
- **Have you got enough material for your essay?** If not, gather more material or develop your existing points further.

The final plan should contain three distinct stages: an introduction, the main development of ideas, and a conclusion.

2. CONSTRUCTING AN ARGUMENT

Many essays involve presenting an argument. This should be a carefully constructed and well-developed expression of a point of view, and one which persuades the reader that what you are saying is correct. An argument should be:

- **Objective**: you should assure the reader that you are not influenced by personal prejudices, and that you have not allowed your emotions to intrude.
- **Fair**: you should consider a range of possible points of view and treat each one seriously. If you do not agree with a point of view, make it clear what your reasons are for rejecting it. Accept that there may be valid points against your argument.
- **Clear**: you will be more likely to convince the reader that you are right by being clear, precise and direct. Don't waste space on detail that does not help your argument.
- **Logical**: make sure your points are not put down at random but follow an order that makes sense. What might seem an obvious connection to you and not worth mentioning might not be so to others. Make sure it is clear how you have arrived at your conclusion.

In developing an argument, take the reader through a series of stages:

- **Introduce the subject**: provide the reader with any background information they need to follow your train of thought.
- **Introduce supporting evidence**: this might be statistics, facts or quotations. The reader might not believe you if you simply say something is true. If you can present evidence then you are more likely to be taken seriously.
- **Analyse the evidence**: look at what information the evidence provides.
- **Draw a conclusion from the evidence**: show that the evidence leads you to a natural conclusion.
- **Introduce any contrasting evidence**: mention any statistics, examples, documents, etc that might be used against your conclusion.
- **Argue against the contrasting evidence**: explain why you do not think that it affects the truth of your argument. Perhaps the evidence is unreliable, or perhaps there is a reason why it does not apply in this case.

Presenting evidence

Your arguments will be more persuasive if the evidence you bring forward is clearly presented:

- Statistics are often easier to take in if they are presented in the form of tables. However, make sure that you explain the tables so that the reader can see how the information in them relates to your argument.
- Similarly, make sure that you label any diagrams or pictures so that their connection to the argument is obvious.
- Facts and statistics are more impressive if they have a reliable source. For example, writing *A third of all marriages in Britain end in divorce* is not as impressive as writing *A government survey published in 2004 showed that a third of all marriages in Britain end in divorce*.
- An occasional quotation from a credible source can be an good way of supporting your argument. Make sure that quotations are reproduced accurately and that you have correctly identified where they come from. (The correct form for presenting quotations is shown on page 8.)

Drawing conclusions

The final part of the essay is one of the most important. A good conclusion will summarize the ideas that you have been developing and leave the reader with a clear impression of your opinions on the subject. Don't be tempted to rush it.

- Briefly remind the reader of your main points, but don't repeat examples.
- Let the reader know your own opinion. You could do this directly by saying what you think, or you could do it indirectly by putting in a quotation or anecdote which highlights your point of view.
- Leave the reader something to think about: an essay that ends with a sentence such as *Thus we see that the statement in the title is not true* attempts to close down the argument and encourages the reader to switch off their mind. It is far better to give the reader something new to take away with them and think about. You might hint at a future development or a problem which is related to the topic. In other words, keep the reader's interest right until the end.

3. WRITING YOUR ESSAY

Paragraphs

Your essay will be divided up into paragraphs consisting of one or more sentences.

- Each paragraph should express an idea which is complete in itself but which also adds something to the whole essay. Try to include just one major point in each paragraph and do not have too many major points in the essay.
- The length of a paragraph depends the significance of the idea in it. Most paragraphs are three sentences or more long, since this is usually what is required to develop a point convincingly. Nevertheless, an occasional short paragraph of two sentences or even one sentence can be effective.
- A particularly important point can be broken down into different aspects and spread over two or more paragraphs – one aspect for each paragraph – in order to make it easier to digest. Do not jam two ideas into one paragraph if they have nothing in common. Deal with them in two separate paragraphs.

The usual structure of a paragraph is basically the same as for the essay as a whole: introduction, main body and conclusion. The introductory sentence is known as a **topic sentence**; the sentence or sentences forming the main body of the paragraph are the **support sentences**; and the paragraph is rounded off by the **concluding sentence**.

Topic sentence

The topic sentence tells the reader the specific topic of the paragraph. A topic sentence will usually be the first sentence of the paragraph, but it could also come after a sentence that has linked the paragraph to the previous one.

Support sentences

These sentences illustrate, develop or argue the paragraph topic as stated in the topic sentence. Be as specific and detailed as possible and check that all examples you give are relevant to this particular topic.

Concluding sentence

This will state a conclusion drawn from the points made in the paragraph and perhaps lead the reader towards a new but related topic. The reader must feel that they have moved on from where they were at the start of the paragraph. However, if you are continuing your current point into the following paragraph you will not need a concluding sentence.

Layout

Each paragraph must begin on a new line, even if it means leaving nearly all of the line above empty. If the line above extends all the way to the right-hand side of the page it is a good idea to indent the paragraph – that is, leave a small gap before starting the first line. If you are using a computer, leave a line of space before the paragraph in order to make it clear to the reader where it begins. Of course, if you do indent or add a line of space, you must do it throughout the essay whenever a paragraph occurs.

Do not think you have to complete a paragraph before moving on. If you get stuck, go on to the next one and come back later. You will then be able to look at it with fresh eyes and perhaps see what needs to be changed.

Sentences

In order to add variety, different forms of sentences should be used in your essay.

Simple sentence

This is the most straightforward form of sentence. It has at least a subject and a verb; for example, *I shouted* or *Big girls don't cry*. Simple sentences are clear and forceful. However, if you were to use only such sentences in your essay, the effect would be repetitive and tedious; for example, *The threat of nuclear war has receded. This has reduced global tension. This has led to discussions between the superpowers. The superpowers have agreed to ...* and so on.

Compound sentence

A compound sentence is essentially two or more sentences joined together by a conjunction, usually *and* or *but*; for example, *The threat of nuclear war has receded and this has reduced global tension,* or (taking an opposing view) *The threat of nuclear war has receded, but this has not reduced global tension.*

Complex sentence

A complex sentence contains a main, or independent, clause and one or more subordinate, or dependent, clauses; for example, *Although the threat of nuclear war has receded, global tension has not been reduced.* Note that the subordinate clause (the first) cannot function as an independent sentence, while the main clause (the second) can. The main clause in each case carries the main emphasis of the sentence. Mentioning something in a subordinate clause lessens its importance.

When writing your sentences, keep the following in mind:

- Usually, only one point should be covered in each sentence. If you find yourself writing a sentence in which two points are made which are not connected, then split it into two sentences.
- Vary the sentences in your essay, mixing the forms listed above.
- From time to time try using a question to liven up your writing. For example, *Did this treaty have any tangible benefits?* You can then go on to answer your own question.
- Meaning has to flow naturally from one sentence to the next throughout the essay, only stopping when the end is reached. This flow can be achieved by using linking devices which bridge the gaps between sentences.

Linking

Linking devices (words, phrases or clauses) take the reader from one sentence or paragraph to the next in a smooth and coherent way, following the line of your argument. Usually they refer back briefly to what has just been said and then perform one of three general functions:

1   move the argument forward – *in addition, consequently, for example, to begin with,* etc
2   counter the argument – *to some degree, nonetheless, in contrast, on the other hand,* etc
3   sum up the argument – *all things considered, in other words, on the whole,* etc

Their more specific functions can be categorized as follows:

- **Adding**: *also, furthermore, in addition, moreover, what is more*
- **Comparing**: *by the same token, likewise, similarly*
- **Consequence**: *accordingly, as a result, consequently, hence, therefore, thus*
- **Contrasting**: *but, conversely, however, in contrast, instead, nevertheless, nonetheless, on the contrary, on the other hand, rather, yet*
- **Illustrating**: *for example, for instance*
- **Restating**: *in brief, in essence, in other words, in short, namely, that is*
- **Sequence**: *at the same time, earlier, first of all, in the first place, in the meantime, meanwhile, next, simultaneously, then, to begin with, while*
- **Summarizing**: *all in all, all things considered, by and large, in any case, in conclusion, on the whole, in the final analysis, on balance, on the whole, to sum up, to summarize*

Linking devices are also used for **signposting**; that is, indicating changes in the direction of the argument and reminding the reader of the place you have reached in the argument. Linking clauses (for example, *Turning our attention to ...* and *As we have seen ...*) are particularly useful for this.

It is not necessary to use a link word, phrase or clause every time you start a sentence. The reader can assume that you are continuing with the same thread of meaning unless tell them otherwise.

Style

Style is the manner in which you express yourself in your writing. It is a matter of personal taste, but you can improve your style by paying attention to certain words, phrases and constructions:

- Do not use contractions (*they've, it's, he'll*), or informal vocabulary (*great, quite good, get started, a bit of research*).
- Use a fairly impersonal style (for example, *this was done* rather than *I did this*). 'Keep your distance' rather than seeming to be too personally involved.
- Avoid expressing strong opinions directly: you should generally aim to offer evidence for consideration, rather than try to persuade directly (for example, *many writers have suggested that ...* rather than *maybe ...*).
- Being formal does not mean that you have to be pompous or difficult to understand.
- Don't use very long sentences if you can avoid them, and where possible use simple language, even – in fact, especially – when discussing complex ideas.

- Avoid beginning sentences in the same way too often.
- Avoid using the conjunction *and* to join clauses too often.
- Avoid using *etc.* Give another example instead.
- *He or she* can be used to refer to a person when it is not specified if they are male or female. For example: *Every householder should be aware that he or she can ... .* However, if it is used too often it can sound clumsy and can be replaced with *they*.
- Words such as *really, very, quite* and *extremely* are often redundant and can be left out.
- Do not use words such as *thing* and *do* too often. Try to find less general words that will add varierty and precision to your writing.
- Be careful with the following words and phrases:
  And also *And* is enough on its own.
  The reason why is because *The reason is that* reads better.
  Due to the fact that *Because* is enough.
  It seems/appears that This can often be left out.
  Interesting Rather than just say that something is interesting, you show more understanding of your subject if you explain it in a way that makes an interesting point.

References and quotations

If you are writing an essay in which you present information taken from other sources, you must be sure to give references which say where you found the information. References should appear at two places: in the essay itself and at the end.

In the text

There are different ways of marking a reference within the text:

- a superscript number; that is, higher than the normal position on the line: *as Jones[1] maintains*
- a number in brackets: *as Jones (1) maintains*
- naming the author and using brackets: *... as Jones maintains (1995, p.20)*, or *... as has been recently maintained (JONES, 1995, p.20).* The reader can then check the source by looking up the author's name in the list of references at the end.

Whichever method you use, the reference should be placed immediately after the passage or quotation.

At the end

You need to give details of each source in a separate section entitled 'References' at the end of your essay.

Give the following information: author's last name, author's initial or initials, title, place of publication, publisher, date of publication, and page number (if necessary). Here are two acceptable ways of presenting this information:

JONES, K., *Truth in Modern Politics*, New York, Simon and Simon, 1995, p.20.
JONES, K. (1995) *Truth in Modern Politics*, New York, Simon and Simon.

If you are giving a reference to a website, you should give the following information: author's last name, author's initial or initials, title of text, and URL (Web address):

JONES, K., 'Truth in Modern Politics', http://www.xyz.ac.uk/

Quotations

- **Punctuation** For guidelines on how to use punctuation with quotations, see the section on **Punctuation** in **What you need to know about English**.
- **Long quotations** If you want to include a quotation that is three lines or more long, then you should present it as a separate block of text without inverted commas, leaving a line above and below it, for example:

The book tells us:

Meaning has to flow naturally from one sentence to the next throughout the essay, only stopping when the end is reached. This flow can be achieved by using linking devices which bridge the gaps between sentences.

Rewriting

Once you have written the first draft of your essay:

- **Read over your first draft**. Do you find the essay convincing yourself? You may need to rewrite some of your arguments, developing some points more fully.
- **Ask yourself if you have dealt with the question in the essay title**. Have you gone off at a tangent or answered a different question?
- **Check your paragraphs**. Are they in the best order for putting your points across effectively? Is the signposting clear? Can you perhaps improve a paragraph by moving the sentences around?
- **Check your sentences**. Do you need to restructure some so you have a variety of sentence forms?
- **See if you can improve on your choice of words**. If you find you have used the same word a lot in a few lines, look for some synonyms (words with similar meanings) in a thesaurus such as *Chambers Thesaurus*.
- **Do not be afraid to cut items out**. Delete anything that is repetitive or unnecessary.

Did you know?

George Orwell is best known for his novels *Animal Farm* and *Nineteen Eighty-Four*, but he was also a great essay-writer. In 1946 he gave the following advice in his essay *Politics and the English Language*. It is as relevant now as it was then:

1. Never use a metaphor, simile, or other figure of speech which is quite often seen in print.
2. Never use a long word where a short one will do.
3. Always cut a word out if it is possible to do so.
4. Never use the passive voice where the active voice will do.
5. Never use a foreign phrase, a scientific word, or jargon if an everyday English equivalent will suffice.
6. Break any of these rules sooner than say anything outright barbarous.

4. CHECKING THE FINISHED ESSAY

Once you have finished writing your essay, and you have the written or printed version in your hands, you need to look over it again to make sure everything is in order before you hand it over to the person or people who will read it.

It is important that you do this – it is the last chance you will have!

It is a good idea to read through your document at least twice, looking at it in different ways. The first time you read through your work you can skim through it quickly to make sure it is properly organized and succeeds in meeting its aims. When you have done this, you can **proofread** it to check for spelling mistakes and errors in grammar or punctuation.

Proofreading

When you are proofreading, you read through a text with the sole intention of checking spelling, punctuation and grammar, and alphabetical and numerical order. You should not be thinking about whether the information is accurate or clearly expressed.

It is advisable to take a break between the end of the writing process and the start of the reading process so that you can give your eyes and brain a rest and allow yourself to switch from 'write mode' to 'read mode'.

Five proofreading tips

Proofreading involves actively looking for mistakes in the way that something is written, so look out for:

1   words that you find difficult to spell – it is a good idea to keep a list of these
2   easily confused words, eg *hoard* and *horde*
3   the sequence of any numerical ordering
4   the sequence of any alphabetical ordering
5   correct and consistent use of punctuation marks

Computerized spelling checks

A word processor with a spelling check function (or spellchecker) may help to identify some keying errors and simple spelling mistakes. However, it will <u>not</u> pick up cases of a correct word being used in the wrong place. For example, if I had just typed *the right word in the wrong plaice*, a spelling check would not detect that *plaice* was an error – even though it I did not intend to write about the fish – because the computer recognizes it as an acceptable word.

Moreover, a spelling check cannot identify nonsense, as keying *ice cream juggernaut over the green horizon drinks furry mandolin* will confirm.

Finally, spelling checks and grammar checks are only as good as the programming behind them, and sometimes make suggestions which are simply wrong.

For all these reasons, you should always read your finished document carefully yourself.

5. WRITING ESSAYS UNDER EXAM CONDITIONS

You might have to write essays in an examination. The difference here is that you have a lot less time, so you need to know your material well enough to make the relevant points quickly. A few tips:

- Make sure you are familiar with the key facts. Memorize important figures and good quotations beforehand so that you can reproduce them quickly.
- Trying to dredge half-remembered information up from your memory wastes valuable time and can be stressful, so stick to what you know.
- Write an introduction, main body and conclusion as for a regular essay, but keep each part short. This will show that you know what the most important points are, and also that you can organize your information well.
- Before you start writing the essay itself, write an outline of what your structure will be, listing the key points in note form. This helps you to gather and organize your information before you start, and is useful to refer back to as you write. Once you start writing, you should have a lot to say and will not want to stop. It is also important that your examiner can see what you meant to do, even if you did not have quite enough time to finish your essay. This can even gain you valuable extra marks!
- Divide your time up between the questions you have to answer, and stick rigidly to this. Try to make sure that you are finishing your conclusion as the time allocated for the essay finishes. If you have not made all your points in this time, mention them briefly as part of your conclusion and then move on.
- Keep an eye on the time as you work. Make sure that you don't spend too much time on any one part of the question or too much time making notes before you start writing.

Five Points to Remember

1. Make sure you read the question properly and answer the one you've been asked rather than the one you would like to be asked.

2. Carefully plan your essay first before you start writing.

3. An essay should have an introduction, followed by the main body, with your arguments summed up in a conclusion at the end.

4. Always be balanced and objective.

5. Read over your essay carefully after you finish writing it as there will probably be a number of mistakes to correct.

Getting information

1. **Getting help from dictionaries**
2. **Getting help from thesauruses**
3. **Getting help from other reference books**
4. **Searching the Internet**
      Search tools
      Performing searches

The amount of information that anybody can carry around in their head is limited, so it is a good idea to know where you can turn to for help when you are writing. You should have access to works of reference, which can provide you with information and give you an answer if you are not sure about the correct way of expressing something. These sources of help might include:

- a dictionary
- a thesaurus
- specialist reference books
- the Internet

If you do not have access to these at home, they should be available at your local or school library.

I. GETTING HELP FROM DICTIONARIES

A dictionary will allow you to:

- check the correct spelling of a word
- look up the definition of a word in order to find its exact meaning

Many dictionaries have additional features, such as:

- information about the origin or 'etymology' of a word
- information about the correct pronunciation of a word
- examples of how a word is used in a sentence
- advice about how to use difficult words correctly
- miscellaneous useful information, often collected at the back of the book

2. GETTING HELP FROM THESAURUSES

A thesaurus is a book that contains lists of **synonyms** – that is, words that have a similar meaning to another word. A thesaurus allows you to look up a common word and find a range of words that have the same or nearly the same meaning. Looking up a word in a thesaurus may help you to find a more exact term or a livelier phrase than you had.

A thesaurus is not the same thing as a dictionary. Synonyms listed in a thesaurus are not precise definitions of the word under which they are found, and there will be many subtle differences between the words. Therefore it is a good idea to use a dictionary along with your thesaurus so you can check the exact meaning of any words you are not quite sure of.

How to use a thesaurus

There are two main ways in which a thesaurus can be arranged:

1   Some thesauruses – notably the famous *Roget's Thesaurus* – are arranged by theme. These books have an index, and you need to look up a word in the index to know where to find synonyms for the word.
2   More modern thesauruses are arranged in an 'A-to-Z' style, like a dictionary. If you are using an A-to-Z thesaurus, you can go straight to the word you are looking for without having to search in an index.

The lists of synonyms in a thesaurus might be arranged in alphabetical order, or they might be grouped so that the most common words or the ones closest in meaning to the entry word are shown first. You will need to get used to the style of the particular thesaurus in order to make the most of it.

Not every synonym of a word will be useful for what you want to say, and so thesauruses often indicate when a synonym is restricted in use to certain occasions. A label might tell you that a word is only appropriate in informal contexts and so it should not be used in an essay. Similarly, it might point out formal or technical words that are not appropriate for more general use. A label might also indicate that a word is restricted to a certain regional variety of English, such as American or Australian English.

3. GETTING HELP FROM OTHER REFERENCE BOOKS

Besides a dictionary and a thesaurus, there are several other books that may help you. Your school library should contain a reference section where you can go to consult these books (although they cannot usually be taken away). If you find that you need to consult a particular book regularly, it might be worth investing in your own copy.

*   **Subject dictionaries**, covering subjects such computing, law, music and science, explain the meanings of words that might not be covered in a general dictionary. They are also likely to give more detail about the meanings of words than a general dictionary.
*   A **dictionary of quotations** will allow you to look up the author and source of a famous quotation and check the exact words.
*   Another useful resource is a **biographical dictionary**, which allows you to look up a famous or historical person to find information about their life and check details such as birth and death dates.
*   **Encyclopedias** are useful places to go to look up factual information on a wide range of subjects. The largest, such as the *Encyclopedia Britannica*, have many volumes, but it is also possible to get single-volume encyclopedias for home use. You might need to be a little careful when looking up information about subjects such as sport and politics in an older encyclopedia, as this sort of information can quickly become out of date.
*   For completely up-to-date information you might want to consult *Whittaker's Almanack*. This is a book published every year that contains information about the year ahead, including astronomical data and tide charts. It also contains details about government, organizations and current events.
*   An **atlas** is an essential source of information about geography. As is the case with encyclopedias, you may find that information in older books has become out of date. The names of places may have changed and some countries may have been reorganized.

4. SEARCHING THE INTERNET

Spending a lot of money on building up a library of reference books is largely unnecessary thanks to the Internet, which allows you instant access to a vast amount of information.

The Internet is especially useful if you need information that is up to date. You are more likely to find current information online than in a library of books that were printed years ago. However, not all websites are regularly updated, so you have to be quite careful.

One thing to keep in mind when using the Internet for research is that information posted on the Internet is not always guaranteed to be accurate. It is advisable to use reliable websites provided by people who have reputations to maintain: organizations, companies, universities and academics. The type of organization that maintains a site on the Internet can be seen from the sequence of letters in its address:

1 .ac or .edu indicates that the website belongs to a university or college.
2 .com or .co indicates a company.
3 .gov indicates a government department.
4 .net indicates a network provider.
5 .org indicates a non-commercial organization.

> ── Did you know? ──
>
> Although the World Wide Web is part of our everyday lives, it has been around for a surprisingly short time. Its co-creator, British scientist Tim Berners-Lee, put the world's first website online in August 1991.

Search tools

If you want to use the Internet to find information, you have to decide which of the various 'search tools' will best suit your purpose. There are three basic types of tool:

1 search engines
2 directories
3 bots

Search engines

A search engine will search its database of web pages for a specific word and display a list of websites containing the word. The database is compiled by a program which trawls the Internet on the lookout for new sites. A search engine is therefore very comprehensive and useful for finding specific or obscure information.

Directories

A directory is a selection of websites arranged according to subject. Unlike a search engine, the database of a directory is created by people rather than computer programs. As a result you will find fewer sites featured, but these will often be more relevant. A review of each site will help you to make your choice.

The sites in a directory are listed according to a branching system, starting with a general subject and branching into specific categories. This means that you can quickly find sites on a topic that interests you, and you can also see related sites on similar topics.

Bots

A bot (short for 'robot') collects and compares up-to-date information from a number of search engines and directories, carrying out so-called 'metasearches'. These give you fewer sites to choose from than a search engine, but the sites are more likely to be useful.

Performing searches

Whether you are using a search engine, a directory or a bot, the searching process is similar. You type a keyword or keywords into the box provided and press 'return'. You can also type in various signs and symbols which will help you to narrow down your search:

1   Type **AND** between two words to restrict the search to sites containing both words.
2   Type **OR** between two words to restrict the search to sites which contain either one word or the other, or both.
3   Type **NOT** in front of a word to restrict the search to sites which do not contain that word.
4   Type **NEAR** between two words to restrict the search to sites where the two words are fairly close (say within 20 words of each other).
5   Type a plus sign (+) between two words to achieve the same result as typing **AND**. This symbol can also be used in front of a so-called 'stop word' (a common word such as *the, of* or *how* that is normally ignored in the search, or a single letter such as the initial in a name) to ensure that the 'stop word' will be included in the search.
6   Type a minus sign (–) between two words to achieve the same result as typing **NOT**.
7   Put **double quotation marks** around a phrase to restrict the search to sites containing exactly that phrase rather than the individual words. You use **brackets** instead of double quotation marks in some search tools.

So, for example, typing in *"william shakespeare" AND plays OR sonnets* will bring up websites about William Shakespeare's plays and sites about his sonnets, whereas typing in *"william shakespeare" AND plays AND sonnets* will only bring up sites mentioning both plays and sonnets.

However, the exact method of searching and the devices used for searches can vary from tool to tool. Some use the plus and minus signs, but some do not; some automatically include every word in the search, so AND and NOT do not apply. Each search tool should contain instructions under a heading such as 'Help' or 'Search tips' or 'Refine your search'. It is well worth spending a few minutes reading these instructions.

You will usually also be given the option of an advanced search, which will allow you to restrict your search even more.

Six tips for successful Internet searching

1. Speed up your search by restricting your search to the UK Web (this is usually an option in search engines). On the other hand, if you cannot find what you want, it may be because you are restricting your search to the UK Web instead of taking advantage of the whole of the World Wide Web.

2. Speed up your search by restricting it to one language.

3. If you are unsuccessful with one search engine, try a different one. Some engines search more web pages than others or have a different database.

4. If one keyword does not give you the result you want, try a different keyword related to the same subject.

5. Add especially helpful sites to your 'Favourites' menu or 'bookmark' them, so that you can easily return to them by clicking on the 'Favourites' or 'Bookmarks' menu on your toolbar.

6. Print out or save to disk any web pages you are really interested in.

Writing for science

1. **The conventions of scientific writing**
    Using numbers
    SI units
    Biological classification
    The use of Latin and Greek
2. **Experiment reports**

1.THE CONVENTIONS OF SCIENTIFIC WRITING

Look at the **Essay Writing** section in this supplement: the hints given there are valid for science essays too. In addition, scientific writing style has some rules of its own:

- Be *particularly* clear and concise.
- 'Keep your distance' by remaining as neutral as possible. If you have to express a personal view, you should state clearly that it is your own view, and why you are presenting it.
- Make sure that any figures or tables you give follow the guidelines set out under **Results** above.
- If you refer to a published work in your essay, give a paraphrase of the information rather than an exact quotation. The precise words do not matter (as they might do in a literature essay); what matters is that you show you understand the material by presenting it in your own words.
- Use metric measurements always, and use the standard abbreviations for them.

Using numbers

Scientific and technical writing uses some conventions about numbers that are different from those of non-technical writing.

- When writing large numbers use spaces rather than commas:

    23 678
    167 983
    2 569 746

- However, no space is needed if the number contains only four figures:

    9765

- You can abbreviate amounts of more than a million using whole or decimal numbers together with *m*:

    a population of 6.2m

- However, if you are using other abbreviations, such as *km* meaning *kilometres*, it is better to give the number in full to prevent confusion:

    6 200 000 km from the sun

- Very large or very small numbers can be shown as decimal numbers multiplied by powers of ten:

    $8000 = 8 \times 10^3$ $6\,000\,000 = 6 \times 10^6$
    $0.007 = 7 \times 10^{-3}$ $7\,750\,000 = 7.75 \times 10^6$

- Numbers below ten should be written out in words, for example *The experiment was repeated three times*, unless they are part of a measurement (for example, *4g* or *5cm*).

- Avoid starting sentences with a number. Either write out the number in words or change the structure of the sentence. So, for example, a sentence beginning *25 of those questioned said that ...* could be rewritten as *Twenty-five of those questioned said that ...* or *Of those questioned, 25 said that ...*

- The word *billion* (sometimes abbreviated to *bn*) is understood to mean one thousand million (one and nine zeroes, which is 1,000,000,000 or 10^9). Formerly, in British English a billion was one million million (one and twelve zeroes, which is 1,000,000,000,000 or 10^{12}). Similarly, *trillion* is understood to be one million million (the former British billion), rather than one million million million (one and eighteen zeroes, or 10^{18}). If you need to use these terms, it is still a good idea to indicate the number in figures to avoid confusion about which definition of the word you are following.

SI units

The SI (*Système International*) units are the internationally recognized units for scientific measurement.

- Always use SI units of measurement, and make sure you give the units using the accepted symbols for them. (An exception to this rule is the *litre*, which is not an SI unit, but is used as a measure of volume in biology and chemistry.)
- Names of SI units are always lower case, even when they are come from a proper name, for example *newton*, *ampere* and *kelvin*.
- You do not need full stops after abbreviations for units of measurement, and they should not be pluralized.

There are seven base units, from which the others are derived:

quantity	unit	symbol
length	*metre*	*m*
mass	*kilogram*	*kg*
time	*second*	*s*
electric current	*ampere*	*A*
temperature	*kelvin*	*K*
luminous intensity	*candela*	*cd*
amount of substance	*mole*	*mol*

Some of the most common derived SI units are shown in the table below:

quantity	unit	symbol
force	*newton*	*N*
pressure	*pascal*	*Pa*
energy	*joule*	*J*
power	*watt*	*W*
frequency	*hertz*	*Hz*
conductance	*siemens*	*S*
electrical charge	*coulomb*	*C*

quantity	unit	symbol
potential difference/ voltage	volt	V
capacitance	farad	F
resistance	ohm	Ω
radioactivity	becquerel	Bq

Did you know?

The importance of using only metric measurements is illustrated by the sorry tale of an expensive spacecraft. In 1999, the Mars Climate Orbiter was due to send vital data about the red planet back to Earth when it mysteriously burned up in the atmosphere. It was later discovered by embarrassed NASA officials that the demise of the $125 million craft was due to one set of engineers using metric measurements and another using the older imperial system.

Biological classification

If you are writing about an organism, make sure you use the standard conventions for biological classification:

- Classification names should be given in italics.
- Classification names have two parts, the **genus name** or **generic name**, which begins with a capital letter, followed by the **species name** or **specific name**, which begins with a lower case letter (*Homo sapiens, Rattus norvegicus*).
- Classification names behave like proper nouns, so you do not need the or a: *isolated populations of Arnoglossus laterna*.
- Always write out the classification name in full the first time that you use it. You can then abbreviate the genus name if you use it again (*A. laterna*).
- If the organism also has a widely used common name, give both the common name and the classification name the first time you mention the organism, and then use the common name on subsequent occasions: *We observed colonies of the brown rat (Rattus norvegicus) in several locations. The behaviour of the brown rat can vary* ...

The use of Latin and Greek

Scientific language contains many words that come from Latin and Greek. Take care to distinguish between **singular** and **plural forms** of nouns. In Latin-based words the singular form is often shown by the ending *-us, -a, -um* or *-is* and the plural form by the ending *-i, -ae, -a* or *-es*. Sometimes the same form is used for both singular and plural, for example, *species*.

Here is a list of some common scientific words that have Latin or Greek plurals:

singular	plural
analysis	analyses
bacterium	bacteria
criterion	criteria
datum	data
diagnosis	diagnoses
focus	foci (but often focuses)
fungus	fungi
genus	genera
hypothesis	hypotheses
index	indices
larva	larvae
locus	loci
matrix	matrices
medium	media
nucleus	nuclei
ovum	ova
phylum	phyla
pupa	pupae
spectrum	spectra

2. EXPERIMENT REPORTS

The conventions for scientific writing apply for experiment reports, too. Experiment reports use the following format:

Title
Abstract
Introduction
Materials and Methods
Results
Discussion
References

After the title, each section should be preceded by the appropriate heading in bold, in capitals or underlined.

Title

The title should be clear, informative and as specific as possible, so that the reader can see at a glance what the report is about. Make sure you include:

- the name of the substance, organism, situation, etc being studied
- the aim of the experiment

Abstract

An abstract is an at-a-glance summary for people who may not wish to read the whole report. It is usually only required at university level. As it is a summary, it is written last of all. The abstract should be short (no more than one paragraph) and should not go into detail. It usually includes:

- a description of the topic
- a summary of the methods used
- a summary of the results
- a summary of the main conclusion (the most important part)

Introduction

In the introduction you should include:

- how the experiment is relevant to your topic of study.
- what the aim of the experiment is. If the aim is to test a hypothesis, then state the hypothesis, the thinking behind it and the predictions that you are testing.
- any relevant assumptions you are making. For example, *In investigating the acceleration due to gravity of a falling ball, I will assume that air resistance is negligible.*
- any relevant background information on the topic. Briefly discuss any important experiments carried out by others.

Materials and methods

In this section you should describe what you actually did in the experiment without mentioning the results. You need to write clearly and in detail. It should be possible for someone else to repeat the experiment simply from reading your description. Be sure to include information on:

- the materials and equipment you used
- how you used the materials
- sizes, measurements, concentrations, etc
- any special reasons why you chose particular materials or methods
- any methods you used to analyse the data
- the location and date, if it is a field study

Take care to:
- give only necessary details. For example, do not give the size of a beaker unless it is absolutely vital to an understanding of the experiment.
- avoid mentioning irrelevant matters such as how to clean up after the experiment or details specific to your circumstances such as 'the assignment that our class was given'.
- explain the reasons why you carried out a particular action. For example, you might write: *In order to test whether … , I … .*
- show how you made the experiment as accurate as possible. For example, an unexpected result may have prompted you to take extra readings.
- use the first person (*I, we*) or the third person (*he, she, it, they*). Using the second person (*you*) sounds as though you are giving instructions to the reader. You can also use the passive occasionally, for example, *The experiment was repeated three times*.

- write in the past tense. A report describes what you have actually done, not what you intend to do.

Results

In this section you should give the results of the experiment without referring to their significance. Bear in mind the following:

- You must describe the main trends of your results. Refer in your description to the appropriate figures (diagrams, graphs, charts, etc) and/or tables in the order in which they appear in the report.
- Do not repeat data in the text that you have already given in a figure or table. Instead, refer to the figure or table by its number; for example, either *Figure 1 shows that ...* or *... as shown in Figure 1* or *... is shown to fluctuate (fig.1)*.

There are standard ways of presenting figures and tables:

- Figures and tables must be given a number followed by a title.
- They should be numbered separately; so, for example, if you had two figures and one table, they would be presented as: *Figure 1, Figure 2,* and *Table 1*.
- Make sure that the title is clear and informative, so that the reader can understand the figure or table on its own without having to read through the report.
- Put the number and title at the bottom of a figure and at the top of a table.
- Remember to give a scale for each figure, if appropriate.
- Each graph axis must be labelled with what is being measured measured and the unit of measurement (for example, *length/m*).
- If you are able to quantify the margin of error in your data, then put this information on your graphs as error bars (for example, *length to nearest 0.5 cm*), and in your tables as, for example, *length = 25cm (0.5)*.

Discussion

This section splits into two distinct elements: **Analysis** and **Evaluation**.

Under the heading **Analysis** you need to consider the evidence and analyse the results in relation to what you identified as the aim of the experiment. You should:

- explain the patterns and relationships exhibited by your results.
- explain how far the results support your hypothesis and/or predictions about what would happen.

In the **Evaluation** section you need to evaluate your experiment and discuss how valid the conclusions you have reached are. You need to:

- discuss how your assumptions and analysis of errors might have an effect on your interpretation of the results.
- identify any results that were unlikely in the circumstances, and give reasons for accepting or rejecting them.
- take into account alternative interpretations of your results which might be equally valid. What hypothesis or hypotheses other than your own might account for the results you obtained?
- explain to what extent the results have helped you understand of your topic of study.

- if you can think of any, make recommendations for better methods or further experiments which might help to achieve the aim of the experiment or test the hypothesis.

Five Points to Remember

1. Always use metric measurements.

2. Be very clear and concise. Use short sentences and paragraphs.

3. Write up only the necessary details of your experiment.

4. Classification names for organisms should be given in italics.

5. Familiarize yourself with the singular and plural forms of Latin and Greek words commonly used in science.

Other forms of writing

1. **Letters**
   Two ways of setting out a letter
   Standard parts of a letter
   Letters of application
2. **CVs**
3. **E-mail**
4. **Text messages**

I. LETTERS

Because we have electronic forms of communication, it is not surprising that people spend less time writing letters and more time on their mobile phone or at the computer. However, even though it is no longer the fastest or necessarily the most convenient way of communicating, there are still many occasions when writing a letter is preferable to using the telephone or sending an e-mail or text message:

* Sometimes information needs to be exchanged so that everyone who is involved in something understands exactly what is being agreed.
* There are still some people who do not have access to e-mail and text messages, and a letter may be the only way of sending a written message to them.
* Sometimes the time and effort spent writing a letter expresses the personal relationship you have with someone.

The first of these reasons generally relates to formal letters, and the second and third relate to personal letters. These two kinds of letter tend to be written in different styles.

> **Did you know?**
>
> Madhu Agrawal of India certainly knows how to write a good letter. In 2003 she had 334 of her letters published in over twenty prominent newspapers, which is the most ever by one person in a single year.

Two ways of setting out a letter

There are two common ways of setting out a letter:

1 **Blocked** or **fully blocked layout** is best for formal letters.
2 **Indented layout** is a style that can be used for more informal letters.

Blocked layout (for formal letters)

If you are writing a formal letter, for example to a potential employer, you should use **blocked layout**.

* All paragraphs and headings are against the left-hand margin, except for the top part of the letter, which is set on right-hand side of the page.
* The top part of the letter contains the address of the sender, and any other contact details.
* Below this, but on the left-hand side, is the address of the recipient (the person to whom the letter is being sent).

- Each new line and each new paragraph starts against the margin of the page, rather than being moved in slightly or 'indented'.
- At least one line of clear space appears between each paragraph.
- Often a 'minimal' style of punctuation is used, so there are no commas in the address, in the date, or in the opening and closing lines of the letter.
- Full stops are not generally used for abbreviations.

Indented layout (for informal letters)

For more informal letters, including those that are handwritten, the format most widely used is known as **indented** or **semi-blocked**.

- The sender's address is on the right, as in a fully blocked letter, but you do not generally include the recipient's address.
- The opening and closing lines of the letter are against the left hand margin, but all other first lines are usually indented.
- Because the indenting shows where paragraphs begin and end, there are not usually clear lines between paragraphs. However, you can also include clear lines if you wish.
- You can use commas in the date and after the opening and close if you like.
- You can use full stops in abbreviations if you wish.

Standard parts of a letter

A formal letter contains six parts:

1   address
2   other contact details
3   date
4   greeting
5   main part of the letter
6   ending

Address

When you write the address:

- Put the separate parts of the address on separate lines.
- You can shorten words such as *Road* and *Street* to *Rd* and *St* even in formal letters.
- Add the postcode in capitals on a separate line at the end.
- No commas are needed to mark the separate parts of the address in formal letters.

Other contact details

After the address you may wish to include your telephone number and other contact details:

- Make it clear what the number refers to by writing *Tel:* or *Phone:* in front of it.
- You might also include a mobile phone number on a separate line. Indicate that this is a mobile and not a land phone by writing *Mobile:* in front of it.
- Place your regional code in brackets, or put a dash between the regional code and your personal number, for example *(0131) 123 …*
- You may also wish to give your e-mail address (*E-mail:*) or a website address (*Web:*).

64 Plockenden Road
Islington
LONDON
N1 0ZZ
Tel: 01234 567 8910

Alexander Maxwell
Personnel Manager
Sellers Department Store
Kingsway Shopping Centre
Walford
LONDON
N2 0ZZ

12 October 2006

Dear Mr Maxwell

<u>Part-time Seasonal Staff</u>

I am writing in response to your advertisement in this week's 'London Jobs News' for part-time sales staff over the festive period.

I am seventeen years old, and I am studying for my A levels at Thames School. This year I gained five GCSEs, including English and Maths.

During holidays and at weekends, I have worked in a clothes shop as a sales assistant, and recently in a newsagent's, where I was often left in charge. I am keen to follow a career in the retail industry, as I enjoy working with the public in this environment.

Should you consider me suitable for a post, I can provide the names of three referees.

I look forward to hearing from you, and should you wish to, please do not hesitate to contact me at home at the above number.

Yours sincerely

Jonathan Lee

Jonathan Lee

A blocked formal letter

25 Laburnum Road
ABERDEEN
AB6 6FW

17ʰ October

Dear Anne

It was great to get your long letter yesterday. I hadn't expected to hear from you so soon after you moved. I honestly thought you'd be too busy getting settled in your new school (and arranging your new room).

I hope that your new neighbours are nice, and that you like the school you are at now. I know you miss all your old friends right now, but I am sure you will make some good new friends soon. You have so many hobbies and interests, no doubt you'll soon belong to as many clubs there as you did here, and you'll meet new people.

We are all missing you, and I am really missing our chats! Please promise me you will come back to visit soon, perhaps in the holidays. I'm sure you'd like to come back to Scotland near the New Year, and my mum says you can stay with us if you do.

I'll phone you some time next week, and we can catch up!

Love,

Deirdre

An indented formal letter

Dates

For formal letters, write the month in words and the year in full, without using a suffix (such as -th) for the number of the day, and without using commas:

13 October 2004

If you want to include the date in an informal letter, you can include the day and miss out the year, and you can include a comma if you wish:

Monday, 27th January
Monday 27 January

Beginnings

The beginning of a letter, where you greet and 'speak' directly to the recipient of the letter, is called the **salutation**. There are various forms of words that are used:

- If you can, address the person by name (*Dear Dr Steadman*).
- If you do not know the name of the person or are not sure of how to address them, use *Dear Sir*, *Dear Madam* or *Dear Sir/Madam*.
- You want to avoid getting to off to a bad start, so take care to get the name and style of address correct. Watch out for unusual spellings and for people who are called *Dr*, *Lord*, *Lady*, etc rather than *Mr* or *Ms*. Remember that people do not like having their names spelt incorrectly!
- There are certain formal ways of addressing people in authority. It is worth checking the correct form of address if you want to make a good impression.
- In more informal letters, you might prefer a greeting such as *My dear Joe*, or *Dearest Mary*.

The main part of the letter

The aim of a letter is to communicate effectively. As you would with any piece of writing, think about what you are trying to say and what is the best way to achieve your aims:

- Make sure that your letter has a clear structure so that the reader has no problem in understanding any information.
- Think about the tone you would like to create. Do you want to appear businesslike, or is a more friendly tone called for?
- Being formal is not the same as being long-winded or elaborate. There is no need to write long complex sentences for the sake of it. Aim for a direct and easy-to-read style.

Endings

The ending of a letter, where you 'sign off' is called the **complimentary close**. The wording of the salutation at the beginning of the letter determines the wording of the close:

- *Dear Sir*, *Dear Madam* or *Dear Sir/Madam* is followed by *Yours faithfully*.
- If you mention the person by name (*Dear Janice* or *Dear Dr Steadman*), you use *Yours sincerely*.
- In more informal letters, you might prefer to close with, for example, *Regards*, *Best wishes*, *Yours*, or *Kind regards*.

Letters of application

A letter in which you apply for a job should be written with care, even if it is a part-time or summer job. First impressions count, and a potential employer will base his or her first impression of you on your letter.

The person who reads your letter will probably have read hundreds of other letters over the months or years, so it is worth taking a bit of time to try and get things right.

- Your letter should be written on A4 paper, usually a single sheet of good quality white paper.

- You should write only on one side of the paper.
- Create a good impression by keeping the paper clean and using a matching envelope.
- As with any other formal letter, put your information across clearly and concisely, using correct, consistent language and making sure you include all the necessary information.
- At the same time, try include some memorable or interesting detail in order to attract the reader's attention and provide something to talk about at a later stage.
- Unless a job advertisement specifically asks for the application to be handwritten, send a printed letter with a signature at the bottom.

Letters of application without a CV

If you are sending a letter without a CV, you need to make sure that your letter is complete and includes all the necessary details, including:

- your home address
- your telephone number (or numbers)
- your e-mail address, if appropriate
- a clear indication of which job you are applying for
- where you heard about the job or saw it advertised
- your age (if relevant)
- your education and any training you have
- your present job, or details of any voluntary or other work you are currently involved in
- any other experience, qualifications or interests that might be relevant or make you an attractive applicant
- the names and addresses of at least one referee

Covering letters accompanying a CV

Job advertisements often ask applicants to send a CV and a covering letter. It is also common for people to write speculative or 'spec' letters asking about whether or not work is available.

Here are some useful points to remember:

- If you are replying to an advertisement, unless it asks for a handwritten letter it is best to print it and then sign it by hand.
- Remember to include your home address, your telephone number and the date.
- Make sure you get correct the name and title of the person you are writing to. If you do not know who to contact, make an effort to find out, as a name is always better than *Dear Sir/Madam*.
- Begin your covering letter with a short paragraph saying where you saw the job advertised, and mentioning that you are enclosing your CV.
- If you are writing a 'spec' letter, say what prompted you to write. Perhaps you have some connection with the company or with someone who works for it.
- In the next paragraph, draw attention to any parts of your CV that might be particularly relevant, and show how these make you a good candidate for employment.
- Finish with a short paragraph saying when you are available for interview.

Because your CV will include all your personal details and your education and work history, you do not need to repeat all this information in the letter that you send.

2. CVS

CV is an abbreviation for **curriculum vitae**. A CV is a summary of your personal details, work history, education, skills and training. It is often required instead of an application form if you apply for a job, and it is usually accompanied by a **covering letter** (see previous section).

Employers often prefer a CV that consists of a single-page summary, with more detailed information provided on extra pages. This allows an employer to get a quick impression without having to read through a long, complicated account.

Although you might have a standard CV stored on your computer, it is always a good idea to change your CV to the specific job you are applying for. This allows you to emphasize particular aspects of the information, and to ignore others if they are not so relevant.

Writing your CV

When preparing a CV, it is important to create a good impression, not just in the content but also through the way it looks. Present information in a clear and concise fashion, using bulleted points – like the ones that appear throughout this supplement – rather than solid paragraphs for lists of information.

The usual way of organizing a CV includes the kind of information that most employers are likely to be interested in:

* personal details
* education and qualifications
* work experience
* skills and achievements
* memberships
* interests
* referees

Personal details

Include all that you think might be relevant:

* name
* full address
* telephone number or numbers
* e-mail address, website, fax number
* date of birth
* nationality

You might like to actually include the words *name: ...* , *address: ...* , as part of the CV, but if the information is displayed clearly at the top this might not be necessary.

Education and qualifications

Name the school you attend, or any you have attended in the past, and the qualifications gained at each one along with the dates.

You do not need to go back too far. Very few employers will be interested in your primary school career!

Work experience

Even if you have only had part-time or seasonal jobs, employers are interested to hear what you have done. Start with your current or most recent job and work backwards from this.

Give details of your responsibilities in each post, and examples of any achievements, rather than just listing names and dates.

Skills and achievements

List any skills you have that you have learned from your leisure-time or extra-curricular activities and voluntary work, together with examples of success or achievement. Many things you do might provide evidence of the skills that employers are looking for, and even if not, will make you more interesting and well developed as a person:

- Mention memberships of school clubs or other organizations, along with any positions of responsibility you have.
- Mention any achievements at school that provide examples of responsibility, teamwork or other skills which could be important in a working environment. For example, did you run a club or manage a tuck shop?

Make sure that you describe the person you *are* rather than the person you think other people *want you to be* – if you are dishonest or misleading, you will soon be found out.

Interests

List two or three leisure-time interests that help to show you as a rounded, balanced person.

- Make sure that you include only what will be viewed positively.
- If you mention particular subjects here, make sure you know enough to be able to talk about them if you are interviewed!

Referees

Give the names and addresses of two people that you trust to be positive about you, or simply state that references are available.

Beverly Roberts

Personal details

Address:	122 Honour Oak Road, Forest Hill, London SE23 4NM
Tel:	669 3439
e-mail:	broberts@goserve.net
Nationality:	British
Date of birth:	4 October 1989

Education and qualifications

2006   Forest Hill Grammar School
GCSEs in Maths (A), Computer Studies (A), English (B), French (B) and Economics (B)

Work experience

2005–2006:   Weekend job as Sales Assistant, Goodfoods, Forest Hill

Summer 2006:   Summer camp assistant, Nottingham
Responsible for tennis tuition

Skills and achievements

- computer literate
- experience of tennis coaching with children
- first aid certificate

Interests

- member of school volleyball team
- keen tennis player
- regular contributor of articles to school magazine

Names of referees available on request.

An example of a CV

3. E-MAIL

It is now common to use **e-mail** (electronic mail) instead of letters as a means of personal communication, although for some more formal types of communication, a letter is still more appropriate.

Whether you use e-mail or traditional letters (often referred to as 'snail mail'), your aims are the same. You still need to think about presenting information clearly, so that the recipient gets the message and knows what is required. You also need to use an appropriate tone, so that you do not cause offence without meaning to.

However, because e-mail is rapid and informal, and is always created using a computer keyboard, it is different from a traditional letter in a few respects, including:

1   addresses
2   headings
3   writing style
4   use of abbreviations and symbols

E-mail addresses

An e-mail address is very often in lower case lettering, with no spaces and with its separate elements separated by full stops, referred to as dots. Sometimes the use of spaces is avoided by using underscores:

> *raj@fishtank.co.uk*
> *marketing_dept@christmas.org*

E-mail headings

In order to send an e-mail, you need to state **the address of the recipient** and **your own address** (this is usually generated automatically). These addresses are written in the heading at the top of an e-mail.

In addition to the addresses of the recipient and sender, you can also include other information in the heading:

*   a **subject heading**, indicating what your message is about. If you are replying to a previous e-mail, your mail tool will create the subject heading using *Re:* and the name of the previous e-mail.
*   the addresses of other people to whom you wish to **copy** the e-mail. An address written in the line called *Cc:* (carbon copy) will be displayed at the top of the e-mail as a recipient of the message; an address written in the line called *Bcc:* (blind carbon copy) will be sent a copy of the message without being displayed at the top as a recipient.
*   **attachments**, files that you wish to include as part of the message.

Writing style for e-mail messages

Because it can be sent quickly and casually, e-mail tends to be fairly informal in style. An e-mail is more like a note than a formal letter, which takes time to be composed, written, posted and delivered.

*   Some people use lower case almost exclusively when writing e-mail.
*   E-mail tends to use a lot of abbreviations and acronyms, some of which are given in the table below.

- People writing e-mail are often less fussy about correcting spelling mistakes when keying at high speed.
- Writing words in upper case is the equivalent of shouting, and is generally frowned upon unless you are using it to express anger.
- There is less use of apostrophes and other punctuation. Colons and semicolons are often replaced by dashes.
- Salutations and complimentary closes are not required. However, many people like to start messages with a greeting of some sort, even if it is only *Hi* or the first name of the person the message is being sent to.

Before you get too relaxed about spelling and use of lower-case letters, it is worth remembering that, although e-mail is more informal than letter writing, you should still be sensitive to what is and is not appropriate, especially with people you do not know. In addition, you still need to be clear about what you are saying: inconsistent or incorrect language can be misunderstood.

Using abbreviations in e-mail

It is customary to use many abbreviations in informal e-mail. These often take the form of a common expression being represented by only the initial letters of the words. Many of these are now widely used, although it is a good idea to make sure those you send messages to are familiar with these before you start to include them in your messages.

Here are some of the more common abbreviations in e-mail:

abbreviation	meaning
AFAIK	as far as I know
ASAP	as soon as possible
ATB	all the best
BTDT	been there done that
BTW	by the way
GAL	get a life
HTH	hope this helps
IMHO	in my humble opinion
IMO	in my opinion
IOW	in other words
LOL	laughing out loud (when someone has written something funny)
MYOB	mind your own business
OMG	Oh my God!
TVM	thanks very much

Another convention used by e-mailers is **emoticons** (also called **smileys**). These are combinations of characters – mainly punctuation marks – which are used to show facial expressions and emotions:

emoticon	meaning
:-)	happy
:-(	sad
;-)	winking
:-o	shocked

4. TEXT MESSAGES

Texting has certain similarities to e-mail in its speed and directness, but it also has some limitations, for example in the length of the message and the speed at which it can be keyed, due to the fact that text messages are sent by mobile phone rather than by computer.

Because of these limitations, text messages have developed their own style:

• Conventional grammar and spelling are often ignored.
• Words are shortened in order to reduce the number of characters, with a single letter or number often used to replace a whole word or syllable.
• Certain conventional abbreviations have now become accepted in text messages.

The most common way to abbreviate words when texting is by omitting vowels, as in the following cases:

abbreviation	meaning
CD	could
FWD	forward
LV	love
MSG	message
PLS	please
PPL	people
SPK	speak
THX	thanks
TXT	text
WD	would
WKND	weekend
XLNT	excellent
YR	your

Numbers are often used to stand for syllables which sound like them, as in the following cases:

abbreviation	meaning
NO1	no one
SUM1	someone
1CE	once
WAN2	want to
2DAY	today
2NITE	tonight
B4	before
4EVER	forever
GR8	great
L8R	later
W8	wait

Letters are often used to stand for whole words, or syllables which sound like the letter, as in the following cases:

abbreviation	meaning
B	be
CU	see you
LO	hello
NE	any
RUOK?	are you okay?
XTRA	extra
Y	why

Informal shortenings and spellings are also used:

abbreviation	meaning
COZ	because
CUM	come
DA	the
LUV	love
RITE	right
SOZ	sorry
THRU	through
W/O	without
WOT	what

Did you know?

If you think you are a speedy text messager then see how quickly you can type out the following message:

The razor-toothed piranhas of the genera Serrasalmus and Pygocentrus are the most ferocious freshwater fish in the world. In reality they seldom attack a human.

In May 2005 the record stood at 48 seconds. Can you do any better?

Five Points to Remember

1. Make sure you date your letters and remember to include all your contact details.

2. Get off to a good start in a letter by making sure that you get the person's name and title right as this will be the first thing they read.

3. Don't use lies or exaggerations in your CV to make it sound more impressive as they will almost certainly be found out sooner or later.

4. Informal English of the sort used in e-mails to friends is not appropriate when communicating with people in authority or people you don't know. If in doubt, always use standard English.

5. Make sure that your e-mail is correctly addressed before clicking the 'send' button! It is all too easy to send an inappropriate message accidentally to the wrong person.

Giving talks and presentations

1. **Preparing your talk**
   Structure
   Essential language for presentations
   Making your talk more memorable
   Using visual aids
2. **Getting ready for your talk**
   Practising
   Looking at the venue
   Dealing with nerves
3. **Getting your message across**

Writing ability is crucial but there will also be times when you will need to use your voice to get a message across. You might never have to make an important speech in parliament or defend a client in court, but there will be occasions when you will require some of the skills of a politician or lawyer to make a point, and so speaking is usually part of the school curriculum.

I. PREPARING YOUR TALK

- There are some similarities between an essay and a talk. Like an essay, a talk should start off with an introduction in which you explain the subject you are going to discuss and what questions you hope to answer. The main body of your argument should be the largest part of your talk and that should end with a summary of the points you have made. You should then end the talk with the conclusions you have arrived at.
- There are also a number of key differences between a talk and an essay. An essay can be read and re-read, so longer sentences are appropriate. Talks are delivered just once so nothing you say should be over-long or complicated. Stick to clear and concise sentences that your audience can understand immediately.
- An essay often contains many facts and details which the reader is able to look at and digest at his or her leisure. Too many facts and figures in a talk, however, will swamp the listener and prevent you from getting your main points across. That is the key difference between a talk and an essay: a talk focuses on a few important points in broad terms while an essay can deal with a greater number of points in more detail.

Structure

Although the audience is most interested in the main body of your presentation, the sections that come before and after it are also important. Below is a useful running order for the different sections of your talk:

Greet your audience
⇓
Introduce yourself
⇓
Outline your talk
⇓

Move to the main body
⇩
Summarize the main points
⇩
Conclude your talk
⇩
Invite questions from the audience
⇩
Accept questions and comments

Essential language for presentations

It is helpful for an audience if you guide it through the structure of your talk. Here is a list of expressions which you can use to signal the different stages.

Introduction

Greeting the audience
Good morning/afternoon/evening.
Hello everybody.

Introducing yourself
My name's [your name] and I'm from [class name].
I think you all know me (*if giving a talk to classmates, for example*)

Explaining the purpose of your talk
Today I want to talk to you about ...
Today I want to explain ...
I'd like to talk to you about ...

Outlining the structure of the talk
I've divided my talk into four parts.
My talk will focus on three main areas.
In the first part I will look at ...
The second part will deal with ...
In the final part I'll show you ...

Saying how long your talk will take
My talk will take about fifteen minutes.
I plan to speak for about ten minutes.

Saying when you prefer to answer questions
I'll be happy to answer your questions at the end of my talk.
Please feel free to interrupt me during my talk if you have a question.

Here is an example of some of these expressions being put to use:

> *Good afternoon everyone. I'm very pleased to be with you today. My name's Marina Potter and I am studying A-level history. I'd like to talk to you about the Russian revolution.*

I've divided my talk into three parts. In the first part I'll look at the political background to the revolution. The second part will deal with the Bolshevik seizure of power, and in the final part I'll describe the response of Russia's wartime allies to the events.

I plan to speak for about thirty minutes. I'll be happy to answer your questions at the end of my presentation.

I'd like to start now by looking at the meaning of the word 'revolution'...

Main body

Moving to the first point
I'd like to start now by looking at ...
In this first part of my talk I want to look at ...

Ending a point
Right, that's all I have to say about ...

Moving to a new point
Moving on now to my next point ...
Now I'd like to look at ...

Describing a sequence
Firstly ...
Secondly ...
Then ...
Next ...
After that ...
Finally ...

Talking about a previous point
In the first part of my talk I mentioned ...
As I've already said ...

Talking about a future point or piece of information
I'll go into this in more detail at a later stage.
I'll come to that later.

Introducing a visual aid
Could you please look at the screen for a moment?
As you can see in the diagram ...
I'd like to show you an example of what I mean ...

Getting back to a main idea
Let me return to what I was saying before.
To get back to my main point ...
As I was saying ...

Involving the audience
As you are aware ...
As you know ...
Can anybody suggest a reason?

Handling interruptions
That's an interesting question. I'll come to that at the end.
If I could just answer that later.

Summarizing
So, what we have looked at here today is ...
I'd like to end now by summarizing the main points of my talk.

Conclusion

Concluding
That's all I have to say about this subject for now.
Thank you very much for your attention.

Inviting questions
I'll be happy to answer your questions now.
Any questions or comments?

Questions and comments

Handling questions
That's an interesting comment. Thank you for that.
I'm afraid I'm not able to answer that question.
I don't think I can answer that just now but I can try to find out for you.

Making your talk more memorable

- Try to open your presentation with something that will grab your audience's attention. A joke, a brief anecdote or a quotation will make them sit up and listen although it should, of course, be relevant to your talk.
- Try to give real examples to illustrate your points as this will give your presentation more impact.
- Use humour where appropriate but only sparingly.
- While you will want to draw on other people's opinions or theories it is important that you express your own views. Personal opinions can be expressed with greater conviction than those of others and will make it clear to the audience that you have thought carefully about the subject.
- Think about involving members of the audience during your talk. Perhaps ask an open question, although make sure not to embarrass anyone by putting them on the spot.
- Finish your talk with a brief summary of the main points you have made, then sum up your argument with a memorable conclusion.
- A good presentation will raise questions as well as answer them so leave time at the end for dealing with points made by your audience. Try to anticipate the kind of questions you might be asked and think about how you would respond to them.

┌───┐
│ ▬ *Did you know?* ▬▬▬▬▬▬▬▬▬▬▬▬▬▬▬▬▬▬▬▬▬▬▬▬▬▬▬▬▬▬▬   │
│   │
│ Keeping your talk concise and to the point is an important consideration │
│ of any speechmaker. Cuban leader Fidel Castro, however, forgot this   │
│ golden rule in 1960 when his speech to the United Nations took a   │
│ staggering 4 hours and 29 minutes to deliver. It is still the longest speech │
│ ever made at the UN.   │
└───┘

Using visual aids

- Provided they are simple and clearly visible from the back of the room, visual aids can add impact to your talk and drive home the points you want to make. Don't use too many, however, as they can distract the audience.
- There are a number of tools you can use: **flipchart**, **whiteboard**, **overhead projector**, **slide projector** and **PowerPoint®**.
- **Handouts** are useful but keep them fairly short. Also, make sure there are enough copies for everyone. Do any printing and photocopying the day before as machines cannot always be relied upon to work when you really need them to.

flipchart
large sheets of paper on a stand

handout
a page or pages distributed among the audience showing information related to a talk, such as the outline, important data or diagrams

overhead projector
a machine which projects images and text from a **transparency** onto a screen

PowerPoint®
a computer application which allows you to prepare slides on your computer that can be projected onto a screen, with graphics and animation if you wish

slide
a small piece of photographic film showing images or text, used with a slide projector

slide projector
a machine which projects photographic images onto a screen

transparency
a sheet of clear plastic, projected onto a screen by an overhead projector

whiteboard
a large white board for writing on, often found in classrooms and offices

Make sure you know how to use electronic presentational tools well in advance! Showing slides upside down or in the wrong order will make you flustered and will not impress the audience. Familiarizing yourself with the technology will mean you can concentrate on giving a good presentation rather than on remembering which buttons you are supposed to press.

2. GETTING READY FOR YOUR TALK

- You don't need to learn your presentation word for word or even write it down as such. Reading from sheets of paper will put off your audience and won't allow you to make eye contact with people or use appropriate hand movements to emphasize your points.
- Instead, summarize your points on index cards and allow yourself to ad-lib so that you sound natural and not stilted.
- Once you have looked at each index card you can easily put it to the back of the pile in your hand so that you don't accidentally repeat yourself. It is much easier to repeat yourself or get lost if you are reading from a long speech.

Practising

- Practice makes perfect. Performing your talk a number of times either on your own or, preferably, in front of someone such as a friend or family member will help you smooth out any rough edges.
- Ask for their feedback. They will tell you if you are speaking too quickly or too softly. They might also notice any distracting mannerisms you have such as playing with your hair or your shirt collar.
- Practising will also give you a good idea of how long your presentation will take when you give it for real. This is important as you might not be the only person giving a talk and you do not want to overrun or finish unexpectedly early.

Looking at the venue

- As well as getting to grips with any computers and overhead projectors you need to use you should also become familiar with the venue for your talk.
- Make sure you know where the light switches are and that there enough power sockets for any electrical equipment you want to use. Cables should be long enough to reach the sockets.
- Look at the size of the room and work out how loud your voice will have to be to ensure that even people at the back will be able to hear you clearly.

Dealing with nerves

- All public performers get nervous before taking centre stage. If you get anxious or short of breath before you start then breathe deeply and count slowly from 1 to 5.
- Before you start your talk smile to yourself and think positive thoughts so that you don't get too worked up.
- Make sure you have a glass of water to hand just in case your mouth goes dry or you get a frog in your throat.

3. GETTING YOUR MESSAGE ACROSS

You might have written the best presentation in the world but if you can't present it properly it won't make the impact it deserves to. Here are a few tips that will help you be an effective communicator:

- Adopt a confident posture by standing up straight and keeping your chin up when you speak. Positive body language will ensure that your audience takes your message seriously. Slouching and speaking into your chest will have the opposite effect.

- Don't speak too quickly. Remember, the best communicators use a measured delivery so that the audience can take in what is being said.
- Remember to pause between sentences. This will allow you to get your breath back and it will also let the audience absorb your message.
- Give eye contact to various people during your talk, and smile too. This will help you to connect to the audience and make you seem less like a recorded announcement at a railway station.
- Accentuate any key points or words and perhaps emphasize them with appropriate gestures.
- If you make any mistakes apologize quickly and move on. You are only human and they will quickly be forgotten.
- It is unlikely that your presentation will be interrupted by standing ovations but do remember to pause for any audience reactions. Something you say might get a response but you wouldn't want your next sentence to be drowned out, so wait for everyone to settle again.

Five Points to Remember

1. Familiarize yourself with the venue for your talk and any equipment you will use.

2. Just like an essay, your talk should have an introduction, a main body, and a conclusion in which you sum up your arguments.

3. Practise your presentation several times before you give it for real.

4. Speak clearly and deliberately. Pause often.

5. Leave time for questions and think about the sort you are likely to be asked.

What you need to know about English

1. **Spelling**
   Twelve spelling rules
   Four tips for learning tricky spellings
2. **Punctuation**
   Punctuation marks
   Punctuation for quotations
3. **Grammar**
   Four grammar rules
4. **Parts of speech**
5. **Abbreviations**
6. **Figures of speech**

I. SPELLING

The idea that spelling is important is sometimes thought of as old-fashioned. However, there are good reasons for using correct spelling as often as you can.

Firstly, correct spelling makes life easy for your readers, whereas incorrect or unconventional spelling can get in the way of your meaning.

Secondly, using correct spelling indicates that you take a pride in your work. Correct and consistent spelling is taken as a sign of a tidy mind at work, and this encourages readers to take you and your writing seriously. An employer who notices a spelling mistake in a letter of application or a CV may throw the application onto the reject pile.

There are several ways that you can ensure your writing is free from spelling mistakes:

- Take note of any incorrect spellings marked by the spellchecker on your computer. However, keep in mind that spellcheckers have limitations (see page 10).
- Check spellings in a dictionary if you are not sure.
- Learn the basic rules of spelling listed below.
- Familiarize yourself with the words you find difficult to spell and make an effort to learn the correct way to spell them.

> *Did you know?*
> Bad spelling can ruin an otherwise good piece of work but it can also damage a career – just ask American politician Dan Quayle. In 1992 the then US Vice-President attended a spelling bee at a school in New Jersey. When a boy correctly spelled the word *potato* Quayle tried to correct the spelling by adding an 'e' to the end of the word. The incident was captured on television and Mr Quayle's reputation immediately took a nose-dive.

Twelve spelling rules

Here are some simple rules, most of them to do with forming words from others. This is not a complete list of such rules, but is good place from which to start.

Rule 1: Adding -*ing*, -*ed*, -*er* and -*s*

If the **base form** of the verb has only one syllable and ends in a single vowel followed by a single consonant, then you have to double the last letter before you add -*ing*, -*ed*, or -*er*:

run – running
pot – potting – potted
stir – stirrer

If the base form of the verb has two or more syllables and ends in a single vowel followed by a single consonant, whether or not you double the final letter depends on the pronunciation. If you pronounce the word with a stress on the final syllable, then you have to double the final letter before you add -*ing*, -*ed*, or -*er*:

regret – regretting – regretted
prefer – preferring – preferred
distil – distiller

But if the stress is not on the final syllable, the final letter is not doubled:

enter – entering – entered
gossip – gossiping – gossiped

Rule 2: Making plurals

Plurals of nouns ending in a consonant followed by -*y* are formed by changing the -*y* to -*ie* and adding -*s*:

berry – berries
hanky – hankies
fly – flies

The plural of nouns that have a vowel before the -*y* are simply formed with -*s*:

boy – boys
day – days

Rule 3: Adding -*ish* and -*y*

If a word ends in a 'silent e', you would usually drop the final -*e* before adding -*ish* or -*y*:

white – whitish
grease – greasy

However, there are a number of exceptions to this rule:

price – pricey
same – samey
mate – matey

Rule 4: Adding -*er* and -*est*

If an adjective has two or more syllables and ends in -*y*, you have to change the -*y* to -*i* before adding -*er* or -*est*:

angry – angrier – angriest
funny – funnier – funniest

But watch out for these one-syllable adjectives ending in *-y*:

dry – drier – driest
sly – slyer – slyest
shy – shier or shyer – shiest or shyest

> Remember that some adjectives have very irregular comparative and superlative forms (eg *good, better, best*).

Rule 5: Adding *-ly*

If an adjective ends in a consonant followed by *-le* you drop the final *-e* before adding *-ly* to make an adverb:

simple – simply
double – doubly

If an adjective ends in *-y*, the *-y* ending is changed to *-i* when *-ly* is added:

happy – happily
weary – wearily

Rule 6: Adding *-able* and *-ible*

The ending *-able* is often added to the end of a verb to make adjectives:

remark – remarkable
respect – respectable

If a word ends in a 'silent e', the final *-e* is dropped before adding *-able*:

advise – advisable
debate – debatable

However, if the word ends in *-ce* or *-ge*, the *-e* is kept when adding *-able*:

notice – noticeable
change – changeable

The ending *-able* is more common than *-ible*, but it is worth remembering some of the common adjectives that end in *-ible*:

audible
comprehensible
credible
edible
eligible
flexible
gullible
illegible
incredible

legible
negligible
permissible
reversible
sensible
visible

Rule 7: Adding *-ful*, *al-* and *-til*

Remember that when the word *full* becomes the suffix *-ful* it drops the final *l*:

hope – hopeful
faith – faithful
colour – colourful

The same rule applies to the words *all* and *till*, which drop the final *l* when used as a prefix or suffix:

all – already – altogether
till – until

If the word to which *-ful* is added ends in *-y*, the *-y* ending is changed to *-i*:

beauty – beautiful
pity – pitiful
fancy – fanciful

> Note that when the ending *-ful* is added to a word for a container of some sort, the resulting word means the amount that the container can hold, but when *full* is used as a separate word it tells us about the container itself. The phrase *a handful of cherries* means 'as many cherries as fit in a hand', whereas *a hand full of cherries* means 'a hand that contains cherries'.

Rule 8: Adding *-ize* or *-ise*

It is acceptable in British English to use either *-ize* or *-ise* for most verbs that end in this sound:

characterize or *characterise*
realize or *realise*
apologize or *apologise*

It is worth learning some of the common words that can only be spelt with *-ise* at the end:

advertise
advise
arise
comprise
compromise
despise
devise
exercise

improvise
revise
rise
supervise
surprise
televise

There are also a few words that are always spelt with **-ize**:

capsize
prize
size

And remember that a few words are spelt with **-yse** in British English:

analyse
breathalyse
catalyse
paralyse
psychoanalyse

Rule 9: The '*i* before *e* except after *c*' rule

You will have probably heard the rule '*i* **before e except after c**'.
Note that this only applies when the word has an 'ee' sound, as in *deep*.

After any letter except *c*, *i* comes before *e*:

bel*ie*ve
ch*ie*f
s*ie*ge
n*ie*ce

But immediately after *c*, *e* comes before *i*:

c*ei*ling
rec*ei*pt
perc*ei*ve
rec*ei*ve

However, there are some very common exceptions to this rule that are worth learning:

weird
seize
caffeine
protein
either
neither
species

Rule 10: Adding endings to -our

When you add the endings -ant, -ary, -ation, -fic, -iferous, -ize or -ise, or -ous to words that end in -our, you take the u out of the -our:

glamour – glamorize
humour – humorous
honour – honorary

You leave the u in if you are adding the endings -able, -er, -ism, -ist, -ite:

honour – honourable
favour – favourite

Rule 11: The endings -ous and -us

The ending -ous is used mainly in adjectives:

famous
anonymous
enormous
poisonous

The ending -us is used mainly in nouns:

cactus
circus
octopus
thesaurus

Rule 12: Words that can end in -se or -ce

Some words, such as *license* and *licence*, are often confused in spelling. The correct spelling depends on whether the word is being used as noun or as a verb. Remember that in British English the ending -se is used in verbs, and the ending -ce is used in nouns:

use -se for verbs	use -ce for nouns
to **practise** juggling	went to football **practice**
I was **advised** to keep quiet	a piece of good **advice**
to **devise** a test	a nuclear **device**
to **license** a drug	a driving **licence**

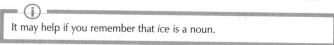

It may help if you remember that *ice* is a noun.

Four tips for learning tricky spellings

There are a number of strategies you can use to help memorize the spelling of a word. Different words are suited to different strategies, so decide which one will be most helpful for each word.

Tip 1: Break down the word

- Try breaking the word down into parts and saying them out loud or to yourself.
- Some words are easiest to learn by sounding out individual letters:
  d-i-a-r-y
- Some words are easiest to learn by sounding out individual syllables:
  re-spon-si-bil-i-ty
- Some words can be broken down into known 'roots' from which the word is created. These roots are spelt the same in every word in which they occur:
  tele-phone
  care-ful-ly

Tip 2: Words within words

- Many tricky words contain common words inside them. For example, the word *favourite* contains *our* and *rite*. Finding and remembering these 'words within words' can help you to learn a difficult spelling.
- The 'words within words' strategy can be very useful for remembering the spelling of silent vowels, for example *get* in ve**get**able or *par* in se**par**ate.

Tip 3: Mnemonics

- A mnemonic is a phrase which helps you to remember something. For example, people learning to read music learn the notes on the lines of treble clef (E, G, B, D and F) by the phrase *Every Good Boy Deserves Favour*.
- Mnemonics can also help you to remember difficult spellings. The best are simple and catchy, and create a vivid picture in your head:
  rhythm **h**elps **y**ou **t**o **h**ear **m**usic
- Mnemonics can help you remember the difficult part of a word:
  the **lie**utenant will **lie** **ut**terly still
- The most helpful mnemonics are often the ones that you make up yourself, creating phrases that have a special meaning for you.

Tip 4: Look – cover – write – check

- *Look – cover – write – check* is a four-stage strategy for learning difficult spellings. First you **look** at the word, then you **cover** it over, try to **write** it down from memory, and uncover it to **check** that you have spelt it correctly.
- When you first look at the word, or if you get the spelling wrong, try to concentrate on the parts that you have problems with, or parts that are not spelt as they sound.

2. PUNCTUATION

As with spelling mistakes, mistakes in punctuation can make reading your work more difficult than it need be and can sometimes result in a different meaning from the one you intended.

Punctuation marks

Here are some of the main punctuation marks and what they should be used for.

Apostrophe

- **Use an apostrophe to show possession.** *The student's books* is correct if you mean one student, and *the students' books* is correct if you mean more than one student. *The children's books* is correct, since the plural form is *children* and the possessive *s* can be added to it.
- **Use an apostrophe in the possessive of names ending in *s*;** for example, *James's calculations* and *Mr Jones's house* are correct. If the word sounds as though it has an extra *s* (Jameses, Joneses) when you say it, then you add an apostrophe and an *s* to the *s* that is already there; if not, you simply add an apostrophe at the end, for example, *Mrs Bridges' books*.
- **Use an apostrophe with periods of time;** for example, *three hours' work* and *five years' wait*.
- **Use an apostrophe to show that a letter has been missed out;** for example, *don't* (= do not), *let's* (= let us), *you're* (= you are), *it's* (= it is) and *who's* (= who is).

Never use an apostrophe if the *s* simply denotes the plural form of the word; for example, *The workers intend to strike* is correct, *The worker's intend to strike* is wrong.

Colon

- **Use a colon to divide an introductory statement and something that explains it;** for example, *There are some things money can't buy: happiness is one of them*.
- **Use a colon to introduce a list;** for example, *You will need: a piece of paper, a ruler and some coloured pencils*.

Comma

- **Use a comma in strings of adjectives and in lists;** for example a *cold, wet, windy day*.
- **Use a comma to separate clauses;** for example, *If people saved energy, the whole world would benefit* and *When people save energy, the whole world benefits*.
- **Use commas around words that give extra information in a sentence but without which the sentence would still make sense;** for example, *She seems nervous but, in those circumstances, you would be*.
- **Use a comma after an introductory phrase** such as *of course, indeed, in fact, now, well,* and so on; for example, *Of course, we do not claim 100% accuracy* or *Now, turning to the question of ...*
- **Use a comma to separate direct speech from the rest of the sentence;** for example, *Peter at once said, 'I want to come too'*.

Do not use a comma instead of a full stop. For example, to write *The economy is doing badly, exports are decreasing* is wrong. *The economy is doing badly, and exports are decreasing* is correct, and so is *The economy is doing badly. Exports are decreasing*.

Hyphen

- **Use a hyphen between words to be read as a single unit;** for example *his mother-in-law, a bunch of forget-me-nots*.
- **Use a hyphen between words that are being used as an adjective before a noun;** for example, *a two-year-old boy, eighteenth-century literature*.

However, if the first element of the compound is an adverb ending in -*ly*, then do not use a hyphen; for example, a *brightly coloured poster* and a *forcefully delivered speech*.

Also, do not use a hyphen if the words are capitalized; for example, a *Northern Ireland spokesman*.

- **Use a hyphen with numbers**; for example, *twenty-five* and *thirty-seventh*.
- **Use a hyphen with fractions**; for example, *two-thirds* and *five-eighths*.
- **Use a hyphen with compass directions**; for example, *south-east* and *north-north-west*.

Inverted commas

- **Use inverted commas to indicate direct speech** (the actual words spoken by someone):

    "I have not yet reached a decision," the head teacher said.

    The head teacher said, *"I have not yet reached a decision."*

    "I have not yet reached a decision," the head teacher said, *"on this matter."*

- **Use inverted commas to indicate titles**, for example *I read an essay called 'The Final Step'.*

Either single or double inverted commas can be used for direct speech, but for all other uses, single quotes should be used.

Question mark

- **Use a question mark only at the end of a sentence that is a question**, and follow it with a new sentence with a capital letter. For example, *Why did it have this result? and was it unavoidable?* should be rewritten as *Why did it have this result, and was it unavoidable?* or *Why did it have this result? Was it unavoidable?*

Semicolon

- **Use a semicolon to join two sentences that are equally important**; for example, *We'll say no more about your behaviour; this subject is closed.*
- **Use a semicolon in lists of longer phrases**; for example, *The area's main industries are shipbuilding, engineering and steel manufacturing; textiles and clothing; coalmining; and brewing.*

Punctuation for quotations

- If there is a quotation within the main quotation, use double inverted commas for the quotation inside; for example, *Ali said, 'We had to keep moving till the man shouted "Stop!", then hold still.'*
- Use **square brackets** around material added to a quotation in order to make it more clear; for example, *'[Shakespeare] was not of an age, but for all time!'* Here, *[Shakespeare]* replaces the unclear *He*.
- Use **ellipsis marks** (three dots) to indicate that something irrelevant to the point has been left out of the quotation, for example *'These facts … speak for themselves.'*
- Use a slash when quoting lines of poetry within a sentence; for example, *'I wandered lonely as a cloud / That floats on high o'er vales and hills'.*

3. GRAMMAR

Correct grammar again ensures your meaning is clear, and makes your work easier to read. If you are not sure about a particular grammatical point, check it in a grammar book or on a grammar website.

Four grammar rules

There are two types of grammar rule: ones that are important because they help you to write clearly, and ones that are obeyed for the sake of tradition. It is important to know about and follow the first type, and the following rules come into this category.

Rule 1: Don't confuse the past tense with past participle

On page 57 it is explained that verbs have a past tense and a past participle. In some cases the same form of the verb is used for both:

> I **cut** my finger.
> The finger was **cut**.

For some verbs there is more than one acceptable form that can be used for the past tense and past participle:

> I **burned** the leaves.
> I **burnt** the leaves.

For some irregular verbs, there are different forms for the past tense and past participle. These should not be used interchangeably. Use the past tense form for main verbs; use the past participle in combination with an auxiliary or 'helping' verb (such as *has* or *was*):

> I **broke** my leg.
> My leg was **broken**.

Some past tenses and past participles are often confused. The table below shows some of the more easily confused ones. Make sure you get these right:

base form	past tense	past participle
begin	began	begun
bite	bit	bitten
go	went	gone
ring	rang	rung
see	saw	seen
show	showed	shown
shrink	shrank	shrunk
take	took	taken
wake	woke	woken

Check in your dictionary if you are not sure of the correct form of the past tense and the past participle.

Rule 2: Make subjects and verbs agree

The form of a verb that you use depends on the subject of the verb. Make sure that the subject and the verb agree in **number** and **person**.

A singular subject is followed by a singular form of the verb, while a plural subject is followed by a plural form of the verb:

> *Vikram **is** arriving today.*
> *Vikram and Fiona **are** arriving today.*

Similarly, there must be agreement between the **person** and the verb. A first-person subject requires a first-person form of the verb, a second-person subject requires a second-person form of the verb, and a third-person subject requires a third-person form of the verb:

> *I **am** arriving today.*
> *You **are** arriving today.*
> *She **is** arriving today.*

Be careful not to write sentences in which it not immediately clear what the subject is. For example:

> *In this country, only one in three children go to school.*

Here, it is only *one child* that goes to school, not *three*, so the verb should be singular:

> *In this country, only one in three children goes to school.*

Rule 3: Use object pronouns after a preposition

Personal pronouns have a different form depending on whether they are a subject or an object:

	subject	object
first person singular	*I*	*me*
second person singular	*you*	*you*
third person singular	*he – she – it*	*him – her – it*
first person plural	*we*	*us*
second person plural	*you*	*you*
third person plural	*they*	*them*

A preposition such as *between, for* or *from* should always be followed by the **object form** of the pronoun (ie *me, you, him, her, them*):

> *There's some sort of feud going on between **them**.*

When a pronoun is one of two words relating to the preposition, take care not to use a subject pronoun:

> *Between **you** and **me**, I think he's gone a little mad.* (not *between **you** and **I***)
> *The sweets were for **Roger** and **me**.* (not *for **Roger** and **I***)

Rule 4: Watch out for 'dangling' participles

A 'dangling' participle is when a participle in an opening phrase relates to the object rather than the subject of the main part of the sentence, making it read oddly:

***Running** out of the house, **a car** knocked him over.*
***Being** a valued customer, **we** would like to make you a very special offer.*

These examples are inaccurate because it is not the car that was running out of the house, nor is it those making the special offer who are the valued customer.

Sometimes the effect of a dangling participle can be comical:

***Cycling** down a road once used by Livingstone, **a leopard** suddenly appeared in front of her.*

The problem can often be resolved by writing a fuller sentence, using a subject and a main verb instead of a participle:

As she was cycling down a road once used by Livingstone, a leopard suddenly appeared in front of her.

4. PARTS OF SPEECH

Words are the building blocks of sentences, but there are different types of building block. For example, the words *dog, red, receive* and *quietly* all perform very different functions.

Just as the engine of a motor vehicle needs to have various components, with each component performing a different function, so too a sentence needs to have different types of words performing various functions. Some types of word (nouns) tell us *what things we are talking about*, others (verbs) express *what is going on*, while others (adverbs) describe *how things are being done*, and so on. The different types of word are called the **parts of speech** (or sometimes **word classes**).

Nouns

A simple definition of a **noun** is that it is a 'naming word'. The words for all of the things you can see if you look around the room or out of the window are nouns. For example *dog, fish, table, phone* and *Peter* are all nouns.

Words such as *tranquillity, courage* and *chaos*, that give names to concepts, ideas or impressions, are also nouns.

A **proper noun** is a name of a particular person, place or thing, and is always spelt with a capital letter. Proper nouns include *David, Saturn, October, Germany, Tokyo, Stonehenge, Rembrandt, Ramadan, Heinz* and *Tuesday*.

Any noun that is not a proper noun is a **common noun**. Whereas proper nouns name particular people and things, common nouns name types of thing of which there may be any number of particular instances. Common nouns are not written with a capital letter.

proper noun	common noun
Saturn	planet
Queen Victoria	monarch
October	month
Germany	country

A **collective noun** refers to a collection of people or objects.

One type of collective noun is **always singular** and can be used with the words *item of* or *article of*. Nouns such as *clothing, furniture, cutlery, equipment* and *luggage* fall into this category:

> an *item of cutlery/The cutlery **is** polished every week.*

Another type of collective noun is **always plural** but has no final *-s*. Nouns such as *cattle, police* and *people* fall into this category:

> *The police **were** looking into the matter.*

Verbs

A simple definition of a **verb** is that it is a 'doing word'. A verb usually denotes an action, such as *jump, sleep, cry* or *eat*, but some verbs denote a state, such as *remain* or *be*.

Verbs may exist in more than one form. If we think of a verb such as *play*, the form of the verb may change depending on:

- **person**: the form may vary according to who is doing the playing. If it is *I* (the so-called **first person**) or *you* (the **second person**) the form of the verb is *play*; if it is someone else (the **third person**) the form is *plays*.
- **number**: the form may vary according to how many are playing. For example, one person *plays* (**singular**), but two people *play* (**plural**).
- **tense**: the form may vary according to when the playing is taking place. For example, yesterday *I played* (**past tense**), but today *I am playing* (**present tense**), and tomorrow *I will play*.
- **voice**: the form may vary according to whether the subject of the sentence is doing the playing or having the playing done to them. For example, *I play* (**active voice**), but *the piano is played* (**passive voice**).

The verb *play* is a **regular verb**: its different forms are created according to predictable patterns. Some common verbs, for example *be*, are **irregular**: their different forms are not predictable.

	present tense	past tense
first person singular	I am	I was
second person singular	you are	you were
third person singular	he/she is	he/she was
first person plural	we are	we were
second person plural	you are	you were
third person plural	they are	they were

Each verb can have up to five different forms:

base form (infinitive)	third person singular of the present tense	present participle	past tense	past participle
jump	*jumps*	*jump**ing***	*jump**ed***	*jump**ed***
sew	*sews*	*sew**ing***	*sew**ed***	*sew**n***

The **base form** is the one from which all the others are formed, and the one that is used to show the present tense after *I*, *you*, *we* and *they*. It is also the form of the verb that you will see if you look it up in a dictionary.

The **present participle** is formed by adding *-ing* to the base form. This part of the verb is often used in combination with another verb such as *is* or *was*:

> *it is cutting*
> *she is finding*
> *he was learning*

The **past participle** of regular verbs (and also many irregular verbs) is often identical in form to the past tense. However, some irregular verbs use different forms for the past tense and past participle:

> *break – broken*
> *forget – forgotten*
> *shrink – shrunk*

The past participle of the verb is often used in combination another verb such as *has* or *was*:

> *it was broken*
> *we had forgotten*
> *it has shrunk*

Adjectives

A simple definition of an **adjective** is that it is a 'describing word'. The role of an adjective is to describe or give information about a noun. For example, in the sentences below, the highlighted words are adjectives:

> The **ginger** cat was drinking milk from a **chipped** saucer.
> The cat was extremely **fat**.
> They saw an **old** house with a **rambling** garden.

Many adjectives are **gradable**, meaning that they have different forms depending on how intense the quality is that you are describing:

> I want a **bigger** glass. (not just a **big** glass)
> That is the **ugliest** dog I've ever seen. (not just an **ugly** dog)

Gradable adjectives can exist in three different forms: the **positive** form, the **comparative** form and the **superlative** form. These different forms are shown below using the adjectives *big* and *beautiful* as examples:

positive	**comparative**	**superlative**
big	*bigger*	*biggest*
beautiful	*more beautiful*	*most beautiful*

Shorter words (words of one syllable and some words of two syllables) form the comparative and superlative in the same way as *big*, by adding -*er* and -*est*:

long – longer – longest
tough – tougher – toughest
happy – happier – happiest

You cannot add -*er* and -*est* to longer words, so the comparative and superlative forms of these are created by using *more* and *most* in front of the positive form:

awkward – more awkward – most awkward
sentimental – more sentimental – most sentimental

The adjectives *good* and *bad* are exceptions to the normal pattern, and have irregular comparative and superlative forms:

positive	**comparative**	**superlative**
good	*better*	*best*
bad	*worse*	*worst*

Adverbs

Adverbs are used to add something extra to the meaning of various parts of speech, and even the meaning of whole sentences.

The most useful way to think about adverbs is that they answer certain questions the writer might want to answer for the reader, such as:

1 how? (*She played **well**; They reacted **sluggishly***)
2 where? where to? where from? (*She's **here**; I'm getting **nowhere***)
3 how far? (*It stretches **endlessly**; He ran **miles***)
4 how long? (*I waited **forever**; I paused **momentarily***)
5 when? (*Are you free **tomorrow**?; I saw him **recently***)
6 how often? (*They are paid **monthly**; We **seldom** discussed it*)
7 to what extent? (*I don't like it **much**; She's **highly** intelligent*)

Some of the most familiar adverbs are formed by adding the ending -*ly* to an adjective:

quick – quickly
sad – sadly
hasty – hastily

Although there are many single-word adverbs, it is also common for a group of words within a sentence to perform the function of an adverb. Such groups of words are known as **adverb phrases** or **adverbials**.

*handle **with care***
*the one **on the left***
*We walked **all the way**.*
*I waited **for ages**.*
*I'll see you **after the party**.*
*We **hardly ever** go there.*
*I agree **with all my heart**.*

Like adjectives, many adverbs are **gradable** and have **positive**, **comparative** and **superlative** forms. There are two kinds of regular gradable adverb.

Words that are adjectives and act as adverbs only because of their position in the sentence use the same forms as adjectives:

*He drives **fast** and works **hard**.* (positive)
*He drove **faster** and worked **harder** than ever.* (comparative)
*He drives **fastest** and works **hardest** when he's angry.* (superlative)

For adverbs that end in *-ly*, the comparative and superlative forms are created by using *more* and *most* in front of the positive form:

closely – more closely – most closely
nervously – more nervously – most nervously

The adverbs *well* and *badly* are exceptions to the normal pattern, and have irregular comparative and superlative forms:

positive	comparative	superlative
well	better	best
badly	worse	worst

Pronouns

Pronouns are short words that can act as substitutes for nouns. Words such as *you*, *them* and *it* are pronouns.

Pronouns save writers from having to spell out names again and again:

*Jim is good worker, but I don't really trust **him**.*
*Sally told me that **she** had forgotten the key.*

Pronouns can act as substitutes not just for a noun, but also for a **noun phrase** – a cluster of words that acts as a noun. This can save a lot of time:

*I fell in love with **the big red sandstone Victorian house with the huge garden that I had seen the previous week**, and decided to buy **it**.*

The use of pronouns is so common that people often overlook them, but they perform a vital function, and without them language soon begins to sound awkward and repetitive.

Personal pronouns stand in place of a person or thing. Different words are used to indicate the **person** and **number**, and whether the pronoun is acting as the **subject** or the **object** of the sentence.

	subject	object
first person singular	*I*	*me*
second person singular	*you*	*you*
third person singular	*he – she – it*	*him – her – it*
first person plural	*we*	*us*
second person plural	*you*	*you*
third person plural	*they*	*them*

Possessive pronouns refer to things that belong to a person or thing:

> *The black pen is **mine**.* (mine = my pen)
> ***Hers** is the red coat.* (hers = her coat)
> ***Ours** are in this box.* (ours = our things)

Reflexive pronouns are used when the person or thing referred to is the same as the subject of the verb:

> *Frank has a high opinion of **himself**.*
> *I had to pinch **myself**.*

Pronouns can be used when asking questions. These are known as **interrogative pronouns**, because you would use them when questioning or interrogating someone:

> ***Who** was on the phone?*
> *To **whom** should I address my correspondence?*
> ***Whose** are these?*
> ***Which** is the least expensive?*
> ***What** is your address?*

Relative pronouns are used to refer back to a person or thing mentioned earlier in the sentence. A relative pronoun follows immediately after the noun to which it refers:

> *the man **who** lives across the street*
> *the person to **whom** I spoke*
> *the people **whose** car was stolen*

Pronouns can be used as the equivalent of pointing to something. Words that do this are known as **demonstrative pronouns**. If the thing is relatively close, you use *this* (or *these* in the plural); if the thing is relatively far away, you use *that* (or *those* in the plural).

> *Do not worry about the notes. **Those** have all been destroyed.*
> *I enclose a map. Please bring **this** with you.*

The **indefinite pronouns** refer to people or things without specifying who they are or which ones they are, or refer to general amounts.

> *I hope you meet **someone** nice.*
> ***Everything** went wrong.*
> ***Many** will try; **most** will fail.*
> *The students were tested and **all** passed.*
> *There is only **half** left.*

Prepositions

Like pronouns, **prepositions** are a fixed set of words. Most of them are short words, such as *in*, *at* or *on*. In addition, some phrases, such as *in front of* or *instead of* act as prepositions. The role of prepositions is to express the relationships between words.

Some prepositions indicate the **place** where something is or the nature of its movement from one place to another:

> the house **near** the park
> She sat **next to** me.
> I saw you **at** the cinema.
> I keep my bike **in** the cellar.

Some prepositions indicate **time**:

> I'll see you **at** nine o'clock.
> I waited **until** Donna arrived.
> It happened **in** July.

Some prepositions indicate the **relationship** between events and items:

> Everything was done **according to** the rules.
> We had a great time **in spite of** the weather.
> There are twelve of us **including** the kids.
> a man **with** white hair

Conjunctions

A simple definition of a **conjunction** is that it is a 'joining word'. The role of a conjunction is to link words or groups of words together. Like pronouns and prepositions, they are a relatively small set of words.

There are only a few **co-ordinating conjunctions**; the main ones are *and, but* and *or*.

> bread **and** butter
> He is very able **but** rather lazy.
> tea **or** coffee

Because their role is to join things together, co-ordinating conjunctions do not generally stand at the start of a sentence. However, you can begin a sentence with a conjunction to indicate a link with the previous sentence:

> We are making the slogan 'Quality is Everything' a way of life. **And** that is not all.

Subordinating conjunctions are used to introduce a piece of information that elaborates on or explains (in a subordinate clause) the main information of the sentence.

Common subordinating conjunctions include *whether, because, if, until, that, in case, as if, unless* and *even though*:

> I wonder **whether** we'll get to meet her.
> Take an umbrella **in case** it rains.
> You should help her **because** she's your sister.

Interjections

Interjections are a special type of word. They are different from other parts of speech because they do not combine with other words in sentences. They stand on their own, and usually express a strong emotion. They are often followed by an exclamation mark:

> **Blast!** *I meant to go the supermarket this afternoon.*
> **Hello!** *I didn't expect to see you.*

Sometimes these words are called **exclamations**.

Determiners

Determiners are often classed as adjectives. The term 'determiner' refers to a small group of words that allow you to be more specific about nouns: to indicate which thing or person is being referred to, and how many of them there are. Words such as *a*, *some* and *several* are determiners.

Articles

The word *a* (or *an*) is known as the **indefinite article**, and the word *the* is known as the **definite article**.

5. ABBREVIATIONS

An abbreviation is a group of letters that represents a word or group of words. Abbreviations may be written using lower-case letters (*pm, mm, oz*), upper-case letters (*BC, EU, CNN*) or a combination of the two (*Hz, pH, BSc*).

You may be unsure whether or not to use full stops in abbreviations. Full stops are not generally used in the following cases:

- after shortened version of a word (*Dr, Mr, Prof, can't*)
- after abbreviations of countries or organizations (*UK, EU*)
- after acronyms (*NATO, UNESCO, NASA*)
- after scientific symbols (*kg, cm*)

Full stops are sometimes used in these cases:

- after strings of letters representing words (*eg* or *e.g.*; *ie* or *i.e.*; *RSVP* or *R.S.V.P.*)
- after people's initials (*H.G. Wells* or *H G Wells*)

If you want to create a plural form of an abbreviation, you may wonder whether it is necessary to add the letter *s* or not. Use the following guidelines:

- Do not add an -*s* to metric units (*76cm, 786g, 500cc*).
- For most other units, it is normal to omit -*s*, but a few always have an -*s* (*100yds, 24hrs*).
- A few abbreviations can be pluralized by doubling the abbreviation instead of adding an -*s* (*pp* = pages).
- You can use an apostrophe when creating a plural of a lower-case abbreviation (*p's and q's*).

6. FIGURES OF SPEECH

A figure of speech is a way of using words to create a striking effect. Here are some of the more widely used figures of speech:

Simile

A simile involves making a comparison between two things, introduced by words such as *like* or *as*:

> She eyed the food **like a hungry lion.**
> He was trembling **like a leaf.**

For a simile to be truly effective it should be original and appropriate. Many similes are so familiar that the reader is not surprised by them:

> *as mad as a hatter*
> *as clean as a whistle*

Metaphor

A metaphor involves using a word or phrase to describe something that it does not literally apply to. This unusual use of the word has the effect of making a comparison, although – unlike a simile – a metaphor does not use words such as *like* or *as*:

> Annie **sailed** into the room.

In this example, the writer does not mean the reader to think that Annie literally travelled into the room in a ship, but that her movement was smooth and impressive, like a ship's.

If you use two metaphors in the same sentence, the result can be a **mixed metaphor** – a combination that creates an absurd image. This is often regarded as a sign of bad writing:

> *There are concrete steps in the pipeline.*

Allusion

An allusion involves using words that makes the reader think of a particular person, object or event:

> *Never in the field of interior design have I seen anything like it.*
> *These are probably the best sandwiches in the world.*

In the first example, the words *never in the field* are an allusion to a famous wartime speech made by Winston Churchill (*Never in the field of human conflict...*); in the second example the phrase *probably the best* might put the reader in mind of advertisements for a certain brand of lager.

Personification

Personification involves giving human qualities to objects or ideas:

> *The computer won't be happy if you don't log out properly.*
> *Fear stalks the corridors of the building.*

In the first example, the computer is pictured as being capable of human emotions such as happiness; in the second example, fear is pictured as a person moving threateningly about a building.

Metonymy

Metonymy is using a term to refer to something that is closely associated with it:

> an oath of allegiance to **the crown** (instead of to the monarch)

Irony

Irony is expressing of a meaning opposite to the one apparently expressed:

> I can't wait!
> Oh, very funny!

Oxymoron

An oxymoron is a phrase composed of words that have contradictory meanings:

> a **horribly good** ghost story

Paradox

A paradox is a statement that, although it seems to be contradictory, contains an element of truth:

> You've got to be cruel to be kind.
> Expect the unexpected.
> Less is more.

Rhetorical question

A rhetorical question is a question that is asked to emphasize a point, without expecting an answer:

> Is the Pope a Catholic?
> Do I have to do everything myself?

Hyperbole

Hyperbole is using extreme exaggeration to make a particular point:

> there are a thousand and one reasons
> not for all the tea in China

Five Points to Remember

1. Bad spelling will ruin an otherwise good piece of work and may even cause you to be marked down.

2. Note down in one place any words you find difficult to spell and try to memorize the correct spelling.

3. Use punctuation correctly – and consistently.

4. Make a mental note of the grammar rules in this section, so you never make these basic mistakes.

5. Familiarize yourself with the different figures of speech as using them will make your writing more interesting.